GREG O'KANE

The Broadview Anthology of Drama:
Plays from the Western Theatre

VOLUME I

From Antiquity Through the Eighteenth Century

The Broadview Anthology of Drama: Plays from the Western Theatre

VOLUME I

From Antiquity through the Eighteenth Century

Jennifer Wise and Craig S. Walker

EDITORS

broadview press

National Library of Canada Cataloguing in Publication

The Broadview anthology of drama : plays from the western theatre / edited by Jennifer Wise and Craig S. Walker.

Contents: v. 1. From antiquity through the eighteenth century
— v. 2. The nineteenth and twentieth centuries
ISBN 1-55111-139-X (v. 1).—ISBN 1-55111-582-4 (v. 2)

1. Drama—Collections.   I. Wise, Jennifer, 1959-   II. Walker, Craig Stewart, 1960-

PN6112.B76 2003   808.82   C2003-902439-3

Broadview Press Ltd. is an independent, international publishing house, incorporated in 1985. Broadview believes in shared ownership, both with its employees and with the general public; since the year 2000 Broadview shares have traded publicly on the Toronto Venture Exchange under the symbol BDP.

We welcome comments and suggestions regarding any aspect of our publications–please feel free to contact us at the addresses below or at broadview@broadviewpress.com.

North America
PO Box 1243,
Peterborough, Ontario
Canada K9J 7H5
3576 California Road,
Orchard Park, NY, USA 14127
Tel: (705) 743-8990;
Fax: (705) 743-8353
email: customerservice@broadviewpress.com

UK, Ireland, and continental Europe
Plymbridge Distributors Ltd.
Estover Road
Plymouth
United Kingdom PL6 7PY
Tel: +44 (0) 1752 202301;
Fax: +44 (0) 1752 202333
email: orders@plymbridge.com

Australia and New Zealand
UNIREPS,
University of New South Wales
Sydney, NSW, 2052
Australia
Tel: 61 2 9664 0999;
Fax: 61 2 9664 5420
email: info.press@unsw.edu.au

www.broadviewpress.com

Broadview Press Ltd. gratefully acknowledges the financial support of the Government of Canada through the Book Publishing Industry Development Program for our publishing activities.

PRINTED IN CANADA

Contents

❦

VOLUME I

❦

❦

Contents of the companion volume
The Broadview Anthology of Drama: Plays from the Western Theatre
Volume II: The Nineteenth and Twentieth Centuries

August Strindberg
The Ghost Sonata (1908)
> Elizabeth Sprigge, trans.
> Craig S. Walker, ed.

Paul Green & Richard Wright
Native Son (1941)
> From the novel by Richard Wright
> Craig S. Walker, ed.

Bertolt Brecht
The Caucasian Chalk Circle (1948)
> Ralph Manheim, trans.
> Craig S. Walker, ed.

Tennessee Williams
Cat on a Hot Tin Roof (1955)
> Craig S. Walker, ed.

Samuel Beckett
Play (1963)
> Craig S. Walker, ed.

Michel Tremblay
Les Belles Soeurs (1968)
> John Van Burek & Bill Glassco, trans.
> Craig S. Walker, ed.

Wallace Shawn
Aunt Dan and Lemon (1985)
> Craig S. Walker, ed.

Tomson Highway
The Rez Sisters (1986)
> Craig S. Walker, ed.

Timberlake Wertenbaker
Our Country's Good (1989)
> Based on the novel *The Playmaker* by Thomas Keneally
> Craig S. Walker, ed.

Caryl Churchill
Mad Forest (1990)
> Craig S. Walker, ed.

Colleen Wagner
The Monument (1995)
> Craig S. Walker, ed.

Acknowledgements

We wish to extend our heartfelt thanks and appreciation to all the delightful people at Broadview Press: to president Don LePan, for his always cheerful encouragement; to Betsy Struthers, for her rights and permissions work; to Kathryn Brownsey, for her exacting inputting and proofreading; to Eileen Eckert, for her meticulous typesetting, copyediting and page layout, as well as for her excellent judgement and patience; and lastly but perhaps above all to Tammy Roberts, who kept us all going.

Jennifer Wise and Craig S. Walker

Introduction

Dramatic writing is designed to be spoken out loud, relished on the tongues of actors, and experienced as something close to music by a listening audience—which may be why plays so often do double duty as great poems. The works included in this anthology are no exception: many are regarded as the pinnacles of literary achievement in their respective languages. But the fact remains that drama, despite its literary pre-eminence, is not a purely literary genre. More than any other language art, drama is also a concrete social activity. It is the lasting manifestation of a tangible (if ephemeral) social practice, the theatre, whose business it is to assemble real living audiences in real public places in real time. Tied in this way to an interactive social event rooted in a precise, unrepeatable moment, drama cannot help but be marked by the extra-literary realities and contingencies of life. Theatre production is an occasion for staging plays, but it is also necessarily an exercise in finance and economics, a response to prevailing laws, an immediate casualty of and contributor to volatile political environments. Often in complete disregard of the literary intentions of the playwright, plays become intertwined through performance with prevailing religious practices and taboos; with the facts of urban planning and architectural design; with interruptions in the flow of goods, services and people because of wars and natural disasters; and with the prejudices and current concerns of the particular group of people who happen to have assembled on a given day to see it. Realism itself is actually very rare in drama and theatre in general, with most plays being constructed according to the logic of the dream, the fantasy, the wish-fulfillment and the cautionary tale. Indeed, playwrights create and transform reality more often than they endeavour simply to "represent" it. But all plays, even the least realistic, are forced nevertheless to contend with the ineluctable substratum of real bodies and things out of which theatre constitutes itself. As a type of real production in real historical time, theatre in consequence does not merely represent but always, to some extent, actually embodies the real world, its changing habits of dress, food and drug consumption, leisure, sex, gender differentiation, deportment, hygiene, marriage, civil disobedience, public speech, and political participation.

Our first principle in assembling this anthology has therefore been to acknowledge drama's special generic status as a type of literature in which meaning is inseparable from real moments in historical time. In practical terms this has meant accompanying each play with plenty of historical background in the form of context-rich introductory essays and detailed explanatory notes. But the principle has also guided our selection of plays. In choosing this particular handful of works to represent a vast literature that spreads over 2,500 years, thirteen different countries and almost as many languages, we aimed to do more than isolate forty-something "great plays" and arrange them in chronological order. Instead, we have tried to tell, as accurately as is possible with such a small sample, the ongoing story of Western theatre and drama—which, when properly understood, is the story of Western civilization. We have therefore chosen plays according to criteria that are not always, strictly speaking, literary. For example, the standard dramatic version of *Uncle Tom's Cabin*—included here for the first time in any major drama anthology—may appear to be a work of dubious quality when judged by literary standards alone. But as an event in world theatre history and in the history of slavery and racism, the play has enormous significance. Besides bringing unprecedented public attention to the atrocity of American slavery, *Uncle Tom's Cabin* was probably the most successful American play ever performed and certainly the most successful melodrama. Since melodrama remains the dominant form of storytelling around the world today and clearly retains its hold on our narrative imagination, it demands its place within any study of Western drama, despite its low reputation as a literary form.

This is not to say that inherent literary quality was not our primary requirement, as will be clear from our inclusion of such acknowledged masterpieces as *Oedipus*, *Hamlet*, *Phèdre*, *Tartuffe*, *The Way of the World*, *The Cherry Orchard*, and many others. But attention was also paid to the context of each play's creation and performance, its effects on audiences or later playwrights, and its role within the "big picture" of drama production generally. We were guided, in short, by a determination to include works whose historical significance was as demonstrable as their literary excellence. And by this we mean demonstrable not only for the country that produced it but internationally, within the whole of the Western theatrical tradition.

Our desire to give students an accurate picture of Western drama overall is also reflected in our inclusion of more plays from non-English-speaking nations than is customary in English-language anthologies. Representative plays from France, Germany, Italy, Spain, Russia, Norway, and Sweden, as well as ancient Greece and Rome, appear here, many in new translations commissioned especially for this anthology.

We were also keen to include a representative sample of plays by women from the pre-modern period. Seventeenth- and eighteenth-century playwrights such as Aphra Behn and Susannah Centlivre were among the most successful playwrights of their time; women have in fact been writing plays since the early Middle Ages, some of which, like the plays of Hroswitha and Hildegard, were among the only dramatic works being written at the time by anybody. Along with recognized gems of medieval drama such as *Everyman* and *The Second Shepherds' Play*, we have also included lesser-known works from the apparent inventors of two of the medieval theatre's most important genres, the saint's play and the morality play.

While hoping to moderate the gender imbalance that must to some degree characterize all historical anthologies such as these, we have also aimed to rectify a common generic imbalance: the preference within university textbooks for "serious" over comic plays. Long gone, we trust, is the old puritanical prejudice against laughter, with its unreasoned assumption that important ideas and experiences are not likely to coexist with amusement. Admittedly, comedy, so dependent on topical references and current events, on ephemeral scandals and passing fashions, even on brand- and street-names, can be a challenging genre to appreciate out of context, and previous anthologizers have understandably tended to shy away from it in favour of more universalist, metaphysical tragedies and "straight" plays. But the resulting picture of Western drama has been a distorted one. If anything, audiences throughout history show a slight preference for laughter over tears, and nothing is more revealing of a person's (or a period's) character than a look at what he or she laughs at. Comedy is the social form *par excellence* within a highly social art, and we have tried to restore it to its proper place by including a number of rarely anthologized comedies, each sufficiently well annotated to ensure that everybody gets all the jokes.

The general orientation of this book ideally suits it for use in theatre history surveys, as well as in literature courses at the undergraduate or graduate level that take a context-sensitive approach to drama. But at the same time, the book was designed with an eye to the needs of multi-genre English courses that approach literary texts thematically. In addition to its other merits, each play was selected for the opportunities it affords for cross-cultural, comparative readings of differing reflections on similar themes. Revenge and forgiveness, master/slave relations, *femmes fatales*, forbidden sex, passion vs. reason, the construction of self within marginalized social groups, the "angry young man," gender stereotyping, marriage, women's empowerment, tyranny and rebellion in the family and the state, law, commerce, role-playing and identity, and the transformative power of theatre itself—these and other perennial dramatic and literary themes can be found in at least two and sometimes several plays. Plays were also selected to ensure representation of a wide range of dramatic sub-genres: tragedy, political satire, situation comedy, morality, farce, tragi-comedy, romance, comedy of manners, fairytale, melodrama, naturalist drama, and allegory.

The anthology consists of six chronologically organised chapters: The Ancient Theatre, Medieval Drama, The Renaissance, and The Enlightenment Stage (Volume One); The Nineteenth Century, and The Twentieth Century: Modernism and After (Volume Two). Each chapter begins with a general introduction that sketches in the main currents of thought and literary practice, as well as the changing trends in theatre production, audience behaviour, and economic and political life that characterize the period. Individual plays are then preceded by their own introduction which locates them more narrowly within the biography and literary output of their author, explains relevant details in their production history, and provides interpretive assistance in approaching them today. As for explanatory footnotes, we have tried to strike a balance between helpfulness and unobtrusiveness, a balance that is more difficult to achieve with some plays than others. Having taught these plays for many years in the classroom, we were guided above all by the needs of our students; in all our annotations, we have tried to anticipate frequently asked questions, to illuminate obscure allusions, and provide translations and glosses that have enriched students' reading experience of these plays in the past. Further assistance and background materials are available on the evolving website of *The Broadview Anthology of Drama* <http://www.broadviewpress.com/drama>. Here may be found production illustrations, historical documents, theoretical statements, and a selection of useful links to theatre and drama websites notable for their academic rigour and comprehensiveness.

The Roman theorist Horace famously said that drama's purpose is to delight and instruct. We hope this book does likewise. We dedicate it to all our students, past, present, and future.

CHAPTER ONE

The Ancient Theatre

The Greek plays that dominate this chapter on the ancient theatre comprise some of the greatest masterpieces ever written for the stage by any nation, in any age. Along with the architectural marvels of the Acropolis, the philosophical works of Plato and Aristotle, and the perfectly inspiring—if imperfectly realized—ideal of Athenian democracy, the tragedies and comedies of Athens in the fifth century B.C.E. represent intellectual and artistic high-water marks against which we have been measuring our accomplishments ever since. This is especially remarkable given that Aeschylus, Sophocles, and Euripides were inventing the art of the stage even as they produced some of its most enduring works. Unlike the best of subsequent playwrights, like Marlowe and Shakespeare, Molière and Racine, and Schiller and Goethe, who benefited from two millennia's worth of drama anthologies like these, the dramatists of fifth-century Athens had nobody to imitate, no preexisting models to work from.

Or rather, they had many—but none that had yet taken on a specifically dramatic form. For when drama first emerged in Athens in the sixth century B.C.E., it did so as the newest addition to a long tradition of poetic composition that stretched back for centuries in the Greek world, possibly as far as the Bronze Age civilization of Mycenae (1600–1125 B.C.E.). At first exclusively oral, this poetic tradition started to be well documented in the seventh century B.C.E., when a fully phonetic writing system was available—or, as some believe, was specifically invented—to record it. Its main genres were epic, lyric, and choral poetry, and unlike today, all three were always performed out loud, to instrumental accompaniment, before a listening audience; this remained the case even in the fifth century, the age of drama, when such poetry was studied at school and memorized from written copies. The first dramatists drew on this exceptionally rich and well-developed poetic legacy in creating a genre that was seen as a "mixture." From epic poetry—which is known to us today mainly through the long narrative poems of Homer, the *Iliad* and the *Odyssey*—theatre borrowed countless mythological stories and characters, as well as poetic methods for imitating their speech and actions. (Athens' first great tragic poet, Aeschylus, is recorded as having said that he wrote his plays by carving thick slices from the banquets of Homer.) From solo lyric—which, like epic poetry, was sung to the lyre or kithara (harp-like guitars)—drama took techniques for writing the kind of subjective monologues perfected by Sappho (b. 7th century), one of Greece's finest lyricists and its best-known female poet. To choral lyric (from the Greek word *chōros*, meaning dance) drama is equally indebted, for all fifth-century tragedies and comedies featured large singing and dancing choruses: eventually fifteen members for tragedy and twenty-four for comedy. (In fact, the earliest sixth-century playwrights, Thespis and Phrynichus, were remembered for their dance steps as much as for their poetry, virtually none of which survives.) Perhaps the most famous form of choral poetry today is the dithyramb, a lofty, formal sort of poem that was originally sung in praise of the Greek wine-god, Dionysus—which is to say, while drunk. Drama incorporated other genres as well, such as iambic poetry, and contributed some poetic techniques of its own, notably *stichomythia*. (This rapid-fire exchange of questions and answers, so suggestive of a witness under cross-examination, and now considered the most 'dramatic' of all compositional styles, was probably borrowed not from any form of poetry but from the type of discourse heard daily in Athens' huge public law courts.) As we move from the dramas of Aeschylus through to those of Euripides later in the fifth century, we see a shift toward ever more iambic dialogue and ever less choral narration. But regardless of the changes ancient drama underwent through time, including the disappearance of the dancing chorus from comedy after Aristophanes, plays continued to be composed in verse.

Of the three kinds of drama written in fifth-century Athens—tragedy, satyr play, and comedy—tragedy emerged first, and helped to shape the others. If we can trust the few surviving scraps of evidence on the subject, it seems that two poets, Arion and Thespis, share responsibility for tragedy's invention. Arion was a late-seventh-century kithara player who is said to have written the first tragedy by adding verse-speaking satyrs to a dithyramb (which he wrote on a subject other than Dionysus). Arion's poetic hybrid—surprisingly, given how serious tragedy was to become—is said to have been funny, even ridiculous: satyrs, the mythic goat-men who accompany Dionysus, were known for their comically perpetual hunger (for sex) and thirst (for wine). Arion's laughable new invention was called *tragōidia*, "the song of the goat-singers." By Aeschylus's time, these goat-men had disappeared from tragedy proper, finding a home in a sub-genre of their own, the satyr play, which made up but one part of a complete tragic tetralogy (one comic satyr play and three tragedies). Only one satyr play has survived in its entirety, Euripides' *Cyclops*, but along with fragments of others it shows that satyr plays were mythological burlesques in which the chorus dressed in satyr costume—that is, in little more than a goat's tail and ears, a *phallus* (artificial penis), and a pair of shaggy goat-skin briefs. If true, this story about Arion's addition of satyrs to a dithyramb could explain how tragedy, satyr play, and their sister-genre, comedy, all came to be performed at festivals celebrating the wine-god. Even though the vast majority of Athenian drama has "nothing to do with Dionysus," as the ancient proverb goes, tragedy's possible roots in an ode to alcohol may have been enough to associate theatre with Dionysus thereafter.

Tragedy's other important innovator was allegedly Thespis, a poet and performer in whose honour actors have been called thespians ever since. After experimenting with white lead and other substances, Thespis is said to have devised a plain linen mask to disguise his face (and enable him to impersonate multiple characters: ancient actors played more than one part in a given play). Masks of animals and deities had probably long existed for religious purposes in the Greek world, but Thespis's use of a human mask in a performance of a poem was evidently a novelty (probably around 534). Along with Arion's satyrs, Thespis's mask shaped tragedy's development in key ways, particularly with respect to women's roles. Athenian women were not considered citizens of the city-state, a privilege that accrued only to land-owning males. As a result, women were barred from participation in all civic activities, including theatre. (Women's public performances were strictly confined to the religious sphere.) With a mask, however, it was no more difficult for a bearded Athenian male to impersonate a queen than a king, and poets accordingly created roles indiscriminately of gender. In contrast to Shakespeare—who likewise worked within a male-only theatre culture, but whose reliance on prepubescent boys for women's parts constrained both the quantity and quality of his female roles—the Greek tragedians, writing for mature men in masks, created as many great roles for female as for male characters.

Thespis's invention also made tragedy into the most "people-pleasing" genre of poetry in Greece. Thanks to the mask, story-telling suddenly had a visual component, an element of illusion, of "seeing" mythological gods and heroes on stage before one's eyes, whereas earlier poets had impersonated them through words alone. Performed in the *theatron*, Greek for "the viewing place," tragedy and subsequent drama were poems whose stories were *seen*. From this first visual aid, innovations in costume design and scenography followed. Aeschylus is credited with creating tragic costumes so exotically impressive that they were imitated by the priests of Greek religious cults. Comedy, by contrast, developed an exaggeratedly undignified costume consisting of a prominent *phallus*, short tunic, and padded, flesh-coloured tights. And whereas tragic masks seem to have been fairly generic—except perhaps for the bloody-eyed mask of Oedipus—those used in Old Comedy sometimes depicted real people: the masks for Aristophanes' *Frogs*, for example, probably featured recognizable likenesses of Aeschylus and Euripides. Other visual aspects of tragedy and comedy included a large circular dancing floor for the chorus (the *orchestra*), and a scene house, called the *skēnē* (from which we get *proskenion*, or proscenium). The *skēnē* served for actors' entrances, exits, and costume changes, as well as for housing the theatre's special-effects machines: a roof-mounted mechanical crane with a harness for flying actors down into (or up and away from) the action, and a wheeled platform for rolling "dead bodies" and other pre-set tableaux out through the *skēnē*'s central doors.

One thing, however, that Arion and Thespis did not change about poetic performance was its competitive aspect: Greek poetry was often performed at large outdoor competitions, like a spectator sport, for prizes. Such festive competitions, which also featured religious parades and rituals, revelry, drinking, and huge state-funded barbeques, had been widely held throughout the Greek world for centuries before drama appeared. Athens' big summer festival, the Panathenaia, specialized in epic poetry, and its spring festivals, held in honour of "wet nature" (the wine and sprouting vines that were Dionysus's domain), were selected as appropriate venues for drama. Tragedy had been an official prize category since at least 534 B.C.E., and comedy was added later, in 486. All of the Greek plays included in this chapter competed at one of Athens' two main spring festivals: either the Great (or City) Dionysia, to whose poetry contests visitors, tourists, colonials, and allies from far and wide were invited; or the Lenaia, the less prestigious of the two, meant for Athenians only.

The entries were written, produced, and performed by some of Athens' most prominent citizens. Rehearsed over months for a single performance, they were staged in the open-air Theatre of Dionysus—which can still be found today, although much rebuilt, on the southern slope of the Acropolis—for noisy, cat-calling, foot-stomping spectators numbering between ten and fourteen thousand, at least some of whom were women. Poets and actors received a token fee from the city, and spectators did have to pay for the fiercely fought-over tickets, of which there were never enough, but nobody earned his living from the theatre in this period (except perhaps the cleaning company: Athenians ate nuts and other snacks throughout the shows). No attempt was made to recoup the huge sums of money that went into mounting these plays. Up to sixty masks and costumes were required for a single tragic tetralogy, and three of these competed each year. Furthermore, new and ever more dazzling masks and costumes had to be conceived and constructed from one year to the next: Greek theatre was an *agōn*, a contest (from which comes prot*agon*ist, "the first contestant," among other words), and the Athenian audience was a demanding and discriminating judge. Neither a profession nor a trade, theatre in fifth-century Athens was a civic institution, and one deemed so vital to the city that rich citizens were pressured into footing the bill, and all citizens received a theatre allowance so that everyone could afford to attend. Athenian theatre may have been an amateur activity, but it brought as much political prestige and social respect as could be gained from participation in any of Athens' highest offices, whether political, juridical, religious, or military.

As for the military, more must be said. In fact there is no way to grasp the essential character of Greek tragedy and comedy without it. Fifth-century Athens was basically a military state, almost perpetually at war. Between 490 and 479 B.C.E. Athens won the battles known collectively as the Persian Wars, and the subsequent development of Athenian society was much indebted to these victories. It was in their immediate aftermath, after Athens' thrillingly, implausibly heroic defeat of the much mightier Persian army, that Athenian drama came into its own. Unlike Athens, which prided itself on its democratic institutions (established by 508), the Persian enemy from the east was, at least in Athenian eyes, a lawless and barbaric monarchy. Athens' triumph over this formidable invader seemed to demonstrate for all Athenians thereafter the superiority of their own egalitarian values and democratic way of life.[1] In addition to growing tremendously nationalistic and confident (or, as some said, obnoxiously arrogant), Athens also became vastly rich and, for a while, almost unchallengeably powerful. The city's enormous political might during the fifth century should be borne in mind when reading the tragedies written for its theatre: their ethical warnings to "count no man happy till his last day is done," their injunctions to remember that "wisdom comes alone through suffering" and that moderation should rule in all things, were delivered to a city intoxicated, above all, by its own greatness.

After repulsing Persia and at its allies' urging, Athens took control of the military alliance against future Persian aggression. Up to 200 states contributed money annually to this alliance, known as the Delian League, whose policies were largely set by Pericles, Athens' military commander. After 454, when its treasury was moved to Athens, Delian League revenues were used—or, as Pericles' critics said, misappropriated—for rebuilding the Acropolis and the theatre, as well as for new construction (of the indoor Odeon, for example, where theatrical previews were staged). Pericles also established the theoric fund to help poorer citizens attend the theatre—a fund that covered not only tickets but expenses related to travelling to the city or ceasing work for the duration of the festival, which for most of the fifth century lasted five days.

The Great Dionysia was in fact timed to coincide with the arrival in town each year of envoys bearing the military dues from Athens' allies. During the festival's opening ceremonies, these pots of silver were carried and displayed upon the stage, a powerful symbol indeed of Athenian military dominance and its resulting wealth. Not only in such pre-performance ceremonies, but throughout the plays themselves, Athenian theatre reflected the city's military values, accomplishments, and in-

---

1 Egalitarian and democratic, that is, in comparison with previous systems of monarchy and tyranny. Athens was a slave-holding state that gave no rights to women. What was radical about Athenian democracy is that all land-owning males had an equal say in political decisions, regardless of wealth or status, and all shared power equally, with civic offices being filled, by lot, with ordinary citizens on a rotating basis. Only the position of military general was by election—an office to which Pericles was re-elected many times.

terests. After Phrynichus's experience with *The Sack of Miletus* in 492, when the poet presented a play about a recent military catastrophe and was indicted and fined for unduly upsetting the audience by reminding them of it, tragedians only rarely treated current events directly, relying instead on ancient myths of topical relevance (Trojan War stories, for example). By contrast, Old Comedy enjoyed almost complete licence to discuss the military situation explicitly and satirize the city's leaders by name. (Aristophanes was repeatedly taken to court by one of the targets of his ridicule on slander and other charges, but he seems to have defended himself successfully each time.) Theatre's strong connection with Athenian military culture was embodied also in the dancing chorus of tragedy, which at some point came to be made up of young men freshly graduated from their military training. To the sounds of the martial *aulos*—a sort of double oboe, probably rather bagpipe-like in timbre—they danced in military rank-and-file across the *orchestra*, displaying for local and far-flung audiences alike the cream of Athens' annual crop of new recruits. Today we may be inclined to think of poets like Aeschylus as men of the theatre, since they wrote, directed, designed, choreographed, and in some cases even danced and acted in their plays. But they are likelier to have thought of themselves as citizen-soldiers, generals, and defenders of Athens' fledgling democracy.

Theatre's central role in Athenian life went beyond the military, of course. In the Theatre of Dionysus, the city communally reflected upon all the political, legal, moral, ethical, and religious dilemmas of the day—and especially on the meaning of its shared cultural inheritance, its ancient myths. The theatre was a place where, in a very concrete way, the city put its democratic ideals into practice, where it questioned, criticized, and updated both its narrative legacy and its own self-image. It has often been said that a small participatory democracy like Athens ultimately invented theatre because it *needed* it, needed a way for citizens to assemble and think through—emotionally, intellectually, and even physically—the issues of central concern to a free and self-governing people.

With the loss of its political autonomy after its defeat in the Peloponnesian War (431–404 B.C.E.), and with the rise of Philip of Macedon and his son Alexander the Great (356–323), Athens became a mere satellite state in an empire ruled from elsewhere. Theatre continued to thrive in Athens through the fourth century, but its nature changed in ways that reflected the new political situation as well as the fact that theatre was now a cultural export rather than primarily a local institution. The *ad hominem*, topical political satire of Aristophanic Old Comedy was replaced by the "New" situation comedy of Menander (342–292), which featured no animal choruses, no bum and penis jokes, no references to local current events, and no life-like masks of Athenians such as Socrates and Euripides. Instead, it focused on familial and marital situations of sufficiently universal appeal to be suitable for the export market. For during this Hellenistic period—when Alexander brought the culture of the Hellenes, or Greeks, to much of the known world as he conquered it as far east as India— Athenian-style theatres were built throughout the Middle East and Asia Minor, and they needed plays. The cultural capital of Greek civilization shifted to Alexandria in Egypt, where librarians and book-copyists catalogued and preserved hundreds of thousands of works of ancient literature, as well as the thousands of plays of classical Athens (now mostly lost). Tragedy continued to compete at the festivals along with New Comedy, but it became an interpreter's, rather than a poet's, art: the Theatre of Dionysus in the fourth century began to stage revivals of fifth-century classics, particularly those of Euripides, the favourite with actors, who for their part were growing increasingly specialized and who soon formed a union (the Artists of Dionysus). It was during this period of remountings by professional actors that Aristotle (384–322) wrote his *Poetics* and his lost treatise on comedy. The former work of dramatic theory contains the most influential definition of tragedy ever written, and one which came to have a huge, albeit largely negative, role in shaping the form tragedy took when it was revived after the Renaissance.

Meanwhile, it was during the Hellenistic period and the following centuries that the Roman Republic emerged as a major power to the west. Along with North Africa, Spain, Britain, and most of the rest of Europe and Asia Minor, Greece was eventually conquered by Rome and absorbed into its empire. Although the more aggressively warlike and stoical Romans were at first suspicious of Greek civilization for its perceived effeminizing effects, the Roman elite came to admire Greek culture for its obviously superior learning—its poetry, philosophy, science, mathematics, and history— and emulated it widely. Romans sent their sons to be educated in Greece or by Greek teachers, learned to read and speak Greek themselves, decorated their homes with images of Athenian drama, and imitated Greek tragedy and comedy on their stages. But because of the very different social and political organization of the Roman Republic, and then the Roman Empire, the theatre of Rome resembled that of Athens in name only.

The sheer size of Rome made it almost ungovernable; it could certainly not be governed by the citizens themselves, who numbered in the millions, rather than in the tens of thousands, as in Athens. Civil wars led by rival political factions, self-aggrandizing military adventurers, and eventually the dictatorship of emperors who claimed to be gods—these and other political realities made Rome too bloated and bloody a place for Athenian-style theatre to thrive. Instead, magistrates and patrician families vied for popularity with, and control over, an ever more unruly and discontented mass of uneducated plebeians, slaves, and subject peoples from around the world. Land shortages, grain shortages, and other serious social problems endemic to Rome's extremely unequal distribution of wealth brought about the "bread and circuses" approach to politics for which Rome has since been infamous. Theatrical events, like so many loaves of bread, were distributed for free in Rome throughout the year—not as a special form of civic participation, eagerly awaited and rehearsed over months, but as an almost daily hand-out to placate the mob, to win its favour and its votes. Whereas actors in Athens had been among the city's best citizens, in Rome they were drawn from the empire's lowest ranks. Like male and female gladiators, who were brought to Rome as slaves and trained to fight and die in Roman amphitheatres for the pleasure of bloodthirsty crowds, actors of both genders were often slaves or criminals and lacked all civil rights, even the right to leave the profession. Like many gladiators, some actors did achieve great fame, but they were also likely to be put to death by the very emperors who had once put gems on their fingers. Murderous anti-slander laws meant that poets, too, took their life into their hands each time they offered a play to the public. In any case, the glut of games and entertainments meant that plays often failed to gain an audience at all. Plays were forced to compete in Rome not against other plays, as in Athens, but against various kinds of nonfictional spectacles. In the pornographic mimes, the animal acts, gladiatorial contests, chariot races, and mock sea-battles that were more to the taste of the audience than plays, public viewing spaces were given over to "reality" shows that featured real suffering, real blood, and real death.

Despite their disconnectedness from the popular taste, tragedies, comedies, and satyr plays were all written in Rome nevertheless. The nine Greek-style tragedies of Seneca (c.4 B.C.E.–65 C.E.) are especially noteworthy, partly because they were to have a more profound influence on Renaissance tragedians than their Greek originals. Comedy, however, was the more popular genre with Roman audiences. The *Miles Gloriosus* of Plautus reproduced here, like all Roman comedy, is essentially a Greek New Comedy rewritten in Latin and adjusted to local tastes, as well as to the long narrow stage of the Roman theatre. Like its Greek model, it features stock character-masks and conventional situations from private life. The other important comic playwright in Rome was Terence (d. 159 B.C.E.), a former North African slave whose lovely style and skill with subplots were widely imitated by such later dramatists as Hroswitha, Shakespeare, and Wycherley.

The theatres built in Rome and across its empire were technically sophisticated, opulent, and almost fully enclosed against the outside world. New technologies of poured concrete allowed for the construction of free-standing semicircular buildings with retractable overhead awnings, air-conditioning systems, and separate tunnel-like entrances for the audience from behind the seats at street level (a method of access that we still call a *vomitorium*). In place of the Greek scene house, which permitted a view of the natural landscape beyond, the Romans erected an elaborately ornamented architectural façade, three stories tall, which served as the permanent backdrop for all plays, generally representing the doorways, windows, and balconies of a number of houses along a street. In keeping with its domestic and largely non-political stories, Roman comedy lacks a chorus; the fully circular dance floor of the Athenian theatre atrophied to a half-moon.

In August of 410 C.E., the city of Rome was entered, plundered, and completely sacked in a matter of days by Alaric, leader of the Visigoths. Greece had already fallen to this Germanic tribe earlier in the decade. After almost a millennium of continuous theatrical activity in Athens and Rome, theatre effectively came to an end in the western world—for the next thousand years. The physical destruction of these great pagan cities might not in itself have caused such a long hiatus. But in the century leading up to the barbarian invasions that reduced them to rubble, another force had arisen in Rome—one so hostile to actors and plays, and so successful at wresting control of all aspects of western culture, that tragedies and comedies would not be written and performed again with any regularity in Europe for nearly ten centuries. This force was Roman Christianity; and its efforts to suppress and eliminate theatre and drama—and occasionally to exploit them—make up the subject matter of the next chapter.

[J.W.]

AESCHYLUS
The Oresteia

As a poet and actor, Aeschylus (525–456 B.C.E.) began competing in the Athenian theatre festival in 499, and winning in 484. But in 468, after some twelve victories, he suffered defeat at the hands of a handsome young upstart, the 27-year-old Sophocles. The *Oresteia* not only restored Aeschylus's supremacy in an art-form he had helped to create, but set standards for tragedy that playwrights have been trying to live up to ever since. Its victory in 458 was to be Aeschylus's last, however; he died two years later in Sicily, having written between 70 and 90 plays.

Like most if not all of Aeschylus's work, the *Oresteia* was performed as a tetralogy: three related tragedies and a comic satyr play (*Proteus*, now lost—along with all but seven of his plays). As the single example of a complete Greek tragic trilogy that has come down to us, and as one of the earliest of all the tragedies that we possess, the *Oresteia* is an unusually important play, affording us a rare glimpse of the sheer magnitude of tragic art in its first flourishing. As we see from Aristophanes' end-of-the-century portrait of him in *Frogs*, Aeschylus was long to remain synonymous with the glory days of tragedy; after his death his stature was such that anyone wanting to revive a play of Aeschylus was automatically given financial support by the city.

Named after Orestes, the son called upon to avenge his father's death and his mother's villainy, the trilogy is based on mythological material that had been familiar to the Greeks for hundreds of years. (It is also the first in a long line of dysfunctional royal family dramas of which *Hamlet* is an obvious later example—complete with an opening scene of watchmen on the roof, exhortations to revenge from the ghost of a slain parent, and the resulting near-madness of the son.) In its basic outline, it is a story of the endless cycle of seduction, betrayal, murder and payback violence that can blight a family through the generations, and it was memorized by every schoolboy of Aeschylus's time by way of the *Odyssey* of Homer.

As Homer tells the story, the victorious general Agamemnon comes home after a decade of fighting in the Trojan war, only to find that his wife Klytemestra has been seduced by Aigisthos, his treason-plotting cousin. Having conspired in his absence, the lovers assassinate the king on his return to Argos—stabbing him during his welcome-home party along with Cassandra, a souvenir from the city he sacked. As is fitting in a monarchy, the murdered king's son Orestes then kills the usurper in turn, restoring himself as rightful heir to his father's throne: "so it is good, when a man has perished, to have a son left after him, since this one took vengeance on his father's killer, the treacherous Aigisthos" (*Od.* Book 3, 196–198).

Like all Greek tragic poets, however, Aeschylus subjects his inherited narrative material to a thorough-going reinterpretation, reshaping it so that the ancient myth becomes, among other things, an occasion for discussing matters of current political concern to the audience in the theatre. Aeschylus's choice of a story about inter-family violence in the House of Pelops was itself a topical one, given that he was writing in the middle of the First Peloponnesian War, a protracted Greek-against-Greek conflict with Sparta that Athens would eventually lose, in 404. By beginning the play with powerful speeches about the suffering and deprivations of battle, Aeschylus seems to be indicting war generally—an impression strongly reinforced by his re-imagining of Klytemestra. In place of the "sluttish" and passive conduit of evil that we find in Homer, Agamemnon's murderer in the *Oresteia* is pointedly reconceived as a civilian casualty, understandably aggrieved by her husband's militarism, his slaughter of her first-born child, his ten-year absence, his infidelity. (Having fought in the famous battles of Marathon and Salamis against the Persians in 490 and 480, Aeschylus knew the costs of soldiering first-hand.) And Argos, where most of the play is set, was not merely a legendary storybook monarchy to Aeschylus and his Athenian audience, but a real-life neighbouring city-state with which they had just, three years earlier, entered into a military alliance against Sparta.

But 461, the year of the Argive alliance, was also an important year for developments within Athens, and these too are reflected in the *Oresteia*. It was the year in which the Athenian statesman Ephialtes successfully implemented a number of radical reforms to the city's legal and political systems, reforms that had the effect of completing the process of democratisation begun in 508, when Aeschylus was 17. Although the Athenian idea of democracy falls far short of ours today, as full citizenship was granted only to land-owning, Athenian-born males, it did represent a major advance, in fairness and accountability, over the systems of monarchy and tyranny that it replaced, and the *Oresteia* is infused with its egalitarian spirit.

Rather than by kings only, the story of Orestes is largely told in the *Oresteia* by Argos's and Athens' least powerful residents: by crippled old war-vets, by captive female slaves, by foreigners.[1] Besides democratizing the point of view in the telling, Aeschylus also rewrites the story itself, transforming it from an exemplary lesson in vengeance for young princes into a celebration of the new democratic legal system of Athens. In the elaborate courtroom drama that serves as the trilogy's climax, Aeschylus proudly displays all the trappings of democratic law, the justice system in which the people (*demos*) have the power (*kratos*) to decide, through public inquiry into the facts of the case, what had previously been determined by the private sword of familial revenge. Orestes' acquittal, despite the weakness of the arguments that Athena uses to secure it, nevertheless marks a victory for democracy over the brute power of kings and tyrants, for justice over vengeance, for civilization over the lawless cycle of retributive violence, curses, murder, and blood-guilt which, in the absence of properly legal remedies, must go on unchecked *ad infinitum*.

Each play in the trilogy represents a stage of Athens' political development, from monarchy (*Agamemnon*) through tyranny (*Libation Bearers*) to the democracy that triumphs in *Eumenides*. In the final play—the costumes for which were said to be so terrifying that women in the audience suffered miscarriages—the bloodthirsty spirit of vengeance is pacified at last in Athena's courtroom, and the trilogy ends with a joyful exit-song in which the audience would have participated. As was perhaps the case in tragic trilogies generally, the *Oresteia* thus ends happily, with a celebration of the establishment of a new era of justice and peace—not only in the mythical royal household of Orestes, but in the real-life democracies at Athens and Argos.

---

[1] The Furies are portrayed as "metics" in Athens, resident aliens.

AESCHYLUS

Agamemnon

translated by Richmond Lattimore

CHARACTERS[1]
WATCHMAN
KLYTEMESTRA
HERALD
AGAMEMNON
CASSANDRA
AIGISTHOS
CHORUS OF ARGIVE ELDERS
ATTENDANTS OF KLYTEMESTRA; OF
   AGAMEMNON; BODYGUARD OF AIGISTHOS
   (all silent parts)

Time: directly after the fall of Troy.

SCENE: *Argos, before the palace of King Agamemnon.*
THE WATCHMAN, who speaks the opening lines, is
posted on the roof of the palace. KLYTEMESTRA's
entrances are made from a door in the center of the
stage; all others, from the wings.

[*THE WATCHMAN, alone.*]

I ask the gods some respite from the weariness
of this watchtime measured by years I lie awake
elbowed upon the Atreidae's[2] roof dogwise to mark
the grand processionals of all the stars of night
burdened with winter and again with heat for men,   5
dynasties in their shining blazoned on the air,
these stars, upon their wane and when the rest
   arise.

I wait; to read the meaning in that beacon light,
a blaze of fire to carry out of Troy the rumour

and outcry of its capture; to such end a lady's[3]   10
male strength of heart in its high confidence ordains.
Now as this bed stricken with night and drenched
   with dew
I keep, nor ever with kind dreams for company:
since fear in sleep's place stands forever at my head
against strong closure of my eyes, or any rest: 15
I mince such medicine against sleep failed: I sing,
only to weep again the pity of this house
no longer, as once, administered in the grand way.
Now let there be again redemption from distress,
the flare burning from the blackness in good   20
   augury.

[*A light shows in the distance.*]

Oh hail, blaze of the darkness, harbinger of
day's shining, and of processionals and dance and
   choirs
of multitudes in Argos for this day of grace.
Ahoy!
I cry the news aloud to Agamemnon's queen,   25
that she may rise up from her bed of state with speed
to raise the rumour of gladness welcoming this
   beacon,
and singing rise, if truly the citadel of Ilium[4]
has fallen, as the shining of this flare proclaims.
I also, I, will make my choral prelude, since   30
my lord's dice cast aright are counted as my own,
and mine the tripled sixes of this torch-lit throw.[5]

May it only happen. May my king come home,
   and I
take up within this hand the hand I love. The rest
I leave to silence; for an ox stands huge upon   35

---

1 For consistency's sake, the English spellings of Greek
  names in the first part of the trilogy have been altered
  slightly.
2 The sons of Atreus: Agamemnon and his brother
  Menelaus.

---

3 Klytemestra, Agamemnon's wife.
4 Troy.
5 Three sixes being a perfect dice throw, the Watchman is
  speaking of his great good luck.

my tongue. The house itself, could it take voice,
  might speak
aloud and plain. I speak to those who understand,
but if they fail, I have forgotten everything.

[*Exit. THE CHORUS enters, speaking.*]

Ten years since the great contestants
of Priam's[6] right,   40
Menelaus and Agamemnon, my lord,
twin throned, twin sceptered, in twofold power
of kings from God, the Atreidae,
put forth from this shore
the thousand ships of the Argives,[7]   45
the strength and the armies.
Their cry of war went shrill from the heart,
as eagles stricken in agony
for young perished, high from the nest
eddy and circle   50
to bend and sweep of the wings' stroke,
lost far below
the fledgelings, the nest, and the tendance.
Yet someone hears in the air, a god,
Apollo, Pan, or Zeus, the high   55
thin wail of these sky-guests, and drives
late to its mark
the Fury upon the transgressors.

So drives Zeus the great guest god
the Atreidae against Alexander:[8]   60
for one woman's promiscuous sake
the struggling masses, legs tired,
knees grinding in dust,
spears broken in the onset.
Danaans[9] and Trojans   65
they have it alike. It goes as it goes
now. The end will be destiny.

---

6 King of Troy.
7 The Greeks who sailed from Argos to sack Troy.
8 Or Paris, prince of Troy, whose theft of Helen from
   Menelaus precipitated the Trojan War. Zeus is described
   as the "guest god" because Paris's abduction took place
   while he was Menelaus's guest, a grave violation of the
   sacred laws of hospitality.
9 Greeks.

You cannot burn flesh or pour unguents,
not innocent cool tears,
that will soften the gods' stiff anger.   70

But we; dishonoured, old in our bones,
cast off even then from the gathering horde,
stay here, to prop up
on staves the strength of a baby.
Since the young vigour that urges   75
inward to the heart
is frail as age, no warcraft yet perfect,
while beyond age, leaf
withered, man goes three footed
no stronger than a child is,   80
a dream that falters in daylight.

[*KLYTEMESTRA enters quietly. THE CHORUS
continues to speak.*]

But you, lady,
daughter of Tyndareus, Klytemestra, our queen:
What is there to be done? What new thing have
  you heard?
In persuasion of what   85
report do you order such sacrifice?
To all the gods of the city,
the high and the deep spirits,
to them of the sky and the market places,
the altars blaze with oblations.   90
The staggered flame goes sky high
one place, then another,
drugged by the simple soft
persuasion of sacred unguents,
the deep stored oil of the kings.   95
Of these things what can be told
openly, speak.
Be healer to this perplexity
that grows now into darkness of thought,
while again sweet hope shining from the flames   100
beats back the pitiless pondering
of sorrow that eats my heart.

I have mastery yet to chant the wonder at the
  wayside
given to kings. Still by God's grace there surges
  within me
singing magic   105

grown to my life and power,
how the wild bird portent
hurled forth the Achaeans'[10]
twin-stemmed power single hearted,
lords of the youth of Hellas,   110
with spear and hand of strength
to the land of Teucrus.
Kings of birds to the kings of the ships,[11]
one black, one blazed with silver,
clear seen by the royal house   115
on the right, the spear hand,
they lighted, watched by all
tore a hare, ripe, bursting with young unborn yet,
stayed from her last fleet running.
Sing sorrow, sorrow: but good win out in the end.   120

Then the grave seer[12] of the host saw through to
    the hearts divided,
knew the fighting sons of Atreus feeding on the hare
with the host, their people.[13]
Seeing beyond, he spoke:
"With time, this foray   125
shall stalk the castle of Priam.
Before then, under
the walls, Fate shall spoil
in violence the rich herds of the people.
Only let no doom of the gods darken   130
upon this huge iron forged to curb Troy—
from inward. Artemis[14] the undefiled
is angered with pity
at the flying hounds of her father[15]
eating the unborn young in the hare and the   135
    shivering mother.
She is sick at the eagles' feasting.

Sing sorrow, sorrow: but good win out in the end.

Lovely you[16] are and kind
to the tender young of ravening lions.
For sucklings of all the savage   140
beasts that lurk in the lonely places you have
    sympathy.
Grant meaning to these appearances
good, yet not without evil.
Healer Apollo,[17] I pray you
let her not with cross winds   145
bind the ships of the Danaans
to time-long anchorage
forcing a second sacrifice unholy, untasted,
working bitterness in the blood
and faith lost. For the terror returns like sickness 150
    to lurk in the house;
the secret anger remembers the child that shall be
    avenged."[18]
Such, with great good things beside, rang out in
    the voice of Calchas,
these fatal signs from the birds by the way to the
    house of the princes,
wherewith in sympathy
sing sorrow, sorrow: but good win out in the end.   155

Zeus: whatever he may be, if this name
pleases him in invocation,
thus I call upon him.
I have pondered everything
yet I cannot find a way,   160
only Zeus, to cast this dead weight of ignorance
finally from out my brain.

He who in time long ago was great,
throbbing with gigantic strength,
shall be as if he never were, unspoken.   165
He who followed him has found

---

10 Greeks.
11 Two eagles, soon to be associated with Zeus, who ripped
   open a pregnant hare and devoured her offspring in full
   view of the assembled army.
12 Calchas, whose job it was to interpret such signs; the
   Greeks viewed the behaviour of birds as significant.
13 I.e., saw the eagles' savagery as symbolic of the kings'
   people-devouring war.
14 Goddess of the hunt and childbirth; Apollo's twin sister
   and Zeus's virgin daughter.
15 Zeus's eagles.

16 Artemis.
17 Major Greek deity, and brother of Artemis. God of
   prophecy, healing, archery, music and painting.
18 Reference to the sacrifice that Artemis demanded of
   Agamemnon: to alter the winds that were holding up the
   expedition to Troy, he would have to sacrifice his first-
   born, Iphigeneia.

his master, and is gone.
Cry aloud without fear the victory of Zeus,
you will not have failed the truth:

Zeus, who guided men to think,   170
who has laid it down that wisdom
comes alone through suffering.
Still there drips in sleep against the heart
grief of memory; against
our pleasure we are temperate.   175
From the gods who sit in grandeur
grace comes somehow violent.

On that day the elder king
of the Achaean ships, no more
strict against the prophet's word,   180
turned with the crosswinds of fortune,
when no ship sailed, no pail was full,
and the Achaean people sulked
fast against the shore at Aulis[19]
facing Chalcis, where the tides ebb and surge: 185

and winds blew from the Strymon,[20] bearing
sick idleness, ships tied fast, and hunger,
distraction of the mind, carelessness
for hull and cable;
with time's length bent to double measure   190
by delay crumbled the flower and pride
of Argos. Then against the bitter wind
the seer's voice clashed out
another medicine
more hateful yet, and spoke of Artemis, so that   195
   the kings
dashed their staves to the ground and could not
   hold their tears.

The elder lord spoke aloud before them:
"My fate is angry if I disobey these,
but angry if I slaughter
this child, the beauty of my house,   200
with maiden blood shed staining
these father's hands beside the altar.
What of these things goes now without disaster?

How shall I fail my ships
and lose my faith of battle?   205
For them to urge such sacrifice of innocent blood
angrily, for their wrath is great—it is right. May
   all be well yet."

But when necessity's yoke was put upon him
he changed, and from the heart the breath came
   bitter
and sacrilegious, utterly infidel,   210
to warp a will now to be stopped at nothing.
The sickening in men's minds, tough,
reckless in fresh cruelty brings daring. He endured
   then
to sacrifice his daughter
to stay the strength of war waged for a woman,   215
first offering for the ships' sake.

Her supplications and her cries of father
were nothing, nor the child's lamentation
to kings passioned for battle.
The father prayed, called to his men to lift her   220
with strength of hand swept in her robes aloft
and prone above the altar, as you might lift
a goat for sacrifice, with guards
against the lips' sweet edge, to check
the curse cried on the house of Atreus   225
by force of bit and speech drowned in strength.

Pouring then to the ground her saffron mantle
she struck the sacrificers with
the eyes' arrows of pity,
lovely as in a painted scene, and striving   230
to speak—as many times
at the kind festive table of her father
she had sung, and in the clear voice of a stainless
   maiden
with love had graced the song
of worship when the third cup was poured.   235

What happened next I saw not, neither speak it.
The crafts of Calchas fail not of outcome.
Justice so moves that those only learn
who suffer; and the future
you shall know when it has come; before then,   240
   forget it.

---

[19] The port from which the Greeks were set to sail to Troy.
[20] River flowing from the north into the Aegean Sea between Macedonia and Thrace.

It is grief too soon given.
All will come clear in the next dawn's sunlight.
Let good fortune follow these things as
she who is here desires,
our Apian land's singlehearted protectress.[21]   245

[*THE CHORUS now turns toward KLYTEMESTRA,
and the leader speaks to her.*]

I have come in reverence, Klytemestra, of your
    power.
For when the man is gone and the throne void,
    his right
falls to the prince's lady, and honour must be given.
Is it some grace—or otherwise—that you have heard
to make you sacrifice at messages of good hope?   250
I should be glad to hear, but must not blame your
    silence.
KLYTEMESTRA: As it was said of old, may the dawn
    child be born
to be an angel of blessing from the kindly night.
You shall know joy beyond all you ever hoped to
    hear.
The men of Argos have taken Priam's citadel.   255
CHORUS: What have you said? Your words escaped
    my unbelief.
KLYTEMESTRA: The Achaeans are in Troy. Is that
    not clear enough?
CHORUS: This slow delight steals over me to bring
    forth tears.
KLYTEMESTRA: Yes, for your eyes betray the loyal
    heart within.
CHORUS: Yet how can I be certain? Is there some   260
    evidence?
KLYTEMESTRA: There is, there must be; unless a
    god has lied to me.
CHORUS: Is it dream visions, easy to believe, you
    credit?
KLYTEMESTRA: I accept nothing from a brain that
    is dull with sleep.
CHORUS: The charm, then, of some rumour, that
    made rich your hope?
KLYTEMESTRA: Am I some young girl, that you   265
    find my thoughts so silly?

---

[21] Klytemestra.

CHORUS: How long, then, is it since the citadel was
    stormed?
KLYTEMESTRA: It is the night, the mother of this
    dawn I hailed.
CHORUS: What kind of messenger could come in
    speed like this?
KLYTEMESTRA: Hephaestus,[22] who cast forth the
    shining blaze from Ida.[23]
And beacon after beacon picking up the flare   270
carried it here; Ida to the Hermaean horn
of Lemnos, where it shone above the isle, and next
the sheer rock face of Zeus on Athos[24] caught it up;
and plunging skyward to arch the shoulders of the
    sea
the strength of the running flare in exultation,   275
pine timbers flaming into gold, like the sunrise,
brought the bright message to Macistus' sentinel
    cliffs,
who, never slow nor in the carelessness of sleep
caught up, sent on his relay in the courier chain,
and far across Euripus' streams the beacon flare   280
carried to signal watchmen on Messapion.
These took it again in turn, and heaping high a pile
of silvery brush flamed it to throw the message on.
And the flare sickened never, but grown stronger yet
outleapt the river valley of Asopus like   285
the very moon for shining, to Cithaeron's scaur
to waken the next station of the flaming post.
These watchers, not contemptuous of the far-
    thrown blaze,
kindled another beacon vaster than commanded.
The light leaned high above Gorgopis' staring   290
    marsh,
and striking Aegyplanctus' mountain top, drove on
yet one more relay, lest the flare die down in speed.
Kindled once more with stintless heaping force,
    they send
the beard of flame to hugeness, passing far beyond
the promontory that gazes on the Saronic strait   295

---

[22] God of fire.
[23] Mount Ida, near Troy, the location of the first fire in the
    queen's series of beacon-flares.
[24] Mt. Athos, and from there to Mt. Macistus on the island
    of Euboia, to Mt. Massapion on the Boiotian coast,
    across the Asopus valley to Mt. Cithaeron.

and flaming far, until it plunged at last to strike
the steep rock of Arachnus near at hand, our
    watchtower.
And thence there fell upon this house of Atreus'
    sons
the flare whose fathers mount to the Idaean beacon.
These are the changes on my torchlight messengers,   300
One from another running out the laps assigned.
The first and the last sprinters have the victory.
By such proof and such symbol I announce to you
my lord at Troy has sent his messengers to me.
CHORUS: The gods, lady, shall have my prayers and   305
    thanks straightway.
And yet to hear your story till all wonder fades
would be my wish, could you but tell it once again.
KLYTEMESTRA: The Achaeans have got Troy, upon
    this very day.
I think the city echoes with a clash of cries.
Pour vinegar and oil into the selfsame bowl,   310
you could not say they mix in friendship, but
    fight on.
Thus variant sound the voices of the conquerors
and conquered, from the opposition of their
fates. Trojans are stooping now to gather in their
    arms
their dead, husbands and brothers; children lean   315
    to clasp
the aged who begot them, crying upon the death
of those most dear, from lips that never will be free.
The Achaeans have their midnight work after the
    fighting
that sets them down to feed on all the city has,
ravenous, headlong, by no rank and file assigned,   320
but as each man has drawn his shaken lot by chance.
And in the Trojan houses that their spears have taken
they settle now, free of the open sky, the frosts
and dampness of the evening; without sentinels set
they sleep the sleep of happiness the whole night   325
    through.
And if they reverence the gods who hold the city
and all the holy temples of the captured land,
they, the despoilers, might not be despoiled in turn.
Let not their passion overwhelm them; let no lust
seize on these men to violate what they must not.   330
The run to safety and home is yet to make; they
    must turn

the pole, and run the backstretch of the double
    course.
Yet, though the host come home without offence
    to high
gods, even so the anger of these slaughtered men
may never sleep. Oh, let there be no fresh wrong   335
    done!

Such are the thoughts you hear from me, a
    woman merely.
Yet may the best win through, that none may fail
    to see.
Of all good things to wish this is my dearest choice.
CHORUS: My lady, no grave man could speak with
    better grace.
I have listened to the proofs of your tale, and I   340
    believe,
and go to make my glad thanksgivings to the gods.
This pleasure is not unworthy of the grief that
    gave it.
O Zeus our lord and Night beloved,
bestower of power and beauty,
you slung above the bastions of Troy   345
the binding net, that none, neither great
nor young, might outleap
the gigantic toils
of enslavement and final disaster.
I gaze in awe on Zeus of the guests   350
who wrung from Alexander such payment.
He bent the bow with slow care, that neither
the shaft might hurdle the stars, nor fall
spent to the earth, short driven.

They have the stroke of Zeus to tell of.[25]   355
This thing is clear and you may trace it.
He acted as he had decreed. A man thought
the gods deigned not to punish mortals
who trampled down the delicacy of things
inviolable. That man was wicked.   360
The curse on great daring
shines clear; it wrings atonement
from those high hearts that drive to evil,
from houses blossoming to pride

---

25   The next few stanzas tell of Zeus's vengeance on Troy for
    Paris's crime of stealing Helen.

and peril. Let there be 365
wealth without tears; enough for
the wise man who will ask no further.
There is not any armour
in gold against perdition
for who spurns the high altar 370
of Justice down to the darkness.

Persuasion the persistent overwhelms him,
she, strong daughter of designing Ruin.
And every medicine is vain; the sin
smolders not, but burns to evil beauty. 375
As cheap bronze tortured
at the touchstone relapses
to blackness and grime, so this man
tested shows vain
as a child that strives to catch the bird flying 380
and wins shame that shall bring down his city.
No god will hear such a man's entreaty,
but whoso turns to these ways
they strike him down in his wickedness.
This was Paris: he came 385
to the house of the sons of Atreus,
stole the woman away, and shamed
the guest's right of the board shared.

She left among her people the stir and clamour
of shields and of spearheads, 390
the ships to sail and the armour.
She took to Ilium her dowry, death.
She stepped forth lightly between the gates
daring beyond all daring. And the prophets
about the great house[26] wept aloud and spoke: 395
"Alas, alas for the house and for the champions,
alas for the bed signed with their love together.
Here now is silence, scorned, unreproachful.
The agony of his loss is clear before us.
Longing for her who lies beyond the sea 400
he shall see a phantom queen in his household.
Her images in their beauty
are bitterness to her lord now
where in the emptiness of eyes

all passion has faded." 405

Shining in dreams the sorrowful
memories pass; they bring him
vain delight only.
It is vain, to dream and to see splendours,
and the image slipping from the arms' embrace 410
escapes, not to return again,
on wings drifting down the ways of sleep.
Such have the sorrows been in the house by the
    hearthside;
such have there been, and yet there are worse than
    these.
In all Hellas, for those who swarmed to the host 415
the heartbreaking misery
shows in the house of each.
Many are they who are touched at the heart by
    these things.
Those they sent forth they knew;
now, in place of the young men 420
urns and ashes are carried home
to the houses of the fighters.

The god of war, money changer of dead bodies,
held the balance of his spear in the fighting,
and from the corpse-fires at Ilium 425
sent to their dearest the dust
heavy and bitter with tears shed
packing smooth the urns with
ashes that once were men.
They praise them through their tears, how this 430
    man
knew well the craft of battle, how another
went down splendid in the slaughter:
and all for some strange woman.
Thus they mutter in secrecy,
and the slow anger creeps below their grief 435
at Atreus' sons and their quarrels.
There by the walls of Ilium
the young men in their beauty keep
graves deep in the alien soil
they hated and they conquered. 440

The citizens speak: their voice is dull with hatred.
The curse of the people must be paid for.
There lurks for me in the hooded night

---

[26] The house of Atreus; the following shifts back to
    Menelaus's grief.

terror of what may be told me.
The gods fail not to mark   445
those who have killed many.
The black Furies stalking the man
fortunate beyond all right
wrench back again the set of his life
and drop him to darkness. There among   450
the ciphers there is no more comfort
in power. And the vaunt of high glory
is bitterness; for God's thunderbolts
crash on the towering mountains.
Let me attain no envied wealth,   455
let me not plunder cities,
neither be taken in turn, and face
life in the power of another.

[*Various members of the CHORUS, speaking severally.*]

From the beacon's bright message
the fleet rumour runs   460
through the city. If this be real
who knows? Perhaps the gods have sent some lie
   to us.

Who of us is so childish or so reft of wit
that by the beacon's messages
his heart flamed must despond again   465
when the tale changes in the end?

It is like a woman indeed
to take the rapture before the fact has shown for
   true.

They believe too easily, are too quick to shift
from ground to ground; and swift indeed   470
the rumour voiced by a woman dies again.

Now we shall understand these torches and their
   shining,
the beacons, and the interchange of flame and flame.
They may be real; yet bright and dreamwise ecstasy
in light's appearance might have charmed our   475
   hearts awry.
I see a herald coming from the beach, his brows
shaded with sprigs of olive; and upon his feet
the dust, dry sister of the mire, makes plain to me
that he will find a voice, not merely kindle flame

from mountain timber, and make signals from the   480
   smoke,
but tell us outright, whether to be happy or—
but I shrink back from naming the alternative.
That which appeared was good; may yet more
   good be given.

And any man who prays that any different things
   befall
the city, may he reap the crime of his own heart.   485

[*THE HERALD enters, and speaks.*]

Soil of my fathers, Argive earth I tread upon,
in daylight of the tenth year I have come back to you.
All my hopes broke but one, and this I have at last.
I never could have dared to dream that I might die
in Argos, and be buried in this beloved soil.   490
Hail to the Argive land and to its sunlight, hail
to its high sovereign, Zeus, and to the Pythian[27]
   king.
May you no longer shower your arrows on our heads.
Beside Scamandrus[28] you were grim; be satisfied
and turn to saviour now and healer of our hurts,   495
my lord Apollo. Gods of the market place
   assembled,
I greet you all, and my own patron deity
Hermes, beloved herald, in whose right all heralds
are sacred; and you heroes that sent forth the host,
propitiously take back all that the spear has left.   500
O great hall of the kings and house beloved; seats
of sanctity; divinities that face the sun:
if ever before, look now with kind and glowing eyes
to greet our king in state after so long a time.
He comes, lord Agamemnon, bearing light in gloom   505
to you, and to all that are assembled here.
Salute him with good favour, as he well deserves,
the man who has wrecked Ilium with the spade of
   Zeus
vindictive, whereby all their plain has been laid
   waste.
Gone are their altars, the sacred places of the gods   510
are gone, and scattered all the seed within the
   ground.

---

27 Apollo.
28 The main river of Troy.

With such a yolk as this gripped to the neck of Troy
he comes, the king, Atreus' elder son, a man
fortunate to be honoured far above all men
alive; not Paris nor the city tied to him   515
can boast he did more than was done him in return.
Guilty of rape and theft, condemned, he lost the
    prize
captured, and broke to sheer destruction all the
    house
of his fathers, with the very ground whereon it
    stood.
Twice over the sons of Priam have atoned their   520
    sins.[29]
CHORUS: Hail and be glad, herald of the Achaean
    host.
HERALD: I am happy; I no longer ask the gods for
    death.
CHORUS: Did passion for your country so strip bare
    your heart?
HERALD: So that the tears broke in my eyes, for
    happiness.
CHORUS: You were taken with that sickness, then,   525
    that brings delight.
HERALD: How? I cannot deal with such words until
    I understand.
CHORUS: Struck with desire of those who loved as
    much again.
HERALD: You mean our country longed for us, as
    we for home?
CHORUS: So that I sighed, out of the darkness of
    my heart.
HERALD: Whence came this black thought to afflict   530
    the mind with fear?
CHORUS: Long since it was my silence kept disaster
    off.
HERALD: But how? There were some you feared
    when the kings went away?
CHORUS: So much that as you said now, even death
    were grace.
HERALD: Well: the end has been good. And in the
    length of time

part of our fortune you could say held favourable,
but part we cursed again. And who, except the gods,   535
can live time through forever without any pain?
Were I to tell you of the hard work done, the nights
exposed, the cramped sea-quarters, the foul
    beds—what part
of day's disposal did we not cry out loud?
Ashore, the horror stayed with us and grew. We lay   540
against the ramparts of our enemies, and from
the sky, and from the ground, the meadow dews
    came out
to soak our clothes and fill our hair with lice. And
    if
I were to tell of winter time, when all birds died,
the snows of Ida past endurance she sent down,   545
or summer heat, when in the lazy noon the sea
fell level and asleep under a windless sky—
but why live such grief over again? That time is gone
for us, and gone for those who died. Never again
need they rise up, nor care again for anything.   550
Why must a live man count the numbers of the
    slain,
why grieve at fortune's wrath that fades to break
    once more?
I call a long farewell to all our unhappiness.
For us, survivors of the Argive armament,
the pleasure wins, pain casts no weight in the   555
    opposite scale.
And here, in this sun's shining, we can boast aloud,
whose fame has gone with wings across the land
    and sea:
"Upon a time the Argive host took Troy, and on
the houses of the gods who live in Hellas nailed
the spoils, to be the glory of days long ago."   560
And they who hear such things shall call this city
    blest
and the leaders of the host; and high the grace of
    God
shall be exalted, that did this. You have the story.
CHORUS: I must give way; your story shows that I
    was wrong.
Old men are always young enough to learn, with   565
    profit.
But Klytemestra and her house must hear, above
others, this news that makes luxurious my life.

---

[29] A more accurate translation here might be "paid a double penalty for their crimes." Note that the language used
throughout the play is legalistic, having to do with crime,
criminal penalties, and justice.

[*KLYTEMESTRA comes forward and speaks.*]

I raised my cry of joy, and it was long ago
when the first beacon flare of message came by night
to speak of capture and of Ilium's overthrow.   570
But there was one who laughed at me, who said:
    "You trust
in beacons so, and you believe that Troy has fallen?
How like a woman, for the heart to lift so light."
Men spoke like that; they thought I wandered in
    my wits;
yet I made sacrifice, and in the womanish strain   575
voice after voice caught up the cry along the city
to echo in the temples of the gods and bless
and still the fragrant flame that melts the sacrifice.

Why should you tell me then the whole long tale
    at large
when from my lord himself I shall hear all the story?   580
But now, how best to speed my preparation to
receive my honoured lord come home again—
    what else
is light more sweet for woman to behold than this,
to spread the gates before her husband home from
    war
and saved by God's hand?—take this message to   585
    the king:
Come, and with speed, back to the city that longs
    for him,
and may he find a wife within his house as true
as on the day he left her, watchdog of the house
gentle to him alone, fierce to his enemies,
and such a woman in all her ways as this, who has   590
not broken the seal upon her in the length of days.
With no man else have I known delight, nor any
    shame
of evil speech, more than I know how to temper
    bronze.

[*KLYTEMESTRA goes to the back of the stage.*]

HERALD: A vaunt like this, so loaded as it is with truth,
    it well becomes a highborn lady to proclaim.   595
CHORUS: Thus has she spoken to you, and well you
    understand,
    words that impress interpreters whose thought is
    clear.

But tell me, herald; I would learn of Menelaus,
    that power beloved in this land. Has he survived
    also, and come with you back to his home again?   600
HERALD: I know no way to lie and make my tale so
    fair
    that friends could reap joy of it for any length of
    time.
CHORUS: Is there no means to speak us fair, and yet
    tell the truth?
    It will not hide, when truth and good are torn
    asunder.
HERALD: He is gone out of the sight of the Achaean   605
    host,
    vessel and man alike. I speak no falsehood there.
CHORUS: Was it when he had put out from Ilium
    in your sight,
    or did a storm that struck you both whirl him away?
HERALD: How like a master bowman you have hit
    the mark
    and in your speech cut a long sorrow to brief stature.   610
CHORUS: But then the rumour in the host that
    sailed beside,
    was it that he had perished, or might yet be living?
HERALD: No man knows. There is none could tell
    us that for sure
    except the Sun, from whom this earth has life and
    increase.
CHORUS: How did this storm, by wrath of the   615
    divinities,
    strike on our multitude at sea? How did it end?
HERALD: It is not well to stain the blessing of this day
    with speech of evil weight. Such gods are honoured
    apart.
    And when the messenger of a shaken host, sad
    faced,
    brings to his city news it prayed never to hear,   620
    this scores one wound upon the body of the people;
    and that from many houses many men are slain
    by the two-lashed whip dear to the War God's
    hand, this turns
    disaster double-bladed, bloodily made two.
    The messenger so freighted with a charge of tears   625
    should make his song of triumph at the Furies' door.
    But, carrying the fair message of our hopes'
    salvation,
    come home to a glad city's hospitality,

how shall I mix my gracious news with foul, and
    tell
of the storm on the Achaeans by God's anger sent?   630
For they, of old the deepest enemies, sea and fire,
made a conspiracy and gave the oath of hand
to blast in ruin our unhappy Argive army.
At night the sea began to rise in waves of death.
Ship against ship the Thracian stormwind   635
    shattered us,
and gored and split, our vessels, swept in violence
of storm and whirlwind, beaten by the breaking
    rain,
drove on in darkness, spun by the wicked
    shepherd's hand.
But when the sun came up again to light the dawn,
we saw the Aegaean Sea blossoming with dead   640
    men,
the men of Achaea, and the wreckage of their ships.
For us, and for our ship, some god, no man, by
    guile
or by entreaty's force prevailing, laid his hand
upon the helm and brought us through with hull
    unscarred.
Life-giving fortune deigned to take our ship in   645
    charge
that neither riding in deep water she took the surf
nor drove to shoal and break upon some rocky
    shore.
But then, delivered from death at sea, in the pale
    day,
incredulous of our own luck, we shepherded
in our sad thoughts the fresh disaster of the fleet   650
so pitifully torn and shaken by the storm.
Now of these others, if there are any left alive
they speak of us as men who perished, must they
    not?
Even as we, who fear that they are gone. But may
it all come well in the end. For Menelaus: be sure   655
if any of them come back that lie will be the first.
If he is still where some sun's gleam can track him
    down,
alive and open-eyed, by blessed hand of God
who willed that not yet should his seed be utterly
    gone,
there is some hope that he will still come home   660
    again.

You have heard all; and be sure, you have heard
    the truth.

[*THE HERALD goes out.*]

CHORUS: Who is he that named you so
    fatally in every way?
    Could it be some mind unseen
    in divination of your destiny   665
    shaping to the lips that name
    for the bride of spears and blood,
    Helen, which is death? Appropriately
    death of ships, death of men and cities
    from the bower's soft curtained   670
    and secluded luxury she sailed then,
    driven on the giant west wind,
    and armoured men in their thousands came,
    huntsmen down the oar blade's fading footprint
    to struggle in blood with those   675
    who by the banks of Simoeis[30]
    beached their hulls where the leaves break.

    And on Ilium in truth
    in the likeness of the name
    the sure purpose of the Wrath drove   680
    marriage with death: for the guest board
    shamed, and Zeus kindly to strangers,
    the vengeance wrought on those men
    who graced in too loud voice the bride-song
    fallen to their lot to sing,   685
    the kinsmen and the brothers.
    And changing its song's measure
    the ancient city of Priam
    chants in high strain of lamentation,
    calling Paris him of the fatal marriage;   690
    for it endured its life's end
    in desolation and tears
    and the piteous blood of its people.

    Once a man fostered in his house
    a lion cub, from the mother's milk   695
    torn, craving the breast given.
    In the first steps of its young life
    mild, it played with children
    and delighted the old.

---

30 A river on the Trojan plain.

Caught in the arm's cradle   700
they pampered it like a newborn child,
shining eyed and broken to the hand
to stay the stress of its hunger.

But it grew with time, and the lion
in the blood strain came out; it paid   705
grace to those who had fostered it
in blood and death for the sheep flocks,
a grim feast forbidden.
The house reeked with blood run
nor could its people beat down the bane,   710
the giant murderer's onslaught.
This thing they raised in their house was blessed
by God to be priest of destruction.

And that which first came to the city of Ilium,
call it a dream of calm   715
and the wind dying,
the loveliness and luxury of much gold,
the melting shafts of the eyes' glances,
the blossom that breaks the heart with longing.
But she turned in mid-step of her course to make   720
bitter the consummation,
whirling on Priam's people
to blight with her touch and nearness.
Zeus hospitable sent her,
a vengeance to make brides weep.   725

It has been made long since and grown old among
      men,
this saying: human wealth
grown to fulness of stature
breeds again nor dies without issue.
From high good fortune in the blood   730
blossoms the quenchless agony.
Far from others I hold my own
mind; only the act of evil
breeds others to follow,
young sins in its own likeness.   735
Houses clear in their right are given
children in all loveliness.

But Pride aging is made
in men's dark actions
ripe with the young pride   740

late or soon when the dawn of destiny
comes and birth is given
to the spirit none may fight nor beat down,
sinful Daring; and in those halls
the black visaged Disasters stamped   745
in the likeness of their fathers.

And Righteousness is a shining in
the smoke of mean houses.
Her blessing is on the just man.
From high halls starred with gold by reeking   750
      hands
she turns back
with eyes that glance away to the simple in heart,
spurning the strength of gold
stamped false with flattery.
And all things she steers to fulfilment.   755

[AGAMEMNON *enters in a chariot, with* CASSANDRA
beside him. THE CHORUS *speaks to him.*]

Behold, my king: sacker of Troy's citadel,
own issue of Atreus.
How shall I hail you? How give honour
not crossing too high nor yet bending short
of this time's graces?   760
For many among men are they who set high
the show of honour, yet break justice.
If one be unhappy, all else are fain
to grieve with him: yet the teeth of sorrow
come nowise near to the heart's edge.   765
And in joy likewise they show joy's semblance,
and torture the face to the false smile.
Yet the good shepherd, who knows his flock,
the eyes of men cannot lie to him,
that with water of feigned   770
love seem to smile from the true heart.
But I: when you marshalled this armament
for Helen's sake, I will not hide it,
in ugly style you were written in my heart
for steering aslant the mind's course   775
to bring home by blood
sacrifice and dead men that wild spirit.
But now, in love drawn up from the deep heart,
not skimmed at the edge, we hail you.
You have won, your labour is made gladness.   780
Ask all men: you will learn in time

which of your citizens have been just
in the city's sway, which were reckless.
AGAMEMNON: To Argos first, and to the gods
    within the land,
I must give due greeting; they have worked with   785
    me to bring
me home; they helped me in the vengeance I have
    wrought
on Priam's city. Not from the lips of men the gods
heard justice, but in one firm cast they laid their
    votes[31]
within the urn of blood that Ilium must die
and all her people; while above the opposite vase   790
the hand hovered and there was hope, but no vote
    fell.
The stormclouds of their ruin live; the ash that dies
upon them gushes still in smoke their pride of
    wealth.
For all this we must thank the gods with grace of
    much
high praise and memory, we who fenced within   795
    our toils
of wrath the city; and, because one woman strayed,
the beast of Argos broke them, the fierce young
    within
the horse, the armoured people who marked out
    their leap
against the setting of the Pleiades. A wild
and bloody lion swarmed above the towers of Troy   800
to glut its hunger lapping at the blood of kings.

This to the gods, a prelude strung to length of
    words.
But, for the thought you spoke, I heard and I
    remember
and stand behind you. For I say that it is true.
In few men is it part of nature to respect   805
a friend's prosperity without begrudging him,
as envy's wicked poison settling to the heart
piles up the pain in one sick with unhappiness,
who, staggered under sufferings that are all his own,
winces again to the vision of a neighbor's bliss.   810

And I can speak, for I have seen, I know it well,
this mirror of companionship, this shadow's ghost,
these men who seemed my friends in all sincerity.
One man of them all, Odysseus,[32] he who sailed
    unwilling,
once yoked to me carried his harness, nor went   815
    slack.
Dead though he be or living, I can say it still.

Now in the business of the city and the gods
we must ordain full conclave of all citizens
and take our counsel. We shall see what element
is strong, and plan that it shall keep its virtue still.   820
But that which must be healed—we must use
    medicine,
or burn, or amputate, with kind intention, take
all means at hand that might beat down
    corruption's pain.
So to the King's house and the home about the
    hearth
I take my way, with greeting to the gods within   825
who sent me forth, and who have brought me
    home once more.
My prize was conquest; may it never fail again.

[*KLYTEMESTRA comes forward and speaks.*]

Grave gentlemen of Argolis assembled here,
I take no shame to speak aloud before you all
the love I bear my husband. In the lapse of time   830
modesty fades; it is human.
                       What I tell you now
I learned not from another; this is my own sad life
all the long years this man was gone at Ilium.
It is evil and a thing of terror when a wife
sits in the house forlorn with no man by, and hears   835
rumours that like a fever die to break again,
and men come in with news of fear, and on their
    heels
another messenger, with worse news to cry aloud
here in this house. Had Agamemnon taken all
the wounds the tale whereof was carried home to   840
    me,
he had been cut full of gashes like a fishing net.

---

31 In the law courts of Aeschylus's time, jurors cast their vot-
    ing-tokens in one of two urns: for acquittal or for guilt.
    Here the gods are voting as one for Troy's destruction.

32 King of Ithaca, whose ten-year voyage home from Troy
    forms the plot of Homer's *Odyssey*.

If he had died each time that rumour told his death,
he must have been some triple-bodied Geryon[33]
back from the dead with threefold cloak of earth
    upon
his body, and killed once for every shape assumed.   845
Because such tales broke out forever on my rest,
many a time they cut me down and freed my throat
from the noose overslung where I had caught it fast.
And therefore is your son, in whom my love and
    yours
are sealed and pledged, not here to stand with us   850
    today,
Orestes. It were right; yet do not be amazed.
Strophius of Phocis,[34] comrade in arms and
    faithful friend
to you, is keeping him. He spoke to me of peril
on two counts; of your danger under Ilium,
and here, of revolution and the clamorous people   855
who might cast down the council[35]—since it lies
    in men's
nature to trample on the fighter already down.
Such my excuse to you, and without subterfuge.

For me: the rippling springs that were my tears
    have dried
utterly up, nor left one drop within. I keep   860
the pain upon my eyes where late at night I wept
over the beacons long ago set for your sake,
untended left forever. In the midst of dreams
the whisper that a gnat's thin wings could winnow
    broke
my sleep apart. I thought I saw you suffer wounds   865
more than the time that slept with me could ever
    hold.

Now all my suffering is past, with griefless heart
I hail this man, the watchdog of the fold and hall;
the stay that keeps the ship alive; the post to grip
groundward the towering roof; a father's single   870
    child;
land seen by sailors after all their hope was gone;

splendor of daybreak shining from the night of
    storm;
the running spring a parched wayfarer strays upon.
Oh, it is sweet to escape from all necessity!

Such is my greeting to him, that he well deserves.   875
Let none bear malice; for the harm that went before
I took, and it was great.
                    Now, my beloved one,
step from your chariot; yet let not your foot, my
    lord,
sacker of Ilium, touch the earth. My maidens there!
Why this delay? Your task has been appointed you,   880
to strew the ground before his feet with tapestries.
Let there spring up into the house he never hoped
to see, where Justice leads him in, a crimson path.

In all things else, my heart's unsleeping care shall
    act
with the gods' aid to set aright what fate ordained.   885

[*Klytemestra's handmaidens spread a bright carpet
between the chariot and the door.*]

AGAMEMNON: Daughter of Leda,[36] you who kept
    my house for me,
there is one way your welcome matched my
    absence well.
You strained it to great length. Yet properly to praise
me thus belongs by right to other lips, not yours.
And all this—do not try in woman's ways to make   890
me delicate, nor, as if I were some Asiatic
bow down to earth and with wide mouth cry out
    to me,
nor cross my path with jealousy by strewing the
    ground
with robes. Such state becomes the gods, and
    none beside.
I am a mortal, a man; I cannot trample upon   895
these tinted splendors without fear thrown in my
    path.
I tell you, as a man, not god, to reverence me.
Discordant is the murmur at such treading down

---

33 A three-bodied monster killed by Heracles.
34 King of Phocis, with whom Orestes grew up.
35 That is, take advantage of the king's absence to overturn
    the existing government of Argos.

36 Mother of both Klytemestra (with Tyndareus) and Helen
    (with Zeus).

of lovely things; while God's most lordly gift to man
is decency of mind. Call that man only blest   900
who has in sweet tranquillity brought his life to
    close.
If I could only act as such, my hope is good.
KLYTEMESTRA: Yet tell me this one thing, and do
    not cross my will.
AGAMEMNON: My will is mine. I shall not make it
    soft for you.
KLYTEMESTRA: It was in fear surely that you vowed   905
    this course to God.
AGAMEMNON: No man has spoken knowing better
    what he said.
KLYTEMESTRA: If Priam had won as you have, what
    would he have done?
AGAMEMNON: I well believe he might have walked
    on tapestries.
KLYTEMESTRA: Be not ashamed before the bitterness
    of men.
AGAMEMNON: The people murmur, and their voice   910
    is great in strength.
KLYTEMESTRA: Yet he who goes unenvied shall not
    be admired.
AGAMEMNON: Surely this lust for conflict is not
    womanlike?
KLYTEMESTRA: Yet for the mighty even to give way
    is grace.
AGAMEMNON: Does such a victory as this mean so
    much to you?
KLYTEMESTRA: Oh yield! The power is yours. Give   915
    way of your free will.
AGAMEMNON: Since you must have it—here, let
    someone with all speed
take off these sandals, slaves for my feet to tread
    upon.
And as I crush these garments stained from the
    rich sea
let no god's eyes of hatred strike me from afar.
Great the extravagance, and great the shame I feel   920
to spoil such treasure and such silver's worth of
    webs.

So much for all this. Take this stranger girl within
now, and be kind. The conqueror who uses softly
his power, is watched from far in the kind eyes of
    God,

and this slave's yoke is one no man will wear from   925
    choice.
Gift of the host to me, and flower exquisite
from all my many treasures, she attends me here.

Now since my will was bent to listen to you in this
my feet crush purple as I pass within the hall.
KLYTEMESTRA: The sea is there, and who shall   930
    drain its yield? It breeds
precious as silver, ever of itself renewed,
the purple ooze wherein our garments shall be
    dipped.
And by God's grace this house keeps full sufficiency
of all. Poverty is a thing beyond its thought.
I could have vowed to trample many splendors   935
    down
had such decree been ordained from the oracles
those days when all my study was to bring home
    your life.
For when the root lives yet the leaves will come again
to fence the house with shade against the Dog
    Star's heat,
and now you have come home to keep your   940
    hearth and house
you bring with you the symbol of our winter's
    warmth;
but when Zeus ripens the green clusters into wine
there shall be coolness in the house upon those days
because the master ranges his own halls once more.

Zeus, Zeus accomplisher, accomplish these my   945
    prayers.
Let your mind bring these things to pass. It is
    your will.

[AGAMEMNON and KLYTEMESTRA enter the house.
CASSANDRA remains in the chariot. THE CHORUS
speaks.]

Why must this persistent fear
beat its wings so ceaselessly
and so close against my mantic heart?
Why this strain unwanted, unrepaid, thus   950
    prophetic?
Nor can valour of good hope
seated near the chambered depth
of the spirit cast it out

as dreams of dark fancy; and yet time
has buried in the mounding sand   955
the sea cables since that day
when against Ilium
the army and the ships put to sea.

Yet I have seen with these eyes
Agamemnon home again.   960
Still the spirit sings, drawing deep
from within this unlyric threnody of the Fury.
Hope is gone utterly,
the sweet strength is far away.
Surely this is not fantasy.   965
Surely it is real, this whirl of drifts
that spin the stricken heart.
Still I pray; may all this
expectation fade as vanity
into unfulfillment, and not be.   970

Yet it is true: the high strength of men
knows no content with limitation. Sickness
chambered beside it beats at the wall between.
Man's fate that sets a true
course yet may strike upon   975
the blind and sudden reefs of disaster.
But if before such time, fear
throw overboard some precious thing
of the cargo, with deliberate cast,
not all the house, labouring   980
with weight of ruin, shall go down,
nor sink the hull deep within the sea.
And great and affluent the gift of Zeus
in yield of ploughed acres year on year
makes void again sick starvation.   985

But when the black and mortal blood of man
has fallen to the ground before his feet, who then
can sing spells to call it back again?
Did Zeus not warn us once
when he struck to impotence   990
that one who could in truth charm back the dead
     men?
Had the gods not so ordained
that fate should stand against fate
to check any man's excess,
my heart now would have outrun speech   995

to break forth the water of its grief.
But this is so; I murmur deep in darkness
sore at heart; my hope is gone now
ever again to unwind some crucial good
from the flames about my heart.   1000

[*KLYTEMESTRA comes out from the house again and
speaks to* CASSANDRA.]

Cassandra, you may go within the house as well,
since Zeus in no unkindness has ordained that you
must share our lustral water, stand with the great
     throng
of slaves that flock to the altar of our household god.
Step from this chariot, then, and do not be so proud. 1005
And think—they say that long ago Alcmena's son[37]
was sold in bondage and endured the bread of slaves.
But if constraint of fact forces you to such fate,
be glad indeed for masters ancient in their wealth.
They who have reaped success beyond their   1010
     dreams of hope
are savage above need and standard toward their
     slaves.
From us you shall have all you have the right to ask.
CHORUS: What she has spoken is for you, and clear
     enough.
Fenced in these fatal nets wherein you find yourself
you should obey her if you can; perhaps you can not.   1015
KLYTEMESTRA: Unless she uses speech
     incomprehensible,
barbarian, wild as the swallow's song, I speak
within her understanding, and she must obey.
CHORUS: Go with her. What she bids is best in
     circumstance,
that rings you now. Obey, and leave this carriage   1020
     seat.
KLYTEMESTRA: I have no leisure to stand outside
     the house and waste
time on this woman. At the central altarstone
the flocks are standing, ready for the sacrifice
we make to this glad day we never hoped to see.
You: if you are obeying my commands at all, be   1025
     quick.
But if in ignorance you fail to comprehend,

---

37 Heracles. It was as a slave to Eurystheus, king of Tiryns,
    that Heracles performed his famous Twelve Labours.

speak not, but make with your barbarian hand
    some sign.
CHORUS: I think this stranger girl needs some
    interpreter
who understands. She is like some captive animal.
KLYTEMESTRA: No, she is in the passion of her own 1030
    wild thoughts.
Leaving her captured city she has come to us
untrained to take the curb, and will not
    understand
until her rage and strength have foamed away in
    blood.
I shall throw down no more commands for her
    contempt.

[*KLYTEMESTRA goes back into the house.*]

CHORUS: I, though, shall not be angry, for I pity her. 1035
    Come down, poor creature, leave the empty car.
      Give way
to compulsion and take up the yoke that shall be
    yours.

[*CASSANDRA descends from the chariot and cries out
loud.*]

    Oh shame upon the earth![38]
    Apollo, Apollo!
CHORUS: You cry on Loxias[39] in agony? He is not 1040
    of those immortals the unhappy supplicate.
CASSANDRA: Oh shame upon the earth!
    Apollo, Apollo!
CHORUS: Now once again in bitter voice she calls
    upon
    this god, who has not part in any lamentation. 1045
CASSANDRA: Apollo, Apollo!
    Lord of the ways, my ruin.
    You have undone me once again, and utterly.
CHORUS: I think she will be prophetic of her own
    disaster.
    Even in the slave's heart the gift divine lives on. 1050
CASSANDRA: Apollo, Apollo!
    Lord of the ways, my ruin.

Where have you led me now at last? What house
    is this?
CHORUS: The house of the Atreidae. If you understand
    not that, I can tell you; and so much at least is true. 1055
CASSANDRA: No, but a house that God hates,
    guilty within
of kindred blood shed, torture of its own,
the shambles for men's butchery, the dripping
    floor.[40]
CHORUS: The stranger is keen scented like some
    hound upon
the trail of blood that leads her to discovered death. 1060
CASSANDRA: Behold there the witnesses to my faith.
    The small children wail for their own death
and the flesh roasted that their father fed upon.
CHORUS: We had been told before of this prophetic
    fame
of yours: we want no prophets in this place at all. 1065
CASSANDRA: Ah, for shame, what can she[41]
    purpose now?
What is this new and huge
stroke of atrocity she plans within the house
to beat down the beloved beyond hope of healing?
Rescue is far away. 1070
CHORUS: I can make nothing of these prophecies.
    The rest
I understood; the city is full of the sound of them.
CASSANDRA: So cruel then, that you can do this thing?
    The husband of your own bed
to bathe bright with water—how shall I speak the 1075
    end?
This thing shall be done with speed. The hand
    gropes now, and the other
hand follows in turn.
CHORUS: No, I am lost. After the darkness of her
    speech
I go bewildered in a mist of prophecies.
CASSANDRA: No, no see there! What is that thing 1080
    that shows?

---

38 Cassandra's words here are actually "barbarian" shrieks:
    "Oi toi toi."
39 One of Apollo's titles, The Riddler, referring to his func-
    tion as the god of prophecy.

40 Reference to the crime of Agamemnon's father, Atreus,
    who, in revenge for the seduction of his wife by his
    brother Thyestes, murdered Thyestes' children and served
    them to their father for dinner. Only Aigisthos, one of
    Atreus's nephews, escaped.
41 Klytemestra.

Is it some net of death?
Or is the trap the woman there, the murderess?
Let now the slakeless fury in the race
rear up to howl aloud over this monstrous death.
CHORUS: Upon what demon in the house do you   1085
    call, to raise
the cry of triumph? All your speech makes dark
    my hope.
And to the heart below trickles the pale drop
as in the hour of death
timed to our sunset and the mortal radiance.
Ruin is near, and swift.   1090
CASSANDRA: See there, see there! Keep from his
    mate the bull.
Caught in the folded web's
entanglement she pinions him and with the black
    horn
strikes. And he crumples in the watered bath.
Guile, I tell you, and death there in the caldron   1095
    wrought.
CHORUS: I am not proud in skill to guess at
    prophecies,
yet even I can see the evil in this thing.
From divination what good ever has come to men?
Art, and multiplication of words
drifting through tangled evil bring   1100
terror to them that hear.
CASSANDRA: Alas, alas for the wretchedness of my
    ill-starred life.
This pain flooding the song of sorrow is mine
    alone.
Why have you brought me here in all unhappiness?
Why, why? Except to die with him? What else   1105
    could be?
CHORUS: You are possessed of God, mazed at heart
to sing your own death
song, the wild lyric as
in clamour for Itys, Itys over and over again
her long life of tears weeping forever grieves   1110
the brown nightingale.
CASSANDRA: Oh for the nightingale's pure song
    and a fate like hers.
With fashion of beating wings the gods clothed
    her about
and a sweet life gave her and without lamentation.
But mine is the sheer edge of the tearing iron.   1115

CHORUS: Whence come, beat upon beat, driven of
    God,
vain passions of tears?
Whence your cries, terrified, clashing in horror,
in wrought melody and the singing speech?
Whence take you the marks to this path of prophecy   1120
and speech of terror?
CASSANDRA: Oh marriage of Paris, death to the
    men beloved!
Alas, Scamandrus, water my fathers drank.
There was a time I too at your springs
drank and grew strong. Ah me,   1125
for now beside the deadly rivers, Cocytus
and Acheron,[42] I must cry out my prophecies.
CHORUS: What is this word, too clear, you have
    uttered now?
A child could understand.
And deep within goes the stroke of the dripping   1130
    fang
as mortal pain at the trebled song of your agony
shivers the heart to hear.
CASSANDRA: O sorrow, sorrow of my city dragged
    to uttermost death.
O sacrifices my father made at the wall.

Flocks of the pastured sheep slaughtered there.   1135
And no use at all
to save our city from its pain inflicted now.
And I too, with brain ablaze in fever, shall go down.
CHORUS: This follows the run of your song.
Is it, in cruel force of weight,   1140
some divinity kneeling upon you brings
the death song of your passionate suffering?
I can not see the end.
CASSANDRA: No longer shall my prophecies like
    some young girl
new-married glance from under veils, but bright   1145
    and strong
as winds blow into morning and the sun's uprise
shall wax along the swell like some great wave, to
    burst
at last upon the shining of this agony.
Now I will tell you plainly and from no cryptic
    speech;

---

[42] Rivers in Hades, the realm of the dead.

bear me then witness, running at my heels upon 1150
the scent of these old brutal things done long ago.
There is a choir that sings as one, that shall not
again
leave this house ever; the song thereof breaks
harsh with menace.
And drugged to double fury on the wine of men's
blood shed, there lurks forever here a drunken rout 1155
of ingrown vengeful spirits never to be cast forth.
Hanging above the hall they chant their song of
hate
and the old sin;[43] and taking up the strain in turn
spit curses on that man who spoiled his brother's
bed.
Did I go wide, or hit, like a real archer? Am I 1160
some swindling seer who hawks his lies from door
to door?
Upon your oath, bear witness that I know by heart
the legend of ancient wickedness within this
house.
CHORUS: And how could an oath, though cast in
rigid honesty,
do any good? And still we stand amazed at you, 1165
reared in an alien city far beyond the sea,
how can you strike, as if you had been there, the
truth.
CASSANDRA: Apollo was the seer who set me to this
work.
CHORUS: Struck with some passion for you, and
himself a god?
CASSANDRA: There was a time I blushed to speak 1170
about these things.
CHORUS: True; they who prosper take on airs of vanity.
CASSANDRA: Yes, then; he wrestled with me, and he
breathed delight.
CHORUS: Did you come to the getting of children
then, as people do?
CASSANDRA: I promised that to Loxias, but I broke
my word.
CHORUS: Were you already ecstatic in the skills of 1175
God?
CASSANDRA: Yes; even then I read my city's destinies.
CHORUS: So Loxias' wrath did you no harm? How
could that be?

CASSANDRA: For this my trespass, none believed
me ever again.
CHORUS: But we do; all that you foretell seems true
to us.
CASSANDRA: But this is evil, see! 1180
Now once again the pain of grim, true prophecy
shivers my whirling brain in a storm of things
foreseen.
Look there, see what is hovering above the house,
so small and young, imaged as in the shadow of
dreams,
like children almost, killed by those most dear to 1185
them,
and their hands filled with their own flesh, as
food to eat.
I see them holding out the inward parts, the vitals,
oh pitiful, that meat their father tasted of ....
I tell you: There is one that plots vengeance for this,
the strengthless lion rolling in his master's bed, 1190
who keeps, all me, the house against his lord's return;
my lord too, now that I wear the slave's yoke on
my neck.
King of the ships, who tore up Ilium by the roots,
what does he know of this accursed bitch, who licks
his hand, who fawns on him with lifted ears, who 1195
like
a secret death shall strike the coward's stroke, nor
fail?
No, this is daring when the female shall strike down
the male. What can I call her and be right? What
beast
of loathing? Viper double-fanged, or Scylla[44] witch
holed in the rocks and bane of men that range the 1200
sea;
smoldering mother of death to smoke relentless hate
on those most dear. How she stood up and
howled aloud
and unashamed, as at the breaking point of battle,
in feigned gladness for his salvation from the sea!
What does it matter now if men believe or no? 1205
What is to come will come. And soon you too
will stand

---

43 For "sin" read "crime."

44 One of two personified sea hazards that wrecked ships
in the strait between Sicily and Italy. Directly opposite
the rocks of Scylla was the whirlpool Charybdis.

beside, to murmur in pity that my words were true.
CHORUS: Thyestes' feast upon the flesh of his own
    children
  I understand in terror at the thought, and fear
  is on me hearing truth and no tale fabricated.   1210
  The rest: I heard it, but wander still far from the
    course.
CASSANDRA: I tell you, you shall look on
    Agamemnon dead.
CHORUS: Peace, peace, poor woman; put those
    bitter lips to sleep.
CASSANDRA: Useless; there is no god of healing in
    this story.
CHORUS: Not if it must be; may it somehow fail to   1215
    come.
CASSANDRA: Prayers, yes; they do not pray; they
    plan to strike, and kill.
CHORUS: What man is it who moves this beastly
    thing to be?
CASSANDRA: What man? You did mistake my
    divination then.
CHORUS: It may be; I could not follow through the
    schemer's plan.
CASSANDRA: Yet I know Greek; I think I know it   1220
    far too well.
CHORUS: And Pythian oracles are Greek, yet hard
    to read.
CASSANDRA: Oh, flame and pain that sweeps me
    once again! My lord,
  Apollo, King of Light, the pain, aye me, the pain!
  This is the woman-lioness, who goes to bed
  with the wolf, when her proud lion ranges far away, 1225
  and she will cut me down; as a wife mixing drugs
  she wills to shred the virtue of my punishment
  into her bowl of wrath as she makes sharp the blade
  against her man, death that he brought a mistress
    home.
  Why do I wear these mockeries upon my body,   1230
  this staff of prophecy, these flowers at my throat?
  At least I will spoil you before I die. Out, down,
  break, damn you! This for all that you have done
    to me.
  Make someone else, not me, luxurious in
    disaster....
  Lo now, this is Apollo who has stripped me here   1235
  of my prophetic robes. He watched me all the time

wearing this glory, mocked of all, my dearest ones
who hated me with all their hearts, so vain, so
    wrong;
called like some gypsy wandering from door to door
beggar, corrupt, half-starved, and I endured it all.   1240
And now the seer has done with me, his prophetess,
and led me into such a place as this, to die.
Lost are my father's altars, but the block is there
to reek with sacrificial blood, my own. We two
must die, yet die not vengeless by the gods. For   1245
    there
shall come one to avenge us also, born to slay
his mother, and to wreak death for his father's blood.
Outlaw and wanderer, driven far from his own land,
he will come back to cope these stones of inward
    hate.
For this is a strong oath and sworn by the high gods,   1250
that he shall cast men headlong for his father felled.
Why am I then so pitiful? Why must I weep?
Since once I saw the citadel of Ilium
die as it died, and those who broke the city, doomed
by the gods, fare as they have fared accordingly,   1255
I will go through with it. I too will take my fate.
I call as on the gates of death upon these gates
to pray only for this thing, that the stroke be true,
and that with no convulsion, with a rush of blood
in painless death, I may close up these eyes, and rest. 1260
CHORUS: O woman much enduring and so greatly
    wise,
  you have said much. But if this thing you know
    be true,
  this death that comes upon you, how can you,
    serene,
  walk to the altar like a driven ox of God?
CASSANDRA: Friends, there is no escape for any   1265
    longer time.
CHORUS: Yet longest left in time is to be honoured
    still.
CASSANDRA: The day is here and now; I can not
    win by flight.
CHORUS: Woman, be sure your heart is brave; you
    can take much.
CASSANDRA: None but the unhappy people ever
    hear such praise.
CHORUS: Yet there is a grace on mortals who so   1270
    nobly die.

CASSANDRA: Alas for you, father, and for your
lordly sons.
Ah!
CHORUS: What now? What terror whirls you
backward from the door?
CASSANDRA: Foul, foul!
CHORUS: What foulness then, unless some horror   1275
in the mind?
CASSANDRA: That room within reeks with blood
like a slaughter house.
CHORUS: What then? Only these victims butchered
at the hearth.
CASSANDRA: There is a breath about it like an open
grave.
CHORUS: This is no Syrian pride of frankincense
you mean.
CASSANDRA: So. I am going in, and mourning as I go   1280
my death and Agamemnon's. Let my life be done.
Ah friends,
truly this is no wild bird fluttering at a bush,
nor vain my speech. Bear witness to me when I die,
when falls for me, a woman slain, another woman,   1285
and when a man dies for this wickedly mated man.
Here in my death I claim this stranger's grace of
you.
CHORUS: Poor wretch, I pity you the fate you see so
clear.
CASSANDRA: Yet once more will I speak, and not
this time my own
death's threnody. I call upon the Sun in prayer   1290
against that ultimate shining when the avengers
strike
these monsters down in blood, that they avenge as
well
one simple slave who died, a small thing, lightly
killed.

Alas, poor men, their destiny. When all goes well
a shadow will overthrow it. If it be unkind   1295
one stroke of a wet sponge wipes all the picture out;
and that is far the most unhappy thing of all.

[CASSANDRA goes slowly into the house.]

CHORUS: High fortune is a thing slakeless
for mortals. There is no man who shall point
his finger to drive it back from the door   1300

and speak the words: "Come no longer."
Now to this man the blessed ones have given
Priam's city to be captured
and return in the gods' honour.
Must he give blood for generations gone,   1305
die for those slain and in death pile up
more death to come for the blood shed,
what mortal else who hears shall claim
he was born clear of the dark angel?

[Agamemnon, inside the house.]

Ah, I am struck a deadly blow and deep within!   1310
CHORUS: Silence: who cried out that he was
stabbed to death within the house?
AGAMEMNON: Ah me, again, they struck again. I
am wounded twice.
CHORUS: How the king cried out aloud to us! I
believe the thing is done.
Come, let us put our heads together, try to find
some safe way out.

[The members of the CHORUS go about distractedly,
each one speaking in turn.]

Listen, let me tell you what I think is best to do.   1315
Let the herald call all citizens to rally here.

No, better to burst in upon them now, at once,
and take them with the blood still running from
their blades.

I am with this man and I cast my vote to him.
Act now. This is the perilous and instant time.   1320

Anyone can see it, by these first steps they have
taken,
they purpose to be tyrants here upon our city.[45]

Yes, for we waste time, while they trample to the
ground
deliberation's honour, and their hands sleep not.

I can not tell which counsel of yours to call my own.   1325

---

45 The word tyrant had a special meaning in ancient
Greece—not, as with us, "an evil despot," but a ruler who
achieved power not by blood inheritance, as a king did,
but through popularity with the people or force of arms.

It is the man of action who can plan as well.

I feel as he does; nor can I see how by words
we shall set the dead man back upon his feet again.

Do you mean, to drag our lives out long, that we
must yield
to the house shamed, and leadership of such as   1330
these?

No, we can never endure that; better to be killed.
Death is a softer thing by far than tyranny.

Shall we, by no more proof than that he cried in
pain,
be sure, as by divination, that our lord is dead?

Yes, we should know what is true before we break   1335
our rage.
Here is sheer guessing and far different from sure
knowledge.

From all sides the voices multiply to make me
choose
this course; to learn first how it stands with
Agamemnon.

[*The doors of the palace open, disclosing the bodies of
AGAMEMNON and CASSANDRA, with KLYTEMESTRA
standing over them.*[46]]

KLYTEMESTRA: Much have I said before to serve
necessity,
but I will take no shame now to unsay it all.   1340
How else could I, arming hate against hateful men
disguised in seeming tenderness, fence high the
nets
of ruin beyond overleaping? Thus to me
the conflict born of ancient bitterness[47] is not
a thing new thought upon, but pondered deep in   1345
time.

---

[46] Use would have been made here of the *ekkyklema*, a
wheeled platform that could be rolled out of the scene
house with actors already positioned on it.

[47] Reference to Agamemnon's slaughter of his and
Klytemestra's daughter, Iphigeneia.

I stand now where I struck him down. The thing
is done.
Thus have I wrought, and I will not deny it now.
That he might not escape nor beat aside his death,
as fishermen cast their huge circling nets, I spread
deadly abundance of rich robes, and caught him fast.   1350
I struck him twice. In two great cries of agony
he buckled at the knees and fell. When he was down
I struck him the third blow, in thanks and reverence
to Zeus the lord of dead men underneath the
ground.
Thus he went down, and the life struggled out of   1355
him;
and as he died he spattered me with the dark red
and violent driven rain of bitter savoured blood
to make me glad, as gardens stand among the
showers
of God in glory at the birthtime of the buds.

These being the facts, elders of Argos assembled   1360
here,
be glad, if it be your pleasure; but for me, I glory.
Were it religion to pour wine above the slain,
this man deserved, more than deserved, such
sacrament.
He filled our cup with evil things unspeakable
and now himself come home has drunk it to the   1365
dregs.
CHORUS: We stand here stunned. How can you
speak this way, with mouth
so arrogant, to vaunt above your fallen lord?
KLYTEMESTRA: You try me out as if I were a
woman and vain;
but my heart is not fluttered as I speak before you.
You know it. You can praise or blame me as you   1370
wish;
it is all one to me. That man is Agamemnon,
my husband; he is dead; the work of this right hand
that struck in strength of righteousness. And that
is that.
CHORUS: Woman, what evil thing planted upon
the earth
or dragged from the running salt sea could you   1375
have tasted now
to wear such brutality and walk in the people's hate?
You have cast away, you have cut away. You shall
go homeless now,

crushed with men's bitterness.

KLYTEMESTRA: Now it is I you doom to be cast out
  from my city
 with men's hate heaped and curses roaring in my ears. 1380
 Yet look upon this dead man; you would not cross
  him once
 when with no thought more than as if a beast had
  died,
 when his ranged pastures swarmed with the deep
  fleece of flocks,
 he slaughtered like a victim his own child, my pain
 grown into love, to charm away the winds of Thrace. 1385
 Were you not bound to hunt him then clear of
  this soil
 for the guilt stained upon him? Yet you hear what I
 have done, and lo, you are a stern judge. But I say
  to you:
 go on and threaten me, but know that I am ready,
 if fairly you can beat me down beneath your hand, 1390
 for you to rule; but if the god grant otherwise,
 you shall be taught—too late, for sure—to keep
  your place.

CHORUS: Great your design, your speech is a
  clamour of pride.
 Swung to the red act drives the fury within your
  brain
 signed clear in the splash of blood over your eyes. 1395
 Yet to come is stroke given for stroke
 vengeless, forlorn of friends.

KLYTEMESTRA: Now hear you this, the right
  behind my sacrament:
 By my child's Justice driven to fulfillment, by
 her Wrath and Fury, to whom I sacrificed this man, 1400
 the hope that walks my chambers is not traced
  with fear
 while yet Aigisthos makes the fire shine on my
  hearth,
 my good friend, now as always, who shall be for us
 the shield of our defiance, no weak thing; while he,
 this other, is fallen, stained with this woman you 1405
  behold,
 plaything of all the golden girls at Ilium;
 and here lies she, the captive of his spear, who saw
 wonders, who shared his bed, the wise in revelations
 and loving mistress, who yet knew the feel as well
 of the men's rowing benches. Their reward is not 1410

unworthy. He lies there; and she who swanlike cried
aloud her lyric mortal lamentation out
is laid against his fond heart, and to me has given
a delicate excitement to my bed's delight.

CHORUS: O that in speed, without pain   1415
 and the slow bed of sickness
 death could come to us now, death that forever
 carries sleep without ending, now that our lord is
  down,
 our shield, kindest of men,
 who for a woman's grace suffered so much, 1420
 struck down at last by a woman.

 Alas, Helen, wild heart
 for the multitudes, for the thousand lives
 you killed under Troy's shadow,
 you alone, to shine in man's memory   1425
 as blood flower never to be washed out. Surely a
  demon then
 of death walked in the house, men's agony.

KLYTEMESTRA: No, be not so heavy, nor yet draw
  down
 in prayer death's ending,
 neither turn all wrath against Helen   1430
 for men dead, that she alone killed
 all those Danaan lives, to work
 the grief that is past all healing.

CHORUS: Divinity that kneel on this house and the two
 strains of the blood of Tantalus,[48]   1435
 in the hands and hearts of women you steer
 the strength tearing my heart.
 Standing above the corpse, obscene
 as some carrion crow she sings
 the crippled song and is proud.   1440

KLYTEMESTRA: Thus have you set the speech of
  your lips
 straight, calling by name
 the spirit thrice glutted that lives in this race.
 From him deep in the nerve is given
 the love and the blood drunk, that before 1445
 the old wound dries, it bleeds again.

CHORUS: Surely it is a huge
 and heavy spirit bending the house you cry;

---

48 Tantalus: son of Zeus, father of Pelops, and grandfather
 of Atreus and Thyestes.

alas, the bitter glory
of a doom that shall never be done with;   1450
and all through Zeus, Zeus,
first cause, prime mover.
For what thing without Zeus is done among
    mortals?
What here is without God's blessing?

O king, my king   1455
how shall I weep for you?
What can I say out of my heart of pity?
Caught in this spider's web you lie,
Your life gasped out in indecent death,
struck prone to this shameful bed   1460
by your lady's hand of treachery
and the stroke twin edged of the iron.
KLYTEMESTRA: Can you claim I have done this?
    Speak of me never
more as the wife of Agamemnon.   1465
In the shadow of this corpse's queen
the old stark avenger
of Atreus for his revel of hate
struck down this man,
last blood for the slaughtered children.   1470
CHORUS: What man shall testify
your hands are clean of this murder?
How? How? Yet from his father's blood
might swarm some fiend to guide you.
The black ruin that shoulders   1475
through the streaming blood of brothers
strides at last where he shall win requital
for the children who were eaten.

O king, my king
how shall I weep for you?   1480
What can I say out of my heart of pity?
Caught in this spider's web you lie,
your life gasped out in indecent death,
struck prone to this shameful bed
by your lady's hand of treachery   1485
and the stroke twin edged of the iron.
KLYTEMESTRA: No shame, I think, in the death given
    this man. And did he not
first of all in this house wreak death
by treachery?   1490
The flower of this man's love and mine,

Iphigeneia of the tears
he dealt with even as he has suffered.
Let his speech in death's house be not loud.
With the sword he struck,   1495
with the sword he paid for his own act.
CHORUS: My thoughts are swept away and I go
    bewildered.
Where shall I turn the brain's
activity in speed when the house is falling?
There is fear in the beat of the blood rain breaking   1500
wall and tower. The drops come thicker.
Still fate grinds on yet more stones the blade
for more acts of terror.

Earth, my earth, why did you not fold me under
before ever I saw this man lie dead   1505
fenced by the tub in silver?
Who shall bury him? Who shall mourn him?
Shall you dare this who have killed
your lord? Make lamentation,
render the graceless grace to his soul   1510
for huge things done in wickedness?
Who over this great man's grave shall lay
the blessing of tears
worked soberly from a true heart?
KLYTEMESTRA: Not for you to speak of such   1515
    tendance.
Through us he fell,
by us he died; we shall bury.
There will be no tears in this house for him.
It must be Iphigeneia
his child, who else,   1520
shall greet her father by the whirling stream
and the ferry of tears
to close him in her arms and kiss him.
CHORUS: Here is anger for anger. Between them
who shall judge lightly?   1525
The spoiler is robbed; he killed, he has paid.
The truth stands ever beside God's throne
eternal: he who has wrought shall pay; that is law.
Then who shall tear the curse from their blood?
The seed is stiffened to ruin.   1530
KLYTEMESTRA: You see truth in the future
at last. Yet I wish
to seal my oath with the Spirit
in the house: I will endure all things as they stand

now, hard though it be. Hereafter   1535
let him go forth to make bleed with death
and guilt the houses of others.
I will take some small
measure of our riches, and be content
that I swept from these halls   1540
the murder, the sin, and the fury.

[*AIGISTHOS enters, followed at a little distance by his
armed bodyguard.*[49]]

AIGISTHOS: O splendor and exaltation of this day
    of doom!
Now I can say once more that the high gods look
    down
on mortal crimes to vindicate the right at last,
now that I see this man—sweet sight—before me   1545
    here
sprawled in the tangling nets of fury, to atone
the calculated evil of his father's hand.
For Atreus, this man's father, King of Argolis—
I tell you the clear story—drove my father forth,
Thyestes, his own brother, who had challenged him   1550
in his king's right—forth from his city and his home.
Yet sad Thyestes came again to supplicate
the hearth, and win some grace, in that he was
    not slain
nor soiled the doorstone of his fathers with blood
    spilled.
Not his own blood. But Atreus, this man's godless   1555
    sire,
angrily hospitable set a feast for him,
in seeming a glad day of fresh meat slain and good
cheer; then served my father his own children's flesh
to feed on. For he carved away the extremities,
hands, feet, and cut the flesh apart, and covered   1560
    them
served in a dish to my father at his table apart,
who with no thought for the featureless meal
    before him ate
that ghastly food whose curse works now before
    your eyes.
But when he knew the terrible thing that he had
    done,

he spat the dead meat from him with a cry, and   1565
    reeled
spurning the table back to heel with strength the
    curse:
"Thus crash in ruin all the seed of Pleisthenes."[50]
Out of such acts you see this dead man stricken here,
and it was I, in my right, who wrought this
    murder, I
third born to my unhappy father, and with him   1570
driven, a helpless baby in arms, to banishment.
Yet I grew up, and justice brought me home again,
till from afar I laid my hands upon this man,
since it was I who pieced together the fell plot.
Now I can die in honour again, if die I must,   1575
having seen him caught in the cords of his just
    punishment.
CHORUS: Aigisthos, this strong vaunting in distress
    is vile.
You claim that you deliberately killed the king,
you, and you only, wrought the pity of this death.
I tell you then: There shall be no escape, your head 1580
shall face the stones of anger from the people's hands.
AIGISTHOS: So loud from you, stooped to the
    meanest rowing bench[51]
with the ship's masters lordly on the deck above?
You are old men; well, you shall learn how hard it is
at your age, to be taught how to behave yourselves.   1585
But there are chains, there is starvation with its pain,
excellent teachers of good manners to old men,
wise surgeons and exemplars. Look! Can you not
    see it?
Lash not at the goads for fear you hit them, and
    be hurt.
CHORUS: So then you, like a woman, waited the   1590
    war out
here in the house, shaming the master's bed with
    lust,
and planned against the lord of war this
    treacherous death?

---

49 The presence of an armed bodyguard was a typical
marker of the tyrant.

50 The house of Atreus.

51 In Athenian ships, the weakest rowers sat on the lowest
benches; a reference to the powerlessness of the members
of the Chorus and also a reminder of the fact that they
were too old and feeble to fight at Troy.

AIGISTHOS: It is just such words as these will make you cry in pain.

Not yours the lips of Orpheus,[52] no, quite otherwise,

whose voice of rapture dragged all creatures in his   1595
train.

You shall be dragged, for baby whimperings sobbed out

in rage. Once broken, you will be easier to deal with.

CHORUS: How shall you be lord of the men of Argos, you

who planned the murder of this man, yet could not dare

to act it out, and cut him down with your own   1600
hand?

AIGISTHOS: No, clearly the deception was the woman's part,

and I was suspect, that had hated him so long.

Still with his money I shall endeavour to control

the citizens. The mutinous man shall feel the yoke

drag at his neck, no cornfed racing colt that runs   1605

free traced; but hunger, grim companion of the dark

dungeon shall see him broken to the hand at last.

CHORUS: But why, why then, you coward, could you not have slain

your man yourself? Why must it be his wife who killed,

to curse the country and the gods within the   1610
ground?

Oh, can Orestes live, be somewhere in sunlight still?

Shall fate grown gracious ever bring him back again

in strength of hand to overwhelm these murderers?

AIGISTHOS: You shall learn then, since you stick to stubbornness of mouth and hand.   1615

Up now from your cover, my henchmen: here is work for you to do.

CHORUS: Look, they come! Let every man clap fist upon his hilted sword.

AIGISTHOS: I too am sword-handed against you; I am not afraid of death.

CHORUS: Death you said and death it shall be; we   1620
take up the word of fate.

KLYTEMESTRA: No, my dearest, dearest of all men, we have done enough. No more

violence. Here is a monstrous harvest and a bitter reaping time.

There is pain enough already. Let us not be bloody now.

Honoured gentlemen of Argos, go to your homes now and give way

to the stress of fate and season. We could not do   1625
otherwise

than we did. If this is the end of suffering, we can be content

broken as we are by the brute heel of angry destiny.

Thus a woman speaks among you. Shall men deign to understand?

AIGISTHOS: Yes, but think of these foolish lips that blossom into leering gibes,

think of the taunts they spit against me daring   1630
destiny and power,

sober opinion lost in insults hurled against my majesty.

CHORUS: It was never the Argive way to grovel at a vile man's feet.

AIGISTHOS: I shall not forget this; in the days to come I shall be there.

CHORUS: Nevermore, if God's hand guiding brings Orestes home again.

AIGISTHOS: Exiles feed on empty dreams of hope. I   1635
know it. I was one.

CHORUS: Have your way, gorge and grow fat, soil justice, while the power is yours.

AIGISTHOS: You shall pay, make no mistake, for this misguided insolence

CHORUS: Crow and strut, brave cockerel by your hen; you have no threats to fear.

KLYTEMESTRA: These are howls of impotent rage; forget them, dearest; you and I

have the power; we two shall bring good order to   1640
our house at least.

[*They enter the house. The doors close. All persons leave the stage.*]

---

52 Legendary musician whose songs enchanted wild animals with their beauty.

AESCHYLUS

Libation Bearers

translated by Geoffrey W. Bakewell[1]

CHARACTERS
    ORESTES
    PYLADES, his friend
    ELECTRA, his sister
    CHORUS OF FOREIGN SERVING WOMEN
    KLYTEMESTRA, his mother
    AIGISTHOS
    CILISSA, his nurse
    DOORKEEPER
    SERVANT

Scene: Argos, with the tomb of Agamemnon in the foreground and the royal palace behind. Statues of Hermes and Apollo are perhaps visible. ORESTES and PYLADES enter from stage right, as travellers.

ORESTES: Hermes, lord of the dead, watcher of
    paternal realms,
be my saviour and ally, I beg you.
I have come to this country, returned from exile,
longing to avenge my father
who at a woman's hand   5
died violently from secret treachery.
Here at the edge of his tomb I call upon my
    father
to hear me, to listen.

Here are two locks of my hair,
one for Inachus, the river of my youth,   10
the second a sign of my grief.

I was not present to lament your fate, father,
Nor to wave farewell as they carried out your
    corpse.

But what do I see? A procession
of women approaches, eye-catching in   15
black robes. What sort of misfortune does this
    mean?
Does some new grief befall the house,
or do these women bring to my father
liquid offerings, propitiation for the dead below?
That must be it. I think my sister Electra comes   20
    this way,
splendid in her wretched grief. O Zeus, let me
    avenge
my father's fate: be my willing ally.
Pylades, let's get out of the way, so that I
may clearly learn what the women pray for.
CHORUS: Sent forth from the house, escorting the   25
    offerings,
I match each step with a sharp-handed blow.
My cheek runs red with the scratchings of my
    nails in a new-torn furrow,
For a long time now my heart subsists on shrieks,
and in my grief I tear my clothes:
the rippings echo loudly.   30
Upon my chest droop the folds of my robes,
stretched and shorn amid ghastly misfortune.

Piercing, hair-raising was the cry of the house's
dream-prophet, startled from sleep by anger,
from deep within the dwelling   35
barking out a midnight cry of fear
which smote the women's quarters.

---

[1] Translator's note: The text is largely that of M.L. West, *Aeschylus Tragoediae* (Stuttgart, 1990).

And the interpreters of these divine dreams
in turn shouted and swore that
those below the ground blamed   40
and hated their killers.

O mother Earth! The godless woman eagerly
    sends me
with a thankless thank-offering to turn away evils.
But I fear to accomplish her prayer.
For what atonement is there for blood fallen upon   45
    the ground?
O most wretched hearth!
O destruction of the house!
Sunless, mortal-hating darkness hides the house
with the deaths of its masters.

Once an unconquerable, untamable,   50
insurmountable respect touched the people's ears
    and hearts.
But now it has departed, and *someone* is afraid.
For mortals, prosperity is divine, indeed more
    than divine.
But the balance scale of Justice swiftly casts
    shadows
on those who look upon the light;   55
sorrows bide their time and wait to burst forth
on others in gloomy twilight;
and endless night engulfs the rest.

As for the blood drunk down by the nurturing
    ground,
the vengeful clots have hardened and do not vanish.   60
Endless folly and all-powerful sickness
    string the guilty one along.
Nor is there any cure for one who breaches bridal
    beds.
All streams, rushing together in a single channel
to wash away the hand-defiling stain,
    strive in vain.

But since the gods brought force   65
to bear against my city, and led me from
my father's house into slavery,
I must praise those who now rule my life,
just or not, despite my better judgement,
controlling my bitter hatred.   70

And I weep underneath my cloak
for the senseless deaths of my late masters
shivering in secret sorrow.

ELECTRA: Servant women, housemaids,
    since you are here to escort my supplication,   75
    give me advice about these matters.
    What should I say while pouring out these
        offerings at the tomb?
    How might I speak kind words, how should I
        pray to my father?
    Should I say I bring a loving wife's offerings to her
        beloved husband,
    even though they come from my mother?   80
    I don't dare do this, nor do I know what to say
    as I pour the honeyed mixture on my father's
        tomb.
    Should I mouth the customary formula,
    asking the dead to return the favour to those
    sending these honours … with a gift worthy of   85
        their crimes?
    Or should I keep silent as I pour the liquid for the
        earth to drink,
    with dishonour for my father, just as he died, and
    depart with my eyes fixed forward, throwing
    behind me the offering urn, like someone
    discarding the remains of a sacrifice?   90
    Friends, take part in my deliberations:
    we share a common hatred within the house.
    Do not hide within your heart what you think for
        fear of anyone.
    That which is fated awaits both free and slave alike.
    Please speak if you have any ideas better than mine.   95
CHORUS: I respect your father's tomb as an altar,
    and will speak from the heart, since you urge it.
ELECTRA: Please speak, since you honoured my
    father's tomb.
CHORUS: As you pour the offerings, ask good
    things for his well-wishers.
ELECTRA: And which of my friends wish him well?   100
CHORUS: First of all, you yourself, and anyone who
    hates Aigisthos.
ELECTRA: So I should make these prayers for myself
    and you?
CHORUS: You yourself know the answer; say it.
ELECTRA: Who else should I add to our group?

CHORUS: Even if Orestes is far away, nevertheless remember him. 105

ELECTRA: Good idea—you instruct me well here.

CHORUS: And as for those guilty of the killing, as you remember …

ELECTRA: What shall I say? Teach and explain it to me; I don't know.

CHORUS: Pray for some god or mortal to come against them.

ELECTRA: Do you mean to judge or to avenge? 110

CHORUS: Simply say, someone who will kill them in return.

ELECTRA: Is it pious for me to ask the gods for this?

CHORUS: How could it be impious to repay your enemy with evils?

ELECTRA: Greatest herald of gods above and below, lord of the dead, help me, Hermes, 115
summon the divinities below the earth to
hear my prayers, for they watch over my father's house.
Summon too Earth herself, who gives birth to all things
and, after she has nourished them, reclaims them full-grown.
Meanwhile, I begin to pour these offerings 120
and speak, addressing my father. Pity me
and kindle beloved Orestes as a light in the house.
We have been sold by our mother and now wander about;
her payment was Aigisthos, who shared in your murder.
I am all but a slave, Orestes is in exile far from his 125
possessions,
while they carouse amid the fruits of your hard work.
I pray that by some good fortune Orestes may come here:
hear me, father. Grant that I may be more chaste
than my mother, and have a holier hand.
I ask these prayers for us. As for our enemies— 130
Father, may your avenger appear to them.
Let those who killed you die in return. It is just.
This evil curse upon them I insert
into the middle of my prayer for good.
Be for us the bringer of good things, together 135
with

the gods above and Earth and triumphant Justice.
With these prayers I complete my offerings.

Now it is time for your laments to blossom
as you cry out the dead man's paean.

CHORUS: Shed a tear, splashing, falling for your 140
fallen master
upon this fortress of the good which keeps evil pollution at bay,
now that the libations have been poured.
Hear me, your majesty,
hear me, O master, with your mind in darkness.
Aieeeeeee! 145
Let some strong spear-man come to liberate the house,
brandishing in his hands a Scythian bow bent taut
for warlike deed, waving a sword well-forged for hand-to-hand.

ELECTRA: My father now has his offerings; the earth has drunk them.
But now share your thoughts on a strange new 150
matter....

CHORUS: Speak. My heart leaps in fear.

ELECTRA: I see this shorn lock of hair on the tomb.

CHORUS: Is it from some man, or from a slim-waisted girl?

ELECTRA: This is easy for anyone to figure out.

CHORUS: How should my old age learn from your 155
youth?

ELECTRA: No one except me could cut it.

CHORUS: You mean that those who should cut their hair in grief oppose us.

ELECTRA: A glance shows that it feathers like my own.

CHORUS: With what sort of strands? This I want to know.

ELECTRA: It's just like mine in appearance. 160

CHORUS: Surely it wasn't a secret gift from Orestes?

ELECTRA: It certainly looks like his curls.

CHORUS: How did Orestes dare to come here?

ELECTRA: He sent a cropped tuft in honour of my father.

CHORUS: This possibility also makes me weep, 165
if he will never set foot in this land again.

ELECTRA: A wave of bitterness surged towards my heart too,
and I was struck, as if an arrow swept through me.

Salty, bitter drops fall from my eyes in a
   dangerous flood,
I cannot hold them off as I gaze upon this hair.   170
How can I imagine that any other citizen was
   owner of this lock?
The woman who killed him certainly didn't clip it,
I mean my unmaternal mother, who has become
   hostile
to her children.
But how can I say it out loud, that this   175
   magnificent gift
is from Orestes, whom I love beyond all others?
My hope is teasing me, alas.
If only the hair had the clear voice of a messenger
so that my mind might not be swayed back and
   forth,
whether to throw away this lock,   180
if in fact it was trimmed from an enemy's head,
or whether it is kin and shares my sorrow,
a tomb offering in my father's honour.
I call upon the gods who know
by what storms we are tossed like sailors.   185
But if salvation is to come, a great tree-trunk
may develop from a small seed.
Wait. Here's a second sign, tracks
like footsteps, similar to my own.
In fact two sets of marks are here,   190
those of the man himself, and those of a
   companion.
The heels and soles, when measured,
match my own tracks.
This pain—like the pangs of childbirth.
I must be losing my mind.   195
ORESTES: Pray that we may fare well in what
   follows;
tell the gods your prayers have been answered.
ELECTRA: Why, what do I now receive from the
   gods?
ORESTES: You look upon those for whom you just
   prayed.
ELECTRA: Do you know which people I called   200
   upon?
ORESTES: I know that you admire Orestes.
ELECTRA: And how then are my prayers answered?
ORESTES: I am he—do not search for another
   dearer than me.

ELECTRA: What? Are you weaving some trick about
   me, stranger?
ORESTES: Then I stitch together a plot against   205
   myself.
ELECTRA: Or do you wish to laugh amidst my
   misfortunes?
ORESTES: I also mock myself, if I mock you.
ELECTRA: Am I really to greet you as if you were
   Orestes?
ORESTES: You are slow to recognize me in the
   flesh,
yet seeing this lock of hair cut for the dead   210
and examining my tracks
you flew into joy and thought you saw me.
Place the clipped curls next to the cut and look at
   them;
they belong to your brother, and are distinctly like
   your own.
And look at this garment on which you yourself   215
   wove
a hunting scene with your thrusts of the batten.
Shhh—control yourself. Do not be foolish in your
   joy.
I know that our nearest are not our dearest.
ELECTRA: O fondest care of our father's house,
wept-for hope of a seed to save our family tree,   220
trusting in your might you will reclaim our
   father's house.
O sight for sore eyes, you play a quadruple role
   for me.
Father I must call you; and my affection for my
   mother
falls to you—the woman herself I have every right
   to hate—
as does my love for our sister,[2]   225
ruthlessly sacrificed.
And you were also the faithful brother who
   respected me.
Now if only Force and Justice, together with a third,
Zeus, the greatest of all, will be with me!
ORESTES: Zeus, Zeus, witness these doings.   230
Look upon the offspring deprived of their eagle
   father

_____
2 Iphigeneia.

who perished in the twists and coils
of a horrible viper.
Ravenous hunger squeezes the orphans,
who are not grown-up enough   235
to carry their father's prey to the nest.
You can gaze upon me and this woman,
I mean Electra, in the same way,
as offspring missing a father,
both sharing the same exile from his house.   240
If you destroy the fledglings of a father
who sacrificed and honoured you greatly,
where will you find a like hand
to do you honour at banquets?
If you destroy the eagle's descendants   245
mortals would no longer believe the birdsigns you
    send,
nor would this royal tree-trunk, everywhere
    withered,
assist at your altars on days when cattle are
    sacrificed.
Care for this scion, and you would raise up to
    greatness
a house which now seems to have plunged into   250
    the depths.
CHORUS: O children, saviours of your father's hearth,
    keep quiet so that none may learn this news
    and happily blab it all to those in power.
    How I long to see them dead, oozing
    pitchy sap amid a flame!   255
ORESTES: The great-hearted oracle of Loxian Apollo
    will never betray me. It commands me
    to run this risk, shouting often,
    speaking of ruin to freeze my warm heart
    unless I go after those guilty of my father's death   260
    in the same manner, meaning that I should
    kill them in return.
    Otherwise I will pay with my own life,
    made savage, impoverished and punished,
    after suffering countless evils.   265
    And in speaking the oracle showed the rage
    of things below the ground hostile to mortals[3]

and set forth the diseases which clamber upon
human flesh, growths eating away at the body
with their savage jaws, white pus flowering on the   270
    sores.
And the god spoke of other assaults of the Furies,
assaults taking shape from the blood of fathers.

There he sits, seeing clearly,
moving his eyebrow in the gloom.
The shadowy weapon of those below ground   275
comes from family members who have fallen
and beg for vengeance.
Madness and phantom fear in the night
disturb, shake, and chase the surviving kin,
his back torn by the bronze whip of the city.   280
For such exiles there is no share of a common cup,
no pouring of libations, and the invisible anger of
    a father
excludes them from altars. No one is permitted
to house or to stay with them. Honourless, friendless,
at last they die, evilly shriveled up by all-   285
    consuming fate.
Isn't it necessary to trust such statements from the
    oracle?
Even if I didn't believe them, the deed must still
    be done.
For many of my desires converge here,
the commands of the god and my great grief for
    my father.
The lack of money also weighs upon me,   290
and the wish that the most famous citizens alive,
those who with righteous heart destroyed Troy,
may not be enslaved to a pair of women.
For Aigisthos is a woman at heart. He will soon
    find out
what he is made of.   295
CHORUS: Great Goddesses of Fate, see this matter
    through
    to its divine end, where justice reestablishes itself.
    Let hateful speech match hateful speech.
    Justice shouts greatly, demanding her due.
    Let bloody blow atone for bloody blow.   300
    "The doer must suffer": thus runs the age-old tale.

---

3 The Furies, sometimes euphemistically called
  Eumenides, "the kindly ones." Female powers of the
  chthonic realms, they were imagined to pursue murderers with disease and madness, or, as in this case, to stimu-

late surviving male relatives to exact vengeance on behalf
of the murder victim.

ORESTES: Father, unhappy father, what might I say or do
  to help you float in from afar
  where your bed holds you?
  Light is an antidote to darkness,   305
  and noble weeping is likewise welcome
  to the descendants of Atreus here before the house.
CHORUS: Child, the raging jaw of fire does not conquer
  the spirit of one who dies:
  he shows his anger later.   310
  Dead, he is lamented
  and exposes the guilty to harm.
  The mourning for fathers and parents,
  righteous, all-embracing, stirred into motion,
  always hunts them down.   315
ELECTRA: Father, now it is my turn.
  Listen to my much-wept griefs.
  Your two children stand at your tomb
  and wail in loud lament.
  Your tomb has welcomed   320
  suppliants and exiles alike.
  In these matters what is good, what is free from evil?
  Doesn't ruin remain standing in the ring?
CHORUS: But from this mess the god
  could make more melodious music   325
  if he wanted to. Instead of tombside laments
  a victory song might welcome
  a new-found friend in the royal halls.
ORESTES: Father, you should have died at Troy,
  spear-struck by one of the Lycians.[4]   330
  Then you would have left fame to your house
  and the whole town would have envied your
    children's lives,
  and you would have had a towering tomb across
    the sea.
  This the house could have endured.
CHORUS: Your father has a distinguished role below   335
    the earth,
  friend to his friends
  who died noble deaths at Troy.
  Imposing monarch, he attends
  the awesome lords of the underworld.

For while alive he was a king, filling   340
  the office which destiny assigned him,
  wielding in his two hands the scepter which men
    obey.
ELECTRA: Father, I would not have had you dead,
  not even if you had perished beneath
  the walls of Troy and lay buried   345
  with the rest of your spear-slain folk
  beside Scamander's ford.
  Better for those who killed him
  to have died thus themselves,
  and for someone far away,   350
  who had no part in the fighting,
  to learn of the deadly fate of our enemies.
CHORUS: Child, what you wish for is finer than
    gold,
  greater than great good fortune beyond the lot of
    mortals.
  It's easy to wish.   355
  But then the crack of this double whip strikes home:
  Orestes' helpers lie below the ground,
  while our hateful masters have unclean hands
  and misery has come to these children.
ORESTES: Your words pierce those who hear,   360
  just like an arrow.
  Zeus, Zeus,
  send up from below the ground
  late-avenging destruction
  against the daring, shameless hand of mortals.   365
  My parents' payment will be made together:
  to my father, by my mother.
CHORUS: May I be the one to sing the piercing cry
  as the sacrifice is performed,
  the man struck, the woman destroyed.   370
  Why should I conceal within me
  what sort of hatred rushes to the surface?
  My bitter feelings are tossed by head-winds
  blowing from my heart.
ELECTRA: And when might Zeus strike   375
  with violent hand—
  Yes! Yes!—
  shattering their heads?
  Let him make a promise to the land.
  From injustice I demand justice.   380
  Hear me, Earth, and you Powers of the
    underworld.

---

4 Inhabitants of Asia Minor with a reputation for bravery;
  allies of the Trojans, they were led by Sarpedon.

CHORUS: Indeed, the law is that bloody drops
  which fall to the ground
  demand more blood.
  Death shouts aloud for a Fury,   385
  an avenger from those who have already perished,
  and she piles destruction upon destruction.
ORESTES: Alas! You realms of the dead.
  Look about you, powerful Curses of those who
      have faded.
  Look at the remnants of Atreus' descendants: 390
  desperate, dishonoured, deprived of their house.
  Zeus, where might one turn?
CHORUS: My own heart has in turn been shaken
  as I listen to this grieving.
  Sometimes hope leaves me,   395
  and my insides blacken
  as I listen to your words.
  But whenever you say something valiant,
  my distress departs,
  and bravery reappears.   400
ELECTRA: What should we say to succeed?
  Those pains which we suffered from those who
      bore us?
  She may fawn and wag her tail,
  but the pains are not charmed away.
  Because of my mother   405
  my heart is like a bloody-minded wolf
  and cannot be appeased.
CHORUS: I struck myself in oriental fashion
  and wailed aloud like a Persian woman.
  My hands were visible, ceaselessly stretching   410
      upward,
  upward, one after the other, roaming here and
      there,
  and my head rang with the blows.
ELECTRA: Alas, alas, mother, cruel, shameless,
  you dared to bury the king your husband
  unwept, unmourned, carried out like an enemy   415
  with none of his subjects present.
ORESTES: It was all without honour, you say.
  Well then she will pay for my father's dishonour—
  the gods and my own two hands
  will see to that.   420
  Once I've slaughtered her I can die.
CHORUS: His corpse was also mutilated, you should
      know.

The one who did it was she
who buried him thus. She wanted to make his death
unbearable for you to live with.   425
You hear the dishonourable anguish of your
    father.
ELECTRA: You speak of father's death. As for me,
  I was kept away in dishonour, undeservedly,
  locked inside the house like a savage dog,
  far quicker to cry than to laugh,   430
  mixing weeping and wailing in secret.
  Listen and do not forget—
  engrave it in your mind.
CHORUS: Record it. Drill the story into your head,
  down to the calm depths of your heart.   435
  This is how it stands.
  But he himself burns to see
  what comes next.
  It's up to you to do your duty
  with unflinching might.   440
ORESTES: Father, I call you, stand with your loved
    ones.
ELECTRA: I too lend my voice; I have wept.
CHORUS: All of us here shout in support.
  Hear us! Ascend to the light!
  Be with us against your enemies!   445
ORESTES: Violence will clash with violence, claims
    to justice will contend.
ELECTRA: Gods, see that our justice prevails.
CHORUS: Trembling creeps over me as I hear our
    prayers.
  Destiny has long stood in wait;
  now it may come to those who pray for it.   450

  Oh! Inborn pain
  and discordant bloody blow
  of destruction!
  Alas for the lamentable, unendurable mourning!
  Alas for the sorrow which never stops!   455

  It is up to the house to bandage and cure
  these wounds; no outsiders can do it,
  only they themselves, through
  savage, bloody conflict.
  This is the hymn of the gods below the earth.   460

  Blessed beings underground, hear our prayer.

Be kind and send help to the children.
Let them triumph.
ORESTES: Father, you did not die in a kingly fashion.
Give me the authority over your house, I ask you.   465
ELECTRA: Father, I too have need of you.
Help me to escape great hardship, inflicting it on
Aigisthos instead.
ORESTES: Then the customary banquets could be
held in your honour.
Otherwise your underground companions will be
well-fed,
but you will lack honour as the steam rises from   470
burnt victims.
ELECTRA: And on my wedding day I will bring you
liquid offerings
out of my share of the inheritance from your
house.
I will honour this tomb of yours above all else.
ORESTES: Earth, release my father to watch over
our battle.
ELECTRA: Persephone, give us his beautiful power.   475
ORESTES: Remember the bath in which you were
slaughtered, father.
ELECTRA: Remember how they snared you in a
strange new net.
ORESTES: You were caught with chains that were
not bronze.
ELECTRA: And tangled up in wickedly twisted plots.
ORESTES: Doesn't this shame rouse you, father?   480
ELECTRA: Do you raise your head and give a
welcome nod?
ORESTES: Either send Justice as an ally to your
loved ones,
or let us wrestle them down the same way they
pinned you.
They bested you—don't you wish to triumph in
turn?
ELECTRA: And hear this final cry, father.   485
Look upon us, fledglings perched at your tomb.
Take pity on the cry which rises from female and
male alike.
ORESTES: Do not blot out this seed of Pelops'[5]
descendants.

Through them you live, even though you die.
For children preserve a man's glory even after   490
he is gone. They are like cork buoys which float a
fishing net,
preserving the linen line rising from the deep.
Listen. We make these laments on your behalf.
You will be saved if you honour our plea.
CHORUS: Indeed, you two have given this speech its   495
proper length,
honour to compensate for the tearless burial.
But now that you have rightly decided to act,
it's time for deeds, Orestes: test your destiny.
ORESTES: Agreed. But it is not a detour to ask
why, for what reason she[6] sent libations,   500
trying after the fact to atone for the incurable
suffering.
He is dead, and has contempt for her pitiful
offering.
This doesn't make sense—
her gifts are worse than her crime.
One could pour out everything for having   505
shed blood once, but as they say, it doesn't work.
If you know, tell me. I want to know.
CHORUS: I do know, my child; I was there.
Quaking from dreams and fears in the night
the godless woman sent these libations.   510
ORESTES: Really? Do you know enough about the
dream to tell me everything?
CHORUS: She says she seemed to give birth to a
serpent.
ORESTES: And how did the story end?
CHORUS: It slept wrapped in baby clothes, just like
a real child.
ORESTES: What food did it seek with its baby fangs?   515
CHORUS: In the dream, she suckled it with her breast.
ORESTES: Wasn't her breast torn by the hateful
creature?
CHORUS: Yes—it sucked clots of blood along with
the milk.
ORESTES: This vision is not an empty one.
CHORUS: Frightened, she cried out in her sleep,   520
and many torches, blinded by the gloom,
flared up in the house for its mistress.

---

5 Son of Tantalus, father of Atreus and Thyestes, and
grandfather of Agamemnon and Menelaus.

6 Klytemestra.

Now she sends these libations to his tomb,
hoping they will be a cure to cut short her distress.
ORESTES: I pray to Earth and to my father's grave   525
    that her dream may come true for me.
I interpret it to fit together like this:
if the snake came from the same place I did
and was wrapped in baby clothes like me
and strained at the breast that nursed me   530
and drank clots of blood with its mother's milk
while she wailed in fear and pain,
then it must be that she will die violently,
since she raised a frightful monster.
I become the snake and slay her: thus says this   535
    dream.
CHORUS: I choose you as my interpreter in these
    matters:
may they turn out as you say. Now explain the
    rest to your friends,
assigning the various duties, what to do and what
    not to do.
ORESTES: The plan is simple. I ask that Electra go
    inside,
and that you all conceal these agreements of mine,   540
so that those who killed a man of note by
    treachery
may themselves be taken by treachery,
dying in the same noose, as the Loxian said,
king Apollo, whose prophecies never yet have lied.
I shall arrive at the courtyard gates dressed as a   545
    traveller,
having the whole outfit, posing as a guest-friend
and military ally, together with this man here,
    Pylades.
The two of us will put on a Parnassian[7] accent,
mimicking the speech of those from Phokis.[8]

But it could be that the gatekeepers frown and   550
don't let us in, since the house is possessed by
    evils, after all.
We will wait in such a way that anyone
walking past the house will wonder and say

"Why do Aigisthos' gates lock out the suppliant
if the man himself is at home and knows about it?"   555
And if I then cross the threshold of the gates
and find him sitting on my father's throne,
or if he in fact shows up later and speaks to me
face to face—believe me, he will get a look at
    me—
before he can say "Where does the stranger come   560
    from?"
I'll make him a corpse, swiftly impaling him on
    my sword.
And the Fury, who has had plenty of murder,
will down a third drink of blood straight-up.
And you, Electra, take good care of things inside,
so that our plans come off without a hitch.   565
As for you women, I ask that you watch your
    tongues,
keeping quiet when necessary,
yet speaking up when it will help.
As to the rest: let it be his[9] job to watch over me,
steadying me for the fencing match to come.   570
CHORUS: The earth nurses many strange and
    terrible things,
frightful sorrows;
the arms of the sea teem,
filled with hostile monsters;
even the torches hung between heaven and earth   575
do harm.
Birds and beasts alike
know the windy anger of storms.

But who could adequately express
the audacious arrogance of men,   580
the brazen passions of
reckless-hearted women,
passions bound to human ruin?
Loveless love in which women rule
ruins the yoke which binds   585
animal with animal, man with woman.

---

7 Mountain that rises above Delphi, home of Apollo's oracle.
8 Region in central Greece.

9 Ambiguous; could refer to Agamemnon, Apollo,
Hermes, or even Pylades (see A.F. Garvie, *Choephoroi*
[Oxford, 1986], xlvi).

Those without winged wits should learn this.
Consider Althaea,[10] the wretched, child-killing
daughter of Thestius.
Aflame, she made careful plans   590
and set the bloody brand of her boy ablaze.
It had been his companion ever since
he emerged bawling from his mother,
and grew older with him until
the fateful day when both were consumed.   595

Legend provides another woman to hate,
the murderous maiden Scylla.
She destroyed a man
she should have loved,
helped those she should have hated.   600
Trusting in Minos' gift of golden necklaces from
    Crete,
the bitch cut off the immortal hair of her father
    Nisos
who lay relaxed in heedless sleep.[11]
Now Hermes meets and leads him down.

And since I've brought to mind relentless sorrows,   605
what about the unwelcome wedding hated by our
    house
and the womanish cunning brought to bear
against a man in arms?
I honour cool hearths unheated by passion,
and women who don't wield brazen spears.   610

When it comes to evils, the story of Lemnos[12]
takes precedence. This abominable tale
is known throughout the world;

Lemnian calamities serve again and again
as a benchmark for what is terrible.   615

The Lemnian people vanish,
dishonoured among mortals
and despised by the gods for their deed.
No one honours that which is hateful to the gods.
Which of these examples do I choose unjustly?   620

This sword pushes sharp-pointed
on through the lungs of those
who have unlawfully violated
the utter majesty of Zeus.
The sword is driven by Justice,   625
Justice trampled and trodden lawlessly to the ground.
But Justice's foundation is shored up,
and Fate the swordsmith
already stands at the forge.
A deep-thinking, splendid Fury   630
brings into the house
the child of earlier bloodshed.
In time comes payment for pollution.
ORESTES: Slave! Slave! Do you hear me pounding
    the courtyard gate?
Is anyone inside? Slave!   635
Again I say: Slave!
Is anybody home?
Yet a third time I call for someone
to come out from the house.
Does Aigisthos make his house   640
hospitable to guests?
DOORKEEPER: Enough! I hear you. Where are you
    from, stranger?
Who are you?
ORESTES: Tell the lords of the house
that I have come bringing them news.   645
And hurry, since the dark chariot of night is
coming on quickly; it is time for travellers
to drop anchor in houses which welcome strangers.
Let someone with authority in the house come to
    the door,

---

10 Mother of Meleager. It was prophesied that her son
    would live no longer than a brand that was burning on
    the hearth at the time of his birth. To prolong his life
    Althaea snatched the brand from the fire and locked it
    away. But when Meleager killed her brothers in a quar-
    rel, she rekindled the brand and let him die.
11 The result of this betrayal of her father was the capture
    of her city, Megara, by the Cretans under Minos of
    Knossos.
12 Large Aegean island legendary for marital strife: after
    their husbands all take mistresses, the island's women kill
    all of Lemnos's men—and then marry members of Jason's

crew, the Argonauts. In another story, Lemnian men kill
their Athenian-born concubines, together with their offspring, when the women begin to raise these "Lemnian"
children as Athenians (see Garvie 1986:217–18).

either a woman in charge here, or better yet, a man.   650
For in talking with women one's words are
       politely vague.
But when a man talks with a man
he's encouraged, and speaks clearly what he means.
KLYTEMESTRA: *[appearing in the doorway]*
       Strangers, please speak if you need anything.
You will find all that you might expect   655
in a house like this: warm baths,
a bed to charm away your aches,
and honest folks standing by to keep an eye on
       things.
If you need anything else more complicated,
that is an issue for men: I will let them know.   660
ORESTES: I am a stranger from Daulis in Phokis.
I was striding towards Argos, carrying my own gear,
just after I'd laced up my boots to come here,
when I met a stranger, someone I didn't know.
He asked about my journey and told me of his own.   665
He was Strophius, from Phokis—he told me as
       we walked.
"Stranger," he said, "since you are already bound
       for Argos,
you must remember to tell the parents of Orestes
that he is dead. Don't forget!
Whether his family will decide to bring him home,   670
or whether they want to bury him there as an alien,
a stranger forever, bring their instructions back
       with you.
Right now the sides of a bronze urn conceal
the ashes of a man who has been well-lamented."
Now I have told you all I heard. Whether I   675
       happen
to be talking to the lords of the house and his
       relatives,
I don't know—the one who bore him would.
KLYTEMESTRA: Aiee! You mean that we are
       destroyed from top to bottom.
O Curse of this house, you are hard to wrestle
       with!
Even from afar your gaze strikes many tranquil   680
       things.
Putting your hand to your unerring bow
you strip me, a poor wretch, of those I love.
And now Orestes too—even though he was smart
to keep his foot clear of the deadly muck here.

As for that recent hope that he would be the doctor   685
to cure the evil frenzy in this house:
you can write it off. It has betrayed us.
ORESTES: I would have preferred to have good
       news in hand
when meeting and staying with such prosperous
       hosts.
For what bond is kinder than that between host   690
       and guest?
But I thought it would be impious
not to see this through for his loved ones
after my promise and your kind welcome.
KLYTEMESTRA: You will not receive less than you
       deserve,
nor would you be any less dear to our house.   695
Another man might well have come
to announce these things just as you did.
But now it is time for strangers who have travelled
       far
to receive their due.
Lead him to the comfortable quarters   700
where we lodge the men who visit.
The same holds for the companion who stands
       behind him.
There let them enjoy what the house has to offer.
See to them well; I shall hold you accountable.
Meanwhile I will share the news with those   705
who rule the house, and together with our loved
       ones
we will discuss this turn of events.
CHORUS: Dear servants of this house,
when will we lend a strong voice in support of
       Orestes?
O Lady Earth, majestic tomb mound,   710
you who now lie atop
the body of our kingly admiral,
now hear us; now help us.
Now it is high time
for treacherous Persuasion to join the fray;   715
now is the moment
for Hermes, lord of the dead, to preside over
these dark struggles in which swords slay.

The stranger seems to be stirring up trouble.
I see this woman, the nurse of Orestes, has been   720
       weeping.

Old woman, where are you off to, trudging before
    the house?
Grief accompanies you, unbidden.
NURSE: My mistress orders me to summon Aigisthos
    to the strangers as quickly as possible, so that he
    may come and learn the new tidings more clearly,   725
    man from man. In front of the servants
    she put on a sad face, but inside she hides
    her laughter about the deeds that have worked out
    beautifully for her. For this house, though,
    things are terrible, given the clear report the   730
        strangers made.
    As for him, he'll rejoice when he learns the story.
    Alas, I am wretched. The mix of ancient woes
    which took place in this house of Atreus was
    difficult enough to bear, and grieved the heart in
        my breast.
    But never yet did I endure suffering like this.   735
    The other evils I patiently bore.
    But my beloved Orestes! That sweet labour which
        wore me out,
    whom I accepted from his mother and raised as
        my own,
    his cries which had me pacing to and fro in the night,
    the many burdensome things I endured—all   740
        come to naught.
    The little thing can't think for itself, and you have
        to
    raise it with your own judgement: there's no other
        way.
    A child still in diapers doesn't speak a word
    when hunger or thirst or a full bladder takes over:
    a baby's stomach has a mind of its own.   745
    I tried to predict these things in advance, but I know
    I often guessed wrong, and washed diapers till
        they shone.
    I was both laundry-woman and nurse all in one.
    Doing the chores of two women,
    I raised Orestes for his father.   750
    And now I find out he is dead. Woe is me!
    I now go to a man who has defiled this house.
    He will be glad to learn the news.
CHORUS: How does she command him to come?
NURSE: What do you mean, 'how'? Say it again, so   755
    I understand more clearly.
CHORUS: With bodyguards, or walking by himself?

NURSE: She tells him to bring spear-bearing
    comrades.
CHORUS: Do not announce this to our hated master;
    instead, tell him to come alone as swiftly as possible,
    so that without fear he may hear the news and   760
    rejoice.
    It is the messenger's job to straighten a crooked tale.
NURSE: Wait—you are encouraged by the recent news?
CHORUS: Suppose Zeus one day sets an end to our
    evils.
NURSE: And how might he do that? Orestes, our
    house's hope, is gone.
CHORUS: Not yet: only a bad prophet would think   765
    so.
NURSE: What do you mean? Do you have some
    separate news?
CHORUS: Go and make the announcement,
    perform your duties.
    The gods will do as they see fit.
NURSE: Alright—I will go and obey your words.
    And may all turn out for the best, with the gods'   770
    blessing.
CHORUS: Now, Zeus, father of the Olympian gods,
    grant my prayer
    that the rightful rulers of the house
    may succeed,
    striving to see good order again.   775
    All that I ask is just.
    Zeus, please protect them.

    Hear me, Zeus, and bring the man inside the house
    face to face with our enemies.
    If you are willing to exalt him,   780
    you will be repaid two and three times over.

    Behold the colt of a man you loved,
    yoked to a chariot, alone;
    set some limit to his race of troubles
    and preserve his gait   785
    so that we see
    the lunge of his steps
    as they finish the course.

    And you gods who within the house
    tend the wealth-loving storeroom,   790
    listen to me with kindness.

Use fresh justice running with blood
to resolve the blood from deeds of old.
Let old man Murder make no more children
in this house.   795

O Apollo, inhabiting the great and well-built cavern,
let the man's house lift its gaze,
and emerging from the veil of darkness
let him look with loving eyes
upon the bright light of freedom.   800
Maia's child Hermes might also
justly take part since, when he wishes,
he blows most favourably for action.
He willingly reveals many things,
and speaks obscurely about those which are hidden.   805
At night he brings gloom upon the eyes,
while by day he is in no way more visible.

And then we women will hurl forth
the glorious cry of triumph
a house-saving,   810
fair-winded, sharply struck,
keening melody. These matters sail smoothly on.
My gain, mine increases here,
and ruin stands distant from our friends.

And you, be courageous when the time comes for   815
    deeds.
When she cries to you "Child,"
shout back "Yes! My father's!"
and complete her doom.
No one will blame you.

Hold the bravery of Perseus[13] in your heart: endure.   820
Delight your loved ones,
both those below the ground
and those above it.
Lodge the bloody destruction of the evil Gorgon
inside the house; fulfill the blameless   825
destiny foretold by Apollo.

---

13 Son of Danaë and Zeus, Perseus twice suffered banish-
    ment by parental figures, but with help from Athena and
    Hermes, he was able to kill the Gorgon Medusa, the sight
    of whose horrifying face turned men to stone.

AIGISTHOS: I have come, called by a messenger's
    summons.
    I understand that certain strangers have arrived
    with scarcely welcome news to tell:
    the death of Orestes. This too would be   830
    a bloody burden to bear for the house,
    already bitten and slow to heal from prior death.
    How shall I judge if it is really true?
    Perhaps the story springs forth from women's
        fright,
    dying unfulfilled. What could you say about these 835
        things
    to clarify them for me?
CHORUS: We did hear, but go inside
    and ask the strangers. Messengers are
    nowhere near as reliable as when a man
    himself questions other men.   840
AIGISTHOS: I very much want to see and question
        the messenger,
    whether he was there beside the dying man,
    or whether his knowledge is second-hand, based
        on vague report.
    He won't steal away my clear-sighted mind. [exits]
CHORUS: Zeus, Zeus, what shall I say?   845
    How shall I begin this prayer and invocation to
        the gods?
    And when I have spoken enough in support, how
        shall I end it?
    Even now the blood-stained blades of murderous
        axes
    will destroy Agamemnon's house
    utterly and forever,   850
    or else Orestes, kindling a flaming light for freedom,
    will rule the city with law
    amid the prosperity of his fathers.
    These are the stakes as god-like Orestes
    steps into the ring, one against two.   855
    May he conquer!
(AIGISTHOS, within) Aaaaaaaaai!
CHORUS: What? What then?
    How does it stand?
    What is the result for the house?   860
    Let's distance ourselves from the business afoot,
    so that we may seem unconnected to these evils.
    The outcome of the struggle has already been
        decided.

SERVANT: Horrible, terrible—my master struck down!
   I say it again: it's ghastly! 865
   Aigisthos is no more. Quick, open up!
   Undo the bars on the women's gates!
   We need someone young and strong!
   Even so, he can't help a dead man.
   Hey! Hey! 870
   I shout to the deaf, and waste my breath
   on those who are asleep.
   Where is Klytemestra? What is she doing?
CHORUS: Now it seems her neck will fall
   near the chopping block, whacked by Justice. 875
KLYTEMESTRA: What's going on? What was that
   cry you raised in the house?
SERVANT: The dead strike down the living, I say!
KLYTEMESTRA: Alas! I understand what you mean
   from your riddles.
   We will be slain treacherously, just as we slew.
   Someone hand me the man-killing axe, quickly. 880
   [servant exits]
   Let's find out whether we win or lose.
   I've come to the brink of this evil.
ORESTES: *[enters with Pylades and a bloodied sword]*
   I've been looking for you. He's had his fill.
KLYTEMESTRA: Alas! You're dead, my dearest
   Aigisthos.
ORESTES: You love the man? Well, then, you'll lie in 885
   the same tomb.
   Now that he's dead you'll never leave his side.
KLYTEMESTRA: Son, wait! My child, have pity for
   this breast,
   at which you often dozed
   and sucked out nourishing milk with your gums.
ORESTES: Pylades, what shall I do? Should I shrink 890
   from killing my mother?
PYLADES: Then what about the rest of Apollo's
   prophecies
   chanted at Delphi, and the oaths sworn there?
   Better to have all men as your enemies rather than
   the gods.
ORESTES: I say that you are right, and advise me
   well.
   You, this way. I want to slaughter you atop your 895
   man.
   While he was alive you thought him better than
   my father.

Then die and sleep together with him, since you
   love him,
   and hate the man you should have loved.
KLYTEMESTRA: I raised you, and want to grow old
   with you.
ORESTES: What? You would live with me, though 900
   you killed my father?
KLYTEMESTRA: Fate was also responsible for these
   things, my child.
ORESTES: As she is for your impending doom.
KLYTEMESTRA: Have you no respect for your
   parent's curses, child?
ORESTES: No: you hurled me into misfortune after
   you bore me.
KLYTEMESTRA: I didn't cast you out, but sent you 905
   to friends' homes.
ORESTES: I was shamefully sold, though born of a
   free father.
KLYTEMESTRA: Where then is the price I took for
   you?
ORESTES: I shrink from naming your disgrace
   aloud.
KLYTEMESTRA: What about your father's infidelities?
   Give them equal time.
ORESTES: Don't scrutinize a man who toiled while 910
   you idled indoors.
KLYTEMESTRA: It's a hard thing for women to be
   kept apart from a man, my child.
ORESTES: And yet a man's labour feeds women
   seated inside.
KLYTEMESTRA: My child, it seems you will kill
   your mother.
ORESTES: It is you who kill yourself, not I.
KLYTEMESTRA: Careful—think of your mother's 915
   vengeful hounds.
ORESTES: There's no fleeing my father's if I falter here.
KLYTEMESTRA: I think I sing my dirge to a tomb in
   vain.
ORESTES: Yes: my father's fate marks out your own.
KLYTEMESTRA: Alas! This is the viper I bore and
   raised.
   The fear from my dreams was all too good a 920
   prophet.
ORESTES: You killed the man you shouldn't have.
   Now suffer what you shouldn't. *[goes with
   Klytemestra and Pylades into the house]*

CHORUS: I sigh at the double misfortune of even
    these two.
  Although steadfast Orestes has topped many acts
  of bloodshed, we nevertheless prefer this,   925
  that he, the eye of the house, not perish in utter ruin.
  Justice came for the sons of Priam in time,
  the belated penalty falling heavier.
  And into the house of Agamemnon came
  a double lion, a double curse.   930
  The exile sent by Apollo sped through the course,
  driven on by divine advice.

  Raise a cry of triumph! Our master's house
  has escaped from evils, and from the two
    criminals
  who squandered its possessions   935
  along an evil path of fate.

  And in came crafty Punishment,
  whose skill is hidden battle.
  In the combat his hand was grasped by
  the true daughter of Zeus—we mortals who   940
  understand rightly call her Justice—
  and she breathed out angry destruction upon his
    enemies.

  This same justice, treacherously injured,
  was truthfully supported by Apollo the Loxian,
  who holds the great crevasse[14] in the land around   945
    Parnassus.
  After a time, she attacks.
  One way or another, the divine prevails.
  One should not serve the wicked.
  It is right to honour those who rule in heaven.

  Light is visible; a great chain   950
  has been removed from the house.
  Rise up, O House! For too long now
  you have lain prostrate on the ground.

  Soon our champion, crowned at last,
  will cross the threshold,   955
  once he has driven all pollution from the house
  with cleansings that banish ruin.
  Our fortunes are a sight for sore eyes
  and music to the ears:
  the strangers who dwelt here   960
  will again be outcast.

ORESTES: [revealed on the ekkyklema with the bodies
    of Aigisthos and Klytemestra; the robe used in
    Agamemnon's murder is also present]
  Behold the double tyranny of the land,
  the patricidal destroyers of my house.
  Once they were majestic, seated on their thrones,
  and even now they love one another,   965
  as their end suggests: to their oath they remained
    true.
  They swore to kill my poor father,
  and that they would die together:
  no perjury here.

  As you listen to the sordid tale,   970
  behold their clever trick,
  the fetter they used on my poor father,
  bindings for his hands and yoke for his feet.
  Stretch it out, and standing about in a circle
  show the robe, so that father may see—   975
  not my father, but the father who watches over all,
  Helios[15]—may see the unholy deeds of my mother,
  so that he may someday be my witness at judgement,
  that I rightly brought about my mother's doom.
  About Aigisthos' fate I have nothing to say: 980
  he got what adulterers deserve under the law.

  But what euphemism can I use and yet describe
    the robe correctly?
  Net of a wild beast? Bath-covering to wrap a
    corpse's feet?
  You might call it a snare, a noose, a foot-binding
    cloak.
  It's the sort of thing a thief might possess,   985
  a trick to make a living from strangers' silver.
  Often might he gladden his heart,
  killing many men with this trap.
  And the woman who thought up this abomination
  against her husband, from whom she bore   990

---

14 The oracle at Delphi.

15 God of the sun.

children in her womb—a sweet burden once,
but now an evil one, as she shows—
what do you think? If she had been an eel or a viper,
could she have been any more venomous,
making someone rot away at her touch alone,   995
  unbitten,
relying on her daring and wicked cunning?
May I never have such a mate in my house!
By the gods, I'd rather die childless.
CHORUS: Alas, alas for the wretched deeds.
  You died a hateful death. Aieeeeeee!   1000
  But suffering also blooms for the one who waits.
ORESTES: Did she do it or didn't she?
  This cloak proves it, dyed by Aigisthos' blade.
  With time the gore from the slaughter
  has marred and stained the cloth's bright hues.   1005
  Now I praise my father, now mourn him in person,
  as I address the garment which killed him.
  I grieve over the deeds, the suffering, and our
    whole family.
  No one envies the pollution this victory has
    brought me.
CHORUS: No mortal can go through life unharmed   1010
  and not pay a price.
  Alas! One hardship is already here,
  and another is on the way.
ORESTES: I want you all to know
  that I can't predict where it will end—   1015
  I am like a charioteer pulled by his horses
  from the racetrack. My wits rebel
  and drag me off into defeat.
  Near my heart Fear prepares to sing;
  my heart itself waits to dance to anger's tune.   1020
  While I am still lucid, friends, I'll proclaim it aloud:
  I say I killed my mother justly;
  she was polluted with patricide, hated by the gods.
  The urgings of the prophet at Delphi, Loxian
    Apollo,
  were the chief cause of my bold act.   1025
  He promised me that if I did these things
  I would be innocent of the evil charge,
  but if I ignored him—I will not speak of the
    punishment.
  No one could begin to describe those afflictions.
  Now look at me.   1030

Equipped with this branch and tuft of wool[16]
I will flee the kindred blood I shed
and arrive as a suppliant at the shrine
at the middle of the earth, the navel-stone,
the plain of Loxian Apollo,   1035
where his holy fire is said to burn undying.
Apollo instructed me to turn to no other hearth.
And I urge all the Argives to remember these things
as time passes, what sort of evils were done,
and to speak in my defense if Menelaus comes.   1040
I will be a wanderer, banished from this land,
in life and death leaving this reputation behind.
CHORUS: But you acted well. Do not yoke your
  mouth
with harmful speech, and do not give voice to evils.
You freed the entire city of the Argives,   1045
calmly beheading the two serpents.
ORESTES: *[the madness coming upon him]* Ai! Ai!
  These women are sullen-faced, like Gorgons,
clad in black and thickly wreathed with snakes.
I cannot stay any longer.
CHORUS: What hallucinations whirl you about?   1050
  You are dearest of all
to your father. Wait, don't be afraid; you have
  won a great victory.
ORESTES: My troubles are no hallucinations.
  These women are clearly my mother's vengeful
    hounds.[17]
CHORUS: The blood is still fresh on your hands.
  This is the source of your mind's disturbance.   1055

---

16 Objects traditionally carried by suppliants.

17 Orestes is beginning to suffer the madness of guilt, embodied in the fearsome Furies, who will be represented on stage by the Chorus in the final play of the trilogy. They are not literally hounds, but hideous, foul-smelling women, the spirits of vengeance. In mythology they were conceived as daughters of Earth, born from Uranus's blood, which was spilled when his son Cronos castrated him. Older than Olympians like Athena and Apollo, the Furies were thought of as chthonic, or underworld, gods. They punished a variety of crimes after the fact, such as perjury and murder, and did so with such savage indifference to human suffering that they were superstitiously addressed as "Eumenides," Kindly Ones, rather than as Furies.

ORESTES: Lord Apollo, these women come in swarms,
and evil streams drip from their eyes.
CHORUS: There is one cleansing cure for you.
Laying his hands upon you, Loxian Apollo
will set you free from these afflictions.   1060
ORESTES: You do not see these women; I do.
I am driven out; I can no longer stay. *[exits]*
CHORUS: May you fare well, and may god watch over
you kindly, protecting you with timely fortunes.

This, the third successive storm in the royal house,
has run its course and blown itself out.   1065
First came the horrible, child-devouring
sufferings of Thyestes.
Next were the sufferings of a regal husband:
the chief warrior of the Achaeans perished,
struck down in his bath.   1070
And now again, third, from somewhere has come
a saviour—or should I say doom?
For where will it end? Where will the might of
Destruction
take its rest, lulled at last to sleep?

AESCHYLUS

Eumenides

translated by Geoffrey W. Bakewell[1]

CHARACTERS
PYTHIA, PRIESTESS OF APOLLO
APOLLO
HERMES
GHOST OF KLYTEMESTRA
ORESTES
ATHENA
CHORUS OF EUMENIDES/WOMEN OF ATHENS

Scene: Delphi, in front of Apollo's Oracle. After line 234, the Acropolis at Athens.

PYTHIA: Of the gods, I first pay homage in this prayer
   to Earth, the original oracular deity.
   Then comes her daughter Themis,
   the next to seat herself at her mother's oracle,
   as some say. The third to take a turn   5
   was another daughter of Earth, the Titan Phoebe.
   She took the seat with her mother's blessing,
   and without violence on anyone's part.
   She then gave it[2] as a birthday present to Apollo,
   who added her name to his own, becoming   10
      Phoebus.
   He left pool and rock behind on the island Delos,
   came ashore on the Attic coast busy with ships,
   and made his way to this land and his throne at
      Parnassos.

The children of Hephaistos[3] escorted and
   honoured him greatly,
blazing a trail and taming the savage land.   15
Upon his arrival the people worshipped him
   fervently,
as did king Delphos, the helmsman of this land.
Zeus fired Apollo's mind with divine inspiration,
and seated him as the fourth prophet on the
   tripod here:
the Loxian[4] serves as the spokesman for his father   20
   Zeus.
These are the gods with which I begin my prayers.
In my speech I also give Athena Pronaia[5] her due.
And I honour the nymphs who frequent the
   Korykian[6] cave,
home to birds and haunt of gods.
Dionysus too holds sway in the region—I do not   25
   forget him—
ever since he, a god, led his maenads to destroy
   Pentheus,[7]

---

1 Translator's note: The text is largely that of M.L. West, *Aeschylus Tragoediae* (Stuttgart, 1990). I am particularly indebted to the commentary of A.H. Sommerstein, *Aeschylus Eumenides* (Cambridge, 1989).

2 She is speaking here of the oracle itself, passed down from Earth, or Ge, through to Apollo, the current custodian deity.

3 Athenians, via their legendary king Erechthonius and his father Hephaistos.

4 Apollo as the riddler, or the crooked one, since his prophesies were notoriously difficult to interpret.

5 Major Greek goddess Athena, patron deity of the city of Athens, especially her law courts, was called this at Delphi, where she was worshipped "before the great temple" of Apollo.

6 A cave on Mt. Parnassos above Delphi.

7 King of Thebes who denied the divinity of Dionysus when he came to that city. Dressing up as a woman to spy on the religious rites of Dionysus' maenads, Pentheus was savagely dismembered by these frenzied Bacchantes—of whom his mother Agave was one. See Euripides' *Bacchai*.

planning his destruction as if he were a hare.
Invoking the streams of Pleistos,[8] the power of
    Poseidon,
and loftiest Zeus who brings fulfillment,
I shall now take my seat as prophet upon the tripod: 30
may the gods grant me success far beyond my
    previous entries.
If any Greeks are present, let them draw lots
and come forth, as custom dictates.
I prophesy in whatever way the god leads me.

Unspeakable horrors, affronts to the eyes 35
sent me reeling back from the Loxian's dwelling
strengthless, unable to stand upright.
I scramble on my hands; swiftness has left my legs.
A frightened old woman is nothing, or rather,
    childlike.
I went into the inner chamber decorated with 40
    many garlands.
And there I saw a man, seated at the navelstone[9]
    like a suppliant,
polluted, hateful to the gods, his hands running
    with blood,
holding a newly drawn sword and a tall olive branch
appropriately wrapped in a great fleecy tuft of
    white wool.
I will be proven to have spoken clearly here. 45
And in front of this man slept
an astonishing band of women seated on chairs.
I shouldn't call them women: they were gorgons.
Even gorgons aren't the right comparison:
I once saw a painting of the harpies 50
who carried off Phineus'[10] food. But these creatures
are wingless, and black, and entirely loathsome.
Their fetid snortings render them unapproachable
and a hateful ooze drips from their eyes.
Their clothing is not fit to wear 55
before the statues of the gods or into men's homes.
I have not laid eyes on the race to which this
    company belongs,

nor do I know what land boasts that it raised this
    brood
safely, without regretting its labour later on.
From here on out let this be the concern 60
of the master of this shrine, the mighty Loxian.
He is a prophet with healing powers, an
    interpreter of omens,
and has cleansed the homes of others.
ORESTES: Lord Apollo, you know how not to
    commit injustice.
And since you know this, learn also not to be 65
    indifferent.
Your strength is sufficient to help me.
APOLLO: I will not betray you. I will be your guard
    to the end,
both standing beside you and watching from afar:
I will not become gentle to your enemies.
Even now you see that these crazed females 70
have themselves been caught. Sunk in sleep,
the repulsive maidens are at once old women and
    yet girls:
neither god nor man nor beast ever mingles with
    them.
They were born for evil, since they inhabit
the evil gloom of Tartaros[11] below the earth, 75
objects of hatred for men and the Olympian gods.
Nevertheless flee; and do not weaken.
For they will drive you over the vast mainland
throughout the earth with wandering footsteps,
past the sea and cities surrounded by water. 80
Do not tire too quickly; shepherd yourself in this
    labour.
And when you come to the citadel of Pallas
    Athena[12]
sit down as a suppliant, embracing her ancient
    cult-statue.
There, having jurors for these matters,
and persuasive arguments, we will find a way 85
to free you from these toils forever.
For it was I who persuaded you to slay your mother.
Remember this; do not let fear defeat your wits.

---

8 The river in the gorge below Delphi.
9 The oracle, said to be located on "the navel of the earth"
   because of the dramatic mountain landscape at Delphi.
10 A Thracian seer who, in punishment for his unjust treat-
    ment of his sons, was blinded by the gods.

---

11 Underworld realm, sometimes conceived as far below
    Hades, or sometimes synonymous with Hades, land of
    the dead.
12 The city of Athens.

And you, Hermes, blood brother, my own father's
      son,
protect him and escort him well,   90
shepherding this suppliant of mine.
For Zeus respects the rights of the stranger;
Speed him with good fortune back among men.

[exit Apollo, Orestes and Hermes]

GHOST OF KLYTEMESTRA: Sleeping, are you?
      What use do I have for sleepers?
Thanks to you I have been greatly dishonoured   95
among the other spirits of the dead,
the taunts of those I killed ring incessantly among
      the shades,
and I wander in disgrace. I tell you,
they blame me greatly.
And although I suffered terrible things from my   100
      family,
no deity is angered on my behalf
even though I was slaughtered by matricidal hands.
Look at these wounds; fix them in your heart.
Indeed, you have licked up many of my offerings.
Wineless libations, honeyed offerings, grand   105
      nocturnal banquets
I made at a hearthfire, at an hour shared by no
      other gods.
And I see all these offerings trampled underfoot,
while he escapes like a fawn.
He easily sprang free
from the middle of the nets, mocking you greatly.   110
Hear me, for I have spoken about my life, my soul.
Heed me, O goddesses below the ground.
In a dream I, Klytemestra, call upon you.

[Members of the Chorus move and moan in their sleep]

KLYT.: Go ahead, moan. The man is gone and flees
      farther.
There are no suppliants among my friends.   115
CHORUS: Unhhhh.
KLYT.: You sleep too much, and do not pity my
      suffering.
Orestes is gone, who killed me, his mother.
CHORUS: Arhhhh.
KLYT.: You cry out, you sleep; why won't you swiftly   120
      get up?
What fate has been dealt you, save to cause harm?

CHORUS: Arhhhh.
KLYT.: Sleep and toil, powerful conspirators,
      have sapped the strength of the horrible she-
      dragon.
CHORUS: Aieeee. Aieeee.   125
      Seize. Seize. Seize. Seize. Show me where.
KLYT.: In a dream you chase your prey, barking like
      a dog
bent on thoughts of slaughter.
What are you doing? Get up. Don't let weariness
overcome you; don't ignore our suffering,   130
      charmed by sleep.
Rebuke yourself, drive yourself on with just
      reproaches,
for these act as spurs to the wise.
After him, fill his sails with a bloody wind,
shrivel him with your breath, the fire of your belly,
wear him out with new pursuit.   135
CHORUS: Wake up. And wake her too, the way I
      did you.
Are you sleeping? Get up, shake your sleep aside.
Let's see whether this premonition is false or true.
Alas, alas! Woe! We have suffered, friends.
Much have I suffered, and all in vain.   140
We have suffered a painful blow, alas,
an unbearable evil.
He has escaped from the nets, the beast is gone.
Conquered by sleep, I lost my prey.

O son of Zeus, you are a thief; a young man, you   145
trampled us venerable divinities under your
      horse's hooves.
All to honour your suppliant, a godless man,
savage to his parents.
Although a god, you stole from us a mother-killer.
Who will say that any of this is just?   150

Reproach came to me in my dreams,
striking like a charioteer
with crop in hand
underneath my mind and heart.
I can feel the frigid, icy sting   155
of the violent public flogger.

The younger gods do things like this
and have absolute power, more than is just.

I can see that the seat drips with gore
from head to foot,   160
and that the navel of the world
has won for itself a fearsome pollution of blood.

Although a prophet, Apollo has defiled his inner
    chamber
with pollution from his own hearth.
He set it in motion, himself invited it in,   165
by honouring mortals and slighting ancient
    prerogatives
contrary to the law of the gods.

He offends me. Moreover, he will never free Orestes.
Even in death the man shall never find release.
Still unpurified, seeking help, he will arrive in a   170
    place
where another avenger will weigh upon his head.
APOLLO: Out, I command you, swiftly leave this
    building.
Depart from the prophetic chambers
or you will receive a gleaming, winged snake
speeding from my golden bowstring   175
and in pain spit up the black foam,
vomit the clots of men's blood which you gulped
    down.
It is wrong for you to come near this building.
You belong where beheadings and blindings
count as justice, where the freshness of youth   180
is marred by castration, where there is mutilation
and stoning, and those spitted along their spines
wail greatly. Do you hear how the gods reject
the sort of feast-day you favour? Every aspect
of your appearance shows what you are.   185
Creatures like you should inhabit the cave of a
    bloodthirsty lion
instead of polluting visitors to my oracle.
Depart, you shepherdless flock:
not a single god is friendly to a herd like this.
CHORUS: Lord Apollo, now in turn listen to me.   190
You are more than an accessory here:
you brought it all to pass, and are fully responsible.
APOLLO: What do you mean? Speak this much and
    no more.
CHORUS: Did you tell Orestes to pose as a stranger
    and kill his mother?

APOLLO: Yes I did, to send vengeance for his father.   195
    What of it?
CHORUS: And did you then offer to accept him
    fresh with slaughter?
APOLLO: Yes, and I told him to come as a suppliant
    to my shrine here.
CHORUS: And do you then abuse us, his escorts?
APOLLO: Yes, because you are not fit to approach
    this house.
CHORUS: But this is the task assigned to us.   200
APOLLO: What honour is this? Go ahead, boast
    about your noble privilege.
CHORUS: We drive matricides from their homes.
APOLLO: And what about a woman who eliminates
    her husband?
CHORUS: Her crime does not count as murdering kin.
APOLLO: Then you greatly dishonour and disregard   205
    the marriage pledges
of Zeus and Hera, who brings fulfillment.
Your view scorns and casts aside Kypris,[13]
the source of the dearest things to mortals.
For husband and wife the marriage bed which is
    their lot
is greater than any oath, and guarded by justice.   210
If you slack off when spouses murder one
    another—
not taking vengeance, not watching with anger—
I say you drive Orestes from his home unjustly.
For I know that you take his crime very seriously,
but treat hers more gently.   215
The goddess Pallas[14] will preside over a trial of
    these matters.
CHORUS: I will never leave that man in peace.
APOLLO: Pursue him then, make more trouble for
    yourselves.
CHORUS: Don't try to curtail my rights with your
    argument.
APOLLO: I wouldn't agree to accept those "rights" of   220
    yours.
CHORUS: Of course not: you are said to be mighty
    beside Zeus' throne.
    But I will pursue and punish this man, I will track
    him down:

---

13 Aphrodite.
14 Athena.

his mother's blood leads me on. *[Chorus exits, stage right]*

APOLLO: And I will assist and rescue my suppliant.
Men and gods alike fear the rage of the suppliant   225
whom anyone willingly betrays. *[exit, stage right]*

[The scene here shifts to the Acropolis of Athens. An image or statue of Athena is visible. Enter Orestes, from stage right]

ORESTES: Queen Athena, at the commands of the Loxian
I have come; receive me kindly as a suppliant.
I do not seek purification for hands unwashed by Apollo,
but am blunted, worn down by travelling and   230
staying with others.
Crossing land and sea alike,
following the instructions of the Loxian's oracle
I approach your house and sacred image, goddess.
Keeping watch here, I await a just result.

CHORUS: Excellent. Here is a clear sign of the man.   235
Follow these hints of the voiceless informer.
Like a dog after a wounded fawn
we track the dripping blood.
Insides pant with the hard, man-killing labour.
I have roamed the whole earth,   240
and came spanning the sea in wingless flight
pursuing as swiftly as a ship.
And now the man is here somewhere, hunkered down.
The scent of human blood brings a smile to my lips.

Look, look: and again!   245
Keep an eye on him; don't let
the mother-killer flee unpunished.
Wrapped about the statue of an immortal goddess
he takes sanctuary and seeks a trial for his bloody hands.
But this is impossible. It is difficult to collect   250
maternal blood scattered upon the earth. Aieeee!
The moisture has been poured on the ground and is gone.
But you must pay in return: I will slurp down
the red broth from your living limbs. What a meal
I shall make of that undrinkable drink!   255
And when I've withered you alive I'll drag you below

to atone for the miseries of your slaughtered mother.
And if any other mortal has done wrong,
committing impiety against any god, stranger,
or his own dear parents,   260
you will see him getting his just deserts.
For Hades is a great examiner of mortals
below the ground;
he oversees all, and writes it on the tablets of his mind.

ORESTES: Taught by evils, I know the proper occasion   265
for many things, and in particular when to speak,
when to keep quiet. In this matter
I was told to speak by a wise teacher.
For the blood from my hand grows tired and fades;
the pollution of killing my mother has been   270
washed away.
While still fresh it was driven out in gory baths
by the sacrifice of pigs at the hearth of the god Phoebos.
It would be a long story for me to name
all those whom I met and left unharmed by my presence.
And now in all piety, with pure speech I call upon   275
Athena, the queen of this land, to come
and be my helper. Without a spearfight
she will acquire me, my land, and the Argive people
as an ally, justly trustworthy forever.
But whether she now marches, assisting her friends,   280
with straight or covered leg,[15]
in the reaches of the Libyan land
around the streams of Triton, the spring where she was born,
or whether she watches over the plain of Phlegra[16]
like a brave man in command, may she come—   285
for a god hears, even when far away—
to release me from these evils.

---

[15] See Sommerstein 1989, 134: "a soldier moved with 'straight leg' when marching rapidly forward unopposed; he moved with 'covered leg' when advancing cautiously under attack. … Athena is thus presented as fighting at the side of her [friends] when they are carrying all before them and also when they are hard pressed."

[16] Near Pallene, on the westernmost peninsula of the Khalkidike.

CHORUS: Neither Apollo nor the might of Athena
    can save you.
  You will wander neglected,
  all thought of joy gone from your mind,   290
  a bloodless meal for grazing gods, a shadow.
  What? Nothing to say? Do you reject my claims,
  my fatted calf?
  I'll feast on your living flesh, not slaughter you at
     an altar.
  Now hear this song which will bind you.   295
  Come, strike up a dance
  since we have decided to display
  our hateful music,
  and to set forth how our group
  administers its lots among mortals.   300

  We claim that we deal justly.
  Our anger moves against no one
  who shows that his hands are clean:
  he goes through life unharmed.
  But when someone transgresses   305
  and hides his bloody hands
  just like this man here,
  we stand by the deceased as upright witnesses
  and punish his bloodshed forever.

  Mother, mother Night, you who bore me   310
  to punish blind and seeing alike,[17]
  hear me. For Leto's son[18]
  dishonours me, deprives me
  of this hare, a proper sacrifice
  to purge a mother's murder.   315

  This is a song
  That breaks on the victim
  slamming the mind with
  frenzy of madness:
  binding the wits,   320
  consuming the life,
  cacophonous hymn of the Furies.

  Fate which pierces to the quick spun it
  for this duty of ours to last forever,

to hound those mortals who undertake   325
empty acts of wickedness
until they go beneath the earth.
And even in death
they find no freedom.

This is a song   330
That breaks on the victim
slamming the mind with
frenzy of madness:
binding the wits,
consuming the life,   335
cacophonous hymn of the Furies.

These privileges were awarded us at our birth.
As for the immortals, we are to keep our hands off
    them.
We do not even keep the same dinner company.
Not for me the all-white garments.[19]   340

I chose the overthrow of houses.
Whenever violence is nurtured in a home
and a dear one dies,
we hunt down the perpetrator, yes.
However strong he is, nevertheless   345
we blot him out with new bloodshed.

We hasten to free everyone from these worries.
Our actions give the gods immunity;
they need not even attend the preliminary hearing.
Zeus thought our race blood-dripping and hateful,   350
and barred us from his company.

Men's notions, grandiose in the open air,
melt and fade into dishonour in the nether world
under our black-clad attack
and the beat of our angry feet.   355

Leaping high,
we bring down the heavy might
of our foot from above,
trip up runners in the homestretch,
encompass their doom.   360

---

[17] I.e., the dead and the living.
[18] Apollo.

---

[19] A line is missing from the text here.

Even as he falls he does not know why:
our blow takes away his wits.
Darkness of pollution hovers over the man,
groaning voices tell of the dark mist above the
    house.

For we alone are resourceful,   365
we alone have the final say,
we remember evils,
majestic, indifferent to men's pleas,
pursuing our thankless tasks
in sunless gloom far apart from the gods,   370
making the paths rocky and steep
for the living and the eyeless dead alike.

What mortal, therefore,
does not tremble in fear
as he hears our dictates,   375
the powers allotted us by the Fates
and confirmed by the gods forever?
It is our age-old right, and we have met
with no dishonour, although our station
is the sunless darkness below the earth.   380
ATHENA: Far away I heard a cry for help
as I claimed Skamander's land[20] as my own,
a great portion of the captive booty
which the Achaian commanders and leaders
awarded to me, root and branch, forever,   385
a choice gift for the children of Theseus.
From there I came, speeding my tireless foot,
wingless, carried airborne in the fold of my aegis.[21]
And seeing these strange new visitors to the land
I feel no fear, but marvel at the sight.   390
Who on earth are you? I speak to all of you at once,
both this foreigner seated at my statue,
and you too. You are unlike any breed of begotten
    things,
nor do gods behold you among the goddesses,
nor are you similar to mortal shapes.   395
But to speak badly of one's neighbours without
    cause
is inappropriate, and far from just.

CHORUS: You will learn all this quickly, daughter of
    Zeus.
  We are the eternal daughters of Night;
  we are called Curses among houses underground.   400
ATHENA: Now I know your family and true name.
CHORUS: You will learn our honoured role in short
    order.
ATHENA: Indeed, if someone will set it forth clearly.
CHORUS: We drive murderers from their homes.
ATHENA: And where does the killer's flight end?   405
CHORUS: Where rejoicing is never heard.
ATHENA: And do you howl this kind of exile
    against him?
CHORUS: Yes: he chose to become his mother's
    slayer.
ATHENA: Was he forced to do it? Did he fear
    someone's anger?
CHORUS: What motive could suffice to drive a man   410
    to matricide?
ATHENA: I've only heard one side of the story,
    although two are present.
CHORUS: But he won't take an oath, nor offer one.
ATHENA: You prefer to seem just rather than be just.
CHORUS: What do you mean? Explain—you don't
    lack wisdom.
ATHENA: I say that injustice should not triumph   415
    through the mere searing of oaths.[22]
CHORUS: Then you investigate, and pronounce a
    just verdict.
ATHENA: Would you entrust the result of your
    accusation to me?
CHORUS: Of course. We respect you, since you
    have respected us.
ATHENA: So, stranger, what do you want to say in
    response to this?
  Tell me your country and your family and your   420
    misfortunes,

---

20 Troy.
21 Athena's trademark shield, sometimes adorned with the
   image of the Gorgon Medusa's head.

---

22 Customary legal practices in Athens allowed for the settling of some types of disputes if the accused agreed to
   swear an oath of innocence—on the assumption that fear
   of the gods would discourage a false oath. Athena seems
   to be saying that justice is not served through such potentially meaningless rituals, but only through a full investigation of the facts of the alleged crime.

and then try to refute these women's claim.
If faith in justice persuaded you
to sit at my hearth clutching my statue,
a suppliant deserving respect just like Ixion,[23]
give me a clear answer to all these charges.   425

ORESTES: Queen Athena, first I will remove a great
      concern
   expressed in your most recent words.
   I am not a suppliant, nor did I take my seat
   beside your statue with blood-guilt on my hands.
   I will give you a great proof of this.   430
   It is the law for the suppliant to remain silent
   until a man who can cleanse bloodshed
   drenches him with the slaughtered gore of a
      young beast.
   Long ago I was purified in this way in others' homes,
   by beast-sacrifices and running streams.   435
   This is no longer a worry, I tell you.
   As to my family, you will learn about it in short
      order.
   I am an Argive, and am glad you ask about my
      father,
   Agamemnon, commander of ship-riding men.
   Together with him you destroyed Troy,   440
   the city of Ilium. He himself perished
   in a poor homecoming. My black-hearted mother
   slew him, draping him with colourful nets
   that testify to the murder, done in the bath.
   An exile until then, I came back   445
   and slew the woman who bore me, I don't deny it,
   in a murder to avenge my dearest father's death.
   Loxian Apollo is also partly responsible,
   for he foretold griefs, goading my heart,
   unless I did something to the guilty.   450
   Now you decide the case, whether I acted justly
      or not.
   It is in your hands: I accept the verdict, whatever
      it may be.

ATHENA: The matter is too great for any mortal to
      think
   of deciding it. Nor is it right for me
   to judge cases of angry killings,   455

especially since you are now disciplined
   and came to my dwelling as a purified suppliant,
      harmless.
   Yet the women have a role not easy to dismiss.
   If they do not win their case
   poison will flow from their wounded pride   460
   and coat the ground, an unendurable, dismal
      sickness.
   Thus it stands. I will provoke anger
   whether I allow you to remain or banish you.
   But since this matter has landed here,
   I will choose from this city   465
   faultless jurors, judges of murder who will respect
      their oaths;[24]
   I will establish this law for all time.
   You all gather your testimony and evidence,
   the oaths to buttress your case.
   Having chosen the best of my citizens,   470
   I will come to settle this matter in accordance
      with the truth.

CHORUS: Now the ordained laws crash down,[25]
   if the argument and damage
   done by this mother-killer prevail.
   This deed will quickly unite   475
   all mortals in licentiousness.
   Many real sufferings lie in wait
   for parents, wounds inflicted
   by their children hereafter.
   Nor will the rage of these maenads who oversee   480
      mortals
   pursue anyone because of his actions.
   I will unleash upon them
   every kind of death;
   they will search high and low
   for an ebb, an end to their woes,   485
   as they cite the troubles of those around them.
   In desperation each vainly urges useless remedies.

---

23 The first kin-murderer, who was purified by Zeus and
   later attempted to seduce Hera. Zeus punished him by
   strapping him to a wheel.

24 The six thousand regular citizens who served as jurors in
   Athens' courts every year swore an oath to uphold the
   laws of the land, and to listen fairly and with equal care
   to both sides of the story.

25 The Furies here and in what follows are speaking about
   the *old* legal order, in which bloodshed was punished by
   more bloodshed, the collapse of which system they imagine as catastrophic for human society.

Let no one cry out for Justice
amid the blows of misfortune,
nor call upon the Furies' power.   490
Indeed fathers
and mothers new to suffering
will swiftly learn to lament
when the house of Justice
collapses.   495

There is a place for Fear:
it must remain seated
where it can keep a watchful eye
on mortal minds.
It is a good thing   500
to learn self-restraint under pressure.
What person or city
would respect Justice
without nourishing
fear in his heart?   505

Praise neither the life of anarchy
nor that of subjection.
God always gives sovereignty
to the in-between, and keeps watch in many ways.
What I say now fits in: 510
hubris[26] is truly the child of impiety;
the prosperity yearned for
and kind to all
springs from healthy thoughts.

Once and for all I say to you: 515
respect the altar of Justice.
Do it no dishonour. Do not trample it
with godless foot as you watch your advantage.
For punishment will follow; the appointed end
    will come.
Given this, let each person   520
choose to honour his parents
and respect the guests
who move about his house.

Choosing justice leads to happiness;
learning it the hard way does not.   525
The just man does not face ruin.

Yet the bold and lawless man
whose ship teems with unjust cargo
will in time lose his sail
when the yard-arm shatters   530
and grief seizes him.

Caught in the whirlpool he struggles in vain:
his cries fall on deaf ears.
The gods laugh at the sight of this hothead,
who swore it would never happen to him,   535
sinking beneath the waves of the strong surge.
He has steered his past prosperity
straight onto the reef of Justice;
and now he goes down, unwept and unseen.

[enter Athena, followed by 12 citizens and a herald;
benches and two urns, and perhaps a water-clock, are
brought]

ATHENA: Speak, herald; call the people to order.   540
    Let human lungs fill the shrill Tyrrhenian[27]
        trumpet
    and show how its voice stretches to heaven.
    This court is now convened.
    It is proper for the whole city and for these jurors
    to be silent and to learn my laws,   545
    for time everlasting,
    so that Justice may be done.

[enter Apollo]

    King Apollo, keep to your own domain.
    Tell me, how is this affair any business of yours?
APOLLO: I too come to testify. This man seated   550
        himself at my hearth
    as a suppliant according to custom.
    I cleansed him of murder and will stand beside him.
    I am responsible for the killing of his mother.
    Open the case, and render judgement as you see fit.
ATHENA: I hereby open the case; now it is your   555
        turn to speak;
    For when the prosecutor speaks first and starts
        from the beginning,
    he serves as a good tutor in the details of the
        dispute.

---

26 Lawless, disdainful violence.

27 From Etruria, home of the Etruscans, or Tuscans, in cen-
    tral Italy.

CHORUS: We are numerous, but will speak briefly.
And you, answer point by point in turn.
Tell me first: did you kill your mother? 560
ORESTES: Yes, I did. There's no denying it.
CHORUS: Round one goes to us.[28]
ORESTES: Why boast? I'm still on my feet.
CHORUS: Now tell us how you killed her.
ORESTES: I will. Sword in hand, I slit her throat. 565
CHORUS: Who persuaded you? Who planned it?
ORESTES: The one beside me, with his prophecies.
He'll swear to it.
CHORUS: The prophet directed you to kill your
mother?
ORESTES: Yes, and so far I have no regrets.
CHORUS: If the verdict goes against you, you'll 570
quickly change your tune.
ORESTES: I have faith. And my father sends
assistance from his tomb.
CHORUS: Go ahead, trust the grave; you put your
mother there.
ORESTES: Yes, because she was guilty, polluted
twice over.
CHORUS: How so? Explain it to the jurors.
ORESTES: Her victim was her husband and my 575
father.
CHORUS: So what? You're alive; and her death has
freed her.
ORESTES: Why didn't you hunt her down while she
was alive?
CHORUS: She was not related to the one she killed.
ORESTES: And do I share my mother's blood?
CHORUS: How else did she nurture you within her 580
loins, you murderer?
Do you reject the blood nearest and dearest you?
ORESTES: You, Apollo, bear witness for me now,
explain whether I slew her with justice.
For I don't deny that I did it: I did.
But evaluate this act of bloodshed for me, say 585
whether in your mind
I acted justly or not, so that I can tell these jurors.
APOLLO: I say to you, great lawcourt of Athena,
he acted justly. As a prophet, I cannot lie.
Never yet have I spoken from my sacred seat

anything uncommanded by Zeus, father of the 590
Olympian gods,
whether about a man, a woman, or a city.
I urge you all to learn how strong his claim to
justice is,
and to obey the will of the Father.
For not even an oath is stronger than Zeus.
CHORUS: So you're saying that Zeus gave you the 595
oracle
to tell this man here, Orestes,
to avenge his father's murder but to disregard his
mother?
APOLLO: Yes. But the two cases are entirely different.
He who died was a noble man, honoured with
god-given scepters;
and he perished at the hand of a woman 600
who did not strike nobly with a wild bowshot, as
an Amazon would,
but as you will hear, Pallas—
you and those seated beside you
to decide this matter with their vote.
She welcomed him with kindly smiles 605
as he returned from a campaign, all in all successful;
he had a bath; and from the edge of the tub
she draped a robe around him, and binding her
husband
in its endless woven folds she struck.
There: I have now recounted the demise 610
of this majestic man, this commander of men and
ships.
And I have told it thus to arouse the indignation
of those who have been assigned to hear this case.
CHORUS: You claim that Zeus takes the father's side;
yet he himself shackled his own father, old man 615
Kronos.
A bit inconsistent, don't you think?
I call you jurors to witness: you heard this
exchange.
APOLLO: You disgusting animals! The gods loathe you.
Zeus could always remove those shackles; mere
imprisonment
has a cure, and many means of resolution. 620
But let the dust suck up the blood of a man's death
just once, and there is no turning back.
My father never made any magic antidotes for
death,

---

28 In ancient Greece a wrestler won by throwing his opponent three times.

although he arranges all other things according to
  his whim,
turning them topsy-turvy without breaking a sweat.   625
CHORUS: Yet look how you strain to defend this man.
  He poured the kindred blood of his mother on
    the ground;
  will he now succeed to his father's estate in Argos?
  Which public altars will he use?
  What brotherhood[29] will receive him at their   630
    sacred waters?
APOLLO: I will also make this point; note that I
  speak truly.
  The person called "mother" is not a child's parent;
  she is only the "nurse" of a newly sown embryo.
  The parent is the male, who mounts; the female is
    a stranger
  who with divine help preserves a stranger's offspring. 635
  I will show you proof of this claim.
  A father may give birth without a mother—
  witness the child of Olympian Zeus who stands
    beside you.
  She was not raised in the gloom of the womb,
  yet is a child such as no goddess could bring forth.   640

  I will do what I can, Pallas, in many ways,
  to make your city and your people great.
  I sent this man as a suppliant to your temple
  to become a trustworthy friend for all time,
  that he and his descendants might be your allies,   645
  and that the children of these men here
  might cherish this bond forever.[30]
ATHENA: Has enough been said? Shall I now order
  these judges
  to vote for justice, in accordance with their
    understanding?
APOLLO: I have already shot all my arrows;   650
  I wait to hear the outcome of the contest.
ATHENA: And you? How shall I arrange things to
  avoid your censure?

---

29 Lit., *phratries,* civic organizations made up of men from
    related aristocratic families.
30 The city of Argos had just allied itself with Athens against
    Sparta in 461, three years before Aeschylus wrote the
    play. He is here using the ancient mythology to legiti-
    mate and celebrate this new military pact.

CHORUS: You heard what you heard; keep your
  oath
  fixed in your hearts as you cast your ballots,
    strangers.
ATHENA: Now hear my decree, people of Attica,   655
  as you choose between the pleas in this court's
    first case of bloodshed.
  This council of judges will belong
  to the nation of Aegeus[31] always and forevermore.
  It will meet on this hill of Ares,
  camp and quarters for the Amazons once,   660
  when they brought an army here in envy at
    Theseus,
  piled up this new, high-towered city against the
    Acropolis,
  and sacrificed to the war-god: now rock and hill
    alike
  bear his name. And in this place
  civic respect and innate fear   665
  will prevent injustice by day and night alike,
  provided the citizens themselves do not mess with
    the laws.
  If you mar a sparkling spring with foul
  and muddy streams you will never find a drink.
  Citizens, I advise you to maintain and honour   670
  the mean between anarchy and subjection:
  do not drive all fear from the city.
  For what mortal is just without fear?
  If you properly fear the authority of the laws
  you will have a fortress protecting   675
  your land and city alike, a thing no other men
    have,
  not even those in Scythia and the Peloponnese.
  I establish this council as free from bribes,
  august, quick to anger, wakeful on behalf of those
    who sleep,
  a guardian of the land.   680

  I dwelt at length on this advice for my citizens
  with an eye to the future. But now it is necessary
  for them to stand and raise their ballots and
    decide the case,
  all the while respecting their oath. I have spoken.

---

31 Athenians.

[Throughout the following exchange the jurors rise, one by one, and cast their ballot-pebbles]

CHORUS: I suggest that you not dishonour us,   685
dangerous visitors to your land.
APOLLO: And I urge you to fear the oracles
from me and Zeus: do not render them fruitless.
CHORUS: You meddle in bloody deeds that aren't
your business;
you will hand out polluted prophecies hereafter.   690
APOLLO: Did my father make some mistake
with his suppliant Ixion,[32] the first killer?
CHORUS: You brought it up. But if I don't win my case
I'll be back, with pain for this land.
APOLLO: Among both younger and older gods   695
you are outcasts: I'll win this case.
CHORUS: You also acted like this in Pheres' house;
you persuaded the Fates to make mortals
deathless.[33]
APOLLO: Wasn't it right to help a man who
honoured me,
especially in his time of need?   700
CHORUS: You destroyed the age-old balance of powers
and cheated the ancient goddesses with wine.
APOLLO: You won't get what you're after in this trial;
the poison you'll soon spit up won't harm your
enemies a bit.
CHORUS: Upstart, you trample me, your elder,   705
under your horse's hooves;
therefore I wait to hear the outcome of the case,
still of two minds whether to hate this city.
ATHENA: This is my work; I am the last to make
my choice.[34]

I will cast this ballot for Orestes.
For no mother bore me, and I always approve   710
the male with all my heart, except when it comes
to marriage:
above all, I am my father's child.
Therefore I will not give greater weight to the
death of a woman
who killed her husband, the lord of the house.
Orestes wins even if the votes are equal.   715
You jurors to whom this task has been assigned,
shake the ballots from the urns as swiftly as possible.
ORESTES: Phoebos Apollo, what will the outcome be?
CHORUS: Night, dark mother, are you watching this?
ORESTES: Now end it with a noose, or live to see   720
the light.
CHORUS: Now vanish in disgrace, or maintain our
rights hereafter.
APOLLO: Use care: separate the cast ballots into
groups, strangers,
and remember, do not cheat in the sorting.
Mistakes made here have grave consequences.
A single vote can restore the fortunes of a whole   725
house.
ATHENA: This man has been acquitted of bloodshed:
the vote is a tie.
ORESTES: Pallas, you have saved my house
and restored me to my father's land
of which I was deprived. And the Greeks will say   730
"This man is an Argive again, and he dwells
amid his father's estate, thanks to Pallas and the
Loxian
and the Third, the Saviour Zeus, who brings all
things to pass."
Zeus paid heed to my father's fate and saved me,
gazing upon my mother's advocates.   735
I will now depart for home,
once I have sworn an oath
to this country and your people for all eternity,
that never will any leader from my land
lead a host of well-armed hoplites against you.[35]   740
For even when I am in the grave
I will beset with baffling failures
those who violate my oath,

---

32 Zeus spirited Ixion up among the gods and purified him
of the murder of his father-in-law, whom Ixion had killed
rather than pay promised wedding gifts. But Ixion was
eventually punished for ungratefully trying to seduce
Zeus's wife, Hera, and was strapped by Hermes to an
eternally rotating wheel.
33 Cf. Euripides' *Alcestis*. Apollo got the Fates drunk and
convinced them to give Admetos, son of Pheres, the option of outliving his time if he could find someone to die
in his place. His wife Alcestis volunteered.
34 Whether Athena's ballot is the eleventh or twelfth is both
controversial and important: See Sommerstein 1989,
222–26.

---

35 See above, note 30.

making their journeys dispiriting, their marches
　　ill-omened,
their labours a source of regret. 745
But if they keep my oath and always
honour this city of Pallas by sending troops as allies
I will be kind to them.
And now farewell to you and your city's people alike.
May you pin all your opponents to the mat; 750
may your spearwork bring salvation and victory.
CHORUS: Younger gods, you have crushed underfoot
　　ancient laws, taken them from my hands.
　　I am dishonoured in this land, wretched, furious.
　　Alas! I will release poison, evil poison from my 755
　　　　heart in retaliation,
　　a dripping blight the land cannot
　　endure. It will rush
　　over the fields (o Justice, Justice!)
　　stunting growth, killing offspring,
　　raising sores and bringing doom to men. 760
　　I groan. What shall I do?
　　I am mocked. I have suffered unendurably
　　in these citizens' hands.
　　Alas, grief-stricken daughters of Night,
　　terrible is your misery. 765
ATHENA: Trust me; do not take it so hard.
　　For you have not been defeated; the vote resulted
　　in a tie, and truly brought you no dishonour.
　　On the contrary, you faced clear evidence from
　　　　Zeus,
　　and the speaker of the oracle testified 770
　　he promised Orestes immunity if he did these deeds.
　　Do not hurl your heavy rage against this land,
　　do not be angry, do not cause infertility
　　by releasing your deep-held venom,
　　the wild foam that devours seeds. 775
　　For I promise you, with full sincerity,
　　that you shall sit on shining thrones
　　Beside our altars, underground,
　　dwelling in this land
　　Well honoured by these citizens. 780
CHORUS: Younger gods, you have crushed underfoot
　　ancient laws, taken them from my hands.
　　I am dishonoured in this land, wretched, furious.
　　Alas! I will release poison, evil poison from my
　　　　heart in retaliation,
　　a dripping blight the land cannot 785

endure. It will rush over the fields (o Justice, Justice!)
stunting growth, killing offspring,
raising sores and bringing doom to men.
I groan. What shall I do?
I am mocked. I have suffered unendurably 790
in these citizens' hands.
Alas, grief-stricken daughters of Night,
terrible is your misery.
ATHENA: You are not dishonoured. You are
　　goddesses, they're only mortals—
　　do not trouble the land in your rage. 795
　　I put my trust in Zeus, and—need I say more?—
　　I alone among the gods control the key to the
　　　　chamber
　　in which he keeps his thunderbolt.
　　But there is no need for that. Take my advice
　　and reign your threats: cast no curse 800
　　upon the earth for fruitfulness to end.
　　Soothe the black and bitter squall that rages
　　in your breast; instead dwell here with me,
　　in honour and in majesty.
　　What I'm offering should earn your praise: 805
　　That this abundant land will henceforth give
　　its first-fruits to you in sacrifice
　　whenever children are born and weddings
　　　　celebrated.
CHORUS: That I should suffer this!
　　alas! 810
　　I, old and wise, must live underground,
　　dishonoured and despised?
　　alas!
　　I'll pour out all my hate and rage!
　　No, no, alas! 815
　　What grief pierces my chest?
　　Mother Night, look at me!
　　The dirty tricks of these gods have stripped away
　　my ancient honours, reduced me to nothing.
ATHENA: I will put up with your anger. You are older, 820
　　and for this reason much wiser than I;
　　but Zeus also gave me no mean intelligence.
　　If you depart for foreign climes
　　you will long for this land like a lover—I know it
　　　　well.
　　For onrushing time will bring 825
　　greater fame to these citizens of mine; and if your
　　　　honoured abode

stands next to the shrine of Erechtheus,[36]
men and women in long procession will give you
more than you would get from any other mortals.
So do not throw your bloody, sharpening stones   830
here in my land, nor harmful passions in my
    young men,
inflaming them in wineless fury; plant no civil war
among my citizens, no brazen daring against one
    another.
Do not make their hearts seethe like fighting cocks.
Let there be war only with our enemies, and let it   835
    be abundant
for those who long for such fierce glory.
But the bird that battles in its nest, at home—this
    I hate.
Here is what you may obtain from me:
act well and you will fare well and share well
in honour in this land so dear to the gods.   840
CHORUS: That I should suffer this!
    alas!
I, old and wise, must live underground,
dishonoured and despised?
    alas!   845
I'll pour out all my hate and rage!
No, no, alas!
What grief pierces my chest?
Mother Night, look at me!
The dirty tricks of these gods have stripped away   850
my ancient honours, reduced me to nothing.
ATHENA: I will not tire of repeating these benefits
    to you,
so that you may not say that you, an older god,
have been forced from your land into exile,
    dishonoured
by me, your junior, and by my citizens.   855
If you honour Persuasion at all,
if my tongue can soothe and charm:
well, you'll stay. Should you still refuse,
it would be unjust for you to mete out to this city
any anger or rage, any harm to the people.   860
For it is possible for you to be a shareholder in
    this land,
honoured forever, as you deserve.

---

36 The temple of Athena Polias on the Acropolis.

CHORUS: Queen Athena, what home do you say I'll
    have?
ATHENA: A painless one, free from every grief. Take it.
CHORUS: Suppose I do. What privilege awaits me?   865
ATHENA: No house may flourish without you.
CHORUS: You will do this, make me so strong?
ATHENA: Yes. I will prosper only those who honour
    you.
CHORUS: And will you give me a guarantee of this
    for time everlasting?
ATHENA: Yes. I speak only of what I intend to do.   870
CHORUS: You start to bring me round; my anger fades.
ATHENA: Remain here and you'll find new friends.
CHORUS: What blessings shall I sing over this land?
ATHENA: Songs befitting splendid victory:
    for blessings from earth and liquid sea   875
    and heaven, for breaths of sun-splashed winds
    to waft through the land;
    for abundant fruit of soil and beasts
    to flourish for my citizens, never weakening;
    for the well-being of human offspring too,   880
    that more may worship you, and that you be
      kindly to those who do.
For I am like a gardener: I love the race
to which these just men belong, wish it free from
    grief.
That is up to you. My task is to ensure
that this city, proudly victorious in tests of war,   885
finds fame among men.
CHORUS: I will dwell here, together with Athena;
    I will not dishonour a city
    that all-powerful Zeus and Ares
    also inhabit; for it is a bastion of immortals,   890
    a defender of altars,
    source of the Greek gods' delight.
    I pray and make kind prophecies for the city,
    that the brilliant light of the sun
    cause life-giving blessings   895
    to spring forth from the soil in abundance.
ATHENA: Out of affection for my citizens have I
    done this,
settling these great and stern divinities here.
For it is their prerogative
to arrange all human affairs.   900
Whoever incurs their wrath
does not even see

the blows that strike him down.
Earlier offenses bind him, drag him off
before these goddesses; silent doom   905
flows from their savage rage,
and levels him mid-boast.
CHORUS: Let no ill wind bring harm to trees—
I speak my benediction:
let heat that sears the buds from plants   910
halt beyond the borders here;
let no grievous blight
creep up, destroying any crops;
let Pan ensure the flocks will thrive,
gracing all with twin kids   915
at the appointed time;
and let future generations thank the gods
for wealth hid deep in dirt: an unexpected gift.[37]
ATHENA: Do you hear this, guardians of the city,
what these blessings entail?   920
The Furies have great power to rule
among both immortals and those beneath the
    ground;
it is also clear how decisively they act
when it comes to the living:
some they move to songs of joy;   925
to others they give lives dimmed with tears.
CHORUS: I command man-slaying, premature deaths
to keep away.
Let lovely young women
live and find husbands,   930
you gods who have the power, and you too,
Fates, my sisters, born from my mother,
straight-dealing divinities
who share in every house
and give weight to every moment,   935
far the most honoured of the gods
because you bring justice in your train.
ATHENA: I rejoice at what these goddesses
bring to pass, blessings for my land.
I love and thank Persuasion,   940
because she guided my tongue and mouth
in dealing with these women and their savage
    objections.

But Zeus prevailed, ruler of council and
    marketplace,
and now our rivalry in doing good works
will bring victory forever.   945
CHORUS: I pray that civil strife,
source of endless evils,
may never roar in this city;
may the dust not drink down
the black blood of citizens, and then in anger   950
snatch up vengeance, retaliation,
the destruction of the city.
Instead, may they delight one another in turn,
resolved to love in common
and hate with a single heart.   955
For this is the cure for many human ills.
ATHENA: Do they have the wisdom to choose the path
of wholesome speech?
I see these frightful faces
as a huge benefit for these citizens.   960
By treating these kindly goddesses with kindness,
honouring them greatly and forever,
you will be a glorious sight,
administering your land and city justly.
CHORUS: Farewell, farewell, people of the city,   965
enjoy the wealth you have earned,
seated close to the virgin daughter of Zeus,
cherishing her as she cherishes you,
learning wisdom through the ages.
The Father admires those   970
who shelter under his daughter's wings.
ATHENA: Farewell to you too.
I shall go in front
to show you your chambers
by the holy light of these escorts.   975
These majestic sacrifices honour your descent
beneath the earth; go and eagerly
keep ruin far from the land,
sending gain that the city may triumph.
And you, city-keeping descendants of Kranaos,   980
lead these metics.[38]
May the citizens appreciate
the goods they receive.

---

37 This may be a reference to silver mined in the area
  around Laureion.

38 Metics were 'resident aliens,' i.e., free non-citizens resid-
  ing in Greek cities. The Eumenides are thus likened to
  'landed immigrants,' new-comers to Athens.

CHORUS: Farewell, farewell again, I repeat,
all you gods on the Acropolis   985
and you mortals who dwell
throughout the city of Pallas.
Honour my residence here
and you will never fault
the fortunes of your life.   990

ATHENA: I thank you for your words and prayers
and will send you with the glow of brilliant torches
to the realms deep beneath the earth,
with these women, who serve my image
justly, as attendants,[39] escorting you down to the   995
    most treasured
place in all the land of Theseus.
Maidens, matrons, grandmothers,
dress these goddesses in crimson robes,
and honour them in procession: let the torchlight
    advance!
Their presence here, kindly to the land,   1000
from now on brings glory, manliness, and fortune.

ESCORTS:[40] This way to your home, childless
    children of Night;
great and worthy, you have our kindly escort.
Countrymen, keep a holy silence.

In the primeval depths of Earth   1005
receive our reverence, our honours and sacrifices.
All dwellers in the city, keep a holy silence.

This way, mighty goddesses,
gracious and kindly to the land.
Delight in the torch-devouring firelight along the   1010
    way.
Now shout for joy and crown our song.

The peace between Athena's people and these
    guests
shall last forever: Zeus who watches over all
and Fate have sworn a pact to make it so.
Now shout for joy and crown our song.   1015

[exit all]

---

[39] The women are the sacred household of Athena Polias.

[40] The final song is probably sung by a chorus composed
    of Athena's attendants.

SOPHOCLES

Oedipus Tyrannos

S ophocles was a master of irony, and *Oedipus Tyrannos* is saturated with it, even in its very title. A tyrant in ancient Greece was not an evil overlord, in the modern sense, but merely a man who ascended to rulership through popular acclaim rather than through blood-inheritance. When the play begins, Oedipus believes himself to be a tyrant, as do his Theban subjects; by the play's catastrophic end, he has come to see himself for what he is: not Thebes' tyrant but her true king, Oedipus the King—but also, necessarily, Oedipus the regicide, the patricide, the incestuous lover of his own mother the queen. His metaphorical blindness to the truth of his own identity is replaced by a cruel, clear vision, and in but one of the many ironic reversals that this entails, Oedipus's sudden insight condemns him to a literal blindness, for it takes him beyond the limits of what a man can bear to see.

Sophocles (c.496–406/5 B.C.E.) was a friend of Herodotus, the historian, and Pericles, the general and statesman, and twice served as general himself, although he was said to have avoided acting in his own plays on account of a weak voice. He survived the horrendous plague of 430, which killed one out of every four Athenians, including Pericles. In choosing to dramatize the old Homeric tale of Oedipus against the backdrop, and in the immediate aftermath, of a calamitous ebola-like viral epidemic, Sophocles not only transformed a current civic misery into an occasion for profound thinking about the nature of crime and guilt, but created a tragedy which has probably done more to shape the history of the art-form than any other single play. Yet *Oedipus Tyrannos*, unlike the vast majority of Sophocles' more than 100 plays, did not win first prize in the year of its presentation.[1]

In Homer's version of the myth, Oedipus's crimes come to light yet he continues to rule Thebes regardless. For Sophocles, on the contrary, crimes are crimes, even if committed in ignorance by an exemplary king. He revises the tale accordingly, making the story of Oedipus into the first "who-dunnit" of the Western theatre, a murder mystery in which a prosecutor sets out to find a murderer, only to discover, through cross-examination of all available witnesses, that the criminal he's been seeking all along is himself. Unlike in Homer, where the regicidal king gets off scot-free, Sophocles the democrat imposes upon his tyrant-king a fate even worse than had been decreed for ordinary men: not only exile, but self-mutilation, a permanent and visceral reminder of the limits of his knowledge. And Oedipus's name adds further levels of irony here, suggesting not only "swollen-foot" in Greek, but also *oida,* "I know...." Remaining willfully ignorant of the first meaning of his name—the mutilation of his ankles in infancy by his parents—Oedipus focusses only on the second, his grown-up knowingness and mastery. Knowledgeable enough to solve the riddle of the Sphinx and

---

1   It is not known whether *Oedipus Tyrannos* (c.429) was performed as part of a trilogy, nor what its accompanying plays might have been. Contrary to common belief, it was *not* performed with either *Antigone* or *Oedipus Coloneus.* The former was probably staged around 441, the later posthumously, by Sophocles' grandson, c. 401.

save the city, he ironically ignores the meaning of the answer: the feet of man, i.e., his own crippled feet, the key to the riddle of *his* identity.

Above the gates of the Temple at Delphi, their most sacred oracle, the Greeks engraved the motto "Know Thyself." It is an injunction very much honoured in this play, which raises questions about hidden crimes, self-deception, and the need to bring the truth to light, even at the cost of one's self-image, even into destruction. *Oedipus* is perhaps the archetypal tragedy of self-knowledge, and it is no coincidence that it has served as the lynch-pin, not only of the most influential theory of tragedy in the Western tradition, the *Poetics* of Aristotle, but also of what is arguably its most significant theory of self-knowledge, too: Freud's ideas about the mechanisms of unconscious repression, in which the Oedipus complex takes pride of place.

SOPHOCLES
Oedipus Tyrannos
Translated by Thomas Gould[1]

DRAMATIS PERSONAE
  OEDIPUS
  PRIEST
  CREON
  CHORUS
  TIRESIAS
  JOCASTA
  MESSENGER
  HERDSMAN
  2ND MESSENGER

OEDIPUS: My children, ancient Cadmus'[2] newest care,
  why have you hurried to those seats, your boughs
  wound with the emblems of the suppliant?
  The city is weighed down with fragrant smoke,
  with hymns to the Healer and the cries of mourners.   5

I thought it wrong, my sons, to hear your words
through emissaries, and have come out myself,
I, Oedipus, a name that all men know.[3]
Old man—for it is fitting that you speak
for all—what is your mood as you entreat me,   10
fear or trust? you may be confident
that I'll do anything. How hard of heart
if an appeal like this did not rouse my pity!
PRIEST: You, Oedipus, who hold the power here,
you see our several ages, we who sit   15
before your altars—some not strong enough
to take long flight, some heavy in old age,
the priests, as I of Zeus, and from our youths
a chosen band. The rest sit with their windings
in the markets, at the twin shrines of Pallas,[4]   20
and the prophetic embers of Ismēnos.[5]

---

1 Annotations for this play are indebted throughout to Gould's commentary, as published in *Oedipus the King by Sophocles: A Translation with Commentary* (Prentice-Hall, 1970).
2 Cadmus was the founder and first king of Thebes; his "newest care" is thus the plague-stricken citizenry of present-day Thebes.

3 Oedipus's name had many resonances that will be crucial to the meaning of the play overall. It evokes both "swollen foot" (*oiden + pous*) and "I know" (*oida*).
4 The two temples of Athena, patron deity of Athens, who was also worshipped at Thebes.
5 A river in Thebes. At the nearby Temple of Apollo (Ismenios was Apollo's son), offerings were burnt for the purposes of prophesy.

Our city, as you see yourself, is tossed
too much, and can no longer lift its head
above the troughs of billows red with death.
It dies in the fruitful flowers of the soil,   25
it dies in its pastured herds, and in its women's
barren pangs. And the fire-bearing god
has swooped upon the city, hateful plague,
and he has left the house of Cadmus empty.
Black Hades is made rich with moans and weeping.   30
Not judging you an equal of the gods,
do I and the children sit here at your heart,
but as the first of men, in troubled times
and in encounters with divinities.
You came to Cadmus' city and unbound   35
the tax we had to pay to the harsh singer,[6]
did it without a helpful word from us,
with no instruction; with a god's assistance
you raised up our life, so we believe.
Again now Oedipus, our greatest power,   40
we plead with you, as suppliants, all of us,
to find us strength, whether from a god's response,
or learned in some way from another man.
I know that the experienced among men
give counsels that will prosper best of all.   45
Noblest of men, lift up our land again!
Think also of yourself: since now the land
calls you its Saviour for your zeal of old,
oh let us never look back at your rule
as men helped up only to fall again!   50
Do not stumble! Put our land on firm feet!
The bird of omen was auspicious then,
when you brought that luck: be that same man
    again!

The power is yours; if you will rule our country,
rule over men, not in an empty land.   55
A towered city or a ship is nothing
if desolate and no man lives within.
OEDIPUS: Pitiable children, oh I know, I know
the yearnings that have brought you. Yes, I know
that you are sick. And yet, though you are sick,   60
there is not one of you so sick as I.
For your affliction comes to each alone,
for him and no one else, but my soul mourns
for me and for you, too, and for the city.
You do not waken me as from a sleep,   65
for I have wept, bitterly and long,
tried many paths in the wanderings of thought,
and the single cure I found by careful search
I've acted on: I sent Menoeceus' son,
Creon, brother of my wife, to the Pythian   70
halls of Phoebus,[7] so that I might learn
what I must do or say to save this city.
Already, when I think what day this is,
I wonder anxiously what he is doing.
Too long, more than is right, he's been away.   75
But when he comes, then I shall be a traitor
if I do not do all that the god reveals.
PRIEST: Welcome words! But look, those men
    have signaled that it is Creon who is now
    approaching!
OEDIPUS: Lord Apollo! May he bring Saviour Luck,   80
    a Luck as brilliant as his eyes are now!
PRIEST: His news is happy, it appears. He comes,
    forehead crowned with thickly berried laurel.
OEDIPUS: We'll know, for he is near enough to hear
    us.
    Lord, brother in marriage, son of Menoeceus!   85
    What is the god's pronouncement that you bring?
CREON: It's good. For even troubles, if they chance
    to turn out well, I always count as lucky.
OEDIPUS: But what was the response? You seem
    to say I'm not to fear—but not to take heart either. 90
CREON: If you will hear me with these men present,
    I'm ready to report—or go inside.
OEDIPUS: Speak out to all! The grief that burdens me
    concerns these men more than it does my life.

---

6 The Sphinx, a winged creature with the body of a lion
and the head and breasts of a woman. She "taxed" the
Thebans by destroying all the males of the city who were
unable to solve her riddle (for an eighteenth-century version of this theme, see Gozzi's *Turandot* later in this volume). The riddle, about what single creature walks on
four feet, two feet, and three feet, was solved by Oedipus, the brainy man with the swollen feet—a highly
ironic outcome. He saves Thebes by identifying the creature as "man"; yet Oedipus's legendary knowingness fails
when it comes to a riddle closer to home, i.e., his own
identity, the meaning of his own crippled childhood,
upright youth, and cane-assisted old age.

7 Apollo's temple at Delphi, which housed the most famous and widely-consulted oracle in the ancient world.

CREON: Then I shall tell you what I heard from the god. 95

The task Lord Phoebus sets for us is clear:
drive out pollution sheltered in our land,
and do not shelter what is incurable.

OEDIPUS: What is our trouble? How shall we
cleanse ourselves?

CREON: We must banish or murder to free ourselves 100
from a murder that blows storms through the city.

OEDIPUS: What man's bad luck does he accuse in this?

CREON: My Lord, a king named Laius ruled our land
before your came to steer the city straight.

OEDIPUS: I know. So I was told—I never saw him. 105

CREON: Since he was murdered, you must raise
your hand against the men who killed him with
their hands.

OEDIPUS: Where are they now? And how can we
ever find the track of ancient guilt now hard to read?

CREON: In our own land, he said. What we pursue, 110
that can be caught; but not what we neglect.

OEDIPUS: Was Laius home, or in the countryside—
or was he murdered in some foreign land?

CREON: He left to see a sacred rite, he said;
He left, but never came home from his journey. 115

OEDIPUS: Did none of his party see it and report—
someone we might profitably question?

CREON: They were all killed but one, who fled in fear,
and he could tell us only one clear fact.

OEDIPUS: What fact? One thing could lead us on 120
to more if we could get a small start on our hope.

CREON: He said that bandits chanced on them and
killed him—with the force of many hands, not
one alone.

OEDIPUS: How could a bandit dare so great an act—
unless this was a plot paid off from here! 125

CREON: We thought of that, but when Laius was
killed,
we had no one to help us in our troubles.

OEDIPUS: It was your very kingship that was killed!
What kind of trouble blocked you from a search?

CREON: The subtle-singing Sphinx asked us to turn 130
from the obscure to what lay at our feet.

OEDIPUS: Then I shall begin again and make it plain.
It was quite worthy of Phoebus, and worthy of you,
to turn our thoughts back to the murdered man,
and right that you should see me join the battle 135

for justice to our land and to the god.
Not on behalf of any distant kinships,
it's for myself I will dispel this stain.
Whoever murdered him may also wish
to punish me—and with the selfsame hand. 140
In helping him I also serve myself.
Now quickly, children: up from the altar steps,
and raise the branches of the suppliant!
Let someone go and summon Cadmus' people:
say I'll do anything. Our luck will prosper 145
if the god is with us, or we have already fallen.

PRIEST: Rise, my children; that for which we came,
he has himself proclaimed he will accomplish.
May Phoebus, who announced this, also come
as Saviour and reliever from the plague. 150

[*The suppliants exit, and the Chorus, made up of elder
citizens of Thebes, comes dancing into the orchestra.
Oedipus retires into the palace for part of the Chorus's
song.*]

STROPHE 1[8]

CHORUS: *Voice from Zeus, sweetly spoken, what are you
that have arrived from golden
Pytho to our shining
Thebes? I am on the rack, terror
shakes my soul.* 155
Delian Healer, summoned by "iē!"[9]
*I await in holy dread what obligation, something new
or something back once more with the revolving years,
you'll bring about for me.*
Oh tell me, child of golden Hope, 160
deathless Response!

ANTISTROPHE 1

*I appeal to you first, daughter of Zeus,
deathless Athena,
and to your sister who protects this land,
Artemis, whose famous throne is the whole circle* 165
of the marketplace,

---

8 "Strophe" and "antistrophe" refer to the turns and coun-
ter-turns of the choral dance, which was choreographed
with formal and symmetrical patterns.

9 All of this is addressed to Apollo (born on the island of
Delos).

and Phoebus, who shoots from afar: *iō!*
Three-fold defenders against death, appear!
If ever in the past, to stop blind ruin
    sent against the city,   170
you banished utterly the fires of suffering,
    come now again!

STROPHE 2

Ah! Ah! Unnumbered are the miseries
I bear. The plague claims all
our comrades. Nor has thought found yet a spear   175
by which a man shall be protected. What our glorious
earth gives birth to does not grow. Without a birth
from cries of labour
    do the women rise.
One person after another   180
    you may see, like flying birds,
faster than indomitable fire, sped
to the shore of the god that is the sunset.[10]

ANTISTROPHE 2

And with their deaths unnumbered dies the city.
Her children lie unpitied on the ground,   185
spreading death, unmourned.
Meanwhile young wives, and gray-haired mothers
    with them,
on the shores of the altars, from this side and that,
suppliants from mournful trouble,
    cry out their grief.   190
A hymn to the Healer shines,
    the flute a mourner's voice.
Against which, golden goddess, daughter of Zeus,
    send lovely Strength.

STROPHE 3

Cause raging Ares—who,   195
    armed now with no shield of bronze,
burns me, coming on amid loud cries—
to turn his back and run from my land,
with a fair wind behind, to the great
    hall of Amphitritē,[11]
or to the anchorage that welcomes no one,   200

---

[10] I.e., the god of the underworld, Hades.
[11] A nymph of the sea whose "great hall" would have been the Atlantic ocean.

Thrace's troubled sea![12]
If night lets something get away at last,
    it comes by day.
Fire-bearing god......   205
    you who dispense the might of lightning,
Zeus! Father! Destroy him with your thunderbolt!

ANTISTROPHE 3

Lycēan Lord![13] *From your looped*
    bowstring, twisted gold,
I wish indomitable missiles might be scattered   210
and stand forward, our protectors; also fire-bearing
radiance of Artemis,[14] *with which*
    she darts across the Lycian[15] *mountains.*
I call the god whose head is bound in gold,[16]
with whom this country shares its name,   215
Bacchus, wine-flushed, summoned by "euoi!",
    Maenads' comrade,
to approach ablaze
    with gleaming [...][17]
pine, opposed to that god-hated god.   220

OEDIPUS: I hear your prayer. Submit to what I say
and to the labours that the plague demands
and you'll get help and a relief from evils.
I'll make the proclamation, though a stranger
to the report and to the deed. Alone,   225
had I no key, I would soon lose the track.
Since it was only later that I joined you,
to all the sons of Cadmus I say this:
whoever has clear knowledge of the man
who murdered Laius, son of Labdacus,   230
I command him to reveal it all to me—
nor fear if, to remove the charge, he must
accuse himself: his fate will not be cruel—

---

[12] The Black Sea, easternmost marker of the world familiar to the Greeks.
[13] Again, Apollo, whose altar was probably visible on stage in front of the palace.
[14] Twin sister of Apollo.
[15] Coastal region in Western Asia Minor, directly north, across the Mediterranean, of Alexandria.
[16] Dionysus, born in Thebes to Semele, Cadmus's daughter, and thus the grandson of the city's founder.
[17] Missing syllables.

he will depart unstumbling into exile.
But if you know another, or a stranger, 235
to be the one whose hand is guilty, speak:
I shall reward you and remember you.
But if you keep your peace because of fear,
and shield yourself or kin from my command,
hear you what I shall do in that event: 240
I charge all in this land where I have throne
and power, shut out that man—no matter who—
both from your shelter and all spoken words,
nor in your prayers or sacrifices make
him partner, nor allot him lustral water. 245
All men shall drive him from their homes: for he
is the pollution that the god-sent Pythian
response has only now revealed to me.
In this way I ally myself in war
with the divinity and the deceased. 250
And this curse, too, against the one who did it,
whether alone in secrecy, or with others:
may he wear out his life unblest and evil!
I pray this, too: if he is at my hearth
and in my home, and I have knowledge of him, 255
may the curse pronounced on others come to me.
All this I lay to you to execute,
for my sake, for the god's, and for this land
now ruined, barren, abandoned by the gods.
Even if no god had driven you to it, 260
you ought not to have left this stain uncleansed,
the murdered man a nobleman, a king!
You should have looked! But now, since, as it
    happens,
it's I who have the power that he had once,
and have his bed, and a wife who shares our seed, 265
and common bond had we had common children
(had not his hope of offspring had bad luck—
but as it happened, luck lunged at his head):
because of this, as if for my own father,
I'll fight for him, I'll leave no means untried, 270
to catch the one who did it with his hand,
for the son of Labdacus, of Polydōrus,
of Cadmus before him, and of Agēnor.
This prayer against all those who disobey:
the gods send out no harvest from their soil, 275
nor children from their wives. Oh, let them die
victims of this plague, or of something worse.
Yet for the rest of us, people of Cadmus,

we the obedient, may Justice, our ally,
and all the gods, be always on our side! 280
CHORUS: I speak because I feel the grip of your curse:
    the killer is not I. Nor can I point
    to him. The one who set us to this search,
    Phoebus, should also name the guilty man.
OEDIPUS: Quite right, but to compel unwilling gods— 285
    no man has ever had that kind of power.
CHORUS: May I suggest to you a second way?
OEDIPUS: A second or a third—pass over nothing!
CHORUS: I know of no one who sees more of what
    Lord Phoebus sees than Lord Tiresias.[18] 290
    My Lord, one might learn brilliantly from him.
OEDIPUS: Nor is this something I have been slow to
        do.
    At Creon's word I sent an escort—twice now!
    I am astonished that he has not come.
CHORUS: The old account is useless. It told us 295
    nothing.
OEDIPUS: But tell it to me. I'll scrutinize all stories.
CHORUS: He is said to have been killed by
    travellers.
OEDIPUS: I have heard, but the one who did it no
    one sees.
CHORUS: If there is any fear in him at all,
    he won't stay here once he has heard that curse. 300
OEDIPUS: He won't fear words: he had no fear
    when he did it.
CHORUS: Look there! There is the man who will
    convict him!
    It's the god's prophet they are leading here,
    one gifted with the truth as no one else.
OEDIPUS: Tiresias, master of all omens— 305
    public and secret, in the sky and on the earth—
    your mind, if not your eyes, sees how the city
    lives with a plague, against which Thebes can find
    no Saviour or protector, Lord, but you.
    For Phoebus, as the attendants surely told you, 310
    returned this answer to us: liberation
    from the disease would never come unless

---

18 Blind seer whose sightlessness and prophetic powers are
attributed in myth to a number of causes, all having to
do with seeing forbidden sexual acts, or revealing secret
sexual truths (such as that women receive nine times as
much pleasure in lovemaking as men).

we learned without a doubt who murdered Laius—
put them to death, or sent them into exile.
Do not begrudge us what you may learn from birds   315
or any other prophet's path you know!
Care for yourself, the city, care for me,
care for the whole pollution of the dead!
We're in your hands. To do all that he can
to help another is man's noblest labour.   320
TIRESIAS: How terrible to understand and get
no profit from the knowledge! I knew this,
but I forgot, or I had never come.
OEDIPUS: What's this? You've come with very little zeal.
TIRESIAS: Let me go home! If you will listen to me,   325
You will endure your troubles better—and I mine.
OEDIPUS: A strange request, not very kind to the land
that cared for you—to hold back this oracle!
TIRESIAS: I see your understanding comes to you
inopportunely. So that won't happen to me …   330
OEDIPUS: Oh, by the gods, if you understand
about this, don't turn away! We're on our knees to
you.
TIRESIAS: None of you understands! I'll never bring
my grief to light—I will not speak of yours.
OEDIPUS: You know and won't declare it? Is your   335
purpose to betray us and to destroy this land?
TIRESIAS: I will grieve neither of us. Stop this futile
cross-examination. I'll tell you nothing!
OEDIPUS: Nothing? You vile traitor! You could provoke
a stone to anger! You still refuse to tell?   340
Can nothing soften you, nothing convince you?
TIRESIAS: You blamed anger in me—you haven't seen
the one that lives with you!¹⁹
OEDIPUS: Who wouldn't fill with anger, listening
to words like yours which now disgrace this city?   345
TIRESIAS: It will come, even if my silence hides it.
OEDIPUS: If it will come, then why won't you
declare it?
TIRESIAS: I'd rather say no more. Now if you wish,
respond to that with all your fiercest anger!

---

19 The "anger" that Tiresias is here attributing to Oedipus
is a feminine word in the Greek, and hence the meaning of the statement is doubled, as meanings often are
in this play. The seer's accusation consequently refers
both to the temper that lives in Oedipus and to the
woman who lives with him, and to his ignorance of both.

OEDIPUS: Now I am angry enough to come right out   350
with this conjecture: you, I think, helped plot
the deed; you did it—even if your hand
cannot have struck the blow. If you could see,
I should have said the deed was yours alone.
TIRESIAS: Is that right! Then I charge you to abide   355
by the decree you have announced: from this day
say no word to either these or me,
for you are the vile polluter of this land!
OEDIPUS: Aren't you appalled to let a charge like that
come bounding forth? How will you get away?   360
TIRESIAS: You cannot catch me. I have the strength
of truth.
OEDIPUS: Who taught you this? Not your
prophetic craft!
TIRESIAS: You did. You made me say it. I didn't want
to.
OEDIPUS: Say what? Repeat it so I'll understand.
TIRESIAS: I made no sense? Or are you trying me?   365
OEDIPUS: No sense I understood. Say it again!
TIRESIAS: I say you are the murderer you seek.
OEDIPUS: Again that horror! You'll wish you hadn't
said that.
TIRESIAS: Shall I say more, and raise your anger higher?
OEDIPUS: Anything you like! Your words are powerless.   370
TIRESIAS: You live, unknowing, with those nearest
to you in the greatest shame. You do not see the evil.
OEDIPUS: You won't go on like that and never pay!
TIRESIAS: I can if there is any strength in truth.
OEDIPUS: In truth, but not in you! You have no   375
strength,
blind in your ears, your reason, and your eyes.
TIRESIAS: Unhappy man! Those jeers you hurl at
me
before long all these men will hurl at you.
OEDIPUS: You are the child of endless night; it's not
for me or anyone who sees to hurt you.   380
TIRESIAS: It's not my fate to be struck down by you.
Apollo is enough. That's his concern.
OEDIPUS: Are these inventions Creon's or your own?
TIRESIAS: No, your affliction is yourself, not Creon.
OEDIPUS: Oh success!—in wealth, kingship,   385
artistry,
in any life that wins much admiration—
the envious ill will stored up for you!
To get at my command, a gift I did not

seek, which the city put into my hands,
my loyal Creon, colleague from the start,   390
longs to sneak up in secret and dethrone me.
So he's suborned this fortuneteller—schemer!
deceitful beggar-priest!—who has good eyes
for gains alone, though in his craft he's blind.
Where were your prophet's powers ever proved?   395
Why, when the dog who chanted verse was here,[20]
did you not speak and liberate this city?
Her riddle wasn't for a man chancing by
to interpret; prophetic art was needed,
but you had none, it seems—learned from birds   400
or from a god. I came along, yes I,
Oedipus the ignorant, and stopped her—
by using thought, not augury from birds.
And it is I whom you now wish to banish,
so you'll be close to the Creontian throne.   405
You—and the plot's concocter—will drive out
pollution to your grief: you look quite old
or you would be the victim of that plot!
CHORUS: It seems to us that this man's words were
said in anger, Oedipus, and yours as well.   410
Insight, not angry words, is what we need,
the best solution to the god's response.
TIRESIAS: You are the king, and yet I am your equal
in my right to speak. In that I too am Lord.
For I belong to Loxias,[21] not you.   415
I am not Creon's man. He's nothing to me.
Hear this, since you have thrown my blindness at
me:
Your eyes can't see the evil to which you've come,
nor where you live, nor who is in your house.
Do you know your parents? Not knowing, you   420
are
their enemy, in the underworld and here.
A mother's, and a father's double-lashing
terrible-footed curse will soon drive you out.
Now you can see, then you will stare into darkness.
What place will not be harbour to your cry,   425
or what Cithaeron[22] not reverberate

when you have heard the bride-song in your palace
to which you sailed? Fair wind to evil harbour!
Nor do you see how many other woes
will level you to yourself and to your children.   430
So, [go ahead:] at my message, and at Creon, too,
splatter muck! There will never be a man
ground into wretchedness as you will be.
OEDIPUS: Am I to listen to such things from him?
May you be damned! Get out of here at once!   435
Go! Leave my palace! Turn around and go!
TIRESIAS: I wouldn't have come had you not sent
for me.
OEDIPUS: I did not know you'd talk stupidity,
or I wouldn't have rushed to bring you to my
house.
TIRESIAS: Stupid I seem to you, yet to your parents   440
who gave you natural birth I seemed quite shrewd.
OEDIPUS: Who? Wait! Who is the one who gave me
birth?
TIRESIAS: This day will give you birth, and ruin too.
OEDIPUS: What murky, riddling things you always
say!
TIRESIAS: Don't you surpass us all at finding out?   445
OEDIPUS: You sneer at what you'll find has brought
me greatness.
TIRESIAS: And that's the very luck that ruined you.
OEDIPUS: I wouldn't care, just so I saved the city.
TIRESIAS: In that case I shall go. Boy, lead the way!
OEDIPUS: Yes, let him lead you off. Here, underfoot,   450
you irk me. Gone, you'll cause no further pain.
TIRESIAS: I'll go when I have said what I was sent for.
Your face won't scare me. You can't ruin me.
I say to you, the man whom you have looked for
as you pronounced your curses, your decrees   455
on the bloody death of Laius—he is here!
A seeming stranger, he shall be shown to be
a Theban born, though he'll take no delight
in that solution. Blind, who once could see,
a beggar who was rich, through foreign lands   460
he'll go and point before him with a stick.
To his beloved children, he'll be shown
a father who is also brother; to the one
who bore him, son and husband; to his father
his seed-fellow and killer. Go in   465
and think this out; and if you find I've lied,
say then I have no prophet's understanding!

---

20 The Sphinx.

21 Apollo as the riddler, speaker of obscure oracles.

22 A mountain that will echo Oedipus's cries when he learns
the truth about himself; also the mountain on which
Oedipus was abandoned as an infant.

STROPHE 1

CHORUS: *Who is the man of whom the inspired*
  rock of Delphi said
he has committed the unspeakable   470
  with blood-stained hands?
Time for him to ply a foot
mightier than those of the horses
  of the storm in his escape;
upon him mounts and plunges the weaponed   475
son of Zeus,[23] *with fire and thunderbolts,*
and in his train the dreaded goddesses
of Death, who never miss.

ANTISTROPHE 1

The message has just blazed,
  gleaming from the snows   480
of Mount Parnassus: we must track
  everywhere the unseen man.
He wanders, hidden by wild
forests, up through caves
  and rocks, like a bull,   485
anxious, with an anxious foot, forlorn.
He puts away from him the mantic words come from
  earth's
navel,[24] *at its center, yet these live*
forever and still hover round him.

STROPHE 2

Terribly he troubles me,   490
  the skilled interpreter of birds![25]
I can't assent, nor speak against him.
  Both paths are closed to me.
I hover on the wings of doubt,
  not seeing what is here nor what's to come. 495
What quarrel started in the house of Labdacus[26]
or in the house of Polybus,[27]
  either ever in the past
  or now, I never

---

heard, so that … with this fact for my touchstone[28] 500
I could attack the public
  fame of Oedipus, by the side of the Labdaceans
an ally, against the dark assassination.

ANTISTROPHE 2

No, Zeus and Apollo
  understand and know things   505
mortal; but that another man
  can do more as a prophet than I can—
for that there is no certain test,
  though, skill to skill,
one man might overtake another.   510
No, never, not until
  I see the charges proved,
when someone blames him shall I nod assent.
For once, as we all saw, the winged maiden[29] *came*
against him: he was seen then to be skilled,   515
  proved, by that touchstone, dear to the people. So,
never will my mind convict him of the evil.

CREON: Citizens, I hear that a fearful charge
 is made against me by King Oedipus!
 I had to come. If, in this crisis,   520
 he thinks that he has suffered injury
 from anything that I have said or done,
 I have no appetite for a long life—
 bearing a blame like that! It's no slight blow
 the punishment I'd take from what he said: 525
 it's the ultimate hurt to be called traitor
 by the city, by you, by my own people!
CHORUS: The thing that forced that accusation out
 could have been anger, not the power of thought.
CREON: But who persuaded him that thoughts of mine 530
 had led the prophet into telling lies?
CHORUS: I do not know the thought behind his words.
CREON: But did he look straight at you? Was his
 mind right when he said that I was guilty of this
  charge?
CHORUS: I have no eyes to see what rulers do.   535
 But here he comes himself out of the house.

---

23 Apollo.
24 I.e., Apollo's prophesy, which issued from Delphi, said
 to be located at the "navel" of the earth.
25 Tiresias.
26 Creon's family.
27 Believed to be Oedipus's father.

28 A touchstone was used to prove the true quality of gold;
 as a metaphor it was used also in legal contexts to refer
 to the torture that was believed to prove the truth of a
 slave's testimony.
29 The Sphinx.

OEDIPUS: What? You here? And can you really have
  the face and daring to approach my house
  when you're exposed as its master's murderer
  and caught, too, as the robber of my kingship?   540
  Did you see cowardice in me, by the gods,
  or foolishness, when you began this plot?
  Did you suppose that I would not detect
  your stealthy moves, or that I'd not fight back?
  It's your attempt that's folly, isn't it—   545
  tracking without followers or connections,
  kingship which is caught with wealth and numbers?
CREON: Now wait! Give me as long to answer back!
  Judge me for yourself when you have heard me!
OEDIPUS: You're eloquent, but I'd be slow to learn   550
  from you, now that I've seen your malice toward me.
CREON: That I deny. Hear what I have to say.
OEDIPUS: Don't you deny it! You are the traitor here!
CREON: If you consider mindless willfulness
  a prized possession, you are not thinking sense.   555
OEDIPUS: If y[ou think you can wrong a relative]
  and get off [... thinking sense]
CREON: Perfe[ctly just ... and yet]
  what is this [injury you say I've done you?]
OEDIPUS: Di[d ... me yes or no to send]   560
  someone t[o ...]
CREON: An[d ...]
OEDIPUS: H[ow ...]
  Laius [...]
CREON: Lai[us ...]
OEDIPUS: V[...]
CREON: Th[at ...]
OEDIPUS: V[...]
CREON: Ye[s ... and honoured just as he is]
  today[...]
OEDIPUS: [...]
CREON: H[...]
OEDIPUS: [... you did inquire into the murder then]
CREON: We had to, surely, though we discovered
  nothing.
OEDIPUS: But the "skilled" one did not say this then?
  Why not?
CREON: I never talk when I am ignorant.   575
OEDIPUS: But you're not ignorant of your own part.
CREON: What do you mean? I'll tell you if I know.
OEDIPUS: Just this: if he had not conferred with you
  he'd not have told about my murdering Laius.

CREON: If he said that, you are the one who knows.   580
  But now it's fair that you should answer me.
OEDIPUS: Ask on! You won't convict me as the killer.
CREON: Well then, answer. My sister is your wife?
OEDIPUS: Now there's a statement that I can't deny.
CREON: You two have equal powers in this country?   585
OEDIPUS: She gets from me whatever she desires.
CREON: And I'm a third? The three of us are equals?
OEDIPUS: That's where you're treacherous to your
  kinship!
CREON: But think about this rationally, as I do.
  First look at this: do you think anyone   590
  prefers the anxieties of being king
  to untroubled sleep—if he has equal power?
  I'm not the kind of man who falls in love
  with kingship. I am content with a king's power.
  And so would any man who's wise and prudent.   595
  I get all things from you, with no distress;
  as king I would have onerous duties, too.
  How could the kingship bring me more delight
  than this untroubled power and influence?
  I'm not misguided yet to such a point   600
  that profitable honours aren't enough.
  As it is, all wish me well and all salute;
  those begging you for something have me
    summoned,
  for their success depends on that alone.
  Why should I lose all this to become king?   605
  A prudent mind is never traitorous.
  Treason's a thought I'm not enamored of;
  nor could I join a man who acted so.
  In proof of this, first go yourself to Pytho
  and ask if I brought back the true response.   610
  Then, if you find I plotted with that portent
  reader, don't have me put to death by your vote
  only—I'll vote myself for my conviction.
  Don't let an unsupported thought convict me!
  It's not right mindlessly to take the bad   615
  for good or to suppose the good are traitors.
  Rejecting a relation who is loyal
  is like rejecting life, our greatest love.
  In time you'll know securely without stumbling,
  for time alone can prove a just man just,   620
  though you can know a bad man in a day.
CHORUS: Well said, to one who's anxious not to fall.
  Swift thinkers, Lord, are never safe from stumbling.

OEDIPUS: But when a swift and secret plotter moves
    against me, I must make swift counterplot.   625
    If I lie quiet and await his move,
    he'll have achieved his aims and I'll have missed.
CREON: You surely cannot mean you want me exiled!
OEDIPUS: Not exiled, no. Your death is what I want!
CREON: If you would first define what envy is …   630
OEDIPUS: Are you still stubborn? Still disobedient?
CREON: I see you cannot think well.
OEDIPUS: For me I can.
CREON: You should for me as well!
OEDIPUS: But you're a traitor!   635
CREON: What if you're wrong?
OEDIPUS: Authority must be maintained.
CREON: Not if the ruler's evil.
OEDIPUS: Hear that, Thebes!
CREON: It is my city too, not yours alone!   640
CHORUS: Please don't, my Lords! Ah, just in time, I see
    Jocasta there, coming from the palace.
    With her help you must settle your quarrel.
JOCASTA: Wretched men! What has provoked this ill-
    advised dispute? Have you no sense of shame,   645
    with Thebes so sick, to stir up private troubles?
    Now go inside! And Creon, you go home!
    Don't make a general anguish out of nothing!
CREON: My sister, Oedipus your husband here
    sees fit to do one of two hideous things: 650
    to have me banished from the land—or killed!
OEDIPUS: That's right: I caught him, Lady, plotting
    harm
    against my person—with a malignant science.[30]
CREON: May my life fail, may I die cursed, if I
    did any of the things you said I did!   655
JOCASTA: Believe his words, for the god's sake,
    Oedipus,
    in deference above all to his oath
    to the gods. Also for me, and for these men!

STROPHE 1

CHORUS: *Consent, with will and mind,*
    my king, I beg of you!   660
OEDIPUS: *What do you wish me to surrender?*
CHORUS: *Show deference to him who was not feeble*
    in time past

---

[30] I.e., prophesy.

and is now great in the power of his oath!
OEDIPUS: *Do you know what you're asking?*
CHORUS: *Yes.*
OEDIPUS: *Tell me then.*
CHORUS: *Never to cast into dishonoured guilt, with*   665
    an unproved
    assumption, a kinsman who has bound himself by curse.
OEDIPUS: *Now you must understand, when you ask this,*
    you ask my death or banishment from this land.

STROPHE 2

CHORUS: *No, by the god who is the foremost of all gods,*
    the Sun! No! Godless,   670
    friendless, whatever death is worst of all,
    let that be my destruction, if this
    thought ever moved me!
    But my ill-fated soul
    this dying land   675
    wears out—the more if to these older troubles
    she adds new troubles from the two of you!
OEDIPUS: Then let him go, though it must mean my
    death, or else disgrace and exile from the land.
    My pity is moved by your words, not by his—   680
    he'll only have my hate, wherever he goes.
CREON: You're sullen as you yield; you'll be depressed
    when you've passed through this anger. Natures
    like yours are hardest on themselves. That's as it
    should be.
OEDIPUS: Then won't you go and let me be?   685
CREON: I'll go.
    Though you're unreasonable, they know I'm
    righteous.

ANTISTROPHE 1

CHORUS: *Why are you waiting, Lady?*
    Conduct him back into the palace!
JOCASTA: *I will, when I have heard what chanced.*
CHORUS: *Conjectures—words alone, and nothing*   690
    based on thought.
    But even an injustice can devour a man.
JOCASTA: *Did the words come from both sides?*
CHORUS: *Yes.*
JOCASTA: *What was said?*
CHORUS: *To me it seems enough! enough! the land*
    already troubled,
    that this should rest where it has stopped.

OEDIPUS: *See what you've come to in your honest thought,*   695
    in seeking to relax and blunt my heart?

ANTISTROPHE 2

CHORUS: *I have not said this only once, my Lord.*
    That I had lost my sanity,
      without a path in thinking—
    be sure this would be clear   700
      if I put you away
    who, when my cherished land
      wandered crazed
    with suffering, brought her back on course.
    Now, too, be a lucky helmsman!   705

JOCASTA: Please, for the god's sake, Lord, explain to me
    the reason why you have conceived this wrath?

OEDIPUS: I honour you, not them, and I'll explain
    to you how Creon has conspired against me.

JOCASTA: All right, if that will explain how the   710
    quarrel started.

OEDIPUS: He says I am the murderer of Laius!

JOCASTA: Did he claim knowledge or that someone
    told him?

OEDIPUS: Here's what he did: he sent that vicious seer
    so he could keep his own mouth innocent.

JOCASTA: Ah then, absolve yourself of what he charges!   715
    Listen to this and you'll agree, no mortal
    is ever given skill in prophecy.
    I'll prove this quickly with one incident.
    It was foretold to Laius—I shall not say
    by Phoebus himself, but by his ministers—   720
    that when his fate arrived he would be killed
    by a son who would be born to him and me.
    And yet, so it is told, foreign robbers
    murdered him, at a place where three roads meet.
    As for the child I bore him, not three days passed   725
    before he yoked the ball-joints of his feet,
    then cast it, by others' hands, on a trackless
      mountain.
    That time Apollo did not make our child
    a patricide, or bring about what Laius
    feared, that he be killed by his own son.   730
    That's how prophetic words determined things!
    Forget them. The things a god must track
    he will himself painlessly reveal.

OEDIPUS: Just now, as I was listening to you, Lady,
    what a profound distraction seized my mind!   735

JOCASTA: What made you turn around so anxiously?

OEDIPUS: I thought you said that Laius was attacked
    and butchered at a place where three roads meet.

JOCASTA: That is the story, and it is told so still.

OEDIPUS: Where is the place where this was done   740
    to him?

JOCASTA: The land's called Phocis, where a two-
    forked road comes in from Delphi and from Daulia.

OEDIPUS: And how much time has passed since
    these events?

JOCASTA: Just prior to your presentation here
    as king this news was published to the city.   745

OEDIPUS: Oh, Zeus, what have you willed to do to me?

JOCASTA: Oedipus, what makes your heart so heavy?

OEDIPUS: No, tell me first of Laius' appearance,
    what peak of youthful vigour he had reached.

JOCASTA: A tall man, showing his first growth of white.   750
    He had a figure not unlike your own.

OEDIPUS: Alas! It seems that in my ignorance
    I laid those fearful curses on myself.

JOCASTA: What is it, Lord? I flinch to see your face.

OEDIPUS: I'm dreadfully afraid the prophet sees.   755
    But I'll know better with one more detail.

JOCASTA: I'm frightened too. But ask: I'll answer you.

OEDIPUS: Was his retinue small, or did he travel
    with a great troop, as would befit a prince?

JOCASTA: There were just five in all, one a herald.   760
    There was a carriage, too, bearing Laius.

OEDIPUS: Alas! Now I see it! But who was it,
    Lady, who told you what you know about this?

JOCASTA: A servant who alone was saved unharmed.

OEDIPUS: By chance, could he be now in the palace?   765

JOCASTA: No, he is not. When he returned and saw
    you had the power of the murdered Laius,
    he touched my hand and begged me formally
    to send him to the fields and to the pastures,
    so he'd be out of sight, far from the city.   770
    I did. Although a slave, he well deserved
    to win this favour, and indeed far more.

OEDIPUS: Let's have him called back in immediately.

JOCASTA: That can be done, but why do you desire it?

OEDIPUS: I fear, Lady, I have already said   775
    too much. That's why I wish to see him now.

JOCASTA: Then he shall come; but it is right
    somehow
    that I, too, Lord, should know what troubles you.

OEDIPUS: I've gone so deep into the things I feared
    I'll tell you everything. Who has a right 780
    greater than yours, while I cross through this
        chance?
    Polybus of Corinth was my father,
    my mother was the Dorian Meropē.
    I was first citizen, until this chance
    attacked me—striking enough, to be sure, 785
    but not worth all the gravity I gave it.
    This: at a feast a man who'd drunk too much
    denied, at the wine, I was my father's son.
    I was depressed and all that day I barely
    held it in. Next day I put the question 790
    to my mother and father. They were enraged
    at the man who'd let this fiction fly at me.
    I was much cheered by them. And yet it kept
    grinding into me. His words kept coming back.
    Without my mother's or my father's knowledge 795
    I went to Pytho. But Phoebus sent me away
    dishonouring my demand. Instead, other
    wretched horrors he flashed forth in speech.
    He said that I would be my mother's lover,
    show offspring to mankind they could not look at, 800
    and be his murderer whose seed I am.
    When I heard this, and ever since, I gauged
    the way to Corinth by the stars alone,
    running to a place where I would never see
    the disgrace in the oracle's words come true. 805
    But I soon came to the exact location
    where, as you tell of it, the king was killed.
    Lady, here is the truth. As I went on,
    when I was just approaching those three roads,
    a herald and a man like him you spoke of 810
    come on, riding a carriage drawn by colts.
    Both the man out front and the old man himself
    tried violently to force me off the road.
    The driver, when he tried to push me off,
    I struck in anger. The old man saw this, watched 815
    me approach, then leaned out and lunged down
    with twin prongs at the middle of my head!
    He got more than he gave. Abruptly—struck
    once by the staff in this my hand—he tumbled
    out, head first, from the middle of the carriage. 820
    And then I killed them all. But if there is
    a kinship between Laius and this stranger,
    who is more wretched than the man you see?
    Who was there born more hated by the gods?

For neither citizen nor foreigner 825
    may take me in his home or speak to me.
    No, they must drive me off. And it is I
    who have pronounced these curses on myself!
    I stain the dead man's bed with these my hands,
    by which he died. Is not my nature vile? 830
    Unclean?—if I am banished and even
    in exile I may not see my own parents,
    or set foot in my homeland, or else be yoked
    in marriage to my mother, and kill my father,
    Polybus, who raised me and gave me birth? 835
    If someone judged a cruel divinity
    did this to me, would he not speak the truth?
    You pure and awful gods, may I not ever
    see that day, may I be swept away
    from men before I see so great and so 840
    calamitous a stain fixed on my person!
CHORUS: These things seem fearful to us, Lord,
    and yet,
    until you hear it from the witness, keep hope!
OEDIPUS: That is the single hope that's left to me,
    to wait for him, that herdsman—until he comes. 845
JOCASTA: When he appears, what are you eager for?
OEDIPUS: Just this: if his account agrees with yours
    then I shall have escaped this misery.
JOCASTA: But what was it that struck you in my story?
OEDIPUS: You said he spoke of robbers as the ones 850
    who killed him. Now: if he continues still
    to speak of many, then I could not have killed him.
    One man and many men just do not jibe.
    But if he says one belted[31] man, the doubt
    is gone. The balance tips toward me. I did it. 855
JOCASTA: No! He told it as I told you. Be certain.
    He can't reject that and reverse himself.
    The city heard these things, not I alone.
    But even if he swerves from what he said,
    he'll never show that Laius' murder, Lord, 860
    occurred just as predicted. For Loxias
    expressly said my son was doomed to kill him.
    The boy—poor boy—he never had a chance
    to cut him down, for he was cut down first.
    Never again, just for some oracle 865
    will I shoot frightened glances right and left.

---

31 It is not quite clear what Sophocles means by this phrase.
    See Thomas Gould, 1970:105, n. 846.

OEDIPUS: That's full of sense. Nonetheless, send a
man to bring that farm hand here. Will you do it?
JOCASTA: I'll send one right away. But let's go in.
Would I do anything against your wishes? 870

STROPHE 1

CHORUS: *May there accompany me*
the fate to keep a reverential purity in what I say,
in all I do, for which the laws have been set forth
and walk on high, born to traverse the brightest,
highest upper air; Olympus only 875
is their father, nor was it
mortal nature
that fathered them, and never will
oblivion lull them into sleep;
the god in them is great and never ages. 880

ANTISTROPHE 1

The will to violate, seed of the tyrant,
if it has drunk mindlessly of wealth and power,
without a sense of time or true advantage,
mounts to a peak, then
plunges to an abrupt … destiny, 885
where the useful foot
is of no use. But the kind
of struggling that is good for the city
I ask the god never to abolish.
The god is my protector: never will I give that up. 890

STROPHE 2

But if a man proceeds disdainfully
in deeds of hand or word
and has no fear of Justice
or reverence for shrines of the divinities
(may a bad fate catch him 895
for his luckless wantonness!),
if he'll not gain what he gains with justice
and deny himself what is unholy,
or if he clings, in foolishness, to the untouchable
(what man, finally, in such an action, will have 900
strength
enough to fend off passion's arrows from his soul?),
if, I say, this kind of
deed is held in honour—
why should I join the sacred dance?

ANTISTROPHE 2

No longer shall I visit and revere 905
Earth's navel, the untouchable,
nor visit Abae's temple,[32]
or Olympia,[33]
if the prophecies are not matched by events 910
for all the world to point to.
No, you who hold the power, if you are rightly called
Zeus the king of all, let this matter not escape you
and your ever-deathless rule,
for the prophecies to Laius fade … 915
and men already disregard them;
nor is Apollo anywhere
glorified with honours.
Religion slips away.
JOCASTA: Lords of the realm, the thought has come 920
to me to visit shrines of the divinities
with suppliant's branch in hand and fragrant smoke.
For Oedipus excites his soul too much
with alarms of all kinds. He will not judge
the present by the past, like a man of sense. 925
He's at the mercy of all terror-mongers.
Since I can do no good by counselling,
Apollo the Lycēan!—you are the closest—
I come a suppliant, with these my vows,
for a cleansing that will not pollute him. 930
For when we see him shaken we are all
afraid, like people looking at their helmsman.
MESSENGER: I would be pleased if you would help
me, stranger.
Where is the palace of King Oedipus?
Or tell me where he is himself, if you know. 935
CHORUS: This is his house, stranger. He is within.
That is his wife and mother of his children.
MESSENGER: May she and her family find prosperity,
if, as you say, her marriage is fulfilled.
JOCASTA: You also, stranger, for you deserve as much 940
for your gracious words. But tell me why you've
come.
What do you wish? Or what have you to tell us?
MESSENGER: Good news, my Lady, both for your
house and husband.

---

32 Another Apollonian oracle, in the town of Phocis.
33 An oracle of Zeus.

JOCASTA: What is your news? And who has sent
 you to us?
MESSENGER: I come from Corinth. When you have   945
 heard my news
 you will rejoice, I'm sure—and grieve perhaps.
JOCASTA: What is it? How can it have this double
 power?
MESSENGER: They will establish him their king,[34]
 so say the people of the land of Isthmia.
JOCASTA: But is old Polybus not still in power?   950
MESSENGER: He's not, for death has clasped him in
 the tomb.
JOCASTA: What's this? Has Oedipus' father died?
MESSENGER: If I have lied then I deserve to die.
JOCASTA: Attendant! Go in quickly to your master,
 and tell him this. Oracles of the gods!   955
 Where are you now? The man whom Oedipus
 fled long ago, for fear that he should kill him—
 he's been destroyed by chance and not by him!
OEDIPUS: Darling Jocasta, my beloved wife,
 why have you had me called from the palace?   960
JOCASTA: First hear what this man has to say.
 Then see what the god's grave oracle has come to
 now!
OEDIPUS: Where is he from? What is this news he
 brings me?
JOCASTA: From Corinth. He brings news about your
 father: that Polybus is no more! that he is dead!   965
OEDIPUS: What's this, old man? I want to hear you
 say it.
MESSENGER: If this is what must first be clarified,
 please be assured that he is dead and gone.
OEDIPUS: By treachery or by the touch of sickness?
MESSENGER: Light pressures tip agéd frames into   970
 their sleep.
OEDIPUS: You mean the poor man died of some
 disease.
MESSENGER: And of the length of years that he had
 tallied.
OEDIPUS: Aha! Then why should we look to Pytho's
 vapours, or to the birds that scream above our heads?

If we could really take those things for guides,   975
 I would have killed my father. But he's dead!
He is beneath the earth, and here am I,
who never touched a spear. Unless he died
of longing for me and I "killed" him that way!
No, in this case, Polybus, by dying, took   980
 the worthless oracle to Hades with him.
JOCASTA: And wasn't I telling you that just now?
OEDIPUS: You were indeed. I was misled by fear.
JOCASTA: You should not care about this anymore.
OEDIPUS: I must care. I must stay clear of my   985
 mother's bed.
JOCASTA: What's there for man to fear? The realm
 of chance prevails. True foresight isn't possible.
 His life is best who lives without a plan.
 This marriage with your mother—don't fear it.
 How many times have men in dreams, too, slept   990
 with their own mothers! Those who believe such
 things mean nothing
 endure their lives most easily.
OEDIPUS: A fine, bold speech, and you are right,
 perhaps,
 except that my mother is still living,
 so I must fear her, however well you argue.   995
JOCASTA: And yet your father's tomb is a great eye.
OEDIPUS: Illuminating, yes. But I still fear the
 living.
MESSENGER: Who is the woman who inspires this
 fear?
OEDIPUS: Meropē, Polybus' wife, old man.
MESSENGER: And what is there about her that   1000
 alarms you?
OEDIPUS: An oracle, god-sent and fearful, stranger.
MESSENGER: Is it permitted that another know?
OEDIPUS: It is. Loxias once said to me
 I must have intercourse with my own mother
 and take my father's blood with these my hands.   1005
 So I have long lived far away from Corinth.
 This has indeed brought much good luck, and yet,
 to see one's parents' eyes is happiest.
MESSENGER: Was it for this that you have lived in
 exile?
OEDIPUS: So I'd not be my father's killer, sir.   1010
MESSENGER: Had I not better free you from this fear,
 my Lord? That's why I came—to do you service.
OEDIPUS: Indeed, what a reward you'd get for that!

---

34 The messenger uses the word "tyrannos," not "basileus,"
 the expected word for king in a context where the succession is one of blood-inheritance, thus foreshadowing
 the news about Oedipus's true parentage.

MESSENGER: Indeed, this is the main point of my trip, to be rewarded when you get back home. 1015

OEDIPUS: I'll never rejoin the givers of my seed!

MESSENGER: My son, clearly you don't know what you're doing.

OEDIPUS: But how is that, old man? For the gods' sake, tell me!

MESSENGER: If it's because of them you won't go home.

OEDIPUS: I fear that Phoebus will have told the truth. 1020

MESSENGER: Pollution from the ones who gave you seed?

OEDIPUS: That is the thing, old man, I always fear.

MESSENGER: Your fear is groundless. Understand that.

OEDIPUS: Groundless? Not if I was born their son.

MESSENGER: But Polybus is not related to you. 1025

OEDIPUS: Do you mean Polybus was not my father?

MESSENGER: No more than I. We're both the same to you.

OEDIPUS: Same? One who begot me and one who didn't?

MESSENGER: He didn't beget you any more than I did.

OEDIPUS: But then, why did he say I was his son? 1030

MESSENGER: He got you as a gift from my own hands.

OEDIPUS: He loved me so, though from another's hands?

MESSENGER: His former childlessness persuaded him.

OEDIPUS: But had you bought me, or begotten me?

MESSENGER: Found you. In the forest hallows of Cithaeron. 1035

OEDIPUS: What were you doing travelling in that region?

MESSENGER: I was in charge of flocks which grazed those mountains.

OEDIPUS: A wanderer who worked the flocks for hire?

MESSENGER: Ah, but that day I was your saviour, son.

OEDIPUS: From what? What was my trouble when you took me? 1040

MESSENGER: The ball-joints of your feet might testify.

OEDIPUS: What's that? What makes you name that ancient trouble?

MESSENGER: Your feet were pierced and I am your rescuer.

OEDIPUS: A fearful rebuke those tokens left for me!

MESSENGER: That was the chance that names you who you are. 1045

OEDIPUS: By the gods, did my mother or my father do this?

MESSENGER: That I don't know. He might who gave you to me.

OEDIPUS: From someone else? You didn't chance on me?

MESSENGER: Another shepherd handed you to me.

OEDIPUS: Who was he? Do you know? Will you explain! 1050

MESSENGER: They called him one of the men of— was it Laius?

OEDIPUS: The one who once was king here long ago?

MESSENGER: That is the one! The man was shepherd to him.

OEDIPUS: And is he still alive so I can see him?

MESSENGER: But you who live here ought to know that best. 1055

OEDIPUS: Does any one of you now present know about the shepherd whom this man has named? Have you seen him in town or in the fields? Speak out!
The time has come for the discovery!

CHORUS: The man he speaks of, I believe, is the same as the field hand you have already asked to see. 1060
But it's Jocasta who would know this best.

OEDIPUS: Lady, do you remember the man we just now sent for—is that the man he speaks of?

JOCASTA: What? The man he spoke of? Pay no attention! 1065
His words are not worth thinking about. It's nothing.

OEDIPUS: With clues like this within my grasp, give up?
Fail to solve the mystery of my birth?

JOCASTA: For the love of the gods, and if you love your life, give up this search! My sickness is enough. 1070

OEDIPUS: Come! Though my mothers for three generations
were in slavery, you'd not be lowborn!

JOCASTA: No, listen to me! Please! Don't do this thing!

OEDIPUS: I will not listen; I will search out the truth.

JOCASTA: My thinking is for you—it would be best. 1075

OEDIPUS: This "best" of yours is starting to annoy me.

JOCASTA: Doomed man! Never find out who you are!

OEDIPUS: Will someone go and bring that shepherd here?
Leave her to the glory in her wealthy birth!

JOCASTA: Man of misery! No other name   1080
    shall I address you by, ever again.
CHORUS: Why has your lady left, Oedipus,
    hurled by a savage grief? I am afraid
    disaster will come bursting from this silence.
OEDIPUS: Let it burst forth! However low this seed   1085
    of mine may be, yet I desire to see it.
    She, perhaps—she has a woman's pride—
    is mortified by my base origins.
    But I who count myself the child of Chance,
    the giver of good, shall never know dishonour.   1090
    She is my mother, and the months my brothers
    who first marked out my lowness, then my
        greatness.
    I shall not prove untrue to such a nature
    by giving up the search for my own birth.

STROPHE

CHORUS: *If I have mantic power*   1095
and excellence in thought,
by Olympus,
    you shall not, Cithaeron, at tomorrow's
full moon,
fail to hear us celebrate you as the countryman   1100
of Oedipus, his nurse and mother,
or fail to be the subject of our dance,
    since you have given pleasure
to our king.
Phoebus, whom we summon by "i ē!",   1105
may this be pleasing to you!

ANTISTROPHE

Who was your mother, son?
which of the long-lived nymphs
after lying with Pan,
    the mountain roaming.... Or was it a bride   1110
of Loxias?
For dear to him are all the upland pastures.
Or was it Mount Cyllēnē's lord,[35]
or the Bacchic god,
    dweller of the mountain peaks,   1115
who received you as a joyous find
from one of the nymphs of Helicōn,
the favourite sharers of his sport?

---

[35] Hermes.

OEDIPUS: If someone like myself, who never met him,
    may calculate—elders, I think I see   1120
    the very herdsman we've been waiting for.
    His many years would fit with that man's age,
    and those who bring him on, if I am right,
    are my own men. And yet, in real knowledge,
    you can outstrip me, surely: you've seen him.   1125
CHORUS: I know him, yes, a man of the house of Laius,
    a trusty herdsman if he ever had one.
OEDIPUS: I ask you first, the stranger come from
        Corinth:
    is this the man you spoke of?
MESSENGER: That's he you see.   1130
OEDIPUS: Then you, old man. First look at me!
    Now answer: did you belong to Laius' household
        once?
HERDSMAN: I did. Not a purchased slave but raised
    in the palace.
OEDIPUS: How have you spent your life? What is
    your work?
HERDSMAN: Most of my life now I have tended sheep.   1135
OEDIPUS: Where is the usual place you stay with them?
HERDSMAN: On Mount Cithaeron. Or in that district.
OEDIPUS: Do you recall observing this man there?
HERDSMAN: Doing what? Which is the man you
    mean?
OEDIPUS: This man right here. Have you had   1140
    dealings with him?
HERDSMAN: I can't say right away. I don't remember.
MESSENGER: No wonder, master. I'll bring clear
    memory
    to his ignorance. I'm absolutely sure
    he can recall it, the district was Cithaeron,
    he with a double flock, and I, with one,   1145
    lived close to him, for three entire seasons,
    six months long, from spring right to Arcturus,[36]
    Then for the winter I'd drive mine to my fold,
    and he'd drive his to Laius' pen again.
    Did any of the things I say take place?   1150
HERDSMAN: You speak the truth, though it's from
    long ago.
MESSENGER: Do you remember giving me, back then,
    a boy I was to care for as my own?

---

[36] A star whose appearance in September heralds the end
of summer.

HERDSMAN: What are you saying? Why do you ask
   me that?

MESSENGER: There, sir, is the man who was that boy!   1155

HERDSMAN: Damn you! Shut your mouth! Keep
   your silence!

OEDIPUS: Stop! don't you rebuke his words.
   Your words ask for rebuke far more than his.

HERDSMAN: But what have I done wrong, most
   royal master?

OEDIPUS: Not telling of the boy of whom he asked.   1160

HERDSMAN: He's ignorant and blundering toward
   ruin.

OEDIPUS: Tell it willingly—or under torture.

HERDSMAN: Oh god! Don't—I am old—don't
   torture me!

OEDIPUS: Here! Someone put his hands behind his
   back!

HERDSMAN: But why? What else would you find   1165
   out, poor man?

OEDIPUS: Did you give him the child he asks about?

HERDSMAN: I did. I wish that I had died that day!

OEDIPUS: You'll come to that if you don't speak the
   truth.

HERDSMAN: It's if I speak that I shall be destroyed.

OEDIPUS: I think this fellow struggles for delay.   1170

HERDSMAN: No, no! I said already that I gave him.

OEDIPUS: From your own home, or got from
   someone else?

HERDSMAN: Not from my own. I got him from
   another.

OEDIPUS: Which of these citizens? What sort of house?

HERDSMAN: Don't—by the gods!—don't, master,   1175
   ask me more!

OEDIPUS: It means your death if I must ask again.

HERDSMAN: One of the children of the house of
   Laius.

OEDIPUS: A slave—or born into the family?

HERDSMAN: I have come to the dreaded thing, and
   I shall say it.

OEDIPUS: And I to hearing it, but hear I must.   1180

HERDSMAN: He was reported to have been—his son.
   Your lady in the house would tell you best.

OEDIPUS: Because she gave him to you?

HERDSMAN: Yes, my lord.

OEDIPUS: What was her purpose?   1185

HERDSMAN: I was to kill the boy.

OEDIPUS: The child she bore?

HERDSMAN: She dreaded prophecies.

OEDIPUS: What were they?

HERDSMAN: The word was that he'd kill his parents.   1190

OEDIPUS: Then why did you give him up to this
   old man?

HERDSMAN: In pity, master—so he would take him
   home,
   to another land. But what he did was save him
   for this supreme disaster. If you are the one
   he speaks of—know your evil birth and fate!   1195

OEDIPUS: Ah! All of it was destined to be true!
   Oh light, now may I look my last upon you,
   shown monstrous in my birth, in marriage
      monstrous,
   a murderer monstrous in those I killed.

STROPHE 1

CHORUS: *Oh generations of mortal men,*   1200
   while you are living, I will
      appraise your lives at zero!
   What man
   comes closer to seizing lasting blessedness
   than merely to seize its semblance,   1205
   and after living in this semblance, to plunge?
   With your example before us,
   with your destiny, yours,
      suffering Oedipus, no mortal
   can I judge fortunate.   1210

ANTISTROPHE 1

For he, outranging everybody,
shot his arrow and became the lord
   of wide prosperity and blessedness,
oh Zeus, after destroying
the virgin with the crooked talons,[37]   1215
singer of oracles; and against death,
in my land, he arose a tower of defense.
From which time you were called my king
and granted privileges supreme—
   in mighty   1220
Thebes the ruling lord.

---

[37] The Sphinx.

But now—whose story is more sorrowful than yours?
Who is more intimate with fierce calamities
with labours, now that your life is altered?
Alas, my Oedipus, whom all men know: 1225
one great harbour—
one alone sufficed for you,
as son and father,
when you tumbled, plowman of the women's chamber.
How, how could your paternal 1230
  furrows, wretched man,
endure you silently so long?

ANTISTROPHE 2

Time, all-seeing, surprised you living an unwilled life
and sits from of old in judgement on the marriage, not
a marriage, 1235
where the begetter is the begot as well.
Ah, son of Laius …,
would that—oh, would that
I had never seen you!
I wail, 1240
  my scream climbing beyond itself
from my whole power of voice. To say it straight:
  from you I got new breath—
but I also lulled my eye to sleep.

2ND MESSENGER: You who are first among the 1245
  citizens,
what deeds you are about to hear and see!
What grief you'll carry, if, true to your birth,
you still respect the house of Labdacus!
Neither the Ister nor the Phasis river
could purify this house, such suffering 1250
does it conceal, or soon must bring to light—
willed this time, not unwilled. Griefs hurt worst
which we perceive to be self-chosen ones.
CHORUS: They were sufficient, the things we knew
  before, to make us grieve. What can you add to 1255
  those?
2ND MESSENGER: The thing that's quickest said
  and quickest heard:
our own, our royal one, Jocasta's dead.
CHORUS: Unhappy queen! What was responsible?
2ND MESSENGER: Herself. The bitterest of these
  events

is not for you, you were not there to see, 1260
but yet, exactly as I can recall it,
you'll hear what happened to that wretched lady.
She came in anger through the outer hall,
and then she ran straight to her marriage bed,
tearing her hair with the fingers of both hands. 1265
Then, slamming shut the doors when she was in,
she called to Laius, dead so many years,
remembering the ancient seed which caused
his death, leaving the mother to the son
to breed again an ill-born progeny. 1270
She mourned the bed where she, alas, bred double—
husband by husband, children by her child.
From this point on I don't know how she died,
for Oedipus then burst in with a cry,
and did not let us watch her final evil. 1275
Our eyes were fixed on him. Wildly he ran
to each of us, asking for his spear
and for his wife—no wife: where he might find
the double mother-field, his and his children's.
He raved, and some divinity then showed him— 1280
for none of us did so who stood close by.
With a dreadful shout—as if some guide were
  leading—
he lunged through the double doors; he bent the
  hollow
bolts from the sockets, burst into the room,
and there we saw her, hanging from above, 1285
entangled in some twisted hanging strands.
He saw, was stricken, and with a wild roar
ripped down the dangling noose. When she, poor
  woman,
lay on the ground, there came a fearful sight:
he snatched the pins of worked gold from her dress, 1290
with which her clothes were fastened: these he raised
and struck into the ball-joints of his eyes.
He shouted that they would no longer see
the evils he had suffered or had done,
see in the dark those he should not have seen, 1295
and know no more those he once sought to know.
While chanting this, not once but many times
he raised his hand and struck into his eyes.
Blood from his wounded eyes poured down his
  chin,
not freed in moistening drops, but all at once 1300
a stormy rain of black blood burst like hail.

These evils, coupling them, making them one,
have broken loose upon both man and wife.
The old prosperity that they had once
was true prosperity, and yet today,   1305
mourning, ruin, death, disgrace, and every
evil you could name—not one is absent.
CHORUS: Has he allowed himself some peace from
    all this grief?
2ND MESSENGER: He shouts that someone slide
    the bolts and show
to all the Cadmeians the patricide,   1310
his mother's—I can't say it, it's unholy—
so he can cast himself out of the land,
not stay and curse his house by his own curse.
He lacks the strength, though, and he needs a
    guide,
for his is a sickness that's too great to bear.   1315
Now you yourself will see: the bolts of the doors
are opening. You are about to see
a vision even one who hates must pity.

ANAPESTS

CHORUS: *This suffering sends terror through men's eyes,*
terrible beyond any suffering   1320
my eyes have touched. Oh man of pain,
what madness reached you? Which god from far off,
surpassing in range his longest spring,
    struck hard against your god-abandoned fate?
Oh man of pain,   1325
I cannot look upon you—though there's so much
I would ask you, so much to hear,
so much that holds my eyes—
    so awesome the convulsions you send through me.
OEDIPUS: *Ah! Ah! I am a man of misery.*   1330
    Where am I carried? Pity me! Where
is my voice scattered abroad on wings?
    Divinity, where has your lunge transported me?
CHORUS: To something horrible, not to be heard or
    seen.

STROPHE 1

OEDIPUS: *Oh, my cloud*   1335
    of darkness, abominable, unspeakable as it attacks
      me,
not to be turned away, brought by an evil wind!
Alas!

Again alas! Both enter me at once:
    the sting of the prongs, the memory of evils!   1340
CHORUS: I do not marvel that in these afflictions
    you carry double griefs and double evils.

ANTISTROPHE 1

OEDIPUS: *Ah, friend,*
    so you at least are there, resolute servant!
    Still with a heart to care for me, the blind man.   1345
    Oh! Oh!
I know that you are there, I recognize
even inside my darkness, that voice of yours.
CHORUS: Doer of horror, how did you bear to
    quench
    your vision? What divinity raised your hand?   1350

STROPHE 2

OEDIPUS: *It was Apollo there, Apollo, friends,*
    who brought my sorrows, vile sorrows to their
      perfection,
      these evils that were done to me.
But the one who struck them with his hand,
    that one was none but I, in wretchedness.   1355
For why was I to see
when nothing I could see would bring me joy?
CHORUS: *Yes, that is how it was.*
OEDIPUS: *What could I see, indeed,*
    or what enjoy—what greeting   1360
is there I could hear with pleasure, friends?
Conduct me out of the land
    as quickly as you can!
Conduct me out, my friends,
    the man utterly ruined,   1365
supremely cursed,
    the man who is by gods
the most detested of all men!
CHORUS: Wretched in disaster and in knowledge:
    oh, I could wish you'd never come to know!   1370

ANTISTROPHE 2

OEDIPUS: *May he be destroyed, whoever freed the*
    savage shackles
from my feet when I'd been sent to the wild pasture,
    whoever rescued me from murder
and became my saviour—
    a bitter gift: 1375

if I had died then,
I'd not have been such grief to self and kin.
CHORUS: *I also would have had it so.*
OEDIPUS: *I'd not have returned to be my father's*
murderer; I'd not be called by men   1380
my mother's bridegroom.
Now I'm without a god,
child of a polluted parent,
fellow progenitor with him
who gave me birth in misery.   1385
If there's an evil that
surpasses evil, that
has fallen to the lot of Oedipus.
CHORUS: How can I say that you have counselled well?
Better not to be than live a blind man.   1390
OEDIPUS: That this was not the best thing I could
do—
don't tell me that, or advise me any more!
Should I descend to Hades and endure
to see my father with these eyes? Or see
my poor unhappy mother? For I have done,   1395
to both of these, things too great for hanging.
Or is the sight of children to be yearned for,
to see new shoots that sprouted as these did?
Never, never with these eyes of mine!
Nor city, nor tower, nor holy images   1400
of the divinities! For I, all-wretched,
most nobly raised—as no one else in Thebes—
deprived myself of these when I ordained
that all expel the impious one—god-shown
to be polluted, and the dead king's son!   1405
Once I exposed this great stain upon me,
could I have looked on these with steady eyes?
No! No! And if there were a way to block
the source of hearing in my ears, I'd gladly
have locked up my pitiable body,   1410
so I'd be blind and deaf. Evils shut out—
that way my mind could live in sweetness.
Alas, Cithaeron, why did you receive me?
Or when you had me, not killed me instantly?
I'd not have had to show my birth to mankind.   1415
Polybus, Corinth, halls—ancestral,
they told me—how beautiful was your ward,
a scar that held back festering disease!
Evil my nature, evil my origin.
You, three roads, and you, secret ravine,   1420

you oak grove, narrow place of those three paths
that drank my blood from these my hands, from
him
who fathered me, do you remember still
the things I did to you? When I'd come here,
what I then did once more? Oh marriages!   1425
Marriages!
You gave us life and when you'd planted us
you sent the same seed up, and then revealed
fathers, brothers, sons, and kinsman's blood,
and brides, and wives, and mothers, all the most
atrocious things that happen to mankind!   1430
One should not name what never should have been.
Somewhere out there, then, quickly, by the gods,
cover me up, or murder me, or throw me
to the ocean where you will never see me more!
Come! Don't shrink to touch this wretched man!   1435
Believe me, do not be frightened! I alone
of all mankind can carry these afflictions.
CHORUS: Tell Creon what you wish for. Just when
we need him he's here. He can act, he can advise you.
He's now the land's sole guardian in your place.   1440
OEDIPUS: Ah! Are there words that I can speak to him?
What ground for trust can I present? It's proved
that I was false to him in everything.
CREON: I have not come to mock you, Oedipus,
nor to reproach you for your former falseness.   1445
You men, if you have no respect for sons
of mortals, let your awe for the all-feeding
flames of lordly Hēlius[38] prevent
your showing unconcealed so great a stain,
abhorred by earth and sacred rain and light.   1450
Escort him quickly back into the house!
If blood kin only see and hear their own
afflictions, we'll have no impious defilement.
OEDIPUS: By the gods, you've freed me from one
terrible fear, so nobly meeting my unworthiness: 1455
grant me something—not for me; for you!
CREON: What do you want that you should beg me so?
OEDIPUS: To drive me from the land at once, to a place
where there will be no man to speak to me!
CREON: I would have done just that—had I not   1460
wished
to ask first of the god what I should do.

---

[38] The sun.

OEDIPUS: His answer was revealed in full—that I,
　the patricide, unholy, be destroyed.
CREON: He said that, but our need is so extreme,
　it's best to have sure knowledge what must be done. 1465
OEDIPUS: You'll ask about a wretched man like me?
CREON: Is it not time you put your trust in the god?
OEDIPUS: But I bid you as well, and shall entreat you.
　Give her who is within what burial
　you will—you'll give your own her proper rites; 1470
　but me—do not condemn my fathers' land
　to have me dwelling here while I'm alive,
　but let me live on mountains—on Cithaeron
　famed as mine, for my mother and my father,
　while they yet lived, made it my destined tomb, 1475
　and I'll be killed by those who wished my ruin!
　And yet I know: no sickness will destroy me,
　nothing will: I'd never have been saved
　when left to die unless for some dread evil.
　Then let my fate continue where it will! 1480
　As for my children, Creon, take no pains
　for my sons—they're men and they will never lack
　the means to live, wherever they may be—
　but my two wretched, pitiable girls,
　who never ate but at my table, never 1485
　were without me—everything that I
　would touch, they'd always have a share of it—
　please care for them! Above all, let me touch
　them with my hands and weep aloud my woes!
　Please, my lord! 1490
　Please, noble heart! Touching with my hands,
　I'd think I held them as when I could see.
　What's this?
　Oh gods! Do I hear, somewhere, my two dear ones
　sobbing? Has Creon really pitied me 1495
　and sent to me my dearest ones, my children?
　Is that it?
CREON: Yes, I prepared this for you, for I knew
　you'd feel this joy, as you have always done.
OEDIPUS: Good fortune, then, and, for your care, 1500
　be guarded far better by divinity than I was!
　Where are you, children? Come to me! Come here
　to these my hands, hands of your brother, hands
　of him who gave you seed, hands that made
　these once bright eyes to see now in this fashion. 1505
　He, children, seeing nothing, knowing nothing,
　he fathered you where his own seed was plowed.

I weep for you as well, though I can't see you,
　imagining your bitter life to come,
　the life you will be forced by men to live. 1510
　What gatherings of townsmen will you join,
　what festivals, without returning home
　in tears instead of watching holy rites?
　And when you've reached the time for marrying,
　where, children, is the man who'll run the risk 1515
　of taking on himself the infamy
　that will wound you as it did my parents?
　What evil is not here? Your father killed
　his father, plowed the one who gave him birth,
　and from the place where he was sown, from there 1520
　he got you, from the place he too was born.
　These are the wounds: then who will marry you?
　No man, my children. No it's clear that you
　must wither in dry barrenness, unmarried.
　Son of Menoeceus![39] You are the only father 1525
　left to them—we two who gave them seed
　are both destroyed: watch that they don't become
　poor, wanderers, unmarried—they are your kin.
　Let not my ruin be their ruin, too!
　No, pity them! You see how young they are, 1530
　bereft of everyone, except for you.
　Consent, kind heart, and touch me with your hand!
　You, children, if you had reached an age of sense,
　I would have counselled much. Now, pray you
　may live always where it's allowed, finding a life 1535
　better than his was, who gave you seed.

TROCHEES

CREON: Stop this now. Quiet your weeping. Move
　away, into the house.
OEDIPUS: Bitter words, but I obey them.
CREON: There's an end to all things.
OEDIPUS: I have first this request. 1540
CREON: I have heard it.
OEDIPUS: Banish me from my homeland.
CREON: You must ask that of the god.
OEDIPUS: But I am the gods' most hated man!
CREON: Then you will soon get what you want. 1545
OEDIPUS: Do you consent?
CREON: I never promise when, as now, I'm
　ignorant.

---

[39] Creon.

OEDIPUS: Then lead me in.

CREON: Come. But let your hold fall from your
  children.

OEDIPUS: Do not take them from me, ever!   1550

CREON: Do not wish to keep all of the power.
  You had power, but that power did not follow
    you through life.

CHORUS: People of Thebes, my country, see: here is
  that Oedipus—

he who "knew" the famous riddle, and attained
  the highest power,
whom all citizens admired, even envying his luck!   1555
See the billows of wild troubles which he has
  entered now!
Here is the truth of each man's life: we must wait,
  and see his end,
scrutinize his dying day, and refuse to call him happy
till he has crossed the border of his life without pain.

EURIPIDES

Hippolytus

I n 428 B.C.E., the year after Pericles' death, Euripides won first prize for his *Hippolytus* trilogy. It was a rare victory for the poet, one of only three that Euripides earned in his life, though he wrote over 90 plays.[1] But if he was perhaps underappreciated in his time, history has compensated him well: more of his plays have survived into the present than those of Aeschylus and Sophocles put together.

From Aristophanes' hilarious portrayal of him in *Frogs* we can deduce that Euripides was, if not a willfully iconoclastic writer, then at least a controversial one. He was known for his large private library, a rarity at the time, for his avoidance of public life, and for his many poetic and musical innovations. His 19 surviving plays are laced with subversive declarations, some of which were said to have provoked near-riots of outrage from the audience: denials of the divinity and even the existence of the gods, accusations of fraudulence at the Delphic oracle, and praise of money as the ultimate good in life. And because Euripides' characters routinely break their oaths, spy, slander the innocent, and get away with murder, Aristotle declared that, unlike Sophocles, who tended to idealize people, Euripides portrayed them just the way they are. Perhaps it was this psychological realism that led Aristotle to call the last of the three great Attic tragedians the "most tragic" of all, most successful in eliciting pity and fear and effecting a catharsis of these emotions: his characters are most like ourselves.

The world of *Hippolytus* is one of malignant gods and moral uncertainty where humans are manipulated like puppets and the innocent are destroyed along with the guilty. Aphrodite, goddess of lust, makes no secret of the pettiness of her grudge against Hippolytus and feels no remorse for the shambles of human anguish and death that she desires, plots, and brings about. Hippolytus may be an insufferably self-righteous prude, a twisted holy man whose denial of the flesh and hatred of women make him ripe for a lesson in moderation and acceptance of all things human. But Phaedra, properly respectful of Aphrodite's power, is pitilessly humiliated and destroyed along with him, mere "collateral damage" in Aphrodite's mission to trample Hippolytus underfoot. While Euripides goes out of his way to depict Phaedra's love-sickness with deep sympathy, he nevertheless portrays her as an out-and-out liar, willing to trade Hippolytus's life for her good name.

For its focus on love and domestic life, for the reduced role it gives to the Chorus, and for its use of such narrative conventions as the tell-all prologue and the falsely incriminating letter, *Hippolytus* seems in retrospect to be laying the groundwork for New Comedy, a genre which, unbeknownst to anybody in the fifth century, was about to replace both tragedy and Old Comedy in the fourth century and for centuries to come (see Plautus's *Miles Gloriosus* in this chapter). But in equally significant ways, *Hippolytus* also carries on the tradition of Attic tragedy as practised by Aeschylus and

---

[1] He also won a posthumous fourth victory for the *Bacchae* trilogy.

Sophocles, particularly with respect to tragic irony. Like the destruction of Oedipus, which is unexpected only by the hero and only until it reveals itself as absolutely fitting and inevitable, Hippolytus's fate is an unforseen catastrophe only to Hippolytus himself. To everyone else, it is the logical and even necessary outcome of his fanatical puritanism, his gravely mistaken attempt to deny Aphrodite, whose power is sexual desire.

Born in 485, Euripides died in 406 while a guest of the king of Macedon—the neighbouring monarchy that would arise to conquer Athens in the following century. Sophocles, who was himself to die later that same year, solemnly announced Euripides' death to the Athenians at the theatre festival, during the preview, or *proagon*, reportedly reducing them to tears.

EURIPIDES

Hippolytus

Translated by Gilbert and Sarah Lawall

CHARACTERS
 APHRODITE (APH.)
 HIPPOLYTUS (HIPP.)
 HUNTSMEN
 SERVANT OF HIPPOLYTUS (SERV.)
 NURSE OF PHAEDRA (NUR.)
 CHORUS OF WOMEN (CH.)
 CHORUS-LEADER (CH.-L.)
 PHAEDRA (PH.)
 THESEUS (TH.)
 ARTEMIS (ART.)

[*The scene for the whole play is the open space before the double doors of the royal palace of Trozen. Directly beside the doors is a statue of Aphrodite. Also on stage is a statue of Artemis; possibly it should be to one side of the stage, in a wooded setting suggested by scene painting. APHRODITE comes into sight above the scene building and begins her soliloquy.*]

APH.: Powerful among mortals and not without name,
 I am the goddess called Cypris—this also in heaven.

Of all the men who live between the Pontic Sea
 and the boundaries of Atlas, seeing the light
 of the sun,
I put first those who reverence my power but trip and
 throw down those who think big before me.
For this holds true for gods as well as men: 5
 they like people to honour them.

I will soon show how true this is.

Hippolytus, the son of Theseus[1] and offspring of the
 Amazon,[2] was raised by chaste Pittheus.[3]

---

1 King of Athens and Trozen.
2 Hippolyte, sometimes identified in myth as Antiope, queen of the Amazons. Before being defeated in battle by Theseus and made his captive concubine, this warrior, according to legend, lived in an all-female society free of marriage. Like her "illegitimate" son Hippolytus she would have been an expert and passionate rider of horses.
3 Former king of Trozen, and Hippolytus's great-grandfather (Theseus's maternal grandfather).

He alone of the citizens in this land of Trozen   10
says that I am worst of the gods—*by nature*.
He refuses to make love and won't touch marriage.
Instead, he honours Phoebus' sister Artemis,[4] the
    maiden daughter of Zeus,
and thinks her the greatest of gods.
Throughout the green woods he's always   15
    consorting with that virgin,
hunting down the land's wild animals with his
    swift dogs
and falling in with a companionship more than
    mortal.

They don't make me jealous. Why should I care?
But for his sins[5] against me I will take vengeance
    on Hippolytus this very day. I have been
    preparing for this
a long time now, and not much is left to be done.   20
Once when he went from Pittheus' house
to participate in the holy mysteries
of Pandion's land,[6] his father's nobly-born wife
Phaedra[7] saw him, and her heart was seized
with a terrible love—just as I planned.   25
Then before coming to this Trozenian land
she set up, close by the rock of Pallas,[8]
a temple to Cypris that looked out upon this land,
since she loved a love away from home. Men will
    ever after say
that this goddess was erected for Hippolytus.   30
But now that Theseus has left Cecropian[9] soil,
fleeing the pollution of Pallantid[10] blood,
and, sailing with his wife to this land,

has accepted a year's exile away from home,
now she is groaning and struck out of her wits   35
by the goads of love. The miserable woman is
dying in silence, and no-one in the household
    understands her illness.

But this is not the way her love must end.
I will reveal the situation to Theseus, and
    everything will be made clear.
That young man who battles against me   40
will be killed by his father, with curses that the
    sea-god
Poseidon once granted Theseus as a gift of honour:
the right to call upon the god[11] three times, and
    not in vain.
She will die with her good name, but nonetheless
Phaedra will die. For I will not honour her   45
    misfortune
higher than paying back my own enemies
with just such reckoning as seems good to me.

But here I see Theseus' son
coming, just back from the hunt—
Hippolytus. I'll be leaving now.   50
A large band of servants follows his footsteps
And shouts along with him, honouring the
    goddess Artemis
with hymns.

For he does not know that the gates of Hades
    stand open, and that this day's light is the last
    that he will see. [*Exit*]

[*HIPPOLYTUS enters from stage right, indicating an
entrance from the country. He is followed by hunting
companions and servants. They all arrive directly from
the hunt and proceed toward the statue of Artemis.
HIPPOLYTUS sings as he exhorts his followers.*]

HIPP.: Follow me, follow me, singing   55
    of Zeus' heavenly daughter
Artemis, for we are in her care.
HIPP. and HUNTSMEN [*singing a traditional cult
    song as they approach the statue.*]

---

4 Goddess of the Hunt, here ridiculed as a virgin, i.e., not
much of a "consort" for Hippolytus.

5 Literally, "mistakes" or "errors," a key concept here and
in tragedy generally, conveyed by the Greek term "hamar-
tia" and related words.

6 Athens, to which city Hippolytus would have travelled
for the celebration.

7 Daughter of King Minos of Crete, she married Theseus
after Hippolyte's death.

8 Pallas Athena's "rock" is the Acropolis in Athens.

9 Attica. Athens' first King was Cecrops.

10 Theseus'ss cousins, sons of Pallas (and hence "the
Pallantidae"), rebelled against Theseus's reign, and were
killed by him.

---

11 According to some versions of the myth, Poseidon was
Theseus's father.

Mistress, most holy mistress,
offspring of Zeus,
hail, hail, virgin daughter   60
of Leto and Zeus: Artemis,
most beautiful of maidens,
you who dwell
in the great heaven
in your noble father's halls,   65
the richly golden house of Zeus.
Hail, O most beautiful, most
beautiful of those on Olympus.

[*The song over, HIPPOLYTUS stands in front of the
statue of Artemis and addresses the goddess.*]

HIPP.: I have arranged this woven garland for you,
mistress, and I bring it from an untouched meadow   70
where no shepherd dares pasture his flock
and iron has not yet come, an untouched
meadow where only the bee in springtime passes.
Aidos, goddess of self-restraint, tends it with
        streams of clear water
for those whose wisdom is not taught, but in   75
        whose very nature
virtue is rooted, assigned a place in all things forever.
These may pluck flowers there, but it is not right
        for the wicked. [*placing a wreath on the gilded
        hair of the statue of Artemis*]
Dear mistress, on your golden hair
I place this wreath with my pious hand.
For I alone of mortals have this privilege: 80
I consort with you and we exchange words;
I can hear your voice although I cannot see your
        face.
May I round the goal of my life just as I began it.

[*His offering and prayer made, HIPPOLYTUS turns
away from the statue of Artemis. As he moves toward
the palace doors, an older servant steps forward from
among Hippolytus's hunting companions and addresses
him.*]

SERV.: Prince—for only the gods should be called
        masters—would you take some well-meant
        advice from me?
HIPP.: Of course—otherwise I would not appear   85
        wise.
SERV.: Do you know the custom among mortals?

HIPP.: No, I don't. What are you getting at?
SERV.: They hate pride, and not being everyone's friend.
HIPP.: Rightly so. Is there a proud man who is not
        tiresome?
SERV.: Do you think speaking politely with people   90
        wins you any thanks?
HIPP.: A great deal; and profit too, with little effort.
SERV.: Don't you expect the same is true among the
        gods?
HIPP.: Certainly, since we mortals observe their
        customs.
SERV.: [*with a gesture toward the statue of Aphrodite*]
        Then why don't you address a proud goddess?
HIPP.: [*pretending not to notice his gesture*] Which   95
        one? Watch out that your tongue doesn't slip.
SERV.: [*pointing*] This one, standing right beside
        your door: Cypris.
HIPP.: [*turning away*] I greet her from a distance,
        pure as I am.
SERV.: She is proud, nonetheless, and widely known
        among mortals.
HIPP.: No god who is worshipped at night suits me.   100
SERV.: My child, the gods must have their honours.
HIPP.: Each has his own likes and dislikes, in gods
        as well as men.
SERV.: I wish you luck and as much good sense as
        you need.

[*HIPPOLYTUS turns abruptly away from the old servant
and addresses his other companions and servants.*]

HIPP.: Get along, men. Enter the house and see to
        the food. There's no pleasure after the hunt
        like a big meal. And you'll have to rub down
        the horses so that when I've eaten enough I
        can yoke them to my chariot and exercise
        them properly.
    [*to the servant, with a glance toward the statue of
        Aphrodite*] But as for your Cypris—I bid her a   105
        fond farewell! [*Exit into the palace*]
SERV.: [*pausing before the statue of Aphrodite on his
        way into the palace*] But I—for young people
        should not be imitated
    when they think like that—will speak as a slave
        should
    and pray to your image,
    mistress Cypris. One must understand and forgive.

If someone is young and high-strung   110
and talks nonsense, pretend not to hear him.
Gods ought to be wiser than mortals. [*Exit*]

[*As the old servant exits, the* CHORUS *of fifteen
Trozenian women enters from stage-left, that is, from
the direction of the city. They are young married
women from respectable families who, having heard the
gossip that something is wrong with Phaedra, have
come now to find out what the trouble is.*]

CH.: [*singing as it enters the circular dance floor*]

STROPHE 1

They say it is Ocean's water that drips from the rock
whose steep sides send forth a flowing stream, to
   be dipped up in our pitchers.
There a friend of mine   115
was washing purple robes
in the stream's clear water
and was laying them out on the back of a rock
warm from the sun. From her I
first heard the news about the queen.   120

ANTISTROPHE 1

Worn out with illness she lies there, staying inside
the house, light robes shading her blonde head.
By taking no food to her mouth
for three days, so I hear,
she now keeps her body   125
pure of Demeter's grain.
Suffering in secret she wishes
To beach her ship on the wretched shore of death.

STROPHE 2

Are you possessed, princess,
by Pan or Hecate   130
or the sacred Corybantes or the Mountain Mother
that your mind is wandering?[12]
Or have you offended Dictynna,[13]

great goddess of wild animals
by neglecting her rites and offerings, and now   135
   waste away unhallowed?
For she wanders even through this lagoon
and over the sandbar along the sea
in wet swirls of brine.

ANTISTROPHE 2

Or is your husband, the Erechthids'
nobly born ruler,   140
tended by someone else in the house? Does he lie
   secretly
with another, away from your bed?
Or has some sailor
setting out from Crete sailed into the
harbour friendliest to seamen,   145
bringing news to the queen,
so that in grief over her misfortunes
her soul is anchored fast to her bed?

EPODE

Along with the dissonant harmony
of being a woman   150
there dwells a wretched helplessness
before birth pains and irrational feelings.
Through my womb this chill breeze once
darted. I called on the heavenly easer of
   childbirth, the mistress of the arrows,
Artemis, and now (heaven willing) she always   155
comes to me, greatly envied.

[*The double doors of the palace open, and* PHAEDRA *is
brought out. She is lying on her sick-bed which is
carried out and set down by her servants in full view of
the audience. Her hair is arranged on top of her head,
and folds of her light robe are drawn up over her head
to shade her face. Her old* NURSE *accompanies her and
removes the folds of her robe from her head as she
brings her out of doors.*]

CH.: [*declaiming in a manner half way between
         singing and ordinary speech*] But here is her old
         nurse in front of the doors
bringing her out of the house.
The gloomy cloud on her brow only grows larger.
My very soul desires to learn what the trouble   160
   is—

---

12 All possible sources of divine derangement: Pan was sup-
    posed to cause 'panic' with his loud shouts; Hecate was
    a goddess of the underworld associated with night ter-
    rors; Corybantes worshiped the great Mother Goddess
    Cybele with frenzied dances.
13 Dictynna is the form in which Artemis was worshipped
    on Phaedra's home island of Crete.

what has harmed
The queen's body and changed her colour.

[*The CHORUS retires to the sides of the orchestra as the NURSE and PHAEDRA hold the centre of the stage. This scene is declaimed in the same way as the chorus's lines above.*]

NUR.: [*to herself*] O troubles of mortal men, and
    hated illnesses!
    [*turning to PHAEDRA*] What should I do with
      you? What should I *not* do?
    Here is your sunlight; here is the bright open air.   165
    Your sick-bed is now
    outside the house.
    All you could talk about was coming out here;
    soon you'll be rushing back to your bedroom.
    You're quickly upset and don't enjoy anything.   170
    Nothing at hand pleases you, and you think
    anything far off is better.
    [*to herself again*] I would rather be sick than tend
      the sick;
    one is a simple matter, but along with the other
    comes grief in the mind and work for the hands.   175

    Man's whole life is painful,
    and there's no rest from labour.
    But if there is anything better than life
    it's covered with clouds and concealed in darkness.
    We seem to be madly in love   180
    with what glitters here on earth,
    through our ignorance of any other life,
    and because we've never been shown what's
      beneath the earth.
    Mere tales carry us aimlessly about.
PH.: [*to her servants*] Lift up my body; hold up my head.   185
    My limbs feel weak in the joints.
    Take hold of my hands and my pretty arms,
      servants.
    This thing on my head is heavy—
    take it off, and let my hair curl down over my
      shoulders.
NUR.: [*as she loosens PHAEDRA'S hair*] Steady, child,   190
    and don't shift your body about so violently.
    You'll bear your illness more easily
    with a calm and noble spirit.
    Besides, suffering is forced on mortals.

PH.: [*delirious*] Ah!
    If I only could take a drink   195
    from a clear spring of pure water,
    lie in the tall grass of the meadow
    under black poplars, and find rest.
NUR.: [*shocked*] Child, what are you saying?
    Won't you stop talking this way in front of   200
      everybody,
    shouting words that ride forth on madness?
PH.: [*still delirious*] Take me to the mountains; I'll
      go to the woods
    among the pines, where hunting dogs run
    in pursuit of spotted deer.
    O gods, hear my prayer! I long to shout to the dogs,   205
    throw the Thessalian javelin
    from beside my blonde hair and hold a barbed
      lance in my hand.
NUR.: Why these troubled thoughts, child?
    What do you care about hunting?
    Why do you long for flowing springs?   210
    There's clear water right here on the slope
    next to the city walls. You could drink there.
PH.: [*still delirious*] Artemis, mistress of the lagoon
      by the sea
    and of the courses resounding to horses' hooves,
    I wish I were on your sacred grounds,   215
    taming Venetian colts.
NUR.: Now what nonsense are you shouting?
    A minute ago you were in the mountains, setting
      out
    on the hunting you longed for; but now you
      desire colts
    on the sands beside the waves.   220
    This needs a prophet's insight, and lots of it,
    to tell what god draws you back by the reins
    and strikes your wits astray, child.
PH.: [*suddenly coming to her senses*] Oh misery! What
      have I done?
    Where have I strayed from my right mind?   225
    I went mad. A god clouded my mind, and I fell.
    [*groaning*] Oh—Oh—miserable me!
    Nurse, cover up my head again.
    I'm horrified at what I've said.
    Cover me! Tears fall from my eyes;   230
    shame has come to my face.

Keeping my mind straight is painful,
but this madness is evil. It would be best of all
to die with no awareness of either.

NUR.: [*replacing the robe over PHAEDRA'S head*] I'm   235
   covering you. But when will death cover my
   body?
[*to herself*] A long life has taught me many things.
We mortals should mix our friendships
with one another moderately,
and not to the inner marrow of the soul.
Our hearts' affections ought to be loosely tied,   240
easy to push aside or to draw tight.
It's a heavy burden when one soul suffers
for two, as I'm agonizing over this woman.

A rigid way of life, they say,
trips and throws us instead of bringing pleasure,   245
and wars against health.
I admire excess less
than moderation,
and wise men agree with me.

[*The CHORUS-LEADER steps forward and addresses the
nurse. The lines of this scene are spoken in ordinary
conversational tones.*]

CH.-L.: Old woman, our queen's trusted nurse, we   250
   see Phaedra's miserable condition, but it's
   unclear to us what her illness is. We want to
   learn about it from you.
NUR.: I don't know. I've tried to find out, but she
   won't tell.
CH.-L.: Not even what started her troubles?
NUR.: It's the same thing. She keeps quiet about
   everything.
CH.-L.: How feeble and wasted her body is!
NUR.: And why not? She hasn't eaten for three days.   255
CH.-L.: Because she's lost her mind? Or is she trying
   to die?
NUR.: Yes, to die. For this fasting will soon end her life.
CH.-L.: It's amazing if what you say satisfies her
   husband.
NUR.: She hides her pain and doesn't admit she's ill.
CH.-L.: Can't he tell by looking at her face?   260
NUR.: As it happens, he's out of the country.
CH.-L.: Can't you force her to tell you about her
   illness and wandering mind?

NUR.: I've tried everything and have got nowhere.
   But even now I won't slacken my efforts, so
   that you who are here may see what kind of   265
   person I am toward masters in trouble.
[*to PHAEDRA*] Come, dear child, let's both forget
what has been said, and you be more pleasant.
Relax your gloomy frown and way of thinking,
and I, if I didn't say the right things to you,   270
will pass to other and better words.
If your illness is one we don't talk about,
these people here are women to help cure your
   trouble.
If your condition may be revealed to men,
speak, so that doctors may be told of the case.   275

[*pause*] Well then, why are you quiet? You mustn't
   be silent, child,
but either correct me if I have said something wrong,
or agree if what I have said is right.

[*pause*] Say something! Look at me! [*pause*] Oh,
   I'm miserable,
women, for all my work is wasted,   280
and I'm right back where I was before. She wasn't
softened by my words then, nor is she won over now.
[*to PHAEDRA*] But know this at least, and then be
   more stubborn
than the sea itself. If you die, you will betray your
children, who will not share in their father's estate: 285
I swear by that horse-riding Amazon queen,
who gave birth to a master for your children,
a bastard who thinks high-born thoughts. You
   know very well whom I mean:
Hippolytus—
PH.: Oh!   290
NUR.: Does this touch you?
PH.: You've destroyed me, nurse! By the gods I beg
   you not to mention that man again.
NUR.: You see? You can think clearly, but still
   you don't want to help your children and save
   your own life.
PH.: I love my children. But I am tossed by a   295
   different storm of fate.
NUR.: I assume your hands, child, are clean of blood?
PH.: My hands are clean, but my mind is polluted.
NUR.: From harmful spells cast by an enemy?

PH.: A loved one destroys me against my will and against his. 300

NUR.: Has Theseus wronged you?

PH.: No, and may I never be seen wronging him!

NUR.: What then is this terrible thing that urges you on to die?

PH.: Leave me to my error. I'm not wronging you.

NUR.: Not on purpose, but you will make me a failure. 305

[*The NURSE falls at PHAEDRA'S feet and takes hold of her hand in a gesture of supplication.*]

PH.: What are you doing? Using force, gripping my hand?

NUR.: [*taking hold of her knees*] And your knees, and I will never let you go.

PH.: All this will seem evil to you too, woman, if you learn about it—evil!

NUR.: What evil is greater for me than not reaching you?

PH.: It will ruin you. And yet it brings me honour. 310

NUR.: Then why do you hide it, if I am begging for your own good?

PH.: Out of shameful things I am making noble ones.

NUR.: If you tell, won't you appear more honoured?

PH.: Go away, by the gods! Let go my right hand!

NUR.: Certainly not, since you don't give me the gift you should. [*pause*] 315

PH.: I will give it. For I yield in reverence of your suppliant hand.

NUR.: Then I'll be quiet. It's your turn to speak now. [*pause*]

PH.: O my wretched mother, what a love you loved!

NUR.: The one she had for the bull, child?[14] Or what is this you say!

PH.: And you also, my luckless sister, bride of Dionysus![15] 320

NUR.: Child, what's happened to you? Are you slandering your relatives?

PH.: And I a third! How miserably I am perishing!

NUR.: I'm stunned. Where is this talk leading?

PH.: My misfortune comes from them and is no recent thing.

NUR.: I still know no better what I want to hear. 325

PH.: If only you could say for me the things I have to say.

NUR.: I'm no seer to know obscure things clearly.

PH.: What is meant when they say people are in love?

NUR.: Pleasure, child, but also pain at the same time.

PH.: It's the latter I feel. 330

Nur.: What are you saying? Are you in love, child? With what man?

PH.: Whoever he is—the son of the Amazon—

NUR.: Hippolytus, you say?

PH.: You heard it from yourself, not me.

NUR.: [*shocked*] No! No! What do you mean, child? You have destroyed me! 335

[*to the chorus*] Women, this is unbearable! I can't bear living! Hateful is the day and hateful the light I see! [*throwing herself on the ground*]

I will throw myself down—hurl away my body. Dying, I will free myself from life. Farewell! I am already dead.

For virtuous people love evil things—against their will,

but nonetheless they do! Cypris is no god,

but something greater than a god, if such there be, 340

who has destroyed this woman, myself, and the household.

Ch.-L.: [*singing to another member of the chorus*]

STROPHE

Did you hear?
Did you hear
these unspeakable things
that the queen shrieked aloud—her wretched misfortunes? 345
[*to PHAEDRA*] I would rather die than ever come to have
feelings like yours, dear lady. [*groaning sadly*]
O miserable woman with such sorrows!
O troubles that rear mortals!

---

14 Phaedra's mother was Pasiphae, Queen of Crete, whose love for a bull produced the Minotaur, a mythological hybrid of man and bull.

15 Ariadne, another of Phaedra's disgraced relatives, who helped Theseus kill the Minotaur and outwit the Laby- rinth. Accounts of her life vary in mythology. The "luck- lessness" Phaedra is referring to here is either Ariadne's subsequent abandonment by Theseus on the island of Naxos, or her murder by Artemis for leaving her first husband, the god Dionysus, for the mortal Theseus.

You are ruined; you have revealed your ills to the light. 350
What awaits you in the course of this day?
Something terrible will happen to this house.
No longer is it unclear where the fatal star
of Cypris wanes and sets, O luckless child of Crete.

Having risen from her bed, PHAEDRA approaches the CHORUS and calmly addresses its members.

PH.: Women of Trozen, you who live on this 355
furthest threshold of Pelops' land,
already and in other circumstances during the
long hours of the night
I pondered how the lives of mortals are ruined.
It doesn't seem to me that they fail
because of the way they think, for most people 360
think rightly
enough. But this is how it must be seen:
we understand and recognize what is good,
but we don't carry it through: some from laziness,
others by giving preference not to virtue but to
some other
pleasure, and life has many pleasures, such as 365
long gossiping and leisure—a delightful evil—
and modesty, and these pleasures are of two
kinds, one harmless,
the other a burden on the household. If every case
were clear,
there would not be two kinds with the same name.
Since this is what I had come to think,
not even a magic charm could have made me change 370
and fall into the opposite way of thinking.

I will tell you the path my thoughts have taken.
When love first wounded me, I looked to see how
I might best bear it. I began by
keeping silence about my illness and hiding it. 375
For the tongue is not to be trusted; it knows
how to advise the thoughts of other men,
but when it speaks for itself it gets only trouble.
Second, I planned to bear my senseless passion
properly
by overcoming it with virtuous restraint. 380
And third, since I did not succeed in conquering
Cypris by these means, I resolved to die—
the best of all plans, as no-one will deny.

May it be my luck not to go unnoticed if I do
good deeds,
and not to have many witnesses if I do shameful 385
ones.
And moreover, being a woman—I was well aware
of that!—
I knew that both the deed and the illness were
disreputable,
things hated by all. May she die a horrible death,
whoever begins to shame her marriage bed in the
eyes of men.
And I hate women who talk virtuously and enjoy 390
a good reputation
but commit daring crimes in secret.

[*glancing toward the statue near the door*]

How, sea-born mistress Cypris, do they ever
look their husbands in the face
and not shudder at the darkness that shared their
deeds
and at the walls of the house, fearing they might 395
speak?
It is this that is causing my death, friends,
that I may never be caught shaming my husband
nor the children I have born. But may they live
in the famous city of Athens as free men
thriving amid free speech, with a good reputation 400
from their mother.
For it enslaves a man, no matter how bold his
spirit, when he knows of his mother's or
father's misdeeds.
They say that one good thing lets you get the
better of life:
having a good and just mind.
For time sooner or later reveals base men,
Setting its mirror before them as before a young 405
maiden.
May I never be seen among them!
CH.-L.: What a fine thing virtue is in all our actions,
and what a noble reputation it reaps among
mortals!
NUR.: Mistress, just now your misfortune suddenly
gave me a terrible fright.
But now I realize I was foolish. Among mortals 410
second thoughts are somehow wiser.

It's nothing out of the ordinary or unreasonable
    that you've
experienced, and now the goddess's resentment
    has fallen on you.
You're in love. Is that any surprise? Many people are.
Are you going to kill yourself because of love?   415
A bad bargain for lovers
now and in the future, if they have to kill themselves!
Cypris is an unbearable thing when she comes in
    full flood.
She comes gently to anyone who yields,
but if she finds someone out of the ordinary and   420
    thinking big,
she seizes him, and you can imagine how she
    humbles his pride!
She passes through the sky; she lives in the waves
of the sea; Cypris gives birth to all things.
It is she who sows and gives desire,
and all of us on earth are her offspring.   425

Now those who possess writings of ancient authors
and themselves live with poetry all the time
know that Zeus once desired to marry
Semele, and they know also that radiant Dawn once
snatched Cephalus up among the gods,   430
because of love. But just the same they dwell
in heaven and don't flee from the other gods—
Content, as I think, to be conquered by their fate.
Won't you endure yours? Your father should have
    begotten you
on special terms or with other gods as   435
masters, if you are not content with these laws.
How many completely sensible men, do you think,
see that their marriages are sick but don't seem to
    see it?
How many fathers help their erring sons
come by love? One of the wise things for   440
mortals is this: hiding what doesn't look good.
Mortals should not strive to achieve excessive
    perfection in life;
nor would you make the roof over a house
exactly perfect. In a situation such as
you have fallen into, how would you expect to   445
    swim out?
If you have more good things than bad,
you are doing quite well for a human being.

Dear child, stop this wicked thinking.
Stop being so proud. For your wishing to be greater
than the gods is nothing but pride.   450
Endure it, if you are in love! A god willed it.
Since you are sick, find some good way to subdue
    your sickness.
There are incantations and charms that cast spells.
Some remedy for this sickness will come to light.
Men would be late indeed in finding a way if we   455
    women cannot find one.
CH.-L.: Phaedra, what she says is more useful
    in your present circumstances, but I praise you.
    Still my praise is more difficult to take than
    her words and more painful for you to hear.
PH.: It is this that destroys men's well-governed   460
    cities and homes, these fine speeches!
    One should not say what pleases the ears
    but rather what will bring a good name.
NUR.: Why these proud words? It's not nobly
    phrased speeches
    that you need, but the man! Let's get to the point   465
    quickly,
    and speak the straight truth about you.
    If your life were not in danger over this,
    or if you had self-control,
    I would never have gone so far for the sake of
    love's pleasures. But the stakes are high—   470
    saving your life. No-one would begrudge this.
PH.: What horrible things you're saying! Shut your
    mouth
    and don't let out such shameful words again!
NUR.: Shameful, but better than virtuous words for
    you.
    And the deed is better, if it saves your life,   475
    than the mere name for which you die so proudly.
PH.: No, stop! in the name of the gods, you speak
    too cleverly
    about shameful things. Don't go any further! I'm
    overwrought
    with desire, and if you continue to use fine words
    about shameful deeds
    I'll be consumed in what I now flee.   480
NUR.: If that is how it is—[pausing] You shouldn't
    have gone astray,
    but since you have, obey me. This favour is
    second best.

At home I have magic charms
for love (I just remembered them).
They will end your illness with no shame   485
or harm to your mind—if you don't turn coward.
But we need something from the man you desire,
some token—either a lock of hair or a scrap of his
        cloak—
to take and join the two for one good end.
PH.: Is the charm a salve or a drink?   490
NUR.: I don't know. Try to profit by it, and don't ask
        questions, child.
PH.: I'm afraid you may turn out to be too clever
        for me.
NUR.: You're afraid of everything! What are you
        worrying about?
PH.: That you might pass any of this on to Theseus'
        son.
NUR.: Enough, child. I'll arrange everything well.   495
    [moving toward the door and addressing the statue of
        Aphrodite] All I ask, sea-born mistress Cypris,
    is that you be my helper. The other things I have
        in mind
    need only be told to my friends within.

[Exit into the house.]

CH.: [singing and dancing, at first solemnly, but with
        increasing agitation in the second strophe and
        antistrophe.]

STROPHE 1

Eros, Eros, you who distill desire
over the eyes, bringing sweet   500
delight to the hearts of those against whom you
        campaign,
may you never bring harm when you appear to me,
or ever come with discord.
For neither the shafts of fire nor those of the stars
        are more powerful
than the arrows of Aphrodite, shot from the   505
        hands of Eros, child of Zeus.

ANTISTROPHE 1

In vain, in vain by the Alpheus[16]

and by the Pythian temple of Phoebus[17]
the Grecian land increases its slaughter of cattle,
while Eros, the tyrant of men,
doorkeeper of Aphrodite's   510
dearest bridal chambers, goes unworshipped by us,
although he ravages mortals and hurls them
        through all disasters
when he comes.

STROPHE 2

The girl of Oechalia,[18]
a filly unyoked before,   515
manless and unwed, was yoked by Cypris
from the palace of Eurytus,
and like a running nymph or bac-
chante, amid blood and smoke,
she was given to the son of Alcmene[19]   520
in a marriage filled with murder. O
unhappy bride!

ANTISTROPHE 2

O holy wall
of Thebes, O mouth of the fountain of Dirce,
you also could tell how Cypris comes.   525
For to the fork-flamed thunder
she gave in marriage the mother-to-be of twice-
        born Bacchus and bedded her down
to a murderous fate.[20]
Cypris blows furiously upon everything, and like
        a bee she flies about.

[PHAEDRA, standing near the palace doors and
listening to voices which begin to be heard within,
addresses the CHORUS.]

---

16 A river associated with the site of Olympic games, where
    a temple of Olympian Zeus was set up.

17 The Oracle at Delphi, called Pythian after the python
    that guarded the site before Phoebus Apollo killed it and
    established his temple there.
18 Iole was promised in marriage to whoever could beat her
    father Eurytus in archery. Heracles succeeded, but Iole
    was denied him—until he returned and took her by
    force, destroying the city.
19 Heracles, son of Zeus and a mortal, Alcmene.
20 Semele, daughter of Cadmus, king of Thebes, was im-
    pregnated by Zeus and then killed by his thunderbolt.
    Zeus extracted her offspring, Dionysus, from her womb
    and sewed it into his thigh for a "second" birth.

PH.: Silence, women! We are ruined, completely 530
    ruined!

CH.-L.: What's going on inside, Phaedra, that
    terrifies you so?

PH.: Quiet! Let me hear what they are saying inside.

CH.-L.: I'll be quiet. But this is a bad beginning.

PH.: [*screaming*] O wretched me, what must I suffer?

CH.-L.: [*chanting or singing excitedly*] What are you 535
    screaming about? Why are you shrieking? Tell
  us, woman, what you have heard that rushes upon
    your mind
  and terrifies you so.

PH.: It's all over. Come over here by the doors and
    listen to the shouting that rises in the palace.

CH.-L.: [*chanting or singing excitedly*] You are by the
    doors. You should report
  any words from the palace. 540
  Tell me, tell me, what is the matter?

PH.: Hippolytus, the son of the horse-loving
    Amazon, is shouting and cursing my servant.

CH.-L.: [*still chanting or singing*] I hear voices, but
    nothing clear.
  You can hear better, where the shouting
  comes to you through the doors. 545

Ph.: Yes, I can hear clearly now; he calls her 'wicked
    matchmaker,' 'betrayer of your master's bed!'

CH.-L.: [*chanting or singing*] How terrible! You've
    been betrayed, my friend.
  How can I help you?
  Your secrets are revealed; you are ruined,
  [*moaning*] betrayed by your friends! 550

PH.: She has ruined me by telling of my troubles; as
    a friend would,
  she tried to cure me of my illness, but she didn't
    do it well.

CH.-L.: [*calmer now*] Now what will you do in this
    impossible situation?

Ph.: I don't know, except for one thing: die as
    quickly as possible!
  This is the only remedy for the disaster now upon 555
    me.

[*HIPPOLYTUS rushes from the house onto the stage
followed by the NURSE who attempts to restrain him.
PHAEDRA shrinks back and listens; HIPPOLYTUS
deliberately ignores her.*]

HIPP.: [*shouting*] O mother earth and spreading
    light of the sun,
  what unspeakable words I have heard!

NUR.: Be quiet, child, before someone hears you
    shouting.

HIPP.: No! I have heard terrible things and cannot
    be silent.

NUR.: [*grasping at his hand and then falling at his feet* 560
    in an attempt at supplication] Yes! I beg of you
  by this right hand and its strong arm.

HIPP.: Keep your hand away and don't touch my
    clothes.

NUR.: By your knees I implore you, don't ruin me.

HIPP.: What do you mean, if, as you say, you have
    said nothing bad?

NUR.: This story, my child, is not for everyone to hear.

HIPP.: But surely fine things are better told to the 565
    multitude.

NUR.: My child, don't dishonour your oaths.

HIPP.: My tongue swore; my mind took no oath.

NUR.: Child, what will you do? Ruin your friends?

HIPP.: 'Friends'? I spit out the word! No wicked
    person is a friend of mine.

NUR.: Try to understand and forgive; to err is 570
    human, my child.

HIPP.: [*turning away from the nurse and raising his
    face and hands to the sky*] O Zeus, why did
    you send women—a counterfeit coin
  and a bane for me—to live in the light of the sun?
  If you wanted to sow a mortal race,
  you should not have had it come from women.
  Instead, mortals should go to your temples 575
  and pay bronze or iron or a weight of gold
  to buy the seed of children, each man paying
  according to the worth of his estate, and they
    should
  live at liberty in their homes without women.
  [*soliloquizing*]
  It is clear from the following that woman is a 580
    great evil:
  the father who begets her and rears her adds
  a dowry and sends her from home—to be rid of
    an evil!
  Her husband in turn takes the ruinous creature
    into his house
  and rejoices. He puts jewelry on his idol

(fine things for the wicked) and dresses her up   585
    with pretty clothes:
the poor wretch, undermining his own prosperity.
It's easiest to have an empty-headed woman, but
    even she is
worse than useless, enshrined at home in her
    silliness.
And I hate the clever one. May my home never
    have a woman
who thinks bigger than a woman should.   590
Cypris spawns more wickedness
in clever women, while the mindless woman's
stunted wits keep her out of trouble.
And no servant should ever go in to a woman,
but voiceless, biting beasts should dwell with them   595
so that they would speak to no-one
and hear no voices in reply.
But as it is, wicked women make wicked plots
    indoors
and their servants bring them out into the open—
[to the nurse]
just as you have come to me about my father, you   600
    evil creature,
to arrange an affair in his untouchable marriage bed.
I'll clean these things away with streams of pure
    water
and wash out my ears. How could I ever *be* wicked,
when I feel defiled merely hearing such things?
Be sure that it is this same piety of mine that saves   605
    you, woman.
If I had not been caught off guard and trapped
    into oaths by the gods,
I would never have kept from telling all this to
    my father.
But now I will leave home for as long as
Theseus is out of the country, and I will keep
    silent.
But I will come back when my father returns, and   610
    I will be watching
to see how you look at us—both you and your
    mistress!

[*The words above are spoken with a glance toward
PHAEDRA as HIPPOLYTUS moves toward the side of
the stage to depart. Before he exits, he delivers a last
tirade.*]

May you both perish! I will never have my fill of
    hating
women, not even if people say I am always talking
    about them—
for they are always evil!
Let someone teach them restraint,   615
Or let me trample them under foot, forever!

[*HIPPOLYTUS exits, and PHAEDRA, who has been
listening in silence, moves forward and sings the
following lament.*]

PH.: [*singing sorrowfully*]

ANTISTROPHE

Oh, how miserable
and unfortunate
are the destinies of women!
What means do we have or what words can we use   620
to loosen this knot of words, now we are snared
    and have fallen?
We have got what we deserved. O earth and light
    of day!
Where can I escape from what's happened?
How can I conceal my misery, friends?
What god or mortal would be seen aiding me,   625
sitting beside me, or helping me cope with these
    unjust deeds?
My suffering carries me across
the hardest of all crossings to the other shore of life.
I am the most unfortunate of women.
CH.-L.: [*sorrowfully*] It's all over. Your servant's schemes,   630
    mistress, did not succeed. Everything's gone wrong.
PH.: [*to her nurse*] O wickedest of women and
    corrupter of your friends,
see what you've done to me! May Zeus, my
    grandfather,
strike you with his fire-bolts and destroy you root
    and branch!
Didn't you see what was in your mind? Didn't I   635
    tell you
to keep silent about these things which now
    disgrace me?
But you had no restraint, and so I will no longer
    die with a good reputation.

I need new plans now.

For he, now that his mind is whetted with rage,
will denounce me to his father for what you did   640
    wrong,
and fill the whole earth with shameful tales.
I wish you were dead—both you and whoever else
    is eager
to help friends by evil means—and without their
    consent!
NUR.: Mistress, you can blame me for my mistakes,
for shock overpowers your judgement.   645
    But I can speak against these charges, if you will
    listen.
    I brought you up and am fond of you. I sought a
    remedy
    for this sickness of yours, but found—something
    I hadn't intended.
    If I had succeeded, I would certainly have been
    counted among the wise.
    It's by our luck that we get known for intelligence.   650
PH.: Do you think this is fair and what I deserve—
    Wounding me and then smoothing it over with
    words?
NUR.: We're talking too much. I didn't act with
    restraint,
but there is a way to save you even now, child.
PH.: Stop talking! You did not advise me well in the   655
    past, and you set your hand to evil deeds. Get
    out of my way and try—thinking about
    yourself. I'll arrange my own affairs, and I'll
    do it well.

[*Exit nurse.*]

PH.: [*to the chorus*] And you, noble daughters of
    Trozen, grant me this request,
cover with silence what you have heard here.
CH.-L.: I swear by holy Artemis, Zeus' daughter,
    never to reveal any of your troubles to the light of
    day.
PH.: Thank you. There is one thing more I have to say: 660
    I have thought of something for my misfortunes,
    something to give my children a reputable life
    and to benefit myself even as things have turned
    out.
    For I will never shame my Cretan home
    nor will I come to face Theseus   665
    amid shameful deeds because of one life.

CH.-L.: What are you about to do? What uncurable
    evil?
PH.: Die. But how, is something I will decide.
CH.-L.: Hush! Use words of good omen!
PH.: And you,   670
    give me good advice!
    [*turning to the statue by the door*]
    I will delight Cypris, who is destroying me,
    when I depart from life this very day,
    and a bitter love will have conquered me.
    Yet will I give trouble to someone else   675
    when I die, so that he will know not to be haughty
    over my troubles. When he shares equally in this
    sickness of mine,
    he will learn restraint. [*Exit into the palace.*]
CH.: [*singing and dancing*]

STROPHE 1

I wish I were among the steep rocks in
sheltering recesses   680
and that a god
would make me into a feathered bird
among winged flocks.
I wish I were lifted up over the sea
waves of the Adrian   685
shore,[21] and over Eridanus' water,[22]
into whose dark swells
the wretched girls
lamenting in grief for Phaethon[23] drip the
amber-gleaming radiance of their tears.   690

ANTISTROPHE 1

I wish to end my journey on the shores, sown
    with apples
where the Hesperides[24] sing,

---

21 In the gulf of Venice.
22 The River Po in Italy, believed to be the source of am-
    ber.
23 Phaethon, son of the sun god Helios, took his father's
    chariot for a dangerous joyride and was dashed to earth
    by Zeus. He landed in the Eridanus river, on the banks
    of which his sisters, turned into poplar trees, shed their
    tears of amber.
24 Nymphs who guarded golden apples at the far western
    limit of the world.

where the sea-lord
of the dark shallows[25]
no longer gives passage to sailors,   695
but sets the sacred boundary of
heaven, which Atlas holds,
and where ambrosial springs flow
near Zeus' marriage bed,[26]
and holy earth, abundantly bountiful,   700
increases the gods' happy lot.

STROPHE 2

Oh white-winged Cretan
ship, who through the briny
salt-crashing sea wave
ferried my queen from her bountiful home,   705
and gave her the gift of a disastrous marriage!
Truly it flew
a bird ill-omened for both sides,
from the land of Minos to famous Athens.
On the shores of Munichus[27]   710
they bound fast the twisted rope-ends,
and stepped onto the mainland.

ANTISTROPHE 2

And for this an unholy desire,
the terrible sickness of Aphrodite,
crushed her inside.   715
Now she, foundering in her hard misfortune,
will fasten a hanging noose to beams of her bridal
      chamber
fitting it around her white neck,
ashamed of her hateful lot,
choosing instead a good   720
reputation, and ridding her heart
of its grievous passion.

[*PHAEDRA has hanged herself inside the palace, and
one of her servants shouts for help.*]

---

25 Poseidon, at the westernmost entrance to the Mediter-
    ranean, the Straits of Gibraltar.
26 Zeus and his wife Hera were said to have started their
    marriage in a western paradise where the earth gave
    golden apples as wedding gifts.
27 The harbour of Athens.

VOICE OF SERVANT FROM INSIDE THE PALACE:
[*Screams are heard, then—*] Come and help—
      everyone who's near the house!
   She's strangled in a noose—the queen—Theseus'
      wife!
CH.-L.: [*sorrowfully*] It's all over. The queen is   725
   alive no longer; she hangs suspended in a noose.
VOICE OF SERVANT FROM INSIDE THE PALACE:
   Won't you hurry? Won't someone bring a double-
      edged
   sword to loosen the knot from her neck?
ANOTHER MEMBER OF THE CHORUS:
   [*to her companions*] Friends, what should we do?
      Do you think we should enter
   the house and loosen the queen from the tight   730
      noose?
CH.-L.: [*in reply*] Why? Aren't there young servants
      near by?
   Meddling doesn't make for a safe life.

[*Inside the palace, the queen's body has been lowered
from the noose and is being arranged, perhaps on the
same bed on which she was brought out from the house
earlier in the play.*]

VOICE OF SERVANT FROM INSIDE THE PALACE:
   [*to other servants inside*] Lay out her body and
      straighten her limbs.
   This is a better housekeeping for my masters.
CH.-L.: She is dead then, I hear, the poor woman,   735
   For they are already laying out her body.

[*Enter THESEUS, just arrived from Delphi, where he
has been consulting the prophetic god Apollo. As he
comes on stage, his head is wreathed with garlands that
indicate a favourable reply from the oracle.*]

THESEUS: Women, do you know why they are
      shouting in the house?
   What is the noise that I hear through the doors?
   My house does not see fit to open its doors
   and address me graciously as an envoy from the god.   740
   Nothing wrong has happened to aged Pittheus,
      has it?
   His life is already far along, but nonetheless
   it would grieve me if he left us.
CH.-L.: What has happened to you here does not
      concern old people,

Theseus; it is the young that are dead and bring   745
     you grief.
TH.: [*anguished*] Surely my children haven't been
     robbed of their lives?
CH.-L.: They live, but their mother has died—most
     painfully for you.
TH.: What are you saying? My wife is dead? How
     did it happen?
CH.-L.: She fastened up a noose and hanged herself.
TH.: Frozen with grief, or what happened to her?   750
CH.-L.: That's as much as we know, for we, too,
     have just now come
   to your house, Theseus, to mourn your ills.
TH.: [*tearing the garlands from his head and speaking
     sorrowfully*] Why is my head wreathed with these
   woven leaves? Disaster has struck me—just as I
     return from the oracle!
   Unbar the doors, servants; undo the bolts,   755
   so that I may see the bitter sight
   of my wife, whose death has destroyed me.

[*The doors are opened; PHAEDRA'S body, laid out on
the bed, is brought onto the stage; a tablet hangs from
her wrist.*]

CH.-L.: [*singing pitifully*] Miserable woman and
     piteous woes!
   You have suffered and done
   enough to confound this house.   760
   What recklessness was yours!—
   a violent death in an unholy
   act, through the wrestling of your own piteous hand!
   Who, miserable woman, has darkened your life?
TH.: [*lamenting in anguished song which alternates
     with calm speech*]

STROPHE

[*anguished*] Oh what troubles are mine! I have   765
     suffered, miserable that I am,
   the greatest of my ills! O misfortune!
[*calm*] How heavily you have descended upon me
     and my house—
   some inexplicable pollution coming from a
     vengeful power.
[*anguished*] A destruction of life that I cannot
     survive;
   miserable, I behold a sea of troubles   770

[*calm*] too great ever to swim back out of,
   or ever to cross its waves of disaster.
[*anguished*] How can I, so miserable, explain your
     fateful calamity
   and hit on the truth, O miserable wife?
[*calm*] For like a bird you have vanished from my   775
     hand
   rushing to Hades with a swift leap.
[*anguished*] Piteous, piteous are these sufferings;
   from some time long ago I must have been
     gathering upon myself
   this god-sent calamity because of the sins of
     someone before my time.
CH.-L.: [*speaking calmly*] You are not the only one   780
     to whom such woes have come, king;
   many others have lost their dear wives.
TH.: [*continuing his lament*]

ANTISTROPHE

[*anguished*] I wish I were under the earth, in the
     gloom under the earth,
   dwelling in darkness, dead myself, wretched as I am,
[*calm*] bereaved of your dear companionship:
   for you have destroyed me even more than yourself.   785
[*anguished*] What happened? How did such a
   deadly misfortune come to your heart, wretched
     woman?
[*calm*] Won't someone tell me what happened, or
     does the mob
   of my servants guard their ruler's house in vain?
[*anguished*] ....[*line missing*]........   790
   wretched me, what grief I see in my house!
[*calm*] Unbearable and unspeakable! Oh, I am
     ruined!
   My house is empty, my children orphaned!
[*anguished*] You have left, you have left us,
   O my dear, the best of all women whom the light   795
     of the sun
   and the star-faced brightness of night behold!
CH.-L.: [*singing*] O wretched man, what trouble
     your house has!
   My eyes moisten and
   flood with tears over your misfortune.
   But I have long shuddered with fear of the   800
     calamity to follow.

[*The CHORUS and THESEUS notice the tablet attached to PHAEDRA's wrist. THESEUS, speaking more calmly now, takes it in his hands.*]

TH.: Ah!
What is this tablet fastened to her hand?
Does it mean to tell me something new?
Did she write me a letter to plead with me
about remarriage and the children, poor woman? 805
Be assured, wretched wife. There is no woman
who will enter Theseus' bed and home.
[*inspecting the tablet*]
These marks of the hammered gold seal that belonged
to my wife, who no longer lives—they revive my affection.
Come, let us unfold the sealed coverings 810
and see what this tablet has to tell me.
CH.-L.: [*singing*] Here is a new evil that a god sends in upon us
to take the place of the old . . . .[*lines missing*] . . .
. . . .
Ruined, destroyed, I say, 815
is the house of my rulers.
TH.: [*speaking*] Another disaster added to disaster!
CH.-L.: [*speaking*] What is it? Tell me, if I may know.
Th.: [*singing*] It cries aloud, this tablet cries aloud abominable things!
How can I flee the weight of my woes? I am dead! 820
I am gone!
Such a song—such a song of woe I have seen given voice
in these words! Wretched me!
CH.-L.: [*speaking*] Your words are the beginning of trouble.
TH.: [*first singing and then speaking*]
I can no longer hold back this ruinous woe
in the gates of my mouth, painful as it is to let out. 825
[*Shouting to summon citizens to witness the
denunciation and cursing of his son.*]
Ho! City! [*A group of men gathers and listens.*]
Hippolytus has dared touch my bed
by force, dishonouring the sacred eye of Zeus.
Now, O my father Poseidon, with one of the
three curses that you once promised me, 830
destroy my son, and may he not escape
this day, if you really gave me true curses.

CH.-L.: King, pray to the gods and take back your words.
In time you will know you have made a mistake, believe me.
TH.: Impossible! And furthermore, I will drive him 835
out of this land.
He will be struck by one of these two fates.
Either Poseidon will send him dead
to the house of Hades, honouring my curses,
or wandering in exile from this land
he will scrape together a wretched life on foreign 840
soil.
CH.-L.: [*seeing Hippolytus approach*] Here he is now,
your son himself coming just in time,
Hippolytus.
Relax your harsh anger, king Theseus, and
consider what is best for you and your family.
HIPP.: [*rushing onto the stage followed by his
companions*] I heard your shout and came right
away, father.
I don't know what made you shout, though, and I 845
wish you would tell me.
[*catching sight of Phaedra's body*]
Ah! What is this? I see your wife, father,
but she's dead. This is a great surprise,
for I left her just now, looking on the light of this
very day—only a little while ago!
What happened to her? How did she die?
[*perplexed at his father's silence*]
Father, I want to know, and from you! 850
Why are you silent? Silence is no help in times of trouble.
Although someone who wants to hear about everything,
even in times of trouble, is caught as over-eager,
still it isn't right to hide your misfortunes from
your friends, father, and from those who are more 855
than friends.
TH.: [*soliloquizing and refusing to look at his son*]
O men, you who make many mistakes and all for nothing,
Why do you teach thousands of skills,
contriving and discovering all things,
when there is one thing you don't understand and
have never tracked down:
teaching brainless people right thinking. 860

HIPP.: [*perplexed yet further at his father's behaviour*]
You're speaking of a terribly clever person, if he
could
pound thought into the thoughtless.
But this is no time for theorizing, father.
I fear your tongue is running wild in your troubles.
TH.: [*continuing to soliloquize*] Men should have 865
been given some sure sign
of their friends and a means of judging their
minds:
to know who is a true friend and who is not.
And all men ought to have two voices,
one honest and the other whatever it happened to
be,
so that a tongue plotting unjust deeds might be 870
refuted
by the honest one, and we would not be
deceived.
HIPP.: [*still perplexed*] Has one of my friends
slandered me to your ears,
and am I in trouble, although in no way to blame?
I am astonished, for your words dumbfound me
by straying so far from the seat of intelligence. 875
TH.: [*still soliloquizing and looking away from his son*]
The mind of man! How far will it go?
What limit will there be to its daring and
recklessness?
For if it swells up throughout a man's lifetime,
and he who comes after will be more villainous
than he who went before, then the gods 880
will have to cast another land alongside this earth
to receive those men who are unjust and born
evil-doers.

[*THESEUS turns toward his son and gestures with the
accusing tablet.*]

Look at him there! Although begotten by me,
he shamed my bed and is clearly convicted
by the dead woman of being utterly evil. 885
Look at me now! Since I am caught up in your
pollution
anyway, you can look your father in the face.
So *you* consort with the gods as if you were more
than
man! You're chaste and untainted by evil?
No boasting of yours would induce me 890

to made the mistake of attributing such ignorance
to the gods.
Keep your pretensions! Put on a good show
with your vegetarian diet, and let Orpheus lead
you in your
frenzied dances as you bow down to the smoke of
wordy doctrines!
For you are caught! I proclaim to everyone: shun 895
such men! For they hunt you down with saintly
words
while concocting shameful deeds.

This woman is dead. Do you think this will save
you?
It convicts you most of all, you wicked man.
For what oaths, what words would have more effect 900
than this woman, and allow you to escape blame?

Will you say she hated you and that the bastard
is a natural enemy of legitimate children?
You make her a poor bargainer in life
if she gave up what was dearest to her out of 905
hatred for you!

Or will you say that promiscuous behaviour is
natural for women
but not for men? I know young men
who are no more stable than women
when Cypris stirs up their young hearts,
and the fact that they're men helps too. 910

But now why am I competing with your words,
when the body is here as the clearest witness?
Get out of this land as fast as you can and go into
exile.
And don't go to god-built Athens
nor to the frontiers of the land my spear rules. 915
For if I give in to you after you have done this to
me,
Sinis of the Isthmus will never acknowledge
that I killed him, but he will call it an empty
boast.[28]

---

28 Sinis was a legendary bad guy who killed his victims by
tying them to bent pine trees and catapulting them into
the air.

Nor will the Scironid cliffs bordering the sea
say that I am hard on evil-doers.[29]   920
CH.-L.: I don't think I could call any mortal really
    fortunate, when even the foremost are
    overthrown.
HIPP.: Father, you are angry and under a terrible
    strain. But this affair, which looks so reasonable,
    will look quite different if you spread it out and
        examine it.
I am not clever at making speeches before a crowd   925
but am better before a few people of my own age.
This is perfectly natural, for those who make a
    poor showing
among the wise speak more to the tune of the
    crowd.
However, since this calamity has come, I must
speak out. I will begin with your first point,   930
when you attacked me and thought you could
        destroy me
without my answering back. You can see this
    sunlight
and this earth; they contain no man—even if you
        deny it—
with a more virtuous nature than mine.
For first I know how to reverence the gods   935
and to have friends who do not try to do wrong
and who would be ashamed to commission evil
    deeds
and pay back friendly treatment with shameful
    things.
I don't laugh at my companions, father,
but am the same to my friends both present and   940
    absent.
And I've never touched the one thing in which
    you think you have caught me now.
Up to this minute my body is pure of sexual love.
I know nothing of the act itself except what I have
    heard people say
and seen in pictures. And I'm not eager to look at
    them, since my soul is virgin. [*THESEUS
    winces with disbelief.*]

---

29 Another mythological villain defeated by Theseus. Sciron
    tripped his victims at the edge of a cliff, making them
    fall to their deaths.

But perhaps my virtue itself doesn't persuade you.   945
Well then, you must show how it could have been
    corrupted.
Was her body more beautiful than those
of other women? Or did I hope to receive
an inheritance along with her bed and thus dwell
    in your palace?
Then I was a fool, and not in my right mind.   950
Or is ruling pleasant for sane men?
Not at all, unless the monarchy that pleases them
has first of all destroyed their common sense.
I would like to be first as victor in the Greek
    games,
but second man in the city,   955
always living happily with the best men as my
    friends.
For the power to act is there, and the absence of
    danger
gives more pleasure than any ruler has.

[*THESEUS attempts to break in.*]

One of my points has not been mentioned; you
    have all the others.
If I had a witness as virtuous as I am to attest to   960
    my nature
and if I were making my plea while this woman
    still saw the light of day,
you would know the wicked by examining their
    deeds.
But now I swear by Zeus protector of oaths
and by the ground beneath our feet
that I have never touched your wife   965
nor wanted to nor even had it in mind.
May I perish without fame or even memory of my
    name,
without city or home, wandering in exile over the
    earth,
and may neither sea nor earth receive my dead
flesh, if I am evil by nature.   970
I don't know what it was she feared that made
her end her life; for it is not right for me to speak
    further.
She acted virtuously though she had no virtue,
while I, having virtue, did not use it well.
CH.-L.: You have said enough to turn aside his   975
    accusation,

and have added oaths by the gods: no small
    pledge of good faith.
TH.: Isn't this fellow a born charlatan and spell-binder,
    who is so sure his smooth manners will
    overpower my spirit, after he has dishonoured his
        father?
HIPP.: And I am amazed at the same thing in you,   980
        father,
    For if you were my son and I were your father,
    I would have killed you and not punished you
        with exile
    if I thought you had touched my wife.
TH.: A fitting suggestion! But you will not die
    according to this law you have decreed for yourself.   985
    For a quick death is easy for a man in misfortune.
    Instead you will wander in exile from your
        fatherland
    and scrape together a wretched life on foreign soil.
HIPP.: What are you going to do? Won't you wait
        for time
    to proclaim the truth about me? Will you drive   990
        me from the land?
TH.: Beyond the Pontic Sea and the regions of Atlas,
    if I could. I hate your presence so much!
HIPP.: Will you test neither my oath nor my pledge
        nor yet
    what the prophets say? Will you throw me out of
        the land without trial?
TH.: [holding out the tablet] This tablet doesn't need   995
        any drawing of lots to
    condemn you on good evidence. As for the birds
        flying
    above our heads—I bid them a fond farewell!
HIPP.: O gods, why don't I open my mouth,
    I who am being destroyed by you whom I reverence?
    No, that's not it. I would not persuade those   1000
        whom I must,
    and I would break my sworn oaths for nothing.
TH.: Oh, how your saintliness kills me!
    Won't you get out of your fatherland as fast as you
        can?
HIPP.: Where will I turn in my misery? What
    friend's house will I enter, exiled on this charge?   1005
TH.: Whoever enjoys entertaining friends who
        violate wives
    and share in corrupting households.

HIPP.: Alas, this cuts to the quick! It brings me close
        to tears,
    if indeed I appear corrupt and seem so to you.
TH.: Then was the time to groan, and you should   1010
        have thought ahead
    before you dared violate your father's wife.
HIPP.: O house, if only you could speak
    and witness whether I have a corrupt nature.
TH.: How clever of you to flee to voiceless
        witnesses.
    But the deed itself needs no speech to proclaim   1015
        you wicked.
HIPP.: If only I could stand apart and look at
    myself, so that I could cry over what I suffer.
TH.: You have always practised worshipping yourself
        far more
    than being just and acting piously toward your
        parents.
HIPP.: O wretched mother, O bitter childbirth!   1020
    May none of my friends be a bastard!
TH.: Won't you drag him off, servants? Didn't you hear
    me proclaiming him an exile long ago?
HIPP.: If any one of them touches me, he'll be sorry!
    Do it yourself, if that's what you want. *You* throw   1025
    me out of the land!
TH.: I'll do it, if you don't obey my commands.
    For no pity comes over me for your exile. [*Exit.*]
HIPP.: [*soliloquizing*]
    It's all settled, apparently. O wretched me!
    I know what this is all about, but I know no way
        to reveal it.
    [*addressing the statue of Artemis*]
    O maiden daughter of Leto, my dearest goddess,   1030
    my comrade, my fellow-hunter, we will indeed be
        exiled
    from famous Athens. Farewell, city
    and land of Erechtheus.
    [*to the landscape around him*]
    O plain of Trozen,
    what divine happiness you hold for those who   1035
        grow up here!
    Farewell! This is the last time I will look at you or
        speak to you.
    [*to his companions*]
    Come along, my young companions of this land,
    speak to me and send me forth from this soil.

You will never see another man more virtuous
even if it doesn't seem so to my father. [*Exit with*   1040
    his companions.]
CH.: [*singing and dancing*]

STROPHE 1

Whenever I think of how the gods care for us,
my sorrow is greatly lightened. But anyone who
    keeps within him hope of understanding
is disappointed when he looks at what happens to
    men and at their deeds,
For things come and go by turns. Men's lives
    change course
and wander about forever.   1045

ANTISTROPHE 1

And thus I pray that divine fate grant me
a prosperous good fortune and a heart unbroken
    by grief.
May my opinions be neither rigid nor counterfeit.
May I have an easy disposition changing always
    with tomorrow's time,
and in this way may I live my life happily   1050

STROPHE 2

My mind is no longer clear; what I see is contrary
    to all expectation.
We have seen the brightest star of Greece and
    Athens,
seen him sent forth to another land
by his father's anger.
O sands of our city's shores!   1055
O mountain woods, where he used to kill
wild beasts with his swift-footed dogs,
accompanying holy Dictynna!

ANTISTROPHE 2

No longer will you mount your chariot with its
    Venetian colts
nor keep to the track around the lagoon with your 1060
    well-trained horse.
The sleepless music from the strings of your lyre
will cease in your father's house.
The resting place of Leto's virgin daughter[30]

_____

30 Artemis.

will have no garlands throughout the thick green
    meadows.
The young girls' competition for your wedding bed 1065
is ended by your exile.

EPODE

And for your misfortune
I will live out my ill-fated fate
in tears. O miserable mother,
you bore a child for nothing!   1070
I rage at the gods!
Graces, you who link couples in marriage, since
    this
wretched man does not deserve his doom, why
do you send him away from his home and
    fatherland?
CH.-L.: [*in normal speaking tones*] I see one of   1075
    Hippolytus' servants looking sad
    and hurrying earnestly toward the palace.
SERV.: [*entering from stage right*] Where should I go
    to find Theseus, the king
    of this land, women? If you know,
    tell me. Is he inside the palace here?   1080
CH.-L.: Here he is himself, coming out of the palace.
SERV.: Theseus, I bring a message that deserves your
    attention
    and that of the citizens who live in the city of Athens
    and within the boundaries of the Trozenian land.
TH.: What is it? Has some strange calamity   1085
    seized upon our two neighbouring cities?
SERV.: Hippolytus no longer lives—or almost so.
    He still sees the light of day, but his life is poised
    on a slim balance.
TH.: From what? Did he make someone his enemy
    by shamefully dishonouring his wife, just as he   1090
    violated his father's?
SERV.: His own team of horses destroyed him—
    and also the curses that you called down upon
        your son with your own mouth
    when you prayed to your father who rules the sea.
TH.: O gods—and Poseidon! You really were my
    father, for you listened to my prayers!   1095
    How was he destroyed? Tell me! How did the
        dead weight
    of Justice's trap strike him for putting me to
        shame?

SERV.: We were near the wave-beaten shore
   currying the horses' hair with combs,
   and we were weeping, for someone had come and   1100
      told us
   that Hippolytus would never again set foot in this
      land
   since you had sentenced him to a miserable life in
      exile.
   And he came to us on the shore with the same
      tearful tale, and an immense group
   of friends and companions was following along
      behind him.
   And finally, when he had stopped groaning, he said,   1105
   "Why am I so upset? My father's words must be
      obeyed.
   Get the horses yoked and ready for the chariot,
   servants, for this is no longer my city."
   Then each man hurried,
   and quicker than you could say it we had   1110
      harnessed
   the colts and brought them to stand right next to
      our master.
   He seizes the reins from the chariot rail
   and fits his feet right into the shoe frames.
   Then, opening his hands to the gods,
   he prays, "Zeus, may I no longer live if I am an   1115
      evil-natured man.
   May my father come to see how he has
      dishonoured me,
   whether I die or continue to see the light of day."
   With this, he took the goad into his hands and
      struck it
   against all the colts at the same time. We servants
      followed
   our master beside the chariot near the bridles,   1120
   along the road straight to Argos and Epidaurus.
   When we entered open country,
   there was a certain promontory
   lying just beyond this land toward the Saronic Sea.
   At that moment an earthly rumble like Zeus'   1125
      thunder
   rose into a mighty roar, horrible to hear.
   The horses pricked up their heads and ears
   toward heaven, and we were terribly afraid over
   where the noise was coming from. Looking off
   toward the sea-beaten shore we saw an awesome   1130

wave standing fixed in the sky, so that my eye
      could not
see Sciron's shore, and the Isthmus
and the rock of Asclepius were hidden.
And then it swelled up and bubbled deep
foam all around, and as the sea spurted high   1135
the wave comes toward the shore where the four
      horses were drawing the chariot.
And as it broke with a triple surge,
it gave forth a bull—a fierce monster.
The whole earth was filled with his roaring,
and the echoes made you shudder. And for us   1140
      who saw it,
the sight was more than our eyes could stand.
Instantly a terrible fear gripped the colts,
and our master, thoroughly at home with the
      ways
of horses, snatched the reins in his hands
and pulled like a seaman on an oar,   1145
hanging his body backward against the reins.
The colts clamped their jaws on the forged bits
and bore him along in spite of his efforts, heeding
      neither the hand
of the helmsman, nor the reins, nor the
well-built chariot. Whenever he gripped the tiller   1150
and set his course straight toward smooth ground,
the bull appeared in front to head them off,
maddening the four horses with fear.
Whenever they rushed with raging spirits toward
      the rocks
the bull approached in silence and followed   1155
      alongside the chariot's rim
until he tipped it and tossed it
by smashing its wheels against a rock.
Everything was thrown together. The wheel hubs
and the axle pins leaped up in the air,
and he himself, the wretched man, tangled in the   1160
      reins,
is dragged along bound in a knot hard to loosen.
Battering his head against the rocks
and ripping his flesh he shouted with terror in his
      voice,
"Stop! You were raised in my own stables!
Don't destroy me! Damned curse of my father!   1165
Don't any of you here want to save me, the best of
      men?"

Many of us wanted to but our feet could not keep
    up
and we were left behind. And yet somehow or other
he was set loose from the cut leather thongs that
    bound him,
and he fell, breathing only a little bit of life now.   1170
His horses, and that monster of a
bull that brought such misery were hidden
    somewhere in the rocky earth.
I am only a slave in your palace, king,
but I will never be able to believe
that your son is evil,   1175
not even if the whole race of women hanged
    themselves
and if someone filled all the pinewood on Mount
    Ida
with writing. For I know that he is good.
CH.-L.: [*mournfully*] A new disaster has taken place
    and there is no escaping fate and what must be.   1180
TH.: In my hatred for the man who has suffered
    these things,
    I was pleased with this report. But now, out of
        respect
    for the gods and also for him (since he is of my
        blood),
    I will neither rejoice nor be distressed at what has
        happened.
SERV.: Well then, should we bring him in or what   1185
    should we do
    with the wretched man to please you?
    Think about it. If you want my advice,
    you won't be hard on your unfortunate son.
TH.: Bring him in! So that I may see with my own eyes
    the man who denies he violated my bed,   1190
    and so that I may refute him with words and with
        this god-sent disaster.

[*Exit SERVANT of Hippolytus: THESEUS waits while
the CHORUS sings a hymn to Aphrodite.*]

CH.: You subdue the unbending will of gods and
    mortal men,
    Cypris, and along with you
    the bright-feathered one[31] attacks from all sides
    with swiftest wing.   1195

_____
31 Eros.

He flies about over the earth and the echoing
salt sea.
Eros enchants those on whose maddened hearts
he rushes gleaming with his golden wings—
young creatures of the mountains and the seas,   1200
and all those whom earth nurtures,
and those the blazing sun beholds,
and men. Over all of these you hold the honour
    of a queen,
Cypris, and alone wield power.

[*ARTEMIS suddenly appears above the palace, moved
into sight by a mechanical contrivance. She carries her
bow and arrows.*]

ARTEMIS: [*addressing THESEUS, first declaiming and
    then speaking*] You, the nobly born son of Aegeus,   1205
        I command to listen:
    I, Artemis, the maiden daughter of Leto, address
        you.
    Why, wretched Theseus, are you pleased at these
        things
    when you have impiously slain your son
    and believed the lying stories of your wife
    while things were unclear? Clear is the ruin you   1210
        have suffered now.
    Why don't you hide your body in the depths of
        the earth
    in shame,
    or take wing and soar to a life in the sky,
    lifting your foot out of this trouble?
    For among good men there is no   1215
    possible place in life for you.

    Hear, Theseus, the state of your woes.
    I bring you no further troubles, but I will cause
        you grief.

    Now I have come for this: to reveal your son's honest
    mind, so that he may die with a good name,   1220
    and to reveal your wife's mad passion, or, in a way,
    her nobility. For the goddess most hated
    by us who take pleasure in virginity
    stung her with goads, and she fell in love with
        your son.
    While trying to overcome Cypris by the power of   1225
        her will,

she was ruined by what her nurse did without her
  consent.
For she put your son under oath and told him
  about Phaedra's sickness.
As was right, he did not take up
her suggestion, nor again when you called him
  wicked
did he retract his sworn pledge, since he was pious   1230
  in his very nature.
But she, fearing to face a cross-examination,
wrote a lying letter and destroyed
your son with treachery: lies, but nonetheless she
  persuaded you. [*THESEUS groans*]
Does that tale sting you, Theseus? Quiet now,
so that you can hear the rest and groan yet more.   1235

You know the three powerful curses your father
  gave you?
You took one of them, O most wicked man,
for use against your son, while it could have been
  used on an enemy.
Your father, the sea-god, though wishing you well,
granted your prayer as he had to, since he had   1240
  promised;
it is you who clearly appear to have done wrong
  against both him and me.
You did not delay over the pledge or await the voice
of prophets, nor did you refute him, nor permit
  time to make
a lengthy examination. Instead, acting faster than
  you should have,
you sent curses upon your son and killed him.   1245
TH.: Mistress, I wish I were dead!
ART.: You did terrible things, but nonetheless
  you can still receive pardon even for them,
  for Cypris wished these things to happen,
  to glut her anger. This law holds among the gods;   1250
  no-one of us is willing to oppose the will
  of a god who wishes to do something, but we
    always stand aside.
For you can be certain that if I had not feared Zeus
I would never have come to this degree of shame
and let one who is dearest to me of all mortals   1255
perish. First, your ignorance of
your mistake releases you from baseness.
And then your wife in dying took away

the chance of refuting her words: so your mind
  was persuaded.
These evils have broken forth upon you most of   1260
  all,
but I also have my grief. For gods do not rejoice
when pious men die, but we destroy wicked men
entirely—themselves, their children, and their
  homes.
CH.-L.: [*declaiming*] Here comes the wretched
  fellow,
his youthful flesh and blond head   1265
battered. O troubles of the house!
A double misfortune has come about,
sent by the gods to seize upon this roof.
HIPP.: [*first screaming with pain, then declaiming,
  and finally breaking into song*] Wretched that I am,
    battered by the
unjust curses of an unjust father.   1270
I am miserably dead, unhappy me!
Pains rush through my head,
and spasms leap in my brain.
[*to his servants, who are carrying or supporting him*]
Stop! Let me rest my worn-out body.
O hateful team of horses,   1275
reared by my own hand,
you destroyed me, you killed me. [*cry of pain*]
In the gods' name, gently, servants,
when you touch my wounded flesh with your
  hands. [*making an effort to see*]
Who stands to the right of my body?   1280
Lift me gently and pull me along carefully—
me, the ill-fated and cursed,
through my father's errors. Zeus, Zeus, do you see
  this?
Here I am, the pious and god-fearing,
the one who surpassed all in virtue.   1285
I am walking to a death I foresee, my life
destroyed completely and for nothing
have I struggled at works
of piety toward men. [*sounds of pain, then singing*]
Aaaaah, aaaah!   1290
And now pain, pain comes over me.
Let me go, wretched me,
and may healing death come to me.
Destroy me completely, destroy me the ill-fated
  one.

I long for a double-edged sword   1295
to cut through
and put my life to rest.
O wretched curse of my father!
Some murderous evil inherited
from ancient ancestors   1300
is spilling over against me
and doesn't stop.
It comes upon me—why me?
I deserve no evil! [*groans of pain*]
What should I say? How can I   1305
release my life and free it from the pain
of this suffering?
May the night-black
force of Hades put me, ill-fated, to rest!
ART.: [*addressing HIPPOLYTUS*] Unhappy boy,   1310
      yoked to such a misfortune!
The nobility of your mind has destroyed you.
HIPP.: [*recognizing the voice and presence of ARTEMIS*]
      O divine breath of fragrance! Even in my troubles
      I feel your presence, and my body's pains are
          eased.
      The goddess Artemis is present in this place.
ART.: Unhappy boy! She is indeed, the goddess you   1315
      love the most.
HIPP.: Do you see me, mistress, how miserable I am?
ART.: I see. But it is not lawful to shed tears from
      my eyes.
HIPP.: Your master of hunting dogs and your
      servant no longer lives.
ART.: No. And yet you die still dearest of all to me.
HIPP.: Your keeper of horses and the guardian of   1320
      your statues no longer lives.
ART.: For Cypris, who would do anything, schemed
      it all.
HIPP.: Alas, well do I know the goddess who has
      destroyed me.
ART.: She blamed you for not honouring her, and
      she was angry at your chastity.
HIPP.: One goddess, I realize now, has destroyed the
      three of us.
ART.: Yes, your father, you, and his wife as the third. 1325
HIPP.: I begin to pity my father too, for his mistakes.
ART.: He was tricked by a goddess's plans.
HIPP.: How miserable you are over what has
      happened, father.

TH.: I am ruined, my son, and have no pleasure left
      in life.
HIPP.: I grieve more for you than for myself,   1330
      because of your mistake.
TH.: If only I might die instead of you, my son.
HIPP.: O bitter gifts from your father Poseidon!
TH.: I wish they had never come to my lips!
HIPP.: Why? You would have killed me anyway,
      since you were so angry then.
TH.: My judgement was overturned by the gods!   1335
HIPP.: Alas! If only the human race could curse the
      gods!
ART.: Enough! For even in the darkness of earth
      this wilful wrath of the goddess Cypris
      will not fall upon your body unrevenged,
      thanks to your piety and noble mind.   1340
      For with my own hand I will take vengeance on
          another man,
      whoever happens to be the dearest of mortals to her,
      with these inescapable arrows.
      And to you, wretched youth, to make up for your
          misfortune,
      I will give the greatest honours in the city of Trozen. 1345
      Unwed maids before their marriages
      will shear their locks for you, and through the
          long ages
      you will enjoy their fullest mourning and tears.
      And the maidens will always think of you when
          composing their
      songs, and Phaedra's love for you   1350
      will not fall nameless into silence.
      And you, son of aged Aegeus, take
      your son into your arms and draw him close to you.
      For you killed him without knowing what you
          did, since it is natural
      for men to make mistakes when the gods so grant. 1355
      And I advise you not to hate your father,
      Hippolytus, for you have your lot in life and
          perish with it.
      Farewell! It is not right for me to behold the dead
      nor defile my sight with the last breaths of the
          dying.
      I see that you are already close to that misfortune. 1360
HIPP.: [*to ARTEMIS, as she departs*] Farewell as you
      leave, blessed maiden.
      You leave our long companionship with ease.

I will stop quarrelling with my father, since you so
 wish.
For I always obeyed your words in the past.
[*turning toward his father*]
Hipp.: Alas, alas, darkness is already coming over   1365
 my eyes.
Take hold of me, father, and straighten up my body.
Th.: [*supporting his son*] Alas, child, what are you
 doing to me, the ill-fated?
Hipp.: I have perished and see the gates of the
 underworld.
Th.: Leaving behind my blood-defiled hands?
Hipp.: No, no, for I free you from this murder.   1370
Th.: What do you say? Do you release me and free
 me from guilt?
Hipp.: Yes, and I call to witness Artemis who kills
 with her bow.

Th.: Dearest son, how noble you have shown
 yourself to your father!
Hipp.: Dearest father, farewell, a fond farewell, father!
Th.: Alas, your pious and noble mind!   1375
Hipp.: Pray that you may have such luck with your
 legitimate sons!
Th.: Don't abandon me now, son, but endure.
Hipp.: My enduring is over. I am dead, father.
 Cover my face with robes as quickly as possible.
Th.: O famous boundaries of Athens and Pallas,   1380
 you will regret the loss of this man! O wretched me!
[*addressing the statue of Aphrodite*]
How fully I will remember your evil deeds,
 Cypris!

[*THESEUS exits into the palace as servants carry in the
bodies of PHAEDRA and HIPPOLYTUS; the CHORUS
exits stage left.*]

ARISTOPHANES

Frogs

—~—

Besides being one of the great comic masterpieces of the Western theatre, *Frogs* is an extra-ordinary historical document. For a start, it is practically unique in providing us with a sustained eyewitness account of the practice of fifth-century tragedy. While the author was arguably in the business of making jokes, not recording history, Aristophanes' knowledgeable appreciation of the work of his predecessors and co-workers in the Athenian theatre was such that even his most outlandish parodies contain priceless information about the nature of theatre in ancient Greece. But the play also provides us with an almost unparalleled example of how serious a business comedy can be. No less than tragedy, comedy engages a community in a discussion of matters of the utmost concern to all, and for the festival audience that assembled in 405 B.C.E. to see *Frogs*, the matter at hand was, literally, the city's survival.

Performed exclusively for Athenians at the "local" Lenaia competition, the play was presented on the eve of the city's devastating loss of the Peloponnesian War. Although one would barely know it from the wackiness of his comedy, Aristophanes was speaking to an audience that was exhausted, frightened, and demoralized. The Spartan blockade had already ruined countless Athenians; many were on state relief and nearing starvation. Never, perhaps, in its history had Athens felt so rudderless and depleted. Not only had the city already suffered the accumulated casualties, refugees, and plague deaths from 27 years of fighting, but all its great leaders and generals were either dead, exiled, or looked upon with paranoid suspicion. Populist demagogues were whipping up the desperate citizenry to ever more irrational and self-destructive acts. Spartan offers of peace were being rejected by the radical democrats, heedless of the consequences; and as *Frogs* took the stage in 405, the enemy, thanks to the bottomless financial support of Persia, was encamped within a few miles of the city, preparing the spring offensive that would bring the Athenians to total defeat.

As if these weren't grounds enough to fear that the end of Attic culture was near, the year in which Aristophanes composed *Frogs* was also the year in which Athens, the city of theatre, had lost its last two remaining first-rate tragedians, Euripides and Sophocles. With Aeschylus, the master, long gone, this double blow of 406 must have felt ominously symbolic of the end of an era—as indeed it was.

Thus in *Frogs,* Dionysus, god of theatre, goes down to Hades for help, for only among the dead will he find a playwright wise enough to save the city with his good advice. Setting his sights at first upon the populist poet Euripides, Dionysus comes to realize, however, that the city is *already* in the grip of talk-obsessed politicians and lawless relativists (like Euripides), and that salvation lies elsewhere: in the civic ideals, high standards, and serious moral purpose equivalent with both the glory days of Athenian democracy and with the poet who best exemplified them, Aeschylus.

For the good advice he gave his audience in *Frogs*, Aristophanes was awarded the highest civic honours. The specific political recommendations he put forward in the play were enacted in reality, and upon his comedy was bestowed an extraordinary privilege never yet enjoyed at Athens by any playwright: a second performance in his lifetime. But while the play triumphed, the worst came true for Athens. Not only *did* tragedy effectively die at Athens with Euripides, but *Frogs* was to stand as the last great monument of the fearless artistic genre of Attic Old Comedy. After the decline of Athenian democratic institutions that followed on the loss of the war, the public performance of a play like *Frogs*—with its earthy humour, *ad hominem* insults, and genuine political satire—would not be possible anywhere in Europe for the next two thousand years.

ARISTOPHANES

Frogs

Translated by Jennifer Wise[1]

DRAMATIS PERSONAE
  DIONYSUS
  XANTHIAS
  HERACLES
  DEAD GUY
  CHARON
  ÆACUS
  PERSEPHONÉ'S MAID
  TWO FEMALE INNKEEPERS
  CHORUS OF FROGS/INITIATES
  EURIPIDES
  ÆSCHYLUS
  PLUTO
  MUSE OF EURIPIDES (silent)

Scene: In front of the house of Heracles, and on the banks of Acheron in Hades. Enter Dionysus, on foot, with his slave Xanthias riding on a donkey and laden with baggage. Dionysus, wearing a saffron-yellow woman's dress and effeminate theatrical footwear, is "disguised" as Heracles, with a lion-skin and club.

XANTHIAS: Hey, master, can I give 'em one of the classic slave gags?

---

1 This English version and its annotations are based on and indebted throughout to the texts, literal translations, and commentaries of Alan H. Sommerstein (*Frogs*, Aris and Phillips, 1996) and Kenneth Dover (*Frogs*, Oxford, 1993).

DIONYSUS: Sure, any one you like, except "Oof! What a load!" Please. I'm sick to death of that one...   5

XANTHIAS: OK, no problem. How about—

DIONYSUS: —whatever you want, as long as it's not "Oh, my aching back."

XANTHIAS: Hm. What about that really killer one, about—   10

DIONYSUS: —any joke will do, I told you, except the one I said—

XANTHIAS: Which was...?

DIONYSUS: ...where you shift your "load" from side to side and moan that you need to take a dump.   15

XANTHIAS: [*crestfallen*] Can't I even say that I'm so weighted down by this load that I might just have to....fart?

DIONYSUS: Not unless you're trying to make *me* gag.

XANTHIAS: [*exasperated*] Well, what's the point of my   20 carrying all this stuff, then, if I don't get to make any luggage jokes? Every comedy's got *some* baggage-handling schtick—Phrynichus's got some, and Lycis, and Ameipsias....

DIONYSUS: Well, you don't. Whenever I'm served up   25 one of those old "witticisms" in the theatre, I get home feeling.....old myself.

XANTHIAS: Great. Just great. My neck's killing me and I'm not even allowed to try to get a laugh out of it.   30

DIONYSUS: Will you just listen to his outrageous lip? Here I am, *moi*, Dionysus, son of a...wine-bottle, walking on my own two feet, so that this spoiled brat can ride on the donkey and not have to carry his load. 35

XANTHIAS: But I am carrying it, aren't I?

DIONYSUS: No, you're riding.

XANTHIAS: Yeah, but I'm carrying this...

DIONYSUS: How?

XANTHIAS: ...with difficulty! 40

DIONYSUS: No, your "burden" is being carried by the donkey.

XANTHIAS: Not *this*! I'm carrying *this* myself, by gods!

DIONYSUS: But...how can you claim to be carrying 45 it, when you are *being carried*?

XANTHIAS: Beats me....My shoulder's dislocated?

DIONYSUS: Fine, have it your own way. If you think the animal's so useless, trade places with him.

XANTHIAS: Oh, why didn't I agree to fight in that 50 sea battle?[2] I would have won my freedom...and then I could really tell you where to go....

DIONYSUS: Dismount, swine. We're here. This is the very door at which I want to make my first stop. Hey! Boy! [*getting no response, he uses his club as a* 55 *knocker*] Hey! Slave!

HERACLES: [*from within*] Who's there? Knocks like a Centaur. Must be for me. [*opens door and collapses in helpless laughter at the sight of Dionysus's get-up*] What the.....? [*convulsions*] 60

DIONYSUS: [*whispering*] Hey, Xanthias...

XANTHIAS: Huh?

DIONYSUS: Did you see that?

XANTHIAS: What?

DIONYSUS: How scared he was? 65

XANTHIAS: Yeah, scared you might be wacko.

HERACLES: Help, by Demeter! Help me stop laughing! It's no use, I gotta laugh.

DIONYSUS: Come out for a minute, will you? I've got something to ask you. 70

HERACLES: My lion's-skin? Over a prom dress?[3] What's going on here? A club, and those faggy shoes?[4] What's the meaning of this? Where have you been in this absurd get-up?

DIONYSUS: Well, you see, it all began aboard the 75 good ship Cleisthenes[5]...

HERACLES: That explains it...[*camping*] "You-hoo, sailors; all hands on dick!"

DIONYSUS: We sank twelve or thirteen enemy ships!

HERACLES: [*lisping*] What, just you two? 80

DIONYSUS: By Apollo, yes!

XANTHIAS: ....And then I woke up.

DIONYSUS: Seriously, there I was, on deck, reading this great tragedy by Euripides, *Andromeda*, when suddenly I was struck with a powerful longing, I 85 can't tell you how...big it was.

HERACLES: A longing? How...big *was* it?

DIONYSUS: Like Molon.[6]

HERACLES: For a woman?

DIONYSUS: No, actually. 90

HERACLES: For a boy, then?

DIONYSUS: No, no.

HERACLES: A man?

DIONYSUS: Eurghch!

HERACLES: I guess that leaves...Cleisthenes? 95

DIONYSUS: Listen to me; this is no laughing matter. I'm really not well; this passion is consuming me!

HERACLES: What sort of passion are we talking about, bro?

DIONYSUS: I dare not speak its name; but I can give 100 you an analogy you'll understand: have you ever in your life been suddenly seized by a longing for...I don't know, a bowl of...soup?

HERACLES: A bowl of soup? Well, yes, yes, I have, by god! 105

DIONYSUS: So...you see what I'm saying?

---

2 The naval battle of Arginousai, which was fought and won in the summer of 406 B.C.E. with the help of slaves. This was the first time slaves were used by the Athenian navy, and they were rewarded for their participation with their liberty.

3 Lit., a saffron-yellow gown, expensive and believed to be sexy, and typically worn by women on special occasions.

4 Lit., *kothurnoi*, soft leather boots, wearable on either foot, with pointed toes. Associated both with women and with Dionysus, they were later regarded as the footwear of the tragic actor.

5 Used by Aristophanes throughout his plays as a homosexual joke.

6 An actor known for his size.

HERACLES: Oh! as far as a bowl of soup goes, I understand you perfectly.

DIONYSUS: Well, that's the kind of desire that's been devouring me...but for Euripides. 110

HERACLES: Ugh! He's dead!

DIONYSUS: And nothing's going to stop me from going after him.

HERACLES: To the bottom of Hades?

DIONYSUS: Even *lower* than the bottom, if necessary. 115

HERACLES: But what do you want with him?

DIONYSUS: I need a great poet; for as Euripides says, "some are dead and gone, and those that live are bad."[7]

HERACLES: What about Iophon,[8] Sophocles' son? 120

DIONYSUS: He's the only good one left...but I've got my doubts even about him.

HERACLES: Well what about Sophocles himself? If you must bring someone back from Hades, why not him? He was way better than Euripides. 125

DIONYSUS: No, I want to give Iophon a chance to prove himself first, without his father's help, see what he's capable of. Anyway, Euripides is much more likely to go A.W.O.L.—he was always a bit of a sneak, whereas Sophocles was so easy-going...he's 130 probably as content in Hades as he was on earth.

HERACLES: And what about Agathon?[9]

DIONYSUS: He's left me as well;[10] a good poet, too, sorely missed by his...friends.[11]

HERACLES: Sad. Where did he go? 135

DIONYSUS: To Macedonia. Or was that Macaronia? Macademia?[12] Anyway, he's eating well there, apparently.

HERACLES: And Xenocles?

DIONYSUS: Still alive, unfortunately! 140

HERACLES: And Pythangelus?

XANTHIAS: Notice how nobody ever mentions me? Or my shoulder, which is now destroyed.

HERACLES: But come on—there are dozens of young kids around, churning out tragedies by the 145 thousands. For sheer verbiage, they beat Euripides by a mile.

DIONYSUS: Withered little raisins, all of them, cacophonous wankers, piss-artists to a man. Sure, they might be granted a tragic Chorus once; but 150 what do they do? Shoot their whole wad on the first date, never to be heard from again. No, look where you will these days, you won't find a single poet with enough balls to utter a truly noble phrase.

HERACLES: How...many balls? 155

DIONYSUS: Ballsy enough to dare such lines as, "Heaven, Zeus's flop-house,"[13] or "the foot of Time,"[14] or "a heart that will not swear by the sacred...things, a tongue that takes an oath, while the soul remains...out of it."[15] 160

HERACLES: You *like* that sort of thing?

DIONYSUS: I love it.

HERACLES: But it's idiotic—and you know it!

DIONYSUS: "Don't come trespassing in my mind; you have a brain of your own to keep thoughts 165 in."[16]

HERACLES: ....garbage, pure unadulterated crap!

DIONYSUS: Listen, Mr. Suddenly-an-Expert-on-Art, stick to food, OK?

XANTHIAS: Me? They couldn't care less... 170

DIONYSUS: Look, I've dolled myself up to look like you for a reason. I was hoping you might have some travel tips—maybe the names of some of the people you stayed with down there in Hades? You

---

7 A quotation from Euripides' *Oeneus*.

8 Tragic poet, said to have written 50 plays, one of which competed against Euripides' *Hippolytus* in 428.

9 Tragic poet and lover of Pausanias, known for his physical beauty, distinctive poetic style, and many artistic innovations.

10 Agathon left Athens for Macedonia sometime after 408, invited there by King Archelaus.

11 "Friends" here might also mean "lovers," for Agathon was open about his "passive homosexuality." (See A. Sommerstein, *Frogs*, 1996:163–164.)

12 An untranslatable pun, lit. "the banquets of the blest,"

where "of the blest" (Greek *makaron*) sounds like "of the Macedonians" (Gr. *Makedonon)*. Macedonian feasts were famous for their lavishness.

13 Misquoted by Dionysus from Euripides' *Wise Melanippe*. Euripides actually wrote "dwelling-house."

14 Appears both in *Alexandros* (frag. 42) and *Bacchae* (889).

15 An inept paraphrase of *Hippolytus*, 1044: "My tongue has sworn; my mind remains unpledged."

16 Another mangled paraphrase, possibly from *Andromache* or *Andromeda* (frag. 144).

know, when you were down there getting that dog, Cerberus? I could really use the names of the best ports, pie-shops, prostitutes, highways, rest-stops, turn-offs, and hotels with the fewest bedbugs.... 175

XANTHIAS: Am I...invisible?

HERACLES: You? Go to Hades? Have you lost your mind? 180

DIONYSUS: Just tell me the best way to get there; I want a route that's neither too hot, nor too cold.

HERACLES: Oh, well, let's see....um...the best route....Ah, yes! You could go via the Rope and Stool—if you don't mind getting "hung up" a bit on the way.... 185

DIONYSUS: No. I'd feel a bit choked up by that one.

HERACLES: There is another path, very short and "well-beaten." Get it? Well-beaten, as in mortar and pestle? 190

DIONYSUS: You mean hemlock?

HERACLES: Exactly.

DIONYSUS: Too cold. Your legs go all frozen.

HERACLES: Well, there's a super-quick and easy route. Downhill all the way. 195

DIONYSUS: Now you're talking. I'm not really much of a walker....

HERACLES: Great; then just run on over to the Potters' Quarter. 200

DIONYSUS: And...?

HERACLES: Climb up the observation tower...

DIONYSUS: [confused] To watch the races?

HERACLES: ...keep your eye on the torch, the starting signal. And when they yell "on your mark, get set, go!" Well, you go. 205

DIONYSUS: Where?

HERACLES: Down.

DIONYSUS: Splat? Humpty Dionysus omelette?[17] No thanks. 210

HERACLES: Which way, then?

DIONYSUS: [whining] The one you took.

HERACLES: Ah! That's the long way. First you come to the edge of a huge, bottomless lake.[18]

DIONYSUS: Do I...swim? 215

HERACLES: There's an old ferry operator who'll take you across in his little boat. Two obols.[19]

DIONYSUS: Two obols? [to audience] Don't leave home without 'em, right? [to Heracles] Do they really take obols down there? 220

HERACLES: Theseus introduced them.[20] Anyway, next you'll see snakes and monsters.

DIONYSUS: Don't try to frighten me...I am going, you know.

HERACLES: ...then this giant sea of mud, the Eternal Dung-flats, where they keep the people who insulted a guest, or bounced a cheque on a call-boy; the people who beat their mother, or punched their father, or swore a false oath, or copied out any of those shitty song lyrics of Morsimus[21].... 225 230

DIONYSUS: Or, while they're at it, anyone who's learned that stupid line-dance of Kinesias.[22]

HERACLES: Then the sound of pipes will surround you, and you'll see a beautiful light, just like we have here, and fragrant meadows, and happy bands of men and women, clapping hands. 235

DIONYSUS: Happy, clapping bands?

HERACLES: Mystic initiates—a spiritual cult.

XANTHIAS: So what am I? The sacrificial cow? That's it; I've had it. [puts down bags] 240

HERACLES: They'll explain everything else you need to know. They live close to Pluto's palace, too, on the same road. Goodbye, brother. Good luck. [exits]

DIONYSUS: And good health to you too. [to Xanthais] You! Pick up those bags! 245

XANTHIAS: But I was just putting them down...

DIONYSUS: And hurry up about it!

---

17 Untranslatable pun, depending on the Gr. word *thrion*, which refers both to a delicious dish (stuffed fig-leaf), and to a hemisphere of the human brain.

18 Acheron, the body of water that must be crossed by the souls of the dead, sometimes represented as a river.

19 Exactly what the members of the audience paid to get into the theatre.

20 Having visited Hades to abduct Persephone, Theseus was released from imprisonment there by Heracles. An Athenian in mythology, Theseus might have brought Athenian customs down with him.

21 Eye-doctor, great-nephew of Aeschlyus, and tragic poet whom Aristophanes often ridiculed.

22 Another frequent target of Aristophanes. A sickly dithyrambic poet, Kinesias was ridiculed, among other things, for his work in the *pyrrhikhe*, a competitive group dance performed naked with full military gear.

XANTHIAS: [*the donkey is gone*] Please, master, I beg you. Can't you hire someone? [*a corpse is being carried on a litter across the stage*] What about some dead guy, who's being carried down there anyway?   250

DIONYSUS: And if I can't find one…?

XANTHIAS: Then I'll go.

DIONYSUS: All right; fine. Ah! here comes one now.   255
Hey, there! You…yes, I'm talking to you, dead guy.
Would you mind carrying some of my stuff down to Hades with you?

DEAD GUY: How many pieces?

DIONYSUS: Just this.   260

DEAD GUY: That'll be two drachma.

DIONYSUS: Are you kidding!?

DEAD GUY: Fine. [*to his bearers*] Move on.

DIONYSUS: Wait a minute, wait a minute. I'm sure we can work something out…   265

DEAD GUY: Flat rate, two drachma, or no deal.

DIONYSUS: Hold on. [*counting out spare change*]
Here's….nine obols.

DEAD GUY: Nine obols!? No thanks—I'd rather live….[*is carried off*]   270

XANTHIAS: Damned unions! All right, I'll go.

DIONYSUS: You're a good man. Let's get to the boat.

CHARON: Ahoy, there! Pull 'er along shore.

XANTHIAS: What's that? A lake?

DIONYSUS: Holy Poseidon, it's the one Heracles   275
mentioned, and I see the boat.

XANTHIAS: Hey! there's Charon.

DIONYSUS: Ahoy, Charon!

XANTHIAS: Ahoy, Charon!

BOTH: Ahoy, Charon![23]   280

CHARON: [*calling to no-one in particular*] Anyone for an end to trouble and misfortune? Anyone for the Plains of Oblivion? The infernal rope factory? Pet Cemetery, Purgatory, and Port Alberni[24]—all aboard!   285

DIONYSUS: Oh, that's me.

CHARON: Get aboard then, on the double.

DIONYSUS: Um…would you mind repeating the um….what did you say your first stop was?

CHARON: [*generic annoyance*] Ah, go to hell…   290

DIONYSUS: Excellent. For two, please.

CHARON: I don't take slaves—unless he's a veteran.[25]

XANTHIAS: But I couldn't enlist! I had pink-eye.

CHARON: Sorry, you'll have to run around the lake.

XANTHIAS: And where exactly am I going?   295

CHARON: Just past The Rock of Deadly Thirst, there's a juicebar.

DIONYSUS: Have you got that?

XANTHIAS: Yes, I've got it alright—bad luck!

CHARON: Come, sit to your oar. [*calling out*] Anyone   300
else for the other side? This is your final boarding call. Hey. What are you doing?

DIONYSUS: What am I doing? I am sitting on the oar, as you said.

CHARON: Not *on* it, fatso, *at* it.[26]   305

DIONYSUS: Oh. There.

CHARON: Well? Put your hands out. Come on, stretch your arms.

DIONYSUS: [*does so, too literally*] There.

CHARON: Enough of this nonsense—come on, feet   310
against the—right. Now row! Like you mean it!

DIONYSUS: Row! How am I supposed to know how to row? I'm a fair-weather, land-lubbery sea-virgin!

CHARON: It's not difficult; and as soon as you start, you'll hear some gorgeous singing.   315

DIONYSUS: Who…sings?

CHARON: The Frogs. With voices of swans; beautiful.

DIONYSUS: All right, set the rhythm.

CHARON: Ewwww-one! Aaaand two! Aaaand…

FROGS: Brekekekex, ko-ax, ko-ax,   320
Brekekekex, ko-ax.
Slime-covered offspring of the bog,
Raising sweet voices from the fog,
Melodious hymns of musical frogs
To Lord Dionysus, he's our god: 325
Ko-ax, ko-ax.

---

23 Comic allusion to a well-known triple invocation from a satyr-play by Achaeus, *Aethon*; in performance, some bit of business should make this funny.

24 Lit., Tainaron, an actual geographical location. Dover suggests that its function might be to "give a sour topical twist" to the otherwise mythological catalogue of hellish destinations. Any well-known local hell-hole may be substituted in performance.

---

25 Already immortalized himself by serving in the fleet at Arginousai.

26 Dressed in the padding of the comic actor's costume, Dionysus would have a fat belly.

On holiday feasts, when drinking grog
In honour of Zeus' son they throng
Drunk and hung-over, stumbling along,
Towards our pagan synagogue.   330
    Ko-ax, ko-ax.
DIONYSUS: Listen to me, ko-ax, ko-ax,
  my bum's gone numb, ko-ax, ko-ax.
FROGS: Brekekekex, ko-ax, ko-ax.
DIONYSUS: They don't give a damn.   335
FROGS: Ko-ax, ko-ax.
DIONYSUS: I hope you get warts, you boring
  amphibians!
FROGS: [*faster*] You think we're boring, imbecile?
  The Muses love our domicile   340
  Where grows the reedy chlorophyll,
  Which is so very versatile—
  Makes Pan-pipes sing like whippoorwills.
  We also make the marshy quills
  That make the lyre Apollo trills!   345
  Brekekekex, ko-ax, ko-ax.
DIONYSUS: There're blisters oozing from my hole
  Because of all this rigmarole!
  I think they're going to burst and say:
FROGS: Brekekekex, ko-ax, ko-ax.   350
DIONYSUS: *I beg you*, kermits, stop it, eh?
FROGS: [*faster still*] No no we won't,
  We will not stop
  But louder sing, if anything!
  On sunny days   355
  We love to hop
  Through galingale
  And marshy mop
  And join as Zeus' rain goes drop:
  Kerplunketsplishsplashdribbleplop.[27]   360
  Brekekekex, ko-ax, ko-ax.
DIONYSUS: [*taking over the song and the rhythm*]
    Now I forbid you toads to sing!
FROGS: Oh, what a cruel and heartless thing!
DIONYSUS: I'm looking out for Number One.   365
FROGS: Brekekekex, ko-ax, ko-ax.
DIONYSUS: Oh, croak away; see if I care.
FROGS: And so we will,
  The live-long day,
  You'll see our tonsils   370

As we say:
  "Brekekekex, ko-ax, ko-ax."
DIONYSUS: [*taking over, and winning*]
  You will not get the best of me:
  Brekekekex, ko-ax, ko-ax.   375
FROGS: Oh, no! Oh, no! We cannot lose!
DIONYSUS: Oh, yes, oh yes, you're history;
  Cuz' I'll keep up my verbal blast
  Till I'm the victor in this match!
  [*He somehow vanquishes them, probably by blowing*   380
  an enormous fart.[28] *The song abruptly ends.*] Ha! I
  knew I'd put a stop to you; your "ko-ax" is toast.
CHARON: Enough, enough already! Ship oars! Pull
  alongside; and out you get. Hey! Aren't you
  forgetting something?   385
DIONYSUS: Take your lousy two obols. Now, where's
  Xanthias? Xanthias? Ahoy, Xanthias!
XANTHIAS: [*from a distance*] Ahoy!
DIONYSUS: Get over here.
XANTHIAS: Hi there, master.   390
DIONYSUS: So, what'dya see on the walk around?
XANTHIAS: Darkness and mud....
DIONYSUS: Did you see any of those people Heracles
  was telling us about, the father-beaters and
  perjurers?   395
XANTHIAS: What, didn't you? [*nods to audience*]
DIONYSUS: Ha! by Poseidon! You're right; the place
  is crawling with them. Well, what do we do now?
XANTHIAS: Get going, if you ask me. This is the
  place where Heracles said there'd be all those lions   400
  and tigers and bears.
DIONYSUS: He's such a show-off! I bet he was
  exaggerating, just to scare me off. In fact, I think
  he's secretly jealous of me—afraid that everybody
  might discover that I'm more macho than he is!   405
  Ha, what would *that* do to his reputation? But he'll
  be sorry he messed with Dionysus! I hope we *do*
  meet some monster. Bag a couple of beasts. I'll
  show him who's boss around here.
XANTHIAS: Sure, whatev—Listen! I hear something.   410
DIONYSUS: [*terrified*] Where, where?
XANTHIAS: Behind you!
DIONYSUS: I'll lead the way.
XANTHIAS: No! It's in front.

---

27 An eight-syllable Greek word, full of "p"-sounds.

28 See G. Wills, *Hermes* 97, 1969:313–15.

DIONYSUS: Ok, you lead then.　415

XANTHIAS: Oh my god! It's an enormous....monster!

DIONYSUS: What's it look like?

XANTHIAS: Dreadful, terrible! But the thing is, it keeps changing shape; now it's a bull, now a mule; now, now it's....[*whistles*] an amazing babe!　420

DIONYSUS: That does it; I'm going in there...

XANTHIAS: No, no; she's changed again....Now she's.....a bit of a dog.

DIONYSUS: Ah! It's Empusa!

XANTHIAS: [*madly improvising*] Yes, that's it! And her　425 whole...face is on fire!

DIONYSUS: And is one of her legs made of bronze?

XANTHIAS: Yes! and the other one is made of horseshit![29]

DIONYSUS: Ah! Help! Get me out of here!　430

XANTHIAS: With pleasure!

DIONYSUS: [*flees into the audience*[30]] Help, help, Priest, save me, please; you want me to come to the cast party after the show, don't you?

XANTHIAS: Help! We're going to die! Heracles!　435

DIONYSUS: Don't, *don't* say that name.

XANTHIAS: OK. Help, Dionysus!

DIONYSUS: Shhh! Not that one either!

XANTHIAS: [*to the imaginary ghost, making hocus-pocus gestures*] "I banish thee, I banish thee, I　440 banish thee." Master. Get over here.

DIONYSUS: .....yes?

XANTHIAS: You can relax now; everything's fine, and I can say, like Hegelochus, "Ask not what your country can do for you, but what you can do for　445 your cunt...."[31]

DIONYSUS: —try!

XANTHIAS: Empusa's gone.

DIONYSUS: You swear?

XANTHIAS: I swear.　450

DIONYSUS: Swear by Zeus?

XANTHIAS: I swear by Zeus.

DIONYSUS: Say it again.

XANTHIAS: "It." OK, OK, I swear by Zeus.

DIONYSUS: Boy oh boy! I tell you, one look at that　455 Empusa's face, and I went white!

XANTHIAS: Interesting [*pointing to the seat of Dionysus' dress*] how *this* went such a lovely brown!

DIONYSUS: [*tragic pose*] Ahhhh! Why all these slings and arrows of fortune? What god can I accuse of　460 tormenting me like this?

XANTHIAS: Maybe it was "Zeus's flop-house" or "Time's Foot." [*noise off*] Hist!

DIONYSUS: What's the matter now?

XANTHIAS: Don't you hear?　465

DIONYSUS: What?

XANTHIAS: The sound of pipes.

DIONYSUS: Yes, I certainly do, and I detect a most mystical whiff of incense, if I'm not mistaken. But Shhh! let's be quiet; if we hide we might be able　470 to spy on them.

CHORUS: Iacchus, oh! Iacchus! Iacchus, oh! Iacchus!

XANTHIAS: Listen, Master; yes, it must be the initiates, the ones he told us about: they're singing that sacred hymn, by Marilyn Manson.[32]　475

DIONYSUS: I think you're right, but let's just watch from here for another few minutes.

CHORUS: [*enters in procession, all carrying incense—or literally, torches—and wearing extremely grungy old clothes*[33]] Iacchus, my Lord, Iacchus!　480
Iacchus, my Lord, Iacchus!
Join our company, O-oh.
In your sacred grove, O-oh!
Come and dance with us, O-oh
Oh Iacchus, won't you come back home.　485

Toss your head, my lord, O-oh,
Crowned with myrtle-boughs, O-oh,
Feet dance on the ground, O-oh,
Oh, Iacchus, won't you get on down.

---

29 Lit., cow dung.

30 To the front row, reserved for dignitaries, where the Priest of Dionysus sat.

31 Reference to an untranslatable slip of the tongue made in the theatre by an actor named Hegelochus. During a performance of Euripides' *Orestes*, he gave the world *galen* the wrong pitch, changing its meaning from "calm" to "a skunk." The original is "After the stormy waves, I see 'tis calm again." For the Greeks, the skunk, or pole-cat, was a particularly bad omen.

32 Lit., Diagoras, an infamously militant atheist, and hence, a joke.

33 It was traditional for initiates to wear their oldest clothes for the ceremony.

Lead the sacred dance, O-oh, 490
Taught by Graces three, O-oh,
Whirling wild and free, O-oh,
Oh, Iacchus, won't you dance with me.

XANTHIAS: Holy daughter of Demeter, I smell rump
roast![34] 495

DIONYSUS: Can't you keep your mind off your
sausage for five minutes?

CHORUS: Brandish the torches; spread the light.
Iacchus, Iacchus! Our delight!
Meadows shine like starry seas 500
When you ignite our mysteries!
Old folks lose the weight of years;
The careworn shed their anxious fears;
And all grow young when dancing here.
Let's join in holy ecstasy 505
Upon this flowery water-lea.

CHORUS LEADER: [addressing the audience] Silence
brethren, and listen up. Are there any unbelievers
out there, any blasphemers who have never
witnessed or partaken of an authentic theatre festival 510
before? Anyone not initiated into the Dionysian
revels of that drunken head-banger, Cratinus?[35] If
so, be gone; you are not wanted here—You, who
love to snicker at serious things, you bad citizens
you! You selfishly let civil strife consume us all, you 515
corrupters of public office, who line your pockets
while the city flounders; and that includes anyone
who surrenders his fort or his ship, or who's a
damned tax-collector like Thorycion, who nevertheless makes money on the black market exporting 520
sanctioned natural resources from Ægina to
Epidaurus, and who brokers secret arms deals for the
enemy, for example, or shits on the altar of Hecaté[36]
while headlining in some dithyramb.[37] Be gone,

you politicians who nibble away at the subsidies of 525
the playwrights, just because you've always been
their favourite target of ridicule on this illustrious
platform, the stage; to all such people I say, and I
repeat, you are not welcome here; be gone, and
make room for our initiates. [to Chorus] Now lift 530
your voices up, and start your all-night ecstasy.

CHORUS: Through the flowery meadows wide
We kick our feet up—we've imbibed!
We've got courage to deride:
Satire is our only guide. 535

Goddess, saviour, let us raise
Voices up in grateful praise;
She will save us from perdition,
Even despite that creep Thorycion.

CHORUS LEADER: Let's address our hymns now to 540
Demeter, Queen of the Harvest, who makes the
land fruitful.

CHORUS: Demeter, goddess of the corn,
Keep your chorus safe till morn.
May we play, cavort and dance 545
With no disasters, no ill-chance.

And may we say hilarious things:
Some that tickle, some that sting;
And while you're at it, gracious lord,
Let me win the academy award! 550

CHORUS LEADER: All right, then. Now it's time to
summon a certain pretty young god...Dionysus!
Lord of the Dance!

CHORUS: Dionysus, glory be!
Join our festive company. 555
Meet the goddess,
Show us how
To make our moves
Without fatigue.
[refrain] Dionysus, Lord of the dance, Iacchus will 560
accompany me!
You cleverly thought of making a gag
Of dressing us all in tatters and rags;
You steered us through a comic strait
Without ruining our financial state.[38]

---

34 Literally, pork, which was roasted at such festivals in
honour of Demeter, but with a *double entendre*, also implying "vulva."

35 Comic poet who in 423 beat Aristophanes' *Clouds*, possibly for sentimental reasons, as it seems he was making
a sort of comeback after a long career as an alcoholic.

36 On the offerings of food left at a shrine of the goddess.

37 Again, the joke targets Kinesias, both literally (on account of his well-known problems with diarrhea), and
figuratively (exploiting his undisguised impiety).

38 By choosing to dress the members of the chorus as Initiates, Aristophanes solved what could have been a crip-

[*refrain*] Dionysus, Lord of the dance, Iacchus will 565
    accompany me!
I just stole a little peek—
A luscious beauty, feet so neat—
As her ripped-up rag-holes rippled,
What did I see but a cute little nipple!
[*refrain*] Dionysus, Lord of the dance, Iacchus will 570
    accompany me!

DIONYSUS: Hey, I'd love to join this throng;
    She's the one—I'll tag along...
XANTHIAS: They're playing my song...
CHORUS: Now, shall we, all of us,
    Satirize Archidemus? 575
    Still without his adult teeth,
    He can't join up with the élite,[39]
    But what a first-rate politician!
    Number one with slobs and cretins!

    Cleisthenes, he lost his chum, 580
    Pulls the cheek-hairs from his bum,
    Weeping at the grave all day,
    Keening with a tear-stained face,
    Bending over, just in case,
    Howling Studley Do-Right's name. 585

    As for Callias, they say,
    He squandered dad's big dick away;
    Every battle he begins:
    Lion loses, pussy wins.[40]

---

pling financial problem during wartime, when money
was scarce, while at the same time preparing for his later
jokes about Euripides' taste for dressing tragic characters
in rags.

[39] Notorious politician, ridiculed for many things, among
them his alleged foreign descent and "bleary-eyed"
squint. The joke hinges on an untranslatable pun on the
word *phrateres,* suggesting in this context both "gaining
admission into an aristocratic religious guild" and "growing permanent teeth."

[40] Hereditary priest of the Eleusinian Mysteries, addict of
Sophistic education, and all-round profligate, Callias was
often ridiculed in comedy and elsewhere for the speed
with which he relieved himself of his enormous inheritance. The literal meaning here seems to be something
like: "fighting at sea dressed in a lion-skin of/with cunt."

DIONYSUS: Um, excuse me, could you please tell us 590
    where Pluto lives? We're strangers to these
    parts....and have just arrived.
CHORUS: You're there; his door is right here.
DIONYSUS: Slave? Baggage.
XANTHIAS: Again with the bug-infested luggage.... 595
CHORUS LEADER: As for me, I'll go with you,
    Dishy girls, and women too
    With my sacred torch upheld
    To your dances on the veld.
CHORUS: To the flowered fields we go, 600
    Sprinkled with the blooming rose;
    Dancing lovely special rites
    Blessed by the Fates tonight.
    For we alone will see the light,
    Having led a righteous life. 605
    We're religious, we're most dear—
    To foreigners, and those right here.
DIONYSUS: Let's see! How should I knock? I wonder
    if there's a correct way...do you know how the
    natives do it around here? 610
XANTHIAS: Stop stalling, Heracles. Why don't you
    show us some of that great bravery you were
    bragging about?
DIONYSUS: [*thumping with club*] Hey! Boy!
ÆACUS: Who's there? 615
DIONYSUS: Mighty Heracles.
ÆACUS: Oh! It's you! You impudent, shameless dog-
    napper, you awful, awful, awful man! You stole our
    dog, Cerberus, when I was on duty—you nabbed
    him and grabbed him and almost strangled him, 620
    you fiend! But I've got you in my clutches now,
    puppy-poacher! And the black stones of Styx, the
    rocks of blood-soaked Acheron, and all the horrid
    howling hounds of Hell will have their way with
    you now; our hundred-headed Hydra will....hurt 625
    you, hard, by tearing you limb from limb; our
    Spanish Sere-Sucker will liquify your lungs and the
    Bitches of Burnaby will hack out your kidneys and
    grind up your bloody guts; just hold on a second,
    while I go get them...[*exits*] 630
XANTHIAS: Master, what are you doing down there?
DIONYSUS: [*having peed himself in terror*] I'm making
    some....holy water. Call the initiates!
XANTHIAS: Get up, you twit, before somebody sees
    you. 635

DIONYSUS: [*rising*] No, really, I don't feel well. I think I'm going to faint. Give me a cold compress, for my heart.

XANTHIAS: [*from luggage*] Here.

DIONYSUS: Could you apply it yourself? 640

XANTHIAS: [*Dionysus gestures oddly*] Well, Golden Gods! So that's where you keep your heart!

DIONYSUS: It slithered down, with fear.

XANTHIAS: You really are the most cowardly god alive. 645

DIONYSUS: What! Me? Cowardly! I, who had the presence of mind to ask you for a compress! Who else would have thought of that!

XANTHIAS: Meaning?

DIONYSUS: A *real* coward would have just laid there, 650 overcome by the fumes; whereas I stood up—and what's more, I even wiped myself!

XANTHIAS: Oh, Poseidon, a miraculous feat of bravery.

DIONYSUS: Yes it was. Anyway, tell me that you 655 weren't scared shitless at the sound of all those terrifying threats.

XANTHIAS: No, actually, I wasn't.

DIONYSUS: Really. Well then, since you claim to have such intestinal fortitude, I think you should 660 become me—here, take my club and lion-skin.....if you're so brave and fearless, and I'll play the baggage-carrier.

XANTHIAS: [*resignedly*] OK, all right, hand 'em over...you're the master [*puts costume on*]. And 665 voila—Xanthi-acles! You think I've got what it takes to play the part of a god?

DIONYSUS: The god of Village Idiots....Here, I'll take the bags.

PERSEPHONÉ'S MAID: Heracles! Darling! is it really 670 you? Come in. As soon as my mistress Persephoné heard you were coming, she started baking buns, making cakes and rolls and barbequing an entire bull—she even whipped up two or three batches of your favourite soup! Hurry! Come on in! 675

XANTHIAS: No, thanks, really, I'm fine.

ATTENDANT: By Apollo, you will come in. She's stewed a chicken with her own two hands, and baked some sweets, and right now she's mixing up some first-rate wine. Come on.... 680

XANTHIAS: Really; thanks, I'm fine, honest.

ATTENDANT: Don't be ridiculous! You must! The after-dinner entertainment is already waiting for you....the flute-girl's gorgeous, and there's two or three dancing girls who— 685

XANTHIAS: —wait....did you say....dancing girls?

ATTENDANT: And young ones, too, freshly plucked ...all over. So get in there; the cook's about to take the fish off the fire; the table's already being set.

XANTHIAS: Fine. Yes. Well, then! Why don't you, ah, 690 run along then, and tell those dancing-girls that the big kahuna is on his way. Slave! Come on; follow me. And pick up that baggage!

DIONYSUS: Just a minute, buster. You're not telling me that you took this little costume-switching joke 695 seriously? Really! Now stop this silliness and pick up those bags, and carry them inside, alright?

XANTHIAS: How can you even *think* about taking this back—you *gave* it to me!

DIONYSUS: I'm not thinking about it, I'm doing it. 700 Gimme that skin....

XANTHIAS: See how I am treated? Ye gods, be my judges!

DIONYSUS: Gods? What gods? Are you so stupid, such an utter fool as to imagine that you, a slave 705 and a mortal, could be the son of Alcmene?[41]

XANTHIAS: Fine—take them! But just remember that one day, you might need me—maybe not today, maybe not tomorrow, but soon, god willing.

CHORUS: We've just seen the act of a sensible man; 710
A politician like him never lacks for a plan.
He'll always cross over, come danger or sleet,
To walk on the sunnier side of the street;
He's not paralyzed by a change in conditions,
Won't stick to his guns or a principled position; 715
Call him a genius, or call him a sleaze—
Hell, just call him Theramenes![42]

---

41 This is funny because, as the audience well knew, Heracles himself *was* a slave and a mortal before becoming a god.

42 A politician notorious for changing his politics to suit his career—fiercely oligarchic during the anti-democratic coup of 411, outspokenly democratic when this regime fell—Theramenes was called "the *kothurnos*," the boot that fits either foot. The metaphors in this passage refer to changing sides on a ship, not the street.

DIONYSUS: Well wouldn't it really be just too absurd
    For my slave to get lucky with one of those birds?
    Picture my Xanthias, reclined on a cushion,   720
    Kissing that dancer in blissful seclusion;
    He'd ache for a piss and he'd call for the pottle,
    And catch me at work—giving willy a throttle;[43]
    Sweet vengeance he'd take, now he'd be in my place,
    And punch me decisively right in the face.   725
    What a scoundrel this slave is. He'd sock me a blow,
    Putting both of my lights out—and stopping this
      show![44]

INNKEEPER: Plathané, Plathané! Come quick! It's
    that nut-case, the one who barged into our inn that
    time and ate up sixteen of loaves of bread.   730

PLATHANE: My god, it's him all right!

XANTHIAS: Somebody's going to get in trou-ble...

INNKEEPER: And not only that, but twenty helpings
    of beef—worth half an obol apiece.

XANTHIAS: Somebody's going to get a beat-ing....   735

INNKEEPER: And I don't even *know* how much
    garlic.

DIONYSUS: You're raving, good woman, you don't
    know what you're saying.

INNKEEPER: So you thought I wouldn't recognize   740
    you in those shoes, did you? Remember all that
    salted fish?

PLATHANE: And all of that fresh cheese he devoured,
    containers and all...

INNKEEPER: But when I gave him the bill, he just   745
    shot me this *look*, and started...roaring!

XANTHIAS: Yup; sounds like him alright; he does
    that everywhere.

PLATHANE: And then he drew his sword, like some
    kind of maniac.   750

INNKEEPER: That's right, he did.

PLATHANE: And we were so terrified that we
    practically flew up to the rafters, while he just
    stormed right out of there like a tornado, tearing
    up all the carpets along with him.[45]   755

XANTHIAS: Yup; pure Heracles.

INNKEEPER: We can't let him get away with this.
    Quick; call that famous lawyer, Cleon.[46]

PLATHANE: Or whatshisname, that ambulance-
    chaser, Hyperbolus.[47] He'll indict him on all   760
    charges and clobber him in the courts.

INNKEEPER: You disgusting pig! [*making a fist*] Oh,
    how I'd love to knock your teeth out, the ones you
    used to gobble up my stock—

PLATHANE: —and throw you in the slammer—[48]   765

INNKEEPER: —and slit open your sausage-
    swallowing throat with a...sickle. I'm going to get
    Cleon; he'll haul your sorry ass to court this very
    day and force you to cough up the evidence.

DIONYSUS: Xanthias, may I die on this very spot if   770
    you're not my absolute best friend.

XANTHIAS: No way. Forget it. I'm not going to
    pretend to be Heracles again.

DIONYSUS: Oh, don't say that, sweet, lovely
    Xanthias.   775

XANTHIAS: [*mimicking Dionysus obnoxiously*] But I'm
    just a slave and a mortal; how could I be the son
    of Alcmeme?

DIONYSUS: You're right, you're right. I know you're
    angry, and I don't blame you. Here; hit me; go   780
    ahead; I deserve it. Look, I swear this is the last
    time: if I ever take this costume back from you
    again, may I die in disgusting agony[49]—myself,
    my wife, my children, all of my friends, and I'll
    even throw in....Archidemus' squint.[50]   785

---

46 Leading populist politician and the main satyric target
    of Aristophanes' *Knights* (and appearing in many other
    plays as well). Here the joke hinges on the fact that Cleon
    repeatedly harassed Aristophanes with lawsuits, and had
    a reputation for vexatious litigation generally.

47 Another famous prosecutor, much derided throughout
    Aristophanes' works, and the central figure in at least
    three separate comedies by non-Aristophanic play-
    wrights. Banished from Athens in 417, he was eventu-
    ally assassinated in exile by the opponents of democracy.

48 Lit., the Barathron, a rocky pit just outside Athens into
    which criminals were thrown.

49 A conventional oath made hilarious by the fact that
    Heracles did, in fact, end up dying in unspeakable agony
    thanks to a certain (poisoned) garment his wife gave him
    to wear by accident. See Sophocles' *Women of Trachis*.

50 See above, n. 39.

---

43 Lit., "rubbing my chickpea."

44 Lit., knock out the front row of my chorus singers, i.e.,
    teeth.

45 Lit., "rush-mats."

XANTHIAS: Hm....tempting. OK, done. I accept your oath, and your terms. [*They exchange clothes/props*]

CHORUS: Now is the time to perfect your act,
Get your roar up and running, your gestures exact;   790
To play Heracles you've got to get it all right—
Flash your courage around, flex your terrible might;
But *if* you show weakness, make errors or flub it,
It'll be off with the club and back on with the luggage.

XANTHIAS: Thank-you, dear Chorus, your counsel is clever;   795
Could not put it better myself whatsoever;
If there's any benefit he stands to gain,
He's sure to defraud me all over again.
But I'll do my best to put on a brave front,
Fake some murderous glances, and confident grunts.   800
And it looks like the timing is good for a roar—
I think I hear someone approaching the door.

ÆACUS: Grab that dog-thief, and tie him up! He's going to pay for his crimes.

DIONYSUS: [*mimicking Xanthias obnoxiously*]   805
Somebody's going to get in trou-ble....

XANTHIAS: [*using club*] The hell I will. Back! Back!

ÆACUS: Oh, you *would* put up a fight...Spartacus, Thugasus, Ruffianicus,[51] get him!

DIONYSUS: Yes, hit him! He's a disgraceful thief—   810

ÆACUS: Absolutely!

DIONYSUS: An *absolutely* disgraceful thief.

XANTHIAS: By god, I swear, I never stole so much as a hair from you—I've never even been here before! Let me die on the spot if I'm lying. If you   815
don't believe me, take my slave here—he knows the whole story. If you beat him hard enough I'm sure he'll tell you the truth. And if you're still not satisfied, then you can kill me.[52]

ÆACUS: [*with intense relish*] Exactly how should I torture him?   820

XANTHIAS: Any way you want: tie him to the rack, hang him up by his toes, flog him with the cat-o-nine-tails, flay him alive, break him on the wheel, pour vinegar up his nose, squish him under a pile   825
of bricks, whatever. [*Æacus excitedly produces a stalk of leeks*] No, I'm sorry, but no leeks.[53]

ÆACUS: Excellent advice; and if I happen to maim him....permanently, I'll pay fair compensation.

XANTHIAS: Nah, don't worry about it; he's all yours;   830
just take him and...torture away.

ÆACUS: No, I want him to testify right here. Come on, you, put those bags down and prepare to squeal....

DIONYSUS: Um, excuse me, I'm afraid you're not   835
actually allowed to torture me because I'm a god and if you try it, well, you'll be sorry.

ÆACUS: What?

DIONYSUS: I said, I'm an immortal, I'm Dionysus—you know, son of Zeus? This guy's the slave.   840

ÆACUS: [*to Xanthias*] Did you hear that?

XANTHIAS: Yes, I did. Go ahead and flog him; if he's really a god, he won't feel it.

DIONYSUS: [*to Xanthias*] Well, that would apply to you too, then, wouldn't it, *Heracles*? Maybe he   845
should beat you too?

XANTHIAS: Good idea; [*to Æacus*] pummel us both, and see who flinches first. Whoever cries loudest is *not* a god.

ÆACUS: That's a gentleman for you; always takes the   850
high road. Now, strip.

XANTHIAS: Um, small question? You're going to make this...equal, right?

ÆACUS: Don't worry; I'll hit you both, one after the other.   855

XANTHIAS: Great.

ÆACUS: There! [*He strikes Xanthias*]

XANTHIAS: Just see if I flinch.

ÆACUS: I just hit you.

---

51 Lit., Pardocas, Ditylas, Sceblyas, three very foreign-sounding names, suggesting the Scythian archers whom the Athenians kept as slaves and used as policemen.

52 Rules of evidence at Athens stipulated that the testimony of slaves could be admitted into the record only if it had been extracted under torture. The assumption was that slaves could not be counted on to tell the truth other-wise. A litigant who said, as Xanthias does, "Go ahead,

torture my slaves if you don't believe me," normally didn't expect to be taken up on it.

53 Lit., leeks and green onions, which were used in some kind of ceremonial beating of young boys in an initia-tion ritual. See Sommerstein, *Frogs*,1996:210, n. 621–2.

XANTHIAS: No, you didn't. 860

ÆACUS: Interesting. Now the other—

DIONYSUS: [*imitating Xanthias' strategy*] Whenever you're ready....

ÆACUS: You didn't feel anything?

DIONYSUS: Not even a sneeze. Do you know why? 865

ÆACUS: I've no idea. Back to the first one...

XANTHIAS: Hurry up; get it over with. Aaaaaaah!

ÆACUS: What does "ahhhhh" mean? Feel any....pain?

XANTHIAS: No no no—I was just...thinking how sad it was that I missed my big festival again this year, 870 the Diomeia-aaaah.....

ÆACUS: I commend your piousness. Back to the other.....

DIONYSUS: Ow-wow-wow!

ÆACUS: What's wrong ? 875

DIONYSUS: [*pointing off*] Wow! Lookit those horsemen go!

ÆACUS: So why are you crying?

DIONYSUS: They're...peeling onions...

ÆACUS: You're not feeling these blows at all? 880

DIONYSUS: Not in the slightest.

ÆACUS: Hmmm. The mortal must be this one, then.

XANTHIAS: Help!

ÆACUS: What's the matter?

XANTHIAS: Pull this thorn out, would you? 885

ÆACUS: Ah. Well, try the other one again....

DIONYSUS: Aaaaaaaapollo!..."lord of Delos and Pytho!"

XANTHIAS: He felt that. Didn't you?

DIONYSUS: Sheesh!...You illiterate, don't you 890 recognize that line from Hipponax? I was just reciting...

XANTHIAS: Look, you're not doing it right; give him a good one, right in the—

ÆACUS: Let's see your stomach. [*hits him hard*] 895

DIONYSUS: Poseidon...!

XANTHIAS: Someone's getting hur-urt...

DIONYSUS: "...who reigns over the cape of the Ægean, over the windy blue-grey sea."

ÆACUS: Oh, Demeter, I still can't tell which of you 900 is the god. Come inside; the master and Persephoné will know which is which, being gods themselves.

DIONYSUS: Brilliant; I wonder why you didn't think of that *before* you beat us.[*they go into the house*] 905

CHORUS: Oh, sacred Muse: inspire our chorus!
  Check out this sea of wise faces before us!
  Are they any better than our politicians—
  Short on integrity, long on ambition?
  They deafen us with their cacophonous shouts 910
  About keeping the babbling foreigners out;
  But they *should* be lamenting for their own agendum:
  'Cuz "fifty-plus-one" is a lost referendum![54]

CHORUS LEADER: [*to audience*] It is the sacred duty of the chorus to give good advice and instruction 915 to the city. First, equality must be restored to all citizens, so that nobody has any reason to worry. Whoever was led astray by Phrynichus[55] and his tricks, or was tripped up by him—I say we must allow these people to clear themselves and be 920 forgiven their mistake. Second, we can't have a city in which some of us are deprived of our rights. It's disgraceful to see men who helped fight in a single naval battle be changed from slaves to masters overnight—not that I disapprove of this; on the 925 contrary, I applaud you for it; in fact it's the only sensible thing you've done. But at the same time it's only fair that you pay equal attention to those other men, and to their fathers, who fought in so many battles and are our blood relatives—that you 930 listen to these men when they ask for forgiveness, and that you pardon them. You're people of great natural wisdom—use it! Cool your anger and

---

54 This passage is all about Cleophon, perhaps the most topical politician of the day, and the subject of one of the comedies that competed against *Frogs*. A series of political and mythological puns—revolving around Philomela, the word *amphilalos*, double-talking, and the fact that Cleophon owned a shop for making musical instruments—makes this passage untranslatable. I have, however, retained some of the main ideas: the reference to a politician's obnoxious verbal harangues, his foreignness, his lamentation, and the final joke, which literally says that he's doomed anyway, even if the votes come out equal. (Cleophon was in fact tried, condemned, and executed in 404.)

55 Not the playwright referred to earlier, but the demagogue and chief architect of the oligarchic coup carried by the "Four Hundred"; he was assassinated in 411, and democracy restored.

accept as fellow-citizens *everyone* who's fought with us in our ships, and let's all live together, enjoying equal rights. But I warn you: if we're too proud to do this, and continue to be petty and uncompromising, especially at a time when our city is imperilled in the high seas of a desperate war,[56] the time will come when people will say that we were not wise.   935 940

CHORUS: "If I can see right the shape of a man's life,"[57]
You are doomed, tiny mortals, with danger and
    strife!
You're all bathhouse attendants, you're
    laundromat flunkies,
Whose goods are still filthy, you miserable monkeys.   945
You're always defensive, you know you're in shit,
You can't leave the house but with a big stick;
For you're scared if one night you decide to get
    drunk
You'll be stripped of your clothes on the street by
    some punk.

CHORUS LEADER: I've often thought that we've been treating the best and brightest citizens of Athens as if they were pieces of old currency: now this old silver, as we all know, is the genuine article, beautifully made and accepted with confidence everywhere, both here in Greece and among the barbarians as well....but do we trust these coins? No. We prefer vile copper-alloys, freshly minted but worthless. And we deal with our citizens in the same way: if they happen to be well born, well educated, physically fit and cultured in music and the arts, we treat them with utter contempt. We only have use for the basest trash, emigres, fair-haired peasants, fresh off the boat, scum of the earth that the city would once have judged unworthy to serve even as scapegoats. You morons! It isn't too late—you can still mend your ways and learn how to value what's valuable again. With this policy, you win either way: if you succeed, all's well; but even if you fail, even if something does   950 955 960 965

go wrong, at least you'll gain the respect of intelligent people, who'll say yes, you fell, but you fell with honour.   970

ÆACUS: [*coming back out, now chummy*] By our saviour Zeus, I'll say one thing for your master: he's a true gentleman.   975

XANTHIAS: *Of course* he's a gentleman—at least I think that's why he doesn't know how to do anything except drink and screw.

ÆACUS: But he resisted the temptation to beat you, even though you were caught red-handed, pretending to be the master when you're really the slave.   980

XANTHIAS: Oh, yeah, I would like to have seen him try it....!

ÆACUS: That's exactly the kind of slavish sentiment I love to hear.   985

XANTHIAS: What do you mean?

ÆACUS: I mean, like, I, like, practically *see god* when I curse my master behind his back.

XANTHIAS: Yeah, and what about, after getting thrashed, when you leave the house in a huff, grumbling under your breath?   990

ÆACUS: Oh yes, yes, yes, I love that too.

XANTHIAS: And what about meddling in everybody's business?   995

ÆACUS: The best! The absolute best!

XANTHIAS: [*giving a high-five*] Brother! By Zeus, we're *blood*, man. And listening in on the masters' conversations?

ÆACUS: [*ecstatic; sexual*] Yes! Yes! Yes!   1000

XANTHIAS: And then blabbing everything you heard to your friends?

ÆACUS: Oh Zeus. When I do this? Actually, I, like, *have an orgasm.*

XANTHIAS: Phœbus Apollo! [*with great sincerity*] Thanks for sharing, man....Hug? [*they do*] But what in the name of Our Whipped Lord is all this noise?....what's all that shouting about?   1005

ÆACUS: It's Æschylus and Euripides.

XANTHIAS: Get out....!   1010

ÆACUS: No, it's extremely serious business, very serious indeed; a major conflict has broken out among the dead—divisive as hell.

XANTHIAS: What are they fighting about?

ÆACUS: We have a law here, you see, that stipulates   1015

---

56 Lit., "in the arm of the waves," a line from Archilochus, c. seventh century B.C.E.

57 A near-quotation of a line from a tragedy by Ion of Chios. This stanza addresses a politician named Cleigenes. See Sommerstein, p. 218, n. 108–16.

that, in all the professions, or at least in all the worthwhile, intellectual professions, which is to say, the fine arts, the best practitioner in each field gets to eat for free for all eternity at City Hall, and sit on a throne beside Pluto… 1020

XANTHIAS: I know *that*...

ÆACUS: ...*unless* someone even more expert comes along, at which point the first artist is supposed to step down.

XANTHIAS: So what could Aeschylus be so upset 1025 about?

ÆACUS: Well, he *was* holding the chair for tragedy, *obviously*, being the greatest tragedian ever...

XANTHIAS: But....?

ÆACUS: But when Euripides got here, he started 1030 doing these soap-box recitations for all the robbers and criminals and father-beaters who live down here; and they got one whiff of his sneaky rhetoric and evasive logic, and they went wild for him, proclaiming him the greatest poet that's ever lived. 1035 And this got Euripides so riled up that he went and just took possession of the throne.

XANTHIAS: And nobody stoned him to death?

ÆACUS: No, but there were cries for a trial...And so they're taking it to court, to get a decision about 1040 who's the better playwright.

XANTHIAS: Wait—who wanted a trial? That mob of criminals you were talking about, the ones who like Euripides?

ÆACUS: You got it. [*indicating the spectators.*] I'm 1045 afraid they wouldn't take no for an answer.

XANTHIAS: But didn't Æschylus have any supporters?

ÆACUS: Nah. Good people are no easier to come by down here than they are on earth. 1050

XANTHIAS: So, what's Pluto going to do?

ÆACUS: Start the contest as soon as possible; put their skills on trial, and declare a winner.

XANTHIAS: Does this mean that Sophocles doesn't even want to be considered for the chair? 1055

ÆACUS: Not exactly. The second he got down here? Aeschylus went right up to him, shook his hand, embraced him, and said "Sophocles, take it. The throne is yours." Sophocles declined. But now that Euripides is challenging, Sophocles said that, like 1060 a boxer, he'd "sit this round out"; if Aeschylus wins,

great; but if not, Sophocles vowed to fight to the death rather than let the title go to *Euripides*.

XANTHIAS: When's it starting?

ÆACUS: Right away! And what a fight it's going to 1065 be— tragic art itself will be weighed in the scales!

XANTHIAS: What, like a slice of baloney?[58]

ÆACUS: No—they're bringing rulers and yardsticks, and t-squares and plumb-lines and compasses, because Euripides says he's going to put their plays 1070 to the test word by word.

XANTHIAS: Really? Æschylus must be furious.

ÆACUS: Pawing the ground and glowering like a *bull*....

XANTHIAS: Who's going to be the judge?

ÆACUS: Ah, that wasn't an easy decision; neither of 1075 them thought that anyone was qualified. Æschylus in particular objected to being judged by [*indicating audience*] them, the Athenians...

XANTHIAS: Too many crooks, eh?

ÆACUS: ...And if not crooks, then philistines who 1080 don't appreciate real art. But they finally agreed on a compromise, your master, because at least he's got a lot of stage experience. But let's get out of here; when the masters are agitated about something, it's the slaves who get knocked around! 1085

CHORUS: Oh! what a wrath, what a terrible rage
In the heart of the thunderer, high on his throne,
As the fast-talking artist, his rival, begins
To sharpen his tusks on the whetting stone.
In the crashing-helmet struggle of his lofty-crested 1090
     speech
See the sparks ignite, shards of shrapnel screech,
As our man beats back at the galloping lines
Of a cunning master craftsman with a verbose mind.
Then, with the mane of his shaggy mount a-bristle
And his brow contracted, with a fearsome roar 1095
He will bellow forth his word-storms, hammered
     up with rivets,
Tearing up his verses like a wrecked ship's boards.
Then will the blabbermouth, like himself, uncurl
     his slippery tongue,
And in his jaw, clamped tight the bit of envy,
Will he slice, and dice, and reduce to quibbled 1100
     nothing
The monumental labour of our hero's lungs.

---

58 Lit., like an animal weighed at an Apaturia festival.

EURIPIDES: [*To Dionysus*] No, I will not let go of this chair; it's mine. I'm a better artist than he is any day.

DIONYSUS: Æschylus, why are you keeping so quiet? Do you hear what he's saying? 1105

EURIPIDES: He's starting off all distant and dignified and aloof....but it's just a trick; we've seen it a million times in his plays.

DIONYSUS: Hey, hey, hey, cool your jets, bud. 1110

EURIPIDES: I know this guy's style, figured out his trip a long time ago: he's nothing but a bombast machine, a bloated, self-indulgent monster-mouth who spews forth piles of savage rant without any subtlety at all.... 1115

ÆSCHYLUS: How dare you! You, son of a cabbage-vendor! Who do you think you are to talk to me like that—you, you, scrounger of stupidities, you rag-stitching beggar-maker, you bag-man? You shall regret those words, my friend. 1120

DIONYSUS: That's enough, Æschylus; remember what you once said about "calming the wild wrath that like a furnace roasts your innards?"

ÆSCHYLUS: No, I won't, not until I've unmasked this creator of cripples and shown up his arrogance 1125 for what it is.

DIONYSUS: Quick, boys! Batten down the hatches,[59] the storm-cloud is about to burst.

ÆSCHYLUS: You collector of cretinous melodies,[60] you've corrupted our art-form, with your filthy 1130 sexual perversions, and your—

DIONYSUS: —Ok, Ok, easy does it, Æschylus, let's be gentlemen, shall we? And as for you, Euripides, you naughty boy, I suggest you move back just a bit, out of his line of fire, or in his anger he might 1135 knock you out cold with a block of big words, and we don't want any spilling of brains here, do we?[61] And Æschylus, no hissy-fits, please. Just argue the matter rationally, with a cool head; you're famous artists, not barmaids,[62] and yet you start screaming 1140

at the drop of a hat, as if your hair was on fire.[63]

EURIPIDES: No, let him do his worst; I can handle anything he can dish out. Let him trash whatever he wants—my dialogue, my choruses, my tragic fundamentals, and sure, my *Peleus, Æolus, Meleager* 1145 and even my *Telephus*, if he dares.

DIONYSUS: Æschylus? Any rebuttal?

ÆSCHYLUS: Actually, I was just thinking how unequal this competition is, and that, in all fairness, I should withdraw... 1150

DIONYSUS: How so?

ÆSCHYLUS: Because my poetry lived on after me, whereas his didn't, and so he's got it all down here with him, to recite from. But, if that's how you want it, fine; it's your call. 1155

DIONYSUS: [*calling backstage*] Hey, can somebody get me some candles and incense? I'd better pray to the gods that, when I decide between these two geniuses, I give the impression that I know what the hell I'm talking about. And while I'm doing 1160 that, you could sing a hymn to the Muses.

CHORUS: Oh Zeus' daughters, Muses nine,
Who read the thoughts of clever minds
When they enter the ring of argumentation
Armed with gimmicks and sharp cogitations— 1165
Look down on them, Muses, inspire their prowess:
One with mighty mega-words,
The other with scraps and roll-ends of verse.
Let the great cerebral battle begin!

DIONYSUS: [*gesturing toward the incense plate, and* 1170 *Aeschylus*] Now you too: offer your prayer to the gods before starting the match.

ÆSCHYLUS: Oh, Demeter! who nurtured my mind, help me to be worthy of thy Mysteries!

DIONYSUS: Your turn, Euripides; take some incense. 1175

EURIPIDES: I'll pass, thanks; not my kind of thing...

DIONYSUS: What, have you coined some new gods of your own?

EURIPIDES: Basically.

DIONYSUS: Well go ahead then; pray to your gods. 1180

EURIPIDES: Heaven, my grub, Twisting Tongue, Genius, and Shit-detecting Nostrils, help me trash any argument he throws at me.

CHORUS: How curious we are to watch them lock horns,

---

59 Lit., bring a black lamb, an offering to placate the storm god, Typhos.

60 Lit., monodies, or arias, from Crete.

61 The end of this line features an untranslatable pun on the similarity in sound between *Telephus*, the title of an Euripidean tragedy, and *enkephalos*, the word for brains.

62 Lit., baker-women.

63 Lit, like a *prinos*, a wood that burned loudly.

These mighty tongue-tilters, these mouth matadors; 1185
From one we'll get elegance, wit and finesse;
While the other will rip up great words by the roots,
Will fall on the foe, with his storm and his stress,
And flatten his rhetoric with Seven League boots.

DIONYSUS: Alrighty, right off the top—let's start 1190
with some speeches....Now, we're looking for clever
word-play right down the line—no clichés, no false
analogies, no speaking below the belt.

EURIPIDES: Friends, Mr. Speaker, I will in due time
discuss my own work; but I'd like to begin today 1195
with my opponent. I will show to you all what a
fraud and a phoney he is, and unmask all the
bogus methods he used to fool his poor audiences
who, after a lifetime spent in the theatre watching
those boring old plays of Phrynichus, had grown 1200
stupid, lazy, and easy to trick. First, my opponent
here would start off with some silent figure, like
Achilles or Niobé, who'd sit there for an eternity
under some....scarf, her head totally hidden, and
monopolize the action for hours without saying a 1205
bloody thing!

DIONYSUS: Gosh, he's right...

EURIPIDES: Meanwhile, the Chorus would fire off
fifty rounds of continuous lyrics,[64] while the actors
just sat there, mute. 1210

DIONYSUS: Actually, I kinda liked those silent
characters...better than the endless yadada-yadada
of the talking heads we get today....

EURIPIDES: If you liked that stuff, it's because it
hypnotised you—froze your brains. 1215

DIONYSUS: Come to think of it, you might be
right....What did that.....little so-and-so think he
was doing?

EURIPIDES: Pure voodoo quackery—the idea is that
the audience gets all tense and expectant, waiting, 1220
waiting for Niobé to finally open her
mouth...and....say....*something*.

DIONYSUS: Oh, the sneak! How could he deceive
me like that! Æschylus, why are you twitching and
squirming like that? 1225

EURIPIDES: Because I'm showing him up for what
he is, and he knows it. Then, when the play is

already half over because the chorus has been
blathering on like that for hours, he'll suddenly toss
in a dozen gigantic words, these massive, armour- 1230
plated apparitions with monstrous shaggy helmets
that nobody's ever heard before in their life.

ÆSCHYLUS: Give me patience...!

DIONYSUS: Shhhh!

EURIPIDES: When he finally did open up his mouth, 1235
you couldn't understand a single word the man
said—

DIONYSUS: [*to Æschylus*] Stop grinding your
teeth.

EURIPIDES: —all these Scamanders, and Trojan 1240
moats, and griffin-eagle-forged brazen
breastplates—every word a towering precipice,
dangerous to hear and virtually impossible to
understand.

DIONYSUS: Hmm, now that you say it.....I spent an 1245
entire sleepless night trying to figure out what a
"tawny horse-cock" was.[65]

ÆSCHYLUS: You idiot, it's an image painted on the
side of a ship.

DIONYSUS: Oh! One of those bird-things. I thought 1250
it might be some kind of dildo.[66]

EURIPIDES: But what was a half-chicken doing in a
tragedy anyway?

ÆSCHYLUS: Oh, look who's talking, you
blasphemous slime. What did *you* write about? 1255

EURIPIDES: Well, at least not about cock-headed
horses, or antlered deer-goats, things that exist only
in Persian tapestries. No, when I took tragedy over
from you, it was so bloated with bombast and
overstuffed words, the first thing I had to do was 1260
put it on a diet: I had to slim down the excess,
cutting out all fatty phrases with a regimen of
sensible little versicles, plenty of exercise,[67] stewed-

---

64 Lit., four strings of lyrics.

65 Lit., "before now I have lain awake through the long
watches of the night," a quotation from *Hippolytus*.

66 Lit., Philoxenus's son Eryxis. The allusion is obscure; possibly connected with gluttony.

67 Possibly also a humourous reference to Euripides' supposed preference for an acting style that involved more
moving about the stage, in contrast to the immobility of
Aeschylean heroes. See J.D.Denniston, *CQ* 21,
1927:117.

beet laxatives, and health-food distillations of high-fibre book-juice.[68] Then I fed it back up again with a mixture of organic monologues with a dash of adultery.[69] I never had my characters just start jabbering away, saying whatever drivel came into my head so that nobody had a chance to figure out what the hell was going on; no, in the opening scene I always made everything clear right away, explaining all the narrative antecedents— 1265 1270

ÆSCHYLUS: —better than talking about your own antecedents, like your mother, who—

EURIPIDES: In my plays nobody just sat there; I gave everybody an equal chance to have their say: women, slaves, masters, daughters, even the old crones. 1275

ÆSCHYLUS: And you deserve to be executed for it!

EURIPIDES: No, I don't—ever heard of democracy? 1280

DIONYSUS: Ah, let's not go there, shall we, pal? Your record is not exactly spotless on that score.[70]

EURIPIDES: Well, anyway, I taught people how to talk, really talk—

ÆSCHYLUS: Oh god, if only you'd croaked first... 1285

EURIPIDES: —how to make distinctions, and computations, how to see, imagine, grasp, cogitate, plan, tie everything up in love-knots, and be suspicious, always, of everything...

ÆSCHYLUS: Exactly....! 1290

EURIPIDES: ...I brought everyday life on stage, life as we live it, things the audience is familiar with, and could actually call me on, if I got it wrong. I didn't try to mesmerize them with mumbo-jumbo, or distract them with exotic spectacle, like Kyknos and Memnon riding on stage with those ridiculous musical horses.[71] All you have to do is compare our followers. He's got Phormisius and that air- 1295

head Megaenetus, big-bearded, trumpet-playing soccer-hooligans who crack tree-trunks and humans for breakfast, whereas I've got the smart ones, Kleitophon and Theramenes. 1300

DIONYSUS: Theramenes? A genius, you're right: rather than ever admit his guilt, he just keeps manipulating the words till a carnal *cigar* is made to sounds like a mere *canard*![72] 1305

EURIPIDES: Exactly! I put the spirit of rational inquiry and criticism into my plays. I got the audience thinking, analysing, especially about their private lives, which they're living much better now thanks to me, because now they ask questions, like "what does this mean?," and "where does this come from?," and "where does that go?" 1310

DIONYSUS: My god, it's true! Athenians these days *have* started asking questions, like "Slave, where have all the pots gone? Who bit the head off this anchovy? *Why* must such a new pie-plate...die? Where has all the garlic gone? Who's been siphoning off the olive-oil?" Whereas, in the bad old days, they used to just sit there, in silence, gaping like inbred half-wits with their jaws hanging open like Melitides.[73] 1315 1320

CHORUS: [*to Aeschylus*] "Glorious Achilles, these things thou dost see..."[74]
How will you reply to this sharp repartee?
Watch out for your anger, for if it takes hold
You'll be ruled out of bounds by the referee;
His charges are tough, so beware, noble one,
That you rein in your sails, and proceed cautiously,
Letting slack, giving out, bit by bit, till you're sure
That your wind's in control, your sheets safe in the breeze. 1325 1330

DIONYSUS: And now, the man who took the art of tragedy and made it into such a magnificent monument of mumbo-jumbo—Aeschylus! Open 'yer floodgates and let 'er rip.

ÆSCHYLUS: That I should be reduced to debating with this creature is a disgusting offence to my very soul. But just in case he ever tries to claim that he 1335

---

68 Euripides was famed for his extensive private library, a rarity in his age.

69 Lit, a dash of Kephisophon. He was a friend and collaborator of Euripides, said in some sources to have been a slave, and to have had an affair with Euripides' wife.

70 For leaving Athens for a monarchy, Macedonia, in the last year of his life, Euripides could have been seen as betraying the democratic cause.

71 Lit., with bells on the cheek-plates of their horses' harnesses.

72 Untranslatable pun, literally, "not a Chian but a Kian."

73 Proverbial half-wit.

74 A line quoted from Aeschylus's *Myrmidons*, likening the playwright to his hero Achilles.

beat me, answer this one question: by what criteria should we judge a playwright?

EURIPIDES: Poetic technique, good advice, and an ability to make people better citizens. 1340

ÆSCHYLUS: And what if you've in fact done the opposite, taken fine, upstanding, well-behaved people, and ruined them completely—what would you say a poet deserved for doing this? 1345

DIONYSUS: Death—why are you asking him?

ÆSCHYLUS: Then consider if you will what he inherited from me: were my characters all noble, selfless, six-foot heroes? Or were they lazy, decadent slobs? No. My characters were all lance-and-spear-snorting warriors with high-crested helmets, strong greaves and seven-layer ox-hide shields. 1350

DIONYSUS: I wish he wouldn't clang all those helmets around...

EURIPIDES: Oh really? And how did they *get* so heroic, pray tell? [*silence*] 1355

DIONYSUS: Come on Aeschylus, enough with the portentous silences.

ÆSCHYLUS: Thanks to a play of mine, full of the spirit of war... 1360

EURIPIDES: [*dryly*] Which one?

ÆSCHYLUS: Well, take *Seven Against Thebes* for example. Nobody can come away from *that* play without wanting to go right out and fight.

DIONYSUS: Yes, I've been meaning to complain to you about that: our Theban enemies have been practically invincible in battle ever since that play, and it's all your fault! 1365

ÆSCHYLUS: Look, you Athenians might have become invincible yourselves, but you didn't even try. And then I did *Persians*, a lesson about the love of victory—a brilliant achievement, if I do say so myself— 1370

DIONYSUS: Oh, yeah, I loved that part where they called up the ghost of Darius and the Chorus clapped its hands like this and went "Yiaou-oi!"[75] 1375

ÆSCHYLUS: —which is just what playwrights are supposed to do. Look, all our best poets, from time immemorial, have been the ones who've had something useful to teach. Orpheus taught us about Mystery cults and the evils of murder; Musaeus about foretelling the future and curing disease; Hesiod about farming, and when to plough, and plant, and harvest the fields. As for *Homer*—why do you think he's considered the most divine poet of all, hm? It's because of all the good practical advice he gave about the training and arming of soldiers. 1380 1385

DIONYSUS: Well, he didn't get through to that klutz Pantakles, I can tell you that much. I was watching him the other day in the parade, trying to do up his shoes—while he was marching![76] 1390

ÆSCHYLUS: Well I can name plenty of men who have been inspired to greatness—like Lamachus, for example, a true hero.[77] Following Homer's example, I created characters worthy of emulation, like Patroclus, and Teucer, men with the courage of lions, heroes intended to fire the heart of every Athenian male with a single desire: to live up to such examples every time they hear the trumpet calling them to war. I did *not* create sluts like Phaedra,[78] god forbid; in fact, I challenge anyone to find a single love-sick female in any of my plays. 1395 1400

EURIPIDES: How could there be? You've probably never even seen one! 1405

ÆSCHYLUS: Thankfully, no. Whereas you're an expert on the passions of adulterous women, aren't you Euripides?

DIONYSUS: My god, how interesting....the very thing that you wrote about in your plays actually did end up happening under your own roof—your own wife—! 1410

EURIPIDES: [*to Aeschylus*] Wait one minute, you contemptible savage, are you accusing my Phaedra of actually harming the city in some way? 1415

---

75 Meant to sound exaggerated and ridiculous. Aeschylus in fact has the barbarian Persians cry "ee" and "oi" at various points in the play, which was exotic enough; Aristophanes takes the outlandishness one step further.

76 Lit., "trying to attach the crest to his helmet—when it was already on his head."

77 One of Athens' best fighters, a general revered after his death for his tremendous courage.

78 Along with Phaedra, whose passion for her stepson Hippolytus is the subject of one of Euripides' tragedies, Stheneboea is also named here (and later her illicit love-object, Bellerophon).

ÆSCHYLUS: Of course! Women of quality, good citizens' wives, have been popping themselves left, right and centre thanks to all your unrequited Hippolytus-passions.

EURIPIDES: What, do you think I made up the story of Phaedra? It existed long before I got here. 1420

ÆSCHYLUS: No, you didn't invent it, but it's your duty, as an artist, not to parade such filth on the stage. Children are taught by schoolmasters; but adults depend on us poets: they need us to show them what's *good*. 1425

EURIPIDES: Oh, so spewing out words the size of Mount Parnassus is your idea of teaching? Wouldn't people learn a little more if you used a language actually spoken by.....*humans*? 1430

ÆSCHYLUS: Look, you pathetic fool, glorious thoughts and ideas *must* be expressed in appropriately glorious language. It's only fitting for demi-gods to use bigger words than we do, just as they should dress better than we do—a fact which 1435 I understood.....before you totally debased it.

EURIPIDES: What do you mean?

ÆSCHYLUS: Well, for example, by dressing all your kings in rags, making them look pathetic....

EURIPIDES: And what's wrong with that? 1440

ÆSCHYLUS: For one thing it's taught the rich people how to shirk their responsibilities: now, when the city goes to them, cap in hand, desperate for money for the war effort, they put on their rags and wail about their poverty! 1445

DIONYSUS: Rags, ha!—and cashmere undergarments underneath. No, they can't possibly shell out the money for a ship, but didn't you just see them in the seafood shop, placing a big order for imported oysters? 1450

ÆSCHYLUS: Yes, you've taught people how to talk all right—but they should be in training for the war! You've emptied all the gyms, you've flattened every bum-muscle in town! Young men nowadays do nothing but sit, chattering away. *And* they've 1455 started talking back to their superior officers, like the men did on the *Paralus*. In my day, the only thing soldiers knew how to do was holler for their rations and sing "yo-ho-ho and a bottle of rum."

DIONYSUS: [*nostalgically*] Yes, by Apollo, and blow 1460 farts in the face of the guys in the bottom galleys,

fling shit around the mess-hall, and steal each other's clothes when on shore-leave. But now all they know how to do is debate the merits of their orders...."Should we sail this way, Should we sail 1465 that way....?"

ÆSCHYLUS: But that's not the worst of it. He's shown women as pimps, women giving birth in temples, having sex with their brothers, and claiming that life is not really life! Why else do you think that the city 1470 is so over-run with civil servants and politicians, demagogues and media monkeys? You can't find a single person in the whole city anymore who's physically fit enough to carry a goddamned torch in the opening ceremonies of the Olympics! 1475

DIONYSUS: [*laughing*] You got that right! At the Pan-Athenian games? I nearly died—there was this pudgy little piglet, huffing and puffing as he brought up the rear.....and when he went through the stands in the Potters' Quarter, everyone started 1480 slapping and smacking him as he went by, till they knocked a fart right out of him—almost blew out his torch!

CHORUS: The fight is intense and the outcome unsure,
For each in his way is a true connoisseur: 1485
One has got power and force on his side,
The other's got speed and the know-how to slide
Out of difficult corners with acid replies.
This is no time to lean back on your laurels,
This is the time to put forth *all* your quarrels, 1490
So many arguments left to try out,
Old ones and new, in this brain-boxing bout;
Attack with the left, and dissect with the right,
And risk all your cleverness, wit and insight!

And if you're inhibited, have any fears 1495
That the audience won't understand what it hears,
Will not be able to fathom the gist
Of the subtlest points of your brainy lit-crit—
Worry not, champions, they're no idiots,
They've trained in the trenches, they're schooled 1500
    literates—
Each has a book and can check your allusions;
Big-brained by nature, they've had highbrow
    infusions.
So don't hesitate to pull out all yer quips;
The audience here is as smart as a whip!

EURIPIDES: All right, I'd like to go right to the beginning: your prologues. I allege that in this most basic component of tragedy, the "great man" over here was inept; his prologues explained nothing. 1505

DIONYSUS: Example? 1510

EURIPIDES: Dozens. Okay, start with your *Oresteia*.

DIONYSUS: Silence, everyone. Go ahead Aeschylus; recite one.

ÆSCHYLUS: "Chthonic Hermes, who protects the
    fatherly realm with a benevolent eye,
Be my friend and saviour I pray; 1515
For to this land I do return and remigrate."

DIONYSUS: Well? Anything wrong with that?

EURIPIDES: Dozens of things.

DIONYSUS: In three lines?!

EURIPIDES: Yeah, he's made at least four mistakes in each one. 1520

DIONYSUS: Aeschylus, calm down. Don't lose the whole war over three measly verses!

ÆSCHYLUS: [*spluttering rage*] Me! To him! How—

DIONYSUS: Trust me.... 1525

EURIPIDES: In fact he's made a colossal mistake in the very first sentence....

ÆSCHYLUS: [*to Dionysus, still in a fit*] Do you hear this crap?! [*controlling himself*] OK, what the hell. What "mistake" have I made? 1530

EURIPIDES: Let's hear it again?

ÆSCHYLUS: "Chthonic Hermes, who protects the fatherly realm with a benevolent eye"—

EURIPIDES: —tell me: is it or is it not correct that Orestes says these words at his father's tomb? 1535

ÆSCHYLUS: That's right.

EURIPIDES: So you're saying that Orestes' dad—who was slaughtered in cold blood by his wife—had been *benevolently protected*?!

ÆSCHYLUS: No, the speaker here is referring to Hermes, usually known as a thief and a messenger, as an *underworld* god, implying that this quality was inherited from *his* father... 1540

EURIPIDES: Then your mistake is even worse than I thought, because if he inherited an underworld quality from his father Zeus— 1545

DIONYSUS: —then he'd be a natural-born body-snatcher! Ha ha ha!

ÆSCHYLUS: Dionysus, your breath stinks of booze.

DIONYSUS: Let's have a bit more, Aeschylus; Euripides, listen carefully. 1550

ÆSCHYLUS: "....be my friend and saviour
    I pray; for to this land I do return and remigrate."

EURIPIDES: Hear that? The great Aeschylus tells us the same thing twice. 1555

DIONYSUS: What do you mean, twice?

EURIPIDES: Look: "I do return and remigrate"— What's the difference between returning and remigrating? Same thing.

DIONYSUS: By god he's right; it would be like saying to a neighbour "Can I borrow a bread-basket—or rather, a loaf-receptacle?"[79] 1560

ÆSCHYLUS: You twittering idiot! It's *not* the same thing at all—the line is perfect.

DIONYSUS: How so? 1565

ÆSCHYLUS: Because anyone can "return" to his homeland, if he's been away. But Orestes was not just away, but in *exile*—and so he both returns *and* remigrates.

DIONYSUS: Brilliant. Euripides? 1570

EURIPIDES: Well I say, no, he couldn't have "remigrated," because he came home secretly, without permission from the immigration authorities.

DIONYSUS: Also brilliant! [*to Euripides*] What?? 1575

EURIPIDES: Let's move on. Aeschylus, do another one.

DIONYSUS: Yes, on we go. You know the drill. Aeschylus speaks, Euripides criticizes.

ÆSCHYLUS: "And here beside this burial mound I call upon my father/To harken and to hear." 1580

EURIPIDES: There he goes again—"To harken *and* to hear?" Same damned thing.

DIONYSUS: But he's speaking to the dead, you ninny; everybody knows you have to call them at least three times if you want to get an answer. But let's move on to *your* prologue technique. 1585

EURIPIDES: Fine. Listen up. And if I repeat myself, even once, or you hear a single word of irrelevant padding—pinch my bum and call me Nancy. 1590

DIONYSUS: Alrighty, recite away—and let's hear how a *real* wordsmith does it.

---

79 Lit., two Greek synonyms used to describe a kneading-trough.

EURIPIDES: "Oedipus at the start was a lucky man—"

ÆSCHYLUS: —he was not! He was unlucky from the day he was born—before he was born! When Apollo said he'd grow up to kill his father—he wasn't even conceived yet! Lucky!? 1595

EURIPIDES: "—but then he became the most wretched of all."

ÆSCHYLUS: He did *not* "become" wretched; he always was! How can yo—look, the first thing that happened to him when he was born was that they put him in a broken pot and left him outside all winter so that he wouldn't grow up to kill his father; then off he wanders on his two gimp feet to Corinth; and then, while he's still young, he marries this old bag, who turns out to be his mom, and then he pokes his eyes out! 1600 1605

DIONYSUS: Yeah, great life...almost as lucky as Erasinides....[80] 1610

EURIPIDES: You're so full of it. My prologues are excellent.

ÆSCHYLUS: In fact, I don't even have to analyse your prologues separately; with the gods' help, I can demolish them all at once with a simple little water-bottle.[81] 1615

EURIPIDES: ....a water-bottle....?

ÆSCHULUS: Just one. You see, the thing is, you have this formulaic pattern in your writing, so that just about anything fits—"bit of wool," "little bag" "water-bottle." You'll see; I'll prove it. 1620

EURIPIDES: Oh, really?

ÆSCHYLUS: Go ahead; recite one.

EURIPIDES: Okay..."*As* the story dis*sem*inates, Ae*gyp*tus travelled to Argos by ship And *with* his sons of *fifty strong* he—" 1625

ÆSCHYLUS:—*lost* his *wa*-ter-*bo*ttle.

DIONYSUS: Damn that water-bottle! Try another one. That's too weird...

EURIPIDES: "Dionysus, ar*ray*ed in his *skins*, And his *rit*ual wand on the *pine*-flaming *Mount*ain of *Parn*assus' height, *Leaps* as he dances with sacred delight For he—" 1630

ÆSCHYLUS: —lost his water-bottle. 1635

DIONYSUS: [*mimes being stabbed by it*] Ah! We're hit, hit by a water-bottle![82]

EURIPIDES: Mere coincidence. Here's one he can't possibly put a water-bottle on: "No man's possessed by a perfect bliss For he's either well-born with no means to live Or he's—" 1640

ÆSCHYLUS:—lost his water-bottle.

DIONYSUS: Euripides?

EURIPIDES: What? 1645

DIONYSUS: Pack it in; this is one powerful little water-bottle.[83]

EURIPIDES: Absolutely not! It's a joke. Here; I've got one that'll put a leak in his bottle.

DIONYSUS: All right, go ahead—but watch out... 1650

EURIPIDES: "Cadmus, son of Agenor, Left his home in Sidon's town And—"

ÆSCHYLUS: —lost his water-bottle.

DIONYSUS: Listen, pal, why don't you just...make him an offer on the damned bottle? Okay? He's shredding all your prologues with it. 1655

EURIPIDES: What?! You want me to *buy* it from him?

DIONYSUS: Trust me....

EURIPIDES: Not a chance. I could recite lots of prologues that he can't strap water-bottles to. Here: "Pelops, son of Tantalus/to Pisa rode on mares so swift/And—" 1660

ÆSCHYLUS: —lost his water-bottle.

DIONYSUS: See? I warned you. Seriously, why don't you just cough up for it—I bet he'd let you have it for an obol....they're really great things to have... 1665

---

80 One of the commanders at the battle of Arginousai, he was arrested on his return to Athens, charged with embezzlement, and executed (with five others) for abandoning shipwrecked men.

81 Lit., oil-flask, of the kind a man would have taken to the gym with him, for oiling his body down, and might easily misplace. Since this meaning of "oil-flask" is lost today, and fitness addicts today are always seen with water-bottles instead, "water-bottle" perhaps better carries the original connotations.

---

82 Lit, "alack, we are struck again," allusion to Agamemnon's cries when stabbed by his wife.

83 Lit., "lower your yard-arm; this oil-flask is blowing hard"—conventional sailor's talk for "pull back; danger."

EURIPIDES: Not so fast; I've got lots left: "Once Oineus from his fields—"

ÆSCHYLUS:—lost his water-bottle. 1670

EURIPIDES: Will you let me finish the sentence first!? "Once Oineus from his fields/A healthy harvest reaped;/Preparing first-fruits for the gods/He—"

ÆSCHYLUS:—lost his water-bottle.

DIONYSUS: In the middle of a sacrifice? Who could 1675 have taken it...?

EURIPIDES: Never mind. Ha! Try this: "Zeus, as Truth the story tells—"

DIONYSUS: —Okay, we get the idea, Zeus lost his water-bottle too. Look, this is getting you nowhere. 1680 That bottle's popping everywhere like a contagious disease. I think you should turn to his lyrics.

EURIPIDES: Good idea. I can easily prove that his lyrics suck—they're all the same.

CHORUS: Oh dear, what's going to happen now? 1685
How can he dare to have the gall
To criticize the best of all
The man whose lyrics far eclipse
All other writers' penmanship?

EURIPIDES: [sneering] The best songwriter of all? 1690 We'll see about that. I think I can cut his lyrics down to size—one size fits all.

DIONYSUS: Here, give me some pebbles. I'll keep count.

EURIPIDES: [singing, to pipe accompaniment] 1695
"Pythian Achilles, you hear our men dying:
How stricken we are, how we call for your help.
Hermes our forebear, we call from the lakeshore:
How stricken we are, how we call for your help."

DIONYSUS: Ooops. That's two strikes against you, 1700 Aeschylus.

EURIPIDES: "Most glorious Achean, great ruler and scion
Of Atreus, harken to me as I say:
How stricken we are, how we call for your help."

DIONYSUS: Third strike, Aeschylus. 1705

EURIPIDES: "Hush now, the Bee-girls arrive at the Temple
Of Artemis there to unlock all the doors;
How stricken we are, how we call for your help.
I have the power to speak like a prophet of
Auspicious journeys, commandments of men; 1710
How stricken we are, how we call for your help."

DIONYSUS: Well, there sure is a whole lot of stricken' goin' on. Speaking about needing some help, I could use the bathroom....[84]

EURIPIDES: You're not going anywhere; I'd like to do 1715 some of his lyre songs now.

DIONYSUS: Fine. But can they not be whacking themselves so much in this one?

EURIPIDES: [singing, to real or imaginary lyre]
Two-throned power of Achaea,
Greece's youthful manhood joined 1720
[strumming sound] phlat-o-thrat-o phlat-o-thrat
Sphinx, that bitch of evil fortune,
Lorded over days that sped
phlat-o-thrat-o phlat-o-thrat
With a spear and hand avenging, 1725
By a martial-omened bird
phlat-o-thrat-o phlat-o-thrat
Who handed them to serve as prey for
Brutal, air-borne, roaming hounds
phlat-o-thrat-o phlat-o-thrat 1730
And who inclined, as one together,
Gath'ring round the great Ajax
phlat-o-thrat-o phlat-o-thrat.

DIONYSUS: What's all this "phlat-o-thrat?" Some hillbilly work-song[85] you picked up serving at 1735 Marathon, or what?

ÆSCHYLUS: Well at least that's a respectable source, used respectably; and at least nobody can accuse me of just recycling old gems from the Phrynichus songbook.[86] But this guy, he collects his chestnuts 1740 from any old place at all—whorehouses, frat party booze-ups, blues pipes, dance-bands, the graveyard wailing of Carian slaves! Let me show you what I

---

84 Lit., I could use a bath; all those strokes have made my groin sore.

85 Lit., rope-winder's song, i.e., verse sung while turning the ropes that hauled water buckets up from wells. Aeschylus's service at Marathon, where the Athenians defeated the Persians, was a great symbol of his, and Athens', illustrious military history (although Marathon itself was probably a rustic backwater).

86 Rather than 'gems' and 'chestnuts,' the Greek uses metaphors of honey and sacred meads of the Muses, with the poet as the collecting bee—a conventional image often used to describe the artist's collecting of sources and inspiration.

mean. Somebody get me a lyre—or no, on second
thought, where's that girl who plays the spoons?[87]   1745
Come on down, O Muse of Euripides! [*she
materializes from backstage; she is perhaps an old
prostitute*] Yes, you're perfect.
DIONYSUS: Hey, I know her! She used to be—well,
she was not one of the *Lesbian* muses, anyway.   1750
ÆSCHYLUS: [*singing, to spoon accompaniment*]
Ye halcion-birds, who twitter away
In the ever-blowing spume of the sea,
Wetting your wings and your feathery skin
With besprinkling drops in its watery waves—   1755
Ye spiders that hang in the angles of roofs
Who twi-i-i-i-st with their fe-e-e-et
The thread in the bobbin, over the loom,
Where melodious shuttles pick out their songs—
Where pipe-loving dolphins leap at the darkblue   1760
Prows with their rams-heads, bound for the
      racetrack,
Oracular. Delight of the grape-vine,
Flowering tendrils that banish all care, and
Throw your arms around me, baby![88]

See? Did you notice that foot?   1765
DIONYSUS: [*misunderstanding, watching the dancing
foot of the Muse*] Mmmm, yes.
ÆSCHYLUS: And the other one, about the fe-e-e-et?
DIONYSUS: [*as before*] Mmmmm, yes.
ÆSCHYLUS: And you have the nerve to criticize *my*   1770
lyrics!? Your poetic tricks remind me of the twelve
positions listed in Cyrene's *Confessions of a
Legendary Whore.*[89] sick, twisted, and hard to get
into! Anyway, enough of your choruses. Let's look
at your solos.   1775

---

87 Lit., who clacks together potsherds, a parodic allusion to
    a scene in Euripides' *Hypsipyle,* in which a former prin-
    cess, reduced to slavery, comforts a baby by playing cas-
    tanets.
88 From *Hypsipyle,* uttered when the title character is reu-
    nited with her son.
89 Lit., "you who manipulate your parts into The Twelve
    Tricks of Cyrene." Cyrene was a courtesan famous for
    possessing a "broad and varied sexual repertoire"
    (Sommerstein 1996:267, n. 1327–8).

[*singing*]
Blackest darkness of the night,
What is this dream you sent to me,
Fearful out of grim Hades?
A life that is no life,   1780
But a child of ghastly night,
Makes me shudder at the sight,
Its corpse wrapped in a gruesome shroud of black.
Its eyes were dripping deadly gore
And boy it sure had big ugly claws.   1785
So light the lamp my servants, please,
Fetch limpid water from the stream
In buckets, heat it till it steams,
That I may wash away this fearful dream.

Poseidon of the sea,   1790
Oh my god, what's happening—
You there, neighbours! Lo, behold
These signs and portents, it's my chicken
Yes my chicken's really stolen,
Glyce's nabbed it, now she's gone.   1795
O Ye nymphs of mountaintops
And you Manya, help me to arrest her.

I, oh woe is me,
was doing my embroidery
twi-i-i-i-i-i-i-i-sting   1800
the flax to spin a ske-e-ein,
So I could take it to the Agora,
Lo, to sell it on the morrra',
When he took flight, flew up high
On gossamer wings up to the sky   1805
Leaving me in grief and tears.
Oh sorrow, sorrow, misery,
I shed I shed these tragic tears,
Oh, unhappy, and sa-a-ad, me.

Now ye Cretan sons of Ida   1810
Seize your weapons, hurry, please,
Stir your leaping legs neatly
And put that bitch's house under surveillance.

With Dictynna, and her dogs,
Comb the building, top to bottom;   1815
And thou, Hecate, child of Zeus,
Illuminate your brightest flame

Hold aloft your torches twain;
Light my way to Glyce's place,
So I can go in and mount a search. 1820
DIONYSUS: Okay, that's enough singing.
ÆSCHYLUS: More than enough. But if you want me
to really settle this thing, once and for all....I've got
to take him to the scales. We'll weigh in, and our
words themselves will decide it. 1825
DIONYSUS: Well, if that's really what it's come down
to, that I'm reduced to weighing up poetry like a
grocer selling cheese....
CHORUS: Of all of the wonders that I've ever seen
This is the cream de la crème de la cream! 1830
Only great minds could have thought up this
scheme—
If I'd only *heard* such a rumour were true,
I'd never have believed such cock-a-doodle-doo!
DIONYSUS: Okay, you two, come and stand here
beside the scales. [*they do*] 1835
BOTH: There.
DIONYSUS: Now, hold on, and speak your line, and
don't let go till I say..."cuckoo."
BOTH: Holding!
DIONYSUS: And........Go! 1840
EURIPIDES: "If only the *Argo*'s prow had never sailed
away—"
ÆSCHYLUS: "River Spercheios and cattle-grazing
fields—"
DIONYSUS: Cuckoo!
BOTH: Stop!
DIONYSUS: [*seeing Aeschylus's side*] Whoa! This side's 1845
gone *way* down!
EURIPIDES: What!!?
DIONYSUS: Well, he threw in a river, and water-
logged beef always weighs more, whereas you put
in a line that just...sailed away! 1850
EURIPIDES: Hm. OK, OK, let's try another one.
DIONYSUS: All right; positions.....
BOTH: Ready!
DIONYSUS: Go!
EURIPIDES: "Persuasion's only temple is the spoken 1855
word—"
ÆSCHYLUS: "Death's the only god who will not
accept gifts—"
DIONYSUS: Cuckoo!
BOTH: Released!

DIONYSUS: Aeschylus again! I think it was because
he put in Death that time. That's a real "heavy." 1860
EURIPIDES: But I put in Persuasion, a magnificent
word.
DIONYSUS: Nah, Persuasion's a featherbrained,
lightweight thing, no good. You've got to try to
think of something heavy, you know, bulky, dense, 1865
get the scale down..
EURIPIDES: Hrmmm, what have I got along those
lines? Oh, what, what, what....
DIONYSUS: I know—what about Achilles'
mighty....dice? Three throws and you're out![90] Ha 1870
ha ha! Now, gentlemen, get ready; this is your last
weigh-in. And...go!
EURIPIDES: "He seized, right-handed, his iron-
heavy spear—"
ÆSCHYLUS: "Chariot on chariot and corpse upon
corpse—"
DIONYSUS: Foiled again! 1875
EURIPIDES: How did he *do* that!?
DIONYSUS: He threw in a pile of chariots and two
dead bodies—a hundred Egyptians couldn't lift
that!
ÆSCHYLUS: But enough of this line-by-line 1880
quibbling—let him climb in there himself, along
with his children, his wife, his wife's lover
Kephisophon—sure, and he can take all his books
in with him too, and I can still outweigh him,
easily, with just two lines! 1885
DIONYSUS: [*to Pluto*] I really love them both....I
don't see how I can choose....I don't want to upset
either one. I think one's a really great poet, but I
like the other one too.
PLUTO: But isn't that why you came down here in 1890
the first place?
DIONYSUS: Yes...What if....I do make a choice?
PLUTO: Then you can take him back up with you
when you go; it's all arranged.
DIONYSUS: Bless you. All right you two, listen up. I 1895
came down here for a playwright—and why? To save
the city, so my theatre festivals won't come to an end.

90 Lit., "two ones and a four," i.e., spots on the surface of
the tossed dice. The joke is not clear. Dover notes that
the phrase appears in a comedy by Eupolis (frag. 372)
See Dover, 1993:368, n. 1400.

So it comes down to this: whoever gives me the best advice is the one I'll take back with me. OK, start with this: what should we do about that traitor, Alcibiades? The city is agonizing over this question. 1900

ÆSCHYLUS: What does the city think?

DIONYSUS: The city? Oh, it pines for him, but it hates him, but it wants him back. What do you think?

EURIPIDES: I hate a citizen who proves so slow 1905
To help his land, so swift to do her woe
For selfish ends, while harming those at home.

DIONYSUS: Nice, by Poseidon, very nice. And you?

ÆSCHYLUS: It's never wise, within your state,
To rear a baby lion cub; 1910
But if you have, and he grows up,
You're best to cater to his taste.

DIONYSUS: Oh help me Zeus if I know what to do!
One was so clear, but the other so wise! All right, one more: what can the city do to save itself? 1915

EURIPIDES: If we could get old tub-o'-guts Kleocritus[91] airborne, say, on a pair of wings made out of that fairy Kinesias, he could fly over the sea—

DIONYSUS: —what, so that the enemy dies 1920 laughing?

EURIPIDES: No, because he'd be armed with bottles of vinegar, and he'd spray-bomb the enemy's eyes!

DIONYSUS: You're a genius. What a brilliant invention. Did you think this up all by yourself, 1925 or did your wife's boyfriend help you?

EURIPIDES: No! it was all mine—except the vinegar part was Kephisophon's idea. Actually, I have an idea of my own which I'd like to share.

DIONYSUS: Go ahead. 1930

EURIPIDES: When we regard as trustworthy what we do not trust now, and as untrustworthy that which we now do trust—

DIONYSUS: What? Wait, can you be a little clearer and...just a bit...stupider? 1935

EURIPIDES: If we were to shift our trust from the ones we trust now, and put it instead in those we ignore—

DIONYSUS: —then we'd be saved?

EURIPIDES: It's only logical that if we're failing with 1940 what we're doing now, we should do the opposite.

DIONYSUS: And what do you think?

ÆSCHYLUS: First, tell me this: who *is* the city trusting right now? Her best citizens?

DIONYSUS: Are you kidding? She loathes them. 1945

ÆSCHYLUS: Who does she like then—her worst?

DIONYSUS: Well, no, she doesn't actually like them either, but she's stuck with 'em.

ÆSCHYLUS: Well if she turns her nose up at both caviar and cod, how does she expect to keep herself 1950 alive?[92]

DIONYSUS: If you can think of a solution, you can come back up with me....

ÆSCHYLUS: Me? I'll....tell you when I get up there.

DIONYSUS: Ohho, no you don't; you've got to come 1955 up with the goods right here.

ÆSCHYLUS: "When they treat their enemy's soil as their own, and their own as the enemy's; when they see their ships as their wealth, and their riches as dross." 1960

DIONYSUS: I wouldn't worry about the riches part; the lawyers get it all anyway.[93]

PLUTO: Please; the time has come. You must decide.

DIONYSUS: Okay.....I'm going to go with....the one my inner soul tells me.... 1965

EURIPIDES: —and don't forget the gods, the ones you swore by to come after me....And hey, who loves you, man?

DIONYSUS: "It was only my tongue that swore....."[94] I'm going with Aeschylus. 1970

EURIPIDES: You miserable traitor!

DIONYSUS: What, for choosing Aeschylus? What's wrong with that?

EURIPIDES: How can you look me in the face and ask me that? You should be ashamed![95] 1975

---

91 Identity uncertain.

92 Lit., won't accept either a woollen cloak or a goat-skin coat, seemingly proverbial for self-destructive pickiness.

93 Lit., the jurors, who were paid three obols a day for judging lawsuits.

94 From Euripides' *Hippolytus*. See above, n. 13.

95 See Sophocles' *Philoctetes*, l. 108–110.

DIONYSUS: Hey, you're the one who always said that shame is an outdated emotion![96]

EURIPIDES: [*tragic diction*] Oh, you villain, you heartless wretch, how can you leave me so....dead?

DIONYSUS: How? I think you put it quite well 1980 yourself: "Who really knows if death is death, or life is life"—or breath is brunch, or sleep a flannel shirt?

PLUTO: Dionysus, and you too, Aeschylus, please, come with me... 1985

DIONYSUS: But...

PLUTO: I'd like to offer you some hospitality before you set sail.

DIONYSUS: Oh! Great! Thanks! [*they exit*]

CHORUS: How lucky and rare it is to find 1990
A man with a precision mind;
From him we learn by wise example;
Thus he, his wisdom judged so ample,
Returns again, back home to bring
His blessings to his friends and kin— 1995
That is to say, *all* citizens,
For we all gain from his intelligence.

The moral, my friends?
It *isn't* so cool, in the end, to sit
At the bare feet of Socrates, picking nits, 2000
Sophisticating your life away,
Neglecting the matters that go to the heart
Of the ancient and noble tragedian's art.
To idle one's time in such talk idiotic
Is to risk being seen as an utter psychotic. 2005

PLUTO: Well, farewell then, Aeschylus, and good luck. Take your wise advice, and use it to save the city; try to educate the fools there, numerous though they are. And you, Xanthias, take this sword, and give it to Cleophon; and give these 2010 nooses to Inland Revenue and also to Myrmex and Nicomachus; and give this hemlock here to Archenomus; and tell them all to hurry up and get down here immediately, because if they don't, I'll come for 'em myself, brand 'em, cuff 'em, and 2015 transport 'em six feet under where they belong.[97]

ÆSCHYLUS: I'll do my best. And, would you mind doing me a favour? Give my chair to Sophocles to look after for me while I'm gone? He's the second-greatest poet there is. And make sure above all that 2020 that filthy lying pervert never sits in my chair—ever, even by mistake.

PLUTO: Now, if we could have the Chorus bring out their torches and sing a hymn of praise in this man's honour, escorting him out of Hades with an 2025 example of his own art.

CHORUS: You under-world gods: grant this artist safe passage.
Guide him up to the light with good thoughts and good blessings
That the city see an end to its painful misfortune
Of fearful encounters on water and earth; 2030
And if Cleophon or anyone else still wants to fight,
They're free to go do it—on *their* native turf![98]

---

[96] Lit., "What's shameful, if it doesn't seem that way to those...[who do it]." Quoted from Euripides' *Aeolus*, and a particularly scandalous utterance in its original context: a brother defending the incestuous rape of his sister with the idea that morality is a matter of personal taste.

---

[97] Appended to the end of this line, possibly for the second production of *Frogs* in 404, are the words "along with Adeimantus, son of Leucolophus." Cousin of Alcibiades and general of the fleet, Adeimantus tried (unsuccessfully) to prevent the mutilation of prisoners of war in 405; after the disastrous battle of Aigospotamoi, he came to be seen as traitor. See Dover 1993:76 and Sommerstein 1996:297 n. 1512.

[98] Cleophon's mother, often ridiculed in comedy as a babbling foreigner, was evidently from Thrace. Cleophon and his "non-Athenian" cohorts are being attacked here for their reckless refusal to accept the peace-treaty offered by Sparta, for perpetuating the war and, as was to be the case, for sealing Athens' doom.

PLAUTUS

Miles Gloriosus (The Braggart Warrior)

Based on an unknown Greek New Comedy called *Braggart*, *Miles Gloriosus* introduces us to some of the most enduring stock elements of ancient situation comedy: the braggart soldier and his crafty slave, the stupid slave, the drunken slave, the bloodthirsty cook, prostitutes with hearts of gold, and, as always in such domestic sitcoms, the sincere young lovers whose union is blocked by the old masters but abetted by their clever slaves. Through a succession of cunning plans involving deception, disguise, and role-playing, slave outwits master and the lovers are united in the end. Whether in the travelling improv troupes of the commedia dell'arte, the thwarted lovers' plays of Shakespeare, or the crafty servant comedies of Molière and Beaumarchais, the theatrical conventions manifested in *Miles Gloriosus* will resurface across Europe during the Renaissance, down to and including the standard location for such intrigues: the city street with its "two houses divided."

Pyrgopolynices and Palaestrio in particular show Plautus as a bridge between the comic theatre of Greece and that of post-Renaissance Italy, England and France. This master-servant duo is both a direct descendant of the comic pairing of Dionysus and Xanthias in *Frogs*, and the prototype for many later comic couples such as The Count and Figaro, and Don Giovanni and Leporello (including the famous list of conquests by the thousands). Individually, too, Palaestrio has fathered countless successors in the literature, while deluded swaggering dolts like Pygopolynices are ubiquitous in Western performance media, from Renaissance figures like Il Capitano and Ralph Roister Doister to twentieth-century sitcom characters by the score.

Plautus's play is also, however, an exuberant comic creation in its own right. Performed around 206 B.C.E. in Rome, it seems to have succeeded in drawing an audience and actually keeping it in the theatre—an achievement in itself given that plays in Plautus's time had to compete with such sensational spectacles as gladiatorial combat, animal acts, chariot races and mock sea battles, all involving real blood, agony, and death.[1] Unfortunately, the appeal of *Miles Gloriosus* to its first audiences can scarcely be imagined from reading alone, for its performance depended on a number of features not recorded in the text: nearly constant music and songs, broad clowning and physical comedy, fast-paced chaotic action, and the ebullient word-play, punning and alliteration that are always somewhat lost in translation. Above all, the long stage of the Roman theatre made continual running a virtual necessity, especially for the scheming slaves who were the main attractions in this type of theatre. Clad in funny red wigs and fat with the padding of traditional Greek comedy costume, the actors who played the slaves seem in fact to have been famous for their own particular

---

[1] Terence tells of two attempts, a few decades later, to perform his play *The Mother-in-Law,* both of which were foiled by the audience's flight to more spectacular entertainments.

trademark running styles, refined and perfected over the course of their careers and doubtless fondly anticipated by audiences. With its doors and balconies and decorative alcoves, the long and narrow Roman stage would also have provided many opportunities for comic hiding, asides, mistaken identities, entrances and exits and bumping into other running slaves.

Although beatings, threats of beatings, and the tendency for the slave to be cleverer than the master are already present as comic conventions in Athenian Old Comedy, all are ratcheted up several notches in Rome. Gruesome death by public crucifixion did indeed lie perpetually in wait for rebellious slaves, and Roman playwrights, for their part, laboured under savage censorship laws that specified death as the penalty for slander. Under such violent and repressive circumstances, not only did slaves need to be crafty to survive—so too did playwrights like Plautus.

Note on character-names. Intentionally long and difficult to pronounce, the names of Plautus's characters are Greek coinages which convey the main attributes of the person named: Pyrgopolynices means roughly "Many City Sacker," Palaestrio is a "Wrestler," Artotrogus a "Bread-Gobbler," Philocomasium a "Party Lover;" Acroteleutium is the "Ultimate End," i.e., the best, and Pleusicles denotes "Sailing to Glory."

PLAUTUS

Miles Gloriosus (The Braggart Warrior)

Translated by Peter L. Smith

CHARACTERS

PYRGOPOLYNICES, a vainglorious soldier, (resident in Ephesus)
ARTOTROGUS, his parasite
PALAESTRIO, a cunning slave of Pyrgopolynices
PLEUSICLES, a young Athenian (Palaestrio's former master)
PHILOCOMASIUM, a young Athenian courtesan (Pyrgopolynices' concubine, in love with Pleusicles)
SCELEDRUS, a stupid slave of Pyrgopolynices (Philocomasium's guard)
PERIPLECTOMENUS, a pleasant old man (Pleusicles' host in Ephesus)
ACROTELEUTIUM, a courtesan, client of Periplectomenus
MILPHIDIPPA, her alluring maid
LURCIO, a bibulous slave of Pyrgopolynices

CARIO, a bloodthirsty cook of Periplectomenus
Various attendant slaves, all minor parts or silent roles

ACT I

[*The stage represents a street, ostensibly in Ephesus, but in fact not unlike a typical street in Rome. We see two houses, side by side. Although they are attached to each other by a common wall, it is clear that they are two distinct residences. The house on stage left belongs to Pyrgopolynices, the braggart warrior; its neighbor belongs to Periplectomenus, an urbane and elderly bachelor. Each house has a prominent door opening onto the street. Downstage center there is a low altar; otherwise the street is clear. Enter PYRGOPOLYNICES, preceded by several weird and dismally incompetent slaves; he is followed at a short distance by his parasite ARTOTROGUS, who is well fed and well oiled.*]

ACT I, SCENE 1

PYRGO.: [*striking a pose and addressing his slaves*]
    Shine my shield till it glows and glitters and gleams
    Like the radiant rays of the sun from a summer sky;
    So, when its hour has come and the foe's at hand,
    Its dazzling light will dizzy the enemy line.
    My task will be to comfort this pining sword: 5
    My gay blade mustn't despair or get down in the
        mouth.
    Poor lad, he's lived so long with his nose in my belt
    That now he longs to give someone a belt in the
        nose.
    Where's Artotrogus?
ARTOT.:   Here, beside a hero
    Audacious, tenacious, sagacious; good gracious, a   10
        king!
    And a warrior! Even Mars would hesitate
    To match his deeds of courage against yours.
PYRGO.: Was he the one I saved on Cockroach Plains,
    Where the commander-in-chief was Neptune's
        grandson,
    Bumbomachides Clytomestoridysarchides?[1]   15
ARTOT.: I remember. The one with golden armour,
    Whose troops you puffed apart with a breath of air,
    As the wind blows leaves or scatters a house of straw.
PYRGO.: Great Pollux, that was nothing.
ARTOT.:   Great Hercules,
    It was nothing compared to other deeds   20
    I could describe—[*aside*] except you never did them.
    [*speaking directly to the audience*]
    If anyone knows a more colossal liar,
    A man more stuffed with pride and vanity,
    Then call me your slave; I'll put myself on the block.
    Why do I stay? His cheese sauce is divine!   25
PYRGO.: Where are you?
ARTOT.:   Here, sir. Remember, sir,
    That poor elephant we met in India?
    You forcefully flung your fist and fractured his arm!
PYRGO.: His "arm"?
ARTOT.:   I actually meant to say his "leg."
PYRGO.: But I hit him a careless blow.   30

---

[1] Bumbomachides means "son of roaring battle";
    Clytomestoridysarchides is obscure but clearly meant to
    denote a very grandiose opponent.

ARTOT.:   By Pollux, if only
    You'd really tried, you'd have transpenetrated your
        arm
    Through hide and guts clear down to elephant
        marrow.
PYRGO.: Let's not discuss it now.
ARTOT.:   Heavens-to-Hercules,
    It's a waste of valuable breath for you to tell me:
    I know what a great, strong man you are.   35
    [*aside*] This painful role is strictly from hunger,
        friends:
    I've got to get an earful to keep my stomach cheerful,
    So I'm forced to nod my head to all his lies.
PYRGO.: Now what was I saying?
ARTOT.:   Aha! I know what you want
    To say. It's a fact, sir, you did! I remember, you did!   40
PYRGO.: Did what?
ARTOT.:   Well, whatever it was that you did.
PYRGO.: Have you got—
ARTOT.:   Wax tablets? Yes, and a stylus, too.
PYRGO.: How intelligent of you to read my mind!
ARTOT.: I'm a student of all your ways; that's only right.
    My mission is to sniff your every whim.   45
PYRGO.: How good's your memory?
ARTOT.: [*madly improvising*] In Cilicia, I recall,
    A hundred and fifty, a hundred in Babblebaloneya,
    Thirty Sards, three score from Macedon—
    All men that you . . . killed off one afternoon.   50
PYRGO.: And what's the total sum?
ARTOT.: [*after a rapid mental calculation*] Seven
        thousand.
PYRGO.: That should be right. First-class arithmetic!
ARTOT.: It's not written down, but I still remember it.
PYRGO.: Great Pollux, I love your memory!
ARTOT.:   It runs on food.
PYRGO.: If you never change, you'll never miss a meal;   55
    You'll always be my table's closest friend.
ARTOT.: [*with renewed enthusiasm*]
    In Cappadocia, five hundred at once (if your sword
    Had not gone dull) you'd have slain with a single
        slice.
PYRGO.: Poor nonentities, I let them live.
ARTOT.: Why should I tell you what every mortal   60
        knows?
    Pyrgopolynices, you alone on earth
    In courage and beauty and action stand invincible.

All the girls adore you, naturally,
Because you're so handsome.
Yesterday some of them   65
Caught me by the sleeve.
PYRGO.:   And what did they say?
ARTOT.: They grilled me. "Is he Achilles?" said one
    to me.
    "No," I replied; "his brother." Then the second
    Said, "Merciful Castor, what a gorgeous man!
    A real gentleman! Look at his dreamy hair!   70
    I envy the girls that climb into bed with him!"
PYRGO.: That's what they said?
ARTOT.:   Didn't they both implore me
    To march you past on parade over there today?
PYRGO.: It's a pain to be painfully handsome.
ARTOT.: You're telling me.   75
    The girls are pests: they plead and badger and beg
    To see you, ordering me to bring you round.
    I can't attend to your business affairs.
PYRGO.: I think it's time for us to go to the forum,
    Where I ought to pay the salary   80
    Of those recruits I signed up yesterday.
    King Seleucus is awfully keen for me
    To round up and enlist recruits for him.
    [solemnly] This day is dedicated to the King.
ARTOT.: Let's go then, sir.   85
PYRGO.:   Follow on, attendant lords.
    [They march out toward the forum, stage left.]

ACT II

[The door of the house on stage left opens, and
PALAESTRIO steps forward to address the audience.
Although he is Pyrgopolynices' slave, his prior loyalty is
to the young Athenian Pleusicles, as he will explain.
PALAESTRIO is ingratiating and shrewd, a paragon
of the tricky slave.]

ACT II, SCENE 1

PALAE.: To tell you the plot of our play is my kind
    intention,
    If you'll be so good as to listen with total attention.
    If you're not in the mood, get up and go out for a
    walk;
    Make room for someone who wants to hear me
    talk. [a defiant pause]

So you'll know why you're present in this place of   5
    joy,
I'll tell you the name and the plot (a thumbnail
    sketch)
Of the comedy that we're about to play.
In Greek it's called *Alazon* (or *The Braggart*);
Our Latin title is *Miles Gloriosus.*
This town is Ephesus. That soldier is my master—   10
He's on his way to the forum: boastful, shameless,
Slimy, full of lies and lechery.
He says the girls all chase him, out of control;
The truth is, he's a laughing-stock wherever he goes.
Our hookers pucker up to egg him on,   15
Their every smooch a smirk of ridicule.
I haven't been his faithful slave for long.
I want you to know the story—how I came
From my old service into this new servility.
Pay attention! Now I'll begin to weave the plot.   20
I had a master in Athens, a fine young man;
He was hot for a harlot (maid-in-Athens brand)
And she loved him—a romantic situation.
He was sent to Naupactus as an ambassador
On behalf of our great and glorious government.   25
Meanwhile, this soldier comes along to Athens,
And snakes his way in beside my master's girl.
He went ahead by playing up to her mother
With baubles and bottles of bubbly and fabulous
    food.
Soon the old girl and the soldier were thick as   30
    thieves.
The moment our soldier saw his golden chance,
He bamboozled that bitch—the mother of the girl
My master loved; for unbeknownst to mom
He whisked her daughter off to a boat and
    brought her
Here to Ephesus, against her will.   35

When I knew my master's girl was filched from
    Athens,
Quick as a wink I got hold of a ship myself,
And set out for Naupactus to bring my master the
    news.
But when we were far at sea, as luck would have it,
Pirates seized the boat I was sailing on.   40
I had no chance; the message never arrived.
They gave me as a present to this soldier.

After he brought me home into his household,
I saw my master's love, the Athenian girl.
When she caught sight of me, she winked and   45
    gave a sign
Not to speak her name; then, when the chance
    arose,
Upon my shoulder poured out her tale of woe:
She told me she longed to fly from here to Athens,
Said she still loved my young Athenian master,
And hated no one worse than that soldier of ours.   50

As for me, when I learned the woman's heart,
I scribbled a message, signed it, secretly
Passed it to a certain merchant to take to Athens
To my master, who'd loved this girl, in order to
    tell him
To come here. He didn't ignore my note;   55
You see, he's come, and is staying here next door
With a close friend of the family, a charming old
    man.
This old man's trying to help his love-struck guest;
He's pitching in with advice and encouragement.

And so, inside, I've hit on a staggering stunt   60
For the lovers to have a private rendezvous.
The soldier had given a room to his little lady,
Her own retreat—no one else allowed inside—
And in that room I chopped a hole in the wall
To grant her secret access to this house;   65
The old man knows I did it: he gave advice.

I've got a fellow slave—a worthless type;
The soldier ordered *him* to guard the girl.
With the help of a slick sort of confidence trick
And a clever disguise, we'll throw dust in his eyes!   70
We'll make the man unsee what he plainly saw.
Don't get confused: today this woman will play
Two roles as she passes back and forth. She'll be
One and the same girl, whatever she may pretend.
With her help we'll make an ass of the slave on   75
    guard.

I hear a noise from the old man's house next door.
That's him: the charming old man I told you about.

ACT II, SCENE 2

[*The old man PERIPLECTOMENUS emerges
through the door of his own house, stage right. He is
furiously berating his slaves.*]

PERIP.: From this time on, by Hercules,
    If you see a stranger up on the roof,
    And let him escape without broken bones,
    I'll cut you to pieces! I'll skin you alive!

My neighbours here have a grandstand view   5
Of all that's happening in my house:
They simply peer through the open skylight!

Here's my public proclamation:
If you see any man from that soldier's house
Cavorting or sporting on top of our roof   10
(Except Palaestrio, of course),
Then give him a shove down into the street.
Whether he claims to be chasing a chicken,
Pursuing a pigeon or hunting a monkey,
All you slaves are as good as dead   15
Unless you pummel and pound him to pulp.
And while you're at it, check that house
For any infraction of gambling laws;
If they've been rolling dice, make sure
They've got no bones to party with.   20
PALAE.: Some kind of crime has been committed,
    By a man from our house—this much I've heard;
    And so the old man's told his boys
    To fracture all my fellow slaves.
    But I heard him say he didn't mean me;   25
    Who gives a damn what he does to the rest?
    I'll go up to him.
PERIP.: Who's this?
    Is that you coming, Palaestrio?
PALAE.: What's going on, Periplectomenus?   30
PERIP.: You're just the man I want to see.
PALAE.: What is it? Why are you ranting and roaring
    Against our house?
PERIP.:   Our goose is cooked!
PALAE.: What's the trouble?
PERIP.:   It's out in the open.
PALAE.: What's out in the open?   35
PERIP.:   From the roof
    A moment ago some man looked down—

One of the people who live in your house—
And through our skylight caught a glimpse
Of Philocomasium and my young guest
Kissing each other.   40
PALAE.:   Who was the man?
PERIP.: Your fellow slave.
PALAE.:   .   Which one do you mean?
PERIP.: I've no idea: he took to his heels
In a hell of a hurry.
PALAE.:   I've a hunch
It's all over with me.
PERIP.:   When he ran, I bellowed:
"Hey, what are you doing up there on the roof?"   45
He shouted back without slowing down;
He said he was on a monkey chase.
PALAE.: Ye gods, to think my life's been ruined
All on account of a wandering ape!
Look, is the girl Philocomasium still here   50
In your house?
PERIP.:   When I came out, she was.
PALAE.: Please go, tell her to cross to our house
Quick as she can, and let the whole household
See her at home, unless she wants
Her love affair to give all us slaves   55
A swinging party up on the cross.[2]
PERIP.: I've told her that; if you've nothing to add—
PALAE.: But I have. You've got to tell her this:
On no account must she lose her grip
On woman's instinctive genius;   60
And she must cultivate all the acquired
Skills of her sex.
PERIP.:   How do you mean?
PALAE.: To confute that confounded spy on the roof
And convince him he couldn't have seen her there.
What if he's seen her a hundred times?   65
She must deny it all the same.
She's got good looks and a treacherous tongue,
She's brash and bold and brassy;

She trusts herself, she can lean on herself,
She's sneaky and snake-in-the-grass-y.   70
Let her face her accuser and talk him down
By swearing a solemn and sacred oath.
She's well supplied with lies and perjuries,
Fibs and frauds and fabrications,
Diabolical machinations,   75
Hypocritical falsifications,
A slippery woman needn't shop
For fresh chicanery at the store;
Her garden at home produces a crop
Of lies by the bushel beside her door.   80
PERIP.: If she's here, I'll pass the message.
What do you think, Palaestrio?
What trick are you tossing now in your brain?
PALAE.: Just keep quiet a little while,
While I muster all my plans,   85
While I ponder what to do,
While I think of a wily trick
To dupe my wily fellow slave,
Who saw her kissing here just now.
I'll make him unsee what he saw.   90
PERIP.: Ponder away! I'll back off
To give you room. [*to audience*]
Just look at the man!
The way he stands with his face screwed up,
Stern and worried and full of thought!   95
He knocks on his head with his fist. I think
He's calling his brain to come out and join in.
Look! He's turning; his left hand now
Is propped in position on his left leg,
While his right hand acts as an adding machine,   100
Pounding out sums on the other leg.
Ouch! What a slap! This infant plan
Is having a dreadfully difficult birth.
He's snapped his fingers; he's working away;
He's shifting position again and again.   105
Oh, look now! He shakes his head:
He doesn't seem to like what he's found.
Whatever comes out, it'll be well done:
He'll never produce a half-baked plan.

Hey! Now he's entered the building trade: 110
He's propped a column under his chin.
Go on! I take no pleasure at all
In that kind of architectural style:

---

2 Crucifixion had been practised in Rome as an ordinary,
   if especially gruesome, form of capital punishment for
   hundreds of years before Christ. It was used on slaves particularly, but also on Jews and other rebels. When slaves
   throughout the play refer to "the cross," they are speaking of an everyday and highly visible form of torture and
   murder.

I've heard of a poet—a foreign type—
Who holds a similar propped-up pose,   115
While languishing inside the lock-up,
Doubly guarded all day long.[3]
Ah, how pretty! He's standing there gracefully,
Just like a slave in a comedy.
He'll never get a moment's rest   120
Until he gains his heart's desire.
I think he's found it.

PALAE.: [*adopting an attitude of self-harangue*]
Come! if you've got it,
Wake up, don't let yourself fall asleep,
Unless you want to do sentry duty,   125
Bruised and battered and black and blue.
I'm speaking to *you*. Have you been drinking?
Hey! I'm talking to you, Palaestrio!
Come on, wake up! Come on, get up!
Come on, *it's morning*!   130

[*replying to the voice of his alter ego*] I hear you.

[*first voice continues*]
You see? The enemy's close at hand;
Your back is under siege; take thought!
Bring in reinforcements; summon aid.
It's time for haste; no time to waste.   135
Take the offensive! Some way, somehow,
Circle and cut them off in the rear!
Lay down a blockade to foil the foe,
Put up a stockade to guard our men.
Destroy the enemy's line of supply,   140
Then build a road that will make it safe
For food and provisions and army divisions
To be transported wherever you go.
Look after this business! It calls for speed.
Come on, be quick, be calm, be cool,   145
Produce and perfect a practical plan
To force the seen to become unseen
And make what's done come all undone.

---

[3] Slander of Roman citizens was a crime punishable by
death, and as a result topical jokes about actual individuals were exceedingly rare in the theatre. This, however,
seems to be a reference to Gnaeus Naevius (270–190s
B.C.E.), an imprisoned and later exiled dramatist who got
in trouble with a powerful family for naming it in a play.

PERIP.: [*to audience*] This fellow's launching a great
    campaign,
He's building bulging battlements.   150
PALAE.: Just give the word that you'll take charge,
And our hearts will soar with hope that we
Can crush our enemies.
PERIP.:   Here's the word:
I'll take charge.
PALAE.:   I say you'll get
Whatever you're after.   155
PERIP.:   Jupiter
Bless you, friend! Could you please
Let me share in your bold invention?
PALAE.:   Shhh!
I'll lead you into the secret realm
Of dark skulduggery. Soon you'll know
My plans as well as I do myself.   160
PERIP.: I promise they'll be safe with me.
PALAE.: My boss—this soldier—hasn't got human
Skin; he's surrounded with elephant hide.
And no more brains than a pile of rocks.
PERIP.: I won't argue with you on this!   165
PALAE.: Here's the scheme I've got in mind;
I'm contemplating a pleasant plot.
I'll tell him that Philocomasium's sister
(I'll say that she's an identical twin)
Has just arrived in town from Athens,   170
Bringing along her fiancé.
As like her sister as peas in a pod!
And I'll tell him they're both staying as guests
Here in your house.
PERIP.:   Magnificent!
Delightful! A spectacular invention!   175
PALAE.: As a result, if my fellow slave
Brings a charge before the soldier
And claims he's seen her over here,
Kissing a stranger, I'll calmly prove
It was really her sister the fellow saw   180
Hugging and kissing her lover.
PERIP.:   Superb!
I'll tell the same story if the soldier
Questions me.
PALAE.:   But be sure to say
They're identical; and Philocomasium
Must be forewarned, so she won't slip   185
When the soldier questions her.

PERIP.:   Brilliant!
    But say if the soldier gets the urge
    To see them both, hand in hand,
    What then?
PALAE.:   That's easy. Anyone clever
    Can bang together a thousand excuses: 190
    "She's not at home, she's out for a walk,
    She's doing her face, she's taking a nap,
    She's in the tub, she's at supper, she's busy.
    She hasn't the time—too bad, old chap."
    You can put him off as much as you want,   195
    If only we're careful, right at the start,
    To make him believe our lies are true.
PERIP.: A lovely plan!
PALAE.:   Please go in, then,
    And tell the woman, if she's there,
    To cross to our house at once. And look—   200
    Teach her, train her, school her well
    To use our plan the way we wove it:
    She's her twin sister.
PERIP.:   I'll send her home
    Schooled like a scholar. Anything else?
PALAE.: Just go in.   205
PERIP.:   I'm going. [*exit into his own house*]
PALAE.:   It's home
    For me too: I've got a man to track.
    I'll go under cover and snoop around,
    To find out which of my fellow slaves
    Was chasing a monkey over the roof.
    The man would be bound to spread the word   210
    That he'd seen our master's light-of-love
    Here, next door, in the fond embrace
    Of some young punk from out of town.
    I know the type: "Have I got *news*!
    I've got to tell someone before I burst!"   215
    If I learn who saw her, he'll be faced
    With catapults and battering rams.
    My plans are ready, my aim is fixed:
    To storm his camp and seize the man.
    If I can't find him, I'll follow my nose   220
    And sniff his tracks like a hungry hound
    Until I've chased the fox to his den.
    Listen! Our doors are creaking open;
    I'd better lower my voice a bit.
    A fellow slave is coming out;   225
    This man is Philocomasium's guard.

ACT II, SCENE 3

[*Enter SCELEDRUS through the door of the soldier's
house. Palaestrio's fellow slave is not very bright.*]

SCELE.: Unless I've just been having a nightmare,
    Walking around on top of the roof,
    Honest-to-Pollux I'd swear I saw
    Philocomasium, master's girlfriend,
    Here, next door, up to no good.   5
PALAE.: He's the one who saw her kissing—
    I've heard him say that much himself.
SCELE.: Who's that?
PALAE.:   Your fellow slave. What is it, Sceledrus?
SCELE.: Oh, Palaestrio,
    I'm so happy to see you!   10
PALAE.:   Why?
    What's the trouble? Give me a clue.
SCELE.: I'm afraid—
PALAE.:   Of what?
SCELE.:   O Herc! I'm afraid
    That today all the slaves in our house
    Will get lifted up to hang from the cross.
PALAE.: Go lift yourself! I don't much care   15
    For these uplifting thoughts of yours.
SCELE.: Probably you don't know the amazing
    Thing that has just happened in here.
PALAE.: What thing do you mean?
SCELE.:   It's wicked and awful!
PALAE.: Keep it to yourself, then. Don't tell me;   20
    I've no desire to know.
SCELE.:   Well,
    I won't allow you not to know.
    Today I chased our little monkey
    Over onto this man's roof.
PALAE.: Great Pollux, Sceledrus, why in the world   25
    Would a chimp be chased by a chump like you?
SCELE.: Oh, go to hell!
PALAE.:   Well, my advice
    To you, my friend, is go—on speaking.
SCELE.: As luck would have it, through the skylight
    I looked down to the house next door.   30
    There I saw Philocomasium kissing
    Some young fellow I didn't know.
PALAE.: Sceledrus! A scandalous, slanderous lie!
SCELE.: I definitely saw her.
PALAE.:   You?

SCELE.:   Yes, me.
  I saw her with these two eyes of mine.   35
PALAE.: Go on, you didn't! A likely story!
SCELE.: Do you think there's something wrong with
      my eyes?
PALAE.: I don't give medical advice.
  But if the gods are on your side,
  You'll have the sense to drop that tale.   40
  I warn you not to lose your head:
  You might not get it back again.
  Unless you stop that stupid talk
  A double death's in store for you.
SCELE.: Why do you say double?   45
PALAE.:   I'll explain.
  In the first case, if you falsely charge
  Our Philocomasium, you're a goner!
  In the second, if your facts are right
  And you were the guard, you're a goner again.
SCELE.: I don't know what'll become of me: 50
  I only know I really saw it.
PALAE.: Do you still insist, you idiot?
SCELE.:   What
  Do you want me to say except what I saw?
  Anyhow, she's still inside right here,
  At the house next door.   55
PALAE.:   What, not at home?
SCELE.: Take a look, go inside yourself;
  I don't ask you to take my word.
PALAE.: All right, I'll go. [exit into soldier's house]
SCELE.:   I'll wait for you here.
  [to audience] While I'm at it, I'll set a trap;
  I'll catch that heifer and tan her hide,   60
  As soon as she tries to return to the barn.

  What am I going to do? The soldier
  Put me in charge of guarding her.
  If I accuse her now, I'm through;
  I'm through all the same if I shut up   65
  And the news gets out. What in the world's
  More shameless and depraved than women?
  While I was up on the roof, that girl
  Just left her room and went outside.
  Pollux! What a brazen bitch!   70
  If the soldier finds this out,
  I swear to Herc he'll hang the house
  And hoist yours truly on the cross.

Whatever happens, I'll keep mum
Rather than die in agony.   75
How can I possibly guard a woman
Who's always got herself for sale?
PALAE.: [emerging from the soldier's house]
  Sceledrus, Sceledrus, what other man
  Is such a barefaced liar as you?
  When you were born the gods above   80
  Must've groaned with anger!
SCELE.:   What is it?
PALAE.: Do you want to get your eyes gouged out,
  When they're seeing things that don't exist?
SCELE.: That don't exist?
PALAE.:   I wouldn't buy
  Your claim to life for a worm-eaten walnut!   85
SCELE.: What's the trouble?
PALAE.:   What's the trouble,
  You're asking me?
SCELE.:   Why not ask you?
PALAE.: Wouldn't it be a good idea
  To get your tattletale tongue cut out?
SCELE.: My what?   90
PALAE.: Look! Philocomasium's
  At home—the girl you saw next door,
  Kissing and hugging another man.
SCELE.: I'm surprised you can't afford
  To drink a better grade of wine.   95
PALAE.: Come again?
SCELE.: There's something wrong with your eyes.
PALAE.: Well, as for you, my squinting friend,
  You're blind: that's all that's wrong with *your* eyes.
  That woman's definitely at home.   100
SCELE.: At home, you say?
PALAE.:   At home, I say.
SCELE.: You're pulling my leg, Palaestrio.
PALAE.: Then I'd better go home and wash my hands.
SCELE.: How's that?
PALAE.:   'Cause you're a muddy mess.
SCELE.: You go to hell!   105
PALAE.:   You'll go to hell,
  Sceledrus, I promise you,
  Unless you get a new pair of eyes
  And learn to sing another tune.
  But look! Our door is opening here.
SCELE.: [indicating Periplectomenus's house]
  Well, *this* is the door I'm looking at;   110

There's no way that she can cross
From here to here, except by the door.
PALAE.: Look! She's home! Oh, Sceledrus,
Some bee in your bonnet is bugging you.
SCELE.: I see for myself, I think for myself, 115
I trust myself more than anyone else:
No man is going to frighten me off
From knowing she's inside this house.
I'll plant myself here, in case that girl
Crawls to her home while I'm off guard. 120
PALAE.: [aside] I've got him now; I'll whirl him about
And hurl him down from his towering fort.
[to Sceledrus] Do you want me to try to make you admit
You're feeble-sighted?
SCELE.:   Go ahead and try.
PALAE.: That you haven't got a brain in your head— 125
That your eyes are useless?
SCELE.:   That I'd love!
PALAE.: I believe you said our master's girl
Was over here?
SCELE.:   Yes. Furthermore,
I say I saw her playing around,
Inside the house, with another man. 130
PALAE.: You know there isn't a passageway
From here to our house.
SCELE.:   Yes, I know.
PALAE.: No balcony or garden route
Unless you fly through the skylight.
SCELE.:   I know.
PALAE.: Well then, if she's home, and if 135
I make you see her leaving our house,
Have you earned a thumping?
SCELE.:   All right.
PALAE.: Watch that door. Don't let her sneak out
Secretly to cross this way.
SCELE.: That's just my plan. 140
PALAE.:   I'll soon produce
Her here, in person, on the street.
[exit again into soldier's house]
SCELE.: Go ahead and try. I want to know
Whether I saw what I think I saw,
Or whether he'll do what he says he'll do
To prove the girl is really home. 145
The eyes I've got are perfectly good,
I'm not in the market for any more.

This fellow's always sniffing around,
He's always playing up to her;
He's the first to be called to dinner, 150
He's the first to be given a bite;
He's been in our house for just three years,
Yet no one else within our walls
Wallows in greater luxury.

But I'd better do what I've got to do: 155
I'll just stand and watch this door.
I'll guard it this way. Here's one time
That no one'll make a fool of me.

[SCELEDRUS stations himself in front of the old man's house, facing the audience. From PALAESTRIO's crucifixion taunt in the next scene, we can assume that he stands with his arms spread out to block the door.]

ACT II, SCENE 4

[PALAESTRIO and PHILOCOMASIUM emerge stealthily from the soldier's house.]

PALAE.: [sotto voce] Obey your orders; don't forget.
PHILO.: Stop nagging: you surprise me.
PALAE.: Well, I'm afraid you're not too bright.
PHILO.: Give me ten empty-headed girls
Without a scheming thought among them: 5
I'll train them and still have tricks to spare.
Come on, get on with your clever games.
I'll move away from you a little.
PALAE.: [aloud] What do you say, Sceledrus?
SCELE.: I'm busy here. I've ears, just speak your wishes. 10
PALAE.: I suspect you're doomed to die
Outside the gate, in that position:
Hands spread out and nailed to the crossbar.
SCELE.: Why in the world do you think that?
PALAE.: Look to your left. Who is that woman? 15
SCELE.: Holy heavenly gods almighty!
This is master's concubine!
PALAE.: That's my own opinion, too.
Come on now, since you're so eager—
SCELE.: What shall I do? 20
PALAE.:   Prepare to die.
PHILO.: Where's that honest slave of yours
Who was spreading ugly libellous lies
About poor little me?

PALAE.:   Here you are!
He told *me* what *I* told *you*.
PHILO.: You big crook, do you claim you saw   25
Me here next door, in the act of kissing?
PALAE.: "With some unknown young fellow," he said.
SCELE.: That's what I said, by Hercules!
PHILO.: *You* saw *me*?
SCELE.:   With my very own eyes!
I think—   30
PHILO.:   —You won't have those eyes for long,
If they see more than there is to see.
SCELE.: So help me Herc, you'll never stop me
From having seen what I said I saw.
PHILO.: Really, it's not very bright of me
To stand and chat with this lunatic: 35
I'll merely have him put to death.
SCELE.: Threaten away! I'm sure the cross
Will be my final resting place.
All my family settled there:
Great-grandfather, Grandpa, Dad.   40
Just the same, these threats of yours
Can't do a thing to hurt my eyes.
But I'd like a word or two with you,
Palaestrio. [*to* PALAE.*, sotto voce*] I want to know,
Where did she come from?   45
PALAE.:   Where else but home?
SCELE.: *Home?*
PALAE.:   Am I standing here?
SCELE.:   I think so.
It's simply amazing how she can move:
There she *was*; here she *is*....where she *wasn't!*
I know there's no balcony on our house,
There's no garden route to cross by,   50
There's no window that isn't barred.
[*he turns to Philocomasium.*]
Damn it, I *did* see you inside here.
PALAE.: Hold on, you scoundrel, are you still trying
To accuse this woman?
PHILO.:   Merciful Castor,
I think my dream has just come true—   55
A dream I had this very night.
PALAE.: What did you dream?
PHILO.:   I'll tell you now.
Pay very close attention, please.
Last night as I slept, I seemed to learn
That my dear sister—she's my twin—   60

Had come from Athens to Ephesus,
Bringing her lover along with her.
Both of them, it seemed to me,
Had come to stay in this house next door.
PALAE.: [*aside*] The story you hear is really Palaestrio's   65
Dream. [*aloud*] Go on, continue.
PHILO.: My sister's arrival had made me happy,
So it seemed; but on her account
I felt I was heavily weighted down
With a load of grave suspicion.   70
For one of my household seemed to me,
In my sleep, to be accusing me
(Exactly as you're doing now)
Of having kissed some strange young man,
Because that sister of mine (my twin)   75
Had kissed her very own dear love.
I was the victim, so I dreamt,
Of such a false and groundless charge.
PALAE.: [*with reverent awe*]
And now you're awake, the same events
Are happening as you saw in your sleep?   80
Sweet Hercules! A dream come true!
Go inside and pray to the gods.
I feel we must relate this news
To the soldier.
PHILO.:   That's what I intend;
I certainly could never bear   85
To be slandered with immorality.
[*exit into the soldier's house*]
SCELE.: I'm a little afraid what I've done;
I've got an itch all over my back.
PALAE.: Do you know you're finished?
SCELE.:   [*bemused*] Now, at least,
She's certainly home. My mind's made up   90
To guard our doorway now, right here,
Wherever *she* is.
PALAE.:   Sceledrus, hey!
How strangely similar her dream
To the pattern you revealed in life,
When you suspected you saw her kissing!   95
SCELE.: I don't know what I should believe.
It's reached the point that what I've seen
I no longer think I really saw.
PALAE.: Great Herc, it'll be too late, I think,
When you come to. If this news gets   100
To our master first, you're sweetly screwed.

SCELE.: Now I've got the funny feeling
  I'm walking around inside a fog.
PALAE.: Obviously that was true just now
  Since she was home here all the time.   105
SCELE.: I really don't know what to say.
  I didn't see her, and yet I did.
PALAE.: Honest to Pollux, you're such a fool
  I think you've almost ruined us:
  Wanting to play the faithful slave   110
  For master, you've almost been swallowed up.
  But listen! That was a creaking sound
  From our neighbour's door. I'll keep quiet.

ACT II, SCENE 5

[*PHILOCOMASIUM appears from the old man's
house, hastily disguised as her twin sister. Her attitude
is melodramatically reverent and gravely heroic.*]

PHILO.: Fire the altar! Praise and joy!
  I thank thee, Diana of Ephesus!
  O incense, arise to her in the skies,
  O sweet-smoke odour of Araby.
  Yea, when I rode in the realm of Neptune,   5
  Tossed by the tempest's turbulent tide,
  She saved me—saved me from sore affliction,
  While the baleful billows boiled.
SCELE.: Palaestrio, O Palaestrio!
PALAE.: O Sceledrus, Sceledrus, what is it?   10
SCELE.: This woman, who's just come out from here,
  Is she our master's concubine,
  Philocomasium, or isn't she?
PALAE.: By heaven, I think so; yes, she seems so.
  But it's simply amazing how she can move: 15
  There she *was*; here she *is*... where she *wasn't*!
  (If it's her.)
SCELE.:   Have you got any doubt
  That this is her?
PALAE.:   She seems to be.
SCELE.: Let's go near, let's speak her name.
  Hey there, Philocomasium!   20
  What business have you in that house,
  And what're you up to over there?
  Why are you silent? I'm talking to you!
PALAE.: No, by Pollux, you're all on your own;
  This girl is making no reply.   25
SCELE.: I'm talking to *you*, you sneaky slut,
  Who wander around the neighbourhood.

PHILO.: [*icily*] With whom are you conversing?
SCELE.: With *whom*? With *youm*!
PHILO.:   But who are you,
  And what have you got to do with me?   30
SCELE.: You ask me who I am?
PHILO.:   Why not?
  Why shouldn't I ask what I don't know?
PALAE.: Who am I, then, if you don't know him?
PHILO.: You're an awful nuisance, whoever you are,
  Both you and he.   35
SCELE.:   You don't know us?
PHILO.: Neither of you.
SCELE.:   Oh dear, I'm afraid—
PALAE.: Afraid of what?
SCELE.:   Afraid that somewhere
  We've lost our own identity!
  She says she doesn't know you or me.
PALAE.: I want to follow this up, Sceledrus,   40
  (Whether we're us or someone else):
  It could be that a neighbour of ours,
  While we were looking the other way,
  Has made some change in you and me.
SCELE.: Damn it, I'm certainly me!   45
PALAE.:   And I
  Am I. You're looking for trouble, wench!
  I'm speaking to you. Hey! Philocomasium!
PHILO.: What's got into your crazy mind
  That you make up silly names to call me?
PALAE.: Aha! And what are you normally called?   50
PHILO.: My name's Justine.
SCELE.:   Like hell it is!
  To trick us, Philocomasium,
  You want to have a made-up name.
  You're not Justine, you're *un*-Justine,
  And you're out to do my master harm.   55
PHILO.: I?
SCELE.:   Yes, you.
PHILO.:   Who yesterday
  Came from Athens to Ephesus,
  Just at nightfall, with my lover,
  A young Athenian?
PALAE.:   Tell me, please,
  What's your business in Ephesus?   60
PHILO.: My dear twin sister I heard was living
  Here; I've come to find her.
SCELE.:   Slut!

PHILO.: Well, I swear to Castor, I'm a fool
  To talk with you. I'm leaving now.
SCELE.: But I don't intend to let you leave.   65
PHILO.: Let go!
SCELE.:   Ah, no! You're caught in the act.
  I won't let go.
PHILO.: You'll get a slap like a thunderclap
  If you don't let go!
SCELE.: [to PALAE., *who hasn't moved*]
                          Damn it, get with it!
  Hold her by the other arm.   70
PALAE.: I'm not anxious to have my back
  Exposed to trouble. For all I know
  She may not be Philocomasium
  But another woman just like her.
PHILO.: Will you let me go or won't you?   75
SCELE.:   No!
  By force and strength, against your will,
  If you won't come gladly, I'll drag you home.
PHILO.: This is my home, when I'm abroad;
  My real home base is back in Athens.
  I don't care for that home of yours,   80
  And I don't know who you people are.
SCELE.: Get a lawyer and sue me! I'll never release you
  Unless you give your solemn pledge
  That, if I do, you'll go inside.
PHILO.: You're forcing me, whoever you are.   85
  I give my pledge: let me go, and then
  I'll go inside where you command.
SCELE.: All right, you're free.
PHILO.:   All right, I'm gone!
  [*exit into the old man's house*]
SCELE.: There's a woman's word for you!
PALAE.: Sceledrus, you've let our prize   90
  Slip through your fingers. There's no doubt
  That she's our master's concubine.
  Do you want to give this all you've got?
SCELE.: What should I do?
PALAE.:   Bring me a sword
  Out here.   95
SCELE.:   What will you do with it?
PALAE.: [*heroically*] First I'll burst into the house:
  If I've spied a man inside
  Kissing Philocomasium,
  I'll lop off his head—and he'll be dead!
SCELE.: Did it seem to be her?   100

PALAE.:   Great Pollux, yes,
  Without a doubt.
SCELE.:   But oh, the way
  She pretended!
PALAE.:   Go! Bring out the sword!
SCELE.: I'll see that it's here immediately.
  [*exit into the soldier's house*]
PALAE.: [*to audience*] The infantry and the cavalry
  Are manned by men in their prime;   105
  But for sheer pluck or derring-do,
  The girls win every time!
  The way she managed both her roles:
  Didn't you find her clever?
  She made that idiotic guard   110
  Look sillier than ever!
  What fun to have a space to crawl
  From house to house right through the wall!

[*Enter SCELEDRUS, stunned, from the soldier's house.*]

SCELE.: Oh, Palaestrio, the sword's
  Not necessary.   115
PALAE.:   What? Why not?
SCELE.: She's there at home: master's girl.
PALAE.: At home?
SCELE.:   She's lying on her couch.
PALAE.: Holy Pollux, if this is true,
  You've got yourself in a lovely mess.
SCELE.: How's that?   120
PALAE.:   Because you dared to touch
  That lady from the house next door.
SCELE.: I feel sick.
PALAE.:   There can't be any
  Other explanation:
  That person is our girl's twin sister.
  It was she that you saw kissing.   125
SCELE.: Obviously she's the one,
  Just as you say. I would have been
  On the brink of death, if I'd spoken out.
PALAE.: If you're wise, you'll keep it under your hat:
  A slave may know, but mustn't tell.   130
  I'm leaving now; I've no desire
  To get mixed up with all your plans.
  I'm going to visit my neighbour here;
  Your meddling muddles make me tired.
  If master comes and asks for me,   135
  Look for me here; here's where I'll be.
  [*exit into the old man's house*]

ACT II, SCENE 6

SCELE.: So he's gone, has he? Couldn't care less for
    his master's
    Business! Plays the part of a part-time slave!
    Well, she's at home inside here now, for sure,
    'Cause I just found her lying on her bed.
    My mind's made up to be a watchdog now.   5

[*Enter PERIPLECTOMENUS, from his own house.
He pretends to be unaware of SCELEDRUS, but speaks
for his benefit.*]

PERIP.: So help me Hercules, these slaves next door
    Must think I've had a sudden change of sex:
    They mock me like a woman! And my guest,
    The girl who came from Athens yesterday,
    To be tricked and treated like a common slut!   10
SCELE.: Oh, help! He's heading headlong straight
    for me.
    I'm afraid I may be in a mighty mess,
    To judge from what I heard this old man say.
PERIP.: [*aside*] I'll take him on.
    [*aloud*] Hey, numbskull Sceledrus,   15
    Did you make fun of that girl who's staying with me?
SCELE.: Dear neighbour, sir, please listen.
PERIP.: Me listen to you?
SCELE.: I want to clear myself.
PERIP.: You clear yourself?   20
    After doing a deed so wild and wicked?
    Do you think your precious army connections
    Give you the right to do what you want, jailbird?
SCELE.: May I speak?
PERIP.: So help me gods and goddesses,   25
    I'm going to see you flogged and flayed alive,
    Tormented all day long, from dawn to dusk.
    You broke the tiles and gutters on my roof,
    While you were trying to catch your monkey friend.
    Next, you spied on my house and on my guest,   30
    Who had his dear beloved in his arms;
    You dared to charge your master's blameless girl
    With foul behaviour, me with infamy;
    Abused my lady guest at my front door!
    Unless I see you punished with the lash,   35
    I'll cram that master of yours more full of shame
    Than the sea is full of waves in a winter storm.
SCELE.: I'm so confused, Periplectomenus, I don't
    know

Whether I ought to get annoyed with you...
    But maybe your girl isn't ours and she's not her,   40
    And then I ought to clear myself with you.
    In fact, right now, I don't know what I saw:
    That girl of yours is so much like our own,
    If she isn't the same.
PERIP.: Take a look inside: you'll see.   45
SCELE.: You'd let me?
PERIP.: No, I order you. Take your time.
SCELE.: That's just what I'll do. [*exit into old man's
    house*]
PERIP.: [*rushing to the door of the soldier's house*]
    Quick, Philocomasium,
    Action stations! Run to my house on the run!   50
    Later, when Sceledrus leaves my house, double
    quick
    Make your run on the run back home again.
    Ye gods, I'm sure she's bungled it.
    If he doesn't see the girl—he's at the door.
SCELE.: [*returning from the old man's house*]
    Holy gods almighty! For heaven to make   55
    Two different women more identical:
    Impossible!
PERIP.:   Well?
SCELE.:   I've made a mess of things.
PERIP.: Is she the one?
SCELE.:   She is, and yet she isn't.
PERIP.: Did you see her?
SCELE.:   Yes, I saw her and your guest
    Hugging and kissing.   60
PERIP.:   Is she the one?
SCELE.:   I don't know!
PERIP.: Do you want to know for sure?
SCELE.:   Of course.
PERIP.:   Go inside
    Your house at once; see if your girl's in there.
SCELE.: Fine. That's good advice. I'll be right back.
    [*exit into the soldier's house*]
PERIP.: Great Pollux! I've never seen any man
    Duped and doped in such a funny way!   65
    Look: here he comes.
SCELE.: [*returning from the soldier's house*]
    Periplectomenus, I beg you
    In the name of gods and men, by my lack of brains
    And by your knees—
PERIP.:   To do what?

SCELE.:   To forgive
   My ignorance and stupidity. Now at last   70
   I know I was a blind and brainless idiot.
   Philocomasium's there inside.
PERIP.:   What now,
   Jailbird? Have you seen both girls?
SCELE.:   Yes, I have.
PERIP.: I want you to produce your master.
SCELE.: I've earned a dreadful drubbing, I confess,   75
   And I admit I wronged that guest of yours.
   But I thought she was master's concubine,
   The girl our soldier'd given me to guard.
   Two pails of water from a single well
   Aren't more alike than this girl and your guest.   80
   Yes, and I peeked through your skylight at you,
   I confess.
PERIP.:   You confess! I was a witness!
   And while my two young guests were kissing
       there,
   You saw them?
SCELE.:   I saw them. Why deny what I saw?
   But I thought I'd seen Philocomasium.   85
PERIP.: So! Did you think I was such a worthless man
   That I'd knowingly allow that girl to do
   Such horrible harm to my neighbour, in my house?
SCELE.: Now, when I see the truth, I realize
   I acted foolishly; I meant no harm.   90
PERIP.: You meant no good! A slave should always keep
   His eyes and hands and tongue in firm control.
SCELE.: If I so much as mumble from now on,
   Even about a thing I know for sure,
   Then have me tortured: I'll submit to you.   95
   This time, forgive me, please.
PERIP.:   I'll try my best
   To think you meant no harm in this affair.
   I'll forgive you this time.
SCELE.:   May the gods love you!
PERIP.: By Herc, if the gods love you, you'll hold
       your tongue;
   Henceforth, you'll not know even what you know,   100
   You'll not see what you've seen.
SCELE.:   Superb advice.
   That's just my plan. Have I begged enough?
PERIP.:   Yes, go!
SCELE.: Nothing else I can do for you?
PERIP.:   Stay out of my life!

SCELE.: [*to himself, as he begins to leave*] He's fooling
       me. How wonderfully kind and generous
   Not to get angry! I know what he's doing: 105
   As soon as the soldier comes back home from town,
   I'll be arrested. He and Palaestrio
   Are out to get me: I've known for quite a while.
   They'll never lure me into that fishy trap;
   I'll run away somewhere and hide for a couple of   110
       days,
   Until this row dies down and tempers cool.
   For I'm more damned than a whole damned city
       of sin.

   Oh, hell! Come what may, I'll just go home.
   [*exit into the soldier's house*]
PERIP.: He's gone. I swear to Pollux, I'm quite sure
   That any squealing pig has far more brains!   115
   He's been deprived of seeing what he saw!
   His eyes and ears and even his mind have fled
   To our side. So far, things have gone just fine.
   This woman's done a quite delightful job.

   I'll go back to our senate; for Palaestrio's   120
   At my house now, with Sceledrus away:
   A full-scale senate meeting can be held.
   I'll enter: mustn't miss the muster call.
   [*exit into his own house*]

ACT III

[*Enter PALAESTRIO through Periplectomenus's door,
stage right. As he emerges, he is talking over his
shoulder to his fellow-conspirators, who do not appear
at once.*]

ACT III, SCENE 1

PALAE.: Keep back, you two, inside the doorway
   (Just for a moment, Pleusicles),
   Let me scout first to make sure
   That there's no one here to spy on us
   When we hold our secret council.   5
   Our need now is for safe ground
   Where no enemy can attack
   And plunder this wonderful plan of ours.

[*to audience*]
A well-planned scheme looks badly planned

If your enemies can use it,   10
And if your enemies can use it,
It never fails to ruin you.
You see, however well contrived,
A plan is often snatched away
If you're not careful to take some thought   15
In choosing the place to hatch the plot.
In fact, if somehow your enemies
Come to learn your clever scheme,
They'll put that scheme of yours to work:
They'll tie your tongue and bind your hands   20
And in the end they'll do to you
What you had meant to do to them.

I'll check on the left side and the right,
Then look all round to make quite sure
That there's no hunter lying low   25
To fold his ears around our plan.
From here the outlook's beautifully barren,
All the way to the end of the street.
I'll call them. Periplectomenus!
Hey, Pleusicles! Come on outside.   30

[*Enter PERIPLECTOMENUS and PLEUSICLES.
Palaestrio's original master is an attractive and well-
mannered young man, but he is not very quick on the
uptake.*]

PERIP.: Here we are, at your command.
PALAE.: It's easy to command good men like you.
  What I want to know is this: do we use
  The same plan we thought up inside?
PERIP.: It seems perfect for our needs.   35
PALAE.: What do you say, Pleusicles?
PLEUS.: If you two like it, would I object?
  Could I get a better friend than you?
PALAE.: There's a polite and pleasant statement!
PERIP.: A very appropriate thing to say!   40
PLEUS.: But there's one circumstance that racks
  My heart with agonizing pain.
PERIP.: What circumstance is that? Speak out!
PLEUS.: That I should trouble a man like you
  (At your age!) with this childishness!   45
  It's beneath your virtue and dignity.
  You're using all your energy
  In working for my selfish ends;
  Assisting in my love affair!

And all the while you're doing things   50
That men of your age, as a rule,
Would sooner shun than undertake.
I'm so ashamed to be causing you
So much distress in your old age.
PALAE.: As lovers go, you're very strange   55
  If you feel shame for what you've done.
  You can't be a lover, Pleusicles;
  You're the shadow of a man in love!
PLEUS.: Does being a lover make it right
  For me to bother this old man?   60
PERIP.: What do you mean? Do you really think
  That I've got both feet in the grave?
  Am I fit for the coffin? Do I appear
  To have spent so many years on earth?
  As a matter of fact, my age right now   65
  Is a hale and hearty fifty-four:
  My eyesight's fine; I'm not so fragile;
  My feet are quick; my hands are agile.
PALAE.: His hair is white as white can be:
  But old at heart? No sir, not he!   70
  Since birth, he's lived in prime condition,
  Blessed with a tranquil disposition.
PLEUS.: Honest to Pollux, I've seen that;
  You are quite right, Palaestrio.
  When it comes to kindness, this man here   75
  Is every bit as young as I.
PERIP.: Yes, my friend, the more you test me,
  All the more you'll come to know
  My friendliness toward your love.
PLEUS.: Why test you when I know it now?   80
PERIP.: Reliable experience
  Is never gained at second hand.
  Unless you've been in love yourself,
  You'll scarcely read a lover's heart.
  I too have sparks of love still glowing,   85
  All my juices still are flowing,
  I'm not quite as dry as dust—
  I've had a pleasant life of lust.

I can be witty, gay, and bright,
Or play the tactful guest all night,   90
Whichever you want. I'm never the galling
Type who contradicts a host:
Tactless manners I find appalling;
Tact and taste are uppermost.

I always deliver, with fine elocution,   95
My conversational contribution.
Likewise, I know how to keep quiet
When it's another man's turn to try it.
You'll never see me spit or cough
Or fail to blow my nose—not me!   100
After all, I was born in Ephesus,
Not in southern Italy!

PALAE.: What a delightfully young old man,
If he's as good as he says he is.
It's obvious, he was raised as a child   105
In the tender care of the Goddess of Charm.

PERIP.: I'll prove what a charming man I am;
You'll see—I'll be better than my word.

At banquets, I am never found
Seducing someone else's girl,   110
Or grabbing choicest chunks of meat,
Or gulping down a glass of wine.
When partying, I'm never first
To start a drunken argument:
If anyone's annoying me,   115
I shut my mouth and head for home.
Whenever I'm dining I'm always a shining
Example of love and loveliness.

PALAE.: Heavenly Pollux! Your character
Is simply blossoming with charm!   120
I'd be willing to pay their weight in gold
To get three men as good as you.

PLEUS.: I can tell you, you won't find
Another man at his ripe age
Who's more urbane in all respects   125
Or friendlier to every friend.

PERIP.: I'll make you admit that I'm still young
When it comes to personality:
Whatever you're doing, I'll show up
Teeming with little favours for you.   130

Do you need a witness in court
Who's stern and angry? Look, it's me!
A gentle one, maybe? You'll say that I
Am gentler far than the ocean calm,
That I'm more limpid and liquid smooth   135
Than the caress of the western breeze.
To suit your needs, I can make myself
An entertaining dinner guest,

Or a practically perfect parasite,
Or a butler—the best in the business.   140
As for dancing, no prancing fairy
Has steps as neat and sweet as mine.

PALAE.: [to Pleusicles] What do you think you'd
    choose to crown
These talents, if you had the choice?

PLEUS.: I'd like to be able to show him all   145
The gratitude he's earned from me.
You've earned it, too; I'm well aware
What a terrible nuisance I am to you.
But for me to cause you such expense—
It hurts me.   150

PERIP.: You're an idiot.
What a man spends on a bad wife
Or on an enemy—that's real expense;
On a good guest and on a friend
Money spent is money saved;   155
And whatever is spent on the gods' account
The wise man reckons as capital gain.
It's thanks to the gods I've got the means
To be such a generous host to you;
Eat and drink, relax yourself,   160
Get loaded with laughter along with me.
My house is a free one, I'm a free one,
Too: I like to live for myself.
With all my wealth and influence
(Thank heaven for it, I may say)   165
I could have found a wife with a dowry,
Married a girl from the upper crust;
But I don't want to have a spouse
Who'll yap and bitch around the house.

PALAE.: Come now! To have a little son   170
And to be a father: that's nice.

PERIP.: Ye gods! To have a little fun
And be free from bother: much nicer.

PALAE.: Sir, you have that rare ability
To guide yourself and your fellow man!   175

PERIP.: Now, a good wife's a thing of joy,
If there's any place on the face of the earth
Where such a creature can be found;
But I know that the sort of bride I'd get
Would never be likely to say to me: 180

"Please, dear husband, buy me some wool,
And I'll knit you a sweater that's soft and warm;

I'll make you a lovely overcoat
So you won't shiver when winter comes."

(You'd never hear that from any wife!) 185
If I had a wife, her voice would wake me
At dawn, before the cocks were crowing:

"Please, dear husband, give me some money,
Mother needs a little present.
Give me some cash to buy some candy; 190
Give me some money to give next Sunday
To the sorceress, the dream-diviner,
The psychic, and the entrail-gazer;
If I don't have cash, I'll enrage the lady
Who tells the future from my eyebrows. 195
There's no diplomatic way
Of avoiding a gift for the laundry maid;
For days on end, the girl in the pantry
Has fumed because she's had no tip.
The midwife, too, is extremely cross 200
Because I've been ungenerous.
Aren't you going to give anything
To the nurse who looks after the little slaves?"

All these feminine expenses
(And you can be sure of many others) 205
Keep me from wanting to wed a wife
Who'd always be weaving words like these.
PALAE.: I hope the gods are on your side!
Great Herc! If ever you chase away
That freedom of yours, you'll find it hard 210
To get it safely reinstated!
PLEUS.: But it's a guarantee of fame
In a great and wealthy family
To bring up children; they provide
A living self-memorial. 215
PERIP.: When I've got so many relatives
Why in the world should I need children?
As it is, I'm a happy man,
And I live my life the way I want.
I'll give all I've got to my relatives 220
When I die: I'll divide it among them all.
Meanwhile, they'll flock to me, constantly talk to
     me,
Watch what I'm doing, ask what I want.
Long before dawn they'll all be here

Wanting to know how I slept last night. 225
Those who send me lovely gifts
Will substitute for real sons.
When they roast a sacrificial calf
My share is bigger than their own.
They drag me to the feast! They're always 230
Inviting me to lunch or dinner;
The one who serves me the poorest supper
Feels most miserable of men.
My relatives are rivals with their gifts,
And me—I murmur quietly: 235
"Though it's my money they're gaping at,
It's me they're making rich and fat."
PALAE.: What insight's here! What foresight clear!
How well you furnish the needs of life!
You're so well off, it's just like having 240
Twins or triplets in the house!
PERIP.: Holy Pollux, if I'd had a real son,
I'd have had an endless supply of trouble.
I'd feel continual mental anguish:
If he was sick in bed with a fever 245
I'd think he was dying; if he fell down
Drunk or tumbled from a horse,
I'd become a nervous wreck,
Afraid he'd broken his leg or neck.
PLEUS.: This man deserves enormous wealth 250
And the longest life the gods can give:
He guards what he has, he enjoys himself,
And he's most obliging to his friends.
PALAE.: A delightful personality!
So help me heaven, if heaven were fair 255
The gods would not have been content
With one design for all our lives.
Compare how merchandise is priced
By an honest government inspector:
When the stuff is decent, he sets a price 260
That will get it sold for its proper worth;
When the stuff is poor, he fines the owner
The full face value of the goods!
Well, honest gods would have divided
Human life on a similar scheme: 265
To a man of delightful personality
They'd give a long and lasting life;
But those who were wicked and criminal
Would die a swift and speedy death.

If the gods had followed this simple plan,   270
(a) There'd be far fewer bad men around;
(b) When they did commit their crimes, they'd act
With far less swagger, and finally,
(c) For all the honest types
The cost of living would come down!   275
PERIP.: To find fault with the plans of the gods
Is foolish and ignorant; it is
The equivalent of blasphemy.
You'd better stop that kind of talk.

Now I want to buy provisions,   280
My guest, to welcome you into my house
As you deserve and as I desire:
With good face, with good grace, and with good
    food.
PLEUS.: Please, I'm certainly not unhappy
At what you've spent on me so far.   285
No one can possibly hope to have
A friend so warm and generous
That he can stay three days on end
Without becoming a bit of a pain;
But when he's stayed ten days on end   290
Well, that's a downright siege of Troy!
Even if the host is holding out
Without bad grace, the slaves will grumble.
PERIP.: I've taken steps to guarantee
My slaves all slave away for me;   295
They're not inclined to boss me around,
My friend; you won't see me kowtow.
If they're upset at what I want,
I steer the ship and crack the whip;
If they hate a job they've got to do it   300
Willy-nilly, like it or not.
Now I'm off to do the shopping
I said I'd do.
PLEUS.:   If your mind's made up,
Shop moderately—no great expense:
Anything at all's enough for me.   305
PERIP.: Come on, come off it, take away
That old and rusty platitude.
My dear young friend, you mustn't repeat
The tired clichés of the men in the street.
You'll hear them say, when they come to dinner,   310
When the main course has been served:
"Why did you go to all this trouble?

Such extravagance just for me?
Holy Herc, you must be crazy,
This would be enough for ten!"   315
Whatever food you've bought for them,
They groan and frown—and gulp it down.
PALAE.: That's exactly how it happens.
What a shrewd and keen intelligence!
PERIP.: But these same people never say,   320
However high the table's piled:
"Have that removed; take out this dish;
Oh, no ham, please, I don't care for it;
Away with that juicy slice of pork;
This lovely eel will be better cold,   325
Off, out, away!"
                    You'd never hear
These pronouncements from any of them;
No, they hurl themselves onto the table,
Feet off the ground, as they glut themselves.
PALAE.: A good description of bad manners!   330
PERIP.: I haven't delivered a hundredth part
Of the total lecture I could give,
If only we had sufficient time.
PALAE.: Yes. Well, then, the matter at hand:
This should be our first concern.   335
Now please pay attention, both of you.
I need your help, Periplectomenus.
I've thought up a delicious little trick
To get our soldier clipped and shorn,
Of all his lovely locks—and give   340
Our Philocomasium's lover here
An ideal opportunity
To spirit her away and keep her.
PERIP.: I'd love to share that plan of yours.
PALAE.: Well I would love to share that ring   345
Of yours.
PERIP.:   What in the world for?
PALAE.: When I've got it, then I'll give
A full account of my little scheme.
PERIP.: Use it, take it!
PALAE.:   Take from me
In return the trick that I've devised.   350
PERIP.: We're both listening, ears wide open.
PALAE.: My master likes to play around with women,
More, I believe, than any man
Who ever was or ever will be.
PERIP.: I share that belief myself.   355

PALAE.: He says, moreover, he's *so* handsome—
　Far better looking than Alexander.
　All the women in Ephesus
　Are chasing him—or so he claims.
PERIP.: Holy Pollux, many husbands　　　　360
　Wish that claim were really true!
　But I know perfectly well that he's
　This way. Get on, Palaestrio,
　Weigh me a few of your shortest words
　And wrap them up as fast as you can.　365
PALAE.: All right. Can you find me a woman,
　Absolutely beautiful,
　Well stacked and well stocked
　With a sense of fun and trickery?
PERIP.: Freeborn or the daughter of a slave?　370
PALAE.: I couldn't care less, provided
　You get me a professional,
　The type that's always self-employed;
　She must have a clever breast (I can't
　Say "brain": no woman has one of those!)　375
PERIP.: Do you want her green, or fully ripened?
PALAE.: Just like this: luscious, juicy,
　The most delicious you can find,
　And young—oh, young, especially.
PERIP.: I've got the girl: a client of mine,　380
　Who's young, eye-filling, and bed-willing.
　But what use will we make of her?
PALAE.: You'll conduct her now to your house,
　Then you'll bring her here dressed up
　In the fashion of a noble matron　385
　(You know: hair swept up and bound
　In a roll), and have her pretend that she's
　Your wife. She must be taught this story.
PLEUS.: I seem to have lost your train of thought.
PALAE.: You'll find it again. [*to* PERIP.] But has she a　390
　　maid,
　Perhaps?
PERIP.:　　Yes, and sharp as a tack.
PALAE.: We need her too. You must tell this story
　To the woman and her little maid:
　She's to pretend that she's your wife
　And dying of love for our soldier here;　395
　That she gave this ring to her loyal slave,
　The maid, who gave it next to me,
　As a kind of middleman, to pass
　Along to the soldier.
PERIP.:　　　　　I hear you.
　Please don't pound me until I'm deaf;　400
　My ears are really very good.
PALAE.: I'll give it to him, saying it's
　Been offered to me by your wife,
　To win him over to her cause.
　The way he is, he'll fall, poor sap:　405
　His dirty mind is never set
　On anything but adultery.
PERIP.: If you gave the job to the sun in the sky
　To search for girls, he couldn't find
　Two lovelier women for this job　410
　Than I have. Keep your spirits up!
PALAE.: All right, look after it, but be quick!
　[*exit* PERIPLECTOMENUS]
　Now listen to me, Pleusicles.
PLEUS.: Your obedient servant, sir.
PALAE.:　　　　　　Do this:
　When the soldier reaches the house,　415
　Remember not to call Philocomasium
　By her right name.
PLEUS.:　　　　What name shall I use?
PALAE.: Justine.
PLEUS.:　　Of course. The very name
　We chose before.
PALAE.:　　　　Enough! Please go.
PLEUS.: I'll remember. But why it matters　420
　To remember, I'd still like to know.
PALAE.: I'll tell you at the moment when
　The need demands. Meanwhile, keep quiet!
　[*nodding after* PERIPLECTOMENUS]
　Exactly as he's acting now,
　Play your part actively as well.　425
PLEUS.: I'm going inside, then.[*exit into old man's house*]
PALAE.:　　　　　Only try
　To keep your head and follow orders.

ACT III, SCENE 2

PALAE.: What a commotion! What a mighty plan!
　Today I'll kidnap the soldier's concubine,
　If the men in the ranks keep battle discipline.
　I'll call my friend. Hey, Sceledrus, if you're not
　　too busy,
　Step outside the house. Palaestrio wants you.　5

[*LURCIO, a drunken slave, enters staggering from the
soldier's house.*]

LURCIO: Sceledrus 'sbusy.

PALAE.: How?

LURCIO: He's asleep and snoring.

PALAE.: What do you mean, "snorting"?

LURCIO: I meant to say "snoring."
But somehow 'sall the same, you snore, you snort—

PALAE.: Ah! Is Sceledrus sleeping inside?

LURCIO: Not his nose!
It's roaring away. He snitched a cup on the sly...   10
Back in the cellar....spicing the jars.... wine-steward.

PALAE.: Haha. You crook! All right, assistant
steward—

LURCIO: What do you want?

PALAE.: How did he manage to fall asleep?

LURCIO: With his eyes, I guess.   15

PALAE.: That's not my question, stupid!
Go on. You're done for unless I hear the truth.
Did you pour out wine for him?

LURCIO: No.

PALAE.: You deny it?

LURCIO: Of course I deny it; he ordered me not to
speak.
I didn't pour out eight half-pints into a jug   20
And he didn't drink it hot for his lunch, either.

PALAE.: And you didn't drink?

LURCIO: I'll be damned if I drank!
I couldn't drink!

PALAE.: Why not?

LURCIO: I had to gulp it down.
It was so hot, my throat was getting burned.

PALAE.: *They* get tight and *we* drink vinegar-water!   25
What a pair of cellar bottle-openers!

LURCIO: You'd do the same, if you had charge of
the cellar.
You're jealous because you can't keep up to us.

PALAE.: Hey! Did he ever open wine before?
Answer me, you good-for-nothing!   30
And to help you remember, I'll tell you this:
If you lie, Lurcio, you'll get crucified!

LURCIO: Oh yeah? You want to give public evidence.
And when I'm fired from my cellar sinecure,
You and some friend will wangle the wine detail.   35

PALAE.: Holy Pollux, no! Buck up, speak out!

LURCIO: I swear I never saw him pour it. It was this
way:
He'd give the word, then I'd pour out the wine.

PALAE.: That's why those jars were standing on their
heads!

LURCIO: No! This is why the jars were tipping over: 40
In the cellar there were little slippery spots,
And a two-quart jug was close to the jars (like this)
And it got filled up ten times! I saw it
Filling up and getting empty. The jug kept rolling
On the floor in ecstasy, and the jars kept tipping.   45

PALAE.: Go on, get inside! While you play holy roller
In the cellar, I'll get master from the forum.

LURCIO: I'm through! He'll torture me if he comes
home
And hears about this from someone else.
I'll run away somewhere and postpone my fate.   50
[*to audience*]
Don't tell this fellow, please, word of honour!

PALAE.: Where are *you* going?

LURCIO: I'm on an errand; I'll be back soon.

PALAE.: Who sent you?

LURCIO: Philocomasium.

PALAE.: Well, hurry back!

LURCIO: By the way, if he's handing out punishments   55
When I'm not around, I'd like you to have my
share. [*exit*]

PALAE.: I've just realized what the girl has done:
Sceledrus fell asleep, so she sent away
This other guard, to have a chance to cross over.
Good!

Here's Periplectomenus with the woman I asked   60
him
To bring. She's gorgeous! The gods are helping us.
What dignity and class! Not at all like a courtesan!
This business is starting to shape up beautifully.

ACT III, SCENE 3

[*Enter PERIPLECTOMENUS with the two women that
he has promised to bring, the luscious courtesan ACRO-
TELEUTIUM and her maid MILPHIDIPPA. PAL-
AESTRIO stands to one side and watches unobserved.*]

PERIP.: I've told you, Acroteleutium,
And you too, Milphidippa;
I explained the plan at your house.
If you have the slightest doubt about
This flimflam and skulduggery,   5

I'd like you to hear it all again;
But if you understand it, we've
Got better things to chat about.
ACROT.: My dearest patron, I would look
A fool—an utter idiot— 10
If I took on a job for someone,
Promising to give my all,
And then when I was on the job
I couldn't be both loose and sly.
PERIP.: It's always best to have advice. 15
ACROT.: Advice? A professional like me?
That's hardly needed, heaven knows!
Didn't I tell you, on my own,
After my ears were merely washed
By the first wave of your appeal, 20
Just how the soldier should be trimmed?
PERIP.: No one alone can know it all.
I've seen a lot of people sail
Right past the land of good advice
And never set foot on the shore. 25
ACROT.: If a woman has to do a job
That's wicked and malicious,
She needs no reminder or advice—
Her memory's eternal;
But if she must take on a task 30
That's good or honest, suddenly
She's troubled by forgetfulness
And can't remember anything!
PERIP.: That's why I'm frightened. You've a job
To do that's good and wicked both: 35
When you two work your worst upon
The soldier, that will help my cause.
ACROT.: Just as long as we don't know
We're doing a good deed, have no fear.
PERIP.: You do deserve some dire disaster! 40
ACROT.: Hey! Don't worry, we can take it.
PERIP.: That's the spirit! Follow me.
PALAE.: [aside] Why should I wait to go and meet
them?
[to PERIP.] I'm so glad to see you back,
With the lovely equipment you've got there. 45
PERIP.: Ah, you've come at the right moment,
Palaestrio. Look! Here they are,
The girls you asked me to bring along,
All dressed up.
PALAE.:   Hurrah! My friend for life!

I'm Palaestrio, Acroteleutium. 50
ACROT.: Who is he, I'd like to know?
He uses my name like an old friend.
PERIP.: This man's our master craftsman.
ACROT.: Hi, master craftsman.
PALAE.:   Hi, yourself.
Tell me, has he loaded you 55
With your instructions?
PERIP.:   These two girls
Have both been perfectly rehearsed.
PALAE.: I want to hear exactly how;
I'm scared you may have made a slip.
PERIP.: I've now transmitted your instructions, 60
Adding nothing of my own.
ACROT.: Do you really want your boss, the soldier,
Made a laughingstock?
PALAE.:   You said it!
ACROT.: All is delightfully, ever so cleverly,
Beautifully, dutifully ready. 65
PALAE.: I want you to pretend that you're
The wife of this man here.
ACROT.:   So be it.
PALAE.: Making believe you're head over heels
In love with the soldier.
ACROT.:   You'll see it done!
PALAE.: And that this affair is being arranged 70
By your maid, with me as middleman.
ACROT.: You could have been a professional prophet:
You tell the future perfectly.
PALAE.: And that your lovely little maid
Has brought this ring along to me, 75
So I can give it to the soldier
With your message.
ACROT.:   Right again!
PERIP.: What's the point of dismembering
Their memorized plans?
ACROT.:   It's a good idea.
Dearest patron, you must realize 80
That when there's a proper master craftsman,
Once he gets the keel of a boat
Lined up absolutely straight,
It's easy to build the rest of the ship
On his firmly laid foundation. 85
Now this keel's been truly laid,
Carpenters are all at hand,
And a foreman, skilled in supervision.

If we're not kept waiting by the man
Who's supplying the raw material,   90
From what I know of our enterprise
And skill, the ship will soon be launched.
PALAE.: I suppose you know my master, the soldier?
ACROT.: What a silly question!
How could I help but know that   95
Widely dreaded, curly-headed,
Loud-speaking, perfume-reeking lecher?
PALAE.: And he doesn't know you?
ACROT.:   He's never seen me:
How should he know who I am?
PALAE.: Oh, what a lovely piece of news!   100
Our game will be lovelier than ever.
ACROT.: Can't you simply hand me the man
And then keep quiet and relax?
If I fail to trick him marvellously,
Please lay all the blame on me.   105
PALAE.: Come on then, go along inside,
Get after this business with all your wits.
ACROT.: O.K. Your worries are over.
PALAE.: Periplectomenus, take these girls
Inside for now. I'm off to the forum   110
To find him and present this ring;
I'll tell him that your wife gave it to me
And that she's dying with love for him.
I want you two to send this girl
To us, as soon as we come back.   115
She'll play the secret messenger.
PERIP.: We'll do it, don't you worry.
PALAE.: Attend to your job; I'll bring him here
Loaded, primed, and ready to go. [exit stage left]
PERIP.: Have a good walk, do a good job!   120
[to Acrot.] If I can work out all the details
Of this affair, so that today
My guest can have the soldier's mistress
And take her away from here to Athens—
If only we can trip this trap,   125
Oh, what a gift you'll get from me!
ACROT.: Is the girl providing help herself?
PERIP.: Charmingly and disarmingly.
ACROT.: The future's well assured, I know.
When our wicked talents have been combined,   130
Never fear, we'll be triumphant
Through underhanded treachery.
PERIP.: Well, then, we should go inside

To think this through with cool minds,
And carefully and properly   135
Rehearse the job we've got to do,
So, when the soldier comes, there'll be
No slip-up.
ACROT.:   Let's get going, then!

[*The two women accompany PERIP. into his house.*]

ACT IV

[*Enter PYRGOPOLYNICES, stage left, from the forum, accompanied by PALAESTRIO and other slaves.*]

ACT IV, SCENE 1

PYRGO.: What a joy, when you're doing a job,
And it turns out nicely, the way you want!
Today I sent my parasite
On a trip to visit King Seleucus,
So that Seleucus could be shown   5
The fine recruits I signed up here:
Enough to keep his kingdom safe
And let me take a little rest.
PALAE.: Why not look after your own affairs
And forget Seleucus? I've got something   10
New and dazzling arranged for you!
I am acting as middleman.
PYRGO.: All other matters will have to wait:
I give you my absolute attention.
[*he dismisses the other slaves*]
Speak: I now surrender my ears   15
Into your sole authority.
PALAE.: Look around: we don't want a spy
To pounce on our conversation.
This affair was entrusted to me
To be handled with utter secrecy.   20
PYRGO.: There's no one here.
PALAE.:   This little token
Of love—first, take it from me.
PYRGO.: What's this? Where's it from?
PALAE.:   It comes
From a dazzling lady who's fond of fun;
She loves you and is lusting for   25
Your pure and perfect pulchritude.[4]

---

4 Beauty.

It's her ring. Just now her maid
  Gave it to me to bring to you.
PYRGO.: What's her status? Freeborn or only
  A wave of the wand away from slavery?   30
PALAE.: Come on! Would I dare to speak to you
  As a go-between from a former slave,
  You, who can never find the time
  For the freeborn girls who are after you?
PYRGO.: Is she married or unattached?   35
PALAE.:   She's married
  And unattached.
PYRGO.:   How can she be
  At the same time married and unattached?
PALAE.: She's a young bride with an old husband.
PYRGO.: Hurray!
PALAE.:   She's lovely, luscious, and
  Refined!   40
PYRGO.:   Be careful to tell the truth!
PALAE.: Her beauty's almost a match for yours.
PYRGO.: Holy Herc, she must be gorgeous!
  But who is she?
PALAE.:   The wife of Periplectomenus,
  This old gentleman next door.
  She's dying for you and dearly wants   45
  To leave him: she detests the fellow.
  Now she's ordered me to beg
  And implore you to give her the power
  And the opportunity to do it.
PYRGO.: Sweet Hercules, I want it if she does!   50
PALAE.: She? *Want* it?
PYRGO.:   But what shall we do
  With that concubine who's in the house?
PALAE.: Why not tell her to go away
  Wherever she wants? In fact, her mother
  And twin sister have just arrived   55
  Here in Ephesus, looking for her.
PYRGO.: *What*? Here in Ephesus, her mother?
PALAE.: I've got it on good authority.
PYRGO.: Holy Herc, what a lovely chance
  To kick that woman out of the house!   60
PALAE.: Wait! Would you like to do the job
  In a lovely way?
PYRGO.:   Speak. What's your plan?
PALAE.: Do you want to remove her double quick,
  And have her leave without bad will?
PYRGO.: Yes.   65

PALAE.:   Then this is what you should do.
  You've absolutely loads of money;
  Tell the girl to keep as gifts
  The gold and trinkets you've piled on her.
  Tell her to leave you and go away,
  Taking them wherever she wants.   70
PYRGO.: Good advice; but be careful to see
  That I don't lose her and then have this girl
  Change her mind.
PALAE.:   Hah! You're a fine one!
  She loves you as if you were her own eyes.
PYRGO.: It's Venus who loves me.   75
PALAE.:   Shh! Be quiet!
  The door's opening. Come here quietly.
  That little cruiser coming this way
  Is the woman's go-between.
PYRGO.: What little cruiser?
PALAE.:   Her maid,
  Who's coming out of the house this way.   80
  She brought me that ring I gave you.
PYRGO.: Holy Pollux, she's not bad
  Herself!
PALAE.:   Compared to the other girl
  She's like a crow or a chimpanzee.
  Look at her eyes! She's on the track;   85
  She's listening, waiting to attack.

ACT IV, SCENE 2

[*MILPHIDIPPA, who has been visible for some time,
speaks first to the audience.*]

MILPH.: In front of the house is the arena
  Where now I must hold my little circus.
  I'll pretend that I don't see them
  Or even know that they're about.
PYRGO.: Quiet, let's be eavesdroppers   5
  To hear if she mentions me at all.
MILPH.: [*in a loud "soliloquy"*]
  I hope there's no one near who meddles
  In matters that aren't his own concern,
  Someone who'd spy on what I'm doing,
  Some loafer from the idle rich.   10
  They're the people I'm afraid of:
  They'd be a nuisance or get in the way,
  If they're out here while she's in there.
  She wants this fellow desperately,

My poor, unhappy mistress. And now   15
Her heart is all aflutter for him,
That simply lovely, simply gorgeous
Soldier, Pyrgopolynices.
PYRGO.: Has *she* fallen for me as well?
She's praising my looks. Holy Pollux,   20
Her conversations needs no wax!
PALAE.: How so?
PYRGO.:   Because she speaks
With shining polish and spotless elegance.
PALAE.: She's got *you* to talk about:
A shining topic of conversation!   25
PYRGO.: Well, she herself is a simply
Lovely, simply sparkling girl.
Holy Hercules, she's starting
To please me a little, Palaestrio.
PALAE.: Before you've even seen the other?   30
PYRGO.: I can take the other on faith.
Besides, she's absent, and this little cruiser
Is forcing me to love her.
PALAE.:   Great Herc,
Don't fall for her; she's engaged to me!
If the other girl marries you today,   35
This one will become my wife.
PYRGO.: Then why do you wait to talk to her?
PALAE.: All right, follow me.
PYRGO.:   Your humble servant.
MILPH.: [*continuing her "soliloquy"*]
How I wish I could have a chance
To meet the gentleman on whose   40
Account I've come outside the house.
PALAE.: [*to her*] That wish of yours will soon come true;
Keep up your spirits, have no fear.
There's a certain man who knows where to find
What you want.   45
MILPH.:   Who was that I heard?
PALAE.: A partner who shares and bears your plans.
MILPH.: Oh, my! Then my secret isn't a secret.
PALAE.: I'd say it's both secret and un-secret.
MILPH.: How so?
PALAE.: You keep secrets from those you don't trust: 50
I am your loyal, trusty friend.
MILPH.: Pass me the password, brother in Bacchus!
PALAE.:"A certain woman loves a certain man."
MILPH.: That's true of many girls.
PALAE.:   But not

So many send a gift from their finger.   55
MILPH.: Ah, I recognize you now,
You've got me back on level ground.
Is the man not here?
PALAE.:   Maybe yes, maybe no.
MILPH.: Let me have you all alone.
PALAE.: A short conversation or a long one?   60
MILPH.: A word or two.
PALAE.: [*to* PYRGO] I'll be back in a moment.
PYRGO.: What of me? Shall I stand here all the while,
A handsome hero going to waste?
PALAE.: Stand there and stand it; I'm working for you. 65
PYRGO.: Hurry up! Waiting tortures me.
PALAE.: Easy does it—you know that!—
It's the rule for this kind of merchandise.
PYRGO.: All right, have it your own sweet way.
PALAE.: [*aside*] I've never seen a stone so stupid. 70
[*to* MILPH.] Here I am again. What did you want
me for?
MILPH.: To have a little conference
On how you want this Troy to be sacked.
PALAE.: Say she's crazy for him—
MILPH.:   I've got that.
PALAE.: Praise his face, praise his physique,   75
And mention his heroic deeds.
MILPH.: I'm all sharpened for that job;
I showed you just a moment ago.
PALAE.: Then keep your wits and look around:
Follow the trail and track my words.   80
PYRGO.: Could you give me some small share of your
Attention today?
                At last! Here you are.
PALAE.: Yours to command.
PYRGO.:   What has she told you?
PALAE.: She says her mistress is suffering torture,
Wailing, weeping, all worn out,   85
Because she wants you, because she needs you.
This is why she's been sent to you.
PYRGO.: Have her approach.
PALAE.:   You know what to do,
I hope. Fill yourself with scorn
And act displeased; criticize   90
My offering you for mass consumption.
PYRGO.: I remember. I'll follow instructions.
PALAE.: [*aloud*] Am I to summon the woman who
wants you?

PYRGO.: Have her approach and state her wish.
PALAE.: Woman, approach, state your wish. 95
MILPH.: Hello, handsome.
PYRGO.: She actually knows my middle name!
  May the gods grant you all you ask.
MILPH.: To spend a lifetime alone with you—
PYRGO.: That's asking too much!
MILPH.: Not me, silly,
  But my mistress who's dying for you. 100
PYRGO.: Many other women share that desire.
  Demand exceeds supply.
MILPH.: Holy Castor,
  No wonder you value yourself so highly!
  You're so handsome, so distinguished
  In accomplishments and manly beauty. 105
  Was there ever a human who more deserved
  To be a god?
PALAE.: By God, he's not really
  Human. [aside to MILPH.] I think a vulture has more
  Humanity.
PYRGO.: [aside to PALAE.] I'll preen myself now, 110
  Seeing that she's so high in my praise.
PALAE.: [to MILPH.] Do you see how this no-good
    carries on?
  [to PYRGO.] Why not answer this woman? She's
    come
  From the girl I mentioned a while ago.
PYRGO.: Which one you mentioned? So many girls 115
  Run after me: I can't remember them.
MILPH.: From the woman who robs her fingers
  And gives your fingers something to wear.
  I took this ring from one who desires you;
  Brought it to him; he gave it to you. 120
PYRGO.: What do you want now, woman? Speak!
MILPH.: She wants you so much: don't reject her.
  Her very life depends on you:
  Her hope and despair are in your hands.
PYRGO.: What does she want? 125
MILPH.: To whisper in your ear,
  To melt in your arms, to seethe in your embrace.
  Unless you're willing to help her now,
  She'll soon be pushed to utter despair.
  Come, dear Achilles, say you'll do it,
  In fairness save that lady fair; 130
  Show your kind and generous nature,
  Sacker of cities, slayer of kings!

PYRGO.: Holy Herc, what a nuisance!
  How often have I told you, you good-for-nothing,
  Not to keep promising my charms 135
  To all and sundry?
PALAE.: Do you hear that, woman?
  I told you once and I'm telling you again:
  If this wild boar isn't brought a gift
  He's not likely to act as stud
  For every pretty passing piglet. 140
MILPH.: He'll get whatever price he asks.
PALAE.: He'll need three thousand golden drachmas:
  His absolute rock-bottom price.
MILPH.: Merciful Castor, that's too cheap!
PYRGO.: I've never been a greedy man. 145
  I've quite a bit of wealth already:
  Over a thousand bushels of golden drachmas.
PALAE.: Not counting his cash reserves! And his silver:
  Not merely masses, but mountains of it!
  Mount Etna isn't half as high. 150
MILPH.: [aside to PALAE.] Sweet Castor, what
    an awful liar!
PALAE.: How am I doing?
MILPH.: What about me?
  Am I spreading it on?
PALAE.: You know what you're doing.
MILPH.: [to PYRGO.] Please send me to get her
    right away.
PALAE.: Can't you give her some reply? 155
  Say you either will or won't.
MILPH.: Why torment that heartsick girl?
  She's never done you any harm.
PYRGO.: Tell her to come out here to us.
  Say I'll do everything she wants. 160
MILPH.: Now you're acting the way you should,
  When you go for a woman who goes for you—
PALAE.: [aside] This girl was born with a sense of fun!
MILPH.: —When you don't heap scorn upon my plea,
  When you treat my entreaty so generously. 165
  [aside to Palae.] How's that? Am I doing well?
PALAE.: Holy Herc, I can't stop laughing!
MILPH.: That's why I had to hide my face!
PYRGO.: By Pollux, woman, I hope you know
  What a great honour I'm doing her. 170
MILPH.: I know it and I'll tell her that.
PALAE.: To another woman he could have sold
  This favour for money.

MILPH.:   I believe you.

PALAE.: Perfect warriors are produced
　From women he's made pregnant;   175
　Every child lives eight hundred years!

MILPH.: Come on, you're making fun of me!

PYRGO.: Actually, they live a thousand years,
　From millennium to millennium.

PALAE.: [to Pyrgo.] I cut the total down a bit   180
　In case she thought I was lying to her.

MILPH.: I'm staggered! How many years will he live
　Himself, if his sons all live so long?

PYRGO.: My dear woman, I was born
　Just one day after Jupiter.   185

PALAE.: If his birthday had been the day before,
　This man would hold royal sway in heaven!

MILPH.: Please, please, enough! If I can,
　Let me get away from you alive!

PALAE.: Then why not go, since you've got your   190
　answer?

MILPH.: I'll go and bring her here—the woman
　I'm acting for. Anything you want?

PYRGO.: To be no more handsome than I am:
　My beauty takes up so much time!

PALAE.: Are you still here? Be off!   195

MILPH.:   I'm gone.

PALAE.: One more thing—do you hear? Speak to her
　With skill and art; thrill her heart—
　[aside] Tell Philocomasium, if she's there,
　To cross home; let her know he's here.

MILPH.: She's here with my mistress; both of them   200
　Have secretly overheard our talk.

PALAE.: Wonderful! If they've heard us talk
　They'll be able to steer a perfect course.

MILPH.: [as if outraged] Out of my way, I'm leaving.

PALAE.: I'm not in your way, I'm not touching you,   205
　I'm not—saying another word.

PYRGO.: Tell her to hurry and come out here.
　We'll give her top priority.

[Exit MILPHIDIPPA into the old man's house.]

ACT IV, SCENE 3

PYRGO.: What's your advice to me now, Palaestrio,
　About my concubine? I certainly can't
　Bring this one into the house before she goes.

PALAE.: Why ask me what to do? I've already told you

How to manage it most mercifully.   5
　Let her have the gold and all the fancy clothes
　You've lavished on her—keep them, pack them off.
　Tell her it's really high time she went home:
　Her mother and twin sister have arrived;
　She ought to head back in their company.   10

PYRGO.: How do you know they're here?

PALAE.:   With my own eyes
　I saw her sister here.

PYRGO.:   Did they meet each other?

PALAE.: Yes.

PYRGO.: Did her sister seem....well-built?

PALAE.:   You want
　Everything!   15

PYRGO.: Where's their mother? Did her sister say?

PALAE.: On the ship, in bed, with sore and swollen
　eyes;
　The captain told me, the man who brought them
　here.
　He's next door—the captain—staying as a guest.

PYRGO.: Is he well-built?   20

PALAE.:   Go way! I must admit,
　You'd be the perfect all-round stallion:
　Male or female, all's alike to you.
　Back to business!

PYRGO.:   That advice you gave me:
　I want you to speak to Philocomasium.
　You talk the same kind of language, you and she.   25

PALAE.: It's better for you to tell her face to face.
　Say you simply have to find a wife.
　Your family want it; your friends are forcing you.

PYRGO.: You think that's best?

PALAE.:   Of course I think it's best.

PYRGO.: All right, I'll go in. Meanwhile, you wait here;   30
　Keep watch and call to me when she comes out.

PALAE.: Just get on with the job.

PYRGO.:   It's as good as done.
　If she won't go willingly, I'll kick her out!

PALAE.: No, no, no! Be careful! She must leave you
　With good grace. And give her what I said: 35
　Have her take the gold and trinkets you piled on her.

PYRGO.: I will!

PALAE.:   I think you'll easily get your way.
　Go in. Don't stand around.

PYRGO.:   Your wish is my command.
　[exit into house]

PALAE.: [*to audience*]
  Well, he doesn't seem to change much, does he?
  Didn't I tell you what a lecherous fellow he was?   40
  Now I need Acroteleutium
  Or her maid or Pleusicles. Holy Jupiter,
  Opportunity's always on my side!
  The very people I wanted most to see
  Are coming out together from the house next door.   45

ACT IV, SCENE 4

[*PLEUSICLES, ACROTELEUTIUM, and
MILPHIDIPPA emerge from the old man's house.*]

ACROT.: Follow me, look in every direction:
  We don't want any witnesses.
MILPH.: I don't see anyone except him,
  And we want him.
PALAE.:   And he wants you.
MILPH.: How are you doing, master craftsman?   5
PALAE.: Me, master craftsman? Rubbish!
MILPH.:   Why?
PALAE.: Because, compared to you, I'm not
  Fit to hammer a nail in the wall!
ACROT.: Oh, come now! Really!
PALAE.:   This girl's wicked:
  She's got wit and a smooth, sharp tongue.   10
  What a sight to see her plane the soldier
  Down to size!
MILPH.:   But he's not finished yet.
PALAE.: Don't you worry: the whole affair's
  Beginning to shape up beautifully.
  I hope all of you will just continue   15
  Giving your helpful cooperation.
  The soldier himself has gone inside
  To ask his little concubine
  To leave him and go away with her sister
  And mother to Athens.   20
PLEUS.:   Oh, great!
PALAE.: Then, too, there's the gold and the jewelry
  That he himself piled on the girl:
  He's giving it all as a present, for her
  To take away—it was my idea!
PLEUS.: The whole thing should be very easy   25
  If she's willing and he's eager.
PALAE.: Don't you know, when you're near the top,
  As you're climbing out of a deep well,

That's the time of greatest danger?
From the top you can fall straight down again.   30
This plan of ours has now arrived
At the top of the well; but if the soldier
Comes to his senses, there's no chance
Of saving it. Now most of all
We must be tricky.   35
PLEUS.:   Our side clearly
  Has plenty of raw material:
  The girls make three....you, four....
  I'm five....the old man, six.
PALAE.: The six of us, I'm quite convinced,
  Have such a fund of treachery   40
  That we can tackle any town,
  Assault the walls, and lay it low.
  Just pay attention.
ACROT.:   Well, that's why
  We're here, to see if you want anything.
PALAE.: Wonderful! You, my dear, I now   45
  Appoint Lieutenant-General.
ACROT.: In general, General, as far as I can,
  I'll help you get whatever you want.
PALAE.: I want the soldier to be duped
  With cleverness, wit, and elegance.   50
ACROT.: Sweet Castor, General, your commands
  Are fun!
PALAE.:   But do you know how?
ACROT.: Of course! By pretending that
  I'm racked with love for him.
PALAE.:   That's it.
ACROT.: And pretending, because of that love,   55
  To have divorced this husband of mine,
  Yearning for marriage with him.
PALAE.:   O.K.
  Just one thing more: say that this house
  Belongs to you as part of your dowry,
  And that the old man went away   60
  From here after your divorce.
  So, when the time comes, *he* won't be afraid
  To enter someone else's house.
ACROT.: A good idea.
PALAE.:   But when he comes out,
  I'd like you to stand over there a little;   65
  Pretend to scorn your loveliness,
  To feel so ugly compared to him;
  Make believe you're overawed

By his magnificence; then go on
  To praise his handsome body, his face,   70
  His charming manner, his perfect looks.
  Enough instructions?
ACROT.:   Yes. Will you
  Be satisfied if I hand you back
  My piece of work so well worked over
  That you can't find any fault?   75
PALAE.: Fair enough. Now, Pleusicles,
  Learn the orders I've got for you.
  As soon as this job's done and she's
  Disappeared inside, that's the time
  For you to come along to our house   80
  All dressed up like a sea-captain.
  Wear a rusty-coloured hat,
  A woolen patch over one eye,
  And also a rusty-coloured cloak
  (That's a favourite colour with sailors)   85
  Hitched up on your left shoulder,
  With your other arm waving free.
  Be neat and tidy: you must pretend
  You're the owner and master of the ship.
  This old man will provide the costume;   90
  He's got slaves who are fishermen.
PLEUS.: What then? When I'm all dressed up,
  Tell me, what do you want me to do?
PALAE.: Come here and call for Philocomasium
  As if you're acting for her mother.   95
  Tell her, if she's going to Athens,
  To go with you quickly to the harbour;
  Anything she wants placed aboard
  She must have carried to the ship.
  Unless she comes, you'll give orders   100
  To sail: the wind is favourable.
PLEUS.: This picture pleases me. Go on!
PALAE.: At once our friend will encourage her
  To go, to hurry up, not keep
  Her mother waiting.   105
PLEUS.:   You think of everything!
PALAE.: I'll tell her to ask for me as a porter
  To carry her luggage to the harbour.
  He'll order me to go with her
  To the harbour. And then (please realize)
  I'll leave with you at once for Athens.   110
PLEUS.: And when you've arrived there, before
  You've passed three days in slavery,

  I'll see that you're a free man.
PALAE.: Go quickly and get dressed.
PLEUS.:   Anything else?
PALAE.: Remember what I've said.   115
PLEUS.: Goodbye. [*exit stage right*]
PALAE.: [*to the women*] You two go inside here
  Right now; I'm pretty sure that he
  Will soon be coming out this way.
ACROT.: We just *adore* taking orders from you.   120

[*The women move toward the old man's door.*]

PALAE.: Go on, get out of here. Look!
  The door's opening right on schedule.
  Here he comes, smiling: he's got his way.
  He's panting for a fantasy, poor fellow!

ACT IV, SCENE 5

[*As the women disappear from sight,
PYRGOPOLYNICES emerges from his own house.*]

PYRGO.: I got my way the way I wanted,
  In a spirit of friendship and goodwill,
  With Philocomasium.
PALAE.:   Why
  Were you so long inside the house?
PYRGO.: I've never seen her so in love: 5
  That girl adores me more than ever!
PALAE.: What happened?
PYRGO.:   Oh, how I pleaded with her,
  And oh, what stubborn stuff she was!
  But finally I got my way.
  I gave her all those special presents: 10
  Some she wanted, some she demanded;
  I made her a present of you as well.
PALAE.: Me too? How will I ever
  Live without you?
PYRGO.:   Come, cheer up.
  At the same time I'll give you your freedom.   15
  I tried hard to see if I could
  Persuade the girl in any way
  To leave me without taking you.
  But she overwhelmed me.
PALAE.:   I put my trust
  In the gods and you. At any rate,   20
  Though your news is bitter to me, because
  I must forego you, the best of masters,

Still I'm glad that your beauty
And my help have led to a victory
Over this woman from next door.   25
I'm winning her over for you now.
PYRGO.: Why waste words? I will make you
A free man and a wealthy man
If you can do it.
PALAE.:   I'll see it's done.
PYRGO.: I'm burning to get her.   30
PALAE.:   Easy does it!
Control yourself; don't be so passionate!
Look! Here she is, coming outside.

ACT IV, SCENE 6

[*Enter ACROTELEUTIUM and MILPHIDIPPA
from the old man's house.*]

MILPH.: [*sotto voce*] Mistress, look! The soldier's here.
ACROT.: Where?
MILPH.:   To our left.
ACROT.:   I see him.
MILPH.: Glance out of the corner of your eye,
So he won't know we've spotted him.
ACROT.: I see him. Oh, Jupiter! Now's the time   5
For us to stoop even lower than usual!
MILPH.: You go first.
ACROT.: [*aloud*] I want to know,
Did you actually meet the man in person?
[*aside*] Keep your voice up, let him hear.   10
MILPH.: [*aloud*] Yes, by Pollux, I spoke to *him*
Calmly, for as long as I wanted,
Taking my time, pleasing myself.
PYRGO.: [*sotto voce*] Do you hear what she says?
PALAE.:   Yes, I hear it.
How happy she is to have been with you!   15
ACROT.: Oh, what a lucky woman you are!
PYRGO.: They all seem to love me.
PALAE.:   You deserve it.
ACROT.: Sweet Castor, that's amazing news:
You walked up to him with your request!
They say he's usually approached like a king,   20
By letter or by courier.
MILPH.: Well, I swear I barely had a chance
To approach him with my request.
PALAE.: What fame you enjoy among the women!
PYRGO.: I'll endure it; it's the will of Venus.   25

ACROT.: To Venus I express my thanks,
To her I speak this heart-felt prayer:
Dear goddess, let me have a chance at him,
The man I love, the man I burn for;
Please make him kind to me, I pray,   30
Don't let him be cross at what I yearn for.
MILPH.: I hope it'll happen, though many girls
Have already set their sights on him.
He spurns them and shuts himself away
From all of them. You're the only exception.   35
ACROT.: That's why I'm devoured with dread—
Because he's hard to satisfy.
His eyes may cause a change of heart
As soon as he catches sight of me,
Perhaps his savoir-faire will make him   40
Scorn my appearance on the spot.
MILPH.: It won't happen; don't be discouraged!
PYRGO.: See how she belittles herself!
ACROT.: I'm worried that your description of me
Made me prettier than I am.   45
MILPH.: I was careful to see that you'd
Be lovelier than he thinks you are.
ACROT.: Ye gods, if he doesn't want to have me
As his wife, I'll kiss his knees,
Imploring him; otherwise,   50
If I fail in my request,
I'll kill myself! Life without him?
For me, it's quite impossible.
PYRGO.: I've got to save this girl from death,
I see. Shall I approach?   55
PALAE.:   No, no!
Don't you see, you'll cheapen yourself
If you lavish yourself before you're asked.
Let *her* do the asking, let her come
To enquire, to desire, to wait for you.
Let her! Do you want to tarnish   60
That glory of yours? Please be careful.
This situation's happened only
Twice in human history:
You and Sappho's lover, Phaon—
Both desired to the *n*th degree.[5]   65

_____

5 The great lyric poet Sappho (7th century B.C.E.) was said,
perhaps originally in a comedy, to have jumped to her
death from a cliff when Phaon, a ferryboat operator, rejected her love.

ACROT.: Shall I go in, or do you prefer
 To call him out, Milphidippa?
MILPH.: Neither. We should wait here
 Till someone comes out.
ACROT.:   I can't last
 Without going in.   70
MILPH.:   The door's shut.
ACROT.: I'll break it down!
MILPH.:   You're out of your mind!
ACROT.: If he has ever been in love,
 Or if he's as wise as he is handsome,
 Whatever I do in the name of love,
 He'll forgive and be merciful.   75
PALAE.: Look how this unhappy girl
 Is ruined by love!
PYRGO.:   The feeling's mutual.
PALAE.: Quiet, she'll hear you.
MILPH.:   Why have you stopped?
 You're looking stunned! Why don't you knock?
ACROT.: [*slowly, in a trance*] Not within is the one I   80
  want.
MILPH.: How do you know?
ACROT.:   My nose . . . knows.
 It would sniff . . . a whiff . . . if
 He were there.
PYRGO.:   Now she's psychic!
 Because she loves me, therefore Venus
 Has made her the gift of prophecy!   85
ACROT.: Somewhere here, not far away,
 Is the man I long to see: he smells!
PYRGO.: Holy Pollux, her nose has better
 Vision than her eyes!
PALAE.:   She's blind with love.
ACROT.: [*in distress*] Hold me up, please!   90
MILPH.:   Why?
ACROT.:   So I won't fall.
MILPH.: What is it?
ACROT.:   I can't stand up;
 My eyes have caused my mind to fail.
MILPH.: Holy Pol, you must have seen . . .
 The soldier!
ACROT.:   Yes.
MILPH.:   I don't see him. Where is he?
ACROT.: Oh, you'd see him if you loved him.   95
MILPH.: I swear you don't love him any more
 Than I would, dear lady, if you'd let me.

PALAE.: All the girls certainly love you,
 The moment they get a glimpse of you.
PYRGO.: I may have told you some time or other: 100
 Venus is my father's mother.
ACROT.: Dear Milphidippa, please go up
 To him and meet him.
PYRGO.:   She's afraid of me!
PALAE.: [*aloud*] She's coming to *us*.
MILPH.:   It's *you* I want.
PYRGO.: And *we* want *you*!   105
MILPH.:   Just as you ordered,
 I've brought my mistress out of doors.
PYRGO.: So I see.
MILPH.:   Well, tell her to approach.
PYRGO.: I've taught my heart not to despise her
 Like other women; you asked so nicely.
MILPH.: Mercy, she won't be able to speak   110
 A word, if she comes near you.
 While she merely gazed from afar,
 Her eyes cut off the tip of her tongue.
PYRGO.: This woman's illness must be cured,
 I see.   115
MILPH.: Look! She's trembling: terror struck her
 When she caught a glimpse of you.
PYRGO.: Even brave warriors act that way;
 Don't be surprised that a woman should.
 But what does she want me to do?   120
MILPH.: To come to her house: with you
 She wants to live and spend a lifetime.
PYRGO.: I, come to her house? Well, she's married!
 Her husband would catch me in the act.
MILPH.: No! For your sake she drove out her   125
  husband.
PYRGO.: How in the world could she do that?
MILPH.: This house is part of her dowry.
PYRGO.:   Is it?
MILPH.: Yes.
PYRGO.:   Tell her to go inside.
 I'll be there presently.
MILPH.:   Just see
 That you don't keep her waiting long: 130
 It would be mental cruelty.
PYRGO.:   I won't,
 Believe me. Get going.
MILPH.:   We're going.
 [*they hurry into the old man's house*]

PYRGO.: What's this I see?

PALAE.: What do you see?

PYRGO.: Somebody's coming along here
(Look!) in the uniform of a sailor.   135

PALAE.: He's coming to us; he must want you.
This is the ship's captain.

PYRGO.: I suppose
He's coming to fetch *her* now.

PALAE.: I guess so.

ACT IV, SCENE 7

[*Enter PLEUSICLES, stage right, supposedly from the
harbour. He speaks first to the audience.*]

PLEUS.: If I didn't know that love had caused other men
To act disgracefully, I'd be more ashamed
To be parading here, for love, in this get-up.
But I've been told that many men, for love,
Have done many things dishonourable and   5
unworthy.
Take Achilles: the way he let his friends get killed—
But there's Palaestrio, standing with the soldier;
Now I must declaim a different speech. [*in a loud
"soliloquy"*]
Women are born daughters of Delay,
When you're waiting for a woman, all other   10
Kinds of delay, however long, seem trivial.
I think they practise being slow!

I'll call for this Philocomasium. I'll knock
On the door. Hey! Anyone here?

PALAE.: Young man, what is it?
Why are you knocking?   15

PLEUS.: I'm looking for Philocomasium.
I'm from her mother. She'd better come, if she's
coming.
She's holding everyone up: we want to sail.

PYRGO.: Things have been ready for ages. Palaestrio,
Take the gold, jewelry, clothing, all her treasures,
And get slaves to help you carry them to the ship.   20
All the presents I gave are packed: let her take them!

PALAE.: Yes sir. [*exit into the soldier's house*]

PLEUS.: Oh Herc, please hurry.

PYRGO.: He won't delay.
What's that thing there? What happened to your
eye?

PLEUS.: My eyes all *right*.

PYRGO.: I mean your *left*.

PLEUS.: I'll tell you.
Because of my love, I can't see out of this eye;   25
If I'd steered away from my love, it would see
quite well.
They're holding me up too long.

PYRGO.: Look, here they are.

ACT IV, SCENE 8

[*Enter PALAESTRIO and PHILOCOMASIUM from
the soldier's house. PHILOCOMASIUM is in tears,
and continues to sob as the scene develops.*]

PALAE.: Oh please, won't you ever stop your crying
Today?

PHILO.: How can I help crying?
I'm leaving the place where my life was most
Beautiful.

PALAE.: See! Here's the man
Who's come from your mother and your sister.   5

PHILO.: I see him.

PYRGO.: Palaestrio, do you hear?

PALAE.: What do you want?

PYRGO.: Get those things
Brought out: all the presents I gave her.

PLEUS.: How do you do, Philocomasium.

PHILO.: How do you do.   10

PLEUS.: Your mother and sister
Asked me to give their love to you.

PHILO.: Then give them my love, too.

PLEUS.: They ask you to come, while the wind
Is right, so they can get under way;
If your mother hadn't been sick,   15
They would have come along with me.

PHILO.: I'll go, though it's not what I want to do:
My sense of duty—

PLEUS.: Wise girl!

PYRGO.: If she hadn't lived with me,
She'd still be a stupid girl today.   20

PHILO.: I'm simply tortured by the fact
That I'll be removed from the sort of man
Who can make any girl in the world
Overflow with cleverness.
Also, because I was close to you,   25
My heart got wilder all the time.

And now, it seems, I must give up
That glory.
PYRGO.:   Don't cry.
PHILO.:   I can't help it
When I look at you.
PYRGO.:   Come on, cheer up!
PHILO.: I'm the only one who knows how it hurts!   30
PALAE.: I don't wonder, Philocomasium,
That you were glad to be in this house,
Or that *his* beauty, character, courage
Won your heart and held you here.
I'm just a slave; but I weep too   35
At the sight of him, because we're parting.
PHILO.: Please, may I have a last embrace
Before I leave you?
PYRGO.:   Yes, you may.
PHILO.: Oh, my dearest! Oh, my darling!

[*Hurling herself at* PYRGOPOLYNICES, *she "faints"
into* PLEUSICLES' *arms.*]

PALAE.: Watch out there! Catch the woman,   40
Don't let her hurt herself.
PYRGO.:   What's going on?
PALAE.: Because she's leaving you, she's fainted
Suddenly, unhappy girl.
PYRGO.: Run inside and bring some water!
PALAE.: Water's no good; rest is what   45
She needs. Don't interfere, please,
Until she comes around again.
PYRGO.: They've got their heads too close together.
I don't like it! Take your lips away
From hers, sailor; you're looking for trouble!   50
PLEUS.: I was checking to see if she was breathing.
PYRGO.: Well, you should have used your ear!
PLEUS.: If you prefer, I'll drop her.
PYRGO.:   Oh, no!
Hang on!
PALAE.: [*aside*] I'm getting uncomfortable.
PYRGO.: Slaves! Go and fetch from the house   55
All the presents I gave this girl.
PALAE.: [*to the statue of* PYRGO.*'s Lar* [6]]
Hail to thee, dear household god!
Take my last greeting before I go.

---

[6] Guardian spirit entrusted with the safe care of a household, worshipped regularly and on special occasions.

Dear fellow slaves, both men and women,
Goodbye, good luck to all of you!   60
I pray you'll all speak well of me,
Even when I'm far away.
PYRGO.: Come, Palaestrio, cheer up!
PALAE.: Oh dear, I can't help crying
Now that I'm leaving!   65
PYRGO.:   Take it easy!
PALAE.: I'm the only one who knows how it hurts!
PHILO.: *Oh!* What happened? What's going on?
What do I see? Hail, light of day!
PLEUS.: Hail, yourself! Are you better now?
PHILO.: Oh, tell me, whom have I embraced?   70
What man? I'm ruined! Am I myself?
PLEUS.: Don't be frightened....my lovely one!
[*they embrace again*]
PYRGO.: What does that business mean?
PALAE.:   Remember,
The woman has recently been unconscious.
[*aside to Pleusicles*]
I'm very much afraid that this   75
Will finally get too obvious.
PYRGO.: [*overhearing*] What will?
PALAE.: [*improvising*] Having all these presents
Carried behind us through the city;
I'm afraid you'll be criticized for this.   80
PYRGO.: It's my stuff, not theirs, I'm giving away.
I couldn't care less for them! All right,
Go, and may all the gods attend you!
PALAE.: I mention it only for your sake.
PYRGO.:   Of course.
PALAE.: And now, goodbye.   85
PYRGO.:   Goodbye to you.
PALAE.: Go ahead, I'll follow you soon;
I want a few words with master.

[*PLEUSICLES, PHILOCOMASIUM, and the slaves
leave for the harbour, stage right.* PALAESTRIO *is
alone with* PYRGOPOLYNICES.]

PALAE.: Though you've always held other
Slaves more faithful to you than me,
All the same, for you I feel   90
Nothing but thanks for everything.
If you had willed it so, I'd much
Prefer to be a slave for you
Than to live free with someone else.

PYRGO.: Please keep your courage up.   95

PALAE.: Ohhh, when the thought occurs to me
    How I'll have to change my habits:
    Learning a woman's way of life,
    Forgetting military routine!

PYRGO.: There, there, be a good fellow!   100

PALAE.:   I can't
    Do it; I've lost all desire.

PYRGO.: Go on, follow them, don't delay.

PALAE.: Goodbye.

PYRGO.:   Goodbye to you.

PALAE.: And please (you will remember, won't you?),
    If I do obtain my freedom   105
    I'll send word to you—don't
    Let me down.[7]

PYRGO.:   That's not in my nature.

PALAE.: Keep reflecting, whatever you do,
    How faithful I've always been to you.
    In this way you'll come to know   110
    Who's your friend and who's your foe.

PYRGO.: Yes, in the past I've often seen it;
    Now I know you really mean it.

PALAE.: You know? Well, sir, after today
    You'll swear to the truth of what I say.   115

PYRGO.: I can scarcely refrain from ordering you
    To stay.

PALAE.:   Oh, you mustn't do that!
    People would say that you're a liar,
    That you have no sense of honour,
    That I'm the only one of your slaves   120
    With any real loyalty.
    If I thought that there was a way
    Of doing it honourably, I'd urge you;
    But it's quite impossible. Please don't do it.

PYRGO.: Well, go.   125

PALAE.:   I'll endure whatever comes.

PYRGO.: Goodbye, then.

PALAE.:   I really must
    Go . . . quickly. [*exit, stage right*]

PYRGO.:   Goodbye, goodbye.
    Before he did this, I always thought

---

7 Former masters were expected to continue to help their
   freed slaves through the convention of the "patron-
   client" relationship.

This fellow was my very worst slave;
Now I discover he's faithful to me.   130
When I think a bit about it,
I was a fool to send him off!
But now I'll go inside the house
To my lovely lady. Just a moment:
I think I heard a noise at the door.   135

ACT IV, SCENE 9

[*A youthful SLAVE comes out of the old man's house.*]

SLAVE: [*over his shoulder*] Don't keep prompting me,
    I remember my job.
    I'll go and find him now, wherever he is;
    I'll track him down, I won't spare any pains.

PYRGO.: He's looking for me. I'll go and meet the lad.

SLAVE: Ah, there you are. Hail, loveliest of men,   5
    Abounding in astounding charm, uniquely
    Loved by two gods.

PYRGO.:   Which two?

SLAVE: Mars and Venus.

PYRGO.: A clever lad!

SLAVE: She begs you to go inside.
    She wants you, needs you, waits with bated breath.
    Help one who loves you. Don't stand there, go in!   10

PYRGO.: I will! [*exit into the old man's house*]

SLAVE: All by himself he's snared himself in the net.
    The trap is ready: The old man's manning his
       post,
    To attack our battle-shy adulterer,
    Who thinks all women adore him at first sight,   15
    Though in fact he's loathed by men and women
       alike.
    Now I'll enter the turmoil; I hear shouting. [*exit
       into the old man's house*]

ACT V

[*Amid great commotion, enter PERIPLECTOMENUS,
followed from his house by PYRGOPOLYNICES, who
is threatened by burly slaves and by a menacing cook
named CARIO.*]

ACT V, SCENE 1

PERIP.: Bring him here! If he won't come
    Pick him up and throw him out!

Hang him up half way between
Heaven and earth! Tear him apart!
PYRGO.: I beg you, Periplectomenus, by Hercules! 5
PERIP.: By Hercules, you're wasting breath.
Cario, how's your carving knife?
You must be sure it's really sharp.
CARIO: Oh, it's been itching to get this lecher!
Lippety-lop: loin chop! 10
I'll slice away and hang the bits
Like babies' beads around his neck.
PYRGO.: I'm finished!
PERIP.:   Not yet! There's more to come.
CARIO: Now do you want me to fly at the fellow?
PERIP.: No. First he should be pounded 15
With clubs.
CARIO: Yes. Repeatedly!
PERIP.: How dare you! Why did you try to seduce
Another man's wife? Shame on you!
PYRGO.: So help me god, I didn't invite her;
She just came. 20
PERIP.:   He's lying; hit him.
PYRGO.: Wait! Let me speak!
PERIP.: [to his slaves] What are you waiting for?
PYRGO.: Please may I say something?
PERIP.: Say it.
PYRGO.:   I was asked to go to her.
PERIP.: And you dared to go? This will teach you! 25
PYRGO.: Oh! ow! Now I'm pounded
Enough! Oh, please!
CARIO: How soon do I slice?
PERIP.: Whenever you like. With all your strength,
Strain him and stretch him out full length.
PYRGO.: Holy Hercules! Listen to me 30
Before you let him cut me up.
PERIP.: Speak.
PYRGO.:   I had some justification.
I thought that she was unattached.
This is what the woman told me,
Her maid, who was our go-between. 35
PERIP.: Say you won't take vengeance (swear!)
On any man in this affair,
For beatings you've received today,
Or future beatings, come what may,
If we don't perform this operation, 40
Venus's darling little relation.
PYRGO.: By Jupiter and Mars I swear

I'll hurt no man in this affair
Merely because I'm black and blue:
Justice demanded it of you. 45
If my testimonials aren't attacked,
I'll be getting off easily, in fact.
PERIP.: And if you break your oath, what then?
PYRGO.: May they never testify again!
CARIO: I think he should be beaten up 50
And then we ought to let him go.
PYRGO.: May all the gods in heaven bless you!
My dearest friend! My advocate!
CARIO: O.K., my fee: a hundred drachmas.
PYRGO.: What for? 55
CARIO: To let you leave today
With good testimonials,
Darling little grandson of Venus.
You won't get away otherwise,
Make no mistake.
PYRGO.:   All right.
CARIO: You're learning.
In case you're worried about your tunic, 60
Cloak, and sword, they'll be safe with us.
Slave: Do I keep on pounding, or have I hit him
Often enough?
PYRGO.:   I've been softened enough
With those clubs of yours. Please!
PERIP.: Release this man. 65
PYRGO.:   Oh, thank you, sir.
PERIP.: If, at any time in the future,
I catch you here: no testimonials!
PYRGO.: I'm not arguing with that!
PERIP.: Let's go inside, Cario.

[*Exit PERIPLECTOMENUS, with CARIO and the
slaves. PYRGOPOLYNICES is left alone momentarily,
until his SLAVES enter from the harbour.*]

PYRGO.: Look! Here are my slaves. Tell me, 70
Has Philocomasium left already?
SLAVE: Long ago.
PYRGO.:   Ah! oh!!
SLAVE: You'd say much more
Than that, if you knew what I know.
You see, the man who had the patch 75
Over his eye wasn't really a sailor.
PYRGO.: Then who was he?
SLAVE: Philocomasium's lover.

PYRGO.: How do you know?
SLAVE: I know.
   As soon as they passed the city gate,
   Right there, without a moment's pause,   80
   They were kissing in each other's arms.
PYRGO.: *Alas!* Unhappy me!
   I can see that I've been tricked.
   That crook of a man, Palaestrio—
   He swindled me and sucked me in.   85

[*directly to the audience*]
I find that justice has been done:
If more adulterers met my fate,
There'd be less adultery in the state;
Illicit affairs wouldn't even be planned!   90

Let's all go home now. Give us a hand.

[*Exeunt omnes.*]

CHAPTER TWO

Medieval Drama

I n 312 C.E., Emperor Constantine was marching with his army to Rome to defeat a rival emperor when he saw a vision in the sky: a crucifix, accompanied by the words "Under this sign, conquer." He affixed Christian symbols to his soldiers' armaments, and conquer he did. The odds had been against him, and Constantine was impressed—so impressed that he adopted Christianity as the official state religion. What had once been seen by Roman writers like Tacitus, Suetonius, and Pliny as a "pernicious superstition"—a "depraved...contagion" originating in the rebellious province of Judaea and deserving of swift suppression in the capital—was suddenly institutionalized as the only legal and legitimate religion for the entire Roman Empire.

By the middle of the following century, the western half of the Roman Empire would be in ruins, and continual incursions by the Goths, Vandals and Huns would keep it plunged in violent chaos for centuries to come. Constantine had long since relocated to the Eastern Empire, however, to Byzantium, which he renamed Constantinople. There a Greek-speaking Christian culture would remain until the fifteenth century, when the city fell to the Ottoman Turks and its Christian scholars fled with their books to Italy, helping to launch the Renaissance there. But at the time of Constantine's vision and despite the Western Empire's imminent collapse, most of Europe had already been conquered by Rome—by Roman militarism, Roman roads, and Rome's paper-based bureaucracy—and was easily retooled to receive the new religion. Constantine and his successors placed the Empire's administrative infrastructure in the hands of the Christian bishops, who retained its hierarchies and its use of Latin for administration of subject-peoples who didn't speak it, as well as its expansionist, world-dominating ambitions. Just as the peoples of Europe had paid tribute to Rome under its emperors, they would continue to pay obeisance to Rome under its popes, who like the emperors before them were seen as divine, inviolable, and above all human laws. Under threat of damnation and hellfire in the next world, to say nothing of torture, live cremation, and decapitation in this one, Europeans of many languages were bound, from the Dark through the Middle Ages and beyond, to follow the dictates of Roman religious policy, which endeavoured to control all aspects of life and thought from the cradle to the grave, and from one extremity of the known globe to the other.

As each leader of Europe's barbarian tribes was converted, all the members of his tribe were considered Christian. This hardly represented the truth of the situation, as most Europeans were in fact still pagan, meaning that they recognized many gods. Christianity on the contrary tolerated one only, called the one "true" god. According to the radically binary thinking of the early Church Fathers, all that does not belong to God belongs to the Devil; thus all non-Christian gods and religions were branded as satanic, the work of devils in disguise. Efforts were made through the following centuries not only to convert (or kill) the Jews, pagans, and later, the Muslims, but also to obliterate pre-Christian institutions and influences in general. Works of Greek and Roman literature were burnt, the thousand-year-old philosophy academy of Plato and Aristotle was closed, the Olympic games were banned, and all theatres shut down. In 601 Pope Gregory the Great instructed the clergy to "destroy" remaining pagan religious artifacts, "purify" their shrines, and install Christian relics there, so that the people, who were still pagan in their sympathies despite the conversion of their leaders, "will have no need to change their place of concourse." The Christian calendar of holy days was superimposed over the existing calendar of pagan festivals, which were outlawed in favour of Christmas, Easter, Corpus Christi, and others.

Aiding the missionary activities of the early Dark Ages (fifth to seventh centuries) was a series of continent-wide catastrophes: major earthquakes, widespread famine and an accompanying pestilence, the constant terrorism of barbarian and then Viking attacks, and a virulent plague epidemic that cut the population of Europe in half. In a time of general ignorance and superstition, these natural and man-made calamities may well have seemed to confirm the preachers' apocalyptic sermonizing about judgement day, the sinfulness of mankind, and the omnipresence of devils. In any case, in the six centuries between Constantine and Hroswitha, whose tenth-century *The Conversion of Thais the Whore* begins this chapter, Christian missionaries in Europe, like Pafnutius in this play, succeeded in convincing their pagan subjects to fear Hell, hold their earthly desires in contempt, and invest their love and longing in the spiritual realm instead, in the promise of salvation and a blissful transfiguration in the afterlife.

As for theatre, it was perceived from the beginning as a diabolical threat to Christianity because of its continued popularity in Rome even among new converts. Largely in reaction to the murderous spectacles that passed for theatre under the decadent Empire, Church Fathers such as Tatian, Tertullian, and Augustine wrote with fanatical zeal against the stage, which they characterized as an instrument in the devil's fiendish plot to corrupt men's souls and damn them to hell for all eternity. Acting, role-playing, costumes, make-up, cross-dressing, the representation of fictional stories, even the wearing of platform shoes, were considered sinful, a cruel mockery of the truth of God's creation. To represent something, even in speech, was described as equivalent with actually doing it: thus the ancient Greek theatre, in which the violence was fictional and merely narrated, was no better than a real bloodbath in the Roman coliseum. To represent an evil act like murder or incest in a play was necessarily to be advocating it; but if theatre on the contrary represented angels and goodness, it was equally guilty, since such a representation was by definition feigned, a blasphemous lie. Under the influence of such polemics, the Church set about trying to suppress theatrical spectacles, first by heaping fresh woes upon the already miserable lives of Roman actors in the form of prohibitions and exclusions. In the sixth century, Emperor Justinian finally closed down the theatres for good—albeit not before marrying a famous actress, Theodora, known for her striptease act. For centuries thereafter, clerics were warned against allowing the now-homeless, travelling actors to perform in their jurisdictions. Actors were forbidden to have contact with Christian women, hold slaves, or wear gold. They were officially excommunicated, were denied the sacraments, including marriage and burial, and in general were defamed and debased throughout Christendom. This Church-sanctioned persecution of actors lasted in some places well into the eighteenth century, when French priests were still refusing to admit into their graveyards the bodies of even the most distinguished theatre artists.

Such policies were especially hypocritical given how dependent on theatre and drama Christian worship itself was and remained. In sharp contrast to outlawed forms of pagan worship—which focussed on seasonal cycles and nature-deities and thus involved various ambulatory activities outdoors in forests and fields—early Christian services consisted of an indoor, sedentary, seated audience, applause in the form of hand-clapping, and a purpose-built structure with benches, aisles, and galleries. But like Judaism, which provided Christianity's basic moral teachings only to then be demonized as filthy and abominable, theatre was vilified as a ruse of the Evil One rather than credited as a model—although the great anti-theatrical writer St. Augustine, an ardent theatre-goer in his youth, did acknowledge the similarities. In the fourth century, Emperor Constantine had dozens of magnificent churches constructed in Rome, Jerusalem, and elsewhere to rival the grandest of Roman theatres, and in the following centuries members of the clergy only increased the presence of dramatic and theatrical elements within them. Faced with the task of explaining the new religion to illiterate slaves and then illiterate barbarians, clerics came to depend on illustrative playlets, costumes, and special effects, eventually writing full-scale plays for performance both inside and outside the church.

The Christian campaign to replace theatre with church-going was not, however, the only reason for the near-disappearance of drama in the Dark and early Middle Ages. With classical schools closed and Christian instruction limited to doctrine and faith (and often hostile to knowledge and inquiry), literacy declined. Latin was virtually the only written language available, and few understood it; even among the clergy, illiteracy was the norm. In the absence of a technology for collecting and dramatizing stories, any troupes that had managed to survive from pre-Christian times would eventually have resorted to forms of entertainment not dependent on the ability to read and write: juggling, acrobatics, songs and dances, animal wrangling, magic tricks and epic monologues. As in pre-literate Greece, it was not the actor but the minstrel or troubadour who was the best-known type of storyteller in this period. Consequently, the earliest known plays of Christian Europe were written in monasteries, practically the only bastions of literacy left. By the medieval period (twelfth to fourteenth centuries), this would begin to change: greater peace and stability in Europe allowed for the re-establishment of regular trade, the growth of manufacturing towns, the consolidation of national entities, and the founding of the first universities and trade guilds. These phenomena, especially the last two, stimulated a resurgence of literacy, which in turn supported the emergence of a few semi-regular theatre traditions and dramatic genres. Some of these were religious and didactic, some purely secular and comic, while others, particularly the mystery plays that dramatized stories from the Bible, combined elements of both.

Of the four main religious genres of the Middle Ages, three originally emerged from monasteries: the miracle or saint's play, liturgical drama, and the morality play. All were written at first in Latin; as literacy spread outside monastery walls, all would eventually be written in Europe's various spoken languages, or vernaculars. In keeping with their monastic origins, miracle plays, liturgical dramas, and morality plays remained genres of Christian instruction, although their didacticism came to be accompanied by ever more spectacular and inventive staging techniques. The miracle play, which in the Middle Ages was performed outdoors in churchyards, dramatized the persecution, suffering, and martyrdom of Christian saints, whose steadfastness under truly macabre forms of physical torture was meant to demonstrate the truth and saving power of their faith. At roughly the same time as Hroswitha was developing this (at times luridly realistic) genre in her Germanic monastery, Benedictine monks in England, Switzerland, and France were taking the first steps toward liturgical drama, a genre performed inside the church itself. From the tenth century, Benedictine monks were required by the rules of their order to act out a certain section of the church service in dumb-show. The "Quem Quaeritis" trope—a sung section of the Easter Mass depicting an exchange between an angel and the Marys who have come looking for Jesus' body at the sepulchre—is the first portion of the Latin liturgy known to have been illustrated by clerics' gestures. Over the next three centuries, spurred on no doubt by the efflorescence of secular literary activity in the Gothic age of chivalry and courtly romances, enactments of key moments of the church service blossomed into semi-autonomous plays. Some featured comic episodes (the Marys go shopping), over-the-top perform-ances (the raging villain Herod was always a favourite), and elaborate costumes, props, and special effects: rising stars and angels on pulleys, fireworks, even live animals. Lastly, Abbess Hildegard's twelfth-century *Play of the Virtues* inaugurated the morality play, an allegorical depiction of the struggle between virtue and vice for possession of the soul. Meant to teach clear moral lessons, moralities often represented life as a journey and abstract spiritual qualities as characters met along the way. Eventually staged on a grand scale—*The Castle of Perseverance*, for example, was performed as an outdoor tournament between competing armies for a fortress in which the soul of Mankind resides—the morality play is also represented here by *Everyman*, perhaps its finest example.

As for secular forms of medieval theatre, some may have preserved traditions that went all the way back to pagan Rome. They included the variety acts of the travelling professionals referred to above; the farces and interludes of students and other amateurs; and large-scale mysteries, also prob-ably performed in the main by amateurs. The activities of the professionals remain shadowy through-out the Middle Ages; in fact we often know such performers were active only because of edicts published against them. They evidently provided entertainment for the nobility in their banquet halls, during or after dinner, as well as for the clergy, in the refectories of their monasteries (despite repeated prohibitions against the practice). When not shooed away by local officials, such troupes also set up stages in the market squares and at the fairs of growing medieval towns. Literacy allowed such performers to expand their repertoire beyond songs, jigs, and tricks with monkeys; but most of their written works, which took the form of little palm-sized rolls (from which we get the actor's "role"), have not survived. Even after the advent of written plays, however, they continued to sing, dance, juggle, and play instruments: the first professional performers known to us by name, from the Italian and English Renaissance, were dancers and musicians as well as actors (a term that scarcely existed in the Middle Ages). In medieval England, small numbers of these travelling performers were also occasionally auditioned, hired, and paid by the trade guilds of manufacturing towns to provide a little professional polish to their otherwise amateur Bible-cycle plays (see below).

Secular forms of theatre also emerged out of student life. With the founding of universities in Bologna (c.1000), Paris (1150), Oxford (1160), Cambridge (1209)—and, in 1218, the only secular university in all of Europe, in Salamanca, Spain (under the Moors)—young people and scholars from all over Europe began to congregate in such urban centres, which grew rapidly under their influence. A Middle-English comedy called *The Interlude of the Student and His Girlfriend* (1260), written for three actors and a puppy, is perhaps the oldest surviving secular play of the Christian era. (An interlude, as its name suggests, was performed between other featured activities, such as a religious morality play or the courses of a meal.) Paris soon became an especially vibrant centre for students in general—whose knowledge of Latin gave to Paris's university district the name it still bears today, the "Latin Quarter"—and secular theatre in particular. For in Paris were founded Europe's two oldest theatrical societies. The Basoche was a theatre-producing guild of law clerks founded in the 1200s; the *Enfants Sans Souci*, a group which may have overlapped with the former, was evidently made up of students, who performed satirical, politically charged *sotties* (from *sot*, French for fool) on scaffold-stages in the street or market, wearing fools' caps (hoods with asses' ears). The Basochians were famous for monopolizing Paris's Law Courts every year with their irreverent and uproarious moot courts, mock trials, and farces—in defiance of perpetual orders to cease and desist. *The Farce of Pierre Pathelin* is a superb example of this secular tradition of the medieval farceur. (Like the English interlude, the French farce, from *farcie*, meaning "stuffing," was the savoury filling between heavier works.)

Medieval universities also contributed important experiments in Greek- and Roman-style drama. Although isolated, "one-off" events, landmark steps in the re-emergence of tragedy were taken by academics in Florence and Padua, where in 1315 Albertino wrote a play inspired by Seneca. Like Hroswitha's much earlier rewritings of Terence, classroom imitations of ancient tragedy in the Middle Ages were still undertaken in Latin; not until the Renaissance would tragedies and comedies be written in the vernacular or performed with any regularity in public.

The last category of medieval secular theatre is the *jeu*, mumming, or mystery play, an often outdoor enactment of a story first popularized as a narrative poem. An oral bardic tradition like that of Homer in ancient Greece existed in nearly all European countries in the Dark and Middle Ages. As literacy spread, a few attempts were made to write down and dramatize the legends and courtly romances that had initially been sung by minstrels, troubadours, and jongleurs. Plays about Robin and Marion, King George and the Dragon, even one about the Sack of Troy, were performed in France and England in the thirteenth and fourteenth centuries. Minstrels also sang of contemporary events, and a story brought back from the Crusades about the conquest of Jerusalem was dramatized at a French nobleman's banquet in 1377 or 1378; a mystery about Joan of Arc, *Le Mystère du Siège d'Orleans*, produced by and featuring the real-life Bluebeard, the famous serial killer, was presented in 1435 and involved hundreds of performers, perhaps the inhabitants of an entire village.

The mystery play, however, is much better known today in its religious form, the form it took for dramatizing Bible stories from the mid-fourteenth to the mid-sixteenth century.[1] Such mysteries were part of church-sponsored holiday celebrations at Christmas, Easter, and on Corpus Christi Day, took place all across Europe, and hence are much better documented than their secular counterparts. They were not typically performed every year, however, nor were new plays written from one year to the next. Texts were edited as religious dogmas changed—references to the cult of the Virgin Mary, for example, were expurgated from English mysteries after the Reformation—but in general the same plays were performed over and over again for years, possibly centuries, sometimes on the exact same sets. Staging methods varied widely from one country to the next, but most surviving

---

1 The mystery plays of Spain, called *autos*, only really got underway during the Renaissance, by which time they were written for professional, unionized acting troupes who performed secular plays in permanent public theatres the rest of the year.

mysteries share a surprisingly freewheeling approach to dramatizing the Bible. Their earthy language, comic exuberance, and city-wide involvement made these cycles in many places a genuine form of populist "street-theatre" despite their apparent authorship by clerics.

In England, many (though not all) mysteries were written for performance on the Thursday after Trinity Sunday, or Corpus Christi Day (late May/early June). The particular vitality of English mysteries owes something to the fact that they were performed by the trade guilds of larger market and manufacturing towns such as York, Chester, and Coventry. On pain of a fine, each of the town's main craft guilds was required to take responsibility for preparing and performing one episode of the entire biblical narrative, according to their skills: the Plasterers took Creation; the Shipwrights, Noah's Ark; the Nailers, the Massacre of the Innocents; the Goldsmiths, the Three Kings; the Bakers, the Last Supper; and the Butchers, the *Mortificacio Christi*. The plays of the Wakefield cycle, to which *The Second Shepherds' Play* belongs, were performed on wheeled floats called pageant-wagons that were rolled one by one along the town's parade-route, stopping at pre-appointed audience locations long enough for the play to be performed, then moving on to the next location to perform it again. At each successive stopping-place, another audience awaited: ordinary folk standing in the streets or sitting on bleachers, aristocrats and visiting dignitaries sheltering in the upper-story windows of surrounding buildings. All seem to have enjoyed the festival atmosphere and the succession of glittering pageants, as well as the alcoholic drinks for sale by those who had successfully bid on the right to erect bleachers and operate a concession at one of the performance locales. Given the physical proximity (and occasional traffic back-ups) between one pageant and the next—Wakefield featured 32 pageants, and the plays were of various lengths—there must have been lively competition between the guilds; certainly every opportunity was taken to advertise the tradesmen's skills. Spectacular elements included life-sized wickerwork animals, dazzling pyrotechnics, exploding blood-sacs, horses, devils emerging from hell and angels from heaven, musicians, sheep, and, of course, the ever-popular Herod, who in one play is instructed to descend from his pageant-wagon and rage in the street.

In France and Germany, mysteries commonly took the form of passion plays, which also dramatized the Bible but focussed more narrowly on Christ's life and death. These were performed on the Continent even less frequently than in England—Germany's *Oberammergau Passion Play*, for example, was (and still is) performed only once every ten years—and often for superstitious reasons (to avert a Turkish attack, the plague, etc.). Some extended over many weeks, however: *The Acts of the Apostles*, performed in Bourges in the sixteenth century, took forty days; the passion play of Valenciennes took twenty-five. Like some saints' plays, passion plays were performed on a single fixed set representing several different Biblical locations simultaneously: Heaven on the left, Hell on the far right, and Nazareth, the Temple, Jerusalem, and various other locales, called "mansions," in between. (This "unified" approach to staging the Bible seems to have been typical in France, whereas a multiplicity of moving locales seems to have been preferred in England.[2]) On such simultaneous fixed sets, the star of the show was undoubtedly the mansion of the cavernous, gaping Hell-Mouth. Belching flames and spewing grotesquely-clad winged devils, who gyrated in delicious evil to tempt

---

2 Compare the French and English approaches to "unity of action" in the Renaissance, discussed in the introduction to Chapter 3.

the crowd and scare the children, Hell-Mouth exemplified a fascinating irony of didactic theatre: Vice is more entertaining than Virtue. Far from being hampered by this fact, the creators of medieval drama exploited it to the fullest, even in morality plays. Stage directions in *The Castle of Perseverance*, for example, instruct the Vice figure, Belial, to go into battle with "gunpowder burning in pipes, in his hands, in his ears, and in his arse."

As secular offerings multiplied in the later Middle Ages (fourteenth to sixteenth centuries), theatre-producing clerics and religious brotherhoods tried hard to compete, adding ever more sensational elements to their mysteries, miracles and moralities, sometimes even collaborating with secular groups. Such survival tactics could not prevent and may even have hastened their demise. For even during the heyday of religious drama, the Reformation and Renaissance were already underway. Beginning in 1400 in Prague, revolts against the Roman Church swept through central and northern Europe, giving violent birth to independent new national churches, monarchies, and systems of art-patronage; by the mid-1400s, printing presses had begun disseminating millions of books across Europe, bringing the Church's millennium-long control of information to an end. For a number of reasons—not least of which was the incendiary atmosphere of religious hatred ignited by the Reformation, to which religious plays were suspected of contributing—opposition to religious plays was mounting. Protestants objected to the representation of God on stage, Catholics feared that religious plays were discrediting religion itself. By the mid-sixteenth century in England and France, religious plays were banned altogether. The intermittent, Church-sponsored, largely amateur performing traditions of the Middle Ages were about to give way to the permanent, professional, secular and crown-sponsored theatrical institutions of the Renaissance—but not before shaping the latter in key ways. In England, for example, Bible cycles gave many members of the public their first taste of what semi-regular theatre-going might be like, in effect cultivating the audience that would soon be filling the public playhouses of Shakespeare's London. As a boy Shakespeare certainly saw the last mysteries performed at nearby Coventry, and refers in his plays to their tradesmen-actors, their ranting Herods, their old Vice figures, their swarms of devils emerging from the ubiquitous Hell-Mouth—a set-piece that professional companies of the Elizabethan period still had on hand in their stockrooms. The goriness of the saint's play would live on in many blood-splattered Renaissance tragedies, as would the dramatic structure of the morality play, which is plainly evident in such works as *Dr. Faustus* and *Macbeth*. In fact, the clear-cut moralism of medieval religious theatre in general, its division into virtuous good and devilish evil, would continue to exert a powerful influence on Western drama, both theory and practice, for a long time to come.

[J.W.]

HROSWITHA OF GANDERSHEIM

The Conversion of Thais the Whore

After centuries of neglect, Hroswitha of Gandersheim (c. 930?–c.1000) has at last received due recognition, not only as the first important dramatist of Christian Europe, but as the first female playwright of the entire Western tradition. An aristocratic poet, historian, and canoness of an Imperial Abbey in Saxony, Hroswitha wrote six plays during the second half of the tenth century, a mildly astonishing accomplishment given the darkness of the age. Although she benefitted from the burst of literary and intellectual activity associated with the Carolingian (and Ottonian) Renaissance, she was nevertheless writing at a time when theatre and drama were still suffering under the opprobrium heaped upon them by the early Church Fathers, who saw such activities as part of the Devil's fiendish plot to destroy mankind.

Perhaps therefore to preempt criticism, Hroswitha prefaced her collection of plays by emphasizing her moral purpose: to save Christians from the guilt they must feel when reading Classical literature, particularly the Roman comedies of Terence (193?–159 B.C.E.). Terence's six gentle sitcoms were widely read in the monastery schools of Hroswitha's time for educational reasons, as examples of spoken Latin. But how sinful this was! Like those of Plautus, Terence's heroines are often clever, alluring courtesans, and his plays unapologetic celebrations of such ordinary human (and therefore ungodly) pursuits as sex, love, and marriage. As Hroswitha puts it, such is Terence's beauty and "pagan guile" that Catholic readers must be stained by the wickedness of his subject matter even while delighting in his style.

Hroswitha's declared solution is to imitate Terentian comedy, but to focus on the "laudable" rather than on the "shameless" deeds of women. And indeed her borrowing of an ancient comedy style is readily apparent, particularly in the device of the "cunning plan." As do characters in *Frogs* and *Miles Gloriosus*, the ascetic old hermit in *Thais*, when faced with an impediment, resorts to role-playing and disguise: in order to gain access to a famous courtesan, he dresses up as a handsome young lover—not, of course, for the worldly purpose of procuring her body, but for the sacred one of saving her soul. Just how funny the author intended this incongruous scene to be is uncertain. Elsewhere, however, her humorous aim is unmistakable. For example, Hroswitha takes pains to portray Pafnutius as something of a laughing-stock to his students, who exaggerate their ignorance as a way of egging him on, and who are clearly more interested in his obsession with the whore than in his painfully abstract lesson in music theory. (And notice, too, that Hroswitha has chosen to characterize Thais as a sort of female mirror-image of the teacher Pafnutius: as she prepares to light the fire that will consume all her worldly riches, she is shown surrounded by worshipful but uncomprehending "disciples" in a scene that parallels Pafnutius's music lesson almost exactly.)

But *The Conversion of Thais the Whore*, like Hroswitha's other plays, is most interesting not as a Christian rewriting of Terence, but as the prototype of a whole new genre, the miracle or saint's play. This was a didactic form that went on to flourish across Europe well into the sixteenth century and in some places beyond, and which, in its focus on the martyrdom and suffering of saints, emerged as one of the most theatrical, if often the goriest, forms of theatre in the Middle Ages. These saints' plays, such as the much later *Martyrdom of St. Apollonia,* were said to have been performed in church-yards by "foolish clergy," and they enacted gruesome scenes of torture and death, sometimes with such fervour that real injury and fatality occurred: extraction of teeth, scalding with hot irons and helmets, burnings at the stake, and hangings from the cross. Hroswitha's plays were probably not given full outdoor public performances of this type. But in writing them she did make free dramatic use of the many grisly scenes of martyrdom that enlivened popular legends of the lives of saints from the earliest days of Christianity: boilings in oil, breast mutilations, floggings, beheadings, breakings on the wheel. In *Thais,* however, this violence against women, so relished throughout Christian hagiography, seems to have been put to bitterly ironic ends. For here the torturer is Saint Pafnutius, a holy father whose care for Thais' soul leads him to conceive a particularly disgusting method for debasing and ruining her body.

Although care must be taken to resist reading modern feminist ideas into this play in an un-warranted way, there is no avoiding the fact that the particular penance decreed for Thais is laden with gendered symbolism. She is described by her male reformers as diabolically beautiful, irresist-ible to men in a way that endangers their lives, a "vicious serpent," a *femme fatale.*[1] And the Christian fathers' view and treatment of her is coloured throughout with sexual sadism: Pafnutius desires that she be "pierced through all [her] flesh with pain," and Antonius, on hearing that Thais has at last been locked up, confesses that his "veins are bursting" with excitement at the prospect. Pafnutius's zeal to cure Thais' lust through incarceration eventually abates, but too late. Her earlier fear—that being sealed up for years in a tiny cell with her own ever-mounting excrement might be too severe a punishment—proves justified; she is released from her penance after three years but presently dies. While her death is glorified in doctrinal Christian fashion as a desirable release from the burdens of the flesh, the contrast between St. Thais' abject physical defilement and St. Pafnutius's unstained pious self-satisfaction cannot fail to stand as a perennial reproach to the moralizing, paternalistic confinement of women throughout the ages.

Thais was such a common name for prostitutes in the Greek and Roman worlds that it is diffi-cult to say whether the saint about which Hroswitha writes was a real or merely a legendary martyr. Her name was used by Terence for one of his most famous courtesans (*Eunuch,* 161 B.C.E.), and in later literature she reappears in Dryden (1697) and Massenet (1894). For biblical and ideological reasons, Christian hagiography was particularly fond of "harlot saints" (St. Pelagia, St. Afra, and of course Mary Magdalene, patron saint of repentant whores). But Hroswitha may well have been in-terested in Thais for other reasons. For prostitutes in the ancient world were not just common street-walkers; many were rich, powerful and witty companions who enjoyed more social respect than the average wife. Indeed, the most telling irony of this play is that courtesans like Thais were in some ways the ancient equivalent of nuns like Hroswitha herself: they were among the only materially independent, free-minded, and well-educated women of their time.

---

[1] Compare the use of serpent imagery in the portrayal of Klytemestra in the *Oresteia.* Looking forward, one also finds the same character archetype of the *femme fatale* in Gozzi's *Turandot.*

HROSWITHA OF GANDERSHEIM

The Conversion of Thais the Whore

translated by Katharina M. Wilson

*The conversion of Thais, the whore,/ whom the hermit Pafnutius converted, like Abraham before,/
disguised as a lover. After assigning her penance, Pafnutius had her confined to a narrow cell for five full years/
until, duly reconciled to God through her worthy penance and tears,/ fifteen days thereafter in Christ she died.*

CHARACTERS

  DISCIPLES
  PAFNUTIUS
  YOUNG MEN
  THAIS
  LOVERS
  ABBESS
  ANTONIUS
  PAUL

DISCIPLES: Father Pafnutius, why is your countenance beclouded and dark, lacking its customary serenity?

PAFNUTIUS: The man whose heart is grieved/ shows in his countenance, too, that he is bereaved./ 5

DISCIPLES: Why are you grieved?/

PAFNUTIUS: Because of the wrong perpetrated against our Maker.

DISCIPLES: What wrong?

PAFNUTIUS: The wrong perpetrated by His creatures 10 Whom He created in His own image.

DISCIPLES: Your words frighten us.

PAFNUTIUS: Even though His Majesty,/ incapable of suffering, cannot be affected by injury,/ yet when I transfer our own human weakness metaphorically 15 to God, then what greater injury could there be than that the microcosm alone resists the power of Him to Whose rule the macrocosm obediently submits?/

DISCIPLES: What is the microcosm? 20

PAFNUTIUS: Man.

DISCIPLES: Man?/

PAFNUTIUS: Man, indeed.

DISCIPLES: What man?/

PAFNUTIUS: All men./ 25

DISCIPLES: But how is that possible?

PAFNUTIUS: Because the Creator wills it so./

DISCIPLES: We don't understand that, though./

PAFNUTIUS: Many people have difficulty in understanding./ 30

DISCIPLES: Explain it for us, notwithstanding./

PAFNUTIUS: Listen, carefully./

DISCIPLES: We pay attention, eagerly and fully./

PAFNUTIUS: Just as the macrocosm consists of four elements, contrary to each other but still/ made 35 concordant through the Creator's will/ according to the regular arrangements of harmony so, too, man is made up not only of those selfsame elements mentioned afore/ but also of parts much more contrary than those four./ 40

DISCIPLES: And what can be more contrary than the elements?

PAFNUTIUS: The body and the soul: because, even though the elements are contrary to each other, they are still made of matter;/ the soul, however,/ 45 is not mortal like the body at all/ neither is the body mortal like the soul./

DISCIPLES: So it is, indeed./

PAFNUTIUS: But if we follow the rules of dialectic, then we must concede/ that not even these two are 50 contrary to each other./

DISCIPLES: But who could deny that, father?/

PAFNUTIUS: He who knows the dialectic method of argument; for nothing is contrary to the essential substance,/ which contains within itself all 55 contraries' expanse./

DISCIPLES: What did you have in mind when you said "according to the regular arrangement of harmony"?

PAFNUTIUS: I meant this: just as high and low tones, 60

joined harmoniously, produce music, so, too, the contrary elements, brought together in concordance, produce one single world.[1]

DISCIPLES: What an extraordinary thing it is that dissonant things can be said to be concordant/ or that concordant things can be called dissonant!/ 65

PAFNUTIUS: That is because nothing seems to be composed entirely of similar parts, nor from parts that are entirely unrelated by some numerical relationship but are differentiated from each other by their substance and nature. 70

DISCIPLES: What is music?

PAFNUTIUS: Music is one of the subjects of philosophy in the *quadrivium*./

DISCIPLES: What is it that you call the *quadrivium*?/ 75

PAFNUTIUS: Arithmetic, geometry, music, and astronomy.

DISCIPLES: Why are they called the quadrivium which in Latin means the crossroads?

PAFNUTIUS: Because just as roads emanate from a crossing, so, too, the straight (because emanating from the study of philosophy) roads of these four disciplines originate from philosophy./ 80

DISCIPLES: We hesitate to ask questions about the other three as we can barely grasp with our mind's faculty/ the difficulty/ of the subject at hand./ 85

PAFNUTIUS: Indeed, it is difficult to understand./

DISCIPLES: Explain for us the subject of which we just spoke superficially a little./

PAFNUTIUS: I can not say much because to hermits this subject is a riddle./ 90

DISCIPLES: What does it concern?/

PAFNUTIUS: Of music you wish to learn?/

DISCIPLES: Yes.

PAFNUTIUS: It deals with sound./ 95

DISCIPLES: Are there many kinds or can just one be found?/

PAFNUTIUS: Three are reported to exist, but every one of them is joined in arithmetical relationship to the other,/ so that what characterizes one, does not lack in the other./ 100

DISCIPLES: And what distinction exists between the three?/

PAFNUTIUS: The first is called cosmic, or rather celestial,/ the second human; and the third is instrumental./ 105

DISCIPLES: What makes celestial music appear?/

PAFNUTIUS: The seven planets and the celestial sphere./

DISCIPLES: How? 110

PAFNUTIUS: In the same manner as instrumental music, because the same number of intervals, the same lengths, and the same agreement of sounds can be found in it as in chords.

DISCIPLES: What are intervals? 115

PAFNUTIUS: They are distances measured between the planets/ and also between the chords of instruments./

DISCIPLES: And what are lengths?

PAFNUTIUS: The same as tones. 120

DISCIPLES: We don't know anything about tones either.

PAFNUTIUS: Tone is produced by two sounds, and their relationship can be expressed by numbers such as 9:8. 125

DISCIPLES: The faster we attempt to grasp the concepts you teach us, the more you increase the difficulty of the matter./

PAFNUTIUS: The nature of this discussion necessitates that manner./ 130

DISCIPLES: So tell us something, however little, of harmony so that we understand the word at least better./

PAFNUTIUS: Harmony means an agreement of sounds./ 135

DISCIPLES: Why?

PAFNUTIUS: Because it is produced sometimes by four, five, or eight sounds.

DISCIPLES: Since we now know these three, we would also like to learn their names. 140

PAFNUTIUS: The first is called *diatessaron* denoting four tones and their mathematical relationship to each other such as the *epitriton*, that is 4:3. The second, *diapente*, consists of five tones, their

---

1 As Katharina M. Wilson (*The Plays of Hrotsvit of Gandersheim*, Garland Press, 1989) points out, the following "music lesson" is based on Boethius's *Institutio Musica* I.4. Here, as in *The Second Shepherds' Play*, music serves as a key metaphor for the basic Christian drama which moves from discordant conflict (suffering, sin, pagan fallenness etc.) to harmonious resolution (repentance, salvation, and union with the divine).

relationship, the *hemioleos*, being 3:2. The third, *diaposon*, its ratio being 2:1, consists of eight tones. 145

DISCIPLES: Do the spheres and the planets produce a sound so that they deserve to be compared with instrumental chords?/

PAFNUTIUS: Very much so, indeed. 150

DISCIPLES: Why is it not heard then?

PAFNUTIUS: There are many explanations. Some assert that this music cannot be heard because it never ceases; some say it is because the air is too thick for us to hear;/ but others say that the sound 155 is of such magnitude that it cannot enter the narrow passages of our ear;/ there are others, who suggest that the music of the spheres produces such a joyful, such a sweet sound/ that if it could be heard, spellbound/ all people would neglect and 160 abandon themselves and their occupation and would only follow the sound from East to West.

DISCIPLES: Then it is better that it cannot be heard./

PAFNUTIUS: This the Creator of all, long ago discerned./ 165

DISCIPLES: Let that be enough of this. Proceed to tell us about human music./

PAFNUTIUS: What do you want to know about human music?/

DISCIPLES: Where and how can it be observed? 170

PAFNUTIUS: Not only, as I said before/ in the union of body and soul,/ and not only in the emission of sound high and low,/ but also in the pulse of our veins and in the measures of our limbs as in the parts of our fingers where we find the same 175 mathematical proportions of measure as we mentioned in harmonies, because music is not only the agreement of sounds but also that of other dissimilar entities./

DISCIPLES: Had we known beforehand that the 180 solving of the knot of our question would pose such a degree of difficulty for us ignorant students, then we would have preferred not knowing anything about the microcosm, to undergoing such a difficult lesson. 185

PAFNUTIUS: There was no harm in your efforts to learn more/ because now you know some things of which you were ignorant before./

DISCIPLES: That is true, but we are weary of this philosophical explanation, because our minds are 190 incapable of following the subtlety of your reasoning.

PAFNUTIUS: Why do you make fun of me, I who am clearly ignorant and no philosopher?

DISCIPLES: Then how did you come to have this 195 knowledge which you just demonstrated, tiring us out?

PAFNUTIUS: I was eager to share with you the tiny drop of knowledge which I drank from the overflowing cup of philosophers—not stopping to 200 collect but by chance passing by.

DISCIPLES: We thank you for your kindness but we fear the words of the Apostle who says: God has chosen the foolish to confound the wise./[2]

PAFNUTIUS: Whoever deals in sinful things, whether 205 foolish or wise/ deserves punishment and God's reprise./

DISCIPLES: That is true.

PAFNUTIUS: It is not the knowledge of knowable things which offends God, but the wrongdoing of 210 the knower.

DISCIPLES: True.

PAFNUTIUS: And in Whose praise could the knowledge of the disciplines be used more worthily and justly than in His Who made things knowable 215 and gave us the sciences?/

DISCIPLES: In no one else's./

PAFNUTIUS: The more one recognizes how miraculously God had arranged everything according to number, measure and weight,/ the more he will 220 burn with ardent love for God, which will not abate./

DISCIPLES: And rightly so with love that is beyond measure./

PAFNUTIUS: But why do I dwell on these things that 225 give you not the least bit of pleasure?/

DISCIPLES: Tell us then the reason for your grief so that we no longer burst with curiosity to hear./

PAFNUTIUS: When you learn of it, you will not be pleased by what you hear./ 230

DISCIPLES: He who gives in to curiosity, is not seldom saddened but we cannot overcome our curiosity, because it is an aspect of our human weakness.

---

2 I. Corinthians 1:27.

PAFNUTIUS: A certain shameless woman dwells in this land./ 235
DISCIPLES: For all citizens a grave peril at hand./
PAFNUTIUS: She shines forth in wondrous beauty, but threatens men with foul shame./
DISCIPLES: How misfortunate. What is her name?/ 240
PAFNUTIUS: Thais.
DISCIPLES: Thais, the whore?
PAFNUTIUS: That is her name./
DISCIPLES: No one is unaware of her sordid fame./
PAFNUTIUS: No wonder, because she is not satisfied 245 with leading only a few men to damnation/ but is ready to ensnare all men with the allurement of her beauty and drag them along with her to eternal perdition./
DISCIPLES: A doleful situation./ 250
PAFNUTIUS: And not only frivolous youths dissipate their family's few possession on her,/ but even respected men waste their costly treasures by lavishing gifts on her./ Thus they harm themselves.
DISCIPLES: We are horrified to hear./ 255
PAFNUTIUS: Crowds of lovers flock to her, wishing to be near./
DISCIPLES: Damning themselves in the process.
PAFNUTIUS: These fools that come to her are blind in their hearts; they contend and quarrel and fight 260 each other./
DISCIPLES: One vice gives birth to another./
PAFNUTIUS: Then, when the fight has started they fracture each other's faces and noses with their fists; they attack each other with their weapons and 265 drench the threshold of the brothel with their blood gushing forth./
DISCIPLES: What detestible wrong!/
PAFNUTIUS: This is the injury to our Maker which I bewail./ This is the cause of my grief and ail./ 270
DISCIPLES: Justifiably you grieve thereof, and doubtlessly the citizens of heaven grieve with you.
PAFNUTIUS: What if I visit her, disguised as a lover, to see if perchance she might be recovered from her worthless and frivolous life? 275
DISCIPLES: He who instilled the desire for this undertaking in you,/ may He make this worthy desire come true./
PAFNUTIUS: Stand by me with your constant prayers all the while/ so that I won't be overcome by the 280 vicious serpent's guile./

DISCIPLES: He who overcame the prince of the dark, may He grant you triumph over the fiend.

* * *

PAFNUTIUS: Here I see some young men in the forum. First I will go to them and ask, where I may 285 find her whom I seek./
YOUNG MEN: Hm, a stranger approaches; let's enquire what he wants.
PAFNUTIUS: Young men, who are you?/
YOUNG MEN: Citizens of this town. 290
PAFNUTIUS: Greetings to you./
YOUNG MEN: Greetings to you whether you are from these parts or a stranger./
PAFNUTIUS: I just arrived. I am a stranger./
YOUNG MEN: Why did you come? What do you 295 seek?/
PAFNUTIUS: Of that, I cannot speak./
YOUNG MEN: Why not?
PAFNUTIUS: Because that is my secret.
YOUNG MEN: It would be better if you told us,/ 300 because as you are not one of us,/ you will find it very difficult to accomplish your business without the inhabitants' advice.
PAFNUTIUS: What if I told you and by telling an obstacle for myself procured? 305
YOUNG MEN: Not from us—rest assured!/
PAFNUTIUS: Then, trusting in your promise I will yield,/ and my secret no longer shield./
YOUNG MEN: We will not betray our promise; we will not lay an obstacle in your way./ 310
PAFNUTIUS: Rumours reached my ear/ that a certain woman lives here/ who surpasses all in amiability,/ surpasses all in affability./
YOUNG MEN: Do you know her name?/
PAFNUTIUS: I do. 315
YOUNG MEN: What is her name?/
PAFNUTIUS: Thais.
YOUNG MEN: For her, we too are aflame./
PAFNUTIUS: They say she is the most beautiful woman on earth,/ greater than all in delight and 320 mirth./
YOUNG MEN: Whoever told you that, did not tell a lie.
PAFNUTIUS: It was for her sake that I decided to make this arduous journey; I came to see her 325 today./

YOUNG MEN: There are no obstacles in your way./

PAFNUTIUS: Where does she stay?/

YOUNG MEN: In that house, quite near./

PAFNUTIUS: The one you are pointing out to me here?/ 330

YOUNG MEN: Yes.

PAFNUTIUS: I will go there.

YOUNG MEN: If you like, we'll go along./

PAFNUTIUS: No, I'd rather go alone./ 335

YOUNG MEN: As you wish.

* * *

PAFNUTIUS: Are you inside, Thais, whom I'm seeking?/

THAIS: Who is this stranger speaking?/

PAFNUTIUS: One who loves you. 340

THAIS: Whoever seeks me in love/ finds me returning his love./

PAFNUTIUS: Oh Thais, Thais, what an arduous journey I took to come to this place/ in order to speak with you and to behold your face./ 345

THAIS: I do not deny you the sight of my face nor my conversation./

PAFNUTIUS: The secret nature of our conversation/ necessitates the solitude of a secret location./

THAIS: Look, here is a room well furnished for a pleasant stay./ 350

PAFNUTIUS: Isn't there another room, where we can converse more privately, one that is hidden away?/

THAIS: There is one so hidden, so secret, that no one besides me knows its inside except for God./ 355

PAFNUTIUS: What God?/

THAIS: The true God./

PAFNUTIUS: Do you believe He knows what we do?/

THAIS: I know that nothing is hidden from His view./ 360

PAFNUTIUS: Do you believe that He overlooks the deeds of the wicked or that He metes out justice as its due?/

THAIS: I believe that He weighs the merits of each person justly in His scale/ and that, each according to his deserts receives reward or travail./ 365

PAFNUTIUS: Oh Christ, how wondrous is the patience, of Thy great mercy! Thou seest that some sin with full cognition,/ yet Thou delay their deserved perdition./ 370

THAIS: Why do you tremble? Why the change of colour? Why all these tears?

PAFNUTIUS: I shudder at your presumption,/ I bewail your sure perdition/ because you know all this so well,/ and yet you sent many a man's soul to Hell./ 375

THAIS: Woe is me, wretched woman!

PAFNUTIUS: You deserve to be damned even more,/ as you offended the Divine Majesty haughtily, knowing of Him before./ 380

THAIS: Alas, alas, what do you do? What calamity do you sketch?/ Why do you threaten me, unfortunate wretch?/

PAFNUTIUS: Punishment awaits you in Hell/ if you continue in sin to dwell./ 385

THAIS: Your severe reproach's dart/ pierces the inmost recesses of my heart./

PAFNUTIUS: Oh, how I wish you were pierced through all your flesh with pain/ so that you wouldn't dare to give yourself to perilous lust again./ 390

THAIS: How can there be place now for appalling lust in my heart when it is filled entirely with the bitter pangs of sorrow/ and the new awareness of guilt, fear, and woe?/ 395

PAFNUTIUS: I hope that when the thorns of your vice are destroyed at the root,/ the winestock of penitence may then bring forth fruit./

THAIS: If only you believed/ and the hope conceived/ that I who am so stained,/ with thousands and thousands of sins enchained,/ could expiate my sins or could perform due penance to gain forgiveness! 400

PAFNUTIUS: Show contempt for the world, and flee the company of your lascivious lovers' crew./ 405

THAIS: And then, what am I to do?/

PAFNUTIUS: Withdraw yourself to a secret place,/ where you may reflect upon yourself and your former ways/ and lament the enormity of your sins. 410

THAIS: If you have hopes that I will succeed,/ then I will begin with all due speed./

PAFNUTIUS: I have no doubt that you will reap benefits.

THAIS: Give me just a short time to gather what I long saved:/ my wealth, ill-gotten and depraved./ 415

PAFNUTIUS: Have no concern for your treasure,/ there'll be those who will use them for pleasure./

THAIS: I was not planning on saving it for myself nor giving it to friends. I don't even wish to give it to the poor because I don't think that the prize of sin is fit for good.[3] 420

PAFNUTIUS: You are right. But how do you plan to dispose of your treasure and cash?/

THAIS: To feed all to the fire, until it is turned to ash./ 425

PAFNUTIUS: Why?

THAIS: So that nothing is left of what I acquired through sin,/ wronging the world's Maker therein./

PAFNUTIUS: Oh how you have changed from your prior condition/ when you burned with illicit passions/ and were inflamed with greed for possessions./ 430

THAIS: Perhaps, God willing,/ I'll be changed into a better being./ 435

PAFNUTIUS: It is not difficult for Him, Himself changeable, to change things according to His will./

THAIS: I will now leave and what I planned fulfill./

PAFNUTIUS: Go forth in peace and return quickly. 440

* * *

THAIS: Come, hurry along,/ my worthless lovers' throng!/

LOVERS: The voice of Thais calls us, let us hurry, let us go/ so that we don't offend her by being slow./

THAIS: Be quick, come here, and don't delay,/ there is something I wish to say./ 445

LOVERS: Oh Thais, Thais, what do you intend to do with this pile, why did you gather all these riches around the pyre yonder?/

THAIS: Do you wonder?

LOVERS: We are much surprised./ 450

THAIS: You'll be soon apprised./

LOVERS: That's what we hope for.

THAIS: Then watch me!

LOVERS: Stop it Thais; refrain!/ What are you doing? Are you insane?/ 455

THAIS: I am not insane, but savouring good health again./

_____
[3] Matthew 27:6.

LOVERS: But why this destruction of four-hundred pounds of gold,/ and of these treasures manifold?/ 460

THAIS: All that I extorted from you unjustly, I now wish to burn,/ so that no spark of hope is left that I will ever again return/ and give in to your lust.

LOVERS: Wait for a minute, wait,/ and the cause of your distress relate! 465

THAIS: I will not stay,/ for I have nothing more to say./

LOVERS: Why do you dismiss us in obvious disgust?/ Do you accuse any one of us of breaking trust?/ Have we not always satisfied your every desire,/ and yet you reward us with hate and with ire!/ 470

THAIS: Go away, depart!/ Don't tear my robe apart./ It's enough that I sinned with you in the past;/ this is the end of my sinful life, it is time to part at last./ 475

LOVERS: Whereto are you bound?/

THAIS: Where I never can be found./

LOVERS: What incredible plight/ …that Thais, our only delight,/ the same Thais who was always eager to accumulate wealth, who always had lascivious things on her mind,/ and who abandoned herself entirely to voluptuousness of every kind,/ has now destroyed her jewels and her gold and all of a sudden scorns us,/ and wants to leave us./ 480

* * *

THAIS: Here I come, father Pafnutius, eager to follow you. 485

PAFNUTIUS: You took so long to arrive here,/ that I was tortured by grave fear/ that you may have become involved once again in worldly things.

THAIS: Do not fear; I had different things planned namely to dispose of my possessions according to my wish and to renounce my lovers publicly. 490

PAFNUTIUS: Since you have abandoned those/ you may now make your avowals/ to the Heavenly Bridegroom. 495

THAIS: It is up to you to tell me what I ought to do. Chart my course as if drawing a circle.

PAFNUTIUS: Then, come along./

THAIS: I shall follow you, I'm coming along:/ Oh, how I wish to avoid all wrong,/ and imitate your deeds! 500

* * *

PAFNUTIUS: Here is the cloister where the noble company of holy virgins stays./ Here I want you to spend your days/ performing your penance.

THAIS: I will not contradict you. 505

PAFNUTIUS: I will enter and ask the abbess, the virgins' leader, to receive you./

THAIS: In the meantime, what shall I do?

PAFNUTIUS: Come with me./

THAIS: As you command, it shall be./ 510

PAFNUTIUS: But look, the abbess approaches. I wonder who told her so promptly of our arrival./

THAIS: Some rumour, bound by no hindrance and in speed without a rival./

* * *

PAFNUTIUS: Noble abbess, Providence brings you,/ 515 for I came to seek you./

ABBESS: Honoured father Pafnutius, our most welcome guest,/ your arrival, beloved of God, is manifoldly blest./

PAFNUTIUS: May the felicity of eternal bliss/ grant 520 you the Almighty's grace and benefice./

ABBESS: For what reason does your holiness deign to visit my humble abode?/

PAFNUTIUS: I ask for your aid; in a situation of need I took to the road./ 525

ABBESS: Give me only a hint of what you wish me to do, and I will fulfill it forthright./ I will try to satisfy your wish with all my might.

PAFNUTIUS: I have brought you a half-dead little she-goat, recently snatched from the teeth of 530 wolves. I hope that by your compassion its shelter will be ensured,/ and that by your care, it will be cured,/ until, having cast aside the rough pelt of a goat, she will be clothed with the soft wool of the lamb. 535

ABBESS: Please, explain it more./

PAFNUTIUS: She whom you see before you, led the life of a whore./

ABBESS: What a wretched life she bore!/

PAFNUTIUS: She gave herself entirely to vice./ 540

ABBESS: At the cost of her salvation's sacrifice!/

PAFNUTIUS: But now urged by me and helped by Christ, she renounced her former frivolous way of life and seeks to embrace chastity./

ABBESS: Thanks be to the Lord for the change./ 545

PAFNUTIUS: But because the sickness of both body and soul must be cured by the medicine of contraries, it follows that she must be sequestered from the tumult of the world,/ obscured in a small cell, so that she may contemplate her sins 550 undisturbed./

ABBESS: That cure will work very well./

PAFNUTIUS: Then have them build such a cell./

ABBESS: It will be completed promptly./

PAFNUTIUS: Make sure it has no entry and no exit, 555 only a tiny window through which she may receive some modest food on certain days at set hours and in small quantity./

ABBESS: I fear that the softness of her delicate disposition/ will find it difficult to suffer such 560 harsh conditions./

PAFNUTIUS: Do not fear; such a grave offense certainly requires a strong remedy.

ABBESS: That is quite plain./

PAFNUTIUS: I am loath to delay any longer, because 565 I fear she might be seduced by visitors again./

ABBESS: Why do you worry? Why don't you hurry/ and enclose her? Look, the cell you ordered is built./

PAFNUTIUS: Well done. Enter, Thais, your tiny cell, 570 just right for deploring your sins and guilt./

THAIS: How narrow, how dark is the room!/ For a tender woman's dwelling, how full of gloom!/

PAFNUTIUS: Why do you complain about the place?/ Why do you shudder and your steps retrace?/ It is 575 only proper that you who for so long were wandering unrestrained/ in a solitary place should be detained./

THAIS: A mind used to comfort and luxury,/ is rarely able to bear such austerity./ 580

PAFNUTIUS: All the more reason to restrain it by the reins of discipline, until it desist from rebellion.

THAIS: Whatever your fatherly concern prescribes for my reform,/ my wretched self does not refuse to perform;/ but in this dwelling there is one 585 unsuitable thing however/ which would be difficult for my weak nature to bear./

PAFNUTIUS: What is this cause of care?/

THAIS: I am embarrassed to speak./

PAFNUTIUS: Don't be embarrassed, but speak!/ 590

THAIS: What could be more unsuitable/ what could

be more uncomfortable, than that I would have to perform all necessary functions of the body in the very same room? I am sure that it will soon be uninhabitable because of the stench. 595

PAFNUTIUS: Fear rather the eternal tortures of Hell,/ and not the transitory inconveniences of your cell./

THAIS: My frailty makes me afraid.

PAFNUTIUS: It is only right/ that you expiate the evil sweetness of alluring delight/ by enduring this 600 terrible smell./

THAIS: And so I shall./ I, filthy myself, do not refuse to dwell/ in a filthy befouled cell/ —that is my just due./ But it pains me deeply that there is no spot left dignified and pure,/ where I could invoke the 605 name of God's majesty.

PAFNUTIUS: And how can you have such great confidence that you would presume to utter the name of the unpolluted Divinity with your polluted lips? 610

THAIS: But how can I hope for grace, how can I be saved by His mercy if I am not allowed to invoke Him, against Whom alone I sinned, and to Whom alone I should offer my devotion and prayer?

PAFNUTIUS: Clearly you should pray not with words 615 but with tears; not with your tinkling voice's melodious art/ but with the bursting of your penitent heart./

THAIS: But if I am prohibited from praying with words, how can I ever hope for forgiveness?/ 620

PAFNUTIUS: The more perfectly you humiliate yourself, the faster you will earn forgiveness./ Say only: Thou Who created me,/ have mercy upon me!/

THAIS: I will need His mercy not to be overcome in 625 this uncertain struggle.

PAFNUTIUS: Struggle manfully so that you may gloriously attain your triumph.

THAIS: You must pray for me so that I may deserve the palm of victory./ 630

PAFNUTIUS: No need to admonish me./

THAIS: I hope so.

PAFNUTIUS: Now it is time that I return to my longed-for retreat and visit my dear disciples. Noble abbess,/ I commit my charge to your care 635 and kindness,/ so that you may nourish her delicate body with a few necessities occasionally/ and nourish her soul with profitable admonitions frequently./

ABBESS: Don't worry about her, because I will look 640 after her, and my maternal affections will never cease./

PAFNUTIUS: I will then leave.

ABBESS: Go forth in peace!/

* * *

DISCIPLES: Who knocks at the door? 645

PAFNUTIUS: Hello!/

DISCIPLES: Our father's, Pafnutius' voice!

PAFNUTIUS: Unlock the door!

DISCIPLES: Oh father, greeting to you!/

PAFNUTIUS: Greetings to you, too./ 650

DISCIPLES: We were worried about your long stay./

PAFNUTIUS: It was good that I went away./

DISCIPLES: What happened with Thais?

PAFNUTIUS: Just the event for which I was praying./

DISCIPLES: Where is she now staying?/ 655

PAFNUTIUS: She is bewailing her sins in a tiny cell, quite nigh./

DISCIPLES: Praise be to the Trinity on High./

PAFNUTIUS: And blessed be His formidable name, now and forever. 660

DISCIPLES: Amen.

* * *

PAFNUTIUS: Behold, three years of Thais' penitence have passed and I don't know whether or not her penance was deemed acceptable. I will rise and go to my brother Antonius, so that through his 665 intercession I may find out.

* * *

ANTONIUS: What unexpected pleasure, what surprising delight:/ it is my brother and co-hermit Pafnutius whom I sight!/ He is coming near./

PAFNUTIUS: I am here./ 670

ANTONIUS: How good of you to come, brother, your arrival gives me great joy.

PAFNUTIUS: I am as delighted in seeing you as you are with my visit.

ANTONIUS: And what happy and for both of us 675 welcome cause brings you here away from your solitary domain?/

PAFNUTIUS: I will explain./

ANTONIUS: I'd like to know./

PAFNUTIUS: Three years ago/ a certain whore/ by the name of Thais lived in this land/ who not only damned herself but dragged many a man to his miserable end./ 680

ANTONIUS: What an abominable way one's life to spend!/ 685

PAFNUTIUS: I visited her, disguised as a lover, secretly/ and won over her lascivious mind first with kind admonitions and flattery,/ then I frightened her with harsh threats.

ANTONIUS: A proper measure,/ necessary for this whore of pleasure./ 690

PAFNUTIUS: Finally she yielded,/ scorning the reprehensible way of life she formerly wielded/ and she chose a life of chastity consenting to be enclosed in a narrow cell./ 695

ANTONIUS: I am delighted to hear what you tell/ so much so that my veins are bursting, and my heart beats with joy.

PAFNUTIUS: That becomes your saintliness, and while I am overjoyed by her change of heart,/ I am still disturbed by a decision on my part:/ I fear that her frailty/ can bear the long penance only with great difficulty./ 700

ANTONIUS: Where true affection reigns,/ kind compassion never wanes./ 705

PAFNUTIUS: Therefore I'd like to implore you that you and your disciples pray together with me until Heaven reveals to our sight or ears/ whether or not Divine Mercy has been moved to forgiveness by the penitent's tears./ 710

ANTONIUS: We are happy to comply with your request./

PAFNUTIUS: I have no doubt that God will graciously listen and grant your behest./

* * *

ANTONIUS: Look, the Gospel's promise is fulfilled in us. 715

PAFNUTIUS: What promise?

ANTONIUS: The one that promises that communal prayer can achieve all./

PAFNUTIUS: What did befall?/ 720

ANTONIUS: A vision was granted to my disciple, Paul./

PAFNUTIUS: Call him!

ANTONIUS: Come hither, Paul, and tell Pafnutius what you saw. 725

PAUL: In my vision of Heaven, I saw a bed/ with white linen beautifully spread/ surrounded by four resplendent maidens who stood as if guarding the bed./And when I beheld the beauty of this marvelous brightness I said to myself: This glory belongs to no one more than to my father and my lord Antonius. 730

ANTONIUS: I am not worthy to such beautitude to soar./

PAUL: After I spoke, a Divine voice spoke: "This glory is not as you hope for Antonius, but is meant for Thais the whore."/ 735

PAFNUTIUS: Praised be Thy sweet mercy, Oh Christ, only begotten Son of God, for Thou hast deigned to deliver me from my sadness' plight./ 740

ANTONIUS: To praise Him is meet and right./

PAFNUTIUS: I shall go and visit my prisoner.

ANTONIUS: It is proper to give her hope for forgiveness without further remiss,/ and assure her of the comfort of Heavenly bliss./ 745

* * *

PAFNUTIUS: Thais, my adoptive daughter, open your window so I may see you and rejoice./

THAIS: Who speaks? Whose is this voice?

PAFNUTIUS: It is Pafnutius, your father.

THAIS: To what do I owe the bliss of such great joy that you deign to visit me, poor sinful soul?/ 750

PAFNUTIUS: Even though I was absent in body for three years, yet I was constantly concerned about how you would achieve your goal./

THAIS: I do not doubt that at all./ 755

PAFNUTIUS: Tell me of these past three years' course,/ and how you practised your remorse./

THAIS: That is all I can tell:/ I have done nothing worthy of God, and that I know full well./

PAFNUTIUS: If God would consider our sins only/ no one would stand up to scrutiny./ 760

THAIS: But if you wish to know how I spent my time, in my conscience I enumerated my manifold sins and wickedness and gathered them as in a bundle of crime./ Then I continuously went over them in my mind,/ so that just as the nauseating 765 smell here never left my nostrils, so the fear of Hell never departed from my heart's eyes.

PAFNUTIUS: Because you punished yourself with such compunction/ you have earned forgiveness' unction./ 770

THAIS: Oh, how I wish I did!

PAFNUTIUS: Give me your hand so I can lead you out.

THAIS: Venerable Father, do not take me, stained and foul wretch, from this filth; let me remain in this place/ appropriate for my sinful ways./ 775

PAFNUTIUS: It is time for you to lessen your fear/ and to begin to have hopeful cheer./

THAIS: All angels sing His praise and His kindness, because He never scorns the humility of a contrite soul. 780

PAFNUTIUS: Remain steadfast in fearing God, and continue to love Him forever. After fifteen days you will leave your human body/ and, having completed your happy journey,/ by the favour of Heavenly grace you will reach the stars. 785

THAIS: Oh, how I desire to avoid Hell's tortures, or rather how I aspire/ to suffer by some less cruel fire!/ For my merits do not suffice/ to secure me the bliss of paradise./ 790

PAFNUTIUS: Grace is God's gift and a free award,/ and not human merit's reward;/ because if it were simply a payment for merits, it wouldn't be called grace. 795

THAIS: Therefore praise Him all the company of heaven, and on earth the least little sprout or bush,/ not only all living creatures but even the waterfall's crush/ because He not only suffers men to live in sinful ways/ but rewards the penitent with the gift of grace./ 800

PAFNUTIUS: This has been His custom from time immemorial, to have mercy on sinners rather than to slay them.

* * *

THAIS: Do not leave, venerable father, but stand by me with consolation in my hour of death. 805

PAFNUTIUS: I am not leaving,/ I am staying/ until your soul rejoices in Heaven's gains/ and I bury your earthly remains./

THAIS: Death is near./ 810

PAFNUTIUS: Then we must begin our prayer./

THAIS: Thou Who made me, Have mercy upon me/ and grant that my soul which Thou breathed into me,/ may return happily to Thee.

PAFNUTIUS: Thou Who art created by no one, Thou only art truly without material form, one God in Unity of Substance,/ Thou Who created man, unlike Thee, to consist of diverse substances;/ grant that the dissolving, diverse parts of this human being/ may happily return to the source of their original being; that the soul, divinely imparted, live on in heavenly bliss,/ and that the body may rest in peace/ in the soft lap of earth, from which it came,/ until ashes and dirt combine again/ and breath animates the revived members; that Thais be resurrected exactly as she was,/ a human being, and joining the white lambs may enter eternal joys./ Thou Who alone art what Thou art, one God in the Unity of the Trinity who reigns and is glorified, world without end. 815 820 825 830

HILDEGARD OF BINGEN

The Play of the Virtues

P oet, composer, artist, visionary, theologian and public preacher, Hildegard (1098–1179) was one of the most dazzling intellectuals of her age. Consulted by kings, popes and noble house-holds across Western Europe and England, she produced an immense corpus of works on subjects ranging from religion to natural science and medicine. Author of some three hundred sur-viving letters and over seventy gorgeous and highly original works of vocal music, Hildegard was a convent founder and administrator, undertook four major lecture tours throughout Germany, and, despite what seems to have been a lifelong struggle with migraines, remained an active public figure in Church affairs right up to her death at the age of 81. Like Hroswitha before her, she was also the inventor of a new dramatic genre that would go on to flower across Europe throughout the Middle Ages: the morality play. Like Hroswitha, she wrote in Latin, virtually the only written language then in use in Western Europe but not her native tongue.

Her "play," or more literally, "order" or dance of the virtues, was written for performance at her newly established convent at Rupertsberg near Bingen (c. 1150). With the exception of the role of the Devil, which was taken by her secretary, the monk Volmar, the parts were performed by the women of Hildegard's cloister. And, again with the exception of the Devil's part, which was merely spoken, the parts were sung; *The Play of the Virtues* is a musical composition, and cannot be appre-ciated without being heard. Although musical imagery and occasional songs are conspicuous in many plays of this period (see particularly *Thais* and *The Second Shepherds' Play*), it is only in Hildegard's morality play that real singing comprised as integral a part of the performance as it had in the thea-tre of ancient Athens. But since virtually no Greek musical notation has survived, Hildegard also has the distinction of being the earliest known theatre composer whose music is still enjoyed today.

Typical of such later morality plays as *Everyman*, *The Play of the Virtues* is an allegory. From the Greek for "speaking otherwise," an allegory tells its often didactic story in a disguised form. The battle that the play portrays, between the Virtues and the Devil for possession of the soul, is in-tended to be experienced as a symbolic account of the essential struggle of a Christian life. Charac-ters are conceived as generic embodiments of spiritual values, their names taking the form of abstract nouns: Chastity, Charity, Love, Obedience. Anima, the central figure, represents the human soul; no individuation is attempted, nor is any necessary, for the values taught in such plays are supposed to apply universally. Note, however, that the characterization of the Devil is something of an excep-tion, far exceeding in realism that of any of the Virtues. That evil is inherently more theatrical than virtue is a fascinating paradox of Christian theatre that would eventually be exploited in the moral interludes of the High Middle Ages and early Renaissance, in which a flamboyant Vice figure often starred as one of the newly professionalized actor's most crowd-pleasing stocks-in-trade.

In order to grasp the appeal of the play in its time, it should be remembered that the Medieval world-view was itself deeply allegorical: *everything* was believed to be a symbol for something else—

the Old Testament was "really" a coded prediction of the New, natural events were the messages of God, the devil was everywhere. In fact Hildegard herself was viewed as an otherworldly Sybil, a direct mouthpiece for the divine, a notion she promulgated in all her visionary art and for which she received an official stamp of approval from Pope Eugenius himself.

HILDEGARD OF BINGEN

The Play of the Virtues

translated by Peter Dronke

CHARACTERS
  PATRIARCHS AND PROPHETS
  VIRTUES
    KNOWLEDGE OF GOD
    HUMILITY
    CHARITY
    FEAR OF GOD
    OBEDIENCE
    FAITH
    HOPE
    CHASTITY
    INNOCENCE
    WORLD-REJECTION
    HEAVENLY LOVE
    DISCIPLINE
    SHAMEFASTNESS
    VICTORY
    MERCY
    DISCRETION
    PATIENCE
  ANIMA
  DEVIL
  CHORUS

PROLOGUE

PATRIARCHS AND PROPHETS: Who are these, who
    are like clouds?
VIRTUES: You holy ones of old, why do you marvel
    at us?

The Word of God grows bright in the shape of 5
    man, and thus we shine with him,
building up the limbs of his beautiful body.
PATRIARCHS AND PROPHETS: We are the roots,
    and you, the boughs,
fruits of the living eye,
and in that eye we were the shadow.

SCENE 1

THE LAMENT OF (A CHORUS OF) EMBODIED
    SOULS: Oh, we are strangers here!
    What have we done, straying to realms of sin?
    We should have been daughters of the King,
    but we have fallen into the shadow of sins.
    Oh living Sun, carry us on your shoulders 5
    back to that most just heritage we lost in Adam!
    King of kings, we are fighting in your battle.
ANIMA:[1] (*happily*) Oh sweet divinity, oh gentle life,
    in which I shall wear a radiant robe,
    receiving that which I lost in my first manifestation– 10
    I sigh for you, and invoke all the Virtues.
VIRTUES: You happy Soul, sweet and divine creation,
    fashioned in the deep height of the wisdom of God,
    you show great love.
ANIMA: (*happily*) Oh let me come to you joyfully, 15
    that you may give me the kiss of your heart.
VIRTUES: We must fight together with you, royal
    daughter.

---

[1] In Latin, the Soul.

ANIMA: (*depressed, laments*)[2] Oh grievous toil, oh harsh weight
    that I bear in the dress of this life:
    it is too grievous for me to fight against my body.   20
VIRTUES: (*to Anima*) Anima, you that were given your place by the will of God,
    you instrument of bliss, why are you so tearful
    in the face of the evil God crushed in a maidenly being?
    You must overcome the devil in our midst.
ANIMA: Support me, help me to stay firm!   25
KNOWLEDGE OF GOD: Look at the dress you are wearing, daughter of salvation:
    be steadfast, and you'll never fall.
ANIMA: (*unhappily*) I don't know what to do
    or where to flee.
    Woe is me, I cannot complete   30
    this dress I have put on.
    Indeed I want to cast it off!
VIRTUES: Unhappy state of mind,
    oh poor Anima,
    why do you hide your face in the presence of   35
    your Creator?
KNOWLEDGE OF GOD: You do not know or see or taste the One who has set you here.
ANIMA: God created the world:
    I'm doing him no injury—
    I only want to enjoy it!   40
DEVIL: (*shouting to Anima*) What use to you is toiling foolishly, foolishly? Look to the world: it will embrace you with great honour.
VIRTUES: Is this not a plangent voice, of utmost sorrow?
    Ah, a certain wondrous victory already   45
    rose in that Soul, in her wondrous longing for God,
    in which a sensual delight was secretly hidden,
    alas, where previously the will had known no guilt
    and the desire fled man's wantonness.
    Mourn for this, mourn, Innocence,   50
    you who lost no perfection in your fair modesty,
    who did not devour greedily, with the gullet of the serpent of old.

DEVIL: What is this power—as if there were no one but God? I say, whoever wants to follow me and do my will, I'll give him everything. As for you,   55 Humility, you have nothing that you can give your followers: none of you even know what you are!
HUMILITY: My comrades and I know very well
    that you are the dragon of old
    who craved to fly higher than the highest one: 60
    but God himself hurled you in the abyss.
VIRTUES: As for us, we dwell in the heights.

SCENE 2

HUMILITY: I, Humility, queen of the Virtues, say:
    come to me, you Virtues, and I'll give you the skill
    to seek and find the drachma that is lost
    and to crown her who perseveres blissfully.
VIRTUES: Oh glorious queen, gentlest mediatrix,   5
    gladly we come.
HUMILITY: Because of this, beloved daughters,
    I'll keep your place in the royal wedding-chamber.[3]
CHARITY: I am Charity, the flower of love—
    come to me, Virtues, and I'll lead you   10
    into the radiant light of the flower of the rod.
VIRTUES: Dearest flower, with ardent longing we run to you.
FEAR OF GOD: I, Fear of God, can prepare you, blissful daughters,
    to gaze upon the living God and not die of it.
VIRTUES: Fear, you can help us greatly: 15
    we are filled with the longing never to part from you.
DEVIL: Bravo! Bravo! What is this great fear, and this great love? Where is the champion? Where the prize-giver? You don't even know what you are worshipping!   20
VIRTUES: But you, you were terrified at the supreme Judge,
    for, swollen with pride, you were plunged into Gehenna.[4]

---

2 In a very swift transition, Anima suddenly loses her resolve to live virtuously and to deny her body, and feels overcome by the weight of the corporeal world.

3 For spiritual union with Christ the Bridegroom.

4 From the Hebrew *gê' hinnōm*, the valley of the son of Himmon, where children were said to have been burnt as offerings to Baal (Jer. 19:5); used figuratively for a place of fiery agony.

OBEDIENCE: I am Obedience, the shining one—
    come to me, lovely daughters, and I'll lead you
    to your homeland and to the kiss of the King.   25

VIRTUES: Sweetest summoner,
    it is right for us to come, most eagerly, to you.

FAITH: I am Faith, the mirror of life:
    precious daughters, come to me
    and I shall show you the leaping fountain.   30

VIRTUES: Serene one, mirror-like, we trust in you:
    we shall arrive at the fountain through you.

HOPE: I am the sweet beholder of the living eye,
    I whom no dissembling torpor can deceive.
    Darkness, you cannot cloud my gaze!   35

VIRTUES: Living life, gentle, consoling one,
    you overcome the deadly shafts of death
    and with your seeing eye lay heaven's gate open.

CHASTITY: Maidenhood, you remain within the
    royal chamber.
    How sweetly you burn in the King's embraces,   40
    when the Sun blazes through you,
    never letting your noble flower fall.
    Gentle maiden, you will never know the shadow
    over the falling flower!

VIRTUES: The flower in the meadow falls in the
    wind, the rain splashes it,
    But you, Maidenhood, remain in the symphonies   45
    of heavenly habitants:
    you are the tender flower that will never grow dry.

INNOCENCE: My flock, flee from the Devil's taints!

VIRTUES: We shall flee them, if you give us aid.

WORLD-REJECTION: I, World-rejection, am the
    blaze of life.
    Oh wretched, exiled state on earth,   50
    with all your toils—I let you go.
    Come to me, you Virtues,
    and we'll climb up to the fountain of life!

VIRTUES: Glorious lady, you that always fight
    Christ's battles,
    great power that tread the world under your feet,   55
    you thereby dwell in heaven, victoriously.

HEAVENLY LOVE: I am the golden gate that's fixed
    in heaven:
    whoever passes through me
    will never taste bitter rebelliousness in her mind.

VIRTUES: Royal daughter, you are held fast in the   60
    embraces the world shuns:

how tender is your love in the highest God!

DISCIPLINE: I am the one who loves innocent ways
    that know nothing ignoble;
    I always gaze upon the King of kings
    and, as my highest honour, I embrace him.

VIRTUES: Angelic comrade, how comely you are   65
    in the royal nuptials!

SHAMEFASTNESS: I cover over, drive away or tread
    down all the filths of the Devil.

VIRTUES: Yours is a part in the building of heavenly
    Jerusalem,
    flowering among shining lilies.

MERCY: How bitter in human minds is the harshness   70
    that does not soften and mercifully ease pain!
    I want to reach out my hand to all who suffer.

VIRTUES: Matchless mother of exiles
    you are always raising them up
    and anointing the poor and the weak.   75

VICTORY: I am Victory, the swift, brave champion:
    I fight with a stone, I tread the age-old serpent
    down.

VIRTUES: Oh gentlest warrior, in the scorching
    fountain
    that swallowed up the voracious wolf—
    glorious, crowned one, how gladly   80
    we'll fight against that trickster, at your side!

DISCRETION: I am Discretion, light and moderator
    of all creatures—
    the impartiality of God, that Adam drove away
    by acting wantonly.

VIRTUES: Fairest mother, how sweet you are, how
    gentle—
    in you no one can be confounded.   85

PATIENCE: I am the pillar that can never be made
    to yield,
    as my foundation is in God.

VIRTUES: You that stay firm in the rocky cavern,
    you are the glorious warrior who endures all.

HUMILITY: Daughters of Israel, God raised you   90
    from beneath the tree,
    so now remember how it was planted.
    Therefore rejoice, daughters of Jerusalem.

SCENE 3

VIRTUES: Alas, alas, let us lament and mourn,
    because our master's sheep has fled from life!

ANIMA: (*laments, penitent and calling upon the Virtues*) You royal Virtues, how graceful,
how flashing-bright you look in the highest Sun,
and how delectable is your home, 5
and so, what woe is mine that I fled from you!
VIRTUES: You who escaped, come, come to us, and God will take you back.
ANIMA: Ah, but a burning sweetness swallowed me up in sins,
so I did not dare come in.
VIRTUES: Don't be afraid or run away: 10
the good Shepherd is searching for his lost sheep—it is you.
ANIMA: Now I need your help to gather me up—
I stink of the wounds
that the age-old serpent has made gangrenous.
VIRTUES: Run back to us, retrace those steps 15
where you'll never falter, in our company:
God will heal you.
ANIMA: (*penitently, to the Virtues*) I am the sinner who fled from life:
riddled with sores I'll come to you—
you can offer me redemption's shield. 20
All of you, warriors of Queen Humility,
her white lilies and her crimson roses,
stoop to me, who exiled myself from you like a stranger,
and help me, that in the blood of the Son of God I may arise.
VIRTUES: Fugitive Anima, now be strong: 25
put on the armour of light.
ANIMA: And you, true medicine, Humility, grant me your help,
for pride has broken me in many vices,
inflicting many scars on me.
Now I'm escaping to you—so take me up! 30
HUMILITY: All you Virtues, lift up this mournful sinner,
with all her scars, for the sake of Christ's wounds,
and bring her to me.
VIRTUES: We want to bring you back—we shan't desert you,
the whole of heaven's host will have joy in you: 35
thus it is right for us now to play our symphony.
HUMILITY: Oh unhappy daughter, I want to embrace you:

the great surgeon has suffered harsh and bitter wounds for your sake.
VIRTUES: Living fountain, how great is your sweetness:
you did not reject the gaze of these upon you— 40
no, acutely you foresaw
how you could avert them from the fall the angels fell,
they who thought they possessed a power
which no law allows to be like that.
Rejoice then, daughter Jerusalem, 45
for God is giving you back many
whom the serpent wanted to sunder from you,
who now gleam in a greater brightness
than would have been their state before.

SCENE 4

DEVIL: Who are you? Where are you coming from?
You were in my embrace, I led you out. Yet now
you are going back, defying me—but I shall fight
you and bring you down!
ANIMA: (*penitently*) I recognized that all my ways 5
were wicked, so I fled you.
But now, you trickster, I'll fight you face to face.
Queen Humility, come with your medicine, give me aid!
HUMILITY: Victory, you who once conquered this creature in the heavens,
run now, with all your soldiery,
and all of you bind this Fiend! 10
VICTORY: Bravest and most glorious warriors, come,
help me to vanquish this deceitful one!
VIRTUES: Oh sweetest warrior, in the scorching fountain
that swallowed up the voracious wolf—
glorious, crowned one, how gladly 15
we'll fight against that trickster, at your side!
HUMILITY: Bind him then, you shining Virtues!
VIRTUES: Queen of us all, we obey—
we'll carry out your orders totally.
VICTORY: Comrades, rejoice: the age-old snake is bound! 20
VIRTUES: Praise be to you, Christ, King of the angels!
CHASTITY: In the mind of the Highest, Satan, I trod on your head,
and in a virgin form I nurtured a sweet miracle
when the Son of God came into the world;

therefore you are laid low, with all your plunder;   25
and now let all who dwell in heaven rejoice,
because your belly has been confounded.

DEVIL: You don't know what you are nurturing, for
your belly is devoid of the beautiful form that
woman receives from man; in this you transgress   30
the command that God enjoined in the sweet act
of love; so you don't even know what you are!

CHASTITY: How can what you say affect me?
Even your suggestion smirches it with foulness.
I did bring forth a man, who gathers up mankind   35
to himself, against you, through his nativity.

VIRTUES: Who are you, God, who held
such great counsel in yourself,
a counsel that destroyed the draught of hell
in publicans and sinners,   40
and now shine in paradisal goodness!
Praise to you, King, for this!
Almighty Father, from you flowed a fountain in
fiery love:
guide your children into a fair wind, sailing the
waters,
so that we too may steer them in this way   45
into the heavenly Jerusalem.

FINALE

VIRTUES AND SOULS: In the beginning all creation
was verdant,
flowers blossomed in the midst of it;
later, greenness sank away.
And the champion saw this and said:
"I know it, but the golden number is not yet full.   5
You then, behold me, mirror of your fatherhood:
in my body I am suffering exhaustion,
even my little ones faint.
Now remember that the fullness which was made
in the beginning
need not have grown dry,   10
and that then you resolved
that your eye would never fail
until you saw my body full of jewels.
For it wearies me that all my limbs are exposed to
mockery:
Father, behold, I am showing you my wounds."   15
So now, all you people,
bend your knees to the Father,
that he may reach you his hand.

ANONYMOUS (THE "WAKEFIELD MASTER")

The Second Shepherds' Play

T*he Second Shepherds' Play* (c. 1450?) was the thirteenth of thirty-two spectacular "mystery" plays that were performed in the streets of the English market-town of Wakefield as part of an annual Spring religious festival. Like its companion pieces in the Wakefield cycle—which spanned the entire story of the Bible from Creation to The Hanging of Judas—it was charged with the task of teaching, to a mixed and probably rather rowdy outdoor festival audience, both the facts and the Christian significance of a single episode of the Bible.

Its basic narrative comes from Luke 2:7–16, which describes Jesus' nativity in Bethlehem and the shepherds who, watching their flocks by night, are invited by an angel to witness the birth of their saviour in a nearby stable. In a country whose economy was as dependent on sheep, shepherds, and wool as England's was in the fifteenth century, this biblical episode was almost guaranteed to strike a personal note with the tradesmen who performed it and their audience. And indeed the episode is vividly animated with local details throughout. In effect, the play presents us with supposedly ancient Semitic shepherds who spend their time bemoaning the freezing snow of a bitter English winter and bewailing the cruelty of the English upper classes. In addition, these complaints are often accompanied by colourful curses on Christ's Cross and all his saints—phenomena that would hardly have existed on the day before Christ's birth. Not that there's anything unusual about this sort of anachronism in plays; the deliberate (and sometimes comical) updating of old stories was the essence of Greek tragedy, too. But the degree of irreverent contemporizing in *The Second Shepherds' Play* is striking in a piece ostensibly intended to teach religious doctrine, and in one meant for performance on Corpus Christi Day with the official cooperation and approval of the Church.

Striking, too, is the fact that the dramatizers of Luke 2:7–16 evidently saw fit to parody the whole idea of the nativity. Like Mary at the play's end, Mak's wife Gill also gives birth to a "lamb of god" in a humble shack; but rather than producing the body of a divine saviour, as Mary does, Gill offers up to the shepherds' inspection a stinking long-nosed sheep with a tattoo on its ear. And far from being, like Mary, a holy virgin chosen by God as his sacred vessel, Gill is a screaming drunkard with bad breath who has already conceived a great number of children by the standard human method. And just in case anyone has missed the biblical allusions, the anonymous playwright has Gill at one point pray to "God so mild" that if she's lying, she'll "eat" the child—an outrageous joke at the expense of the whole Corpus Christi festival, which celebrated the gift of Christ's body to the world, and which began with a parade of his symbolically edible body, the communion wafer, through the streets.

And yet, despite all the seemingly impious humour, the play is also a sincere illustration of the nativity story and all the abstract spiritual values that it contains. Beginning with images of suffering, winter, ugliness and dissonance, the play ends with release, rebirth, harmony and salvation, not only in the forgiving of Mak, the rewarding of the shepherds, and the redemption of everyone with the birth of Jesus, but also in the images of springtime cherries, the playfulness of tennis, and the celestial perfection of the angel's song. Given that the ordinary punishment for sheep-stealing in the fifteenth century was death, the shepherds' decision to toss Mak in a blanket—perhaps a common hazing ritual for initiation into a tradesman's guild—functions as a clear endorsement of the virtue of forgiveness. When read side-by-side with such popular secular farces of the period as *Pierre Pathelin*, *The Second Shepherds' Play* emerges as a fascinating hybrid, and one that's absolutely typical of the mystery plays of the Middle Ages: an earnest species of religious indoctrination grafted onto an earthily ebullient comedy of the deprivations, discords, and dishonesties of everyday life.

ANONYMOUS (THE "WAKEFIELD MASTER")
The Second Shepherds' Play[1]

CHARACTERS
FIRST SHEPHERD
SECOND SHEPHERD
THIRD SHEPHERD
MAK
GILL
AN ANGEL
MARY

[*A field near Bethlehem. Enter First Shepherd.*]

1 SHEP. Lord! what, these weathers are cold! and I
    am ill-happed;[2]
I am near-hand dold,[3] so long have I napped;
My legs they fold, my fingers are chapped;
It is not as I would, for I am all lapped
    In sorrow. 5
In storms and tempest,
Now in the east, now in the west,

Woe is him who never has rest,
    Mid-day nor morrow!

But we seely[4] shepherds, that walk on the moor, 10
In faith, we are near-hands out of the door;
No wonder, as it stands, if we be poor,
For the tilth of our lands lies fallow as the floor,
    As ye ken.[5]
We are so lamed, 15
O'ertaxed and shamed,[6]
We're made hand-tamed
    By these gentlery men.

Thus they reave[7] us our rest, Our Lady them wary![8]
These men that are lord-fast,[9] they cause the 20
    plough tarry.
What men say is for the best, we find it contrary;
Thus are husbands[10] oppressed, in point to miscarry
    In life.

---

1 This translation is based on the Towneley text of Rick Cherewko et al. (www.acs.ucalgary.ca). I am also indebted to the version of Sylvan Barnet et al. (Penguin/ Mentor, 1962).
2 Poorly wrapped, dressed.
3 Practically numb.
4 Simple.
5 Know.
6 MS: "ramyd," meaning perhaps oppressed.
7 Rob of.
8 Curse.
9 In the service of lords, nobles.
10 Husbandmen, i.e., shepherds.

Thus hold they us under,
Thus they bring us in blunder;   25
It were great wonder,
    If ever should we thrive.

For may he get a painted sleeve, or a brooch
    nowadays,
Woe is him that him grieves, or once against-says![11]
Dare no man him reprieve,[12] what mastery he makes;   30
And yet may no man believe one word that he says,
    No letter.
He can make purveyance,[13]
With boast and bragance,
And all is through maintenance   35
    Of men that are greater.

There shall come a swain, as proud as a po,[14]
He must borrow my wain,[15] my plough also;
Then I am full fain[16] to grant ere he go.
Thus live we in pain, anger and woe,   40
    By night and day.
He must have if he longed,
If I should forego it;
I were better be hanged
    Than once say him nay.   45

It does me good, as I walk thus by mine own,
Of this world for to talk in manner of moan.
To my sheep will I stalk and hearken anon,
There abide on a balk,[17] or sit on a stone
    Full soon.   50
For I trow,[18] pardie,[19] true men if they be,
We get more company 'ore[20] it be noon.

_____

[11] Speaks against him.
[12] Censure, condemn.
[13] Privileged right of the crown to buy goods for the royal
household at prices immune from the fluctuations of the
ordinary economy, and to commandeer horses and vehicles for the collection of such provisions.
[14] Peacock.
[15] Waggon.
[16] Delighted.
[17] A ridge or mound of unplowed land in a field.
[18] Know, believe, trust.
[19] *Par Dieu*, by god.
[20] Before.

[*Enter Second Shepherd.*]

2 SHEP. Benste[21] and Dominus! what may this
    bemean?
Why fares this world thus? Oft have we not seen,
Lord, these weathers are spiteous, and the   55
    weathers full keen;
And the frost so hideous they water mine eeyen,[22]
    No lie.
Now in dry, now in wet,
Now in snow, now sleet,
When my shoes freeze to my feet   60
    It is not all easy.

But as far as I ken, or yet as I go,
We seely wed-men[23] endure much woe;
We have sorrow then and then, it falls oft so.
Seely Capel, our hen, both to and fro   65
    She cackles;
But begins she to croak,
To groan or to cluck,
Woe is him, our cock,
    For he is in shackles.[24]   70

These men that are wed have not all their will;
When they are full hard stead,[25] they sigh full still;
God knows they are led full hard, full ill,
In bower nor in bed they say nought theretill,[26]
    This tide.[27]   75
My part have I found—
I know my lesson:
Woe is him that is bound,
For he must abide.

But now late in our lives—a marvel to me,   80
That I think my heart rives[28] such wonders to see,
What that destiny drives, it should so be!—

_____

[21] *Benedicte*, bless me.
[22] Eyes.
[23] Poor married men.
[24] The husband, not only enslaved to the nobles, is also in
servitude to his wife, the hen.
[25] Bestead, i.e., beset or surrounded (by ill fortune, etc.).
[26] To that.
[27] Time.
[28] Cleaves, splits open.

Some men will have two wives, and some men three,
    In store.
Some are woe that have any;   85
But so far can I,
Woe is him that has many,
For he feels sore.

But young men of wooing, for God that you
    bought,
Be well ware of wedding, and think in your thought: 90
"Had I known" is a thing that serves of nought;
Much endless mourning has wedding home
    brought,
    And griefs,
With many a sharp shower,
For thou may catch in an hour   95
What shall sow thou full sour
    As long as thou lives.

For, as ever read I epistle, I have one to my fere[29]
As sharp as a thistle, as rough as a brier;
She is browed like a bristle, with a sour- [looking][30] 100
    cheer;
Had she once wet her whistle she could sing full
    clear
    Her pater-noster.
She is as great as a whale,
She has a gallon of gall;
By him that died for us all,   105
    I would I had run till I had lost her!
1 SHEP. God
    Look over the row! full deafly ye stand.
2 SHEP. Yea, the devil in thy maw, so tarrying!
    Saw thou anywhere of Daw?   110
1 SHEP. Yea, on a lea[31] land
    Heard I him blow; he comes here at hand,
        Not far;
    Stand still.
2 SHEP. Why?   115
1 SHEP. For he comes, hope I.

2 SHEP. He will make us both a lie
    Unless we beware.

[*Enter Third Shepherd. At first he doesn't see the
others.*]

3 SHEP. Christ's cross me speed, and Saint Nicholas!
    Thereof had I need, it is worse than it was.   120
    Whoso could, take heed, and let the world pass:
    It is ever in dread and brittle as glass,
        And slithers.[32]
    This world fared never so,
    With marvels more and more,   125
    Now in wealth, now in woe,
        And all is awry.

Was never since Noah's flood such floods seen,
Winds and rains so rude, and storms so keen;
Some stammered, some stood in doubt, as I ween; 130
Now God, turn all to good! I say as I mean.
        For ponder:
These floods so they drown
Both in fields and in town,
And bear all down,   135
        And that is a wonder.

We that walk in the nights, our cattle to keep,
We see sudden sights, when other men sleep.
Yet methink my heart lights—I see shrews[33] peep.
Ye are two tall wights[34]: I will give my sheep 140
    A turn.
But full ill have I meant;
As I walk on this bent,[35]
I may lightly repent
    My toes if I spurn.[36]   145

Ah, sir, God you save, and master mine!
A drink fain would I have, and somewhat to dine.

---

29 Mate.
30 The MS has "loten."
31 Fallow, not in use.

32 Slippery, undependable.
33 Rascals, villains.
34 People, creatures; tall wights would be big, hearty fellows.
35 Field, grassy place.
36 Trip, stumble.

1 SHEP. Christ's curse, my knave, thou art a lither
    hind![37]
2 SHEP. What, the boy does rave!
    Abide some time;
        We have made it.[38]   150
Ill thrift on thy pate![39]
Though the shrew came late,
Yet is he in state
    To dine, if he had it.   155
3 SHEP. Such servants as I, that sweats and swinks,[40]
Eats our bread full dry, and that me forthinks;[41]
We are oft wet and weary when mastermen winks,[42]
Yet comes full lately both dinners and drinks
    But naitly.[43]   160
Both our dame and our sire,
When we have run in the mire,
They can nip at our hire,[44]
    And pay us full lately.

But hear my truth, master: for the fare that ye make,   165
I shall do thereafter work as I take;[45]
I shall do a little, sir, and now and then fake,[46]
For yet lay my supper never on my stomach
    In fields.
Whereto should I threap?[47]   170
With my staff can I leap,
And men say "light cheap
    Litherly foryields."[48]
1 SHEP. Thou were an ill lad—to ride a-wooing
With a man that had but little for spending—   175

2 SHEP. Peace, boy, I bade; no more jangling,
    Or I shall make thee afraid, by the heaven's king,
        With thy gauds![49]
    Where are our sheep, boy? We scorn—
3 SHEP. Sir, this same day at morn   180
    I left them in the corn,
        When they rang Lauds;[50]
    They have pasture good—they cannot go wrong.
1 SHEP. That is right. By the rood,[51] these nights are
    long!
    Yet I would, ere we yode,[52] one gave us a song.   185
2 SHEP. So I thought as I stood, for mirth us
    among.[53]
3 SHEP. I grant.
1 SHEP. Let me sing the tenory.
2 SHEP. And I the treble so high.
3 SHEP. Then the mean falls to me;   190
    Let's see how ye chant.

[*Enter Mak, with a cloak thrown over his smock.*]

MAK. Now, Lord, for thy names seven, that made
    both moon and stars,
    Well more than I can neven,[54] thy will, Lord,
    fails me far;[55]
    I am all uneven,[56] that moves oft my harns;[57]
    Now would God I were in heaven, for there weep   195
    no bairns[58]
        So still!
1 SHEP. Who is that pipes so poor?
MAK. Would God ye wist how I fared!
    Lo, a man that walks on the moor,
        And has not all his will!   200
2 SHEP. Mak, where has thou gone? Tell us tidings.
3 SHEP. Is *he* come? Then each one take heed to his
    thing.

---

37 Lewd or wicked farm hand.
38 We've already prepared the meal.
39 Bad luck on your head!
40 Labours, toils.
41 And I regret that.
42 Sleep.
43 Nevertheless? Thoroughly? Editors are not agreed on the
    meaning of this word.
44 That is, chip away at our wages.
45 For what you pay me, I'll work only insofar as I'm re-
    warded for it.
46 The MS says "among ever lake," i.e., "now and then play/
    fool around."
47 Argue.
48 Cheap goods yield little or, "You get what you pay for."

49 Tricks, pranks.
50 Church service held in early morning.
51 The cross.
52 Went.
53 That is, for mirth in our midst.
54 Name.
55 MS: "of me tharns," or, lacks toward me.
56 Upset.
57 Brains; confuses my wits?
58 Children.

[Takes his cloak from him.]

MAK. What! *Ich*[59] be a yeoman, I tell you, of the king;
　　The self and the same, sent from a great lording,
　　　　Und *sich*.　　　　　　　　　　　　　　　　　205
　　Fie on you! Go hence!
　　Out of my presence!
　　I must have reverence.
　　　　Why, who be *Ich*?
1 SHEP. Why make ye it so quaint? Mak, ye do wrong.　210
2 SHEP. But, Mak, play ye the saint? I trow[60] that ye
　　long.
3 SHEP. I trow the shrew can feint,[61] the devil might
　　him hang!
MAK. I shall make complaint, and make you all to
　　thwang[62]
　　　　At a word.
　　And tell even how ye doth.[63]　　　　　　　215
1 SHEP. But, Mak, is that truth?
　　Now take out that southern tooth,[64]
　　　　And set in a turd!
2 SHEP. Mak, the devil in your eye! a stroke would I
　　lend you.
3 SHEP. Mak, know ye not me? By God, I could　　220
　　teen[65] you.
MAK. God look you all three! methought I had seen
　　you.
　　Ye are a fair company.
1 SHEP.　Can ye now mean you?[66]
2 SHEP. Shrew, peep!
　　Thus late as thou goes,　　　　　　　　225
　　What will men suppose?
　　And thou has an ill noise
　　　　Of stealing of sheep.[67]
MAK. And I am true as steel, all men relate!
　　But a sickness I feel, that holds me full hate　230

My belly fares not well, it is out of estate.
3 SHEP. Seldom lies the devil dead by the gate.[68]
MAK. Therefore
　　Full sore am I and ill,
　　If I stand stone still;　　　　　　　　235
　　I eat not a needle
　　　　This month and more.
1 SHEP. How fares thy wife? By my hood, how fares
　　she?
MAK. Lies weltering,[69] by the rood, by the fire, lo!
　　And a house full of brood; she drinks well, too;　240
　　Ill speed other good that she will do
　　　　But so!
　　Eats as fast as she can,
　　And each year that comes to man,
　　She brings forth a brat,[70]　　　　　　245
　　　　And some years two.

But were I not more gracious, and richer by far,
I were eaten out of house and of harbour;
Yet is she a foul douce, if ye come near.[71]
There is none that trows nor knows a worse　　250
　　　　Than ken I.
Now will ye see what I proffer?
To give all in my coffer
To-morn next to offer
　　Her head-mass penny.[72]　　　　　　255
2 SHEP. I know so forwaked is none in this shire:[73]
　　I would sleep if I took less to my hire.[74]
3 SHEP. I am cold and naked, and would have a fire.
1 SHEP. I am weary, for-raked,[75] and run in the mire.
　　　　Wake thou!　　　　　　　　　　260
2 SHEP. Nay, I will lie down-by,
　　For I must sleep, truly.
3 SHEP. As good a man's son was I
　　　　As any of you.
　　But, Mak, come hither! between shall thou lie down.　265

59　Mak briefly puts on a false Southern dialect with the "ich" and "sich," but not consistently.
60　Trust.
61　"Paint" in the MS, i.e., dissemble, counterfeit.
62　Be whipped.
63　Perhaps, "And how are you?"
64　Southern speech.
65　Beat, vex.
66　Remember.
67　A reputation as a sheep-stealer.

68　Proverbial; it's wise to be suspicious of some things.
69　Wallowing, in a bloated and senseless way.
70　MS: "lakin," a baby.
71　That is, his "sweet" wife reeks.
72　Will pay tomorrow for her funeral mass.
73　Wearied with being awake and watching.
74　I'd take less wages if only I could sleep.
75　Tired of walking.

MAK. Then might I hinder your whispering round
    me;[76]
        No dread.
From my top to my toe
Manus tuas commendo,
Pontio Pilate![77]   270
    Christ's cross me speed!

Then he rises, while the shepherds are asleep, and
    says:

Now were time for a man that lacks what he would,
To stalk privily then into a fold,
And nimbly to work then, and be not too bold,
For he might pay high for the bargain, if it were   275
    told,
        At the ending.
Now is the time for a spell;[78]
But he needs good counsel
That fain would fare well,
        And has but little spending.   280

[Mak casts a spell on the sleeping shepherds.]

But about you, a circle as round as a moon!
Till I have done that I will, till that it be noon,
That ye lie stone-still, till that I have done.
And I shall say there-till of good words a few
      On height: 285
Over your heads my hand I lift,
Out go your eyes, fordo your sight!
But yet I must make better shift,[79]
       If it be right.

[Shepherds snore.]

Lord, what, they sleep hard! that may ye all hear.   290
I never was a shepherd, but now will I lere.[80]
If the flock be scared, yet shall I nip near.

How! Draw hitherward! now mends our cheer
    From sorrow.
A fat sheep, I dare say,   295
A good fleece, dare I say.
Requite when I may,
    But this will I borrow.

[Carries the sheep to the door of his house.]

MAK. How, Gill, art thou in? Get us some light.
WIFE. Who makes such din this time of the night?   300
    I am set for to spin; I doubt that I might
    Rise a penny to win. I shrew them on height!
       So fares
    A housewife that has been
    Run off her feet thus between![81]   305
    Here may no coin[82] be seen
       For such small chares.[83]
MAK. Good wife, open the heck! Sees thou not what
    I bring?
WIFE. I allow thee, draw the sneck.[84]
    Ah, come in, my sweeting!   310
MAK. Yea, thou there not reck of my long standing?
WIFE. By the naked neck art thou like for to hang!
MAK. Away!
    I am worth my meat,
    For in a strait can I get   315
    More than they that swink and sweat
       All the long day.
    Thus it fell to my lot, Gill: I had such grace!
WIFE. It were a foul blot to be hanged for the case.
MAK. I have scaped, Gillot, oft as hard a glace.[85]   320
WIFE. But so long goes the pot to the water, men says,
      At last
    Comes it home broken.
MAK. Well know I the token,
    But let it never be spoken.   325
       But come and help fast.
    I would he were slain; I list well eat:

---

76 MS: "Then might I lett you bedene of that you would
    round."
77 Luke 23:46: "Father, into thy hands I commend my
    spirit"; here Mak substitutes Pontius Pilate for God.
78 MS has "time for to reel," i.e., time to get busy, or mov-
    ing.
79 Have a better strategy, device?
80 Learn.

81 Instead of "run off her feet," MS reads "to be raced."
82 MS has "note" rather than "coin."
83 Chores.
84 Latch.
85 Beating.

This twelvemonth was I not so fain of one sheep-
    meat.

WIFE. Come they ere he be slain, and hear the sheep
    bleat—

MAK. Then might I be ta'en: that were a cold sweat!   330
            Go bar
  The gate door.

WIFE. Yes, Mak,
  For if they come at thy back—

MAK. Then might I pay, for all the pack,   335
      The devil of the worse!

WIFE. A good trick have I spied, since thou can none:
  Here shall we him hide till they be gone,
  In my cradle abide—let me alone—
  And I shall lie beside in childbed and groan.   340

MAK.   Good head![86]
  And I shall say thou was lighted
  Of a knave-child[87] this night.

WIFE. Now, well is me! Day bright,
      That ever I was bred!   345
  This is a good guise and a fair cast;
  Yet a woman's advice helps at the last!
  I wonder who spies; again, go thou fast!

MAK. But I come ere they rise, else blows a cold blast!
      I will go sleep.   350

[*Mak returns to the Shepherds.*]

  Yet sleeps all this company,
  And I shall go stalk privily,
  As if it had never been I
      That carried their sheep.

1 SHEP. *Resurrex a mortruis!*[88] Have hold my hand!   355
  Judas carnas dominus![89] I may not well stand.
  My foot sleeps, by Jesus! and I water fasting.
  I thought that we laid us full near England.

2 SHEP. Ah, yea!
  Lord, what, I have slept well!   360
  As fresh as an eel,
  As light I me feel
      As leaf on a tree.

3 SHEP. Benste[90] be herein! So me quakes,
  My heart is out of skin; what a din it makes!   365
  To the door will I win. Hark, fellows, wake!
      We were four:
  See ye anywhere of Mak now?

1 SHEP. We were up ere thou.

2 SHEP. Man, I give God a vow,   370
      That went he nowhere.

3 SHEP. Methought he was lapt in a wolfskin.

1 SHEP. So are many happed now: namely, within.

3 SHEP. When we had long napped, methought
    with a spin
  A fat sheep he trapped, but he made no din.   375

2 SHEP. Be still!
  Thy dream makes thee wood,[91]
  It is but phantom, by the rood.

1 SHEP. Now God turn all to good,
      If it be his will!   380

2 SHEP. Rise, Mak, for shame! thou lies right long.

MAK. Now Christ's holy name be us among!
  What is this? For Saint James, I may not well go!
  I trow I be the same. Ah, my neck has lain wrong
      Enough,   385
  Many thanks, since yester-even!
  Now, by Saint Stephen,
  I was scared by a dream!
      My heart's out of puff![92]
  I thought Gill began to croak, and travail full sad,   390
  Well near at the first cock, of a young lad
  For to mend our flock. Then be I never glad;
  More cradles to rock,[93] more than ever I had.
      Ah, my head!
  A house full of young tharms,[94]   395
  The devil knock out their harns![95]
  Woe is him has many bairns,
      And so little bread!
  I must go home, by your leave, to Gill, as I thought.
  Pray you: look up my sleeve, that I steal nought: 400

---

[86] MS has "Thou rede," you advise well.
[87] Boy.
[88] Bad Latin: Resurrection from the dead.
[89] As above: Judas, god of the flesh.
[90] God's blessing.
[91] Crazy.
[92] Last two lines of the MS reads "I was flayed with a swevyn /my heart out of slough."
[93] MS has "I have tow on my rock."
[94] Stomachs.
[95] Brains.

I am loth you to grieve, or from you take aught.
    [*Exits*]

3 SHEP. Go forth, ill might thou 'chieve!
    Now would I we sought,
        This morn,
    That we had all our store.   405

1 SHEP. But I will go before.
    Let us meet.

2 SHEP.   Where?

3 SHEP. At the crooked thorn.

[*Mak's house.*]

MAK. [*knocking*] Undo this door! Who is here? How 410
    long shall I stand?

WIFE. Who makes such a bere?[96] Go walk in the
    waniand![97]

MAK. Ah, Gill, what cheer? It is I, Mak, your husband.

WIFE. Then may we see here the devil in a band.
        Sir Guile!   415
    Lo, he comes with a late,
    As he were holden in the throat.
    I may not sit at my note[98]
        A hand-long while.

MAK. Will ye hear what fare she makes to get her a 420
    gloze?[99]
    And does nought but fakes, and picks her toes.[100]

WIFE. Why, who wanders, who wakes, who comes,
    who goes?
    Who brews, who bakes? What makes me thus hose?
        And then
    It is sad to behold,   425
    Now in hot, now in cold—
    Full woeful is the household
        That wants a woman!
    But what end hast thou made with the
        shepherds, Mak?

MAK. The last word that they said when I turned 430
    my back:
    They would look that they had their sheep, all
    the pack.
    I hope they will not be well paid when they their
    sheep lack,
        Pardie!
    But howso the game goes,
    It's me they will suppose,[101]   435
    And make a foul noise,
        And cry out upon me.
    But thou must do as thou hight.[102]

WIFE.   I accord me thereto:
    I shall swaddle him right in my cradle.   440
    If it were a greater sleight, yet could I help till.
    I will lie down straight; come hap[103] me.

MAK.   I will.

WIFE.   Behind!
    Come Coll and his marrow,[104]   445
    They will nip us full narrow.

MAK. But I may cry out "Harrow!"
        The sheep if they find.

WIFE. Hearken, aye, when they call: they will come
    anon.
    Come and make ready all, and sing by thine own; 450
    Sing "Lullay!" thou shall, for I must groan,
    And cry out by the wall on Mary and John,
        Full sore.
    Sing "Lullay" on fast
    When thou hears at the last;   455
    And if I play a false cast,
        Trust me no more.

[*The field.*]

3 SHEP. Ah, Coll, good morn! Why sleeps thou not?

1 SHEP. Alas, that ever was I born! We have a foul blot!
    A fat wether have we lorn.[105]   460

3 SHEP.   Marry, Gods forbid!

2 SHEP. Who would do us that scorn?
        That were a foul spot.

---

96 Noise.

97 Waning of the moon, an unlucky time to be out doing
    things. The phrase would be roughly equivalent to "Go
    play in traffic."

98 Work, or perhaps milking?

99 An excuse, that is, not to come to the door.

100 MS has "And does nought but lakes [plays] /and claws
    her toes."

101 Suspect.

102 Promised.

103 Dress, wrap up.

104 Mate.

105 Lost.

1 SHEP. Some shrew.
   I have sought with my dogs   465
   All Horbury Shrogs,[106]
   And of fifteen hogs
      Found I but one ewe.
3 SHEP. Now trow me if ye will: by Saint Thomas of
      Kent,[107]
   Either Mak or Gill was at that assent!   470
1 SHEP. Peace, man, be still! I saw when he went.
   Thou slanders him ill; thou ought to repent,
      Good speed.
2 SHEP. Now as ever might I thrive,
   If I should even here die,   475
   I would say it were he
      That did that same deed.
3 SHEP. Go we thither instead, and run on our feet;
   Shall I never eat bread, the sooth till I wit.
1 SHEP. Nor drink in my head with him till I meet.   480
2 SHEP. I will rest in no stead till that I him greet.
      My brother,
   One thing I hight:[108]
   Till I see him in sight
   Shall I never sleep one night   485
      Where I do another.

[*Mak's house.*]

3 SHEP. Will ye hear how they hack?[109] our sire list
      croon.
1 SHEP. Heard I never none crack so clear out of tune.
   Call on him.
2 SHEP.   Mak! undo your door soon.   490
MAK. Who is it that spake, as it were noon,
      On loft?[110]
   Who is that, I say?
3 SHEP. Good fellows, were it day!
MAK. As far as ye may,   495
      Good, speak soft,
   Over a sick woman's head that is at malease;
   I had liefer be dead than she had any disease.

WIFE. Go to another stead; I may not well quease.
   Each foot that ye tread goes through my nose,   500
      So high!
1 SHEP. Tell us, Mak, if ye may,
   How fare ye, I say?
MAK. But are ye in this town today?
      Now how fare ye?   505
   Ye have run in the mire, and are wet yet?
   I shall make you a fire, if ye will sit.
   A nurse would I hire—know ye one yet?
   Well quit is my hire—my dream, this is it!—
      A season.   510
   I have bairns, if ye knew,
   Well more than a few;
   But we must drink as we brew,
      And that is but reason.
   I would ye dined as ye went; methink that ye sweat.   515
2 SHEP. Nay, neither mends our mood, drink nor meat.
MAK. Why, sir, ails you aught but good?
3 SHEP.   Yea, our sheep that we get
   Are stolen as they went; our loss is great.
MAK. Sirs, drink!   520
   Had I been there,
   Some should have bought it full sore.
1 SHEP. Marry, some men trows that ye *were*,
      And that us forthinks.
2 SHEP. Mak, some men trows that it should be ye.   525
3 SHEP. Either ye or your spouse; so say we.
MAK. Now, if ye have suspicion of Gill or of me,
   Come and rip our house, and then may ye see
      Who had her!
   If I any sheep got,   530
   Either cow or stot[111]—
   And Gill, my wife, rose not
      Here since she laid her—
   As I am both true and leal, to God here I pray,
   That this be the first meal that I shall eat this day.   535
1 SHEP. Mak, as I have zeal, watch out, I say;
   He learned timely to steal, that could not say nay.
WIFE.   I swelt![112]
   Out, thieves, from my house!
   Ye come to rob us, for the nonce.   540

---

106 An area near Wakefield—that is, a locale well known
    to the audience of this play.
107 Thomas à Becket, Archbishop of Canterbury, mur-
    dered 1170, canonized shortly thereafter.
108 Promise.
109 Sing badly.
110 With full volume.

---

111 Bull.
112 I faint!

MAK. Hear ye not how she groans?
    Your hearts should melt.
WIFE. Out, thieves, from by bairn! Nigh him not there!
MAK. Wist ye how she had fared, your hearts would
    be sore.
    Ye do wrong, I you warn, that thus comes before   545
    To a woman that has fared—but I say no more!
WIFE.   Ah, my middle!
    I pray to God so mild,
    If ever I you beguiled,
    That I eat this child   550
        That lies in this cradle.
MAK. Peace, woman, for God's pain, and cry not so:
    Thou spills thy brain, and makes me full woe.
2 SHEP. I trow our sheep be slain. What find ye two?
3 SHEP. All work we in vain; as well may we go.   555
        But hatters![113]
    I can find no flesh,
    Hard nor nesh,[114]
    Salt nor fresh,
        But two bare platters....   560
    [peers into cradle, sees "baby"]
    Live cattle like this, tame nor wild,
    None, as I have bliss, as loud as he smiled.
WIFE. No, so God bless, and give me joy of my child!
1 SHEP. We have marked amiss; I hold us beguiled.
2 SHEP. Sir, done!   565
    Sir, Our Lady him save!
    Is your child a knave?[115]
MAK. Any lord might him have,
        This child, as his son.
    When he wakens, he grips—what joy to see.   570
3 SHEP. In good time to his hips, and in seel![116]
    But who were his gossips,[117] so soon ready?
MAK. So fair fall their lips![118]
1 SHEP.   [aside] Hark now, a lie!
MAK. So God them thank,   575
    Parkin, and Gibbon Waller, I say,
    And gentle John Horne, in good faith—

He made all the hooray,
    With his great shanks.
2 SHEP. Mak, friends will we be, for we are all one.   580
MAK. We! now I hold for me, for amends get I none.
    Farewell all three! all glad were ye gone.

[They leave the house.]

3 SHEP. Fair words may there be, but love is there none
        This year.
1 SHEP. Gave ye the child anything?   585
2 SHEP. I trow, not one farthing.
3 SHEP. Fast again will I fling—
        Abide ye me there.
    [goes back into the house]
    Mak, take it to no grief, if I come to thy bairn.
MAK. Nay, thou does me great mischief, and foul   590
    has thou fared.
3 SHEP. The child will it not grieve, that little day-star.
    Mak, with your leave, let me give your bairn
        But sixpence.
MAK. Nay, go way: he sleeps.
3 SHEP. Methinks he peeps.   595
MAK. When he wakens he weeps.
        I pray you go hence.

[First and Second Shepherds return.]

3 SHEP. Give me leave him to kiss, and lift up the
        clout. [lifts the cloth]
    What the devil is this? He has a long snout!
1 SHEP. He is marked amiss. We wait ill about.[119]   600
2 SHEP. Ill-spun weft, I wis, ay comes foul out.[120]
        Aye, so?
    He is like to our sheep!
3 SHEP. How, Gib, may I peep?
1 SHEP. I trow, kind will creep   605
        Where it may not go.[121]
2 SHEP. This was a quaint gaud,[122] and a far cast—
    It was a high fraud!
3 SHEP.   Yea, sirs, was't.

---

113 An exclamation, like "Drat!"
114 Soft.
115 A boy.
116 The best of luck to him, future happiness, etc.
117 Godparents.
118 Bless their hearts!

119 He is malformed; let's get out of here.
120 Proverb, meaning that the bad genes of the parents
     comes out in the offspring.
121 Also proverbial, meaning that the truth of nature will
     reveal itself somehow in the end.
122 Trick.

Let burn this bawd, and bind her fast. [*to Gill*]   610
A false scold hangs at the last;
    So shall thou.
Will ye see how they swaddle
His four feet in the middle?
Saw I never in a cradle   615
    A horned lad ere now.
MAK. Peace, bid I! What, let go your blare!
I am he that him got, and yond woman him bare.
1 SHEP. What devil shall he hight?[123] Mak?
    Lo, God, Mak's heir!   620
2 SHEP. Let be all that. Now God give him care,
    I say.
WIFE. A pretty child is he,
    As sits on a woman's knee;
    A dilly-down pardie,   625
        To make a man laugh.
3 SHEP. I know him by the ear-mark—that is a good
    token.
MAK. I tell you, sirs, hark, his nose was broken.
    Afterwards, he was forspoken.[124]
1 SHEP. This is a false work—I would fain be   630
    wroken:[125]
        Get a weapon!
WIFE. He was taken by an elf,
    I saw it myself;
    When the clock struck twelve,
        Was he misshapen.   635
2 SHEP. Ye two plot so deft, as with one head.[126]
1 SHEP. Since they maintain their theft, let's do
    them to dead.
MAK. If I trespass eft,[127] lop off my head!
    With you will I be left.
1 SHEP.   Sirs, do my rede: 640
    For this trespass,
We will neither ban nor flyte,[128]
Fight nor chide,

---

123 What devil's name will he be called?
124 Bewitched.
125 Revenged.
126 MS has "Ye two are well feft sam in a stead," are in
    agreement together.
127 Again.
128 Curse nor fight.

But have done as tight,
    And cast him in canvas.   645

[*They toss and bounce Mak in a sheet, then leave his
house*]

1 SHEP. Lord, what! I am sore, in point for to burst;
    In faith, I may no more; therefore will I rest.
2 SHEP. As a sheep of seven score he weighed in my fist.
    For to sleep anywhere, methink that I list.
3 SHEP. Now I pray you,   650
    Lie down on this green.
1 SHEP. Of these thieves yet I believe—
3 SHEP. Whereto should ye grieve?
    Do as I say you.

An Angel sings "Gloria in Excelsis;" then let him say:

    Rise, herdmen kind, for now is he born   655
    Who shall take from the fiend that which Adam
        had lorn:
    That warlock to end, this night is he born.
    God is made your friend now at this morn.
        He behests
    To Bethlehem go see,   660
    There lies that Free[129]
    In a crib full poorly,
        Betwixt two beasts.
1 SHEP. This was a quaint voice that ever yet I heard.
    To name it is to rejoice, thus to be scared.   665
2 SHEP. Of God's son of heaven, he spake upward.
    All the wood in a levin,[130] methought that he made
        Appear.
3 SHEP. He spake of a bairn
    In Bethlehem, I you warn.   670
1 SHEP. That betokens yond star;
    Let us seek him there.
2 SHEP. Say, what was his song? Heard ye not how
    he cracked it,
    Three breves to a long?[131]
3 SHEP. Yea, marry, he hacked[132] it.   675
    Was no crochet wrong, nor nothing that lacked it.

---

129 Freeborn, noble child.
130 Lightning flash.
131 Three short notes to a long one.
132 Sang.

1 SHEP. For to sing us among, right as he knacked
   it,[133]
    I can.
2 SHEP. Let see how ye croon.
  Can ye bark at the moon?   680
3 SHEP. Hold your tongues, have done!
1 SHEP. Hark after, then.
2 SHEP. To Bethlehem he bade that we should gang;[134]
  I am full feared that we tarry too long.
3 SHEP. Be merry and not sad; of mirth is our song: 685
  Everlasting gladness may we earn without noise.
1 SHEP. Hie we thither, therefore,
  If we be wet and weary,
  To that child and that lady:
    We have it not to lose.   690
2 SHEP. We find by the prophecy—let be your din!—
  Of David and Isaiah, and more than I mind,
  They prophesied by clergy, that in a virgin
  Should be light and lie, to remove our sin
    And slake it,   695
  Our kind from woe;
  For Isaiah said so:
  Ecce virgo
    Concipiet a child that is naked.[135]
3 SHEP. Full glad may we be and abide that day, 700
  That Lovely One to see that all might may.[136]
  Lord, well were me for once and for ay,
  Might I kneel on my knee some word for to say
    To that child.
  But the angel said: 705
  In a crib was he laid,
  He was poorly arrayed,
    Both meek and mild.
1 SHEP. Patriarchs that have been, and prophets before,
  They desired to have seen this child that is born. 710
  They are gone full clean; they were forlorn.
  We shall see him, I ween, ere it be morn,
    As a token.
  When I see him and feel,
  Then wot I full well   715
  It is true as steel

  What prophets have spoken:
  To so poor as we are that he would appear,
  First find, and declare by his messenger.
2 SHEP. Go we now, let us fare; the place is us near. 720
3 SHEP. I am ready and yare—go we in cheer
    To that Bright.
  Lord, if thy will it be,
  We are unlearned, all three;
  Thou grant us somekind glee,   725
    To comfort thy wight.

[*The stable in Bethlehem.*]

1 SHEP. Hail, comely and clean! hail, young child!
  Hail, Maker, as I mean, of a maiden so mild!
  Thou has waried, I ween, the warlock so wild,
  The false beguiler of spleen,[137] now goes he 730
    beguiled.
    Lo, he merries!
  Lo, he laughs, my sweeting!
  A well-fared meeting!
  My promise I'm keeping—
    Have a bob of cherries!   735
2 SHEP. Hail, sovereign saviour, for thou has us sought!
  Hail, noble child and flower, that all-things has
    wrought!
  Hail, full of favour, that made all of nought!
  Hail! I kneel and I cower. A bird have I brought
    To my bairn.   740
  Hail, little tiny mop,
  Of our creed thou art crop!
  I would drink in thy cup,
    Little day-star!
3 SHEP. Hail, darling dear, full of godhead! 745
  I pray thee be near, when that I have need.
  Hail! sweet is thy cheer! My heart would bleed
  To see thee sit here in so poor weed,
    With no pennies.
  Hail! put forth thy dall![138]   750
  I bring thee but a ball;
  Have and play thee with all,
    And go to tennis.
MARY. The Father of Heaven, God omnipotent,
  That made all in seven, his son has he sent. 755

---

133 Trilled, ornamented the note.
134 Go.
135 Isaiah, 7:14: "Behold, a virgin shall conceive...."
136 That god who will have all might, all power.

---

137 MS has "teen," or woe.
138 Hand.

My name did he neven,[139] and alighted ere he went.
I conceived him full even, through might, as he
    meant;
      And now he is born.
He keep you from woe!
I shall pray him so;   760
Tell forth as ye go,
      And mind on this morn.
1 SHEP. Farewell, lady, so fair to behold,
  With thy child on thy knee.

2 SHEP.   But he lies full cold.   765
  Lord, well is me! now we go, thou behold.
3 SHEP. Forsooth, already it seems to be told
    Full oft.
1 SHEP. What grace we have found!
2 SHEP. Come forth, now have we won.   770
3 SHEP. To sing we are bound:
    Let ring aloft! [*Exeunt, singing*]

---

[139] Name.

ANONYMOUS

The Farce of Master Pierre Pathelin

L ike *The Second Shepherds' Play*, with which it has much in common, *The Farce of Master Pierre Pathelin* (c.1460?) cannot easily be assigned a precise date. Both works have come down to us through copies written or published in the mid-to-late fifteenth century, but by this time both may already have been known to audiences for decades or more. What is certain about *Pathelin* is that it was one of the most popular farces of the French Middle Ages. So great was its fame that many of its words and phrases took up residence in everyday speech: to *patheliner* was to feign illness; *revenons à nos moutons*, or "getting back to our sheep...," was to return to the matter at hand after endless irrelevant digressions. Not only did the details of the play enter the French language, but it was the dying wish of the greatest farce actor of the period that he be committed to earth with his body wrapped in a copy of *Pierre Pathelin*[1]—a fanciful last will whose comical intent does nothing to counteract the impression it leaves that *Pathelin* was to the medieval farceur what *Hamlet* was soon to become for generations of tragedians: a holy writ.

And its high reputation is deserved. Practically everyone in this play is a scam-artist, and most get scammed in return. Continuing a long theatrical tradition begun by the Watchman in *Agamemnon* and continued by the shepherds in *The Second Shepherds' Play*, the play begins with the "life is hard" trope, the litany of hardships endured by the little man. In Pierre's case, as in Mak's, his hunger and poverty are compounded by his reputation for petty larceny; like Mak he is berated by his long-suffering wife as a hopeless provider, and like Mak he is helped immeasurably by her in conceiving and carrying out a cunning plan—which in both cases involves some version of taking to bed and pretending to be ill. Whereas Gill feigns the groans of childbirth to disguise the stolen sheep, Pierre whips himself into a fake delirium to put the clothier off the scent of the filched cloth. A chaos of demented non-sequiturs, phoney dialects, hallucinations, and obscenely blasphemous curses combine to make the scene of Pierre's confinement a sustained comic *tour-de-force* that, for sheer lunacy, is matched by few plays in the repertory. And yet, as much as the play celebrates Pierre's mastery of language and the arts of deception, his crooked virtuosity is ultimately eclipsed by that of the shepherd who, for all the seeming simplicity of his monosyllabic replies, manages to dupe the duper in the end.

This play dates from a period in European history when an independent justice system (under the patronage of the crown) was just beginning to emerge after centuries of the perversion of law by

---

[1] The anecdote appears in a play and may be entirely fictional, but it nevertheless conveys a good sense of the play's stature in its time.

religious superstition and the power of the Church. *Pierre Pathelin* is accordingly but one of many plays of the era that deal with matters of litigation, judges, lawyers and their clients—an unsurprising fact when we realize that, in medieval France, more plays were staged by members of the burgeoning legal profession than by any other group. Perhaps developing originally out of the need to practise cross-examination techniques by holding mock trials, theatre groups were established during this period within law societies across the country. In Paris alone, law clerks numbered in the thousands, and they were well known throughout the city for their performances in such comedy groups as the *Enfants Sans Souci*.[2] Pathelin, however, is satirized here not as one of their number—that is, as a real lawyer—but as an unethical village fraud, a holdover of the "bad old days" of ecclesiastical or otherwise unprofessional jurisprudence.

_____

2 Roughly, "The Carefree Kids." Their motto about the actor's life, which took the form of a clever pun on their name, retains its wit today: "it's a life *sans souci*, but oftentimes *sans six sous*" ("without even six cents").

ANONYMOUS
The Farce of Master Pierre Pathelin
Translated by Alan E. Knight

CHARACTERS
    PATHELIN, a village pettifogger
    GUILLEMETTE, his wife
    GUILLAUME JOCEAULME, the clothier
    THIBAULT AIGNELET, the shepherd
    THE JUDGE

[*Pathelin's house.*]

PATHELIN: Holy Mary, Guillemette, for all the trouble I take to scrimp and save we just can't get ahead. I've seen the day, though, when I was a real attorney.

GUILLEMETTE: By Our Lady of the Law Trade! I was just thinking about that. But now people don't think you're nearly as clever as they used to. I remember when everybody wanted you to take his case. Now they all call you a prattling pettifogger.

PATHELIN: And I don't mean to brag, of course, but there's not a sharper fellow in the whole circuit, except maybe the mayor.

GUILLEMETTE: Yes, but he's studied his Latin grammar and he knows how to conjure his verbs.

PATHELIN: Whose case don't I expedite if I decide to take it on? It's true I don't know much Latin, but when I chant with our priest from the mass-book, it sounds like I've studied for as long as Charlemagne stayed in Spain.

GUILLEMETTE: But what's it worth to us? Not a thing! We're starving to death, our clothes have as many holes as a sieve, and we have no idea how we can get new ones. So, what's all your knowledge worth to us?

PATHELIN: Hold your tongue! I swear, if I really put my mind to it, I'll find out where to get some clothes—and some headgear too. God willing, we'll pull out of this and be back on our feet in no time. "God does a deed with all due speed," they say. If I really have to apply myself to further my practice, you won't be able to find my equal.

GUILLEMETTE: By Saint James, certainly not in swindling. At that you're a past master.

PATHELIN: By God, you mean a master of proper lawyering.[1]

GUILLEMETTE: By my faith, you're a master deceiver. I know, because despite your little learning and less common sense, you're taken for one of the slyest wits in the parish.

PATHELIN: Nobody knows the finer points of the law the way I do.

GUILLEMETTE: Or the finer points of cheating, by God. At least that's the reputation you have.

PATHELIN: And so have those who wear fine clothes of silk and velvet, who claim to be lawyers, but aren't. Enough of this chatter, I'm off to the fair.

GUILLEMETTE: To the fair?

PATHELIN: Yes, by Saint John! (*He sings*) "To the fair, my pretty maid . . ." Would it displease you if I bought some cloth or some other little thing that we need? Our clothes are nothing but rags.

GUILLEMETTE: But you don't have a penny to bless yourself with. What'll you do there?

PATHELIN: Don't ask too many questions, my lady. But if I don't bring back enough cloth to outfit us both, then call me a liar to my face. What colour would you like? A gray-green, a Brussels black, or what? I need to know.

GUILLEMETTE: Whatever you can get. Beggars can't be choosers.

PATHELIN: [*counting on his fingers*] Two and a half yards for you and three for me, or maybe four. That makes . . .

GUILLEMETTE: You count off the yards very generously, but who the Devil will give you that much cloth on credit?

PATHELIN: What do you care who? Somebody will give it to me and with payment due on Judgement Day, because it won't be paid for any sooner.

GUILLEMETTE: Very well then. In that case, no matter what happens, we'll be covered.

PATHELIN: I'll buy some gray or green, Guillemette, and for a waistcoat I'll need three quarters of a yard of fine black cloth . . . or maybe a yard.

---

1 Pathelin is not a *real* lawyer; he is meant to represent a typical phenomenon of the later Middle Ages: an obviously incompetent hold-over from the days, before the rise of the legal profession, when disputes were handled by clerics and village priests.

GUILLEMETTE: Indeed! God help me! Go ahead then and don't forget to drink on the bargain if you find a gullible creditor.

PATHELIN: Take care of things here. [*He leaves*]

GUILLEMETTE: Oh God! But what merchant . . .? Whoever it is, I just pray he's blind as a bat.

[*At the Clothier's shop.*]

PATHELIN: Isn't that the one there? No, I don't think so. Yes it is, by Saint Mary. He deals in cloth goods. [*To the Clothier*] God be with you.

GUILLAUME JOCEAULME, CLOTHIER: And God give you joy.

PATHELIN: So help me, you're just the person I wanted to see. How's your health, Guillaume? Are you hale and hearty?

THE CLOTHIER: Yes, thank God.

PATHELIN: Here, shake. How are things going?

THE CLOTHIER: Pretty well. [*They shake*] At your service. And how are you?

PATHELIN: By Saint Peter, I'm as well as ever. So, you're enjoying life?

THE CLOTHIER: Yes, but believe me, merchants can't always do as they please.

PATHELIN: And how's business? Are you able to keep the wolf from the door?

THE CLOTHIER: So help me God, Master Pierre, it's hard to say. It's always work, work, work.

PATHELIN: Ah, what a wise man your father was! God rest his soul. By Our Lady, it seems to me that you're like him in every way. What a good and clever merchant he was. [*He stares at the Clothier*] Your face resembles his, by God, like a perfect picture. If God ever had mercy on one of his creatures, may he grant true pardon to his soul.

THE CLOTHIER: Amen! And to us too if it please him.

PATHELIN: By my faith, he often predicted in great detail the times we live in now; and I often think of what he said, for he was considered one of the best.

THE CLOTHIER: Please sit down, sir. It's high time I remembered my manners.

PATHELIN: I'm fine like this. By heaven, your father had . . .

THE CLOTHIER: Truly, you must sit down.

PATHELIN: Very well. [*he sits down*] "Ah," he used to say to me, "you will see great marvels." [*He stares at the Clothier again*] Look at those eyes, those ears, that nose, that mouth! So help me God, never did a son more closely resemble his father! And look at that dimpled chin; you're really a chip off the old block. If anyone should say to your mother that you're not your father's son, he'd just be itching for a quarrel. Truly I can't imagine how nature in all her works formed two faces so much alike that one is blemished exactly like the other. Why, it's as if somebody had spit you both out in the same way, like two gobs against a wall. You're the very spit and image of your father. By the way, what about the good Laurence, your lovely aunt? Did she pass away?

THE CLOTHIER: No, certainly not.

PATHELIN: How beautiful she was when I saw her, tall and straight and graceful. By the precious Mother of God, you resemble her in shape as if someone had made you both of snow. I think there's not a family in the whole region whose members look so much alike. [*He gets up and stares more intently at the Clothier*] By God, the more I look at you, the more I see your father. You're more alike than two drops of water, without a doubt. What a gentleman he was, what an honest man, who would sell his goods on credit to anyone who asked. May God have mercy on him. He always used to give me a hearty laugh. Would to Christ the worst in the world were like him; then people wouldn't rob and steal from one another the way they do. [*He feels a piece of cloth*] What a fine piece of cloth this is, so soft and smooth, and so attractive.

THE CLOTHIER: I had it specially made from the wool of my own sheep.

PATHELIN: Ah, what a good businessman you are! But you wouldn't be your father's son, if you weren't. You just never stop working.

THE CLOTHIER: So what do you expect? If a man wants to make a living, he's got to toil and sweat.

PATHELIN: [*feeling another piece of cloth*] And this cloth, is it dyed in the wool? It's as strong as leather.

THE CLOTHIER: It's a very good fabric from Rouen, and well made I assure you.

PATHELIN: Well, I'm really tempted. By the Lord's passion, I had no intention of buying cloth when I came. I've saved up 80 gold pieces to pay off a debt, but I can see you're going to get 20 or 30 of them. I like that colour so much it hurts.

THE CLOTHIER: Gold pieces? Indeed! Is it possible that the people you're indebted to would take some other coinage instead?

PATHELIN: Oh yes, if I wanted them to. It doesn't matter to me how it's paid. [*He feels another piece of cloth*] And what cloth is this? The more I look at it, the crazier I am about it. I'll have to have a coat made of it, and another for my wife.

THE CLOTHIER: As you know, cloth is very expensive these days. I'll sell you some if you wish, but 10 or 20 francs won't buy very much.

PATHELIN: That doesn't matter; it's worth the price. Besides, I have a few sous put away that have never seen the light of day.

THE CLOTHIER: God be praised! By Saint Peter, that doesn't displease me a bit.

PATHELIN: To be brief, I'm so taken with this cloth that I just have to have some of it.

THE CLOTHIER: All right. First you must decide how much you need. Take as much as you want. In fact, I could let *you* take the entire bolt even if you didn't have a sou.

PATHELIN: That's kind of you. Thanks very much.

THE CLOTHIER: Do you want some of this light blue?

PATHELIN: First, how much will a yard cost me? Wait, here's a penny. God's share should be paid first; it's only right. "Let no bargain be made before God's share is paid." [*He puts a coin in a collection box*]

THE CLOTHIER: By God, that's the talk of an honest man; you've really cheered me up. Do you want my last word on the price?

PATHELIN: Yes.

THE CLOTHIER: It will cost *you* only 24 sous per yard.

PATHELIN: Never! 24 sous? Holy Mother!

THE CLOTHIER: That's just what it cost me, by my soul! I'll have to charge at least that, if you take it.

PATHELIN: The Devil take it! It's too much.

THE CLOTHIER: But you don't realize how much

cloth has gone up. All the sheep died last winter in the great freeze.

PATHELIN: Twenty sous! Twenty sous!

THE CLOTHIER: I swear to you I have to charge 24. Just wait till market day on Saturday and you'll see what it costs. A fleece that used to cost 20 pence when they were plentiful cost me 40 pence last July.

PATHELIN: By God, if that's the way it is, then without more haggling, I'll buy. Come on, measure it.

THE CLOTHIER: How much do you need?

PATHELIN: That's easy to figure out. What's the width?

THE CLOTHIER: The standard Brussels width.

PATHELIN: Three yards for me and two and a half yards for my wife—she's tall. That makes six yards, doesn't it? . . . No it doesn't. How stupid of me!

THE CLOTHIER: It only lacks half a yard of being six exactly.

PATHELIN: Then I'll round it off at six. Anyway, I need a hat.

THE CLOTHIER: Take that end and we'll measure it. I'm sure we've got a good six yards here. One . . . two . . . three . . . four . . . five . . . and six.

PATHELIN: Saint Peter's gut! It's six on the nose.

THE CLOTHIER: Shall I measure it again?

PATHELIN: No, for Pete's sake! There's always a little gain or loss in business deals. How much is that altogether?

THE CLOTHIER: Let's see. At 24 sous a yard and six yards, it comes to nine francs.

PATHELIN: That makes six gold pieces, right?

THE CLOTHIER: That's right, by God.

PATHELIN: Then, Sir, will you give me that much credit for the short time it takes to come to my house? It's not really credit. You'll have your money, in gold or in francs, as soon as you reach the door.

THE CLOTHIER: By our Lady! I'd have to go far out of my way to get there.

PATHELIN: I swear to God, not a word has passed your lips since you failed to speak the gospel truth. You say it's far out of your way. The thing is, you've never wanted to find an occasion to come drink at my house. But this time you will have a drink there.

THE CLOTHIER: By Saint James, I hardly do anything but drink to seal the bargain with my customers. I'll go, but it's bad luck, you know, to give credit on the first sale of the day.

PATHELIN: Isn't it worth it if I pay you in gold coins instead of the common currency? By God, we'll even eat the goose that my wife is roasting.

THE CLOTHIER: [aside] This man is driving me crazy! [To Pathelin] Go ahead then. I'll come later and bring the cloth.

PATHELIN: There's no need for that. Will it burden me if I just tuck it under my arm? Not in the least.

THE CLOTHIER: No, don't bother. It would be more fitting and proper if I carried it.

PATHELIN: May Mary Magdalene send me misfortune if I put you to that trouble. As I said, under the arm. It'll give me a nice hump. [He puts the cloth under his arm inside his robe] There, that's perfect. You'll have plenty of drink and good cheer before you leave my house.

THE CLOTHIER: Please give me my money as soon as I arrive.

PATHELIN: Of course I will. No, I won't, by God— not until you've been well fed! And I'm glad I didn't have any money on me. At least you'll come sample my wine. Your late father, when he passed my house, used to call out: "Hi there, friend," or "What do you say?" or "What's new?" But now you rich people don't care a straw about us poor people.

THE CLOTHIER: God in heaven, I'm a lot poorer than you are.

PATHELIN: Well, so long; goodbye. Come to my house as soon as you can and we'll drink well, I promise you.

THE CLOTHIER: I'll do that. Go on ahead, but see that I get the gold.

PATHELIN: Gold? I give you my word. And the Devil take me if I ever broke my word. [He leaves the shop] Gold, indeed! Well, hang him! He wouldn't sell to me at my price, only at his. But he'll be paid at mine. He needs gold, does he? Fool's gold he'll get. By God, if he had to run from now till he's paid, he'd get to the end of the world first.

THE CLOTHIER: Those gold pieces he gives me won't see daylight for a whole year, I swear, unless somebody steals them. Well, there's no buyer so clever that he won't find a seller who can outwit him. That would-be trickster was stupid enough to pay 24 sous a yard for cloth that's not even worth 20! 305

[*Pathelin's house.*]

PATHELIN: Well, did I get it?

GUILLEMETTE: What?

PATHELIN: What happened to your old worn-out dress?

GUILLEMETTE: That's just what it was. What do you 310 want with it?

PATHELIN: Nothing. Nothing. So, did I get it? I told you I would. [*He takes the cloth from beneath his robe*] How's that for a piece of cloth?

GUILLEMETTE: Holy Mother! I'll stake my salvation 315 there's been a swindle. Oh, God! What have you gotten us into now? Alas! Alas! Who'll pay for it?

PATHELIN: Who'll pay for it, you ask? By Saint John, it's paid for. The draper that sold it to me wasn't as crazy as all that, my love. May I be hanged if I 320 didn't bleed him as white as a sack of plaster. The thieving ragpicker got what he deserved.

GUILLEMETTE: How much did it cost?

PATHELIN: I owe nothing. He's been paid, so don't worry. 325

GUILLEMETTE: He's been paid? But you didn't have a penny. What did you use for money?

PATHELIN: I swear to you, woman, I did have money. I had one Paris penny.

GUILLEMETTE: You either signed a note or used a 330 magic formula; that's how you got it. And when the note comes due, they'll come and seize all our goods. Everything we have will be taken away.

PATHELIN: I swear to God, the whole thing cost only a penny. 335

GUILLEMETTE: *Benedicite Maria!* Only a penny? That can't be.

PATHELIN: You can pluck out this eye if he got more than that or ever does get more, no matter what tune he sings. 340

GUILLEMETTE: Who's the merchant?

PATHELIN: It's a certain Guillaume whose last name is Joceaulme, if you must know.

GUILLEMETTE: But how did you get it for one penny? What was the trick? 345

PATHELIN: It was God's penny that sealed the bargain. If I had asked him to drink on it instead, I could have kept the penny. Still, it was a pretty good deal. He and God can divide that penny if they want to, because it's all they'll get from me, 350 no matter how much they rant and rave.

GUILLEMETTE: How did he decide to let you have the cloth on credit? He's so bullheaded.

PATHELIN: By Saint Mary, I flattered him and his whole family tree so much that he almost *gave* it 355 to me. I told him that his late father was such a worthy man. "Oh, my friend," says I, "what good stock you come from! Your lineage," says I, "is the purest in the whole district." But I swear to God that guy comes from the scurviest lot of scoundrels 360 and the vilest riffraff in the country. "Guillaume, my friend," says I, "how much you resemble your good father in looks and in every other way!" God knows I piled on the flattery, and all the while I was throwing in remarks about his cloth. "Holy 365 Mary," says I, "how easily he gave his merchandise on credit, and without pretense! I can see," says I, "that you're his spit and image." But you could pull all the teeth of that sea-hog of a father and that baboon of a son before they'd give you anything 370 on credit or even give you the time of day. Anyway, I talked so fast that he finally gave me six yards on credit.

GUILLEMETTE: Really? And you never have to return it? 375

PATHELIN: That's right. If I return anything to him, it'll be the Devil.

GUILLEMETTE: That reminds me of the fable of the crow, who was sitting up on a high cross with a piece of cheese in his beak. A fox came by and, 380 seeing the cheese, thought to himself, "How can I get that?" Then he sat directly beneath the crow and said, "Ah, you have such splendid feathers and your song is so melodious." The vain and foolish crow, hearing his song praised like that, opened his 385 beak to sing. His cheese fell to the ground and Master Fox grabbed it in his teeth and ran. That's just the way it was I'm sure, with this cloth. You got it by flattery and sweet-talk, the same way the fox got the cheese. You really put one over on him. 390

PATHELIN: He's supposed to come eat goose with us, so here's what we have to do. I know he'll come whining to have his money immediately and I've planned a good reception for him. I'll go get into bed and pretend to be sick and when he comes 395 you'll say, "Shh! Speak softly," and you'll moan and put on a long face. "Alas," you'll say, "he's been sick for the past six or eight weeks." And if he says to you, "That's a lot of nonsense! He just left my shop a few minutes ago," you'll say, "Alas! This is a poor 400 time to be making jokes." Then we'll make him think he's on a wild goose chase, because that's the only kind of goose or anything else he'll ever get here.

GUILLEMETTE: I swear I'll play the role to perfec- 405 tion. But if you get caught again and brought to justice, I'm afraid it'll be twice as bad as it was be- fore.

PATHELIN: Quiet. I know what I'm doing; we have to do exactly what I said. 410

GUILLEMETTE: But, for God's sake, think of that Saturday they put you in the pillory. You know how everybody jeered at you for your shady dealings.

PATHELIN: Enough of such talk. He'll be here any 415 minute now and we've got to keep this cloth. I'm going to get into bed.

GUILLEMETTE: Go ahead.

PATHELIN: Now don't laugh.

GUILLEMETTE: Of course I won't. I'll be crying hot 420 tears.

PATHELIN: We both have to be serious so he won't suspect anything.

[*Clothier's shop.*]

THE CLOTHIER: I think it's time for me to have a little drink before I leave. Oh, no, I won't. I'll soon 425 be drinking and eating goose at Master Pierre Pathelin's house. By the patron saint of fools, I'll get my money there and the special treat they're preparing, and it won't cost me a sou. I can't sell anything more here, so I'll be going. 430

[*In front of Pathelin's house.*]

THE CLOTHIER: Hey There! Master Pierre!

GUILLEMETTE: [*opening the door*] Please sir, for the love of God, if you have something to say, speak softly.

THE CLOTHIER: God be with you, Madame. 435

GUILLEMETTE: Shh! Softer.

THE CLOTHIER: What's the matter?

GUILLEMETTE: Bless my soul . . .

THE CLOTHIER: Where is he?

GUILLEMETTE: Alas! Where should he be? 440

THE CLOTHIER: Who . . . ?

GUILLEMETTE: Ah, that was ill-spoken, my good sir. "Where is he," indeed! May God in his mercy have pity on him. The poor suffering man is in the same place he's been without budging for eleven weeks 445 now.

THE CLOTHIER: But who . . . ?

GUILLEMETTE: Pardon me, but I don't dare speak louder. I think he's resting now; he was a little drowsy. Alas, he's so sick, the poor man. 450

THE CLOTHIER: Who?

GUILLEMETTE: Master Pierre.

THE CLOTHIER: What? Didn't he come to my shop to get six yards of cloth just now?

GUILLEMETTE: Who? Him? 455

THE CLOTHIER: He just left there, not ten minutes ago. Hurry up! Devil take me, I've stayed too long already. Quick, give me my money and no more foolishness.

GUILLEMETTE: Hey! No more of *your* foolishness! 460 This is no time to joke around.

THE CLOTHIER: Are you crazy? My money! Now! You owe me nine francs.

GUILLEMETTE: Ah, Guillaume, are you making fun of me? This is no asylum for lunatics. Go tell your 465 nonsense to fools like yourself and play your tricks on them.

THE CLOTHIER: May I renounce God if I don't get my nine francs!

GUILLEMETTE: Alas, Sir, not everyone is as eager to 470 laugh and gossip as you are.

THE CLOTHIER: Please, I beg of you, no more joking. Just have Master Pierre come here, for the love of—

GUILLEMETTE: Misfortune strike you down! Will 475 this go on all day?

THE CLOTHIER: But isn't this the house of Master Pierre Pathelin?

GUILLEMETTE: Of course! May the patron saint of lunatics [*crosses herself*] addle your brain! Speak low! 480

THE CLOTHIER: The Devil take your "speak low"! Shouldn't I ask for what's mine?

GUILLEMETTE: God help me! Speak low, if you don't want him to wake up.

THE CLOTHIER: How "low" do you want? In the ear? In the cellar? Or in the bottom of the well? 485

GUILLEMETTE: My God, how you drivel on! But that's always been your way.

THE CLOTHIER: The Devil it has! [*Calming down*] Now that I think about it, if you want me to speak low, just say so. I'm really not used to arguments like this. The truth is that Master Pierre took six yards of cloth today. 490

GUILLEMETTE: What is this? Will this go on all day? The Devil take it! Now, just what do you mean by "took"? Oh, may the one who's lying be hanged! That poor man is in such a pitiful state that he hasn't left his bed in eleven weeks. Then you come along with your wild ideas. Now is that right? By God's passion, you'll leave my house at once. Oh, what misery! 495 · 500

THE CLOTHIER: You asked *me* to speak so low. Now, by the Holy Virgin, you're screaming.

GUILLEMETTE: So help me, you're the one who can't speak without quarrelling. 505

THE CLOTHIER: Look, so I can go, just give me—

GUILLEMETTE: [*shouting*] Are you going to speak low?

THE CLOTHIER: But you're going to wake him yourself. Damn it all, you're yelling four times louder than I am. I insist that you pay me. 510

GUILLEMETTE: What is this? Are you drunk or just out of your mind? God in heaven!

THE CLOTHIER: Drunk! Saint Peter curse you! What a question! 515

GUILLEMETTE: Please! Speak lower!

THE CLOTHIER: By Saint George, I demand payment for six yards of cloth!

GUILLEMETTE: You must have been dreaming. And just who did you give it to? 520

THE CLOTHIER: To him.

GUILLEMETTE: He's in fine shape to be buying cloth. Alas, he can't even move. He has no need for new clothes. He'll never get dressed again, except in graveclothes; and he'll never leave his room again, except feet first. 525

THE CLOTHIER: Then this happened since early this morning, because I spoke to him for sure.

GUILLEMETTE: Your voice is so loud! For the love of God, speak lower! 530

THE CLOTHIER: You're the one shouting, damn it all, you and nobody else. God help me, this is agony. Will somebody pay me so I can go! By God, every time I've given credit, I've had nothing but trouble. 535

PATHELIN: [*from his bed*] Guillemette, a little rose water. Prop me up. Tuck me in behind. Damn! Who was I talking to? The water jar! Give me a drink! Rub my feet!

THE CLOTHIER: I hear him in there. 540

GUILLEMETTE: Yes.

PATHELIN: [*delirious*] Ah, wicked woman! Come here! Did I tell you to open these windows? Come cover me up. Get rid of these people in black! *Marmara carimari carimara!*[2] Take them away from me, away! 545

GUILLEMETTE: What's the matter? You're tossing about so. Have you lost your senses?

PATHELIN: You don't see what I see. There's a monk in black flying around the room. Catch him. Get a stole to exorcise him! The cat! Get the cat! Look how he rises up! 550

GUILLEMETTE: What is all this? Aren't you ashamed? This is too much stirring about, for heaven's sake.

PATHELIN: Those doctors are killing me with all the vile potions they make me drink. And yet we have to believe them; we're like putty in their hands. 555

GUILLEMETTE: (*to the Clothier*) Alas! Come and see him, good sir. He's suffering terribly.

THE CLOTHIER: Was he taken so ill on returning from the fair? 560

GUILLEMETTE: The fair?

THE CLOTHIER: Yes, by Saint John! I'm sure he was there. Master Pierre! I need the money for the cloth I gave you on credit. 565

PATHELIN [*pretending to take the Clothier for a doctor*]: Ah, Doctor John! I shat two tiny black turds, round as balls and hard as rocks. Should I take another enema?

---

2 Vaguely Latin or Italianate nonsense-words.

THE CLOTHIER: How should I know? What've I got 570
to do with enemas? I want my nine francs or six
gold pieces.

PATHELIN: Those three black sharp things—you call
those pills? They nearly busted my jaws. For God's 575
sake don't make me take any more of them, Doctor
John. There's nothing in the world more bitter, and
they made everything come up again.

THE CLOTHIER: No they didn't, by God. My nine
francs haven't appeared yet.

GUILLEMETTE: Hang such tiresome people. Go away, 580
by all the devils, since it can't be on God's part.

THE CLOTHIER: I swear to God, I'll get my cloth
before I leave, or my nine francs.

PATHELIN: And my urine specimen, doesn't it show
that I'm dying? For God's sake, whatever happens, 585
don't let me die.

GUILLEMETTE [to the Clothier]: Be off with you! It's
terrible to torment him like this.

THE CLOTHIER: Lord God in heaven! Six yards of
cloth! Tell me, do you think it's right that I should 590
lose it?

PATHELIN: Oh, Doctor John! Do you think you
could loosen my bowels? I'm so constipated I don't
know how I stand to sit on the throne.

THE CLOTHIER: I want my nine francs now or by 595
Saint Peter of Rome—

GUILLEMETTE: Alas! You're tormenting this man so.
How can you be so cruel? You can see plain as day
that he thinks you're his doctor. Alas! The poor
soul has had such misfortune. He's been in that 600
bed for eleven straight weeks, the poor man!

THE CLOTHIER: By God, I don't know how this
sickness came about, because today he was in my
shop and we did business together—at least it
seems we did. Otherwise I don't know what could 605
have happened.

GUILLEMETTE: By Our Lady, I think your memory
is slipping, my friend. If you take my advice, you'll
go get some rest. Besides, there are a lot of gossips
around who'll think you came in here to see *me*. 610
Go on now; his doctors will be here soon.

THE CLOTHIER: I don't care if others do think evil
of it, because I have no such thoughts. Damn it
all, how'd I get into this mess? I swear to God, I
thought . . . 615

GUILLEMETTE: Again?

THE CLOTHIER: And don't you have a goose
cooking?

GUILLEMETTE: What a question! Sir, that's not a
dish for sick people. Go chase your own goose and 620
don't come here making fun of us. You've got some
nerve to do that.

THE CLOTHIER: Please excuse me, but I really
thought . . .

GUILLEMETTE: Still? 625

THE CLOTHIER: By the sacrament! Goodbye! [*He
leaves the house*] Now I've got to figure this out. I
know I should have six yards of cloth in one piece.
But that woman addles my brain so much I can't
think. He really did take the cloth. . . . No, he 630
couldn't have, damn it! It just doesn't fit. I saw
Death coming to strike him down—at least he so
pretended. . . . Yes he did! He did take the cloth
and he put it under his arm, by Saint Mary! . . . No,
he didn't. Maybe I'm dreaming. But even in my 635
sleep I'd never give my cloth away to anybody, no
matter how much I liked him. I just wouldn't have
given credit. . . . By God, he did take the cloth! . . .
No, damn it all, he didn't. I know he didn't. But
where does that leave me! . . . Yes he did, by Our 640
Lady's passion! . . . Misfortune take me, body and
soul, if I know who could decide who got the best
of this deal, them or me. I just can't figure it out.

PATHELIN: Is he gone?

GUILLEMETTE: Quiet, I'm listening. I don't know 645
what he was muttering, but he left grumbling so
much that he was almost hysterical.

PATHELIN: Isn't it time for me to get up? We sure
pulled that one off.

GUILLEMETTE: I don't know if he's coming back or 650
not. [*Pathelin starts to get up*] No, don't get up yet!
Everything would be ruined if he found you out
of bed.

PATHELIN: He's always so suspicious of others, but
by God he met his match this time. The joke was 655
on him and it fit like a cross on a steeple.

GUILLEMETTE: No greedy shark ever took the bait
quicker than he did. It serves him right. He never
gives a thing in church on Sundays. [*She laughs.*]

PATHELIN: For God's sake, don't laugh. If he came 660
back and heard you, it would spoil everything. I'm
sure he'll be back.

GUILLEMETTE: Hold in your laughter if you can, but I swear I can't help myself.

THE CLOTHIER: By the sacred sun that shines, I'm going back to that backwoods barrister, I don't care what anybody says. Oh, God! That phoney financial fraud would fleece his own family! Now, by Saint Peter, I know he has my cloth, the sneaky swindler. I gave it to him right on this spot. 670

GUILLEMETTE: When I think of the face he made looking at you, I can't help laughing. He was so greedy in asking you for—

PATHELIN: Peace, you cackler! I swear to God, if he came back and heard you, we might as well start running. He's such a sour old bastard. 675

THE CLOTHIER: [*returning to Pathelin's house*] That addlepated advocate, that bibulous barrister, does he take us all for fools? By damn, the only doctor he needs is a good hangman. I'll renounce God if he doesn't have my cloth. And he played this trick on me, too. [*At the door*] Hey, in there! Where are you hiding? 680

GUILLEMETTE: On my oath, he heard me and he seems to be raving mad. 685

PATHELIN: I'll pretend to be delirious. Go to the door.

GUILLEMETTE: [*to the Clothier*] My, how you're shouting.

THE CLOTHIER: By God, you were laughing! My money—now! 690

GUILLEMETTE: Holy Mary! What do you think I have to laugh about? There's no sadder person in town. He's fading fast. Never did you hear such an uproar or such raving. He's still delirious. His mind wanders, he sings, he jabbers in so many languages and jumbles them all together. He won't live half an hour longer. I swear, I laugh and cry at the same time. 695

THE CLOTHIER: I don't know what you mean about laughing and crying. But to put it bluntly, I must be paid now! 700

GUILLEMETTE: For what? Are you insane? Are you going to start that again?

THE CLOTHIER: I'm not used to being paid with words when I sell my cloth. Would you have me believe the moon is made of green cheese? 705

PATHELIN: [*delirious*] Arise! Make way for the Queen of Guitars. Let her approach without delay. I know she gave birth to four and twenty guitarlings, sired by the Abbot of Iverneaux. I'll have to be the godfather. 710

GUILLEMETTE: Alas! Think about God the father, my dear, not about guitars.

THE CLOTHIER: What a pair of con artists you are! Quick, now give me my money in gold or silver for the cloth you took. 715

GUILLEMETTE: Good God! You were mistaken once, isn't that enough?

THE CLOTHIER: Do you know what's going on, woman? So help me, I don't know what you mean by "mistaken." But never mind, you'll either pay up or be strung up. How do I wrong you by coming here to ask for what's mine? By Saint Peter of Rome— 720 725

GUILLEMETTE: Alas! How you torment this poor man! Truly, I can see in your face that you're losing your wits. If only I had help, sinner that I am, I'd have you tied up. You're a raving lunatic.

THE CLOTHIER: I'm raving because I don't have my money. 730

GUILLEMETTE: Oh, what madness! Cross yourself. *Benedicite!* Make the sign of the cross.

THE CLOTHIER: May I renounce God if I ever again sell cloth on credit. [*Pathelin stirs*] What an invalid! 735

PATHELIN: [*in Limousin dialect*][3] Mother of God, crowned [Queen of heaven], by my faith, I want to go, or I'll renounce God, to the other side of the sea. God's belly, I say *gigone!* [*points to Clothier*] That one there steals money and gives nothing. Toll not the bell. Take your nap. Let him not speak 740

---

[3] In what follows, Pierre adopts a succession of dialects from several regions of medieval France. Such dialects were fundamentally different from one another, even at times mutually incomprehensible, but at the time of the play's performance they were what most residents of France actually spoke. From here to the end of the scene, Pierre not only accomplishes a feat of astonishing linguistic ventriloquism, but speaks in rhymed verse as well. The translator, Alan E. Knight, has opted for a plain literal prose translation, as far as that was possible here, rather than a series of inappropriate English dialects that would in any case fail to do justice to the original.

to me of money! [*To the Clothier.*] Did you understand, cousin?

GUILLEMETTE: He had an uncle from Limousin, the brother of his aunt by marriage. I'll bet that's what makes him babble in the Limousin dialect. 745

THE CLOTHIER: Damn it, he stole out of my shop with the cloth under his arm.

PATHELIN: [*Picard dialect*] Come in, sweet damsel. What does that pack of scoundrels want? Get back, you shitten knaves! Quick! I want to become a priest! Now, may the Devil be part of that ancient priesthood. And must the priest laugh when he should be chanting his mass? 750

GUILLEMETTE: Alas! Alas! The hour draws near when he'll need the last sacraments. 755

THE CLOTHIER: But how does he speak the Picard dialect so well? And why all this silliness?

GUILLEMETTE: His mother was from Picardy. That's why he speaks it now. 760

PATHELIN: [*to the Clothier*] Where did you come from, you carnival clown? [*garbled Flemish*] Arms, to arms, good man! Fortunately, I know several books. Henry! Henry! Come to sleep. I shall be well armed. Foolishness, foolishness! Crazy inventions! A run! Ar un! A nun is bound! There are distichs in these verses. But great feasting disturbs the brain. Wait a minute! Come quick! Something to drink, I beg of you! Come, look: a gift of God. And put some water in it for me. But wait a while because of the frost. 765

Quick, call Father Thomas so I can be shriven. 770

THE CLOTHIER: What's going on? Will he never stop jabbering in different languages? If he'd just give me my money, or even a deposit, I'd be on my way. 775

GUILLEMETTE: By God's passion, I'm tired of this. You're the weirdest man I ever met. Just what do you want? I don't know how you can be so obstinate. 780

PATHELIN: [*Norman dialect*] Come here! Renouart au Tiné! [*He looks into his gown*] What the devil! How hairy my balls are! They're furry as a caterpillar or a honeybee. Hey! Speak to me, Gabriel. God's wounds! What's biting my ass? Is it a fly, a dungbeetle, or a cockchafer? [*He puts his hand into his gown*] What the Devil? I've got 785

dysentery! Am I one of the loose-bowelled of Bayeux? Jean du Quemin would be glad to know that I am. Well, by St. Michael, I'll gladly drink to his health. 790

THE CLOTHIER: How can he stand to talk so much? He's going stark raving mad.

GUILLEMETTE: His schoolmaster was from Normandy. Now at the end he's remembering him. He's sinking fast. 795

THE CLOTHIER: Holy Mary! This is the craziest mess I've ever gotten myself into. Never would I have doubted that he was at the fair today.

GUILLEMETTE: You really believed it? 800

THE CLOTHIER: I did, by Saint James. But now I see it wasn't so.

PATHELIN: Is that an ass I hear braying? [*To the Clothier*] Alas and alack, good cousin, they all shall bray in great sorrow the day that I see thee no more. And yet I must needs detest thee, for thou hast played false with me. Thy work is naught but deceit. [*Breton dialect*] May he go to the Devil, body and soul. 805

GUILLEMETTE: [*to Pathelin*] May God have mercy on you. 810

PATHELIN: May you have dizzy spells all night with much lamenting and with all your relatives praying for you, for fear that you'll vomit your guts out. There will be such weeping and wailing that even the starving dogs will take pity on you. May you receive a coffin as alms out of much love and courtesy. 815

THE CLOTHIER: Alas! For God's sake, listen to him. He's going fast. How he rattles on! But what the Devil is he jabbering about? Holy Mary, how he mutters! God's bodkin, he babbles and quacks his words so you can't understand a thing. It's no Christian tongue he's speaking, nor any that makes sense. 820

825

GUILLEMETTE: His father's mother came from Brittany. But he's dying, and all this indicates that it's time for the last sacraments.

PATHELIN: [*Lorraine dialect*] Hey, by St. Gengoux, you're lying! I swear to God! Great balls, may God send you misfortune! You're not worth an old door-mat! Get out of here, you bloody old boot; fuck off! Leave, you low-life lecher! You're too 830 malicious, by God! You there! Come have a drink and give me a peppercorn; I'll eat it and, by George, I'll drink to you. What do you expect me to say? Say, are you by chance from Picardy? The peasants there are dumbfounded. [*Here he shifts from Lorraine dialect to Latin*] Good day to you, beloved master, most reverend father. How are you burning? What's new? There are no eggs in Paris. What does that merchant want? Let him say to himself that the swindler, the one lying in bed, wants to give him, if he will, some goose to eat. If it's good, ask for some without delay. 835 840 845

GUILLEMETTE: I swear, he's going to die making speeches. My, how he Latinizes! Don't you see how highly he esteems the divinity? His humanity is ebbing away. Now I'll remain poor and miserable.

THE CLOTHIER: It would be better for me to go before he breathes his last. If he has some secret things to confide in you before he dies, I doubt that he would want to say them in front of me. Please forgive me, but I swear to you that I truly believed he had taken my cloth. Farewell, good woman. I beg you in God's name to forgive me. 850 855

GUILLEMETTE: May this day be blessed for you and also for me in my sorrow.

THE CLOTHIER: [*leaving the house*] By the gracious Virgin, I'm more confused now than ever. The Devil, in his shape, took my cloth to tempt me. [*Crosses himself*] *Benedicite.* May he leave me in peace. But since that's the way it is, I give the cloth, in God's name, to whoever took it. 860

PATHELIN: [*getting up*] Now then, didn't I instruct you well? There he goes, the gullible simpleton. Now he's really got some confused ideas under that bonnet of his. I bet he'll have nightmares when he goes to bed tonight. 865

GUILLEMETTE: We really put him in his place. Didn't I play my part well? 870

PATHELIN: By God, you played it to perfection. Now at least we have enough cloth to make some clothes.

[*Clothier's shop.*]

THE CLOTHIER: Damn it all! Everybody feeds me lies; everybody steals from me and takes all he can get. I feel like I'm the king of the wretched. Even 875

the shepherds of the field defraud me. And my own shepherd, to whom I've always been generous, will not get away with cheating me. He'll be begging for mercy, by the Blessed Virgin! 880

THIBAULT AIGNELET, THE SHEPHERD: [*entering the shop*] God grant you a blessed day and a good evening, gentle Master.

THE CLOTHIER: Aha! There you are, you dung-covered scoundrel! What a good fellow you are! Good for nothing! 885

THE SHEPHERD: Begging your pardon, Sir, but some guy, I don't know who, with stripes on his sleeve, and all kind of excited, and carrying a whip handle without a cord, came up and said to me— But I don't rightly recollect what it was he said. He talked about you, Master, and some kind of summons, but, Holy Mary, I couldn't make heads or tails out of it. He mixed me up so with his talk about "sheep," and "afternoon session," and he made a great fuss about things you had said against me, Sir. 890 895

THE CLOTHIER: If I don't haul you before the judge in two shakes, I pray to God to strike me with storm and flood. Never again will you get away with killing my sheep, I swear. And no matter what happens, you'll pay me for those six yards . . . I mean, for killing my sheep and for all the losses you've caused me in the last ten years. 900

THE SHEPHERD: You shouldn't believe those poison tongues, good Master, for by my soul— 905

THE CLOTHIER: And by Our Lady you'll pay me on Saturday for my six yards of cloth—I mean, for what you stole of my sheep.

THE SHEPHERD: What cloth? Ah, Sir, I believe you are upset about something else. By Saint Lupus,[4] Master, I'm afraid to say anything when I see you like this. 910

THE CLOTHIER: Go and leave me in peace. And answer your summons, if you know what's good for you. 915

THE SHEPHERD: But Sir, let's settle this now. For God's sake, don't take me to court.

---

4 Latin for wolf, the enemy of sheep; there were at least six French saints by this name.

THE CLOTHIER: Go! The matter is in good hands. Go on, now! I won't make a settlement, by God, and I won't agree to anything but what the judge decides. Damn it all, everybody will cheat me from now on if I don't put a stop to it. 920

THE SHEPHERD: Goodbye, Sir. May God give you joy. So now I have to defend myself. 925

[*Pathelin's door.*]

THE SHEPHERD: [*knocking*] Is anybody here?

PATHELIN: I'll be hanged if he hasn't come back.

GUILLEMETTE: No it can't be! Saint George preserve us. That would be the end.

THE SHEPHERD: God be with you and keep you. 930

PATHELIN: God save you, my good fellow. What is it you want?

THE SHEPHERD: They're going to fine me for not showing up, if I don't answer my summons, Sir, this afternoon, and if you please, would you, good Master, plead my case for me, 'cause I don't know nothing about it, and I can pay you good, even though I'm dressed so poor. 935

PATHELIN: Come here and speak up. Which are you, plaintiff or defendant? 940

THE SHEPHERD: Well, Sir, I work for a certain merchant, you know, and for a long time I've taken his sheep out to graze and I guard 'em, and I swear when I think about him paying me next to nothing . . . Do I have to tell everything? 945

PATHELIN: Certainly. A client should hide nothing from his counsel.

THE SHEPHERD: It's true, Sir, it's the truth, I struck 'em down, so that many of 'em were knocked out and fell down dead, even though they were strong and healthy, and then I made him think, so's he wouldn't punish me, that they died of the scab. "Oh," he'd say, "don't leave a diseased one with the others; get rid of it." "I'll be glad to," I'd say; and I'd get rid of it all right, but not the way he thought, for, by Saint John, I ate every one of 'em, 'cause I knew what they really died of. What else can I tell you? I kept doin' this so long and struck down and killed so many that he noticed it, and when he found out he had been deceived, so help me God, he sent somebody to spy on me 'cause you could hear 'em cry out, you know, when you 950 955 960

hit 'em. So I was caught red-handed, I can never deny it, and now I come to ask if there ain't some way we can put the old hound off the scent, and don't worry about money, I got enough to pay you good. I know he's got a good case, but you can find some loophole, if you will, to make it worthless. 965

PATHELIN: I promise you you'll be satisfied with the results. What will you give me if I overturn the claim of your accuser and get you a full pardon? 970

THE SHEPHERD: Instead of payin' in sous, I'll pay you in solid gold crowns.

PATHELIN: Then you'll have an unbeatable case even if it's twice as weak as you say. The stronger the case I argue against, the quicker I can render it null, when I put my mind to it. You'll hear how well I can spiel it off after he's presented his argument. Come over here. By God, you're wily enough to understand the trick. Now tell me, what's your name? 975 980

THE SHEPHERD: By Saint Maurus, it's Thibault Aignelet.

PATHELIN: Aignelet, did you appropriate many lambs from your master? 985

THE SHEPHERD: On my oath, I may have eaten thirty or more in three years.

PATHELIN: That makes an income of ten a year— the equivalent of a few games at the tavern. [*He thinks for a moment*] I believe I have a good ruse here. Do you think he can readily find a witness to prove his allegation? That's the most important part of the trial. 990

THE SHEPHERD: Prove, Sir? Holy Mary! By all the saints in paradise, instead of one, he'll find ten to testify against me. 995

PATHELIN: That's almost enough to ruin your case. Here's what I had in mind. I'll pretend that I'm not on your side and that I've never seen you before. 1000

THE SHEPHERD: For God's sake, don't do that!

PATHELIN: No, that's no good. But here's what we have to do. If you speak, they'll trap you one by one on all counts of the indictment, and in such cases, confessions are as prejudicial and harmful as the Devil himself. So here's what will make our case: as soon as they call you to appear before the court, you'll answer only with "baa," no matter what they 1005 say to you. And if they should curse you, saying, "Hey, you stinking yokel! May God plunge you into misery! Are you making fun of the court?" just answer "baa." "Ha!" I'll say, "he's a poor simpleton who thinks he's talking to his sheep." But even if they knock themselves out yelling at you, make sure no other word comes out of your mouth. 1010

THE SHEPHERD: Seein' as how this touches me close, I'll make sure I don't say nothin' else and I'll do it right, I promise.

PATHELIN: Now make sure you stick to your promise. And even to me, no matter what I say or ask, don't answer any other way. 1020

THE SHEPHERD: Me? Never, by the sacrament! You can cry out that I'm crazy, if I say another word today, to you or anybody else, no matter what they say to me, except "Baa," just like you told me. 1025

PATHELIN: If you do that, by Saint John, your accuser will be caught in our trap. But also make sure, when it's over, that I get a payment I'll be proud of.

THE SHEPHERD: Sir, if I don't pay you at your word, 1030 then never believe me again. But please work hard on my case.

PATHELIN: By Our Lady, I'll bet the judge is already on the bench; he always holds court around six o'clock. Now you come along after me; we won't 1035 both go together.

THE SHEPHERD: That's a good idea, so nobody sees you're my lawyer.

PATHELIN: And God help you if you don't pay generously. 1040

THE SHEPHERD: I swear I'll pay at your word; really, Sir, have no fear. [exits]

PATHELIN: Well now, it may not be raining money, but it's sprinkling. At least I'll get a little something out of this. If everything falls into place, I'll have 1045 a gold piece or two for my trouble.

[Courtroom.]

PATHELIN: [removing hat, bowing] Your Honour, God grant you success and whatever your heart desires.

THE JUDGE: Welcome, Sir. Please don your hat and 1050 take your place over there.

PATHELIN: [seeing the Clothier] Damn! [To the Judge] I'm fine here, Your Honour; I'll have more room to manoeuver.

THE JUDGE: If there is business before the court, let 1055 it be done quickly so I can adjourn.

THE CLOTHIER: My lawyer is coming, Your Honour. He's finishing up some other business. If the court please, we had better wait for him.

THE JUDGE: Wait? I have cases to hear elsewhere. If 1060 the offending party is present, then state the case yourself without delay. Are you not the plaintiff?

THE CLOTHIER: I am.

THE JUDGE: Where is the defendant? Is he here in person? 1065

THE CLOTHIER: Yes, there he is, not saying a word. God only knows what he's thinking.

THE JUDGE: Since you're both here, state your case.

THE CLOTHIER: Then here's my complaint against him, Your Honour. The truth is that for the love 1070 of God and in charity I fed and clothed him in his childhood; and, to be brief, when I saw that he was strong enough to go to the fields, I made him my shepherd and set him to watching my flock. But as sure as you're sitting there, Your 1075 Honour, he wrought such carnage among my wethers and ewes that without a doubt—

THE JUDGE: Just a minute! Wasn't he hired by you?

PATHELIN: That's a good point! Because if he had finagled to employ him without a contract— 1080

THE CLOTHIER: [seeing Pathelin] May I disavow God if it isn't you! You, without a doubt!

THE JUDGE: Why are you holding your hand to your face, Master Pierre? Do you have a toothache?

PATHELIN: Yes, and the pain is so excruciating that 1085 never before have I been in such agony. I can't even look up. For God's sake, make him get on with it.

THE JUDGE: Proceed! Finish your deposition. Come on, be brief about it.

THE CLOTHIER: It's him and nobody else! By God's 1090 cross, it really is! Master Pierre, it was you that I sold six yards of cloth to.

THE JUDGE: What's he saying about cloth?

PATHELIN: He's rambling. He thinks he's getting to his opening statement, but he doesn't know how 1095 because he isn't used to this.

THE CLOTHIER: May I be hanged by the bloody neck if anybody else took my cloth.

PATHELIN: Look how this unworthy man goes to extremes to build his case. He means, and he's very stubborn about it, that his shepherd has sold the wool—that's what I understood—from which the cloth of my robe was made. He seems to be saying that the shepherd's a thief and has been stealing the wool of his sheep.

THE CLOTHIER: God send me misfortune if you haven't got it!

THE JUDGE: Silence! The Devil take you for running off at the mouth! Can't you get back to your deposition without delaying the court with such drivel?

PATHELIN: Oh, my tooth aches, but I can't help laughing! He's already so rushed he doesn't know where he left off. We'll have to lead him back to the subject.

THE JUDGE: Come now, let's get back to those sheep. What happened next?

THE CLOTHIER: He took six yards of it, worth nine francs.

THE JUDGE: Do you take us for fools or simpletons? Where do you think you are?

PATHELIN: I swear to God, he's trying to make an ass of you! And he looks like such a decent man. But I suggest you examine his adversary.

THE JUDGE: That's a good idea. He sees him often, so he must know him. [*To the Shepherd*] Step forward! Speak!

THE SHEPHERD: Baa!

THE JUDGE: Another vexation! What do you mean, "baa"? Am I a goat! Speak to me!

THE SHEPHERD: Baa!

THE JUDGE: The bloody pox take you! Are you trying to make a fool of me!

PATHELIN: He must be either crazy or pigheaded; or maybe he thinks he's among his sheep.

THE CLOTHIER: I'll renounce God if you aren't the one that got my cloth—you and nobody else! [*To the Judge*] Oh, you don't know, Your Honour, by what malice—

THE JUDGE: What? Hold your tongue! Are you dense? Set aside this accessory matter and let's get back to the principal.

THE CLOTHIER: Very well, Your Honour, but the case concerns me. Nevertheless, I promise I won't say another word about it for the rest of the day. Some other time it may be different; right now I'll just have to swallow it. Now, I was saying in my complaint that I had given six yards—I should say, my sheep—Please forgive me, Your Honour. This good Master—I mean, my shepherd, when he was supposed to be in the fields—He told me I would get six gold pieces when I came . . . I mean to say, three years ago my shepherd made an agreement that he would faithfully guard my sheep and would cause me no loss nor do me any wrong, and then—Now he brazenly refuses to give me either cloth or money! [*To Pathelin*] Ah, Master Pierre, I swear . . . [*To the Judge*] This scoundrel here was stealing the wool from my sheep, and he was killing healthy ones by clubbing them on the head.—when he put my cloth under his arm, he took off in a great hurry, saying that I should go collect my six gold pieces at his house!

THE JUDGE: There's neither rime nor reason in any of your railing and ranting. What is this? You mix in one thing and then another. In short, by God, I can't make heads or tails of it. [*To Pathelin*] He prattles about cloth, then he jabbers about sheep and jumbles it all up. Nothing he says makes sense.

PATHELIN: I'll bet anything he's keeping this poor shepherd's wages for himself.

THE CLOTHIER: You can shut your mouth, by God! It's the gospel truth that he stole my cloth! I know better than you or anybody else where my shoe pinches, and by God in heaven, I know you have it!

THE JUDGE: What does he have?

THE CLOTHIER: Nothing, Your Honour. But I swear he's the biggest swindler—OK, I'll try to control my tongue and I won't say another word about it today, no matter what happens.

THE JUDGE: Very well, but remember your promise. Now conclude quickly.

PATHELIN: This shepherd cannot answer the charges against him without counsel, and he's afraid or doesn't know how to ask for it. I would be willing to counsel him, Your Honour, if you so ordered.

THE JUDGE: Him? I should think that would be a wasted effort. He's as poor as a church mouse.

PATHELIN: I swear I have no thought of gain. Let it be for love of God. Now I'll try to find out from the poor lad what he has to say, and I'll see if he can instruct me as to how to reply to the charges against him. He'd have a hard time getting out of this, if nobody helped him. [*To the Shepherd*] Come over here, my friend. Now, if we could find—do you understand? 1190

THE SHEPHERD: Baa!

PATHELIN: What is this "baa"? By the Holy Blood, are you crazy? Tell me about your case. 1200

THE SHEPHERD: Baa!

PATHELIN: What is this "baa"? Do you hear the ewes bleating? Try to understand, this is for your own good.

THE SHEPHERD: Baa! 1205

PATHELIN: Come on! Answer yes or no. [*Softly*] That's good. Keep it up. [*Aloud*] Will you do that?

THE SHEPHERD: Baa!

PATHELIN: Speak up, or you'll find yourself in real trouble, I'm afraid. 1210

THE SHEPHERD: Baa!

PATHELIN: It takes a real ass to bring such a poor fool to trial. Your Honour, send him back to his sheep. He's just a natural-born fool.

THE CLOTHIER: You call him a fool? By Saint Saviour of Asturias, he's smarter than you are. 1215

PATHELIN: [*to the Judge*] Send him back to watch his sheep, *sine die*,[5] never to return. A plague on him who brings charges against such natural-born fools. 1220

THE CLOTHIER: Will he be sent back before I can be heard?

THE JUDGE: So help me, since he's a born fool, yes. Why shouldn't he be?

THE CLOTHIER: But Your Honour, at least allow me to sum up my case first. This isn't something I dreamed up or just idle discourse. 1225

THE JUDGE: Nothing but vexation comes of bringing suit against fools and simpletons. Now hear this: to stop this senseless babble, the court will be adjourned. 1230

_____

5 Without specifying a particular day; indefinitely.

THE CLOTHIER: Will they go without obligation to return?

THE JUDGE: And why not?

PATHELIN: Return! You never saw a greater fool in word or deed. [*Pointing to the Clothier*] And this other one isn't an ounce better. They're both brainless boneheads. By the Blessed Virgin, their brains together wouldn't weigh a carat. 1235

THE CLOTHIER: You took my cloth by deceit, Master Pierre, without paying. As I'm a poor sinner, that wasn't the deed of an honest man. 1240

PATHELIN: May I renounce Saint Peter of Rome if he isn't an insidious fool, or well on his way to being one. 1245

THE CLOTHIER: I recognize you by your speech, by your clothes, and by your face. And I'm not crazy! I'm sane enough to know what's good for me. [*To the Judge*] I'll tell you the whole story, Your Honour, upon my conscience. [*The Judge grimaces. Laughter in the court, or in the audience*] 1250

PATHELIN: Please, Your Honour, bring them to order. [*To the Clothier*] Aren't you ashamed to haul this poor shepherd into court for three or four grubby old sheep that aren't worth two buttons? [*To the Judge*] His litany gets longer and more tedious. 1255

THE CLOTHIER: What sheep? It's always the same old song! It's you I'm talking to and, by God, you'll give me back my cloth. 1260

THE JUDGE: [*to court or audience*] You see that? I really get the cases, don't I? He won't stop braying for the rest of the day.

THE CLOTHIER: I'll bring suit—!

PATHELIN: Make him shut up! [*To the Clothier*] You prattle too much, by God. Let's say he did knock off six or seven sheep, or even a dozen, and ate them—Holy Christmas, you weren't crippled by it. You still earned a lot more than that in the time he's been watching your flock. 1265 1270

THE CLOTHIER: Look at that, Your Honour, just look! I talk to him about cloth and he answers me in sheep. [*To Pathelin*] Those six yards of cloth that you stuck under your arm, where are they? Don't you intend to give them back to me? 1275

PATHELIN: Oh, Sir, would you have him hanged for six or seven sheep? At least think it over. Don't be so harsh on this poor, unfortunate shepherd, who hasn't a thing to his name.

THE CLOTHIER: You're an expert in changing the subject! The Devil himself made me sell cloth to such a customer. Please, Your Honour, I charge him— 1280

THE JUDGE: (*thinks he means the Shepherd*) I absolve him of your charges and forbid you to proceed. A fine thing it is to bring suit against a fool. [*To the Shepherd*] Go back to your sheep. 1285

THE SHEPHERD: Baa!

THE JUDGE: [*to the Clothier*] By our Lady, you've certainly shown what kind of person you are, Sir. 1290

THE CLOTHIER: But Your Honour, I swear, I want him to—

PATHELIN: Can't he shut up?

THE CLOTHIER: But it's *you* I have a case against! You tricked me with your eloquent speeches and carried my cloth away like a thief! 1295

PATHELIN: Your Honour, I solemnly appeal. Are you going to listen to this?

THE CLOTHIER: So help me God, you're the biggest swindler! Your Honour, let me say— 1300

THE JUDGE: It's a three-ring circus with you two— nothing but wrangling and squabbles. So help me, I've got to be going. [*To the Shepherd*] Go, my son, and don't ever come back, even if an officer serves you with a warrant. The court grants you a full pardon. 1305

PATHELIN: Say "thank you."

THE SHEPHERD: Baa!

THE JUDGE: Is that clear? Go now and don't worry about a thing. It's all right. 1310

THE CLOTHIER: But is it right for him to go like that?

THE JUDGE: Bah! I have business elsewhere. You're both outrageous mockers and you won't detain me a moment longer. I'm leaving. Will you come to supper with me, Master Pierre? 1315

PATHELIN: I can't. [*Judge exits*]

THE CLOTHIER: You're an outright thief! Tell me, will I ever be paid?

PATHELIN: For what? Are you crazy? Who do you think I am anyway? By God, I've been trying to figure out who it is you take me for. 1320

THE CLOTHIER: Indeed!

PATHELIN: No just a minute, my good man. I'll tell you right now who it is you take me for. It's the town fool, isn't it? But look! [*He lifts his hat*] That can't be, because he's not bald on top of his head like me. 1325

THE CLOTHIER: Do you think I'm an imbecile? It was you in person; you, yourself, and nobody but you. Your voice proves it and don't think it doesn't. 1330

PATHELIN: Me, myself, and I? No it wasn't, I swear. Get that out of your head. It was probably John from Noyon; he's about my size.

THE CLOTHIER: The Devil it was! He doesn't have that besotted, witless face of yours. Didn't I leave you sick a while ago at your house? 1335

PATHELIN: Now there's a fine bit of evidence! Me, sick? And what was I sick with? Come on, admit your stupidity; it's quite clear now. 1340

THE CLOTHIER: I'll renounce Saint Peter if it wasn't you—you and nobody else. I know that to be absolutely true.

PATHELIN: Well don't you believe it, because it positively wasn't me. I never took a yard or even half a yard of cloth from you. I don't have that kind of reputation. 1345

THE CLOTHIER: Damn it all, I'm going to go back to your house to see if you're there. We won't have to squabble here any more if I find you there. 1350

PATHELIN: By Our Lady, that's a good idea! That way you'll know for sure. [*Clothier exits*]

PATHELIN: Hey, Aignelet!

THE SHEPHERD: Baa!

PATHELIN: Come here. Was your case well disposed of? 1355

THE SHEPHERD: Baa!

PATHELIN: Your accuser has gone, so you don't have to say "baa" anymore. I really cooked his goose, didn't I? And didn't I counsel you just right? 1360

THE SHEPHERD: Baa!

PATHELIN: Hey, don't worry. Nobody'll hear you. Speak up.

THE SHEPHERD: Baa!

PATHELIN: It's time for me to go now, so pay me. 1365

THE SHEPHERD: Baa!

PATHELIN: To tell the truth, you played your part very well; you looked good. But what really fooled him was that you kept from laughing.

THE SHEPHERD: Baa! 1370

PATHELIN: Why "baa"? You mustn't say it any more. Just pay me generously.

THE SHEPHERD: Baa!

PATHELIN: Why do you keep saying "baa"? Speak normally and pay me so I can go. 1375

THE SHEPHERD: Baa!

PATHELIN: You know what? I'll tell you. I'm asking you, please, without any more bleating around the bush, to think about paying me. I've had enough of your baas. Pay up quickly. 1380

THE SHEPHERD: Baa!

PATHELIN: Is this some kind of joke? Is this all you're going to do? I swear to God, if you don't escape, you're going to pay me, understand? The money! Now! 1385

THE SHEPHERD: Baa!

PATHELIN: You've got to be kidding. Is this all I'm going to get from you?

THE SHEPHERD: Baa!

PATHELIN: You're running this into the ground. And 1390 just who are you trying to fool? Do you know who you're dealing with? Don't babble your baas to me anymore today; just pay me.

THE SHEPHERD: Baa!

PATHELIN: Is this the only pay I'll get? Who do you 1395 think you're playing games with? I was taking such pride in your performance; now really make me proud of you.

THE SHEPHERD: Baa!

PATHELIN: Are you trying to pull the wool over my 1400 eyes? God's curse! Have I lived so long that a shepherd, a sheep in human clothing, a churlish knave can make a fool of me?

THE SHEPHERD: Baa!

PATHELIN: Will I get no other word? If you're doing 1405 this for a joke, say so and don't make me argue any more. Come and have supper at my house.

THE SHEPHERD: Baa!

PATHELIN: By Saint John, you're right: the goslings lead the geese to pasture. [*To himself*] I thought I 1410 was the master in these parts of all the cheaters and swindlers and those who give their word in payment, collectible on Judgement Day; and now a shepherd of the fields outwits me. [*To the Shepherd*] By Saint James, if I could find an officer, 1415 I'd have you arrested.

THE SHEPHERD: Baa!

PATHELIN: Baa, yourself! May I be hanged if I don't go find me a good policeman! And misfortune seize him if he doesn't throw you in jail. 1420

THE SHEPHERD: [*running away*] If he finds me, I'll give him a full pardon.

ANONYMOUS

Everyman

*E*veryman (written after 1485) is one of the great surprises of medieval drama and a rarity in all theatrical literature: an allegory that really works. If read merely as an example of the appropriation of theatre by the Church, it might seem little more than a heavy-handed, repetitive instruction manual for preparing for the afterlife according to Christian doctrine: renounce worldly goods, go to confession, mortify your flesh, repent, take the seven sacraments, and accept the promise of eternal life in heaven. But the play manages almost completely to transcend its surface didacticism because Everyman's real struggle has less to do with achieving a proper Christian death than with acknowledging the all-too-human state of denial in which he has been living. And because what he has been denying is nothing less than the single most basic and ineluctable fact of all human life, the fact that we die, his journey to the grave truly does represent the life of every one of us.

Written at a time when the Black Death was a familiar agent of mortality for the people of Europe, the play shares its central personified Death-figure with many other artworks of the period. But *Everyman* is not really about the plague, disease, or premature death at all, but about life—the life of every person without exception, to whom death comes sooner or later and often without warning. Given that we do die, and may die soon, how should we be living? What is worthwhile? Where can we find the comfort that assures us that we haven't wasted our lives? What thoughts will accompany us into our final minutes, a time of reckoning that we all, even the socialites among us, will face utterly alone? This morality play is certainly the product of a period of widespread and doctrinaire religious belief. Paradoxically, however, its inquiry into the ultimate value of material wealth, physical beauty, and other lifestyle attainments, far from being any less pertinent today, is perhaps even more urgent in a consumerist, materialist age like ours than it was in the fifteenth century. Religious beliefs may come and go, but the fact of death remains.

Along with the play's touchingly sweet poetic style, it is the very rigour of *Everyman*'s allegorical structure that has enabled the play to speak with equal potency to audiences of all types, of all religions, in every epoch. Everyman's surprising run-in with Death expresses, in an unsurpassingly clear and concrete form, the basic tension that animates all the great religions of the world and even human spirituality itself: the apparent contrast between the material side of life—which weighs down, and disappoints, and fades; which decays, is lost, and disappears—and the less tangible but ultimately more lasting components of our experience, those that live on after us because they live in others. In *Everyman,* Good Deeds is the name given to this sphere of human action, but the self-transcending, world-improving behaviours to which it refers could go by many other names as well.

Since the rediscovery of *Everyman* as a work for the stage by William Poel in 1901, it has proved itself an attractive and versatile theatrical vehicle. In addition to the annual performance of

Hofmannsthal's version at the Salzburg Festival in Austria,[1] *Everyman* has been staged around the world in the last hundred years from China to Chicago, from Italy to the Philippines. Beginning with Peter Arnott's famous production of the 1960s, which refashioned the work as a puppet-play and revealed its inherent stylistic kinship with the many non-realistic presentational styles of twentieth-century modernism and postmodernism, *Everyman* has appeared in countless diverse incarnations: in a Hispanic version as *El Hombre*; in a multiple-religion version as *EveryOne*; as an Appalachian musical; it has been staged as an AIDS play, and as a play about cancer, set in Hungary with Everywoman as its central figure. In Frank Galati's production with Steppenwolf Theatre in 1995, the existentialist drama at the heart of the play was brought out with especial power. The performance began each night with a lottery; each night one member of the multi-racial cast drew the death straw, and that night, without warning, was chosen to play Everyman and confront his or her death—an inspired piece of theatrical randomness and inevitability that effectively conveys the essential moral truth, as well as the main call to action, of this potentially transformative play: Death is coming. Live accordingly.

---

[1] Performed there every year since 1925, with the exception of the Hitler years.

ANONYMOUS
Everyman

CHARACTERS
GOD
DEATH
EVERYMAN
FELLOWSHIP
KINDRED
COUSIN
GOODS
GOOD DEEDS
KNOWLEDGE
CONFESSION
BEAUTY
STRENGTH
DISCRETION
FIVE-WITS
ANGEL
MESSENGER
DOCTOR

Here beginneth a treatise how the High Father of Heaven sendeth Death to summon every creature to come and give account of their lives in this world and is in manner of a moral play.

MESSENGER. I pray you all give your audience,
  And hear this matter with reverence,
    By figure a moral play:
  The *Summoning of Everyman* called it is,
  That of our lives and ending shows   5
    How transitory we be all day.
  This matter is wondrous precious,
  But the intent of it is more gracious,
    And sweet to bear away.
  The story saith: Man, in the beginning,   10
  Look well, and take good heed to the ending,
    Be you never so gay;
  Ye think sin in the beginning full sweet,
  Which in the end causeth the soul to weep,

When the body lieth in clay.   15
Here shall you see how Fellowship and Jollity,
Both Strength, Pleasure, and Beauty,
Will fade from thee as flower in May.
For ye shall hear, how our heaven king
Calleth Everyman to a general reckoning.   20
Give audience, and hear what he doth say.

God speaketh.

GOD. I perceive here in my majesty,
   How that all creatures be to me unkind,
   Living without dread in worldly prosperity;
   Of ghostly sight the people be so blind,[1]   25
   Drowned in sin, they know me not for their
      God;
   In worldly riches is all their mind.
   They fear not my righteousness, the sharp rod;
   My law that I showed, when I for them died,
   They forget clean, and shedding of my blood red; 30
   I hanged between two, it cannot be denied;
   To get them life I suffered to be dead;
   I healed their feet, with thorns hurt was my head;
   I could do no more than I did truly.
   And now I see the people do clean forsake me: 35
   They use the seven deadly sins damnable,
   As pride, covetise, wrath, and lechery,
   Now in the world be made commendable,
   And thus they leave of angels the heavenly
      company;
   Every man liveth so after his own pleasure,   40
   And yet of their life they be nothing sure.
   I see—the more that I them forbear,
   The worse they be from year to year;
   All that liveth appaireth[2] fast;
   Therefore I will, in all the haste,   45
   Have a reckoning of every man's person.
   For if I leave the people thus alone
   In their life and wicked tempests,
   Verily they will become much worse than beasts,
   For now one would by envy another up eat;   50
   Charity they all do clean forget.
   I hoped well that every man
   In my glory should make his mansion,

---

[1] Blind, that is, to things of the spirit.
[2] Degenerates.

And thereto I had them all elect;
   But now I see, like traitors deject,   55
   They thank me not for the pleasure that I to
      them meant,
   Nor yet for their being that I them have lent.
   I proffered the people great multitude of mercy,
   And few there be that ask it heartily.
   They be so cumbered with worldly riches   60
   That needs on them I must do justice,
   On every man living without fear.
   Where art thou, Death, thou mighty messenger?
DEATH. Almighty God, I am here at your will,
   Your commandment to fulfil.   65
GOD. Go thou to Everyman,
   And show him in my name
   A pilgrimage he must on him take,
   Which he in no wise may escape;
   And that he bring with him a sure reckoning   70
   Without delay or any tarrying.
DEATH. Lord, I will in the world go run over all,
   And cruelly out search both great and small.
   Every man will I beset that liveth beastly
   Out of God's laws, and dreadeth not folly.   75
   He that loveth riches I will strike with my dart,
   His sight to blind, and from heaven to depart,
   Except that alms be his good friend,
   In hell for to dwell, world without end.
   Lo, yonder I see Everyman walking;   80
   Full little he thinketh on my coming;
   His mind is on fleshly lusts and his treasure,
   And great pain it shall cause him to endure
   Before the Lord, Heaven King.

Enter Everyman.

   Everyman, stand still! Whither art thou going   85
   Thus gaily? Hast thou thy Maker forgot?
EVERYMAN. Why askest thou?
   Wouldest thou wit?[3]
DEATH. Yea, sir, I will show you;
   In great haste I am sent to thee   90
   From God, out of his majesty.
EVERYMAN. What, sent to me?
DEATH. Yea, certainly.
   Though thou have forgot him here,

---

[3] Know.

He thinketh on thee in the heavenly sphere,   95
As, ere we depart, thou shalt know.
EVERYMAN. What desireth God of me?
DEATH. That shall I show thee:
    A reckoning he will needs have,
    Without any longer respite.   100
EVERYMAN. To give a reckoning longer leisure I crave;
    This blind matter troubleth my wit.
DEATH. On thee thou must take a long journey;
    therefore thy book of 'count with thee thou bring,
    For turn again thou can not by no way;   105
    And look thou be sure of thy reckoning,
    For before God thou shalt answer, and show
    Thy many bad deeds and good but a few,
    How thou hast spent thy life, and in what wise,
    Before the chief lord of paradise.   110
    Have ado that we were in that way,
    For, wit thou well, thou shalt make none attorney.
EVERYMAN. Full unready I am such reckoning to give.
    I know thee not; what messenger art thou?
DEATH. I am Death, that no man dreadeth.   115
    For every man I rest,[4] and no man spare;
    For it is God's commandment
    That all to me should be obedient.
EVERYMAN. O Death, thou comest when I had
        thee least in mind!
    In thy power it lieth me to save;   120
    Yet of my good will I give thee, if thou will be kind,
    Yea, a thousand pound shalt thou have,
    And defer this matter till another day.
DEATH. Everyman, it may not be by no way.
    I set not by gold, silver, nor riches,   125
    Nor by pope, emperor, king, duke, nor princes;
    For if I would receive gifts great,
    All the world I might get,
    But my custom is clean contrary.
    I give thee no respite; come hence, and not tarry.   130
EVERYMAN. Alas, shall I have no longer respite?
    I may say Death giveth no warning.
    To think on thee, it maketh my heart sick,
    For all unready is my book of reckoning,
    But twelve year and I might have abiding,   135
    My counting book I would make so clear,
    That my reckoning I should not need to fear.

_____
4 Arrest.

Wherefore, Death, I pray thee, for God's mercy,
    Spare me till I be provided of remedy.
DEATH. Thee availeth not to cry, weep, and pray,   140
    But haste thee lightly that thou were gone that
        journey,
    And prove thy friends if thou can.
    For, wit thou well, the tide abideth no man,
    And in the world each living creature
    For Adam's sin must die of nature.   145
EVERYMAN. Death, if I should this pilgrimage take,
    And my reckoning surely make,
    Show me, for saint charity,
    Should I not come again shortly?
DEATH. No, Everyman; and thou be once there,   150
    Thou mayst never more come here,
    Trust me verily.
EVERYMAN. O gracious God, in the high seat celestial,
    Have mercy on me in this most need!
    Shall I have no company from this vale terrestrial   155
    Of mine acquaintance that way me to lead?
DEATH. Yea, if any be so hardy,
    That would go with thee and bear thee company.
    Hie thee that thou were gone to God's magnificence,
    Thy reckoning to give before his presence.   160
    What, weenest[5] thou thy life is given thee,
    And thy worldly goods also?
EVERYMAN. I had wend[6] so, verily.
DEATH. Nay, nay; it was but lent thee;
    For as soon as thou art gone,   165
    Another a while shall have it, and then go therefrom,
    Even as thou hast done.
    Everyman, thou art mad! Thou hast thy wits five,
    And here on earth will not amend thy life!
    For suddenly I do come.   170
EVERYMAN. O wretched caitiff, whither shall I flee,
    That I might scape this endless sorrow?
    Now, gentle Death, spare me till to-morrow,
    That I may amend me
    With good advisement.   175
DEATH. Nay, thereto I will not consent,
    Nor no man will I respite;
    But to the heart suddenly I shall smite
    Without any advisement.

_____
5 Think.
6 Thought.

And now out of thy sight I will me hie; 180
See thou make thee ready shortly,
For thou mayst say this is the day
That no man living may scape away.
EVERYMAN. Alas! I may well weep with sighs deep;
Now have I no manner of company 185
To help me in my journey, and me to keep;
And also my writing is full unready.
How shall I do now for to excuse me?
I would to God I had never been got!
To my soul a full great profit it had been, 190
For now I fear pains huge and great.
The time passeth; Lord, help, that all wrought!
For though I mourn, it availeth nought.
The day passeth, and is almost agone;
I wot not well what for to do. 195
To whom were I best my complaint to make?
What if I to Fellowship thereof spake,
And showed him of this sudden chance?
For in him is all mine affiance;[7]
We have in the world so many a day 200
Been good friends in sport and play.
I see him yonder, certainly;
I trust that he will bear me company;
Therefore to him will I speak to ease my sorrow.
Well met, good Fellowship, and good morrow! 205

Fellowship speaketh.

FELLOWSHIP. Everyman, good morrow! By this day,
Sir, why lookest thou so piteously?
If any thing be amiss, I pray thee me say,
That I may help to remedy.
EVERYMAN. Yea, good Fellowship, yea, 210
I am in great jeopardy.
FELLOWSHIP. My true friend, show to me your mind;
I will not forsake thee, to my life's end,
In the way of good company.
EVERYMAN. That was well spoken, and lovingly. 215
FELLOWSHIP. Sir, I must needs know your heaviness;
I have pity to see you in any distress.
If any have you wronged ye shall revenged be,
Though I on the ground be slain for thee,
Though that I know before that I should die. 220
EVERYMAN. Verily, Fellowship, gramercy.

FELLOWSHIP. Tush! by thy thanks I set not a straw.
Show me your grief, and say no more.
EVERYMAN. If I my heart should to you break,
And then you do turn your mind from me, 225
And would not me comfort, when ye hear me speak,
Then should I ten times sorrier be.
FELLOWSHIP. Sir, I say as I will do indeed.
EVERYMAN. Then be you a good friend at need.
I have found you true here before. 230
FELLOWSHIP. And so ye shall evermore;
For, in faith, and thou go to hell,
I will not forsake thee by the way.
EVERYMAN. Ye speak like a good friend, I believe
you well;
I shall deserve it, if I may. 235
FELLOWSHIP. I speak of no deserving, by this day.
For he that will say and nothing do
Is not worthy with good company to go.
Therefore show me the grief of your mind,
As to your friend most loving and kind. 240
EVERYMAN. I shall show you how it is:
Commanded I am to go a journey,
A long way, hard and dangerous,
And give a strait count without delay
Before the high judge Adonai.[8] 245
Wherefore I pray you, bear me company,
As ye have promised, in this journey.
FELLOWSHIP. That is matter indeed! Promise is duty,
But if I should take such a voyage on me,
I know it well, it should be to my pain; 250
Also it makes me afeard, certain.
But let us take counsel here as well as we can,
For your words would fear[9] a strong man.
EVERYMAN. Why, ye said, if I had need,
You would me never forsake, quick nor dead, 255
Though it were to hell, truly.
FELLOWSHIP. So I said, certainly.
But such pleasures be set aside, the sooth to say;
And also, if we took such a journey,
When should we come again? 260
EVERYMAN. Nay, never again till the day of doom.
FELLOWSHIP. In faith, then will not I come there!
Who hath you these tidings brought?

---

7 Trust.

8 Hebrew for God.
9 Frighten.

EVERYMAN. Indeed, Death was with me here.

FELLOWSHIP. Now, by God that all hath bought, 265
    If Death were the messenger,
    For no man that is living to-day
    I will not go that loath journey—
    Not for the father that begat me!

EVERYMAN. Ye promised otherwise, pardie![10] 270

FELLOWSHIP. I wot well I say so, truly;
    And yet if thou wilt eat, and drink, and make
      good cheer,
    Or haunt to women the lusty company,
    I would not forsake you while the day is clear,
    Trust me verily! 275

EVERYMAN. Yea, thereto ye would be ready!
    To go to mirth, solace, and play,
    Your mind will sooner apply,
    Than to bear me company in my long journey.

FELLOWSHIP. Now, in good faith, I will not that way. 280
    But if thou will murder, or any man kill,
    In *that* I will help thee with a good will!

EVERYMAN. Oh, that is a simple advice indeed!
    Gentle Fellow, help me in my necessity;
    We have loved long, and now I need; 285
    And now, gentle Fellowship, remember me.

FELLOWSHIP. Whether ye have loved me or no,
    By Saint John, I will not with thee go!

EVERYMAN. Yet I pray thee, take the labour and do
    so much for me
    To bring me forward, for saint charity, 290
    And comfort me till I come without the town.

FELLOWSHIP. Nay, if thou would give me a new
    gown,
    I will not a foot with thee go;
    But if thou had tarried, I would not have left
      thee so.
    And as now, God speed thee in thy journey! 295
    For from thee I will depart as fast as I may.

EVERYMAN. Whither away, Fellowship? will thou
    forsake me?
    Yea, by my fay![11] To God I betake thee.

EVERYMAN. Farewell, good Fellowship; for thee my
    heart is sore.
    Adieu for ever, I shall see thee no more. 300

---

[10] *Par Dieu,* by God.
[11] Faith.

FELLOWSHIP. In faith, Everyman, farewell now at
    the end;
    For you I will remember that parting is mourning.

EVERYMAN. Alack! shall we thus depart indeed?
    Ah, Lady, help! without any more comfort,
    Lo, Fellowship forsaketh me in my most need. 305
    For help in this world whither shall I resort?
    Fellowship here before with me would merry make,
    And now little sorrow for me doth he take.
    It is said, "In prosperity men friends will find,
    Which in adversity be full unkind." 310
    Now, whither for succor shall I flee,
    Since Fellowship hath forsaken me?
    To my kinsmen I will truly,
    Praying them to help me in my necessity;
    I believe that they will do so, 315
    For kind will creep where it may not go.[12]
    I will go say, for yonder I see them go.
    Where be ye now, my friends and kinsmen?

KINDRED. Here be we now at your commandment.
    Cousin, I pray you show us your intent 320
    In any wise, and not spare.

COUSIN. Yea, Everyman, and to us declare
    If ye be disposed to go any whither,
    For wit you well, we'll live and die together.

KINDRED. In wealth and woe we will with you hold, 325
    For over his kin a man may be bold.

EVERYMAN. Gramercy, my friends and kinsmen kind;
    Now shall I show you the grief of my mind.
    I was commanded by a messenger,
    That is an high king's chief officer: 330
    He bade me go a pilgrimage to my pain,
    And I know well I shall never come again;
    Also I must give a reckoning, straight,
    For I have a great enemy that hath me in wait,
    Which intendeth me to hinder. 335

KINDRED. What account is that which ye must
    render?
    That would I know.

EVERYMAN. Of all my works I must show
    How I have lived and my days spent;
    Also of ill deeds, that I have used 340
    In my time, since life was me lent;
    And of all virtues that I have refused.

---

[12] Family can be depended upon.

Therefore, I pray you, go thither with me,
  To help to make mine account, for saint charity.
COUSIN. What, to go thither? Is that the matter?   345
  Nay, Everyman, I had liefer[13] fast bread and water
  All this five year and more.
EVERYMAN. Alas, that ever I was born!
  For now shall I never be merry
  If that you forsake me.   350
KINDRED. Ah, sir! What? Ye be a merry man!
  Take good heart to you, and make no moan.
  But one thing I warn you, by Saint Anne:
  As for me, ye shall go alone.
EVERYMAN. My Cousin, will you not with me go?   355
COUSIN. No, by our Lady! I have the cramp in my toe.
  Trust not to me, for, so God me speed,
  I will deceive you in your most need.
KINDRED. It availeth not us to entice.
  Ye shall have my maid with all my heart;   360
  She loveth to go to feasts, there to be nice,
  And to dance, and abroad to start:
  I will give her leave to help you in that journey—
  If that you and she may agree.
EVERYMAN. Now show me the very effect of your   365
     mind—
  Will you go with me, or abide behind?
KINDRED. Abide behind? yea, that will I, if I may!
  Therefore farewell till another day.
EVERYMAN. How should I be merry or glad?
  For fair promises men to me make,   370
  But when I have most need, they me forsake.
  I am deceived; that maketh me sad.
COUSIN. Cousin Everyman, farewell now,
  For verily I will not go with you.
  Also of mine own an unready reckoning   375
  I have to account; therefore I make tarrying.
  Now, God keep thee, for now I go.
EVERYMAN. Ah, Jesus, is all come hereto?
  Lo, fair words make fools fain;[14]
  They promise, and nothing will do certain.   380
  My kinsmen promised me faithfully
  For to abide with me steadfastly,
  And now fast away do they flee—
  Even so Fellowship promised me.

---

13 Rather.
14 Happy.

What friend were best for me to provide?   385
  I lose my time here longer to abide.
  Yet in my mind a thing there is....
  All my life I have loved riches.
  If that my Good now help me might,
  He would make my heart full light.   390
  I will speak to him in this distress.
  Where art thou, my Goods and Riches?
GOODS. Who calleth me? Everyman? what hast
    thou haste?
  I lie here in corners, trussed and piled so high,
  And in chests I am locked so fast,   395
  Also sacked in bags, thou mayst see with thine eye
  I cannot stir; in packs low I lie.
  What would ye have, lightly me say.
EVERYMAN. Come hither, Good, in all the haste
    thou may,
  For of counsel I must desire thee.   400
GOODS. Sir, if ye in the world have sorrow or adversity,
  That can I help you to remedy shortly.
EVERYMAN. It is another disease that grieveth me;
  In this world it is not, I tell thee so.
  I am sent for another way to go,   405
  To give a strait count general
  Before the highest Jupiter of all.
  And all my life I have had joy and pleasure in thee;
  Therefore, I pray thee, go with me—
  For, peradventure, thou mayst before God   410
    almighty
  My reckoning help to clean and purify,
  For it is said ever among,
  That money maketh all right that is wrong.
GOODS. Nay, Everyman, I sing another song!
  I follow no man in such voyages;   415
  For if I went with thee,
  Thou shouldst fare much the worse for me!
  For because on me thou did set thy mind,
  Thy reckoning I have made blotted and blind,
  That thine account thou cannot make truly;   420
  And that hast thou for the love of me.
EVERYMAN. That would grieve me full sore,
  When I should come to that fearful answer.
  Up, let us go thither together!
GOODS. Nay, not so; I am too brittle, I may not   425
    endure;
  I will follow no man one foot, be ye sure.

EVERYMAN. Alas, I have thee loved, and had great
    pleasure
    All my life-days in goods and treasure.
GOODS. That is to thy damnation without lesing,[15]
    For my love is contrary to the love everlasting.   430
    But if thou had me loved moderately during,
    And to the poor given part of me,
    Then shouldst thou not in this dolour be,
    Nor in this great sorrow and care.
EVERYMAN. Lo, now was I deceived ere I was ware,   435
    And all I may blame on my spending of time.
GOODS. What, weenest thou that I am thine?
EVERYMAN. I had wend so.
GOODS. Nay, Everyman, I say no;
    As for a while I was lent thee,   440
    A season thou hast had me in prosperity.
    My condition is man's soul to kill;
    If I save one, a thousand do I spill.
    Weenest thou that I will follow thee?
    Nay, from this world not verily.   445
EVERYMAN. I had wend otherwise.
GOODS. Therefore to thy soul Goods are a thief;
    For when thou art dead, this is my guise—
    Another to deceive in the same wise
    As I have done thee, and all to his soul's reprief.[16]   450
EVERYMAN. O false Good, cursed thou be!
    Thou traitor to God, that hast deceived me,
    And caught me in thy snare.
GOODS. Marry, thou brought thyself in care—
    Whereof I am glad!   455
    I must needs laugh; I cannot be sad.
EVERYMAN. Ah, Good, thou hast had long my
    heartly love;
    I gave thee that which should be the Lord's above.
    But wilt thou not go with me, indeed?
    I pray thee truth to say.   460
GOODS. No, so God me speed.
    Therefore farewell, and have good day.
EVERYMAN. Oh, to whom shall I make my moan
    For to go with me in that heavy journey?
    First Fellowship said he would with me go;   465
    His words were very pleasant and gay,
    But afterward he left me alone.

Then spake I to my kinsmen, all in despair,
And also they gave me words fair—
They lacked no fair speaking,   470
But all forsake me in the ending.
Then went I to my Goods, that I loved best,
In hope to have comfort, but there had I least;
For my Goods sharply did me tell
That he bringeth many into hell!   475
Then of myself I was ashamed,
And so I am worthy to be blamed;
Thus may I well myself hate.
Of whom shall I now counsel take?
I think that I shall never speed   480
Till that I go to my Good Deed.
But alas, she is so weak,
That she can neither go nor speak;
Yet will I venture on her now.
My Good Deeds, where be you?   485
GOOD DEEDS. Here I lie, cold in the ground;
    Thy sins have me so bound
    That I cannot stir.
EVERYMAN. O Good Deeds, I stand in fear;
    I must you pray of counsel,   490
    For help now should come right well.
GOOD DEEDS. Everyman, I have understanding
    That ye be summoned account to make
    Before Messias, of Jerusalem King;
    If you do by me,[17] that journey with you will I take.   495
EVERYMAN. Therefore I come to you, my moan to
    make;
    I pray you that ye will go with me.
GOOD DEEDS. I would full fain, but I cannot
    stand, verily.
EVERYMAN. Why, is there anything on you fallen?
GOOD DEEDS. Yea, sir, I may thank you of all;   500
    If ye had perfectly cheered me,
    Your book of 'count now full ready had been.
    Look, the books of your works and deeds eke[18]—
    Ah, see how they lie under the feet,
    To your soul's heaviness.   505
EVERYMAN. Our Lord Jesus, help me!
    For one letter here I cannot see.

---

15 Lying.
16 Reproof.

17 That is, do what I advise.
18 As well.

GOOD DEEDS. There is a blind reckoning in time
    of distress!
EVERYMAN. Good Deeds, I pray you, help me in
    this need,
    Or else I am forever damned indeed.   510
    Therefore help me to make reckoning
    Before the redeemer of all thing,
    That king is, and was, and ever shall.
GOOD DEEDS. Everyman, I am sorry of your fall,
    And fain would I help you, and I were able.   515
EVERYMAN. Good Deeds, your counsel I pray you
    give me.
GOOD DEEDS. That shall I do verily;
    Though that on my feet I may not go,
    I have a sister, that shall with you also,
    Called Knowledge, which shall with you abide,   520
    To help you to make that dreadful reckoning.
KNOWLEDGE. Everyman, I will go with thee, and
    be thy guide,
    In thy most need to go by thy side.
EVERYMAN. In good condition I am now, in everything,
    And am wholly content with this good thing;   525
    Thanked be God my creator!
GOOD DEEDS. And when he hath brought you there,
    Where thou shalt heal thee of thy smart,
    Then go you with your reckoning and your
        Good Deeds together,
    For to make you joyful at heart   530
    Before the blessed Trinity.
EVERYMAN. My Good Deeds, gramercy;
    I am well content, certainly,
    With your words sweet.
KNOWLEDGE. Now go we together lovingly,   535
    To Confession, that cleansing river.
EVERYMAN. For joy I weep; I would we were there.
    But, I pray you, give me cognition
    Where dwelleth that holy man, Confession.
KNOWLEDGE. In the house of salvation: 540
    We shall find him in that place,
    That shall us comfort by God's grace.

Enter Confession.

    Lo, this is Confession. Kneel down and ask mercy,
    For he is in good conceit with God almighty.
EVERYMAN. O glorious fountain that all   545
    uncleanness doth clarify,

Wash me from the spots of vice unclean,
    That on me no sin may be seen.
    I come with Knowledge for my redemption,
    Redempt with hearty and full contrition;
    For I am commanded a pilgrimage to take,   550
    And great accounts before god to make.
    Now, I pray you, Shrift,[19] mother of salvation,
    Help my good deeds for my piteous exclamation.
CONFESSION. I know your sorrow well, Everyman.
    Because with Knowledge ye come to me,   555
    I will you comfort as well as I can,
    And a precious jewel I will give thee,
    Called penance, voider of adversity;
    Therewith shall your body chastised be,
    With abstinence and perseverance in God's service: 560
    Here shall you receive that scourge of me,
    Which is penance strong, that ye must endure,
    To remember thy Saviour was scourged for thee
    With sharp scourges, and suffered it patiently;
    So must thou, ere thou scape that painful   565
        pilgrimage.
    Knowledge, keep him in this voyage,
    And by that time Good Deeds will be with thee.
    But in any wise, be certain of mercy,
    For your time draweth fast; and ye will saved be.
    Ask God mercy, and He will grant truly.   570
    When with the scourge of penance man doth
        him bind,
    The oil of forgiveness then shall he find.
EVERYMAN. Thanked be God for his gracious work,
    For now I will my penance begin;
    This hath rejoiced and lighted my heart,   575
    Though the knots be painful and hard within.
KNOWLEDGE. Everyman, look your penance that
    ye fulfil,
    What pain that ever it to you be,
    And Knowledge shall give you counsel at will,
    How your account ye shall make clearly.   580
EVERYMAN. O eternal God, O heavenly figure,
    O way of righteousness, O goodly vision,
    Which descended down in a virgin pure
    Because he would Everyman redeem,
    Which Adam forfeited by his disobedience,   585
    O blessed Godhead, elect and high-divine,

---

[19] Penance, absolution.

Forgive my grievous offence;
Here I cry thee mercy in this presence.
O ghostly treasure, O ransomer and redeemer,
Of all the world hope and conductor,   590
Mirror of joy, founder of mercy,
Which illumineth heaven and earth thereby,
Hear my clamorous complaint, though it late be!
Receive my prayers; unworthy in this heavy life
Though I be, a sinner most abominable,   595
Yet let my name be written in Moses' table.
O Mary, pray to the Maker of all thing,
Me for to help at my ending,
And save me from the power of my enemy,
For Death assaileth me strongly;   600
And, Lady, that I may by means of thy prayer
Of your Son's glory to be partner,
By the means of his passion I it crave,
I beseech you, help my soul to save!
Knowledge, give me the scourge of penance,   605
My flesh therewith shall give acquaintance.
I will now begin, if God give me grace.
KNOWLEDGE. Everyman, God give you time and space:
Thus I bequeath you in the hands of our Saviour,
Now may you make your reckoning sure.   610
EVERYMAN. In the name of the Holy Trinity,
My body sore punished shall be:
[*Scourges himself*]
Take this, body, for the sin of the flesh;
Also thou delightest to go gay and fresh,
And in the way of damnation thou did me bring;   615
Therefore suffer now strokes of punishing.
Now of penance I will wade the water clear,
To save me from purgatory, that sharp fire.
GOOD DEEDS. [*rises up from prostrate posture*]
I thank God, now I can walk and go,
And am delivered of my sickness and woe.   620
Therefore with Everyman I will go, and not spare;
His good works I will help him to declare.
KNOWLEDGE. Now, Everyman, be merry and glad;
Your Good Deeds cometh now, ye may not be sad;
Now is your Good Deeds whole and sound,   625
Going upright upon the ground.
EVERYMAN. My heart is light, and shall be evermore;
Now will I smite faster than I did before.
GOOD DEEDS. Everyman, pilgrim, my special friend,
Blessed be thou without end;   630

For thee is prepared the eternal glory.
Ye have me made whole and sound,
Therefore I will bide by thee in every stound.[20]
EVERYMAN. Welcome, my Good Deeds! Now I
hear thy voice,
I weep for very sweetness of love.   635
KNOWLEDGE. Be no more sad, but ever rejoice:
God seeth thy living in his throne above.
Put on this garment to thy behoof,[21]
Which is wet with your tears,
Or else before God you may it miss,   640
When ye to your journey's end come shall.
EVERYMAN. Gentle Knowledge, what do ye it call?
KNOWLEDGE. It is a garment of sorrow,
From pain it will you borrow;
Contrition it is,   645
That getteth forgiveness;
It pleaseth God passing well.
GOOD DEEDS. Everyman, will you wear it for your
heal?
EVERYMAN. [*puts on robe of contrition*] Now blessed
be Jesu, Mary's Son,
For now have I on true contrition.   650
And let us go now without tarrying.
Good Deeds, have we clear our reckoning?
GOOD DEEDS. Yes, indeed I have [it] here.
EVERYMAN. Then I trust we need not fear.
Now, friends, let us not part in twain.   655
KNOWLEDGE. Nay, Everyman, that will we not,
certain.
GOOD DEEDS. Yet must thou lead with thee
Three persons of great might.
EVERYMAN. Who should they be?
GOOD DEEDS. Discretion and Strength they hight,[22]   660
And thy Beauty may not abide behind.
KNOWLEDGE. Also ye must call to mind
Your Five-wits as for your counsellors.
GOOD DEEDS. You must have them ready at all hours.
EVERYMAN. How shall I get them hither?   665
KNOWLEDGE. You must call them all together,
And they will hear you incontinent.[23]

---

20 Hour, or a difficult, painful time.
21 Benefit.
22 Are called.
23 Instantly.

EVERYMAN. My friends, come hither and be present,
    Discretion, Strength, my Five-wits, and Beauty.
BEAUTY. Here at your will we be all ready.   670
    What will ye that we should do?
GOOD DEEDS. That ye would with Everyman go,
    And help him in his pilgrimage.
    Advise you: will ye with him or not in that voyage?
STRENGTH. We will bring him all thither,   675
    To his help and comfort, ye may believe me.
DISCRETION. So will we go with him all together.
EVERYMAN. Almighty God, loved might thou be!
    I give thee laud that I have hither brought
    Strength, Discretion, Beauty, and Five-wits; lack   680
      I nought.
    And my Good-Deeds, with Knowledge clear,
    All be in my company at my will here;
    I desire no more to my business.
STRENGTH. And I, Strength, will by you stand in
      distress,
    Though thou would in battle fight on the ground.   685
FIVE-WITS. And though it were through the world
      round,
    We will not depart for sweet nor sour.
BEAUTY. No more will I unto death's hour,
    Whatsoever thereof befall.
DISCRETION. Everyman, advise you first of all;   690
    Go with a good advisement and deliberation.
    We all give you virtuous 'monition
    That all shall be well.
EVERYMAN. My friends, hearken what I will tell:
    I pray God reward you in his heavenly sphere.   695
    Now hearken, all that be here,
    For I will make my testament
    Here before you all present.
    In alms, half my good I will give with my hands
      twain
    In the way of charity, with good intent;   700
    And the other half still shall remain
    In bequest to be returned where it ought to be.
    This I do in despite of the fiend of hell,
    To go quite out of his peril
    Ever after and this day.   705
KNOWLEDGE. Everyman, hearken to what I say:
    Go to Priesthood, I you advise,
    And receive of him in any wise
    The holy sacrament and ointment together,

Then shortly see ye turn again hither.   710
    We will all abide you here.
FIVE-WITS. Yea, Everyman, hie you that ye ready were.
    There is no emperor, king, duke, nor baron,
    That of God hath commission,
    As hath the least priest in the world being;   715
    For of the blessed sacraments pure and benign
    He beareth the keys, and thereof hath the cure
    For man's redemption, it is ever sure,
    Which God for our soul's medicine
    Gave us out of his heart with great pain.   720
    Here in this transitory life, for thee and me
    The blessed sacraments seven there be:
    Baptism, confirmation, with priesthood good,
    And the sacrament of God's precious flesh and
      blood;
    Marriage, the holy extreme unction, and penance.   725
    These seven be good to have in remembrance—
    Gracious sacraments of high divinity.
EVERYMAN. Fain would I receive that holy body,
    And meekly to my ghostly[24] father I will go.
FIVE-WITS. Everyman, that is the best that ye can do.   730
    God will you to salvation bring,
    For priesthood exceedeth all other thing;
    To us Holy Scripture they do teach,
    And convert man from sin, heaven to reach.
    God hath to them more power given   735
    Than to any angel that is in heaven.
    With five words[25] he may consecrate
    God's body in flesh and blood to make,
    And handleth his Maker between his hands.
    The priest bindeth and unbindeth all bands,   740
    Both in earth and in heaven.
    Thou ministers all the sacraments seven.
    Though we kiss thy feet thou were worthy.
    Thou art surgeon that cureth sin deadly:
    No remedy we find under God   745
    But all only priesthood.
    Everyman, God gave priests that dignity,
    And setteth them in his stead among us to be;
    Thus be they above angels in degree.

[*Everyman goes to receive sacraments.*]

---

24 Spiritual.
25 The words spoken during the Eucharist ceremony: "For
    this is my body" (*hoc est enim corpus meum*).

KNOWLEDGE. If priests be good, it is so surely.   750
    But when Jesus hanged on the cross with great
       smart,
    There he gave, out of his blessed heart,
    The same sacrament in great torment;
    He sold them not to us, that Lord omnipotent.
    Therefore Saint Peter the apostle doth say   755
    That Jesus' curse have all they
    Which God their Saviour do buy or sell,
    Or they for any money do take or tell.
    Sinful priests give the sinners example bad,
    Their children sit by other men's fires, I have heard,   760
    And some haunt women's company,
    With unclean life, as lusts of lechery;
    These be with sin made blind.
FIVE-WITS. I trust to God no such may we find.
    Therefore let us priesthood honour,   765
    And follow their doctrine for our souls' succour;
    We be their sheep, and they shepherds be,
    By whom we all be kept in surety.
    Peace, for yonder I see Everyman come,
    Which hath made true satisfaction.   770

[*Re-enter Everyman.*]

GOOD DEEDS. Methink it is he indeed.
EVERYMAN. Now Jesu be your alder speed.[26]
    I have received the sacrament for my redemption,
    And then mine extreme unction:
    Blessed be all they that counselled me to take it!   775
    And now, friends, let us go without longer respite;
    I thank God that ye have tarried so long.
    Now set each of you on this rod[27] your hand,
    And shortly follow me.
    I go before; there I would be. God be your guide.   780
STRENGTH. Everyman, we will not from you go,
    Till ye have done this voyage long.
DISCRETION. I, Discretion, will bide by you also.
KNOWLEDGE. And though this pilgrimage be never
    so strong,
    I will never part you from.   785
    Everyman, I will be as sure by thee
    As ever I did by Judas Maccabee.[28]

---

[26] May Jesus aid you all.
[27] Cross.
[28] "The Hammerer," great Jewish leader and warrior who
    in 164 B.C.E. repulsed the Syrian invasion of Jerusalem.

EVERYMAN. Alas, I am so faint I may not stand,
    My limbs under me do fold.
    Friends, let us not turn again to this land,   790
    Not for all the world's gold,
    For into this cave must I creep,
    And turn to earth, and there to sleep.
BEAUTY. What, into this grave? alas!
EVERYMAN. Yea, there shall ye consume more and less. 795
BEAUTY. And what, should I smother here?
EVERYMAN. Yea, by my faith, and never more appear.
    In this world live no more we shall,
    But in heaven before the highest Lord of all.
BEAUTY. I cross out all this! Adieu, by Saint John!   800
    I take my tap in my lap and am gone.[29]
EVERYMAN. What, Beauty, whither will ye?
BEAUTY. Peace! I am deaf, I look not behind me,
    Not if thou wouldest give me all the gold in thy
    chest.
EVERYMAN. Alas, whereto may I trust?   805
    Beauty goeth fast away from me—
    She promised with me to live and die.
STRENGTH. Everyman, I will thee also forsake and
    deny;
    Thy game liketh me not at all.
EVERYMAN. Why, then ye will forsake me all!   810
    Sweet Strength, tarry a little space.
STRENGTH. Nay, sir, by the rood of grace,
    I will hie me from thee fast,
    Though thou weep to thy heart tobrast.[30]
EVERYMAN. Ye would ever bide by me, ye said.   815
STRENGTH. Yea, I have you far enough conveyed;
    Ye be old enough, I understand,
    Your pilgrimage to take on hand.
    I repent me that I hither came.
EVERYMAN. Strength, you to displease I am to blame;   820
    Will you break promise that is debt?
STRENGTH. In faith, I care not;
    Thou art but a fool to complain.
    You spend your speech and waste your brain;
    Go, thrust thee into the ground!   825
EVERYMAN. I had wend surer I should you have found.
    He that trusteth in his Strength,
    She him deceiveth at the length.

---

[29] Proverbial for a quick departure.
[30] Break to pieces.

Both Strength and Beauty forsake me,
Yet they promised me fair and lovingly.   830
DISCRETION. Everyman, I will after Strength be gone;
As for me, I will leave you alone.
EVERYMAN. Why, Discretion, will ye forsake me?
DISCRETION. Yea, in faith, I will go from thee,
For when Strength goeth before,   835
I follow after evermore.
EVERYMAN. Yet, I pray thee, for the love of the Trinity,
Look in my grave once, piteously.
DISCRETION. Nay, so nigh will I not come.
Farewell, every one!   840
EVERYMAN. Oh, all thing faileth, save God alone,
Beauty, Strength, and Discretion;
For when Death bloweth his blast,
They all run from me full fast.
FIVE-WITS. Everyman, my leave now of thee I take;   845
I will follow the other, for here I thee forsake.
EVERYMAN. Alas! then may I wail and weep,
For I took you for my best friend.
FIVE-WITS. I will no longer thee keep;
Now farewell, and there an end.   850
EVERYMAN. O Jesu, help! all have forsaken me!
GOOD DEEDS. Nay, Everyman, I will bide with thee,
I will not forsake thee indeed;
Thou shalt find me a good friend at need.
EVERYMAN. Gramercy, Good Deeds, now may I   855
true friends see;
They have forsaken me every one;
I loved them better than my Good Deeds alone.
Knowledge, will ye forsake me also?
KNOWLEDGE. Yea, Everyman, when ye to death
shall go;
But not yet for no manner of danger.   860
EVERYMAN. Gramercy, Knowledge, with all my heart.
KNOWLEDGE. Nay, yet I will not from hence depart,
Till I see where ye shall be come.
EVERYMAN. Methink, alas, that I must be gone,
To make my reckoning and my debts pay,   865
For I see my time is nigh spent away.
Take example, all ye that this do hear or see,
How they that I love best do forsake me,
Except my Good Deeds that bideth truly.
GOOD DEEDS. All earthly things is but vanity: 870
Beauty, Strength, and Discretion, do man
forsake,

Foolish friends and kinsmen that fair spake,
All flee save Good Deeds, and that am I.
EVERYMAN. Have mercy on me, God most mighty,
And stand by me, thou Mother and Maid, holy   875
Mary.
GOOD DEEDS. Fear not, I will speak for thee.
EVERYMAN. Here I cry God mercy.
GOOD DEEDS. Short our end, and minish[31] our pain;
Let us go and never come again.
EVERYMAN. Into thy hands, Lord, my soul I   880
commend;
Receive it, Lord, that it be not lost!
As thou me boughtest, so me defend,
And save me from the fiend's boast,
That I may appear with that blessed host
That shall be saved at the day of doom.   885
In manus tuas—of might's most,
Forever—*commendo spiritum meum.*[32]

[*Dies.*]

KNOWLEDGE. Now hath he suffered that we all
shall endure;
The Good Deeds shall make all sure.
Now hath he made ending;   890
Methinketh that I hear angels sing
And make great joy and melody
Where Everyman's soul received shall be.
ANGEL. Come, excellent elect spouse to Jesu;
Here above thou shalt go,   895
Because of thy singular virtue.
Now the soul is taken the body from,
Thy reckoning is crystal-clear.
Now shalt thou into the heavenly sphere,
Unto the which all ye shall come   900
That live well before the day of doom.
DOCTOR. This moral men may have in mind;
Ye hearers, take it of worth, old and young,
And forsake Pride, for he deceiveth you in the end.
And remember Beauty, Five-wits, Strength, and   905
Discretion—
They all at the last do Everyman forsake,
Save his Good Deeds; there doth he take.
But beware: if they be small

---

31 Diminish.
32 Luke 23:46: "Into thy hands I commend my spirit."

Before God, he hath no help at all.
None excuse may be there for Everyman. 910
Alas, how shall he do, then?
For after death, amends may no man make,
For then mercy and pity do him forsake.
If his reckoning be not clear when he doth come,
God will say—*Ite maledicti in ignem Æternum.*[33] 915

And he that hath his account whole and sound,
High in heaven he shall be crowned;
Unto which place God bring us all thither,
That we may live, body and soul together.
Thereto help the Trinity! 920
Amen, say ye, for saint charity.

THUS ENDETH THIS MORAL PLAY OF EVERYMAN.

---

[33] Matthew 25:41: "Depart from me, ye cursed, into everlasting fire."

CHAPTER THREE

The Renaissance

R*enaissance*, French for "rebirth," alludes to a putative reawakening of the spirit and energy of the Classical age—with all its enthusiasm for learning, science, and art—which took place in Europe after the Middle Ages. The use of the word to describe a period of history dates back only to the nineteenth century. However, the general *concept* of a "rebirth" can be found in Vasari, whose *Lives of the Artists* (1550) identified a continuous tradition in Italian painting that led from Giotto to Michelangelo, and which stood in contrast to medieval art (which Vasari believed was severely limited by ignorance). The concept is even detectable in the writings of the fourteenth-century Italian poet Petrarch, who was one of the first to suggest that between the Classical Age and his own time had fallen a Middle Age of darkness—implying, naturally, that his own age was already in recovery from that period. Perhaps what best defines "the Renaissance" is less a strict set of dates than a certain self-consciousness about the enterprise of reviving the spirit of the Classical age. Wherever one chooses to date the beginnings of the Renaissance, there is little question that such a self-conscious creative revival was well underway in Italy by 1453, when the fall of Constantinople brought an influx of Greek scholars and Classical texts into Italy.

The central thrust of this creative and intellectual revival was a scholarly movement known as "Humanism," based in the idea that the human in all its manifestations is a proper subject of study. This idea represented a strong contrast to prior assumptions that the only legitimate scholarly pursuits were those trained on a better understanding of the nature of God. This scholarly change was cognate with a shift in general outlook: from the idea of humanity as ultimately inconsequential relative to God and the church, to the notion of an inherent human dignity and a readiness to set spiritual and material accomplishments side by side.

One of the major engines of this cultural transformation was the rapid advance of science and technology. To take but one example, the shift in astronomy from a Ptolemaic to a Copernican universe improved navigation, abetted the spread of commercial trade—which in turn accelerated the economic changes that were making feudalism obsolete—and encouraged the exploration of regions of the world unknown to Europeans. These changes in the understanding of the physical universe helped to transform people's understanding of their spiritual place within a metaphysical universe. Meanwhile, the invention or distribution of other basic technologies, such as the printing press, paper, the compass, and above all, the growth of literacy, enabled a more efficient exchange of ideas, thus amplifying the aforementioned effects.

An important indirect effect of the advances in science and technology was to win further prestige for the notion that "truth" was a commodity to be found in many places, not solely in the domain of conventional theological doctrine and church authority. This more liberal understanding of the nature of truth is closely related to two of the most important influences on Renaissance theatre: one of these was the Reformation, and the other the recovery of classical models of art and literature. As the Roman Catholic Church became ever more riven with political factions, discredited by corruption and an unseemly lust for worldly power, the notion of one true, universal faith began to be challenged. The Reformation revolts of the early sixteenth century led by Martin Luther, Henry VIII, John Calvin, and others brought a number of new Protestant sects into existence. Whereas religion had once been the great unifying force throughout the continent, it was now a force of division. Perhaps the most obvious effect of this on the theatre is in the suppression of religious dramas throughout much of Europe. Religious controversy was perceived as so overheated that the performance of religious dramas might easily become an incendiary act, contributing to civil unrest. But another effect had to do with the erosion of the Catholic Church's political influence. As the central authority represented by the Roman Church's hegemony became fragmented, the sense of national and regional identity grew stronger. Latin had already begun to be supplanted by vernacular languages (those spoken by the people in any given region), and its demise was hastened by the schisms within Christianity. Accordingly, one of the main characteristics of European Renaissance theatre is its newly secular and regional nature.

Renaissance theatre was also shaped by a revival of interest in Greek and Roman models of art and literature. To Humanist scholars, the Classical world represented a source of truth and authority that was prior to and therefore stood apart from the Church; the legitimacy inferred from this historical precedence provided vital leverage for the process of detaching Renaissance culture from the religiosity of the medieval outlook. By the fifteenth century there were many Humanists in Italy engaged in the serious study of Greek and Roman texts, probing the question of the applicability of these texts to their own world. In their view, Classical models exemplified a kind of universal truth that had since been lost. While these scholars were still for the most part Christian despite their admiration of the ancients, they felt that a careful, scientifically minded integration of Classical ideas into the modern Christian world would lead to greater wisdom than any achieved to that point. It was out of this scholarly attempt to create a confluence of modern sensibilities and Classical ideas and forms that many of the most important elements of Renaissance theatre emerged.

Italy became the starting point for the Renaissance for several reasons. Because of its central location in the Mediterranean as a trading juncture between East and West, vast amounts of wealth passed through the region, which led to the creation in the fourteenth century of the world's first major banking system. The resulting superfluity of wealth created leisure for the upper classes and raised the question of how best to order a society freed from most of life's exigencies. Nationalism also played a part in the rise of Renaissance civilization here. Italy did not yet exist as a nation, but consisted rather of a number of rich, prince-ruled city-states, the most powerful of which were Venice, Milan, Florence, the Papal states, and Naples. These city-states were strongly competitive, and with their ruling families eager to demonstrate their prestige, the conditions were ideal for the creation of a strong patronage system that encouraged art and scholarship. In fact, many of the most outstanding artistic products of Renaissance Italy were actually initiated as exercises in self-aggrandizement by the princes and their families. Finally, because Renaissance Italians lived among the ruins of Roman architecture, they were faced with constant reminders of the heights achieved by the civilization that preceded theirs. For the Italian Humanists these material remains of what Augustine had called the City of Man embodied a persuasive alternative to the idea of the City of God and thus served as literal touchstones for Humanism's ultimate goal: to equal the greatest accomplishments of the ancient Romans.

Theatrical activity in the Italian Renaissance is often divided into two categories, *commedia erudita* and *commedia dell'arte*. The former was the theatre that emerged from the work of scholars, based on classical models and performed by amateurs; the latter was the theatre of professional actors, who improvised performances based on stock character-masks and formulaic scenarios. The two groups did not, however, operate in isolation from one another. The *commedia dell'arte* troupes often performed at court, for example, and sometimes even performed scripted comedies, such as Machiavelli's *Mandragola*. It is also possible to identify exceptions, such as the playwright Beolco, whose "Ruzzante" plays appear to fall somewhere between the two categories. In a general way, though, the division between the scholarly, literary-based theatre of the amateurs who performed for the elites and the largely improvisational theatre of the professionals who performed for general audiences was nonetheless real, and perhaps explains why so many of the extant dramas of the Italian Renaissance seem to be addressed to audiences of peculiarly refined sensibilities.

If the dramatic literature of the Italian Renaissance has little presence in today's repertoire, many of its theatrical innovations are still very much in evidence. A lasting contribution was made by the improvised *commedia dell'arte* companies. Although rooted partly in the conventions of Greek and Roman New Comedy, Atellan farce and roving mime troupes, Italian comedy was developed substantially by the professional actors of the Renaissance, who refined character types, comic business, dialogue rhythms and performance techniques. As *commedia dell'arte* troupes began performing throughout Europe, their robust style had a positive effect on the vitality of Renaissance comedy in general. More specifically, their comic formulas began to show up in the plots and characters of Molière, Shakespeare and Ben Jonson, among other playwrights. (Indeed, Molière's company at one time shared a theatre with—and undoubtedly learned from—the *commedia dell'arte* company then resident in Paris.)

The *commedia erudita* is perhaps less immediately appealing to our modern sensibilities, but it bequeathed three main innovations to subsequent theatre. First, there are the dramatic theories, which, in attempting to forge a union of Aristotle with Horace and ensure that this alloy evinced sound scientific principles, ended up developing a new set of neoclassic dramatic principles, including the notorious unities of action, space and time (i.e., the concept that a play should tell a single continuous story that takes place in a single location during a period of not more than 24 hours). The actual relationship of these theories to the drama written in Italy during the Renaissance is dubious; however, they were to have a direct effect on French drama in the seventeenth century, and they reopened the general critical discussion of the theatre that has been ongoing ever since.

The second major area has to do with theatre architecture and scenic design. In this, the biggest single influence was a 15 B.C.E. Roman work, Vitruvius's *De Re Architectura*, which was discovered in 1414 and printed in 1486. Vitruvius had made a study of Roman architecture, including Greco-Roman theatres, stressing the symmetry and proportion of Classical design. To the Italian scholars, the work articulated ideals of form that seemed consonant with the universal philosophic ideals they sought, and Vitruvius's work became a source-book for ideas about how to design the perfect theatre—though these were accommodated to Renaissance values in the same way that Aristotle's theories had been. For instance, most new theatres were built indoors, within existing structures at royal courts. Another important accommodation had to do with the newly discovered principles of representing perspective in painting, discoveries which, to the Italian Renaissance mind, seemed to have disclosed the hidden scientific principles of nature itself. Altering the Classically inspired theatre to accommodate perspective scenery resulted in the proscenium stage, which used a picture-frame-like arch to divide the theatre into two parts, with the stage (and concealed scenic machinery) on one side, and the audience on the other. This became the most permanent contribution of the Italian Renaissance to Western theatre, as the proscenium stage is by far the most common kind found today. The Italians further enhanced the perspective illusion behind the picture-frame by devising ingenious methods of shifting the scenery, such as chariot-and-pole systems, hinged flats, and so forth.

The third area of innovation lay in the plays performed in these theatres; here again, invention consisted of a combination of creative misreading and imperfect understanding of Greek and Roman theatre practices. One major outcome was pastoral drama—plays featuring highly refined shepherds and nymphs in an idyllic setting—which seems to have been intended by its inventors to fill the place which they understood the satyr play to have held in Greek theatre. The most famous pastorals were Torquato Tasso's *Aminta* (1573) and Giambattista Guarini's *The Faithful Shepherd* (1590), which were much imitated throughout Europe, and whose influence can be seen in Shakespeare's *As You Like It* and *The Winter's Tale*. But perhaps the most enduring of all the dramatic forms introduced by the *commedia erudita* is opera, which was intended to capture the union of music and drama found in Greek tragedy. In effect, a new dramatic form was created, one which quickly became enormously popular in Italy and has continued to thrive and undergo development to the present day.

In England and Spain, Renaissance drama emerged in cultures that had retained many elements of the popular medieval theatre, such as an open-air stage, the habit of representing multiple locations without set changes, and the mixing of comic and serious matter. In Spain, the theatre of the so-called "Golden Age" was influenced to an extent by the Moorish rule that had ended only in 1492, an influence evident in the music, dance, and prevalence of the theme of honour, especially in the *comedia capa y espada* ("cape and sword plays"). Spanish theatre was also shaped by the Inquisition, which in reaction to the Moorish occupation, fanatically and often tyrannically reasserted the authority of the Catholic Church, and thus strongly distinguished the culture of Spain from those countries in which the Reformation had taken a firm hold. The effects of the Counter-Reformation culture in Spain are most evident in the *autos sacramentales*, the large-scale religious plays that continued to be performed in Spain long after similar works had been banned elsewhere in Europe. In Spain, theatre was usually performed in one of two places: in public squares on *carros*—large wagons hitched together to create an enormous outdoor stage—and in the *corrales*—theatres built inside existing courtyards open to the sky but surrounded by walls, enabling the charging of admission.

Spaces like the Spanish *corrales* also existed in the yards of English inns, which provided a common site for public theatre until more permanent structures were built. 1576 is a watershed year for English theatre: the first permanent public theatre, known simply as "The Theatre," was built in Shoreditch just north of London's city walls; the first permanent "private" indoor theatre was also built that year in Blackfriars, on the Thames. The founding of these two theatres is important because, from this time, plays were performed under circumstances much more conducive to the sustained development of dramaturgical skill. Playwrights like Marlowe and Shakespeare had the advantage of writing not for a band of roving players, but for and with permanent companies of actors performing for regular, and increasingly sophisticated, audiences. Playwrights, players and spectators all found themselves joined in a creative partnership through which they rapidly taught one another about the craft of theatre.

Perhaps the most remarkable thing about English and French drama of the Renaissance is the extraordinarily high literary quality of so many of the plays. In both countries, a uniquely rich literary context assured that careful attention would be paid to the use of language in the plays, and accordingly, playwrights such as Marlowe and Shakespeare, Racine and Molière created works that continue to stand as the outstanding monuments of the felicitous use of their respective languages. Both nations were experiencing crucial periods of linguistic development, though these manifested themselves in radically different ways.

The English language had developed very rapidly in the five centuries between the Norman Conquest and the foundation of the first permanent theatres. If rules of grammar and spelling had not yet been settled, there was a good deal of excitement about the possibilities of the language, which had integrated words from various sources to create a massive vocabulary—a great gift to a writer such as Shakespeare, and one to which he freely added. The seemingly limitless wealth and variety of language found in Shakespeare further augmented the expansive effect of the broad emotional range, the fast-moving action, and the rapidly changing locales of his plays, all of which provided a stark contrast to the drama of France, where playwrights were developing a deliberately finite neoclassical dramaturgy of restraint, purity and rationality. And yet, these expansive plays of Shakespeare were performed with very little scenery, and most often upon the open thrust stage of the public theatres of London. Italianate scenery could be found in England, but generally only in the masques performed for audiences at court.

In France, the situation was different in that the language was actually shrinking as the vocabulary was purged of words regarded as inelegant and unnecessary, and as the rules of rhetoric were refined to the most dignified degree possible. Theatrical conditions were also quite different; in Paris, the proscenium theatre had became the norm for public as well as court performances, though there were significant variations between one theatre and the next. For instance, the elaborate Italianate machinery made possible by the proscenium arch was further developed and improved in France, a trend that culminated in the *Salle des machines*, a royal theatre designed expressly for the display of scenic wonders. At the other end of the scale were the theatres built in indoor tennis courts (a practice that would also be adopted in Restoration England). On these and other proscenium stages, plays would be presented with a simplicity comparable to that of the thrust stage of the English public theatre. Whereas in London this simplicity was intended as a sort of blank slate on which to imaginatively project the setting of each scene, the austerity of the Parisian stage provided a static, abstract backdrop for the characters and text. The members of the *Académie française* (the distinguished literary experts assembled by Cardinal Richelieu to pronounce on matters of literary etiquette) were all agreed that the "barbarity" of using the same space for multiple settings and times, as Shakespeare did, had no place in the French theatre. Instead, French drama was mainly set in an elegantly decorated but largely bare room, in which both private and public meetings might plausibly take place. As for dramatic action, certain plays, such as Molière's *Le Bourgeois gentilhomme,* might feature lots of spectacular dance, music, and moving scenery, but a serious poetic drama such as *Phèdre* was expected to be austerely presented with minimal action and spectacle.

In retrospect, it seems inevitable that the period of intense creativity that defined the Renaissance would eventually burn itself out. In Italy, while the *commedia dell'arte* continued to be popular, the literary drama became increasingly repetitive and lifeless during the seventeenth century. In Spain, the popular theatre of the Golden Age began its decline after the death of Pedro Calderón, Lope de Vega's great successor. For a time, as the court theatre grew more lucrative, the public theatre was sapped of vitality; then, with the war of the Spanish succession, it more or less fell into dormancy. In England, after a period of growing cynicism, the definite end of the Renaissance theatre came swiftly with the closing of the public playhouses by the Puritans in 1642. There was some small amount of theatrical activity during the interregnum, but the tradition of the Tudor and Stuart periods had been disrupted, and when the new public theatres opened in London in 1660, they would have a very different character. But by that point, the theatre of France was entering its prime, and the neoclassical conventions being perfected in that country would set new standards for theatre throughout Europe.

[C.S.W.]

CHRISTOPHER MARLOWE

Doctor Faustus

T he life of Christopher Marlowe (1564–1593) was short, scandalous, violent and brilliantly creative. The best known today of a group of Elizabethan writers known as the "university wits," Marlowe was not shy about showing his learning in his plays, and yet his mind seems never to have been unduly constrained by academic proprieties—of any kind. Indeed, during his lifetime there was an attempt by Cambridge University to disown association with the man who was to become one of its most famous graduates. After Marlowe completed his B.A., university officials suggested that he should be denied his M.A., citing not only his poor record of attendance, but also rumours that he privately practiced Roman Catholicism (which was at that time enduring a period of political suspicion). It is difficult to know how accurate such rumours are, especially when we hear that Marlowe was subsequently accused of atheism and also of homosexuality (technically a serious criminal offence at the time, though the law was enforced only capriciously). In any case, the Privy Council intervened on Marlowe's behalf at Cambridge, asking for lenience because Marlowe, they claimed, had been engaged "on matters touching the benefit of his country." This lent credence to another set of rumours: that Marlowe was working as an agent in the Queen's secret service. Indeed, some believe that it may have been the latter occupation—as opposed to mere drunkenness and belligerence (to which vices Marlowe was apparently no stranger)—that resulted in the violent manner of Marlowe's death: stabbed in the head in the course of a tavern brawl with some dubious characters with whom Marlowe had been drinking all day, until, allegedly, the rather large bill arrived and a quarrel began.

The notorious aspects of Marlowe's biography would be of little interest, however, were it not that these reinforce our impression of the daring originality and rather dangerous independence of thought evident in his plays. As befits a career that spanned barely six years, Marlowe's output was not especially prodigious; yet those few works he left behind show such a startling advance in many ways over the preceding English drama that he occupies a place of honour among English playwrights second only to that of his peer and successor, Shakespeare. Indeed, the heights which Marlowe's own work reaches, embracing technical achievements theretofore unknown in English drama, lends support to the notion that Faustus is an alter ego for the playwright: a sort of Icarus of the mind who dares to aspire well beyond the bounds of what had been readily possible—or permissible. This theme of "over-reaching" runs, in variations, throughout Marlowe's work: *Tamburlaine the Great* (1587–88) tells the story of a shepherd who becomes a world conqueror, singlemindedly seeking omnipotence through military domination until his destiny turns toward self-destruction. Similarly, in *The Jew of Malta* (c. 1590), Barabas seek vengeance with a singlemindedness that finds him eventually outside any restraints of morality or conscience, and the title character of *Edward II* (c. 1592) is a homosexual monarch who is determined to pursue his personal preference despite the violent political consequences.

But the most memorable and influential of all such characters found in Marlowe's work is certainly Faustus, who pursues personal knowledge and power in defiance of the explicit warnings of heaven itself. Indeed, one of the reasons that *Doctor Faustus* is so memorable, and has assumed such a central place in the imagination of Western civilization is that, despite all the passages that reiterate conventional Christian doctrine and spell out the consequences of Faustus's disobedience, his curiosity and aspirations emerge as somewhat heroic (however foolhardy) qualities. For in declining to heed religious admonition and instead pursuing personal ambition, Faustus can be seen as an embodiment of that intellectual passion which carried Western civilization out of the Middle Ages and through the Renaissance, and which, in a sense, continues to characterize our culture in the twenty-first century: the turning away from the strict observance of religious pieties to embrace instead the humanist aspiration to fulfill and even expand human potential.

Of course, Faustus achieves little of value as a result of his transgressions. But even in this irony, we may see parallels to the paths taken by Western civilization. We may observe that, for all the staggering advances we have made in technical prowess and the accumulation of knowledge over the last thousand years, and for all the progress we have made in ensuring that such knowledge is readily accessible to the vast majority of the population, on the whole, we human beings still find ourselves occupied more often than not in trivial, mindless, wasteful and destructive enterprises. From this perspective, however disappointing it may be, we should perhaps not be surprised to see Faustus drift into sensual indulgences and the playing of practical jokes. For, although Faustus is made virtually omnipotent (at least, within the limits of what is Lucifer's to bestow), he is, finally, still profoundly human.

Leaving aside the frustration that the actions of Faustus the character may arouse in us, it has always been frustrating to modern readers and audiences that, although many passages of *Doctor Faustus* show Marlowe working at the peak of his talents, the text that has come down to us is badly corrupt, containing some sections that most scholars doubt were written by Marlowe himself. Furthermore, the play exists in two distinct versions, one published in 1604 and one published in 1616. Both of these emerged well after the play was written, and neither appears to be wholly complete. However, it is the special virtue of Michael Keefer's outstanding edition, from which the following text has been adapted, that, while using the 1604 version as a basis, it also draws on the 1616 version. The result is the most plausible reconstruction of Marlowe's play yet published.

[C.S.W.]

CHRISTOPHER MARLOWE

The Tragical History of Doctor Faustus

DRAMATIS PERSONAE

  JOHN FAUSTUS, doctor of theology.
  WAGNER, a student, and Faustus's servant; also
    speaks the part of CHORUS.
  GOOD ANGEL.
  EVIL ANGEL.
  VALDES and CORNELIUS, magicians.
  THREE SCHOLARS, colleagues of Faustus at
    Wittenberg University.
  MEPHASTOPHILIS, a devil.
  CLOWN (ROBIN).
  RAFE, another clown.
  LUCIFER.
  BELZEBUB.
  THE SEVEN DEADLY SINS.
  POPE.
  CARDINAL OF LORRAINE.
  FRIAR.
  VINTNER.
  CHARLES V, Emperor of Germany.
  KNIGHT.
  ALEXANDER THE GREAT and his
    PARAMOUR, spirits.
  HORSE-COURSER.
  DUKE OF VANHOLT and his DUCHESS.
  HELEN OF TROY, a spirit.
  OLD MAN.
  Devils, Friars, Attendants.

PROLOGUE.

Enter Chorus.

Chorus. Not marching now in fields of Thracimene
  Where Mars did mate the Carthaginians,[1]

Nor sporting in the dalliance of love
In courts of kings where state is overturn'd,
Nor in the pomp of proud audacious deeds   5
Intends our muse to vaunt his heavenly verse.[2]
Only this, gentlemen: we must perform
The form of Faustus' fortunes, good or bad.
To patient judgments we appeal our plaud,[3]
And speak for Faustus in his infancy: 10
Now is he born, his parents base of stock,
In Germany, within a town call'd Rhodes;[4]
Of riper years to Wittenberg he went,[5]
Whereas his kinsmen chiefly brought him up.
So soon he profits in divinity,   15
The fruitful plot of scholarism grac'd,
That shortly he was grac'd with doctor's name,[6]
Excelling all whose sweet delight disputes[7]

---

    defeat upon the Romans at the battle of Lake Trasummenus in 217 B.C. The mention of Mars is an allusion to Livy's *Historiae* XXII. i. 8–12, according to which the battle was preceded by terrifying portents in which the war-god figured prominently. Since these portents demoralized the Romans, Livy's text could suggest either that Mars had allied himself with the Carthaginians or that he had rivalled them in destroying the Roman army.

[2] vaunt] display proudly.

[3] appeal our plaud] appeal for our applause.

[4] Rhodes] Roda (now Stadtroda), near Weimar.

[5] Wittenberg] The University of Wittenberg was famous under Martin Luther and Philipp Melanchthon as a Protestant centre of learning.

[6] grac'd] At Cambridge it was and still is by the "grace" or decree of the university Senate that degrees are conferred; Marlowe's name appears in the Grace Book in 1584 and 1587 for the B.A. and M.A. degrees respectively.

[7] whose sweet delight disputes] It is possible to construe "disputes" as a verb; more probably the expression is elliptical and means "whose sweet delight consists in disputes...."

---

[1] Mars did mate] Mars "allied himself with" or "rivalled." Hannibal's Carthaginian army inflicted a crushing

In heavenly matters of theology,
Till swoll'n with cunning of a self-conceit,[8]   20
His waxen wings did mount above his reach[9]
And melting heavens conspir'd his overthrow.
For falling to a devilish exercise,[10]
And glutted now with learning's golden gifts,   25
He surfeits upon cursed necromancy;[11]
Nothing so sweet as magic is to him,
Which he prefers before his chiefest bliss:
And this the man that in his study sits.

Exit.

ACT I

ACT I, SCENE I.

Faustus in his study.

Faustus. Settle thy studies Faustus, and begin
To sound the depth of that thou wilt profess.[12]
Having commenc'd, be a divine in show,[13]
Yet level at the end of every art,[14]
And live and die in Aristotle's works: 5
Sweet *Analytics*, 'tis thou hast ravish'd me—[15]

---

8 cunning] knowledge, erudition, cleverness; sometimes with negative connotations.

9 waxen wings] an allusion to the story of Icarus (cf. Ovid, *Metamorphoses* VIII. 183–235): escaping with his father Daedalus from Minos's island kingdom of Crete, Icarus ignored his father's warning about the wings he had made for them and flew too close to the sun. The episode was a favourite of Renaissance moralists and emblem writers.

10 falling to] These words link the metaphors of an Icarian (or Luciferian) fall and that of gluttonous surfeit.

11 necromancy] The A-text spelling ("Negromancy," corrected in B to "Necromancie") reflects a common medieval and early modern corruption of *necromantia* (divination by consultation of the dead) into *nigro-* or *negromantia* (black magic).

12 profess] affirm faith in or allegiance to.

13 commenc'd] taken a degree.

14 level at the end of every art] take aim at the final purpose or limit of every discipline.

15 *Analytics*] the name of two treatises on logic by Aristotle, whose works still dominated the university curriculum.

Bene disserere est finis logices.[16]
Is to dispute well logic's chiefest end?
Affords this art no greater miracle?
Then read no more, thou hast attain'd the end.   10
A greater subject fitteth Faustus' wit:[17]
Bid *on kai me on* farewell; Galen come,[18]
Seeing *ubi desinit philosophus, ibi incipit medicus.*[19]
Be a physician Faustus, heap up gold,
And be eterniz'd for some wondrous cure!   15
Summum bonum medicinae sanitas:[20]
The end of physic is our bodies' health.[21]
Why Faustus, hast thou not attain'd that end?
Is not thy common talk sound aphorisms?[22]
Are not thy bills hung up as monuments,   20
Whereby whole cities have escap'd the plague,
And thousand desperate maladies been eas'd?
Yet art thou still but Faustus, and a man.
Couldst thou make men to live eternally,
Or being dead, raise them to life again,   25
Then this profession were to be esteem'd.
Physic farewell; where is Justinian?
*Si una eademque res legatur duobus,
alter rem, alter valorem rei, etc.*[23]

---

16 *bene ... logices*] "To argue well is the end or purpose of logic" (a definition derived not from Aristotle but from Cicero).

17 wit] understanding.

18 *on kai me on*] a transliteration of Greek words meaning "being and not being." Again, the phrase is not Aristotelian; its source is a text of the sophist Gorgias, *On Nature or that which is not*, as preserved by the sceptic Sextus Empiricus in his *Adversus mathematicos*; Galen] Claudius Galenus (c. 130–200), a Greek who served as the personal physician of several Roman emperors, including Marcus Aurelius, is the most famous of ancient writers on medicine.

19 *ubi ... medicus*] "Where the philosopher leaves off, there the physician begins." Freely translated from Aristotle, *Sense and Sensibilia* 436a.

20 *Summum ... sanitas*] "The supreme good of medicine is health." Translated from Aristotle, *Nicomachean Ethics* 1094a.

21 physic] medicine.

22 sound aphorisms] reliable medical precepts.

23 *Si ... rei*] "If one and the same thing is bequeathed to two persons, one of them shall have the thing, the other the value of the thing." Derived in part from II.xx of

A petty case of paltry legacies! 30
Exhereditare filium non potest pater, nisi—[24]
Such is the subject of the *Institute*[25]
And universal body of the law.
This study fits a mercenary drudge
Who aims at nothing but external trash— 35
Too servile and illiberal for me.[26]
When all is done, divinity is best:
Jerome's Bible, Faustus, view it well.[27]
Stipendium peccati mors est. Ha! *Stipendium, etc.*[28]
The reward of sin is death? That's hard. 40
Si peccasse negamus, fallimur,
et nulla est in nobis veritas.[29]
If we say that we have no sin
We deceive ourselves, and there's no truth in us.
Why then belike we must sin, 45
And so consequently die.
Ay, we must die, an everlasting death.
What doctrine call you this? *Che sarà, sarà,*

What will be, shall be? Divinity, adieu![30]
These metaphysics of magicians[31] 50
And necromantic books are heavenly!
Lines, circles, seals, letters and characters:[32]
Ay, these are those that Faustus most desires,
O, what a world of profit and delight,
Of power, of honor, of omnipotence, 55
Is promis'd to the studious artisan![33]
All things that move between the quiet poles[34]
Shall be at my command. Emperors and kings
Are but obey'd in their several provinces,
Nor can they raise the wind, or rend the clouds;[35] 60
But his dominion that exceeds in this[36]
Stretcheth as far as doth the mind of man!
A sound magician is a mighty god:
Here tire, my brains, to get a deity![37]

Enter Wagner.

Wagner, commend me to my dearest friends, 65
The German Valdes and Cornelius;
Request them earnestly to visit me.
Wagner. I will, sir.

Exit.

---

the *Institutes*, a compilation of Roman law carried out at the command of the emperor Justinian in the sixth century.

[24] *Exhereditare … nisi*—] "A father cannot disinherit his son except—." An incomplete formulation of a rule from Justinian's *Institutes* II.xii.

[25] *Institute*] "Institute" here means "founding principle," and may refer also to Justinian's *Institutes*.

[26] Too servile] A contrast between the liberal arts and "servile" or "mechanical" studies and practices is an Elizabethan commonplace.

[27] Jerome's Bible] The Vulgate, prepared mainly by St. Jerome in the fourth century, was the Latin text of the Bible used by the Roman Catholic church.

[28] *Stipendium … est*] the first half of Romans 6:23, a verse which in the Geneva Bible is translated as follows: "For the wages of sin is death: but the gift of God is eternal life through Jesus Christ our Lord."

[29] *Si peccasse … veritas*] 1 John 1:8. Faustus has again quoted only the first half of an antithetical statement: he notices the condemnation of sinners by the law of God, but not the conditional promise of divine mercy which immediately follows in 1 John 1:9. In the Geneva Bible, 1 John 1:8–9 is rendered as follows: "If we say that we have no sin, we deceive our selves, and truth is not in us. If we acknowledge our sins, he is faithful and just, to forgive us our sins, and to cleanse us from all unrighteousness."

---

[30] What … adieu] Making a "despairing reference to the difficulties of the doctrine of predestination" (A.W. Ward), these words amount to a reprobate's version of the Calvinist teaching on this subject.

[31] metaphysics] the science of the supernatural.

[32] lines] a reference to the occult art of geomancy, or divination by means of astrologically determined patterns of points and lines; circles] A primary function of magic circles was to protect the practitioner of ceremonial magic from evil spirits; seals, letters and characters] talismanic symbols of the planets and of the angels, spiritual intelligences, and daemons that were believed to govern them.

[33] artisan] practitioner of an art.

[34] quiet poles] This could refer either to the poles of the outermost celestial sphere or, more probably, to those of the earth.

[35] raise the wind, or rend the clouds] a blasphemous echo of Jeremiah 10:13 (which speaks of God's power over clouds, lightning and wind).

[36] exceeds] excels.

[37] get] beget.

Faustus. Their conference will be a greater help to me[38]
    Than all my labors, plod I ne'er so fast.   70

Enter the Good Angel and the Evil Angel.

Good Ang. O Faustus, lay that damned book aside,
    And gaze not on it, lest it tempt thy soul
    And heap God's heavy wrath upon thy head!
    Read, read the Scriptures; that is blasphemy.
Evil Ang. Go forward, Faustus, in that famous art   75
    Wherein all nature's treasury is contain'd:
    Be thou on earth as Jove is in the sky,[39]
    Lord and commander of these elements![40]

Exeunt Angels.

Faustus. How am I glutted with conceit of this![41]
    Shall I make spirits fetch me what I please,   80
    Resolve me of all ambiguities,
    Perform what desperate enterprise I will?
    I'll have them fly to India for gold,[42]
    Ransack the ocean for orient pearl
    And search all corners of the new found world   85
    For pleasant fruits and princely delicates;
    I'll have them read me strange philosophy
    And tell the secrets of all foreign kings;
    I'll have them wall all Germany with brass
    And make swift Rhine circle fair Wittenberg;   90
    I'll have them fill the public schools with silk
    Wherewith the students shall be bravely clad;[43]
    I'll levy soldiers with the coin they bring,

And chase the Prince of Parma from our land[44]
And reign sole king of all our provinces;   95
Yea, stranger engines for the brunt of war[45]
Than was the fiery keel at Antwerp's bridge[46]
I'll make my servile spirits to invent.
Come, German Valdes and Cornelius,
And make me blest with your sage conference!   100

Enter Valdes and Cornelius.

    Valdes, sweet Valdes, and Cornelius,
    Know that your words have won me at the last
    To practise magic and concealed arts:
    Yet not your words only, but mine own fantasy,
    That will receive no object, for my head   105
    But ruminates on necromantic skill.[47]
    Philosophy is odious and obscure;
    Both law and physic are for petty wits;

---

38 conference] conversation.

39 Jove] The substitution of the supreme god of the pagan Roman pantheon for the Christian God is common in Renaissance humanist texts and in Elizabethan poetry.

40 these elements] earth, water, air and fire, here used as a metonymy for the world contained by the sphere of the moon which these elements were thought to constitute.

41 conceit of this] the thought, the notion of this.

42 India] a name applied to "both th'Indias of spice and mine" (Donne, "The Sun Rising"); here it seems to refer to the East Indies, as opposed to the Spanish conquests in "the new found world."

43 bravely] splendidly. University regulations forbade students to wear fine clothing: their scholars' gowns were to be made of woolen cloth in sombre colours, and silk-lined hoods could only be worn by the holders of doctoral degrees.

44 the Prince of Parma] Alessandro Farnese, Duke of Parma, a grandson of the emperor Charles V and the foremost general of his time. Parma served as Spanish governor of the Netherlands from 1578 until his death in 1592; he was hated by Protestants as a tyrant. He commanded the force that the Spanish Armada was to have transported across the Channel in 1588 for the invasion of England.

45 brunt] assault, onset.

46 fiery ... bridge] On April 4, 1585 the Netherlanders sent two fire-ships loaded with explosives against the pontoon bridge over the river Scheldt which formed part of Parma's siegeworks around Antwerp; one of them reached its target and destroyed part of the bridge, killing many Spanish soldiers. Parma had the bridge rebuilt, and Antwerp subsequently surrendered.

47 Yet ... skill] According to the influential theory of natural magic set out in Marsilio Ficino's *De vita coelitus comparanda* (1489), fantasy or imagination is the chief magical faculty; acting both internally and outside of the body, it links corporeal objects to the incorporeal subject, soul, or mind. The view that knowledge which comes to the body through the senses is assembled by the *sensus communis* (common sense) and passed upward to the faculty of fantasy or imagination was widely accepted in the sixteenth century. Faustus is saying that his ruminations on necromancy block his perceptions of external objects—a category which presumably includes the four chief academic disciplines, as *objecta intellectionis.*

Divinity is basest of the three,
Unpleasant, harsh, contemptible and vile; 110
'Tis magic, magic, that hath ravish'd me.
Then, gentle friends, aid me in this attempt,
And I, that have with concise syllogisms
Gravell'd the pastors of the German church[48]
And made the flowering pride of Wittenberg 115
Swarm to my problems as the infernal spirits
On sweet Musaeus when he came to hell,[49]
Will be as cunning as Agrippa was,
Whose shadows made all Europe honor him.[50]
Valdes. Faustus, these books, thy wit, and our 120
        experience
Shall make all nations canonize us.
As Indian Moors obey their Spanish lords,[51]
So shall the subjects of every element[52]
Be always serviceable to us three:
Like lions shall they guard us when we please, 125
Like Almain rutters with their horsemen's staves,[53]
Or Lapland giants trotting by our sides;
Sometimes like women, or unwedded maids,
Shadowing more beauty in their airy brows[54]
Than has the white breasts of the queen of love. 130
From Venice shall they drag huge Argosies,[55]

And from America the golden fleece
That yearly stuffs old Philip's treasury,[56]
If learned Faustus will be resolute.
Faustus. Valdes, as resolute am I in this 135
        As thou to live, therefore object it not.
Cornelius. The miracles that magic will perform
Will make thee vow to study nothing else.
He that is grounded in astrology,[57]
Enrich'd with tongues, well seen in minerals,[58] 140
Hath all the principles magic doth require.
Then doubt not, Faustus, but to be renown'd
And more frequented for this mystery[59]
Than heretofore the Delphian oracle.[60]
The spirits tell me they can dry the sea 145
And fetch the treasure of all foreign wrecks,
Ay, all the wealth that our forefathers hid
Within the massy entrails of the earth.[61]
Then tell me Faustus, what shall we three want?
Faustus. Nothing, Cornelius. O, this cheers my soul! 150
Come, show me some demonstrations magical,
That I may conjure in some lusty grove
And have these joys in full possession.
Valdes. Then haste thee to some solitary grove,
And bear wise Bacon's and Albanus' works,[62] 155

---

48 Gravell'd] confounded, embarrassed.
49 Musaeus] the legendary pre-Homeric Greek poet, a pupil of Orpheus. In Virgil's *Aeneid*, Musaeus is represented as standing in the midst of a crowd of spirits in the underworld, head and shoulders above the rest.
50 Agrippa … Whose shadows] Henricus Cornelius Agrippa of Nettesheim (1486–1535), said to be "the greatest conjurer in christendom." Agrippa distinguished in *De occulta philosophia* III.xlii between two kinds of necromancy: *necyomantia*, the reviving of corpses by means of a blood sacrifice, and *scyomantia*, in which only the *umbra* or shadow of a dead person is invoked.
51 Indian Moors] native peoples of the Americas.
52 subjects] a word close in meaning to the B-text's "spirits." "Subjects" carries the additional implication of obedience or subjection to a sovereign will (here, that of the magician).
53 Almain rutters] German cavalrymen; staves] lances.
54 shadowing] harbouring.
55 Argosies] ships of the city of Ragusa (now Dubrovnik), on the Dalmatian coast, known to the English as

Argouse, Argusa or Aragosa; by the late sixteenth century the word was generally applied to richly laden merchant ships.
56 golden … treasury] An annual plate-fleet shipped gold and silver from the Americas to Spain.
57 grounded in] firmly established in.
58 enrich'd with tongues] improved by knowledge of (ancient) languages. Latin was the common language of educated people in sixteenth-century Europe, while advanced humanist scholars, following the examples of Giovanni Pico, Johannes Reuchlin and Desiderius Erasmus, would be expected to study Greek, Hebrew, and possibly Aramaic and other languages as well; well seen in minerals] well versed in the properties of minerals.
59 frequented] sought out.
60 Delphian oracle] The oracle of Apollo at Delphi was the most famous and authoritative of ancient Greek oracles.
61 massy] heavy, massive.
62 wise Bacon's and Albanus's works] Roger Bacon (c. 1214–1294), an English Franciscan philosopher, was reputed also to have been a magician (cf. Robert

The Hebrew Psalter, and New Testament;
And whatsoever else is requisite
We will inform thee ere our conference cease.
Cornelius. Valdes, first let him know the words of art,
And then, all other ceremonies learn'd,   160
Faustus may try his cunning by himself.
Valdes. First I'll instruct thee in the rudiments,
And then wilt thou be perfecter than I.
Faustus. Then come and dine with me, and after meat
We'll canvas every quiddity thereof.[63]   165
For ere I sleep I'll try what I can do;
This night I'll conjure though I die therefore.

Exeunt.

ACT I, SCENE II.

Enter two scholars.

1 Sch. I wonder what's become of Faustus, that was
wont to make our schools ring with *sic probo*.[64]
2 Sch. That shall we presently know, for see: here
comes his boy.[65]

Enter Wagner.

1 Sch. How now sirrah, where's thy master?[66]   5
Wagner. God in heaven knows.
2 Sch. Why, dost not thou know?
Wagner. Yes, I know, but that follows not.

1 Sch. Go to sirrah, leave your jesting, and tell us
where he is.   10
Wagner. That follows not necessary by force of
argument, which you, being licentiate, should
stand upon; therefore acknowledge your error and
be attentive.[67]
2 Sch. Why, didst thou not say thou knew'st?   15
Wagner. Have you any witness on't?
1 Sch. Yes, sirrah, I heard you.
Wagner. Ask my fellow if I be a thief!
2 Sch. Well, you will not tell us.
Wagner. Yes sir, I will tell you; yet if you were not   20
dunces you would never ask me such a question,
for is not he *corpus naturale*, and is not that
mobile?[68] Then wherefore should you ask me such
a question? But that I am by nature phlegmatic,
slow to wrath and prone to lechery (to love I would   25
say), it were not for you to come within forty foot
of the place of execution—although I do not
doubt but to see you both hanged the next
sessions.[69] Thus having triumphed over you, I will
set my countenance like a precisian, and begin to   30
speak thus:[70] Truly, my dear brethren, my master
is within at dinner with Valdes and Cornelius, as
this wine if it could speak would inform your

Greene's play *Friar Bacon and Friar Bungay*). "Albanus"
is an error for Pietro d'Abano or Petrus de Aponus
(c. 1250–1316), a physician who was posthumously
convicted of sorcery and burned in effigy by the Inquisition, and whose *Heptameron* was printed together with
other works on magic in editions of Agrippa's *De occulta
philosophia*, beginning in 1567.
63 canvass every quiddity] discuss every essential particular.
64 *sic probo*] "Thus I prove"; the cry of triumph with which
Faustus, in "gravelling" one or another Lutheran theologian (I.i.114) in a scholastic disputation, would have
clinched his argument.
65 presently] at once.
66 sirrah] a term of address that expresses the speaker's contempt, the addressee's social inferiority, or both.

67 licentiate] licensed by an academic degree to proceed to
further studies; stand upon] insist on.
68 dunces] Renaissance humanists opposed both the hair-
splitting complexity of scholastic logic and the non-clas-
sical Latin of scholastic writers. As a result, the name of
Johannes Duns Scotus (c. 1265–1308), one of the most
subtle medieval logicians, came to denote sophistical
quibbling and, by extension, stupidity; *corpus naturale
... mobile*] "a body that is natural or subject to
change"—an adaptation of Aristotle's statement of the
subject-matter of physics.
69 place of execution] the scene of action; in this case, the
dining-room where (as Wagner will shortly reveal)
Faustus is conferring with Valdes and Cornelius. "To do
execution" could mean to eat heartily. Wagner at once
reverts to the more obvious meaning of the expression.
70 precisian] a puritan, one who is precise and scrupulous
about religious observances. Having parodied the logic
of scholastic disputation, Wagner proceeds to parody the
discourse of priestly or ministerial piety.

worships; and so the Lord bless you, preserve you, and keep you, my dear brethren, my dear brethren.[71]   35

Exit.

1 *Sch.* Nay then, I fear he is fallen into that damned art, for which they two are infamous through the world.

2 *Sch.* Were he a stranger, and not allied to me, yet should I grieve for him. But come, let us go and inform the Rector, and see if he by his grave counsel can reclaim him.   40

1 *Sch.* O, but I fear me nothing can reclaim him.

2 *Sch.* Yet let us try what we can do.   45

Exeunt.

ACT I, SCENE III.

Enter Faustus to conjure.

Faustus. Now that the gloomy shadow of the earth,
   Longing to view Orion's drizzling look,[72]
   Leaps from th'antarctic world unto the sky[73]
   And dims the welkin with her pitchy breath,
   Faustus, begin thine incantations,   5
   And try if devils will obey thy hest,
   Seeing thou hast pray'd and sacrific'd to them.
   Within this circle is Jehovah's name,

Forward and backward anagrammatiz'd,[74]
   The breviated names of holy saints,   10
   Figures of every adjunct to the heavens,[75]
   And characters of signs and erring stars[76]
   By which the spirits are enforc'd to rise;
   Then fear not, Faustus, but be resolute,
   And try the uttermost magic can perform.   15
Sint mihi dei Acherontis propitii! Valeat numen triplex Iehovae! Ignei, aerii, aquatici spiritus salvete! Orientis princeps Belzebub, inferni ardentis monarcha, et Demogorgon, propitiamus vos ut appareat et surgat Mephastophilis. Quid tu moraris?   20
Per Iehovam, Gehennam et consecratam aquam quam nunc spargo, signumque crucis quod nunc facio, et per vota nostra, ipse nunc surgat nobis dicatus Mephastophilis.[77]

Enter a devil.

I charge thee to return and change thy shape.   25
   Thou art too ugly to attend on me;
   Go, and return an old Franciscan friar:
   That holy shape becomes a devil best.

Exit devil.

---

71 the Lord bless you … and keep you] Numbers 6:24. This is the first verse of the priestly benediction delivered by God to Moses for transmission to Aaron and his sons as a formula with which they are to bless the Israelites. In quoting these words as an exit line, Wagner is mocking the language with which religious services were (and are) commonly brought to a close.

72 Orion's drizzling look] The constellation of Orion was associated in classical poetry with winter storms.

73 th'antarctic world] The thought that Marlowe held the view that night comes not from the east but from the southern hemisphere has troubled commentators. For observers in the northern hemisphere of a geocentric world, however, it is a matter of simple observation that after the sun sets in the west it sinks into the lower hemisphere, from which the shadow of the earth is therefore projected.

74 anagrammatiz'd] Cabalist mystics believed that hidden meanings were present in every possible recombination of letters in the Hebrew scriptures, and practitioners of Cabalistic magic saw the names of God in particular as containing occult secrets of divine power and knowledge.

75 adjunct to] heavenly body attached to.

76 characters of signs and erring stars] diagrams representing the constellations of the zodiac (one Latin term for which was *signa*) and the planets.

77 *Sint … Mephastophilis*] "May the gods of Acheron be propitious to me. Away with the threefold divinity of Jehovah! Hail, spirits of fire, air, and water! Belzebub, Prince of the East, monarch of burning hell, and Demogorgon, we invoke your favour that Mephastophilis may appear and ascend. Why do you delay? By Jehovah, Gehenna, and the holy water which I now sprinkle, by the sign of the cross which I now make, and by our vows, may Mephastophilis himself now rise to serve us!"; *Mephastophilis*] a compound of three Greek words indicating negation (*me*), light (*phos*), and loving (*philis*); in its original form, the name thus means "not-light-loving"—perhaps parodying the Latin Lucifer, "light-bearer."

I see there's virtue in my heavenly words,[78]
Who would not be proficient in this art?   30
How pliant is this Mephastophilis,
Full of obedience and humility:
Such is the force of magic and my spells!
Now, Faustus, thou art conjurer laureate[79]
That canst command great Mephastophilis!   35
Quin redis, Mephastophilis, fratris imagine![80]

Enter Mephastophilis.

Meph. Now, Faustus, what wouldst thou have me do?
Faustus. I charge thee wait upon me whilst I live
     To do whatever Faustus shall command,
     Be it to make the moon drop from her sphere   40
     Or the ocean to overwhelm the world.
Meph. I am a servant to great Lucifer,[81]
     And may not follow thee without his leave;
     No more than he commands must we perform.
Faustus. Did not he charge thee to appear to me?   45
Meph. No, I came hither of my own accord.
Faustus. Did not my conjuring speeches raise thee?
     Speak.
Meph. That was the cause, but yet *per accidens*,[82]
     For when we hear one rack the name of God,[83]
     Abjure the Scriptures and his saviour Christ,   50
     We fly, in hope to get his glorious soul;[84]
     Nor will we come unless he use such means
     Whereby he is in danger to be damn'd.
     Therefore the shortest cut for conjuring
     Is stoutly to abjure the Trinity,[85]   55
     And pray devoutly to the prince of hell.

Faustus. So Faustus hath already done,
     And holds this principle:
     There is no chief but only Belzebub,
     To whom Faustus doth dedicate himself.   60
     This word "damnation" terrifies not him,
     For he confounds hell in Elysium:[86]
     His ghost be with the old philosophers!
     But leaving these vain trifles of men's souls,
     Tell me, what is that Lucifer thy lord?   65
Meph. Arch-regent and commander of all spirits.
Faustus. Was not that Lucifer an angel once?
Meph. Yes Faustus, and most dearly lov'd of God.
Faustus. How comes it then that he is prince of devils?
Meph. O, by aspiring pride and insolence,   70
     For which God threw him from the face of heaven.
Faustus. And what are you that live with Lucifer?
Meph. Unhappy spirits that fell with Lucifer,
     Conspir'd against our God with Lucifer,
     And are for ever damn'd with Lucifer.   75
Faustus. Where are you damn'd?
Meph.   In hell.
Faustus. How comes it then that thou art out of hell?
Meph. Why this is hell, nor am I out of it:
     Think'st thou that I who saw the face of God
     And tasted the eternal joys of heaven   80
     Am not tormented with ten thousand hells
     In being depriv'd of everlasting bliss?
     O Faustus, leave these frivolous demands,
     Which strike a terror to my fainting soul.
Faustus. What, is great Mephastophilis so passionate[87]   85
     For being deprived of the joys of heaven?
     Learn thou of Faustus manly fortitude
     And scorn those joys thou never shalt possess.
     Go, bear these tidings to great Lucifer:
     Seeing Faustus hath incurr'd eternal death   90
     By desperate thoughts against Jove's deity,
     Say he surrenders up to him his soul,
     So he will spare him four and twenty years,[88]
     Letting him live in all voluptuousness,

---

78   virtue] power; also, ironically, moral virtue.
79   laureate] crowned with laurel; of proved distinction.
80   *Quin ... imagine*] "Why do you not return, Mephastophilis, in the shape of a friar!"
81   Lucifer] The name appears in Isaiah 14:12.
82   *per accidens*] The scholastics distinguished between an efficient cause, i.e., an agent which itself produced an effect, and a cause *per accidens*, which was related to the final effect only in the sense of having provided an occasion for the intervention of some external agent.
83   rack] torture.
84   glorious] splendid; possibly also boastful (the root meaning of *gloriosus*).
85   stoutly] courageously, resolutely.

---

86   confounds hell in Elysium] identifies hell with Elysium; confuses the two; undoes hell through belief in Elysium (in ancient Greece, the place in the afterworld reserved for heroes).
87   passionate] subject to strong emotion.
88   So] on condition that.

Having thee ever to attend on me 95
To give me whatsoever I shall ask,
To tell me whatsoever I demand,
To slay mine enemies and aid my friends,
And always be obedient to my will.
Go, and return to mighty Lucifer, 100
And meet me in my study at midnight,
And then resolve me of thy master's mind.
Meph. I will, Faustus.

Exit.

Faustus. Had I as many souls as there be stars
I'd give them all for Mephastophilis! 105
By him I'll be a great emperor of the world,
And make a bridge thorough the moving air[89]
To pass the ocean with a band of men;
I'll join the hills that bind the Afric shore,
And make that country continent to Spain,[90] 110
And both contributory to my crown;
The emperor shall not live but by my leave,
Nor any potentate of Germany.
Now that I have obtain'd what I desire,
I'll live in speculation of this art 115
Till Mephastophilis return again.

Exit.

ACT I, SCENE IV.

Enter Wagner and the Clown.[91]

Wagner. Sirrah boy, come hither.
Clown. How, "boy"? Swowns boy, I hope you have
seen many boys with such pickadevaunts as I
have.[92] "Boy," quotha?

Wagner. Tell me sirrah, hast thou any comings in?[93] 5
Clown. Ay, and goings out too, you may see else.[94]
Wagner. Alas, poor slave: see how poverty jesteth in
his nakedness. The villain is bare, and out of
service, and so hungry that I know he would give
his soul to the devil for a shoulder of mutton, 10
though it were blood raw.[95]
Clown. How, my soul to the devil for a shoulder of
mutton though 'twere blood raw? Not so, good
friend: b'urlady I had need have it well roasted, and
good sauce to it, if I pay so dear.[96] 15
Wagner. Well, wilt thou serve me, and I'll make thee
go like *Qui mihi discipulus?*[97]
Clown. How, in verse?
Wagner. No sirrah, in beaten silk and stavesacre.[98]
Clown. How, how, knave's acre? Ay, I thought that 20
was all the land his father left him. Do ye hear, I
would be sorry to rob you of your living.
Wagner. Sirrah, I say in stavesacre!
Clown. Oho, oho, stavesacre! Why then belike, if I
ere your man I should be full of vermin.[99] 25
Wagner. So thou shalt, whether thou beest with me
or no. But sirrah, leave your jesting, and bind
yourself presently unto me for seven years, or I'll
turn all the lice about thee into familiars, and they
shall tear thee to pieces.[100] 30

---

89 thorough] The distinction between "through" and "thorough", like that between "travail" and "travel", is a modern one.

90 continent to] continuous with.

91 *Clown*] a boorish rustic, a fool. This character is presumably to be identified with the Robin of II.ii and III.ii.

92 Swowns] a contraction of "God's wounds"; picka-
devaunt] a short beard trimmed to a point; apparently
from the French *piqué devant*, "peaked in front" (although the compound word is unknown in French). In
this passage one may suspect an obscene *double entendre*.

93 comings in] earnings.

94 goings out] expenses; a punning reference to the fact
that the Clown is bursting out of his tattered clothes.

95 out of service] unemployed.

96 b'urlady] a contraction of "by Our Lady."

97 *Qui mihi discipulus*] "You who are my pupil." The opening words of *Ad suos discipulus monita paedagogica, seu
carmen de moribus* ("Teacherly admonition to his pupils,
or poem of conduct"), a didactic poem by William Lily
(c. 1466–1522) which appears in all of the many editions of *A Shorte Introduction of Grammar*, the standard
elementary Latin textbook used in Elizabethan schools.

98 beaten silk] embroidered silk; with a punning suggestion that Wagner will thrash his servant; stavesacre] a
preparation against lice made from the seeds of a plant
related to the delphinium.

99 belike] in all likelihood.

100 seven years] the standard period of time for an appren-
ticeship or a contract of indentured labour; famil-
iars] Witches and sorcerers were commonly believed to
have attendant spirits who took the form of animals.

Clown. Do you hear, sir? You may save that labor: they are too familiar with me already, swowns they are as bold with my flesh as if they had paid for my meat and drink.

Wagner. Well, do you hear, sirrah? Hold, take these guilders. 35

Clown. Gridirons, what be they?

Wagner. Why, French crowns.

Clown. Mass, but for the name of French crowns, a man were as good have as many English counters.[101] And what should I do with these? 40

Wagner. Why now, sirrah, thou art at an hour's warning whensoever or wheresoever the devil shall fetch thee.

Clown. No, no; here, take your gridirons again. 45

Wagner. Truly, I'll none of them.

Clown. Truly, but you shall.

Wagner. Bear witness I gave them him!

Clown. Bear witness I give them you again!

Wagner. Well, I will cause two devils presently to fetch thee away. Baliol, and Belcher![102] 50

Clown. Let your Balio and Belcher come here, and I'll knock them, they were never so knocked since they were devils! Say I should kill one of them, what would folks say? "Do ye see yonder tall fellow 55

in the round slop, he has killed the devil": so I should be called "kill-devil" all the parish over.[103]

Enter two devils, and the clown runs up and down crying.

Wagner. Balio and Belcher, spirits away!

Exeunt.

Clown. What, are they gone? A vengeance on them, they have vile long nails. There was a he-devil and 60 a she-devil. I'll tell you how you shall know them: all he-devils has horns, and all she-devils has clefts and cloven feet.[104]

Wagner. Well sirrah, follow me.

Clown. But do you hear: If I should serve you, would 65 you teach me to raise up Banios and Belcheos?

Wagner. I will teach thee to turn thyself to anything: to a dog, or a cat, or a mouse, or a rat, or any thing.

Clown. How? A Christian fellow to a dog or a cat, a 70 mouse or a rat? No, no, sir. If you turn me into anything, let it be in the likeness of little pretty frisking flea, that I may be here and there and everywhere: O, I'll tickle the pretty wenches' plackets, I'll be amongst them i'faith![105] 75

Wagner. Well sirrah, come.

Clown. But do you hear, Wagner?

Wagner. How? Baliol and Belcher!

Clown. O Lord! I pray sir, let Banio and Belcher go sleep. 80

Wagner. Villain, call me Master Wagner, and see that you walk attentively, and let your right eye be always diametrally fixed upon my left heel, that thou mayest *quasi vestigiis nostris insitere.*[106]

Exit.

---

101 guilders … French crowns … English counters] Wagner professes to give the Clown Dutch guilders. Observing, it would seem, that the coins have holes punched in them, the Clown mis-hears the word as "gridirons"— whereupon Wagner re-identifies the coins as French crowns. A proclamation of 1587 authorized members of the public to strike holes in French crowns, which in the late 1580s and early 1590s were notoriously debased, and often counterfeit. From the sixteenth until the early nineteenth century, English merchants issued privately minted counters or tokens which circulated without of course having any officially accepted value; "counter" often denoted a debased or counterfeit coin; Mass] an oath: "by the Mass."

102 Baliol] a deformation of "Belial," a name which occurs in the Bible (e.g., 2 Cor. 6:15) with a possible pun on Belly-all. If the name of Belcher helps to activate the same pun, then the demons' names in this scene resonate with the motif of surfeiting that appears elsewhere in the play.

---

103 tall] valiant, handsome; round slop] baggy breeches.

104 horns] standard demonic equipment, perhaps with an overtone of cuckoldry. The pairing of "horns" with "clefts" may also give the word phallic overtones; clefts] vulvas.

105 placket] pocket in a woman's skirt; metaphorically a woman's genitals.

106 *quasi vestigiis nostris insitere*] "as if walking in our footsteps."

Clown. God forgive me, he speaks Dutch fustian.[107]   85
  Well, I'll follow him, I'll serve him, that's flat.

Exit.

ACT II

ACT II, SCENE I.

Enter Faustus in his study.

Faustus. Now Faustus, must thou needs be damn'd,
  And canst thou not be saved.
  What boots it then to think of God or heaven?[108]
  Away with such vain fancies, and despair,
  Despair in God, and trust in Belzebub.   5
  Now go not backward: no Faustus, be resolute.
  Why waverest thou? O, something soundeth in
    mine ears:
  "Abjure this magic, turn to God again."
  Ay, and Faustus will turn to God again.
  To God? He loves thee not;   10
  The god thou serv'st is thine own appetite,
  Wherein is fix'd the love of Belzebub:
  To him I'll build an altar and a church,
  And offer lukewarm blood of new-born babes!

Enter Good Angel, and Evil.

Good Ang. Sweet Faustus, leave that execrable art.   15
Faustus. Contrition, prayer, repentance: what of these?
Good Ang. O, they are means to bring thee unto heaven.
Evil Ang. Rather illusions, fruits of lunacy,
  That makes men foolish that do trust them most.
Good Ang. Sweet Faustus, think of heaven and
    heavenly things.   20
Evil Ang. No Faustus, think of honor and of wealth.

Exeunt Angels.

Faustus. Of wealth?
  Why, the signory of Emden shall be mine![109]

When Mephastophilis shall stand by me
What God can hurt me? Faustus, thou art safe;[110]   25
Cast no more doubts. Come, Mephastophilis,[111]
And bring glad tidings from great Lucifer![112]
Is't not midnight? Come Mephastophilis,
Veni, veni, Mephastophilis![113]

Enter Mephastophilis.

  Now tell me, what says Lucifer thy lord?   30
Meph. That I shall wait on Faustus whilst he lives,
  So he will buy my service with his soul.
Faustus. Already Faustus hath hazarded that for thee.
Meph. But now thou must bequeath it solemnly,
  And write a deed of gift with thine own blood,   35
  For that security craves great Lucifer.
  If thou deny it I will back to hell.
Faustus. Stay Mephastophilis, and tell me,
  What good will my soul do thy lord?
Meph. Enlarge his kingdom.   40
Faustus. Is that the reason why he tempts us thus?
Meph. Solamen miseris socios habuisse doloris.[114]
Faust. Why, have you any pain that tortures others?
Meph. As great as have the human souls of men.
  But tell me, Faustus, shall I have thy soul?   45
  And I will be thy slave and wait on thee,
  And give thee more than thou hast wit to ask.
Faustus. Ay Mephastophilis, I give it thee,
Meph. Then stab this arm courageously,
  And bind thy soul, that at some certain day   50
  Great Lucifer may claim it as his own:
  And then be thou as great as Lucifer!
Faustus. Lo Mephastophilis, for love of thee
  I cut mine arm, and with my proper blood[115]
  Assure my soul to be great Lucifer's,   55

---

107 fustian] bombast, nonsense. Fustian was a coarse cloth made of cotton and flax; the word was metaphorically applied to inflated or inappropriately lofty language.
108 boots] avails.
109 signory] lordship, rule; Emden] a prosperous port in northwest Germany which conducted an extensive trade with England.

---

110 When … me?] a blasphemous distortion of Romans 8:31: "If God be on our side, who can be against us?"
111 Cast] emit, ponder.
112 glad tidings] Compare Luke 2:10: "I bring you glad tidings of great joy."
113 *Veni, veni, Mephastophilis!*] "Come, O come, Mephastophilis!"—a blasphemous echo of the twelfth-century Advent hymn *Veni, veni, Emmanuel.*
114 *Solamen … doloris*] "It is a comfort to the wretched to have had companions in misfortune."
115 proper] own.

Chief lord and regent of perpetual night.
View here the blood that trickles from mine arm,
And let it be propitious for my wish.
Meph. But Faustus, thou must
  Write it in manner of a deed of gift.[116]   60
Faustus. Ay, so I will. But Mephastophilis,
  My blood congeals, and I can write no more.
Meph. I'll fetch thee fire to dissolve it straight.

Exit.

Faustus. What might the staying of my blood portend?
  Is it unwilling I should write this bill?[117]   65
  Why streams it not, that I may write afresh?
  "Faustus gives to thee his soul": ah, there it stay'd.
  Why should'st thou not? Is not thy soul thine own?
  Then write again: "Faustus gives to thee his soul."

Enter Mephastophilis with a chafer of coals.[118]

Meph. Here's fire: come Faustus, set it on.   70
Faustus. So: now the blood begins to clear again;
  Now will I make an end immediately.
Meph. [*aside*] O, what will not I do to obtain his soul!
Faustus. Consummatum est: this bill is ended,[119]
  And Faustus hath bequeath'd his soul to Lucifer.   75
  But what is this inscription on mine arm?
  Homo fuge! Whither should I fly?[120]
  If unto God he'll throw thee down to hell.
  My senses are deceiv'd: here's nothing writ.
  O yes, I see it plain! Even here is writ   80
  Homo fuge; yet shall not Faustus fly.

---

116 deed] a legally binding document.

117 bill] contract.

118 *chafer*] a kind of saucepan or chafing-dish, in this case
    apparently with a grate over which other dishes could
    be heated.

119 *Consummatum est*] "It is finished." According to the gos-
    pel of John, these were the last words of Jesus on the
    cross (John 19:30).

120 *Homo fuge*] "Man, flee!" The Latin words occur in the
    Vulgate text of 1 Timothy 6:11, but this line as a whole
    alludes more distinctly to Psalm 139:7–8: "Whither
    shall I go from thy spirit? or whither shall I flee from
    thy presence? If I ascend into heaven, thou art there: if
    I lie down in hell, thou art there."

Meph. I'll fetch him somewhat to delight his mind.

Exit.

*Enter with devils, giving crowns and rich apparel to
Faustus, and dance, and then [the devils] depart.*

Faustus. Speak Mephastophilis: what means this show?
Meph. Nothing, Faustus, but to delight thy mind,
  And let thee see what magic can perform.   85
Faustus. But may I raise such spirits when I please?
Meph. Ay Faustus, and do greater things than these.
Faustus. Then there's enough for a thousand souls!
  Here Mephastophilis, receive this scroll,
  A deed of gift, of body and of soul: 90
  But yet conditionally, that thou perform
  All articles prescrib'd between us both.
Meph. Faustus, I swear by hell and Lucifer
  To effect all promises between us made.
Faustus. Then hear me read them.   95
  On these conditions following:
  *First, that Faustus may be a spirit in form and
    substance;*
  *Secondly, that Mephastophilis shall be his servant,
    and at his command;*
  *Thirdly, that Mephastophilis shall do for him, and
    bring him whatsoever;*
  Fourthly, that he shall be in his chamber or house   100
    invisible;
  *Lastly, that he shall appear to the said John Faustus
    at all times, in what form or shape soever he please;*
  *I, John Faustus of Wittenberg, Doctor, by these
    presents*[121] *do give both body and soul to Lucifer,*
  Prince of the East, and his minister Mephastophilis,   105
  *and furthermore grant unto him that four and twenty
    years being expired, and these articles above written
    being inviolate, full power to fetch or carry the said
    John Faustus, body and soul, flesh, blood, or goods,
    into their habitation wheresoever.*   110
            By me, John Faustus.
Meph. Speak Faustus, do you deliver this as your deed?
Faustus. Ay, take it, and the devil give thee good on't.
Meph. So. Now, Faustus, ask me what thou wilt.
Faustus. First will I question with thee about hell.   115
  Tell me, where is the place that men call hell?

---

121 *these presents*] the legal articles.

Meph. Under the heavens.

Faustus. Ay, so are all things else; but whereabouts?

Meph. Within the bowels of these elements,[122]
   Where we are tortur'd and remain forever.   120
   Hell hath no limits, nor is circumscrib'd
   In one self place, but where we are is hell,[123]
   And where hell is there must we ever be;
   And to be short, when all the world dissolves
   And every creature shall be purify'd,   125
   All places shall be hell that is not heaven.

Faustus. Come, I think hell's a fable.

Meph. Ay, think so still, till experience change thy
   mind.

Faustus. Why, think'st thou then that Faustus shall
   be damn'd?

Meph. Ay, of necessity, for here's the scroll   130
   Wherein thou hast given thy soul to Lucifer.

Faustus. Ay, and body too, but what of that?
   Think'st thou that Faustus is so fond to imagine[124]
   That after this life there is any pain?
   Tush, these are trifles and mere old wives' tales.   135

Meph. But I am an instance to prove the contrary,
   For I tell thee I am damn'd, and now in hell.

Faustus. Nay, and this be hell, I'll willingly be damn'd!
   What, sleeping, eating, walking and disputing?
   But leaving this, let me have a wife, the fairest maid   140
   in Germany, for I am wanton and lascivious, and
   cannot live without a wife.

Meph. How, a wife? I prithee Faustus, talk not of a
   wife.

Faustus. Nay, sweet Mephastophilis, fetch me one, for   145
   I will have one.

Meph. Well, thou wilt have one. Sit there till I come;
   I'll fetch thee a wife in the devil's name.

Enter a devil dressed like a woman, with fireworks.[125]

Meph. Tell, Faustus: how dost thou like thy wife?

Faustus. A plague on her for a hot whore!   150

[Exit devil.]

Meph. Tut Faustus, marriage is but a ceremonial toy.[126]
   If thou lov'st me, think no more of it.
   I'll cull thee out the fairest courtesans
   And bring them every morning to thy bed.
   She whom thine eye shall like, thy heart shall have,   155
   Be she as chaste as was Penelope,[127]
   As wise as Saba, or as beautiful[128]
   As was bright Lucifer before his fall.
   Hold, take this book: peruse it thoroughly.
   The iterating of these lines brings gold;   160
   The framing of this circle on the ground
   Brings whirlwinds, tempests, thunder and
     lightning.
   Pronounce this thrice devoutly to thyself,
   And men in armor shall appear to thee,
   Ready to execute what thou desir'st.   165

Faustus. Thanks, Mephastophilis; yet fain would I
   have a book wherein I might behold all spells and
   incantations, that I might raise up spirits when I
   please.

Meph. Here they are in this book.   170

They turn to them.

Faustus. Now would I have a book where I might see
   all characters and planets of the heavens, that I
   might know their motions and dispositions.[129]

Meph. Here they are too.

Turn to them.

Faustus. Nay, let me have one book more, and then   175
   I have done, wherein I might see all plants, herbs,
   and trees that grow upon the earth.

Meph. Here thy be.

---

122 these elements] earth, water, air and fire, which were
   held to make up the world up to the sphere of the
   moon.
123 self] single, particular.
124 fond] foolish.
125 *fireworks*] In the comic sequences of sixteenth-century
   pageants and plays, fireworks were often attached to the
   costumes of devils and clowns in ways designed to make
   fun of sexual and excretory functions.

---

126 toy] trifle.
127 Penelope] the faithful wife of Odysseus.
128 Saba] the Queen of Sheba, who in 1 Kings 10:1–13
   comes to Jerusalem to test King Solomon's knowledge
   of God with "hard questions."
129 characters] talismanic symbols of the planets and of the
   spiritual powers that govern them.

Faustus. O, thou art deceived.
Meph. Tut, I warrant thee.[130]   180

Turn to them.

Exeunt.

ACT II, SCENE II.

Enter Robin the ostler with a book in his hand.

Robin. O, this is admirable! Here I ha' stolen one of Doctor Faustus' conjuring books, and i'faith I mean to search some circles for my own use: now will I make all the maidens in our parish dance at my pleasure stark naked before me, and so by that means I shall see more than I ever felt, or saw yet.[131]   5

Enter Rafe, calling Robin.

Rafe. Robin, prithee come away! There's a gentleman tarries to have his horse, and he would have his things rubbed and made clean: he keeps such a chafing with my mistress about it, and she has sent me to look thee out; prithee come away!   10

Robin. Keep out, keep out, or else you are blown up, you are dismembered. Rafe! Keep out, for I am about a roaring piece of work.[132]   15

Rafe. Come, what dost thou with that same book? Thou canst not read.

Robin. Yes, my master and mistress shall find that I can read: he for his forehead, she for her private study.[133] She's born to bear with me, or else my art fails.[134]   20

Rafe. Why Robin, what book is that?

Robin. What book? Why, the most intolerable book for conjuring that e'er was invented by any brimstone devil!   25

Rafe. Canst thou conjure with it?

Robin. I can do all these things easily with it: first, I can make thee drunk with hippocras at any tavern in Europe for nothing; that's one of my conjuring works.[135]   30

Rafe. Our master parson says that's nothing.

Robin. True, Rafe. And more, Rafe, if thou hast any mind to Nan Spit our kitchen maid, then turn her and wind her to thine own use, as often as thou wilt, and at midnight.[136]   35

Rafe. O brave Robin, shall I have Nan Spit, and to mine own use? On that condition I'll feed thy devil with horse-bread as long as he lives, of free cost.[137]

Robin. No more, sweet Rafe: let's go and make clean our boots which lie foul upon our hands; and then to our conjuring, in the devil's name!   40

Exeunt.

ACT II, SCENE III.

Enter Faustus in his study, and Mephastophilis.

Faustus. When I behold the heavens then I repent
And curse thee, wicked Mephastophilis,
Because thou hast depriv'd me of those joys.

Meph. Why Faustus,
Think'st thou heaven is such a glorious thing?   5
I tell thee 'tis not half so fair as thou
Or any man that breathes on earth.

---

130 I warrant thee] I assure you (that the book contains all that I say it does).

131 circles] magic circles, and also women's vaginas.

132 roaring] noisy, riotous.

133 forehead] A deceived husband or cuckold was said to wear horns on his forehead; private study] with a quibble on private parts.

134 to bear with] to put up with; also (another bawdy quibble) to lie under, to bear the weight of his body.

135 hippocras] wine flavoured with spices.

136 Nan Spit … turn her and wind her] One of the humblest occupations in the kitchen of a large household or inn was that of the turnspit, whose job was to stand by the open fireplace and crank the horizontally mounted spit on which roasting meat was impaled. Robin tempts Rafe with the thought of sexually impaling and "turning" this kitchen maid—of treating her, in effect, as she treats a roast of meat.

137 horse-bread] bread made of beans, bran, etc. for horses—but apparently sometimes eaten also by the very poor. Rafe seems to be aware of the popular superstition according to which familiar spirits took the form of animals, and were fed like pets by the witches to whom they attached themselves.

Faustus. How prov'st thou that?

Meph.   'Twas made for man,
  Therefore is man more excellent.

Faustus. If it were made for man, 'twas made for me: 10
  I will renounce this magic and repent.[138]

Enter Good Angel and Evil Angel.

Good Ang. Faustus, repent yet, God will pity thee.

Evil Ang. Thou art a spirit, God cannot pity thee.

Faustus. Who buzzeth in mine ears I am a spirit?[139]
  Be I a devil, yet God may pity me.   15
  Ay, God will pity me if I repent.

Evil Ang. Ay, but Faustus never shall repent.

Exeunt Angels.

Faustus. My heart's so harden'd I cannot repent.[140]
  Scarce can I name salvation, faith, or heaven,
  But fearful echoes thunders in mine ears,   20
  "Faustus, thou art damn'd!" Then swords and
    knives,
  Poison, guns, halters, and envenom'd steel[141]
  Are laid before me to dispatch myself,
  And long ere this I should have done the deed
  Had not sweet pleasure conquer'd deep despair.   25
  Have I not made blind Homer sing to me

Of Alexander's love and Oenon's death?[142]
And hath not he that built the walls of Thebes
With ravishing sound of his melodious harp[143]
Made music with my Mephastophilis?   30
Why should I die, then, or basely despair?
I am resolv'd: Faustus shall ne'er repent.
Come Mephastophilis, let us dispute again,
And reason of divine astrology.[144]
Speak, are there many spheres above the moon?[145]   35

---

[138] lines 1–10.] These exchanges between Faustus and Mephastophilis reflect the movement of Psalm 8:3–6, in which a contemplation of the creation leads first to a recognition of divine majesty ("When I behold thine heavens, even the work of thy fingers … What is man, say I, that thou art mindful of him?"), and then to what might be read as a contrasting emphasis upon human dignity ("thou hast made him a little lower than God … Thou hast made him to have dominion over the works of thy hands"). If Mephastophilis makes sophistical use of this pattern, Faustus seems inclined rather to recognize that "The heavens declare the glory of God, and the firmament showeth the work of his hands" (Psalm 19:1).

[139] buzzeth] whispers.

[140] My heart's so harden'd] Taking their cue from God's hardening of Pharaoh's heart in Exodus 4:21; 7:3, 13; and 10:1, 20, 27, Calvinists understood an impenitent hardness, whether wavering or obdurate, as a condition determined by the will of God.

[141] halters] hangman's nooses.

[142] Alexander's love and Oenon's death] These are matters which Homer left unsung; Faustus would have been the first to hear them from his lips. Paris (also named Alexandros), a son of King Priam and Queen Hecuba of Troy, was cast out by his parents (for it was prophesied that he should cause the destruction of Troy) and brought up among the shepherds of Mount Ida, where he won the love of Oenone. Asked by Hera, Athena, and Aphrodite to award a golden apple to the most beautiful goddess, he succumbed to Aphrodite's bribe of the love of the fairest woman alive, abandoned Oenone and abducted Helen from Sparta, thus provoking the Trojan War. Later, having been wounded by a poisoned arrow he could have been healed only by Oenone; after jealously refusing to cure him, she was overwhelmed by remorse and threw herself onto his funeral pyre.

[143] he … harp] Amphion and his brother built the walls of Thebes; the music of Amphion's lyre magically moved huge stones into place.

[144] astrology] not clearly distinguished from astronomy until the seventeenth century.

[145] lines 35–62.] The elements (earth, water, air, and fire) that make up "the substance of this centric earth" were thought to be concentrically disposed; so also, in the old geocentric cosmology, were the spheres that governed the motions of those wandering or "erring" stars, the planets. Mephastophilis says there are nine spheres: those of the planets, including the moon and the sun; the firmament, to which the fixed stars are attached; and the empyrean, the outermost and motionless sphere of the universe. (He apparently conflates the *primum mobile*, thought of by some astronomers as a distinct sphere that imparts motion to the heavens, with the firmament.) All of this is utterly commonplace. The systems developed by ancient astronomers were enormously more complex: Eudoxus (fourth century B.C.) required twenty-seven, and Ptolemy (second century A.D.) more than eighty variously revolving spheres, including epicyclic and eccentric ones, to explain the motions of the planets.

Are celestial bodies but one globe,
As is the substance of this centric earth?
Meph. As are the elements, such are the heavens,
    Even from the moon unto the empyreal orb,
    Mutually folded on each other's spheres,   40
    And jointly move upon one axle-tree
    Whose termine is term'd the world's wide pole.
    Nor are the names of Saturn, Mars, or Jupiter
    Feign'd, but are erring stars.
Faustus. But tell me, have they all one motion, both   45
    situ et tempore?[146]
Meph. All jointly move from east to west in four and
    twenty hours upon the poles of the world, but
    differ in their motions upon the poles of the
    zodiac.
Faustus. These slender questions Wagner can decide: 50
    Hath Mephastophilis no greater skill?
    Who knows not the double notion of the planets?[147]
    The first is finish'd in a natural day,
    The second thus: Saturn in thirty years,
    Jupiter in twelve, Mars in four, the Sun, Venus, and   55
    Mercury in a year, the Moon in twenty-eight
    days.[148] Tush, these are freshmen's suppositions!
    But tell me, hath every sphere a dominion or
    intelligentia?[149]

Meph. Ay.   60
Faustus. How many planets or spheres are there?
Meph. Nine: the seven planets, the firmament, and
    the empyreal heaven.
Faustus. But is there not *coelum igneum, et crystal-*
    linum?[150]   65
Meph. No Faustus, they be but fables.
Faustus. Resolve me then in this one question: Why
    are not conjunctions, oppositions, aspects, eclipses
    all at one time, but in some years we have more,
    in some less?[151]   70
Meph. Per inaequalem motum respectu totius.[152]
Faustus. Well, I am answered. Now tell me who made
    the world.
Meph. I will not.
Faustus. Sweet Mephastophilis, tell me.   75
Meph. Move me not, Faustus.[153]
Faustus. Villain, have I not bound thee to tell me
    any thing?
Meph. Ay, that is not against our kingdom.
    This is. Thou are damn'd, think thou of hell.
Faustus. Think, Faustus, upon God that made the   80
    world!
Meph. Remember this.

Exit.

Faustus. Ay, go accursed spirit to ugly hell:
    'Tis thou hast damn'd distressed Faustus' soul.
    Is't not too late?

Enter Good Angel and Evil Angel.

Evil Ang.   Too late.
Good Ang. Never too late, if Faustus can repent.[154]   85

---

[146] *situ et tempore*] "in position and time"; i.e., in the direction of their revolutions around the earth and in the
time these take.

[147] poles of the world … poles of the zodiac … the double
motion of the planets] The apparent diurnal motion of
the planetary spheres "upon one axle-tree" (the northern "termine" of which nearly coincides with the star Po-
laris) is of course due, in post-Copernican terms, to the
earth's rotation upon its axis. The second component of
the planets' apparent "double motion" is an effect of the
differences between the earth's period of revolution
around the sun and theirs.

[148] first … days] The periods of planetary revolution given
by Faustus correspond for the most part to the then-ac-
cepted figures: Saturn 28 years, Jupiter 12 years, Mars
2 years, Venus, Mercury, and, of course, the sun 1 year,
and the moon 1 month. The actual—as opposed to apparent—periods for the inner planets are of course
much less: 7½ and 3 months respectively.

[149] dominion or *intelligentia*] It was widely believed that the
planets were moved or guided by angels or intelligences.

[150] *coelum igneum, et crystallinum*] "a fiery, and a crystalline
heaven."

[151] conjunctions, oppositions, aspects] astrological terms referring respectively to the apparent proximity of two
planets, to their positioning on opposite sides of the sky,
and to any other angular relation between their positions.

[152] *Per inaequalem motum respectu totius*] "through an unequal motion with respect to the whole."

[153] move] anger.

[154] if Faustus can repent] This condition raises the issue of
Calvinist double predestination: if Faustus *is* able to

Evil Ang. If thou repent, devils shall tear thee in pieces.
Good Ang. Repent, and they shall never raze thy
skin.[155]

Exeunt Angels.

Faustus. Ah Christ, my Saviour,
Seek to save distressed Faustus' soul![156]

Enter Lucifer, Belzebub, and Mephastophilis.

Lucifer. Christ cannot save thy soul, for he is just;   90
There's none but I have interest in the same.[157]
Faustus. O, what art thou that look'st so terribly?
Lucifer. I am Lucifer, and this is my companion
prince in hell.
Faustus. O Faustus, they are come to fetch away thy
soul!
Lucifer. We come to tell thee thou dost injure us.   95
Thou talk'st of Christ, contrary to thy promise.
Belzebub. Thou should'st not think of God.
Lucifer.   Think of the devil.
Belzebub. And of his dam too.
Faustus. Nor will I henceforth: pardon me in this,[158]
And Faustus vows never to look to heaven,   100
Never to name God or to pray to him,
To burn his Scriptures, slay his ministers,
And make my spirits pull his churches down.
Lucifer. So shalt thou show thyself an obedient
servant, and we will highly gratify thee for it.   105
Belzebub. Faustus, we are come from hell to show
thee some pastime. Sit down, and thou shalt
behold the Seven Deadly Sins appear to thee in
their own proper shapes and likeness.
Faustus. That sight will be as pleasing unto me as   110
Paradise was to Adam, the first day of his creation.

Lucifer. Talk not of Paradise, or creation, but mark
the show.
Go, Mephastophilis, fetch them in.

Enter the Seven Deadly Sins.

Belzebub. Now Faustus, question them of their names
and dispositions.   115
Faustus. That shall I soon: what art thou, the first?
Pride. I am Pride. I disdain to have any parents. I
am like Ovid's flea, I can creep into every corner
of a wench: sometimes like a periwig I sit upon
her brow; next like a necklace I hang about her   120
neck; then like a fan of feathers I kiss her lips; and
then, turning myself to a wrought smock, do what
I list.[159] But fie, what a smell is here? I'll not speak
a word more, unless the ground be perfumed and
covered with a cloth of arras.[160]   125
Faustus. Thou art a proud knave indeed. What art
thou, the second?
Covet. I am Covetousness, begotten of an old churl
in an old leathern bag; and might I have my wish,
I would desire that this house and all the people   130
in it were turned to gold, that I might lock you
up in my good chest. O, my sweet gold!
Faustus. What art thou, the third?
Wrath. I am Wrath. I had neither father nor mother;
I leapt out of a lion's mouth when I was scarce half   135
an hour old, and ever since I have run up and
down the world with this case of rapiers, wounding
myself when I had nobody to fight withal.[161] I was
born in hell, and look to it: for some of you shall
be my father.   140
Faustus. What art thou, the fourth?
Envy. I am Envy, begotten of a chimney-sweeper and
an oyster wife.[162] I cannot read, and therefore wish
all books were burned; I am lean with seeing others

---

repent, i.e., if he is one of the elect, then it is never too
late to do so—but if he is one of the reprobate, and cannot repent, then it is always too late.
[155] raze] graze.
[156] seek] According to the Calvinist orthodoxy of Elizabethan England, the process of salvation had to be initiated by God. Faustus's "seek" suggests that he lacks
faith in Christ's ability to save him.
[157] interest in] a legal claim upon.
[158] Nor will I henceforth] i.e., think of God.

---

[159] Ovid's flea] The *Elegia de pulice*, a poem written in imitation of Ovid's amatory elegies, was wrongly ascribed
to him. In it is a line addressed to the flea: "You go wherever you wish; nothing, savage, is hidden from you."
[160] cloth of arras] tapestry fabric of the kind woven at Arras in Flanders; to use it as a floor covering would be
grossly ostentatious.
[161] case] pair.
[162] begotten … wife] and therefore filthy and foul-smelling.

eat. O, that there would come a famine through all the world, that all might die, and I live alone: then thou should'st see how fat I would be. But must thou sit and I stand? Come down, with a vengeance![163] 145

Faustus. Away, envious rascal! What art thou, the fifth? 150

Gluttony. Who I, sir? I am Gluttony. My parents are all dead, and the devil a penny they have left me, but a bare pension, and that buys me thirty meals a day and ten bevers: a small trifle to suffice nature.[164] O, I come of a royal parentage: my grandfather was a gammon of bacon, my grandmother a hogshead of claret wine.[165] My godfathers were these: Peter Pickleherring and Martin Martlemas-beef.[166] O, but my godmother she was a jolly gentlewoman, and well-beloved in every good town and city: her name was Mistress Margery March-beer.[167] Now, Faustus, thou hast heard all my progeny, wilt thou bid me to supper? 155 160

Faustus. No, I'll see thee hanged: thou wilt eat up all my victuals. 165

Gluttony. Then the devil choke thee.

Faustus. Choke thyself, glutton! What art thou, the sixth?

170

Sloth. I am Sloth. I was begotten on a sunny bank, where I have lain ever since, and you have done me great injury to bring me from thence. Let me be carried thither again by Gluttony and Lechery. I'll not speak another word for a king's ransom. 175

Faustus. What are you, mistress minx, the seventh and last?[168]

Lechery. Who I, sir? I am one that loves an inch of raw mutton better than an ell of fried stock-fish, and the first letter of my name begins with Lechery.[169] 180

Lucifer. Away, to hell, to hell.

Exeunt the Sins.

Now Faustus, how dost thou like this?

Faustus. O, this feeds my soul.

Lucifer. Tut, Faustus, in hell is all manner of delight. 185

Faustus. O, might I see hell, and return again, how happy were I then!

Lucifer. Thou shalt. I will send for thee at midnight. In mean time, take this book, peruse it thoroughly, and thou shalt turn thyself into what shape thou wilt. 190

Faustus. Great thanks, mighty Lucifer: This will I keep as chary as my life.[170]

Lucifer. Farewell, Faustus, and think on the devil.

Faustus. Farewell, great Lucifer. Come, Mephastophilis. 195

Exeunt omnes.

---

163 with a vengeance] with a curse on you. The phrase was used as a vehement intensifier.

164 bevers] drinks; also light meals or snacks.

165 hogshead] a wine-barrel of a standard size, holding (in modern terms) 225 litres or 63 American gallons—the equivalent of 25 cases of a dozen bottles of wine; claret] light red wine from the Bordeaux region (in the sixteenth century claret was made in the manner of a modern rosé).

166 Pickleherring] a clown figure associated (like Jack a Lent and Steven Stockfish) with carnival festivities and popular farces; Martlemas-beef] Martinmas, or St. Martin's day (November 11), was the traditional time to slaughter cattle that could not be fed over the winter and to commence the production of salt beef; it was therefore also a time for feasting on "green" or unsalted beef.

167 March-beer] a strong beer brewed in March.

---

168 minx] hussy, wanton woman.

169 raw mutton] a metaphor for prostitutes; the expression here takes on a phallic meaning; ell] a measure of length (equal in England to some forty-five inches), commonly contrasted to an inch; stockfish] unsalted dried fish, sometimes abusively associated with the male organ, as in *1 Henry IV* II.v. 227: "you bull's pizzle, you stockfish," and more generally with sexual coldness or impotence, as in *Measure for Measure* III.i. 353–4: "he was begot between two stockfishes." Roma Gill remarks: "Lechery is saying in effect that she prefers a small amount of virility to a large quantity of impotence."

170 chary] carefully.

ACT III

ACT III, CHORUS.

Enter the Chorus [Wagner].

Wagner. Learned Faustus,
  To know the secrets of astronomy
  Graven in the book of Jove's high firmament,
  Did mount him up to scale Olympus' top,[171]
  Where sitting in a chariot burning bright,[172]   5
  Drawn by the strength of yoked dragons' necks,
  He views the clouds, the planets and the stars,
  The tropics, zones, and quarters of the sky,[173]
  From the bright circle of the horned moon
  Even to the height of *primum mobile*;[174]   10
  And whirling round with this circumference
  Within the concave compass of the pole,
  From east to west his dragons swiftly glide,
  And in eight days did bring him home again.
  Not long he stay'd within his quiet house   15
  To rest his bones after his weary toil,
  But new exploits do hale him out again,
  And mounted then upon a dragon's back
  That with his wings did part the subtle air,[175]
  He now is gone to prove cosmography,[176]   20

---

171 to scale Olympus' top] i.e., to ascend to the dwelling-place of the gods.
172 a chariot burning bright] a parodic echo of the vision of the divine chariot-throne in Ezekiel 1:13–28.
173 tropics, zones … quarters] The tropics of Cancer and Capricorn, the arctic and antarctic circles and the equator divided the celestial sphere into five belts or zones; traditional astronomy also quartered the celestial sphere with two other circles that passed through its north and south poles: the solstitial colure, which intersects the two tropics at the solstitial points (those at which the ecliptic meets the tropics); and the equinoctial colure, which intersects the equator at the equinoctial points (those at which the ecliptic crosses the equator).
174 From … *mobile*] from the lowest to the highest of the spheres.
175 subtle] rarified.
176 to prove cosmography] to put geography to the test. Cosmography was sometimes thought of as a science that maps the universe as a whole, thus incorporating geography and astronomy.

That measures coasts and kingdoms of the earth.
And as I guess, will first arrive at Rome
To see the Pope, and manner of his court,
And take some part of holy Peter's feast,
The which this day is highly solemniz'd.   25

Exit.

ACT III, SCENE I.

Enter Faustus and Mephastophilis.

Faustus. Having now, my good Mephastophilis,
  Pass'd with delight the stately town of Trier,[177]
  Environ'd round with airy mountain tops,
  With walls of flint, and deep entrenched lakes,
  Not to be won by any conquering prince;   5
  From Paris next, coasting the realm of France,
  We saw the river Main fall into Rhine,
  Whose banks are set with groves of fruitful vines;
  Then up to Naples, rich Campania,[178]
  Whose buildings, fair and gorgeous to the eye   10
  (The streets are straightforth and pav'd with finest brick),
  Quarters the town in four equivalents.
  There saw we learned Maro's golden tomb,[179]
  The way he cut, an English mile in length,[180]

---

177 Trier] a city on the Moselle River, capital of an electoral state of the Holy Roman Empire, which under the rule of Elector-Archbishop Johann von Schönenburg was subjected during the 1580s and 1590s to a violent wave of witch-hunts.
178 Campania] in ancient usage, the plain surrounding the city of Capua; since medieval times, Naples has been the principal city of this region. (In modern Italy the name Campania is applied to a much larger area.)
179 Maro] Virgil, or Publius Vergilius Maro, died at Naples in 19 B.C. In part because his fourth Eclogue was interpreted as a prophecy of the coming of Christ, he acquired a reputation during the medieval period as a necromancer. His supposed tomb stands on the promontory of Posilipo on the Bay of Naples, at the Naples end of a tunnel, nearly half a mile in length, which cuts through the promontory—and which, as Petrarch wrote, "the insipid masses conclude was made by Virgil with magical incantations."
180 way] road. The tunnel is in fact some seven yards wide.

Thorough a rock of stone in one night's space.   15
From thence to Venice, Padua, and the rest,
In midst of which a sumptuous temple stands,
That threats the stars with her aspiring top.[181]
Thus hitherto hath Faustus spent his time.
But tell me now, what resting place is this?   20
Hast thou, as erst I did command,
Conducted me within the walls of Rome?

Meph. Faustus, I have, and because we will not be
    unprovided,
I have taken up his Holiness' privy chamber for
    our use.[182]

Faustus. I hope his Holiness will bid us welcome.   25

Meph. Tut, 'tis no matter, man, we'll be bold with
    his good cheer.
And now my Faustus, that thou may'st perceive
What Rome containeth to delight thee with,
Know that this city stands upon seven hills
That underprop the groundwork of the same;   30
Just through the midst runs flowing Tiber's stream,
With winding banks that cut it in two parts,
Over the which four stately bridges lean,
That make safe passage to each part of Rome.
Upon the bridge call'd Ponte Angelo   35
Erected is a castle passing strong,[183]

Within those walls such stores of ordnance are,
And double cannons, fram'd of carved brass,[184]
As match the days within one complete year—
Besides the gates and high pyramides[185]   40
Which Julius Caesar brought from Africa.

Faustus. Now, by the kingdoms of infernal rule,
Of Styx, Acheron, and the fiery lake
Of ever-burning Phlegethon, I swear[186]
That I do long to see the monuments   45
And situation of bright splendent Rome.
Come therefore, let's away.

Meph. Nay Faustus, stay: I know you'd fain see the
    Pope,
And take some part of holy Peter's feast,[187]
Where thou shalt see a troop of bald-pate friars   50
Whose *summum bonum* is in belly-cheer.[188]

Faustus. Well, I am content to compass then some
    sport,[189]
And by their folly make us merriment.
Then charm me, that I may be invisible,
To do what I please   55
Unseen of any whilst I stay in Rome.

[Mephastophilis charms him.][190]

Meph. So, Faustus: now
Do what thou wilt, thou shalt not be discern'd.

Sound a sennet.[191] *Enter the Pope and the Cardinal of Lorraine to the banquet, with Friars attending.*[192]

---

181 sumptuous temple … That threats the stars] Saint Mark's in Venice. The "aspiring top" would have to be that of the campanile, which stands at some distance from the church.

182 privy chamber] a synonym in the late Middle Ages for a privy, jakes, or latrine in the private suite of rooms of the master or mistress of a great house; the term was subsequently applied to a bedchamber adjoining the privy; only the most privileged guests would pass beyond the more public reception rooms into this room. The term may retain overtones of scatological intimacy, since prior to the development of the flush toilet, the lord of a great house might use a portable privy stool or close stool in the privy chamber.

183 bridge … strong] The papal fortress of Castel San Angelo, which incorporates the ancient mausoleum of the emperor Hadrian, stands a short distance from the north end of the Ponte San Angelo; this bridge, originally named the Pons Aelius, was built by Hadrian in 134 to provide a connection between his circular mausoleum and the Campus Martius.

184 double cannons] cannons of very large calibre.

185 pyramides] an obelisk, in this case the one brought to Rome from Egypt by the emperor Caligula (not Julius Caesar), and moved to its present site in the Piazza San Pietro in 1586. The word is singular, not plural.

186 Styx, Acheron … Phlegethon] three of the four rivers of Hades.

187 of] in.

188 *summum bonum*] highest good.

189 compass] contrive.

190 *Mephastophilis charms him*] According to Henslowe's *Diary* the Admiral's Men owned a "robe for to go invisible," a prop which may have been used here.

191 *sennet*] a flourish on the trumpet to announce a ceremonial entrance.

192 *Cardinal of Lorraine*] This position was held during the sixteenth century by several members of the powerful

Pope. My lord of Lorraine, will't please you draw near? 60

Faustus. Fall to, and the devil choke you and you spare.[193]

Pope. How now, who's that which spake? Friars, look about!

Friar. Here's nobody, if it like your Holiness.[194] 65

Pope. My lord, here is a dainty dish was sent me from the Bishop of Milan.

Faustus. I thank you, sir.

[Snatch it.]

Pope. How now, who's that which snatched the meat from me? Will no man look? My lord, this dish 70 was sent me from the Cardinal of Florence.

Faustus. You say true, I'll ha'it.

[Snatch it.]

Pope. What, again! My lord, I'll drink to your grace.

Faustus. I'll pledge your grace.

[Snatch it.]

Lorraine. My lord, it may be some ghost newly crept 75 out of purgatory come to beg a pardon of your Holiness.

Pope. It may be so. Friars, prepare a dirge to lay the fury of this ghost.[195] Once again, my lord, fall to.

The Pope crosseth himself.

Guise family: Jean de Guise (1498–1550); Charles de Guise (1524–1574), who helped foment the wars of religion that convulsed France for decades after 1562 and acquired a reputation for dissimulation and cruelty; and Louis de Guise (1555–1588), who along with his brother, Henri, third Duc de Guise (1550–1588), was assassinated by King Henri III. As leaders of the pro-Spanish and ultra-Catholic Ligue, and thus major figures in the Spanish-led campaign against Protestantism, Louis and Henri de Guise were feared and detested in England.

193 and you spare] if you eat sparingly.

194 like] please.

195 dirge] originally "dirige", the first word of the antiphon at matins in the Office of the Dead ("Dirige, Domine, Deus meus, in conspectu tuo viam meum": "Direct, O Lord, my God, my way in thy sight").

Faustus. What, are you crossing your self? Well, use 80 that trick no more, I would advise you.

Cross again.

Faustus. Well, there's the second time. Aware the third, I give you fair warning.

Cross again, and Faustus hits him a box of the ear, and they all run away.

Come on, Mephastophilis, what shall we do?

Meph. Nay, I know not; we shall be cursed with bell, 85 book and candle.[196]

Faustus. How? Bell, book and candle, candle, book and bell,
Forward and backward, to curse Faustus to hell.
Anon you shall hear a hog grunt, a calf bleat, and an ass bray,
Because it is Saint Peter's holy day! 90

Enter all the Friars to sing the dirge.

Friar. Come brethren, let's about our business with good devotion.

[They] sing this:

Cursed be he that stole away his Holiness' meat from the table.
     Maledicat dominus![197]
Cursed be he that struck his Holiness a blow on the face. 95
     Maledicat dominus!
Cursed be he that took Friar Sandelo a blow on the pate.
     Maledicat dominus!
Cursed be he that disturbeth our holy dirge.
     Maledicat dominus! 100
Cursed be he that took away his Holiness' wine.
Maledicat dominus! Et omnes sancti! Amen.[198]

[Faustus and Mephastophilis] beat the Friars and fling fireworks among them, and so exeunt.

---

196 bell, book and candle] At the end of the ritual of excommunication, the bell is tolled, the book closed, and the candle extinguished. That ritual is confused here with the office of exorcism.

197 *Maledicat dominus*] "May the Lord curse him."

198 *et omnes sancti*] and (may) all the saints (curse him).

ACT III, SCENE II.

Enter Robin and Rafe with a silver goblet.

Robin. Come Rafe, did I not tell thee we were for ever made by this Doctor Faustus' book? *Ecce signum,* here's a simple purchase for horse-keepers![199] Our horses shall eat no hay as long as this lasts.   5

Enter the Vintner.

Rafe. But Robin, here comes the Vintner.
Robin. Hush, I'll gull him supernaturally. Drawer, I hope all is paid.[200] God be with you; come Rafe.
Vintner. Soft, sir; a word with you.[201] I must yet have a goblet paid from you ere you go.   10
Robin. I a goblet? Rafe, I a goblet? I scorn you, and you are but a etc. I a goblet? Search me![202]
Vintner. I mean so, sir, with your favor.

[Searches Robin.]

Robin. How say you now?
Vintner. I must say somewhat to your fellow. You,   15
sir.
Rafe. Me, sir? Me, sir! Search your fill! Now, sir, you may be ashamed to burden honest men with a matter of truth.
Vintner. Well, t'one of you hath this goblet about   20
you.
Robin. You lie, drawer, 'tis afore me. Sirrah you, I'll teach ye to impeach honest men: stand by, I'll scour you for a goblet.[203] Stand aside, you had best, I charge you in the name of Belzebub! Look   25
to the goblet, Rafe.[204]
Vintner. What mean you, sirrah?
Robin. I'll tell you what I mean.

He reads.

Sanctabulorum periphrasticon—Nay, I'll tickle you, Vintner! Look to the goblet, Rafe. *Polypragmos*   30
Belseborams framanto pacostiphos tostu Mephas-tophilis, etc.[205]

Enter Mephastophilis; sets squibs at their backs; they run about.[206]

Vintner. O nomine Domine! What mean'st thou, Robin? Thou hast no goblet!
Rafe. Peccatum peccatorum! Here's thy goblet, good   35
Vintner!
Robin. Misericordia pro nobis![207] What shall I do? Good devil, forgive me now, and I'll never rob thy library more!
Meph. Monarch of hell, under whose black survey   40
Great potentates do kneel with awful fear,
Upon whose altars thousand souls do lie,
How am I vexed with these villains' charms!
From Constantinople am I hither come
Only for pleasure of these damned slaves.   45
Robin. How, from Constantinople? You have had a great journey, will you take sixpence in your purse to pay for your supper, and be gone?
Meph. Well villains, for your presumption, I transform thee into an ape, and thee into a dog,   50
and so be gone!

Exit.

Robin. How, into an ape? That's brave, I'll have fine sport with the boys; I'll get nuts and apples enow.
Rafe. And I must be a dog.

---

199 *Ecce signum*] "Behold the sign."
200 Drawer] an insult: Robin pretends to mistake the Vintner (or innkeeper) for his employee, the tapster or drawer who serves the customers.
201 Soft] softly, slowly; here carrying an imperative force, as in "not so fast!"
202 etc.] a substitute for a scatological or obscene expression.
203 impeach] accuse.
204 Look to the goblet, Rafe] Robin and Rafe are apparently passing the goblet back and forth between them.

205 lines 24–26.] Robin's incantation is gibberish, though some of it comes close to deviating into sense. The Greek *periphrastikos* means "circumlocutory" (*periphrasticon* could be a genitive plural, like the Latinate nonsense-word *sanctabulorum*). In Greek *Polypragmosyne* means "curiosity" or "meddlesomeness," and a *polypragmon* is a "busybody." The first four words of the invocation might then be translated as "Busy-body Belseborams … of beating-around-the-bush holy-molydoms …!"
206 *squibs*] fireworks. The action indicated here was a popular element in low comedy.
207 lines 27–30.] garbled scraps of liturgical Latin.

Robin. I'faith, thy head will never be out of the   55
pottage pot.

Exeunt.

ACT IV

ACT IV, CHORUS.

Enter Chorus.

Chorus. When Faustus had with pleasure ta'en the view
　Of rarest things and royal courts of kings,
　He stay'd his course, and so returned home,
　Where such as bare his absence but with grief,
　I mean his friends and nearest companions,   5
　Did gratulate his safety with kind words,
　And in their conference of what befell
　Touching his journey through the world and air
　They put forth questions of astrology,
　Which Faustus answer'd with such learned skill   10
　As they admir'd and wonder'd at his wit.[208]
　Now is his fame spread forth in every land;
　Amongst the rest of Emperor is one,
　Carolus the Fifth, at whose palace now[209]
　Faustus is feasted 'mongst his noblemen.   15
　What there he did in trial of his art
　I leave untold, your eyes shall see perform'd.

Exit.

ACT IV, SCENE I.

Enter Emperor, Faustus, and a Knight, with attendants.

Emperor. Master Doctor Faustus, I have heard strange
report of thy knowledge in the black art, how that
none in my empire, nor in the whole world, can
compare with thee for the rare effects of magic:
they say thou hast a familiar spirit, by whom thou   5
canst accomplish what thou list.[210] This therefore
is my request: that thou let me see some proof of
thy skill, that mine eyes may be witnesses to
confirm what mine ears have heard reported; and
here I swear to thee, by the honor of mine imperial   10
crown, that whatever thou doest, thou shalt be no
ways prejudiced or endamaged.[211]

Knight. [aside] I'faith, he looks much like a conjurer.

Faustus. My gracious sovereign, though I must confess myself far inferior to the report men have   15
published, and nothing answerable to the honor
of your imperial Majesty, yet for that love and duty
binds me thereunto, I am content to do whatsoever your Majesty shall command me.[212]

Emperor. Then Doctor Faustus, mark what I shall say.   20
　As I was sometime solitary set
　Within my closet, sundry thoughts arose[213]
　About the honor of mine ancestors:
　How they had won by prowess such exploits,
　Got riches, subdu'd so many kingdoms,   25
　As we that do succeed, or they that shall[214]
　Hereafter possess our throne shall,
　I fear me, never attain to that degree
　Of high renown and great authority;
　Amongst which kings is Alexander the Great,   30
　Chief spectacle of the world's pre-eminence,[215]
　The bright shining of whose glorious acts
　Lightens the world with his reflecting beams,
　As when I hear but motion made of him[216]
　It grieves my soul I never saw the man.   35
　If therefore thou, by cunning of thine art,
　Canst raise this man from hollow vaults below
　Where lies entomb'd this famous conqueror,
　And bring with him his beauteous paramour,[217]

208　As] that.
209　Carolus the Fifth] Charles V (1500–1558), King of
　Spain and Holy Roman Emperor from 1518 and 1519
　respectively until his abdication in 1555. The histori-
　cal Doctor Faustus never made an appearance at the
　imperial court. Contemporary *magi*, however, had con-
　nections with the courts of both the emperor
　Maximilian (Charles V's grandfather and immediate
　predecessor) and Charles V.

210　rare] remarkable, extraordinary;　what thou list] what-
　ever you wish.
211　endamaged] harmed.
212　nothing answerable] quite unequal;　for that] because.
213　closet] study, inner chamber.
214　succeed] follow in dynastic succession.
215　pre-eminence] pre-eminent people.
216　motion] mention.
217　paramour] mistress, consort (i.e., Roxane of Oxyartes).

Both in their right shapes, gesture, and attire   40
They us'd to wear during their time of life,
Thou shalt both satisfy my just desire
And give me cause to praise thee whilst I live.

Faustus. My gracious lord, I am ready to accomplish
your request, so far forth as by art and power of   45
my spirit I am able to perform.

Knight. [aside] I'faith that's just nothing at all.

Faustus. But if it like your Grace, it is not in my
ability to present before your eyes the true
substantial bodies of those two deceased princes,   50
which long since are consumed to dust.

Knight. [aside] Ay, marry Master Doctor, now there's a
sign of grace in you when you will confess the truth.

Faustus. But such spirits as can lively resemble
Alexander and his paramour shall appear before   55
your Grace, in that manner that they best lived in,
in their most flourishing estate, which I doubt not
shall sufficiently content your imperial Majesty.

Emperor. Go to, Master Doctor, let me see them
presently.[218]   60

Knight. Do you hear, Master Doctor? You bring
Alexander and his paramour before the Emperor?

Faustus. How then, sir?

Knight. I'faith, that's as true as Diana turned me to
a stag.   65

Faustus. No sir, but when Actaeon died, he left the
horns for you.[219] Mephastophilis, be gone.

Exit Mephastophilis.

Knight. Nay, and you go to conjuring, I'll be gone.[220]

Exit Knight.

Faustus. I'll meet with you anon for interrupting me
so.[221] Here they are, my gracious lord.   70

Enter Mephastophilis with Alexander and his paramour.

Emperor. Master Doctor, I heard this lady while she
lived had a wart or mole in her neck. How shall I
know whether it be so or no?

Faustus. Your highness may boldly go and see.

[Emperor does so; then spirits exeunt.]

Emperor. Sure these are no spirits, but the true   75
substantial bodies of these two deceased princes.

Faustus. Will't please your highness now to send for the
knight that was so pleasant with me here of late?

Emperor. One of you call him forth.

Enter the Knight with a pair of horns on his head.

How now, sir knight? Why, I had thought thou   80
had'st been a bachelor, but now I see thou hast a
wife, that not only gives thee horns but makes thee
wear them. Feel on thy head!

Knight. Thou damned wretch and execrable dog,
Bred in the concave of some monstrous rock,   85
How dar'st thou thus abuse a gentleman?
Villain, I say, undo what thou hast done!

Faustus. O not so fast, sir; there's no haste but
good.[222] Are you remembered how you crossed
me in my conference with the Emperor? I think I   90
have met with you for it.

Emperor. Good Master Doctor, at my entreaty release
him. He hath done penance sufficient.

Faustus. My gracious lord, not so much for the injury
he offered me here in your presence, as to delight   95
you with some mirth, hath Faustus worthily re-
quited this injurious knight; which being all I desire,
I am content to release him of his horns.[223] And sir
knight, hereafter speak well of scholars. Mephastophilis, transform him straight.[224] Now, my good   100
lord, having done my duty, I humbly take my leave.

Emperor. Farewell, Master Doctor; yet ere you go,
expect from me a bounteous reward.

Exeunt Emperor, Knight, and attendants.

---

218 Go to] Normally an expression of incredulity, it appears
here to express mild demurral, or perhaps encouragement, with the same range of meanings as "Come,
come"; presently] at once.

219 Diana ... Actaeon] Actaeon, a hunter, witnessed the
goddess Diana and her nymphs bathing; the goddess
transformed him into a stag and he was torn to pieces
by his own dogs.

220 and] if.

221 meet with] get even with.

---

222 there's ... good] a common proverb: "No haste but good
(speed)."

223 injury] insult.

224 straight] at once.

ACT IV, SCENE II.

Faustus. Now Mephastophilis, the restless course
That time doth run with calm and silent foot,
Shortening my days and thread of vital life,
Calls for the payment of my latest years.
Therefore, sweet Mephastophilis,   5
Let us make haste to Wittenberg.
Meph. What, will you go on horseback, or on foot?
Faustus. Nay, till I am past this fair and pleasant green
I'll walk on foot.

Enter a Horse-courser.[225]

Hor. I have been all this day seeking one Master   10
Fustian; mass, see where he is.[226] God save you,
Master Doctor.
Faustus. What, horse-courser, you are well met.
Hor. Do you hear, sir? I have brought you forty
dollars for your horse.   15
Faustus. I cannot sell him. If thou lik'st him for fifty,
take him.
Hor. Alas sir, I have no more. I pray you, speak for
me.
Meph. I pray you, let him have him. He is an honest   20
fellow, and he has a great charge, neither wife not
child.[227]
Faustus. Well, come, give me your money. My boy
will deliver him to you. But I must tell you one
thing before you have him: ride him not into the   25
water at any hand.[228]
Hor. Why sir, will he not drink of all waters?
Faustus. O yes, he will drink of all waters, but ride
him not into the water. Ride him over hedge or
ditch, or where thou wilt, but not into the water.   30

Hor. Well, sir, now am I a made man for ever! I'll
not leave my horse for forty.[229] If he had but the
quality of hey ding ding, hey ding ding, I'd make
a brave living on him: he has a buttock so slick as
an eel.[230] Well, God-bye sir, your boy will deliver   35
him me.[231] But hark ye sir, if my horse be sick or
ill at ease, if I bring his water to you, you'll tell
me what it is?[232]
Faustus. Away, you villain! What, dost thou think I
am a horse-doctor?   40

Exit Horse-courser.

What art thou, Faustus, but a man condemn'd to die?
Thy fatal time doth draw to final end;[233]
Despair doth drive distrust into my thoughts.
Confound these passions with a quiet sleep:
Tush, Christ did call the thief upon the cross.[234]   45
Then rest thee, Faustus, quiet in conceit.[235]

Sleeps in his chair.

Enter Horse-courser all wet, crying.

Hor. Alas, alas, Doctor Fustian, quotha? Mass,
Doctor Lopus was never such a doctor: has given
me a purgation, has purged me of forty dollars, I
shall never see them more.[236] But yet like an ass   50

---

225 *Horse-courser*] Although "courser" may suggest the ex-
ercising or racing of horses, the term appears to mean
primarily a horse-dealer.

226 Fustian] a clownish deformation of "Faustus"; bombast,
nonsense; mass] a contraction of "By the Mass."

227 charge] burden (of family responsibilities). Mephastophilis promptly contradicts this claim, thereby
mocking transparent falsehoods of the kind used by
horse-dealers.

228 at any hand] under any circumstances.

229 leave] sell.

230 hey ding ding ... eel] "hey ding-a-ding" is a common
refrain in popular songs; compare *As You Like It* V.iv.18–
19 ("When birds do sing, hey ding-a-ding ding, / Sweet
lovers love the spring"). The phrase has sexual overtones,
and "buttock so slick as an eel" implies sexual potency;
thus, the "brave living" that the horse-courser anticipates
will presumably come from stud fees.

231 God-bye] a contraction of "God be with you."

232 water] urine.

233 fatal time] time allotted by fate.

234 the thief upon the cross] See Luke 23:43 (which is contradicted, however, by Matt. 27:44). St. Augustine
wrote: "Do not despair—one of the thieves was saved;
do not presume—one of the thieves was damned."

235 conceit] state of mind.

236 Doctor Lopus] Doctor Roderigo Lopez, a Portuguese
marrano and personal physician to Queen Elizabeth.
Lopez incurred the enmity of the Earl of Essex, who in
January 1594 accused him of high treason; he was tried

as I was, I would not be ruled my him, for he bade me I should ride him into no water. Now I, thinking my horse had some rare quality that he would not have had me know of, I like a venturous youth rid him into the deep pond at the town's end. I was no sooner in the middle of the pond, but my horse vanished away, and I sat upon a bottle of hay, never so near drowning in my life![237] But I'll seek out my doctor, and have my forty dollars again, or I'll make it dearest horse.[238] O, yonder is his snipper-snapper.[239] Do you hear? you, hey-pass, where's your master?[240]

Meph. Why sir, what would you? You cannot speak with him.

Hor. But I will speak with him.

Meph. Why, he's fast asleep; come some other time.

Hor. I'll speak with him now, or I'll break his glass windows about his ears.[241]

Meph. I tell thee, he hath not slept this eight nights.

Hor. And he have not slept this eight weeks I'll speak with him.

Meph. See where he is, fast asleep.

Hor. Ay, this is he. God save ye Master Doctor! Master Doctor, Master Doctor Fustian, forty dollars, forty dollars for a bottle of hay!

Meph. Why, thou seest he hears thee not.

Hor. So ho, ho! So ho, ho![242] (*Hallow in his ear.*) No, will you not wake? I'll make you wake ere I go!

Pull him by the leg, and pull it away.

Alas, I am undone! What shall I do?

Faustus. O my leg, my leg! Help, Mephastophilis! Call the officers, my leg, my leg!

Meph. Come villain, to the constable.

Hor. O Lord, sir: let me go, and I'll give you forty dollars more.

Meph. Where be they?

Hor. I have none about me; come to my ostry, and I'll give them you.[243]

Meph. Be gone, quickly.

Horse-courser runs away.

Faustus. What, is he gone? Farewell he, Faustus has his leg again, and the horse-courser, I take it, a bottle of hay for his labor. Well, this trick shall cost him forty dollars more.

Enter Wagner.

How now, Wagner, what's the news with thee?

Wagner. Sir, the Duke of Vanholt doth earnestly entreat your company.

Faustus. The Duke of Vanholt! An honorable gentleman, to whom I must be no niggard of my cunning.[244] Come Mephastophilis, let's away to him.

Exeunt.

ACT IV, SCENE III.

Enter to them the Duke, and the Duchess; the Duke speaks.[245]

Duke. Believe me, Master Doctor, this merriment hath much pleased me.

Faustus. My gracious lord, I am glad it contents you so well. But it may be, madam, you take no delight in this. I have heard that great-bellied women do long for some dainties or other: what is it, madam? Tell me, and you shall have it.

(and convicted) on February 28 on charges that included attempting to poison the queen, and was executed on June 7—more than a year after Marlowe's death. Although Lopez was well-known even before his appointment as the queen's physician in 1586 (he had previously been household physician to the Earl of Leicester), the past-tense allusion to him suggests that in its present form this scene must be post-Marlovian; a purgation] an emetic: the horse-dealer has been cleansed of money.

237 bottle] from the French "botte," meaning bundle.

238 dearest] most expensive. If the horse-courser can't have his money back, he'll take revenge.

239 snipper-snapper] conceited young fellow, smart-aleck.

240 hey-pass] an expression used by fairground conjurors or jugglers.

241 glass windows] spectacles.

242 So ho, ho] a huntsman's cry.

243 ostry] hostelry, inn.

244 niggard] a parsimonious person, one who shares only grudgingly.

245 *Enter to them*] Faustus and Mephastophilis must leave the stage after IV.ii to indicate the passage of time—and must then immediately re-enter. An intervening scene may have been lost.

Duchess. Thanks, good Master Doctor, and for I see your courteous intent to pleasure me, I will not hide from you the thing my heart desires; and were it now summer, as it is January, and the dead time of winter, I would desire no better meat than a dish of ripe grapes.[246]

Faustus. Alas, madam, that's nothing. Mephastophilis, be gone.[247]

Exit Mephastophilis.

Were it a greater thing than this, so it would content you, you should have it.

Enter Mephastophilis with the grapes.

Here they be, madam, will't please you to taste on them?

Duke. Believe me, Master Doctor, this makes me wonder above the rest, that being in the dead time of winter, and in the month of January, how you should come by these grapes.

Faustus. If it like your Grace, the year is divided into two circles over the whole world, that when it is here winter with us, in the contrary circle it is summer with them, as in India, Saba, and farther countries in the east; and by means of a swift spirit that I have, I had them brought hither, as ye see.[248] How do you like them, madam, be they good?

Duchess. Believe me, Master Doctor, they be the best grapes that e'er I tasted in my life before.

Faustus. I am glad they content you so, madam.

Duke. Come, madam, let us in, where you must well reward this learned man for the kindness he hath showed to you.

Duchess. And so I will, my lord, and whilst I live rest beholden for this courtesy.

Faustus. I humbly thank your Grace.

Duke. Come Master Doctor, follow us, and receive your reward.

Exeunt.

---

246 meat] food.
247 Mephastophilis, be gone] Mephastophilis is presumably invisible to the Duke and Duchess.
248 two circles … east] The two "circles" should of course be the northern and southern hemispheres. Saba is the land of the Queen of Sheba, now Yemen.

ACT V

ACT V, SCENE I.

Enter Wagner solus.

Wagner. I think my master means to die shortly,
For he hath given to me all his goods;
And yet methinkes if that death were near[249]
He would not banquet and carouse and swill
Amongst the students, as even now he doth,
Who are at supper with such belly-cheer
As Wagner ne'er beheld in all his life.
See where they come: belike the feast is ended.

Exit.

Enter Faustus with two or three Scholars.

1 Sch. Master Doctor Faustus, since our conference about fair ladies, which was the beautiful'st in all the world, we have determined with our selves that Helen of Greece was the admirablest lady that ever lived.[250] Therefore, Master Doctor, if you will do us so much favor as to let us see that peerless dame of Greece, whom all the world admires for majesty, we should think ourselves much beholding unto you.

Faustus. Gentlemen,
For that I know your friendship is unfeign'd[251]
(And Faustus' custom is not to deny
The just requests of those that wish him well),
You shall behold that peerless dame of Greece
No otherways for pomp and majesty
Than when Sir Paris cross'd the seas with her
And brought the spoils to rich Dardania.[252]
Be silent then, for danger is in words.

Music sounds, and Helen passeth over the stage.

2 Sch. Too simple is my wit to tell her praise,
Whom all the world admires for majesty.

---

249 methinkes] Modernized spelling would upset the rhythm of this line.
250 determined with] settled among.
251 for that] because.
252 Dardania] Troy, referred to here by the name of the founder of the Trojan dynasty, Dardanus.

3 Sch. Not marvel though the angry Greeks pursu'd[253]
  With ten years' war the rape of such a queen,[254]
  Whose heavenly beauty passeth all compare.   30
1 Sch. Since we have seen the pride of nature's works,
  And only paragon of excellence,

Enter an Old Man.

  Let us depart, and for this glorious deed
  Happy and blest be Faustus evermore.
Faustus. Gentlemen, farewell, the same I wish to you.   35

Exeunt Scholars.

Old Man. Ah Doctor Faustus, that I might prevail
  To guide thy steps unto the way of life,
  By which sweet path thy may'st attain the goal
  That shall conduct thee to celestial rest.
  Break heart, drop blood, and mingle it with tears,   40
  Tears falling from repentant heaviness
  Of thy most vile and loathsome filthiness,
  The stench whereof corrupts the inward soul
  With such flagitious crimes of heinous sins[255]
  As no commiseration may expel   45
  But mercy, Faustus, of thy Saviour sweet,
  Whose blood alone must wash away thy guilt.[256]
Faustus. Where art thou, Faustus? wretch, what hast
    thou done?[257]
  Damn'd art thou, Faustus, damn'd, despair and die!
  Hell claims his right, and with a roaring voice   50
  Says, "Faustus, come, thine hour is almost come!"

Enter Mephastophilis, who gives him a dagger.

  And Faustus now will come to do thee right.
Old Man. Ah stay, good Faustus, stay thy desperate
    steps:
  I see an angel hovers o'er thy head,
  And with a vial full of precious grace[258]   55
  Offers to pour the same into thy soul:
  Then call for mercy and avoid despair.
Faustus. Ah my sweet friend, I feel thy words
  To comfort my distressed soul.
  Leave me awhile to ponder on my sins.   60
Old Man. I go, sweet Faustus, but with heavy cheer,
  Fearing the ruin of thy hopeless soul.

Exit.

Faustus. Accursed Faustus, where is mercy now?
  I do repent, and yet I do despair:
  Hell strives with grace for conquest in my breast;   65
  What shall I do to shun the snares of death?
Meph. Thou traitor, Faustus, I arrest thy soul
  For disobedience to my sovereign lord.
  Revolt, or I'll in piece-meal tear thy flesh![259]
Faustus. I do repent I e'er offended him.   70
  Sweet Mephastophilis, entreat thy lord
  To pardon my unjust presumption,
  And with my blood again I will confirm
  My former vow I made to Lucifer.
Meph. Do it then quickly, with unfeigned heart,   75
  Lest greater danger do attend thy drift.[260]
Faustus. Torment, sweet friend, that base and
    crooked age

---

253 pursu'd] sought to punish or avenge (*OED*, v. I.i.b).
254 rape] abduction.
255 flagitious] extremely wicked, infamous.
256 no ... guilt] Compare Revelation 1:5: "Jesus Christ ...
    loved us, and washed us from our sins in his own
    blood." *The Prayer-Book of Queen Elizabeth* (1559)
    specifies that if a person in "extremity of sickness ... do
    truly repent him of his sins, and steadfastly believe that
    Jesus Christ ... shed his blood for his redemption"
    (135), this is the equivalent of taking communion.
    Faustus is unable so to believe; one interpretation of the
    blood-pact that he made in II.i (and renews in this
    scene) is that it amounts to a self-exclusion, through the
    shedding of his own blood, from the number of those
    for whom Christ's redeeming blood was shed.
257 Where art thou, Faustus?] Cf. Genesis 3:9: "the Lord God
    called to the man, and said unto him, Where art thou?"

258 a vial full of previous grace] The Old Man here individu-
    alizes an image from Revelation 5:8, in which elders
    worshipping before the throne of God carry "golden vi-
    als full of odours, which are the prayers of saints." (This
    image undergoes an apocalyptic transformation when
    seven angels are given "seven golden vials full of the
    wrath of God" [Rev. 15:7], which they pour out as
    plagues upon the earth [Rev. 16:1–21].)
259 Revolt] reverse your course of action (*OED*, v. I.2b); in
    religious contexts, the word carries the implication of
    departing from the truth (*OED*, v. I.2a, 2c).
260 drift] conscious or unconscious tendency or aim (*OED*,
    sb. 3, 4).

That durst dissuade me from thy Lucifer,
With greatest torments that our hell affords.
Meph. His faith is great, I cannot touch his soul.   80
But what I may afflict his body with
I will attempt, which is but little worth.
Faustus. One thing, good servant, let me crave of thee
To glut the longing of my heart's desire:
That I might have unto my paramour[261]   85
That heavenly Helen which I saw of late,
Whose sweet embracings may extinguish clean
These thoughts that do dissuade me from my vow,
And keep mine oath I made to Lucifer.
Meph. Faustus, this, or what else thou shalt desire   90
Shall be perform'd in the twinkling of an eye.

Enter Helen.

Faustus. Was this the face that launch'd a thousand
          ships
And burnt the topless towers of Ilium?[262]
Sweet Helen, make me immortal with a kiss;
Her lips suck forth my soul, see where it flies![263]   95
Come Helen, come, give me my soul again;
Here will I dwell, for heaven be in these lips,
And all is dross that is not Helena.

Enter Old Man.

I will be Paris, and for love of thee
Instead of Troy shall Wittenberg be sack'd,   100
And I will combat with weak Menelaus[264]

And wear thy colours on my plumed crest;
Yea, I will wound Achilles in the heel
And then return to Helen for a kiss.
O, thou art fairer than the evening air   105
Clad in the beauty of a thousand stars;
Brighter art thou than flaming Jupiter
When he appear'd to be hapless Semele,[265]
More lovely than the monarch of the sky
In wanton Arethusa's azur'd arms,[266]   110
And none but thou shalt be my paramour.

Exeunt.

Old Man. Accursed Faustus, miserable man,
That from thy soul exclud'st the grace of heaven
And fliest the throne of his tribunal seat!

Enter the devils.

Satan begins to sift me with his pride;[267]   115
As in this furnace God shall try my faith,
My faith, vile hell, shall triumph over thee!
Ambitious fiends, see how the heaven smiles
At your repulse, and laughs your state to scorn:
Hence, hell, for hence I fly unto my God.   120

Exeunt.

---

261 unto] as.
262 topless] immensely high; Ilium] Troy.
263 kiss … flies] Compare the apocryphal Wisdom of Solomon, 7:25–26, 29, 8:2: Wisdom "is the breath of the power of God, and a pure influence that floweth from the glory of the Almighty: therefore can no defiled thing come unto her. For she is the brightness of the everlasting light, the undefiled mirror of the Majesty of God, and the image of his goodness. [...] For she is more beautiful than the Sun, and is above all the order of the stars, and the light is not to be compared unto her. [...] I have loved her, and sought her from my youth: I desired to marry her, such love had I unto her beauty."
264 weak Menelaus] Book III of Homer's *Iliad* recounts the duel between Alexandros or Paris and Menelaus. Paris challenged all the best of the Achaeans to single combat, but recoiled in fear from Menelaus. Having agreed

that Helen and her possessions should go to the victor, Paris was defeated, but saved from death by Aphrodite, who carried him in a mist into his own bedchamber. There, although shamed in Helen's eyes as in everyone else's, he promptly took her to bed.
265 hapless Semele] One of Jupiter's human mistresses, she was persuaded by Juno to ask him to come to her in the same form in which he embraced Juno in heaven, and was consumed by fire.
266 Arethusa] a nymph who, bathing in the river Alpheus, aroused the river-god's lust; fleeing from him, she was transformed into a fountain. No classical myth links her with Jupiter or the sun-god.
267 sift me] Compare Christ's words to Peter at the last supper: "Simon, Simon, behold, Satan hath desired to have you, and he may sift you as wheat" (Luke 22:31, Authorized Version).

ACT V, SCENE II.

Enter Faustus with the Scholars.

Faustus. Ah, gentlemen!

1 Sch. What ails Faustus?

Faustus. Ah, my sweet chamber-fellow, had I lived with thee, then had I lived still, but now I die eternally. Look, comes he not, comes he not? 5

2 Sch. What means Faustus?

3 Sch. Belike he is grown into some sickness, by being over-solitary.

1 Sch. If it be so, we'll have physicians to cure him. 'Tis but a surfeit, never fear, man.[268] 10

Faustus. A surfeit of deadly sin, that hath damned both body and soul.

2 Sch. Yet Faustus, look up to heaven; remember, God's mercies are infinite.

Faustus. But Faustus' offence can ne'er be pardoned: 15 the serpent that tempted Eve may be saved, but not Faustus. Ah gentlemen, hear me with patience, and tremble not at my speeches. Though my heart pants and quivers to remember that I have been a student here these thirty years, O would I had 20 never seen Wittenberg, never read book: and what wonders I have done, all Germany can witness, yea all the world, for which Faustus hath lost both Germany and the world, yea heaven itself, heaven the seat of God, the throne of the blessed, the 25 kingdom of joy, and must remain in hell for ever— hell, ah, hell, for ever! Sweet friends, what shall become of Faustus, being in hell for ever?

3 Sch. Yet Faustus, call on God.

Faustus. On God, whom Faustus hath abjured? on 30 God, whom Faustus hath blasphemed? Ah my God, I would weep, but the devil draws in my tears. Gush forth blood instead of tears, yea life and soul! Oh, he stays my tongue; I would lift up my hands, but see, they hold them, they hold them! 35

All. Who, Faustus?

Faustus. Lucifer and Mephastophilis. Ah, gentlemen, I gave them my soul for my cunning.[269]

All. God forbid!

Faustus. God forbade it indeed, but Faustus hath done 40 it: for the vain pleasure of four and twenty years hath Faustus lost eternal joy and felicity. I writ them a bill with mine own blood, the date is expired, the time will come, and he will fetch me![270]

1 Sch. Why did not Faustus tell of this before, that 45 divines might have prayed for thee?

Faustus. Oft have I thought to have done so, but the devil threatened to tear me in pieces if I named God, to fetch both body and soul if I once gave ear to divinity, and now 'tis too late: gentlemen, 50 away, lest you perish with me.

2 Sch. O what may we do to save Faustus?

Faustus. Talk not of me, but save yourselves, and depart.

3 Sch. God will strengthen me, I will stay with 55 Faustus.

1 Sch. Tempt not God, sweet friend, but let us into the next room, and there pray for him.

Faustus. Ah, pray for me, pray for me; and what noise soever ye hear, come not unto me, for nothing can 60 rescue me.

2 Sch. Pray thou, and we will pray that God may have mercy upon thee.

Faustus. Gentlemen, farewell. If I live till morning, I'll visit you; if not, Faustus is gone to hell. 65

All. Faustus, farewell.

Exeunt Scholars.

The clock strikes eleven.

Faustus. Ah Faustus,
Now hast thou but one bare hour to live,
And then thou must be damn'd perpetually.
Stand still, you ever-moving spheres of heaven. 70
That time may cease, and midnight never come!
Fair nature's eye, rise, rise again, and make
Perpetual day, or let this hour be but a year,
A month, a week, a natural day,
That Faustus may repent, and save his soul. 75
O lente lente currite noctis equi![271]

---

268 surfeit] an excessive indulgence in food or drink, and the resulting disorder of the system.

269 cunning] knowledge.

270 bill] deed.

271 *O lente … equi*] "O gallop slowly, slowly, you horses of the night!" Faustus is quoting from Ovid, *Amores*

The stars move still, time runs, the clock will strike,
The devil will come, and Faustus must be damn'd.
O, I'll leap up to my God: who pulls me down?
See, see where Christ's blood streams in the   80
  firmament:
One drop would save my soul, half a drop! Ah,
  my Christ,
Ah rend not my heart for the naming of my
  Christ,²⁷²
Yet I will call on him, oh spare me Lucifer!
Where is it now? 'tis gone,
And see where God stretcheth out his arm   85
And bends his ireful brows!
Mountains and hills, come, come, and fall on me
And hide me from the heavy wrath of God.²⁷³
No, no?
Then will I headlong run into the earth.   90
Earth, gape! O no, it will not harbor me.
You stars that reign'd at my nativity,
Whose influence hath allotted death and hell,
Now draw up Faustus like a foggy mist

Into the entrails of yon laboring cloud,   95
That when you vomit forth into the air
My limbs may issue from your smoky mouths,
So that my soul may but ascend to heaven.²⁷⁴

*The watch strikes.*²⁷⁵

Ah, half the hour is past: 'twill all be past anon.
Oh God, if thou wilt not have mercy on my soul,   100
Yet for Christ's sake, whose blood hath ransom'd me,
Impose some end to my incessant pain:
Let Faustus live in a hell a thousand years,
A hundred thousand, and at last be sav'd.
O, no end is limited to damned souls.²⁷⁶   105
Why wert thou not a creature wanting soul?
Or why is this immortal that thou hast?
Ah, Pythagoras' metempsychosis, were that true²⁷⁷
This soul should fly from me, and I be chang'd
Unto some brutish beast.   110
All beasts are happy, for when they die
Their souls are soon dissolv'd in elements,
But mine must live still to be plagu'd in hell.
Curst be the parents that engender'd me;
No Faustus, curse thyself, curse Lucifer   115
That hath depriv'd thee of the joys of heaven!

The clock striketh twelve.

I.xiii. 40. The tone of Ovid's request to Aurora, goddess of the dawn, to hold back her horses so that he can remain longer in bed with his beloved is deliberately teasing. The playfully erotic associations of the line make it especially poignant in this context.

272 rend … Christ] Cf. Joel 2:12–13, where, faced by a terrifying prospect of destruction that makes the earth quake and the heavens tremble, and that darkens the sun, moon and stars, the Israelites are exhorted to repentance: "Turne you unto me with all youre hertes, with fastynge, wepynge, and mourning: rente ["rend" in the Authorized Version] your hertes, and not your clothes. Turn you unto the LORD your God: for he is gracious and mercyfull, longe sufferynge and of greate compassyon, and ready to pardon wickednes." There are multiple ironies in Faustus's plea to the devil not to rend his heart, when according to Joel he himself should be rending it in a penitent turning to God.

273 Mountains … God] This is a recurrent motif in apocalyptic writings, e.g., Luke 23:30: "Then shall they begin to say to the mountains, Fall on us; and to the hills, Cover us"; Revelation 6:16: "And said to the mountains and rocks, Fall on us, and hide us from the face of him that sitteth on the throne, and from the wrath of the Lamb." See also Hosea 10:8.

274 lines 92–98.] Having aspired initially to "rend the clouds" (I.i. 60) and to beget himself in divine form (I.i. 63–64), Faustus now begs to undergo a bizarrely literalized reversal of the process of rebirth that was central to Renaissance Hermetic-Cabalistic magic. The bargain proposed—of resorption into a dismembering womb and of the regurgitation and dispersal of his body in exchange for the salvation of his soul—is the most violent expression of despair in the play.

275 *watch*] clock.

276 no end is limited to damned souls] i.e., damnation is endless. But "end" here suggests purpose and finality as well as temporal conclusiveness. Faustus, who challenged "the end of every art" (I.i. 4) and set out to transgress the limits fixed by his human state and his despair, here seems to recognize an absence of limit (and a corresponding emptying out of purposefulness and temporality) as the defining conditions of damnation.

277 metempsychosis] the doctrine of the transmigration of souls.

[V.ii]

O it strikes, it strikes, now body, turn to air
Or Lucifer will bear thee quick to hell![278]

Thunder and lightning.

O soul, be changed into little water drops
And fall into the ocean, ne'er be found;   120
My God, my God, look not so fierce on me!

Enter devils.

Adders and serpents, let me breathe awhile!
Ugly hell gape not, come not Lucifer,
I'll burn my books, ah Mephastophilis!

Exeunt with him.

EPILOGUE.

Enter Chorus.

Chorus. Cut is the branch that might have grown
    full straight,
  And burned is Apollo's laurel bough
  That sometime grew within this learned man:
  Faustus is gone, regard his hellish fall,
  Whose fiendful fortune may exhort the wise   5
  Only to wonder at unlawful things,[279]
  Whose deepness doth entice such forward wits
  To practice more than heavenly power permits.

Exit.

    Terminat hora diem, terminat Author opus.[280]

---

278 quick] alive.

279 Only to wonder] to be content with wondering.
280 *Terminat ... opus*] "The hour ends the day; the author
    ends his work."

WILLIAM SHAKESPEARE

Hamlet

It is not strictly true that we know little of the life of William Shakespeare (1564–1616). However disappointed we may feel in the quantity of information, given his unparalleled celebrity as a writer, we know far more about his life than we do of most middle-class people and many other writers in the Elizabethan and Jacobean ages. Shakespeare (also spelt Shakspere or Shakespear) was baptized in Stratford-upon-Avon on April 26, 1564, and reasonable conjecture (given the customs of the time) suggests that he was born three days earlier, April 23, the same day of the year on which he died fifty-two years later. His father, John, was first an alderman and then Stratford's bailiff (a position which was then equivalent to mayor). The good local grammar school, paid for by the town, would certainly have provided William's early education. Not surprisingly, he did not go on to university, which at the time would have been unusual for someone of his social class.

Exactly when Shakespeare joined the theatre in London as an actor and playwright is unknown, but in 1592, the first mention of him appears: a sarcastic expression of resentment by a slightly older playwright, Robert Greene. Shakespeare is called "an upstart crow beautified with our feathers." The comment probably refers to Shakespeare's taking over work on the series of *Henry VI* plays; this may well have involved the revision of the material of other playwrights who had originally worked on the story. In any case, from 1594 on, he is listed as a member of the company called The Lord Chamberlain's Men (later The King's Men). Shakespeare was a shareholder in the company, so, given the total lack of control over copyright at the time, it is unsurprising that he was reluctant to publish his plays and allow them into the hands of other theatre troupes, which would thereby have compromised the profits of his own company. That Shakespeare was also an actor in the company for which he wrote, and that he would therefore have the opportunity of forging and refining his written work in the heat of performance, no doubt goes far in explaining how he was able to make such substantial advances in theatricality over the work of more strictly literary playwrights. This fact is also one reason (among many) to doubt theories which argue that someone else, such as Edward de Vere, 17th Earl of Oxford, authored the plays. Anyone who has worked on a new play alongside its author will know how difficult it would be for the putative playwright to conceal his non-authorship from the rest of the company. If Shakespeare's company knew that he was not the author of the plays that bore his name, and yet no member of the company—not even an actor bitter over a sudden dismissal—ever revealed this secret, even long after de Vere's and Shakespeare's deaths, this was a better kept conspiracy than any other known to history. That such a singular event should occur in the notoriously gossipy theatre world seems most improbable indeed.

Shakespeare wrote thirty-seven or thirty-eight plays (depending on whether *Two Noble Kinsmen*, a collaboration with John Fletcher, is included in the total). These, taken as a whole, evince mastery of virtually every major type of play that was popular in his time—something that can hardly be claimed for any other playwright. A few representative titles can illustrate the point: the history play: *Richard III, Henry IV (Parts 1 & 2), Henry V*; the comedy: *Twelfth Night, A Midsummer Night's Dream, Much Ado About Nothing*; the romance: *Cymbeline, The Winter's Tale, The Tempest*; and the tragedy: *Romeo and Juliet, Othello, King Lear, Antony and Cleopatra*, and, of course, *Hamlet*.

Whether or not *Hamlet* is, as many people believe, Shakespeare's best play, it is certainly the most famous play ever written. Not only is it the most performed, filmed, read and discussed of all Shakespeare's works, but the title character has spread well beyond the confines of his play to achieve iconic status in Western culture. Even those who have never seen or read the play can recognize certain allusions to *Hamlet*: the image of a man dressed in black and scrutinizing a human skull held in the palm of his hand, or the phrase "to be or not to be." Yet, despite this accretion of clichés, the play is somehow able to transcend familiarity to emerge fresh and still enigmatic with each encounter.

When we read a story—any story—we always develop some anticipation about its outcome which we build and revise as we go on reading. When we re-read a well-written story, much of our interest turns to observing and interrogating the mechanisms that have informed that earlier anticipation of the outcome. In re-reading *Hamlet*, or in seeing it performed after having read it, one cannot help but be impressed at the fantastic complexity of all the mechanisms influencing our expectations, and at how certain subtle details, perhaps unnoticed in earlier readings, can suddenly rise to prominence to change our expectations—even when we know how the story actually turns out. *Hamlet* is a play with so many facets, it has been said, that even the worst production will manage in the course of a performance to achieve something of interest, however fleetingly; a little gesture might offer new insights into Polonius's relationship to his children, for instance, or an emphasized phrase might imply something previously unconsidered about Gertrude's first marriage. This feature of *Hamlet*—that it is a play which many of us think we know so well and yet is still able provide a field for new discoveries—certainly accounts for much of the play's enduring appeal. But we can go further, and say that this ability to suddenly reveal unexpected ideas rising against a familiar horizon also makes an essential contribution to the meaning of the play. For *Hamlet*, above all else, is a play that finds its meanings in the distance between notions of "what should happen" and "what does happen." Indeed, Hamlet himself spends most of the play weighing this question of what is being done against what should be done, and the leading actor's delineation of the variations in the tension between those factors is what usually provides the main dramatic interest for audiences during a performance. Moreover, that is a version of the same tension lying behind many of the most intriguing discussions of the play: at the story's end, has Hamlet done what he should have done? How do we know? Who can we trust to tell us? Why should we doubt what we are told?

However we decide the answers to such questions, it is clear enough that Shakespeare wanted his audiences to ask them, for his extant sources—so far as we have been able to identify them—tell a much simpler story. Saxo Grammaticus, in his *Gesta Danorum*, a history of Denmark written about 1200, tells the story of one Amleth (which has no clear historical basis, but which we may imagine taking place around 1050). Saxo's story was freely translated by François de Belleforest in Volume 5 of his *Histoires tragiques* (1570); this, in turn, seems to have been Shakespeare's main source for his play (although many believe that there was also an earlier play, possibly by Thomas Kyd, based on the same story). In Belleforest's version of the story, the characters of Polonius and his children do not exist; the murder of the old King by his brother is widely known among the Danish subjects, but the brother persuades the people that he was defending the Queen; Hamlet, being quite young and frightened, decides to feign madness for self-protection, but, when he gradually becomes more vindictive and accusatory, he is sent into exile, where he marries the King of Britain's daughter; meanwhile, the Queen repents her part in the murder of the old King; Hamlet returns after a year's exile and, while his uncle celebrates the false news of his nephew's death, Hamlet burns down the palace.

Naturally, then, Belleforest's version of the story does not open itself to questions such as how mad Hamlet is, or what Gertrude knew, or how passionate was the love affair between Ophelia and Hamlet, or about the moral status of the ghost. But, when we ask ourselves such questions of Shakespeare's *Hamlet*, these point not to weaknesses, but to the real essence of the play. For these are, in a sense, Hamlet's own questions, and by asking them ourselves, we move closer to sharing Hamlet's own most momentous dilemma: does it (as he puts it) "stand upon" him—that is, is it rightly his responsibility—to kill Claudius? Different readers will have different answers to this question; indeed, many readers will change their answer according to what they have derived from a particular reading or viewing of the play.

In short, to read *Hamlet* for the first time is to enter into one of the key conversations of Western civilization.

[C.S.W.]

WILLIAM SHAKESPEARE
The Tragedy of Hamlet, Prince of Denmark

CHARACTERS

HAMLET, Prince of Denmark.
CLAUDIUS, King of Denmark, Hamlet's Uncle.
GERTRUDE, Queen of Denmark, Hamlet's Mother.
GHOST of Hamlet's Father.

POLONIUS, Lord Chamberlain.
LAERTES, his Son.
OPHELIA, his Daughter.

HORATIO, Friend to Hamlet.

VOLTIMAND, ⎤ Courtiers,
CORNELIUS, ⎦ ambassadors to Norway.
ROSENCRANTZ, ⎤ Courtiers,
GUILDENSTERN, ⎦ schoolmates of Hamlet.
OSRIC, a Courtier.

MARCELLUS, ⎤ Officers.
BERNARDO, ⎦
FRANCISCO, a Soldier.
REYNALDO, Servant to Polonius.

FORTINBRAS, Prince of Norway.

A PRIEST.
A CAPTAIN.
ENGLISH AMBASSADORS.
PLAYERS,
A GENTLEMAN,
Two CLOWNS: a Grave-digger and his companion.

LORDS, LADIES, OFFICERS, SOLDIERS, SAILORS, MESSENGERS, and ATTENDANTS.

ACT I

SCENE I.—ELSINORE.[1]

A guard platform before the Castle.
FRANCISCO at his post. Enter BERNARDO.

BERNARDO. Who's there?

FRANCISCO. Nay, answer me. Stand and unfold
    yourself.[2]

BERNARDO. Long live the King!

FRANCISCO. Bernardo?

BERNARDO. He.   5

FRANCISCO. You come most carefully upon your hour.

BERNARDO. 'Tis now struck twelve; get thee to bed,
    Francisco.

FRANCISCO. For this relief much thanks. 'Tis bitter
    cold,

  And I am sick at heart.

BERNARDO. Have you had quiet guard?   10

FRANCISCO.   Not a mouse stirring.

BERNARDO. Well, good night.

  If you do meet Horatio and Marcellus,

  The rivals of my watch, bid them make haste.[3]

FRANCISCO. I think I hear them. Stand, ho! Who is
    there?

Enter HORATIO and MARCELLUS.

HORATIO. Friends to this ground.   15

MARCELLUS.   And liegemen to the Dane.[4]

FRANCISCO. Give you good-night.

MARCELLUS.   O! farewell, honest soldier:

  Who hath relieved you?

FRANCISCO.   Bernardo hath my place.

  Give you good night. [*Exit.*]

MARCELLUS.   Holla, Bernardo!

BERNARDO.   Say,

  What, is Horatio there?

HORATIO.   A piece of him.

BERNARDO. Welcome, Horatio, welcome, good   20
    Marcellus.

MARCELLUS. What, has this thing appeared again
    to-night?

BERNARDO. I have seen nothing.

MARCELLUS. Horatio says 'tis but our fantasy,

  And will not let belief take hold of him

  Touching this dreaded sight, twice seen of us: 25

  Therefore I have entreated him along

  With us to watch the minutes of this night;

  That, if again this apparition come,

  He may approve our eyes and speak to it.

HORATIO. Tush, tush! 'twill not appear.   30

BERNARDO.   Sit down awhile,

  And let us once again assail your ears,

  That are so fortified against our story,

  What we two nights have seen.

HORATIO.   Well, sit we down,

  And let us hear Bernardo speak of this.

BERNARDO. Last night of all,   35

  When yond same star that's westward from the pole[5]

  Had made his course to illume that part of heaven

  Where now it burns, Marcellus and myself,

  The bell then beating one,—

MARCELLUS. Peace! break thee off! Look where it   40
    comes again!

Enter GHOST.

BERNARDO. In the same figure, like the king that's
    dead.

MARCELLUS. Thou art a scholar; speak to it, Horatio.

BERNARDO. Looks it not like the king? Mark it,
    Horatio.

HORATIO. Most like. It harrows me with fear and
    wonder.

BERNARDO. It would be spoke to.   45

MARCELLUS.   Question it, Horatio.

HORATIO. What art thou that usurp'st this time of
    night,

  Together with that fair and warlike form

  In which the majesty of buried Denmark[6]

---

[1] Elsinore (Helsingor) was the capital of Denmark until
  1170.

[2] Nay, answer me] Francisco is on watch and Bernardo
  has come to relieve him, so rightly it is Francisco who
  should make the demand; unfold] disclose.

[3] rivals] partners.

[4] liegemen to the Dane] loyal subjects of the King of
  Denmark.

[5] pole] polestar.

[6] buried Denmark] the late King of Denmark.

Did sometimes march? By heaven I charge thee
  speak!
MARCELLUS. It is offended.   50
BERNARDO.   See, it stalks away!
HORATIO. Stay! Speak, speak! I charge thee speak!

[*Exit Ghost.*]

MARCELLUS. 'Tis gone, and will not answer.
BERNARDO. How now, Horatio? You tremble and
  look pale.
  Is not this something more than fantasy?
  What think you on't?   55
HORATIO. Before my God, I might not this believe
  Without the sensible and true avouch
  Of mine own eyes.
MARCELLUS.   Is it not like the king?
HORATIO. As thou art to thyself.
  Such was the very armour he had on   60
  When he the ambitious Norway combated.
  So frowned he once when, in an angry parle,[7]
  He smote the sledded Polacks on the ice.
  'Tis strange.
MARCELLUS. Thus twice before, and jump at this 65
  dead hour,[8]
  With martial stalk hath he gone by our watch.
HORATIO. In what particular thought to work I
  know not;
  But, in the gross and scope of my opinion,
  This bodes some strange eruption to our state.
MARCELLUS. Good now, sit down, and tell me he 70
  that knows,
  Why this same strict and most observant watch
  So nightly toils the subject of the land;[9]
  And why such daily cast of brazen cannon
  And foreign mart for implements of war;[10]
  Why such impress of shipwrights, whose sore task[11] 75
  Does not divide the Sunday from the week.
  What might be toward, that this sweaty haste
  Doth make the night joint-labourer with the day?

Who is't that can inform me?
HORATIO.   That can I;
  At least, the whisper goes so. Our last king, 80
  Whose image even but now appeared to us,
  Was, as you know, by Fortinbras of Norway,[12]
  Thereto pricked on by a most emulate pride,
  Dared to the combat; in which our valiant
    Hamlet—[13]
  For so this side of our known world esteemed him— 85
  Did slay this Fortinbras; who, by a sealed compact,
  Well ratified by law and heraldry,[14]
  Did forfeit with his life all those his lands
  Which he stood seized of, to the conqueror;[15]
  Against the which a moiety competent[16] 90
  Was gaged by our king; which had returned
  To the inheritance of Fortinbras,
  Had he been vanquisher, as, by the same covenant,
  And carriage of the article designed,[17]
  His fell to Hamlet. Now, sir, young Fortinbras,[18] 95
  Of unimprovéd mettle hot and full,
  Hath in the skirts of Norway here and there[19]
  Sharked up a list of lawless resolutes,[20]
  For food and diet, to some enterprise
  That hath a stomach in't; which is no other— 100
  As it doth well appear unto our state—
  But to recover of us, by strong hand
  And terms compulsatory, those foresaid lands
  So by his father lost. And this, I take it,[21]

---

7 parle] parley, encounter.
8 jump] precisely.
9 toils the subject of the land] makes the Danish people toil.
10 mart for] trade in.
11 impress] forced service.

---

12 Fortinbras] i.e., Old Fortinbras, father to the present Prince of Norway.
13 Hamlet] i.e., Old Hamlet, father to the present Prince of Denmark.
14 law and heraldry] heraldic law governing the combat.
15 stood seized of] had taken possession of. Apparently, the principal states were not included in the agreement, for Norway continues as an independent kingdom.
16 a moiety competent] an equal portion.
17 by the … designed] by the reciprocal provisions of the agreement.
18 young Fortinbras] i.e., the present Prince of Norway.
19 skirts] outskirts, border regions.
20 sharked up a list of lawless resolutes] with an appetite like a shark's, enlisted a troop of desperadoes.
21 Young Fortinbras intends to avenge the defeat and death of his father, Old Fortinbras, and take back the lands he lost.

Is the main motive of our preparations,   105
The source of this our watch, and the chief head
Of this post-haste and rummage in the land.[22]
BERNARDO. I think it be no other but e'en so;
Well may it sort that this portentous figure[23]
Comes arméd through our watch, so like the King   110
That was and is the question of these wars.
HORATIO. A mote it is to trouble the mind's eye.
In the most high and palmy state of Rome,[24]
A little ere the mightiest Julius fell,
The graves stood tenantless, and the sheeted dead[25]   115
Did squeak and gibber in the Roman streets;
As stars with trains of fire, and dews of blood,
Disasters in the sun; and the moist star
Upon whose influence Neptune's empire stands
Was sick almost to doomsday with eclipse.   120
And even the like precurse of fierce events,
As harbingers preceding still the fates
And prologue to the omen coming on,
Have heaven and earth together demonstrated
Unto our climatures and countrymen.[26]   125
But soft! Behold! Lo, where it comes again.

Re-enter GHOST.

I'll cross it, though it blast me. Stay, illusion!
If thou hast any sound, or use of voice,
        Speak to me.
If there be any good thing to be done,   130
That may to thee do ease, and, race to me,
        Speak to me:
If thou art privy to thy country's fate,
Which happily foreknowing may avoid,
O, speak;   135
Or if thou hast uphoarded in thy life
Extorted treasure in the womb of earth,
For which, they say, you spirits oft walk in death,
        [*Cock crows.*]
Speak of it: stay, and speak! Stop it, Marcellus.
MARCELLUS. Shall I strike at it with my partisan?[27]   140

HORATIO. Do, if it will not stand.
BERNARDO.   'Tis here!
HORATIO.   'Tis here!

[*Exit GHOST.*]

MARCELLUS. 'Tis gone!
We do it wrong, being so majestical,
To offer it the show of violence;
For it is as the air, invulnerable,   145
And our vain blows malicious mockery.[28]
BERNARDO. It was about to speak, when the cock
    crew.
HORATIO. And then it started, like a guilty thing
Upon a fearful summons. I have heard,
The cock, that is the trumpet to the morn,   150
Doth with his lofty and shrill-sounding throat
Awake the god of day; and at his warning,
Whether in sea or fire, in earth or air,[29]
The extravagant and erring spirit hies
To his confine; and of the truth herein   155
This present object made probation.[30]
MARCELLUS. It faded on the crowing of the cock.
Some say that ever 'gainst that season comes
Wherein our Saviour's birth is celebrated,[31]
The bird of dawning singeth all night long;   160
And then, they say, no spirit dare stir abroad;
The nights are wholesome; then no planets strike,[32]
No fairy takes, nor witch hath power to charm,[33]
So hallowed and so gracious is the time.
HORATIO. So have I heard and do in part believe it.   165
But, look, the morn, in russet mantle clad,
Walks o'er the dew of yon high eastward hill.
Break we our watch up; and by my advice
Let us impart what we have seen to-night
Unto young Hamlet; for, upon my life,   170
This spirit, dumb to us, will speak to him.

---

[22] rummage] commotion.
[23] Well may it sort] it makes sense.
[24] palmy] flourishing with the palms of many victories.
[25] sheeted dead] dead in their shrouds.
[26] climatures] climes, weather.
[27] partisan] a long-handled spear.

[28] our vain … mockery] The futility of our attempts to strike it make a mockery of us.
[29] sea, fire, earth, air] the four elements.
[30] probation] proof. The notion that the ghost might be evil is carefully emphasized.
[31] i.e., just before Christmas.
[32] no planets strike] There are no malevolent astrological influences.
[33] takes] bewitches.

Do you consent we shall acquaint him with it,
As needful in our loves, fitting our duty?
MARCELLUS. Let's do't, I pray; and I this morning
    know
Where we shall find him most conveniently.   175

[*Exeunt.*]

SCENE II.

A ROOM OF STATE IN THE CASTLE.

Flourish. Enter Claudius KING *of Denmark, Gertrude
the* QUEEN, *Council including* POLONIUS, *his son*
LAERTES, HAMLET *and Others.*[34]

KING. Though yet of Hamlet our dear brother's death
    The memory be green, and that it us befitted
    To bear our hearts in grief, and our whole kingdom
    To be contracted in one brow of woe,
    Yet so far hath discretion fought with nature   5
    That we with wisest sorrow think on him,
    Together with remembrance of ourselves.
    Therefore, our sometime sister, now our queen,[35]
    The imperial jointress of this war-like state,[36]
    Have we, as 'twere with a defeated joy,   10
    With one auspicious and one dropping eye,
    With mirth in funeral and with dirge in marriage,
    In equal scale weighing delight and dole,
    Taken to wife: nor have we herein barred
    Your better wisdoms, which have freely gone   15
    With this affair along. For all, our thanks.
    Now follows that you know: young Fortinbras,
    Holding a weak supposal of our worth,
    Or thinking by our late dear brother's death
    Our state to be disjoint and out of frame,   20
    Colleagued with this dream of his advantage,
    He hath not failed to pester us with message,
    Importing the surrender of those lands
    Lost by his father, with all bands of law,
    To our most valiant brother. So much for him.   25

Enter VOLTEMAND *and* CORNELIUS.[37]

    Now for ourself and for this time of meeting.
    Thus much the business is: we have here writ
    To Norway, uncle of young Fortinbras—
    Who, impotent and bed-rid, scarcely hears
    Of this his nephew's purpose—to suppress   30
    His further gait herein, in that the levies,
    The lists and full proportions, are all made
    Out of his subject.[38] And we here dispatch
    You, good Cornelius, and you, Voltimand,
    For bearers of this greeting to old Norway,   35
    Giving to you no further personal power
    To business with the king more than the scope
    Of these dilated articles allow.[39]
    Farewell and let your haste commend your duty.
CORNELIUS.   ⎤
VOLTEMAND. ⎦ In that, and all things, will we show   40
    our duty.
KING. We doubt it nothing: heartily farewell.

[*Exeunt* VOLTIMAND *and* CORNELIUS.]

    And now, Laertes, what's the news with you?
    You told us of some suit; what is't, Laertes?
    You cannot speak of reason to the Dane,
    And lose your voice; what wouldst thou beg, Laertes,   45
    That shall not be my offer, not thy asking?
    The head is not more native to the heart,
    The hand more instrumental to the mouth,
    Than is the throne of Denmark to thy father.
    What wouldst thou have, Laertes?   50
LAERTES.   Dread my lord,
    Your leave and favour to return to France;
    From whence, though willingly I came to Denmark,
    To show my duty in your coronation,
    Yet now, I must confess, that duty done,
    My thoughts and wishes bend again toward France   55
    And bow them to your gracious leave and pardon.

---

34 Hamlet may be mentioned last because he is dramati-
    cally isolated from the others. He may even have entered
    separately.
35 sister] i.e., sister-in-law.
36 jointress] joint ruler.

37 Voltemand and Cornelius enter at this late point accord-
    ing to the *Folio*, possibly because the actors playing them
    were doubling as Marcellus and Bernardo and needed
    time to change.
38 the levies … subject] Young Fortinbras is building his
    forces out of Norway's subjects and property.
39 dilated articles] detailed documents.

KING. Have you your father's leave? What says
    Polonius?
POLONIUS. He hath, my lord, wrung from me my
    slow leave
  By laboursome petition, and at last
  Upon his will I sealed my hard consent.[40]   60
  I do beseech you, give him leave to go.
KING. Take thy fair hour, Laertes; time be thine,
  And thy best graces spend it at thy will.
  But now, my cousin Hamlet, and my son.—
HAMLET. [*Aside.*] A little more than kin, and less   65
  than kind.[41]
KING. How is it that the clouds still hang on you?
HAMLET. Not so, my lord; I am too much i' the
  sun.[42]
QUEEN. Good Hamlet, cast thy nighted colour off,
  And let thine eye look like a friend on Denmark.
  Do not for ever with thy vailéd lids[43]   70
  Seek for thy noble father in the dust:
  Thou know'st 'tis common; all that lives must die,
  Passing through nature to eternity.
HAMLET. Ay, madam, it is common.[44]
QUEEN.   If it be,
  Why seems it so particular with thee?   75
HAMLET. Seems, madam! Nay, it is. I know not "seems."
  'Tis not alone my inky cloak, good mother,
  Nor customary suits of solemn black,
  Nor windy suspiration of forced breath,
  No, nor the fruitful river in the eye,   80
  Nor the dejected haviour of the visage,
  Together with all forms, moods, shapes of grief,
  That can denote me truly. These indeed seem,
  For they are actions that a man might play:
  But I have that within which passeth show;   85
  These but the trappings and the suits of woe.
KING. 'Tis sweet and commendable in your nature,
  Hamlet,
  To give these mourning duties to your father:

But, you must know, your father lost a father;
That father lost, lost his; and the survivor bound   90
In filial obligation for some term
To do obsequious sorrow. But, to persevere
In obstinate condolement is a course
Of impious stubbornness; 'tis unmanly grief:
It shows a will most incorrect to heaven,   95
A heart unfortified, a mind impatient,
An understanding simple and unschooled.
For what we know must be and is as common
As any the most vulgar thing to sense,
Why should we in our peevish opposition   100
Take it to heart? Fie! 'tis a fault to heaven,
A fault against the dead, a fault to nature,
To reason most absurd, whose common theme
Is death of fathers, and who still hath cried,
From the first corse till he that died to-day,[45]   105
"This must be so." We pray you, throw to earth
This unprevailing woe, and think of us
As of a father; for let the world take note,
You are the most immediate to our throne;
And with no less nobility of love   110
Than that which dearest father bears his son
Do I impart toward you. For your intent
In going back to school in Wittenberg,[46]
It is most retrograde to our desire;
And we beseech you, bend you to remain   115
Here in the cheer and comfort of our eye,
Our chiefest courtier, cousin, and our son.
QUEEN. Let not thy mother lose her prayers, Hamlet:
  I pray thee stay with us; go not to Wittenberg.
HAMLET. I shall in all my best obey you, madam.   120
KING. Why, 'tis a loving and a fair reply.
  Be as ourself in Denmark. Madam, come;
  This gentle and unforced accord of Hamlet
  Sits smiling to my heart; in grace whereof,
  No jocund health that Denmark drinks to-day,   125
  But the great cannon to the clouds shall tell,
  And the king's rouse the heavens shall bruit again,
  Re-speaking earthly thunder. Come away.

[*Exeunt all except HAMLET.*]

---

[40] hard consent] reluctant consent.
[41] kin … kind] Hamlet has been made more than Clau-
    dius's nephew (kin) but is not his offspring (kind). There
    is also a pun on "kind."
[42] sun] a pun on "son."
[43] vailéd lids] lowered eyelids.
[44] common] both universal and vulgar.

[45] corse] corpse.
[46] Wittenberg] i.e., the Protestant university associated
    with Martin Luther, founded in 1502.

HAMLET. O! that this too too solid flesh would melt,
  Thaw and resolve itself into a dew; 130
  Or that the Everlasting had not fixed
  His canon 'gainst self-slaughter! O God! O God!
  How weary, stale, flat, and unprofitable
  Seem to me all the uses of this world.
  Fie on't, ah fie! 'tis an unweeded garden, 135
  That grows to seed; things rank and gross innature
  Possess it merely. That it should come to this!
  But two months dead—nay, not so much, not
    two—
  So excellent a king; that was, to this,
  Hyperion to a satyr; so loving to my mother[47] 140
  That he might not beteem the winds of heaven[48]
  Visit her face too roughly. Heaven and earth!
  Must I remember? why, she would hang on him,
  As if increase of appetite had grown
  By what it fed on; and yet, within a month— 145
  Let me not think on't—Frailty, thy name is
    woman—
  A little month—or ere those shoes were old
  With which she followed my poor father's body,
  Like Niobe, all tears—why she, even she—[49]
  O God! a beast, that wants discourse of reason, 150
  Would have mourned longer—married with my
    uncle—
  My father's brother, but no more like my father
  Than I to Hercules—within a month,
  Ere yet the salt of most unrighteous tears
  Had left the flushing in her gallèd eyes, 155
  She married. O most wicked speed, to post
  With such dexterity to incestuous sheets.
  It is not nor it cannot come to good;
  But break, my heart, for I must hold my tongue!

Enter HORATIO, MARCELLUS, AND BERNARDO.

HORATIO. Hail to your lordship! 160
HAMLET. I am glad to see you well. Horatio, or I do
  forget myself.

HORATIO. The same, my lord, and your poor
  servant ever.
HAMLET. Sir, my good friend; I'll change that name
  with you.
  And what make you from Wittenberg, Horatio?
    Marcellus.[50]
MARCELLUS. My good lord. 165
HAMLET. I am very glad to see you. [*To BERNARDO.*]
  Good even, sir.
  But what, in faith, make you from Wittenberg?
HORATIO. A truant disposition, good my lord.
HAMLET. I would not hear your enemy say so,
  Nor shall you do my ear that violence, 170
  To make it truster of your own report
  Against yourself. I know you are no truant.
  But what is your affair in Elsinore?
  We'll teach you to drink deep ere you depart.
HORATIO. My lord, I came to see your father's funeral. 175
HAMLET. I prithee, do not mock me, fellow-student;
  I think it was to see my mother's wedding.
HORATIO. Indeed, my lord, it followed hard upon.
HAMLET. Thrift, thrift, Horatio! the funeral baked
  meats
  Did coldly furnish forth the marriage tables.[51] 180
  Would I had met my dearest[52] foe in heaven
  Ere I had ever seen that day, Horatio!
  My father—methinks I see my father—
HORATIO. Where, my lord?
HAMLET.   In my mind's eye, Horatio.
HORATIO. I saw him once; he was a goodly king. 185
HAMLET. He was a man, take him for all in all;
  I shall not look upon his like again.
HORATIO. My lord, I think I saw him yesternight.
HAMLET. Saw, who?
HORATIO. My lord, the king your father. 190
HAMLET.   The king my father!
HORATIO. Season your admiration for a while
  With an attent ear, till I may deliver,
  Upon the witness of these gentlemen,
  This marvel to you.
HAMLET.   For God's love, let me hear.

---

47 Hyperion to a satyr] the sun god as compared to a part-goat creature known for its lascivious appetite.
48 beteem] permit.
49 Niobe] in Ovid's *Metamorphoses*, a mother who wept inconsolably for her murdered children; she turned to stone.

---

50 what make you from] what brings you away from.
51 funeral baked … tables] the leftover meat pies from the funeral were re-served cold at the wedding.
52 dearest] most heartily hated.

HORATIO. Two nights together had these gentlemen,   195
    Marcellus and Bernardo, on their watch,
    In the dead vast and middle of the night,
    Been thus encountered: a figure like your father,
    Armed at point exactly, *cap-à-pe*,[53]
    Appears before them, and with solemn march   200
    Goes slow and stately by them: thrice he walked
    By their oppressed and fear-surprisèd eyes,
    Within his truncheon's length; whilst they, distilled
    Almost to jelly with the act of fear,
    Stand dumb and speak not to him. This to me   205
    In dreadful secrecy impart they did,
    And I with them the third night kept the watch;
    Where, as they had delivered, both in time,
    Form of the thing, each word made true and good
    The apparition comes. I knew your father;   210
    These hands are not more like.[54]
HAMLET.   But where was this?
MARCELLUS. My lord, upon the platform where we
    watched.
HAMLET. Did you not speak to it?
HORATIO.   My lord, I did;
    But answer made it none; yet once methought
    It lifted up its head and did address   215
    Itself to motion, like as it would speak;
    But even then the morning cock crew loud,
    And at the sound it shrunk in haste away
    And vanished from our sight.
HAMLET.   'Tis very strange.
HORATIO. As I do live, my honoured lord, 'tis true;   220
    And we did think it writ down in our duty
    To let you know of it.
HAMLET. Indeed, indeed, sirs, but this troubles me.
    Hold you the watch to-night?
MARCELLUS.⎤
BERNARDO. ⎦   We do, my lord.
HAMLET. Armed, say you?   225
MARCELLUS.⎤
BERNARDO. ⎦   Armed, my lord.
HAMLET. From top to toe?
MARCELLUS.⎤
BERNARDO. ⎦   My lord, from head to foot.

HAMLET. Then saw you not his face?
HORATIO. O yes, my lord; he wore his beaver up.[55]
HAMLET. What looked he, frowningly?
HORATIO. A countenance more in sorrow than in   230
    anger.
HAMLET. Pale or red?
HORATIO. Nay, very pale.
HAMLET.   And fixed his eyes upon you?
HORATIO. Most constantly.
HAMLET.   I would I had been there.
HORATIO. It would have much amazed you.
HAMLET. Very like, very like. Stayed it long?   235
HORATIO. While one with moderate haste might
    tell a hundred.
MARCELLUS.⎤
BERNARDO. ⎦ Longer, longer.
HORATIO. Not when I saw it.
HAMLET. His beard was grizzled, no?[56]
HORATIO. It was, as I have seen it in his life,   240
    A sable silvered.
HAMLET.   I will watch to-night;
    Perchance 'twill walk again.
HORATIO.   I warrant it will.
HAMLET. If it assume my noble father's person,
    I'll speak to it, though hell itself should gape
    And bid me hold my peace. I pray you all,   245
    If you have hitherto concealed this sight,
    Let it be tenable in your silence still;
    And whatsoever else shall hap to-night,
    Give it an understanding, but no tongue:
    I will requite your loves. So, fare you well.   250
    Upon the platform, 'twixt eleven and twelve,
    I'll visit you.
ALL   Our duty to your honour.
HAMLET. Your loves, as mine to you. Farewell.

Exeunt HORATIO, MARCELLUS, and BERNARDO.

    My father's spirit in arms! all is not well;
    I doubt some foul play: would the night were come!   255
    Till then sit still, my soul: foul deeds will rise,
    Though all the earth o'erwhelm them, to men's eyes.

[*Exit.*]

---

53 Armed at point exactly, *cap-à-pe*] armed precisely in the
    manner of Old Hamlet from head to foot.
54 These hands … like] Horatio's hands do not resemble one
    another more than the ghost resembled Old Hamlet.

---

55 beaver] visor, face-guard.
56 grizzled] gray.

SCENE III

A ROOM IN THE CASTLE.

Enter LAERTES and OPHELIA.

LAERTES. My necessaries are embarked; farewell:
  And, sister, as the winds give benefit
  And convoy is assistant, do not sleep,
  But let me hear from you.
OPHELIA.   Do you doubt that?
LAERTES.For Hamlet, and the trifling of his favour,   5
  Hold it a fashion and a toy in blood,[57]
  A violet in the youth of primy nature,[58]
  Forward, not permanent, sweet, not lasting,
  The perfume and suppliance of a minute;[59]
  No more.   10
OPHELIA.   No more but so?
LAERTES.   Think it no more:
  For nature crescent does not grow alone[60]
  In thews and bulk; but, as this temple waxes,[61]
  The inward service of the mind and soul
  Grows wide withal. Perhaps he loves you now,
  And now no soil nor cautel doth besmirch[62]   15
  The virtue of his will; but you must fear,
  His greatness weighed, his will is not his own;
  For he himself is subject to his birth;
  He may not, as unvalued persons do,[63]
  Carve for himself, for on his choice depends   20
  The safety and health of this whole state;
  And therefore must his choice be circumscribed
  Unto the voice and yielding of that body
  Whereof he is the head. Then if he says he loves you,
  It fits your wisdom so far to believe it   25
  As he in his particular act and place
  May give his saying deed; which is no further
  Than the main voice of Denmark goes withal.
  Then weigh what loss your honour may sustain,

If with too credent ear you list his songs,[64]   30
Or lose your heart, or your chaste treasure open
To his unmastered importunity.
Fear it, Ophelia, fear it, my dear sister;
And keep you in the rear of your affection,
Out of the shot and danger of desire.[65]   35
The chariest maid is prodigal enough[66]
If she unmask her beauty to the moon;
Virtue herself 'scapes not calumnious strokes;
The canker galls the infants of the spring
Too oft before their buttons be disclosed,[67]   40
And in the morn and liquid dew of youth
Contagious blastments are most imminent.
Be wary then; best safety lies in fear:
Youth to itself rebels, though none else near.
OPHELIA. I shall th' effect of this good lesson keep,   45
  As watchman to my heart. But, good my brother,
  Do not, as some ungracious pastors do,
  Show me the steep and thorny way to heaven,
  Whiles, like a puffed and reckless libertine,
  Himself the primrose path of dalliance treads,   50
  And recks not his own rede.[68]
LAERTES.   O! fear me not.
  I stay too long. But here my father comes.

Enter POLONIUS.

  A double blessing is a double grace;
  Occasion smiles upon a second leave.
POLONIUS. Yet here, Laertes! aboard, aboard, for   55
    shame!
  The wind sits in the shoulder of your sail,
  And you are stayed for. There, my blessing with thee!
  And these few precepts in thy memory
  Look thou character.[69] Give thy thoughts no tongue,
  Nor any unproportioned thought his act.[70]   60
  Be thou familiar, but by no means vulgar;
  Those friends thou hast, and their adoption tried,
  Grapple them to thy soul with hoops of steel;

---

57 a toy in blood] an amorous sport.
58 primy] early, in the springtime. Laertes' choice of imagery in this scene suggests a rather youthful Hamlet.
59 suppliance] diversion.
60 crescent] in a state of growth.
61 thews and bulk] sinews and flesh; temple] the body.
62 cautel] deceit.
63 unvalued] of low social rank.

64 credent] credulous; list] listen to.
65 shot and danger] a military metaphor.
66 chariest] most modest.
67 buttons] buds.
68 recks not his own rede] heeds not his own counsel.
69 Look thou character] Be sure to inscribe.
70 unproportioned] unbalanced, ill-judged.

But do not dull thy palm with entertainment
Of each new-hatched, unfledged comrade. Beware   65
Of entrance to a quarrel; but, being in,
Bear't that th' opposed may beware of thee.
Give every man thine ear, but few thy voice;
Take each man's censure, but reserve thy judgment.[71]
Costly thy habit as thy purse can buy,[72]   70
But not expressed in fancy; rich, not gaudy;
For the apparel oft proclaims the man,
And they in France of the best rank and station
Are of a most select and generous chief in that.[73]
Neither a borrower, nor a lender be;   75
For loan oft loses both itself and friend,
And borrowing dulls the edge of husbandry.[74]
This above all: to thine own self be true,
And it must follow, as the night the day,
Thou canst not then be false to any man.   80
Farewell; my blessing season this in thee!
LAERTES. Most humbly do I take my leave, my lord.
POLONIUS. The time invites you; go, your servants
    tend.[75]
LAERTES. Farewell, Ophelia; and remember well
    What I have said to you.   85
OPHELIA.   'Tis in my memory locked,
    And you yourself shall keep the key of it.
LAERTES. Farewell. [*Exit.*]
POLONIUS. What is't, Ophelia, he hath said to you?
OPHELIA. So please you, something touching the
    Lord Hamlet.
POLONIUS. Marry, well bethought: 90
    'Tis told me, he hath very oft of late
    Given private time to you; and you yourself
    Have of your audience been most free and
        bounteous.
    If it be so—as so 'tis put on me,
    And that in way of caution—I must tell you,   95
    You do not understand yourself so clearly
    As it behooves my daughter and your honour.
    What is between you? Give me up the truth.

OPHELIA. He hath, my lord, of late made many
    tenders
    Of his affection to me.   100
POLONIUS. Affection! pooh! You speak like a green
    girl,
    Unsifted in such perilous circumstance.[76]
    Do you believe his tenders, as you call them?
OPHELIA. I do not know, my lord, what I should think,
POLONIUS. Marry, I'll teach you: think yourself a baby,   105
    That you have ta'en these tenders for true pay,
    Which are not sterling. Tender yourself more dearly;
    Or—not to crack the wind of the poor phrase,
    Running it thus—you'll tender me a fool.
OPHELIA. My lord, he hath importuned me with love   110
    In honourable fashion.
POLONIUS. Ay, fashion you may call it: go to, go to.
OPHELIA. And hath given countenance to his
    speech, my lord,
    With almost all the holy vows of heaven.
POLONIUS. Ay, springes to catch woodcocks. I do   115
    know,[77]
    When the blood burns, how prodigal the soul
    Lends the tongue vows: these blazes, daughter.
    Giving more light than heat, extinct in both,
    Even in their promise, as it is a-making,
    You must not take for fire. From this time   120
    Be something scanter of your maiden presence;
    Set your entreatments at a higher rate[78]
    Than a command to parley. For Lord Hamlet,
    Believe so much in him, that he is young,
    And with a larger tether may he walk   125
    Than may be given you: in few, Ophelia,
    Do not believe his vows, for they are brokers,
    Not of that dye which their investments show,[79]
    But mere implorators of unholy suits,[80]
    Breathing like sanctified and pious bonds,[81]   130
    The better to beguile. This is for all:

71 censure] opinion (not necessarily disapprobation).
72 habit] clothing.
73 Are of a most select and generous chief in that] belong
    to the very cream of a well-born elite in that respect.
74 husbandry] thriftiness.
75 tend] attend, wait.

76 Unsifted] inexperienced.
77 springes to catch woodcocks] snares to catch proverbi-
    ally stupid birds.
78 entreatments] negotiations—another military metaphor.
79 investments] garments.
80 implorators] solicitors.
81 bonds] pledges.

I would not, in plain terms, from this time forth,
Have you so slander any moment's leisure,
As to give words or talk with the Lord Hamlet.
Look to't, I charge you; come your ways.   135
OPHELIA. I shall obey, my lord. [*Exeunt.*]

SCENE IV.

THE GUARD PLATFORM.

Enter HAMLET, HORATIO, and MARCELLUS.

HAMLET. The air bites shrewdly; it is very cold.
HORATIO. It is a nipping and an eager air.
HAMLET. What hour now?
HORATIO.   I think it lacks of twelve.
MARCELLUS. No, it is struck.
HORATIO.   Indeed? I heard it not.
It then draws near the season   5
Wherein the spirit held his wont to walk.

A flourish of trumpets, and cannon go off.

What does this mean, my lord?
HAMLET. The king doth wake to-night and takes his
    rouse,[82]
Keeps wassail, and the swagg'ring up-spring reels;[83]
And, as he drains his draughts of Rhenish down,[84]   10
The kettle-drum and trumpet thus bray out
The triumph of his pledge.[85]
HORATIO.   Is it a custom?
HAMLET. Ay, marry, is't:
But to my mind—though I am native here
And to the manner born—it is a custom   15
More honoured in the breach than the observance.
This heavy-headed revel east and west
Makes us traduced and taxed of other nations;
They clepe us drunkards, and with swinish phrase[86]
Soil our addition; and indeed it takes[87]   20

From our achievements, though performed at height,
The pith and marrow of our attribute.[88]
So oft it chances in particular men,
That for some vicious mole of nature in them,
As, in their birth—wherein they are not guilty,   25
Since nature cannot choose his origin,—
By the o'ergrowth of some complexion,
Oft breaking down the pales and forts of reason,
Or by some habit that too much o'er-leavens
The form of plausive manners; that these men,   30
Carrying, I say, the stamp of one defect,
Being nature's livery, or fortune's star,
Their virtues else, be they as pure as grace,
As infinite as man may undergo,
Shall in the general censure take corruption   35
From that particular fault: the dram of evil
Doth all the noble substance of a doubt,
To his own scandal.[89]

Enter GHOST.

HORATIO.   Look, my lord, it comes.
HAMLET. Angels and ministers of grace defend us!
Be thou a spirit of health or goblin damned,   40
Bring with thee airs from heaven or blasts from hell,
Be thy intents wicked or charitable,
Thou com'st in such a questionable shape
That I will speak to thee. I'll call thee Hamlet,[90]
King, father; royal Dane, O! answer me: 45
Let me not burst in ignorance; but tell
Why thy canonizéd bones, hearsed in death,
Have burst their cerements; why the sepulchre,[91]
Wherein we saw thee quietly interred,

---

82 wake to-night and takes his rouse] stays up and carouses.
83 swagg'ring up-spring] a wild dance.
84 Rhenish] wine from the Rhine region.
85 The triumph of his pledge] the achievement of down-
   ing a cup at one draught.
86 clepe] call.
87 with swinish … addition] turn their titles of distinction
   into allusions to swine.

88 attribute] reputation.
89 the dram of evil … scandal] Where even a drop of evil
   exists, it makes one doubt whether any noble qualities
   are present, and thus corrupts the reputation of the
   whole.
90 I'll call thee Hamlet] The existence of ghosts was generally accepted in Shakespeare's age; however, whereas
   some doctrine (usually Roman Catholic) held that a
   ghost was probably the spirit of a deceased person, other
   doctrine (usually Protestant) held that a ghost was more
   likely a demonic spirit who had taken on the dead person's features.
91 cerements] waxed linen shroud.

Hath op'd his ponderous and marble jaws,   50
To cast thee up again. What may this mean,
That thou, dead corse, again in complete steel
Revisits thus the glimpses of the moon,
Making night hideous; and we fools of nature[92]
So horridly to shake our disposition   55
With thoughts beyond the reaches of our souls?
Say, why is this? wherefore? what should we do?

[*The GHOST beckons HAMLET.*]

HORATIO. It beckons you to go away with it,
  As if it some impartment did desire
  To you alone.[93]   60
MARCELLUS.   Look, with what courteous action
  It waves you to a more removéd ground:
  But do not go with it.
HORATIO.   No, by no means.
HAMLET. It will not speak; then will I follow it.
HORATIO. Do not, my lord.
HAMLET.   Why, what should be the fear?
  I do not set my life at a pin's fee;   65
  And for my soul, what can it do to that,
  Being a thing immortal as itself?
  It waves me forth again. I'll follow it.
HORATIO. What if it tempt you toward the flood,
  my lord,[94]
  Or to the dreadful summit of the cliff   70
  That beetles o'er his base into the sea,[95]
  And there assume some other, horrible form,
  Which might deprive your sovereignty of reason
  And draw you into madness? Think of it;
  The very place puts toys of desperation,   75
  Without more motive, into every brain
  That looks so many fathoms to the sea
  And hears it roar beneath.
HAMLET.   It waves me still.
  Go on. I'll follow thee.
MARCELLUS. You shall not go, my lord.   80
HAMLET.   Hold off your hands!
HORATIO. Be ruled; you shall not go.

HAMLET.   My fate cries out,
  And makes each petty artery in this body
  As hardy as the Nemean lion's nerve.[96]

[*GHOST beckons.*]

  Still am I called. Unhand me, gentlemen,

[*Breaking from them.*]

  By heaven! I'll make a ghost of him that lets me![97]   85
  I say, away! Go on, I'll follow thee.

[*Exeunt GHOST and HAMLET.*]

HORATIO. He waxes desperate with imagination.[98]
MARCELLUS. Let's follow; 'tis not fit thus to obey him.
HORATIO. Have after. To what issue will this come?
MARCELLUS. Something is rotten in the state of   90
  Denmark.
HORATIO. Heaven will direct it.
MARCELLUS.   Nay, let's follow him.

[*Exeunt.*]

SCENE V.

ANOTHER PART OF THE PLATFORM.

Enter GHOST and HAMLET.

HAMLET. Whither wilt thou lead me? speak; I'll go
  no further.
GHOST. Mark me.
HAMLET.   I will.
GHOST.   My hour is almost come,
  When I to sulph'rous and tormenting flames
  Must render up myself.
HAMLET.   Alas! poor ghost.
GHOST. Pity me not, but lend thy serious hearing   5
  To what I shall unfold.
HAMLET.   Speak; I am bound to hear.
GHOST. So art thou to revenge, when thou shalt hear.
HAMLET. What?
GHOST. I am thy father's spirit;

---

92 fools of nature] playthings of the natural world (as the
     Ghost, being supernatural, is not).
93 impartment] communication.
94 the flood] the ocean.
95 beetles] overhangs.

96 Nemean lion's nerve] sinews of the mythical giant lion
     slain by Hercules.
97 lets] hinders.
98 waxes] grows.

Doomed for a certain term to walk the night,   10
And for the day confined to fast in fires,
Till the foul crimes done in my days of nature
Are burnt and purged away. But that I am forbid
To tell the secrets of my prison-house,
I could a tale unfold whose lightest word   15
Would harrow up thy soul, freeze thy young blood,
Make thy two eyes, like stars, start from their spheres,
Thy knotted and combinéd locks to part,
And each particular hair to stand on end,
Like quills upon the fretful porpentine.[99]   20
But this eternal blazon must not be
To ears of flesh and blood. List, list, O, list!
If thou didst ever thy dear father love—
HAMLET. O God!
GHOST. Revenge his foul and most unnatural murder.   25
HAMLET. Murder!
GHOST. Murder most foul, as in the best it is;
  But this most foul, strange, and unnatural.
HAMLET. Haste me to know't, that I, with wings as swift
  As meditation or the thoughts of love,
  May sweep to my revenge.   30
GHOST.   I find thee apt;
  And duller shouldst thou be than the fat weed
  That rots itself in ease on Lethe wharf,[100]
  Wouldst thou not stir in this. Now, Hamlet, hear:
  'Tis given out that, sleeping in my orchard,   35
  A serpent stung me; so the whole ear of Denmark
  Is by a forgéd process of my death[101]
  Rankly abused; but know, thou noble youth,
  The serpent that did sting thy father's life
  Now wears his crown.   40
HAMLET.   O my prophetic soul!
  My uncle!
GHOST. Ay, that incestuous, that adulterate beast,
  With witchcraft of his wits, with traitorous gifts—
  O wicked wit and gifts, that have the power
  So to seduce!—won to his shameful lust   45
  The will of my most seeming-virtuous queen.
  O Hamlet! what a falling-off was there;

From me, whose love was of that dignity
That it went hand in hand even with the vow
I made to her in marriage; and to decline   50
Upon a wretch whose natural gifts were poor
To those of mine!
But virtue, as it never will be moved,
Though lewdness court it in a shape of heaven,
So lust, though to a radiant angel linked,   55
Will sate itself in a celestial bed,
And prey on garbage.
But, soft! methinks I scent the morning air;
Brief let me be. Sleeping within my orchard,
My custom always of the afternoon,   60
Upon my secure hour thy uncle stole,[102]
With juice of cursed hebona in a vial,[103]
And in the porches of my ears did pour
The leperous distilment; whose effect
Holds such an enmity with blood of man   65
That swift as quicksilver it courses through
The natural gates and alleys of the body,
And with a sudden vigour it doth posset[104]
And curd, like eager droppings into milk,[105]
The thin and wholesome blood. So did it mine,   70
And a most instant tetter barked about,[106]
Most lazar-like, with vile and loathsome crust,[107]
All my smooth body.
Thus was I, sleeping, by a brother's hand,
Of life, of crown, of queen, at once dispatched;   75
Cut off even in the blossoms of my sin,
Unhouseled, disappointed, unaneled,[108]
No reckoning made, but sent to my account[109]
With all my imperfections on my head:
O, horrible! O, horrible! most horrible!   80

---

[99] fretful porpentine] frightened porcupine.

[100] Lethe] the river of forgetfulness in Hades, the underworld.

[101] forgéd process] false account.

[102] secure] carefree, unsuspecting.

[103] hebona] a poisonous plant of some kind (not specifically identifiable).

[104] posset] curdle.

[105] eager] sour.

[106] a most instant tetter barked about] an instantaneous eruption of the skin spread with a bark-like effect.

[107] lazar-like] like leprosy.

[108] Unhouseled, disappointed, unaneled] respectively: not having received the housel or eucharist, spiritually unprepared for a divine appointment, not having been anointed with holy oil—in short, deprived of last rites.

[109] reckoning] confession; cf. *Everyman*.

If thou hast nature in thee, bear it not;
Let not the royal bed of Denmark be
A couch for luxury and damned incest.[110]
But, howsoever thou pursuest this act,
Taint not thy mind, nor let thy soul contrive   85
Against thy mother aught. Leave her to heaven,
And to those thorns that in her bosom lodge,
To prick and sting her. Fare thee well at once!
The glow-worm shows the matin to be near,[111]
And 'gins to pale his uneffectual fire;   90
Adieu, adieu, adieu. Remember me. [*Exit.*]
HAMLET. O all you host of heaven! O earth! What else?
   And shall I couple hell? O fie! Hold, hold, my
      heart![112]
   And you, my sinews, grow not instant old,
   But bear me stiffly up! Remember thee?   95
   Ay, thou poor ghost, while memory holds a seat
   In this distracted globe. Remember thee?[113]
   Yea, from the table of my memory [114]
   I'll wipe away all trivial fond records,[115]
   All saws of books, all forms, all pressures past,[116]   100
   That youth and observation copied there;
   And thy commandment all alone shall live
   Within the book and volume of my brain,
   Unmixed with baser matter: yes, by heaven!
   O most pernicious woman!   105
   O villain, villain, smiling, damnéd villain!
   My tables: meet it is I set it down,
   That one may smile, and smile, and be a villain—
   At least I'm sure it may be so in Denmark. [*Writing.*]
   So, uncle, there you are. Now to my word;   110
   It is, "Adieu, adieu! remember me."
   I have sworn't.

Enter HORATIO and MARCELLUS.

HORATIO. My lord! my lord!
MARCELLUS.   Lord Hamlet!

---

[110] luxury] lust.
[111] matin] morning.
[112] Hamlet is aware that his task may embrace evil as well
   as good.
[113] globe] his head, the world, Shakespeare's theatre.
[114] table] tablet, notebook.
[115] fond] foolish.
[116] saws] maxims; pressures] impressions.

HORATIO.   Heaven secure him!
HAMLET. So be it.
HORATIO. Hillo, ho, ho, my lord!   115
HAMLET. Hillo, ho, ho, boy! come, bird, come.[117]
MARCELLUS. How is't, my noble lord?
HORATIO.   What news, my lord?
HAMLET. O! wonderful.
HORATIO.   Good my lord, tell it.
HAMLET. No; you will reveal it.
HORATIO. Not I, my lord, by heaven!   120
MARCELLUS.   Nor I, my lord.
HAMLET. How say you, then; would heart of man
   once think it?
   But you'll be secret?
MARCELLUS. ⎤
HORATIO.   ⎦   Ay, by heaven, my lord.
HAMLET. There's never a villain dwelling in all
   Denmark
   But he's an arrant knave.
HORATIO. There needs no ghost, my lord, come   125
   from the grave,
   To tell us this.
HAMLET.   Why, right; you are i' the right;
   And so, without more circumstance at all,
   I hold it fit that we shake hands and part;
   You, as your business and desires shall point you—
   For every man hath business and desire,   130
   Such as it is—and, for mine own poor part,
   Look you, I'll go pray.
HORATIO. These are but wild and whirling words,
   my lord.
HAMLET. I am sorry they offend you, heartily;
   Yes, faith, heartily.   135
HORATIO.   There's no offence, my lord.
HAMLET. Yes, by Saint Patrick, but there is, Horatio,[118]
   And much offence too. Touching this vision here,
   It is an honest ghost, that let me tell you;
   For your desire to know what is between us,
   O'ermaster't as you may. And now, good friends,   140
   As you are friends, scholars, and soldiers,
   Give me one poor request.
HORATIO. What is't, my lord? we will.

---

[117] Hillo … come] a falconer's cry.
[118] Saint Patrick] known as the keeper of Purgatory.

HAMLET. Never make known what you have seen
  tonight.
HORATIO. ⎤
MARCELLUS. ⎦ My lord, we will not.   145
HAMLET.   Nay, but swear't.
HORATIO.   In faith,
  My lord, not I.
MARCELLUS.   Nor I, my lord, in faith.
HAMLET. Upon my sword.
MARCELLUS. We have sworn, my lord, already.
HAMLET. Indeed, upon my sword, indeed.
GHOST. [*beneath the stage.*] Swear.   150
HAMLET. Ah, ha boy! sayst thou so? art thou there,
  true-penny?[119]
  Come on,—you hear this fellow in the cellarage—
  Consent to swear.
HORATIO.   Propose the oath, my lord.
HAMLET. Never to speak of this that you have seen,
  Swear by my sword.   155
GHOST. [*beneath.*] Swear.
HAMLET. *Hic et ubique?*[120] Then we'll shift our
  ground. Come hither, gentlemen, and lay your
  hands again upon my sword. Swear by my sword
  never to speak of this that you have heard.   160
GHOST. [*beneath.*] Swear.
HAMLET. Well said, old mole! Canst work i' the earth
  so fast? A worthy pioner![121] Once more remove,
  good friends.
HORATIO. O day and night, but this is wondrous   165
  strange!
HAMLET. And therefore as a stranger give it welcome.
  There are more things in heaven and earth, Horatio,
  Than are dreamt of in your philosophy.
  But come;
  Here, as before, never, so help you mercy,   170
  How strange or odd soe'er I bear myself—
  As I perchance hereafter shall think meet
  To put an antic disposition on—[122]
  That you, at such times seeing me, never shall,
  With arms encumbered thus, or this head-shake,[123]   175

Or by pronouncing of some doubtful phrase,
As, "Well, well, we know," or, "We could, an if we
  would";
Or, "If we list to speak," or, "There be, an if they
  might";
Or such ambiguous giving out, to note
That you know aught of me—this do swear,   180
So grace and mercy at your most need help you.
GHOST [*Beneath*]. Swear.   [*They swear.*]
HAMLET. Rest, rest, perturbéd spirit! So, gentlemen,
  With all my love I do commend me to you:[124]
  And what so poor a man as Hamlet is   185
  May do, to express his love and friending to you,
  God willing, shall not lack. Let us go in together;
  And still your fingers on your lips, I pray.
  The time is out of joint; O curséd spite,
  That ever I was born to set it right!   190
  Nay, come, let's go together. [*Exeunt.*]

ACT II

SCENE 1

A ROOM IN POLONIUS' QUARTERS.

Enter POLONIUS and REYNALDO.

POLONIUS. Give him this money and these notes,
  Reynaldo.
REYNALDO. I will, my lord.
POLONIUS. You shall do marvellous wisely, good
  Reynaldo,
  Before you visit him, to make inquiry
  Of his behaviour.   5
REYNALDO.   My lord, I did intend it.
POLONIUS. Marry, well said, very well said. Look
  you, sir,
  Inquire me first what Danskers are in Paris;[125]
  And how, and who, what means, and where they
  keep,
  What company, at what expense; and finding
  By this encompassment and drift of question   10
  That they do know my son, come you more nearer
  Than your particular demands will touch it.

---

119 true-penny] honest fellow.
120 *Hic et ubique*] here and everywhere (Latin).
121 pioner] pioneer, miner.
122 antic disposition] mad behaviour.
123 encumbered] folded.

---

124 commend me] entrust myself.
125 Danskers] Danes.

Take you, as 'twere, some distant knowledge of him;
As thus, "I know his father, and his friends,
And, in part, him"—do you mark this, Reynaldo?   15
REYNALDO. Ay, very well, my lord.
POLONIUS. "And, in part, him—but," you may say,
    "not well,
But if't be he I mean, he's very wild,
Addicted so and so." And there put on him
What forgeries you please; marry, none so rank[126]   20
As may dishonour him; take heed of that;
But, sir, such wanton, wild, and usual slips
As are companions noted and most known
To youth and liberty.
REYNALDO.   As gaming, my lord?
POLONIUS. Ay, or drinking, fencing, swearing,   . 25
    quarrelling—
Drabbing; you may go so far.[127]
REYNALDO. My lord, that would dishonour him.
POLONIUS. Faith, no; as you may season it in the
    charge.
You must not put another scandal on him,
That he is open to incontinency;   30
That's not my meaning; but breathe his faults so
    quaintly
That they may seem the taints of liberty,
The flash and outbreak of a fiery mind,
A savageness in unreclaiméd blood,
Of general assault.   35
REYNALDO.   But, my good lord,—
POLONIUS. Wherefore should you do this?
REYNALDO.   Ay, my lord,
I would know that.
POLONIUS.   Marry, sir, here's my drift;
And, I believe, it is a fetch of warrant,[128]
You laying these slight sullies on my son
As 'twere a thing a little soiled i' the working,   40
Mark you,
Your party in converse, him you would sound,
Having ever seen in the prenominate[129] crimes
The youth you breathe of guilty, be assured,
He closes with you in this consequence;   45

"Good sir," or so; or "friend," or "gentleman,"
According to the phrase or the addition[130]
Of man and country.
REYNALDO.   Very good, my lord.
POLONIUS.   And then, sir, does he this—he
does—what was I about to say? By the mass I was   50
about to say something. Where did I leave?
REYNALDO. At "closes in the consequence."
POLONIUS. At "closes in the consequence" —Ay,
    marry!
He closes with you thus: "I know the gentleman;
I saw him yesterday, or t'other day,   55
Or then, or then, with such, or such; and, as you say,
There was "a gaming; there o'ertook in's rouse;[131]
There falling out at tennis"; or perchance,
"I saw him enter such a house of sale,"
Videlicet, a brothel, or so forth.[132]   60
See you now;
Your bait of falsehood takes this carp of truth;
And thus do we of wisdom and of reach,[133]
With windlasses, and with assays of bias,[134]
By indirections find directions out: 65
So by my former lecture and advice
Shall you my son. You have me, have you not?
REYNALDO. My lord, I have.
POLONIUS.   God be wi' you; fare you well.
REYNALDO. Good my lord!
POLONIUS. Observe his inclination in yourself.[135]   70
REYNALDO. I shall, my lord.
POLONIUS.   And let him ply his music.
REYNALDO.   Well, my lord.

Exit REYNALDO. Enter OPHELIA.

POLONIUS. Farewell! How now, Ophelia? What's
    the matter?
OPHELIA. Alas! my lord, I have been so affrighted.
POLONIUS. With what, in the name of God?

---

126 forgeries] fabrications.
127 Drabbing] whoring, going to brothels.
128 fetch of warrant] justifiable trick.
129 prenominate] aforementioned.

130 addition] formal title.
131 o'ertook in's rouse] having had too much to drink.
132 *Videlicet*] namely.
133 of reach] of foresight.
134 windlasses] roundabout approaches; assays of bias] in-
    direct attempts (a metaphor taken from lawn bowling).
135 in yourself] for yourself.

OPHELIA. My lord, as I was sewing in my closet,[136]   75
  Lord Hamlet, with his doublet all unbraced;[137]
  No hat upon his head; his stockings fouled,
  Ungartered, and down-gyvéd to his ankle;[138]
  Pale as his shirt; his knees knocking each other;
  And with a look so piteous in purport   80
  As if he had been loosed out of hell
  To speak of horrors, he comes before me.
POLONIUS. Mad for thy love?
OPHELIA.   My lord, I do not know;
  But truly I do fear it.
POLONIUS.   What said he?
OPHELIA. He took me by the wrist and held me hard,   85
  Then goes he to the length of all his arm,
  And, with his other hand thus o'er his brow,
  He falls to such perusal of my face
  As he would draw it. Long stayed he so;
  At last, a little shaking of mine arm,   90
  And thrice his head thus waving up and down,
  He raised a sigh so piteous and profound
  As it did seem to shatter all his bulk
  And end his being. That done, he lets me go,
  And with his head over his shoulder turned,   95
  He seemed to find his way without his eyes;
  For out o' doors he went without their help,
  And to the last bended their light on me.
POLONIUS. Come, go with me; I will go seek the king.
  This is the very ecstasy[139] of love,   100
  Whose violent property fordoes[140] itself
  And leads the will to desperate undertakings
  As oft as any passion under heaven
  That does afflict our natures. I am sorry.
  What! have you given him any hard words of late?   105
OPHELIA. No, my good lord: but, as you did command,
  I did repel his letters and denied
  His access to me.
POLONIUS.   That hath made him mad.
  I am sorry that with better heed and judgment
  I had not quoted him; I feared he did but trifle,[141]   110

And meant to wrack thee; but, beshrew my
    jealousy![142]
By heaven, it is as proper to our age
To cast beyond ourselves in our opinions[143]
As it is common for the younger sort
To lack discretion.Come, go we to the king: 115
This must be known; which, being kept close,
    might move
More grief to hide than hate to utter love.[144]
Come.   [*Exeunt.*]

SCENE II

A ROOM IN THE CASTLE.

Enter KING, QUEEN, ROSENCRANTZ,
GUILDENSTERN, and Attendants.

KING. Welcome, dear Rosencrantz and Guildenstern.
  Moreover that we much did long to see you,[145]
  The need we have to use you did provoke
  Our hasty sending. Something have you heard
  Of Hamlet's transformation; so I call it,   5
  Since nor the exterior nor the inward man
  Resembles that it was. What it should be
  More than his father's death, that thus hath put him
  So much from the understanding of himself,
  I cannot dream of: I entreat you both,   10
  That, being of so young days brought up with him,
  And since so neighboured to his youth and humour,
  That you vouchsafe your rest here in our court[146]
  Some little time; so by your companies
  To draw him on to pleasures, and to gather,   15
  So much as from occasion you may glean,[147]

---

136 closet] private room.
137 doublet all unbraced] jacket all undone.
138 down-gyved] hanging down like a prisoner's fetters.
139 ecstasy] madness.
140 property fordoes] quality destroys.
141 quoted] observed.

---

142 wrack] ruin (i.e., by taking her virginity without mar-
    rying her); jealousy] mistrust, suspicions.
143 as proper … opinions] as natural for old men to sup-
    pose they know more than they have evidence for ("to
    cast" is a hunting term for finding the prey's scent).
144 might move … love] might cause more grief by conceal-
    ment than it would cause hatred at having the matter
    spoken of openly.
145 Moreover that] besides the fact that.
146 vouchsafe your rest] consent to stay.
147 glean] acquire (knowledge), infer.

Whether aught to us unknown afflicts him thus,
That, opened, lies within our remedy.
QUEEN. Good gentlemen, he hath much talked of
    you;
And sure I am two men there are not living   20
To whom he more adheres. If it will please you
To show us so much gentry and good will[148]
As to expend your time with us awhile,
For the supply and profit of our hope,
Your visitation shall receive such thanks   25
As fits a king's remembrance.
ROSENCRANTZ.   Both your majesties
Might, by the sovereign power you have of us,
Put your dread pleasures more into command[149]
Than to entreaty.
GUILDENSTERN.   But we both obey,
And here give up ourselves, in the full bent,[150]   30
To lay our service freely at your feet,
To be commanded.
KING. Thanks, Rosencrantz and gentle Guildenstern.
QUEEN. Thanks, Guildenstern and gentle Rosencrantz;
And I beseech you instantly to visit   35
My too much changed son. Go, some of you,
And bring these gentlemen where Hamlet is.
GUILDENSTERN. Heavens make our presence, and
    our practices
Pleasant and helpful to him!
QUEEN.   Ay, amen!

*Exeunt ROSENCRANTZ, GUILDENSTERN and
Attendant(s).*

Enter POLONIUS.

POLONIUS. The ambassadors from Norway, my   40
    good lord,
Are joyfully returned.
KING. Thou still[151] hast been the father of good news.
POLONIUS. Have I, my lord? Assure you, my good
    liege,
I hold my duty, as I hold my soul,

Both to my God and to my gracious king;   45
And I do think—or else this brain of mine
Hunts not the trail of policy so sure
As it hath used to do—that I have found
The very cause of Hamlet's lunacy.
KING. O, speak of that; that do I long to hear.   50
POLONIUS. Give first admittance to the ambassadors;
My news shall be the fruit to that great feast.[152]
KING. Thyself do grace to them, and bring them in.

[*Exit POLONIUS.*]

He tells me, my sweet queen, that he hath found
The head and source of all your son's distemper.   55
QUEEN. I doubt it is no other but the main;[153]
His father's death and our o'erhasty marriage.
KING. Well, we shall sift him.

*Re-enter POLONIUS, with VOLTIMAND and
CORNELIUS.*

              Welcome, my good friends!
Say, Voltimand, what from our brother Norway?
VOLT. Most fair return of greetings, and desires.   60
Upon our first, he sent out to suppress[154]
His nephew's levies; which to him appeared
To be a preparation 'gainst the Polack;
But, better looked into, he truly found
It was against your highness: whereat grieved,   65
That so his sickness, age, and impotence
Was falsely borne in hand, sends out arrests[155]
On Fortinbras; which he, in brief, obeys,
Receives rebuke from Norway, and, in fine,[156]
Makes vow before his uncle never more   70
To give the assay of arms against your majesty.[157]
Whereon old Norway, overcome with joy,
Gives him three thousand crowns in annual fee,
And his commission to employ those soldiers,
So levied as before, against the Polack;   75
With an entreaty, herein further shown,

[*Giving a paper.*]

---

148 gentry] courtesy.
149 dread] venerable.
150 in the full bent] to the furthest limit (as far as a bow
    might be bent).
151 still] always.

152 fruit] i.e., for dessert.
153 doubt] suspect.
154 first] first words.
155 falsely borne in hand] deceived.
156 in fine] finally.
157 give the assay] make an attempt.

That it might please you to give quiet pass
Through your dominions for this enterprise,
On such regards of safety and allowance[158]
As therein are set down.   80
KING.   It likes us well;
And at our more considered time we'll read,[159]
Answer, and think upon this business:
Meantime we thank you for your well-took labour.
Go to your rest; at night we'll feast together:
Most welcome home.   85

Exeunt VOLTIMAND and CORNELIUS.

POLONIUS.   This business is well ended.
My liege, and madam, to expostulate
What majesty should be, what duty is,
Why day is day, night night, and time is time,
Were nothing but to waste night, day, and time.
Therefore, since brevity is the soul of wit,   90
And tediousness the limbs and outward flourishes,
I will be brief. Your noble son is mad:
Mad call I it; for, to define true madness,
What is't but to be nothing else but mad?
But let that go.   95
QUEEN.   More matter, with less art.[160]
POLONIUS. Madam, I swear I use no art at all.
That he is mad, 'tis true; 'tis true 'tis pity;
And pity 'tis 'tis true: a foolish figure;
But farewell it, for I will use no art.
Mad let us grant him, then; and now remains   100
That we find out the cause of this effect,
Or rather say, the cause of this defect,
For this effect defective comes by cause;
Thus it remains, and the remainder thus.
Perpend.[161]   105
I have a daughter, have while she is mine;
Who, in her duty and obedience, mark,
Hath given me this: now, gather, and surmise.
    To the celestial, and my soul's idol, the most
    beautified Ophelia.—

That's an ill phrase, a vile phrase; "beautified"[162]   110
is a vile phrase; but you shall hear these:
    In her excellent white bosom, these...etc.[163]
QUEEN. Came this from Hamlet to her?
POLONIUS. Good madam, stay awhile; I will be
    faithful.[164]
    Doubt thou the stars are fire;   115
        Doubt that the sun doth move;
    Doubt truth to be a liar;[165]
        But never doubt I love.
    O, dear Ophelia! I am ill at these numbers.[166]
I have not art to reckon my groans; but that I love   120
thee best—O, most best!—believe it. Adieu.
    Thine evermore, most dear lady, whilst this
        machine is to him,[167]

                              HAMLET.
This in obedience, hath my daughter shown me;
And more above, hath his solicitings,[168]   125
As they fell out by time, by means, and place,
All given to mine ear.
KING.   But how hath she
Received his love?
POLONIUS.   What do you think of me?
KING. As of a man faithful and honourable.
POLONIUS. I would fain prove so. But what might   130
    you think,
When I had seen this hot love on the wing—
As I perceived it, I must tell you that,
Before my daughter told me—what might you,
Or my dear majesty your queen here, think,
If I had played the desk or table-book,[169]   135

158 regards] conditions.
159 considered time] when the time to consider has been taken.
160 More matter, with less art] Give us more substance and less display of cleverness.
161 Perpend] consider carefully.

162 beautified] Polonius's pedantic objection to the phrase is that it could be taken to mean "made beautiful by make-up."
163 *In her excellent white bosom, these, etc.*] a formal beginning to a love letter—i.e., let the recipient keep these verses close to her heart, within her dress and between her breasts.
164 stay awhile; I will be faithful] hang on a moment; I won't disappoint you.
165 Doubt] suspect.
166 numbers] poetic skills.
167 machine] i.e., his body.
168 and more above] and moreover.
169 played the desk or table-book] i.e., remained passive and said nothing.

Or given my heart a winking, mute and dumb,
Or looked upon this love with idle sight;
What might you think? No, I went round to work,
And my young mistress thus I did bespeak:
"Lord Hamlet is a prince, out of thy star;[170]   140
This must not be": and then I precepts gave her,
That she should lock herself from his resort,
Admit no messengers, receive no tokens.
Which done, she took the fruits of my advice;
And he, repulsed—a short tale to make—   145
Fell into a sadness, then into a fast,
Thence to a watch, thence into a weakness,[171]
Thence to a lightness; and by this declension[172]
Into the madness wherein now he raves,
And all we wail for.   150
KING.   Do you think 'tis this?
QUEEN. It may be, very likely.
POLONIUS. Hath there been such a time—I'd fain
    know that—
    That I have positively said, "'Tis so,"
    When it proved otherwise?
KING.   Not that I know.
POLONIUS. Take this from this, if this be otherwise: 155

[*Pointing to his head and shoulder.*]

    If circumstances lead me, I will find
    Where truth is hid, though it were hid indeed
    Within the centre.[173]
KING.   How may we try it further?
POLONIUS. You know sometimes he walks four
    hours together
    Here in the lobby.   160
QUEEN.   So he does indeed.
POLONIUS. At such a time I'll loose my daughter to
    him;
    Be you and I behind an arras then;[174]
    Mark the encounter; if he love her not,
    And be not from his reason fall'n thereon,[175]

Let me be no assistant for a state,   165
    But keep a farm, and carters.
KING.   We will try it.

Enter HAMLET, *reading.*[176]

QUEEN. But look, where sadly the poor wretch
    comes reading.
POLONIUS. Away! I do beseech you, both away.
    I'll board him presently.[177]

Exeunt KING, QUEEN, *and Attendants.*

                    O! give me leave.
    How does my good Lord Hamlet?   170
HAMLET. Well, God a-mercy.[178]
POLONIUS. Do you know me, my lord?
HAMLET. Excellent well; you are a fishmonger.[179]
POLONIUS. Not I, my lord.
HAMLET. Then I would you were so honest a man.   175
POLONIUS. Honest, my lord?
HAMLET. Ay, sir. To be honest, as this world goes, is
    to be one man picked out of ten thousand.
POLONIUS. That's very true, my lord.
HAMLET. For if the sun breed maggots in a dead dog,   180
    being a god kissing carrion—[180] Have you a
    daughter?
POLONIUS. I have, my lord.
HAMLET. Let her not walk i' the sun; conception is
    a blessing, but not as your daughter may con-   185
    ceive.[181] Friend, look to 't.

---

176 *Enter Hamlet*] Some editors put this stage direction af-
    ter line 170, though the earliest texts that specify his
    entrance, the Folio edition and the Second Quarto edi-
    tion, place it here. The point is important, for this earlier
    entrance allows the possibility that Hamlet overhears
    Polonius's last speech, thus warranting a suspicion that
    he is being spied upon in III.i.
177 board] address.
178 God a-mercy] thank-you (God have mercy).
179 fishmonger] slang term for a procurer or a pimp.
180 if the sun … dog] The ancients believed that the sun
    created new life from dead matter; good kissing carrion]
    an attractive piece of flesh with which to pleasure one-
    self.
181 the sun] Apart from its literal sense, the sun is an em-
    blem of royalty; conception] forming ideas; becoming
    pregnant.

---

170 out of thy star] not of your destiny.
171 a watch] insomnia.
172 lightness] giddiness.
173 centre] centre of the earth.
174 arras] a hanging tapestry.
175 thereon] because of that.

POLONIUS. [*Aside.*] How say you by that? Still harping on my daughter: yet he knew me not at first; he said I was a fishmonger: he is far gone, far gone: and truly in my youth I suffered much extremity for love—very near this. I'll speak to him again. What do you read, my lord? 190

HAMLET. Words, words, words.

POLONIUS. What is the matter, my lord?

HAMLET. Between who?[182] 195

POLONIUS. I mean the matter that you read, my lord.

HAMLET. Slanders, sir: for the satirical rogue says here that old men have grey beards, that their faces are wrinkled, their eyes purging thick amber and plum-tree gum, and that they have a plentiful lack of wit, together with most weak hams: all which, sir, though I most powerfully and potently believe, yet I hold it not honesty to have it thus set down; for you yourself, sir, should be old as I am, if, like a crab, you could go backward.[183] 200 205

POLONIUS. [*Aside.*] Though this be madness, yet there is a method in 't. Will you walk out of the air, my lord?[184]

HAMLET. Into my grave? 210

POLONIUS. Indeed, that is out o' the air. [*Aside.*] How pregnant sometimes his replies are—a happiness that often madness hits on, which reason and sanity could not so prosperously be delivered of.[185] I will leave him, and suddenly contrive the means of meeting between him and my daughter.[186] My honourable lord, I will most humbly take my leave of you. 215

HAMLET. You cannot, sir, take from me any thing that I will more willingly part withal; except my life, except my life, except my life.[187] 220

POLONIUS. Fare you well, my lord.

HAMLET. These tedious old fools!

Enter ROSENCRANTZ and GUILDENSTERN.

POLONIUS. You go to seek the Lord Hamlet; there he is. 225

Exit POLONIUS.

ROSENCRANTZ. God save you, sir!

GUILDENSTERN. Mine honoured lord!

ROSENCRANTZ. My most dear lord!

HAMLET. My excellent good friends! How dost thou, Guildenstern? Ah, Rosencrantz! Good lads, how do ye both? 230

ROSENCRANTZ. As the indifferent children of the earth.[188]

GUILDENSTERN. Happy in that we are not over happy;
On Fortune's cap we are not the very button.[189]

HAMLET. Nor the soles of her shoe? 235

ROSENCRANTZ. Neither, my lord.

HAMLET. Then you live about her waist, or in the middle of her favours?

GUILDENSTERN. Faith, her privates we.[190]

HAMLET. In the secret parts of Fortune? O! most true; she is a strumpet.[191] What news? 240

ROSENCRANTZ. None, my lord, but that the world's grown honest.

HAMLET. Then is doomsday near; but your news is not true.[192] Let me question more in particular: what have you, my good friends, deserved at the hands of Fortune, that she sends you to prison hither? 245

---

182 Between who?] Hamlet wilfully misunderstands "matter" as a problem or quarrel between two people.

183 honesty] fairness.

184 out of the air] i.e., out of the fresh air, where there might be draughts that would bad for a sick person.

185 pregnant] full of meaning; happiness] aptness of speech; delivered of] refers back to the figurative use of "pregnant"—i.e., such interesting notions would be unlikely to emerge from a sane person. Much of what Hamlet says in his supposed "madness" may be interpreted as cryptic but sensible utterance.

186 suddenly] immediately.

187 withal] with.

188 indifferent] ordinary.

189 Fortune's cap … button] i.e., they are not at the very top of fortune (hence, they are therefore not likely to make an imminent fall into misfortune). They are making silly banter.

190 privates] ordinary subjects; genitals.

191 strumpet] whore (i.e., because she is so promiscuous and fickle with her favours).

192 Then is doomsday near] i.e., because people must have suddenly become honest in fear of divine judgement.

GUILDENSTERN. Prison, my lord!

HAMLET. Denmark's a prison.

ROSENCRANTZ. Then is the world one. 250

HAMLET. A goodly one; in which there are many confines, wards, and dungeons, Denmark being one o' the worst.

ROSENCRANTZ. We think not so, my lord.

HAMLET. Why, then 'tis none to you; for there is 255 nothing either good or bad, but thinking makes it so: to me it is a prison.

ROSENCRANTZ. Why, then your ambition makes it one; 'tis too narrow for your mind.

HAMLET. O God! I could be bounded in a nutshell, 260 and count myself a king of infinite space, were it not that I have bad dreams.

GUILDENSTERN. Which dreams, indeed, are ambition, for the very substance of the ambitious is merely the shadow of a dream. 265

HAMLET. A dream itself is but a shadow.

ROSENCRANTZ. Truly, and I hold ambition of so airy and light a quality that it is but a shadow's shadow.[193]

HAMLET. Then are our beggars bodies, and our 270 monarchs and outstretched heroes the beggars' shadows.[194] Shall we to the court? for, by my fay, I cannot reason.[195]

ROSENCRANTZ. ⎫
GUILDENSTERN. ⎭ We'll wait upon you.[196]

HAMLET. No such matter; I will not sort you with 275 the rest of my servants, for, to speak to you like an honest man, I am most dreadfully attended.[197]

But, in the beaten way of friendship, what make you at Elsinore?[198]

ROSENCRANTZ. To visit you, my lord; no other 280 occasion.

HAMLET. Beggar that I am, I am even poor in thanks; but I thank you: and sure, dear friends, my thanks are too dear a halfpenny.[199] Were you not sent for? Is it your own inclining? Is it a free 285 visitation? Come, come deal justly with me: come, come; nay, speak.

GUILDENSTERN. What should we say, my lord?

HAMLET. Anything but to the purpose.[200] You were sent for; and there is a kind of confession in your 290 looks, which your modesties have not craft enough to colour.[201] I know the good king and queen have sent for you.

ROSENCRANTZ. To what end, my lord?

HAMLET. That you must teach me. But let me conjure 295 you, by the rights of our fellowship, by the consonancy of our youth, by the obligation of our ever-preserved love, and by what more dear a better proposer could charge you withal, be even and direct with me, whether you were sent for or no![202] 300

ROSENCRANTZ. [Aside to GUILDENSTERN.] What say you?

HAMLET. [Aside.] Nay then, I have an eye of you. If you love me, hold not off.

GUILDENSTERN. My lord, we were sent for. 305

HAMLET. I will tell you why; so shall my anticipation prevent your discovery, and your secrecy to the

---

193 ambition ... shadow] Rosencrantz and Guildenstern boastfully suggest they are above vulgar material considerations.

194 Then are ... shadows] If social ambition makes for lack of realism, then the most real are those with the least social standing, the beggars; all those of higher rank are the shadows cast by beggars. outstretched] elongated, like shadows.

195 fay] faith; reason] debate.

196 wait upon] a courtly way of saying "accompany," though Hamlet takes the phrase in the sense we use in a restaurant.

197 sort] classify; dreadfully attended] possessed of very poor servants; haunted by disturbing spirits.

198 beaten way] well-traveled path (i.e., the relationship more familiar to them).

199 beggar that I am] perhaps recalls the suggestion that beggars are more real (see note 194 above); my thanks are too dear a halfpenny] ambiguous—humbly, worth less than the smallest coin or, scathingly, a more expensive gratuity than Rosencrantz and Guildenstern deserve, if they have ulterior motives.

200 Anything but to the purpose] Q2. As such, Hamlet is sarcastically remarking on their evasiveness. The Folio reads "Why, anything, but to the purpose": in which case, he is persuading them to speak the truth. The difference is less in Hamlet's meaning than in his attitude.

201 colour] disguise.

202 conjure] solemnly urge; consonancy] similarity of age.

king and queen moult no feather.[203] I have of
late,—but wherefore I know not,—lost all my
mirth, forgone all custom of exercises; and indeed
it goes so heavily with my disposition that this
goodly frame, the earth, seems to me a sterile
promontory; this most excellent canopy, the air,
look you, this brave o'erhanging firmament, this
majestical roof fretted with golden fire, why, it
appears no other thing to me but a foul and
pestilent congregation of vapours.[204] What a piece
of work is a man![205] How noble in reason! how
infinite in faculty! in form, in moving, how express
and admirable! in action how like an angel! in
apprehension how like a god! the beauty of the
world! the paragon of animals![206] And yet, to me,
what is this quintessence of dust?[207] man delights
not me; no, nor woman neither, though, by your
smiling, you seem to say so.

ROSENCRANTZ. My lord, there was no such stuff in
my thoughts.

HAMLET. Why did you laugh then, when I said,
"man delights not me"?

ROSENCRANTZ. To think, my lord, if you delight not
in man, what lenten entertainment the players shall
receive from you.[208] We coted them on the way;
and hither are they coming, to offer you service.

HAMLET. He that plays the king shall be welcome;
his majesty shall have tribute of me; the adventur-
ous knight shall use his foil and target; the lover
shall not sigh gratis; the humorous man shall end
his part in peace; the clown shall make those laugh
whose lungs are tickle o' the sear; and the lady shall
say her mind freely, or the blank verse shall halt
for't.[209] What players are they?

ROSENCRANTZ. Even those you were wont to take
such delight in, the tragedians of the city.

HAMLET. How chances it they travel? Their
residence, both in reputation and profit, was better
both ways.[210]

ROSENCRANTZ. I think their inhibition comes by
the means of the late innovation.[211]

HAMLET. Do they hold the same estimation they did
when I was in the city? Are they so followed?

ROSENCRANTZ. No, indeed are they not.

HAMLET. How comes it? Do they grow rusty?

ROSENCRANTZ. Nay, their endeavour keeps in the
wonted pace: but there is, sir, an aery of children,
little eyases, that cry out on the top of question,
and are most tyrannically clapped for't.[212] These

---

203 prevent your discovery] anticipate your disclosure;
moult no feather] be uncompromised.

204 frame] structure; sterile promontory] a barren piece of
land jutting into the sea; firmament] the sky (imagined
as a dome-like structure in which planets and stars are
affixed); fretted] adorned with ornamental fret-work.

205 a man] a human being of either sex (though gender-
specific use is made later).

206 paragon] finest example.

207 quintessence] (alchemical) fifth or last essence, out of
which the other four elements were made; matter in its
most refined state.

208 lenten entertainment] meagre and inhospitable reception of one disinclined to be amused—an allusion to
Lent, the pre-Easter forty-day period of fasting and self-
denial.

209 Hamlet's emphatically warm regard for those who acknowledge they are playing at being royalty is perhaps
rooted in part in his contrasting resentment of royal hypocrisy; foil and target] sword and shield; gratis] without
recompense; humorous man … peace] ironic, the unbalanced and troubled character ruled by one of the
"humours," or moods, will be made happy when the actor is paid; those laugh whose lungs … sere] those who
will laugh at the least provocation, those with hair-trigger
lungs ("sear" is the part of a gunlock which holds the
hammer back); the lady … halt for't] the boy playing the
lady's role will say whatever he wants—if he doesn't, it will
be only because he has forgotten his lines, in which case,
the blank verse will limp ("halt") as he tries to improvise
his way through the part. (Improvising in blank verse—
a highly valued skill in a company as under-rehearsed as
Shakespeare's was—requires great experience.)

210 Their residence … ways] Being a residential theatre
company in the city was both more prestigious and
more profitable.

211 inhibition] being forced to stop their performances; in-
novation] new fashion. At the time he was writing,
Shakespeare's own company was facing just such a rival
company of boy actors.

212 aery] a nest (of an eagle or hawk); eyases] baby hawks
(a predatory bird); who cry out on top of the question]
whose shrill voices shout down all debate; tyrannically]
ruthlessly, violently.

are now the fashion, and so berattle the common stages—so they call them—that many wearing rapiers are afraid of goose-quills, and dare scarce come thither.[213]   360

HAMLET. What! are they children? who maintains 'em? how are they escotted? Will they pursue the quality no longer than they can sing? will they not say afterwards, if they should grow themselves to common players—as it is most like, if their means   365
are no better—their writers do them wrong, to make them exclaim against their own succession?[214]

ROSENCRANTZ. Faith, there has been much to-do on both sides; and the nation holds it no sin to   370
tarre them to controversy: there was, for a while, no money bid for argument, unless the poet and the player went to cuffs in the question.[215]

HAMLET. Is it possible?

GUILDENSTERN. O! there has been much throwing   375
about of brains.

HAMLET. Do the boys carry it away?

ROSENCRANTZ. Ay, that they do, my lord; Hercules and his load too.[216]

HAMLET. It is not very strange; for my uncle is King   380
of Denmark, and those that would make mows at him while my father lived, give twenty, forty, fifty, a hundred ducats a-piece for his picture in little.

'Sblood, there is something in this more than natural, if philosophy could find it out.[217]   385

A flourish of trumpets.

GUILDENSTERN. There are the players.

HAMLET. Gentlemen, you are welcome to Elsinore. Your hands, come then; the appurtenance of welcome is fashion and ceremony: let me comply with you in this garb, lest my extent to the   390
players—which, I tell you must show fairly outward—should more appear like entertainment than yours. You are welcome; but my uncle-father and aunt-mother are deceived.[218]

GUILDENSTERN. In what, my dear lord?   395

HAMLET. I am but mad north-north-west: when the wind is southerly I know a hawk from a hand-saw.[219]

Enter POLONIUS.

POLONIUS. Well be with you, gentlemen!

HAMLET. Hark you, Guildenstern; and you too—at   400
each ear a hearer. That great baby you see there is not yet out of his swaddling-clouts.[220]

ROSENCRANTZ. Happily he's the second time come to them; for they say an old man is twice a child.

HAMLET. I will prophesy he comes to tell me of the   405
players; mark it.—You say right, sir; o' Monday morning; 'twas so indeed.

---

213 berattle] noisily assail; the common … them] There is resentment here of the contemptuous overtones of the word "common"—as if boys' companies were deemed more refined; many … goose-quills] Supposedly courageous gentlemen are cowed into acquiescing to fashion by critics.

214 escotted] financially supported; pursue the quality] presume to rival the professional actors; no longer than they can sing] i.e., until their soprano voices break; if their means are no better] if they do not have better means of making a living; exclaim against … succession] speak out against the position they will eventually take over.

215 tarre] incite; no money … question] No one would pay for any play unless the plot contained some new sally in the quarrel between the men and the boy actors.

216 Hercules and his load too] The logo of Shakespeare's Globe theatre was Hercules bearing the globe on his shoulders.

217 make mows] make faces, scorn; picture in little] miniature portrait; 'Sblood] God's blood—an oath.

218 appurtenance] that which belongs; garb] manner; extent] extension of civility.

219 north-north-west] in very specific ways or moments; hawk from a handsaw] a pun—hawk refers to a type of pickaxe as well as the bird; handsaw not only refers to the tool but plays upon "hernshaw" or heron, a bird often found hunting with the hawk. There may also be a recollection here of the "little eyases," the boy actors, and hence a contrast being made between the threat that skillful performers or dissemblers, as opposed to Rosencrantz and Guildenstern's crude approach, would represent to Hamlet.

220 clouts] clothes. If Hamlet's previous reference to the "hawk" alludes to the boy players, he may be suggesting that Polonius is the most naive of the predatory dissemblers he faces.

POLONIUS. My lord, I have news to tell you.

HAMLET. My lord, I have news to tell you. When Roscius was an actor in Rome —221   410

POLONIUS. The actors are come hither, my lord.

HAMLET. Buzz, buzz!222

POLONIUS. Upon my honour —

HAMLET. Then came each actor on his ass—223

POLONIUS. The best actors in the world, either for   415
tragedy, comedy, history, pastoral, pastoral-comical, historical-pastoral, tragical-historical, tragical-comical-historical-pastoral; scene individable, or poem unlimited: Seneca cannot be too heavy, nor Plautus too light. For the law of writ   420
and the liberty, these are the only men.224

HAMLET. O Jephthah, judge of Israel, what a treasure hadst thou!225

POLONIUS. What treasure had he, my lord?

HAMLET. Why   425

> One fair daughter and no more,
> The which he loved passing well.226

POLONIUS. [Aside.] Still on my daughter.

HAMLET. Am I not i' the right, old Jephthah?

POLONIUS. If you call me Jephthah, my lord, I have   430
a daughter that I love passing well.

HAMLET. Nay, that follows not.

POLONIUS. What follows, then, my lord?

HAMLET. Why,

> As by lot, God wot.   435

And then, you know,

> It came to pass, as most like it was.—

The first row of the pious chanson will show you more; for look where my abridgment comes.227

Enter the Players.

You are welcome, masters; welcome, all.—I am   440
glad to see thee well—Welcome, good friends. O, my old friend! Thy face is valanced since I saw thee last: comest thou to beard me in Denmark? What! my young lady and mistress! By 'r lady, your ladyship is nearer to heaven than when I saw you   445
last, by the altitude of a chopine. Pray God, your voice, like a piece of uncurrent gold, be not cracked within the ring.228

Masters, you are all welcome. We'll e'en to 't like French falconers, fly at anything we see: we'll have   450
a speech straight. Come, give us a taste of your quality; come, a passionate speech.

1ST PLAYER. What speech, my good lord?

HAMLET. I heard thee speak me a speech once, but it was never acted; or if it was, not above once; for   455
the play, I remember, pleased not the million; 'twas caviare to the general: but it was—as I received it, and others, whose judgments in such matters cried in the top of mine—an excellent play, well digested in the scenes, set down with as much modesty as   460
cunning. I remember one said there were no sallets in the lines to make the matter savoury, nor no matter in the phrase that might indict the author of affectation; but called it an honest method, as

---

221 Roscius] the most famous actor of Classical Rome. Hamlet is satirizing Polonius's long-winded style by suggesting that his message would begin with the most ancient piece of pedantry he could muster.

222 Buzz, buzz!] a contemptuous dismissal of stale news.

223 Upon … his ass] i.e., if the actors came "upon [Polonius's] honour," then, according to Hamlet, they came upon a stupid beast of burden; for Polonius places his honour at the beck and call of those in power.

224 The pedantry of this advertisement suggests that Polonius is its author; scene individable] a play observing the neo-classical unities of time and place; poem unlimited] an epic or romantic work that disregards the neo-classical unities; Seneca] a Roman tragic playwright; Plautus] a Roman comic playwright.

225 Jephthah was compelled, because of a foolish vow he made in exchange for power, to sacrifice his daughter. Judges 11.30–40.

226 A quote from a popular ballad on the subject.

227 the first row … will show you more] The first stanza ("row") will show you more (of the story; of personal power and wealth). The first stanza continues: "*Great wars there should be, /and who should be the chief but he…*"

228 valanced] fringed (with a beard); young lady and mistress] the boy actor of the company who plays female parts; chopine] a thick-soled shoe; cracked within the ring] pun on ring as vocal tone and the ring around a sovereign's head on a coin—which, if cracked through, would make the coin non-legal tender.

wholesome as sweet, and by very much more
handsome than fine.[229] 465

One speech in it I chiefly loved; 'twas Æneas'
tale to Dido; and thereabout of it especially, where
he speaks of Priam's slaughter.[230] If it live in your
memory, begin at this line: let me see, let me see:— 470
The rugged Pyrrhus, like the Hyrcanian beast—[231]
'tis not so, it begins with Pyrrhus—
The rugged Pyrrhus, he, whose sable arm,
Black as his purpose, did the night resemble
When he lay couched in the ominous horse,[232] 475
Hath now this dread and black complexion smeared
With heraldry more dismal; head to foot[233]
Now is he total gules; horridly tricked[234]
With blood of fathers, mothers, daughters, sons,
Baked and impasted with the parching streets,
That lend a tyrannous and a damnéd light 480
To their vile murders. Roasted in wrath and fire,
And thus o'er-sized with coagulate gore,[235]
With eyes like carbuncles, the hellish Pyrrhus[236]
Old grandsire Priam seeks. 485
So, proceed you.

POLONIUS. 'Fore God, my lord, well spoken, with
good accent and good discretion.

1ST PLAYER.   *Anon he finds him,*
Striking too short at Greeks. His antique sword, 490

Rebellious to his arm, lies where it falls,
Repugnant to command. Unequal matched,
Pyrrhus at Priam drives; in rage strikes wide;
But with the whiff and wind of his fell sword[237]
The unnerved father falls. Then senseless Ilium,[238] 495
Seeming to feel this blow, with flaming top
Stoops to his base, and with a hideous crash
Takes prisoner Pyrrhus' ear. For lo! his sword,
Which was declining on the milky head
Of reverend Priam, seemed i' the air to stick: 500
So, as a painted tyrant, Pyrrhus stood,[239]
And, like a neutral to his will and matter,
Did nothing.
But, as we often see, against some storm,
A silence in the heavens, the rack stand still,[240] 505
The bold winds speechless, and the orb below
As hush as death, anon the dreadful thunder
Doth rend the region; so, after Pyrrhus' pause,
Aroused vengeance sets him new a-work;
And never did the Cyclops' hammers fall 510
On Mars's armour, forged for proof eterne,[241]
With less remorse than Pyrrhus' bleeding sword
Now falls on Priam.
Out, out, thou strumpet, Fortune! All you gods,
In general synod, take away her power;[242] 515
Break all the spokes and fellies from her wheel,[243]
And bowl the round nave down the hill of heaven,[244]
As low as to the fiends!

POLONIUS. This is too long.

HAMLET. It shall to the barber's, with your beard. 520
Prithee, say on: he's for a jig or a tale of bawdry,
or he sleeps. Say on; come to Hecuba.[245]

1ST PLAYER. *But who, O! who, had seen the mob-led*
queen—[246]

---

229 caviare to the general] for a more refined appetite than
that of the general public; modesty as cunning] restraint
as skill; sallets] spicy bits; handsome than fine] well-pro-
portioned rather than fancy.

230 Æneas, the Trojan hero of Virgil's *Æneid*, survived the
Trojan war and, while seeking a new home, stopped in
Carthage, where he met Queen Dido; Priam] King of
Troy.

231 *Pyrrhus*] (also called Neoptelemus) son of Achilles,
whose father had been killed earlier in the Trojan War
by Priam's son, Paris; Hyrcanian beast] a tiger found on
the shores of the Caspian Sea.

232 horse] i.e., the hollow wooden horse in which the
Greeks concealed themselves to enter Troy.

233 heraldry] coat of arms decoration.

234 gules] heraldic term for red; tricked] heraldic term for
represented with colours.

235 o'er-sized] smeared all over; coagulate gore] clotting
blood.

236 carbuncles] a precious stone, deep red in colour.

237 fell] cruel.

238 senseless Ilium] the inanimate citadel of Troy.

239 painted tyrant] a painting of a tyrant.

240 rack] the storm clouds.

241 for proof eterne] to hold up throughout eternity.

242 synod] council.

243 fellies] rims.

244 round nave] hub of the wheel.

245 jig] a silly musical sketch usually performed after the
main drama; Hecuba] Queen of Troy, Priam's wife.

246 mob-led queen] Most editors follow Dryden in changing the original "mobled" to read "mobbled" (an obscure

HAMLET. "The mob-led queen."

POLONIUS. That's good. "Mob-led queen" is good.   525

1ST PLAYER. *Run barefoot up and down, threat'ning*
    the flames
    With bisson rheum; a clout upon that head[247]
    Where late the diadem stood; and, for a robe,
    About her lank and all o'er-teemed loins,[248]
    A blanket, in the alarm of fear caught up;   530
    Who this had seen, with tongue in venom steeped,
    'Gainst Fortune's state would treason have
       pronounced:
    But if the gods themselves did see her then,
    When she saw Pyrrhus make malicious sport
    In mincing with his sword her husband's limbs,   535
    The instant burst of clamour that she made—
    Unless things mortal move them not at all—
    Would have made milch the burning eyes of
       heaven,[249]
    And passion in the gods.

POLONIUS. Look where he has not turned his colour   540
    and has tears in 's eyes. Prithee, no more.

HAMLET. 'Tis well; I'll have thee speak out the rest
    of this soon.—Good my lord, will you see the
    players well bestowed?[250] Do you hear, let them
    be well used; for they are the abstract and brief   545
    chronicles of the time: after your death you were
    better have a bad epitaph than their ill report while
    you live.[251]

POLONIUS. My lord, I will use them according to
    their desert.   550

HAMLET. God's bodikins, man, much better; use
    every man after his desert, and who should 'scape
whipping?[252] Use them after your own honour
and dignity: the less they deserve, the more merit
is in your bounty. Take them in.   555

POLONIUS. Come, sirs.

HAMLET. Follow him, friends: we'll hear a play tomorrow. [*To FIRST PLAYER.*] Dost thou hear me,
old friend? Can you play the Murder of Gonzago?

1ST PLAYER. Ay, my lord.   560

HAMLET. We'll ha't to-morrow night. You could, for
a need, study a speech of some dozen or sixteen
lines, which I would set down and insert in't, could
you not?[253]

1ST PLAYER. Ay, my lord.   565

HAMLET. Very well. Follow that lord; and look you
mock him not. My good friends, I'll leave you till
night; you are welcome to Elsinore.

Exeunt POLONIUS and Players.

ROSENCRANTZ. Good my lord.

HAMLET. Ay, so, God buy t' ye.   570

Exeunt ROSENCRANTZ and GUILDENSTERN.

    Now I am alone.
    O, what a rogue and peasant slave am I![254]
    Is it not monstrous that this player here,
    But in a fiction, in a dream of passion,
    Could force his soul so to his own conceit[255]   575
    That from her working all his visage wanned,
    Tears in his eyes, distraction in 's aspect,
    A broken voice, and his whole function suiting
    With forms to his conceit? and all for nothing![256]
    For Hecuba!   580
    What's Hecuba to him or he to Hecuba
    That he should weep for her? What would he do
    Had he the motive and the cue for passion
    That I have? He would drown the stage with tears,
    And cleave the general ear with horrid speech,   585
    Make mad the guilty and appal the free,[257]

---

word meaning "muffled"); but it is more likely, thematically, dramatically and typographically, that Shakespeare
meant the word as spelled: i.e., a neologism suggesting
a loss of leadership and inversion of civic order so cata-
clysmic that, paradoxically, the Queen was led by the
mob in her panic and dismay. The hyphen added here
merely emphasizes that this is a compound word.

247 bisson rheum] blinding tears; clout] rag.

248 o'er-teemed] worn-out with bearing children (she was
    mother to nineteen).

249 milch] weep — literally "give milk."

250 bestowed] lodged.

251 abstract] synopsis.

252 God's bodikins] an oath—literally God's little body, the
    holy wafer taken at communion.

253 for a need] were it necessary.

254 peasant] base.

255 to his own conceit] according to his own conception.

256 whole … conceit] his entire physicality in accord with
    his conception.

257 free] i.e., guilt-free.

[II.ii]

Confound the ignorant, and amaze indeed
The very faculties of eyes and ears.
Yet I,
A dull and muddy-mettled rascal, peak,[258]   590
Like John-a-dreams, unpregnant of my cause,[259]
And can say nothing; no, not for a king,
Upon whose property and most dear life
A damned defeat was made. Am I a coward?
Who calls me villain? breaks my pate across?   595
Plucks off my beard and blows it in my face?
Tweaks me by the nose? gives me the lie i' the throat,
As deep as to the lungs? Who does me this, Ha?
Swounds, I should take it, for it cannot be
But I am pigeon-livered and lack gall[260]   600
To make oppression bitter, or ere this
I should have fatted all the region kites[261]
With this slave's offal. Bloody, bawdy villain![262]
Remorseless, treacherous, lecherous, kindless
     villain![263]
O! vengeance!   605
Why, what an ass am I! This is most brave
That I, the son of a dear father murdered,
Prompted to my revenge by heaven and hell,
Must, like a whore, unpack my heart with words,
And fall a-cursing like a very drab,[264]   610
A scullion! Fie upon't! foh! About, my brain![265]
Hum—I have heard,
That guilty creatures, sitting at a play
Have by the very cunning of the scene
Been struck so to the soul that presently   615
They have proclaimed their malefactions.
For murder, though it have no tongue, will speak

With most miraculous organ. I'll have these players
Play something like the murder of my father
Before mine uncle; I'll observe his looks;   620
I'll tent him to the quick: if he but blench,[266]
I know my course. The spirit that I have seen
May be a devil: and the devil hath power
To assume a pleasing shape; yea, and perhaps
Out of my weakness and my melancholy—   625
As he is very potent with such spirits—
Abuses me to damn me. I'll have grounds
More relative than this: the play's the thing[267]
Wherein I'll catch the conscience of the king.

[*Exit.*]

ACT III

SCENE I

A ROOM IN THE CASTLE.

*Enter KING, QUEEN, POLONIUS, OPHELIA,
ROSENCRANTZ, and GUILDENSTERN.*

KING. And can you, by no drift of circumstance,[268]
     Get from him why he puts on this confusion,
     Grating so harshly all his days of quiet
     With turbulent and dangerous lunacy?
ROSENCRANTZ. He does confess he feels himself   5
     distracted;[269]
     But from what cause he will by no means speak.
GUILDENSTERN. Nor do we find him forward to be
     sounded,[270]
     But, with a crafty madness, keeps aloof
     When we would bring him on to some confession
     Of his true state.   10
QUEEN.   Did he receive you well?

---

258 peak] mope.
259 John-a-dreams] a nickname for a daydreamer;
     unpregnant] not fertilized by indignation in a way that
     would give birth to vengeance.
260 pigeon-livered … gall] The pigeon, as the epitome of
     meekness, was thought to have a liver empty of gall—
     the source of rancour.
261 kites] scavenger birds.
262 offal] rotting flesh.
263 kindless] unnatural, without kind.
264 drab] prostitute.
265 scullion] a kitchen menial; foh!] an exclamation of dis-
     gust; About] get going.

266 tent] examine, probe (a "tent" was a medical instrument
     used for examining wounds); blench] flinch, blink (not
     blanch).
267 relative] pertinent; material, relating the crime to the
     suspect.
268 drift of circumstance] in the course of matters; inciden-
     tally.
269 distracted] disordered in his mind.
270 forward to be sounded] amenable to being examined.

ROSENCRANTZ. Most like a gentleman.

GUILDENSTERN. But with much forcing of his
    disposition.

ROSENCRANTZ. Niggard of question, but of our
    demands
    Most free in his reply.[271]

QUEEN.   Did you assay him
    To any pastime?   15

ROSENCRANTZ. Madam, it so fell out that certain
    players
    We o'erraught on the way; of these we told him,[272]
    And there did seem in him a kind of joy
    To hear of it: they are about the court,
    And, as I think, they have already order   20
    This night to play before him.

POLONIUS.   'Tis most true;
    And he beseeched me to entreat your majesties
    To hear and see the matter.

KING. With all my heart; and it doth much content me
    To hear him so inclined.   25
    Good gentlemen, give him a further edge,
    And drive his purpose on to these delights.

ROSENCRANTZ. We shall, my lord.

[Exeunt ROSENCRANTZ and GUILDENSTERN.]

KING.   Sweet Gertrude, leave us too;
    For we have closely sent for Hamlet hither,
    That he, as 'twere by accident, may here   30
    Affront[273] Ophelia.
    Her father and myself, lawful espials,[274]
    Will so bestow ourselves that, seeing, unseen,
    We may of their encounter frankly judge,
    And gather by him, as he is behaved,   35
    If 't be the affliction of his love or no
    That thus he suffers for.

QUEEN.   I shall obey you.
    And for your part, Ophelia, I do wish
    That your good beauties be the happy cause
    Of Hamlet's wildness; so shall I hope your virtues   40
    Will bring him to his wonted way again,
    To both your honours.

OPHELIA.   Madam, I wish it may.

[Exit QUEEN.]

POLONIUS. Ophelia, walk you here. Gracious, so
    please you,[275]
    We will bestow ourselves. [To OPHELIA.] Read on
    this book;
    That show of such an exercise may colour   45
    Your loneliness. We are oft to blame in this,[276]
    'Tis too much proved, that with devotion's visage
    And pious action we do sugar o'er
    The devil himself.

KING. [Aside.]   O! 'tis too true;
    How smart a lash that speech doth give my   50
    conscience!
    The harlot's cheek, beautied with plastering art,
    Is not more ugly to the thing that helps it
    Than is my deed to my most painted word:
    O heavy burden!

POLONIUS. I hear him coming; let's withdraw, my   55
    lord.

[Exeunt KING and POLONIUS.]

Enter HAMLET.

HAMLET. To be, or not to be: that is the question:
    Whether 'tis nobler in the mind to suffer
    The slings and arrows of outrageous fortune,
    Or to take arms against a sea of troubles,
    And by opposing end them. To die: to sleep,   60
    No more; and, by a sleep to say we end[277]
    The heart-ache and the thousand natural shocks
    That flesh is heir to: 'tis a consummation[278]
    Devoutly to be wished. To die, to sleep;
    To sleep; perchance to dream—ay, there's the   65
    rub:[279]

---

271 Cf. II.ii.215ff.
272 o'erraught] overtook.
273 Affront] meet face to face.
274 espials] spies.

275 Gracious] i.e., Gracious king.
276 that show … loneliness] so that the sight of you read-
    ing will offer a plausible explanation for you being alone
    here.
277 To die … more] i.e., to die is no more than to sleep.
278 consummation] pun—obliteration of being; sexual
    climax.
279 the rub] the tricky part, the obstacle (a metaphor from
    lawn bowling).

For in that sleep of death what dreams may come
When we have shuffled off this mortal coil,[280]
Must give us pause. There's the respect[281]
That makes calamity of so long life;
For who would bear the whips and scorns of time,[282]   70
The oppressor's wrong, the proud man's
    contumely,[283]
The pangs of despised love, the law's delay,
The insolence of office, and the spurns[284]
That patient merit of the unworthy takes,[285]
When he himself might his quietus make[286]   75
With a bare bodkin? who would these fardels
    bear,[287]
To grunt and sweat under a weary life,
But that the dread of something after death,
The undiscovered country, from whose bourn[288]
No traveller returns, puzzles the will,   80
And makes us rather bear those ills we have
Than fly to others that we know not of?
Thus conscience does make cowards of us all;[289]
And thus the native hue of resolution
Is sicklied o'er with the pale cast of thought,[290]   85
And enterprises of great pith and moment[291]
With this regard their currents turn awry,[292]

And lose the name of action. Soft you now!
    The fair Ophelia! Nymph, in thy orisons[293]
    Be all my sins remembered.[294]   90
OPHELIA.   Good my lord,
    How does your honour for this many a day?[295]
HAMLET. I humbly thank you; well, well, well.
OPHELIA. My lord, I have remembrances of yours,
    That I have longéd long to re-deliver;
    I pray you, now receive them.   95
HAMLET.   No, not I;
    I never gave you aught.
OPHELIA. My honoured lord, you know right well
    you did;
    And, with them, words of so sweet breath composed
    As made these things more rich: their perfume lost,
    Take these again; for to the noble mind   100
    Rich gifts wax poor when givers prove unkind.
    There, my lord.
HAMLET. Ha, ha! Are you honest?[296]
OPHELIA. My lord!
HAMLET. Are you fair?   105
OPHELIA. What means your lordship?
HAMLET. That if you be honest and fair, your honesty
    should admit no discourse to your beauty.[297]
OPHELIA. Could beauty, my lord, have better
    commerce than with honesty?   110
HAMLET. Ay, truly; for the power of beauty will
    sooner transform honesty from what it is to a bawd
    than the force of honesty can translate beauty into
    his likeness: this was sometime a paradox, but now
    the time gives it proof.[298] I did love thee once.   115
OPHELIA. Indeed, my lord, you made me believe so.
HAMLET. You should not have believed me; for virtue
    cannot so inoculate our old stock but we shall
    relish of it.[299] I loved you not.

---

280 shuffled … mortal coil] i.e., cast off the flesh which
    encircles the soul, or cast off corporeal life as if it were
    a coil of rope mooring the soul to the living world as a
    ship is moored to a harbour.
281 For … pause] For the thought of the dreams that might
    come after death must make us reconsider; respect] con-
    sideration.
282 of time] i.e., inherent to living in time, rather than be-
    ing in timelessness, eternity.
283 contumely] contempt.
284 insolence of office] the rudeness of those with official
    power.
285 of] from.
286 quietus] quittance of debt, clear account.
287 bare bodkin] mere (or unsheathed) dagger; fardels] bur-
    dens.
288 bourn] border, region.
289 conscience] inner reflection.
290 sicklied o'er] given a sick appearance; cast] colour.
291 pith] vigour, strength; moment] importance.
292 regard] consideration.

---

293 orisons] prayers.
294 Be … remember'd] i.e., I hope your prayers include me.
295 for this many a day] in the few days since I last saw you.
296 honest] truthful; chaste.
297 your honesty … beauty] Your modesty should allow no
    approach to your beauty; your truthfulness should not
    allow others to be deceived by your appearances.
298 sometime] once.
299 inoculate] graft; for virtue … of it] for a graft of virtue
    to our original sinful nature will not wipe away all fla-
    vour of that nature.

OPHELIA. I was the more deceived.   120

HAMLET. Get thee to a nunnery: why wouldst thou be
a breeder of sinners? I am myself indifferent honest;
but yet I could accuse me of such things that it were
better my mother had not borne me.300 I am very
proud, revengeful, ambitious; with more offences at   125
my beck than I have thoughts to put them in,
imagination to give them shape, or time to act them
in.301 What should such fellows as I do crawling
between earth and heaven? We are arrant knaves, all;
believe none of us. Go thy ways to a nunnery.302   130
Where's your father?

OPHELIA. At home, my lord.

HAMLET. Let the doors be shut upon him, that he
may play the fool nowhere but in 's own house.
Farewell.   135

OPHELIA. O! help him, you sweet heavens!

HAMLET. If thou dost marry, I'll give thee this plague
for thy dowry: be thou as chaste as ice, as pure as
snow, thou shalt not escape calumny. Get thee to
a nunnery, go; farewell. Or if thou wilt needs   140
marry, marry a fool; for wise men know well
enough what monsters you make of them.303 To
a nunnery, go; and quickly too. Farewell.

OPHELIA. O heavenly powers, restore him!

HAMLET. I have heard of your paintings too, well   145
enough; God hath given you one face, and you
make yourselves another: you jig, you amble, and
you lisp, and nickname God's creatures, and make
your wantonness your ignorance.304 Go to, I'll no
more on 't; it hath made me mad. I say, we will   150
have no more marriages; those that are married
already—all but one—shall live; the rest shall keep
as they are. To a nunnery, go. [Exit.]

OPHELIA. O what a noble mind is here o'erthrown:
The courtier's, soldier's, scholar's, eye, tongue, sword,   155
The expectancy and rose of the fair state,305
The glass of fashion and the mold of form,306
The observed of all observers, quite, quite down!
And I, of ladies most deject and wretched,
That sucked the honey of his music vows,   160
Now see that noble and most sovereign reason,
Like sweet bells jangled, out of tune and harsh;
That unmatched form and feature of blown
youth307
Blasted with ecstasy: O! woe is me,
To have seen what I have seen, see what I see!   165

Re-enter KING and POLONIUS.

KING. Love! his affections do not that way tend;308
Nor what he spake, though it lacked form a little,
Was not like madness. There's something in his soul
O'er which his melancholy sits on brood;309
And I do doubt the hatch and the disclose310   170
Will be some danger; which for to prevent,
I have in quick determination
Thus set it down: he shall with speed to England,
For the demand of our neglected tribute:311
Haply the seas, and countries different312   175
With variable objects, shall expel313
This something-settled matter in his heart,
Whereon his brains still beating puts him thus
From fashion of himself. What think you on 't?314

POLONIUS. It shall do well: but yet do I believe   180
The origin and commencement of his grief

---

300 indifferent honest] of average virtue.

301 at my beck] within reach, bidding.

302 nunnery] convent. The use of "nunnery" as a slang term
for brothel was not in common use until well after the
date of this play.

303 monsters] cuckolds (a husband with an adulterous wife
was said to wear horns).

304 jig … amble] dance, stroll in a provocative manner; lisp]
affect babyish speech; make your … ignorance] pretend
that you are too innocent to understand the implications
of your speech and actions.

305 expectancy and rose] greatest hope and finest ornament.

306 glass of fashion] mirror by which fashion assessed itself;
mold of form] model of manners.

307 feature of blown] image of fully-matured.

308 affections] inclinations.

309 sits on brood] as a hen broods, or incubates, her eggs.

310 doubt] fear.

311 neglected tribute] Evidently Denmark extorts an annual
payment from England which is now overdue.

312 Haply] perhaps.

313 variable objects] a change in scenery.

314 shall expel … fashion of himself] shall dislodge this
deep-rooted preoccupation on which his brain keeps
hammering away, thereby making him so unlike his
usual self.

Sprung from neglected love. How now, Ophelia!
You need not tell us what Lord Hamlet said;
We heard it all. My lord, do as you please;
But, if you hold it fit, after the play,   185
Let his queen mother all alone entreat him
To show his griefs. Let her be round with him;315
And I'll be placed, so please you, in the ear
Of all their conference. If she find him not,316
To England send him, or confine him where   190
Your wisdom best shall think.

KING.   It shall be so:
Madness in great ones must not unwatched go.

[*Exeunt.*]

SCENE II

A HALL IN THE CASTLE.

Enter HAMLET and Players.

HAMLET. Speak the speech, I pray you, as I
pronounced it to you, trippingly on the tongue;317
but if you mouth it, as many of our players do, I
had as lief the town-crier spoke my lines. Nor do
not saw the air too much with your hand, thus;   5
but use all gently; for in the very torrent, tempest,
and—as I may say—whirlwind of your passion,
you must acquire and beget a temperance, that
may give it smoothness. O, it offends me to the
soul to hear a robustious, periwig-pated fellow tear   10
a passion to tatters, to very rags, to split the ears
of the groundlings, who for the most part are
capable of nothing but inexplicable dumb-shows
and noise: I would have such a fellow whipped for
o'er-doing Termagant; it out-herods Herod:318   15
pray you, avoid it.

1ST PLAYER. I warrant your honour.319

HAMLET. Be not too tame neither, but let your own
discretion be your tutor: suit the action to the
word, the word to the action; with this special ob-   20
servance, that you o'erstep not the modesty of
nature. For anything so overdone is from the purpose of playing, whose end, both at the first and
now, was and is, to hold, as 'twere, the mirror up
to nature; to show virtue her own feature, scorn   25
her own image, and the very age and body of the
time his form and pressure. Now this overdone,
or come tardy off, though it make the unskillful
laugh, cannot but make the judicious grieve; the
censure of which one must in your allowance   30
o'erweigh a whole theatre of others.320 O, there
be players that I have seen play, and heard others
praise, and that highly, not to speak it profanely,
that, neither having the accent of Christians nor
the gait of Christian, pagan, nor man, have so   35
strutted and bellowed that I have thought some of
nature's journeymen had made men and not made
them well, they imitated humanity so abomina-
bly.321

1ST PLAYER. I hope we have reformed that indiffer-   40
ently with us.322

HAMLET. O, reform it altogether. And let those that
play your clowns speak no more than is set down
for them; for there be of them that will themselves
laugh, to set on some quantity of barren spectators   45
to laugh too, though in the mean time some
necessary question of the play be then to be
considered.323 That's villainous, and shows a most
pitiful ambition in the fool that uses it. Go, make
you ready. [*Exeunt Players.*]   50

*Enter POLONIUS, ROSENCRANTZ, and
GUILDENSTERN.*

How now, my lord; will the king hear this piece
of work?

---

315 show his griefs] reveal his grievances; round] blunt.
316 find him not] does not discover what he has got on his
    mind.
317 trippingly] lightly, dextrously.
318 robustious, periwig-pated] boisterous, wig-headed; capa-
    ble of] capable of appreciating; Termagant … Herod]
    tyrannical, violent-tempered characters in the mysteries.
319 warrant] assure.

320 come tardy off] done lackadaisically; unskillful] undis-
    criminating; one] i.e., one judicious person.
321 Christian, pagan, nor man] those of our culture, exotic
    foreigners, nor indeed any human being at all; journey-
    men] assistants who have not yet mastered the craft.
322 indifferently] moderately.
323 necessary question] essential point.

POLONIUS. And the queen too, and that presently.
HAMLET. Bid the players make haste.

[*Exit POLONIUS.*]

   Will you two help to hasten them?   55
ROSENCRANTZ. ⎤
GUILDENSTERN. ⎦ We will, my lord.

[*Exeunt ROSENCRANTZ and GUILDENSTERN.*]

HAMLET. What, ho! Horatio!

Enter HORATIO.

HORATIO. Here, sweet lord, at your service.
HAMLET. Horatio, thou art e'en as just a man
   As e'er my conversation coped withal.[324]   60
HORATIO. O! my dear lord,—
HAMLET.   Nay, do not think I flatter;
   For what advancement may I hope from thee,
   That no revenue hast but thy good spirits
   To feed and clothe thee? Why should the poor be
      flattered?
   No; let the candied tongue lick absurd pomp,[325]   65
   And crook the pregnant hinges of the knee[326]
   Where thrift may follow fawning. Dost thou
      hear?[327]
   Since my dear soul was mistress of her choice
   And could of men distinguish, her election
   Hath sealed thee for herself; for thou hast been[328]   70
   As one, in suffering all, that suffers nothing,[329]
   A man that fortune's buffets and rewards
   Hast ta'en with equal thanks; and blessed are those
   Whose blood and judgment are so well co-mingled

That they are not a pipe for fortune's finger[330]   75
To sound what stop she please. Give me that man
That is not passion's slave, and I will wear him
In my heart's core, ay, in my heart of heart,
As I do thee. Something too much of this.[331]
There is a play to-night before the king;   80
One scene of it comes near the circumstance,
Which I have told thee of my father's death:
I prithee, when thou seest that act afoot,
Even with the very comment of thy soul[332]
Observe mine uncle; if his occulted guilt[333]   85
Do not itself unkennel in one speech,
It is a damnéd ghost that we have seen,[334]
And my imaginations are as foul
As Vulcan's stithy. Give him heedful note;[335]
For I mine eyes will rivet to his face,   90
And after we will both our judgments join
In censure of his seeming.[336]
HORATIO.   Well, my lord:
If he steal aught the whilst this play is playing,
And 'scape detecting, I will pay the theft.
HAMLET. They are coming to the play; I must be   95
   idle.[337] Get you a place.

*Danish march. A Flourish. Enter KING, QUEEN,
POLONIUS, OPHELIA, ROSENCRANTZ,
GUILDENSTERN, and Others.*

KING. How fares our cousin Hamlet?
HAMLET. Excellent, i' faith; of the chameleon's dish:
   I eat the air, promise-crammed. You cannot feed
   capons so.[338]   100

---

324 As e'er … withal] as I have ever met.
325 candied] sugar-coated, flattering; lick absurd pomp]
   fawn upon absurdly pompous persons.
326 pregnant hinges] joints full of readiness to bend.
327 Where thrift … fawning] where material gain will come
   from sycophancy.
328 Since my dear soul … herself] Ever since I have been
   capable of choice and of telling the difference between
   men, my soul has placed its distinctive mark (seal) upon
   you.
329 as one … suffers nothing] like a person who, despite
   having suffered all manner of misfortune, never thinks
   of himself as a victim.

330 pipe] e.g., a recorder or flute (cf. the upcoming exchange
   with Rosencrantz and Guildenstern).
331 Something too much of this] That's more than enough
   of that.
332 the very comment of thy soul] your most profound consideration.
333 occulted] concealed.
334 damnéd ghost] a demon rather than a benevolent spirit.
335 Vulcan's stithy] the sooty smithy of the notorious god
   of blacksmiths.
336 both our judgments … seeming] compare our judgments of his appearance.
337 be idle] act the fool.
338 of the chameleon's dish] playing upon "fares" as "eats,"
   Hamlet alludes to the ancient belief that chameleons fed

KING. I have nothing with this answer, Hamlet; these words are not mine.

HAMLET. No, nor mine now. [*To POLONIUS.*] My lord, you played once i' the university, you say?

POLONIUS. That did I, my lord, and was accounted a good actor. 105

HAMLET. What did you enact?

POLONIUS. I did enact Julius Caesar: I was killed i' the Capitol; Brutus killed me.

HAMLET. It was a brute part of him to kill so capital a calf there. Be the players ready?[339] 110

ROSENCRANTZ. Ay, my lord; they stay upon your patience.

QUEEN. Come hither, my dear Hamlet, sit by me.

HAMLET. No, good mother, here's metal more attractive.[340] 115

POLONIUS. [*To the KING.*] O, ho! do you mark that?

HAMLET. Lady, shall I lie in your lap?

OPHELIA. No, my lord.

HAMLET. I mean, my head upon your lap. 120

OPHELIA. Ay, my lord.

HAMLET. Do you think I meant country matters?[341]

OPHELIA. I think nothing, my lord.

HAMLET. That's a fair thought to lie between maids' legs. 125

OPHELIA. What is, my lord?

HAMLET. Nothing.[342]

OPHELIA. You are merry, my lord.

HAMLET. Who, I?

OPHELIA. Ay, my lord. 130

HAMLET. O God, your only jig-maker.[343] What should a man do but be merry? For, look you, how cheerfully my mother looks, and my father died within 's two hours.

OPHELIA. Nay, 'tis twice two months, my lord. 135

HAMLET. So long? Nay then, let the devil wear black, for I'll have a suit of sables.[344] O heavens! die two months ago, and not forgotten yet? Then there's hope a great man's memory may outlive his life half a year; but, by 'r lady, he must build churches then, 140 or else shall he suffer not thinking on, with the hobby-horse, whose epitaph is, "For, O! for, O! the hobby-horse is forgot".[345]

The trumpets sound. A dumb-show follows.[346]

Enter a KING and a QUEEN, very lovingly; the QUEEN embracing him, and he her. She kneels, and makes show of protestation unto him. He takes her up, and declines his head upon her neck. He lays him down upon a bank of flowers: she, seeing him asleep, leaves him. Anon comes in another MAN, takes off his crown, kisses it, pours poison in the sleeper's ears, and exit. The QUEEN returns, finds the KING dead, and makes passionate action. The POISONER, with some two or three MUTES, comes in again, seeming to lament with her. The dead body is carried away. The POISONER woos the QUEEN with gifts; she seems loath and unwilling awhile, but in the end accepts his love. [Exeunt.]

OPHELIA. What means this, my lord?

HAMLET. Marry, this is miching mallecho; it means mischief.[347] 145

---

on air; I eat … so] Having been stuffed full of promises, I have room for nothing but air; even capons (castrated cocks, raised for food) would require more. Hamlet may be implying that he is resentful about disappointed ambition, that, as the denied heir to the throne, he feels castrated.

339 so capital a calf] such a fine fool (the phrase "kill a calf" refers to the killing of a fool enacted in the mummers' entertainments).

340 attractive] punning on "magnetic."

341 country matters] rustic behaviour; also punning on "cunt."

342 Nothing] i.e., no obstacle.

343 jig-maker] creator of bawdy jokes.

344 suit of sables] luxurious dark furs, more opulent than mere black clothing.

345 suffer not thinking on] endure not being thought of; For … hobby-horse is forgot] the refrain from a popular song. The hobby-horse was used in mummer's entertainments—a horse costume usually worn around the rider's waist and used in a playful enactment of ritual death and resurrection.

346 *dumb-show*] A mimed performance presenting an emblematic version of the action which would follow was common in the Elizabethan theatre. Whether Claudius sees and understands the dumb show is debatable.

347 miching mallecho] sneaking mischief.

OPHELIA. Belike this show imports the argument of
the play.

Enter PROLOGUE.

HAMLET. We shall know by this fellow. The players
cannot keep counsel; they'll tell all.[348]   150

OPHELIA. Will he tell us what this show meant?

HAMLET. Ay, or any show that you'll show him. Be
not you ashamed to show, he'll not shame to tell
you what it means.

OPHELIA. You are naught, you are naught. I'll mark   155
the play.[349]

PRO. *For us, and for our tragedy,*
  Here stooping to your clemency,
  We beg your hearing patiently.

HAMLET. Is this a prologue, or the posy of a ring?[350] 160

OPHELIA. 'Tis brief, my lord.

HAMLET. As woman's love.

Enter the PLAYER KING and PLAYER QUEEN.

P.KING. *Full thirty times hath Phoebus' cart gone round*
  Neptune's salt wash and Tellus' orbéd ground,[351]
  And thirty dozen moons with borrowed sheen   165
  About the world have times twelve thirties been,
  Since love our hearts and Hymen did our hands[352]
  Unite commutual in most sacred bands.

P.QUEEN. *So many journeys may the sun and moon*
  Make us again count o'er ere love be done!   170
  But woe is me! you are so sick of late,
  So far from cheer and from your former state,
  That I distrust you. Yet, though I distrust,[353]
  Discomfort you, my lord, it nothing must;
  For women's fear and love holds quantity,   175
  In neither aught, or in extremity.[354]

Now what my love is, proof hath made you know;
And as my love is sized, my fear is so.
Where love is great, the littlest doubts are fear;
Where little fears grow great, great love grows there. 180

P.KING. *Faith, I must leave thee, love, and shortly too;*
  My operant powers their functions leave to do:[355]
  And thou shalt live in this fair world behind,[356]
  Honoured, beloved; and haply one as kind
  For husband shalt thou—   185

P.QUEEN.   *O! confound the rest;*
  Such love must needs be treason in my breast:
  In second husband let me be accurst;
  None wed the second but who killed the first.

HAMLET. [*Aside.*] That's wormwood.[357]

P.QUEEN. *The instances that second marriage move,*[358] 190
  Are base respects of thrift, but none of love;
  A second time I kill my husband dead,
  When second husband kisses me in bed.

P.KING. *I do believe you think what now you speak;*
  But what we do determine oft we break.   195
  Purpose is but the slave to memory,
  Of violent birth, but poor validity;
  Which now, like fruit unripe, sticks on the tree,
  But fall unshaken when they mellow be.[359]
  Most necessary 'tis that we forget   200
  To pay ourselves what to ourselves is debt;
  What to ourselves in passion we propose,
  The passion ending, doth the purpose lose.
  The violence of either grief or joy
  Their own enactures with themselves destroy;[360]   205
  Where joy most revels grief doth most lament,

348 counsel] a secret.
349 naught] lit., of no worth, indecent (the origin of
  naughty); mark] watch.
350 posy of a ring] a motto inscribed on the inside of a ring
  (i.e., because it is so short).
351 *Phoebus*] the sun-god; *Neptune*] the ocean; *Tellus*] the
  earth.
352 *Hymen*] god of marriage and chastity.
353 *distrust*] am worried about.
354 *For women's ... extremity*] i.e, women have great fears
  where they have great love; where they have no love,
  they are fearless.

355 *My operant ... do*] My physical faculties must fail.
356 *thou ... behind*] you will live on.
357 wormwood] a bitter herb (that will not be easily swallowed by Claudius and Gertrude).
358 *instances ... move*] considerations that motivate second
  marriages.
359 *Purpose is ... mellow be*] i.e., intentions last no longer
  than they are remembered; they are begotten with enthusiasm, but no lasting strength; they are like fruit
  which holds fast to the tree only until it is ripe, at which
  point it falls off without even needing to be shaken.
360 *The violence ... destroy*] The very extremity or violence
  of emotion inherent in grief and joy destroys that which
  we intend to enact under their inspiration.

Grief joys, joy grieves, on slender accident.
This world is not for aye, nor 'tis not strange,[361]
That even our loves should with our fortunes change;
For 'tis a question left us yet to prove   210
Whether love lead fortune or else fortune love.
The great man down, you mark his favourite flies;
The poor advanced makes friends of enemies.[362]
And hitherto doth love on fortune tend,
For who not needs shall never lack a friend;   215
And who in want a hollow friend doth try
Directly seasons him his enemy.[363]
But, orderly to end where I begun,
Our wills and fates do so contrary run
That our devices still are overthrown,   220
Our thoughts are ours, their ends none of our own:
So think thou wilt no second husband wed;
But die thy thoughts when thy first lord is dead.

P.QUEEN. *Nor earth to me give food, nor heaven light!*
Sport and repose lock from me day and night!   225
To desperation turn my trust and hope!
An anchor's cheer in prison be my scope![364]
Each opposite that blanks the face of joy[365]
Meet what I would have well, and it destroy!
Both here and hence pursue me lasting strife,   230
If, once a widow, ever I be wife!

HAMLET. If she should break it now!*[366]

P.KING. *'Tis deeply sworn. Sweet, leave me here awhile;*
My spirits grow dull, and fain I would beguile
The tedious day with sleep. [*Sleeps.*]   235

P.QUEEN.   *Sleep rock thy brain;*
And never come mischance between us twain! [*Exit.*]

HAMLET. Madam, how like you this play?

QUEEN. The lady doth protest too much, methinks.[367]

HAMLET. O! but she'll keep her word.   240

KING. Have you heard the argument?[368] Is there no
offence in't?

HAMLET. No, no! They do but jest, poison in jest;
no offence i' the world.

KING. What do you call the play?   245

HAMLET. *The Mousetrap.* Marry, how? Tropically.[369]
This play is the image of a murder done in Vienna:
Gonzago is the duke's name; his wife, Baptista. You
shall see anon; 'tis a knavish piece of work: but
what of that? your majesty and we that have free   250
souls, it touches us not: let the galled jade wince;
our withers are unwrung.[370]

Enter PLAYER as LUCIANUS.

This is one Lucianus, nephew to the king.

OPHELIA. You are a good chorus, my lord.

HAMLET. I could interpret between you and your   255
love, if I could see the puppets dallying.[371]

OPHELIA. You are keen, my lord, you are keen.

HAMLET. It would cost you a groaning to take off
my edge.[372]

OPHELIA. Still better, and worse.[373]   260

HAMLET. So you must take your husbands. Begin,
murderer; pox, leave thy damnable faces, and
begin.[374] Come; the croaking raven doth bellow
for revenge.

LUCIANUS. *Thoughts black, hands apt, drugs fit, and*   265
time agreeing;
Confederate season, else no creature seeing;[375]
Thou mixture rank, of midnight weeds collected,

---

361 *aye*] ever.
362 *The great man … advanced*] When a rich person is down
on his luck, he suddenly has only flies for companions;
whereas a poor man who has suddenly come into a fortune …
363 *And who … enemy*] Someone in need who turns to a
hollow friend immediately turns him into an enemy
with the "seasoning" of need.
364 *An anchor's cheer*] the life of an anchorite, a hermit.
365 *opposite that blanks*] adverse event that pales.
366 If she … now] What if she breaks her promise now.
367 protest] promise, swear.

368 argument] plot.
369 how? Tropically] How does it come by that title? By a
trope, metaphorically.
370 let the galled jade … unwrung] Let the old horse rubbed
raw by its saddle wince when it is ridden, our sides are
unchafed.
371 interpret … dallying] The "interpreter" of a puppet
show narrated the show.
372 a groaning … edge] Hamlet puns on keen—a sharp
edge, and his sexual desire, the relief of which would
cause her to groan as she lost her maidenhead.
373 better and worse] sharper-witted and more offensive.
374 pox … begin] dammit, stop mugging and get to work.
375 *Confederate … seeing*] time being co-operative, and
nothing else but time watching.

With Hecate's ban thrice blasted, thrice infected,[376]
Thy natural magic and dire property,[377]
On wholesome life usurp immediately. 270

[*Pours the poison into the Sleeper's ears.*]

HAMLET. He poisons him i' the garden for's estate.
His name's Gonzago; the story is extant, and writ
in very choice Italian.[378] You shall see anon how
the murderer gets the love of Gonzago's wife.
OPHELIA. The king rises. 275
HAMLET. What! frighted with false fire?[379]
QUEEN. How fares my lord?
POLONIUS. Give o'er the play.
KING. Give me some light: away!
ALL. Lights, lights, lights! 280

[*Exeunt all except HAMLET and HORATIO.*]

HAMLET. Why, let the stricken deer go weep,
The hart ungallèd play;[380]
For some must watch, while some must sleep:
So runs the world away.
Would not this, sir, and a forest of feathers, if the 285
rest of my fortunes turn Turk with me, with two
Provincial roses on my razed shoes, get me a
fellowship in a cry of players, sir?[381]
HORATIO. Half a share.[382]
HAMLET. A whole one, I. 290
For thou dost know, O Damon dear,[383]

---

376 *Hecate's ban*] curse of the goddess of witchcraft.

377 *dire property*] fatal attribute.

378 His] the murdered king's; extant] If the story once was
extant, it is not now. It is likely that Shakespeare invented it.

379 false fire] blank shots.

380 Why, let … play] Let the deer that has been struck by
the hunter creep off to weep and die while the others
continue to frolic.

381 feathers] such as actors might wear in their hats; turn
Turk] prove treacherous (being non-Christians, Turks
were assumed to be inherently immoral); cry] pack (as
of hounds).

382 Half a share] Shakespeare was one of several sharehold-
ers in his company; some less important members were
allowed half a share.

383 Damon] In Greek legend, Damon and Pythias had an
ideal friendship.

This realm dismantled was
Of Jove himself; and now reigns here
A very, very—pajock.[384]
HORATIO. You might have rhymed.[385] 295
HAMLET. O good Horatio! I'll take the ghost's word
for a thousand pound. Didst perceive?
HORATIO. Very well, my lord.
HAMLET. Upon the talk of the poisoning?
HORATIO. I did very well note him. 300
HAMLET. Ah ha! Come, some music! come, the
recorders!
For if the king like not the comedy,
Why then, belike he likes it not, perdie.[386]
Come, some music!

Re-enter ROSENCRANTZ and GUILDENSTERN.

GUILDENSTERN. Good my lord, vouchsafe me a 305
word with you.
HAMLET. Sir, a whole history.
GUILDENSTERN. The king, sir,—
HAMLET. Ay, sir, what of him?
GUILDENSTERN. Is in his retirement marvelous 310
distempered.
HAMLET. With drink, sir?
GUILDENSTERN. No, my lord; rather with choler.[387]
HAMLET. Your wisdom should show itself more
richer to signify this to the doctor; for me to put 315
him to his purgation would perhaps plunge him
into far more choler.[388]
GUILDENSTERN. Good my lord, put your discourse
into some frame, and start not so wildly from my
affair.[389] 320
HAMLET. I am tame, sir; pronounce.
GUILDENSTERN. The queen, your mother, in most
great affliction of spirit, hath sent me to you.
HAMLET. You are welcome.

---

384 pajock] either "patchock," a boorish contemptible person, or "peacock," a bird reputed to be cruel and lustful.

385 rhymed] i.e., "ass" instead of "pajock."

386 perdie] by God (corruption of French, *par dieu*).

387 choler] anger (but Hamlet pretends to understand it literally, as an attack of bile).

388 signify] report.

389 frame] logical order.

GUILDENSTERN. Nay, good my lord, this courtesy   325
is not of the right breed. If it shall please you to
make me a wholesome answer, I will do your
mother's commandment; if not, your pardon and
my return shall be the end of my business.

HAMLET. Sir, I cannot.   330

GUILDENSTERN. What, my lord?

HAMLET. Make you a wholesome answer; my wit's
diseased. but, sir, such answer is I can make, you
shall command; or rather, as you say, my mother.
Therefore no more, but to the matter: my mother,   335
you say,—

ROSENCRANTZ. Then thus she says: your behaviour
hath struck her into amazement and admira-
tion.390

HAMLET. O wonderful son, that can so astonish a   340
mother! But is there no sequel at the heels of this
mother's admiration? Impart.

ROSENCRANTZ. She desires to speak with you in her
closet391 ere you go to bed.

HAMLET. We shall obey, were she ten times our   345
mother. Have you any further trade with us?

ROSENCRANTZ. My lord, you once did love me.

HAMLET. And do still, by these pickers and
stealers.392

ROSENCRANTZ. Good my lord, what is your cause   350
of distemper? You do surely bar the door upon
your own liberty, if you deny your griefs to your
friend.

HAMLET. Sir, I lack advancement.393

ROSENCRANTZ. How can that be, when you have   355
the voice of the king himself for your succession
in Denmark?

HAMLET. Ay, sir, but "While the grass grows"—the
proverb is something musty.394

Enter PLAYERS, with recorders.

O, the recorders: let me see one. To withdraw with   360

you: why do you go about to recover the wind of
me, as if you would drive me into a toil?395

GUILDENSTERN. O, my lord, if my duty be too
bold, my love is too unmannerly.396

HAMLET. I do not well understand that. Will you   365
play upon this pipe?

GUILDENSTERN. My lord, I cannot.

HAMLET. I pray you.

GUILDENSTERN. Believe me, I cannot.

HAMLET. I do beseech you.   370

GUILDENSTERN. I know no touch of it, my lord.

HAMLET. 'Tis as easy as lying; govern these ventages
with your finger and thumb, give it breath with
your mouth, and it will discourse most eloquent
music.397 Look you, these are the stops.   375

GUILDENSTERN. But these cannot I command to
any utterance of harmony; I have not the skill.

HAMLET. Why, look you now, how unworthy a thing
you make of me. You would play upon me; you
would seem to know my stops; you would pluck   380
out the heart of my mystery; you would sound me
from my lowest note to the top of my compass;
and there is much music, excellent voice, in this
little organ, yet cannot you make it speak. 'Sblood,
do you think I am easier to be played on than a   385
pipe? Call me what instrument you will, though
you can fret me, you cannot play upon me.398

Enter POLONIUS.

God bless you, sir!

POLONIUS. My lord, the queen would speak with
you, and presently.399   390

HAMLET. Do you see yonder cloud that's almost in
shape of a camel?

POLONIUS. By the mass, and 'tis like a camel, indeed.

HAMLET. Methinks it is like a weasel.

---

390 admiration] astonishment.

391 closet] private room.

392 pickers and stealers] i.e., hands (slang, from the Church
catechism, "keep my hands from picking and stealing").

393 advancement] promotion.

394 musty] too stale to quote (though not so now: "While
the grass grows, the horse starves").

---

395 withdraw] speak privately; recover the wind … toil] a
hunting metaphor: move upwind of the prey so that the
hunter's scent drives it into the net (toil).

396 if my duty … unmannerly] If I seem impudent it is because I love you too much.

397 ventages] wind holes.

398 fret] a pun: irritate; play the frets of a musical instrument.

399 presently] immediately.

POLONIUS. It is backed like a weasel.   395
HAMLET. Or like a whale?
POLONIUS. Very like a whale.
HAMLET. Then will I come to my mother by and
    by. [*Aside.*] They fool me to the top of my bent.[400]
    [*Aloud.*] I will come by and by.   400
POLONIUS. I will say so. [*Exit.*]
HAMLET. By and by is easily said. Leave me, friends.

[*Exeunt all but HAMLET.*]

    'Tis now the very witching time of night,
    When churchyards yawn and hell itself breathes out
    Contagion to this world: now could I drink hot   405
      blood,
    And do such bitter business as the day
    Would quake to look on. Soft! now to my mother!
    O heart! lose not thy nature; let not ever
    The soul of Nero enter this firm bosom.[401]
    Let me be cruel, not unnatural;   410
    I will speak daggers to her, but use none;
    My tongue and soul in this be hypocrites;
    How in my words soever she be shent,[402]
    To give them seals never, my soul, consent![403] [*Exit.*]

SCENE III

A ROOM IN THE CASTLE.

Enter KING, ROSENCRANTZ, and GUILDENSTERN.

KING. I like him not, nor stands it safe with us
    To let his madness range. Therefore prepare you;
    I your commission will forthwith dispatch,
    And he to England shall along with you.
    The terms of our estate may not endure[404]   5
    Hazard so near us as doth hourly grow
    Out of his brows.[405]
GUILDENSTERN.   We will ourselves provide.[406]

---

[400] fool me … bent] treat me as if I were a fool to the limit
    of my endurance.
[401] Nero] who had his mother executed.
[402] shent] rebuked.
[403] give them seals] make good those words with action.
[404] terms of our estate] position as king.
[405] brows] i.e., mad ideas from his head.
[406] we … provide] we will get ready.

Most holy and religious fear it is
    To keep those many many bodies safe
    That live and feed upon your majesty.   10
ROSENCRANTZ. The single and peculiar life is bound
    With all the strength and armour of the mind
    To keep itself from noyance; but much more[407]
    That spirit upon whose weal depends and rests
    The lives of many. The cease of majesty   15
    Dies not alone, but like a gulf doth draw[408]
    What's near it with it; it is a massy wheel,
    Fixed on the summit of the highest mount,
    To whose huge spokes ten thousand lesser things
    Are mortised and adjoined; which, when it falls,   20
    Each small annexment, petty consequence,
    Attends the boisterous ruin. Never alone
    Did the king sigh, but with a general groan.[409]
KING. Arm you, I pray you, to this speedy voyage;[410]
    For we will fetters put upon this fear,   25
    Which now goes too free-footed.
ROSENCRANTZ.   ⍳
GUILDENSTERN.   ⍳   We will haste us.

Exeunt ROSENCRANTZ and GUILDENSTERN.

Enter POLONIUS.

POLONIUS. My lord, he's going to his mother's closet.
    Behind the arras I'll convey myself
    To hear the process. I'll warrant she'll tax him
      home;[411]
    And, as you said, and wisely was it said,   30
    'Tis meet that some more audience than a mother,
    Since nature makes them partial, should o'er-hear
    The speech, of vantage. Fare you well, my liege:[412]
    I'll call upon you ere you go to bed
    And tell you what I know.   35
KING.   Thanks, dear my lord.

[*Exit POLONIUS.*]

    O! my offence is rank, it smells to heaven;
    It hath the primal eldest curse upon 't;

---

[407] noyance] harm.
[408] gulf] whirlpool.
[409] general] shared by all of his society.
[410] Arm you] Prepare yourselves.
[411] process] proceedings; tax him home] rebuke him sharply.
[412] of vantage] in addition.

A brother's murder! Pray can I not,[413]
Though inclination be as sharp as will:
My stronger guilt defeats my strong intent;   40
And, like a man to double business bound,
I stand in pause where I shall first begin,
And both neglect. What if this cursèd hand
Were thicker than itself with brother's blood,
Is there not rain enough in the sweet heavens   45
To wash it white as snow? Whereto serves mercy
But to confront the visage of offence?
And what 's in prayer but this two-fold force,
To be forestallèd, ere we come to fall,
Or pardoned, being down? Then, I'll look up;   50
My fault is past. But, O! what form of prayer
Can serve my turn? "Forgive me my foul murder"?
That cannot be; since I am still possessed
Of those effects for which I did the murder,
My crown, mine own ambition, and my queen.   55
May one be pardoned and retain the offence?
In the corrupted currents of this world
Offence's gilded hand may shove by justice,[414]
And oft 'tis seen the wicked prize itself
Buys out the law; but 'tis not so above;   60
There is no shuffling, there the action lies
In his true nature, and we ourselves compelled[415]
Even to the teeth and forehead of our faults
To give in evidence. What then? what rests?
Try what repentance can: what can it not?   65
Yet what can it, when one cannot repent?
O wretched state! O bosom black as death!
O limed soul, that struggling to be free[416]
Art more engaged! Help, angels! make assay;[417]
Bow, stubborn knees; and heart with strings of steel,   70
Be soft as sinews of the new-born babe.
All may be well. [*He kneels.*]

Enter HAMLET.

HAMLET. Now might I do it pat, now he is praying;
And now I'll do 't. And so he goes to heaven;

And so am I revenged. That would be scanned.[418]   75
A villain kills my father; and for that,
I, his sole son, do this same villain send
To heaven.
Why, this is hire and salary, not revenge.[419]
He took my father grossly, full of bread,[420]   80
With all his crimes broad blown, as flush as May;
And how his audit stands, who knows save heaven?
But in our circumstance and course of thought[421]
'Tis heavy with him. And am I then revenged,
To take him in the purging of his soul,   85
When he is fit and seasoned for his passage?
No.
Up, sword, and know thou a more horrid hent;[422]
When he is drunk asleep, or in his rage,
Or in the incestuous pleasure of his bed,   90
At gaming, swearing, or about some act
That has no relish of salvation in 't;
Then trip him, that his heels may kick at heaven,
And that his soul may be as damned and black
As hell, whereto it goes. My mother stays.[423]   95
This physic but prolongs thy sickly days. [*Exit.*]

The KING rises and advances.

KING. My words fly up, my thoughts remain below:
Words without thoughts never to heaven go.

[*Exit.*]

SCENE IV

THE QUEEN'S APARTMENT.

Enter QUEEN and POLONIUS.

POLONIUS. He will come straight. Look you lay
home to him;[424]
Tell him his pranks have been too broad to bear with,

---

413 primal ... murder] i.e., Cain and Abel.
414 gilded] lined with gold.
415 shuffling] trickery; the action lies in his true nature] The
    deed is exposed in its true nature.
416 limed] trapped (like a bird, with lime).
417 make assay] make an attempt.

418 scanned] looked into.
419 hire and salary] payment for the deed.
420 grossly] unpurified by repentance; full of bread] "the
    iniquity ... of Sodom, pride, fulness of bread" (Ezekiel
    16:49).
421 in our circumstance] as far as we mortals can see.
422 hent] occasion for seizure.
423 stays] awaits.
424 lay home] speak bluntly.

And that your Grace hath screened and stood
   between
Much heat and him. I'll silence me even here.[425]
   Pray you be round with him.   5

HAMLET. [*Within.*] Mother, mother, mother!
QUEEN.   I'll warrant you;
   Fear me not. Withdraw, I hear him coming.

POLONIUS hides behind the arras.

HAMLET. Now, mother, what's the matter?
QUEEN. Hamlet, thou hast thy father much offended.
HAMLET. Mother, you have my father much offended.   10
QUEEN. Come, come, you answer with an idle
   tongue.[426]
HAMLET. Go, go, you question with a wicked tongue.
QUEEN. Why, how now, Hamlet!
HAMLET.   What's the matter now?
QUEEN. Have you forgot me?
HAMLET.   No, by the rood, not so:[427]
   You are the queen, your husband's brother's wife;   15
   And,—would it were not so!—you are my mother.
QUEEN. Nay, then I'll set those to you that can speak.
HAMLET. Come, come, and sit you down; you shall
   not budge;
   You go not, till I set you up a glass[428]
   Where you may see the inmost part of you.   20
QUEEN. What wilt thou do? Thou wilt not murder me?
   Help, help, ho!
POLONIUS. [*Behind.*] What, ho! help! help! help!
HAMLET. [*Draws.*] How now! a rat? Dead, for a
   ducat, dead![429]

[*Makes a pass through the arras.*]

POLONIUS. [*Behind.*] O! I am slain.   25
QUEEN. O me! what hast thou done?
HAMLET. Nay, I know not: is it the king?
QUEEN. O! what a rash and bloody deed is this!
HAMLET. A bloody deed! almost as bad, good mother,
   As kill a king, and marry with his brother.   30

---

[425] I'll silence … here] I'll be quiet now.
[426] idle] foolish.
[427] rood] holy cross.
[428] glass] mirror.
[429] Dead for a ducat] i.e., the cheap price of exterminating
   vermin.

QUEEN. As kill a king!
HAMLET.   Ay, lady, 'twas my word.

[*Lifts up the arras and discovers POLONIUS.*]

[*To POLONIUS.*]

Thou wretched, rash, intruding fool, farewell!
I took thee for thy better; take thy fortune;[430]
Thou find 'st to be too busy is some danger.[431]
Leave wringing of your hands: peace! sit you down,   35
And let me wring your heart; for so I shall
If it be made of penetrable stuff,
If damnéd custom have not brassed it so
That it is proof and bulwark against sense.[432]
QUEEN. What have I done that thou dar'st wag thy   40
   tongue
   In noise so rude against me?
HAMLET.   Such an act
   That blurs the grace and blush of modesty,
   Calls virtue hypocrite, takes off the rose
   From the fair forehead of an innocent love
   And sets a blister there, makes marriage vows[433]   45
   As false as dicers' oaths; O! such a deed[434]
   As from the body of contraction plucks
   The very soul, and sweet religion makes[435]
   A rhapsody of words: heaven's face doth glow,[436]
   Yea, this solidity and compound mass,   50
   With tristful visage, as against the doom,
   Is thought-sick at the act.[437]
QUEEN.   Ay me! what act,
   That roars so loud and thunders in the index?[438]

---

[430] better] superior in rank.
[431] busy] i.e., a busy-body, meddlesome.
[432] proof] armoured.
[433] sets a blister] brands, as a harlot.
[434] dicers' oaths] i.e., promises that gamblers make to
   heaven on condition that they win.
[435] from the … soul] destroys the spirit of the whole concept of honouring contracts.
[436] rhapsody] nonsensical outburst; glow] blush.
[437] Yea, this solidity … act] The entire solid earth, compounded of various elements, with a sorrowful
   expression like that it would bear at judgment day, is
   thought-sick at the act.
[438] index] table of contents (i.e., the text before the main
   story begins).

HAMLET. Look here upon this picture, and on this;
  The counterfeit presentment of two brothers.[439]   55
  See, what a grace was seated on this brow;
  Hyperion's curls, the front of Jove himself,[440]
  An eye like Mars, to threaten and command,[441]
  A station like the herald Mercury[442]
  New-lighted on a heaven-kissing hill,   60
  A combination and a form indeed,
  Where every god did seem to set his seal,
  To give the world assurance of a man.[443]
  This was your husband: look you now, what follows.
  Here is your husband; like a mildewed ear,   65
  Blasting his wholesome brother. Have you eyes?[444]
  Could you on this fair mountain leave to feed,
  And batten on this moor? Ha! have you eyes?[445]
  You cannot call it love, for at your age
  The hey-day in the blood is tame, it's humble,   70
  And waits upon the judgment; and what judgment
  Would step from this to this? Sense, sure, you have,
  Else could you not have motion; but sure, that sense
  Is apoplexed;for madness would not err,[446]
  Nor sense to ecstacy was ne'er so thralled   75
  But it reserved some quantity of choice,
  To serve in such a difference. What devil was 't
  That thus hath cozened you at hoodman-blind?[447]
  Eyes without feeling, feeling without sight,
  Ears without hands or eyes, smelling sans all,   80
  Or but a sickly part of one true sense
  Could not so mope.[448]
  O shame! where is thy blush? Rebellious hell,
  If thou canst mutine in a matron's bones,

To flaming youth let virtue be as wax,   85
  And melt in her own fire: proclaim no shame
  When the compulsive ardour gives the charge,[449]
  Since frost itself as actively doth burn,
  And reason panders will.[450]
QUEEN.   O Hamlet! speak no more;
  Thou turn'st mine eyes into my very soul;   90
  And there I see such black and grainéd spots
  As will not leave their tinct.[451]
HAMLET.   Nay, but to live
  In the rank sweat of an enseaméd bed,[452]
  Stewed in corruption, honeying and making love
  Over the nasty sty—[453]   95
QUEEN.   O! speak to me no more;
  These words like daggers enter in mine ears;
  No more, sweet Hamlet!
HAMLET.   A murderer, and a villain;
  A slave that is not twentieth part the tithe[454]
  Of your precedent lord; a vice of kings;[455]
  A cut-purse of the empire and the rule,[456]   100
  That from a shelf the precious diadem stole,[457]
  And put it in his pocket!
QUEEN.   No more!
HAMLET. A king of shreds and patches,—

Enter GHOST.

  Save me, and hover o'er me with your wings,
  You heavenly guards! What would your gracious   105
    figure?
QUEEN. Alas, he's mad!
HAMLET. Do you not come your tardy son to chide,
  That, lapsed in time and passion, lets go by
  The important acting of your dread command?
  O! say!   110
GHOST.   Do not forget: this visitation
  Is but to whet thy almost blunted purpose.

---

439 counterfeit presentment] portrait.
440 Hyperion] the Titan who fathered the Sun, Moon and
  Dawn; front] forehead; Jove] the supreme Roman god,
  Jupiter.
441 Mars] god of war.
442 station] stance; Mercury] the winged messenger god.
443 assurance of a man] certain evidence of what a man
  should be.
444 mildewed ear … brother] like a rotting ear of corn, infecting the healthy one next to it.
445 batten] grow fat.
446 apoplexed] paralyzed.
447 cozened] hoodwinked; hoodman-blind] blind-man's
  bluff.
448 not so mope] not be so dull-witted.

---

449 gives the charge] sounds the attack.
450 panders] acts as a pimp to.
451 leave their tinct] lose their colour.
452 enseamed] greasy (seam = lard).
453 sty] i.e., a place fit for pigs.
454 tithe] one tenth part.
455 vice] villainous fool in morality plays.
456 cut-purse] pickpocket.
457 diadem] the crown.

But look; amazement on thy mother sits;
O step between her and her fighting soul;
Conceit in weakest bodies strongest works:[458]
Speak to her, Hamlet.   115
HAMLET.   How is it with you, lady?
QUEEN. Alas! how is 't with you,
  That you do bend your eye on vacancy
  And with the incorporal air do hold discourse?[459]
  Forth at your eyes your spirits wildly peep;
  And, as the sleeping soldiers in the alarm,   120
  Your bedded hairs, like life in excrements,[460]
  Start up and stand on end. O gentle son!
  Upon the heat and flame of thy distemper
  Sprinkle cool patience. Whereon do you look?
HAMLET. On him, on him! Look you, how pale he   125
    glares!
  His form and cause conjoined, preaching to stones,
  Would make them capable. Do not look upon
    me;[461]
  Lest with this piteous action you convert
  My stern effects: then what I have to do
  Will want true colour; tears perchance for blood.[462] 130
QUEEN. To whom do you speak this?
HAMLET. Do you see nothing there?
QUEEN. Nothing at all; yet all that is I see.
HAMLET. Nor did you nothing hear?
QUEEN.   No, nothing but ourselves.
HAMLET. Why, look you there! look, how it steals   135
    away;
  My father, in his habit as he lived;[463]
  Look! where he goes, even now, out at the portal.
      [Exit GHOST.]
QUEEN. This is the very coinage of your brain:
  This bodiless creation, ecstasy
  Is very cunning in.[464]   140
HAMLET.   Ecstasy!

My pulse, as yours, doth temperately keep time,
And makes as healthful music. It is not madness
That I have uttered. Bring me to the test,
And I the matter will re-word, which madness
Would gambol from. Mother, for love of grace,[465]   145
Lay not that flattering unction to your soul,[466]
That not your trespass but my madness speaks;
It will but skin and film the ulcerous place,
Whiles rank corruption, mining all within,
Infects unseen. Confess yourself to heaven;   150
Repent what's past; avoid what is to come;
And do not spread the compost on the weeds
To make them ranker. Forgive me this my virtue;
For in the fatness of these pursy[467] times
Virtue itself of vice must pardon beg,   155
Yea, curb[468] and woo for leave to do him good.
QUEEN. O Hamlet! thou hast cleft my heart in twain.
HAMLET. O! throw away the worser part of it,
  And live the purer with the other half.
  Good night; but go not to my uncle's bed;   160
  Assume a virtue, if you have it not.[469]
  That monster, custom, who all sense doth eat,
  Of habits devil, is angel yet in this,
  That to the use of actions fair and good
  He likewise gives a frock or livery,   165
  That aptly is put on. Refrain to-night;[470]
  And that shall lend a kind of easiness
  To the next abstinence: the next more easy;
  For use almost can change the stamp of nature,
  And master ev'n the devil or throw him out   170
  With wondrous potency. Once more, good-night;
  And when you are desirous to be blessed,
  I'll blessing beg of you.

[Of POLONIUS.]

                          For this same lord,
  I do repent: but heaven hath pleased it so,

---

[458] Conceit] imagination.
[459] incorporal] without body.
[460] excrements] excrescences, outgrowths.
[461] capable] i.e., of responding, of action.
[462] convert … effects] divert my stern deeds.
[463] habit as he lived] clothed as he customarily was when
    alive.
[464] This bodiless … cunning in] Ecstasy, or madness, is very
    cunning in creating such bodiless apparitions.

[465] gambol] leap, shy away (like a horse).
[466] unction] emollient, ointment.
[467] pursy] bloated.
[468] curb] bow, on bended knee.
[469] Assume] pretend, put on a disguise.
[470] That monster … put on] While custom may annihilate
    all reasoned thought of right and wrong in habitual acts
    of evil, it can similarly create in us a habit of doing good.

To punish me with this, and this with me,   175
That I must be their scourge and minister.[471]
I will bestow him, and will answer well[472]
The death I gave him. So, again, good-night.
I must be cruel, only to be kind:
Thus bad begins and worse remains behind.   180
One word more, good lady.

QUEEN.   What shall I do?

HAMLET. Not this, by no means, that I bid you do:
Let the bloat king tempt you again to bed,[473]
Pinch wanton on your cheek, call you his mouse;[474]
And let him, for a pair of reechy[475] kisses,   185
Or paddling in your neck with his damned fingers,
Make you to ravel all this matter out;[476]
That I essentially am not in madness,
But mad in craft, 'twere good you let him know;[477]
For who that 's but a queen, fair, sober, wise,   190
Would from a paddock, from a bat, a gib,[478]
Such dear concernings hide? who would do so?
No, in despite of sense and secrecy,
Unpeg the basket on the house's top,
Let the birds fly, and, like the famous ape,   195
To try conclusions, in the basket creep,
And break your own neck down.[479]

QUEEN. Be thou assured, if words be made of breath,
And breath of life, I have no life to breathe
What thou hast said to me.   200

HAMLET. I must to England; you know that?[480]

QUEEN.   Alack!
I had forgot: 'tis so concluded on.

HAMLET. There's letters sealed; and my two school-
fellows,[481]
Whom I will trust as I will adders fanged,
They bear the mandate; they must sweep my way,   205
And marshal me to knavery. Let it work;
For 'tis the sport to have the enginer[482]
Hoist with his own petard: and it shall go hard[483]
But I will delve one yard below their mines,
And blow them at the moon. O! 'tis most sweet,   210
When in one line two crafts directly meet.[484]
This man shall set me packing;[485]
I'll lug the guts into the neighbour room.
Mother, good night. Indeed, this counsellor
Is now most still, most secret, and most grave,   215
Who was in life a foolish prating knave.
Come, sir, to draw toward an end with you.
Good-night, mother.

[*Exeunt severally; HAMLET dragging the body of
POLONIUS.*]

ACT IV

SCENE 1

A ROOM IN THE CASTLE.

*Enter KING, QUEEN, ROSENCRANTZ, and
GUILDENSTERN.*

KING. There's matter in these sighs. These profound
heaves
You must translate. 'Tis fit we understand them.
Where is your son?

---

471 their] i.e., the heavens'.

472 bestow] dispose of.

473 bloat king] bloated with indulgence, or falsely puffed up
to appear majestic.

474 pinch wanton on your cheek] leave marks upon your
cheek that show you to be licentious.

475 reechy] filthy.

476 Make you … out] persuade you to divulge all the details we have discussed.

477 Hamlet is still speaking negatively; these are the things
Gertrude should not do.

478 paddock, bat, gib] frog, bat, tom-cat (all three being
associated with witches).

479 Unpeg the basket … down] allusion to a parable about
an ape who released birds from a basket; after they flew
off, he climbed into the basket, hoping this would enable him to fly himself, but he fell and broke his neck.

480 I must to England …] It is not clear how Hamlet came
by this knowledge.

481 schoolfellows] Rosencrantz and Guildenstern.

482 enginer] inventor.

483 hoist … petard] blown up with his own bomb—a petard was an explosive device used for gaining access
through gates, etc.

484 crafts] vessels, crafty plots.

485 packing] moving; loading the body.

QUEEN. [*To ROSENCRANTZ and GUILDENSTERN.*]
 Bestow this place on us a little while.

[*Exeunt ROSENCRANTZ and GUILDENSTERN.*]

 Ah, mine own lord, what have I seen to-night!   5
KING. What, Gertrude? How does Hamlet?
QUEEN. Mad as the sea and wind, when both contend
 Which is the mightier. In his lawless fit,
 Behind the arras hearing something stir,
 Whips out his rapier, cries "A rat! a rat!"   10
 And, in this brainish apprehension, kills[486]
 The unseen good old man.
KING.   O heavy deed!
 It had been so with us, had we been there.
 His liberty is full of threats to all;
 To you yourself, to us, to every one.   15
 Alas! how shall this bloody deed be answered?
 It will be laid to us, whose providence[487]
 Should have kept short, restrained, and out of
  haunt,[488]
 This mad young man. But so much was our love,
 We would not understand what was most fit,   20
 But, like the owner of a foul disease,
 To keep it from divulging, let it feed
 Even on the pith of life. Where is he gone?
QUEEN. To draw apart the body he hath killed;
 O'er whom—his very madness, like some ore   25
 Among a mineral of metals base,
 Shows itself pure—he weeps for what is done.
KING. O Gertrude! come away.
 The sun no sooner shall the mountains touch
 But we will ship him hence; and this vile deed   30
 We must, with all our majesty and skill,
 Both countenance and excuse. Ho! Guildenstern!

Re-enter ROSENCRANTZ and GUILDENSTERN.

 Friends both, go join you with some further aid.
 Hamlet in madness hath Polonius slain,
 And from his mother's closet hath he dragged him.   35
 Go seek him out; speak fair, and bring the body
 Into the chapel. I pray you, haste in this.

[*Exeunt ROSENCRANTZ and GUILDENSTERN*].

 Come, Gertrude, we'll call up our wisest friends;
 And let them know both what we mean to do,
 And what's untimely done. So, haply, slander,   40
 Whose whisper o'er the world's diameter,
 As level as the cannon to his blank[489]
 Transports his poisoned shot, may miss our name.
 And hit the woundless air. O! come away;
 My soul is full of discord and dismay.   45

[*Exeunt.*]

SCENE II

ANOTHER ROOM IN THE SAME.

Enter HAMLET.

HAMLET. Safely stowed.
ROSENCRANTZ. ⎤
GUILDENSTERN. ⎦ [*Within.*] Hamlet! Lord Hamlet!
HAMLET. What noise? Who calls on Hamlet? O, here
 they come.

Enter ROSENCRANTZ, GUILDENSTERN and OTHERS.

ROSENCRANTZ. What have you done, my lord,   5
 with the dead body?
HAMLET. Compounded it with dust, whereto 'tis kin.
ROSENCRANTZ. Tell us where 'tis, that we may take
 it thence
 And bear it to the chapel.
HAMLET. Do not believe it.
ROSENCRANTZ. Believe what?   10
HAMLET. That I can keep your counsel and not mine
 own. Besides, to be demanded of a sponge![490]
 What replication should be made by the son of a
 king?[491]
ROSENCRANTZ. Take you me for a sponge, my lord?   15
HAMLET. Ay, sir, that soaks up the king's countenance, his rewards, his authorities.[492] But such
 officers do the king best service in the end. He

---

486 brainish apprehension] mad delusion.
487 providence] foresight.
488 haunt] free access (to the court).

489 blank] point-blank target.
490 demanded of] questioned by.
491 replication] reply.
492 countenance] favour; authorities] delegated powers.

keeps them, like an ape, in the corner of his jaw; first mouthed, to be last swallowed. When he needs what you have gleaned, it is but squeezing you, and, sponge, you shall be dry again.

ROSENCRANTZ. I understand you not, my lord.

HAMLET. I am glad of it: a knavish speech sleeps in a foolish ear.

ROSENCRANTZ. My lord, you must tell us where the body is, and go with us to the king.

HAMLET. The body is with the king, but the king is not with the body.[493] The king is a thing—

GUILDENSTERN. A thing, my lord!

HAMLET. Of nothing: bring me to him. Hide fox, and all after![494] [*Exeunt.*]

SCENE III

ANOTHER ROOM IN THE SAME.

Enter KING, attended.

KING. I have sent to seek him, and to find the body.
How dangerous is it that this man goes loose!
Yet must not we put the strong law on him:
He's loved of the distracted multitude,[495]
Who like not in their judgment, but their eyes;
And where 'tis so, the offender's scourge is weighed,[496]
But never the offence. To bear all smooth and even,
This sudden sending him away must seem
Deliberate pause. Diseases desperate grown.[497]
By desperate appliance are relieved,
Or not at all.

Enter ROSENCRANTZ.

How now! what hath befall'n?

ROSENCRANTZ. Where the dead body is bestowed, my lord,
We cannot get from him.

KING.   But where is he?

ROSENCRANTZ. Without, my lord; guarded, to know your pleasure.

KING. Bring him before us.

ROSENCRANTZ. Ho! Bring in the lord.

Enter HAMLET and GUILDENSTERN.

KING. Now, Hamlet, where's Polonius?

HAMLET. At supper.

KING. At supper! Where?

HAMLET. Not where he eats, but where he is eaten. A certain convocation of politic worms are e'en at him. Your worm is your only emperor for diet.[498] We fat all creatures else to fat us, and we fat ourselves for maggots. Your fat king and your lean beggar is but variable service; two dishes, but to one table. That's the end.

KING. Alas, alas!

HAMLET. A man may fish with the worm that hath eat of a king, and eat of the fish that hath fed of that worm.

KING. What dost thou mean by this?

HAMLET. Nothing, but to show you how a king may go a progress through the guts of a beggar.[499]

KING. Where is Polonius?

HAMLET. In heaven; send thither to see: if your messenger find him not there, seek him i' the other place yourself. But, indeed, if you find him not within this month, you shall nose him as you go up the stairs into the lobby.

KING. [*To SOME ATTENDANTS.*] Go seek him there.

HAMLET. He will stay till you come.

[*Exeunt ATTENDANTS.*]

KING. Hamlet, this deed, for thine especial safety,
Which we do tender, as we dearly grieve[500]
For that which thou hast done, must send thee hence
With fiery quickness. Therefore prepare thyself.
The bark is ready, and the wind at help,[501]

---

493 The body ...] Perhaps he means that Polonius's body is with Old Hamlet, but Claudius is not (yet) with Polonius.

494 Hide fox ... after] a cry of challenge in a game like hide and seek.

495 distracted multitude] bewildered masses.

496 scourge] punishment.

497 pause] planning.

498 In the German city of Worms, Emperor Charles V presided over a famous Diet, an assembly of representatives, which condemned the teachings of Martin Luther in 1521.

499 progress] formal royal tour.

500 tender] hold dear.

501 bark] ship.

The associates tend, and every thing is bent[502]
For England.

HAMLET.   For England?[503]

KING.   Ay, Hamlet.

HAMLET.   Good.

KING. So is it, if thou knew'st our purposes.   50

HAMLET. I see a cherub that sees them.[504] But,
  come; for England! Farewell, dear mother.

KING. Thy loving father, Hamlet.

HAMLET. My mother: father and mother is man and
  wife, man and wife is one flesh, and so, my   55
  mother. Come, for England! [Exit.]

KING. Follow him at foot. Tempt him with speed
    aboard.[505]
  Delay it not; I'll have him hence to-night.
  Away! for every thing is sealed and done
  That else leans on the affair. Pray you, make   60
    haste.[506]

Exeunt ROSENCRANTZ and GUILDENSTERN.

  And England if my love thou hold'st at aught—[507]
  As my great power thereof may give thee sense,
  Since yet thy cicatrice looks raw and red[508]
  After the Danish sword, and thy free awe
  Pays homage to us—thou mayst not[509] coldly set   65
  Our sovereign process, which imports at full,[510]
  By letters conjuring to that effect,[511]

---

502 tend] attend, wait; bent] in readiness, like a bent bow.
503 Cf. III.iv.202.
504 cherub] an angel with special insight.
505 at foot] closely, at heel.
506 leans on] appertains to.
507 England] King of England.
508 cicatrice] scar.
509 Danish sword … homage] In the ninth and tenth centuries, England was repeatedly invaded by Vikings.
  Ethelred the Unready, King of England, tried paying
  Denmark to desist, but in 1002 decided to massacre all
  the Danes in his kingdom. In response, the King of
  Denmark, Sweyn Forkbeard, conquered England in
  1013. England was ruled by Danes until 1042 and remained a tributary to Denmark until 1066.
510 coldly … process] regard with indifference our royal
  will; imports at full] gives the utmost importance to.
511 conjuring] solemnly entreating (usually by invoking sacred obligation).

The present death of Hamlet. Do it, England;[512]
For like the hectic in my blood he rages,[513]
And thou must cure me. Till I know 'tis done,   70
Howe'er my haps, my joys were ne'er begun.[514]

[*Exit.*]

SCENE IV

A PLAIN IN DENMARK.

*Enter FORTINBRAS, a CAPTAIN, and Soldiers,
marching.*

FORTINBRAS. Go, captain, from me greet the
    Danish king;
  Tell him that, by his license, Fortinbras
  Claims the conveyance of a promised march[515]
  Over his kingdom. You know the rendezvous.
  If that his Majesty would aught with us,   5
  We shall express our duty in his eye,[516]
  And let him know so.

CAPTAIN.   I will do 't, my lord.

FORTINBRAS. Go softly on.[517]

Exeunt all but CAPTAIN.

Enter HAMLET, ROSENCRANTZ and OTHERS.

HAMLET. Good sir, whose powers are these?

CAPT. They are of Norway, sir.   10

HAMLET. How purpos'd, sir, I pray you?

CAPT. Against some part of Poland.

HAMLET. Who commands them, sir?

CAPT. The nephew to old Norway, Fortinbras.

HAMLET. Goes it against the main of Poland, sir,   15
  Or for some frontier?

CAPT. Truly to speak, and with no addition,[518]
  We go to gain a little patch of ground
  That hath in it no profit but the name.

---

512 present] immediate.
513 hectic] fever.
514 haps] chances, fortune.
515 conveyance] escort; promised] as requested through
  Voltemand in II.ii.
516 express … eye] pay our respects in person.
517 softly] slowly, carefully.
518 with no addition] plainly.

To pay five ducats, five, I would not farm it; 20
Nor will it yield to Norway or the Pole
A ranker rate, should it be sold in fee.[519]
HAMLET. Why, then the Polack never will defend it.
CAPT. Yes, 'tis already garrison'd.
HAMLET. Two thousand souls and twenty thousand 25
    ducats
  Will not debate the question of this straw![520]
  This is the imposthume of much wealth and
      peace,[521]
  That inward breaks, and shows no cause without
  Why the man dies. I humbly thank you, sir.
CAPT. God be wi' you, sir. [*Exit.*] 30
ROSENCRANTZ. Will 't please you go, my lord?
HAMLET. I'll be with you straight. Go a little before.

[*Exeunt all except HAMLET.*]

  How all occasions do inform against me,
  And spur my dull revenge! What is a man,
  If his chief good and market of his time[522] 35
  Be but to sleep and feed? A beast, no more.
  Sure he that made us with such large discourse,
  Looking before and after, gave us not
  That capability and godlike reason
  To fust in us unus'd. Now, whether it be[523] 40
  Bestial oblivion, or some craven scruple[524]
  Of thinking too precisely on the event—
  A thought, which, quartered, hath but one part
      wisdom,
  And ever three parts coward—I do not know
  Why yet I live to say "This thing 's to do," 45
  Sith I have cause, and will, and strength and means
  To do 't. Examples gross as earth exhort me.[525]
  Witness this army of such mass and charge[526]
  Led by a delicate and tender prince,[527]

Whose spirit with divine ambition puff'd 50
Makes mouths at the invisible event,[528]
Exposing what is mortal and unsure
To all that fortune, death, and danger dare,
Even for an egg-shell. Rightly to be great
Is not to stir without great argument, 55
But greatly to find quarrel in a straw
When honour's at the stake. How stand I then,[529]
That have a father kill'd, a mother stain'd,
Excitements of my reason and my blood,
And let all sleep, while to my shame, I see 60
The imminent death of twenty thousand men,
That for a fantasy and trick of fame,
Go to their graves like beds, fight for a plot
Whereon the numbers cannot try the cause,[530]
Which is not tomb enough and continent[531] 65
To hide the slain? O! from this time forth,
My thoughts be bloody, or be nothing worth!
    [*Exit.*]

SCENE V

ELSINORE. A ROOM IN THE CASTLE.

Enter QUEEN, HORATIO, and a GENTLEMAN.

QUEEN. I will not speak with her!
GENTLEMAN. She is importunate, indeed distract.[532]
  Her mood will needs be pitied.
QUEEN.   What would she have?
GENTLEMAN. She speaks much of her father; says
    she hears

---

519 ranker] higher; in fee] outright.
520 Two thousand … straw] i.e., given the involvement of
    two armies, even these numbers will prove insufficient.
521 imposthume] abscess, infection.
522 market] exchange for profit.
523 fust] become moldy.
524 Bestial oblivion] brute forgetfulness.
525 gross] large, obvious.
526 charge] expense.
527 tender] young.

---

528 Makes … event] scornfully makes faces at the unknown
    outcome of his project.
529 Rightly … stake] "It is true that a great person should
    never be provoked without a great cause; however, any
    cause which involves honour, however apparently mi-
    nor, is inherently a great cause well worth a fight." The
    common editorial suggestion that the "not" should be
    read as a double negative (not not) is unnecessary.
530 a plot … cause] a piece of land not big enough to hold
    those who are fighting for it.
531 continent] sufficient container.
532 distract] out of her mind.

There's tricks i' the world; and hems, and beats
  her heart;[533]   5
Spurns enviously at straws; speaks things in
  doubt,[534]
That carry but half sense. Her speech is nothing,
Yet the unshapéd use of it doth move
The hearers to collection. They aim at it,[535]
And botch the words up fit to their own thoughts;   10
Which, as her winks, and nods, and gestures yield
  them,[536]
Indeed would make one think there might be
  thought,
Though nothing sure, yet much unhappily.
HORATIO. 'Twere good she were spoken with, for
  she may strew
Dangerous conjectures in ill-breeding minds.[537]   15
QUEEN. Let her come in. [*Exit GENTLEMAN.*]
  [*aside*] To my sick soul, as sin's true nature is,
Each toy seems prologue to some great amiss.[538]
So full of artless jealousy is guilt,[539]
It spills itself in fearing to be spilt.[540]   20

Re-enter GENTLEMAN, with OPHELIA.

OPHELIA. Where is the beauteous majesty of Denmark?
QUEEN. How now, Ophelia!
OPHELIA. *How should I your true love know*
    From another one?
By his cockle hat and staff,   25
    And his sandal shoon.[541]

QUEEN. Alas! sweet lady, what imports this song?
OPHELIA. Say you? nay, pray you, mark.
  He is dead and gone, lady,
    He is dead and gone;   30
  At his head a grass-green turf,
    At his heels a stone.
  O, ho!
QUEEN. Nay, but Ophelia,—
OPHELIA. Pray you, mark.   35
  White his shroud as the mountain snow,—

Enter KING.

QUEEN. Alas! look here, my lord.
OPHELIA. *Larded all with sweet flowers;*[542]
  Which bewept to the grave did go
    With true-love showers.   40
KING. How do you, pretty lady?
OPHELIA. Well, God 'ild you![543] They say the owl
  was a baker's daughter.[544] Lord! we know what we
  are, but know not what we may be. God be at your
  table!   45
KING. Conceit upon her father.[545]
OPHELIA. Pray you, let's have no words of this; but
  when they ask you what it means, say you this:
  To-morrow is Saint Valentine's day,
    All in the morning bedtime,   50
  And I a maid at your window,
    To be your Valentine:
  Then up he rose, and donned his clothes
    And dupped the chamber door;[546]
  Let in the maid, that out a maid   55
    Never departed more.
KING. Pretty Ophelia—
OPHELIA. Indeed, la! without an oath, I'll make an
  end on 't!

---

533 hems] clears her throat (onomatopoeic).
534 Spurns ... straws] takes offence at trifles.
535 collection] gathering fragments (of her ideas); aim] try to guess (her meaning).
536 Which] i.e., her words; yield] convey.
537 ill-breeding] evil-minded.
538 toy] trifle; amiss] misfortune.
539 artless jealousy] impulsive anxiety.
540 spills ... spilt] Guilt betrays itself through its very fear of being found out (e.g., the Queen's initial anxious refusal to speak to Ophelia reveals her guilty conscience more than anything Ophelia could possibly say in conversation).
541 *cockle ... shoon*] hat, staff and shoes which signified a Christian pilgrim: a common convention for depicting a lover—approaching the beloved as if religiously approaching a shrine.

542 *Larded*] garnished.
543 God 'ild you] God yield (have mercy on) you.
544 owl ... daughter] A folk tale tells of a baker's daughter who, because she refused charity when Christ, in disguise, asked for bread in her father's shop, was transformed into an owl. Perhaps Ophelia is thinking of the awful consequences she believes followed her rejection of Hamlet on her father's instructions.
545 Conceit upon] playing with ideas about.
546 *dupped*] opened up.

By Gis and by Saint Charity,[547]   60
    Alack, and fie for shame!
Young men will do 't if they come to 't;
    By Cock they are to blame.[548]
Quoth she, before you tumbled me,
    You promised me to wed.   65

KING. How long hath she been thus?

OPHELIA. I hope all will be well. We must be patient: 70
but I cannot choose but weep, to think they should
lay him i' the cold ground. My brother shall know
of it. And so I thank you for your good counsel.
Come, my coach![549] Good-night, ladies; good-
night, sweet ladies; good-night, good-night. [*Exit.*]   75

KING. Follow her close; give her good watch, I pray
you. [*Exit HORATIO.*]
O! this is the poison of deep grief; it springs
All from her father's death. O Gertrude, Gertrude!
When sorrows come, they come not single spies,
But in battalions. First, her father slain;   80
Next, your son gone, and he most violent author
Of his own just remove; the people muddied,[550]
Thick and unwholesome in their thoughts and
    whispers,
For good Polonius' death; and we have done but
    greenly,[551]
In hugger-mugger to inter him; poor Ophelia[552]   85
Divided from herself and her fair judgment,
Without the which we are pictures, or mere beasts;
Last, and as such containing as all these,
Her brother is in secret come from France,
Feeds on his wonder, keeps himself in clouds,[553]   90
And wants not buzzers to infect his ear[554]
With pestilent speeches of his father's death—

Wherein necessity, of matter beggar'd,[555]
Will nothing stick our person to arraign[556]
In ear and ear. O my dear Gertrude! this,[557]   95
Like to a murdering-piece, in many places[558]
Give me superfluous death.[559]

[*A noise within.*]

QUEEN.   Alack! what noise is this?

Enter a GENTLEMAN.

KING. Where are my Switzers? Let them guard the
door.[560]
What is the matter?

GEN.   Save yourself, my lord;
The ocean, overpeering of his list,[561]   100
Eats not the flats with more impetuous haste
Than young Laertes, in a riotous head,[562]
O'erbears your officers. The rabble call him lord;
And, as the world were now but to begin,
Antiquity forgot, custom not known—   105
The ratifiers and props of every word—[563]
They cry, "Choose we! Laertes shall be king!"
Caps, hands, and tongues applaud it to the clouds,
"Laertes shall be king, Laertes king!"[564]

QUEEN. How cheerfully on the false trail they cry!   110
O! this is counter, you false Danish dogs![565]

[*Noise within.*]

KING. The doors are broke.

Enter LAERTES, armed, with DANES following.

---

547 *Gis*] slang abbreviation of Jesus.
548 *Cock*] corruption of God; penis.
549 coach] In Marlowe's *Tamburlaine*, the mad Zabina calls
for her coach to take her to her dead husband.
550 muddied] clouded, confused.
551 greenly] foolishly.
552 hugger-mugger] secrecy and haste.
553 wonder] bewilderment.
554 buzzers] insect-like gossips.

555 of matter beggared] bereft of facts.
556 Will nothing stick] will not hesitate.
557 in ear and ear] in both of Laertes' ears, or in one ear after another.
558 murdering-piece] scattershot cannon.
559 Give … death] Kill me many times over.
560 Switzers] Swiss mercenaries often served as royal guards.
561 overpeering … list] rising above shore.
562 in a riotous head] leading a mob.
563 ratifiers … word] i.e., custom and antiquity are what test
and give meaning and context to every word we utter.
564 Although Denmark was an elective monarchy, this is
nothing like due process.
565 counter] following the scent in a direction opposite to
that taken by the prey.

LAERTES. Where is the king? Sirs, stand you all without.

DANES. No, let's come in!

LAERTES.   I pray you, give me leave.

DANES. We will, we will.   115

[*They retire without the door.*]

LAERTES.   I thank you. Keep the door.
O thou vile king! Give me my father.

QUEEN.   Calmly, good Laertes.

LAERTES. That drop of blood that 's calm proclaims
  me bastard,
  Cries cuckold to my father, brands the harlot
  Even here, between the chaste unsmirchéd brow
  Of my true mother.   120

KING.   What is the cause, Laertes,
  That thy rebellion looks so giant-like?[566]
  Let him go, Gertrude; do not fear our person:[567]
  There 's such divinity doth hedge a king,
  That treason can but peep to what it would,[568]
  Acts little of his will. Tell me, Laertes,   125
  Why thou art thus incensed. Let him go, Gertrude.
  Speak, man.

LAERTES. Where is my father?

KING.   Dead.

QUEEN.   But not by him!

KING. Let him demand his fill.

LAERTES. How came he dead? I'll not be juggled with.   130
  To hell, allegiance! vows, to the blackest devil!
  Conscience and grace, to the profoundest pit!
  I dare damnation. To this point I stand,
  That both the worlds I give to negligence,[569]
  Let come what comes; only I'll be revenged   135
  Most throughly for my father.

KING.   Who shall stay you?

LAERTES. My will, not all the world:
  And, for my means, I'll husband them so well,[570]
  They shall go far with little.

KING.   Good Laertes,
  If you desire to know the certainty   140
  Of your dear father's death, is't writ in your revenge,
  That, swoopstake, you will draw both friend and
    foe,[571]
  Winner and loser?

LAERTES.   None but his enemies.

KING.   Will you know them then?

LAERTES. To his good friends thus wide I'll ope my
    arms;
  And like the kind life-rendering pelican,   145
  Repast them with my blood.[572]

KING.   Why, now you speak
  Like a good child and a true gentleman.
  That I am guiltless of your father's death,
  And am most sensibly in grief for it,[573]
  It shall as level to your judgment pierce   150
  As day does to your eye.

DANES: [*Within.*] Let her come in.

LAERTES. How now! What noise is that?

Re-enter OPHELIA.

O heat, dry up my brains! tears seven times salt,
  Burn out the sense and virtue of mine eye![574]   155
  By heaven, thy madness shall be paid by weight,
  Till our scale turn the beam. O rose of May![575]
  Dear maid, kind sister, sweet Ophelia!
  O heavens! is 't possible a young maid's wits
  Should be as mortal as an old man's life?   160
  Nature is fine in love, and where 'tis fine,[576]
  It sends some precious instance of itself
  After the thing it loves.

OPHELIA. *They bore him barefaced on the bier;*
  Hey non nonny, nonny, hey nonny;   165

---

566 giant-like] a reference to the Titans who attempted to
  overthrow the Olympian gods.

567 fear] be afraid for.

568 peep … would] look from a distance at what it would
  like to do.

569 both … negligence] I don't care what happens in this
  world or the next.

570 husband] use economically.

571 swoopstake] sweeping up all the stakes on the table.

572 kind … blood] The pelican was reputed to feed its
  young on blood from its own breast.

573 most sensibly in] keenly felt.

574 virtue] power.

575 paid … beam] avenged until the weight of vengeance
  shifts the scales the other way.

576 Nature … loves] fine = "delicate" and "ended," so: nature is delicate in love, and where it meets death, it sends
  a precious part of itself (e.g., Ophelia's sanity) after the
  dead beloved.

[IV.v]

And in his grave rained many a tear;
Fare you well, my dove!

LAERTES. Hadst thou thy wits, and didst persuade
   revenge,
  It could not move thus.

OPHELIA. You must sing: 170
   A-down a-down!
  —and you—
   Call him a-down-a!
  O how the wheel becomes it!577 It is the false
  steward that stole his master's daughter.578   175

LAERTES. This nothing's more than matter.579

OPHELIA. There's rosemary; that's for remembrance.
  Pray, love, remember. And there is pansies; that's
  for thoughts.

LAERTES. A document in madness, thoughts and   180
  remembrance fitted.

OPHELIA. There 's fennel for you, and columb-
  ines.580 There 's rue for you; and here 's some for
  me. We may call it herb of grace o' Sundays.581
  O! you must wear your rue with a difference.   185
  There's a daisy.582 I would give you some violets,
  but they withered all when my father died.583
  They say he made a good end—
  *For bonny sweet Robin is all my joy.*584

LAERTES. Thought and affliction, passion, hell itself, 190
  She turns to favour and to prettiness.585

OPHELIA. *And will he not come again?*
  And will he not come again?

---

577 wheel becomes it] The round, or alternating refrain,
   suits the song very well.
578 false … daughter] She may mean that the refrain, which
   is supposed to serve the song, is so catchy it steals the
   focus. In any case, Ophelia's mind is still preoccupied
   with thoughts of violated maidens.
579 nothing's … matter] This nonsense tells more than a
   factual account.
580 fennel, columbines] perhaps symbolizing flattery and
   marital infidelity, presented to Gertrude.
581 rue, herb o'grace] perhaps symbolizing repentance, for
   herself and Claudius.
582 daisy] perhaps symbolizing dissembling, added to Claudius's rue.
583 violets] symbolize faithfulness.
584 *For … joy*] a line from a popular song, the lyrics of
   which are not extant.
585 favour] charm.

No, no, he is dead;
  Go to thy death-bed,   195
He never will come again.
His beard was as white as snow
*All flaxen was his poll,*586
  He is gone, he is gone,
  *And we cast away moan:*587   200
  God ha' mercy on his soul!
And of all Christian souls, I pray God. God be
  wi', ye! [*Exit.*]

LAERTES. Do you see this, O God?

KING. Laertes, I must commune with your grief,
  Or you deny me right. Go but apart,   205
  Make choice of whom your wisest friends you will,
  And they shall hear and judge 'twixt you and me.
  If by direct or by collateral hand588
  They find us touched, we will our kingdom give,589
  Our crown, our life, and all that we call ours,   210
  To you in satisfaction; but if not,
  Be you content to lend your patience to us,
  And we shall jointly labour with your soul
  To give it due content.

LAERTES.   Let this be so.
  His means of death, his obscure burial—   215
  No trophy, sword, nor hatchment o'er his bones,590
  No noble rite nor formal ostentation—
  Cry to be heard, as 'twere from heaven to earth,
  That I must call't in question.591

KING.   So you shall;
  And where the offence is, let the great axe fall.   220
  I pray you go with me. [*Exeunt.*]

SCENE VI

ANOTHER ROOM IN THE SAME.

Enter HORATIO and a SERVANT.

HORATIO. What are they that would speak with me?

---

586 *poll*] head.
587 *cast away moan*] waste our crying.
588 collateral] indirect, collaborative.
589 touched] implicated.
590 hatchment] a cover for the tomb that bears the coat of
   arms of the deceased.
591 Cry … That] demand examination to such an extreme
   degree that …

SERVANT. Sailors, sir; they say, they have letters for
    you.
HORATIO. Let them come in. [*Exit SERVANT.*]
    I do not know from what part of the world
    I should be greeted, if not from Lord Hamlet.   5

Enter SAILORS.

1ST SAILOR. God bless you, sir.
HORATIO. Let him bless thee too.
2ND SAILOR. He shall, sir, an't please him. There 's a
    letter for you, sir—it comes from the ambassador
    that was bound for England—if your name be   10
    Horatio, as I am let to know it is.
HORATIO. [*reads the letter*] *Horatio, when thou shalt*
    have overlooked this, give these fellows some means
    to the King.[592] *They have letters for him. Ere we were*
    two days old at sea, a pirate of very war-like   15
    appointment gave us chase.[593] *Finding ourselves too*
    slow of sail, we put on a compelled valour; and in
    the grapple I boarded them: on the instant they got
    clear of our ship, so I alone became their prisoner.
    They have dealt with me like thieves of mercy, but   20
    they knew what they did; I am to do a turn for
    them.[594] *Let the king have the letters I have sent; and*
    repair thou to me with as much haste as thou wouldst
    fly death. I have words to speak in thine ear will make
    thee dumb; yet are they much too light for the bore   25
    of the matter.[595] *These good fellows will bring thee*
    where I am. Rosencrantz and Guildenstern hold their
    course for England: of them I have much to tell thee.
    Farewell.
        He that thou knowest thine,   30
                HAMLET.
Come, I will give you way for these your letters,[596]
And do 't the speedier that you may direct me
To him from whom you brought them. [*Exeunt.*]

---

[592] *overlooked*] looked over; *means*] i.e., of access.
[593] *pirate*] i.e., pirate ship; *appointment*] outfitting, equipment.
[594] *thieves of mercy*] i.e., instead of "angels of mercy."
[595] *too light for the bore*] inadequate to the seriousness, lit. a calibre of shot too small for the barrel of the gun.
[596] *way*] the means of access requested.

SCENE VII

ANOTHER ROOM IN THE SAME.

Enter KING and LAERTES.

KING. Now must your conscience my acquittance seal,
    And you must put me in your heart for friend,
    Sith you have heard, and with a knowing ear,
    That he which hath your noble father slain
    Pursued my life.   5
LAERTES.   It well appears. But tell me
    Why you proceeded not against these feats,
    So crimeful and so capital in nature,[597]
    As by your safety, wisdom, all things else,
    You mainly were stirred up.[598]
KING.   O, for two special reasons,
    Which may to you, perhaps, seem much   10
        unsinewed,[599]
    But yet to me th'are strong. The queen his mother
    Lives almost by his looks, and for myself—
    My virtue or my plague, be it either which—
    She's so conjunctive to my life and soul,[600]
    That, as the star moves not but in his sphere,   15
    I could not but by her. The other motive,
    Why to a public count I might not go,[601]
    Is the great love the general gender bear him;[602]
    Who, dipping all his faults in their affection,
    Would, like the spring that turneth wood to   20
        stone,[603]
    Convert his gyves to graces; so that my arrows,[604]
    Too slightly timbered for so loud a wind,[605]
    Would have reverted to my bow again,
    And not where I had aimed them.
LAERTES. And so have I a noble father lost;   25
    A sister driven into desperate terms,[606]

---

[597] *capital*] punishable by death.
[598] *mainly*] powerfully.
[599] *unsinewed*] feeble.
[600] *conjunctive*] united, like planets.
[601] *count*] account, reckoning.
[602] *general gender*] common sort of people.
[603] When a natural spring contains a high concentration of lime, it will petrify wood.
[604] *gyves*] fetters.
[605] *slightly timbered*] lightly shafted.
[606] *terms*] conditions.

Whose worth, if praises may go back again,[607]
Stood challenger on mount of all the age
For her perfections. But my revenge will come.
KING. Break not your sleeps for that; you must not   30
    think
That we are made of stuff so flat and dull
That we can let our beard be shook with danger
And think it pastime. You shortly shall hear more;
I loved your father, and we love ourself,
And that, I hope, will teach you to imagine—   35

Enter a MESSENGER.

How now! What news?
MESSENGER.   Letters, my lord, from Hamlet.
    This to your majesty; this to the queen.
KING. From Hamlet! who brought them?
MESSENGER. Sailors, my lord, they say; I saw them
    not.
    They were given me by Claudio, he received them   40
    of him that brought them.
KING. Laertes, you shall hear them. Leave us. [*Exit
    MESSENGER.*]
    *High and mighty, You shall know I am set naked on
    your kingdom.*[608] *To-morrow shall I beg leave to see
    your kingly eyes; when I shall, first asking your pardon*   45
    *thereunto, recount the occasions of my sudden and
    more strange return.*
                                    HAMLET.
    What should this mean? Are all the rest come back?
    Or is it some abuse, and no such thing?[609]   50
LAERTES. Know you the hand?
KING. 'Tis Hamlet's character.[610] "Naked."
    And in a postscript here, he says "alone."
    Can you advise me?
LAERTES. I'm lost in it, my lord. But let him come: 55
    It warms the very sickness in my heart,
    That I shall live and tell him to his teeth,
    "Thus diest thou."
KING.   If it be so, Laertes—
    As how should it be so? How otherwise?—
    Will you be ruled by me?   60

LAERTES.   Ay my lord;
    So you will not o'er-rule me to a peace.
KING. To thine own peace. If he be now returned,
    As checking at his voyage, and that he means[611]
    No more to undertake it, I will work him
    To an exploit, now ripe in my device,   65
    Under the which he shall not choose but fall;
    And for his death no wind of blame shall breathe,
    But even his mother shall uncharge the practice[612]
    And call it accident.
LAERTES.   My lord, I will be ruled;
    The rather, if you could devise it so   70
    That I might be the organ.
KING.   It falls right.
    You have been talked of since your travel much,
    And that in Hamlet's hearing, for a quality
    Wherein, they say, you shine. Your sum of parts
    Did not together pluck such envy from him   75
    As did that one, and that, in my regard,
    Of the unworthiest siege.[613]
LAERTES.   What part is that, my lord?
KING. A very ribbon in the cap of youth,
    Yet needful too; for youth no less becomes
    The light and careless livery that it wears   80
    Than settled age his sables and his weeds,[614]
    Importing health and graveness. Two month since
    Here was a gentleman of Normandy.
    I've seen myself, and served against, the French,
    And they can well on horseback; but this gallant   85
    Had witchcraft in 't. He grew into his seat,
    And to such wondrous doing brought his horse,
    As had he been incorpsed and demi-natured
    With the brave beast. So far he topped my
        thought,[615]
    That I, in forgery of shapes and tricks,[616]   90
    Come short of what he did.
LAERTES.   A Norman was 't?

---

[611] checking at] turning away from (a term from falconry).
[612] uncharge the practice] exonerate the event of any sus-
    picion.
[613] siege] rank, seat.
[614] sables, weeds] black fur, sober attire.
[615] incorpsed, demi-natured] of one body and a split nature,
    like a centaur.
[616] forgery … tricks] invention of postures and feats.

---

[607] go back again] revert to the past.
[608] *naked*] without any belongings.
[609] abuse] deception.
[610] character] handwriting.

KING. A Norman.
LAERTES. Upon my life, Lamord.
KING.   The very same.
LAERTES. I know him well; he is the broach indeed
    And gem of all the nation.   95
KING. He made confession of you,[617]
    And gave you such a masterly report
    For art and exercise in your defence,
    And for your rapier most especially,
    That he cried out, 'twould be a sight indeed   100
    If one could match you. The scrimers of their
        nation,[618]
    He swore, had neither motion, guard, nor eye,
    If you opposed them. Sir, this report of his
    Did Hamlet so envenom with his envy
    That he could nothing do but wish and beg   105
    Your sudden coming o'er, to play with you.
    Now, out of this—
LAERTES.   What out of this, my lord?
KING. Laertes, was your father dear to you?
    Or are you like the painting of a sorrow,
    A face without a heart?   110
LAERTES.   Why ask you this?
KING. Not that I think you did not love your father,
    But that I know love is begun by time,[619]
    And that I see, in passages of proof,[620]
    Time qualifies the spark and fire of it.[621]
    There lives within the very flame of love   115
    A kind of wick or snuff that will abate it,[622]
    And nothing is at a like goodness still,
    For goodness, growing to a pleurisy,[623]
    Dies in his own too-much. That we would do,
    We should do when we would, for this "would"   120
        changes,
    And hath abatements and delays as many
    As there are tongues, are hands, are accidents;

And then this "should" is like a spendthrift sigh,[624]
    That hurts by easing. But, to the quick o' the
        ulcer;[625]
    Hamlet comes back; what would you undertake   125
    To show yourself your father's son in deed
    More than in words?
LAERTES.   To cut his throat i' the church.
KING. No place, indeed, should murder sanctuarize;[626]
    Revenge should have no bounds. But, good Laertes,
    Will you do this: keep close within your chamber. 130
    Hamlet returned shall know you are come home;
    We'll put on those shall praise your excellence,[627]
    And set a double varnish on the fame
    The Frenchman gave you; bring you, in fine,
        together,[628]
    And wager on your heads. He, being remiss,   135
    Most generous and free from all contriving,
    Will not peruse the foils; so that, with ease—
    Or with a little shuffling—you may choose
    A sword unbated, and, in a pass of practice[629]
    Requite him for your father.   140
LAERTES.   I will do 't;
    And, for that purpose, I'll anoint my sword.
    I bought an unction of a mountebank,[630]
    So mortal that, but dip a knife in it,
    Where it draws blood no cataplasm so rare,[631]
    Collected from all simples that have virtue[632]   145
    Under the moon, can save the thing from death[633]
    This is but scratched withal. I'll touch my point
    With this contagion, that, if I gall him slightly,
    It may be death.

617 confession] report.
618 scrimers] *escrimeurs*, fencers.
619 begun by time] has a beginning in time (rather than
    being primordially ordained).
620 passages of proof] proven cases.
621 qualifies] diminishes.
622 snuff] residue of burnt wick.
623 pleurisy] fullness, excess (the disease was thought to be
    caused by an excess of blood).
624 spendthrift sigh] Sighing was thought to provide relief
    from discomfort at the expense of shortening one's life
    span.
625 quick o' the ulcer] heart of the matter.
626 murder sanctuarize] provide sanctuary for a murderer.
627 put on those shall] enlist some people who will.
628 in fine] finally.
629 sword unbated] as opposed to a foil with a blunted or
    buttoned point.
630 unction] ointment (poison); mountebank] itinerant
    quack pharmacist.
631 cataplasm] bandage, plaster.
632 simples] medicinal herbs.
633 virtue … moon] power (which was thought to be en-
    hanced by the effect of the moon).

KING.   Let's further think of this;
   Weigh what convenience both of time and means   150
   May fit us to our shape. If this should fail,[634]
   And that our drift look through our bad
      performance,[635]
   'Twere better not assayed. Therefore this project
   Should have a back or second, that might hold,[636]
   If this should blast in proof. Soft! Let me see.[637]   155
   We'll make a solemn wager on your cunnings...
   I ha 't!
   When in your motion you are hot and dry—
   As make your bouts more violent to that end—
   And that he calls for drink, I'll have prepared him   160
   A chalice for the nonce; whereon but sipping,[638]
   If he by chance escape your venomed stuck,[639]
   Our purpose may hold there. But stay! what noise,

Enter QUEEN.

   How now, sweet queen!
QUEEN. One woe doth tread upon another's heel,   165
   So fast they follow. Your sister's drowned, Laertes.[640]
LAERTES. Drowned! O, where?
QUEEN. There is a willow grows aslant a brook,
   That shows his hoary leaves in the glassy stream.
   Therewith fantastic garlands did she make,[641]   170
   Of crow-flowers, nettles, daisies, and long
      purples,[642]
   That liberal shepherds give a grosser name,[643]
   But our cold maids do dead men's fingers call
      them.[644]
   There, on the pendant boughs her coronet weeds

Clambering to hang, an envious sliver broke,[645]   175
When down her weedy trophies and herself
Fell in the weeping brook. Her clothes spread wide
And, mermaid-like, awhile they bore her up;
Which time she chanted snatches of old lauds,[646]
As one incapable of her own distress,[647]   180
Or like a creature native and indued
Unto that element. But long it could not be
Till that her garments, heavy with their drink,
Pulled the poor wretch from her melodious lay
To muddy death.   185
LAERTES.   Alas! then, she is drowned?
QUEEN. Drowned, drowned.
LAERTES. Too much of water hast thou, poor Ophelia,
   And therefore I forbid my tears. But yet
   It is our trick, nature her custom holds,[648]
   Let shame say what it will. When these are gone   190
   The woman will be out. Adieu, my lord![649]
   I have a speech of fire, that fain would blaze,
   But that this folly douts it.[650] [*Exit.*]
KING.   Let's follow, Gertrude.
   How much I had to do to calm his rage!
   Now fear I this will give it start again.   195
   Therefore let's follow. [*Exeunt.*]

ACT V

SCENE I

A CHURCHYARD.

Enter two CLOWNS, a Sexton and another.[651]

1ST CLOWN. Is she to be buried in Christian burial
   when she wilfully seeks her own salvation?[652]

---

634 shape] role (a theatrical metaphor).
635 drift look through] intent show through.
636 back or second] back-up or plan B.
637 blast in proof] fall apart when tried.
638 nonce] moment.
639 stuck] thrust.
640 In 1579, a young woman named Katherine Hamlett
    drowned in the Avon River near Stratford. Shakespeare
    was 15 at the time.
641 Therewith … make] i.e., by weaving the flowers into a
    circlet of willow twigs.
642 long purples] a kind of wild orchid.
643 liberal] free-speaking; grosser name] presumably some-
    thing phallic.
644 cold] chaste.

---

645 sliver] limb.
646 lauds] hymns.
647 incapable] i.e., of understanding.
648 trick] way.
649 When these … out] When these tears are gone, the
    womanly part of me will be cried out.
650 douts] douses.
651 Sexton] gravedigger; another] the Second Clown is of-
    ten played as a second gravedigger, but the part is not
    specified as such, and he addresses the First Clown not
    as an employer or partner, but as an acquaintance.
652 salvation] mistake for damnation.

2ND CLOWN. I tell thee she is; therefore make her grave straight. The crowner hath sat on her, and finds it Christian burial.653 5

1ST CLOWN. How can that be, unless she drowned herself in her own defence?

2ND CLOWN. Why, 'tis found so.

1ST CLOWN. It must be *se offendendo*; it cannot be else.654 For here lies the point: if I drown myself 10 wittingly it argues an act; and an act hath three branches; it is, to act, to do, and to perform: argal, she drowned herself wittingly.655

2ND CLOWN. Nay, but hear you, Goodman Delver— 15

1ST CLOWN. Give me leave. Here lies the water— good. Here stands the man—good. If the man go to this water, and drown himself, it is, will he nill he, he goes; mark you that. But if the water come to him, and drown him, he drowns not himself. 20 Argal, he that is not guilty of his own death shortens not his own life.

2ND CLOWN. But is this law?

1ST CLOWN. Ay, marry, is 't; crowner's quest law.656

2ND CLOWN. Will you ha' the truth on 't? If this had 25 not been a gentlewoman she should have been buried out o' Christian burial.

1ST CLOWN. Why, there thou sayest; and the more pity that great folk should have countenance in this world to drown or hang themselves more than 30 their even Christen.657 Come, my spade. There is no ancient gentlemen but gardeners, ditchers, and grave- makers; they hold up Adam's profession.

2ND CLOWN. Was he a gentleman?

1ST CLOWN. A' was the first that ever bore arms.658 35

2ND CLOWN. Why, he had none.

1ST CLOWN. What, art a heathen? How dost thou understand the Scripture? The Scripture says Adam

digged. Could he dig without arms? I'll put another question to thee; if thou answerest me not 40 to the purpose, confess thyself—

2ND CLOWN. Go to.

1ST CLOWN. What is he that builds stronger than either the mason, the shipwright, or the carpenter?

2ND CLOWN. The gallows-maker; for that frame 45 outlives a thousand tenants.

1ST CLOWN. I like thy wit well, in good faith; the gallows does well. But how does it well? It does well to those that do ill. Now thou dost ill to say the gallows is built stronger than the church; argal, 50 the gallows may do well to thee. To 't again, come.

2ND CLOWN. Who builds stronger than a mason, a shipwright, or a carpenter?

1ST CLOWN. Ay, tell me that, and unyoke.659

2ND CLOWN. Marry, now I can tell. 55

1ST CLOWN. To 't.

2ND CLOWN. Mass, I cannot tell.

Enter HAMLET and HORATIO at a distance.

1ST CLOWN. Cudgel thy brains no more about it, for your dull ass will not mend his pace with beating.660 And when you are asked this question 60 next, say, "a grave-maker": the houses that he makes lasts till doomsday. Go, get thee to Yaughan; fetch me a stoup of liquor.661 [*Exit 2ND CLOWN.*]

[*1ST CLOWN digs, and sings.*]

In youth, when I did love, did love,
Methought it was very sweet, 65
To contract —O—the time for—a—my behove,
*O—Methought there—a—was nothing meet.*662

HAMLET. Has this fellow no feeling of his business, that he sings at grave-making?

HORATIO. Custom hath made it in him a property 70 of easiness.

---

653 crowner] coroner.
654 *se offendendo*] mistake for *se defendendo*—in self-defence. The subsequent argument parodies a case from 1560, Hales vs. Pettit, which tried whether Hales' suicide was a wilful act that entailed forfeiture of his lease.
655 argal] mistake for *ergo*, therefore.
656 quest] inquest.
657 countenance] privilege; even Christen] equal Christians.
658 bore arms] i.e., a coat of arms.

---

659 unyoke] unburden yourself.
660 your] colloquially used in a general sense—i.e., not the Second Clown's but any dull ass—though the insult is, of course, specific.
661 Yaughan] presumably the name of a local tavern-keeper; stoup] tankard.
662 *O, a*] grunts, as he digs.

HAMLET. 'Tis e'en so; the hand of little employment
   hath the daintier sense.

1ST CLOWN. *But age, with his stealing steps,*
   Hath clawed me in his clutch,   75
And hath shipped me into the land,
   As if I had never been such.

[*Throws up a skull.*]

HAMLET. That skull had a tongue in it, and could
   sing once. How the knave jowls it to the ground,
   as if it were Cain's jaw-bone, that did the first   80
   murder![663] This might be the pate of a politician
   which this ass now o'er-offices, one that would
   circumvent God, might it not?[664]

HORATIO. It might, my lord.

HAMLET. Or of a courtier, which could say, "Good   85
   morrow, sweet lord! How dost thou, good lord?"
   This might be my Lord Such-a-one, that praised
   my Lord Such-a-one's horse, when he meant to beg
   it, might it not?

HORATIO. Ay, my lord.   90

HAMLET. Why, e'en so! and now my Lady Worm's;
   chopless, and knocked about the mazzard with a
   sexton's spade.[665] Here's fine revolution, and we
   had the trick to see't. Did these bones cost no more
   the breeding but to play at loggets with 'em?[666]   95
   Mine ache to think on 't.

1ST CLOWN. *A pick-axe and a spade, a spade,*
   For and a shrouding sheet;[667]
O, a pit of clay for to be made
   For such a guest is meet.   100

[*Throws up another skull.*]

HAMLET. There's another; why may not that be the
   skull of a lawyer? Where be his quiddities now, his
   quillets, his cases, his tenures, and his tricks?[668]

Why does he suffer this rude knave now to knock
him about the sconce with a dirty shovel, and will   105
not tell him of his action of battery?[669] Hum! This
fellow might be in 's time a great buyer of land,
with his statutes, his recognizances, his fines, his
double vouchers, his recoveries.[670] Is this the fine
of his fines, and the recovery of his recoveries, to   110
have his fine pate full of fine dirt?[671] Will his
vouchers vouch him no more of his purchases, and
double ones too, than the length and breadth of a
pair of indentures?[672] The very conveyances of his
lands will scarcely lie in this box, and must the   115
inheritor himself have no more, ha?[673]

HORATIO. Not a jot more, my lord.

HAMLET. Is not parchment made of sheep-skins?

HORATIO. Ay, my lord, and of calf-skins too.

HAMLET. They are sheep and calves which seek out   120
   assurance in that.[674] I will speak to this fellow.
   Whose grave's this, sir?

1ST CLOWN. Mine, sir.
   O! a pit of clay for to be made
      For such a guest is meet.   125

HAMLET. I think it be thine, indeed; for thou liest
   in't.

1ST CLOWN. You lie out on't, sir, and therefore it is
   not yours; for my part, I do not lie in't, and yet it
   is mine.   130

HAMLET. Thou dost lie in't, to be in't and say it is
   thine: 'tis for the dead, not for the quick; therefore
   thou liest.[675]

1ST CLOWN. 'Tis a quick lie, sir; 'twill away again,
   from me to you.   135

HAMLET. What man dost thou dig it for?

1ST CLOWN. For no man, sir.

---

663 jowls] hurls.

664 o'er-offices] lords it over; one … God] someone who
   had tried to usurp God's powers.

665 chopless] jawless; mazzard] head.

666 Did … breeding] were these bones bred for nothing
   better; loggets] a game similar to horseshoes, played with
   small pieces of wood.

667 *For and*] and moreover.

668 quiddities, quillets] quibbling arguments, fine legal distinctions; tenures] terms of property leases.

669 sconce] head.

670 statutes … recoveries] mechanisms for collateralizing
   and claiming the land of a debtor.

671 fine] (pun) end, legal action, delicate.

672 pair of indentures] two halves of a contract, cut (indentured) in such a way that, brought together, they formed
   a single sheet (the size of the plot of earth the skull has
   now).

673 conveyances] land transfer documents.

674 assurance] (pun) confidence, deed.

675 quick] living.

HAMLET. What woman, then?

1ST CLOWN. For none, neither.

HAMLET. Who is to be buried in 't?   140

1ST CLOWN. One that was a woman, sir; but, rest her soul, she's dead.

HAMLET. How absolute the knave is!⁶⁷⁶ We must speak by the card, or equivocation will undo us.⁶⁷⁷ By the Lord, Horatio, these three years I have 145 taken note of it; the age is grown so picked that the toe of the peasant comes so near the heel of the courtier, he galls his kibe.⁶⁷⁸ How long hast thou been a grave-maker?

1ST CLOWN. Of all the days i' the year, I came to 't 150 that day that our last king Hamlet overcame Fortinbras.

HAMLET. How long is that since?

1ST CLOWN. Cannot you tell that? Every fool can tell that. It was the very day that young Hamlet 155 was born; he that is mad, and sent into England.

HAMLET. Ay, marry, why was be sent into England?

1ST CLOWN. Why, because he was mad. He shall recover his wits there; or, if 'a do not, 'tis no great matter there. 160

HAMLET. Why?

1ST CLOWN. 'Twill not be seen in him there; there the men are as mad as he.

HAMLET. How came he mad?

1ST CLOWN. Very strangely, they say. 165

HAMLET. How strangely?

1ST CLOWN. Faith, e'en with losing his wits.

HAMLET. Upon what ground?

1ST CLOWN. Why, here in Denmark. I have been sexton here, man and boy, thirty years.⁶⁷⁹ 170

HAMLET. How long will a man lie i' the earth ere he rot?

1ST CLOWN. Faith, if he be not rotten before he die —as we have many poxy corses now-a-days that will scarce hold the laying in—he will last you 175

some eight year or nine year.⁶⁸⁰ A tanner will last you nine year.

HAMLET. Why he more than another?

1ST CLOWN. Why, sir, his hide is so tanned with his trade that he will keep out water a great while, and 180 your water is a sore decayer of your whoreson dead body.⁶⁸¹ Here 's a skull now; this skull hath lain you i' the earth three-and-twenty years.

HAMLET. Whose was it?

1ST CLOWN. A whoreson mad fellow's it was: whose 185 do you think it was?

HAMLET. Nay, I know not.

1ST CLOWN. A pestilence on him for a mad rogue! A' poured a flagon of Rhenish on my head once.⁶⁸² This same skull, sir, was Yorick's skull, the 190 king's jester.

HAMLET. This!

1ST CLOWN. E'en that.

HAMLET. Let me see. [*Takes the skull.*] Alas, poor Yorick! I knew him, Horatio; a fellow of infinite 195 jest, of most excellent fancy. He hath borne me on his back a thousand times, and now—how abhorred in my imagination it is! My gorge rises at it. Here hung those lips that I have kissed I know not how oft. Where be your gibes now? your gam- 200 bols? your songs? your flashes of merriment, that were wont to set the table on a roar? Not one now, to mock your own grinning? quite chopfallen?⁶⁸³ Now get you to my lady's chamber, and tell her, let her paint an inch thick, to this favour she must 205 come.⁶⁸⁴ Make her laugh at that. Prithee, Horatio, tell me one thing.

HORATIO. What's that, my lord?

HAMLET. Dost thou think Alexander looked o' this fashion i' the earth?⁶⁸⁵ 210

HORATIO. E'en so.

HAMLET. And smelt so? Pah! [*Puts down the skull.*]

HORATIO. E'en so, my lord.

---

676 absolute] strictly literal.

677 by the card] according to strict rules (a sailor would use a card with compass points marked on it to navigate).

678 picked] finical; kibe] chilblain or corn on the heel.

679 By the Gravedigger's reckoning, then, Hamlet is thirty years old.

680 poxy corses] corpses of those who died of syphilis.

681 whoreson] expresses rough familiarity.

682 Rhenish] Rhine wine.

683 chopfallen] down-in-the-mouth, jawless.

684 favour] appearance.

685 Alexander] Alexander the Great (356–323 B.C.E.), king of Macedonia and conqueror of the Persian Empire.

[V.i]

HAMLET. To what base uses we may return, Horatio!
    Why may not imagination trace the noble dust of
    Alexander, till he find it stopping a bung-hole?[686]
HORATIO. 'Twere to consider too curiously, to
    consider so.[687]
HAMLET. No, faith, not a jot; but to follow him
    thither with modesty enough, and likelihood to
    lead it.[688] As thus: Alexander died, Alexander was
    buried, Alexander returneth into dust; the dust is
    earth; of earth we make loam, and why of that
    loam, whereto he was converted, might they not
    stop a beer-barrel?
    Imperious Caesar, dead and turned to clay,
    Might stop a hole to keep the wind away:
    O, that that earth, which kept the world in awe,
    Should patch a wall to expel the winter's flaw.
    But soft, but soft awhile! Here comes the king.

*Enter PRIESTS, &c., in procession: the Corpse of
OPHELIA, LAERTES and Mourners following; KING,
QUEEN, their Trains, &c.*

    The queen, the courtiers: who is this they follow?
    And with such maiméd rites? This doth betoken[689]
    The corse they follow did with desperate hand
    Fordo its own life; 'twas of some estate.[690]
    Couch we awhile, and mark.[691]

[Retires with HORATIO.]

LAERTES. What ceremony else?
HAMLET. That is Laertes, a very noble youth; mark.
LAERTES. What ceremony else?
PRIEST. Her obsequies have been as far enlarged
    As we have warranty. Her death was doubtful;
    And, but that great command o'ersways the order,
    She should in ground unsanctified have lodged
    Till the last trumpet: for charitable prayers,
    Shards, flints, and pebbles should be thrown on
        her.[692]

    Yet here she is allowed her virgin crants,[693]
    Her maiden strewments, and the bringing home[694]
    Of bell and burial.
LAERTES. Must there no more be done?
PRIEST.   No more be done:
    We should profane the service of the dead,
    To sing a requiem and such rest to her
    As to peace-parted souls.[695]
LAERTES.   Lay her i' the earth;
    And from her fair and unpolluted flesh
    May violets spring! I tell thee, churlish priest,
    A ministering angel shall my sister be,
    When thou liest howling.[696]
HAMLET.   What! the fair Ophelia?
QUEEN. Sweets to the sweet: farewell!

[Scattering flowers.]

    I hoped thou shouldst have been my Hamlet's wife;
    I thought thy bride-bed to have decked, sweet maid,
    And not have strewed thy grave.
LAERTES.   O! treble woe
    Fall ten times treble on that curséd head
    Whose wicked deed thy most ingenious sense
    Deprived thee of. Hold off the earth awhile,
    Till I have caught her once more in mine arms.
        [Leaps into the grave.]
    Now pile your dust upon the quick and dead,
    Till of this flat a mountain you have made,
    To o'er-top old Pelion or the skyish head[697]
    Of blue Olympus.
HAMLET. [*Advancing.*] What is he whose grief
    Bears such an emphasis? Whose phrase of sorrow
    Conjures the wand'ring stars, and makes them
        stand[698]
    Like wonder-wounded hearers? This is I,
    Hamlet the Dane. [*Leaps into the grave.*]

---

686 bung-hole] hole in a barrel.
687 curiously] minutely.
688 with modesty] without exaggeration.
689 maimed] reduced, incomplete.
690 fordo] destroy; estate] social rank.
691 couch] conceal.
692 shards] broken pottery.

693 crants] garland of maidenhood.
694 strewments] strewn flowers; bringing home] i.e., to the grave.
695 Canon law expressly forbade masses and psalms for suicides.
696 howling] i.e., in Hell.
697 Pelion] a mountain that, in Greek myth, was piled on top of Mount Ossa to enable the gods to scale Mount Olympus.
698 wand'ring stars] planets.

LAERTES.   The devil take thy soul!

[*Grapples with him.*]

HAMLET. Thou pray'st not well.
  I prithee, take thy fingers from my throat;
  For though I am not splenitive and rash[699]   275
  Yet have I in me something dangerous,
  Which let thy wisdom fear. Away thy hand!
KING. Pluck them asunder.
QUEEN. Hamlet! Hamlet!
ALL. Gentlemen!   280
HORATIO. Good my lord, be quiet.

[*The Attendants part them, and they come out of the grave.*]

HAMLET. Why, I will fight with him upon this theme
  Until my eyelids will no longer wag.
QUEEN. O my son! What theme?
HAMLET. I loved Ophelia: forty thousand brothers   285
  Could not, with all their quantity of love,
  Make up my sum. What wilt thou do for her?
KING. O! he is mad, Laertes.
QUEEN. For love of God, forbear him.
HAMLET. 'Swounds, show me what thou'lt do: 290
  Woo't weep? Woo't fight? Woo't fast? Woo't tear
    thyself?
  Woo't drink up eisel? Eat a crocodile?[700]
  I'll do 't. Dost thou come here to whine?
  To outface me with leaping in her grave?
  Be buried quick with her, and so will I: 295
  And, if thou prate of mountains, let them throw
  Millions of acres on us, till our ground,
  Singeing his pate against the burning zone,[701]
  Make Ossa like a wart! Nay, an thou'lt mouth,
  I'll rant as well as thou.   300
QUEEN.   This is mere madness:
  And thus a while the fit will work on him;
  Anon, as patient as the female dove,
  When that her golden couplets are disclosed,[702]

His silence will sit drooping.
HAMLET.   Hear you, sir;
  What is the reason that you use me thus?   305
  I loved you ever. But it is no matter;
  Let Hercules himself do what he may,
  The cat will mew and dog will have his day.[*Exit.*]
KING. I pray you, good Horatio, wait upon him.

[*Exit HORATIO.*]

[*To LAERTES.*] Strengthen your patience in our   310
  last night's speech;
  We'll put the matter to the present push—[703]
  Good Gertrude, set some watch over your son.—
  This grave shall have a living monument.[704]
  An hour of quiet shortly shall we see;
  Till then, in patience our proceeding be.   315

[*Exeunt.*]

SCENE II

A HALL IN THE CASTLE.

Enter HAMLET and HORATIO.

HAMLET. So much for this, sir. Now shall you see
  the other.
  You do remember all the circumstance?
HORATIO. Remember it, my lord?
HAMLET. Sir, in my heart there was a kind of fighting
  That would not let me sleep. Methought I lay   5
  Worse than the mutinies in the bilboes.[705]
  Rashly—
  And praised be rashness for it: let us know,
  Our indiscretion sometime serves us well
  When our deep plots do pall; and that should   10
    teach us[706]
  There 's a divinity that shapes our ends,
  Rough-hew them how we will.
HORATIO.   That is most certain.

---

[699] splenitive] hot-tempered (the spleen was thought to be the seat of anger).

[700] eisel] vinegar.

[701] burning zone] i.e., of the sun.

[702] golden couplets] The dove lays two eggs and her young are covered in golden down.

[703] to the present push] into immediate action.

[704] living monument] an enduring monument, or her death will be memorialized by its effect on the living (e.g., Hamlet's murder).

[705] mutinies … bilboes] mutineers in fetters.

[706] pall] fail.

HAMLET.—Up from my cabin,
  My sea-gown scarfed about me, in the dark
  Groped I to find out them, had my desire,   15
  Fingered their packet, and in fine withdrew[707]
  To mine own room again; making so bold—
  My fears forgetting manners—to unseal
  Their grand commission; where I found, Horatio,
  O royal knavery!, an exact command,   20
  Larded with many several sorts of reasons[708]
  Importing Denmark's health, and England's too,
  With, ho, such bugs and goblins in my life,[709]
  That, on the supervise, no leisure bated,[710]
  No, not to stay the grinding of the axe,   25
  My head should be struck off.
HORATIO.   Is 't possible?
HAMLET. Here's the commission; read it at more
    leisure.
  But wilt thou bear me how I did proceed?
HORATIO. I beseech you.
HAMLET. Being thus be-netted round with villainies—   30
  Ere I could make a prologue to my brains
  They had begun the play—I sat me down,[711]
  Devised a new commission, wrote it fair—
  I once did hold it, as our statists do,[712]
  A baseness to write fair, and laboured much   35
  How to forget that learning; but, sir, now
  It did me yeoman's service. Wilt thou know
  The effect of what I wrote?[713]
HORATIO.   Ay, good my lord.
HAMLET. An earnest conjuration from the king,
  As England was his faithful tributary,   40
  As love between them like the palm should flourish,
  As peace should still her wheaten garland wear,
  And stand a comma 'tween their amities,[714]

And many such-like "As"es of great charge,
  That, on the view and knowing of these contents,   45
  Without debatement further, more or less,
  He should the bearers put to sudden death,
  Not shriving-time allowed.[715]
HORATIO.   How was this sealed?
HAMLET. Why, even in that was heaven ordinant.[716]
  I had my father's signet in my purse,   50
  Which was the model of that Danish seal;
  Folded the writ up in the form of the other,[717]
  Subscribed it, gave't th' impression, placed it safely,
  The changeling never known. Now, the next day
  Was our sea-fight, and what to this was sequent[718]   55
  Thou know'st already.
HORATIO. So, Guildenstern and Rosencrantz go to 't.
HAMLET. Why, man, they did make love to this
    employment.
  They are not near my conscience; their defeat
  Does by their own insinuation grow.[719]   60
  'Tis dangerous when the baser nature comes
  Between the pass and fell incensèd points[720]
  Of mighty opposites.[721]
HORATIO.   Why, what a king is this![722]
HAMLET. Does it not, think thee, stand me now
    upon—[723]
  He that hath killed my king, and whored my mother,   65
  Popped in between the election and my hopes,[724]
  Thrown out his angle for my proper life,[725]

---

[707] Fingered] pick-pocketed; in fine] finally.
[708] Larded] enriched.
[709] such bugs ... life] such threats about the implications
    of allowing me to live.
[710] supervise] first reading; no leisure bated] without allow-
    ing any waste of time.
[711] Ere ... play] Before I could properly assemble my
    thoughts they were in action.
[712] statists] professional politicians (who would have scribes
    write their fair copy).
[713] effect] purport.
[714] comma] link; amities] friendship.

[715] shriving-time] the opportunity to receive absolution
    from a priest.
[716] ordinant] directing events.
[717] Folded ... other] folded the newly written letter in the
    shape of the original.
[718] to ... sequent] occurred after this.
[719] insinuation] intrusion.
[720] pass] thrust; fell] savage; incensèd] angered; points] i.e.,
    of swords.
[721] opposites] antagonists.
[722] Depending on interpretation, Horatio may be remark-
    ing on either Claudius or Hamlet. The ambiguity is
    preserved by his indirect (evasive?) reply to Hamlet's
    subsequent question.
[723] Does ... upon] is it not incumbent on me.
[724] election] i.e., the election of the monarch called for by
    Denmark's constitution.
[725] angle] fishing line.

And with such cozenage—is 't not perfect
  conscience[726]
To quit him with this arm? And is 't not to be
  damned[727]
To let this canker of our nature come   70
In further evil?
HORATIO. It must be shortly known to him from
  England
What is the issue of the business there.
HAMLET. It will be short: the interim is mine;
And a man's life is no more than to say "One." 75
But I am very sorry, good Horatio,
That to Laertes I forgot myself;
For, by the image of my cause, I see
The portraiture of his. I'll count his favours:
But, sure, the bravery of his grief did put me[728] 80
Into a towering passion.
HORATIO.   Peace! who comes here?

Enter OSRIC.

OSRIC. Your lordship is right welcome back to
  Denmark.
HAMLET. I humbly thank you, sir. [*Aside to
  HORATIO.*] Dost know this water-fly?[729] 85
HORATIO. [*Aside to HAMLET.*] No, my good lord.
HAMLET. [*Aside to HORATIO.*] Thy state is the more
  gracious; for 'tis a vice to know him. He hath much
  land, and fertile. Let a beast be lord of beasts, and
  his crib shall stand at the king's mess.[730] 'Tis a 90
  chough; but, as I say, spacious in the possession
  of dirt.[731]
OSRIC. Sweet lord, if your lordship were at leisure, I
  should impart a thing to you from his majesty.
HAMLET. I will receive it, sir, with all diligence of 95
  spirit. Your bonnet to his right use; 'tis for the
  head.
OSRIC. I thank your lordship, it is very hot.

HAMLET. No, believe me, 'tis very cold; the wind is
  northerly. 100
OSRIC. It is indifferent cold, my lord, indeed.[732]
HAMLET. But yet methinks it is very sultry and hot
  for my complexion.[733]
OSRIC. Exceedingly, my lord; it is very sultry, as
  'twere—I cannot tell how. But, my lord, his 105
  majesty bade me signify to you that he has laid a
  great wager on your head. Sir, this is the matter—
HAMLET. I beseech you, remember—

[*HAMLET moves him to put on his hat.*]

OSRIC. Nay, good my lord; for mine ease, in good faith.
  Sir, here is newly come to court Laertes; believe me, 110
  an absolute gentleman, full of most excellent differences, of very soft society and great showing.[734] Indeed, to speak feelingly of him, he is the card or calendar of gentry, for you shall find in him the continent of what part a gentleman would see.[735] 115
HAMLET. Sir, his definement suffers no perdition in
  you; though, I know, to divide him inventorially
  would dizzy the arithmetic of memory, and yet but
  yaw neither, in respect of his quick sail.[736] But,
  in the verity of extolment, I take him to be a soul 120
  of great article, and his infusion of such dearth and
  rareness, as, to make true diction of him, his
  semblable is his mirror; and who else would trace
  him, his umbrage, nothing more.[737]
OSRIC. Your lordship speaks most infallibly of him. 125
HAMLET. The concernancy, sir?[738] Why do we wrap
  the gentleman in our more rawer breath?[739]
OSRIC. Sir?

---

726 cozenage] trickery.
727 quit] repay.
728 bravery] bravado, boastfulness.
729 water-fly] i.e., nervous flapping insect.
730 Let ... mess] If a man possesses property, even if he is
  no better than his livestock, he will be received at court;
  crib] feed-box.
731 chough] jack-daw (chatterer) or churl.

732 indifferent] moderately.
733 complexion] constitution.
734 differences] distinctions.
735 feelingly] with proper feeling, justly; card] chart; con-
  tinent] table of contents.
736 definement] description; perdition] loss; yaw neither]
  not slip from course.
737 article] items (for inventory); infusion] endowment;
  semblable] the only one who can resemble him; um-
  brage] shadow (i.e., anyone who tried to follow in his
  footsteps would be nothing more than his shadow).
738 concernancy] relevance.
739 Why ... breath] Why do we attempt to clothe him with
  our inadequate words?

HORATIO. Is't not possible to understand in another
tongue? You will to't, sir, really.[740]   130

HAMLET. What imports the nomination of this
gentleman?

OSRIC. Of Laertes?

HORATIO. His purse is empty already; all's golden
words are spent.   135

HAMLET. Of him, sir.

OSRIC. I know you are not ignorant—

HAMLET. I would you did, sir; in faith, if you did,
it would not much approve me.[741] Well, sir?

OSRIC. You are not ignorant of what excellence   140
Laertes is—

HAMLET. I dare not confess that, lest I should
compare with him in excellence: but to know a
man well, were to know himself.[742]

OSRIC. I mean, sir, for his weapon; but in the   145
imputation laid on him by them, in his meed he's
unfellowed.[743]

HAMLET. What's his weapon?

OSRIC. Rapier and dagger.

HAMLET. That 's two of his weapons—but, well.   150

OSRIC. The king, sir, hath wagered with him six
Barbary horses; against the which he has imponed,
as I take it, six French rapiers and poniards, with
their assigns, as girdle, hangers, and so.[744] Three
of the carriages, in faith, are very dear to fancy, very   155
responsive to the hilts, most delicate carriages, and
of very liberal conceit.

HAMLET. What call you the carriages?

HORATIO. I knew you must be edified by the margin
ere you had done.[745]   160

OSRIC. The carriages, sir, are the hangers.

HAMLET. The phrase would be more germane to the
matter, if we could carry cannon by our sides; I
would it might be hangers till then.[746] But, on.
Six Barbary horses against six French swords, their   165
assigns, and three liberal-conceited carriages: that's
the French bet against the Danish. Why is this
"imponed," as you call it?

OSRIC. The king, sir, hath laid, that in a dozen passes
between yourself and him, he shall not exceed you   170
three hits; he hath laid on twelve for nine, and it
would come to immediate trial, if your lordship
would vouchsafe the answer.[747]

HAMLET. How if I answer no?

OSRIC. I mean, my lord, the opposition of your   175
person in trial.

HAMLET. Sir, I will walk here in the hall. If it please
his majesty—'tis the breathing time of day with
me—let the foils be brought.[748] The gentleman
willing, and the king hold his purpose, I will win   180
for him an I can; if not, I will gain nothing but
my shame and the odd hits.

OSRIC. Shall I re-deliver you so?

HAMLET. To this effect, sir, after what flourish your
nature will.   185

OSRIC. I commend my duty to your lordship.

HAMLET. Yours, yours. [Exit OSRIC.] He does well
to commend it himself; there are no tongues else
for's turn.

HORATIO. This lapwing runs away with the shell on   190
his head.[749]

HAMLET. He did comply with his dug before he
sucked it.[750] Thus has he—and many more of the

---

[740] Is't ... really] i.e., isn't there a more comprehensible way
of making your point? Give it a good try.

[741] did] i.e., know I was not ignorant; approve] commend.

[742] I dare ... himself] I'd rather not admit knowledge of his
excellence, because that will invite comparisons; saying
one knows another man well implies corresponding self-
knowledge.

[743] but ... unfellowed] To judge solely by what is implied
in his use of weaponry, he has no equal in merit (meed).

[744] imponed] a fancy word for placed or staked; assigns]
accessories; hangers] straps and pads to attach a sword
to a belt or girdle.

[745] margin] i.e., where a word might be glossed with an
explanation like this one.

[746] cannon] i.e., because "carriage" is the word for the frame
in which a cannon rests.

[747] passes] bouts; him] i.e., Laertes; twelve for nine] i.e., that
Laertes will hit twelve times for Hamlet's nine. (It is difficult to see how this will be accomplished within twelve
passes.)

[748] breathing time] period for exercise.

[749] lapwing ... head] (proverb). The lapwing is a bird that
leaves the nest so quickly after being hatched that its
eggshell may be seen on its head—i.e., Osric is a pre-
tentious young man.

[750] He ... it] He paid flattery to his mother's breast before
he suckled.

same bevy that I know the drossy age dotes on— only got the tune of the time and outward habit of encounter, a kind of yeasty collection, which carries them through and through the most fond and winnowed opinions; and do but blow them to their trial, the bubbles are out.[751]   195

Enter a LORD.

LORD. My lord, his majesty commended him to you   200
by young Osric, who brings back to him, that you
attend him in the hall. He sends to know if your
pleasure hold to play with Laertes, or that you will
take longer time.

HAMLET. I am constant to my purposes; they follow   205
the king's pleasure. If his fitness speaks, mine is ready;
now, or whensoever, provided I be so able as now.

LORD. The king, and queen, and all are coming
down.

HAMLET. In happy time.[752]   210

LORD. The queen desires you to use some gentle
entertainment to Laertes before you fall to play.[753]

HAMLET. She well instructs me. [*Exit LORD.*]

HORATIO. You will lose this wager, my lord.

HAMLET. I do not think so; since he went into   215
France, I have been in continual practice; I shall
win at the odds. But thou wouldst not think how
ill all's here about my heart; but it is no matter.

HORATIO. Nay, good my lord,—

HAMLET. It is but foolery; but it is such a kind of   220
gain-giving as would perhaps trouble a woman.[754]

HORATIO. If your mind dislike any thing, obey it; I
will forestall their repair hither, and say you are not
fit.

HAMLET. Not a whit, we defy augury; there's a   225
special providence in the fall of a sparrow.[755] If it
be now, 'tis not to come; if it be not to come, it

will be now; if it be not now, yet it will come. The
readiness is all. Since no man knows aught of what
he leaves, what is't to leave betimes? Let be.   230

Enter KING, QUEEN, LAERTES, LORDS, OSRIC, and ATTENDANTS with foils, &c.

KING. Come, Hamlet, come, and take this hand
    from me.

[*The KING puts the hand of LAERTES into that of HAMLET.*]

HAMLET. Give me your pardon, sir. I've done you
    wrong;
But pardon't, as you are a gentleman.
This presence knows,
And you must needs have heard, how I am   235
    punished
With sore distraction. What I have done,
That might your nature, honour and exception[756]
Roughly awake, I here proclaim was madness.
Was't Hamlet wronged Laertes? Never Hamlet:
If Hamlet from himself be ta'en away,   240
And when he's not himself does wrong Laertes,
Then Hamlet does it not; Hamlet denies it.
Who does it, then? His madness. If 't be so,
Hamlet is of the faction that is wronged;
His madness is poor Hamlet's enemy.   245
Sir, in this audience,[757]
Let my disclaiming from a purposed evil
Free me so far in your most generous thoughts,
That I have shot my arrow o'er the house,
And hurt my brother.   250

LAERTES.   I am satisfied in nature,
Whose motive in this case should stir me most
To my revenge; but in my terms of honour
I stand aloof, and will no reconcilement,
Till by some elder masters, of known honour,
I have a voice and precedent of peace,[758]   255
To keep my name ungored. But till that time,
I do receive your offered love like love,
And will not wrong it.

---

751 bevy] company; drossy] frivolous; tune of the time] fashionable manner of speaking; yeasty collection] build-up of froth; fanned and winnowed] selected and sifted; and … out] if one tests how substantial these words are by blowing, the bubbles (of yeasty froth) will burst.

752 in happy time] opportunely.

753 use … entertainment] speak politely.

754 gain-giving] misgiving.

755 there's … sparrow] Cf. Matthew 10:29.

756 exception] disapproval.

757 The partial lines here and at 229 may indicate that Hamlet pauses briefly.

758 voice and precedent] authoritative pronouncement.

HAMLET.   I embrace it freely;
  And will this brother's wager frankly play.
  Give us the foils. Come on.   260
LAERTES.   Come, one for me.
HAMLET. I'll be your foil, Laertes. In mine
    ignorance[759]
  Your skill shall, like a star i' the darkest night,
  Stick fiery off indeed.[760]
LAERTES.   You mock me, sir.
HAMLET. No, by this hand.
KING. Give them the foils, young Osric. Cousin   265
    Hamlet,
  You know the wager?
HAMLET.   Very well, my lord;
  Your Grace hath laid the odds o' the weaker side.
KING. I do not fear it; I have seen you both;
  But since he is bettered, we have therefore odds.[761]
LAERTES. This is too heavy; let me see another.   270
HAMLET. This likes me well. These foils have all a
    length?
OSRIC. Ay, my good lord.

[*They prepare to play.*]

KING. Set me the stoups of wine upon that table.
  If Hamlet give the first or second hit,
  Or quit in answer of the third exchange,[762]   275
  Let all the battlements their ordnance fire;
  The king shall drink to Hamlet's better breath;
  And in the cup an union shall he throw,[763]
  Richer than that which four successive kings
  In Denmark's crown have worn—give me the cups— 280
  And let the kettle to the trumpet speak,[764]
  The trumpet to the cannoneer without,
  The cannons to the heavens, the heaven to earth:
  "Now the king drinks to Hamlet!" Come, begin;
  And you, the judges, bear a wary eye.   285

---

759 foil] pun on weapon and jewel setting.
760 stick fiery off] appear in bright relief.
761 bettered] adjudged the better swordsman by public
    opinion; odds] betting odds, i.e., the three-hit differ-
    ence.
762 quit] repay, i.e., draw equal in the third bout.
763 an union] a fine (unique) pearl.
764 kettle] kettledrum.

HAMLET. Come on, sir.
LAERTES.   Come, my lord.

[*They play.*]

HAMLET.   One.
LAERTES.   No.
HAMLET.   Judgment!
OSRIC. A hit, a very palpable hit.
LAERTES.   Well, again.
KING. Stay; give me drink. Hamlet, this pearl is thine.
  Here's to thy health.

[*Drinks, then drops pearl into cup. Drum, trumpets,
cannon shot.*]

                    Give him the cup.
HAMLET. I'll play this bout first; set it by awhile.   290
  Come. [*They play.*] Another hit; what say you?
LAERTES. A touch, a touch; I do confess.
KING. Our son shall win.
QUEEN.   He's fat, and scant of breath.[765]
  Here, Hamlet, take my napkin, rub thy brows.[766]
  The queen carouses to thy fortune, Hamlet.   295
HAMLET. Good madam.
KING.   Gertrude, do not drink.
QUEEN. I will, my lord; I pray you pardon me.
  [*She drinks.*]
KING. [*Aside.*] It is the poisoned cup! It is too late.
HAMLET. I dare not drink yet, madam; by and by.
QUEEN. Come, let me wipe thy face.   300
LAERTES. My lord, I'll hit him now.
KING.   I do not think't.
LAERTES. [*Aside.*] And yet 'tis almost against my
    conscience.
HAMLET. Come for the third, Laertes! You but dally;
  I pray you pass with your best violence.
  I am afeard you make a wanton of me.[767]   305
LAERTES. Say you so? Come on. [*They play.*]
OSRIC. Nothing, neither way.
LAERTES. Have at you now!

[*LAERTES wounds HAMLET; then, in scuffling, they
change rapiers, and HAMLET wounds LAERTES.*]

---

765 fat] possibly meaning "sweaty" rather than "overweight."
766 napkin] handkerchief.
767 wanton] spoiled child.

KING.   Part them! They are incensed.

HAMLET. Nay, come, again. [*The QUEEN falls.*]

OSRIC.   Look to the queen there, ho!

HORATIO. They bleed on both sides. How is it, my   310
    lord?

OSRIC. How is it, Laertes?

LAERTES. Why, as a woodcock to mine own springe
    Osric;[768]
  I am justly killed with mine own treachery.

HAMLET. How does the queen?

KING.   She swoons to see them bleed.

QUEEN. No, no, the drink, the drink—O my dear   315
    Hamlet!
  The drink, the drink; I am poisoned. [*Dies.*]

HAMLET. O villany! Ho! Let the door be locked:
  Treachery! Seek it out. [*LAERTES falls.*]

LAERTES. It is here, Hamlet. Hamlet, thou art slain.
  No medicine in the world can do thee good;   320
  In thee there is not half an hour of life.
  The treacherous instrument is in thy hand,
  Unbated and envenomed. The foul practice[769]
  Hath turned itself on me. Lo, here I lie,
  Never to rise again. Thy mother's poisoned.   325
  I can no more. The king—the king's to blame.

HAMLET. The point envenomed too! Then, venom,
  to thy work!

[*Stabs the KING.*]

ALL. Treason! treason!

KING. O, yet defend me, friends; I am but hurt.

HAMLET. Here, thou incestuous, murderous,   330
    damnéd Dane,
  Drink off this potion. Is thy union here?
  Follow my mother. [*KING dies.*]

LAERTES.   He is justly served:
  It is a poison tempered by himself.[770]
  Exchange forgiveness with me, noble Hamlet:
  Mine and my father's death come not upon thee,   335
  Nor thine on me! [*Dies.*]

HAMLET. Heaven make thee free of it! I follow thee.
  I am dead, Horatio. Wretched queen, adieu!
  You that look pale and tremble at this chance,

That are but mutes or audience to this act,[771]   340
Had I but time—as this fell sergeant, death,[772]
Is strict in his arrest—O, I could tell you—
But let it be. Horatio, I am dead;
Thou liv'st; report me and my cause aright
To the unsatisfied.[773]   345

HORATIO.   Never believe it;
  I am more an antique Roman than a Dane:[774]
  Here's yet some liquor left.

HAMLET.   As thou 'rt a man,
  Give me the cup. Let go, by heaven, I'll have't.
  O God! Horatio, what a wounded name,
  Things standing thus unknown, shall live behind me!   350
  If thou didst ever hold me in thy heart,
  Absent thee from felicity awhile,[775]
  And in this harsh world draw thy breath in pain,
  To tell my story.

[*March afar off, and shot within.*]

  What war-like noise is this?   355

OSRIC. Young Fortinbras, with conquest come from
    Poland,
  To the ambassadors of England gives
  This war-like volley.

HAMLET.   O! I die, Horatio;
  The potent poison quite o'er-crows my spirit.[776]
  I cannot live to hear the news from England,   360
  But I do prophesy the election lights[777]
  On Fortinbras. He has my dying voice.[778]
  So tell him, with the occurrents, more and less,[779]
  Which have solicited—The rest is silence. [*Dies.*]

HORATIO. Now cracks a noble heart. Good night,   365
    sweet prince,
  And flights of angels sing thee to thy rest!

[*March within.*]

---

768 woodcock] a stupid bird, easily caught; springe] trap.
769 Unbated] unblunted; practice] plot.
770 tempered] mixed.

771 mutes] performers who have no lines.
772 fell sergeant] dread sheriff's officer.
773 unsatisfied] uninformed.
774 more … Dane] i.e., one who prefers suicide to an un-
    desirable life.
775 felicity] i.e., of death.
776 o'er-crows] triumphs over.
777 election] i.e., of Denmark's new King.
778 voice] recommendation as successor.
779 occurrents] occurrences.

Why does the drum come hither?

*Enter FORTINBRAS, the English Ambassadors, and
Others.*

FORTINBRAS. Where is this sight?

HORATIO.   What is it you will see?
If aught of woe or wonder, cease your search.

FORTINBRAS. This quarry cries on havoc. O proud   370
death![780]
What feast is toward in thine eternal cell,[781]
That thou so many princes at a shot
So bloodily hast struck?

1ST AMBASSADOR.   The sight is dismal;
And our affairs from England come too late.
The ears are senseless that should give us hearing,   375
To tell him his commandment is fulfilled,
That Rosencrantz and Guildenstern are dead.
Where should we have our thanks?

HORATIO.   Not from his mouth,[782]
Had it the ability of life to thank you:
He never gave commandment for their death.   380
But since, so jump upon this bloody question,[783]
You from the Polack wars, and you from England,
Are here arrived, give order that these bodies
High on a stage be placed to the view;[784]
And let me speak to the yet unknowing world   385
How these things came about. So shall you hear
Of carnal, bloody, and unnatural acts,
Of accidental judgments, casual slaughters;[785]
Of deaths put on by cunning and forced cause,
And, in this upshot, purposes mistook   390
Fall'n on the inventors' heads; all this can I
Truly deliver.

FORTINBRAS.   Let us haste to hear it,
And call the noblest to the audience.
For me, with sorrow I embrace my fortune;
I have some rights of memory in this kingdom,[786]   395
Which now to claim my vantage doth invite me.[787]

HORATIO. Of that I shall have also cause to speak,
And from his mouth whose voice will draw on
more.[788]
But let this same be presently performed,
Even while men's minds are wild, lest more   400
mischance
On plots and errors happen.[789]

FORTINBRAS.   Let four captains
Bear Hamlet, like a soldier, to the stage;
For he was likely, had he been put on,[790]
To have proved most royal: and, for his passage,[791]
The soldiers' music and the rites of war   405
Speak loudly for him.
Take up the bodies. Such a sight as this
Becomes the field, but here shows much amiss.[792]
Go, bid the soldiers shoot.

*[A dead march. Exeunt, bearing off the bodies; after
which a peal of ordnance is shot off.]*

---

780 quarry] heap of bodies (as from a hunt); cries on havoc]
proclaims mass slaughter.
781 What feast … cell] i.e., what feast on the bodies of the
dead lies ahead of you in your cave (as if death were a
wild predator).
782 his] i.e., Claudius's—if Hamlet were meant, Horatio
would be lying.
783 so jump … question] so precisely at the moment this
bloody event ended.
784 stage] platform.
785 accidental judgements] just retribution achieved by
chance; casual slaughter] manslaughter (not deliberate
murder).

---

786 rights of memory] traditional rights still recalled.
787 vantage] favourable opportunity.
788 draw on more] encourage the support of others.
789 On] on the basis of.
790 put on] put to the test.
791 passage] death.
792 field] battlefield.

WILLIAM SHAKESPEARE

The Tempest

Scholarly consensus declares *The Tempest* (1611) to be the last play that Shakespeare wrote on his own before retiring to Stratford. *Henry VIII* and *Two Noble Kinsmen*, which appeared later, were collaborations with John Fletcher (and indeed, may represent unfinished projects of Shakespeare's that Fletcher inherited after the older playwright's retirement). The idea that Shakespeare wrote *The Tempest* with his imminent retirement in view has inspired some readers to read it as Shakespeare's farewell to the theatre; indeed, many elements in the play—particularly the epilogue spoken by Prospero—seem hospitable to such a reading.

At the same time, it should be stressed that there are many different ways of looking at *The Tempest*, and to insist on any one at the expense of others is to do a disservice to the play's complexity. For example, some critics have looked to contemporary historical events for a context for the play, pointing to the influence which the accounts of travelers to the New World appear to have had on Shakespeare. In particular, he may have been inspired by accounts of an expedition that took place in 1609. A fleet of nine ships en route to Virginia from Plymouth met with a storm off the coast of Bermuda, and the flagship, the *Sea-Adventure*, was presumed lost with all her passengers, including the admiral and the future governor of Virginia. Nearly a year later, however, the missing passengers turned up in Virginia, explaining that they had been washed ashore in the Bermuda islands, where they had managed to live fairly comfortably while they rebuilt the smaller boats which had been attached to the ship. The written account of this event was not published until 1625, well after *The Tempest* was first produced, but it did circulate in manuscript and it is quite possible that Shakespeare read it shortly before writing his play. Another description of the New World that he might have read was *A Briefe and True Report of the New Found Land of Virginia*, the first original book related to America, written in 1588 by Thomas Hariot (1560–1621), who had accompanied Sir Walter Raleigh as historian and surveyor in the first attempt to found an English colony in North America. Indeed, Hariot, a brilliant polymath who had mastered mathematics, science and astronomy, and with his *Briefe and True Report* became one of the world's first ethnographers, is sometimes named—along with the alchemist, astrologer and mathematician John Dee (1527–1608)—as a possible source for the character of Prospero. Of course, the characters of these men and the accounts of the colonists were inspirational rather than direct sources for Shakespeare, but it does appear that Shakespeare took at least some conscious interest in the theme of colonialism. One of his minor sources that has been identified is Montaigne's essay "On Cannibals," which is a sympathetic account of "natural" as opposed to "artificial" societies. (Caliban, as many people have noticed, is nearly an anagram of the word cannibal.)

But even if we set aside all autobiographical and historical considerations, we find a richly suggestive context for *The Tempest* when we consider its relations to Shakespeare's other plays. When the folio edition of Shakespeare's plays was first published in 1623, the plays were grouped into tragedies, comedies and histories, but there was a group of plays written late in Shakespeare's career that did not fit easily into any of those categories: *Pericles, Cymbeline, The Winter's Tale*, and *The Tempest*. Perhaps it was partly because of the inappropriate categorization and consequent misunderstanding of these plays that they were, for a time, less highly regarded than some of the earlier work—as if they represented a falling off of skill late in Shakespeare's career. In any case, that view no longer persists, for it is recognized that Shakespeare was attempting something different in these four late plays, which are now spoken of as "romances," a genre in which a near-tragedy is averted and contained by a structure of comic fantasy. The overall effect resembles fairytales and folklore, which seem similarly disinterested in observable human behaviour, instead concerning themselves with a realm made of colourful representations of desires and anxieties. So, one of the cardinal rules for approaching *The Tempest* and the other romances is that the reader should try to set aside questions of plausibility and realistic psychological observation, and look instead at questions of meaning and symbolism. Is the storm that opens the play, for instance, perhaps less significant considered as an actual storm than as the representation of a chaotic state of being or morality? And when Prospero says of Caliban, "this thing of darkness I acknowledge mine," how deeply should we understand that identification? Similarly, what does it mean that Prospero has enslaved the spirit, Ariel? As we begin to ask such questions we realize that, as simple as the story told by *The Tempest* seems, it embraces certain complex answers that lie "deeper than e'er plummet sounded."

[C.S.W.]

WILLIAM SHAKESPEARE
The Tempest

CHARACTERS:
  ALONSO, *King of Naples*
  SEBASTIAN, *his brother*
  PROSPERO, *the right Duke of Milan*
  ANTONIO, *his brother, the usurping Duke of Milan*
  FERDINAND, *son to the King of Naples*
  GONZALO, *an honest old councillor*
  ADRIAN & FRANCISCO, *lords*
  CALIBAN, *a savage and deformed slave*
  TRINCULO, *a jester*
  STEPHANO, *a drunken butler*
  MASTER *of the ship*
  BOATSWAIN
  MARINERS
  MIRANDA, *daughter to Prospero*

ARIEL, *an airy spirit*
IRIS, CERES, JUNO, NYMPHS & REAPERS,
  [*presented by*] *spirits*

THE SCENE: *AN UNINHABITED ISLAND*

ACT I.

SCENE I.

The deck of a ship. A tempestuous noise
of thunder and lightning heard.

Enter a SHIPMASTER and a BOATSWAIN.

MASTER. Boatswain!
BOATSWAIN. Here, master. What cheer?

MASTER. Good, speak to the mariners.[1] Fall to't yarely, or we run ourselves aground.[2] Bestir, bestir! [*Exit*] 5

[*Enter MARINERS*]

BOATSWAIN. Heigh, my hearts! Cheerly, cheerly, my hearts! Yare, yare! Take in the topsail. Tend to th'master's whistle![3] —Blow till thou burst thy wind, if room enough![4]

[*Enter ALONSO, SEBASTIAN, ANTONIO, FERDINAND, GONZALO, and others*]

ALONSO. Good boatswain, have care! Where's the master? Play the men.[5] 10

BOATSWAIN. I pray now, keep below.

ANTONIO. Where is the master, boson?

BOATSWAIN. Do you not hear him?[6] You mar our labour: keep your cabins: you do assist the storm. 15

GONZALO. Nay, good, be patient.

BOATSWAIN. When the sea is. Hence! What cares these roarers for the name of king?[7] To cabin! Silence! Trouble us not.

GONZALO. Good, yet remember whom thou hast aboard. 20

BOATSWAIN. None that I more love than myself. You are counsellor: if you can command these elements to silence, and work the peace of the present, we will not hand a rope more.[8] Use your authority: 25 if you cannot, give thanks you have lived so long, and make yourself ready in your cabin for the mischance of the hour, if it so hap.—Cheerly, good hearts!—Out of our way, I say. [*Exit*]

GONZALO. I have great comfort from this fellow. 30 Methinks he hath no drowning mark upon him:

his complexion is perfect gallows.[9] Stand fast, good Fate, to his hanging! make the rope of his destiny our cable, for our own doth little advantage! If he be not born to be hanged, our case is miserable. 35 [*Exeunt*]

Re-enter BOATSWAIN

BOATSWAIN. Down with the topmast! yare! lower, lower! Bring her to try wi' th' maincourse. [*A cry within*] A plague—upon this howling! They are louder than the weather or our office.[10] 40

Re-enter SEBASTIAN, ANTONIO, and GONZALO

Yet again! What do you here? Shall we give o'er, and drown? Have you a mind to sink?

SEBASTIAN. A pox o' your throat, you bawling, blasphemous, incharitable dog!

BOATSWAIN. Work you, then. 45

ANTONIO. Hang, cur, hang! you whoreson, insolent noisemaker, we are less afraid to be drowned than thou art.

GONZALO. I'll warrant him for drowning, though the ship were no stronger than a nutshell, and as 50 leaky as an unstanched wench.[11]

BOATSWAIN. Lay her a-hold, a-hold! Set her two courses! Off to sea again: lay her off![12]

Enter MARINERS, wet

MARINERS. All lost! To prayers, to prayers! All lost! [*Exeunt*] 55

BOATSWAIN. What, must our mouths be cold?[13]

---

1 Good] good boatswain or fellow.
2 yarely] quickly.
3 Tend] attend.
4 Blow … enough] addressed to the storm.
5 Play] meaning either "ply," i.e., "work the sailors"; or "act," i.e., "take manful charge of the ship"; in either case, an uncalled-for reproof.
6 hear him] i.e., his whistle.
7 roarers] i.e., noisy waves considered as bullies.
8 hand] handle.

9 complexion … gallows] His face suggests a criminal character that is destined to die by hanging. Proverb: "He that's born to be hanged need fear no drowning."
10 The dash after "plague" may indicate that a blasphemous curse was censored; our office] the noise of our work.
11 warrant … for] guarantee … against; unstanched] loose.
12 Having lowered the topsail to stop the drift towards the island, the boatswain orders the sails up again to steer clear of the shore.
13 must … cold] Sailors in grave difficulties often drank in the last moments. The boatswain could be making a grim joke, though some productions have him drinking and snarling defiance at the royal party.

GONZALO. The King and Prince at prayers! Let us
    assist them,
  For our case is as theirs.
SEBASTIAN. I am out of patience.
ANTONIO. We are merely cheated of our lives by   60
    drunkards.[14]
  This wide-chapped rascal—would thou might'st
    lie drowning[15]
  The washing of ten tides![16]
GONZALO. He'll be hanged yet,
  Though every drop of water swear against it,
  And gape at wid'st to glut him.[17]   65

*A confused noise within:—'Mercy on us!'—'We split,
we split!'—'Farewell, my wife and children!'—
'Farewell, brother!'—'We split, we split, we split!'—*

ANTONIO. Let's all sink wi' the King.
SEBASTIAN.   Let's take leave of him. [*They exit*]
GONZALO. Now would I give a thousand furlongs
  of sea for an acre of barren ground—long heath,
  brown furze, any thing.[18] The wills above be done!   70
  but I would fain die dry death. [*Exit*]

SCENE II.

The Island. Before the cell of PROSPERO.[19]

Enter PROSPERO and MIRANDA.

MIRANDA. If by your art, my dearest father, you have
  Put the wild waters in this roar, allay them.
  The sky, it seems, would pour down stinking pitch,
  But that the sea, mounting to th' welkin's cheek,[20]
  Dashes the fire out. O, I have suffered   5
  With those that I saw suffer: a brave vessel,[21]

---

14 merely] utterly.
15 wide-chapped] big-mouthed.
16 ten tides] Pirates were often executed by being tied
  down to the shore at low tide until three high tides had
  washed over them.
17 glut] gulp.
18 long heath, brown furze] heather, a weed similar to
  quack grass.
19 cell] any small, close dwelling.
20 welkin's cheek] face of the sky.
21 brave] handsome, impressive.

Who had, no doubt, some noble creatures in her,
Dashed all to pieces! O, the cry did knock
Against my very heart. Poor souls, they perished.
Had I been any god of power, I would   10
Have sunk the sea within the earth, or ere[22]
It should the good ship so have swallowed and
The fraughting souls within her.
PROSPERO.   Be collected.
  No more amazement. Tell your piteous heart[23]
  There's no harm done.   15
MIRANDA.   O, woe the day!
PROSPERO.   No harm.
  I have done nothing but in care of thee,
  Of thee, my dear one, thee, my daughter, who
  Art ignorant of what thou art, nought knowing
  Of whence I am: nor that I am more better
  Than Prospero, master of a full poor cell,   20
  And thy no greater father.
MIRANDA.   More to know
  Did never meddle with my thoughts.[24]
PROSPERO.   'Tis time
  I should inform thee farther. Lend thy hand,
  And pluck my magic garment from me.—So:
  Lie there my art.—Wipe thou thine eyes; have   25
    comfort.[25]
  The direful spectacle of the wrack, which touched
  The very virtue of compassion in thee,[26]
  I have with such provision in mine art[27]
  So safely orderèd that there is no soul—
  No, not so much perdition as an hair— [28]   30
  Betid to any creature in the vessel[29]
  Which thou heard'st cry, which thou saw'st sink.
    Sit down;
  For thou must now know farther.
MIRANDA.   You have often
  Begun to tell me what I am: but stopped,

---

22 or ere] before.
23 amazement] bewilderment; piteous] full of pity.
24 More … thoughts] The desire to know more never disrupted my mind.
25 art] magic robe (symbol of his art).
26 virtue] essence.
27 provision] foresight.
28 perdition] loss.
29 Betid] happened.

And left me to a bootless inquisition,[30]   35
  Concluding, 'Stay; not yet.'
PROSPERO.   The hour's now come,
  The very minute bids thee ope thine ear.
  Obey, and be attentive. Canst thou remember[31]
  A time before we came unto this cell?
  I do not think thou canst: for then thou wast not   40
  Out three years old.[32]
MIRANDA.   Certainly, sir, I can.
PROSPERO. By what? By any other house, or person?
  Of any thing the image, tell me, that
  Hath kept with thy remembrance.
MIRANDA.   'Tis far off,
  And rather like a dream than an assurance   45
  That my remembrance warrants. Had I not[33]
  Four, or five, women once, that tended me?
PROSPERO. Thou hadst, and more, Miranda. But
    how is it
  That this lives in thy mind? What seest thou else
  In the dark backward and abysm of time?[34]   50
  If thou rememb'rest aught ere thou cam'st here,
  How thou cam'st here, thou mayst.
MIRANDA.   But that I do not.
PROSPERO. Twelve year since, Miranda, twelve year
    since,[35]
  Thy father was the Duke of Milan, and
  A prince of power.   55
MIRANDA.   Sir, are not you my father?
PROSPERO. Thy mother was a piece of virtue, and[36]
  She said thou wast my daughter; and thy father
  Was Duke of Milan, and his only heir
  A princess—no worse issuèd.[37]
MIRANDA.   O, the heavens!
  What foul play had we that we came from thence?   60
  Or blessèd was't we did?
PROSPERO.   Both, both, my girl.
  By foul play, as thou say'st, were we heaved thence,

But blessedly holp hither.[38]
MIRANDA.   O, my heart bleeds
  To think o' th' teen that I have turned you to,[39]
  Which is from my remembrance. Please you,   65
    further. [40]
PROSPERO. My brother and thy uncle, called
    Antonio—
  I pray thee, mark me: that a brother should
  Be so perfidious!—he, whom next thyself,
  Of all the world I loved, and to him put
  The manage of my state—as at that time[41]   70
  Through all the signories it was the first,[42]
  And Prospero the prime duke, being so reputed
  In dignity, and for the liberal arts,
  Without a parallel—those being all my study,
  The government I cast upon my brother,   75
  And to my state grew stranger, being transported
  And rapt in secret studies. Thy false uncle—
  Dost thou attend me?
MIRANDA.   Sir, most heedfully.
PROSPERO. —Being once perfected how to grant suits,
  How to deny them, who t' advance, and who   80
  To trash for over-topping; new-created[43]
  The creatures that were mine, I say, or changed
    'em,[44]
  Or else new formed 'em; having both the key[45]
  Of officer and office, set all hearts i' th' state
  To what tune pleased his ear, that now he was   85
  The ivy which had hid my princely trunk,
  And sucked my verdure out on't—Thou attend'st
    not.
MIRANDA. O, good sir! I do.
PROSPERO.   I pray thee, mark me.

---

30 bootless inquisition] useless inquiry.
31 Obey] i.e., the request "ope thine ear."
32 Out] fully.
33 remembrance warrants] memory guarantees.
34 backward] past; abysm] abyss.
35 Miranda is, then, about fifteen years old.
36 piece] masterpiece.
37 no … issuèd] of no lesser birth.

---

38 blessedly holp] providentially helped.
39 teen … to] strife I have made you recall.
40 from] absent from.
41 put … state] entrusted administration of my dukedom.
The fragmented grammar in this section suggests
Prospero's agitation.
42 signories] states in Northern Italy ruled by a signor.
43 trash for over-topping] punish for "getting too big for
their britches"; to "trash" is to use a cord to pull up a
hound in training.
44 or] either.
45 key] pun: key to a lock, musical key.

I, thus neglecting worldly ends, all dedicated
To closeness and the bettering of my mind[46]   90
With that, which, but by being so retired,
O'er-prized all popular rate, in my false brother[47]
Awaked an evil nature; and my trust,
Like a good parent, did beget of him[48]
A falsehood, in its contrary, as great   95
As my trust was—which had indeed no limit:
A confidence sans bound! He, being thus lorded,[49]
Not only with what my revenue yielded,
But what my power might else exact—like one
Who having, into truth, by telling of it,[50]   100
Made such a sinner of his memory,
To credit his own lie: he did believe
He was, indeed, the Duke—out o' the
   substitution,[51]
And executing th'outward face of royalty,
With all prerogative. Hence, his ambition growing—   105
Dost thou hear?

MIRANDA.   Your tale, sir, would cure deafness.

PROSPERO. To have no screen between this part he
   played
And him he played it for, he needs will be
Absolute Milan! Me, poor man—my library[52]
Was dukedom large enough! Of temporal royalties[53]   110
He thinks me now incapable; confederates—[54]
So dry he was for sway—wi' th' King of Naples[55]
To give him annual tribute, do him homage;

Subject his coronet to his crown, and bend[56]
The dukedom, yet unbowed—alas, poor Milan!—   115
To most ignoble stooping.

MIRANDA.   O, the heavens!

PROSPERO. Mark his condition, and the event; then
   tell me[57]
If this might be a brother.

MIRANDA.   I should sin
To think but nobly of my grandmother:
Good wombs have borne bad sons.   120

PROSPERO.   Now the condition:
This King of Naples, being an enemy
To me inveterate, hearkens my brother's suit;
Which was, that he, in lieu o' the premises[58]
Of homage and I know not how much tribute,
Should presently extirpate me and mine[59]   125
Out of the dukedom, and confer fair Milan,
With all the honours on my brother. Whereon,
A treacherous army levied, one midnight
Fated to the purpose, did Antonio open[60]
The gates of Milan; and, i' th' dead of darkness,   130
The ministers for th' purpose hurried thence[61]
Me and thy crying self.

MIRANDA.   Alack, for pity!
I, not rememb'ring how I cried out then,
Will cry it o'er again: it is a hint[62]
That wrings mine eyes to't.   135

PROSPERO.   Hear a little further,
And then I'll bring thee to the present business
Which now's upon us; without the which this story
Were most impertinent.[63]

MIRANDA.   Wherefore did they not
That hour destroy us?

PROSPERO.   Well demanded, wench;
My tale provokes that question. Dear, they durst not,   140
So dear the love my people bore me, nor set

---

46 closeness] secluded study.
47 O'er-prized ... rate] was much more valuable than
   popular opinion held it to be.
48 good parent] refers to a proverbial belief that unusually
   good parents beget unusually inferior offspring.
49 sans bound] without limit.
50 it] i.e., the "lie" of line 102.
51 out ... prerogative] because, in substituting for me, he
   had been assuming all the appearances of royalty and
   enjoying all of its privileges.
52 Absolute Milan] the actual Duke.
53 temporal royalties] royal activities belonging to the
   world (i.e., politics, as opposed to comprehending royalty in a spiritual sense).
54 confederates] verb: joins league with.
55 so dry] so thirsty, desperate (as to treasonously subject
   Milan to a larger rival state).

---

56 his ... his] i.e., Antonio's ... the King's.
57 condition] compact with the King (as see below); event]
   its consequences.
58 in ... premises] in return for assurances.
59 presently] immediately.
60 Fated] designated (i.e., the midnight).
61 ministers] agents.
62 hint] occasion.
63 impertinent] irrelevant.

A mark so bloody on the business; but
With colours fairer painted their foul ends.
In few, they hurried us aboard a bark,[64]
Bore us some leagues to sea, where they prepared   145
A rotten carcass of a butt, not rigged,[65]
Nor tackle, sail, nor mast; the very rats
Instinctively have quit it. There they hoist us,
To cry to th' sea, that roared to us; to sigh
To th' winds, whose pity, sighing back again,   150
Did us but loving wrong.

MIRANDA.   Alack, what trouble
Was I then to you!

PROSPERO.   O, a cherubin
Thou wast, that did preserve me! Thou didst smile,
Infusèd with a fortitude from heaven,
When I have decked the sea with drops full salt,   155
Under my burden groaned: which raised in me
An undergoing stomach, to bear up[66]
Against what should ensue.

MIRANDA. How came we ashore?

PROSPERO.   By Providence divine.
Some food we had and some fresh water that   160
A noble Neapolitan, Gonzalo,
Out of his charity—who being then appointed
Master of this design—did give us, with
Rich garments, linens, stuffs, and necessaries,
Which since have steaded much. So, of his   165
    gentleness,[67]
Knowing I loved my books, he furnished me,
From mine own library with volumes that
I prize above my dukedom.

MIRANDA.   Would I might
But ever see that man![68]

PROSPERO.   Now I arise.
Sit still, and hear the last of our sea-sorrow.   170
Here in this island we arrived: and here
Have I, thy schoolmaster, made thee more profit[69]
Than other princes can, that have more time
For vainer hours, and tutors not so careful.

MIRANDA. Heavens thank you for't! And now, I   175
    pray you, sir—
For still 'tis beating in my mind—your reason
For raising this sea-storm?

PROSPERO.   Know thus far forth.
By accident most strange, bountiful Fortune,
Now my dear lady, hath mine enemies
Brought to this shore; and by my prescience   180
I find my zenith doth depend upon[70]
A most auspicious star, whose influence
If now I court not but omit, my fortunes[71]
Will ever after droop. Here cease more questions;
Thou art inclined to sleep; 'tis a good dulness,   185
And give it way. I know thou canst not choose.

[*MIRANDA sleeps*]

Come away, servant, come! I am ready now.[72]
Approach, my Ariel: come!

[*Enter ARIEL*]

ARIEL. All hail, great master! Grave sir, hail! I come
To answer thy best pleasure; be't to fly,   190
To swim, to dive into the fire, to ride
On the curled clouds; to thy strong bidding, task[73]
Ariel and all his quality.[74]

PROSPERO.   Hast thou, spirit,
Performed to point the tempest that I bade thee?[75]

ARIEL. To every article.   195
I boarded the King's ship; now on the beak,[76]
Now in the waist, the deck, in every cabin,[77]
I flamed amazement; sometime I'd divide,
And burn in many places; on the topmast,[78]
The yards and boresprit, would I flame distinctly,[79]   200
Then meet and join: Jove's lightnings, the precursors
O' th' dreadful thunder-claps, more momentary

---

64 few] i.e., few words; bark] small ship.
65 butt] tub.
66 undergoing stomach] fortitude, guts.
67 steaded] been useful, of good stead; So] in the same way.
68 But ever] only someday.
69 more profit] profit more.

70 zenith] height of fortune.
71 omit] i.e., omit to court.
72 Come away] come here.
73 task] i.e., put to the task.
74 quality] associates, other spirits.
75 to point] in every detail.
76 beak] prow.
77 waist] middle.
78 Cf. St. Elmo's fire.
79 boresprit] bowsprit.

And sight-outrunning were not: the fire and cracks
Of sulphurous roaring the most mighty Neptune
Seem to besiege and make his bold waves tremble,   205
Yea, his dread trident shake.

PROSPERO.   My brave spirit!
Who was so firm, so constant, that this coil[80]
Would not infect his reason?

ARIEL.   Not a soul
But felt a fever of the mad, and played
Some tricks of desperation. All but mariners[81]   210
Plunged in the foaming brine and quit the vessel,
Then all afire with me: the King's son, Ferdinand,
With hair up-staring—then like reeds, not hair—[82]
Was the first man that leapt; cried 'Hell is empty,
And all the devils are here!'   215

PROSPERO.   Why, that's my spirit!
But was not this nigh shore?

ARIEL.   Close by, my master.

PROSPERO. But are they, Ariel, safe?

ARIEL.   Not a hair perished;
On their sustaining garments not a blemish,[83]
But fresher than before: and, as thou bad'st me,
In troops I have dispersed them 'bout the isle.   220
The king's son have I landed by himself,
Whom I left cooling of the air with sighs
In an odd angle of the isle, and sitting,
His arms in this sad knot.[84]

PROSPERO.   Of the King's ship
The mariners, say how thou hast disposed,   225
And all the rest o' th' fleet?

ARIEL.   Safely in harbour
Is the King's ship; in the deep nook where once
Thou call'dst me up at midnight to fetch dew
From the still-vexed Bermoothes, there she's hid;[85]
The mariners all under hatches stowed;   230

Who, with a charm (joined to their suffered
    labour),[86]
I have left asleep; and for the rest o' th' fleet
Which I dispersed, they all have met again,
And are upon the Mediterranean flote[87]
Bound sadly home for Naples,   235
Supposing that they saw the king's ship wracked,
And his great person perish.

PROSPERO.   Ariel, thy charge
Exactly is performed; but there's more work:
What is the time o' th' day?

ARIEL.   Past the mid season.[88]

PROSPERO. At least two glasses. The time 'twixt six   240
    and now[89]
Must by us both be spent most preciously.

ARIEL. Is there more toil? Since thou dost give me pains,
Let me remember thee what thou hast promised,[90]
Which is not yet performed me.

PROSPERO.   How now? moody?
What is't thou canst demand?   245

ARIEL.   My liberty.

PROSPERO. Before the time be out? No more![91]

ARIEL.   I prithee,
Remember I have done thee worthy service;
Told thee no lies, made no mistakings, served
Without or grudge or grumblings: thou didst
    promise
To bate me a full year.[92]   250

PROSPERO.   Dost thou forget
From what a torment I did free thee?

ARIEL.   No.

PROSPERO. Thou dost; and think'st it much to
    tread the ooze
Of the salt deep,
To run upon the sharp wind of the north,
To do me business in the veins o' th' earth[93]   255
When it is baked with frost.[94]

---

80 coil] uproar, confusion.
81 played … tricks] committed foolish acts.
82 up-staring] standing on end.
83 sustaining] either (a) those garments which endured
    (i.e., were not removed prior to abandoning ship); or (b)
    implying that, as with Ophelia, their garments "awhile
    bore [them] up."
84 this] i.e., as Ariel demonstrates.
85 Bermoothes] the Bermudas, which were supposedly
    continually ("still") vexed by storms.

---

86 suffered labour] exhausting struggle.
87 flote] flood, sea.
88 mid-season] noon.
89 glasses] hours, as gauged by an hourglass.
90 remember] remind.
91 time] period of indentured service.
92 bate me] abate my service.
93 veins] subterranean streams.
94 baked] hardened.

ARIEL.   I do not, sir.

PROSPERO. Thou liest, malignant thing! Hast thou
 forgot

 The foul witch Sycorax, who with age and envy[95]

 Was grown into a hoop? Hast thou forgot her?

ARIEL. No, sir.   260

PROSPERO. Thou hast. Where was she born?
 Speak; Tell me.

ARIEL. Sir, in Argier.[96]

PROSPERO.   O, was she so? I must

 Once in a month recount what thou hast been,

 Which thou forget'st. This damned witch Sycorax,

 For mischiefs manifold, and sorceries terrible 265

 To enter human hearing, from Argier,

 Thou know'st, was banished: for one thing she did[97]

 They would not take her life. Is not this true?

ARIEL. Ay, sir.

PROSPERO. This blue-eyed hag was hither brought 270
 with child,[98]

 And here was left by the sailors. Thou, my slave,

 As thou report'st thyself, wast then her servant:

 And, for thou wast a spirit too delicate

 To act her earthy and abhorred commands,

 Refusing her grand hests, she did confine thee,[99] 275

 By help of her more potent ministers,

 And in her most unmitigable rage,

 Into a cloven pine; within which rift

 Imprisoned, thou didst painfully remain

 A dozen years; within which space she died, 280

 And left thee there, where thou didst vent thy groans

 As fast as mill-wheels strike. Then was this
 island—[100]

 Save for the son that she did litter here,

---

[95] Sycorax] possibly derived from the fusion of two Greek
 words: *sys* (sow) and *korax* (raven; curved); Frank
 Kermode conjectures a source in Circe, the mythical
 witch (v. Homer's *Odyssey*) associated with the Coraxi
 tribe in Colchis.

[96] Argier] Algiers.

[97] one thing] possibly her pregnancy; but may allude to a
 witch said to have saved Algiers from invasion by
 Charles V in 1541.

[98] blue-eyed] probably not her irises but her eyelids, the
 blueness of which was regarded as a sign of pregnancy.

[99] hests] behests, demands.

[100] mill-wheels] i.e., the clappers strike water.

A freckled whelp, hag-born—not honoured with[101]

 A human shape.   285

ARIEL.   Yes; Caliban her son.[102]

PROSPERO. Dull thing, I say so; he, that Caliban,

 Whom now I keep in service. Thou best know'st

 What torment I did find thee in; thy groans

 Did make wolves howl, and penetrate the breasts

 Of ever-angry bears: it was a torment 290

 To lay upon the damned, which Sycorax

 Could not again undo; it was mine art,

 When I arrived and heard thee, that made gape

 The pine, and let thee out.

ARIEL.   I thank thee, master.

PROSPERO. If thou more murmur'st, I will rend an oak 295

 And peg thee in his knotty entrails till

 Thou hast howled away twelve winters!

ARIEL. Pardon, master.

 I will be correspondent to command,[103]

 And do my spriting gently.   300

PROSPERO.   Do so;

 And after two days I will discharge thee.

ARIEL. That's my noble master! What shall I do?

 Say what? What shall I do?

PROSPERO.   Go make thyself

 Like a nymph o' th' sea: be subject to

 No sight but thine and mine; invisible 305

 To every eyeball else. Go, take this shape,

 And hither come in't. Go, hence with diligence!

[*Exit ARIEL*]

Awake, dear heart, awake! Thou hast slept well.
 Awake!

MIRANDA. The strangeness of your story put 310
 Heaviness in me.

PROSPERO. Shake it off. Come on;

 We'll visit Caliban my slave, who never

 Yields us kind answer.

MIRANDA.   'Tis a villain, sir,

 I do not love to look on.   315

PROSPERO.   But as 'tis,

 We cannot miss him: he does make our fire,[104]

---

[101] freckled] spotted; whelp] the offspring of a beast, normally used of a bear or dog.

[102] Caliban] an imperfect anagram of "cannibal."

[103] correspondent] compliant.

[104] miss] do without.

Fetch in our wood; and serves in offices
That profit us. What ho! slave! Caliban!
Thou earth, thou! Speak.

CALIBAN. [*Within*] There's wood enough within!   320

PROSPERO. Come forth, I say; there's other business
    for thee.
Come, thou tortoise! When![105]

[*Re-enter ARIEL like a water-nymph*]

Fine apparition! My quaint Ariel,[106]
Hark in thine ear.

ARIEL.   My lord, it shall be done. [*Exit*]

PROSPERO. Thou poisonous slave, got by the devil   325
    himself
Upon thy wicked dam, come forth!

[*Enter CALIBAN*]

CALIBAN. As wicked dew as e'er my mother brushed
With raven's feather from unwholesome fen
Drop on you both! A south-west blow on ye,
And blister you all o'er!   330

PROSPERO. For this, be sure, tonight thou shalt
    have cramps,
Side-stitches that shall pen thy breath up; urchins[107]
Shall, for that vast of night that they may, work[108]
All exercise on thee: thou shalt be pinched
As thick as honeycomb, each pinch more stinging   335
Than bees that made them.

CALIBAN.   I must eat my dinner…
This island's mine, by Sycorax my mother,
Which thou tak'st from me! When thou cam'st first,
Thou strok'st me and made much of me; wouldst
    give me
Water with berries in't; and teach me how   340
To name the bigger light, and how the less,
That burn by day and night: and then I loved thee,

And showed thee all the qualities o' th' isle,
The fresh springs, brine-pits, barren place, and
    fertile.
Cursed be I that did so! All the charms   345
Of Sycorax, toads, beetles, bats, light on you!
For I am all the subjects that you have,
Which first was mine own king; and here you sty me
In this hard rock, whiles you do keep from me
The rest o' th' island.   350

PROSPERO.   Thou most lying slave,
Whom stripes may move, not kindness! I have
    used thee,[109]
Filth as thou art, with human care, and lodged thee
In mine own cell, till thou didst seek to violate
The honour of my child.

CALIBAN. Oh ho! Oh ho! Would it had been done!   355
Thou didst prevent me; I had peopled else
This isle with Calibans.

MIRANDA.[110]   Abhorrèd slave,
Which any print of goodness wilt not take,
Being capable of all ill! I pitied thee,
Took pains to make thee speak, taught thee each   360
    hour
One thing or other. When thou didst not, savage,
Know thine own meaning, but wouldst gabble like
A thing most brutish, I endowed thy purposes[111]
With words that made them known. But thy vile
    race,
Though thou didst learn, had that in't which   365
    good natures
Could not abide to be with; therefore wast thou
Deservedly confined into this rock,
Who hadst deserved more than a prison.[112]

CALIBAN. You taught me language, and my profit
    on't is,
I know how to curse: the red plague rid you,[113]   370
For learning me your language!

---

105 When] an expression of impatience.
106 quaint] ingenuous, pretty. (Ariel takes Prospero's instruc-
    tions literally, assuming a water-nymph disguise; where-
    as Prospero's intention was presumably that Ariel should
    merely become, like a water-nymph, invisible to most
    eyes.)
107 urchins] hedgehogs (or goblins so shaped).
108 vast of night] the long period in which demonic crea-
    tures are able to function.

109 stripes] lashes.
110 Some editors give this speech to Prospero.
111 purposes] meanings.
112 hadst … prison] Here the sense is "otherwise might have
    deserved better than prison"; some editors amend
    "hadst" to "hast," thus suggesting that Caliban deserves
    worse than prison.
113 red plague] bubonic plague; rid] destroy.

PROSPERO.   Hag-seed, hence!
  Fetch us in fuel; and be quick, thou'rt best,[114]
  To answer other business. Shrug'st thou, malice?
  If thou neglect'st, or dost unwillingly
  What I command, I'll rack thee with old cramps,[115]   375
  Fill all thy bones with aches; make thee roar,
  That beasts shall tremble at thy din.
CALIBAN.   No, pray thee.
  [Aside] I must obey. His art is of such power,
  It would control my dam's god, Setebos,[116]
  And make a vassal of him.   380
PROSPERO.   So, slave: hence!

*Exit CALIBAN. Re-enter ARIEL invisible, playing and
singing; FERDINAND following.*[117]

ARIEL'S SONG.

      Come unto these yellow sands,
        And then take hands;
      Curtsied when you have, and kissed
        The wild waves whist; [118]
      Foot it featly here and there;   385
        And sweet sprites bear
        The burden: Hark, hark!
      [*Burden, dispersedly:* Bow, wow.][119]
        The watch dogs bark:
      [*Burden, dispersedly:* Bow, wow.]   390
        Hark, hark! I hear
      The strain of strutting Chanticleer[120]
        Cry: Cock-a-diddle-dow.
FERDINAND. Where should this music be? i' th' air
  or th' earth?

---

[114] thou'rt best] you'd better (be quick).
[115] old] i.e., the sort suffered by the elderly.
[116] Setebos] a god of Patagonia (a region in the southern plateaus of South America).
[117] *invisible*] possibly wearing a conventional black gown to indicate invisibility, possibly just suggested through the acting.
[118] whist] silent.
[119] *Burden*] refrain; *dispersedly*] coming from various directions.
[120] Chanticleer] the cock of folklore, known to Shakespeare's audience through Chaucer's "Nun's Priest's Tale," where he is outwitted by a fox, whom he outwits in turn.

It sounds no more; and sure it waits upon   395
Some god o' th' island. Sitting on a bank,
Weeping again the king my father's wrack,
This music crept by me upon the waters,
Allaying both their fury and my passion[121]
With its sweet air: thence I have followed it—   400
Or it hath drawn me rather—but 'tis gone.
No, it begins again.

ARIEL sings

      Full fathom five thy father lies:
        Of his bones are coral made:
      Those are pearls that were his eyes: 405
        Nothing of him that doth fade
        But doth suffer a sea-change
      Into something rich and strange.
      Sea-nymphs hourly ring his knell:
        [*Burden:* Ding-dong.]   410
      Hark! now I hear them: ding-dong, bell.
FERDINAND. The ditty does remember my drowned
  father.[122]
  This is no mortal business, nor no sound
  That the earth owes. I hear it now above me.[123]
PROSPERO. The fringèd curtains of thine eye   415
  advance,[124]
  And say what thou seest yond.
MIRANDA.   What is't? a spirit?
  Lord, how it looks about! Believe me, sir,
  It carries a brave form. But 'tis a spirit.
PROSPERO. No, wench; it eats and sleeps, and hath
  such senses
  As we have, such. This gallant which thou see'st 420
  Was in the wrack; and, but he's something
  stained[125]
  With grief (that's beauty's canker), thou mightst
  call him[126]
  A goodly person. He hath lost his fellows
  And strays about to find 'em.

---

[121] passion] grief.
[122] remember] commemorate.
[123] owes] owns.
[124] fringèd curtains] eyelids.
[125] but] except that.
[126] that's] which is; canker] a worm that preys upon blossoms.

MIRANDA.   I might call him
  A thing divine; for nothing natural   425
  I ever saw so noble.
PROSPERO. [*Aside*] It goes on, I see,
  As my soul prompts it. Spirit, fine spirit! I'll free thee
  Within two days for this.
FERDINAND.   Most sure, the goddess[127]
  On whom these airs attend! Vouchsafe, my prayer[128]   430
  May know if you remain upon this island;[129]
  And that you will some good instruction give
  How I may bear me here: my prime request,[130]
  Which I do last pronounce, is— O, you wonder!—
  If you be maid or no?   435
MIRANDA.   No wonder, sir;
  But certainly a maid.
FERDINAND.   My language! Heavens!
  I am the best of them that speak this speech,
  Were I but where 'tis spoken.
PROSPERO.   How? the best?
  What wert thou, if the King of Naples heard thee?
FERDINAND. A single thing, as I am now, that   440
    wonders[131]
  To hear thee speak of Naples. He does hear me;
  And, that he does, I weep: myself am Naples,
  Who with mine eyes—never since at ebb—beheld
  The King, my father wracked.
MIRANDA.   Alack, for mercy!
FERDINAND. Yes, faith, and all his lords, the Duke   445
    of Milan,
  And his brave son being twain.
PROSPERO. [*Aside*]   The Duke of Milan,
  And his more braver daughter could control thee,
  If now 'twere fit to do't. At the first sight
  They have changed eyes. Delicate Ariel,
  I'll set thee free for this!—A word, good sir: 450
  I fear you have done yourself some wrong. A
    word![132]
MIRANDA. Why speaks my father so ungently? This

---

127 Most sure] undoubtedly (this is).
128 airs] i.e., the musical airs he has heard.
129 remain] live.
130 bear me] behave.
131 single] solitary, helpless.
132 I fear ... wrong] an ironical or overly polite way of say-
    ing "you're a liar."

Is the third man that e'er I saw; the first
  That e'er I sighed for; pity move my father
  To be inclined my way!   455
FERDINAND.   O, if a virgin,
  And your affection not gone forth, I'll make you
  The Queen of Naples.
PROSPERO.   Soft, sir; one word more— [*Aside*]
  They are both in either's powers; but this swift
    business
  I must uneasy make, lest too light winning
  Make the prize light. —One word more. I charge   460
    thee
  That thou attend me! Thou dost here usurp
  The name thou ow'st not; and hast put thyself[133]
  Upon this island as a spy, to win it
  From me, the lord on't.
FERDINAND.   No, as I am a man!
MIRANDA. There's nothing ill can dwell in such a   465
    temple:
  If the ill spirit have so fair a house,
  Good things will strive to dwell with't.
PROSPERO.   Follow me.
  Speak not you for him; he's a traitor. —Come;
  I'll manacle thy neck and feet together:
  Sea-water shalt thou drink; thy food shall be   470
  The fresh-brook mussels, withered roots, and husks
  Wherein the acorn cradled. Follow.
FERDINAND.   No.
  I will resist such entertainment till[134]
  Mine enemy has more power.

[*He draws, and is charmed from moving*]

MIRANDA.   O, dear father!
  Make not too rash a trial of him, for   475
  He's gentle, and not fearful.[135]
PROSPERO.   What! I say,
  My foot my tutor? Put thy sword up, traitor;[136]
  Who mak'st a show, but dar'st not strike, thy
    conscience
  Is so possessed with guilt. Come from thy ward,[137]

---

133 ow'st] ownest.
134 entertainment] treatment.
135 gentle ... fearful] of noble birth and not a coward.
136 My ... tutor] is an inferior object to be my master.
137 Come ... ward] drop your fighting stance.

For I can here disarm thee with this stick   480
And make thy weapon drop.
MIRANDA.   Beseech you, father!
PROSPERO. Hence! Hang not on my garments.
MIRANDA.   Sir, have pity.
I'll be his surety.
PROSPERO. Silence! One word more
Shall make me chide thee, if not hate thee. What!   485
An advocate for an impostor? Hush!
Thou think'st there is no more such shapes as he,
Having seen but him and Caliban: foolish wench!
To the most of men this is a Caliban,
And they to him are angels.[138]   490
MIRANDA.   My affections
Are then most humble; I have no ambition
To see a goodlier man.
PROSPERO.   Come on; obey:
Thy nerves are in their infancy again,[139]
And have no vigour in them.
FERDINAND.   So they are.
My spirits, as in a dream, are all bound up.   495
My father's loss, the weakness which I feel,
The wrack of all my friends, nor this man's threats,
To whom I am subdued, are but light to me,
Might I but through my prison once a day
Behold this maid. All corners else o' th' earth   500
Let liberty make use of; space enough
Have I in such a prison.
PROSPERO. [Aside]   It works!—Come on.—
Thou hast done well, fine Ariel!—Follow me.—
Hark what thou else shalt do me.
MIRANDA.   Be of comfort;
My father's of a better nature, sir,   505
Than he appears by speech. This is unwonted,
Which now came from him.
PROSPERO.   Thou shalt be as free
As mountain winds; but then exactly do[140]
All points of my command.
ARIEL.   To the syllable.
PROSPERO. —Come, follow.—Speak not for him.   510

[Exeunt]

---

138 to] i.e., compared to.
139 nerves] sinews.
140 then] i.e., until then.

ACT II

SCENE I.[141]

*Enter ALONSO, SEBASTIAN, ANTONIO, GONZALO,
ADRIAN, FRANCISCO, and others.*

GONZALO. Beseech you, sir, be merry; you have cause,
So have we all, of joy; for our escape
Is much beyond our loss. Our hint of woe[142]
Is common: every day, some sailor's wife,
The masters of some merchant—and the   5
    merchant— [143]
Have just our theme; but for the miracle—
I mean our preservation—few in millions
Can speak like us. Then wisely, good sir, weigh
Our sorrow with our comfort.
ALONSO.   Prithee, peace.
SEBASTIAN. He receives comfort like cold porridge.[144]   10
ANTONIO. The visitor will not give him o'er so.[145]
SEBASTIAN. Look, he's winding up the watch of his
wit; by and by it will strike.
GONZALO. Sir—
SEBASTIAN. One: tell.[146]   15
GONZALO. When every grief is entertained that's
    offered,
Comes to the entertainer—
SEBASTIAN. A dollar.
GONZALO. Dolour comes to him, indeed: you have
spoken truer than you purposed.[147]   20
SEBASTIAN. You have taken it wiselier than I meant
you should.

---

141 Another part of the island. (As a rule, when Shakespeare
    has one set of characters clear the stage and another en-
    ter, the scene has changed.)
142 hint] occasion.
143 The ... merchant] the ship masters of some merchant
    vessel, and the merchant whose cargo it carries.
144 porridge] punning on peace/pease (porridge, at that
    time, was usually a sort of pea soup).
145 visitor] (meant sarcastically) spiritual advisor; give him
    o'er so] let him alone so easily.
146 tell] count.
147 dollar] then a continental coin (Sebastian having taken
    the word "entertainer" in its meaning of "innkeeper");
    dolour] grief.

GONZALO. Therefore, my lord—

ANTONIO. Fie, what a spendthrift is he of his tongue!

ALONSO. I prithee, spare. 25

GONZALO. Well, I have done. But, yet—

SEBASTIAN. He will be talking.

ANTONIO. Which, of he or Adrian, for a good wager, first begins to crow?

SEBASTIAN. The old cock. 30

ANTONIO. The cockerel.[148]

SEBASTIAN. Done. The wager?

ANTONIO. A laughter.

SEBASTIAN. A match!

ADRIAN. Though this island seem to be desert— 35

ANTONIO. Ha, ha, ha!

SEBASTIAN. So, you're paid.

ADRIAN. Uninhabitable, and almost inaccessible—

SEBASTIAN. Yet—

ADRIAN. Yet— 40

ANTONIO. He could not miss it.

ADRIAN. It must needs be of subtle, tender, and delicate temperance.

ANTONIO. Temperance was a delicate wench.[149]

SEBASTIAN. Ay, and a subtle; as he most learnedly delivered. 45

ADRIAN. The air breathes upon us here most sweetly.

SEBASTIAN. As if it had lungs, and rotten ones.

ANTONIO. Or, as 'twere perfumed by a fen.

GONZALO. Here is everything advantageous to life. 50

ANTONIO. True; save means to live.

SEBASTIAN. Of that there's none, or little.

GONZALO. How lush and lusty the grass looks! how green!

ANTONIO. The ground indeed is tawny. 55

SEBASTIAN. With an eye of green in't.[150]

ANTONIO. He misses not much.

SEBASTIAN. No; he doth but mistake the truth totally.

GONZALO. But the rarity of it is—which is indeed almost beyond credit— 60

SEBASTIAN. As many vouched rarities are.

GONZALO. That our garments, being, as they were, drenched in the sea, hold notwithstanding their freshness and glosses, being rather new-dyed than stained with salt water. 65

ANTONIO. If but one of his pockets could speak, would it not say he lies?

SEBASTIAN. Ay, or very falsely pocket up his report.

GONZALO. Methinks, our garments are now as fresh as when we put them on first in Afric, at the marriage of the king's fair daughter Claribel to the King of Tunis. 70

SEBASTIAN. 'Twas a sweet marriage, and we prosper well in our return. 75

ADRIAN. Tunis was never graced before with such a paragon to their queen.[151]

GONZALO. Not since widow Dido's time.[152]

ANTONIO. Widow! A pox o' that! How came that widow in? Widow Dido! 80

SEBASTIAN. What if he had said, widower Aeneas too? Good Lord, how you take it!

ADRIAN. Widow Dido said you? You make me study of that; she was of Carthage, not of Tunis.

GONZALO. This Tunis, sir, was Carthage.[153] 85

ADRIAN. Carthage?

GONZALO. I assure you, Carthage.

ANTONIO. His word is more than the miraculous harp.[154]

SEBASTIAN. He hath raised the wall, and houses too. 90

ANTONIO. What impossible matter will he make easy next?

---

[148] old cock] Gonzalo; cockerel] (a young cock) Adrian.

[149] temperance] climate, also a popular girl's name among Puritans.

[150] eye] spot. (Part of the theme of differing perceptions that runs through the scene: Gonzalo and Adrian can see goodness because they are disposed to see it; Sebastian and Antonio see badness because that is their disposition.)

[151] to] for.

[152] Widow Dido] Dido of Carthage was indeed the widow of Sychaeus, as Aeneas was widower of Creusa. The forced merriment is presumably at the idea of two famous lovers (Virgil, *Aeneid*, Bk. 4) labelled by their connection with their previous spouses, or as if they were elderly.

[153] Tunis … was Carthage] close, but not quite; Tunis lies 50 kilometres east of the ruins of Carthage and was built in the ninth century B.C.E. by ancient Libyans who had abandoned Carthage to the Phoenicians.

[154] miraculous harp] Amphion's harp-playing drew the stone walls of Thebes into place.

SEBASTIAN. I think he will carry this island home
    in his pocket, and give it his son for an apple.

ANTONIO. And, sowing the kernels of it in the sea,   95
    bring forth more islands.

GONZALO. I?

ANTONIO. [*To SEBASTIAN*] Why, in good time.

GONZALO. [*To ALONSO*] Sir, we were talking that
    our garments seem now as fresh as when we were   100
    at Tunis at the marriage of your daughter, who is
    now Queen.

ANTONIO. And the rarest that e'er came there.

SEBASTIAN. Bate, I beseech you, widow Dido.155

ANTONIO. O, widow Dido; ay, widow Dido.   105

GONZALO. Is not, sir, my doublet as fresh as the first
    day I wore it? I mean, in a sort.156

ANTONIO. That sort was well fished for.157

GONZALO. When I wore it at your daughter's
    marriage?   110

ALONSO. You cram these words into mine ears against
    The stomach of my sense. Would I had never158
    Married my daughter there! for, coming thence,
    My son is lost; and, in my rate, she too,159
    Who is so far from Italy removed,   115
    I ne'er again shall see her. O thou, mine heir
    Of Naples and of Milan! what strange fish
    Hath made his meal on thee?

FRANCISCO.   Sir, he may live:
    I saw him beat the surges under him,
    And ride upon their backs: he trod the water,   120
    Whose enmity he flung aside, and breasted
    The surge most swoln that met him: his bold head
    'Bove the contentious waves he kept, and oared
    Himself with his good arms in lusty stroke
    To th'shore, that o'er his wave-worn basis bowed,160   125
    As stooping to relieve him. I not doubt161
    He came alive to land.

ALONSO.   No, no; he's gone.

SEBASTIAN. Sir, you may thank yourself for this
    great loss,
    That would not bless our Europe with your daughter,
    But rather lose her to an African;   130
    Where she, at least, is banished from your eye,
    Who hath cause to wet the grief on't.

ALONSO.   Prithee, peace.

SEBASTIAN. You were kneeled to, and importuned
    otherwise
    By all of us; and the fair soul herself
    Weighed between loathness and obedience at   135
    Which end o' th' beam should bow. We have lost
    your son,162
    I fear, for ever. Milan and Naples have
    More widows in them of this business' making,
    Than we bring men to comfort them. The fault's
    Your own—   140

ALONSO.   So is the dearest of the loss.

GONZALO. My lord Sebastian,
    The truth you speak doth lack some gentleness
    And time to speak it in; you rub the sore,
    When you should bring the plaster.

SEBASTIAN.   Very well.

ANTONIO. And most surgeonly.   145

GONZALO. It is foul weather in us all, good sir,
    When you are cloudy.

SEBASTIAN.   Fowl weather?

ANTONIO.   Very foul.

GONZALO. Had I plantation of this isle, my lord—163

ANTONIO. He'd sow 't with nettle-seed.

SEBASTIAN. Or docks, or mallows.   150

GONZALO. And were the king on't, what would I do?

SEBASTIAN. 'Scape being drunk for want of wine.

GONZALO. I'th'commonwealth, I would by
    contraries164
    Execute all things; for no kind of traffic165
    Would I admit; no name of magistrate;   155

---

155 Bate] with the exception of.

156 in a sort] comparatively.

157 sort … fished for] The word "sort," meaning a mass of
    things, was sometimes applied to a catch of fish, the idea
    being that the clothes smell fishy.

158 stomach … sense] disposition of my mind.

159 in my rate] as far as I'm concerned.

160 his] its; basis] i.e., the sand.

161 As] as if it were.

---

162 weighed … bow] like a set of scales, tipped this way and
    that, unsure whether her loathing or sense of obedience
    were stronger.

163 plantation] colonization, though taken by Antonio in
    a literal, agricultural sense.

164 contraries] contrary to usual practice.

165 traffic] trade.

Letters should not be known; riches, poverty,
And use of service, none; contract, succession,[166]
Bourn, bound of land, tilth, vineyard, none;[167]
No use of metal, corn, or wine, or oil;
No occupation; all men idle, all;   160
And women too, but innocent and pure;
No sovereignty—
SEBASTIAN.   Yet he would be king on't.
ANTONIO. The latter end of his commonwealth
    forgets the beginning.
GONZALO. All things in common nature should   165
        produce
    Without sweat or endeavour; treason, felony,
    Sword, pike, knife, gun, or need of any engine,[168]
    Would I not have; but nature should bring forth,
    Of its own kind, all foison, all abundance,[169]
    To feed my innocent people.   170
SEBASTIAN. No marrying 'mong his subjects?
ANTONIO. None, man: all idle; whores and knaves.
GONZALO. I would with such perfection govern, sir,
    To excel the golden age.
SEBASTIAN.   Save his Majesty!
ANTONIO. Long live Gonzalo!   175
GONZALO.   And—Do you mark me, sir?
ALONSO. Prithee, no more: thou dost talk nothing
    to me.
GONZALO. I do well believe your highness; and did
    it to minister occasion to these gentlemen, who are
    of such sensible and nimble lungs that they always   180
    use to laugh at nothing.[170]
ANTONIO. 'Twas you we laughed at.
GONZALO. Who in this kind of merry fooling am
    nothing to you; so you may continue, and laugh
    at nothing still.   185
ANTONIO. What a blow was there given!
SEBASTIAN. An it had not fallen flat-long.[171]
GONZALO. You are gentlemen of brave mettle: you

would lift the moon out of her sphere, if she would
continue in it five weeks without changing.   190

[*Enter ARIEL, invisible, playing solemn music*]

SEBASTIAN. We would so, and then go a-bat-
    fowling.[172]
ANTONIO. Nay, good my lord, be not angry.
GONZALO. No, I warrant you; I will not adventure
    my discretion so weakly.[173] Will you laugh me   195
    asleep, for I am very heavy?
ANTONIO. Go sleep, and hear us.

[*All sleep but ALONSO, SEBASTIAN, and ANTONIO*]

ALONSO. What! all so soon asleep! I wish mine eyes
    Would, with themselves, shut up my thoughts. I find
    They are inclined to do so.   200
SEBASTIAN.   Please you, sir,
    Do not omit the heavy offer of it.[174]
    It seldom visits sorrow; when it doth,
    It is a comforter.
ANTONIO. We two, my lord,
    Will guard your person while you take your rest,   205
    And watch your safety.
ALONSO. Thank you. Wondrous heavy!

[*ALONSO sleeps. Exit ARIEL*]

SEBASTIAN. What a strange drowsiness possesses them!
ANTONIO. It is the quality o' th' climate.
SEBASTIAN.   Why
    Doth it not then our eyelids sink? I find not   210
    Myself disposed to sleep.
ANTONIO.   Nor I: my spirits are nimble.
    They fell together all, as by consent;
    They dropped as by a thunder-stroke. What might,
    Worthy Sebastian—O, what might—? No more!
    And yet methinks I see it in thy face,   215
    What thou should'st be. Th'occasion speaks thee;
        and[175]
    My strong imagination sees a crown

---

166 use of service] employment of servants; succession] in-
     heritance of wealth or office.
167 Bourn] border.
168 engine] i.e., of war.
169 foison] rich harvest.
170 minister occasion] provide opportunity; sensible] sen-
     sitive.
171 An] if; flat-long] with the flat of the sword.

172 a-bat-fowling] hunting birds by night, using a light to
     frighten them, then killing them with a stick or bat.
173 adventure … weakly] lose control of my temper upon
     such feeble provocation.
174 omit] ignore.
175 speaks thee] speaks to, summons.

Dropping upon thy head.

SEBASTIAN.   What? Art thou waking?

ANTONIO. Do you not hear me speak?

SEBASTIAN.   I do: and surely
It is a sleepy language, and thou speak'st   220
Out of thy sleep. What is it thou didst say?
This is a strange repose, to be asleep
With eyes wide open; standing, speaking, moving,
And yet so fast asleep.

ANTONIO.   Noble Sebastian,
Thou let'st thy fortune sleep—die rather: wink'st[176]   225
Whiles thou art waking.

SEBASTIAN.   Thou dost snore distinctly:
There's meaning in thy snores.

ANTONIO. I am more serious than my custom. You
Must be so too, if heed me: which to do
Trebles thee o'er.[177]   230

SEBASTIAN.   Well, I am standing water.[178]

ANTONIO. I'll teach you how to flow.

SEBASTIAN.   Do so. To ebb,
Hereditary sloth instructs me.[179]

ANTONIO.   O,
If you but knew how you the purpose cherish
Whiles thus you mock it! how, in stripping it,[180]
You more invest it! Ebbing men indeed,   235
(Most often), do so near the bottom run
By their own fear or sloth.

SEBASTIAN.   Prithee, say on:
The setting of thine eye and cheek proclaim
A matter from thee, and a birth, indeed
Which throes thee much to yield.[181]   240

ANTONIO.   Thus, sir:
Although this lord of weak remembrance—this[182]
Who shall be of as little memory

When he is earthed—hath here almost persuaded[183]
(For he's a spirit of persuasion, only
Professes to persuade) the King his son's alive,[184]   245
'Tis as impossible that he's undrowned
As he that sleeps here swims.

SEBASTIAN.   I have no hope
That he's undrowned.

ANTONIO.   O, out of that 'no hope'
What great hope have you! No hope that way is
Another way so high a hope, that even   250
Ambition cannot pierce a wink beyond,[185]
But doubts discovery there. Will you grant with me[186]
That Ferdinand is drowned?

SEBASTIAN.   He's gone.

ANTONIO.   Then tell me,
Who's the next heir of Naples?

SEBASTIAN.   Claribel.

ANTONIO. She that is Queen of Tunis; she that dwells   255
Ten leagues beyond man's life; she that from Naples[187]
Can have no note, unless the sun were post—
The Man i' th' Moon's too slow—till newborn chins
Be rough and razorable: she that from whom
We all were sea-swallowed, though some cast again,[188]   260
And by that destiny, to perform an act
Whereof what's past is prologue, what to come
In yours and my discharge.

SEBASTIAN. What stuff is this! How say you?
'Tis true, my brother's daughter's Queen of Tunis;   265
So is she heir of Naples; 'twixt which regions
There is some space.

ANTONIO. A space whose every cubit
Seems to cry out 'How shall that Claribel
Measure us back to Naples? Keep in Tunis,   270
And let Sebastian wake.' Say this were death

---

176 wink'st] have you.

177 trebles thee o'er] increases your status threefold.

178 standing water] still (i.e., waiting); neutral.

179 hereditary sloth] natural laziness and the inherited office of the younger—and therefore idle—brother to the King.

180 If … mock it] if you only knew how perfectly your joking strikes to the heart of my argument.

181 throes … yield] causes you a great deal of labour pain to bring forth.

182 of … remembrance] of the weak memory.

---

183 earthed] buried.

184 only … persuade] His only function (as a royal advisor) is to persuade.

185 wink] glimpse.

186 discovery] what it has discovered.

187 Ten … life] more than a lifetime's trip away.

188 cast again] i.e., cast forth (though the word leads Antonio to pun on its theatrical meaning).

That now hath seized them; why, they were no worse
Than now they are. There be that can rule Naples
As well as he that sleeps; lords that can prate
As amply and unnecessarily   275
As this Gonzalo: I myself could make
A chough of as deep chat. O, that you bore[189]
The mind that I do! What a sleep were this
For your advancement! Do you understand me?
SEBASTIAN. Methinks I do.   280
ANTONIO.   And how does your content
Tender your own good fortune?[190]
SEBASTIAN.   I remember
You did supplant your brother Prospero.
ANTONIO.   True.
And look how well my garments sit upon me;
Much feater than before; my brother's servants[191]
Were then my fellows; now they are my men.[192]   285
SEBASTIAN. But, for your conscience...
ANTONIO. Ay, sir, where lies that? If 'twere a kibe,[193]
'Twould put me to my slipper; but I feel not[194]
This deity in my bosom. Twenty consciences
That stand 'twixt me and Milan, candied be they   290
And melt ere they molest! Here lies your brother,[195]
No better than the earth he lies upon,
If he were that which now he's like, that's dead:
Whom I, with this obedient steel, three inches of it,
Can lay to bed for ever; whiles you, doing thus,   295
To the perpetual wink for aye might put[196]
This ancient morsel, this Sir Prudence, who
Should not upbraid our course. For all the rest,
They'll take suggestion as a cat laps milk;
They'll tell the clock to any business that   300
We say befits the hour.[197]

---

189 chough] jackdaw, a bird that can be taught to mimic
   speech.
190 how ... fortune] i.e., "how do you like your chances?"
191 feater] more suitable.
192 fellows] peers; men] servants.
193 kibe] chilblain.
194 put me to] make me wear.
195 candied ... molest] i.e., conscience, overcome by the
   sweet rewards of the deed, melts before causing any affliction.
196 wink] sleep; aye] ever.
197 tell the clock ... hour] declare that whatever we say is
   opportune.

SEBASTIAN.   Thy case, dear friend,
Shall be my precedent: as thou got'st Milan,
I'll come by Naples. Draw thy sword. One stroke
Shall free thee from the tribute which thou pay'st
And I, the King, shall love thee.   305
ANTONIO.   Draw together:
And when I rear my hand, do you the like,
To fall it on Gonzalo.
SEBASTIAN.   O, but one word.

[*Music. Re-enter ARIEL, invisible*]

ARIEL. My master through his art foresees the danger
That you, his friend, are in, and sends me forth—
For else his project dies—to keep thee living.   310

[*Sings in GONZALO'S ear*]

            While you here do snoring lie,
               Open-eyed Conspiracy
                  His time doth take.
               If of life you keep a care,
            Shake off slumber, and beware.   315
                  Awake! awake!
ANTONIO. Then let us both be sudden.
GONZALO. [*Wakes*]   Now, good angels
Preserve the King!
ALONSO. Why, how now! Ho, awake! Why are you
   drawn?
Wherefore this ghastly looking?   320
GONZALO.   What's the matter?
SEBASTIAN. Whiles we stood here securing your
   repose,[198]
Even now, we heard a hollow burst of bellowing
Like bulls, or rather lions. Did't not wake you?
It struck mine ear most terribly.
ALONSO.   I heard nothing.
ANTONIO. O, 'twas a din to fright a monster's ear,   325
To make an earthquake! Sure, it was the roar
Of a whole herd of lions.
ALONSO.   Heard you this, Gonzalo?
GONZALO. Upon mine honour, sir, I heard a
   humming,
And that a strange one too, which did awake me.
I shaked you, sir, and cried; as mine eyes opened,   330
I saw their weapons drawn. There was a noise,

---

198 securing] keeping watch over.

That's verily. 'Tis best we stand upon our guard,
Or that we quit this place. Let's draw our weapons.
ALONSO. Lead off this ground: and let's make
   further search
   For my poor son.   335
GONZALO. Heavens keep him from these beasts!
   For he is, sure, i'th'island.
ALONSO.   Lead away.
ARIEL. Prospero my lord shall know what I have done.
So, King, go safely on to seek thy son. [*Exeunt*]

SCENE II.

Another part of the island

*Enter CALIBAN, with a burden of wood. A noise of
thunder heard.*

CALIBAN. All the infections that the sun sucks up
   From bogs, fens, flats, on Prosper fall, and make him
   By inch-meal a disease! His spirits hear me,[199]
   And yet I needs must curse. But they'll nor pinch,
   Fright me with urchin-shows, pitch me i' the
      mire,[200]   5
   Nor lead me, like a firebrand, in the dark
   Out of my way, unless he bid 'em; but
   For every trifle are they set upon me:
   Sometime like apes that mow and chatter at me,[201]
   And after bite me; then like hedge-hogs which   10
   Lie tumbling in my bare-foot way, and mount
   Their pricks at my foot-fall; sometime am I
   All wound with adders, who with cloven tongues
   Do hiss me into madness—

[*Enter TRINCULO*]

                    Lo, now, lo!
   Here comes a spirit of his, and to torment me   15
   For bringing wood in slowly. I'll fall flat;
   Perchance he will not mind me.
TRINCULO. Here's neither bush nor shrub to bear off
   any weather at all, and another storm brewing.[202] I

hear it sing i' th' wind. Yond same black cloud, yond   20
huge one, looks like a foul bombard that would shed
his liquor.[203] If it should thunder as it did before, I
know not where to hide my head. Yond same cloud
cannot choose but fall by pailfuls. —What have we
here? a man or a fish? Dead or alive? A fish: he smells   25
like a fish: a very ancient and fish-like smell; a kind
of not of the newest Poor-John.[204] A strange fish!
Were I in England now, as once I was, and had but
this fish painted, not a holiday fool there but would
give a piece of silver.[205] There, would this monster   30
make a man; any strange beast there makes a man.
When they will not give a doit to relieve a lame
beggar, they will lay out ten to see a dead Indian.[206]
Legged like a man! And his fins like arms! Warm, o'
my troth! I do now let loose my opinion, hold it no   35
longer: this is no fish, but an islander, that hath lately
suffered by thunderbolt. [*Thunder*] Alas, the storm
is come again! My best way is to creep under his
gaberdine; there is no other shelter hereabout.[207]
Misery acquaints a man with strange bed-fellows. I   40
will here shroud till the dregs of the storm be past.

[*Crawls under Caliban's cloak. Enter STEPHANO; a
bottle in his hand*]

STEPHANO. [*singing*]
    I shall no more to sea, to sea,
      Here shall I die a-shore—
This is a very scurvy tune to sing at a man's funeral.
Well, here's my comfort. [*Drinks; sings*]   45
    The master, the swabber, the boatswain, and I,
      The gunner, and his mate,
    Loved Mall, Meg, and Marian, and Margery,
      But none of us cared for Kate!
    For she had a tongue with a tang,   50
      Would cry to a sailor 'Go hang!'

---

199 inch-meal] inch by inch.
200 urchin-shows] apparitions resembling hedgehogs or land
    versions of sea-urchins.
201 mow] make mouths, or faces.
202 bear off] ward off.

203 bombard] a large leather vessel, like an oversized wine-
    skin.
204 Poor-John] dried fish similar to cod.
205 painted] i.e., on a signboard outside a fair.
206 doit] small coin; dead Indian] i.e., a Native American,
    many of whom were brought by explorers to Europe,
    where they were exhibited and, usually, died prema-
    turely.
207 gaberdine] cloak.

She loved not the savour of tar nor of pitch,
Yet a tailor might scratch her where'er she did itch!
Then to sea, boys, and let her go hang—!
This is a scurvy tune too: but here's my comfort. 55
[*Drinks*]

CALIBAN. Do not torment me! O!

STEPHANO. What's the matter? Have we devils here?
Do you put tricks upon us with savages and men
of Inde? Ha! I have not 'scaped drowning, to be 60
afeard now of your four legs; for it hath been said,
As proper a man as ever went on four legs cannot
make him give ground: and it shall be said so
again, while Stephano breathes at's nostrils.

CALIBAN. The spirit torments me! O! 65

STEPHANO. This is some monster of the isle with
four legs, who hath got, as I take it, an ague.[208]
Where the devil should he learn our language? I
will give him some relief, if it be but for that. If I
can recover him and keep him tame and get to 70
Naples with him, he's a present for any emperor
that ever trod on neat's-leather.[209]

CALIBAN. Do not torment me, prithee; I'll bring my
wood home faster.

STEPHANO. He's in his fit now and does not talk 75
after the wisest. He shall taste of my bottle: if he
have never drunk wine afore, it will go near to
remove his fit. If I can recover him, and keep him
tame, I will not take too much for him; he shall
pay for him that hath him, and that soundly.[210] 80

CALIBAN. Thou dost me yet but little hurt.
Thou wilt anon, I know it by thy trembling.[211]
Now Prosper works upon thee.

STEPHANO. Come on your ways: open your mouth;
here is that which will give language to you, cat.[212] 85
Open your mouth. This will shake your shaking,
I can tell you, and that soundly. [*Gives CALIBAN a*
drink] You cannot tell who's your friend. Open
your chaps again.[213]

TRINCULO. I should know that voice: it should be— 90

but he is drowned; and these are devils. O, defend
me!

STEPHANO. Four legs and two voices; a most delicate
monster! His forward voice now is to speak well
of his friend; his backward voice is to utter foul 95
speeches, and to detract. If all the wine in my
bottle will recover him, I will help his ague. Come.
Amen! I will pour some in thy other mouth.

TRINCULO. Stephano!

STEPHANO. Doth thy other mouth call me? Mercy! 100
mercy! This is a devil, and no monster: I will leave
him; I have no long spoon.[214]

TRINCULO. Stephano! If thou beest Stephano, touch
me, and speak to me; for I am Trinculo—be not
afeared—thy good friend Trinculo. 105

STEPHANO. If thou beest Trinculo, come forth. I'll
pull thee by the lesser legs. If any be Trinculo's legs,
these are they. Thou art very Trinculo indeed! How
cam'st thou to be the siege of this moon-calf?[215]
Can he vent Trinculos?[216] 110

TRINCULO. I took him to be killed with a thunder-
stroke. But art thou not drowned, Stephano? I hope
now thou are not drowned. Is the storm overblown?
I hid me under the dead moon-calf's gaberdine for
fear of the storm. And art thou living, Stephano? O 115
Stephano, two Neapolitans 'scaped!

STEPHANO. Prithee, do not turn me about: my
stomach is not constant.

CALIBAN. [*Aside*] These be fine things, an if they be
not sprites.[217]
That's a brave god, and bears celestial liquor. 120
I will kneel to him.

STEPHANO. How didst thou 'scape? How cam'st thou
hither? Swear by this bottle how thou cam'st hither.
I escaped upon a butt of sack which the sailors
heaved overboard, by this bottle! —which I made 125
of the bark of a tree, with mine own hands, since
I was cast ashore.[218]

---

208 ague] fever.
209 neat's-leather] cow-hide, i.e., shoes.
210 I will not take too much] no amount will be too large.
211 anon] soon; the trembling is Trinculo's.
212 cat] (proverb) "liquor will make a cat talk."
213 chaps] chops, jaws.

---

214 I have … spoon] (proverb) "He that sups with the devil must have a long spoon."
215 siege] excrement; mooncalf] monstrosity (e.g., a two-headed calf) created by the moon.
216 vent] defecate.
217 an if] if; sprites] spirits.
218 butt of sack] cask of white wine.

CALIBAN. I'll swear upon that bottle to be thy true
subject, for the liquor is not earthly.

STEPHANO. Here: swear then how thou escapedst.   130

TRINCULO. Swum ashore, man, like a duck: I can
swim like a duck, I'll be sworn.

STEPHANO. [*Passing the bottle*] Here, kiss the
book.[219] [*Gives TRINCULO a drink*] Though thou
canst swim like a duck, thou art made like a goose.   135

TRINCULO. O Stephano! hast any more of this?

STEPHANO. The whole butt, man: my cellar is in a
rock by the seaside, where my wine is hid. How
now, moon-calf! How does thine ague?

CALIBAN. Hast thou not dropped from heaven?   140

STEPHANO. Out o' the moon, I do assure thee: I was
the Man in the Moon, when time was.[220]

CALIBAN. I have seen thee in her, and I do adore thee.
My mistress showed me thee, and thy dog and thy
bush.

STEPHANO. Come, swear to that; kiss the book; I   145
will furnish it anon with new contents; swear.

TRINCULO. By this good light, this is a very shallow
monster.—I afeard of him!—A very weak monster.
—he Man i' the Moon? A most poor credulous
monster!—Well drawn, monster, in good sooth!   150

CALIBAN. I'll show thee every fertile inch o' the island;
And I will kiss thy foot. I prithee, be my god.

TRINCULO. By this light, a most perfidious and
drunken monster: when his god's asleep, he'll rob
his bottle.   155

CALIBAN. I'll kiss thy foot: I'll swear myself thy
subject.

STEPHANO. Come on, then; down, and swear.

TRINCULO. I shall laugh myself to death at this
puppy-headed monster. A most scurvy monster! I
could find in my heart to beat him.   160

STEPHANO. Come, kiss.

TRINCULO. But that the poor monster's in drink: an
abominable monster!

CALIBAN. I'll show thee the best springs; I'll pluck
thee berries;
I'll fish for thee, and get thee wood enough.   165
A plague upon the tyrant that I serve!

I'll bear him no more sticks, but follow thee,
Thou wondrous man.

TRINCULO. A most ridiculous monster, to make a
wonder of a poor drunkard!   170

CALIBAN. I prithee, let me bring thee where crabs
grow;[221]
And I with my long nails will dig thee pig-nuts;[222]
Show thee a jay's nest, and instruct thee how
To snare the nimble marmozet; I'll bring thee
To clust'ring filberts, and sometimes I'll get thee   175
Young scamels from the rock. Wilt thou go with
me?[223]

STEPHANO. I prithee now, lead the way without any
more talking. Trinculo, the king and all our
company else being drowned, we will inherit here.
Here, bear my bottle. Fellow Trinculo, we'll fill him   180
by and by again.

CALIBAN. [*Sings drunkenly*]
Farewell, master; farewell, farewell!

TRINCULO. A howling monster, a drunken monster.

CALIBAN.   *No more dams I'll make for fish;*
Nor fetch in firing   185
At requiring,
Nor scrape trenchering, nor wash dish;[224]
'Ban 'Ban, Ca–Caliban,
Has a new master—get a new man.

Freedom, high-day! high-day, freedom! freedom,   190
high-day, freedom!

STEPHANO. O brave monster! lead the way. [*Exeunt*]

ACT III SCENE I.

Before PROSPERO'S cell

[*Enter FERDINAND, bearing a log*]

FERDINAND. There be some sports are painful, and
their labour
Delight in them sets off; some kinds of baseness[225]
Are nobly undergone, and most poor matters

---

219 kiss the book] i.e., drink, but as one takes an oath of
allegiance by kissing the Bible.

220 when time was] once upon a time.

221 crabs] crabapples.

222 pig-nuts] peanuts.

223 scamels] possibly a kind of shellfish: scallops?

224 *trenchering*] wooden plates.

225 There … off] There are some painfully strenuous activities from which we can derive pleasure in the doing.

Point to rich ends. This my mean task
Would be as heavy to me as odious; but   5
The mistress which I serve quickens what's dead,[226]
And makes my labours pleasures: O, she is
Ten times more gentle than her father's crabbèd,
And he's composed of harshness! I must remove
Some thousands of these logs, and pile them up,   10
Upon a sore injunction. My sweet mistress[227]
Weeps when she sees me work, and says such baseness
Had never like executor. I forget.
But these sweet thoughts do even refresh my
     labours—
Most busy least—when I do it.[228]   15

[*Enter MIRANDA: and PROSPERO behind*]

MIRANDA.   Alas, now pray you,
Work not so hard: I would the lightning had
Burnt up those logs that you are enjoined to pile!
Pray, set it down and rest you: when this burns,
'Twill weep for having wearied you. My father[229]
Is hard at study; pray, now, rest yourself: 20
He's safe for these three hours.
FERDINAND.   O, most dear mistress,
The sun will set, before I shall discharge
What I must strive to do.
MIRANDA.   If you'll sit down,
I'll bear your logs the while; pray give me that;
I'll carry it to the pile.   25
FERDINAND. No, precious creature:
I had rather crack my sinews, break my back,
Than you should such dishonour undergo,
While I sit lazy by.
MIRANDA.   It would become me
As well as it does you: and I should do it   30
With much more ease; for my good will is to it,
And yours it is against.
PROSPERO. [*Aside*] Poor worm, thou art infected:
This visitation shows it.[230]

MIRANDA.   You look wearily.
FERDINAND. No, noble mistress; 'tis fresh morning   35
     with me
When you are by at night. I do beseech you—
Chiefly that I might set it in my prayers—
What is your name?
MIRANDA.   Miranda.—O my father!
I have broke your hest to say so.[231]
FERDINAND.   Admired Miranda![232]
Indeed, the top of admiration; worth   40
What's dearest to the world! Full many a lady
I have eyed with best regard, and many a time
The harmony of their tongues hath into bondage
Brought my too diligent ear: for several virtues[233]
Have I liked several women; never any   45
With so full soul but some defect in her[234]
Did quarrel with the noblest grace she owed,[235]
And put it to the foil: but you, O you!—[236]
So perfect and so peerless—are created
Of every creature's best.   50
MIRANDA.   I do not know
One of my sex; no woman's face remember,
Save, from my glass, mine own; nor have I seen
More that I may call men than you, good friend,
And my dear father. How features are abroad,[237]
I am skilless of; but, by my modesty[238]   55
(The jewel in my dower), I would not wish
Any companion in the world but you;
Nor can imagination form a shape,
Besides yourself, to like of. But I prattle[239]
Something too wildly, and my father's precepts   60
I therein do forget.
FERDINAND.   I am, in my condition,
A prince, Miranda; I do think, a king—
I would not so!—and would no more endure
This wooden slavery than to suffer

---

226 quickens] brings to life.
227 sore injunction] stern command.
228 Most busy least] The busier one keeps the mind, the less
     the work seems.
229 weep] as resin is exuded by burning wood.
230 visitation] a play on visit and on the "visitations" of the
     plague upon those infected.

---

231 hest] behest, command.
232 Admired Miranda] The name Miranda means "admi-
     rable (or wonderful) woman."
233 several] various separate.
234 With … soul] so wholeheartedly.
235 owed] owned.
236 put … foil] contrasted it; overthrew.
237 features] human appearances.
238 skilless] ignorant.
239 like of] compare to.

The flesh-fly blow my mouth. Hear my soul   65
    speak:240
The very instant that I saw you, did
My heart fly to your service; there resides,
To make me slave to it; and for your sake
Am I this patient log-man.
MIRANDA.   Do you love me?
FERDINAND. O heaven! O earth! bear witness to   70
    this sound,
And crown what I profess with kind event,241
If I speak true: if hollowly, invert
What best is boded me to mischief! I,
Beyond all limit of what else i' the world,
Do love, prize, honour you.   75
MIRANDA.   I am a fool
To weep at what I am glad of.
PROSPERO. [Aside]   Fair encounter
Of two most rare affections! Heavens rain grace
On that which breeds between them!
FERDINAND.   Wherefore weep you?
MIRANDA. At mine unworthiness, that dare not offer
What I desire to give; and much less take   80
What I shall die to want. But this is trifling;242
And all the more it seeks to hide itself,
The bigger bulk it shows. Hence, bashful cunning,
And prompt me, plain and holy innocence!
I am your wife, if you will marry me;   85
If not, I'll die your maid. To be your fellow243
You may deny me; but I'll be your servant,
Whether you will or no.
FERDINAND.   My mistress, dearest;
And I thus humble ever.
MIRANDA.   My husband, then?
FERDINAND. Ay, with a heart as willing   90
As bondage e'er of freedom: here's my hand.244
MIRANDA. And mine, with my heart in't; and now
    farewell
Till half an hour hence.

FERDINAND.   A thousand thousand!245

[Exeunt FERDINAND and MIRANDA severally]

PROSPERO. So glad of this as they, I cannot be,   95
Who are surprised withal; but my rejoicing246
At nothing can be more. I'll to my book;
For yet, ere supper time, must I perform
Much business appertaining. [Exit]247

SCENE II.

Another part of the island

[Enter CALIBAN, with a bottle, STEPHANO, and TRINCULO]

STEPHANO. Tell not me! When the butt is out we will
drink water; not a drop before: therefore bear up and
board 'em.248 Servant-monster, drink to me!
TRINCULO. Servant-monster! The folly of this island!
They say there's but five upon this isle; we are three   5
of them; if th' other two be brained like us, the
state totters.
STEPHANO. Drink, servant-monster, when I bid
thee. Thy eyes are almost set in thy head.249
TRINCULO. Where should they be set else?250 He   10
were a brave monster indeed, if they were set in
his tail.
STEPHANO. My man-monster hath drowned his
tongue in sack. For my part, the sea cannot drown
me. I swam, ere I could recover the shore, five-and-   15
thirty leagues, off and on, by this light. Thou shalt
be my lieutenant, monster, or my standard.251
TRINCULO. Your lieutenant, if you list; he's no
standard.252
STEPHANO. We'll not run, Monsieur monster.253   20

---

240 flesh-fly] a fly that feeds on carrion and animal waste;
    blow] contaminate.
241 kind event] providential outcome.
242 want] lack.
243 maid] (pun) servant, virgin; fellow] equal.
244 As … freedom] as strongly as slavery always yearns for
    freedom.

---

245 thousand thousand] i.e., farewells.
246 surprised withal] taken unaware.
247 appertaining] related to this matter.
248 bear up and board 'em] a term from naval battle, here
    meaning "get drinking."
249 set in thy head] i.e., like the sun, rolled out of sight.
250 set] (pun) placed.
251 standard] standard-bearer.
252 no standard] (pun) too drunk to stand.
253 run] i.e., from the enemy.

[III.ii]

TRINCULO. Nor go neither: but you'll lie like dogs, and yet say nothing neither.[254]

STEPHANO. Moon-calf, speak once in thy life, if thou beest a good moon-calf.

CALIBAN. How does thy honour? Let me lick thy shoe. I'll not serve him; he is not valiant.

TRINCULO. Thou liest, most ignorant monster: I am in case to justle a constable.[255] Why, thou deboshed fish thou, was there ever man a coward that hath drunk so much sack as I today?[256] Wilt thou tell a monstrous lie, being but half fish and half a monster?

CALIBAN. Lo, how he mocks me! Wilt thou let him, my lord?

TRINCULO. 'Lord' quoth he! That a monster should be such a natural![257]

CALIBAN. Lo, lo again! Bite him to death, I prithee!

STEPHANO. Trinculo, keep a good tongue in your head: if you prove a mutineer, the next tree![258] The poor monster's my subject, and he shall not suffer indignity.

CALIBAN. I thank my noble lord. Wilt thou be pleased to hearken once again to the suit I made to thee?

STEPHANO. Marry, will I. Kneel, and repeat it; I will stand, and so shall Trinculo.

[Enter ARIEL, invisible]

CALIBAN. As I told thee before, I am subject to a tyrant, sorcerer, that by his cunning hath cheated me of the island.

ARIEL. Thou liest.

CALIBAN. Thou liest, thou jesting monkey, thou! I would my valiant master would destroy thee; I do not lie!

STEPHANO. Trinculo, if you trouble him any more in's tale, by this hand, I will supplant some of your teeth.

TRINCULO. Why, I said nothing.

STEPHANO. Mum, then, and no more.—Proceed.

CALIBAN. I say, by sorcery he got this isle; From me he got it: if thy greatness will Revenge it on him—for I know, thou dar'st; But this thing dare not—[259]

STEPHANO. That's most certain.

CALIBAN. Thou shalt be lord of it, and I'll serve thee.

STEPHANO. How now shall this be compassed?[260] Canst thou bring me to the party?[261]

CALIBAN. Yea, yea, my lord: I'll yield him thee asleep, Where thou may'st knock a nail into his head.

ARIEL. Thou liest: thou canst not.

CALIBAN. What a pied ninny's this! Thou scurvy patch![262] I do beseech thy greatness: give him blows, And take his bottle from him. When that's gone He shall drink nought but brine, for I'll not show him Where the quick freshes are.[263]

STEPHANO. Trinculo, run into no further danger: interrupt the monster one word further and, by this hand, I'll turn my mercy out o' doors, and make a stock-fish of thee.[264]

TRINCULO. Why, what did I? I did nothing. I'll go farther off.

STEPHANO. Didst thou not say he lied?

ARIEL. Thou liest.

STEPHANO. Do I so? Take thou that. [Strikes TRINCULO] As you like this, give me the lie another time.

TRINCULO. I did not give the lie! Out o' your wits and hearing too? A pox o' your bottle! This can sack and drinking do. A murrain on your monster, and the devil take your fingers![265]

CALIBAN. Ha, ha, ha!

STEPHANO. Now, forward with your tale.—Prithee stand further off.

---

[254] go] walk; lie (pun) recline; defecate (thus implying also a pun on a secondary meaning of run: urinate).
[255] in case to] in a fit condition to.
[256] deboshed] debauched.
[257] natural] fool (punning on monsters being unnatural).
[258] next tree] i.e., you'll hang from …

[259] this thing] i.e., Trinculo.
[260] compassed] navigated, i.e., accomplished.
[261] party] person.
[262] pied ninny] motley fool; patch] clown.
[263] quick freshes] fresh-water springs.
[264] stock-fish] dried cod, beaten before cooking.
[265] murrain] plague that infects cattle.

CALIBAN. Beat him enough. After a little time,
    I'll beat him too.
STEPHANO.   Stand farther. —Come, proceed.   95
CALIBAN. Why, as I told thee, 'tis a custom with him
    I' th'afternoon to sleep: there thou mayst brain him,
    Having first seized his books; or with a log
    Batter his skull, or paunch him with a stake,[266]
    Or cut his wezand with thy knife. Remember[267]   100
    First to possess his books; for without them
    He's but a sot, as I am, nor hath not[268]
    One spirit to command: they all do hate him
    As rootedly as I. Burn but his books;
    He has brave utensils—for so he calls them—[269]   105
    Which, when he has a house, he'll deck withal:
    And that most deeply to consider is
    The beauty of his daughter; he himself
    Calls her a nonpareil: I never saw a woman
    But only Sycorax my dam and she;   110
    But she as far surpasseth Sycorax
    As great'st does least.
STEPHANO.   Is it so brave a lass?
CALIBAN. Ay, lord: she will become thy bed, I warrant,
    And bring thee forth brave brood.
STEPHANO. Monster, I will kill this man; his   115
    daughter and I will be king and queen—save our
    graces!—and Trinculo and thyself shall be viceroys.
    Dost thou like the plot, Trinculo?
TRINCULO. Excellent.
STEPHANO. Give me thy hand: I am sorry I beat   120
    thee; but while thou livest, keep a good tongue in
    thy head.
CALIBAN. Within this half hour will he be asleep.
    Wilt thou destroy him then?
STEPHANO. Ay, on mine honour.   125
ARIEL. This will I tell my master.
CALIBAN. Thou mak'st me merry; I am full of pleasure.
    Let us be jocund. Will you troll the catch[270]
    You taught me but while-ere?[271]

STEPHANO. At thy request, monster, I will do reason,   130
    any reason. Come on, Trinculo, let us sing. [Sings]
        Flout 'em and scout 'em;
        and scout 'em and flout 'em:
            Thought is free.
CALIBAN. That's not the tune.   135

[ARIEL *plays the tune on a Tabor and Pipe*]

STEPHANO. What is this same?
TRINCULO. This is the tune of our catch, played by
    the picture of Nobody.[272]
STEPHANO. If thou beest a man, show thyself in thy
    likeness: if thou beest a devil, take't as thou list.[273]   140
TRINCULO. O, forgive me my sins!
STEPHANO. He that dies pays all debts. I defy thee.
    Mercy upon us!
CALIBAN. Art thou afeard?
STEPHANO. No, monster, not I.   145
CALIBAN. Be not afeard. The isle is full of noises,
    Sounds and sweet airs that give delight and hurt
        not.
    Sometimes a thousand twangling instruments[274]
    Will hum about mine ears; and sometime voices
    That, if I then had waked after long sleep,   150
    Will make me sleep again: and then, in dreaming,
    The clouds methought would open and show
        riches
    Ready to drop upon me; that, when I waked,
    I cried to dream again.
STEPHANO. This will prove a brave kingdom to me,   155
    where I shall have my music for nothing.
CALIBAN. When Prospero is destroyed.
STEPHANO. That shall be by and by. I remember the
    story.
TRINCULO. The sound is going away. Let's follow   160
    it, and after do our work.
STEPHANO. Lead, monster; we'll follow. I would I
    could see this taborer! He lays it on. Wilt come?
TRINCULO. I'll follow, Stephano. [*Exeunt*

---

266 paunch him] stab his belly.
267 wezand] windpipe.
268 sot, as I am] helpless fool.
269 utensils] instruments, furnishings.
270 troll the catch] sing the song in parts.
271 while-ere] a short while ago.

---

272 picture of Nobody] A popular image of the time showed
    "Nobody" as a figure with head and limbs but no torso.
273 take't as thou list] suit yourself.
274 twangling] twanging and tinkling.

[III.iii]

SCENE III.

Another part of the island

[*Enter ALONSO, SEBASTIAN, ANTONIO, GONZALO, ADRIAN, FRANCISCO, and OTHERS*]

GONZALO. By'r lakin, I can go no further, sir;[275]
  My old bones ache. Here's a maze trod, indeed,
  Through forthrights and meanders! By your
    patience,[276]
  I needs must rest me.
ALONSO.   Old lord, I cannot blame thee,
  Who am myself attached with weariness[277]   5
  To th' dulling of my spirits. Sit down and rest.
  Even here I will put off my hope, and keep it
  No longer for my flatterer: he is drowned
  Whom thus we stray to find; and the sea mocks
  Our frustrate search on land. Well, let him go.   10
ANTONIO. [*Aside to SEBASTIAN*] I am right glad
    that he's so out of hope.
  Do not, for one repulse, forgo the purpose
  That you resolved to effect.
SEBASTIAN. [*Aside to ANTONIO*] The next advantage
  Will we take throughly.
ANTONIO. [*Aside to SEBASTIAN*] Let it be tonight;
  For, now they are oppressed with travel, they   15
  Will not, nor cannot, use such vigilance
  As when they are fresh.
SEBASTIAN. [*Aside to ANTONIO*] I say, tonight:
  no more.

[*Solemn and strange music: and PROSPERO above, invisible. Enter several strange Shapes, bringing in a banquet; they dance about it with gentle actions of salutation, and, inviting the KING, &c., to eat, they depart.*]

ALONSO. What harmony is this? My good friends,
  hark!
GONZALO. Marvellous sweet music!
ALONSO. Give us kind keepers, heavens! What were   20
  these?[278]

SEBASTIAN. A living drollery. Now I will believe[279]
  That there are unicorns; that in Arabia
  There is one tree, the phoenix' throne; one phoenix
  At this hour reigning there.[280]
ANTONIO.   I'll believe both;
  And what does else want credit, come to me,[281]   25
  And I'll be sworn 'tis true. Travellers ne'er did lie,
  Though fools at home condemn them.
GONZALO.   If in Naples
  I should report this now, would they believe me?
  If I should say, I saw such islanders—
  For, certes, these are people of the island—   30
  Who, though they are of monstrous shape, yet note,
  Their manners are more gentle, kind, than of
  Our human generation you shall find
  Many, nay, almost any.
PROSPERO. [*Aside*]   Honest lord,
  Thou hast said well; for some of you there present   35
  Are worse than devils.
ALONSO.   I cannot too much muse[282]
  Such shapes, such gesture, and such sound,
    expressing—
  Although they want the use of tongue—a kind
  Of excellent dumb discourse.
PROSPERO. [*Aside*]   Praise in departing.[283]
FRANCISCO. They vanished strangely.   40
SEBASTIAN.   No matter, since
  They have left their viands behind; for we have
    stomachs.
  Will't please you taste of what is here?
ALONSO.   Not I.
GONZALO. Faith, sir, you need not fear. When we
  were boys,
  Who would believe that there were mountaineers[284]
  Dewlapped like bulls, whose throats had hanging   45
  at them[285]

---

275 By'r lakin] By our ladykin (Virgin Mary).
276 forthrights] straight paths.
277 attached] seized.
278 kind keepers] guardian angels.
279 living drollery] puppet show with live creatures.
280 one tree … there] According to myth, the phoenix was a unique bird said to renew itself from its ashes, and it lived in a unique tree.
281 want credit] lack credibility.
282 muse] wonder at.
283 Praise in departing] save praise for the end.
284 mountaineers] possibly based in accounts of goitrous Swiss mountaineers.
285 dewlapped] having pendulous skin at the throat.

390 THE RENAISSANCE

Wallets of flesh? Or that there were such men[286]
Whose heads stood in their breasts—which now
    we find[287]
Each putter-out of five for one will bring us[288]
Good warrant of?
ALONSO.   I will stand to, and feed,
Although my last; no matter, since I feel   50
The best is past. Brother, my lord the duke,
Stand to and do as we.

[*Thunder and lightning. Enter* ARIEL, *like a harpy;
claps his wings upon the table; and, with a quaint
device, the banquet vanishes.*][289]

ARIEL. You are three men of sin, whom Destiny—
That hath to instrument this lower world
And what is in't—the never-surfeited sea   55
Hath caused to belch up you; and on this island
Where man doth not inhabit, you 'mongst men
Being most unfit to live. I have made you mad;
And even with such-like valour men hang and drown
Their proper selves.   60

[ALONSO, SEBASTIAN, &c., *draw their swords*]

            You fools! I and my fellows
Are ministers of Fate: the elements
Of whom your swords are tempered may as well
Wound the loud winds, or with bemocked-at stabs
Kill the still-closing waters, as diminish[290]
One dowle that's in my plume; my fellow-   65
    ministers[291]
Are like invulnerable. If you could hurt,[292]
Your swords are now too massy for your strengths,
And will not be uplifted. But, remember—

For that's my business to you—that you three
From Milan did supplant good Prospero;   70
Exposed unto the sea—which hath requit it—[293]
Him, and his innocent child: for which foul deed
The powers, delaying, not forgetting, have
Incensed the seas and shores, yea, all the creatures,
Against your peace. Thee of thy son, Alonso,   75
They have bereft; and do pronounce, by me:
Lingering perdition—worse than any death
Can be at once—shall step by step attend
You and your ways; whose wraths to guard you
    from—
Which here, in this most desolate isle, else falls   80
Upon your heads—is nothing but heart's sorrow,
And a clear life ensuing.[294]

[*He vanishes in thunder: then, to soft music, enter the
Shapes again, and dance, with mocks and mows, and
carry out the table*]

PROSPERO. [*Aside*] Bravely the figure of this harpy
    hast thou
Performed, my Ariel; a grace it had, devouring;[295]
Of my instruction hast thou nothing bated[296]   85
In what thou hadst to say. So, with good life[297]
And observation strange, my meaner ministers[298]
Their several kinds have done. My high charms
    work,
And these mine enemies are all knit up
In their distractions; they now are in my power;   90
And in these fits I leave them, while I visit
Young Ferdinand (whom they suppose is drowned)
And his and mine loved darling. [*Exit above*]
GONZALO. I' the name of something holy, sir, why
    stand you
In this strange stare?[299]   95
ALONSO.   O, it is monstrous! monstrous![300]
Methought the billows spoke, and told me of it;

---

286 wallets] wattles.
287 heads … breasts] a traveller's tale also alluded to in
    Othello.
288 putter-out … one] London travellers to dangerous des-
    tinations would deposit a sum with speculators to be
    returned five-fold upon their successful return with
    proof of their visit.
289 *harpy*] a mythological creature with the head and torso
    of a woman, the claws and wings of a bird.
290 still] constantly.
291 dowle] small feather.
292 like] also.

---

293 requit it] avenged the deed.
294 clear] innocent.
295 devouring] i.e., an all-engulfing grace (with a pun on the
    gluttony of harpies).
296 bated] omitted.
297 good life] convincing performance.
298 observation strange] close attention.
299 Gonzalo has not heard Ariel as the harpy.
300 it] i.e., his sin.

The winds did sing it to me; and the thunder,
That deep and dreadful organ-pipe, pronounced
The name of Prosper; it did bass my trespass.[301]
Therefore my son i' th' ooze is bedded; and   100
I'll seek him deeper than e'er plummet sounded,
And with him there lie mudded. [*Exit*]
SEBASTIAN.   But one fiend at a time,
I'll fight their legions o'er.
ANTONIO.   I'll be thy second.

[*Exeunt SEBASTIAN and ANTONIO*]

GONZALO. All three of them are desperate: their
     great guilt,
Like poison given to work a great time after,   105
Now 'gins to bite the spirits. I do beseech you
That are of suppler joints, follow them swiftly
And hinder them from what this ecstasy[302]
May now provoke them to.
ADRIAN.   Follow, I pray you. [*Exeunt*]

ACT IV

SCENE I.

Before PROSPERO'S cell

[*Enter PROSPERO, FERDINAND, and MIRANDA*]

PROSPERO. If I have too austerely punished you,
Your compensation makes amends; for I
Have given you here a third of mine own life,[303]
Or that for which I live; who once again
I tender to thy hand: all thy vexations   5
Were but my trials of thy love, and thou
Hast strangely stood the test. Here, afore Heaven,[304]
I ratify this my rich gift. O Ferdinand!
Do not smile at me that I boast her off,[305]

For thou shalt find she will outstrip all praise,   10
And make it halt behind her.[306]
FERDINAND.   I do believe it
Against an oracle.[307]
PROSPERO. Then, as my gift and thine own acquisition
Worthily purchased, take my daughter. But
If thou dost break her virgin knot before   15
All sanctimonious ceremonies may[308]
With full and holy rite be ministered,
No sweet aspersion shall the heavens let fall[309]
To make this contract grow; but barren hate,[310]
Sour-eyed disdain, and discord, shall bestrew   20
The union of your bed with weeds so loathly
That you shall hate it both: therefore take heed,
As Hymen's lamps shall light you.
FERDINAND.   As I hope
For quiet days, fair issue, and long life,
With such love as 'tis now, the murkiest den,   25
The most opportune place, the strong'st suggestion
Our worser genius can, shall never melt[311]
Mine honour into lust, to take away
The edge of that day's celebration.
When I shall think: or Phoebus' steeds are foundered,   30
Or Night kept chained below.[312]
PROSPERO.   Fairly spoke.
Sit, then, and talk with her; she is thine own.
What, Ariel! My industrious servant, Ariel!

[*Enter ARIEL*]

ARIEL. What would my potent master? Here I am.
PROSPERO. Thou and thy meaner fellows your last   35
     service
Did worthily perform; and I must use you
In such another trick. Go bring the rabble,[313]
O'er whom I give thee power, here to this place;

---

301 bass] proclaimed in deep notes.
302 ecstasy] madness.
303 a third] Prospero's meaning in saying "a third" rather
     than "half" has been variously explained as having an-
     other third in mind represented by his dead wife (a third
     already gone), his magic, or Milan.
304 strangely] exceptionally.
305 boast her off] boast while bargaining her off.

306 halt] limp (the image of praise being feeble by compari-
     son to the reality).
307 Against an oracle] even were an oracle to deny it.
308 sanctimonious] holy.
309 aspersion] grace, blessing.
310 grow] beget life.
311 worser genius can] bad angel can make.
312 When … below] When my mind does think in that
     way, either day or night will be no more.
313 rabble] lesser spirits.

Incite them to quick motion; for I must
Bestow upon the eyes of this young couple   40
Some vanity of mine art; it is my promise,314
And they expect it from me.
ARIEL.   Presently?
PROSPERO. Ay, with a twink.
ARIEL. Before you can say 'Come' and 'Go,'
    And breathe twice; and cry 'so, so,'   45
    Each one, tripping on his toe,
    Will be here with mop and mow.315
    Do you love me, master? No?
PROSPERO. Dearly, my delicate Ariel. Do not approach
    Till thou dost hear me call.   50
ARIEL.   Well I conceive.316 [Exit]
PROSPERO. Look, thou be true; do not give
    dalliance317
    Too much the rein: the strongest oaths are straw
    To th' fire i' the blood. Be more abstemious,
    Or else good night your vow!
FERDINAND.   I warrant you, sir;
    The white-cold virgin snow upon my heart   55
    Abates the ardour of my liver.318
PROSPERO.   Well.
    Now come, my Ariel! Bring a corollary,319
    Rather than want a spirit. Appear, and pertly!320
    No tongue! All eyes! Be silent.

[Soft music. A Masque. Enter IRIS]321

IRIS. Ceres, most bounteous lady: thy rich leas322   60
    Of wheat, rye, barley, vetches, oats, and peas;323
    Thy turfy mountains, where live nibbling sheep,
And flat meads thatched with stover, them to
    keep;324
Thy banks with pioned and twilled brims,325
Which spongy April at thy hest betrims,   65
To make cold nymphs chaste crowns; and thy
    broom groves,326
Whose shadow the dismissèd bachelor loves,
Being lass-lorn; thy pole-clipt vineyard;327
And thy sea-marge, sterile and rocky-hard,328
Where thou thyself dost air: the Queen o' the sky,329   70
Whose watery arch and messenger am I,
Bids thee leave these; and with her sovereign grace,
Here on this grass-plot, in this very place,
To come and sport. Her peacocks fly amain;330
Approach, rich Ceres, her to entertain.   75

[Enter CERES]

CERES. Hail, many-coloured messenger, that ne'er
    Dost disobey the wife of Jupiter;
    Who with thy saffron wings upon my flowers
    Diffusest honey drops, refreshing showers:
    And with each end of thy blue bow dost crown   80
    My bosky acres and my unshrubbed down,331
    Rich scarf to my proud earth; why hath thy queen
    Summoned me hither to this short-grassed green?
IRIS. A contract of true love to celebrate,
    And some donation freely to estate332   85
    On the blest lovers.
CERES.   Tell me, heavenly bow,
    If Venus or her son, as thou dost know,333

---

314 vanity] display.
315 mop and mow] antics and grimaces.
316 conceive] understand.
317 be true] Apparently, Ferdinand and Miranda have been
    embracing.
318 liver] the supposed seat of passion.
319 corollary] plethora, surplus.
320 want] lack; pertly] quickly.
321 Iris] Greek goddess associated with the rainbow and
    with solemn oaths, messenger to the gods.
322 Ceres] Roman goddess of fertility, identified with Greek
    goddess Demeter; leas] grasslands.
323 vetches] legumes used for cattle feed.

324 meads] meadows; stover] eared grain stalks used for win-
    ter cattle feed.
325 pioned and twilled] dug and woven (a process to pre-
    vent bank erosion).
326 spongy April ... crowns] Wet April bedecks (the banks)
    with flowers out of which virgins weave themselves
    crowns for May celebrations.
327 pole-clipt] pruned.
328 sea-marge] seashore.
329 Queen] i.e., Juno.
330 peacocks] Juno's sacred birds, which draw her chariot;
    amain] at full speed.
331 bosky] wooded.
332 estate] bestow.
333 her son] Cupid, often represented as blind.

Do now attend the queen? Since they did plot
The means that dusky Dis my daughter got,[334]
Her and her blind boy's scandaled company   90
I have forsworn.

IRIS.   Of her society
Be not afraid. I met Her Deity[335]
Cutting the clouds towards Paphos and her
    son[336]
Dove-drawn with her. Here thought they to have
    done
Some wanton charm upon this man and maid,   95
Whose vows are, that no bed-rite shall be paid
Till Hymen's torch be lighted; but in vain.[337]
Mars's hot minion is returned again;[338]
Her waspish-headed son has broke his arrows,[339]
Swears he will shoot no more, but play with   100
    sparrows,
And be a boy right out.

CERES.   Highest Queen of State,
Great Juno, comes; I know her by her gait.

[*Enter JUNO*][340]

JUNO. How does my bounteous sister? Go with me
To bless this twain, that they may prosperous be,
And honoured in their issue.   105

SONG

JUNO.

Honour, riches, marriage-blessing,
Long continuance, and increasing,
Hourly joys be still upon you![341]
Juno sings her blessings on you.

CERES.

Earth's increase, foison plenty,[342]   110
Barns and garners never empty;[343]
Vines with clust'ring bunches growing;
Plants with goodly burden bowing;
Spring come to you at the farthest,
    In the very end of harvest!   115
Scarcity and want shall shun you;
    Ceres' blessing so is on you.

FERDINAND. This is a most majestic vision, and
    Harmonious charmingly. May I be bold[344]
    To think these spirits?   120

PROSPERO.   Spirits, which by mine art
    I have from their confines called to enact
    My present fancies.

FERDINAND.   Let me live here ever:
    So rare a wondered father and a wife,[345]
    Makes this place Paradise.

[*JUNO and CERES whisper, and send IRIS on*
employment]

PROSPERO.   Sweet now, silence.[346]
    Juno and Ceres whisper seriously;   125
    There's something else to do: hush, and be mute,
    Or else our spell is marred.

IRIS. You nymphs, called Naiads, of the windring
    brooks,[347]
    With your sedged crowns and ever-harmless
    looks,[348]
    Leave your crisp channels, and on this green land[349]   130
    Answer your summons: Juno does command.
    Come, temperate nymphs, and help to celebrate
    A contract of true love; be not too late.

[*Enter certain NYMPHS*]

---

334 Dis] Pluto, god of the dark underworld (hence "dusky"),
    who abducted Proserpine.
335 Her Deity] i.e., Juno.
336 Paphos] Venus, so named for a centre of her cult based
    at Paphos in Cyprus.
337 Hymen] god of marriage.
338 Mars's hot minion] i.e., Venus, mistress of Mars, the god
    of warfare; returned] i.e., home.
339 waspish-headed] ill tempered, stinging.
340 *Juno*] chief Roman goddess, consort of Jupiter, associ-
    ated with marriage and identified with Greek goddess
    Hera.
341 *still*] constantly.

342 *foison*] rich harvest.
343 *garners*] granaries.
344 charmingly] i.e., the harmonies have a magic power to
    enchant.
345 wondered] wondrous; wife] most editions read "wise."
346 It seems unlikely that Prospero is addressing Ferdinand;
    perhaps Miranda was about to reply.
347 Naiads] water-nymphs of Greek mythology; windring]
    winding and wandering.
348 sedged crowns] crowns of marsh plants.
349 crisp] rippling.

You sun-burned sicklemen, of August weary,
Come hither from the furrow, and be merry: 135
Make holiday: your rye-straw hats put on,
And these fresh nymphs encounter every one
In country footing.[350]

[*Enter certain Reapers, properly habited; they join with
the Nymphs in a graceful dance; towards the end
whereof* PROSPERO *starts suddenly, and speaks; after
which, to a strange, hollow, and confused noise, they
heavily vanish*]

PROSPERO. [*Aside*] I had forgot that foul conspiracy
Of the beast Caliban and his confederates   140
Against my life: the minute of their plot
Is almost come. [*To Spirits*] Well done! Avoid; no
more![351]
FERDINAND. This is strange: your father's in some
passion
That works him strongly.
MIRANDA.   Never till this day
Saw I him touched with anger so distempered.   145
PROSPERO. You do look, my son, in a movèd sort,[352]
As if you were dismayed: be cheerful, sir.
Our revels now are ended. These our actors,[353]
As I foretold you, were all spirits and
Are melted into air, into thin air;   150
And—like the baseless fabric of this vision—[354]
The cloud-capped towers, the gorgeous palaces,
The solemn temples, the great globe itself,
Yea, all which it inherit, shall dissolve[355]
And, like this insubstantial pageant faded,   155
Leave not a rack behind. We are such stuff[356]
As dreams are made on, and our little life[357]
Is rounded with a sleep.—Sir, I am vexed:
Bear with my weakness; my old brain is troubled.
Be not disturbed with my infirmity.   160

If you be pleased, retire into my cell
And there repose. A turn or two I'll walk,
To still my beating mind.
FERDINAND & MIRANDA. We wish your peace.

[*Exeunt*]

PROSPERO.   Come, with a thought—
[*To them*] I thank thee. —Ariel, come!   165

[*Enter* ARIEL]

ARIEL. Thy thoughts I cleave to. What's thy pleasure?
PROSPERO.   Spirit,
We must prepare to meet with Caliban.
ARIEL. Ay, my commander; when I presented
Ceres,[358]
I thought to have told thee of it: but I feared
Lest I might anger thee.   170
PROSPERO. Say again, where didst thou leave these
varlets?[359]
ARIEL. I told you, sir, they were red-hot with
drinking;
So full of valour that they smote the air
For breathing in their faces, beat the ground
For kissing of their feet; yet always bending   175
Towards their project. Then I beat my tabor;
At which, like unbacked colts, they pricked their
ears,[360]
Advanced their eyelids, lifted up their noses[361]
As they smelt music. So I charmed their ears,
That, calf-like, they my lowing followed through   180
Toothed briers, sharp furzes, pricking goss and
thorns,[362]
Which entered their frail shins: at last I left them
I'the filthy-mantled pool beyond your cell,[363]
There dancing up to the chins, that the foul lake
O'erstunk their feet.   185
PROSPERO.   This was well done, my bird.

---

[350] country footing] rural dancing.
[351] avoid] be off.
[352] movèd sort] troubled mood.
[353] revels] masque dances.
[354] baseless] immaterial.
[355] it inherit] occupy it.
[356] rack] wisp of cloud (with a secondary meaning of ship-
    wreck).
[357] on] of.

[358] presented] "introduced" or, possibly, "played" — imply-
    ing that Ariel had played either Iris (who introduces
    Ceres) or Ceres herself.
[359] varlets] base persons, knaves.
[360] unbacked] unbroken.
[361] advanced] raised.
[362] furzes] coarse grass; goss] gorse, a spiny shrub.
[363] mantled] covered with scum.

Thy shape invisible retain thou still.
The trumpery in my house, go bring it hither
For stale to catch these thieves.[364]
ARIEL.   I go, I go. [*Exit*]
PROSPERO. A devil, a born devil, on whose nature
    Nurture can never stick; on whom my pains,   190
    Humanely taken, all, all lost, quite lost;
    And as with age his body uglier grows,
    So his mind cankers. I will plague them all,
    Even to roaring.

[*Enter ARIEL, loaden with glistering apparel, &c.*]

            Come, hang them on this line.[365]

[*PROSPERO and ARIEL remain invisible.*
Enter CALIBAN, STEPHANO, and TRINCULO, all wet]

CALIBAN. Pray you, tread softly, that the blind mole   195
    may not
    Hear a foot fall. We now are near his cell.
STEPHANO. Monster, your fairy, which you say is a
    harmless fairy, has done little better than played
    the Jack with us.[366]
TRINCULO. Monster, I do smell all horse-piss, at   200
    which my nose is in great indignation.
STEPHANO. So is mine. Do you hear, monster? If I
    should take a displeasure against you, look you—
TRINCULO. Thou wert but a lost monster.
CALIBAN. Good my lord, give me thy favour still.   205
    Be patient, for the prize I'll bring thee to
    Shall hoodwink this mischance. Therefore speak
    softly;[367]
    All's hushed as midnight yet.
TRINCULO. Ay, but to lose our bottles in the pool—!
STEPHANO. There is not only disgrace and dis-   210
    honour in that, monster, but an infinite loss.
TRINCULO. That's more to me than my wetting; yet
    this is your harmless fairy, monster.
STEPHANO. I will fetch off my bottle, though I be
    o'er ears for my labour.   215

---

364 stale] decoy.
365 line] a clothesline or perhaps a lime tree (line and lime
     were used interchangeably).
366 Jack] (pun) Jack-o-lantern; knave.
367 hoodwink] cover its head, make it harmless.

CALIBAN. Prithee, my king, be quiet. Seest thou here?
    This is the mouth o' the cell. No noise, and enter.
    Do that good mischief which may make this island
    Thine own for ever, and I, thy Caliban,
    For aye thy foot-licker.   220
STEPHANO. Give me thy hand. I do begin to have
    bloody thoughts.
TRINCULO. O King Stephano! O peer![368] O worthy
    Stephano! Look what a wardrobe here is for thee!
CALIBAN. Let it alone, thou fool; it is but trash.   225
TRINCULO. O, ho, monster! We know what belongs
    to a frippery.[369] O King Stephano!
STEPHANO. Put off that gown, Trinculo; by this
    hand, I'll have that gown.
TRINCULO. Thy Grace shall have it.   230
CALIBAN. The dropsy drown this fool! What do you
    mean
    To dote thus on such luggage? Let't alone,[370]
    And do the murder first. If he awake,
    From toe to crown he'll fill our skins with pinches,
    Make us strange stuff.   235
STEPHANO. Be you quiet, monster. Mistress line, is
    not this my jerkin?[371] Now is the jerkin under the
    line: now, jerkin, you are like to lose your hair, and
    prove a bald jerkin.[372]
TRINCULO. Do, do! We steal by line and level, an't   240
    like your Grace.[373]
STEPHANO. I thank thee for that jest: here's a
    garment for't. Wit shall not go unrewarded while
    I am king of this country! 'Steal by line and level,'
    is an excellent pass of pate.[374] There's another   245
    garment for't.

---

368 peer] an allusion to a popular song, "King Stephen was
     a worthy peer …"
369 frippery] used clothing shop.
370 luggage] junk.
371 jerkin] short, tight, sleeveless jacket.
372 line] (pun) clothesline; equatorial line. The joke is that
     sailors travelling "under the line" to the southern hemi-
     sphere often contracted fevers there, which caused them
     to lose their hair.
373 by line and level] i.e., by the rule.
374 pass of pate] witticism (a term derived from fencing; the
     exact sense is lost, but presumably refers to a pass across
     the top of the head—pate).

TRINCULO. Monster, come, put some lime upon
    your fingers, and away with the rest.[375]
CALIBAN. I will have none on't. We shall lose our
    time,
    And all be turned to barnacles, or to apes[376]   250
    With foreheads villainous low.
STEPHANO. Monster, lay-to your fingers: help to
    bear this away where my hogshead of wine is, or
    I'll turn you out of my kingdom. Go to, carry this.
TRINCULO. And this.   255
STEPHANO. Ay, and this.

[*A noise of hunters beard. Enter divers Spirits, in shape
of hounds, and hunt them about; PROSPERO and
ARIEL setting them on*]

PROSPERO. Hey, Mountain, hey!
ARIEL. Silver! There it goes, Silver!
PROSPERO. Fury, Fury! There, Tyrant, there! Hark,
    hark![377]

[*CALIBAN, STEPHANO, and TRINCULO are driven out*]

    Go, charge my goblins that they grind their joints   260
    With dry convulsions; shorten up their sinews[378]
    With agèd cramps, and more pinch-spotted make
    them
    Than pard, or cat o' mountain.[379]
ARIEL.   Hark, they roar.
PROSPERO. Let them be hunted soundly. At this hour
    Lies at my mercy all mine enemies.   265
    Shortly shall all my labours end, and thou
    Shalt have the air at freedom. For a little
    Follow, and do me service. [*Exeunt*]

---

[375] put … fingers] a phrase used about stealing, meaning,
    roughly, "get your hands dirty"; lime] birdlime, a sticky
    substance used to catch birds.
[376] barnacles] a type of geese, supposed to have been trans-
    formed from shellfish.
[377] Mountain, Silver, Fury, Tyrant] common names for
    hunting dogs.
[378] dry convulsions] palsy supposedly caused by absence of
    vital fluids.
[379] pard, cat o' mountain] leopard, cougar.

ACT V

SCENE I.

Before the cell of PROSPERO.

[*Enter PROSPERO in his magic robes; and ARIEL*]

PROSPERO. Now does my project gather to a head.
    My charms crack not; my spirits obey, and Time
    Goes upright with his carriage. How's the day?[380]
ARIEL. On the sixth hour; at which time, my lord,
    You said our work should cease.   5
PROSPERO.   I did say so,
    When first I raised the tempest. Say, my spirit,
    How fares the King and 's followers?
ARIEL.   Confined together
    In the same fashion as you gave in charge,
    Just as you left them—all prisoners, sir,
    In the lime-grove which weather-fends your cell;[381] 10
    They cannot budge till your release. The king,[382]
    His brother, and yours, abide all three distracted,
    And the remainder mourning over them,
    Brim full of sorrow and dismay; but chiefly
    Him you termed, sir, 'the good old lord, Gonzalo.' 15
    His tears run down his beard, like winter's drops
    From eaves of reeds. Your charm so strongly works
    them[383]
    That if you now beheld them, your affections
    Would become tender.
PROSPERO.   Dost thou think so, spirit?
ARIEL. Mine would, sir, were I human.   20
PROSPERO.   And mine shall.
    Hast thou, which art but air, a touch, a feeling
    Of their afflictions, and shall not myself,
    One of their kind, that relish all as sharply[384]
    Passion as they, be kindlier moved than thou art?
    Though with their high wrongs I am struck to the 25
    quick,
    Yet with my nobler reason 'gainst my fury

---

[380] Time … carriage] Time walks upright, his burden (of
    deeds to be accomplished) light.
[381] weather-fends] acts as a wind-break.
[382] your release] i.e., your release of them.
[383] eaves of reeds] i.e., a thatched roof.
[384] relish all] sense quite.

Do I take part. The rarer action is
In virtue than in vengeance. They being penitent,
The sole drift of my purpose doth extend
Not a frown further. Go, release them, Ariel.   30
My charms I'll break, their senses I'll restore,
And they shall be themselves.
ARIEL.   I'll fetch them, sir. [Exit]
PROSPERO. Ye elves of hills, brooks, standing lakes,
      and groves,[385]
And ye that on the sands with printless foot
Do chase the ebbing Neptune, and do fly him   35
When he comes back; you demi-puppets that[386]
By moonshine do the green sour ringlets make,[387]
Whereof the ewe not bites; and you whose pastime
Is to make midnight mushrooms, that rejoice[388]
To hear the solemn curfew; by whose aid—   40
Weak masters though ye be—I have bedimmed[389]
The noontide sun, called forth the mutinous winds,
And 'twixt the green sea and the azured vault
Set roaring war: to the dread rattling thunder
Have I given fire, and rifted Jove's stout oak[390]   45
With his own bolt; the strong-based promontory
Have I made shake, and by the spurs plucked up[391]
The pine and cedar; graves at my command
Have waked their sleepers, oped, and let 'em forth
By my so potent art. But this rough magic   50
I here abjure; and, when I have required[392]
Some heavenly music—which even now I do—
To work mine end upon their senses that[393]
This airy charm is for, I'll break my staff,

Bury it certain fathoms in the earth,   55
And deeper than did ever plummet sound
I'll drown my book.

[Solemn music. Re-enter ARIEL: after him, ALONSO,
with frantic gesture, attended by GONZALO;
SEBASTIAN and ANTONIO in like manner, attended
by ADRIAN and FRANCISCO: they all enter the circle
which PROSPERO had made, and there stand charmed:
which PROSPERO observing, speaks]

A solemn air, and the best comforter[394]
To an unsettled fancy, cure thy brains,
Now useless, boiled within thy skull! There stand,   60
For you are spell-stopped.
Holy Gonzalo, honourable man,
Mine eyes, even sociable to the show of thine,[395]
Fall fellowly drops. The charm dissolves apace;
And as the morning steals upon the night,   65
Melting the darkness, so their rising senses
Begin to chase the ignorant fumes that mantle
Their clearer reason. O good Gonzalo,
My true preserver, and a loyal sir
To him thou follow'st, I will pay thy graces[396]   70
Home, both in word and deed. Most cruelly
Didst thou, Alonso, use me and my daughter:
Thy brother was a furtherer in the act.
Thou'rt pinched for't now, Sebastian. Flesh and
      blood,
You, brother mine, that entertained ambition,   75
Expelled remorse and nature; who, with
      Sebastian—[397]
Whose inward pinches therefore are most strong—
Would here have killed your king; I do forgive thee,
Unnatural though thou art. Their understanding
Begins to swell, and the approaching tide   80
Will shortly fill the reasonable shore
That now lies foul and muddy. Not one of them
That yet looks on me, or would know me. Ariel,
Fetch me the hat and rapier in my cell.

[Exit ARIEL]

---

385 This speech is adapted from an incantation by the witch
      Medea in Ovid's *Metamorphoses*.
386 demi-puppets] i.e., the doll-like fairies.
387 green … ringlets] circular patches in grass, called "fairy-
      rings," but actually caused by toadstool interference with
      grass roots.
388 mushrooms] because they appear overnight, thought to
      be made by elves.
389 weak masters] i.e., elves have some magical powers, but
      not the dominant power of a magus like Prospero.
390 rifted] split; Jove] Jupiter, chief Roman god, for whom
      the oak was a sacred tree.
391 spurs] roots.
392 required] commanded.
393 their senses that] the senses of those whom.

---

394 and] which is.
395 even … thine] moved by sympathetic feeling at the mere
      sight of your eyes.
396 graces] virtuous acts.
397 nature] i.e., natural feeling.

I will discase me, and myself present,³⁹⁸   85
As I was sometime Milan.—Quickly, spirit;³⁹⁹
Thou shalt ere long be free.

[*ARIEL re-enters, singing, and helps to attire PROSPERO*]

ARIEL.   *Where the bee sucks, there suck I;*
               In a cowslip's bell I lie;
               There I couch when owls do cry.   90
                  On the bat's back I do fly
                     After summer merrily:
               Merrily, merrily shall I live now
               Under the blossom that hangs on the bough.

PROSPERO. Why, that's my dainty Ariel! I shall miss   95
     thee;
  But yet thou shalt have freedom; so, so, so.
  To the king's ship, invisible as thou art:
  There shalt thou find the mariners asleep
  Under the hatches. The master and the boatswain
  Being awake, enforce them to this place,   100
  And presently, I prithee.⁴⁰⁰
ARIEL. I drink the air before me, and return⁴⁰¹
  Or ere your pulse twice beat. [*Exit*]
GONZALO. All torment, trouble, wonder and
     amazement
  Inhabits here. Some heavenly power guide us   105
  Out of this fearful country!
PROSPERO.   Behold, sir king,
  The wronged Duke of Milan, Prospero.
  For more assurance that a living prince
  Does now speak to thee, I embrace thy body;
  And to thee and thy company I bid   110
  A hearty welcome.
ALONSO.   Whe'er thou be'st he or no,
  Or some enchanted trifle to abuse me,⁴⁰²
  As late I have been, I not know. Thy pulse
  Beats, as of flesh and blood; and, since I saw thee,
  Th'affliction of my mind amends, with which,   115
  I fear, a madness held me. This must crave—
  An if this be at all—a most strange story.⁴⁰³

---

³⁹⁸ discase] undress.
³⁹⁹ As ... Milan] as I looked when I was Duke of Milan.
⁴⁰⁰ presently] immediately.
⁴⁰¹ drink the air] consume the intervening space.
⁴⁰² trifle] trick.
⁴⁰³ An if this be at all] if any of this is real.

Thy dukedom I resign, and do entreat⁴⁰⁴
Thou pardon me my wrongs. But how should
     Prospero
Be living and be here?   120
PROSPERO.   First, noble friend,
  Let me embrace thine age; whose honour cannot
  Be measured or confined.
GONZALO.   Whether this be
  Or be not, I'll not swear.
PROSPERO.   You do yet taste
  Some subtleties o' the isle, that will not let you
  Believe things certain. Welcome, my friends all.   125

[*Aside to SEBASTIAN and ANTONIO*]

  But you, my brace of lords, were I so minded,
  I here could pluck his highness' frown upon you,
  And justify you traitors. At this time⁴⁰⁵
  I will tell no tales.
SEBASTIAN. [*Aside*] The devil speaks in him.
PROSPERO.   No.
  For you, most wicked sir, whom to call brother   130
  Would even infect my mouth, I do forgive
  Thy rankest faults—all of them—and require
  My dukedom of thee, which, perforce, I know
  Thou must restore.
ALONSO.   If thou beest Prospero,
  Give us particulars of thy preservation;   135
  How thou hast met us here, whom three hours since
  Were wracked upon this shore; where I have lost—
  How sharp the point of this remembrance is!—
  My dear son, Ferdinand.
PROSPERO.   I am woe for't, sir.
ALONSO. Irreparable is the loss, and Patience   140
  Says it is past her cure.
PROSPERO.   I rather think
  You have not sought her help; of whose soft grace,
  For the like loss I have her sovereign aid,
  And rest myself content.
ALONSO.   You the like loss!
PROSPERO. As great to me as late; and,   145
     supportable⁴⁰⁶
  To make the dear loss, have I means much weaker

---

⁴⁰⁴ Thy dukedom] i.e., my right to tribute from.
⁴⁰⁵ justify] prove.
⁴⁰⁶ late] recent.

Than you may call to comfort you, for I
Have lost my daughter.
ALONSO.   A daughter? O heavens!
That they were living both in Naples,
The king and queen there! That they were, I wish   150
Myself were mudded in that oozy bed
Where my son lies. When did you lose your
    daughter?
PROSPERO. In this last tempest. I perceive, these lords
At this encounter do so much admire[407]
That they devour their reason, and scarce think   155
Their eyes do offices of truth, their words[408]
Are natural breath. But, howsoe'er you have
Been justled from your senses, know for certain[409]
That I am Prospero, and that very duke
Which was thrust forth of Milan; who most strangely   160
Upon this shore, where you were wracked, was
    landed
To be the lord on't. No more yet of this;
For 'tis a chronicle of day by day,
Not a relation for a breakfast nor
Befitting this first meeting. Welcome, sir: 165
This cell's my court. Here have I few attendants
And subjects none abroad. Pray you, look in.
My dukedom since you have given me again,
I will requite you with as good a thing;
At least bring forth a wonder, to content ye   170
As much as me my dukedom.

[*The entrance of the Cell opens, and discovers*[410]
FERDINAND *and* MIRANDA *playing at chess*]

MIRANDA. Sweet lord, you play me false.
FERDINAND. No, my dearest love, I would not for
    the world.
MIRANDA. Yes, for a score of kingdoms you should
    wrangle,
And I would call it fair play.[411]   175

---

407 admire] wonder.
408 do offices of truth] "perform services for Truth" (personi-
    fied).
409 justled] forced, shouldered.
410 *discovers*] reveals.
411 Yes … play] For somewhat less than "the world"—"a
    score of kingdoms"—Ferdinand would be prepared to
    struggle, but Miranda would readily forgive him.

ALONSO.   If this prove
A vision of the island, one dear son
Shall I twice lose.
SEBASTIAN.   A most high miracle!
FERDINAND. Though the seas threaten, they are
    merciful:
I have cursed them without cause.

[*Kneels to* ALONSO]

ALONSO.   Now all the blessings
Of a glad father compass thee about!   180
Arise, and say how thou cam'st here.
MIRANDA.   O, wonder!
How many goodly creatures are there here!
How beauteous mankind is! O brave new world
That has such people in't!
PROSPERO.   'Tis new to thee.
ALONSO. What is this maid, with whom thou wast   185
    at play?
Your eld'st acquaintance cannot be three hours.[412]
Is she the goddess that hath severed us,
And brought us thus together?
FERDINAND.   Sir, she is mortal;
But by immortal Providence she's mine.
I chose her when I could not ask my father   190
For his advice, nor thought I had one. She
Is daughter to this famous Duke of Milan,
Of whom so often I have heard renown,
But never saw before; of whom I have
Received a second life: and second father   195
This lady makes him to me.
ALONSO.   I am hers.
But, O, how oddly will it sound that I
Must ask my child forgiveness!
PROSPERO.   There, sir, stop.
Let us not burden our remembrances with
A heaviness that's gone.   200
GONZALO.   I have inly wept,
Or should have spoke ere this. Look down, you gods,
And on this couple drop a blessèd crown;
For it is you that have chalked forth the way
Which brought us hither.
ALONSO.   I say, Amen, Gonzalo!

---

412 eld'st] longest period of.

GONZALO. Was Milan thrust from Milan, that his issue   205
  Should become kings of Naples? O, rejoice
  Beyond a common joy, and set it down
  With gold on lasting pillars. In one voyage
  Did Claribel her husband find at Tunis,
  And Ferdinand, her brother, found a wife   210
  Where he himself was lost; Prospero his dukedom
  In a poor isle; and all of us ourselves,
  When no man was his own.
ALONSO. [*To FERDINAND and MIRANDA*]
                      Give me your hands:
  Let grief and sorrow still embrace his heart[413]
  That doth not wish you joy.   215
GONZALO.   Be it so! Amen!

[*Re-enter ARIEL, with the Master and Boatswain amazedly following*]

  O look, sir; look, sir! Here are more of us.
  I prophesied, if a gallows were on land,
  This fellow could not drown. Now, blasphemy,
  That swear'st grace o'erboard: not an oath on shore?
  Hast thou no mouth by land? What is the news?   220
BOATSWAIN. The best news is that we have safely found
  Our king and company: the next, our ship—
  Which but three glasses since we gave out split—
  Is tight and yare, and bravely rigged as when[414]
  We first put out to sea.   225
ARIEL. [*Aside to PROSPERO*] Sir, all this service
  Have I done since I went.
PROSPERO. [*Aside to ARIEL*] My tricksy spirit![415]
ALONSO. These are not natural events; they strengthen
  From strange to stranger. Say, how came you hither?   230
BOATSWAIN. If I did think, sir, I were well awake,
  I'd strive to tell you. We were dead of sleep,
  And (how, we know not) all clapped under hatches
  Where, but even now, with strange and several noises[416]
  Of roaring, shrieking, howling, jingling chains,   235
  And mo' diversity of sounds, all horrible,[417]
  We were awaked, straightway at liberty,

Where we—in all her trim—freshly beheld[418]
  Our royal, good, and gallant ship, our master
  Cap'ring to eye her. On a trice, so please you,[419]   240
  Even in a dream, were we divided from them,
  And were brought moping hither.[420]
ARIEL. [*Aside to PROSPERO*]   Was't well done?
PROSPERO. [*Aside to ARIEL*] Bravely, my diligence.
  Thou shalt be free.
ALONSO. This is as strange a maze as e'er men trod;   245
  And there is in this business more than nature
  Was ever conduct of. Some oracle[421]
  Must rectify our knowledge.
PROSPERO.   Sir, my liege,
  Do not infest your mind with beating on[422]
  The strangeness of this business. At picked leisure,   250
  Which shall be shortly, single I'll resolve you—[423]
  Which to you shall seem probable—of every[424]
  These happened accidents. Till when, be cheerful
  And think of each thing well.
  [*Aside to ARIEL*]   Come hither, spirit;
  Set Caliban and his companions free;   255
  Untie the spell.
  [*Exit ARIEL*]   How fares my gracious sir?
  There are yet missing of your company
  Some few odd lads that you remember not.

[*Re-enter ARIEL, driving in CALIBAN, STEPHANO, and TRINCULO, in their stolen apparel*]

STEPHANO. Every man shift for all the rest, and let
  no man take care for himself; for all is but fortune!   260
  Coragio, bully-monster, *coragio*!
TRINCULO. If these be true spies which I wear in
  my head, here's a goodly sight.[425]
CALIBAN. O Setebos, these be brave spirits indeed.[426]
  How fine my master is! I am afraid   265
  He will chastise me.

413 still] continually.
414 yare] seaworthy.
415 tricksy] (pun) magical; appealingly pretty.
416 several] various.
417 mo'] more.

418 trim] sails.
419 Cap'ring to eye] dancing for joy at the sight.
420 moping] dazed.
421 conduct] conductor.
422 infest] torment.
423 single … you] privately, I'll explain to you.
424 every] every one of.
425 spies] eyes.
426 Setebos] the god he mentioned in I.ii.

SEBASTIAN.   Ha, ha!
  What things are these, my lord Antonio?
  Will money buy 'em?
ANTONIO.   Very like. One of them
  Is a plain fish, and, no doubt, marketable.
PROSPERO. Mark but the badges of these men, my   270
    lords,[427]
  Then say if they be true. This mis-shapen knave:[428]
  His mother was a witch; and one so strong
  That could control the moon, make flows and ebbs,
  And deal in her command without her power.[429]
  These three have robbed me; and this demi-devil—   275
  For he's a bastard one—had plotted with them
  To take my life. Two of these fellows you
  Must know and own; this thing of darkness I
  Acknowledge mine.
CALIBAN.   I shall be pinched to death.
ALONSO. Is not this Stephano, my drunken butler?   280
SEBASTIAN. He is drunk now: where had he wine?
ALONSO. And Trinculo is reeling-ripe: where should
    they
  Find this grand liquor that hath gilded them?
  How cam'st thou in this pickle?
TRINCULO. I have been in such a pickle since I saw   285
    you last that, I fear me, will never out of my bones.
    I shall not fear fly-blowing.[430]
SEBASTIAN. Why, how now, Stephano!
STEPHANO. O, touch me not! I am not Stephano,
    but a cramp.
PROSPERO. You'd be king o' the isle, sirrah?   290
STEPHANO. I should have been a sore one, then.[431]
ALONSO. [Of CALIBAN] This is as strange a thing as
    e'er I looked on.
PROSPERO. He is as disproportioned in his manners
  As in his shape. Go, sirrah, to my cell;

Take with you your companions. As you look   295
  To have my pardon, trim it handsomely.
CALIBAN. Ay, that I will; and I'll be wise hereafter,
  And seek for grace. What a thrice-double ass
  Was I, to take this drunkard for a god,
  And worship this dull fool!   300
PROSPERO.   Go to; away!
ALONSO. Hence, and bestow your luggage where
    you found it.
SEBASTIAN. Or stole it, rather.

[*Exeunt CALIBAN, STEPHANO, and TRINCULO*]

PROSPERO. Sir, I invite your Highness and your train
  To my poor cell, where you shall take your rest
  For this one night; which—part of it—I'll waste[432]   305
  With such discourse as, I not doubt, shall make it
  Go quick away—the story of my life
  And the particular accidents gone by
  Since I came to this isle; and in the morn
  I'll bring you to your ship, and so to Naples,   310
  Where I have hope to see the nuptial
  Of these, our dear-beloved, solemnized;
  And thence retire me to my Milan, where
  Every third thought shall be my grave.
ALONSO.   I long
  To hear the story of your life, which must   315
  Take the ear strangely.[433]
PROSPERO.   I'll deliver all;[434]
  And promise you calm seas, auspicious gales,
  And sail so expeditious that shall catch[435]
  Your royal fleet far off. —My Ariel, chick,
  That is thy charge: then to the elements   320
  Be free, and fare thou well!—Please you, draw near.

[*Exeunt*]

---

427 badges] i.e., servants' livery (though here used more
    figuratively, with regard to their muddied and dishev-
    elled appearance in the stolen robes—an image of usur-
    pation).
428 true] i.e., true to their masters.
429 her] the moon's; without] outside of.
430 pickle] (pun) predicament; preservative (the alcohol,
    which will act as an insect repellent).
431 sore] (pun) pained; tyrannical.

432 waste] spend.
433 take] captivate.
434 deliver all] tell everything.
435 sail] sailing.

EPILOGUE

[Spoken by PROSPERO]

Now my charms are all o'erthrown,
And what strength I have's mine own;
Which is most faint. Now 'tis true,
I must be here confined by you,
Or sent to Naples. Let me not,   5
Since I have my dukedom got,
And pardoned the deceiver, dwell
In this bare island by your spell;
But release me from my bands[436]
With the help of your good hands.[437]   10

Gentle breath of yours my sails
Must fill, or else my project fails,
Which was to please. Now I want[438]
Spirits to enforce, art to enchant;
And my ending is despair,   15
Unless I be relieved by prayer,
Which pierces so that it assaults
Mercy itself, and frees all faults.
As you from crimes would pardoned be,
Let your indulgence set me free.   20

---

[436] bands] bonds.
[437] hands] i.e., applauding.

[438] want] lack.

LOPE DE VEGA

Fuenteovejuna

ope Félix de Vega Carpio (1562–1635) was one of the most prolific playwrights in history and the first Spanish playwright to make a living from the theatre. The two facts are not unrelated: at the height of his career, Lope (as he is commonly known in Spain) was paid a flat rate of about 500 reales per play—at a time when the average actor's annual salary was 6,000 reales. Hence, Lope would have had to produce an average of one new play a month to earn the equivalent of the modest salary of an actor. Incredibly, it seems that over the course of the forty-odd years of his active career, he not only met this quota, but often exceeded it. The estimates of his total output run from the absurdly high figure of more than 2,000 plays down to the more modest but still astonishing estimate of 500. The exact number is difficult to fix, because many plays by other authors were produced and published under the name "Lope de Vega" in order to exploit his popularity, and it is probable that Lope sometimes took the work of other playwrights and revised it to a greater or lesser extent before selling the work under his name.

By turns a drop-out, a scholar, a soldier, a sailor, a prisoner, an exile, a lover, a father, a husband, an adulterer and a priest, Lope led a life nearly as eventful as his plays. He began to manifest exceptional energy and abilities early in life; at five, he was writing poetry in both Latin and Spanish. At fourteen, having left school to join the Spanish army marching against Portugal, Lope met the Bishop of Avila, who, recognizing the boy's abilities, coaxed Lope into returning to study at the University of Alcala. After graduating with a bachelor's degree, Lope declined to enter the priesthood because he had fallen in love, but then he promptly left the woman to join a naval expedition to the Azores. When he returned, he fell in love with a different woman: Elena, the married daughter of a theatrical producer, Jerónimo Velázquez. For five years Lope wrote love ballads for Elena (the "Filis" poems) and sold his plays to her father. They then had a falling out and Lope began to write a series of satires about Velázquez, which eventually provoked a libel suit. Lope was imprisoned and then exiled for two years. Only a few weeks later, however, he returned to elope with yet another woman, Isabel de Urbina, daughter to an eminent courtier. Then, abandoning Isabel (who died a few years later), he joined the Spanish Armada for the disastrous naval assault against Britain.

Lope's luck held out, however. His ship was the *San Juan*, one of the few to return from the battle safely. Upon his return, Lope settled down to writing plays at a breathtaking pace, and begetting children—by his mistresses and, simultaneously, a new wife, whom he married in 1598—at a pace which was hardly less remarkable. Yet it seems that Lope remained at least a moderately attentive father to all his children—legitimate and illegitimate alike. When his wife died in 1613, Lope entered the priesthood (which, if only for reasons of security and social advancement, was a common career choice in Spain at that time). This new vocation had little effect on his penchant for conducting illicit affairs or on the pace of his writing of secular plays. In 1627 Pope Urban VIII (who admired Lope despite the church's general disapproval of both the man and his works) made

Lope a Knight of Malta and a doctor of theology. Lope's final years were spent in relative poverty, much of his income having been donated to the church and charity. When he died in 1635, he was given a state funeral that lasted nine days.

Fuenteovejuna (c. 1612–19) is today by far the best known of Lope's works, though we have little idea of how popular the play was in his own time. Sometimes translated as *The Sheep Well*, the play takes its name from a real town in the province of Cordoba in which, in 1476, the main incident on which the play is based occurred. The vassals of Grand Commander Fernán Pérez de Guzmán (called Gomez instead of Pérez in *Chronica de las tres Ordenes y Cavallerias de Sanctiago, Calatrava y Alcantara*, the 1572 chronicle upon which Lope based his play), having suffered many wrongs by their leader, decided "with one consent and will to rise up against him and kill him." When the killing was investigated, all the judge could obtain from the men, women and children of the town (under torture) was the statement that the guilty party was "Fuenteovejuna." The matter was then reported to Queen Isabella and Prince Ferdinand, who ordered that the investigation should cease. The nature of the wrongs committed by the Grand Commander is not specified in the chronicle— Lope uses the dramatically proven tactic of having him commit outrages against the honour of the town's women. However, the death of the Commander is described, and the details, though perhaps slightly more savage than the account Flores offers in his speech to Ferdinand and Isabella— for instance, a few more indignities committed to the corpse, and a more ostentatious show of celebration—are otherwise faithfully represented by Lope. Naturally, having chosen to depict the revolt of the peasants sympathetically, Lope would want to represent the crimes of the Commander more vividly than had the chronicle; it is natural, too, that he would choose to soften the description of their vengeance a little. The wonder is, rather, that in the seventeenth century such an insurrection was represented sympathetically at all.

Part of the answer to our wonder, of course, lies in the play's secondary plot, which represents the seizure of Ciudad Real by Rodrigo Téllez Girón, the Master of Calatrava, in support of the Portuguese claim to the Castilian crown in the war of succession after the death of King Henry, and the ensuing recapture of the city by the Master of Santiago for Ferdinand and Isabella. Like the main plot, this story also has a factual basis and is drawn from the same chronicle. However, whereas historically the two incidents were barely connected, Lope ties them together by showing the Grand Commander as a pernicious, domineering influence, persuading the much younger Rodrigo into the ill-advised venture. While we know that the Grand Commander at the time of the uprising in Fuenteovejuna did indeed support the Portuguese faction, and that Rodrigo eventually (not immediately, as in the play) repented of his support for the Portuguese, claiming the folly of youth and proving afterwards loyal to Ferdinand and Isabella (even dying in their service in 1482), the historical connection between the two incidents apparently goes no further.

Accordingly, many producers of Lope's *Fuenteovejuna* have felt justified over the years in simply cutting the subplot altogether and presenting the play as a fairly straightforward account of an uprising by the oppressed masses against tyrannical authority. Certainly, the tidier political impact to be achieved by editing the play in this way has not gone unnoticed over the years, and in this form the play has often been embraced as a piece of thrilling historical propaganda. However, just as certainly it is clear that, edited in this way, *Fuenteovejuna* becomes a work that is very different from the play that Lope wrote. It essentially becomes a revolutionary socialist work drawn from an age in which such ideas were practically inconceivable. Moreover, to edit the text in this way vitiates the philosophic framework in which Lope has built his play. For Lope, Isabella and Ferdinand were divinely ordained monarchs (the authenticity of whose ordinance was proved by the tremendous growth of Spain under their reign), and their authority is thus an earthly manifestation of divine authority. We may see in this a comparison with Molière's *Tartuffe* and the controversy surrounding that play, wherein Molière endeavoured to contrast aristocratic presumption with royal providence—the latter supposedly lying beyond any motives of personal ambition or petty self-interest. To this idea, Lope adds the suggestion of an idea expressed by Jesus: "Inasmuch as ye have done it unto one of the least of these my brethren, ye have done it unto me" (Matthew 25:40). Reading in this way, we can see an implication not merely that the Grand Commander is both tyrannical *and* insubordinate, but that his actions (and hence the plots) are *unified*—in that he, like Lucifer, is a violator of divine law and order, effectively bent on usurping the rule of God. Naturally, the belief in a divinely ordered and, thus, inherently moral cosmos is not so ingrained in our outlook today as it was in Lope's time; but the play provides a fascinating insight into a Renaissance understanding of the question of what, today, we would call "human rights."

[C.S.W.]

LOPE DE VEGA

Fuenteovejuna

Translated by Richard Sanger

CHARACTERS:

QUEEN ISABEL OF CASTILE
KING FERDINAND OF ARAGON
THE MASTER OF CALATRAVA, don Rodrigo
 Téllez Girón
THE GRAND COMMANDER OF CALATRAVA,
 Fernán Gomez[1]
MANRIQUE, Master of Santiago
A JUDGE
TWO ALDERMEN FROM CIUDAD REAL
ORTUÑO,
FLORES, subordinates of the Commander
ESTEBAN, magistrate, father of Laurencia
ALONSO, magistrate

JUAN ROJO, alderman, uncle to Laurencia
CUADRADO, alderman
PASCUALA,
LAURENCIA,
JACINTA, peasant women
MENGO,
BARRILDO,
FRONDOSO, peasant men
LEONELO, a university graduate
CIMBRANOS, a soldier
BOY
PEASANTS
MUSICIANS

---

[1] Grand Commander] second in rank to the Master.

ACT I

(THE PALACE OF THE
MASTER OF CALATRAVA)[2]

(Enter the Master, the Commander, Flores and Ortuño.)

COMMANDER: Does the Master know I'm in town?[3]
FLORES: He does.
ORTUÑO: Every day he behaves
  More like a man.
COMMANDER: And that my name is
  Don Fernán Gomez de Guzman?
FLORES: Understand: he's a boy still.[4]   5
COMMANDER: Doesn't he know a Grand Commander
  Commands respect?
ORTUÑO: People pander
  To him; they don't advise him well.
COMMANDER: He won't win his men's love like this
  He needs to get us on his side   10
  By showing some manners.

_____

 [2] Palace … Calatrava] Calatrava, on the Guadiana River
   in southwestern Castile (which would be united with
   Aragon in 1479 to become Spain), was the base of the
   Military Order of Calatrava. This military and religious
   order had been founded in the twelfth century, and by
   the fifteenth had grown to be an immensely powerful
   and wealthy force in Castilian politics. Lope does not
   actually specify the location of this scene, but various
   references imply that the setting is Calatrava.
 [3] Lope de Vega uses a wide variety of metrical forms in
   this play, which Richard Sanger, the translator, has
   loosely imitated (often using "partial" or "imperfect"
   rhymes, because rhymes occur with greater natural fre-
   quency in Spanish than in English). This opening scene
   is written (like most of Lope's opening scenes) in
   redondillas—stanzas consisting of four trochaic lines of
   eight syllables each, with a rhyming pattern of ABBA.
 [4] he's a boy still] Don Rodrigo Téllez Girón, the twenty-
   ninth Master of Calatrava, had succeeded his father (and
   was confirmed by election among the Knights and
   Commanders of the Order) in 1466 at the age of eight.
   Accordingly, Pope Pius II had appointed Rodrigo's uncle as a Coadjutor. The uncle died in 1474, and the
   Master thereafter ruled alone. At the time of this scene,
   he would be seventeen or eighteen years old.

ORTUÑO: That's right.
  If one of these arrogant young whips
  Knew what is said behind his back,
  He'd die of shame before behaving
  That thoughtlessly again.   15
FLORES: What pain
  Such men cause! What trouble they make!
  To treat your peers and equals badly
  Is stupid, but to treat the men
  You command with such disdain
  Is the beginning of tyranny.   20
  No, it's not you we're talking about,
  Commander. It's just this boy
  Who doesn't know what love can do.
COMMANDER: Nonsense! On the day he pinned,
    proud,
  To his chest, the symbol of our order,   25
  The great cross of Calatrava,
  He buckled up a sword that has a
  History—that bound him, as a soldier,
  To respect the men he stands beside.
FLORES: We'll soon know if he's turned on us   30
ORTUÑO: Look, he's here.
COMMANDER: Let's see what he says.

(Enter the Master.)

MASTER: I'm so sorry you've had to wait,
  Don Fernán Gomez de Guzman.
  They've just told me you'd arrived.
COMMANDER: Actually, I've been here some time.   35
  I would have expected someone
  With your breeding, someone I love (as
  I do you), to show more manners,
  Seeing as you are the Master
  Of the Order of Calatrava,   40
  And I, your loyal servant.
MASTER: Really,
  Fernando, I had no idea,
  None whatsoever, you were here.
  Let's embrace—this time sincerely.
COMMANDER: Then show me some respect. I've risked   45
  For you my life; I even told
  The Pope that you, though young, were old
  Enough to lead the order.
MASTER: All this
  I know, and by the holy cross

We both wear on our chests, I swear   50
I'll return your love, and honour,
As I would my father, your trust.
COMMANDER: Very well.
MASTER: So: how go the wars?
Anything up?
COMMANDER: Listen closely:
I'll tell you what's happened and how we   55
Should proceed.
MASTER: My friend, I'm all ears.
COMMANDER: Dear Rodrigo Téllez de Girón,[5]
Your father made you our Grand Master
When you were only eight years old;
The Pope, the Kings, and the Commanders   60
All agreed, naming Juan Pacheco
As your advisor. Now he's gone
And you, though still in truth a boy,
Govern our great order alone,
Let me offer you some advice.   65
You know war has divided Spain
Since King Henry the Fourth died.[6]
Your family has supported the claim
Of Alonso of Portugal,
Whose wife is Joan, Henry's daughter.   70
(And not his valet's as some say)
Of course, Ferdinand of Aragon
Whose wife's Isabel, Henry's sister,
Also has designs on the throne
Of our Castile. But since your family[7]   75
Thinks Isabel's claim is uncertain
It's best you ignore the rumours
And support Alonso, your cousin,
After all. Thus I've come to urge you
To call the Knights of Calatrava   80
To assemble in Almagro now

So you may besiege and then capture
The town of Ciudad Real
Which like a fort lies at the pass
That connects Andalusia   85
And Castile. A few men is all
You'll need. The town's only defenders
Are the locals and a lost noble
Or two who sides with Ferdinand
And Isabella. You would do well,   90
Rodrigo, if you could thus silence
All those who say the Cross you wear
Is too big for your boyish shoulders.
Remember the Counts of Uruena
From whose loins you and your stock came;   95
Remember the Marquis of Villena
And the other knights who won fame
And honour on the battlefield.
Unsheathe that still-immaculate sword
Which you, in battle, shall make red[8]   100
As our cross. How can we say you're
Grand Master of the Scarlet Cross,
When the sword you bear is still white?
Both must be red, the one on your chest
And the one that hangs at your side,   105
And you, Girón, shall be the stripes
That fly, proud and sovereign and red,
Above the tomb where your family lies.
MASTER: Fernán Gomez, please rest assured:[9]
I will side with those my family sides   110
And, if need be, like lightning, strike
At Ciudad Real and rage and burn.
Neither my soldiers nor the foe
Shall ever claim I lost my courage
When I lost my uncle. I'll charge   115
And swing this sword, now white as snow,
Until with crimson blood it drips.
And you, I trust, can give me troops?
COMMANDER: A few, but if they take to you,
They'll fight like lions. As you can guess,   120
Fuenteovejuna is poor
And the peasants there better trained
In tending their livestock and grain
Than they are in the art of war.

---

5 Here Lope switches the metre to a more loosely rhymed
   pattern: *romance* verse (in the original, every second line
   rhymes).
6 Henry the Fourth] (1425–1474), half-brother to Isabel
   (or Isabella) and King of Castile, 1454–1474.
7 Ferdinand … designs on … Castile] Ferdinand was at
   this time still Prince of Aragon; upon the death of his
   father, King John of Aragon, in 1479, Ferdinand and
   Isabel would permanently unite the kingdoms of Aragon
   and Castile into Spain.

---

8 make red] i.e., with blood.
9 Here the verse form returns to *redondillas*.

MASTER: That's where you live?   125

COMMANDER: It's where I chose,
  In times like these, to make my base.
  It's a town where you can feel safe
  Gather the men you need—all those
  You can find if you wish.

MASTER: I shall
  And we'll take Ciudad Real.   130

They exit.[10]

THE VILLAGE SQUARE OF FUENTEOVEJUNA.

Enter Laurencia and Pascuala.

LAURENCIA: Well, let's hope he never returns.

PASCUALA: That's funny. I thought you'd be sad
  When I told you he was gone.

LAURENCIA: What?
  I've prayed to every star that burns
  We'll not see his face here again.   135

PASCUALA: Laurencia, I've heard many girls
  Talk like you do now: proud and fierce,
  But one little glance from a man—
  You melt like butter in the sun.

LAURENCIA: I tell you: There is no oak tree   140
  As hardened as my heart.

PASCUALA: Now really,
  Laurencia, strange things can happen:
  You shouldn't say you'll never drink
  From such a cup. You never know.[11]

LAURENCIA: But I swear I do—even though   145
  You and the whole world may think
  Otherwise. What good would it do
  To let Fernando get his way?
  To go along with what he says?
  Would he ever marry me? No.   150
  So I'd be lost—like Alejandra,
  Pilar, Carmen and all the others,

The sweet young village girls he flatters,
  Who once trusted him, the Commander,
  And now must hide their heads in shame.   155

PASCUALA: I'll be surprised if you escape
  His clutches—What he wants, he takes.

LAURENCIA: He won't take me. Since he first came,
  Pascuala, he's chased me around
  And all in vain. His go-between,   160
  Flores, and Ortuño, that sneak,
  Even showed me a fancy gown
  (I think it was silk), a necklace,
  And some jewels they said he'd give me.
  They told me how great and how strong   165
  He is, and his desire for me is,
  And it made me scared but not scared
  Enough to change the way I feel.

PASCUALA: When did this happen?

LAURENCIA: A week ago,
  Down by the river where we go   170
  To wash our clothes.

PASCUALA: Say what you will—
  In the end he shall have his way.

LAURENCIA: With me?

PASCUALA: And I wouldn't blame you if—

LAURENCIA: What? You think I'm young, I won't
    resist?
  I'll show you that behind this face   175
  Men find so soft I'm tough as nails.
  I'd rather rise at dawn to light
  The fire and cook myself a slice
  Of ham cut from the pig I raised,
  Eat it up with the bread I bake   180
  And wash it all down with a tumbler
  Of wine I've stolen from my mother;
  I'd rather cook, for lunch, a steak
  From my cow, stewed with some cabbage,
  Or, if that's too much, wrap a frill   185
  Of bacon round the eggplant I grill,
  And top it all off with a bunch
  Of grapes I've picked from my own vines;
  I'd rather, when it's time for supper,
  Have a hearty stew of red pepper   190
  And olive oil, then pray some lines,
  And fall, not into temptation,
  But bed, fully contented.
  I'd rather that than all they've invented,

---

[10] In Spanish Renaissance drama (as in Shakespeare), a change of time and place is indicated when one group of characters leaves the stage empty and another group enters.

[11] You shouldn't … cup] Pascuala is quoting a Spanish proverb, the gist of which is "Never say never."

These rogues, with their fine conversation 195
And talk of love, their promises
And words of honour—all they wish
Is to spend the night with some warm flesh
Before the cold truth dawns on us.
PASCUALA: What you say, Laurencia, is right: 200
Once they've finished their business
Men are worse than the sparrow is
To the kindly peasant who feeds it.
In winter, when the wheat-fields freeze
And nothing's left to eat, he flies 205
Down from the roof to beg and cries
His little heart out: Please, please, please.
And we give him the crumbs he needs
So he won't starve: but when spring's come
He dances on the roof at dawn 210
And wakes us with a new song: Tease, tease,
tease.[12]
And that's exactly how men are:
When they need us, we're the wheat
That fills their fields, the bread they eat
Their love, their life, the brightest star. 215
But once they've had their way, the breeze
Begins to blow from somewhere else:
They forget all the fine things they felt
And call us names like cheat and tease.
LAURENCIA: Don't trust a single one of them 220
PASCUALA: That's what I say, Laurencia.

(Enter Mengo, Barrildo and Frondoso.)

FRONDOSO: Barrildo, you'll never convince him.
BARRILDO: Look, here are some wise women.
I'm sure they can help us decide.
MENGO: Well, then, why don't we make a deal? 225
If they say I'm right, you each shall
Give me a prize.
BARRILDO: And if we're right?
MENGO: I'll give you something worth more
Than a whole harvest, cut and dried—
The old rosewood fiddle I made. 230

BARRILDO: Then it's a deal.
FRONDOSO: Look, here we are.
Good day, Ladies.
LAURENCIA: Ladies, you call us?
FRONDOSO: It's just the modern turn of phrase.
Anyone who can read these days
Is a "thinker"; if you're bald as 235
A coot, you're "distinguished" or "virile";
If you need glasses to find your seat,
You're clearly a "visionary";
If you're a drunk, you're "sociable"
If you sleep around, you're "lively" 240
If with women you let your passion
Overwhelm you, then you're "dashing";
And you're "strong-willed" if you're a bully.
So this is what I meant, ladies,
When I addressed you as such. 245
I could, ladies, go on and—
LAURENCIA: Enough.
That's the way they talk in the cities.
Where things are so sophisticated.
I know words that are more accurate
But a lot less flattering. 250
FRONDOSO: What?
LAURENCIA: It's the reverse of what you said:
If you work hard and are rewarded,
You're lucky; if you help out friends
You're a show-off; mean, if you don't;
If you speak your mind, you can't be trusted; 255
Boring if you keep your mouth shut;
If you smile at a man, you did it;
If you don't respond, you're frigid;
And if you do, well, you're a… But
That's enough response for you. 260
MENGO: What a wicked tongue you have.
BARRILDO: She's pretty good at speaking bad.
MENGO: I'll bet she ate salt in the womb.[13]
LAURENCIA: Weren't you men having a discussion?
FRONDOSO: Let me explain. 265
LAURENCIA: Tell me your cares.
FRONDOSO: Then, Laurencia, lend me an ear.
LAURENCIA: Lend? I'll give you one.

---

12 Please … Tease] In the original, the sparrow's cry, "*tio*" (a Spanish word meaning "uncle" or, more loosely, "buddy") is replaced by "*judio*" (Spanish for "Jew," which, in antisemitic fifteenth-century Spain, was regarded as an insult).

13 ate salt in the womb] Salt was supposed to be connected to wit.

FRONDOSO: And I'll trust in
  Your good judgement.
LAURENCIA: So who says what?
FRONDOSO: Mengo's wrong, Barrildo and I think.
LAURENCIA: What does he say?   270
BARRILDO: He claims a thing
  We all know must be true is not.
MENGO: I say it's false because that's true.
LAURENCIA: What's true?
BARRILDO: There's no such thing as love,
  Mengo claims.
LAURENCIA: That's saying too much,
  Don't you think?   275
BARRILDO: Too much and much too
  Little. Love makes the world go round.
MENGO: I know I can't speak philosophy;
  If I could just read, I'd be happy.
  But I think if there's conflict found
  Between the things that make up nature   280
  And nature's also in ourselves
  —our humours, our blood, our quarrels—
  I must be right.
BARRILDO: This world and the greater
  World beyond are ruled by harmony,
  And harmony is love, Mengo, my son,   285
  Since love is two hearts beating as one,
  Two chords striking one note.[14]
MENGO: Far from me
  Be it to say there's no such thing
  As desire. We all have wants and needs
  That govern how we act, what we eat,   290
  The tricks we do to save our skin.
  If you try to punch me, up goes
  My arm—it's self-defence, instinct.
  Try to poke my eye and the lids,
  As if of their own accord, close.   295
  It's natural.
PASCUALA: So what new truth
  Are you trying to convince us of?
MENGO: I'm saying that you cannot love
  Anyone but yourself.
PASCUALA: Excuse
  Me, Mengo, but that is a lie.   300

Think of the force that draws a man
  To a woman, that makes the lion,
  Say, pursue his mate.
MENGO: That's exactly
  What I mean. It's all self-interest,
  Not love itself. What would you say   305
  Love is?
LAURENCIA: A desire for beauty.
MENGO: This beauty—why do you want it?
LAURENCIA: So as to enjoy it.
MENGO: I agree.
  But when a man seeks this enjoyment
  Is that not for himself?   310
LAURENCIA: Good point.
MENGO: Therefore, isn't it true that he,
  Above all others, loves himself
  Since he seeks the thing that will allay
  His longing?
LAURENCIA: True.
MENGO: That's why I say
  There's no love but the love I tell   315
  You about, the one I pursue,
  As I wish, to give me pleasure,
  Not someone else.
BARRILDO: But the priest says there
  Was someone called Plato who,
  A long time ago, wrote down how   320
  We should love. And this Plato told
  His girl it was really her soul
  And her virtue he loved.
PASCUALA: Now, now,
  Barrildo, that's the kind of talk
  That the big thinkers in their schools   325
  And colleges spout forth. It fools
  Some girls, not us.
LAURENCIA: That's right. Don't knock
  Yourself out trying to sum up
  Their arguments. And you, Mengo,
  Be grateful that, when they made you,   330
  They didn't claim it was for love.
MENGO: Do you love anything?
LAURENCIA: My good name?
FRONDOSO: May God one day make you jealous
  So you'll know what it's like.
BARRILDO: So tell us:
  Who won the bet?   335

---

14 This world … one note] The influence of Plato's *Symposium* is apparent in this passage and below.

PASCUALA: You want us to say?
  Ask the priest for the answer to that.
  Laurencia's never been in love
  I don't have experience enough
  To say. How could we ever pass
  Judgement on something so serious?   340
FRONDOSO: They're making fun, they're mocking us.

(Enter Flores.)

FLORES: Good day, ladies and gentlemen.
PASCUALA: Why, it's the good commander's help.
LAURENCIA: His dogged retriever: yelp, yelp.
  Where have you come from, countryman?   345
FLORES: Can't you see I've been fighting?
LAURENCIA: So
  Is Don Fernando on his way?
FLORES: The battle's over. What a day:
  We've lost friends and blood.
FRONDOSO: How'd it go?
FLORES: Let me tell you. I saw it all.   350
  To undertake the great campaign[15]
  To capture Ciudad Real
  Our gallant Rodrigo assembled
  Two thousand of his loyal subjects
  To fight on foot; and three hundred   355
  Of the Order riding on horseback
  (For the cross they wear on their chests
  Binds them to take arms against the foe).
  The boy was a sight to behold—
  He rode out in a leaf-green cloak   360
  With his device embroidered in gold
  And so well fastened by six cords
  That only at the sleeves could you see
  The cold armour he wore beneath.
  His horse was a splendid fat beast   365
  Of dappled grey, raised on the grass
  That grows by the Guadalquivir,
  Its tail dressed in fine woven leather,
  Its mane gathered in white ribbons
  That matched the snow flakes on his hide.   370
  Beside him rode Fernán Gomez,
  Your lord, on a powerful steed
  The colour of honey with a black tail

And mane, and a mouth that's white.[16]
Over his coat of armour, a cloak   375
He wore of orange silk, bright
With gold embroidery and pearls;
A helmet topped with ostrich plumes
That seemed blossom to his cloak's fruit.
In one hand, he wields his famous lance—   380
An entire poplar tree in size—
Which he moves and even the Moor
In far Granada shuts his eyes.
We advanced; the town rose in arms,
Proclaimed its loyalty to the crown   385
Of Ferdinand and Isabella,
They fought hard; we beat them down
And the young Master, victorious,
Gave his orders: the rebel leaders
We beheaded and their followers—   390
Low-born plebs and peasants—we treated
To a flogging in the town square.
Young Rodrigo emerged so feared
And so loved that people now say
A boy who with such great aplomb   395
Fights, conquers and deals out justice
(and punishment) must one day become
The scourge of Islam, and eclipse
Their blue crescent with his bright cross.
And to all he's been so generous—   400
Our Commander not the least—
You'd think we'd plundered not the town,
Poor as it is, but his estate.
But listen now. The trumpets start,
Greet your Commander with open heart.   405

Enter the Commander, Ortuño; musicians; Juan Rojo, Esteban and Alonso, magistrates.

MUSICIANS (*singing*): *Let us greet the great Commander*
  He's conquered lands and slaughtered men
  Let us greet the great Commander
  Noble in words, gentle in manner,
  He's come to live in peace again.   410

  Let us greet the great Commander
  He went off to war and no sooner

---

[15] The verse form switches again to *romance*.

[16] a mouth that's white] a sign of a thoroughbred.

Did he make the foe surrender
Than he's home in Fuenteovejuna
Bringing us his glory and his plunder   415
Let us greet the great Commander!
Long live Don Fernándo!

COMMANDER: My good people, I thank you, as I
   should,[17]

   For the love you've shown.

ALONSO: If only we could
   Show what we feel—this is the tiniest bit.   420
   You have our love because you have earned it.

ESTEBAN: Fuenteovejuna and its village council
   Which you've so honoured with your sword, your
      skill,
   Beg you to accept the humble offerings
   Heaped on this cart: not rich and costly things   425
   As you deserve, but simple tokens of our thoughts:
   First, two baskets of smooth earthenware pots,
   Made from local clay; next, geese, a whole flock
   Who sing of your war-like feats with every squawk
   And ten little piglets, preserved in brine-filled tubs   430
   And other meats, tender as a girl's touch;
   And a hundred hens which, to grant your wishes,
   Have left their mates in the neighbouring villages.
   In Fuenteovejuna, we are poor—
   This means we have no great weapons, no horses   435
   To ride, no gold embroidered capes to wear.
   The only gold we have is the love we bear.
   It's pure and strong and comes from our soil too
   Just like the red wine we offer you
   In these dozen wineskins: our best and purest,   440
   A wine that will make your soldiers thirst
   For battle, and brave the coldest winter day.
   Of the cheeses and other gifts, I'll say
   Only that they are the tribute, which is your right,
   From a grateful village. Good appetite!   445

COMMANDER: I'm very grateful. Gentlemen,[18]
   You may leave.

ALONSO: Have a rest, sir,
   And know you're very welcome here.
   We wish the humble wreathes we've done

Your doorway up with were instead   450
   Strings of oriental pearls
   For that's what your Lordship deserves.

COMMANDER: True. Very well put. Well said.
   Now you may leave, gentlemen.

ESTEBAN: Singers, let's hear that song again.   455

MUSICIANS (*singing*): *Let us greet the great Commander.*
   He's conquered lands and slaughtered men
   Let us greet the great Commander.
   He's home to live in peace again.

(The magistrates, the officials and the musicians exit.)

COMMANDER: You two—don't go just yet.   460

LAURENCIA: What is it your Lordship desires?

COMMANDER: The other day you snubbed me—
   Why?

LAURENCIA: Pascuala, you wouldn't do that!

PASCUALA: Not me. Get off!

COMMANDER: You pretty creature,
   You know it's you I'm talking to—   465
   You and this other wench, too—
   Aren't you both in my command?

PASCUALA: We are
   But you can't command such things of us.

COMMANDER: Don't be afraid, just come inside—
   There are men there, and things to try—   470

LAURENCIA: If you'd invited the town's judges
   And my father (who is the mayor)
   We would, yes, but otherwise: no…

(Laurencia and Pascuala begin to leave.)

COMMANDER: Flores!

FLORES: My lord?

COMMANDER: How can they go
   And disobey me?   475

FLORES: Girls, stop there
   And get inside.

LAURENCIA: No, no, hands off!

FLORES: Get inside and stop being stubborn.

PASCUALA: Watch it! You'll lock the door on us

FLORES: The Commander just wants to share
   With you what he's brought from the war.   480

COMMANDER: Once they're inside, throw the bolt.
   Fast.

(Commander exits.)

---

17 At this point the original shifts to *tercets* (stanzas of three
   rhymed lines); the translator has substituted couplets.

18 Here the *redondillas* resume.

[I]

LAURENCIA: Flores, be kind and please let us pass.
ORTUÑO: No, you belong heaped on the cart
  With all the other spoils.
PASCUALA: You say
  Such stupid things. Out of my way!   485
FLORES: Let them go—they're ferocious.
LAURENCIA: Hasn't your lord had enough flesh
  Given to him?
ORTUÑO: It's yours he wants.
LAURENCIA: Let him burst into jealous bits.

(Laurencia and Pascuala exit.)

FLORES: Won't the Commander be thrilled   490
  When he gets this news. He'll be cursing!
ORTUÑO: That's what life is like for a servant:
  Be patient—or choose another field.

(They exit.)

(Enter King Ferdinand, Queen Isabel, Manrique and attendants.)

ISABEL: My Lord, we shouldn't delay—
  Alfonso has gathered his men   495
  And moved them into position.
  We must strike now before he takes
  More cities. Otherwise, we're lost.
FERDINAND: With us are Navarre and Aragon;
  Once I have got Castile in hand,   500
  Victory will be ours.
ISABEL: I trust
  Your majesty's plans will come true
MANRIQUE: Two aldermen have just arrived
  From Ciudad Real, alive—
  Barely—to see you.   505
FERDINAND: Show them through.
FIRST ALDERMAN: Most Catholic King Ferdinand,[19]
  You whom the heavens have wisely sent
  From Aragon to fair Castile
  To save and assuage us, we bend
  Our heads before your great powers   510
  As envoys from a royal city
  (Known as Ciudad Real)
  Humbly seeking royal help. Happy

We were once to be your subjects
And proud as well. But now cruel fate,   515
We find, has stripped us of that honour.
The famous Rodrigo Girón,
Grand Master of Calatrava,
Who, though tender in years, has won
Acclaim for his valour and strength,   520
Hoping, doubtless, to extend
The renown of his order,
Has laid fierce siege to our fair town.
We struck back and so bravely fought
That streams of blood through our streets flowed.   525
In the end, he took the city
But he never would have done it
Without Commander Fernán Gomez,
Who gave him help, advice and soldiers.
Rodrigo took Ciudad Real   530
And will possess it, making us,
To our regret, his vassals
Unless you come soon and save us.
FERDINAND: And where is Commander Gomez?
FIRST ALDERMAN: In Fuenteovejuna, I would guess—   535
  That's the town he's made his headquarters
  And home, and where, so rumour says,
  He takes unspeakable liberties
  With the unhappy folk he rules.
FERDINAND: Do you have someone to lead you?   540
SECOND ALDERMAN: None at all—all our nobles
  Are captured or wounded or dead.
ISABEL: If we delay, they'll just grow bolder
  We must act now so Alfonso
  Won't lead his men from Portugal   545
  In through Extremadura
  And bring great suffering to our soil.
FERDINAND: Don Manrique, take two companies
  And leave for Ciudad Real
  At once. Allow the foe no rest.[20]   550
  The count of Cabra, known by all
  For his bravery in battle,
  Shall go with you. This, I think, best.
MANRIQUE: And very wise, your Majesty—
  I plan to put a sudden end   555

---

[19] The verse form switches to *romance*.

[20] The verse form switches to *redondillas* from here to the end of the scene.

To this boy's string of victories
  Or else die in the attempt.
ISABEL: With you embarked in this endeavour,
  Good fortune could not be surer.

(Exit all. Enter Laurencia and Frondoso.)

LAURENCIA: I've slipped away and left my washing[21]   560
  By the stream so people
  Will have nothing to talk about.
  Frondoso, I have to say stop.
  The whole village is abuzz—
  I'm eying you, you're after me,   565
  They're waiting for us to slip up.
  And since you're a good, strapping boy,
  Sharp-witted, yes, and sharply-dressed
  (Well, sharper than other shepherds)
  Every boy and girl in the parish   570
  Says we might as well be married.
  They're just waiting for the day
  When Father Pedro calls us up
  To the altar. Good luck, I say.
  They'd be better off to fill their barns   575
  With wheat and oats and hay, or crush
  Their grapes and start making their wine.
  I've had enough of all this fuss
  About you and me. I couldn't care less.
FRONDOSO: Look, Laurencia, how cruel you are.   580
  I risk my life just to see you,
  That's my reward. You know my heart
  Is yours—I want to marry you.
  Can't you treat me better?
LAURENCIA: I don't know how.   585
FRONDOSO: Don't you feel something
  When you see how much I suffer?
  When you know I can't eat or drink
  Or tell if I'm asleep or waking?
  How can such a face be so severe?
  So cold? Good Lord, I'm raving!   590
LAURENCIA: Then cure yourself, Frondoso.
FRONDOSO: I want a cure and I'm asking you
  For it. Then, like two turtle doves,
  With our beaks together, we'll coo
  Sweet nothings back and forth… I mean,   595
  Once the priest has blessed our union.

---

21 The verse form switches to *romance.*

LAURENCIA: Then talk to Juan Rojo, my uncle.
  I'm not in love; it's not a game
  I know how to play. Not at all.
FRONDOSO: Laurencia, it's the commander.   600
LAURENCIA: I bet he's stalking deer.
  We'll have to hide.
FRONDOSO: Yes, let's.
LAURENCIA: No, you in those bushes. Me here.

(Enter the Commander.)

COMMANDER: Well, well. This is a piece of luck!
  I come chasing a skittish stag   605
  And what a lovely doe I've found.
LAURENCIA: I was washing clothes on the bank
  And came here for a rest… Good Lord,
  I've left them there! With your permission,
  Your lordship, I'll return to work.   610
COMMANDER: Don't go yet, my lovely Laurencia.
  These rebuffs of yours are so coarse
  They mar the beauty God meant you
  To cherish, and make you monstrous.
  You've slipped between my fingers   615
  A few times now—this time you won't.
  Only this clearing shall know
  The secret we share—you, whose eyes
  Now flee the master of your village,
  Who've scorned and most cruelly snubbed me,   620
  You shall not always be this proud.
  That's not how Pilar behaved,
  The wife of Pedro Redondo,
  When I went to pay a visit;
  Not how Martin del Pozo's wife,   625
  Whatshername, received my gifts
  Just two days after she was wed.
LAURENCIA: They knew how to please you, my
    Lord,
  Because they'd been with other men,
  And shared their generous flesh, before.   630
  Now may God help you catch your stag.
  If you weren't wearing that cross,
  I might think you were the devil
  The way you persecute me.
COMMANDER: Shush!
  Enough of this talk. Let me rest   635
  My cross-bow here and see if my hands
  Can make your body say yes.

LAURENCIA: What's this? Who do you think you are?

(Frondoso enters and picks up the cross-bow.)

COMMANDER: Don't fight back.
FRONDOSO: If I take the bow,
  I swear I'll shoot him in the back.   640
COMMANDER: Give in, girl.
LAURENCIA: Heaven help me now.
COMMANDER: Don't be so scared—We're alone here.
FRONDOSO: Take your hands off her, Commander.
  If not, believe me, I shall make
  Your chest the target of my anger   645
  And pierce that fearful cross you wear.
COMMANDER: You peasant dog!
FRONDOSO: There's no dog here.
  Run, Laurencia!
LAURENCIA: You watch out!
FRONDOSO: Go!

(Laurencia escapes.)

COMMANDER: How stupid of me to have dropped
  My weapon—to think I thought   650
  It might scare her.
FRONDOSO: You know, my Lord,
  If I just press my finger here,
  You'll be finished.
COMMANDER: You let her escape,
  You cretin, you traitor. Give me
  My cross-bow back at once, do you hear, 655
  At once!
FRONDOSO: What? So you can kill me?
  Remember: when it's love's turn
  To rule the heart, it doesn't listen,
  Because love's deaf; and love rules me.
COMMANDER: Do you think a man with my blood 660
  Would really turn his back and flee
  A peasant? Shoot, I dare you!
  Go on, shoot! You can't make me break
  The oaths knights of my order take.[22]
FRONDOSO: No, my Lord, I won't do that—   665
  I'm happy with the job I do.
  But since I want to keep my life,
  I think I'll keep your crossbow too.

---

22 The oaths knights of my order take] the chivalric code
  which would forbid him to flee from a social inferior.

(Frondoso exits.)

COMMANDER: Some turn of events that was!
  But I'm not finished with him yet,   670
  I swear I'll get my sweet revenge.
  Good heavens, what a mess I've made.

He exits.

END OF ACT I.

ACT II

(Enter Esteban and the first Alderman.)

ESTEBAN: We had better stop using up the grain[23]
  In our reserves—there's been hardly a drop of rain
  All spring, and the outlook's none too fair.
  Best to save what we can.
ALDERMAN: I'm with you there:
  Prudence is the best way to rule our town.   5
ESTEBAN: Let's petition the Commander then.
  I can't stand those pompous astrologers
  Who, with their big words and fancy pictures,
  Try to convince us that they know God's own
    secrets—
  Why, some even pretend the future's the past 10
  And the present, well, it doesn't exist—
  It's all circular, wheels within wheels,
  And the man who knows most, knows least.
  Do they keep the rainclouds in a closet
  Along with the stars and each spinning planet? 15
  How else can they know what the heavens
    portend
  And so keep us awake for nights on end?
  Then they tell us what seeds to sow and when:
  Wheat, barley, spinach, cucumber, pumpkin,
  Squashes, zucchini, those gourds and these… 20
  It's them whose brains are really peas.
  And after, just to prove their visionary gifts,
  They'll proclaim a great man will soon perish

---

23 In the original, the first part of this scene is written in
  octavas reales, a pattern of eight lines rhymed:
  ABABABCC. The translator has used a slightly less formal rhyming scheme of approximate couplets here.

And so one does—in Lower Moldavia.[24]
And that there will be tigers in Asia   25
That, in Germany, beer will abound
And there's water in the ocean and snow in the
   mountains…
You see, it's not so hard an art to master:
April ends, and May, I'll predict, comes after.

(Enter Leonelo the Graduate and Barrildo.)

LEONELO: Look, they've beat us to the village salon.   30
BARRILDO: How'd things go in Salamanca?[25]
LEONELO: Up and down.
BARRILDO: You must have learnt a lot by now.
LEONELO: No more than
   Any village barber—it's just that everyone
   At university understands the words I use.
BARRILDO: I'm sure you did well at your studies.   35
LEONELO: I've tried to learn what's really important.
BARRILDO: Nowadays, with so many books in print,
   You'd think everyone thinks themselves a thinker.
LEONELO: That's right. So many books come from
      the printer
   We can't keep track—and since there's no guide   40
   To this inky flood, confusion swamps the mind.
   Just seeing the titles addles those who read best.
   I'm not saying that the printing press
   Hasn't brought to our attention great minds,
   Preserved their works, and spread knowledge far   45
      and wide.
   It was Gutenberg who invented it
   In Germany, around 1386.
   But then what happened was that many men,
   Whom people thought wise, printed their wisdom
   And lost their reputations. And many print   50
   Up their lunacies under the names of famous
      thinkers.
   And others, full of envy, write down the worst mess
   And, with the name of someone they detest,
   Send it out into the world.

BARRILDO: It's not that bad.
LEONELO: Do you think it's right that some illiterate   55
      cad
   Should defame a real thinker?
BARRILDO: Leonelo,
   Printing was a great invention.
LEONELO: You know
   We lived without it for centuries.
   Has it given us anyone as wise
   As Saint Jerome or Augustine?   60
BARRILDO: You're getting worked up. Let's stop
   arguing.

(Enter Juan Rojo and a peasant.)

JUAN ROJO: To marry my daughter off properly,
   The way people expect—feast, wedding, dowry—
   I'd have to sell off all my livestock and lands
   Four times over. That's what no one understands.   65
PEASANT: Have you heard of the Commander's new
      offensive?
JUAN ROJO: I heard what he did to Laurencia.
PEASANT: He talks about us but it's him that's a
      beast.
   I'd like to see him dangling from the olive trees.

(Enter the Commander, Ortuño and Flores.)

COMMANDER: Good evening, my good gentlemen.[26]   70
ALDERMAN: My Lord.
COMMANDER: Please you needn't rise.
MAYOR: Your Lordship may sit where you wish.
   We're more than happy to stand.
COMMANDER: I said I would like you to sit.
ESTEBAN: Those who are good have honour   75
   Which they can bestow on another;
   Those who have none can't impart it.[27]
COMMANDER: Sit down. We have things to discuss
ESTEBAN: Did my Lord see the greyhound race?
COMMANDER: My men told me. They were   80
   amazed.
   They'd never seen a thing that fast.

---

24 Lower Moldavia] i.e., some remote and obscure region
    where the death is effectively meaningless to those who
    heard the prophecy.
25 Salamanca] the location of the University of Salamanca,
    founded in the thirteenth century.

---

26 Here the verse form switches to *redondillas*.
27 Those who … impart it] Esteban's statement is prover-
    bial, and is thus implicitly ironic rather than represent-
    ing an openly defiant insult.

ESTEBAN: Yes, they're extraordinary beasts.
  You know, I'd bet my shirt this one
  Could catch any thief on the run
  Or the quickest coward that flees.   85

COMMANDER: I wish you'd set him on the trail
  Of a hare that keeps escaping me..

ESTEBAN: Of course. Where is it?

COMMANDER: It's a she.

ESTEBAN: What?

COMMANDER: Your daughter.

ESTEBAN: My little girl?

COMMANDER: That's right.   90

ESTEBAN: She's good enough for you?

COMMANDER: Teach her a lesson, for God's sake.

ESTEBAN: What do you mean?

COMMANDER: She won't behave.
  I can name women, ladies too—
  In fact, one whose husband's right here,
  And she, at one wink, came along   95
  To do my bidding.

ESTEBAN: She did wrong
  And you, my Lord, are doing more
  In speaking this way.

COMMANDER: Eloquence!
  Peasant eloquence! Flores,
  Find a copy of Aristotle's   100
  Politics for these learned gents.[28]

ESTEBAN: My lord, we wish you to rule us
  With honour. There are, in this town,
  People of standing and renown.

LEONELO: I've never seen a man this shameless.   105

COMMANDER: I'm sorry. Has some word I uttered
  Upset you?

ALDERMAN: It's the way you talk

That's unfair. It's not right to mock
  The honour of our town.

COMMANDER: Good Lord!
  I didn't know. You, too, have honour?   110
  I suppose you're also knights of the
  Great Order of Calatrava?

ALDERMAN: Some of those who wear that cross on
    their
  Breasts don't exactly have clean blood.

COMMANDER: Mixing my blood and yours, you   115
    mean,
  Dirties you?

ALDERMAN: Evil doesn't clean;
  It leaves a stain.

COMMANDER: Your women should
  Be proud I honour them this way.

MAYOR: The way you speak defames us all.
  The way you act's unspeakable.   120

COMMANDER: What tiresome things you peasants
    say!
  Life is so much more civilized
  In the cities. There, nothing blocks
  Men like me from getting our perks.
  Why, the husbands even take pride   125
  When we service their wives.

ESTEBAN: They don't.
  You're saying this to make us feel
  We're backward, and to have your will.
  The city is also God's home.
  There, he'd punish you much swifter.   130

COMMANDER: Get out of here!

MAYOR: How can he dare
  Speak like this to us?

COMMANDER: Clear the square!

ESTEBAN: We're going.

COMMANDER: Come on now. Go quicker!

FLORES: Please control yourself, sir.

COMMANDER: These louts
  Want to plot behind my back.   135

ORTUÑO: Calm down.

COMMANDER: I'm very calm, in fact.
  Send them all home by separate routes.

LEONELO: What on earth's going on?

ESTEBAN: Goodbye.

(The peasants exit.)

---

28 Aristotle's *Politics*] Presumably, the Commander has in
  mind Aristotle's suggestion—notwithstanding his admiration for democracy—that the most effective form of
  government is that in which supreme power rests in a
  perfect monarch. Thus, the Commander is suggesting
  that these peasants should learn their place in the "natural" hierarchy. However, Aristotle subordinates this idea
  to a more important argument: that ideally power
  should be invested neither in the aristocrats nor in the
  entire citizenry, but rather in the virtuous. Therefore, the
  Commander's allusion is ultimately ironic.

COMMANDER: What do you think of people here?

ORTUÑO: It's obvious that you don't care   140
  About the pain you cause.

COMMANDER: Should I?
  Do you think they're as good as me?

FLORES: It's not equality they want.

COMMANDER: And you think that lovesick peasant
  Should keep my crossbow and go free?   145

FLORES: Last night I was sure I heard him
  Prowling around Laurencia's door.
  I crept up on him, drew my sword
  And carved a nice decoration
  In his face. Then I saw it was   150
  Someone else.

COMMANDER: Where's Frondoso gone?

FLORES: Oh, they say he's somewhere around.

COMMANDER: The man who tried to end my days
  Dares go out?

FLORES: Like a reckless bird,
  Or a fish that can't keep away   155
  From the bait, we'll catch the boy.

COMMANDER: Think: the captain before whose sword
  Cordoba and Granada cringed
  Now lets this mere peasant waif
  Get off with threatening his life.   160
  I tell you: The world's come unhinged.

FLORES: See, what love can do.

ORTUÑO: Since you're alive,
  I'd say you owe him thanks—and more.

COMMANDER: I've controlled myself so far.
  Otherwise, in the blink of an eye,   165
  I would have razed this entire town.
  No, I'll wait till the time is ripe
  And then I'll take revenge… What's up
  With Pascuala?

FLORES: She says that now
  She's getting married—   170

COMMANDER: That shows trust.

FLORES: —And that you should buy your plums
  In the market—not people's homes.

COMMANDER: Does Olalla have news for us?

ORTUÑO: Oh, she's a laugh.

COMMANDER: She's lots of fun.
  What's the story?   175

ORTUÑO: Her fiance's
  Watching her carefully these days.

He's jealous. He knows we've gone
Visiting before—but the minute
He turns his head, she'll let you in.

COMMANDER: Good work! But he keeps his eyes   180
  open.

ORTUÑO: Open—watching for any visit.

COMMANDER: What about, you know, Inez?

FLORES: Which one?

COMMANDER: Antonio's wife.

FLORES: Whenever you wish,
  She's ready and willing. Just push
  The back gate and go through the kitchen.   185

COMMANDER: Easy women! Love them a lot
  But give them little. I tell you,
  Flores, these girls don't know their value.

FLORES: There's nothing as fun as the sport
  Of chasing women and the thrills   190
  It brings. If one gives in too soon,
  We never get to dream and swoon
  And sigh… Though there are also girls—
  Or so our Aristotle claims—[29]
  Who have desires and long for men   195
  Just as badly as we want them.
  Don't be surprised.

COMMANDER: When you're inflamed
  With desire, you welcome relief.
  After, though, it's a different story—
  The things we most quickly forget   200
  Are those that came easy, and cheap.

(Enter Cimbranos, a soldier.)

CIMBRANOS: Isn't Commander Gomez here?[30]

ORTUÑO: He's standing right in front of you.

---

29 Or so our Aristotle claims] One of Aristotle's asides is
here taken out of context and distorted. In his *Physics*
Aristotle argues that matter desires form "as the female
desires the male and the ugly the beautiful" (I.9). The
contextual implication in Aristotle is therefore that the
female looks to the male as the embodiment of mean-
ingful order—clearly not an idea appropriate to the
Commander.

30 Isn't … here?] That the Commander is not immediately
recognizable as the leader is perhaps significant. (Here
the verse form switches to *romance*.)

CIMBRANOS: Oh courageous Fernán Gomez,
   Doff your cap for a helmet's plumes,   205
   Your cloak for a suit of armour.
   The Master of Santiago,
   Along with the Count of Cabra—
   Both supporting Queen Isabel—
   Now lay siege to young Rodrigo.   210
   Ciudad Real may soon fall,
   And the town that cost so much blood
   Belong to the Queen of Castile.
   Already from the high towers
   And ramparts, we can see the shields   215
   Of Castile and Leon, the ensign
   Of Aragon. Though Portugal's
   Alfonso favours our Rodrigo,
   He'll be lucky to return alive.
   Mount your horse, Sir—just seeing you   220
   Should send them all homeward in flight.
COMMANDER: That's enough. Ortuño, tell them
   To sound trumpets in the square.
   How many soldiers do I have?
ORTUÑO: Around fifty, I'd say. No more.   225
COMMANDER: Tell them all to mount their horses.
CIMBRANOS: If we're not quick, Ciudad Real
   Will be Ferdinand and Isabel's.
COMMANDER: Not while I have a sword to wield.

(They exit.)

(Enter Mengo, with Laurencia and Pascuala, fleeing.)

PASCUALA: Don't leave us alone.[31]   230
MENGO: You're scared here?
LAURENCIA: Mengo, it's best we go to town
   Together. The men are all gone
   And he might suddenly appear.
MENGO: Why won't this devil let us breathe?
LAURENCIA: He pursues us in shade and sun.   235
MENGO: I wish a lighting bolt would come
   And strike him down.
LAURENCIA: A bloody beast
   He is, and he's poisoned our town.
MENGO: They tell me our friend Frondoso
   Threatened him with his own crossbow   240

In the clearing, and so freed you from
   His clutching paws.
LAURENCIA: Men, I once said,
   Were silly, vain—a waste of time—
   But since that day I've changed my mind.
   How brave Frondoso was! He saved   245
   My honour—but it may cost his life.
MENGO: There's no question he'll have to flee.
LAURENCIA: That's what I tell him, for all he
   Means to me, and anger fills his eyes.
   He shakes and swears that this Commander   250
   He'll hang up by his feet. Or worse.
PASCUALA: I say we should garrote him first.
MENGO: No, no. A good stoning's the answer.
   You know that sling I keep for fox?[32]
   If I let fly at him with it,   255
   You can bet your flock that I'll split
   His skull open like a nut: Tock!
   Why, Halibut of Ancient Rome
   Wasn't half as cruel as this..
LAURENCIA: Heliogabulus, the name is.[33]   260
   He was a tyrant more loathsome
   Than any beast.
MENGO: Well, this Gabble-loo
   Or however you pronounce it,
   If he and Fernán Gomez met,
   I tell you I know who'd have who.   265
   How could Nature create a man
   As savage as the Commander?
PASCUALA: It's as if the blood of a tiger
   Raged and ran through his every vein.

(Enter Jacinta.)

JACINTA: Help! Save me! Please God, save my soul!   270
LAURENCIA: Jacinta, what's wrong?
PASCUALA: Go on, tell us.
JACINTA: It's the Commander's two helpers:
   They're going to Ciudad Real

---

31 The verse form switches to *redondillas*.

32 for fox] i.e., for protecting livestock from predators.

33 Heliogabulus] (so known, though more correctly Elagabalus), a Roman emperor (218–22 C.E.) who was notorious for his lechery, cruelty, and extravagant wastefulness. He was killed in the end by his own indignant Praetorian Guard.

And armed not with steel but with lust,
They're trying to take me to him.   275
LAURENCIA: Only God can save you, Jacinta:
If the Commander treats you thus,
How will he treat me?

(She exits.)

PASCUALA: A man
Is what you need.

(She exits.)

MENGO: That's what
I'll have to be. Hide behind.   280
JACINTA: But,
Mengo, don't you have a weapon?
MENGO: I have the first weapons God made.
JACINTA: They'll get us!
MENGO: Look, Jacinta, stones—
Plenty of them for us to throw.

(Enter Flores and Ortuño.)

FLORES: Ha! And you thought you had escaped!   285
JACINTA: Mengo, I'm dead!
MENGO: Why do you, sir,
Treat us poor working folk like this?
ORTUÑO: Are you sure you want to stand up
For the lady?
MENGO: I'll defend her
By pleading. She's from my family.   290
I'd like to save her if I could.
FLORES: Let's do him in. Right now.
MENGO: By God,
If you gentlemen make me angry
I'll take out my slingshot and show[34]
How it works! You'll regret each round!   295

(Enter the Commander and Cimbranos.)

COMMANDER: What's this? You want me to dismount
To deal with a matter this low?
FLORES: The people of this wretched village—
Which, by the way, truly deserves
To be swept off the face of the earth   300
Since it has no pleasures to give us—

---

[34] slingshot] The image evokes David versus Goliath.

Have thought—well, this peasant here has—
He should challenge our authority.
MENGO: If you, my Lord, can take pity
On acts of true injustice,   305
Punish these men who, in your name,
Have tried to remove this good wench
From her husband and parents
And allow me now to take her home.
COMMANDER: I'll allow them to take revenge   310
On you.—The sling!
MENGO: My lord, no.
COMMANDER: Tie his hands with it, Ortuño.
MENGO: So is this the way you defend
A woman's honour?
COMMANDER: Now, confess:
What does Fuenteovejuna   315
Think of me?
MENGO: What have we done to you,
Sir, that has caused you such offence?
FLORES: Shall we kill him?
COMMANDER: I wouldn't let
His peasant blood dirty your swords.
Save them for a worthier cause.   320
ORTUÑO: What's my lord's wish?
COMMANDER: Flog him instead—
Tie him to that oak, his clothes off,
And with your horse's reins—
MENGO: Mercy!
You're a nobleman, have mercy on me!
COMMANDER: —Flog him till the steel buckles pop   325
From the leather.
MENGO: Can crimes like these
Dear God, escape your justice?
COMMANDER: And you, my wench, why flee from us?
Is a peasant better than me?
Higher in rank?   330
JACINTA: This is a fine way
To restore the honour I lost
When your soldiers carried me off.
COMMANDER: When they tried to?
JACINTA: That's right. You may
Not think so, but I have a father,
An honest man who goes to church   335
And works his patch of land. In birth,
He may not equal you; however,
In his acts, he's much more noble.

COMMANDER: Such insults won't do much to calm
　My anger. Get moving!　　　　　　　　　340
JACINTA:　　　　　　With whom?
COMMANDER: Why, with me, of course.
JACINTA:　　　　　　　　　Think it over.
COMMANDER: I have—unfortunately for you.
　See, I don't want you any more,
　I'm giving you to the troops, to share.
JACINTA: No power on earth will force me through　345
　Such wrongs, so long as I can breathe.
COMMANDER: You're a peasant. Move!
JACINTA:　　　　　　　　　Have pity!
COMMANDER: Pity? It's not a word which we
　Use here.
JACINTA:　　God shall avenge your deeds.

(They exit with her.)

(Enter Laurencia and Frondoso.)

LAURENCIA: How can you dare come? Don't you fear　350
　For your life?
FRONDOSO:　　　It only shows
　How great the love I bear you is.
　From high up on the hill, I saw
　The Commander set off and, trusting
　In your courage, lost all my fear.　　　　355
　May he set off—and disappear.
LAURENCIA: Hold your tongue. It's the man we most
　　want
　To die that often lives the longest.
FRONDOSO: May he live a thousand years then,
　If that's the case—since wishing him　　360
　Health will hasten his death upon us.
　Laurencia, I wish I knew
　How you really feel about me,
　And if you think my loyalty
　Might win your love. You know it's true　365
　The whole town thinks we belong together,
　They can't understand why we aren't
　Already married… Don't be hard
　And cold like this. Just tell me yes or—
LAURENCIA: Then you and the whole town should　370
　　know
　My answer to you: Know … that it's yes.
FRONDOSO: My lady, mere words can't express
　The joy I feel. Allow me so,

In thanks, to kiss your feet.
LAURENCIA:　　　　　　　Please stop
　This silly speech. You need to chat　　　375
　About these matters with my dad.
　That, as you know, is the next step.
　Look, here he comes now, from the square,
　With my uncle, Juan. Don't worry,
　Frondoso, it's you I will marry,　　　　380
　You I love.
FRONDOSO: God, answer my prayer!

*(They move aside. Enter Esteban, the mayor, and Juan
Rojo, the alderman.)*

ESTEBAN: You know the way he behaved was
　So bad, we nearly had a riot
　On our hands. No one denies that　　　385
　His acts are truly outrageous.
　We're all shocked. Just look how he's ruined
　Poor Jacinta.
ALDERMAN:　　Ferdinand
　And Isabel will make this land
　Fear and obey their laws—and soon.　　390
　They're marching on Ciudad Real,
　Their general Santiago
　Ready to fight young Rodrigo…
　Poor Jacinta, what a nice girl
　She was.　　　　　　　　　　395
ESTEBAN:　　And he had Mengo flogged?
ALDERMAN: You've never seen an ink blotch
　As black and blue as Mengo's flesh.
ESTEBAN: Don't tell me more. It makes my blood
　Boil to hear the way he treats us.
　What's the point of the mayor's post　　400
　If I can't stop this?
ALDERMAN:　　　　Don't reproach
　Yourself—it was his men, Flores
　And Ortuño, who flogged our friend.
ESTEBAN: But there's worse, far worse. They told
　　me
　The other day, down in the valley,　　　405
　Pedro Redondo's wife was found
　Hiding her shame. He'd used her
　The way he does—used her once,
　Then given her to his servants.
ALDERMAN: Stop—I hear voices. Who goes there?　410
FRONDOSO: It's me. I beg your leave to talk, sir.

ESTEBAN: Of course, Frondoso, when you wish.
　I love you as a father does
　His son.
FRONDOSO:　　I know—that's why I dare
　To think you might just grant me what　　　　415
　I'm about to ask. You know who
　My parents are.
ESTEBAN:　　　　Has that mad brute
　Fernán Gomez wronged you?
FRONDOSO:　　　　　　A bit.
ESTEBAN: I could tell.
FRONDOSO:　　　　So, knowing the trust
　You've shown me makes me bold enough　　　420
　To tell you straight out: I'm in love
　With Laurencia, and want to ask
　For her hand. Forgive my rashness—
　I wanted to talk with you first.
ESTEBAN: Frondoso, you make this request　　　425
　At just the right moment to banish
　From my heart its very worst fear.
　I thank heaven that you have come
　To preserve my honour and, son,
　I thank you for how true, and pure　　　　430
　Your intentions are. It's only right,
　Though, that you should tell your father.
　Once he agrees, I'd be honoured
　If you made Laurencia your wife.
ALDERMAN: But shouldn't you ask the girl first?　　435
ESTEBAN: Don't worry: It's all been arranged,
　I'll bet, by them before he came.
　Now, about the dowry; the best,
　I think, would be a sum of gold
　Which I would plan to give you shortly.　　440
FRONDOSO: No, please, I don't need a dowry,
　It's such trouble.
ALDERMAN:　　You should be glad
　He doesn't ask for her naked!
ESTEBAN: Let me ask her what she thinks first
　If you don't mind.　　　　　　445
FRONDOSO:　　　　That would be just
　It's no good to ignore the tastes that
　Others have.
ESTEBAN:　Laurencia!
LAURENCIA:　　　　Yes, sir.
ESTEBAN: There, I'm right. It's a plan they've
　hatched.

　See how quickly she answered us.
　Laurencia, come over here:　　　　　450
　My love, they've just been asking me
　If Gila, your friend, should wed
　Frondoso, who's as good a lad
　As any we have here in Fuente—
LAURENCIA: Gila's marrying him?　　　　455
ESTEBAN:　　　　　　Is there
　Any girl who's a better match?
LAURENCIA: I'd say yes.
ESTEBAN:　　　　Yes? But she's not much
　To look at. He would do better,
　I think, to marry someone else,
　Someone with more appealing looks,　　　460
　Like you perhaps…
LAURENCIA:　　　Still playing tricks
　At your age?
ESTEBAN:　Do you love him as well?
LAURENCIA: I find I like him more and more
　And now because of Fernán Gomez…
ESTEBAN: What shall I say?　　　　465
LAURENCIA:　　　　For me, say yes.
ESTEBAN: That's it then. Let's go to the square
　And see if we can find the priest.
ALDERMAN: Let's go.
ESTEBAN:　　　　Now, son, what did we decide
　About the dowry? As I said,
　I can offer some gold—say, at least　　　470
　Four thousand pieces…
FRONDOSO:　　　I insist
　I'm offended by your offer.
ESTEBAN: Don't be silly. Weddings are over
　In one day—later, you need the gifts.

(They exit, Frondoso and Laurencia remain.)

LAURENCIA: So are you happy now, Frondoso?　　475
FRONDOSO: Happy? The joy I feel inside's
　Enough to make me lose my mind.
　From my heart, great pleasures flow
　And rise as laughter to my eyes—
　To know, Laurencia, you're my prize.　　　480

(They exit.)

(Enter the Master, the Commander, Flores and
Ortuño.)

COMMANDER: There's nothing left to do, sir, but flee.[35]

MASTER: Our walls were too weak; their army too strong.

COMMANDER: It's cost them more lives and blood than they know.

MASTER: At least they can't count among their spoils
Our great banner of Calatrava—   485
To have lost that would have been true defeat.

COMMANDER: And yet all your plans have gone up in smoke.

MASTER: What can I do if one day blind Fortune
Makes a hero, and the next destroys him?

VOICES (off): Victory for Ferdinand and Isabel!   490
Long live the King and Queen of Castile!

MASTER: Look, they're lighting lamps on the battlements
And unfurling from the highest towers
Bright red banners that proclaim their conquest.

COMMANDER: They might dye them with all the   495
blood they've lost—
I'd say it was more tragedy than triumph.

MASTER: Commander, I'm going back to Calatrava.

COMMANDER: And in Fuenteovejuna, I'll stay
Till you choose to fight on with Alfonso
Or to join your forces with Ferdinand.   500

MASTER: I'll tell you by letter what I decide.

COMMANDER: Time will help you choose.

MASTER: I'm young and yet see
Time is already playing tricks on me.

(They exit.)

(Enter the wedding party: Musicians, Mengo, Frondoso, Laurencia, Pascuala, Barrildo, Esteban and Juan Rojo.)

MUSICIANS (singing): *May they live a long life*
As husband and wife—   505
May they live a long life.

MENGO: What kind of song do you call that?[36]

BARRILDO: Go ahead if you can do better.

FRONDOSO: Mengo knows more about beatings
Than poems.   510

MENGO: If you think that's bad,

---

[35] This section is written in *versos sueltos*—blank verse.
[36] The verse form returns to *redondillas* here.

There's a man I could tell you of
Who lives down in the valley—well,
Don Gomez caught him and—

BARRILDO: Don't tell.
That brute's dishonoured us enough.

MENGO: There was a hundred of them at least   515
And they whipped me good that day.
All I had to fight them away
Was my slingshot… So I got beat.
And it hurt. But what they did, think—
I don't want to tell you his name—   520
Yes, an enema: up his bum
They pumped loads of pebbles and ink.
Tell me, how would that feel?

BARRILDO: I'll bet
The Commander thought it a laugh.

MENGO: They're not something to make fun of   525
Though enemas clean you out.
I'd feel like death.

FRONDOSO: Let's hear your ditty,
Barrildo, so long as it's not filthy.

MUSICIANS (singing): *May they live together for many*
years
As man and wife in heavenly bliss   530
May they never be angry or jealous
Nor spoil their lives with cares or tears.
May they end their days together, the dears,
May they live for many years.

MENGO: Now those lines were truly awful.   535

BARRILDO: I wrote them in a rush.

MENGO: Know what
I think of these so-called poets?
Have you seen a man fry dough-nuts?
He drips into the sizzling oil
Bits of batter till the pan's full,   540
He waits a while, and lifts them out:
Some come out swollen, and some flat,
Some all wretched and deformed,
Some nicely fried, some burnt, some raw.
That's how I think that poets work: 545
Each takes his dough (or subject matter),
Throws it into his pan (or paper),
And hopes he can hide what's absurd
Or wrong by coating it with jam.
But when he hands his poems round,   550
No one's hungry; the only one

Who'll eat them's the one who made them.

BARRILDO: Enough nonsense. Let the bride speak.

LAURENCIA: We want to give you all a kiss.

JUAN: Kiss him first.   555

ESTEBAN: And may heaven bless
  This marriage with children and peace.

FRONDOSO: And you bless us with a song.

JUAN: Sing, so that two as one belong.

MUSICIANS *(singing): Down from Fuenteovejuna*
  The young village girl walks;   560
  A knight follows her on horseback
  Wearing a bright red cross.
  She hides behind the bushes,
  Full of shame and fear and shy;
  She pretends she hasn't seen him,   565
  Pulls a branch before her eyes.
  "Why do you hide from me,
  My pretty little doe?
  My desire is a mountain cat
  Which through stone walls can go"   570
  The knight comes closer to her now
  And she, trembling like a leaf,
  Tries to draw across her face
  A curtain of green.
  But since love can easily make a man   575
  Cross great mountains and seas,
  He lifts a branch and says to her
  These words which she repeats:
  "Why do you hide from me,
  My pretty little doe?   580
  My desire is a mountain cat
  Which through stone walls can go."

(The Commander enters, with Flores, Ortuño and Cimbranos.)

COMMANDER: Everyone quiet—Stay where you are.[37]

JUAN: This, sir, is a serious event.
  Shall we stop it just so you can   585
  Show off your military strength?
  By the way, did you win the bat—?
  I'm sorry. I shouldn't have asked.

FRONDOSO: I'm dead. Save me!

LAURENCIA: This way, Frondoso!

---

[37] The verse form from here to the end of the act is *romance*.

COMMANDER: No. Catch him and tie his hands fast.   590

JUAN: Give up, son.

FRONDOSO: So they can kill me?

JUAN: Why would they?

COMMANDER: I'm not the kind of man
  To kill someone that's innocent—
  If I were, those soldiers of mine
  Would have finished him off long ago.   595
  Lock him up in prison, I say.
  His own father shall judge his guilt.

PASCUALA: But today's his wedding day.

COMMANDER: Why should that bother me? Aren't there
  Plenty others to take his place?   600

PASCUALA: If he has offended you, sir,
  Please show, this once, your noble ways
  And forgive him.

COMMANDER: There's not a thing
  I can do. You see, Pascuala,
  It's not me that his actions offend;   605
  They're an offense against the Master
  Rodrigo Girón (God bless him)
  And against the whole of his Order
  Which is the vessel of his honour.
  He must be punished. It's important   610
  To set an example. Some day
  Other men will try to rebel
  And raise a banner against us
  Knowing this loyal subject stole
  The Commander's crossbow and dared   615
  Point it at my chest.

ESTEBAN: As his father-in-law,
  Let me see if I can explain:
  Is it surprising that a boy
  Who's in love gets carried away?
  You tried to take his bride from him—   620
  Are you shocked he tried to save her?

COMMANDER: You're a stupid old fool, Esteban.

ESTEBAN: Sir, your reputation's at stake.

COMMANDER: I never tried to take his bride:
  She wasn't his.   625

ESTEBAN: She was, you did.
  We all know it. We've also heard
  That a King and Queen from Castile
  Are bringing new order and peace
  To their land and grateful subjects

Which will such disorders erase. 630
Once they've finished with their wars,
They'd do well not to permit
Men with such monstrous red Crosses
(As yours) to rule their villages.
Let the King wear one on his breast— 635
He alone deserves such tribute.
COMMANDER: Men! Remove his mayor's staff from
    him!38
ESTEBAN: Here you are. You're welcome to it.
COMMANDER: Now I will use it to beat you
    The way I break a horse that kicks. 640
ESTEBAN: Go on, my lord, I'll bear your blows.
PASCUALA: You're beating an old man like this?
LAURENCIA: If it's because he's my father,
    Why take revenge on him, not me?
    But what have I done to make you 645
    Want revenge?
COMMANDER: Take the girl away
    And set ten soldiers to guard her.

(The Commander and his men exit with Laurencia.)

ESTEBAN: May God send us justice, I pray. *(exits)*
PASCUALA: Their wedding night's become a wake.
    (exits)
BARRILDO: Won't anyone here dare speak up? 650
MENGO: I tried and look what it got me:
    More purple than any bishop
    Could ever wear. Now it's your turn.
JUAN: Let's all speak out.
MENGO: Let's be silent.
    My flesh is red as sliced salmon. 655

(They exit.)

END OF ACT II.

ACT III

(Enter Esteban, Alonso and Barrildo.)

ESTEBAN: Is no one else coming?39
BARRILDO: It looks that way.

---

38 mayor's staff] ceremonial staff of office.
39 The verse form used originally at the beginning of this
    act is *tercets*.

ESTEBAN: Don't they understand what's at play?
BARRILDO: I told everyone in the town
ESTEBAN: Look, they've put Frondoso in irons
    And my Laurencia in such danger 5
    That unless God comes quick to save her—

(Enter Juan Rojo and another alderman.)

JUAN: Why are you making such noise, Esteban?
    This is supposed to be a secret meeting.
ESTEBAN: I think it's a miracle I'm not screaming.

(Enter Mengo.)

MENGO: I thought I'd come too. 10
ESTEBAN: As a man whose hair
    Is white and wet with tears, I have come here
    To ask you, my friends and honest farmers,
    How we should remember this town that's lost
    Itself. How can we honour it with a funeral
    Since this monster has taken from us all 15
    Whatever honour we had to give?
    Answer me: Is there one of you whose life
    And good name has not been destroyed?
    Does the sorrow of others not strike a chord
    In each one of you? Let me tell you: 20
    You have all lost what gave your lives value.
    What are you waiting for? What could be worse?
JUAN: Nothing. There is no misfortune like this.
    But since we've heard Ferdinand and Isabel
    Now rule in peace over Castile 25
    And will shortly in Cordoba hold court
    Let us send two councillors there to report
    Our plight and beg for help.
BARRILDO: King Ferdinand's
    At war, battling enemies on all sides—
    He won't have time to set our village right. 30
ALDERMAN: I say we abandon the town—tonight.
JUAN: There isn't time enough.
MENGO: And if he finds out,
    It may cost us our lives.
ALDERMAN: So we're adrift
    In a ship whose mast this monster's split,
    Sailing lost in an ocean of fear. 35
    They abduct the daughter of our honoured mayor
    In broad daylight, and then on his head break
    The stick he ruled us with! Was any slave
    Treated worse than this?

JUAN: So what shall we do?

ALDERMAN: Die—or make these tyrants die, since   40
    they are few
    And we are many.

BARRILDO: You mean take up arms
    Against our lord?

ESTEBAN: Our only lord on earth's
    The king—and not these subhuman brutes.
    With God on our side, what have we to lose?

MENGO: Be careful. As a simple peasant, sirs,   45
    I speak—Please consider our fears.
    We're the ones who get hurt.

JUAN: We've all suffered—
    Losses of our own—Why wait till they return
    To take our lives? They are razing our vines
    And our houses. They're tyrants. Revenge!   50

(Enter Laurencia, dishevelled.)

LAURENCIA: Let me in. I have every right[40]
    To take my place among you men,
    For a woman, if not a vote,
    Still has a voice. You've forgotten
    Who I am?   55

ESTEBAN: God in heaven
    Aren't you Laurencia?

JUAN: You can't tell
    If it's your own daughter?

LAURENCIA: So changed
    I come, that you may well
    Doubt who I am.

ESTEBAN: Daughter of mine!

LAURENCIA: Don't call me daughter!   60

ESTEBAN: Why not my love?

LAURENCIA: For many reasons—the main one's
    You let tyrants carry me off
    Without seeking revenge, traitors
    Take me without lifting a limb—
    Frondoso hadn't made me his   65
    So you can't say it's up to him
    To avenge me—what happened here
    Is something that you must set right.
    It's only after the wedding night
    That a husband possesses his wife,   70
    For though I may buy a jewel,

---

[40] Here the verse form switches to *romance*.

I can't protect it from thieves
Until it comes into my hands.
Under your eyes, Fernán Gomez
Took me to his house. To the wolf,   75
You coward shepherds left your sheep.
Daggers he placed at my neck,
Madnesses he suggested,
Atrocious crimes, and words, and threats
He plagued me with to make me yield   80
To his desires. Look at this hair—
Doesn't it tell you the story?
Can't you see the bruises I bear,
The blows I took, the blood I spilled?
And you consider yourselves men?   85
You say you're my father—my kin?
Don't your insides burst with grief
To see me in such despair?
Fuenteovejuna—"the well
Where sheep drink"—and that's what you are,   90
Not men, but sheep. Give me weapons,
You're heartless as stone, as bronze,
As wood, as a tiger is—No—
A tigress will at least pursue
And hunt down the hunters who go   95
To India to steal their young.
You are born cowards like the hare,
Not Spaniards, but some other species....
A gaggle of hens is what you are,
Letting your wives go through hell   100
So that other men can enjoy
And mount them. Why bother with swords?
Strap knitting needles to your loins!
Thimbles and rolling pins!
I swear to God I'll make sure it's   105
We women alone who reclaim
This town's honour from these tyrants,
And the blood those traitors owe us.
And you? Let them pelt you with rocks
As you prance and mince down the street—   110
Sissies, pansies, ninnies, eunuchs!
And we'll make you dress as we do
With our headscarves and petticoats,
With painted eyes and powdered cheeks!
Commander Gomez is about   115
To hang Frondoso up alive—
Untried, uncharged, and innocent—

From the castle wall, as a warning.
And he'll do the same to you all,
Half-men. And I'll rejoice, I will,   120
That this once-honourable town's
At least freed of its girls,
And that the age of the Amazons
Has returned to shock again the world.

ESTEBAN: I'm not the kind of man you say,   125
Laurencia, who'll let himself
Be called such vile and hateful names.
I'll fight alone, against the world.

JUAN: And I will too, however strong
And daunting our foe may seem.   130

ALDERMAN: We'll die fighting.

BARRILDO: Unfold a stretch
Of cloth from a stick in the breeze,[41]
And let's put this monster to death!

JUAN: But whose orders shall we obey?

MENGO: No one's—let the whole village rise   135
As one to say what we agree:
It's time that these tyrants should die.

ESTEBAN: Grab your pitchforks, pokers, crossbars,
Your sticks and swords!

MENGO: Long live the King and Queen!

ALL: Long live Ferdinand and Isabel!   140

MENGO: Death to the treacherous tyrants!

ALL: Death to the tyrannous traitors!

(The men all exit.)

LAURENCIA: To arms—God knows our cause is just!
Women of Fuenteovejuna,
Come join your men in rising up   145
To win your honour back! Come one,
Come all!

(Enter Pascuala, Jacinta and other women.)

PASCUALA: What's this? Why all this noise?

LAURENCIA: Can't you see that they're off to kill
Commander Gomez? Little boys,   150
Youths, and men are rushing to join in.
But should they alone have the glory
Of killing him, when we women
Have really suffered so much more?

JACINTA: So what's your plan?   155

LAURENCIA: That we shall commit,
Marching just like soldiers, an act
That will amaze the entire planet.
Jacinta, the great wrongs done you
Mean that you should march at the head.

JACINTA: But you've suffered—just as badly too.   160

LAURENCIA: Pascuala, you'll carry our colours.

PASCUALA: Then let me raise a pretty flag
On this pole—you'll see how nice it looks.

LAURENCIA: There's no time for that. We must attack
While fortune smiles on our efforts.   165
We'll make a flag out of our shawls.

PASCUALA: But we ought to name a captain.

LAURENCIA: Don't dream of it.

PASCUALA: Why not?

LAURENCIA: If all
Of us fight with the strength I feel
We won't need heroes to lead us.   170

(They exit.)

*(Enter Frondoso with his hands tied, Flores, Ortuño,
Cimbranos and the Commander.)*

COMMANDER: With the rope left over from
binding his wrists[42]
I want you to string him up. So it really hurts.

FRONDOSO: How noble of you, my Lord.

COMMANDER: Then dangle him
For all to see from the highest battlement.

FRONDOSO: You remember the day I spared your life?   175

A noise offstage.

FLORES: Wait, I hear something.

COMMANDER: The village?

FLORES: That's right.
And they're coming to interrupt our justice.

ORTUÑO: They're smashing the gates.

COMMANDER: The gates to my house?
The Commander's house?

FLORES: The whole town's come—

JUAN *(off)*: Topple, demolish, flatten, storm, and burn!   180

ORTUÑO: When people riot, it's pretty hard to stop.

COMMANDER: They're rebelling against me?

---

41 Unfold … breeze] i.e., "set up a banner of war."

42 The verse form switches to *octavas reales*.

FLORES: They're so fed up
And so furious they've smashed down the door.
COMMANDER: Untie him. Frondoso, go and restore
Peace among your peasant friends.   185
FRONDOSO: Go I must,
For it's love, my lord, that's led them to this.

(Frondoso's hands are untied and he exits.)

MENGO *(off)*: Long live our Ferdinand and Isabel!
Death to the traitors!
FLORES: Don't let this rabble
Find you here, my lord.
COMMANDER: Let them come if they like—
These walls are strong and we're ready to fight.   190
They'll have to turn back.
FLORES: When whole towns rise up
In arms, enraged, resolved to fight, they never stop
Without claiming their revenge.
COMMANDER: At this door
Like an iron gate, we'll unsheathe our swords
And face their fury.   195
FRONDOSO *(off)*:   Long live Fuenteovejuna!
COMMANDER: That's what they're fighting for! It
makes me want to
Take them all on and see how brave they are.
FLORES: It's your bravery that makes me wonder.
ESTEBAN: Look: Here's the tyrant with his little
henchmen.
Fuenteovejuna! Death to the tyrants!   200

(Enter all the men.)

COMMANDER: Listen, my people—
ALL: Our sufferings can't wait!
COMMANDER: Explain to me what's wrong. We all
make mistakes
And, as a man of honour, I'll pay for mine.
ALL: Fuenteovejuna! Long live Ferdinand the King!
Death to all tyrants! Death to the heathens!   205
COMMANDER: Why don't you listen to me? I'm
speaking!
And I'm your Commander!
ALL: The only commands
We know are Isabel and Ferdinand's.
COMMANDER: Wait!
ALL: Fuenteovejuna! Fernán Gomez
Must die! Down with his name! Off with his head!   210

(They exit. Enter the women, carrying weapons.)

LAURENCIA: Wait here, my daring soldiers, with
your swords
And your hopes—we're not women any more.
PASCUALA: But how we love to take revenge!
We'll drink his blood!
JACINTA: We'll skewer his flesh.
PASCUALA: And slowly braise each piece until we're   215
happy!
ESTEBAN *(off)*: Die, you traitor, die!
COMMANDER *(off)*:   I'm dying—Have pity,
Lord, for I trust in your infinite grace.
BARRILDO *(off)*: Look who's here: Flores.
MENGO *(off)*:   Don't let him escape.
It was him that gave me two thousand lashes.
FRONDOSO *(off)*: I won't be happy till he's breathed   220
his last.
LAURENCIA: Let's go in.
PASCUALA: Wait—we've got to guard the door.
BARRILDO *(off)*: I won't hold back now. The more
you cry, the more
I'll hit you, city boys.
LAURENCIA: Let me inside,
Pascuala—I'll show them I can swing a sword.

(She exits.)

BARRILDO *(off)*: Here's Ortuño.   225
FRONDOSO *(off)*:   Let's have his face rearranged.

(Enter Flores, with Mengo in pursuit.)

FLORES: Have mercy, Mengo. I'm not to blame.
MENGO: On top of pimping for him, you flogged me
And that's reason enough.
PASCUALA: Hand him over, please.
We women will know how to deal with him.
MENGO: Here he is, then. A crueller punishment,   230
I can't imagine.
PASCUALA: He'll pay for your flogging.
MENGO: Go ahead.
JACINTA: Yes, let's do the traitor in.
FLORES: Me killed by women?
JACINTA: That's fair, don't you think?
PASCUALA: Look, he's crying.
JACINTA: Kill the little pimp.
PASCUALA: Kill the traitor.   235

FLORES:　　　　　　　Have mercy on me, dear—

(Enter Ortuño with Laurencia in pursuit.)

ORTUÑO: It's not me you want.
LAURENCIA:　　　　　　I know who you are:
　Come, let's paint our weapons with their blood!
PASCUALA: I'll keep on killing till I'm dead.
ALL:　　　　　　　Long live Ferdinand the great.

(They all exit.)

(Enter King Ferdinand, Queen Isabel, Manrique and the Master of Santiago.)

MANRIQUE: The campaign went extremely well.[43]
　We accomplished our mission　　　　　　240
　With practically no opposition
　And captured Ciudad Real.
　Even if they try to fight back,
　It wouldn't have troubled us much.
　I left the Count of Cabra in charge　　　　245
　Just in case they counterattack.
KING: A wise decision—he'll keep
　The troops in line and hold the pass—
　That way we can be sure that
　Alfonso won't disturb our sleep　　　　　250
　Sneaking in from Portugal…
　And I'm glad it's the Count you chose
　To leave in charge—well he'll serve us,
　As he is valiant and loyal.

(Enter Flores wounded.)

FLORES: Most Catholic King Ferdinand,[44]　　255
　Excellent, valiant and virile,
　On whom Heaven has wisely bestowed
　The glittering crown of fair Castile,
　Listen now to the cruellest act
　Man has ever witnessed on earth.　　　　260
KING: Compose yourself—
FLORES:　　　　　Your Majesty,
　My wounds have brought me to death's door.
　I can't waste words. I've just come from
　The town of Fuenteovejuna
　Where the peasants, in a fit of rage,　　　265

Have slain their military ruler.
Fernán Gomez, my lord, is dead.
Murdered by his faithless subjects
Who, being peasants, decided
To rebel with the slightest cause.　　　　270
Denouncing him as a tyrant,
One after another, they came
To believe their lies and grew bold
Enough to attempt the crime I name—
Storming his house, ignoring his vow　　275
As a nobleman to make up
For any debts he had incurred.
Not only were his words snubbed
But they, filled with a sudden rage,
Smashed his cross and the heart beneath,　280
With a thousand vicious blows
And from the highest balcony
Tossed his body to the ground where,
With the tips of their spears and swords,
The women caught him up and bore　　　285
His body to a nearby house,
Each vying to tear out his hair
And beard, to mutilate his cheeks.
So great was their rage that soon
They'd ripped his face to pieces,　　　　290
The largest of which were his ears.
Then they defaced the coat of arms
Above his door, saying they wished
It replaced with your royal arms
And crest, since his offended them.　　　295
They sacked his house and looted it,
And gleefully between themselves
Divided up the captured booty.
I saw all this from where I hid,
Since, amidst such barbarity,　　　　　300
Cruel fate decided I should live.
And live I did, hiding till dark
When I could escape to bring you
This account. Since you are most just,
My lord, you must punish justly　　　　305
Those who commit such brutal acts.
The Commander's blood demands
They learn how severe you can be.
KING: You can be certain they'll receive
The kind of punishment they must.　　　310
This sad event has so shocked me

---

[43] The verse form switches to *redondillas*.
[44] The verse form switches to *romance*.

That I will now dispatch a judge
To investigate and decide
On an exemplary sentence;
With him, I will send a captain   315
For his protection. Such great sins
Against nature must be punished
So others won't repeat them soon.
Now please tend to this soldier's wounds.

(All exit.)

(Enter women and peasants, with the head of Fernán Gomez on a lance.)

MUSICIANS *(singing)*: *Long live Ferdinand and Isabel—*   320
   And send the tyrants all to hell.
BARRILDO: Let Frondoso recite his verse.[45]
FRONDOSO: Here it is—I've done the best I can.
   If someone thinks it doesn't scan
   They can fix it with their own words.   325

   (singing) Long live the lovely Isabel
   And Ferdinand of Aragon
   Together as one they belong.
   May they live and rule us well
   And leave, when the time has come,   330
   For Heaven, on St. Michael's hand.
   Long live Isabel and Ferdinand.
LAURENCIA: It's your turn, Barrildo.
BARRILDO: Here goes—
   I was up all last night polishing
   The rhymes—   335
PASCUALA: Just say it with conviction
   And we'll think it's great, Heaven knows.
BARRILDO *(singing)*: *Long live the Catholic monarchs.*
   They have conquered far and wide
   To be our rulers and our pride—
   May they always leave their marks,   340
   Fighting giants or fighting dwarves.
MUSICIANS *(singing)*: *Long live Ferdinand and Isabel—*
   And send the tyrants all to hell.
LAURENCIA: Go on, Mengo.
FRONDOSO: Mengo, let's hear.
MENGO: I only write poems for fun.   345

PASCUALA: Like those soldiers who caught someone
   And, for fun, wrote lines on his rear?
MENGO *(singing)*: *A lovely Sunday morn it was*
   That the Commander gave the order.
   I was flogged so much it was torture   350
   And stung like a cloud of hornets.
   But now I've rubbed on bacon grease
   The cure the priest says is best
   Long live our Catholic Kingies
   And may all tyrants bite the dust!   355
MUSICIANS *(singing)*: *Long live Ferdinand and Isabel—*
   And send the tyrants all to hell.
ESTEBAN: Take that head away from here.
MENGO: He looks awful.

(Enter Juan with the Royal Arms on a shield.)

ALDERMAN: Look what he's got.
   It's the King's coat of arms.   360
ESTEBAN: We ought
   Put it on display somewhere.
JUAN: Where?
ALDERMAN: Right by the Town Hall's door.
ESTEBAN: What a nice shield.
BARRILDO: A happy sight!

(The Alderman exits.)

FRONDOSO: Our day has finally arrived.
   This shield heralds the light of dawn.   365
ESTEBAN: Long live the castles of Castile,
   The lions rampant of Leon,
   And the stripes of Aragon!
   And may tyranny be killed!
   Now, villagers, some advice   370
   (Since listening to the words
   Of one's elders never hurts):
   The King will, at the very least,
   Want to investigate this case,
   Especially since he and the Queen   375
   Shall soon be passing through this region.
   We must agree on what we'll say.
FRONDOSO: What do you suggest?
ESTEBAN: When they come,
   Say "Fuenteovejuna did it".
   Be ready to die saying that.   380
FRONDOSO: Yes, that's the way to answer them:
   It was Fuenteovejuna.

---

[45] The *redondillas* resume.

ESTEBAN: Is that what you wish to say?
ALL: Yes!
ESTEBAN: Then let's try a little test.
  I'll play the judge, and I'll choose a   385
  Person—Mengo, say—to question.
MENGO: Why not someone who's really weak?
ESTEBAN: We're just pretending.
MENGO: Then be quick.
ESTEBAN: Who killed the Commander?
MENGO: I'm guessing:
  Fuenteovejuna did it!   390
ESTEBAN: And if I crucify you, hound?
MENGO: Go ahead, and try all you want,
  My lord.
ESTEBAN: Confess, you idiot.
MENGO: All right: I confess.
ESTEBAN: So tell me:
  Who?   395
MENGO: It was Fuenteovejuna.
ESTEBAN: Rip his clothes off. Take horsewhips to him.
MENGO: It won't get you anywhere.
ESTEBAN: We'll see.

(The Alderman reappears.)

ALDERMAN: What are you doing here?
FRONDOSO: What's the story?
ALDERMAN: They've sent a judge and he's arrived.   400
ESTEBAN: Let's get out of here.
ALDERMAN: At his side,
  He's got a captain of the army.
ESTEBAN: Let the devil himself come snoop here.
  You know what to say.
ALDERMAN: We'll be found here.
ESTEBAN: Shh. Mengo: who killed the Commander?   405
MENGO: Why, it was Fuenteovejuna.

(Exit all.)

(Enter the Master and a soldier.)

MASTER: What a horrible way to go!
  I half-think I should take my sword
  To you for bringing such news.
SOLDIER: Lord,
  I'm just the messenger—not the foe.   410
MASTER: Think that a village so inflamed
  Would dare commit such acts. I'll take

Five hundred men and lay it waste.
Not the faintest echo of their names
Will be left—   415
SOLDIER: My lord, contain this rage—
  The village has sworn allegiance
  To the King; the wrath of our regent
  Is not something you want to raise.
MASTER: How can the village be the King's
  If it belongs to our order?   420
SOLDIER: You and he can discuss that matter.
MASTER: But against the King, no one wins.
  For he has special sovereign powers.
  No, I'll calm my anger and seek
  An audience at his royal feet.   425
  I sided with his cousin—now there's
  A good excuse for that: my youth.
  I'll go humbled, knowing I must
  Regain my honour through his trust,
  And be not reviled but renewed.   430

(They exit.)

(Enter Laurencia.)

LAURENCIA: When you're in love and fear some
  danger[46]
  Threatens your love, it makes you suffer
  Even more; Love's pangs get rougher
  The flames hotter, the nights longer
  The strongest, firmest held belief,   435
  When fear attacks, will quickly crumble
  And give way to a pain now double:
  The fear that fear brings love to grief.
  My husband I adore but must,
  Unless good fortune smiles on us,   440
  Spend my nights in fear for his life.
  All I want is him to be safe—
  But if he's here, I twitch and ache;
  If he's away, it's death itself.

(Enter Frondoso.)

FRONDOSO: Laurencia!   445
LAURENCIA: My husband, my love![47]
  How can you dare show your face here?

---

46 This speech is written as a sonnet.
47 The *redondillas* resume until the end of the play.

FRONDOSO: Is this how you repay the care
  I've shown you.
LAURENCIA: I'm frightened of
  What they might do to you. Watch out.
FRONDOSO: Heaven forbid I should ever   450
  Treat you like this?
LAURENCIA: But didn't you shiver
  To see the fury this judge's brought
  To his task, how cruelly he treats
  Everyone he finds. Save your life
  And flee!   455
FRONDOSO: But how? Can't you see I've
  No life to save but these heart beats?
  Is it right I should leave my friends
  To face such danger—and leave you?
  Don't tell me to flee; I can't undo
  The bond we share, I can't pretend   460
  My blood's not yours....

(Cries are heard offstage.)

                    Wait, I hear voices.
  And, if I'm not mistaken—listen!—
  The screams of someone they've dragged in
  To torture… That's where the noise is.

(The judge speaks and the villagers answer offstage.)

JUDGE *(off)*: Tell us the truth, Grandad.   465
FRONDOSO: Good Lord,
  Laurencia, it's an old man
  They've got.
LAURENCIA: They're taking everyone.
ESTEBAN *(off)*: Leave me in peace.
JUDGE *(off)*:   Loosen the cord.
  Now tell me: Who killed the Commander?
ESTEBAN *(off)*: Fuenteovejuna did it.   470
LAURENCIA: Your name, Father, I'll always worship.
FRONDOSO: What a hero!
JUDGE *(off)*:   That boy will answer.
  Tie him up tight—tighter, you dog!
  I know you know. Now tell us who.
  No? We'll stretch your limbs till you're blue.   475
BOY *(off)*: Fuenteovejuna did it.
JUDGE *(off)*: For the love of God, I swear
  I'll hang you all with my own hands.
  Which one of you killed the Commander?
FRONDOSO: They're torturing a child and he dares   480
  To defy them?
LAURENCIA: What a village!
FRONDOSO: What courage!
JUDGE *(off)*:   Bring that girl at once
  And tie her to the rack. Two turns
  On the lever!
LAURENCIA: He's blind with rage.
JUDGE *(off)*: I'll kill each one of you witches   485
  On this rack here, believe you me.
  Who killed the Commander? Now truly…
PASCUALA *(off)*: Fuenteovejuna, it was.
JUDGE *(off)*: One more turn!
FRONDOSO: He'll never break her.
LAURENCIA: That's Pascuala and she won't tell.   490
FRONDOSO: Not even the children will.
JUDGE *(off)*: It's as if they like the rack. Tighter!
PASCUALA *(off)*: Oh, heaven have mercy!
JUDGE *(off)*:   More, you wretch?
  What are you, deaf? That will do her.
PASCUALA *(off)*: It was Fuenteovejuna.   495
JUDGE *(off)*: Bring me the big fat one… That one…
  Yes.
LAURENCIA: That's Mengo, I'll bet.
FRONDOSO: I'm afraid
  They'll break him down.
MENGO *(off)*:   Oh-oh.
JUDGE *(off)*:   Go slow.
MENGO *(off)*: Oh no.
JUDGE *(off)*:   Now turn it tighter.
MENGO *(off)*:   No! NO!
JUDGE *(off)*: Now tell us, peasant, who it was.   500
  Who killed Fernán Gomez de Guzman?
MENGO *(off)*: I'll tell you, sir, I will, if you'll
  Let me go.
JUDGE *(off)*:   Loosen it a little.
FRONDOSO: He's going to tell.
JUDGE *(off)*:   Changed your mind?
  I'll make you speak the truth to me.   505
  Now give the lever a good spin.
MENGO *(off)*: Wait, wait, I'll tell you…
JUDGE *(off)*:   Who killed him?
MENGO *(off)*: A town called Fuenteoveju-nee.[48]

---

48 Fuenteoveju-nee] Mengo names the town with a diminutive.

JUDGE (off): What a pack of headstrong imbeciles!
  They just laugh at the pain we cause   510
  And the one I thought first to confess
  Is the most defiant of all!
  Enough—we'll try again tomorrow.

(Enter Mengo, with the Alderman and Barrildo.)

FRONDOSO: God bless you, Mengo! I stood here
  Terrified, and then your answer   515
  Made me proud and you a hero.
BARRILDO: Bravo Mengo!
ALDERMAN: Mengo stood firm!
BARRILDO: Three cheers for Mengo.
FRONDOSO: Hip-hip-hooray!
MENGO: Hip-hip—
BARRILDO: Here, have a swig, old guy,
  And a bite.   520
MENGO: What's that?
BARRILDO: Lemon jam.
MENGO: My favourite!
FRONDOSO: Now pour him some wine.
BARRILDO: Here you are.
FRONDOSO: Look how it goes down.
  He'll be singing.
LAURENCIA: Give him more to eat.
MENGO: More.
BARRILDO: Try a swig of this. It's mine.
LAURENCIA: Look at him.   525
FRONDOSO: Now he won't say no.
BARRILDO: Good? The grapes are from my vineyard.
MENGO: It's great.
FRONDOSO: Drink up. It's your reward.
LAURENCIA: One glass after another—Whoa!
FRONDOSO: Cover him up. He's cold as ice.
BARRILDO: More?   530
MENGO: Yes, and some more for my horses.
FRONDOSO: But you don't have horses.
BARRILDO: He sure as
  Hell wants some.
FRONDOSO: Wants horses?
BARRILDO: Wants wine!
  Here, Mengo, drink all you can down.
  That must have given you a thirst.
  What's wrong?   535
MENGO: It tastes a little worse.
  My head is starting to spin round.

FRONDOSO: We'd better lie him down a bit.
  Now, Mengo: Who killed the Commander?
MENGO: Was it a man? A woman? No, the answer's
  That Fuenteovejunica did it.   540

(Exit all except Frondoso and Laurencia.)

FRONDOSO: He deserves all the honours we have.
  But tell me now, my little panther,
  Who was it that killed the Commander?
LAURENCIA: Fuenteovejuna, my love.
FRONDOSO: But who killed him?   545
LAURENCIA: Don't torture me—
  The answer's Fuenteovejuna.
FRONDOSO: And I, yes, what have I slain you with?
LAURENCIA: With what? With loving you so purely.

(They exit.)

(Enter King Ferdinand and Queen Isabel.)

ISABEL: I never expected, my lord,
  You would return so quick. What luck.   550
FERDINAND: And how glorious you look.
  I was on my way to Portugal
  And had to pass by here.
ISABEL: I feel
  Your majesty should always make
  Such detours—when the affairs of state   555
  Permit.
FERDINAND: How have you left Castile?
ISABEL: At peace, being quite flat and calm.
FERDINAND: Since you're her Queen, it's no surprise
    that
  She's at peace—and so roundly flat.[49]

(Enter Manrique.)

MANRIQUE: The Master of Calatrava's come   560
  To seek an audience with the Queen.
ISABEL: And I wish to see him.
MANRIQUE: My lady,
  Although he's young in years, his bravery

---

49 roundly flat] Castile is famous for its broad, flat plains;
  translator Richard Sanger argues that Ferdinand's reference to Isabel's anatomy is intended as a husband's loving allusion to what he regards as his wife's very desirable
  combination of flatness and roundness.

Outranks the bravest of our men.

(Enter the Master.)

MASTER: I, Rodrigo Téllez Girón,   565
  The Master of Calatrava
  Come humbly before you to ask for
  Your forgiveness—I was wrong,
  I know, to act the way I have.
  I confess that I was misled   570
  By thoughts of what might lie ahead
  And the advice Fernán Gomez gave.
  And so humble pardon I ask
  And swear, should I receive such grace,
  That I will forthwith undertake   575
  To serve you with the truest heart.
  And when we lay siege to Granada,
  As you plan, I promise you'll see
  How fierce and brave my sword can be,
  Painting red crosses on the Alhambra.   580
  Five hundred soldiers I will bring
  To serve you, and with them, this oath
  I hereby take, with solemn faith,
  Never to offend you again.
FERDINAND: Rise, Master. Since you've come to us,   585
  You needn't fear—we'll treat you well—
MASTER: You soothe my worst fears.
ISABEL: And the skill
  You show in speech can be no less
  Than the daring you've shown in war.
MASTER: My Queen, you are as ravishing   590
  As Esther was, and you, my King,
  As infallible as Xerxes was.[50]

(Enter Manrique.)

MANRIQUE: The judge you sent to investigate
  The case in Fuenteovejuna
  Has returned—he's here to give you a   595
  Full report.
FERDINAND *(to Isabel)*:   You decide their fate
MASTER: If it was up to me, my Lord,

---

50 Esther … Xerxes] The reference is to the proverbially
  wise and beautiful Esther, of the Biblical Book of Esther,
  the Jewish woman who became Queen of Persia, and to
  her husband, Xerxes I (also known as Ahasuerus), King
  of Persia, 486–65 B.C.E.

  I'd teach those peasants a lesson:
  Killing their Commander… Imagine!
FERDINAND: This is not your business. You've erred   600
  A few times in your judgement, Master.
ISABEL: In the future, we should ensure
  That every military order,
  Including that of Calatrava,
  Be brought under the King's command.   605

(Enter the Judge.)

JUDGE: I went to Fuenteovejuna
  As you ordered, and with due care
  And diligence, I there began
  My inquiry into the crime
  That was committed. This being said,   610
  I return without a single shred
  Of evidence: When I came
  To ask the villagers who had
  Done the murder, they just replied,
  As though all speaking with one mind,   615
  "It was Fuenteovejuna."
  Three hundred of them I tortured
  On the rack, showing no mercy:
  I promise you, your Majesty,
  I could not get another word   620
  Out of them. Little boys of ten
  I strapped up and stretched, tried to bribe;
  It did no good. You must decide
  To put to death the entire town,
  Or to pardon them. They've come today   625
  And, for all I've said, will give proof.
  You may question them yourself
FERDINAND: Then show these people in, I say.

(Enter the two Aldermen, Frondoso, the women and the villagers.)

LAURENCIA: That can't be them, the King and Queen!
FRONDOSO: It is and they rule all Castile.   630
LAURENCIA: Good heavens, they're beautiful.
ISABEL: And are these the murderers then?
ESTEBAN: Fuenteovejuna we are
  Madam, arriving here humbly
  To serve you. The cruel tyranny   635
  And excesses the late Commander
  Inflicted on us are the cause
  Of all this: Our daughters he raped,

Our belongings he robbed and laid waste,
Knowing neither pity nor laws.   640
FRONDOSO: And this girl, whom Heaven dropped
    here
To make me the happiest man
On earth, on the first night we planned
Together, the night we were wed,
Do you know what he did? He came   645
And carried her off to his house
Just like that—as if she were his.
If she hadn't fought back, her name
(And our lives) would now be ruined,
MENGO: Can I tell my story now? Please.   650
If you'll just let me, I promise
You'll be shocked to hear how he turned
On me, and all because I tried
To save a village girl from soldiers
Who planned to use her for their pleasure.   655
One after the other—he, like
Some perverse Roman, had my rear-end
Flogged till it was as red and raw
As freshly-sliced salmon, with four

Of his men beat me like a drum.   660
You know, I can still show your Highness
The bruises to prove it. The cure's
Cost me more than my land is worth.
ESTEBAN: Sir, we want you to rule and guide us.
You are the king we call our own,   665
Your arms adorn our village hall,
We seek your pardon, so we all
Entrust ourselves to you, and hope,
In this, you'll find us innocent.
FERDINAND: Since no written proof exists,   670
This crime, though deadly serious,
Must be pardoned. Moreover, since
The village has appealed to me
It shall remain under my care
Until the day a new commander   675
May perhaps appear.
FRONDOSO: Your majesty
Has spoken wisely—just as one
Expects of a king who's achieved
Such great things. So, friends, with your leave,
This Fuenteovejuna's done.   680

MOLIÈRE

Tartuffe

The ironic circumstances of Molière's death are legendary. On February 17, 1673, during the fourth performance of his comedy *L'Invalid Imaginaire* (*The Imaginary Invalid* or *The Hypochondriac*), in which he was playing the title role, Molière suffered a seizure and fell. He was taken to his home in the rue Richelieu in Paris, where, several hours later, he died of tuberculosis. The church refused to give him sanctified burial, on the pretext that, because no priest had been present, Molière had not received sacred rites, nor had he renounced the disreputable life of an actor (though there were exceptions, actors were usually refused burial in sanctified ground at this time). The church authorities undoubtedly felt their arguments had some merit, although it seems likely too that they continued to harbour resentment against Molière for writing *Tartuffe* and producing it to public acclaim despite their best efforts to have it banned. At any rate, only upon the direct intervention of King Louis XIV did the Archbishop of Paris concede to the extent of allowing Molière to be formally buried after sunset among the suicides' and paupers' graves, with the proviso that no requiem masses were to be permitted in any church. Although by the time of his death Molière was acknowledged as the undisputed master of French comedy (a title he has never relinquished), in death as in life he was required to pay a steep price for his art.

Molière was born Jean-Baptiste Poquelin in 1622, the son of an eminent Parisian upholsterer who had attained the prestigious rank of upholsterer to the King. Jean-Baptiste's mother died when he was only ten, an event which, as often happens in such cases, may have prompted his extraordinary determination to prove himself. Having declined his father's plans to have him enter the family business, Jean-Baptiste studied law for a time. However, at twenty-one, he abandoned it to decisively turn his back on his family's social status and enter the theatrical profession. To save his family public embarrassment, he took the stage name Molière.

The company Molière first formed in Paris with a group of nine others, the Illustre-Théâtre, was not a success, to the point that Molière ended up in debtors' prison for a time. Bloodied but unbowed, upon his release he founded a new company with a friend named Madeleine Bejart, and the troupe left to begin what would ultimately become a thirteen-year tour of the provinces. At last, in 1658, the company was offered a crucial opportunity: a performance before King Louis XIV and his brother, the Duke of Orleans, on an improvised stage in the guardroom of the Louvre. The first play the company presented, Corneille's tragedy *Nicomède*, was not judged a success, but the second was one of Molière's own, a comedy called *Le Docteur amoureux*. The King and his brother were amused, and so the company was invited to settle in Paris, where Molière quickly began the task of writing them a repertoire.

During his period of exile, Molière had assimilated many techniques and conventions of theatrical comedy which would become vital components of his work in Paris: the satiric caricatures of obsessive personalities, the wily servants, the rapid-fire exchanges of dialogue, the plots of frustrated then consummated love affairs—all conventions that had been maintained among travelling players, quite possibly without interruption, since the heyday of the New Comedy of Ancient Greece. It was left to Molière to marry the ancient popular techniques to the urbanity of seventeenth-century Paris, thereby creating a new sort of comedy that appealed as much to the taste of the sophisticates of the court audience as to that of the broader public.

Molière's particular gift seems to have been for creating comedy that takes as its premise a set of ordinary social concerns and dramatizes the results of crossing the fine line from normal, sensible, moderate behaviour based on those concerns to unreasonable, obsessive and immoderate behaviour that carries such concerns to the point of absurdity. In many of his plays, such as *Le Miser*, *Le Bourgeois gentilhomme*, *Le Misanthrope*, and *L'Invalid Imaginaire*, the title declares the nature of the obsession which provides the play with its primary theme. *Tartuffe* (or *L'Imposteur*) is obviously a somewhat different case, in that the immoderate behaviour out of which the plot arises is not that of Tartuffe himself. He—as the alternative title suggests, and as is revealed within minutes of the beginning of the play—is an out-and-out imposter who, if he were unconvincing to everyone, would be able to do no harm. Instead, the character whose obsessions drive the plot is the father, Orgon, who has attached his unquestioning faith to Tartuffe and who insists on believing in Tartuffe's goodness to the point of disaster. In suggesting that there is, even in faith and piety, such a thing as immoderation (where the object of it is unworthy), it was predictable that Molière would ruffle a few feathers; in the event, it nearly proved his undoing.

The first three acts of *Tartuffe* were presented at court in 1664. It seems that King Louis XIV was immediately delighted by the play; however, various high-ranking church authorities were in no doubt that the play was suggesting that they themselves were imposters to be distrusted. So vehement were they in their disapproval of the play that they managed to persuade the king to have it banned from the public stage. Molière decided to resist: partly, perhaps, because he believed that the play would be a great success, but partly out of principled anger at having his work interfered with by hypocrites who were far more interested in their own comfortable position than with questions of morality. He sent a series of letters to the king, trying to persuade him to lift the ban: "I have no doubt, your Majesty," he wrote,

> that the persons I portray in my comedy will exert all the influence they can muster against me. But however they represent themselves, it is not God's interest which moves them. They have amply demonstrated this by enthusiastically attending other comedies, which do indeed attack piety and religion—things in which they have little real interest. But they feel that this play, [*Tartuffe*], attacks them personally—that it exposes them for what they are. And this, they find unbearable. This, they can never forgive. Your Majesty, there is no question that I could not so much as dream of continuing to produce my comedies if these Tartuffes were to be allowed to prevail, if you were to permit them to persecute me...

Meanwhile, Molière began a campaign to win influential secular approval for his play, by organizing private readings of it in various salons, and (while the king was away visiting Flanders) having his company perform it under the title *The Imposter*. The church authorities responded by declaring Molière "a demon in human flesh" and having his company's posters torn down. In 1667, the Archbishop of Paris, perhaps desperately sensing that he was losing the battle of opinion, decreed that anyone who performed in, read or saw the play would be excommunicated and he had the chief of police close the theatre down temporarily.

In the meantime, however, Louis XIV's mother, the extremely pious Anne of Austria, through whom the Church had been able to influence the king, had died. Moreover, Molière's campaign had created much of its intended effect on public opinion, so the king—evidently not wanting to find himself playing the role of Orgon in this controversy—had the ban lifted, and the play opened to great acclaim on February 5, 1669.

[C.S.W.]

MOLIÈRE

Tartuffe; or, The Imposter
A Comedy in Five Acts

Translated by Richard Wilbur

CHARACTERS

MME PERNELLE, Orgon's mother
ORGON, Elmire's husband
ELMIRE, Orgon's wife
DAMIS, Orgon's son, Elmire's stepson
MARIANE, Orgon's daughter, Elmire's step-
    daughter, in love with Valère
VALÈRE, in love with Mariane
CLÉANTE, Orgon's brother-in-law
TARTUFFE, a hypocrite
DORINE, Mariane's lady's-maid
M. LOYAL, a bailiff
A POLICE OFFICER
FLIPOTE, Mme Pernelle's maid

THE SCENE THROUGHOUT:
ORGON'S HOUSE IN PARIS

ACT ONE

SCENE ONE

MADAME PERNELLE and FLIPOTE, her maid, ELMIRE, MARIANE, DORINE, DAMIS, CLÉANTE

MADAME PERNELLE. Come, come, Flipote; it's time
    I left this place.
ELMIRE. I can't keep up, you walk at such a pace.
MADAME PERNELLE. Don't trouble, child; no need
    to show me out.
    It's not your manners I'm concerned about.
ELMIRE. We merely pay you the respect we owe.   5
    But, Mother, why this hurry? Must you go?
MADAME PERNELLE. I must. This house appals me.
    No one in it
    Will pay attention for a single minute.
    Children, I take my leave much vexed in spirit.[1]

---

[1] vexed in spirit] In French, Madame Pernelle uses what would have been regarded by Molière's audience as an old-fashioned and fussy mode of expression, something translator Richard Wilbur has hinted at occasionally, as here.

I offer good advice, but you won't hear it.   10
You all break in and chatter on and on.
It's like a madhouse with the keeper gone.
DORINE. If...
MADAME PERNELLE. Girl, you talk too much, and I'm afraid
You're far too saucy for a lady's-maid.
You push in everywhere and have your say.   15
DAMIS. But...
MADAME PERNELLE.   You, boy, grow more foolish every day.
To think my grandson should be such a dunce!
I've said a hundred times, if I've said it once,
That if you keep the course on which you've started,
You'll leave your worthy father broken-hearted.   20
MARIANE. I think...
MADAME PERNELLE.   And you, his sister, seem so pure,
So shy, so innocent, and so demure.
But you know what they say about still waters.
I pity parents with secretive daughters.
ELMIRE. Now, Mother...   25
MADAME PERNELLE.   And as for you, child, let me add
That your behavior is extremely bad,
And a poor example for these children, too.
Their dear, dead mother did far better than you.
You're much too free with money, and I'm distressed
To see you so elaborately dressed.   30
When it's one's husband that one aims to please,
One has no need of costly fripperies.
CLÉANTE. Oh, Madam, really...
MADAME PERNELLE.   You are her brother, Sir,
And I respect and love you; yet if I were
My son, this lady's good and pious spouse,   35
I wouldn't make you welcome in my house.
You're full of worldly counsels which, I fear,
Aren't suitable for decent folk to hear.
I've spoken bluntly, Sir; but it behooves us
Not to mince words when righteous fervor moves us.   40
DAMIS. Your man Tartuffe is full of holy speeches ...
MADAME PERNELLE. And practises precisely what he preaches.
He's a fine man, and should be listened to.
I will not hear him mocked by fools like you.
DAMIS. Good God! Do you expect me to submit   45

To the tyranny of that carping hypocrite?
Must we forgo all joys and satisfactions
Because that bigot censures all our actions?
DORINE. To hear him talk—and he talks all the time—
There's nothing one can do that's not a crime.   50
He rails at everything, your dear Tartuffe.
MADAME PERNELLE. Whatever he reproves deserves reproof.
He's out to save your souls, and all of you
Must love him, as my son would have you do.
DAMIS. Ah no, Grandmother, I could never take   55
To such a rascal, even for my father's sake.
That's how I feel, and I shall not dissemble.
His every action makes me seethe and tremble
With helpless anger, and I have no doubt
That he and I will shortly have it out.   60
DORINE. Surely it is a shame and a disgrace
To see this man usurp the master's place—
To see this beggar who, when first he came,
Had not a shoe or shoestring to his name
So far forget himself that he behaves   65
As if the house were his, and we his slaves.
MADAME PERNELLE. Well, mark my words, your souls would fare far better
If you obeyed his precepts to the letter.
DORINE. You see him as a saint. I'm far less awed;
In fact, I see right through him. He's a fraud.   70
MADAME PERNELLE. Nonsense!
DORINE.   His man Laurent's the same, or worse;
I'd not trust either with a penny purse.
MADAME PERNELLE. I can't say what his servant's morals may be;
His own great goodness I can guarantee.
You all regard him with distaste and fear   75
Because he tells you what you're loath to hear,
Condemns your sins, points out your moral flaws,
And humbly strives to further Heaven's cause.
DORINE. If sin is all that bothers him, why is it
He's so upset when folk drop in to visit?   80
Is Heaven so outraged by a social call
That he must prophesy against us all?
I'll tell you what I think: if you ask me,
He's jealous of my mistress' company.
MADAME PERNELLE. Rubbish!   85
(To Elmire:)   He's not alone, child, in complaining

Of all your promiscuous entertaining.
Why, the whole neighborhood's upset, I know,
By all these carriages that come and go,
With crowds of guests parading in and out
And noisy servants loitering about.   90
In all of this, I'm sure there's nothing vicious;
But why give people cause to be suspicious?
CLÉANTE. They need no cause; they'll talk in any case.
  Madam, this world would be a joyless place
  If, fearing what malicious tongues might say,   95
  We locked our doors and turned our friends away.
  And even if one did so dreary a thing,
  D'you think those tongues would cease their
    chattering?
  One can't fight slander; it's a losing battle;
  Let us instead ignore their tittle-tattle.   100
  Let's strive to live by conscience's clear decrees,
  And let the gossips gossip as they please.
DORINE. If there is talk against us, I know the source:
  It's Daphne and her little husband, of course.
  Those who have greatest cause for guilt and shame   105
  Are quickest to besmirch a neighbor's name.
  When there's a chance for libel, they never miss it;
  When something can be made to seem illicit
  They're off at once to spread the joyous news,
  Adding to fact what fantasies they choose.   110
  By talking up their neighbor's indiscretions
  They seek to camouflage their own transgressions,
  Hoping that others' innocent affairs
  Will lend a hue of innocence to theirs,
  Or that their own black guilt will come to seem   115
  Part of a general shady color-scheme.
MADAME PERNELLE. All that is quite irrelevant. I
  doubt
  That anyone's more virtuous and devout
  Than dear Orante; and I'm informed that she
  Condemns your mode of life most vehemently.   120
DORINE. Oh, yes, she's strict, devout, and has no
  taint
  Of worldliness; in short, she seems a saint.
  But it was time which taught her that disguise;
  She's thus because she can't be otherwise.
  So long as her attractions could enthrall,   125
  She flounced and flirted and enjoyed it all,
  But now that they're no longer what they were
  She quits a world which fast is quitting her,

And wears a veil of virtue to conceal
Her bankrupt beauty and her lost appeal.   130
That's what becomes of old coquettes today:
Distressed when all their lovers fall away,
They see no recourse but to play the prude,
And so confer a style on solitude.
Thereafter, they're severe with everyone,   135
Condemning all our actions, pardoning none,
And claiming to be pure, austere, and zealous
When, if the truth were known, they're merely
  jealous,
And cannot bear to see another know
The pleasures time has forced them to forgo.   140
MADAME PERNELLE *(Initially to Elmire:)* That sort
  of talk is what you like to hear;
Therefore you'd have us all keep still, my dear,
While Madam rattles on the livelong day.
Nevertheless, I mean to have my say.
I tell you that you're blest to have Tartuffe   145
Dwelling, as my son's guest, beneath this roof;
That Heaven has sent him to forestall its wrath
By leading you, once more, to the true path;
That all he reprehends its reprehensible,
And that you'd better heed him, and be sensible.   150
These visits, balls, and parties in which you revel
Are nothing but inventions of the Devil.
One never hears a word that's edifying:
Nothing but chaff and foolishness and lying,
As well as vicious gossip in which one's neighbor   155
Is cut to bits with epee, foil, and saber.
People of sense are driven half-insane
At such affairs, where noise and folly reign
And reputations perish thick and fast.
As a wise preacher said on Sunday last,   160
Parties are Towers of Babylon, because
The guests all babble on with never a pause;[2]
And then he told a story which, I think...
(To Cléante:) I heard that laugh, Sir, and I saw
  that wink!
Go find your silly friends and laugh some more!   165
Enough; I'm going; don't show me to the door.
I leave this household much dismayed and vexed;
I cannot say when I shall see you next.

---

2 Towers of Babylon] a play on Tower of Babel (Genesis
  11).

(Slapping Flipote:) Wake up, don't stand there
   gaping into space!
I'll slap some sense into that stupid face.   170
Move, move, you slut.

SCENE TWO

CLÉANTE, DORINE.

CLÉANTE.   I think I'll stay behind;
   I want no further pieces of her mind.
   How that old lady...
DORINE.   Oh, what wouldn't she say
   If she could hear you speak of her that way!
   She'd thank you for the *lady*, but I'm sure   5
   She'd find the *old* a little premature.
CLÉANTE. My, what a scene she made, and what a din!
   And how this man Tartuffe has taken her in!
DORINE. Yes, but her son is even worse deceived;
   His folly must be seen to be believed.   10
   In the late troubles, he played an able part
   And served his king with wise and loyal heart,
   But he's quite lost his senses since he fell
   Beneath Tartuffe's infatuating spell.
   He calls him brother, and loves him as his life,   15
   Preferring him to mother, child, or wife.
   In him and him alone will he confide;
   He's made him his confessor and his guide;
   He pets and pampers him with love more tender
   Than any pretty mistress could engender,   20
   Gives him the place of honour when they dine,
   Delights to see him gorging like a swine,
   Stuffs him with dainties till his guts distend,
   And when he belches, cries "God bless you, friend!"
   In short, he's mad; he worships him; he dotes;   25
   His deeds he marvels at, his words he quotes,
   Thinking each act a miracle, each word
   Oracular as those that Moses heard.[3]
   Tartuffe, much pleased to find so easy a victim,
   Has in a hundred ways beguiled and tricked him,   30
   Milked him of money, and with his permission
   Established here a sort of Inquisition.[4]

---

[3] words ... Moses heard] i.e., on Mount Sinai, where God
   dictated the ten commandments.
[4] Inquisition] in Roman Catholicism, a ruthless papal judicial institution with a mandate to inquire into and
   combat heresy.

Even Laurent, his lackey, dares to give
Us arrogant advice on how to live;
He sermonizes us in thundering tones   35
And confiscates our ribbons and colognes.
Last week he tore a kerchief into pieces
Because he found it pressed in a *Life of Jesus:*
He said it was a sin to juxtapose
Unholy vanities and holy prose.   40

SCENE THREE

ELMIRE, MARIANE, DAMIS, CLÉANTE, DORINE.

ELMIRE *(To Cléante:)* You did well not to follow; she
     stood in the door
   And said *verbatim* all she'd said before.[5]
   I saw my husband coming. I think I'd best
   Go upstairs now, and take a little rest.
CLÉANTE. I'll wait and greet him here; then I must go.   5
   I've really only time to say hello.
DAMIS. Sound him about my sister's wedding, please.
   I think Tartuffe's against it, and that he's
   Been urging Father to withdraw his blessing.
   As you well know, I'd find that most distressing.   10
   Unless my sister and Valère can marry,
   My hopes to wed *his* sister will miscarry,
   And I'm determined...
DORINE.   He's coming.

SCENE FOUR

ORGON, CLÉANTE, DORINE.

ORGON.   Ah, Brother, good-day.
CLÉANTE. Well, welcome back. I'm sorry I can't stay.
   How was the country? Blooming, I trust, and green?
ORGON. Excuse me, Brother; just one moment.
   (To Dorine:)   Dorine...
   (To Cléante:) To put my mind at rest, I always learn   5
   The household news the moment I return.
   (To Dorine:) Has all been well, these two days I've
     been gone?
   How are the family? What's been going on?
DORINE. Your wife, two days ago, had a bad fever,
   And a fierce headache which refused to leave her.   10

---

[5] *verbatim*] (Latin) to the exact word.

ORGON. Ah. And Tartuffe?

DORINE.   Tartuffe? Why, he's round and red,
     Bursting with health, and excellently fed.

ORGON. Poor fellow!

DORINE.   That night, the mistress was unable
     To take a single bite at the dinner-table.
     Her headache-pains, she said, were simply hellish.   15

ORGON. Ah. And Tartuffe?

DORINE.   He ate his meal with relish,
     And zealously devoured in her presence
     A leg of mutton and a brace of pheasants.

ORGON. Poor fellow!

DORINE.   Well, the pains continued strong,
     And so she tossed and tossed the whole night long,   20
     Now icy-cold, now burning like aflame.
     We sat beside her bed till morning came.

ORGON. Ah. And Tartuffe?

DORINE.   Why, having eaten, he rose
     And sought his room, already in a doze,
     Got into his warm bed, and snored away   25
     In perfect peace until the break of day.

ORGON. Poor fellow!

DORINE.   After much ado, we talked her
     Into dispatching someone for the doctor.
     He bled her, and the fever quickly fell.

ORGON. Ah. And Tartuffe?   30

DORINE.   He bore it very well.
     To keep his cheerfulness at any cost,
     And make up for the blood *Madame* had lost,
     He drank, at lunch, four beakers full of port.

ORGON. Poor fellow!

DORINE.   Both are doing well, in short.
     I'll go and tell *Madame* that you've expressed   35
     Keen sympathy and anxious interest.

SCENE FIVE

ORGON, CLÉANTE.

CLÉANTE. That girl was laughing in your face, and
     though
     I've no wish to offend you, even so
     I'm bound to say that she had some excuse.
     How can you possibly be such a goose?
     Are you so dazed by this man's hocus-pocus   5
     That all the world, save him, is out of focus?
     You've given him clothing, shelter, food, and care;

     Why must you also...

ORGON.   Brother, stop right there.
     You do not know the man of whom you speak.

CLÉANTE. I grant you that. But my judgment's not   10
     so weak
     That I can't tell, by his effect on others ...

ORGON. Ah, when you meet him, you two will be
     like brothers!
     There's been no loftier soul since time began.
     He is a man who...a man who...an excellent man.
     To keep his precepts is to be reborn,   15
     And view this dunghill of a world with scorn.
     Yes, thanks to him I'm a changed man indeed.
     Under his tutelage my soul's been freed
     From earthly loves, and every human tie:
     My mother, children, brother, and wife could die,   20
     And I'd not feel a single moment's pain.

CLÉANTE. That's a fine sentiment, Brother; most
     humane.

ORGON. Oh, had you seen Tartuffe as I first knew him,
     Your heart, like mine, would have surrendered to
     him.
     He used to come into our church each day   25
     And humbly kneel nearby, and start to pray.
     He'd draw the eyes of everybody there
     By the deep fervour of his heartfelt prayer;
     He'd sigh and weep, and sometimes with a sound
     Of rapture he would bend and kiss the ground;   30
     And when I rose to go, he'd run before
     To offer me holy-water at the door.
     His serving-man, no less devout than he,
     Informed me of his master's poverty;
     I gave him gifts, but in his humbleness   35
     He'd beg me every time to give him less.
     "Oh, that's too much," he'd cry, "too much by twice!
     I don't deserve it. The half, Sir, would suffice."
     And when I wouldn't take it back, he'd share
     Half of it with the poor, right then and there.   40
     At length, Heaven prompted me to take him in
     To dwell with us, and free our souls from sin.
     He guides our lives, and to protect my honour
     Stays by my wife, and keeps an eye upon her;
     He tells me whom she sees, and all she does,   45
     And seems more jealous than I ever was!
     And how austere he is! Why, he can detect
     A mortal sin where you would least suspect;

In smallest trifles, he's extremely strict.
Last week, his conscience was severely pricked   50
Because, while praying, he had caught a flea
And killed it, so he felt, too wrathfully.
CLÉANTE. Good God, man! Have you lost your
    common sense—
Or is this all some joke at my expense?
How can you stand there and in all sobriety...   55
ORGON. Brother, your language savours of impiety.
Too much free-thinking's made your faith
    unsteady,
And as I've warned you many times already,
'Twill get you into trouble before you're through.
CLÉANTE. So I've been told before by dupes like   60
    you:
Being blind, you'd have all others blind as well;
The clear-eyed man you call an infidel,
And he who sees through humbug and pretense
Is charged, by you, with want of reverence.
Spare me your warnings, Brother; I have no fear   65
Of speaking out, for you and Heaven to hear,
Against affected zeal and pious knavery.
There's true and false in piety, as in bravery,
And just as those whose courage shines the most
In battle, are the least inclined to boast,   70
So those whose hearts are truly pure and lowly
Don't make a flashy show of being holy.
There's a vast difference, so it seems to me,
Between true piety and hypocrisy:
How do you fail to see it, may I ask?   75
Is not a face quite different from a mask?
Cannot sincerity and cunning art,
Reality and semblance, be told apart?
Are scarecrows just like men, and do you hold
That a false coin is just as good as gold?   80
Ah, Brother, man's a strangely fashioned creature
Who seldom is content to follow Nature,
But recklessly pursues his inclination
Beyond the narrow bounds of moderation,
And often, by transgressing Reason's laws,   85
Perverts a lofty aim or noble cause.
A passing observation, but it applies.
ORGON. I see, dear Brother, that you're profoundly
    wise;
You harbor all the insight of the age.
You are our one clear mind, our only sage,   90

The era's oracle, its Cato too,[6]
And all mankind are fools compared to you.
CLÉANTE. Brother, I don't pretend to be a sage,
Nor have I all the wisdom of the age.
There's just one insight I would dare to claim: 95
I know that true and false are not the same;
And just as there is nothing I more revere
Than a soul whose faith is steadfast and sincere,
Nothing that I more cherish and admire
Than honest zeal and true religious fire,   100
So there is nothing that I find more base
Than specious piety's dishonest face—
Than these bold mountebanks, these *histrios*[7]
Whose impious mummeries and hollow shows
Exploit our love of Heaven, and make a jest   105
Of all that men think holiest and best;
These calculating souls who offer prayers
Not to their Maker, but as public wares,
And seek to buy respect and reputation
With lifted eyes and sighs of exaltation;   110
These charlatans, I say, whose pilgrim souls
Proceed, by way of Heaven, toward earthly goals,
Who weep and pray and swindle and extort,
Who preach the monkish life, but haunt the court,
Who make their zeal the partner of their vice—   115
Such men are vengeful, sly, and cold as ice,
And when there is an enemy to defame
They cloak their spite in fair religion's name,
Their private spleen and malice being made
To seem a high and virtuous crusade,   120
Until, to mankind's reverent applause,
They crucify their foe in Heaven's cause.
Such knaves are all too common; yet, for the wise,
True piety isn't hard to recognize,
And, happily, these present times provide us   125
With bright examples to instruct and guide us.
Consider Ariston and Periandre;
Look at Oronte, Alcidamas, Clitandre;
Their virtue is acknowledged; who could doubt it?
But you won't hear them beat the drum about it.   130

---

6 Cato] Marcus Porcius Cato, the elder (234–149 B.C.E.),
    a notoriously severe Roman censor (i.e., not merely an
    expurgator of texts, but an inspector of general morals
    and conduct).
7 histrios] disreputable stage-players.

They're never ostentatious, never vain,
And their religion's moderate and humane;
It's not their way to criticize and chide:
They think censoriousness a mark of pride,
And therefore, letting others preach and rave,   135
They show, by deeds, how Christians should behave.
They think no evil of their fellow man,
But judge of him as kindly as they can.
They don't intrigue and wangle and conspire;
To lead a good life is their one desire;   140
The sinner wakes no rancorous hate in them;
It is the sin alone which they condemn;
Nor do they try to show a fiercer zeal
For Heaven's cause than Heaven itself could feel.
These men I honour, these men I advocate   145
As models for us all to emulate.
Your man is not their sort at all, I fear:
And, while your praise of him is quite sincere,
I think that you've been dreadfully deluded.
ORGON. Now then, dear Brother, is your speech   150
  concluded?
CLÉANTE. Why, yes.
ORGON.   Your servant, Sir. *(He turns to go.)*
CLÉANTE.   No, Brother; wait.
  There's one more matter. You agreed of late
  That young Valère might have your daughter's hand.
ORGON. I did.
CLÉANTE.   And set the date, I understand.
ORGON. Quite so.   155
CLÉANTE.   You've now postponed it; is that true?
ORGON. No doubt.
CLÉANTE.   The match no longer pleases you?
ORGON. Who knows?
CLÉANTE.   D'you mean to go back on your word?
ORGON. I won't say that.
CLÉANTE.   Has anything occurred
  Which might entitle you to break your pledge?
ORGON. Perhaps.   160
CLÉANTE.   Why must you hem, and haw, and
  hedge?
  The boy asked me to sound you in this affair...
ORGON. It's been a pleasure...
CLÉANTE.   But what shall I tell Valère?
ORGON. Whatever you like.
CLÉANTE.   But what have you decided?
  What are your plans?

ORGON.   I plan, Sir, to be guided
  By Heaven's will.   165
CLÉANTE.   Come, Brother, don't talk rot.
  You've given Valère your word; will you keep it, or
  not?
ORGON. Good day.
CLÉANTE.   This looks like poor Valère's undoing;
  I'll go and warn him that there's trouble brewing.

ACT TWO

SCENE ONE

ORGON, MARIANE.

ORGON. Mariane.
MARIANE.   Yes, Father?
ORGON.   A word with you; come here.
MARIANE. What are you looking for?
ORGON. *(Peering into a small closet:)* Eaves-
  droppers, dear.
  I'm making sure we shan't be overheard.
  Someone in there could catch our every word.
  Ah, good, we're safe. Now, Mariane, my child,   5
  You're a sweet girl who's tractable and mild,
  Whom I hold dear, and think most highly of.
MARIANE. I'm deeply grateful, Father, for your love.
ORGON. That's well said, Daughter; and you can
  repay me
  If, in all things, you'll cheerfully obey me.   10
MARIANE. To please you, Sir, is what delights me best.
ORGON. Good, good. Now, what d'you think of
  Tartuffe, our guest?
MARIANE. I, Sir?
ORGON.   Yes. Weigh your answer; think it through.
MARIANE. Oh, dear. I'll say whatever you wish me to.
ORGON. That's wisely said, my Daughter. Say of   15
  him, then,
  That he's the very worthiest of men,
  And that you're fond of him, and would rejoice
  In being his wife, if that should be my choice.
  Well?
MARIANE.   What?
ORGON.   What's that?
MARIANE.   I...
ORGON.   Well?
MARIANE.   Forgive me, pray.

ORGON. Did you not hear me?   20
MARIANE.   Of *whom*, Sir, must I say
  That I am fond of him, and would rejoice
  In being his wife, if that should be your choice?
ORGON. Why, of Tartuffe.
MARIANE.   But, Father, that's false, you know.
  Why would you have me say what isn't so?
ORGON. Because I am resolved it shall be true.   25
  That it's my wish should be enough for you.
MARIANE. You can't mean, Father...
ORGON.   Yes, Tartuffe shall be
  Allied by marriage to this family,
  And he's to be your husband, is that clear?
  It's a father's privilege...   30

SCENE TWO

DORINE, ORGON, MARIANE.

ORGON *(To Dorine:)*   What are you doing in here?
  Is curiosity so fierce a passion
  With you, that you must eavesdrop in this fashion?
DORINE. There's lately been a rumour going about—
  Based on some hunch or chance remark, no doubt—   5
  That you mean Mariane to wed Tartuffe.
  I've laughed it off, of course, as just a spoof.
ORGON. You find it so incredible?
DORINE.   Yes, I do.
  I won't accept that story, even from you.
ORGON. Well, you'll believe it when the thing is done.   10
DORINE. Yes, yes, of course. Go on and have your fun.
ORGON. I've never been more serious in my life.
DORINE. Ha!
ORGON.   Daughter, I mean it; you're to be his wife.
DORINE. No, don't believe your father; it's all a hoax.
ORGON. See here, young woman   15
DORINE.   Come, Sir, no more jokes
  You can't fool us....
ORGON.   How dare you talk that way?
DORINE. All right, then: we believe you, sad to say.
  But how a man like you, who looks so wise
  And wears a moustache of such splendid size,
  Can be so foolish as to...   20
ORGON.   Silence, please!
  My girl, you take too many liberties.
  I'm master here, as you must not forget.
DORINE. Do let's discuss this calmly; don't be upset.

  You can't be serious, Sir, about this plan.
  What should that bigot want with Mariane?   25
  Praying and fasting ought to keep him busy.
  And then, in terms of wealth and rank, what is he?
  Why should a man of property like you
  Pick out a beggar son-in-law?
ORGON.   That will do.
  Speak of his poverty with reverence.   30
  His is a pure and saintly indigence
  Which far transcends all worldly pride and pelf.
  He lost his fortune, as he says himself,
  Because he cared for Heaven alone, and so
  Was careless of his interests here below.   35
  I mean to get him out of his present straits
  And help him to recover his estates—
  Which, in his part of the world, have no small fame.
  Poor though he is, he's a gentleman just the same.
DORINE. Yes, so he tells us; and, Sir, it seems to me   40
  Such pride goes very ill with piety.
  A man whose spirit spurns this dungy earth
  Ought not to brag of lands and noble birth;
  Such worldly arrogance will hardly square
  With meek devotion and the life of prayer.   45
  ...But this approach, I see, has drawn a blank;
  Let's speak, then, of his person, not his rank.
  Doesn't it seem to you a trifle grim
  To give a girl like her to a man like him?
  When two are so ill-suited, can't you see,   50
  What the sad consequence is bound to be?
  A young girl's virtue is imperilled, Sir,
  When such a marriage is imposed on her;
  For if one's bridegroom isn't to one's taste,
  It's hardly an inducement to be chaste,   55
  And many a man with horns upon his brow[8]
  Has made his wife the thing that she is now.
  It's hard to be a faithful wife, in short,
  To certain husbands of a certain sort,
  And he who gives his daughter to a man she hates   60
  Must answer for her sins at Heaven's gates.
  Think, Sir, before you play so risky a role.
ORGON. This servant-girl presumes to save my soul!
DORINE. You would do well to ponder what I've said.
ORGON. Daughter, we'll disregard this dunderhead.   65

---

8 horns] i.e., cuckold's horns, the (figurative) symbol of
   having an adulterous wife.

Just trust your father's judgment. Oh, I'm aware
That I once promised you to young Valère;
But now I hear he gambles, which greatly shocks me;
What's more, I've doubts about his orthodoxy.
His visits to church, I note, are very few.   70
DORINE. Would you have him go at the same hours
    as you,
And kneel nearby, to be sure of being seen?
ORGON. I can dispense with such remarks, Dorine.
    (To Mariane:) Tartuffe, however, is sure of Heaven's
    blessing,
And that's the only treasure worth possessing.   75
This match will bring you joys beyond all measure;
Your cup will overflow with every pleasure;
You two will interchange your faithful loves
Like two sweet cherubs, or two turtle-doves.
No harsh word shall be heard, no frown be seen,   80
And he shall make you happy as a queen.
DORINE. And she'll make him a cuckold, just wait
    and see.
ORGON. What language!
DORINE.   Oh, he's a man of destiny;
He's *made* for horns, and what the stars demand
Your daughter's virtue surely can't withstand.   85
ORGON. Don't interrupt me further. Why can't you
    learn
That certain things are none of your concern?
DORINE. It's for your own sake that I interfere.

(She repeatedly interrupts Orgon just as he is turning to
speak to his daughter:)

ORGON. Most kind of you. Now, hold your tongue,
    d'you hear?
DORINE. If I didn't love you...   90
ORGON.   Spare me your affection.
DORINE. I'll love you, Sir, in spite of your objection.
ORGON. Blast!
DORINE.   I can't bear, Sir, for your honour's sake,
To let you make this ludicrous mistake.
ORGON. You mean to go on talking?
DORINE.   If I didn't protest
This sinful marriage, my conscience couldn't rest.   95
ORGON. If you don't hold your tongue, you little
    shrew...
DORINE. What, lost your temper? A pious man like
    you?

ORGON. Yes! Yes! You talk and talk. I'm maddened
    by it.
Once and for all, I tell you to be quiet.
DORINE. Well, I'll be quiet. But I'll be thinking hard.   100
ORGON. Think all you like, but you had better guard
That saucy tongue of yours, or I'll...
    (Turning back to Mariane:)   Now, child,
I've weighed this matter fully.
DORINE *(Aside:)*   It drives me wild
That I can't speak.

(Orgon turns his head, and she is silent.)

ORGON.   Tartuffe is no young dandy,
But, still, his person...   105
DORINE *(Aside:)*   Is as sweet as candy.
ORGON. Is such that, even if you shouldn't care
For his other merits...

(He turns and stands facing Dorine, arms crossed.)

DORINE *(Aside:)*   They'll make a lovely pair.
If I were she, no man would marry me
Against my inclination, and go scot-free.
He'd learn, before the wedding-day was over,   110
How readily a wife can find a lover.
ORGON *(To Dorine:)* It seems you treat my orders as
    a joke.
DORINE. Why, what's the matter? 'Twas not to you
    I spoke.
ORGON. What *were* you doing?
DORINE.   Talking to myself, that's all.
ORGON. Ah! *(Aside:)* One more bit of impudence   115
    and gall,
And I shall give her a good slap in the face.

(He puts himself in position to slap her; Dorine, when-
ever he glances at her, stands immobile and silent:)

Daughter, you shall accept, and with good grace,
The husband I've selected...Your wedding-day ...
    (To Dorine:) Why don't you talk to yourself?
DORINE.   I've nothing to say.
ORGON. Come, just one word.   120
DORINE.   No thank you, Sir. I pass.
ORGON. Come, speak; I'm waiting.
DORINE.   I'd not be such an ass.
ORGON *(Turning to Mariane:)* In short, dear Daughter,
    I mean to be obeyed,

And you must bow to the sound choice I've made.

DORINE *(Moving away:)* I'd not wed such a monster, even in jest.

(Orgon attempts to slap her, but misses.)

ORGON. Daughter, that maid of yours is a thorough pest;   125
  She makes me sinfully annoyed and nettled.
  I can't speak further; my nerves are too unsettled.
  She's so upset me by her insolent talk,
  I'll calm myself by going for a walk.

SCENE THREE

DORINE, MARIANE.

DORINE *(Returning:)* Well, have you lost your tongue, girl? Must I play
  Your part, and say the lines you ought to say?
  Faced with a fate so hideous and absurd,
  Can you not utter one dissenting word?

MARIANE. What good would it do? A father's power is great.   5

DORINE. Resist him now, or it will be too late!

MARIANE. But...

DORINE.   Tell him one cannot love at a father's whim;
  That you shall marry for yourself, not him;
  That since it's you who are to be the bride,
  It's you, not he, who must be satisfied;   10
  And that if his Tartuffe is so sublime,
  He's free to marry him at any time.

MARIANE. I've bowed so long to Father's strict control,
  I couldn't oppose him now, to save my soul.

DORINE. Come, come, Mariane. Do listen to reason, won't you?   15
  Valère has asked your hand. Do you love him, or don't you?

MARIANE. Oh, how unjust of you! What can you mean
  By asking such a question, dear Dorine?
  You know the depth of my affection for him;
  I've told you a hundred times how I adore him.   20

DORINE. I don't believe in everything I hear;
  Who knows if your professions were sincere?

MARIANE. They were, Dorine, and you do me wrong to doubt it;
  Heaven knows that I've been all too frank about it.

DORINE. You love him, then?   25

MARIANE.   Oh, more than I can express.

DORINE. And he, I take it, cares for you no less?

MARIANE. I think so.

DORINE.   And you both, with equal fire,
  Burn to be married?

MARIANE.   That is our one desire.

DORINE. What of Tartuffe, then? What of your father's plan?

MARIANE. I'll kill myself, if I'm forced to wed that man.   30

DORINE. I hadn't thought of that recourse. How splendid!
  Just die, and all your troubles will be ended!
  A fine solution. Oh, it maddens me
  To hear you talk in that self-pitying key.

MARIANE. Dorine, how harsh you are! It's most unfair.   35
  You have no sympathy for my despair.

DORINE. I've none at all for people who talk drivel
  And, faced with difficulties, whine and snivel.

MARIANE. No doubt I'm timid, but it would be wrong...

DORINE. True love requires a heart that's firm and strong.   40

MARIANE. I'm strong in my affection for Valère,
  But coping with my father is his affair.

DORINE. But if your father's brain has grown so cracked
  Over his dear Tartuffe that he can retract
  His blessing, though your wedding-day was named,   45
  It's surely not Valère who's to be blamed.

MARIANE. If I defied my father, as you suggest,
  Would it not seem unmaidenly, at best?
  Shall I defend my love at the expense
  Of brazenness and disobedience?   50
  Shall I parade my heart's desires, and flaunt...

DORINE. No, I ask nothing of you. Clearly you want
  To be Madame Tartuffe, and I feel bound
  Not to oppose a wish so very sound.
  What right have I to criticize the match?   55
  Indeed, my dear, the man's a brilliant catch.
  Monsieur Tartuffe! Now, there's a man of weight!
  Yes, yes, Monsieur Tartuffe, I'm bound to state,
  Is quite a person; that's not to be denied;
  'Twill be no little thing to be his bride.   60
  The world already rings with his renown;
  He's a great noble-in his native town;

His ears are red, he has a pink complexion,
And all in all, he'll suit you to perfection.
MARIANE. Dear God! 65
DORINE.   Oh, how triumphant you will feel
At having caught a husband so ideal!
MARIANE. Oh, do stop teasing, and use your cleverness
To get me out of this appalling mess.
Advise me, and I'll do whatever you say.
DORINE. Ah no, a dutiful daughter must obey 70
Her father, even if he weds her to an ape.
You've a bright future; why struggle to escape?
Tartuffe will take you back where his family lives,
To a small town aswarm with relatives—
Uncles and cousins whom you'll be charmed to meet. 75
You'll be received at once by the elite,
Calling upon the bailiff's wife, no less-
Even, perhaps, upon the mayoress,
Who'll sit you down in the *best* kitchen chair.
Then, once a year, you'll dance at the village fair 80
To the drone of bagpipes—two of them, in fact—
And see a puppet-show, or an animal act.
Your husband...
MARIANE.   Oh, you turn my blood to ice!
Stop torturing me, and give me your advice.
DORINE. *(Threatening to go:)* Your servant, Madam. 85
MARIANE.   Dorine, I beg of you...
DORINE. No, you deserve it; this marriage must go
through.
MARIANE. Dorine!
DORINE.   No.
MARIANE.   Not Tartuffe! You know I think him...
DORINE. Tartuffe's your cup of tea, and you shall
drink him.
MARIANE. I've always told you everything, and relied....
DORINE. No. You deserve to be tartuffified. 90
MARIANE. Well, since you mock me and refuse to care,
I'll henceforth seek my solace in despair:
Despair shall be my counsellor and friend,
And help me bring my sorrows to an end.

(She starts to leave.)

DORINE. There now, come back; my anger has 95
subsided.
You do deserve some pity, I've decided.
MARIANE. Dorine, if Father makes me undergo
This dreadful martyrdom, I'll die, I know.

DORINE. Don't fret; it won't be difficult to discover
Some plan of action...But here's Valère, your lover. 100

SCENE FOUR

VALÈRE, MARIANE, DORINE.

VALÈRE. Madam, I've just received some wondrous
news
Regarding which I'd like to hear your views.
MARIANE. What news?
VALÈRE.   You're marrying Tartuffe.
MARIANE.   I find
That Father does have such a match in mind.
VALÈRE. Your father, Madam ... 5
MARIANE.   ...has just this minute said
That it's Tartuffe he wishes me to wed.
VALÈRE. Can he be serious?
MARIANE.   Oh, indeed he can;
He's clearly set his heart upon the plan. 10
VALÈRE. And what position do you propose to take,
Madam?
MARIANE.   Why— I don't know.
VALÈRE.   For heaven's sake—
You don't know?
MARIANE.   No.
VALÈRE.   Well, well!
MARIANE.   Advise me, do.
VALÈRE. Marry the man. That's my advice to you.
MARIANE. That's your advice? 15
VALÈRE.   Yes.
MARIANE.   Truly?
VALÈRE.   Oh, absolutely.
You couldn't choose more wisely, more astutely.
MARIANE. Thanks for this counsel; I'll follow it, of
course.
VALÈRE. Do, do; I'm sure 'twill cost you no remorse.
MARIANE. To give it didn't cause your heart to break.
VALÈRE. I gave it, Madam, only for your sake. 20
MARIANE. And it's for your sake that I take it, Sir.
DORINE. *(Withdrawing to the rear of the stage:)* Let's
see which fool will prove the stubborner.
VALÈRE. So! I am nothing to you, and it was flat
Deception when you...
MARIANE.   Please, enough of that.
You've told me plainly that I should agree 25
To wed the man my father's chosen for me,

And since you've deigned to counsel me so wisely,
I promise, Sir, to do as you advise me.
VALÈRE. Ah, no, 'twas not by me that you were swayed.
No, your decision was already made;   30
Though now, to save appearances, you protest
That you're betraying me at my behest.
MARIANE. Just as you say.
VALÈRE.   Quite so. And I now see
That you were never truly in love with me.
MARIANE. Alas, you're free to think so if you choose.   35
VALÈRE. I choose to think so, and here's a bit of news:
You've spurned my hand, but I know where to turn
For kinder treatment, as you shall quickly learn.
MARIANE. I'm sure you do. Your noble qualities
Inspire affection...   40
VALÈRE.   Forget my qualities, please.
They don't inspire you overmuch, I find.
But there's another lady I have in mind
Whose sweet and generous nature will not scorn,
To compensate me for the loss I've borne.
MARIANE. I'm no great loss, and I'm sure that you'll   45
transfer
Your heart quite painlessly from me to her.
VALÈRE. I'll do my best to take it in my stride.
The pain I feel at being cast aside
Time and forgetfulness may put an end to.
Or if I can't forget, I shall pretend to.   50
No self-respecting person is expected
To go on loving once he's been rejected.
MARIANE. Now, that's a fine, high-minded sentiment.
VALÈRE. One to which any sane man would assent.
Would you prefer it if I pined away   55
In hopeless passion till my dying day?
Am I to yield you to a rival's arms
And not console myself with other charms?
MARIANE. Go then: console yourself; don't hesitate.
I wish you to; indeed, I cannot wait.   60
VALÈRE. You wish me to?
MARIANE.   Yes.
VALÈRE.   That's the final straw.
Madam, farewell. Your wish shall be my law.

(He starts to leave, and then returns: this repeatedly:)

MARIANE. Splendid.
VALÈRE *(Coming back again:)*   This breach,
remember, is of your making;

It's you who've driven me to the step I'm taking.
MARIANE. Of course.   65
VALÈRE *(Coming back again:)* Remember, too, that
I am merely
Following your example.
MARIANE.   I see that clearly.
VALÈRE. Enough. I'll go and do your bidding, then.
MARIANE. Good.
VALÈRE *(Coming back again:)*   You shall never
see my face again.
MARIANE. Excellent.
VALÈRE. *(Walking to the door, then turning about:)*
Yes?
MARIANE.   What?
VALÈRE.   What's that? What did you say?
MARIANE. Nothing. You're dreaming.   70
VALÈRE.   Ah. Well, I'm on my way.
Farewell, *Madame.*

(He moves slowly away.)

MARIANE.   Farewell.
DORINE *(To Mariane:)*   If you ask me,
Both of you are as mad as mad can be.
Do stop this nonsense, now. I've only let you
Squabble so long to see where it would get you.
Whoa there, Monsieur Valère!   75

*(She goes and seizes Valère by the arm; he makes a great
show of resistance.)*

VALÈRE.   What's this, Dorine?
DORINE. Come here.
VALÈRE.   No, no, my heart's too full of spleen.[9]
Don't hold me back; her wish must be obeyed.
DORINE. Stop!
VALÈRE.   It's too late now; my decision's made.
DORINE. Oh, pooh!
MARIANE *(Aside:)*   He hates the sight of me, that's
plain.
I'll go, and so deliver him from pain.   80
DORINE *(Leaving Valère, running after Mariane:)*
And now you run away! Come back.
MARIANE.   No, no.
Nothing you say will keep me here. Let go!

---

9 spleen] i.e., bitterness, melancholy.

VALÈRE *(Aside:)* She cannot bear my presence, I
    perceive.
  To spare her further torment, I shall leave.
DORINE. *(Leaving Mariane, running after Valère:)*   85
    Again! You'll not escape, Sir; don't you try it.
  Come here, you two. Stop fussing, and be quiet.

*(She takes Valère by the hand, then Mariane, and
draws them together.)*

VALÈRE *(To Dorine:)* What do you want of me?
MARIANE *(To Dorine:)*   What is the point of this?
DORINE. We're going to have a little armistice.
  (To Valère:) Now, weren't you silly to get so
    overheated?
VALÈRE. Didn't you see how badly I was treated?   90
DORINE *(To Mariane:)* Aren't you a simpleton, to
  have lost your head?
MARIANE. Didn't you hear the hateful things he said?
DORINE *(To Valère:)* You're both great fools. Her
    sole desire, Valère,
  Is to be yours in marriage. To that I'll swear.
  (To Mariane:) He loves you only, and he wants no   95
  wife
  But you, Mariane. On that I'll stake my life.
MARIANE *(To Valère:)* Then why you advised me so,
  I cannot see.
VALÈRE *(To Mariane:)* On such a question, why ask
  advice of *me?*
DORINE. Oh, you're impossible. Give me your
    hands, you two.
  (To Valère:) Yours first.   100
VALÈRE. *(Giving Dorine his hand:)*   But why?
DORINE *(To Mariane:)*   And now
  a hand from you.
MARIANE. *(Also giving Dorine her hand:)* What are
  you doing?
DORINE.   There: a perfect fit.
  You suit each other better than you'll admit—

*(Valère and Mariane hold hands for some time without
looking at each other.)*

VALÈRE. *(Turning toward Mariane:)* Ah, come, don't
  be so haughty. Give a man
  A look of kindness, won't you, Mariane?

(Mariane turns toward Valère and smiles.)

DORINE. I tell you, lovers are completely mad!   105
VALÈRE *(To Mariane:)* Now come, confess that you
  were very bad
  To hurt my feelings as you did just now.
  I have a just complaint, you must allow.
MARIANE. *You* must allow that you were most
    unpleasant.
DORINE. Let's table that discussion for the present;   110
  Your father has a plan which must be stopped.
MARIANE. Advise us, then; what means must we adopt?
DORINE. We'll use all manner of means, and all at once.
  (To Mariane:) Your father's addled; he's acting like
    a dunce.
  Therefore you'd better humor the old fossil.   115
  Pretend to yield to him, be sweet and docile
  And then postpone, as often as necessary,
  The day on which you have agreed to marry.
  You'll thus gain time, and time will turn the trick.
  Sometimes, for instance, you'll be taken sick,   120
  And that will seem good reason for delay;
  Or some bad omen will make you change the day—
  You'll dream of muddy water, or you'll pass
  A dead man's hearse, or break a looking-glass.
  If all else fails, no man can marry you   125
  Unless you take his ring and say "I do."
  But now, let's separate. If they should find
  Us talking here, our plot might be divined.
  (To Valère:) Go to your friends, and tell them
    what's occurred,
  And have them urge her father to keep his word.   130
  Meanwhile, we'll stir her brother into action,
  And get Elmire, as well, to join our faction.
  Good-bye.
VALÈRE. *(To Mariane:)*   Though each of us will do
    his best,
  It's your true heart on which my hopes shall rest.
MARIANE *(To Valère:)* Regardless of what Father may   135
    decide,
  None but Valère shall claim me as his bride.
VALÈRE. Oh, how those words content me! Come
    what will...
DORINE. Oh, lovers, lovers! Their tongues are never
    still.
  Be off, now.
VALÈRE. *(Turning to go, then turning back:)*
    One last word...

DORINE.   No time to chat:
   You leave by this door; and *you* leave by that.   140

(Dorine pushes them, by the shoulders, toward opposing doors.)

ACT THREE

SCENE ONE

DAMIS, DORINE.

DAMIS. May lightning strike me even as I speak,
   May all men call me cowardly and weak,
   If any fear or scruple holds me back
   From settling things, at once, with that great quack!
DORINE. Now, don't give way to violent emotion.   5
   Your father's merely talked about this notion,
   And words and deeds are far from being one.
   Much that is talked about is left undone.
DAMIS. No, I must stop that scoundrel's machinations;
   I'll go and tell him off; I'm out of patience.   10
DORINE. Do calm down and be practical. I had rather
   My mistress dealt with him—and with your father;
   She has some influence with Tartuffe, I've noted.
   He hangs upon her words, seems most devoted,
   And may, indeed, be smitten by her charm.   15
   Pray Heaven it's true! 'Twould do our cause no harm.
   She sent for him, just now, to sound him out
   On this affair you're so incensed about;
   She'll find out where he stands, and tell him, too,
   What dreadful strife and trouble will ensue   20
   If he lends countenance to your father's plan.
   I couldn't get in to see him, but his man
   Says that he's almost finished with his prayers.
   Go, now. I'll catch him when he comes downstairs.
DAMIS. I want to hear this conference, and I will.   25
DORINE. No, they must be alone.
DAMIS.   Oh, I'll keep still.
DORINE. Not you. I know your temper. You'd start a brawl,
   And shout and stamp your foot and spoil it all.
   Go on.
DAMIS.   I won't; I have a perfect right...
DORINE. Lord, you're a nuisance! He's coming; get   30
   out of sight.

(Damis conceals himself in a closet at the rear of the stage.)

SCENE TWO

TARTUFFE, DORINE.

TARTUFFE *(Observing Dorine, and calling to his
   manservant offstage:)* Hang up my hair-shirt,
   put my scourge in place,[10]
   And pray, Laurent, for Heaven's perpetual grace.
   I'm going to the prison now, to share
   My last few coins with the poor wretches there.
DORINE *(Aside:)* Dear God, what affectation! What   5
   a fake!
TARTUFFE. You wished to see me?
DORINE.   Yes...
TARTUFFE. *(Taking a handkerchief from his pocket:)*
                 For mercy's sake,
   Please take this handkerchief, before you speak.
DORINE. What?
TARTUFFE.   Cover that bosom, girl. The flesh is
   weak,
   And unclean thoughts are difficult to control.
   Such sights as that can undermine the soul.   10
DORINE. Your soul, it seems, has very poor defences,
   And flesh makes quite an impact on your senses.
   It's strange that you're so easily excited;
   My own desires are not so soon ignited,
   And if I saw you naked as a beast,   15
   Not all your hide would tempt me in the least.
TARTUFFE. Girl, speak more modestly; unless you do,
   I shall be forced to take my leave of you.
DORINE. Oh, no, it's I who must be on my way;
   I've just one little message to convey.   20
   Madame is coming down, and begs you, Sir,
   To wait and have a word or two with her.
TARTUFFE. Gladly.
DORINE *(Aside:)*   That had a softening effect!
   I think my guess about him was correct.
TARTUFFE. Will she be long?   25
DORINE.   No: that's her step I hear.
   Ah, here she is, and I shall disappear.

---

10 hair-shirt] a shirt made of rough animal hair, worn next
   to the skin as a penance; scourge] whip, for self-flagel-
   lation.

SCENE THREE

ELMIRE, TARTUFFE.

TARTUFFE. May Heaven, whose infinite goodness
we adore,
Preserve your body and soul forevermore,
And bless your days, and answer thus the plea
Of one who is its humblest votary.

ELMIRE. I thank you for that pious wish. But please, 5
Do take a chair and let's be more at ease.

(They sit down.)

TARTUFFE. I trust that you are once more well and
strong?

ELMIRE. Oh, yes: the fever didn't last for long.

TARTUFFE. My prayers are too unworthy, I am sure,
To have gained from Heaven this most gracious cure; 10
But lately, Madam, my every supplication
Has had for object your recuperation.

ELMIRE. You shouldn't have troubled so. I don't
deserve it.

TARTUFFE. Your health is priceless, Madam, and to
preserve it
I'd gladly give my own, in all sincerity. 15

ELMIRE. Sir, you outdo us all in Christian charity.
You've been most kind. I count myself your debtor.

TARTUFFE. 'Twas nothing, Madam. I long to serve
you better.

ELMIRE. There's a private matter I'm anxious to
discuss.
I'm glad there's no one here to hinder us. 20

TARTUFFE. I too am glad; it floods my heart with bliss
To find myself alone with you like this.
For just this chance I've prayed with all my power—
But prayed in vain, until this happy hour.

ELMIRE. This won't take long, Sir, and I hope you'll be 25
Entirely frank and unconstrained with me.

TARTUFFE. Indeed, there's nothing I had rather do
Than bare my inmost heart and soul to you.
First, let me say that what remarks I've made
About the constant visits you are paid 30
Were prompted not by any mean emotion,
But rather by a pure and deep devotion,
A fervent zeal...

ELMIRE.   No need for explanation.
Your sole concern, I'm sure, was my salvation.

TARTUFFE. *(Taking Elmire's band and pressing her
fingertips:)* Quite so; and such great fervor do I 35
feel...

ELMIRE. Ooh! Please! You're pinching!

TARTUFFE.   'Twas from excess of zeal.
I never meant to cause you pain, I swear.
I'd rather...

(He places his hand on Elmire's knee.)

ELMIRE.   What can your hand be doing there?

TARTUFFE. Feeling your gown; what soft, fine-woven
stuff!

ELMIRE. Please, I'm extremely ticklish. That's enough. 40

(She draws her chair away; Tartuffe pulls his after her.)

TARTUFFE. *(Fondling the lace collar of her gown:)* My,
my, what lovely lacework on your dress!
The workmanship's miraculous, no less.
I've not seen anything to equal it.

ELMIRE. Yes, quite. But let's talk business for a bit.
They say my husband means to break his word 45
And give his daughter to you, Sir. Had you heard?

TARTUFFE. He did once mention it. But I confess
I dream of quite a different happiness.
It's elsewhere, Madam, that my eyes discern
The promise of that bliss for which I yearn. 50

ELMIRE. I see: you care for nothing here below.

TARTUFFE. Ah, well—my heart's not made of stone,
you know.

ELMIRE. All your desires mount heavenward, I'm sure,
In scorn of all that's earthly and impure.

TARTUFFE. A love of heavenly beauty does not preclude 55
A proper love for earthly pulchritude;
Our senses are quite rightly captivated
By perfect works our Maker has created.
Some glory clings to all that Heaven has made;
In you, all Heaven's marvels are displayed. 60
On that fair face, such beauties have been lavished,
The eyes are dazzled and the heart is ravished;
How could I look on you, O flawless creature,
And not adore the Author of all Nature,
Feeling a love both passionate and pure 65
For you, his triumph of self-portraiture?
At first, I trembled lest that love should be
A subtle snare that Hell had laid for me;
I vowed to flee the sight of you, eschewing

A rapture that might prove my soul's undoing; 70
But soon, fair being, I became aware
That my deep passion could be made to square
With rectitude, and with my bounden duty.
I thereupon surrendered to your beauty.
It is, I know, presumptuous on my part 75
To bring you this poor offering of my heart,
And it is not my merit, Heaven knows,
But your compassion on which my hopes repose.
You are my peace, my solace, my salvation;
On you depends my bliss—or desolation; 80
I bide your judgment and, as you think best,
I shall be either miserable or blest.

ELMIRE. Your declaration is most gallant, Sir,
But don't you think it's out of character?
You'd have done better to restrain your passion 85
And think before you spoke in such a fashion.
It ill becomes a pious man like you ...

TARTUFFE. I may be pious, but I'm human too:
With your celestial charms before his eyes,
A man has not the power to be wise. 90
I know such words sound strangely, coming from
me,
But I'm no angel, nor was meant to be,
And if you blame my passion, you must needs
Reproach as well the charms on which it feeds.
Your loveliness I had no sooner seen 95
Than you became my soul's unrivalled queen;
Before your seraph glance, divinely sweet,[11]
My heart's defences crumbled in defeat,
And nothing fasting, prayer, or tears might do
Could stay my spirit from adoring you. 100
My eyes, my sighs have told you in the past
What now my lips make bold to say at last,
And if, in your great goodness, you will deign
To look upon your slave, and ease his pain,
If, in compassion for my soul's distress, 105
You'll stoop to comfort my unworthiness,
I'll raise to you, in thanks for that sweet manna,
An endless hymn, an infinite hosanna.
With me, of course, there need be no anxiety,
No fear of scandal or of notoriety. 110

These young court gallants, whom all the ladies
fancy,
Are vain in speech, in action rash and chancy;
When they succeed in love, the world soon knows it;
No favour's granted them but they disclose it
And by the looseness of their tongues profane 115
The very altar where their hearts have lain.
Men of my sort, however, love discreetly,
And one may trust our reticence completely.
My keen concern for my good name insures
The absolute security of yours; 120
In short, I offer you, my dear Elmire,
Love without scandal, pleasure without fear.

ELMIRE. I've heard your well-turned speeches to the
end,
And what you urge I clearly apprehend.
Aren't you afraid that I may take a notion 125
To tell my husband of your warm devotion,
And that, supposing he were duly told,
His feelings toward you might grow rather cold?

TARTUFFE. I know, dear lady, that your exceeding
charity
Will lead your heart to pardon my temerity; 130
That you'll excuse my violent affection
As human weakness, human imperfection;
And that—O fairest!—you will bear in mind
That I'm but flesh and blood, and am not blind.

ELMIRE. Some women might do otherwise, perhaps, 135
But I shall be discreet about your lapse;
I'll tell my husband nothing of what's occurred
If, in rerum, you'll give your solemn word
To advocate as forcefully as you can
The marriage of Valère and Mariane, 140
Renouncing all desire to dispossess
Another of his rightful happiness,
And...

SCENE FOUR

DAMIS, ELMIRE, TARTUFFE.

DAMIS. *(Emerging from the closet where he has been
hiding:)* No! We'll not hush up this vile affair;
I heard it all inside that closet there,
Where Heaven, in order to confound the pride
Of this great rascal, prompted me to hide.
Ah, now I have my long-awaited chance 5

---

11 seraph] angelic (belonging to the seraphim, an order of
angels).

To punish his deceit and arrogance,
And give my father clear and shocking proof
Of the black character of his dear Tartuffe.
ELMIRE. Ah no, Damis; I'll be content if he
  Will study to deserve my leniency.   10
  I've promised silence—don't make me break my
    word;
  To make a scandal would be too absurd.
  Good wives laugh off such trifles, and forget them;
  Why should they tell their husbands, and upset
    them?
DAMIS. You have your reasons for taking such a course, 15
  And I have reasons, too, of equal force.
  To spare him now would be insanely wrong.
  I've swallowed my just wrath for far too long
  And watched this insolent bigot bringing strife
  And bitterness into our family life.   20
  Too long he's meddled in my father's affairs,
  Thwarting my marriage-hopes, and poor Valère's.
  It's high time that my father was undeceived,
  And now I've proof that can't be disbelieved—
  Proof that was furnished me by Heaven above.   25
  It's too good not to take advantage of.
  This is my chance, and I deserve to lose it
  If, for one moment, I hesitate to use it.
DAMIS. No, I must do what I think. right.
  Madam, my heart is bursting with delight,   30
  And, say whatever you will, I'll not consent
  To lose the sweet revenge on which I'm bent.
  I'll settle matters without more ado
  And here, most opportunely, is my cue.

SCENE FIVE

ORGON, DAMIS, TARTUFFE, ELMIRE.

DAMIS. Father, I'm glad you've joined us. Let us
    advise you
  Of some fresh news which doubtless will surprise
    you.
  You've just now been repaid with interest
  For all your loving kindness to our guest.
  He's proved his warm and grateful feelings toward   5
    you;
  It's with a pair of horns he would reward you.
  Yes, I surprised him with your wife, and heard
  His whole adulterous offer, every word.

She, with her all too gentle disposition,
  Would not have told you of his proposition;   10
  But I shall not make terms with brazen lechery,
  And feel that not to tell you would be treachery.
ELMIRE. And I hold that one's husband's peace of mind
  Should not be spoilt by tattle of this kind.
  One's honour doesn't require it: to be proficient   15
  In keeping men at bay is quite sufficient.
  These are my sentiments, and I wish, Damis,
  That you had heeded me and held your peace.

SCENE SIX

ORGON, DAMIS, TARTUFFE.

ORGON. Can it be true, this dreadful thing I hear?
TARTUFFE. Yes, Brother, I'm a wicked man, I fear:
  A wretched sinner, all depraved and twisted,
  The greatest villain that has ever existed.
  My life's one heap of crimes, which grows each   5
    minute;
  There's naught but foulness and corruption in it;
  And I perceive that Heaven, outraged by me,
  Has chosen this occasion to mortify me.
  Charge me with any deed you wish to name;
  I'll not defend myself, but take the blame.   10
  Believe what you are told, and drive Tartuffe
  Like some base criminal from beneath your roof;
  Yes, drive me hence, and with a parting curse:
  I shan't protest, for I deserve far worse.
ORGON *(To Damis:)* Ah, you deceitful boy, how   15
    dare you try
  To stain his purity with so foul a lie?
DAMIS. What! Are you taken in by such a bluff?
  Did you not hear...?
ORGON.   Enough, you rogue, enough!
TARTUFFE. Ah, Brother, let him speak: you're being
    unjust.
  Believe his story; the boy deserves your trust.   20
  Why, after all, should you have faith in me?
  How can you know what I might do, or be?
  Is it on my good actions that you base
  Your favor? Do you trust my pious face?
  Ah, no, don't be deceived by hollow shows;   25
  I'm far, alas, from being what men suppose;
  Though the world takes me for a man of worth,
  I'm truly the most worthless man on earth.

(To Damis:) Yes, my dear son, speak out now: call
   me the chief
Of sinners, a wretch, a murderer, a thief;   30
Load me with all the names men most abhor;
I'll not complain; I've earned them all, and more;
I'll kneel here while you pour them on my head
As a just punishment for the life I've led.
ORGON *(To Tartuffe:)* This is too much, dear Brother.   35
   (To Damis:)   Have you no heart?
DAMIS. Are you so hoodwinked by this rascal's art
ORGON. Be still, you monster.
   (To Tartuffe:)   Brother, I pray you, rise,
   (To Damis:) Villain!
DAMIS.   But....
ORGON.   Silence!
DAMIS.   Can't you realize...
ORGON. Just one word more, and I'll tear you limb
   from limb.
TARTUFFE. In God's name, Brother, don't be harsh   40
   with him.
   I'd rather far be tortured at the stake
   Than see him bear one scratch for my poor sake.
ORGON *(To Damis:)* Ingrate!
TARTUFFE.   If I must beg you, on bended knee,
   To pardon him...
ORGON. *(Falling to his knees, addressing Tartuffe:)*
                  Such goodness cannot be!
   (To Damis:) Now, there's true charity!   45
DAMIS.   What, you....
ORGON.   Villain, be still!
   I know your motives; I know you wish him ill:
   Yes, all of you—wife, children, servants, all—
   Conspire against him and desire his fall,
   Employing every shameful trick you can
   To alienate me from this saintly man.   50
   Ah, but the more you seek to drive him away,
   The more I'll do to keep him. Without delay,
   I'll spite this household and confound its pride
   By giving him my daughter as his bride.
DAMIS. You're going to force her to accept his hand?   55
ORGON. Yes, and this very night, d'you understand?
   I shall defy you all, and make it clear
   That I'm the one who gives the orders here.
   Come, wretch, kneel down and clasp his blessed feet,
   And ask his pardon for your black deceit.   60
DAMIS. I ask that swindler's pardon? Why, I'd rather...

ORGON. So! You insult him, and defy your father!
   A stick! A stick!
   (To Tartuffe:)   No, no—release me, do.
   (To Damis:) Out of my house this minute! Be off
   with you,
   And never dare set foot in it again.   65
DAMIS. Well, I shall go, but...
ORGON.   Well, go quickly, then.
   I disinherit you; an empty purse
   Is all you'll get from me—except my curse!

SCENE SEVEN

ORGON, TARTUFFE.

ORGON. How he blasphemed your goodness! What
   a son!
TARTUFFE. Forgive him, Lord, as I've already done.
   (To Orgon:) You can't know how it hurts when
   someone tries
   To blacken me in my dear Brother's eyes.
ORGON. Ahh!   5
TARTUFFE.   The mere thought of such ingratitude
   Plunges my soul into so dark a mood...
   Such horror grips my heart...I gasp for breath,
   And cannot speak, and feel myself near death.
ORGON. *(He runs, in tears, to the door through which
   he has just driven his son.)* You blackguard! Why
   did I spare you? Why did I not
   Break you in little pieces on the spot?   10
   Compose yourself, and don't be hurt, dear friend.
TARTUFFE. These scenes, these dreadful quarrels,
   have got to end.
   I've much upset your household, and I perceive
   That the best thing will be for me to leave.
ORGON. What are you saying!   15
TARTUFFE.   They're all against me here;
   They'd have you think me false and insincere.
ORGON. Ah, what of that? Have I ceased believing
   in you?
TARTUFFE. Their adverse talk will certainly continue,
   And charges which you now repudiate
   You may find credible at a later date.   20
ORGON. No, Brother, never.
TARTUFFE.   Brother, a wife can sway
   Her husband's mind in many a subtle way.
ORGON. No, no.

TARTUFFE.   To leave at once is the solution;
  Thus only can I end their persecution.
ORGON. No, no, I'll not allow it; you shall remain.   25
TARTUFFE. Ah, well; 'twill mean much martyrdom
    and pain,
  But if you wish it...
ORGON.   Ah!
TARTUFFE.   Enough; so be it.
  But one thing must be settled, as I see it.
  For your dear honour, and for our friendship's
    sake,
  There's one precaution I feel bound to take.   30
  I shall avoid your wife, and keep away...
ORGON. No, you shall not, whatever they may say.
  It pleases me to vex them, and for spite
  I'd have them see you with her day and night.
  What's more, I'm going to drive them to despair   35
  By making you my only son and heir;
  This very day, I'll give to you alone
  Clear deed and title to everything I own.
  A dear, good friend and son-in-law-to-be
  Is more than wife, or child, or kin to me.   40
  Will you accept my offer, dearest son?
TARTUFFE. In all things, let the will of Heaven be
  done.
ORGON. Poor fellow! Come, we'll go draw up the deed.
  Then let them burst with disappointed greed!

ACT FOUR

SCENE ONE

CLÉANTE, TARTUFFE.

CLÉANTE. Yes, all the town's discussing it, and truly,
  Their comments do not flatter you unduly.
  I'm glad we've met, Sir, and I'll give my view
  Of this sad matter in a word or two.
  As for who's guilty, that I shan't discuss;   5
  Let's say it was Damis who caused the fuss;
  Assuming, then, that you have been ill-used
  By young Damis, and groundlessly accused,
  Ought not a Christian to forgive, and ought
  He not to stifle every vengeful thought?   10
  Should you stand by and watch a father make
  His only son an exile for your sake?
  Again I tell you frankly, be advised:

  The whole town, high and low, is scandalized;
  This quarrel must be mended, and my advice is   15
  Not to push matters to a further crisis.
  No, sacrifice your wrath to God above,
  And help Damis regain his father's love.
TARTUFFE. Alas, for my part I should take great joy
  In doing so. I've nothing against the boy.   20
  I pardon all, I harbor no resentment;
  To serve him would afford me much contentment.
  But Heaven's interest will not have it so:
  If he comes back, then I shall have to go.
  After his conduct—so extreme, so vicious—   25
  Our further intercourse would look suspicious.
  God knows what people would think! Why,
    they'd describe
  My goodness to him as a sort of bribe;
  They'd say that out of guilt I made pretense
  Of loving-kindness and benevolence—   30
  That, fearing my accuser's tongue, I strove
  To buy his silence with a show of love.
CLÉANTE. Your reasoning is badly warped and
    stretched,
  And these excuses, Sir, are most far-fetched.
  Why put yourself in charge of Heaven's cause?   35
  Does Heaven need our help to enforce its laws?
  Leave vengeance to the Lord, Sir; while we live,
  Our duty's not to punish, but forgive;
  And what the Lord commands, we should obey
  Without regard to what the world may say.   40
  What! Shall the fear of being misunderstood
  Prevent our doing what is right and good?
  No, no; let's simply do what Heaven ordains,
  And let no other thoughts perplex our brains.
TARTUFFE. Again, Sir, let me say that I've forgiven   45
  Damis, and thus obeyed the laws of Heaven;
  But I am not commanded by the Bible
  To live with one who smears my name with libel.
CLÉANTE. Were you commanded, Sir, to indulge
    the whim
  Of poor Orgon, and to encourage him   50
  In suddenly transferring to your name
  A large estate to which you have no claim?
TARTUFFE. 'Twould never occur to those who know
    me best
  To think I acted from self-interest.
  The treasures of this world I quite despise;   55

Their specious glitter does not charm my eyes
And if I have resigned myself to taking
The gift which my dear Brother insists on
    making,
I do so only, as he well understands,
Lest so much wealth fall into wicked hands,   60
Lest those to whom it might descend in time
Turn it to purposes of sin and crime,
And not, as I shall do, make use of it
For Heaven's glory and mankind's benefit.
CLÉANTE. Forget these trumped-up fears. Your   65
    argument
Is one the rightful heir might well resent;
It *is* a moral burden to inherit
Such wealth, but give Damis a chance to bear it.
And would it not be worse to be accused
Of swindling, than to see that wealth misused?   70
I'm shocked that you allowed Orgon to broach
This matter, and that you feel no self-reproach;
Does true religion teach that lawful heirs
May freely be deprived of what is theirs?
And if the Lord has told you in your heart   75
That you and young Damis must dwell apart,
Would it not be the decent thing to beat
A generous and honourable retreat,
Rather than let the son of the house be sent,
For your convenience, into banishment?   80
Sir, if you wish to prove the honesty
Of your intentions...
TARTUFFE.   Sir, it is half-past three.
I've certain pious duties to attend to,
And hope my prompt departure won't offend you.
CLÉANTE *(Alone:)* Damn.   85

SCENE TWO

ELMIRE, MARIANE, CLÉANTE, DORINE

DORINE.   Stay, Sir, and help Mariane,
    for Heaven's sake!
She's suffering so, I fear her heart will break.
Her father's plan to marry her off tonight
Has put the poor child in a desperate plight.
I hear him coming. Let's stand together, now,   5
And see if we can't change his mind, somehow,
About this match we all deplore and fear.

SCENE THREE

ORGON, ELMIRE, MARIANE, CLÉANTE, DORINE.

ORGON. Hah! Glad to find you all assembled here.
    (To Mariane:) This contract, child, contains your
    happiness,
And what it says I think your heart can guess.
MARIANE *(Falling to her knees:)* Sir, by that Heaven
    which sees me here distressed, .
    And by whatever else can move your breast,   5
    Do not employ a father's power, I pray you,
    To crush my heart and force it to obey you,
    Nor by your harsh commands oppress me so
    That I'll begrudge the duty which I owe—
    And do not so embitter and enslave me   10
    That I shall hate the very life you gave me.
    If my sweet hopes must perish, if you refuse
    To give me to the one I've dared to choose,
    Spare me at least—I beg you, I implore—
    The pain of wedding one whom I abhor;   15
    And do not, by a heartless use of force,
    Drive me to contemplate some desperate course.
ORGON *(Feeling himself touched by her:)* Be firm, my
    soul. No human weakness, now.
MARIANE. I don't resent your love for him. Allow
    Your heart free rein, Sir; give him your property,   20
    And if that's not enough, take mine from me;
    He's welcome to my money; take it, do,
    But don't, I pray, include my person too.
    Spare me, I beg you; and let me end the tale
    Of my sad days behind a convent veil.   25
ORGON. A convent! Hah! When crossed in their
    amours,
    All lovesick girls have the same thought as yours.
    Get up! The more you loathe the man, and dread him,
    The more ennobling it will be to wed him.
    Marry Tartuffe, and mortify your flesh!   30
    Enough; don't start that whimpering afresh.
DORINE. But why...?
ORGON.   Be still, there. Speak when
    you're spoken to.
    Not one more bit of impudence out of you.
CLÉANTE. If I may offer a word of counsel here...
ORGON. Brother, in counseling you have no peer;   35
    All your advice is forceful, sound, and clever;
    I don't propose to follow it, however.

ELMIRE *(To Orgon:)* I am amazed, and don't know
    what to say;
  Your blindness simply takes my breath away.
  You are indeed bewitched, to take no warning   40
  From our account of what occurred this morning.
ORGON. Madam, I know a few plain facts, and one
  Is that you're partial to my rascal son;
  Hence, when he sought to make Tartuffe the victim
  Of a base lie, you dared not contradict him.   45
  Ah, but you underplayed your part, my pet;
  You should have looked more angry, more upset.
ELMIRE. When men make overtures, must we reply
  With righteous anger and a battle-cry?
  Must we turn back their amorous advances: 50
  With sharp reproaches and with fiery glances?
  Myself, I find such offers merely amusing,
  And make no scenes and fusses in refusing;
  My taste is for good-natured rectitude,
  And I dislike the savage sort of prude   55
  Who guards her virtue with her teeth and claws,
  And tears men's eyes out for the slightest cause:
  The Lord preserve me from such honour as that,
  Which bites and scratches like an alley-cat!
  I've found that a polite and cool rebuff   60
  Discourages a lover quite enough.
ORGON. I know the facts, and I shall not be shaken.
ELMIRE. I marvel at your power to be mistaken.
  Would it, I wonder, carry weight with you
  If I could *show* you that our tale was true?   65
ORGON. Show me?
ELMIRE.   Yes.
ORGON.   Rot.
ELMIRE.   Come, what if I found a way
  To make you see the facts as plain as day?
ORGON. Nonsense.
ELMIRE.   Do answer me; don't be absurd.
  I'm not now asking you to trust our word.
  Suppose that from some hiding-place in here   70
  You learned the whole sad truth by eye and ear—
  What would you say of your good friend, after that?
ORGON. Why, I'd say...nothing, by Jehoshaphat!
  It can't be true.
ELMIRE.   You've been too long deceived,
  And I'm quite tired of being disbelieved.   75
  Come now: let's put my statements to the test,
  And you shall see the truth made manifest.

ORGON. I'll take that challenge. Now do your
    uttermost.
  We'll see how you make good your empty boast.
ELMIRE *(To Dorine:)* Send him to me.   80
DORINE.   He's crafty; it may be hard
  To catch the cunning scoundrel off his guard.
ELMIRE. No, amorous men are gullible. Their conceit
  So blinds them that they're never hard to cheat.
  Have him come down
  (To Cléante & Mariane:)   Please leave us, for a bit.

SCENE FOUR

ELMIRE, ORGON.

ELMIRE. Pull up this table, and get under it.
ORGON. What?
ELMIRE.   It's essential that you be well-hidden.
ORGON. Why there?
ELMIRE.   Oh, Heavens! Just do as you are bidden.
  I have my plans; we'll soon see how they fare.
  Under the table, now; and once you're there,   5
  Take care that you are neither seen nor heard.
ORGON. Well, I'll indulge you, since I gave my word
  To see you through this infantile charade.
ELMIRE. Once it is over, you'll be glad we played.
  (To her husband, who is now under the table:) I'm   10
  going to act quite strangely, now, and you
  Must not be shocked at anything I do.
  Whatever I may say, you must excuse
  As part of that deceit I'm forced to use.
  I shall employ sweet speeches in the task
  Of making that imposter drop his mask;
  I'll give encouragement to his bold desires,
  And furnish fuel to his amorous fires.
  Since it's for your sake, and for his destru
  That I shall seem to yield to his seduc
  I'll gladly stop whenever you decid
  That all your doubts are fully s
  I'll count on you, as soon a
  What sort of man he is.
  And not expose me to
  One moment longer th
  Remember: you're to sa
  Whenever...He's comin

SCENE FIVE

TARTUFFE, ELMIRE, ORGON.

TARTUFFE. You wish to have a word with me, I'm told.
ELMIRE. Yes. I've a little secret to unfold.
  Before I speak, however, it would be wise
  To close that door, and look about for spies.

(Tartuffe goes to the door, closes it, and returns.)

  The very last thing that must happen now   5
  Is a repetition of this morning's row.
  I've never been so badly caught off guard.
  Oh, how I feared for you! You saw how hard
  I tried to make that troublesome Damis.
  Control his dreadful temper, and hold his peace.   10
  In my confusion, I didn't have the sense
  Simply to contradict his evidence;
  But as it happened, that was for the best,
  And all has worked out in our interest.
  This storm has only bettered your position;   15
  My husband doesn't have the least suspicion,
  And now, in mockery of those who do,
  He bids me be continually with you.
  And that is why, quite fearless of reproof,
  I now can be alone with my Tartuffe,   20
  And why my heart—perhaps too quick to yield—
  Feels free to let its passion be revealed.
TARTUFFE. Madam, your words confuse me. Not long ago,
  You spoke in quite a different style, you know.
ELMIRE. Ah, Sir, if that refusal made you smart,   25
  It's little that you know of woman's heart,
  Or what that heart is trying to convey
  When it resists in such a feeble way!
  Always, at first, our modesty prevents
  The frank avowal of tender sentiments;   30
  However high the passion which inflames us,
  Still, to confess its power somehow shames us.
  Thus we reluct, at first, yet in a tone
  Which tells you that our heart is overthrown,
  And what our lips deny, our pulse confesses,   35
  That, in time, all noes will turn to yesses.
  My words are all too frank and free,
  Nor proof of woman's modesty;
  I'm started, tell me, if you will—
  I've tried to make Damis be still,   40

  Would I have listened, calm and unoffended,
  Until your lengthy offer of love was ended,
  And been so very mild in my reaction,
  Had your sweet words not given me satisfaction?
  And when I tried to force you to undo   45
  The marriage-plans my husband has in view,
  What did my urgent pleading signify
  If not that I admired you, and that I
  Deplored the thought that someone else might own
  Part of a heart I wished for mine alone?   50
TARTUFFE. Madam, no happiness is so complete
  As when, from lips we love, come words so sweet;
  Their nectar floods my every sense, and drains
  In honeyed rivulets through all my veins.
  To please you is my joy, my only goal;   55
  Your love is the restorer of my soul;
  And yet I must beg leave, now, to confess
  Some lingering doubts as to my happiness.
  Might this not be a trick? Might not the catch
  Be that you wish me to break off the match   60
  With Mariane, and so have feigned to love me?
  I shan't quite trust your fond opinion of me,
  Until the feelings you've expressed so sweetly
  Are demonstrated somewhat more concretely,
  And you have shown, by certain kind concessions,   65
  That I may put my faith in your professions.
ELMIRE *(She coughs, to warn her husband.)* Why be in such a hurry? Must my heart
  Exhaust its bounty at the very start?
  To make that sweet admission cost me dear,
  But you'll not be content, it would appear,   70
  Unless my store of favours is disbursed
  To the last farthing, and at the very first.
TARTUFFE. The less we merit, the less we dare to hope,
  And with our doubts, mere words can never cope.
  We trust no promised bliss till we receive it;   75
  Not till a joy is ours can we believe it.
  I, who so little merit your esteem,
  Can't credit this fulfilment of my dream,
  And shan't believe it, Madam, until I savour
  Some palpable assurance of your favour.   80
ELMIRE. My, how tyrannical your love can be,
  And how it flusters and perplexes me!
  How furiously you take one's heart in hand,
  And make your every wish a fierce command!
  Come, must you hound and harry me to death?   85

Will you not give me time to catch my breath?
Can it be right to press me with such force,
Give me no quarter, show me no remorse,
And take advantage, by your stern insistence,
Of the fond feelings which weaken my resistance?   90
TARTUFFE. Well, if you look with favour upon my love,
  Why, then, begrudge me some clear proof thereof?
ELMIRE. But how can I consent without offense
  To Heaven, toward which you feel such reverence?
TARTUFFE. If Heaven is all that holds you back,   95
    don't worry.
  I can remove that hindrance in a hurry.
  Nothing of that sort need obstruct our path.
ELMIRE. Must one not be afraid of Heaven's wrath?
TARTUFFE. Madam, forget such fears, and be my pupil,
  And I shall teach you how to conquer scruple.   100
  Some joys, it's true, are wrong in Heaven's eyes;
  Yet Heaven is not averse to compromise;
  There is a science, lately formulated,
  Whereby one's conscience may be liberated,
  And any wrongful act you care to mention   105
  May be redeemed by purity of intention.
  I'll teach you, Madam, the secrets of that science;
  Meanwhile, just place on me your full reliance.
  Assuage my keen desires, and feel no dread:
  The sin, if any, shall be on my head.   110

(Elmire coughs, this time more loudly.)

  You've a bad cough.
ELMIRE.   Yes, yes. It's bad indeed.
TARTUFFE (Producing a little paper bag:) A bit of
    licorice may be what you need.
ELMIRE. No, I've a stubborn cold, it seems. I'm sure it
  Will take much more than licorice to cure it.
TARTUFFE. How aggravating.   115
ELMIRE.   Oh, more than I can say.
TARTUFFE. If you're still troubled, think of things
    this way:
  No one shall know our joys, save us alone,
  And there's no evil till the act is known;
  It's scandal, Madam, which makes it an offense,
  And it's no sin to sin in confidence.   120
ELMIRE (Having coughed once more:) Well, clearly I
    must do as you require,
  And yield to your importunate desire.
  It is apparent, now, that nothing less

Will satisfy you, and so I acquiesce.
To go so far is much against my will;   125
I'm vexed that it should come to this; but still,
Since you are so determined on it, since you
Will not allow mere language to convince you,
And since you ask for concrete evidence, I
See nothing for it, now, but to comply.   130
If this is sinful, if I'm wrong to do it,
So much the worse for him who drove me to it.
The fault can surely not be charged to me.
TARTUFFE. Madam, the fault is mine, if fault there be,
  And...   135
ELMIRE.   Open the door a little, and peek out;
  I wouldn't want my husband poking about.
TARTUFFE. Why worry about the man? Each day he
    grows
  More gullible; one can lead him by the nose.
  To find us here would fill him with delight,
  And if he saw the worst, he'd doubt his sight.   140
ELMIRE. Nevertheless, do step out for a minute
  Into the hall, and see that no one's in it.

SCENE SIX

ORGON, ELMIRE.

ORGON (Coming out from under the table:) That
    man's a perfect monster, I must admit!
  I'm simply stunned. I can't get over it.
ELMIRE. What, coming out so soon? How premature!
  Get back in hiding, and wait until you're sure.
  Stay till the end, and be convinced completely;   5
  We mustn't stop till things are proved concretely.
ORGON. Hell never harbored anything so vicious!
ELMIRE. Tut, don't be hasty. Try to be judicious.
  Wait, and be certain that there's no mistake.
  No jumping to conclusions, for Heaven's sake!   10

(She places Orgon behind her, as Tartuffe re-enters.)

SCENE SEVEN

TARTUFFE, ELMIRE, ORGON.

TARTUFFE (Not seeing Orgon:) Madam, all things
    have worked out to perfection;
  I've given the neighbouring rooms a full inspection;
  No one's about; and now I may at last...

[IV.vii]

ORGON (*Intercepting him:*) Hold on, my passionate
    fellow, not so fast!
  I should advise a little more restraint.   5
  Well, so you thought you'd fool me, my dear saint!
  How soon you wearied of the saintly life—
  Wedding my daughter, and coveting my wife!
  I've long suspected you, and had a feeling
  That soon I'd catch you at your double-dealing.   10
  Just now, you've given me evidence galore;
  It's quite enough; I have no wish for more.
ELMIRE (*To Tartuffe:*) I'm sorry to have treated you
    so slyly,
  But circumstances forced me to be wily.
TARTUFFE. Brother, you can't think...   15
ORGON.   No more talk from you;
  Just leave this household, without more ado.
TARTUFFE. What I intended...
ORGON.   That seems fairly clear.
  Spare me your falsehoods and get out of here.
TARTUFFE. No, I'm the master, and you're the one
    to go!
  This house belongs to me, I'll have you know,   20
  And I shall show you that you can't hurt me
  By this contemptible conspiracy,
  That those who cross me know not what they do,
  And that I've means to expose and punish you,
  Avenge offended Heaven, and make you grieve   25
  That ever you dared order me to leave.

SCENE EIGHT

ELMIRE, ORGON.

ELMIRE. What was the point of all that angry
    chatter?
ORGON. Dear God, I'm worried. This is no laughing
    matter.
ELMIRE. How so?
ORGON.   I fear I understood his drift.
  I'm much disturbed about that deed of gift.
ELMIRE. You gave him...?   5
ORGON.   Yes, it's all been drawn and signed.
  But one thing more is weighing on my mind.
ELMIRE. What's that?
ORGON.   I'll tell you; but first let's see if
    there's
  A certain strong-box in his room upstairs.

ACT FIVE

SCENE ONE

ORGON, CLÉANTE.

CLÉANTE. Where are you going so fast?
ORGON.   God knows!
CLÉANTE.   Then wait;
  Let's have a conference, and deliberate
  On how this situation's to be met.
ORGON. That strong-box has me utterly upset;
  This is the worst of many, many shocks.   5
CLÉANTE. Is there some fearful mystery in that box?
ORGON. My poor friend Argas brought that box to me
  With his own hands, in utmost secrecy;
  'Twas on the very morning of his flight.
  It's full of papers which, if they came to light,   10
  Would ruin him—or such is my impression.
CLÉANTE. Then why did you let it out of your
    possession?
ORGON. Those papers vexed my conscience, and it
    seemed best
  To ask the counsel of my pious guest.
  The cunning scoundrel got me to agree   15
  To leave the strong-box in his custody,
  So that, in case of an investigation,
  I could employ a slight equivocation
  And swear I didn't have it, and thereby,
  At no expense to conscience, tell a lie.   20
CLÉANTE. It looks to me as if you're out on a limb.
  Trusting him with that box, and offering him
  That deed of gift, were actions of a kind
  Which scarcely indicate a prudent mind.
  With two such weapons, he has the upper hand,   25
  And since you're vulnerable, as matters stand,
  You erred once more m bringing him to bay.
  You should have acted in some subtler way.
ORGON. Just think of it: behind that fervent face,
  A heart so wicked, and a soul so base!   30
  I took him in, a hungry beggar, and then...
  Enough, by God! I'm through with pious men:
  Henceforth I'll hate the whole false brotherhood,
  And persecute them worse than Satan could.
CLÉANTE. Ah, there you go—extravagant as ever!   35
  Why can you not be rational? You never
  Manage to take the middle course, it seems,

But jump, instead, between absurd extremes.
You've recognized your recent grave mistake
In falling victim to a pious fake;   40
Now, to correct that error, must you embrace
An even greater error in its place,
And judge our worthy neighbours as a whole
By what you've learned of one corrupted soul?
Come, just because one rascal made you swallow   45
A show of zeal which turned out to be hollow,
Shall you conclude that all men are deceivers,
And that, today, there are no true believers?
Let atheists make that foolish inference;
Learn to distinguish virtue from pretense,   50
Be cautious in bestowing admiration,
And cultivate a sober moderation.
Don't humour fraud, but also don't asperse
True piety; the latter fault is worse,
And it is best to err, if err one must,   55
As you have done, upon the side of trust.

SCENE TWO

DAMIS, ORGON, CLÉANTE.

DAMIS. Father, I hear that scoundrel's uttered threats
Against you; that he pridefully forgets
How, in his need, he was befriended by you,
And means to use your gifts to crucify you.
ORGON. It's true, my boy. I'm too distressed for tears.   5
DAMIS. Leave it to me, Sir; let me trim his ears.
Faced with such insolence, we must not
I shall rejoice in doing you the favor
Of cutting short his life, and your distress.
CLÉANTE. What a display of young hotheadedness!   10
Do learn to moderate your fits of rage.
In this just kingdom, this enlightened age,
One does not settle things by violence.

SCENE THREE

*MADAME PERNELLE, MARIANE, ELMIRE, DORINE,
DAMIS, ORGON, CLÉANTE.*

MADAME PERNELLE. I hear strange tales of very
    strange events.
ORGON. Yes, strange events which these two eyes
    beheld.
The man's ingratitude is unparalleled.

I save a wretched pauper from starvation,
House him, and treat him like a blood relation,   5
Shower him every day with my largesse,
Give him my daughter, and all that I possess;
And meanwhile the unconscionable knave
Tries to induce my wife to misbehave;
And not content with such extreme rascality,   10
Now threatens me with my own liberality,
And aims, by taking base advantage of
The gifts I gave him out of Christian love,
To drive me from my house, a ruined man,
And make me end a pauper, as he began.   15
DORINE. Poor fellow!
MADAME PERNELLE.   No, my son, I'll never bring
    Myself to think him guilty of such a thing.
ORGON. How's that?
MADAME PERNELLE.   The righteous always were
    maligned.
ORGON. Speak clearly, Mother. Say what's on your
    mind.
MADAME PERNELLE. I mean that I can smell a rat,   20
    my dear.
    You know how everybody hates him, here.
ORGON. That has no bearing on the case at all.
MADAME PERNELLE. I told you a hundred times,
    when you were small,
    That virtue in this world is hated ever;
    Malicious men may die, but malice never.   25
ORGON. No doubt that's true, but how does it apply?
MADAME PERNELLE. They've turned you against
    him by a clever lie.
ORGON. I've told you, I was there and saw it done.
MADAME PERNELLE. Ah, slanderers will stop at
    nothing, Son.
ORGON. Mother, I'll lose my temper...For the last time,   30
    I tell you I was witness to the crime.
MADAME PERNELLE. The tongues of spite are busy
    night and noon,
    And to their venom no man is immune.
ORGON. You're talking nonsense. Can't you realize
    I saw it; saw it; saw it with my eyes?   35
    Saw, do you understand me? Must I shout it
    Into your ears before you'll cease to doubt it?
MADAME PERNELLE. Appearances can deceive, my
    son. Dear me,
    We cannot always judge by what we see.

ORGON. Drat! Drat!   40
MADAME PERNELLE.   One often interprets things
    awry;
    Good can seem evil to a suspicious eye.
ORGON. Was I to see his pawing at Elmire
    As an act of charity?
MADAME PERNELLE.   Till his guilt is clear,
    A man deserves the benefit of the doubt.
    You should have waited, to see how things turned   45
    out.
ORGON. Great God in Heaven, what more proof
    did I need?
    Was I to sit there, watching, until he'd...
    You drive me to the brink of impropriety.
MADAME PERNELLE. No, no, a man of such surpassing
    piety
    Could not do such a thing. You cannot shake me.   50
    I don't believe it, and you shall not make me.
ORGON. You vex me so that, if you weren't my mother,
    I'd say to you...some dreadful thing or other.
DORINE. It's your turn now, Sir, not to be listened to;
    You'd not trust us, and now she won't trust you.   55
CLÉANTE. My friends, we're wasting time which
    should be spent
    In facing up to our predicament.
    I fear that scoundrel's threats weren't made in sport.
DAMIS. Do you think he'd have the nerve to go to
    court?
ELMIRE. I'm sure he won't: they'd find it all too crude 60
    A case of swindling and ingratitude.
CLÉANTE. Don't be too sure. He won't be at a loss
    To give his claims a high and righteous gloss;
    And clever rogues with far less valid cause
    Have trapped their victims in a web of laws.   65
    I say again that to antagonize
    A man so strongly armed was most unwise.
ORGON. I know it; but the man's appalling cheek
    Outraged me so, I couldn't control my pique.
CLÉANTE. I wish to Heaven that we could devise   70
    Some truce between you, or some compromise.
ELMIRE. If I had known what cards he held, I'd not
    Have roused his anger by my little plot.
    What is that fellow looking for? Who is he?
    Go talk to him—and tell him that I'm busy.   75

SCENE FOUR

MONSIEUR LOYAL, MADAME PERNELLE, ORGON,
DAMIS, MARIANE, DORINE, ELMIRE, CLÉANTE.

MONSIEUR LOYAL. Good day, dear sister. Kindly let
    me see
    Your master.
DORINE.   He's involved with company,
    And cannot be disturbed just now, I fear.
MONSIEUR LOYAL. I hate to intrude; but what has
    brought me here
    Will not disturb your master, in any event.   5
    Indeed, my news will make him most content.
DORINE. Your name?
MONSIEUR LOYAL.   Just say that I bring greetings
    from
    Monsieur Tartuffe, on whose behalf I've come.
DORINE (To Orgon:) Sir, he's a very gracious man,
    and bears
    A message from Tartuffe, which, he declares,   10
    Will make you most content.
CLÉANTE.   Upon my word,
    I think this man had best be seen, and heard.
ORGON. Perhaps he has some settlement to suggest.
    How shall I treat him? What manner would be best?
CLÉANTE. Control your anger, and if he should   15
    mention
    Some fair adjustment, give him your full attention.
MONSIEUR LOYAL. Good health to you, good Sir.
    May Heaven confound
    Your enemies, and may your joys abound.
ORGON (Aside, to Cléante:) A gentle salutation: it
    confirms
    My guess that he is here to offer terms.   20
MONSIEUR LOYAL. I've always held your family
    most dear;
    I served your father, Sir, for many a year.
ORGON. Sir, I must ask your pardon; to my shame,
    I cannot now recall your face or name.
MONSIEUR LOYAL. Loyal's my name; I come from   25
    Normandy,
    And I'm a bailiff, in all modesty.
    For forty years, praise God, it's been my boast
    To serve with honour in that vital post,
    And I am here, Sir, if you will permit
    The liberty, to serve you with this writ...   30

ORGON. To—*what?*

MONSIEUR LOYAL. Now, please, Sir, let us have
no friction:
It's nothing but an order of eviction.
You are to move your goods and family out
And make way for new occupants, without
Deferment or delay, and give the keys... 35

ORGON. I? Leave this house?

MONSIEUR LOYAL. Why yes, Sir, if you please.
This house, Sir, from the cellar to the roof,
Belongs now to the good Monsieur Tartuffe,
And he is lord and master of your estate
By virtue of a deed of present date, 40
Drawn in due form, with clearest legal phrasing...

DAMIS. Your insolence is utterly amazing!

MONSIEUR LOYAL. Young man, my business here is
not with you,
But with your wise and temperate father, who,
Like every worthy citizen, stands in awe 45
Of justice, and would never obstruct the law.

ORGON. But...

MONSIEUR LOYAL. Not for a million, Sir, would
you rebel
Against authority; I know that well.
You'll not make trouble, Sir, or interfere
With the execution of my duties here. 50

DAMIS. Someone may execute a smart tattoo
On that black jacket of yours, before you're through.

MONSIEUR LOYAL. Sir, bid your son be silent. I'd
much regret
Having to mention such a nasty threat
Of violence, in writing my report. 55

DORINE *(Aside:)* This man Loyal's a most disloyal sort!

MONSIEUR LOYAL. I love all men of upright character,
And when I agreed to serve these papers, Sir,
It was your feelings that I had in mind.
I couldn't bear to see the case assigned 60
To someone else, who might esteem you less
And so subject you to unpleasantness.

ORGON. What's more unpleasant than telling a man
to leave
His house and home?

MONSIEUR LOYAL. You'd like a short reprieve?
If you desire it, Sir, I shall not press you, 65
But wait until tomorrow to dispossess you.
Splendid. I'll come and spend the night here, then,
Most quietly, with half a score of men.

For form's sake, you might bring me, just before
You go to bed, the keys to the front door. 70
My men, I promise, will be on their best
Behaviour, and will not disturb your rest.
But bright and early, Sir, you must be quick
And move out all your furniture, every stick:
The men I've chosen are both young and strong; 75
And with their help it shouldn't take you long.
In short, I'll make things pleasant and convenient,
And since I'm being so extremely lenient,
Please show me, Sir, a like consideration,
And give me your entire cooperation. 80

ORGON *(Aside:)* I may be all but bankrupt, but I vow
I'd give a hundred louis, here and now,[12]
Just for the pleasure of landing one good clout
Right on the end of that complacent snout.

CLÉANTE. Careful; don't make things worse. 85

DAMIS. My bootsole itches.
To give that beggar a good kick in the breeches.

DORINE. Monsieur Loyal, I'd love to hear the whack
Of a stout stick across your fine broad back.

MONSIEUR LOYAL. Take care: a woman too may go
to jail if
She uses threatening language to a bailiff. 90

CLÉANTE. Enough, enough, Sir. This must not go on.
Give me that paper, please, and then begone.

MONSIEUR LOYAL. Well, *au revoir.* God give you all
good cheer!

ORGON. May God confound you, and him who
sent you here!

SCENE FIVE

*ORGON, CLÉANTE, MARIANE, ELMIRE, MADAME
PERNELLE, DORINE, DAMIS.*

ORGON. Now, Mother, was I right or not? This writ
Should change your notion of Tartuffe a bit
Do you perceive his villainy at last?

MADAME PERNELLE. I'm thunderstruck. I'm utterly
aghast.

DORINE. Oh, come, be fair. You mustn't take offense 5
At this new proof of his benevolence.
He's acting out of selfless love, I know.

---

12 louis] i.e., louis d'or, a gold coin introduced in 1740 because of the devalued franc; worth 20 francs, it was im-
printed with an image of King Louis.

Material things enslave the soul, and so
He kindly has arranged your liberation
From all that might endanger your salvation.   10
ORGON. Will you not ever hold your tongue, you
    dunce?
CLÉANTE. Come, you must take some action, and
    at once.
ELMIRE. Go tell the world of the low trick he's tried.
The deed of gift is surely nullified
By such behaviour, and public rage will not   15
Permit the wretch to carry out his plot.

SCENE SIX

VALÈRE, ORGON, CLÉANTE, ELMIRE, MARIANE,
MADAME PERNELLE, DAMIS, DORINE.

VALÈRE. Sir, though I hate to bring you more bad news,
Such is the danger that I cannot choose.
A friend who is extremely close to me
And knows my interest in your family
Has, for my sake, presumed to violate   5
The secrecy that's due to things of state,
And sends me word that you are in a plight
From which your one salvation lies in flight.
That scoundrel who's imposed upon you so
Denounced you to the King an hour ago   10
And, as supporting evidence, displayed
The strong-box of a certain renegade
Whose secret papers, so he testified,
You had disloyally agreed to hide.
I don't know just what charges may be pressed,   15
But there's a warrant out for your arrest;
Tartuffe has been instructed, furthermore,
To guide the arresting officer to your door.
CLÉANTE. He's clearly done this to facilitate
His seizure of your house and your estate.   20
ORGON. That man, I must say, is a vicious beast!
VALÈRE. Quick, Sir; you mustn't tarry in the least.
My carriage is outside, to take you hence;
This thousand louis should cover all expense.
Let's lose no time, or you shall be undone;   25
The sole defence, in this case, is to run....
I shall go with you all the way, and place you!
In a safe refuge to which they'll never trace you.
ORGON. Alas, dear boy, I wish that I could show you
My gratitude for everything I owe you.   30

But now is not the time; I pray the Lord
That I may live to give you your reward.
Farewell, my dears; be careful ...
CLÉANTE.   Brother, hurry.
We shall take care of things; you needn't worry.

SCENE SEVEN

THE OFFICER, TARTUFFE, VALÈRE, ORGON, ELMIRE,
MARIANE, MADAME PERNELLE, DORINE, CLÉANTE,
DAMIS.

TARTUFFE. Gently, Sir, gently; stay right where you are.
No need for haste; your lodging isn't far.
You're off to prison, by order of the Prince.
ORGON. This is the crowning blow, you wretch;
    and since
It means my total ruin and defeat,   5
Your villainy is now at last complete.
TARTUFFE. You needn't try to provoke me; it's no use.
Those who serve Heaven must expect abuse.
CLÉANTE. You are indeed most patient, sweet, and
    blameless.
DORINE. How he exploits the name of Heaven! It's   10
    shameless.
TARTUFFE. Your taunts and mockeries are all for
    naught;
To my duty is my only thought.
MARIANE. Your love of duty is most meritorious,
And what you've done is little short of glorious.
TARTUFFE. All deeds are glorious, Madam, which obey   15
The sovereign prince who sent me here today.
ORGON. I rescued you when you were destitute;
Have you forgotten that, you thankless brute?
TARTUFFE. No, no, I well remember everything;
But my first duty is to serve my King.   20
That obligation is so paramount
That other claims, beside it, do not count;
And for it I would sacrifice my wife,
My family, my friend, or my own life.
ELMIRE. Hypocrite!   25
DORINE.   All that we most revere, he uses
To cloak his plots and camouflage his ruses.
CLÉANTE. If it is true that you are animated
By pure and loyal zeal, as you have stated,
Why was this zeal not roused until you'd sought
To make Orgon a cuckold, and been caught?   30

Why weren't you moved to give your evidence
Until your outraged host had driven you hence?
I shan't say that the gift of all his treasure
Ought to have damped your zeal in any measure;
But if he is a traitor, as you declare,   35
How could you condescend to be his heir?

TARTUFFE (*To the Officer:*) Sir, spare me all this
    clamour; it's growing shrill.
  Please carry out your orders, if you will.

OFFICER. Yes, I've delayed too long, Sir. Thank you
    kindly.
  You're just the proper person to remind me.   40
  Come, you are off to join the other boarders
  In the King's prison, according to his orders.

TARTUFFE. Who? I, Sir?

OFFICER.   Yes.

TARTUFFE.   To prison? This can't be true!

OFFICER. I owe an explanation, but not to you.
  (*To Orgon:*) Sir, all is well; rest easy, and be grateful.   45
  We serve a Prince to whom all sham is hateful,[13]
  A Prince who sees into our inmost hearts,
  And can't be fooled by any trickster's arts.
  His royal soul, though generous and human,
  Views all things with discernment and acumen;   50
  His sovereign reason is not lightly swayed,
  And all his judgments are discreetly weighed.
  He honours righteous men of every kind,
  And yet his zeal for virtue is not blind,
  Nor does his love of piety numb his wits   55
  And make him tolerant of hypocrites.
  'Twas hardly likely that this man could cozen
  A King who's foiled such liars by the dozen.
  With one keen glance, the King perceived the whole
  Perverseness and corruption of his soul,   60
  And thus high Heaven's justice was displayed:
  Betraying you, the rogue stood self-betrayed.
  The King soon recognized Tartuffe as one
  Notorious by another name, who'd done
  So many vicious crimes that one could fill   65
  Ten volumes with them, and be writing still.
  But to be brief: our sovereign was appalled
  By this man's treachery toward you, which he called
  The last, worst villainy of a vile career,
  And bade me follow the impostor here   70

To see how gross his impudence could be,
And force him to restore your property.
Your private papers, by the King's command,
I hereby seize and give into your hand.
The King, by royal order, invalidates   75
The deed which gave this rascal your estates,
And pardons, furthermore, your grave offense
In harboring an exile's documents.
By these decrees, our Prince rewards you for
Your loyal deeds in the late civil war,[14]   80
And shows how heartfelt is his satisfaction
In recompensing any worthy action,
How much he prizes merit, and how he makes
More of men's virtues than of their mistakes.

DORINE. Heaven be praised!   85

MADAME PERNELLE.   I breathe again, at last.

ELMIRE. We're safe.

MARIANE.   I can't believe the danger's past.

ORGON (*To Tartuffe:*) Well, traitor, now you see...

CLÉANTE.   Ah, Brother, please,
  Let's not descend to such indignities.
  Leave the poor wretch to his unhappy fate,
  And don't say anything to aggravate   90
  His present woes; but rather hope that he
  Will soon embrace an honest piety,
  And mend his ways, and by a true repentance
  Move our just King to moderate his sentence.
  Meanwhile, go kneel before your sovereign's throne   95
  And thank him for the mercies he has shown.

ORGON. Well said: let's go at once and, gladly kneeling,
  Express the gratitude which all are feeling.
  Then, when that first great duty has been done,
  We'll turn with pleasure to a second one,   100
  And give Valère, whose love has proven so true,
  The wedded happiness which is his due.

---

13 Prince] here meaning the supreme monarch, the King.

14 late civil war] the 1648–1653 uprisings collectively
  known as the Frondes (the word for the slings used in
  a children's game played in the streets of Paris in defiance of the authorities) in which first the judicial bodies ("Fronde of the Parlement") and then a group of
  rebel aristocrats ("Fronde of the Princes") defied the
  policies of Cardinal Mazarin (1602–1661), the chief
  minister of Louis XIV (1638–1715). Louis was still in
  his minority at the time of the conflicts, but would always carry a painful memory of the sense of betrayal.

JEAN-BAPTISTE RACINE

Phèdre

Orphaned at the age of four, and brought up in the convent at Port-Royal, Jean-Baptiste Racine (1639–1699), it has been suggested, may have become a playwright only because it was the readiest means of elevating his social status. Having first tried and failed to obtain an ecclesiastical benefice, and having no connections that would secure him a royal patronage (a path to success that would have been made difficult by his association with the Jansenists at Port-Royal, who were then regarded by the French monarchy as not only heretical but politically suspect), Racine moved to Paris in his early twenties to try his hand at writing plays. In this, he was able to turn the first-rate classical education he had received from the Jansenist masters at Port-Royal to great advantage, although not in a way of which the anti-theatre Jansenists could have approved. If, while commending his enthusiasm and poetic talents, they had complained of Racine's lack of discipline while under their care, they were dismayed to see the use Racine then made of the classical literature to which they had introduced him. For upon the foundation of those classical models, Racine would eventually build a reputation as one of the greatest of all French dramatists. Whatever his reasons had been for entering the profession, Racine's reputation as a French tragedian is rivalled by only one other playwright: Pierre Corneille, author of *Le Cid*.

Of course, the other great playwright working in Paris at the time was the comedian Molière; and it was through the help of the older man that Racine got his start as a playwright. His first play, *Amasie*, had been left unproduced, but his next two plays, *Les Thébaïdes* (1664) and *Alexandre le grand* (1665) were both produced by Molière's company at the Palais Royal. With this prestigious notice the young playwright's reputation began to rise. However, perhaps feeling that Molière's company was justly more celebrated for comedy than tragedy, Racine secretly negotiated with a rival company for a second production of his *Alexandre*, which opened at the Hôtel de Bourgogne only eleven days after the opening of Molière's production. To add insult to injury, Racine persuaded one of Molière's leading actresses, Therese du Parc, to leave Molière. She became not only the leading actress in Racine's next play, but his mistress as well. The incident caused a rift between the two playwrights that never healed. As for Mlle. du Parc, she was to die the next year in mysterious circumstances. Malicious gossip suggested that Racine had poisoned her to make way for Marie Champmeslé, who would subsequently play the leading roles in many of his greatest works.

At any rate, Racine's choice of the Hôtel de Bourgogne seems to have been providential, for over the next twelve years, the company produced all of the tragedies for which he became famous, including *Andromaque* (1667), *Brittanicus* (1669), *Bérénice* (1670), *Bajazet* (1672), *Mithridate* (1673), and *Iphigenie* (1674). The company also produced Racine's one comedy, *Les Plaideurs* (1668), which was based partly on Aristophanes' *Wasps*, and which—perhaps surprisingly—also became a great success.

However, it was Racine's last tragedy, *Phèdre* (1677), that was, and still is, widely regarded as his supreme accomplishment. *Phèdre* holds a place of honour in the repertoire of French theatre, where it is greatly admired for the elegant simplicity of its structure, the beauty of its language, and the complexity of its psychological portraits. Moreover, although *Phèdre* is not often produced in English, the play is essential reading in any language because it perfectly represents the neo-classical aesthetic.

Naturally, certain aspects of *Phèdre*'s neoclassicism are clearly revealed through a comparison of Racine's play with its classical model, Euripides' *Hippolytus* (though another model was Seneca's *Phaedra*, which was also based on Euripides, and thus marks a sort of middle ground between the Greek and the French tragedy). However, *Phèdre*'s importance as a touchstone for the classical aesthetic within modern literature is perhaps most apparent when the play is contrasted with Elizabethan tragedy, and particularly the work of Shakespeare.

Whereas Shakespeare's tragedies spread themselves out over a variety of locations, *Phèdre* is ostensibly set within a single semi-public room in a palace; whereas the Elizabethans made use of subplots, Racine rigorously confines his scenes to the gradual unfolding of a single story; whereas Elizabethan tragedies are generally full of action and violence, in *Phèdre*, apart from entrances and exits, there is little action between the title character seating herself shortly after her first line and dying after her last; whereas Shakespeare has casts of dozens, Racine's cast is comparatively minimal; whereas Shakespeare uses a variety of styles, interpolates comic incidents into serious plays and mixes verse and prose, Racine sets a sombre tone at the beginning of his play and never wavers from the regular measure of his alexandrine couplets; finally, whereas Shakespeare's polyglot vocabulary is considered one of the glories of English literature, estimated at anywhere in the range of 18,000 to 25,000 words (depending on how variations of root words are counted), Racine makes do in *Phèdre* with about 650 different words, avoiding any word that seemed vulgar or coarse.

Yet for all the economy of its construction, *Phèdre* is a richly conceived piece of literature. Its rigorous structure provides a perfect vehicle for the claustrophobic effect of the story, and various images and allusions ensure that while the deeply conflicted emotions of the central characters are emerging vividly in the pellucid text, an undercurrent of suggestive nuances expands our understanding of the characters' predicament. For example, the sense of tragic inevitability is subtly enhanced by echoes of the past: the false report of Theseus's death echoes the false report of his death earlier in his life, which had resulted in the death of his father, Aegeus; the "unnatural" passion of Phèdre for her stepson echoes her mother's passion for the bull of Minos; and so on. Similarly, while the plotting does not embrace any stories other than the central one, the numerous allusions to other mythological sources amplify that story's implications, so that, like ripples spreading out from a stone thrown into a pond, the drama reverberates outward without ever losing its focus upon the central event.

[C.S.W.]

JEAN-BAPTISTE RACINE

Phèdre

Translated by William Packard[1]

CAST

(In order of their appearance)

HIPPOLYTE, *son of Theseus and Antiope,*
    Queen of the Amazons[2]

THÉRAMÈNE, *mentor to Hippolyte*

OENONE, *nurse and confidante to Phèdre*

PHÈDRE, *wife of Theseus*

PANOPE, *one of Phèdre's women*

ARICIE, *a princess descended from ancient*
    Athenian royalty

THESEUS, *son of Ageus, King of Athens*

ISMÈNE, *confidante to Aricie*

ACT ONE

SCENE ONE

Hippolyte, Théramène

HIPPOLYTE. I have made up my mind: I go, dear
    Théramène,
and leave the loveliness of staying in Trézène.[3]
Each day I have new doubts, they drive me to
    distress,

and I must blush with shame to see my idleness.
For more than six long months I've missed my   5
    father's face,
I do not know his fate, I do not know the place
that could be capable of keeping such a man.
THÉRAMÈNE. In what new place, my lord, will you
    try what new plan?
So far, to satisfy your great uncertainty,
I've sailed the seas each side of Corinth endlessly;[4]   10
I've asked about Theseus of those who, it is said,
saw Acheron descend forever to the dead;[5]
I've visited Elis, and Tenaros, and I[6]
sailed by where Icarus fell screaming from the sky.[7]
And now with what new hope, in what new place   15
    will you

---

1   This translation was first presented by the Institute for Advanced Studies in the Theatre Arts at the Greenwich Mews Theatre, New York City, on February 10, 1966. For amateur performance rights, apply to Samuel French Inc. For all other rights, apply to William Packard, 232 West 14th Street, New York, NY 10011.

2   *Antiope*] According to most sources, Antiope was the sister of Hippolyta (or Hippolyte), who is also called Queen of the Amazons; some, however, suggest that Antiope is another name for Hippolyta herself.

3   Trézène] Troezen, a city in the northeastern Peloponnesian peninsula (the southern part of mainland Greece).

4   each side of Corinth] The Isthmus of Corinth, a thin strip of land connecting the Peloponnese to central Greece, separates the Ionian Sea to the west and the Aegean Sea to the east. The journey described by Théramène in the following lines suggests a circumnavigation of Greece in a counter-clockwise direction.

5   Acheron] Known as "the river of woe" and located in Epirus, a region in northwestern Greece, the Acheron was said by ancient Greeks to descend to Hades, the underworld, because in several places it flows through deep gorges or disappears underground.

6   Elis] (also known as Elea) a city-state in the northwest Peloponnese; Tenaros] a city at the southern tip of the Peloponnese.

7   Icarus] According to legend, he fell from the sky when he flew too close to the sun with the wax-and-feather wings his father, Daedalus, had made so they could escape the Minoan labyrinth. He fell into the Aegean Sea and his body washed up on the island now known as Ikaria, in the northeast Aegean.

listen for his footsteps or look for what new clue?
Now who knows truly if the king your father be
hidden somewhere that must remain a mystery?
Perhaps we fear for what we both know nothing of,
perhaps this hero has discovered some new love,   20
some beautiful young girl he's dying to abuse …
HIPPOLYTE. Stop now, dear Théramène, you've no
    right to accuse.
He's given up that vice, he's long ago outgrown
such bubblings of the blood, he's happier alone;
for Phèdre has made him shed his old inconstancy,[8]   25
so she no longer fears an unknown rivalry.
No no, I only go because I know I must,
and also to escape this place which I distrust.
THÉRAMÈNE. Ah, when did you, my lord, begin to
    hate and fear
this pleasant peaceful place? — for you grew up   30
    right here,
and surely you preferred this quiet rest and sport
to all the pomp and noise of Athens and the court.
What danger made you change, what dread drives
    you away?
HIPPOLYTE. It's not the same, I face a different
    place today,
since this Phèdre, the daughter of Minos and his   35
    wife[9]
Pasiphaë, came here, she has upset my life.
THÉRAMÈNE. I guess at your distress, and I know
    what is true,
For Phèdre weighs on your mind, and she
    depresses you.
The first time she met you, she hardly let you smile

before she ordered your immediate exile.   40
And yet her raging hate, which had you in its hold,
has either disappeared, or grown much more
    controlled.
Besides, what can she do, or bring down on your
    head,
this dying woman who desires to be dead?
This Phèdre, who wastes away from what she will   45
    not say,
grown weary of herself and of the light of day,
can she do anything against you any more?
HIPPOLYTE. I do not fear her hate the way I did
    before.
No, Hippolyte must flee another enemy:
and that is why I fly from this young Aricie,   50
last blood of that bad line which worked against
    us so.
THÉRAMÈNE. What? — even you, my lord, you
    think she is your foe?
She is related to the Pallantides, it's true,[10]
but should she share the blame of that malicious
    crew?
And should you hate her face, which lights the   55
    brightest day?
HIPPOLYTE. If I could hate her face, I would not go
    away.
THÉRAMÈNE. My lord, let me say this before you
    go too far —
you are no longer proud of being what you are:
Hippolyte, the sworn foe of love itself and all
the slavish laws of love that made your father fall.   60
Yet though she may remain cool and aloof in pride,
Venus may still win out, and take your father's side
and, placing you among those men who sigh and
    pine,
she may force you to kneel before her sacred shrine.
My lord: are you in love?   65
HIPPOLYTE.   How can you use that word?
You, who have known my heart since first my
    spirit stirred —
a heart that only knows such distance and disdain,
a heart that hardly can return to earth again.

---

8 old inconstancy] In Plutarch's *Lives*, it is related that
Theseus had wooed and then discarded several women,
"which yet were never represented in the Greek plays.
For he is said to have carried off Anaxo, a Troezenian,
and having slain Sinnis and Cercyon, to have ravished
their daughters; to have married Periboea, the mother
of Ajax, and then Phereboea, and then Iope, the daughter of Iphicles. And further, he is accused of deserting
Ariadne (as is before related), being in love with Aegle,
the daughter of Panopeus, neither justly nor honour-
ably; and lastly, of the rape of Helen, which filled all
Attica with war and blood…" (trans. John Dryden).
9 Minos] the ruler of Crete.

---

10 Pallantides] the fifty sons of Pallas, a former king of Athens; they waged war against Theseus to contest his rule
of the kingdom.

Son of an Amazon, I drank her milk and drew
that strong and stubborn pride which seems to   70
  baffle you;
considering myself, the way a young man does,
I gave myself great praise when I knew who I was.
You who were close to me, who saw to all my
  needs,
you made me learn by heart my famous father's
  deeds.
You told me of his life, and once you had begun,   75
I was on fire to hear whatever he had done:
So you described the way this hero had consoled
mankind for its great loss of Hercules, and told
me how he slew Sinnis, told how he killed Scirron,[11]
and destroyed Procrustes, and slaughtered   80
  Cercyon,[12]
took Epidaurus' bones and spilled them in the
  mud,[13]
then covered over Crete with Minotaur's life blood,[14]
But when you told of deeds that sounded more
  like crimes,
how Theseus used to break his word a hundred
  times —

11 Sinnis] a man who menaced travellers along the Isth-
    mus of Corinth, his favoured method being to tie peo-
    ple between two bent pine trees, then release the trees,
    thereby dismembering his victims; Scirron] a bandit,
    who would compel travellers to wash his feet, then kick
    them over a cliff into the ocean where they would be
    devoured by a huge tortoise.
12 Procrustes] an innkeeper who would make his guests fit
    his bed by racking short people and lopping off the
    limbs of tall ones; Cercyon] a king in Eleusis who would
    challenge those who passed through his city to a wres-
    tling match, in which he would defeat them and kill
    them.
13 Epidaurus's bones] The translation may cause some con-
    fusion here. Apparently Racine means the bones of
    Periphetes, a tyrant who dwelt near Epidaurus, where
    he threatened travellers with his club; Theseus killed him
    and left his bones to be picked by ravens.
14 Minotaur] a monster who was half bull, half man.
    Minos had the architect/inventor Deucalion design a
    labyrinth in which to hide the creature; there, every nine
    years, it was given a sacrifice of seven boys and seven girls
    from Athens, until it was at last slain by Theseus.

Helen is raped away from Sparta by his lies;[15]   85
poor Salamis must sit as Periboëa cries —[16]
and there were many more whose names escape
  me now,
who loved him, and believed that he would keep
  his vow:
Ariadne, weeping in silence by the sea,
Phèdre, too, whom he seduced, although more   90
  happily:
ah, you remember how I begged you to be brief,
such stories made me grave, they stayed and gave
  me grief;
if it were in my will to wrench them from my brain
so only the brave deeds and glories would remain!
Could I be so enslaved and waste my life away?   95
Could some god make me cheat, dissemble and
  betray?
Loose and lascivious, I would have twice the shame
of Theseus — I have none of his great claim to fame
no name, and no strange beasts defeated, and no
  right
to fail as he has failed, or fall from his steep height. 100
And yet suppose my pride should mellow and
  grow mild,
why should it all be for this Aricie, this child?
Surely I sense, deep in the darkness of my heart,
there is a law that says we two must stay apart?
My father disapproves, and by a stern decree,   105
forbids that she enlarge her brother's family:
he fears some bright new life from that guilt-ridden
  line,
therefore each leaf must wilt, and so die on the vine.
This sister must stay chaste forever to the tomb,
and bury their bad name in her own barren womb.   110
Should I stand by her side against my father's laws?
Show off my arrogance by taking up her cause?
Should I let love set sail the madness of my youth …

15 Helen] According to the fables reported by Plutarch,
    Theseus and his friend Pirithous abducted Helen of
    Sparta (later of Troy) while she was still a young girl. She
    must have been very young indeed, for Theseus is said
    to have lived at least a generation before the Trojan War.
16 Periboea] the mother of Ajax and the daughter of
    Salamis and Poseidon.

THÉRAMÈNE. My lord, once fate takes place and
    makes men face the truth,
  not even gods can find what goes on in the mind.   115
  Theseus has made you see, who tried to keep you
    blind;
  his hate has fanned a love, has nurtured a fine fire,
  has lent this enemy a grace which you admire.
  Why are you so afraid of being so in love?
  Perhaps there are strange joys which you know   120
    nothing of:
  or will cruel scruples rule your conscientious days?
  Must you scorn Hercules for his few playful ways?
  What brave courageous soul has Venus never won?
  And you, where would you be if you were not the
    son
  of Antiope, whose breast encouraged a shy fire   125
  for Theseus your father, the thirst of her desire?
  What does it matter now, this high pride when
    you speak?
  Things have already changed, and over this past week
  you were not wild, not free, not as you were before,
  now racing chariots with loud shouts by the shore,   130
  and now perfecting skills with Neptune as your
    guide,[17]
  taking an untamed horse and breaking it to ride.
  The woods do not return the echo of your cries;
  weary with some great weight, you die before my
    eyes.
  Now there can be no doubt: you are in love, you   135
    burn,
  you hide a fatal pain which no man can discern.
  Is it this Aricie has made your spirit bow?
HIPPOLYTE. I go, dear Théramène, to find my father
  now.
THÉRAMÈNE. But will you not tell Phèdre why you
  refuse to stay, my lord?
HIPPOLYTE.You can explain, once I have gone away.   140
  I know I should see her; I shall, before I go.
  But now, why does Oenone seem to be troubled so?

---

[17] Neptune as your guide] In addition to being associated
with the sea, Neptune (the Latin counterpart of Poseidon) was also closely associated with horses and earthquakes.

SCENE TWO

Hippolyte, Oenone, Théramène

OENONE. Alas, my lord, alas: whose troubles are
  like mine?
  The Queen almost begins to end her thin life line.
  Vainly each night and day I stay close by her side:
  she dies of some great pain which she still tries to
    hide.
  Some fatal disarray goes raging through her head,   5
  it keeps her wide awake and takes her from her bed.
  This illness makes her long to see the light of day,
  yet she insists that I turn everyone away …
  She comes.
HIPPOLYTE. Enough, I go: I would not want to wait
  And let her see a face which she has grown to hate.   10

SCENE THREE

Phèdre, Oenone

PHÈDRE. No more, Oenone, no more. Let me stay
  here and wait.
  My strength is so meagre, my weakness is so great.
  My eyes are dazzled by the bright light of the day,
  my knees are trembling as I feel myself give way.
  Alas!   5
OENONE. See how we weep, O gods, and set us free!
PHÈDRE. All these vain ornaments, these veils weigh
  down on me!
  What meddling dreadful hands have tried to tie
    my hair
  in such fine tiny knots with such annoying care?
  All things on every side conspire to do me harm.
OENONE. The way you say these things, you cause   10
  me great alarm!
  When you yourself saw that you were not at your
    best,
  you made me use my hands to get you so well
    dressed;
  and you yourself, because you felt a bit more bright,
  wanted to show yourself and feel the full daylight.
  So here you are, Madam; yet now you try to hide,   15
  you say you hate the day, so you must go inside.
PHÈDRE. Creator of the day, and of my family,
  my mother claimed she came from your fierce clarity;
  O now perhaps you burn with shame to see my pain:

Sun, I shall never gaze on your great face again!   20

OENONE. You choose cruel suicide, is that your last
    desire?

How often must I hear you curse life's famous fire,

stand here as you rehearse the farewells to be made?

PHÈDRE. Why shouldn't I be there, there in the
    forest shade?

Why shouldn't I look out and follow with my eye   25

a cloud of dust, and see a chariot race by?

OENONE. What, Madam?

PHÈDRE.   Where am I? and what did I just say?

Have I gone mad, and have my wits begun to stray?

O I have lost my mind, the great gods are to blame.

Oenone, see how my face must blush with such   30
    great shame:

I let you see too much, my sorrow was too plain;

my eyes, in spite of me, are filled with tears again.

OENONE. Alas, if you must cry, then cry for
    keeping still,

which only aggravates this illness of your will.

So deaf to what we've said, as if you had not heard,   35

will you be pitiless and die without a word?

What fury must obscure the brilliance of the sun?

What poison has dried up your life before it's done?

The darkness of three nights has crept across the skies

since you have slept, and sleep has rested your   40
    sore eyes;

the blazing of three days has chased those nights
    along

since you took food, and ate to make your body
    strong.

Have you dreamed up some scheme, some plot to
    stop your breath?

What pride gave you the right to bring about
    your death?

O, you dismay the gods who gave you your own life,   45

and you betray the man who took you as his wife;

and finally, you cheat your children by this deed,

they will be left to lead a life of endless need.

Suppose on that same day they find their mother
    dead,

their whole inheritance goes somewhere else instead,   50

to someone else's son, some enemy of yours,

son of that Amazon from far-off distant shores,

this Hippolyte …

PHÈDRE.   O god!

OENONE.   That moves you a great deal.

PHÈDRE. Wretched worthless woman, whose name
    did you reveal?

OENONE. Now your great hate is not so hard for   55
    me to gauge;

it is that fatal name that makes you shake with rage.

Live, Lady, live, let love and duty rule in you.

Live, do not leave it to your children to undo

this Scythian's one son; you must keep his caprice[18]

from bleeding the best blood that can be found in   60
    Greece.

Only do not delay, you may die if you wait,

quickly, get back your strength before it is too late,

now, while you still have time, the flame of all
    your days

may be brought back again to a substantial blaze.

PHÈDRE. This has gone on too long: this guile, this   65
    guilty heart.

OENONE. What? tell me what remorse is tearing
    you apart?

What crime obsesses you, that no one understands?

Is there some guilty blood remaining on your hands?

PHÈDRE. Thank god these hands are clean, they've
    nothing to repent.

I only wish my heart were just as innocent.   70

OENONE. Then what appalling thing is still to
    happen here

and why does your poor heart still tremble in its fear?

PHÈDRE. No, no, I've told enough. The rest is best
    unsaid.

I die in silence, so my secret shall be dead.

OENONE. Die then, and try to take your secret to   75
    the skies;

just find some other hand to close your sightless eyes.

Because although your life has almost run its course,

my soul shall be the first to seek its holy source.

So many hopeless roads go headlong to the dead,

and my own sorrow now shall choose the best   80
    deathbed.

Was I untrue to you about some vow I'd sworn?

Remember that these arms held you when you
    were born.

I gave up everything, my home, my family —

Is this the way you pay me for my loyalty?

---

18 Scythian's] i.e., Antiope's (a Scythian Amazon).

PHÈDRE. What can you hope to gain by using so much force? 85
   If I spoke now, you would be frozen with remorse.

OENONE. What evil could exceed what I already see?
   — that you should try to die right here in front of me.

PHÈDRE. If you knew my great guilt, what fate makes me ashamed,
   I would still have to die, but I would die more blamed. 90

OENONE. Madam, by all these tears that I've already shed,
   by these knees I embrace, release me from this dread,
   tell me what deadly doubts have seized you with such fear —

PHÈDRE. It is your wish. Get up.

OENONE.   All right. Speak, I can hear.

PHÈDRE. God! — what am I to say, or where can I begin? 95

OENONE. I do not want to hear your fears that are within.

PHÈDRE. O Venus! Violence! O fatal rage and hate!
   My mother's love cast her in a distracted state![19]

OENONE. Forget such things, Madam, let all such memories
   keep in the secret peace of the eternities. 100

PHÈDRE. Ariadne, sister, O I remember you
   were left by those cold stones to die in silence too!

OENONE. Madam, why must you choose such hateful things to say
   about the blood that moves within your veins today?

PHÈDRE. Since it pleases Venus, this blood which is so base 105
   shall see the last of me and my unhappy race.

OENONE. Are you in love?

PHÈDRE.   I feel that madness in my heart.

OENONE. Who is it?

PHÈDRE.   Who it is, the most shocking part.

---

19 My mother's … state] Phèdre's mother, Pasiphae, under a spell cast by Poseidon (or Neptune), had fallen in love with a prize bull belonging to her husband Minos. She had Deucalion build her a wooden cow and, by hiding within it, persuaded the bull to mount her. The offspring thus begotten was the Minotaur.

I love — (his fatal name makes me become undone)
I love … 110

OENONE.   Who?

PHÈDRE.   — Do you know the Amazon's one son,
   That Prince whom I myself oppressed with hate and shame?

OENONE. Hippolyte? O god, god!

PHÈDRE.   It's you who said his name.

OENONE. O god, how all my blood runs cold and turns to ice.
   O guilt! O great disgrace! O race of hidden vice!
   O joyless voyages, through such great storms and wars, 115
   what fortunes made us land on these tormented shores!

PHÈDRE. My illness goes far back. For I had hardly wed
   the son of Aegeus, and lain down on his bed,
   and tasted the sweet peace of our long reverie
   when Athens made me see my matchless enemy. 120
   I saw him, I was lost — I turned red, I turned pale;
   disturbances occurred; I felt my feelings fail;
   I could no longer see, I could no longer speak;
   my body boiled and froze, then everything grew weak.
   Great Venus can be seen in these few futile fires 125
   with which she plagues my race with passionate desires.
   With reverent strict vows I tried to turn aside;
   I built a shrine for her, and tended it with pride;
   my knife made sacrifice on beasts of every kind;
   I searched through their insides to find my own lost mind. 130
   This was weak treatment for my woeful hopeless love!
   In vain I burned incense and watched it curl above:
   When I prayed to the god, and said her sacred name,
   I still loved Hippolyte; I saw him in the flame,
   and at the altar where my prayers rose to the sky, 135
   I worshipped someone I dared not identify.
   I fled him everywhere — O sickness of despair;
   Seeing his father's face, I even found him there!
   At last I went to war against this lovely lord;
   I persecuted him whom I was so drawn toward. 140
   I banished this bad foe whom I admired so,
   pretending some deep grief, insisting he should go,
   I pressed for his exile, and my persistent cries

removed him from his home and from his father's
   eyes.
Then I could breathe, Oenone; once he had gone   145
   away
I felt freedom and peace with each new passing day.
Beside my husband now, and hiding my past pain,
I could confine myself to my own home again.
O useless cruel outcome! O destiny of men!
My husband brought me here to settle in Trézène —   150
once more I face this foe so fatal to my flesh;
my old wound opened wide, and my breast bled
   afresh.
This is no secret heat concealed within my veins;
this is great Venus now, who plagues me with
   these pains.
This guilt has made me ill, I loathe my waste of days,   155
it makes me hate my life and all its idle ways.
In dying now, at least I leave a noble name,
and I do not expose the full scope of my shame.
I could not bear to see your tears or hear your pleas,
so I told everything, with no apologies.   160
Now leave me to myself, because I choose to die,
and do not lecture me about my reasons why;
now all your foolish pleas to make me live must
   cease;
let me seek my release, and find my final peace.

SCENE FOUR

Phèdre, Oenone, Panope

PANOPE. How I would like to hide the sad news
   which I bring,
   Madam, and yet I know I must say everything.
   Death has been cruel to you, your husband has
      been killed;
   you are the last to know his greatness has been
      stilled.
OENONE. Panope, what did you say?   5
PANOPE.   That the poor Queen must learn
   she cannot pray to god for Theseus to return;
   because the sailing ships that brought this dreadful
      word
   have just told Hippolyte the news of what occurred.
PHÈDRE. God!
PANOPE.   Athens splits itself, in choosing who
   shall rule,

Some choose the Prince your son; but others play   10
   the fool,
forgetting all the law and what the state has done,
they reach beyond their rights and choose a
   foreign son.
It's even rumoured that a ruthless anarchy
is working to restore the race of Aricie.
This may be dangerous, I thought you ought to   15
   know.
Already Hippolyte has made his plans to go;
if he should appear there, there where the storm is
   loud,
then he may be able to sway that coward crowd.
OENONE. Panope, that's quite enough. The Queen,
   having heard you,
will not neglect this news, and your own point of   20
   view.

SCENE FIVE

Phèdre, Oenone

OENONE. Madam, I ceased to plead that you should
   live this through;
   I even could agree that I should die with you;
   I knew you would ignore all tears or talk of force;
   but now this dreadful news dictates a different
      course.
   Your fortune seems to change and wear a strange   5
      new face:
   the King is dead, Madam, so you must take his place.
   His death leaves you one son, you owe him
      everything —
   a slave if you should die; if you should live, a king.
   To what discerning friends could he turn with his
      fears?
   His ancestors would hear his innocent outcries,   10
   and they would shake with rage across the distant
      skies.
   O live! — you still possess the honour of your name.
   Your sordid flame becomes an ordinary flame.
   This passion is no crime, now Theseus has died,
   your guilt has gone away, the knots are all untied.   15
   Now Hippolyte is free and you can see him now,
   and you can let him come as close as you allow.
   Perhaps, because he thinks you are still filled with
      hate,

he leads a faction now to overthrow the state.
Make him see his mistake, help him to understand.   20
He thinks he should be King, Trézène is his
   homeland.
But he knows that the law gives your son all the forts,
all Athens' worldly force, her ramparts and her ports.
Now you both know you have a common enemy,
and so you should unite to fight this Aricie.   25
PHÈDRE. Your words appeal to me: they please me,
   I agree.
Yes, I will live: if life will flow back into me,
and if my feelings for my son can lift my soul
and fill me with new hope, I will again be whole.

END OF ACT ONE

ACT TWO

SCENE ONE

Aricie, Ismène

ARICIE. Hippolyte has told you that this is where
   he'll be?
Hippolyte will come here to say goodbye to me?
Ismène, can this be true? — no one is fooling
   you?
ISMÈNE. Now that Theseus has died, you will see
   much that's new.
Prepare yourself, Madam, to find on every side   5
so many friends of yours whom Theseus tried to
   hide.
Now Aricie is strong, her freedom is complete,
and soon all Greece will be kept captive at her feet.
ARICIE. Ismène, then these are not mere idle
   fantasies —
I cease to be a slave and have no enemies?   10
ISMÈNE. From now on, all the fates are tame and
   will behave;
and brave Theseus has joined your brothers in the
   grave.
ARICIE. Have they said how he died, what led him
   to the dead?
ISMÈNE. Incredible accounts of it are being spread.
Some say that while defiled with infidelity,   15
this fine philanderer was swallowed by the sea.
And others also say, and you will hear them tell,

that with Pirithoüs, descending into hell,[20]
he went to see Cocyte, and through that mood of
   doom,[21]
he showed his own live soul to dead men in the   20
   gloom;
but he could not come back from that disgraceful
   place,
for those were fatal steps which he could not retrace.
ARICIE. Now how could any man, still filled with
   his life breath,
be willing to set forth on the deep sleep of death?
What led him to explore that final finding out?   25
ISMÈNE. Theseus is dead, Madam, there can be no
   more doubt.
Athens is in a storm, Trézène in an uproar,
and all hail Hippolyte as King from shore to shore.
Phèdre is in this palace, and trembling for her son,
seeks counsel from her friends and pleads with   30
   everyone.
ARICIE. Do you think Hippolyte will have more
   love for me
than his own father had, who gave me slavery?
Will he ease my distress?
ISMÈNE.   Madam, I know he will.
ARICIE. This listless Hippolyte may turn against me
   still.
How can you dare to say he pities and adores   35
in me, and me alone, a sex which he ignores?
You know that for some time he has avoided me;
he always finds a place where we will never be.
ISMÈNE. I know the things they say, that Hippolyte
   is cold —
but coming close to you, he was a bit more bold;   40

---

20 Pirithoüs] the best friend of Theseus, who had previously accompanied him in the attempt to abduct Helen. According to myth, Theseus returned the favour by accompanying his friend to the underworld to abduct Persephone, the wife of Hades (or Pluto), god of the underworld. The rest of the story varies, but most versions report that only Theseus returned to the living world. There is, however, a rationalistic version of the story. See note 26.
21 Cocyte] (or Cocytus), the "river of lamentation," is one of the five rivers surrounding Hades (the others being the Styx, the Acheron, the Plegethon, and the Lethe).

I watched him all the while, I tried to find his pride,
and it occurred to me that everyone had lied.
No, he is not so cold as he has been accused:
when you first looked at him, he seemed to be
    confused.
He turned his eyes aside to leave your lovely glance,   45
but they still gazed at you and he was in a trance.
That he should be in love may seem to him absurd;
yet it is in his eyes, if not in his own word.
ARICIE. I listen, dear Ismène, my heart in all its youth
devours what you say, although there's not much   50
    truth!
You who are dear to me, you know my great
    distress:
my heart has only known my own soul's loneliness,
I who have been the toy of accident and chance,
how can I know the joy, the folly of romance?
The daughter of a King from this great ancient   55
    shore,
I only have survived the tragedies of war.
I lost six brothers who were strong and brave and free,
the hope and flower of a famous family!
The sword tore all of them, the earth was wet
    with red,
Erectheus was dead when all these sons had bled.[22]   60
You know that since their death, there was a stern
    decree
forbidding any Greek to fall in love with me:
the flame of my desire might kindle in my womb,
and one day light a fire within my brother's tomb.
Besides, you ought to know with what a haughty   65
    frown
I viewed this conqueror and what he had set down.
For I had hated love through my disdainful days,
and so I thanked Theseus, and even gave him praise
for making me obey the vows I had begun.
But then I had not seen this fearless hero's son.   70
Not that my eyes alone were held by his fair face,
and made to dwell upon his celebrated grace —
those gifts which nature gives, which anyone
    would prize,

he seems to set aside, as something to despise.
I love and value him for what makes him unique: 75
his father's deeds, and not the ways that he was weak:
I love, and I admire the scope of his high pride,
which never yet was tamed, has never yet been tied.
How Phèdre was taken in by Theseus and his sighs!
I have more self-respect, and my affection flies   80
from all these easy vows, passed out to everyone:
such offers leave me cold, they're something that I
    shun.
To teach humility to the inflexible,
to speak of suffering to the insensible,
to chain a prisoner with claims that I would make,   85
which he could strain against, but never really
    break —
that is what I desire, that will make me complete;
and yet strong Hercules fought less than
    Hippolyte;
subdued more often, and seduced more easily,
he gave less glory to each lover he would see.   90
But dear Ismène, alas! — what awful things I dare!
I will come up against more force than I can bear.
Perhaps you may hear me, humble in my despair,
groan under that high pride which now I think so
    fair.
Hippolyte fall in love? — how could my hope or fear   95
affect him in the least ...
ISMÈNE.   Now you yourself shall hear:
    for here he comes.

SCENE TWO

Hippolyte, Aricie, Ismène

HIPPOLYTE.   Madam, before I go away,
    I have some things to say about your fate today.
My father has just died. My fears which were so
    strong
told me the reason why he had been gone so long.
For death, and death alone, could end his   5
    splendid deeds
and hide from all the world the life a hero leads.
The Fates in their great greed have taken from our
    side
this friend of Hercules who shared the same high
    pride.
I think your hatred may ignore his few defects

---

22 Erectheus] a legendary ancestor of Athenian kings (indeed, the great-grandfather of Theseus himself); presumably, his spirit was so aggrieved that he died a second
time.

and grant his memory these fitting last respects. 10
One hope has opened up and pleased me in my
    grief:
I can release your soul and give you some relief.
I can revoke the laws that made you suffer so.
Now you can start to live, your heart is yours to
    know.
And here in this Trézène, which I come to control 15
just as old Pittheus, ancestor of my soul;[23]
which calls for a new King, and recognizes me —
I now proclaim you free and give you liberty.
ARICIE. This is immoderate, your Highness is too kind,
such generosity is madness to my mind; 20
my Lord, it binds me more to all the stern decrees
which you would cast away in an attempt to please.
HIPPOLYTE. In choosing who shall rule, Athens
    becomes undone,
speak first of you, then me, and then the Queen's
    one son.
ARICIE. Of me, my Lord? 25
HIPPOLYTE.   I know, no honour to my name,
an ancient famous law seems to reject my claim.
Greece is displeased with me for my strange
    foreign birth.
But if I could compete against my brother's worth,
Madam, I know so well that my rights would win
    out,
that I would be made Greek and King without a 30
    doubt.
But there are strong restraints which make me rest
    my case.
I therefore say to you: this is your proper place,
your sceptre is the one your ancestors received
from that first son of earth so secretly conceived.
They say that Aegeus once held it in his hands. 35
Athens was satisfied in all of its demands
by my own father, who was hailed as its own King,
and your six brothers were deprived of everything.
But Athens calls you now to come within her walls.
There have been groans enough from all these 40
    hopeless brawls;
there has been blood enough to soak the open fields
and drown the fertile earth with all the life it yields.

---

23 Pittheus] former king of Trézène (or Troezen) and ma-
    ternal grandfather to Theseus.

Trézène will obey me. The countryside of Crete
will give the son of Phèdre a sumptuous retreat.
You will take Attica. Now I must go at last 45
and try to reunite the votes which will be cast.
ARICIE. Astonished and confused by all that I have
    heard,
I have a secret fear that this is all absurd.
Now am I wide awake, or should I trust this dream?
What gracious god, my Lord, made you adopt 50
    this scheme?
How wonderful it is all places know your name!
And how the truth itself exceeds all praise and fame!
Would you betray yourself, like this, all for my sake?
Not hating me may be the greatest gift you make,
and having kept yourself in everything you do 55
from this hostility …
HIPPOLYTE.   Madam, could I hate you?
No matter what they say or how they paint my pride,
do they suppose some beast once carried me inside?
What mind that is unkind, what heart that may
    be hard,
in viewing you, would not grow soft in its regard? 60
Could any man resist the charm of what you are? …
ARICIE. What? My Lord.
HIPPOLYTE.   But I know, now I have gone too far.
Reason, I see, gives way to feelings that are real.
I have already said more than I should reveal,
Madam, so I go on: I must inform you of 65
something which my own heart keeps secret in its
    love.
You see before you here a wretched restless Prince,
epitome of pride too headstrong to convince.
I who fought love and thought my attitude was right;
who laughed at its captives and ridiculed their plight; 70
who scorned the worst shipwrecks, the first one to
    deplore
the storms of mortals which I witnessed from the
    shore;
now I have been bowed down to know the
    common lot,
how I have been estranged and changed to what
    I'm not!
One instant has destroyed my childish arrogance: 75
this soul which was so bold now yields to
    circumstance.
For almost six long months, so hopeless and alone,

and bearing everywhere this torture I have known;
divided in desires, I don't know what to do:
with you, I try to fly; alone, I long for you;   80
far off in the forest, your image follows me;
the brilliance of the day, the night's obscurity,
all show me the sly charm which my high pride
    ignores;
all render Hippolyte a prisoner of yours.
Now through this mad pursuit, I've lost my self-   85
    control,
so I no longer know the scope of my own soul.
I've lost my javelins, my chariot, my bow;
I've lost Neptune's lessons which I learned long
    ago;
the woods no longer hear loud shouts as I rejoice,
and my horses ignore the sound of my own voice.   90
Perhaps the telling of a love so wild and free
might make you blush to see what you have done
    to me.
What foolish things to say from such a captive heart!
And what a sick victim of all your lovely art!
But you should see in me that which is very dear.   95
Imagine that I speak another language here;
do not reject my love for its vague awkward vow,
for I have never tried to say this until now.

SCENE THREE

Hippolyte, Aricie, Théramène, Ismène

THÉRAMÈNE. My Lord, the Queen comes here, and
    I have come before.
  She looks for you.
HIPPOLYTE.   For me?
THÉRAMÈNE.   My Lord, I know no more.
  But I have just been sent to make sure that you stay.
  Phèdre wants to speak to you before you go away.
HIPPOLYTE. Phèdre? — But what can I say? — And   5
    what can she expect …
ARICIE. My Lord, you can't refuse, you owe her this
    respect.
  Although you know too well her old hostility,
  her tears require you to show some sympathy.
HIPPOLYTE. And so you go away. And now I do not
    know
  if I've offended you whom I admire so!   10
  I wonder if this heart which I leave in your hands …

ARICIE. Go, Prince, and carry out your generous
    demands.
  Arrange that Athens be subject to my decree.
  For I accept these things which you bestow on me.
  But this impressive state, although it is so great,   15
  is not the gift you give which I praise with most
    weight.

SCENE FOUR

Hippolyte, Théramène

HIPPOLYTE. Are we all ready now? — But see, the
    Queen draws near.
  Go now, prepare the way, and gather all our gear.
  Set down the plans, the course, the orders, and
    then come
  to free me from this talk which will be tedium.   4

SCENE FIVE

Phèdre, Hippolyte, Oenone

PHÈDRE. There he is. My bad blood refuses to obey.
  Seeing him, I forget what I have come to say.
OENONE. Remember that your son depends on you
    today.
PHÈDRE. They say your plans are made, and you are
    on your way.
  To all your miseries I offer you my tears.   5
  And I have come to you to speak about my fears.
  My son is fatherless; and I can prophesy
  that he shall see the day when I myself must die.
  A thousand enemies attack this child of mine.
  Now you and you alone can keep them all in line.   10
  And yet a new remorse has come before my eyes:
  I fear I may have closed your ears against his cries.
  I tremble when I think he may receive your hate,
  because I am the one you choose to desecrate.
HIPPOLYTE. Madam, I am not base, I could not   15
    cause such pain.
PHÈDRE. If you detested me, then I would not
    complain,
  my Lord. I know you know I tried to injure you;
  but what was in my heart, my Lord, you never knew.
  I took enormous care to make your hatred great.
  I could not let you live so close to my estate.   20
  Aloud and secretly, I was so proud I swore

that I would have you sent to some far distant shore.
I went on to forbid, by an express decree,
that anyone should speak your name in front of me.
Yet weigh my crime against the pain that is my fate,   25
and say that my own hate has only caused your hate;
no woman in this world deserves your pity more,
no woman who you have less reason to abhor.

HIPPOLYTE. A mother's jealousy may make her rarely fair
to some adopted son who comes into her care.   30
Madam, I know this well. Curses which disparage
are the common outcome of a second marriage.
All mothers would scorn me, and find things to deplore;
perhaps they would have tried to make me suffer more.

PHÈDRE. Ah! My Lord, believe me, that this is not the case!   35
I do not fit that law which rules the human race!
A very different care consumes me through and through!

HIPPOLYTE. Madam, I see no need for this to trouble you.
Perhaps your husband still bathes in the light of day;
we weep for his return, and heaven may obey.   40
My father has a god who guards him everywhere;
Neptune will not ignore my father's fervent prayer.

PHÈDRE. One only journeys once to that land of the dead,
my Lord. Since Theseus has been already led
to see those dismal shores, no god restores him now —   45
no freedom or release will Acheron allow.[24]
But still, he is not dead, because he breathes in you.
Always before my eyes, my husband lives anew.
I see him, speak to him; and my heart … O my Lord,
I'm mad, my tortured mind shows its perverse discord.   50

HIPPOLYTE. I see the power now of love that never dies.
Theseus may be dead, yet he lives in your eyes;
I seem to see his face irradiating you.

PHÈDRE. I long for Theseus, yes, Prince, that much is true.
I love him, not the way the shades of Hades must,   55
the driven libertine who lives for his own lust,
who may be making love right now in dead men's beds;
but rather faithful, proud, the haughtiest of heads,
so charming and so young, who won all hearts somehow,
a portrait by a god — or as I see you now.   60
He had your poise, your gaze, your manner and your grace,
a gentle tender smile that lighted his whole face,
when he first sailed the sea without the least conceit,
receiving the sweet vows of the fair maids of Crete.
What were you doing then? Where were you, Hippolyte?   65
Why were you not among the famous Greek elite?
Why were you still too young to join these conquerors
who came on their swift ships to land on our far shores?
Seeing the Cretan beast, you could have gained great praise,
by slaying him within his labyrinthine maze.   70
And so that you would know which way you should be led,
my sister would have come and made you take the thread.
No, wait — I would be there, and well ahead of her,
the love inside of me would be the first to stir.
Prince, I would be the one to help you learn the ways   75
of staying safe and so escaping from the maze.
I would have taken pains to hasten your return!
A thread is not enough to show you my concern.
I'm sure that it would be a peril I could share,
and I myself could walk ahead of you through there;   80
so Phèdre would go with you through that great vacant void,
would have emerged with you, or with you been destroyed.

HIPPOLYTE. Gods! — what words have I heard? — Madam, recall your vow:
Theseus, my father, is your lord and husband now.

---

24 Acheron] one of the rivers of the underworld.

PHÈDRE. My Lord, what makes you say I've placed   85
  this out of mind?
or do I need to have my dignity defined?
HIPPOLYTE. Madam, please forgive me. See how my
  face turns red,
for I misunderstood exactly what you said.
My shame cannot stand here and let you look at me;
I go …   90
PHÈDRE.   You understood too well. O cruelty!
I must have said enough to make it all quite clear.
Well then, prepare to see Phèdre in her fury here.
I am in love. And yet, seeing this sentiment,
do not believe I think that I am innocent,
or that the passion which is poisoning my mind   95
has been encouraged by complacence of some kind.
I am the sick victim of the spite of the skies;
I mightily despise myself in my own eyes.
The gods are my witness, the same great gods
  who lit
a fire in my blood and then kept fanning it;   100
these gods who take delight in their deceit and seek
to seduce and undo a woman who is weak.
Now you yourself know well what happened in
  the past:
I chased you from this place and made you an
  outcast.
I tried to show myself so odious to you,   105
by being hateful and inhuman in your view.
What good was this great war I waged without
  success?
You hated me much more, I did not love you less.
Your sadness gave your face a charm beyond your
  years.
I languished, I burned up, in fire and in tears.   110
Your eyes could witness to the truth of what I say,
if you could lift them up and make them look my
  way.
What am I saying now? — have I become so ill
I could make such a vow, and of my own free will?
I fear for my one son, I must protect this child,   115
and so I had begun to ask you to be mild.
The feeble weakness of a heart too full to speak!
Alas, for it is you and you alone I seek.
Revenge yourself, my Lord, on my disgraceful shame.
Son of a hero who first gave you your own name,   120
here is your chance to kill another beast of Crete:
the wife of Theseus dares to love Hippolyte!
This terrible monster should not escape you now.
Here is my heart, right here, it's waiting for your
  blow.
It is impatient now to pay for its foul lust,   125
it feels your hand reach out and make the fatal thrust.
So strike. Or if you think your hatred should abstain
from granting me at least this last sweet peaceful
  pain,
or if you think my blood would soil your hand,
  my Lord,
then do not make a move, yet let me have your   130
  sword.
Now.
OENONE.   What is this, Madam? By all gods far
  and near!
But someone comes. Quickly, you must not be
  found here;
come, let us leave this place of so much shame
  and dread.

SCENE SIX

Hippolyte, Théramène

THÉRAMÈNE. Is Phèdre fleeing from us, or is she
  being led?
And what are all these signs of suffering, my Lord?
Why do you stand here with no colour, speech or
  sword?
HIPPOLYTE. We must fly, Théramène. I feel such
  wild surprise,
I find that I despise myself in my own eyes.   5
Phèdre … No, by all the gods! — Let this deep
  secret be
kept hidden in the dark through all eternity.
THÉRAMÈNE. If you are going to go, the ship is in
  the port.
My Lord, before you board, listen to this report:
Athens has made her choice, the voices all avow   10
your brother is the one. Phèdre has full power now.
HIPPOLYTE. Phèdre?
THÉRAMÈNE.   An Athenian is coming with a scroll
to put into her hands, which gives complete control.
Her son is King, my Lord.
HIPPOLYTE.   You who look down on us,
is she so virtuous that you reward her thus?   15

THÉRAMÈNE. However, now they say the King is
    still alive,
  that he is in Épire, is well and seems to thrive.[25]
  But I have sought him there, my Lord, and I
    know well …
HIPPOLYTE. We must investigate whatever people tell.
  Let us look into this, and trace it to its source: 20
  if it should prove untrue, I will pursue my course,
  and we will go; and so no matter what it takes,
  we'll choose the ruler who is best for all our sakes.

END OF ACT TWO

ACT THREE

SCENE ONE

Phèdre, Oenone

PHÈDRE. I wish that they would take this fame and
    praise away!
  Now how can you make me see anyone today?
  What have you come to say to comfort my despair?
  I spoke my secret mind, and I should hide
    somewhere.
  My passions all broke out more than I meant to   5
    show.
  I have already said what no one else should know.
  God, how he listened so! — and how he seemed
    to be
  distracted and obtuse, misunderstanding me!
  And how he tried to find some safe way to escape!
  His blushing bothered me and made my shame   10
    take shape!
  Why did you keep me from my fatal last request?
  Alas! when his great sword was resting on my breast,
  did he grow pale for me? — or snatch it from my
    grasp?
  No, no, it was enough for my proud hand to clasp
  the handle, and I made that instrument abhorred   15
  forever in the eyes of this inhuman Lord.
OENONE. Your own misfortunes soar and cause you
    to complain,
  you feed a fire which you must put out again.
  Would it not be discreet and wise as Minos was,

to have much nobler cares than your self-pity does?   20
  Instead of mourning for this wretch who flies his fate,
  be Queen, and concentrate on the affairs of State.
PHÈDRE. Be Queen! — and make the State come
    under my strong rule,
  when I myself stand here, a weak and lawless fool!
  When I have lost control of the whole world of sense!   25
  When I can hardly breathe, my shame is so intense!
  When I am dying.
OENONE.   Fly.
PHÈDRE.   I cannot turn and run.
OENONE. You dared to banish him, whom now you
    dare not shun.
PHÈDRE. There's no more time for that. He knows
    my lust at last.
  All thoughts of modesty and patient tact are past.   30
  I have declared my guilt to this proud hero's eyes;
  hope stole into my heart, I could not hold my sighs.
  And it was you yourself, ignoring my complaint,
  reviving my poor life when I was growing faint,
  with flattery and guile, who told me your grand plan: 35
  you made me seem to see that I could love this man.
OENONE. Alas! — these pains are not something I
    could contrive,
  and what would I not do to make you stay alive?
  If insults have hurt you, and made you try to hide,
  could you forget the scorn of such a haughty pride?   40
  with cruel and stubborn eyes, his obstinate conceit
  watched as you almost fell and lay there at his feet!
  How his great vanity made me hate him again!
  If only you had seen, as I could see him then!
PHÈDRE. Oenone, he could subdue this pride that   45
    bothers you.
  His ways are just as wild as those woods where he
    grew.
  This Hippolyte is rude and savage in his prime,
  and now he heard of love perhaps for the first time.
  Perhaps his great surprise gives rise to his silence,
  and our complaints perhaps have too much violence.   50
OENONE. Remember he was formed and born from
    a strange womb.
PHÈDRE. That Scythian knew well how true love
    could consume.
OENONE. He has a fatal hate which sets our sex apart.
PHÈDRE. Then I shall never see a rival in his heart.
  But all of your advice is overdue and blind.   55

---

25 Épire] Epirus, a region in northwestern Greece.

Now serve my love, Oenone, and never mind my
  mind.
This man opposes love because his heart is hard:
we must find some new way to gain his kind regard.
At least the lure of rule appealed to his high pride;
Athens attracted him, that much he could not hide;   60
already all his ships are turned towards that great
  State,
the sails are in the wind, the men can hardly wait.
Find this ambitious youth whose heart is in the skies,
Oenone; and make the crown shine brightly in
  his eyes.
The sacred diadem is his possession now;   65
I only ask that I might place it on his brow.
Give him the power now which is not in my hands.
He will instruct my son in how to give commands;
perhaps he may consent to play the father's role.
The mother and the son are placed in his control.   70
Use every trick you know to move him to my view:
your words will do more good than mine could
  ever do.
So plead and weep for me; say Phèdre grows weak
  and dies;
and do not be ashamed of begging with your cries.
You can do anything; I send my hopes with you.   75
So go: I will wait here to learn what I must do.

SCENE TWO

Phèdre, alone.

PHÈDRE. O being who can see the shame of my
  rebuff,
  implacable Venus, am I not low enough?
  But you should not prolong this useless cruelty.
  My downfall is complete; for you have wounded me.
  Now if you truly choose your glory should be known,   5
  attack another heart more stubborn than my own.
  This Hippolyte flees you; defying your decrees,
  he never sees your shrine nor kneels down on his
   knees.
  He has a pride of mind your name cannot assuage.
  Goddess, avenge yourself: we share the same outrage!   10
  Let him love — Here you are, you have come
   back to me,
  Oenone? — Then he hates me; he would not hear
   your plea.

SCENE THREE

Phèdre, Oenone

OENONE.   Put out of mind this lust, this
  love that must not be,
  Madam. Instead, recall your virtue instantly.
  The King they said was dead is very much alive;
  they know Theseus is here for they saw him arrive.
  So now they rush and run to see his famous face.   5
  I searched for Hippolyte in almost every place,
  but then a thousand cries went flying to the skies …
PHÈDRE. My husband lives, Oenone, give me no
  more replies.
  I have already sworn a love he must abhor.
  He lives: that is enough, now I must know no more.   10
OENONE. What?
PHÈDRE.   I predicted this; but you preferred to
  doubt.
  My own remorse was weak, and your weeping
   won out.
  If I had only died this morning, all would mourn;
  but I took your advice, so I must die forlorn.
OENONE. You are dying?   15
PHÈDRE.   My god! What did I do today?
  My husband and his son already on their way!
  — this witness who has seen all my deceitful charms
  will watch my features greet his father to my arms,
  my heart still filled with sighs which he would not
   accept,
  my eyes still wet with tears which he could not   20
   respect.
  To keep the self-respect of Theseus clean and free,
  will he now try to hide this love inside of me?
  Will he let me betray his father and his King?
  Can he contain his rage at this dishonouring?
  No, he could not be still. Besides, I know my crime,   25
  Oenone, but I have not grown hard in my lifetime,
  like some who even seem to take delight in blame,
  who wear a smiling face and never blush with shame.
  I know my madness now, I can recall it all.
  I feel the ceiling sees, and each great vacant wall   30
  awaits my husband's face, and when Theseus appears,
  they will speak my disgrace to his astonished ears.
  O let me die, let death deliver me instead.
  I wonder can it be so dreadful to be dead?
  Death is not terrible to those in misery.   35

I only fear the name which I leave after me.
My wretched children shall inherit this chagrin!
The blood of Jupiter should help them to begin;
and yet despite their pride in such a great estate,
a mother's wickedness can be a hateful weight.   40
I fear that they shall hear, alas! the fatal truth,
their mother had such shame when they were in
   their youth.
I fear in later years, when this guilt multiplies,
that neither one of them will dare to lift his eyes.
OENONE. Believe me, I agree, their future makes   45
   me grieve;
I feel you are quite right to fear what you perceive.
But why expose them to such terrible insults?
And why accuse yourself of such grotesque results?
That's that: for they will say that Phèdre, so filled
   with shame,
is racing to escape her husband's rage and blame.   50
And Hippolyte is glad to see the end of you,
for by your dying you support his point of view.
Now how could I reply to these things he accused?
Before him I would be too easily confused.
Then I would have to see this Hippoyte rejoice   55
and tell your tale to all with ears to hear his voice.
I wish I were struck by some fire from the sky!
Now do not lie to me, does he still make you sigh?
How do you see this Prince, so boastful, so upright?
PHÈDRE. I see him as a beast, made frightful to my   60
   sight.
OENONE. Then why should he achieve an easy victory?
You fear him. Then strike first, and have the bravery
to say he did this crime which he may lay to you.
For who will disagree, and claim it is not true?
How fortunate his sword is left here in your hands!   65
All know your present woe, and each man
   understands
his father heard your words whenever you
   complained,
and it was due to you his exile was obtained.
PHÈDRE. How can I injure one so innocent of sin?
OENONE. My purpose only needs your silence to   70
   begin.
I tremble as you do, and I feel some remorse.
To die a thousand times would be a better course.
But I lose you unless you let me have my way,
and your life is to me worth more than I can say.

I will speak out. Theseus, when my fierce tale is done,   75
will limit his revenge to banishing his son.
A father, in great rage, still has a father's mind:
and a light punishment is all that he will find.
But if in spite of all some guiltless blood must spill,
why should your honour put such things beyond   80
   your will?
For your integrity should not be thrown away,
and it has certain laws you know you must obey,
Madam; and so to save your threatened honour, you
must give up everything, perhaps your virtue too.
Who's there? — I see Theseus.   85
PHÈDRE.   Ah! — I see Hippolyte;
in his cruel eyes I see my downfall is complete.
Do what you want with me, my heart is torn and
   sore.
The way things are right now, I can do nothing more.

SCENE FOUR

Theseus, Hippolyte, Phèdre, Oenone, Théramène

THESEUS. I am no longer torn by the strong force
   of fate,
Madam, and to your arms I …
PHÈDRE.   Theseus, you must wait,
do not profane your name by saying anything,
for I do not deserve these greetings that you bring.
You are greatly disgraced. Fate laboured to debase   5
your helpless wife while you were absent from this
   place.
Unworthy of your words, and of your fine high
   pride,
from now on I must find the safest way to hide.

SCENE FIVE

Theseus, Hippolyte, Théramène

THESEUS. Why this excitement now at the mere
   sight of me,
my son?
HIPPOLYTE.   Phèdre is the one to solve this mystery.
Yet if my earnest wish can move your brave heart,
   then
let me, my Lord, depart and not see her again.
Your son is so upset that he must disappear   5
from any place your wife decides she may come near.

THESEUS. My son, you're going to go?
HIPPOLYTE.   I did not search for her:
    you were the one who made her coming here occur.
    When you had left Trézène, my Lord, by your decree,
    you also chose to leave the Queen and Aricie.   10
    I took good care of them according to my vow.
    But what care makes me stay behind in this place
        now?
    Far in the forests, I have wasted each new day
    by chasing frightened game and slaying my small
        prey.
    Why can't I fly from this great laziness I'm in,   15
    and find genuine blood to stain my javelin.
    When you were in your youth, and not yet my
        own age,
    strange beasts were beaten down by your
        enormous rage,
    and tyrants felt the crush of your tremendous bow;
    the innocent were safe, the insolent brought low;   20
    you made peace on the sea, protecting all our shores.
    Travellers did not fear unnecessary wars;
    and Hercules, who heard the ordeals you went
        through,
    could lay his labours down and rest because of you.
    And I, the unknown son who sees my father's fame,   25
    I even envy now my mother's honoured name.
    Allow my courage now to be put to good use.
    If some beast escaped you and is still on the loose,
    then let me try to set its corpse before you feet;
    or if I have to die, then let my death be sweet,   30
    so everyone will praise my days so bravely done,
    and weigh my famous name, and say I was your son.
THESEUS. What madness greets my face? — what
        horror fills this place
    and makes my family fly off in such disgrace?
    If I come back so feared, so little needed here,   35
    gods, why did you help me and make me
        persevere?
    I only had one friend. Desires plagued his life,
    he laboured in Épire to take the tyrant's wife;[26]

I helped him to attain this passion of his mind;
but an outrageous fate dazed us and made us blind.   40
The tyrant stepped aside and took me by surprise.
I saw Pirithoüs destroyed before my eyes
thrown down and torn apart and eaten by strange
    beasts
who feed on human flesh in their atrocious feasts.
I was shut far away in dark abysmal caves,   45
a deep and dismal place, and underneath all graves.
Then after six long months the gods came back to
    me:
and so I could escape by my own subtlety.
The tyrant tried to fight, and when I slaughtered him
his beasts fell on his corpse and tore it limb from   50
    limb.
So when with joy I thought at last I could come near
the gift of all the gods that is to me most dear;
what can I say? — when I myself return all right,
and eagerly expect to satisfy my sight,
my only welcome is a trembling everywhere: 55
all fly, and all refuse the greetings that I bear.
And I, filled with the fear my coming here has
    brought,
wish I were still kept in the cave where I was caught.
Speak to me. Phèdre has said that I have been
    disgraced.
Who betrayed me? — Why has the traitor not   60
    been traced?
Would Greece, whom I have saved and served
    with my brave toil,
protect the guilty one on her own sacred soil?
But you do not reply. Then could my own son be
collaborating with his father's enemy?

---

26 Épire … tyrant's wife] In place of the myth of Pirithoüs
    and Theseus's trip to the underworld (which included
    a confrontation with Cerberus, the three-headed guard
    dog), Plutarch reports a rationalized version of the story
    in which Theseus accompanied his friend "to Epirus, in
order to steal away the king of the Molossians' daughter. The king, his own name being Aidoneus, or Pluto,
called his wife Proserpina, and his daughter Cora, and
a great dog, which he kept, Cerberus, with whom he
ordered all that came as suitors to his daughter to fight,
and promised her to him that should overcome the
beast. But having been informed that the design of
Pirithoüs and his companion was not to court his
daughter, but to force her away, he caused them both
to be seized, and threw Pirithoüs to be torn in pieces
by his dog, and put Theseus into prison, and kept him"
(trans. John Dryden).

My mind is overwhelmed with doubt: I must find 65
out
the criminal and what the crime is all about.
So Phèdre will have to say what has been
troubling her.

SCENE SIX

Hippolyte, Théramène

HIPPOLYTE. Why does my blood run dry and make
my senses blur?
Is Phèdre now giving in to all her inner strife?
Will she accuse herself and lose her right to life?
Gods! — what will the King say? — What fatal
hate has love
spread over all our heads, that we are dying of? 5
And I, fed by a fire which he cannot allow, —
think how he saw me once, and how he sees me now!
Forebodings fill the air and terrify me here.
But then, the innocent should have no cause to
fear.
So let us go, and find some way to state my case 10
and make my father say that I am in his grace,
because although he may despise this love today,
no power in the world can make it go away.

END OF ACT THREE

ACT FOUR

SCENE ONE

Theseus, Oenone

THESEUS. How can I hear these things? What
traitor could betray
his father's famous name in this disgraceful way?
The pain of my great fate keeps on pursuing me!
I don't know where I am or where I ought to be.
O all my tenderness so callously paid back! 5
The bald audacity of such a bad attack!
In order to achieve his evil intercourse,
this proud insolent Prince resorted to cruel force.
That was his weapon there, I recognized his sword:
he swore brave deeds the day I gave it to this Lord. 10
Didn't our common blood give him the least
restraint?

And why did Phèdre delay in voicing her complaint?
Or did her silence try to hide the guilty one?
OENONE. Her silence tried to hide that you had
been undone.
Ashamed that she should be the cause of all his sighs 15
and of the lawless fire that kindles in his eyes,
Phèdre would have lied, my Lord, and killed
herself outright,
so closing both her eyes, extinguishing the light.
I saw her raise her arm, and I ran to her side;
I made her save her life for love of your high pride. 20
Now pitying your shock and her disturbing fears,
I have, despite my vows, interpreted her tears.
THESEUS. Dishonesty! — I see why he became so pale,
and when we met again his feelings had to fail.
I was astonished at his lack of happiness; 25
his cold embraces stole and froze my tenderness.
But how long has his love so hideously grown?
When he was in Athens was it already known?
OENONE. My Lord, remember how the Queen
complained to you.
It was this shameful love, which she already knew. 30
THESEUS. This love began again once back here in
Trézène?
OENONE. I've told you everything, my Lord, that
happened then.
But I have left the Queen alone in her distress;
let me go now and see to her uneasiness.

SCENE TWO

Theseus, Hippolyte

THESEUS. Ah, here he is. Good god! Seeing his
noble air,
what naive eye would not make the same error there?
Why must the forehead of profane adultery
shine with the sacred grace of virtue's simile?
Are there no secret signs, is there no special art 5
to know, with no mistake, a false dishonest heart?
HIPPOLYTE. Now let me ask of you what hideous
disgrace,
my Lord, is on your mind and showing in your face?
Will you not dare to speak this great shame to my
ear?
THESEUS. Traitor and slave! — how dare you stand 10
before me here?

Sky's brightest lightning bolt should throw you to
    the void,
almost the last outlaw of those I have destroyed!
After this ugly lust had come into your head
and led you to defame your father's wedding bed,
you still present yourself, and show your hated face,   15
and so parade your shame throughout this fatal place,
and do not go away, under some foreign sun,
where my own name may be unknown to everyone.
Fly, traitor! — do not try to brave my hatred now,
so go, while my great rage is kept inside somehow.   20
It is enough for me to bear my own despair
for having brought you forth into the living air,
without your death as well dishonouring my name
and spoiling endlessly the splendour of my fame.
Fly; if you do not wish a swift and fatal blow   25
to add you to the beasts that I myself brought low,
make sure that that bright sun which shines up in
    the sky
will never see you breathe beneath its flaming eye.
Fly, I say, forever; now never come back here,
do not let your foul face infect our atmosphere.   30
And you, Neptune, yes, you: if I was ever brave,
if I have ever raged against the slaves that rave,
remember my reward, your promise to obey
whatever I would ask, whatever I would pray.[27]
In the cruel agonies of a crude prison cell,   35
I did not cry for help to free me from that hell.
I held myself in check, I waited in my greed,
until some later day saw some much greater need.
But I implore you now. Revenge a father's heart.
I leave this traitor's life for you to tear apart;   40
stifle his filthy vice in his own blood and lust:
I will worship your worth if you do what you must.
HIPPOLYTE. So Phèdre says Hippolyte is guilty of
    such shame!
Such excellent excess of horror shakes my frame;
so many sudden blows must overthrow me now,   45
they take away my voice and make me dumb
    somehow.
THESEUS. Traitor, you may have thought that by
    your keeping still

poor Phèdre would try to hide your insults and ill
    will?
You made one great mistake, just now when you
    withdrew,
to take away the sword which now accuses you;   50
or rather, you forgot to make your deed complete,
and take away her life to cover your retreat.
HIPPOLYTE. Now irritated by so foul and black a lie,
I feel I should reveal the truth in my reply,
my Lord, yet I suppress something which touches   55
    you.
You should approve my tact, my duty to subdue;
without the slightest wish of stirring up more strife,
remember who I am, and look through my whole
    life.
Always, some minor sins precede great major crimes.
Whoever breaks the law at first for a few times,   60
will finally go on to break all sacred rights;
for crime has its degrees, it has its depths and heights;
thus one has never seen timidity grow strong
and leap to the extreme of evil and vile wrong.
More than a single day is needed to create   65
a monster capable of incest, sin and hate.
Brought up in the chaste gaze of a great heroine,
I never scorned the pride of my own origin.
Old Pittheus, esteemed by all men everywhere,
agreed to teach me when I left my mother's care.   70
I do not seek to see myself in some great light,
but if I have revealed my worth, however slight,
my Lord, above all things I think I have made clear
my hatred for those crimes I am accused of here.
And Hippolyte is known for this in all of Greece.   75
My virtue hurts, and yet I work for its increase.
All know I suffer from so strict and harsh an art.
The light of day is not so pure as my own heart.
Yet they say Hippolyte, obsessed with a strange
    flame …
THESEUS. This is the same high pride that damns   80
    you to your shame.
I see what evil hides behind your cold disguise:
for only Phèdre alone could charm your brazen eyes;
and for all other loves your sly and lifeless soul
would never once catch fire, but kept its self-
    control.
HIPPOLYTE. No, my father, this heart — it's too   85
    much too conceal —

---

27 Neptune … pray] Neptune (or Poseidon), who was ru-
    moured to be the real father of Theseus, had granted
    Theseus three wishes to use at any time.

has not refused a love for someone chaste and real.
Here at your feet I make my great apology:
I love; I love, it's true, what you forbid to me.
For I love Aricie: it is already done;
the daughter of Pallas has overcome your son.   90
I worship her, and I, defying all your laws,
am lost in my own sighs, of which she is the cause.
THESEUS. You love her? God! But no, this trick is to
    distract:
act like a criminal to cover up your act.
HIPPOLYTE. My Lord, for six long months, I fought   95
    this love for her.
I came here trembling now to tell you this news, sir.
But how? Can anything erase this great mistake?
Could any oath I take persuade you for my sake?
"By this earth, by this sky, by nature all in all …"
THESEUS. Always, false hypocrites perjure their own   100
    downfall.
No, do not bore me now with more of your fine lies,
if your dishonesty can find no new disguise.
HIPPOLYTE. You think all this is false and full of
    subtlety.
But Phèdre in her own heart is much more fair to me.
THESEUS. Ah! how your impudence makes me   105
    more angry now!
HIPPOLYTE. Where will I be exiled, and how long is
    your vow?
THESEUS. Far beyond the Pillars of Hercules would
    be[28]
not far enough, and much too near the heart of me.
HIPPOLYTE. Charged with this awful crime, this
    foul atrocity,
what friends will pity me, when you abandon me?   110
THESEUS. Go and invent new friends, whose own
    dishonesty
congratulates incest, applauds adultery —
outlaws without conscience, traitors who know no
    law,
able to care for you and share your brazen flaw.
HIPPOLYTE. You keep on speaking of incest, adultery?   115
I do not speak. But Phèdre comes from her family —

---

28 Pillars of Hercules] i.e., the Rock of Gibraltar and
    Mount Hacho, on either side of the Strait of Gibraltar,
    which separates the Mediterranean Sea from the Atlan-
    tic Ocean.

her mother's blood, my Lord, you know it very well,
is worse than mine, and filled with all the filth of
    hell.
THESEUS. What? — have you lost all sense, that
    you rage to my face?
For the last time, get out, get away from this place: 120
go, traitor, do not wait for your own father's hand
to drive you forcefully before you leave this land.

SCENE THREE

Theseus, alone

THESEUS. Wretched, you are running to your own
    ruin now.
Neptune, god of that sea which all gods fear
    somehow,
has given me his word and he will make it good.
You cannot flee a god, let that be understood.
I loved you; and I sense, in spite of your great crime,   5
the pain you must endure in such a little time.
But you condemned yourself, and now the deed is
    done.
Has any father been so outraged by a son?
O gods, who see the grief which overwhelms me
    here,
how could I ever cause this monster to appear?   10

SCENE FOUR

Phèdre, Theseus

PHÈDRE. My Lord, I come to you, filled with a
    ghastly fear.
I heard your strong loud voice as you were
    speaking here.
I am afraid your threats have ended in something.
If there is still some time, then spare your own
    offspring;
respect your flesh and blood, I dare to beg of you.   5
I cannot hear the cries of what you plan to do;
do not condemn me to this future misery,
that your own hand has killed one of your family.
THESEUS. Madam, there is no blood at all on my
    own hand.
And yet the criminal shall not flee from this land.   10
For an immortal hand is raised in rage right now.
So you will be revenged, Neptune has made the vow.

PHÈDRE. Neptune has made the vow! What? — just
    one angry word ...
THESEUS. What? — now are you afraid that that
    will not be heard?
    Instead, join with me now in prayers of   15
    righteousness.
    Recite his crimes to me in all their foul excess;
    arouse my wrath which is too slow and too
    restrained.
    All of his evil deeds have not yet been explained:
    your world is furious with insults in his eyes:
    your mouth, he says, is full of foul deceits and lies;   20
    he swears that Aricie has all his heart and soul,
    that he loves her.
PHÈDRE.   What's that?
THESEUS.   He spoke with self-control.
    But I know how to scorn this artificial trick.
    May Neptune's justice come, and be most cruel
    and quick.
    Now I myself will go to worship at his shrine,   25
    and urge him to perform that oath that was
    divine.

SCENE FIVE

Phèdre, alone

PHÈDRE. He's gone. What news is this which has
    just struck my ear?
    Now what slow smouldering begins within me here?
    O sky, what thunderbolt! what words that shock
    and stun!
    I came here willingly to save his noble son;
    breaking away, I left Oenone's own frightened arms,   5
    and gave myself to all these torments and alarms.
    What if I were found out, and driven to repent?
    I might have just confessed, admitting my intent;
    if he had not gone on to interrupt my speech,
    I might have let the truth go flying out of reach.   10
    For Hippolyte can feel, and does not feel for me!
    His heart to Aricie! — his soul to Aricie!
    Ah gods! — to my own love this Lord was so unkind,
    with his derisive eye, and his high pride of mind,
    that I imagined he, with such a hardened heart,   15
    would have to hate my sex and be set far apart.
    But now another has attained this famous place;
    in his great scornful gaze another has found grace.

Perhaps he has a heart which some can tempt and
    lure.
I am the only one that he cannot endure;   20
    so why should I defend what he has been about?

SCENE SIX

Phèdre, Oenone

PHÈDRE. Dear Oenone, do you know what I have
    just found out?
OENONE. No, but I tremble now, I must make you
    believe
    I fear for this mad plan which made you try to leave:
    for I distrust the path your fatal passions choose.
PHÈDRE. I have a rival now: this is my bitter news.   5
OENONE. How?
PHÈDRE.   Hippolyte's in love, consumed by a
    great flame.
    That same cold enemy whom no one else could
    tame,
    who praised his own chaste days, and hated
    others' praise —
    this tiger, how I stayed in fear of his wild ways,
    and now he has been tamed he knows a stronger soul,   10
    for Aricie now keeps his heart in her control.
OENONE. Aricie?
PHÈDRE.   Ah, despair which is still unimproved!
    Which way is my own heart still waiting to be
    moved?
    All that I have suffered, my passions and my fears,
    the fury of my love, the horror of my tears,   15
    and the cruel injury of having been refused,
    were all a warning that I would be more abused.
    They are in love! but how? right here before my face?
    how did they meet? and when? and in what secret
    place?
    You knew of it. But then, why didn't you tell me?   20
    Why didn't you describe this dear conspiracy?
    How often have they talked and walked together
    now?
    Far in the forest, did they hope to hide somehow?
    Alas! once they met there, they were completely free.
    There the wide open sky smiled on their ecstasy;   25
    they did whatever they themselves desired to do;
    and each new day was clear and splendid in their
    view.

While I, the sad outcast of everything in sight,
I tried to hide by day and fly from the bright light:
death is the only god I dared to glorify.   30
I waited for the day I could lie down and die:
filled with this bitterness, alone in my despair,
still in my illness watched by all eyes everywhere,
I could not find the time to cry as I desired;
that was a fatal joy I privately acquired;   35
the peaceful features which I wore as my disguise
required that I hide the tears of my own eyes.

OENONE. What true fruit did they taste from their
    vain endeavour?
For they will have to part.

PHÈDRE.   They will love forever.
And right now, as I speak — ah! what a deadly   40
    thought! —
they brave the rage of one who raves and is
    distraught.
Despite the long exile which takes them far apart,
they swear they will remain within each other's heart.
No, no, Oenone, no no, I cannot bear their joy;
take pity on my hate which hastens to destroy.   45
This Aricie must die. My husband must revive
his wrath against that race he said must not survive.
And he must not lay down a few light penalties:
this sister has surpassed her brother's blasphemies.
My jealousy will speak and seek ways to cajole.   50
What am I doing now? have I lost all control?
I, jealous! and Theseus becomes the one I seek!
My husband is alive, and love still makes me weak!
For whom? and for whose heart are all my prayers
    addressed?
Each word I say creates new chaos in my breast.   55
Now all my hopes fly off beyond all scope of crime.
Incest and fraud exist in me at the same time.
My own cold reckless hands, restless for violence,
are burning to disturb the breath of innocence.
Wretched! and still I live? I am still in the sight 60
of that great sacred sun which bore me in its light?
My father is the first of all the gods on high;
and my own ancestors still populate the sky.
Where can I hide? far down in the foul dark of hell.
But how? for even there my father casts a spell;   65
he holds the fatal urn the gods put in his hand:
Minos dooms all who fall to that last ghastly land.
Ah, just imagine how his spirit will despair

when his own daughter comes into his presence
    there,
confessing all her crimes, with shame in every word,   70
and sins the underworld perhaps has never heard!
Father, what will you say when I have said it all?
I know, your hand will drop, the fatal urn will fall;
then you shall have to choose what torment you
    prefer,
so you yourself can be my executioner.   75
Forgive me: a cruel god has damned this family;
and he still takes revenge in my anxiety.
Alas! and my sad heart has never known the taste
of this forbidden love for which I am disgraced.
Pursued by suffering until my dying breath,   80
I leave a painful life as I fly towards my death.

OENONE. Ah, Madam, do reject this insubstantial
    fear.
Do take another look at what has happened here.
You love. And yet we know one cannot conquer fate.
The gods themselves led you into this hateful state.   85
But then are you so sure your story is unique?
Others, equally strong, have grown equally weak.
For flesh is flesh, and frail — unfortunate but true.
Since you are human, you must do what humans do.
Your woe is a great weight imposed so long ago.   90
For the Olympians, the greatest gods we know,
who with a dreadful curse condemn all kinds of
    crime,
have had their own desires and sinned from time
    to time.

PHÈDRE. What do I hear? what words of wisdom do
    you give?
You still will poison me for as long as I live,   95
you wretch! remember that you ruined me this way;
for it was you that made me face the light of day.
Your prayers made me forget the duty that I knew;
I fled from Hippolyte; you forced him in my view.
By what right did your words, which were so full   100
    of shame,
accuse his blameless life and darken his good name?
Perhaps he will be killed, perhaps his father's vow
to strike him down is done and he is dead right now.
I will not hear your words. Get out, you worthless
    beast!
Leave me my last few days and my own fate at least.   105
Let heaven pay you back for all that you have done!

And may your punishment petrify everyone —
all who, like you, may dare to use deceitful speech,
feeding the weakness of each Prince within their
    reach,
luring their hearts to go which way they are inclined,   110
and daring them to do the crimes in their own mind!
O fatal flatterers, the most destructive things
which heaven in its rage inflicts on sinful Kings!

OENONE. (*Alone.*) Ah gods look down on me, my
    faith begins to fade.
So this is what I get. I have been well repaid.   115

END OF ACT FOUR

ACT FIVE

SCENE ONE

Hippolyte, Aricie (Ismène)

ARICIE. Now you are unsafe — Speak out, for your
    own sake!
You leave your father here to make the same mistake?
You are too cruel if you turn from my tears of pain
and easily agree not to see me again;
yet if you go away and leave your Aricie,   5
at least you should assure your own security:
you must defend your name against this shame
    right now,
and force your father to take back his solemn vow —
for there is still some time. Why, and by what caprice,
does your accuser keep her freedom in such peace?   10
You should tell Theseus all.

HIPPOLYTE.   Now what have I not said?
And how could I reveal the shame of his own bed?
Should I describe the truth in all sincerity
and watch my father blush at the indignity?
My heart has only told the gods above and you.   15
For I loved you that much — from you I could
    not hide
what I myself despised and tried to keep inside.
But see the secrecy with which my words are sealed:
forget now, if you can, the things I have revealed,
Madam, because I pray your lips which are so fair   20
may never once repeat this tale of foul despair.
The gods are rational and they deserve our trust;
now for their own sake they shall save me and be just:

unable to escape her punishment in time,
soon Phèdre will pay at last for her most shameful   25
    crime.
Your silence is the thing I ask for, at this stage.
And for all else, I give a free rein to my rage:
fly from this hateful state where you have been a
    slave;
accompany my flight, come with me and be
    brave;
now tear yourself away and leave this fatal place   30
where virtue has to breathe the great stench of
    disgrace;
your hope lies in disguise — to hide your swift
    retreat,
use the confusion which is caused by my defeat.
I can assure you of the safest means of flight:
the guards here are all mine, the only men in sight;   35
now we will take our cause to powerful allies —
Argos holds out its arms, Sparta will sympathize:
we can count on these friends to hear our just appeal;
for Phèdre must not succeed, keeping what she
    can steal,
for she will seize the throne, and once that prize is   40
    won,
she will give everything we have to her own son.
This is our perfect chance, and now we must not
    wait …
But what fear holds you back? you seem to hesitate!
It's only your own cause that moves me to be bold:
when I am all on fire, why do you seem so cold?   45
Does my own banishment fill you so full of fear?

ARICIE. Such a sweet banishment would be to me
    most dear!
What happiness to be tied to your destiny,
forgotten by the rest of sad humanity!
But not united now by any tie so sweet,   50
how could I try to leave this place without deceit?
I know that I can go against all stern commands
and free myself right now out of your father's hands:
this place is not the home of my own family;
and flight is right for those who flee from tyranny.   55
But you love me, my Lord; and there is my good
    name …

HIPPOLYTE. No, you are in my care and you shall
    know no shame.
I have a nobler plan for you and for your life:

fly from your enemies, and join me as my wife.
We shall be free in grief, and under the same sun,   60
our loving vows shall not depend on anyone.
A marriage does not need bright torchlight and
   loud sound.
In the ports of Trézène, in the tombs underground,
great ancient sepulchres of Princes of my race,
there is a temple there which is a sacred place.   65
There men would never dare to make their vows
   in vain:
for perjurers receive a penalty of pain;
and fearing to find there their own predestined
   death,
liars will never try to take that fatal breath.
There, if you believe me, we can declare our love   70
and swear it in the sight of the great gods above;
our witness will be He whom they all worship
   there;
and our father will be all good gods everywhere.
To the great sacred ones I will address our plea,
to chaste Diana, and to Juno's majesty,   75
and all the others there, they see my sweet love now,
and they will guarantee the conscience of my vow.
ARICIE. The King comes now: fly, Prince, you must
   leave right away.
No one must know my plans to go, so I shall stay.
But please leave me someone to show me what to do,   80
to guide my timid steps and lead my love to you.

SCENE TWO

Theseus, Aricie, Ismène

THESEUS. O gods, enlighten me and give me by
   your grace
   the living sight of truth I search for in this place!
ARICIE. Remember everything, Ismène; prepare for   3
   our flight.

SCENE THREE

Theseus, Aricie

THESEUS. You colour now, Madam, and you are
   seized with fright;
   now why did Hippolyte leave here so secretly?
ARICIE. My Lord, he came to say his last farewells to
   me.

THESEUS. Your eyes have overcome the high pride
   of his heart;
   and his first secret sighs are those you made him start.   5
ARICIE. My Lord, I cannot lie and hide the truth
   from you:
   nothing could make him take your hateful point
   of view;
   he never treated me like some lost criminal.
THESEUS. I know: he swore his love would be
   perpetual.
   But do not put your trust in his inconstant mind;   10
   for he swore other loves with vows of the same kind.
ARICIE. My Lord?
THESEUS.   You should have trained this Prince
   to be less vain:
   how could you bear to share his love without
   great pain?
ARICIE. How can you bear to say such evil of his
   ways,
   maligning this fair man and darkening his days?   15
   Have you so little wit to understand his heart?
   Or can you not keep crime and innocence apart?
   Must you see his virtue in some grotesque disguise,
   when it so brightly shines before all other eyes?
   You damn him to slander and scandal everywhere.   20
   Stop it: you should repent of your relentless prayer;
   O you should fear, my Lord, that heaven will fulfill
   its own great hate for you and execute your will.
   Its fatal rage may take away our prey sometimes.
   Sometimes its benefits repay us for our crimes.   25
THESEUS. No, now you cannot hide how he has
   been so lewd:
   your love has made you blind to his ingratitude.
   But I have witnesses who testified right here:
   and I myself have seen fierce tears which are sincere.
ARICIE. Take care, my Lord, take care: for your   30
   heroic hands
   have slain the numberless monsters of many lands;
   but all are not destroyed, because you did not seek
   one … But your son, my Lord, forbids me now to
   speak.
   Informed of the respect which he still holds for
   you,
   I would grieve him too much if I said what I knew.   35
   So I shall be discreet, and leave your presence now;
   if I stayed I might say more than I should somehow.

SCENE FOUR

Theseus, alone

THESEUS. What went on in her mind? what did her
    saying hide —
  begun, and then cut off, unable to confide?
  Were they to baffle me by their hypocrisy?
  Or do the two of them resort to torture me?
  And meanwhile I myself, despite my self-control,   5
  what is the voice I hear cry out in my own soul?
  A secret pity pleads and weeps in my heart's core.
  I must seek out Oenone and question her once more:
  I must find out the truth, my mind must be made
    clear.
  Now guards, go find Oenone alone, and bring her   10
    here.

SCENE FIVE

Theseus, Panope

PANOPE. My Lord, I do not know what the Queen
    means to do,
  but I fear for the state which she now suffers through.
  A fatal pale despair is painted on her face,
  already, the great dread of death has left its trace.
  Already, leaving her and flying shamefully,   5
  Oenone has thrown herself into the raging sea.
  Now no one knows what cruel madness made her
    obey;
  we only know the waves have taken her away.
THESEUS. What do I hear?
PANOPE.   Her death has not disturbed the Queen;
  the anguish of her soul is so grotesquely seen.   10
  Sometimes, as if to ease the torment of her fears,
  she holds her children close and bathes them with
    her tears;
  and then, rejecting them, renouncing tenderness,
  she pushes them away, far from her best caress;
  she walks as if she lived in some oblivion;   15
  and her distracted gaze does not know anyone;
  three times she tried to write; and then, changing
    her mind,
  three times she rose and tore the letter up unsigned.
  See her, my Lord, see her, and listen to her cry.
THESEUS. O gods! Oenone is dead, and Phèdre   20
    desires to die!

Recall my son, he must defend himself somehow;
  now let him speak to me, I want to hear him now.
  The fatal vow must wait, it cannot be begun,
  Neptune; I almost wish my prayer could be undone.
  Perhaps I have believed people I should not trust,   25
  I may have raged too soon and asked you to be just.
  Now into what despair am I led by that vow?

SCENE SIX

Theseus, Théramène

THESEUS. Théramène, is it you? And where is my
    son now?
  I trusted him to you in his most tender years.
  But now I see you weep: what is behind these tears?
  Where is my son?
THÉRAMÈNE.   Too late, this should have come
    before!
  Your suit is useless now: Hippolyte is no more.   5
THESEUS. O gods!
THÉRAMÈNE.   I saw him die, this loveliest of men,
  and this man had no guilt, my Lord, I say again.
THESEUS. My son is no more now! I would have
    been his friend,
  but the impatient gods have rushed him to his end!
  What blow has taken him? What great stroke of   10
    the fates?
THÉRAMÈNE. When he had left Trézène and gone
    beyond the gates,
  he drove his chariot; and with a solemn air,
  his silent grieving guards were all around him there;
  sadly he chose the road to Mycenae, and he
  relaxed the reins so that his horses all ran free;   15
  these handsome animals, which once were his
    own choice,
  and eager to obey the loud sound of his voice,
  now galloped with sad eye and raced with heavy
    head,
  as if responding to his own keen sense of dread.
  A frightful cry, which came from far along the shore, 20
  cut through the quiet sky with an ungodly roar;
  and from the earth itself there came a great loud
    shout
  which terrorized the air and echoed all about.
  Afraid in our stark hearts, our own life blood
    froze cold;

the horses heard and reared and could not be
    controlled.   25
Just then, erupting from the surface of the sea,
there rose a mound of foam which burst ferociously;
the wave approached, and broke, and vomited to
    sight,
amidst the waves of foam, a monster of great height.
Its large forehead was armed with long and   30
    pointed horns;
covered with yellow scales, the beast could be sea-
    born,
a fiery dragon, a wild and raging bull;
the hair along its back was twisted, thick and full;
its shrieking shook the shore and cut across the air.
The sky with horror saw the savage monster there;   35
the earth quaked, and the sight poisoned the
    atmosphere;
the same great wave of foam it came on, fled with
    fear.
Everyone flew, we knew that now no one was
    brave;
we sought the safety that a nearby temple gave.
But Hippolyte remained, true to his origin,   40
halted his horses there, took up his javelin,
threw at the monster's side, and with a perfect aim,
he tore a ghastly wound in its enormous frame.
The great beast leaped ahead and shrieked with
    rage and pain,
came where the horses were, fell to the earth again,   45
rolled over, roared, and showed its throat, began
    to choke,
and bathed the horses there with fire, blood and
    smoke.
Fear overwhelmed them then, none of the horses
    heard
their master shouting out his stern commanding
    word;
he pulled back on the reins, his strength was infinite,   50
but their mouths overflowed with blood around
    the bit.
Through all this violence they say that one could see
a god with a great whip beating them ruthlessly.
Spurred on by their own fear, they raced across
    the rocks;
the axle screeched and broke from such outrageous   55
    shocks:

the chariot flew off its few shattered remains;
but Hippolyte was caught all snarled up in the reins.
Forgive my sorrow now: for knowing what I know,
the sight of this will be a constant source of woe.
For I saw your own son, my Lord, I saw your son   60
dragged by his horses there wherever they would run.
He tried to call a halt, they bolted at the sound,
they ran until he was torn open on the ground.
The field could feel the pain, and our hearts were
    downcast,
and then the mad horse race began to slow at last: 65
and finally they stopped near the great ancient tomb
where all his ancestors are kept in the cool gloom.
I ran there breathlessly, and his guards followed me:
his blood had formed a trail which everyone
    could see;
the rocks were wet with it; there was red everywhere,   70
even the rough thorns bore his bloody shocks of hair.
I reached him, I cried out; and then, trying to rise,
the dying Hippolyte opened and closed his eyes:
"The sky," he said, "has seized a sinless life from me.
When I have died, dear friend, take care of Aricie.   75
If my own father should someday be told the truth,
and pities the sad fate of an insulted youth,
tell him, to please my blood and give my spirit
    peace,
that all these injuries to Aricie must cease;
let him give her …" And then, at last, the hero died,   80
leaving his poor torn form to lie there by my side:
a figure which the gods decided to despise,
which his own father now would never recognize.
THESEUS. My son! My only hope now taken far away!
    O gods! In your high pride you served me well today!   85
I know grief is the fate I must forever face!
THÉRAMÈNE. Then timid Aricie came up to that
    sad place:
she came, my Lord, because you made her try to fly;
she swore to be his wife by all the gods on high.
She came up close; she saw the grass was wet and   90
    bright:
she saw (and what a thing for a sweet lover's sight!)
without colour or form, how Hippolyte stretched
    out.
For a long time she stood, and she had a strong
    doubt;
not knowing her own love who lay there at her feet,

she looked around awhile and called for Hippolyte.   95
But satisfied at last this had to be her love,
she gazed up to the sky and blamed the gods above;
then cold and so alone, and losing all restraint,
she fell there at his feet, insensible and faint.
Ismène was close to her; and lost in tears, Ismène   100
made her come back to life, or back to grief again.
And I myself came here, hating the light of day,
to tell you everything he wanted me to say,
and finishing, my Lord, this last unpleasant task
which his fine dying heart had strength enough to   105
   ask.
But now I seem to see his deadly enemy.

SCENE SEVEN

Theseus, Phèdre, Théramène, Panope (Guards)

THESEUS. My son has lost his life: this is your victory!
   It is no wonder now I tried to see his side,
   deep in my heart I sensed a doubt I could not hide!
   But Madam, he is dead, so you should claim your
     prey;
   enjoy his having died, guilty or not, today: 5
   for I agree my eyes must be forever blind.
   He was a criminal, you proved it to my mind.
   His death gives me enough to occupy my grief,
   without more questions now, to test my disbelief,
   since it would do no good nor cause my son to live —   10
   a greater source of pain is all that it would give.
   Let me go far from here, and far away from you,
   perhaps the sight of death will vanish from my view.
   I choke with memory, and to escape this curse,
   I would exile myself from the whole universe.   15
   Everything rises up against me to complain;
   the fame of my own name increases my great pain:
   if I were less well known, I might hide easily.
   I hate all gifts the gods have ever given me;
   I shall regret their great murderous favours now   20
   and never weary them with any further vow.
   What they have given me, cannot at all repay
   for that which they have now chosen to take away.
PHÈDRE. No, Theseus, let me speak, for I cannot
   keep still;
   I must show you your son in his own guiltless will: 25

for he was innocent.
THESEUS.   Ah! unfortunate son!
   And it was on your word that this damned thing
     was done!
   O cruel! and do you think that I could now
     forgive ...
PHÈDRE. Moments are dear to me, so hear me while
   I live:
   I am the one in whom this passion had begun,   30
   by casting a foul eye on your respectful son.
   The gods lodged him in me until I was obsessed:
   detestable Oenone accomplished all the rest.
   She feared that Hippolyte, informed of my mad lust,
   would tell you of this love which gave him such   35
     disgust:
   and so this meddling wretch, seeing that I was weak,
   hurried to greet you here, and she began to speak.
   Escaping from my rage, she then began to flee
   and sought her judgment in the silence of the sea.
   The sword would have served me, and made me   40
     face my fate,
   but I felt the command of virtue was too great:
   I wanted to come here, to say what I have said,
   so then I could descend more slowly to the dead.
   Medea's poison now runs all along my veins,
   and I can feel it work, I understand these pains.   45
   Already, its cruel death is coming on my heart,
   I feel an unknown cold in every body part;
   already my dim eye no longer comprehends
   my noble husband whom my being here offends;
   and death, which takes away this great disgrace in   50
     me,
   gives back the light of day in all its purity.
PANOPE. She has just died, my Lord.
THESEUS.   If this catastrophe
   could only wipe away the fatal memory!
   I know my error now, and since it has been done,
   I must mingle my tears in the blood of my son!   55
   And I must go embrace his mangled body now,
   to expiate the shame of that great hateful vow.
   He has deserved his name, his honours will increase;
   and so that we are sure his soul will rest in peace,
   I shall, despite the guilt of her whole family,   60
   proclaim to all the world my daughter Aricie!

END OF THE PLAY

CHAPTER FOUR

The Enlightenment Stage

T he hundred or so years covered by this chapter span an unusually dynamic and inspiring period of European history, and one that begins and ends with important revolutions— the Glorious Revolution of 1688 in England, and the American and French Revolutions of 1776 and 1789. Whether bloodlessly, as in England, or otherwise, as in America, these revolutions introduced new models of parliamentary and constitutional democracy that gave rise to our distinctly modern conceptions of human freedom and dignity: the idea that nations are composed of responsible, equal citizens who can govern themselves. In his famous definition of the period, Immanuel Kant wrote that the Enlightenment sweeping Western civilization at this time represented a coming of age, an emergence out of childhood, an era in which individuals were developing the ability and demanding the right to think and act for themselves, independently of the infantilizing mind-control of popes and kings.

It was a coming of age that is confidently expressed by western classical music, nearly all of which was produced during the Enlightenment, otherwise known as the "long" eighteenth century.[1] In the works of Bach, Handel, and Haydn, to name only a few, we can hear the beauty and clarity of Enlightenment optimism, its rationality and fearlessness; in Mozart and Beethoven, its passionate belief in the liberty, fraternity and equality that became the watchwords of the French Revolution. The catastrophic outcome of this particular revolution, however, brought the Enlightenment to a screeching halt. The Reign of Terror into which the Revolution deteriorated horrified the western world with its lawless butchery, sending even once-liberal thinkers into a panicked flight from progressive ideas. After a brief era in which Europe seemed free at last of the fanatical religious slaughter—the wars, crusades, inquisitions, and burnings at the stake—that had bloodied it for centuries, all of Europe became a battleground once again in the Napoleonic Wars. The optimism with which the century began was shattered by its end, with governments and institutions returning in fear to the authoritarian, conservative, emotion-driven modes of government, religion, art and morals that were to prevail throughout the Victorian age. But while it lasted, the Enlightenment was a period of unprecedented free-thinking and social progress, of emancipations and humane liberalism—even of open atheism and neo-paganism.

As usual, theatre in this period reflected and even advanced these trends in social and political life. Although the theatre of each of the four nations represented in this chapter exhibits its own special characteristics, some generalizations can be made. Many of these derive from the overarching fact that the period began with aristocrats in the audience and monarchs upon the stage, but ended with middle-class theatre-goers and ordinary valets like Figaro as the heroes of the day. Reflecting

---

[1] The "long" eighteenth century refers to the period from the restoration of the English monarchy in 1660 to the defeat of Napoleon at the Battle of Leipzig in 1813.

this shift away from aristocratic habits and subjects, theatre gradually became an evening event: whereas afternoon performances had suited the idle habits of the nobility, theatres were catering more and more to professionals, merchants, and other working people, and adjusted their curtain times accordingly. Intermediary measures, like half-price admission after the third act, were adopted in London to please both the elite and the working groups; but the trend toward the latter was not a passing thing. By the end of the eighteenth century, when the streets of most major and even some minor European cities were brightly illuminated by street lamps after dark, theatre was providing a safe and viable evening's entertainment for all but the most destitute.

In London and Venice throughout this period, theatre was a commercial activity, with companies locked in aggressive, mutually sabotaging competition for a demonstrative and often riotously violent audience. In Paris by contrast, the competition for audiences was fought between the one and only state-licenced theatre for French drama, the Comédie Française, which rarely turned a profit, and the more or less illegal popular venues of the fairgrounds, which usually did (and which, after the French Revolution, were allowed to freely mushroom into a bustling theatre district known as the Boulevard). Germany, a late bloomer in continental theatre but quickly the most progressive in many respects, was not a unified country at this time nor did it possess a single capital city. As a result, German drama and theatre came of age in this period within a decentralized network of regional, state-supported, but otherwise autonomous theatres that even today remain the envy of the theatre-producing world. But one thing that can be said of theatre across Europe and England through the century is that, with a few exceptions, the focus gradually shifted away from an emphasis on poetry, word-scenery, and the audible qualities of performance, and toward its visible aspects. If the period begins with the erudite chattiness and verbal double entendres of Restoration comedy, it ends with the French Revolutionary melodrama of Pixerécourt (1773–1844), who built plays around mutes, children, and dogs, and frankly admitted that he created his special-effects-laden Boulevard melodramas for illiterates. Improved technologies of lighting (the Argand oil lamp and centrally controlled gas jets shortly thereafter) made this shift toward a visual style of storytelling possible, and themselves changed further the way that plays were written and performed—perhaps above all diminishing the actor's role from that of undisputed centre of the action to merely one scenic element among many. Whether in the dramatic theories of Diderot and Beaumarchais, or in the visually oriented stage practices of actor-managers and playwrights such as Garrick and Goethe, the trend throughout the period was toward a visually unified stage picture of realistic illusion.

European theatre's shift of focus from monarchs to the middle class, and from poetry to stage pictures, was in many places accompanied by a rejection of French culture and literary style. Having become the most powerful nation in Europe during the seventeenth century, France exported its language, values, cultural and consumer products to the point where, for most of Europe, French culture *was* culture. But France, an absolute monarchy and one of the most hierarchically rigid nations in Europe, championed a dramatic ideal that was correspondingly rule-bound and authoritarian. Consequently, much theatrical theory and practice in the eighteenth century is marked by debates about the legitimacy of French neoclassicism and the appropriateness of its adoption on other national stages. Related to this matter was the question of whether Shakespeare, despite the very low esteem in which he was held by adherents to French aesthetic doctrine, may not in the end have been a better model than Racine, especially for just-developing theatre nations like Germany. The Romanticism with which the century ends, exemplified by plays like Schiller's *The Robbers*, represented a victory for freewheeling English dramaturgy over the unity-enforcing neoclassicism of France, as well as the assertion of native subjects and styles over imported ones. Whereas Greece and Rome had provided the favoured serious subjects for playwrights during the neoclassical age, Romantic-era authors—who in the theatre were likely to be writers of melodrama—turned instead to stories taken from their own national histories, from medieval times, and from current, local news accounts of sensational crimes.

Although it was not until the nineteenth century that theatre became a truly mass-cultural phenomenon, it was in the eighteenth century that theatre, for the first time in the Christian era, ceased to be viewed as a marginal, disreputable activity. Despite valiant efforts made occasionally by monarchs and poets to defend it, acting had continued throughout the Renaissance to be regarded as a shady sort of court-sanctioned prostitution. In the eighteenth century, however, acting came to be seen as an art form, and a socially significant one at that, even as an agent of enlightenment. In England, female actors of the humblest origins were routinely buried in Westminster Abbey from 1730, and chosen as the child-producing consorts of kings, not to mention the legal wives of lords. In France, philosophers wrote about actors and acting with a degree of seriousness formerly reserved for theological or scientific subjects. And in Germany, at least one ruling emperor passed edicts of religious tolerance because of arguments made in its favour from the stage. The advent of periodical journalism and theatre criticism in this period, of countless magazines and newspapers and an entirely new profession, that of the professional writer, brought discussions of plays and players to a rapidly widening audience. The passing of compulsory school-attendance laws in some places in the first decades of the century increased the number of readers, and the age of the celebrity actor was born. In addition to perpetual gossip about actors' private lives, serious analyses of plays and playwrights in the journals gave theatre a high profile in mainstream life and a cultural dominance, even outside the capitals, that it had not enjoyed since ancient Athens.

As with most Enlightenment phenomena, these trends began in England. The Glorious Revolution represented among other things a victory for the business class, and commerce exploded thereafter. The establishment of a national bank, of insurance companies, of personal cheques and credit—all of these innovations stimulated private enterprise, and gave to the stock market an importance in commercial life that it has not lost anywhere since. Soon even servants were trading stock tips, borrowing, investing, speculating, and in some cases making fortunes. Money, as the ancient Greeks noted, is the great equalizer; commerce knows no pedigree, rank, or title, and a commercial England became a model for all Europe of a free and equal society. When Voltaire visited London in the 1720s, it was the stock exchange as well as the theatre that he singled out for praise: here were two places at least in the world where rich and poor, master and servant, Christian and Jew and Muslim all mingled freely and without prejudice, as one man's money is as good as another's in a free-trade system.

In 1695, the law that had required all writings in England to be submitted for pre-publication licencing was allowed to lapse. The above economic developments thus coincided with a brief period in which the English press was free of all censorship. The liberty was not to last; censorship soon returned. In fact, the Licencing Act of 1737 proved particularly repressive for theatre, in effect shutting down a thriving tradition of political satire, closing Henry Fielding's theatre among others, and sending this playwright to the milder genre of the novel (as well as many actors to America). But it was too late; such liberties established precedents for civilized life that inspired artists, intellectuals, lawmakers and statesmen across Europe. As they inspire even today: after the turn of the eighteenth century, England was not to know another period of free, uncensored speech for over 200 years.

London's Restoration and Georgian coffee-house culture also typifies an Enlightenment style of life that was to be emulated elsewhere. In place of the drunken tavern ruffianism of the Renaissance—the kind that killed Christopher Marlowe, and in which women participated only as barmaids or prostitutes—a lucid, witty tradition of coffee-house conversation flourished in the eighteenth century instead. In countless comfortable coffee houses, traders and brokers, actors and booksellers, playwrights and journalists and philosophers, all wired up to various pitches of eloquence by caffeine, discussed politics, plays, the stock market, and ideas of social reform. Out of such coffee-house criticism grew the great periodicals of the day. With the *de facto* leaders of England now ordinary men, rather than divinely protected kings and queens, public dissent and criticism was no longer a treasonous offence, but a legitimate part of the political process. What was said and written in public, whether in the coffee house, in a journal, or on the stage, took on a freedom not enjoyed since the days of Aristophanes. Although things were to change after the Licencing Act of 1737, a smash hit like John Gay's *The Beggar's Opera* (1728) shows the extent to which direct, *ad hominem* abuse of public officials had become a reality in the theatre once again after 2,000 years of politically innocuous sitcom. (In the case of *The Beggar's Opera,* the target was England's so-called first Prime Minister, Robert Walpole—as well as London's short-lived infatuation with Italian opera.)

English theatre began again in the Enlightenment after an eighteen-year hiatus, called the Commonwealth period, during which it was illegal to operate or visit a playhouse. In the wake of the Civil War of 1642, when Cromwell's anti-monarchical, anti-theatrical Puritans gained control of Parliament (and beheaded King Charles I), public theatres were burnt to the ground and acting companies disbanded or scattered to the continent. Some opera and other clandestine entertainment was privately offered during the period, but the lively commercial enterprise of Shakespeare and his followers came to an abrupt end for almost two decades, during which time the boy players grew beards and lost their girlish voices, the apprentices of London lost their theatre-going habits, and the nobility sought asylum in France and elsewhere. (Behn's *The Rover,* reproduced here, gives a good sense of what the exiled young king's loyal courtiers got up to during their years abroad.)

When the English monarchy was restored in 1660, theatre was also restored immediately, although not along the lines it had taken before, during the Elizabethan and Jacobean periods. In imitation of French practices, a theatrical monopoly was put in place, with two royal patents being awarded to King Charles II's friends Killigrew and Davenant, who were thus licenced to operate the only two legal companies in England: the King's, in honour of himself, and the Duke's, in honour of his brother. These royal patents changed hands many times throughout the following century, but continued to regulate the two "legitimate" houses in London, known by mid-century as Drury Lane and Covent Garden (the latter replacing the Restoration-era Lincoln's Inn Fields). In building their theatres, some in tennis courts as had been the custom in Paris, the English reached a compromise between continental and native traditions—the proscenium arch with all its sophisticated Italianate machinery on one hand, and the bare-board thrust stage of the Elizabethan public theatre on the other. The resulting indoor playing spaces featured simplified scene-shifting machinery, a proscenium arch with a number of permanent doors for actors' entrances and exits, and a large forestage, or apron, that extended beyond it into an audience that in effect surrounded the actors on three sides. (In addition to the spectators in side boxes, many dandies took seats on the stage itself, as had long been the custom in both England and France.) By the end of the eighteenth century, these London theatres, sacrificing their thrust stages in the process, were rebuilt to accommodate thousands of spectators each, who now peered from great distances into huge proscenium arches that dwarfed the performers and forced them to adopt ever bigger, less nuanced, more extravagant acting styles. But the early Restoration playhouses were intimate, with roughly 600 patrons all arrayed within remarkably close physical proximity to the actors: on backless benches in the pit, in spacious private and royal boxes, or in crowded galleries above (at first largely populated by seat-reserving, chamber-pot-holding servants of the nobles below).

With the addition of women to the acting profession shortly after the Restoration—partly in imitation of continental practices and partly to forestall Puritan objections to the homoeroticism of the Elizabethan boy-actress tradition—the London theatres took on an even more sexually charged atmosphere than they had had during Shakespeare's time. Sexual alliances between the performers and their atrociously behaved (and often drunk) noble customers became a conspicuous part of the pleasure of theatre-going in this period, at least for the audience, as plays such as *The Country Wife* make clear. In the witty rhyming prologues that accompanied all plays in this period, popular female actors often invited male patrons back to the green room after the show and assured them of a "kind"—that is, a sexually generous—reception.

And after the Puritan austerities of the eighteen-year Commonwealth period, the restored nobility of England indulged in such pleasures with a vengeance, aping many French habits to which they'd become accustomed while abroad. The greatest plays of this period, known as Restoration comedies or comedies of manners, show a strong influence of French theatre with its emphasis on sparkling verbal wit and adultery-related plots. After the Glorious Revolution, Whiggish politics, the rise of business interests and middle-class morality brought about a rapid decline of these aristocratic sex-and-adultery plays, as witnessed by Susannah Centlivre's *A Bold Stroke for a Wife*. Marriage remained a focus of English comedy, but the backlash against the unbridled licentiousness of Charles II's reign, on stage and off, nudged theatre toward sentimental, wholesome plays in which vice is punished and virtue rewarded.

Parisian theatre at the start of this period was marked by the banishment, in 1697, of the Italian comedy troupe that had been resident in one form or another in the capital since the earliest days of professional theatre in France. (Their play *The False Prude*, assumed to be an attack on Louis XIV's second wife, Mme. de Maintenon, seems to have been the culprit.) Before being allowed to reoccupy the Hôtel de Bourgogne in 1716 upon the king's death, these physical comedians took refuge in the Paris fairgrounds, helping its semi-permanent stages to develop into what would become Paris's biggest theatre district after the French Revolution, when state monopolies were (briefly) abolished. In some cases, however, the Italians turned to the fairgrounds of London, where their "night scenes," or mimed Harlequin shows, became very fashionable, inaugurating a 300-year mania in England for harlequinades, or pantomime—a spectacular form of musical entertainment, usually offered as an afterpiece, which in sheer economic terms remained the bread-and-butter of both London theatres throughout the eighteenth century. Meanwhile in Paris, the re-licenced *Théâtre Italien* gradually abandoned Italian-language improv for French literary drama, notably the romantic comedies of Marivaux (1688–1763) and the expatriate Goldoni (1707–1793). In tragedy, the neoclassical ideal as exemplified by Racine continued to reign supreme on the stage of the first self-consciously "national" theatre in Europe, the state-subsidized Comédie Française, which had been created in 1680 through the forced amalgamation of Molière's troupe and two others. Aside from the tragedies of Voltaire and the Beaumarchais comedy reproduced here, the Comédie Française of the 1700s premiered fewer great plays than it had in the previous century. Instead, the acknowledged masterpieces of Corneille, Racine, and Molière continued to ballast the repertory of Paris's sole "legitimate" theatre in the same way that the (radically edited and altered) plays of Shakespeare and his contemporaries continued to provide vehicles for the many stars of the eighteenth-century London stage.

Many German city-states in this period had close political and cultural ties with those in Italy. While there was a perceived need for reform in the theatrical traditions of both language groups, the situation in Germany was dire: there wasn't a single permanent theatre anywhere in Germany at the start of the eighteenth century. Instead, native touring troupes were eking out a miserable living with massive, ill-rehearsed repertories and an ever-present Elizabethan-style clown, known as Hanswurst or Pickelhering. Early reformers such as J.C. Gottsched (1700–1766) began to modernize the German stage by emulating French neoclassical tragedy. With practical on-the-ground support from Caroline Neuber's travelling troupe, this phase of reform brought the first glimmerings of respectability to the German stage, if no perceptible diminution of the public's apparently insatiable appetite for the improvised antics of Hanswurst. But great actors quickly emerged from these early literary efforts, as did a flowering of theatrical writing in comedy, middle-class tragedy, theory, and criticism. G.E. Lessing (1729–1781) produced superb works in all of these genres, as well as two of the Enlightenment's greatest dramatic pleas for religious tolerance, *The Jews* and *Nathan the Wise*. Lessing also deserves the title of father of German theatre for the regular dramaturgical writing he did for the Hamburg National Theatre, in which he championed English models over French, particularly the middle-class novels and plays of Richardson and Lillo. This was a time in Germany when writers and intellectuals had the ear of reform-minded emperors, and by the end of the century most German city-states had permanent theatres with resident companies of actors, each famous for its own house style. The latter part of the century in Germany was dominated by the plays of Goethe and Schiller (as well as by the populist melodramas of Kotzebue, whose assassination by a student radical in 1819 exemplifies the fervour of at least one strain of European Romanticism). Beginning with their early, Shakespeare-inspired *Sturm und Drang* works, *Götz von Berlichingen* and *The Robbers,* Goethe and Schiller emerged as dramatic poets of the first rank, giving the German stage many of its masterpieces. As co-artistic directors of the Weimar Court Theatre, they forged a style thereafter known as Weimar Classicism, noted for its polish and attention to historical accuracy in costume and literary form.

With Italian opera dominating all the opera houses of Europe, and Italian scenic designers having effectively cornered the continental market as well, theatrical reform in Italy concentrated rather on comedy, specifically *commedia dell'arte*. Beloved in Italy and especially in its hometown of Venice since the Renaissance, this improvised form of masked, slapstick comedy was seen as having grown stale over the centuries. Goldoni aimed to reform it with an infusion of realism, an elimination of improvisation and masks, and a shift to contemporary, middle-class subjects and characters. Gozzi, on the other hand, whose fairytale *Turandot* is reproduced here, advocated a return to the fantasy elements and aristocratic values of traditional Italian comedy. As for serious drama, with few exceptions and as befits its origins in Italy's Renaissance academies, opera remained the chief vehicle for tragic subjects in Italian theatre, a role it would retain throughout the following century, during which Verdi gave musical and highly nationalistic expression to the tragedies of Shakespeare and Schiller.

[J.W.]

APHRA BEHN

The Rover[1]

Edited and introduced by Anne Russell[2]

Almost nothing is known with certainty of Aphra Behn's (1640?–1689) early life. From 1671 until her death in 1689, Behn earned her living as a prolific playwright, translator, editor, poet, and novelist. Behn's plays remained a significant part of the theatrical repertoire of the English stage until the middle of the eighteenth century.

The Rover, or The Banished Cavaliers (1677) was one of Behn's most popular plays. Like many of her contemporaries, Behn adapted an earlier play, in this case Thomas Killigrew's *Thomaso, or The Wanderer.* In *The Rover*, Behn examines contemporary issues such as forced marriage and sexual double standards with particular focus on the perspectives of women characters. The complex plot, relying on disguise and mistaken identity, includes many parallels of character and situation. The virginal sisters Hellena and Florinda complain that their brother has arranged Florinda's marriage to an old man and Hellena's admission to a nunnery. In another plot, the courtesan Angellica Bianca argues that wives and prostitutes are treated similarly as commodities. Her thoughtful analysis points to a recurring plot motif—the male characters' difficulty in distinguishing a "maid of quality" from a "harlot."

The Rover is set during the Commonwealth, when Parliament under Oliver Cromwell ruled England and many of the supporters of the monarchy lived in exile; it was performed, however, after the restoration of the monarchy. The Rover of the title, the aptly named Willmore, is a rake and a libertine. He and other "banish'd Cavaliers" arrive in Naples during Carnival, eager to take advantage of the sexual opportunities allowed by the temporary freedom of masks and disguises. At one point Willmore and Angellica Bianca debate the relationship between love and money. Succumbing to Willmore's argument that love ought to be given rather than sold, she gives her love and her money to Willmore, who immediately shifts his attention to the pursuit of the witty Hellena, who is in carnival disguise.

Other characters include Willmore's friend Belvile, who is in love with Florinda. Blunt, a dim-witted comic butt for most of the play, is attracted to a prostitute he thinks to be a young wife;

---

1 The copytext is the first edition, a 1667 quarto (Q1), which exists in three issues. Although the title pages of the first two issues do not name the author, the "Prologue" of all three issues refers to the author as "he." The third issue, however, adds "written by Mrs. A. Behn" to the title page. In some copies of the second issue, and in the third issue, the author's "Postscript" is printed with the addition of the phrase "especially of our sex," an acknowledgment that the author is a woman. Other editions consulted include quartos from 1697 (Q2) and 1709 (Q3); collections of Behn's works published in 1702 (A) and 1724 (B); and modern editions of 1915 (Summers); 1967 (Link); 1995 (Spencer); and 1995 (Todd).

2 The text and annotations are based on Russell's edition as published in J. Douglas Canfield's *Broadview Anthology of Restoration and Early Eighteenth-Century Drama* (2001), with some additional notes of my own. [J.W.]

however, she and her pimp rob and humiliate him. Blunt's desire to take revenge by beating and raping other women endangers Florinda, and also moves the many plots towards closure.

As this brief summary suggests, there are many inconsistencies of tone in this comedy. The plot includes duels, robberies, and rape attempts; many characters make casual anti-Semitic and anti-Catholic slurs. Women characters complain about their subjection to male control, yet seem indulgently tolerant of the men who threaten them. Sexual double standards are criticized in the early parts of the play but deflected in the conclusion. The eloquent Angellica Bianca is silenced; Willmore, the proselytizer of free love, accepts marriage (which conveniently brings Hellena's fortune with it); and the attempted rapes by Willmore, Blunt, and others are instantly forgiven and forgotten.

Critics are divided on how to interpret the conventional round of marriages and forgiveness with which *The Rover* ends. Does the conclusion portray imperfect, but pragmatic, strategies needed for survival in a violent and ruthless society? Or do the final scenes endorse a return to the socio-economic order, socializing the great sexual energy of its lead character? Behn did not let the question settle. Willmore was such a popular character with audiences that Behn wrote a sequel in 1681. As it opens, Willmore offhandedly notes that Hellena has died and that he has spent her money. He then proceeds to pursue free love, just as he had done in *The Rover*.

APHRA BEHN

The Rover; or, The Banished Cavaliers[1]

DRAMATIS PERSONAE
[MEN]
   DON ANTONIO, the Viceroy's son.
   DON PEDRO, a noble Spaniard, his friend.
   BELVILE, an English colonel in love with
      Florinda.
   WILLMORE, the Rover.[2]
   FREDERICK, an English gentleman and friend to
      Belvile and Blunt.
   BLUNT, an English country gentleman.
   STEPHANO, servant to Don Pedro.
   PHILLIPPO, Lucetta's gallant.
   SANCHO, pimp to Lucetta.

BISKEY, AND SEBASTIAN, two bravoes[3] to
   Angellica.
OFFICERS AND SOLDIERS.
[DIEGO,] Page to Don Antonio.
BOY.
WOMEN.
   FLORINDA, sister to Don Pedro.
   HELLENA, a gay young woman designed for a
      nun, and sister to Florinda.
   VALERIA, a kinswoman to Florinda.
   ANGELLICA BIANCA, a famous courtesan.
   MORETTA, her woman.
   CALLIS, governess to Florinda and Hellena.
   LUCETTA, a jilting wench.
   SERVANTS, OTHER MASQUERADERS, MEN AND
      WOMEN.

---

1 *Cavaliers*] supporters of the English monarchy during the English Civil War; many cavaliers left England after the execution of King Charles I in 1649.

2 Rover] wanderer; also pirate.

3 bravoes] hired soldiers; bodyguards.

THE SCENE: NAPLES, IN CARNIVAL TIME.

ACT I, SCENE I. A CHAMBER.

Enter Florinda and Hellena.

FLORINDA. What an impertinent thing is a young
girl bred in a nunnery! How full of questions!
Prithee no more Hellena; I have told thee more
than thou understand'st already.

HELLENA. The more's my grief. I would fain know 5
as much as you, which makes me so inquisitive;
nor is't enough I know you're a lover, unless you
tell me too, who 'tis you sigh for.

FLORINDA. When you're a lover, I'll think you fit
for a secret of that nature. 10

HELLENA. 'Tis true, I never was a lover yet, but I
begin to have a shrewd guess what it is to be so
and fancy it very pretty to sigh, and sing, and
blush, and wish, and dream, and wish, and long
and wish to see the man, and when I do, look pale 15
and tremble; just as you did when my brother
brought home the fine English colonel to see you.
What do you call him, Don Belvile?

FLORINDA. Fie, Hellena.

HELLENA. That blush betrays you. I am sure 'tis 20
so—or is it Don Antonio the viceroy's son? or
perhaps the rich old Don Vincentio whom my
father designs you for a husband? Why do you
blush again?

FLORINDA. With indignation, and how near soever 25
my father thinks I am to marrying that hated
object, I shall let him see I understand better what's
due to my beauty, birth and fortune, and more to
my soul, than to obey those unjust commands.

HELLENA. Now hang me if I don't love thee for 30
that dear disobedience. I love mischief strangely,
as most of our sex do, who are come to love
nothing else. But tell me dear Florinda, don't you
love that fine *Anglese*?[4] For I vow, next to loving
him myself, 'twill please me most that you do so, 35
for he is so gay and so handsome.

FLORINDA. Hellena, a maid designed for a nun
ought not to be so curious in a discourse of love.

HELLENA. And dost thou think that ever I'll be a
nun? or at least till I'm so old, I'm fit for nothing 40
else? Faith no, sister. And that which makes me
long to know whether you love Belvile is because
I hope he has some mad companion or other that
will spoil my devotion. Nay, I'm resolved to
provide myself this carnival, if there be e'er a 45
handsome proper fellow of my humour above
ground, though I ask first.

FLORINDA. Prithee, be not so wild.

HELLENA. Now you have provided yourself of a
man, you take no care for poor me. Prithee, tell 50
me, what dost thou see about me that is unfit for
love? Have I not a world of youth? a humour gay?
a beauty passable? a vigour desirable? well shaped?
clean limbed? sweet breathed? and sense enough
to know how all these ought to be employed to 55
the best advantage? Yes, I do and will; therefore,
lay aside your hopes of my fortune by my being a
devote,[5] and tell me how you came acquainted
with this Belvile, for I perceive you knew him
before he came to Naples. 60

FLORINDA. Yes, I knew him at the siege of
Pamplona.[6] He was then a colonel of French horse,
who when the town was ransacked, nobly treated
my brother and myself, preserving us from all
insolences, and I must own (besides great 65
obligations) I have I know not what that pleads
kindly for him about my heart, and will suffer no
other to enter.—But see, my brother.

*Enter Don Pedro, Stephano with a masquing habit,[7]
and Callis.*

PEDRO. Good morrow, sister. Pray, when saw you
your lover Don Vincentio? 70

FLORINDA. I know not, sir. Callis, when was he here?
For I consider it so little, I know not when it was.

PEDRO. I have a command from my father here to
tell you, you ought not to despise him, a man of
so vast a fortune, and such a passion for you.— 75
Stephano, my things.

---

4 *Anglese*] Englishman (It.).

5 devote] a nun or religious person, devotee.

6 Pamplona] a fortified town in Navarre in the north of
Spain, disputed by France.

7 *masquing habit*] costume worn at carnival.

Puts on his masquing habit.

FLORINDA. A passion for me, 'tis more than e'er I saw, or he had a desire should be known. I hate Vincentio, sir, and I would not have a man so dear to me as my brother follow the ill customs of our country and make a slave of his sister. And sir, my father's will I'm sure you may divert. 80

PEDRO. I know not how dear I am to you, but I wish only to be ranked in your esteem equal with the English Colonel Belvile. Why do you frown and blush? Is there any guilt belongs to the name of that cavalier? 85

FLORINDA. I'll not deny I value Belvile. When I was exposed to such dangers as the licensed lust of common soldiers threatened, when rage and conquest flew through the city, then Belvile, this criminal for my sake, threw himself into all dangers to save my honour. And will you not allow him my esteem? 90

PEDRO. Yes, pay him what you will in honour, but you must consider Don Vincentio's fortune and the jointure he'll make you. 95

FLORINDA. Let him consider my youth, beauty and fortune, which ought not to be thrown away on his age and jointure. 100

PEDRO. 'Tis true, he's not so young and fine a gentleman as that Belvile, but what jewels will that cavalier present you with? those of his eyes and heart?

HELLENA. And are not those better than any Don Vincentio has brought from the Indies? 105

PEDRO. Why, how now! Has your nunnery breeding taught you to understand the value of hearts and eyes?

HELLENA. Better than to believe Vincentio's deserve value from any woman. He may perhaps increase her bags,[8] but not her family. 110

PEDRO. This is fine. Go—up to your devotion; you are not designed for the conversation of lovers.

HELLENA. (*Aside.*) Nor saints yet a while, I hope. Is't not enough you make a nun of me, but you must cast my sister away too, exposing her to a worse confinement than a religious life? 115

PEDRO. The girl's mad! It is a confinement to be carried into the country, to an ancient villa belonging to the family of the Vincentios these five hundred years, and have no other prospect than that pleasing one of seeing all her own that meets her eyes—a fine air, large fields and gardens, where she may walk and gather flowers. 120 125

HELLENA. When, by moonlight? For I am sure she dares not encounter with the heat of the sun; that were a task only for Don Vincentio and his Indian breeding,[9] who loves it in the dog days. And if these be her daily divertissements, what are those of the night, to lie in a wide moth-eaten bed chamber, with furniture in fashion in the reign of King Sancho the First;[10] the bed, that which his forefathers lived and died in. 130

PEDRO. Very well. 135

HELLENA. This apartment (new furbished and fitted out for the young wife) he (out of freedom) makes his dressing room, and being a frugal and jealous coxcomb, instead of a valet to uncase his feeble carcass, he desires you to do that office— signs of favour I'll assure you, and such as you must not hope for, unless your woman be out of the way. 140

PEDRO. Have you done yet?

HELLENA. That honour being past, the giant stretches itself, yawns and sighs a belch or two, loud as a musket, throws himself into bed, and expects you in his foul sheets, and ere you can get yourself undressed, calls you with a snore or two. And are not these fine blessings to a young lady? 145 150

PEDRO. Have you done yet?

HELLENA. And this man you must kiss, nay you must kiss none but him, too, and nuzzle through his beard to find his lips. And this you must submit to for threescore years, and all for a jointure. 155

PEDRO. For all your character[isation] of Don Vincentio, she is as like to marry him as she was before.

HELLENA. Marry Don Vincentio! Hang me, such 160

---

8 bags] wealth.

9 Indian breeding] Presumably Don Vincentio was raised in the Indies.

10 King Sancho the First] a king from long ago.

a wedlock would be worse than adultery with another man. I had rather see her in the Hotel de Dieu,[11] to waste her youth there in vows and be a handmaid to lazars[12] and cripples, than to lose it in such a marriage. 165

PEDRO. You have considered, sister, that Belvile has no fortune to bring you to—banished his country, despised at home, and pitied abroad.

HELLENA. What then? The viceroy's son is better than that old Sir Fifty. Don Vincentio! Don 170 Indian! He thinks he's trading to Gambo[13] still and would barter himself (that bell and bauble[14]) for your youth and fortune.

PEDRO. Callis, take her hence, and lock her up all this Carnival, and at Lent she shall begin her 175 everlasting penance in a monastery.

HELLENA. I care not; I had rather be a nun than be obliged to marry as you would have me, if I were designed for't.

PEDRO. Do not fear the blessing of that choice. You 180 shall be a nun.

HELLENA. Shall I so? You may chance to be mistaken in my way of devotion. A nun! Yes, I am like to make a fine nun! I have an excellent humour for a grate.[15] (Aside.) No, I'll have a saint 185 of my own to pray to shortly, if I like any that dares venture on me.

PEDRO. Callis, make it your business to watch this wild cat. As for you, Florinda, I've only tried you all this while and urged my father's will; but mine 190 is that you would love Antonio. He is brave and young, and all that can complete the happiness of a gallant maid. This absence of my father will give us opportunity to free you from Vincentio by marrying here, which you must do tomorrow. 195

FLORINDA. Tomorrow!

---

11 Hotel de Dieu] hospital run by nuns for the care of the destitute and outcast.
12 lazars] diseased persons, esp. lepers. From Lazarus, Luke 16:20.
13 Gambo] Gambia, on the Slave Coast of Africa.
14 bell and bauble] trifles, but also the signs of a professional fool.
15 grate] bars in the door of a convent, marking the separation of the nun from the world.

PEDRO. Tomorrow, or 'twill be too late. 'Tis not my friendship to Antonio which makes me urge this, but love to thee and hatred to Vincentio. Therefore, resolve upon tomorrow. 200

FLORINDA. Sir, I shall strive to do as shall become your sister.

PEDRO. I'll both believe and trust you. Adieu.

Exeunt Pedro and Stephano.

HELLENA. As becomes his sister! That is to be as resolved your way, as he is his—(*Hellena goes to* 205 *Callis.*)

FLORINDA. I ne'er till now perceived my ruin near. I've no defence against Antonio's love, For he has all the advantages of nature, The moving arguments of youth and fortune. 210

HELLENA. But hark you, Callis, you will not be so cruel to lock me up indeed, will you?

CALLIS. I must obey the commands I have. Besides, do you consider what a life you are going to lead?

HELLENA. Yes, Callis, that of a nun; and till then 215 I'll be indebted a world of prayers to you if you'll let me now see what I never did, the divertissements of a carnival.

CALLIS. What, go in masquerade? 'Twill be a fine farewell to the world, I take it. Pray, what would 220 you do there?

HELLENA. That which all the world does, as I am told: be as mad as the rest and take all innocent freedoms. Sister, you'll go too, will you not? Come, prithee be not sad. We'll outwit twenty brothers 225 if you'll be ruled by me. Come, put off this dull humour with your clothes and assume one as gay and as fantastic, as the dress my cousin Valeria and I have provided, and let's ramble.

FLORINDA. Callis, will you give us leave to go? 230

CALLIS. (*Aside.*) I have a youthful itch of going myself.—Madam, if I thought your brother might not know it, and I might wait on you; for by my troth I'll not trust young girls alone.

FLORINDA. Thou seest my brother's gone already, 235 and thou shalt attend and watch us.

Enter Stephano.

STEPHANO. Madam, the habits are come, and your cousin Valeria is dressed and stays for you.

FLORINDA. 'Tis well. I'll write a note, and if I chance to see Belvile and want an opportunity to speak to him, that shall let him know what I've resolved in favour of him. 240

HELLENA. Come, let's in and dress us.

Exeunt.

SCENE II. A LONG STREET.

Enter Belvile melancholy, Blunt and Frederick.

FREDERICK. Why, what the devil ails the colonel? In a time when all the world is gay, to look like mere Lent thus? Had'st thou been long enough in Naples to have been in love, I should have sworn some such judgment had befallen thee. 5

BELVILE. No, I have made no new amours since I came to Naples.

FREDERICK. You have left none behind you in Paris?

BELVILE. Neither. 10

FREDERICK. I cannot divine the cause, then, unless the old cause, the want of money.

BLUNT. And another old cause, the want of a wench. Would not that revive you?

BELVILE. You are mistaken, Ned. 15

BLUNT. Nay, 'sheartlikins,[16] then thou'rt past cure.

FREDERICK. I have found it out; thou hast renewed thy acquaintance with the lady that cost thee so many sighs at the siege of Pamplona—pox on't, what d'ye call her—her brother's a noble Spaniard—nephew to the dead general— Florinda—ay Florinda—and will nothing serve thy turn but that damned virtuous woman? whom on my conscience thou lovest in spite too, because thou seest little or no possibility of gaining her. 25

BELVILE. Thou art mistaken. I have int'rest enough in that lovely virgin's heart to make me proud and vain, were it not abated by the severity of a brother, who perceiving my happiness—

FREDERICK. Has civilly forbid thee the house? 30

BELVILE. 'Tis so; to make way for a powerful rival, the viceroy's son, who has the advantage of me in being a man of fortune, a Spaniard, and her brother's friend; which gives him liberty to make his court, whilst I have recourse only to letters and distant looks from her window, which are as soft and kind as those which Heaven sends down on penitents. 35

BLUNT. Heyday! 'Sheartlikins, simile! By this light, the man is quite spoiled. Fred, what the devil are we made of that we cannot be thus concerned for a wench? 'Sheartlikins, our cupids are like the cooks of the camp, they can roast or boil a woman, but they have none of the fine tricks to set 'em off, no hogoes[17] to make the sauce pleasant and the stomach sharp. 40 45

FREDERICK. I dare swear I have had a hundred as young, kind and handsome as this Florinda, and dogs eat me, if they were not as troublesome to me i'the morning as they were welcome o'er night. 50

BLUNT. And yet I warrant he would not touch another woman if he might have her for nothing.

BELVILE. That's thy joy, a cheap whore.

BLUNT. Why, ay, 'sheartlikins, I love a frank soul. When did you ever hear of an honest woman that took a man's money? I warrant 'em good ones. But gentlemen, you may be free, you have been kept so poor with Parliaments and Protectors,[18] that the little stock you have is not worth preserving. But I thank my stars, I had more grace than to forfeit my estate by cavaliering.[19] 55 60

BELVILE. Methinks only following the Court[20] should be sufficient to entitle 'em to that.

BLUNT. 'Sheartlikins, they know I follow it to do it no good, unless they pick a hole in my coat for lending you money now and then, which is a 65

---

16 'sheartlikins] God's little heart, a "minced oath" combining "God's heart" and "bodikin."

17 hogoes] from the Fr., *haut goût,* or "high flavour."

18 Protectors] During the period of Parliamentary rule, Oliver Cromwell used the title of Protector of England.

19 cavaliering] During the protectorate, cavaliers who left England could have their estates confiscated. Blunt boasts that he has managed to travel overseas without identifying himself, or being identified, as a cavalier, and hence is not liable to lose his property. There is the connotation that Blunt refused to fight as well.

20 Court] retinue of the exiled Charles II.

greater crime to my conscience, gentlemen, than to the Commonwealth.[21]

Enter Willmore.

WILLMORE. Hah! Dear Belvile! Noble colonel!   70

BELVILE. Willmore! Welcome ashore, my dear rover! What happy wind blew us this good fortune?

WILLMORE. Let me salute my dear Frederick and then command me. How is't, honest lad?

FREDERICK. Faith, sir, the old compliment,   75
infinitely the better to see my dear mad Willmore again. Prithee, why camest thou ashore? And where's the Prince?[22]

WILLMORE. He's well, and reigns still lord of the watery element. I must aboard again within a day   80
or two, and my business ashore was only to enjoy myself a little this carnival.

BELVILE. Pray, know our new friend, sir; he's but bashful, a raw traveller, but honest, stout and one of us.   85

WILLMORE. (*embraces Blunt.*) That you esteem him gives him an int'rest here.

BLUNT. Your servant, sir.

WILLMORE. But well—faith, I'm glad to meet you again in a warm climate, where the kind sun has   90
its god-like power still over the wine and women. Love and mirth are my business in Naples, and if I mistake not the place, here's an excellent market for chapmen[23] of my humour.

BELVILE. See, here be those kind merchants of love   95
you look for.

Enter several men in masquing habits, some playing on music, others dancing after; women dressed like courtesans, with papers pinned on their breasts, and baskets of flowers in their hands.

BLUNT. 'Sheartlikins, what have we here?

FREDERICK. Now the game begins.

WILLMORE. Fine pretty creatures! May a stranger have leave to look and love? What's here? (*Reads   100
the papers.*) "Roses for every month"?

BLUNT. Roses for every month? What means that?

BELVILE. They are, or would have you think, they're courtesans, who here in Naples, are to be hired by the month.   105

WILLMORE. Kind and obliging to inform us. Pray, where do these roses grow? I would fain plant some of 'em in a bed of mine.

WOMEN. Beware such roses, sir.

WILLMORE. A pox of fear: I'll be baked with thee   110
between a pair of sheets, and that's thy proper still;[24] so I might but strew such roses over me, and under me.—Fair one, would you would give me leave to gather at your bush this idle month; I would go near to make some body smell of it all   115
the year after.

BELVILE. And thou hast need of such a remedy, for thou stink'st of tar and rope's ends,[25] like a dock or pest-house.[26]

The woman puts herself into the hands of a man and exeunt.

WILLMORE. Nay, nay, you shall not leave me so.   120

BELVILE. By all means use no violence here.

WILLMORE. Death! Just as I was going to be damnably in love, to have her led off! I could pluck that rose out of his hand, and even kiss the bed the bush grew in.   125

FREDERICK. No friend to love like a long voyage at sea.

BLUNT. Except a nunnery, Frederick.

WILLMORE. Death! But will they not be kind? quickly be kind? Thou know'st I'm no tame fighter,   130
but a rampant lion of the forest.

Advance from the farther end of the scenes two men dressed all over with horns of several sorts, making grimaces at one another, with papers pinned on their backs.

---

21 Commonwealth] name for England during Parliamentary rule.

22 Prince] Charles II.

23 chapmen] brokers, dealers, or traders in some commodity ("love and mirth," in this case).

24 baked ... still] Willmore's double entendre refers to the process by which rose petals are distilled to make rose-water.

25 stink'st...rope's ends] i.e., Willmore has just come off a ship and smells like one.

26 pest-house] hospital for plague victims.

BELVILE. Oh the fantastical rogues, how they're dressed! 'Tis a satire against the whole sex.

WILLMORE. Is this a fruit that grows in this warm country?   135

BELVILE. Yes, 'tis pretty to see these Italians start, swell and stab at the word "cuckold," and yet stumble at horns on every threshold.

WILLMORE. See what's on their back. (*Reads.*) "Flowers of every night." Ah, rogue! and more   140
sweet than roses of every month! This is a gardener of Adam's own breeding.

They dance.

BELVILE. What think you of those grave people? Is a wake in Essex half so mad or extravagant?

WILLMORE. I like their sober grave way; 'tis a kind   145
of legal authorized fornication, where the men are not chid for't, nor the women despised, as amongst our dull English even the monsieurs want that part of good manners.

BELVILE. But here in Italy a monsieur is the hum-   150
blest, best-bred gentleman; duels are so baffled by bravoes, that an age shows not one but between a Frenchman and a hangman, who is as much too hard for him on the piazza, as they are for a Dutch-man on the New Bridge.[27]—But see, another crew.   155

Enter Florinda, Hellena and Valeria, dressed like gypsies; Callis and Stephano; Lucetta, Phillippo and Sancho in masquerade.

HELLENA. Sister, there's your Englishman, and with him a handsome proper fellow. I'll to him, and instead of telling him his fortune, try my own.

WILLMORE. Gypsies, on my life. Sure these will prattle if a man cross their hands.[28] (*Goes to*   160
Hellena.) Dear, pretty (and I hope) young devil, will you tell an amorous stranger what luck he's like to have?

HELLENA. Have a care how you venture with me, sir, lest I pick your pocket, which will more vex   165

---

27 Dutchman on the New Bridge] an anachronistic reference to the French defeat of the Dutch at Niuewerbrug
in 1673.

28 cross their hands] with silver, as payment for telling a
fortune.

your English humour than an Italian fortune will please you.

WILLMORE. How the devil cam'st thou to know my country and humour?

HELLENA. The first I guess by a certain forward   170
impudence, which does not displease me at this time; and the loss of your money will vex you because I hope you have but very little to lose.

WILLMORE. Egad, child, thou'rt i'th' right; it is so little, I dare not offer it thee for a kindness. But   175
cannot you divine what other things of more value I have about me, that I would more willingly part with?

HELLENA. Indeed no, that's the business of a witch, and I am but a Gypsy yet. Yet without looking in   180
your hand, I have a parlous guess 'tis some foolish heart you mean, an inconstant English heart, as little worth stealing as your purse.

WILLMORE. Nay, then thou dost deal with the devil, that's certain. Thou hast guessed as right as   185
if thou had'st been one of that number it has languished for. I find you'll be better acquainted with it, nor can you take it in a better time; for I am come from the sea, child, and Venus not being propitious to me in her own element,[29] I have a   190
world of love in store. Would you would be good-natured and take some on't off my hands.

HELLENA. Why, I could be inclined that way, but for a foolish vow I am going to make—to die a maid.   195

WILLMORE. Then thou art damned without redemption, and as I am a good Christian, I ought in charity to divert so wicked a design; therefore prithee, dear creature, let me know quickly when and where I shall begin to set a helping hand to   200
so good a work.

HELLENA. If you should prevail with my tender heart (as I begin to fear you will, for you have horrible loving eyes), there will be difficulty in't, that you'll hardly undergo for my sake.   205

WILLMORE. Faith, child, I have been bred in dangers and wear a sword that has been employed in a worse cause than for a handsome kind woman.

---

29 Venus … element] Venus, goddess of love, emerged from
the sea.

Name the danger. Let it be anything but a long siege, and I'll undertake it. 210

HELLENA. Can you storm?

WILLMORE. Oh most furiously.

HELLENA. What think you of a nunnery wall? For he that wins me must gain that first.

WILLMORE. A nun! Oh how I love thee for't! 215 There's no sinner like a young saint. Nay, now there's no denying me, the old law[30] had no curse (to a woman) like dying a maid; witness Jepthah's daughter.[31]

HELLENA. A very good text this, if well handled, 220 and I perceive, Father Captain, you would impose no severe penance on her who were inclined to console herself, before she took orders.

WILLMORE. If she be young and handsome.

HELLENA. Ay, there's it. But if she be not— 225

WILLMORE. By this hand, child, I have an implicit faith, and dare venture on thee with all faults. Besides, 'tis more meritorious to leave the world when thou hast tasted and proved the pleasure on't. Then, 'twill be a virtue in thee, which now will be 230 pure ignorance.

HELLENA. I perceive, good Father Captain, you design only to make me fit for heaven, but if on the contrary, you should quite divert me from it and bring me back to the world again, I should 235 have a new man to seek, I find; and what a grief that will be, for when I begin, I fancy I shall love like anything. I never tried yet.

WILLMORE. Egad and that's kind.—Prithee, dear creature, give me credit for a heart, for faith, I'm 240 a very honest fellow. Oh, I long to come first to the banquet of love! And such a swingeing[32] appetite I bring—oh, I'm impatient—thy lodging, sweetheart, thy lodging, or I'm a dead man!

HELLENA. Why must we be either guilty of 245 fornication or murder if we converse with you men? And is there no difference between leave to love me, and leave to lie with me?

WILLMORE. Faith, child, they were made to go together. 250

LUCETTA. Are you sure this is the man? (*Pointing to Blunt.*)

SANCHO. When did I mistake your game?

LUCETTA. This is a stranger, I know by his gazing; if he be brisk, he'll venture to follow me, and then, 255 if I understand my trade, he's mine. He's English too, and they say that's a sort of good-natured loving people, and have generally so kind an opinion of themselves, that a woman of any wit may flatter 'em into any sort of fool she pleases. 260

She often passes by Blunt and gazes on him; he struts and cocks, and walks and gazes on her.

BLUNT. [*Aside.*] 'Tis so. She is taken. I have beauties which my false glass[33] at home did not discover.

FLORINDA. [*Aside.*] This woman watches me so, I shall get no opportunity to discover myself to him and so miss the intent of my coming.—But as I 265 was saying, sir (*Looking in his hand.*), by this line you should be a lover.

BELVILE. I thought how right you guessed, all men are in love, or pretend to be so. Come, let me go, I'm weary of this fooling. 270

[He] walks away. She holds him, he strives to get from her.

FLORINDA. I will not, till you have confessed whether the passion that you have vowed Florinda be true or false.

BELVILE. (*Turns quick towards her.*) Florinda!

FLORINDA. Softly. 275

BELVILE. Thou hast named one will fix me here for ever.

FLORINDA. She'll be disappointed, then, who expects you this night at the garden gate, and if you fail not, as—let me see the other hand—you 280 will go near to do, she vows to die or make you happy. (*Looks on Callis, who observes 'em.*)

BELVILE. What canst thou mean?

FLORINDA. That which I say. Farewell. (*Offers to go.*) 285

---

30 old law] Old Testament law.

31 Jephthah's daughter] Jephthah delayed the sacrifice of his virginal daughter for two months while she "bewailed her virginity"; see Judges 11:30-40.

32 swingeing] enormous or powerful.

33 glass] looking-glass, or mirror.

BELVILE. Oh charming sibyl, stay, complete that joy which as it is will turn into distraction! Where must I be? At the garden gate? I know it. At night you say? I'll sooner forfeit heaven than disobey.

Enter Don Pedro and other masquers, and pass over the stage.

CALLIS. Madam, your brother's here. 290

FLORINDA. Take this to instruct you farther. (*Gives him a letter and goes off.*)

FREDERICK. Have a care, sir, what you promise; this may be a trap laid by her brother to ruin you.

BELVILE. Do not disturb my happiness with 295 doubts. (*Opens the letter.*)

WILLMORE. My dear pretty creature, a thousand blessings on thee! Still in this habit, you say? and after dinner at this place?

HELLENA. Yes, if you will swear to keep your heart 300 and not bestow it between this and that.

WILLMORE. By all the little gods of love, I swear I'll leave it with you, and if you run away with it, those deities of justice will revenge me.

Exeunt all the women.

FREDERICK. Do you know the hand? 305

BELVILE. 'Tis Florinda's.
All blessings fall upon the virtuous maid.

FREDERICK. Nay, no idolatry; a sober sacrifice I'll allow you.

BELVILE. Oh friends, the welcom'st news! the softest 310 letter! Nay, you shall all see it! And could you now be serious, I might be made the happiest man the sun shines on!

WILLMORE. The reason of this mighty joy?

BELVILE. See how kindly she invites me to deliver 315 her from the threatened violence of her brother. Will you not assist me?

WILLMORE. I know not what thou mean'st, but I'll make one at any mischief where a woman's concerned. But she'll be grateful to us for the 320 favour, will she not?

BELVILE. How mean you?

WILLMORE. How should I mean? Thou know'st there's but one way for a woman to oblige me.

BELVILE. Do not profane. The maid is nicely 325 virtuous.

WILLMORE. Whoo, pox, then she's fit for nothing but a husband; let her e'en go, Colonel.

FREDERICK. Peace, she's the colonel's mistress, sir.

WILLMORE. Let her be the devil; if she be thy 330 mistress, I'll serve her. Name the way.

BELVILE. Read here this postscript. (*Gives him a letter.*)

WILLMORE. (*Reads.*) "At ten at night—at the garden gate—of which, if I cannot get the key, I 335 will contrive a way over the wall—come attended with a friend or two." Kind heart, if we three cannot weave a string to let her down a garden wall, 'twere pity but the hangman wove one for us all. 340

FREDERICK. Let her alone for that. Your woman's wit, your fair kind woman, will out-trick a broker or a Jew, and contrive like a Jesuit in chains.—But see, Ned Blunt is stolen out after the lure of a damsel. 345

Exeunt Blunt and Lucetta.

BELVILE. So he'll scarce find his way home again, unless we get him cried by the bellman in the market-place, and 'twould sound prettily—a lost English boy of thirty.

FREDERICK. I hope 'tis some common crafty 350 sinner, one that will fit him; it may be she'll sell him for Peru;[34] the rogue's sturdy and would work well in a mine; at least I hope she'll dress him for our mirth, cheat him of all, then have him well-favouredly hanged and turned out naked at 355 midnight.

WILLMORE. Prithee, what humour is he of that you wish him so well?

BELVILE. Why of an English elder brother's humour, educated in a nursery, with a maid to 360 tend him till fifteen, and lies with his grandmother till he's of age: one that knows no pleasure beyond riding to the next fair, or going up to London with his right worshipful father in Parliament-time, wearing gay clothes, or making honourable love to 365 his lady mother's laundry-maid; gets drunk at a hunting-match, and ten to one then gives some proofs of his prowess. A pox upon him, he's our

---

34 Peru] known for its many mines using slave labour.

banker and has all our cash about him, and if he fail, we are all broke.

FREDERICK. Oh let him alone for that matter, he's of a damned stingy quality that will secure our stock. I know not in what danger it were indeed if the jilt should pretend she's in love with him, for 'tis a kind believing coxcomb; otherwise, if he part with more than a piece of eight—geld[35] him: for which offer he may chance to be beaten, if she be a whore of the first rank.

BELVILE. Nay, the rogue will not be easily beaten, he's stout enough. Perhaps if they talk beyond his capacity, he may chance to exercise his courage upon some of them; else I'm sure they'll find it as difficult to beat as to please him.

WILLMORE. 'Tis a lucky devil to light upon so kind a wench!

FREDERICK. Thou had'st a great deal of talk with thy little Gypsy; could'st thou do no good upon her? For mine was hard-hearted.

WILLMORE. Hang her, she was some damned honest person of quality, I'm sure, she was so very free and witty. If her face be but answerable to her wit and humour, I would be bound to constancy this month to gain her. In the meantime, have you made no kind acquaintance since you came to town? You do not use to be honest so long, gentlemen.

FREDERICK. Faith, love has kept us honest; we have been all fired with a beauty newly come to town, the famous Paduana,[36] Angellica Bianca.

WILLMORE. What, the mistress of the dead Spanish general?

BELVILE. Yes, she's now the only adored beauty of all the youth in Naples, who put on all their charms to appear lovely in her sight, their coaches, liveries, and themselves, all gay as on a monarch's birthday, to attract the eyes of this fair charmer,

while she has the pleasure to behold all languish for her that see her.

FREDERICK. 'Tis pretty to see with how much love the men regard her, and how much envy the women.

WILLMORE. What gallant has she?

BELVILE. None, she's exposed to sale, and four days in the week she's yours—for so much a month.

WILLMORE. The very thought of it quenches all manner of fire in me. Yet prithee, let's see her.

BELVILE. Let's first to dinner, and after that we'll pass the day as you please. But at night ye must all be at my devotion.

WILLMORE. I will not fail you.

ACT II, SCENE I. THE LONG STREET.

Enter Belvile and Frederick in masquing habits, and Willmore in his own clothes, with a vizard in his hand.

WILLMORE. But why thus disguised and muzzled?

BELVILE. Because whatever extravagances we commit in these faces, our own may not be obliged to answer 'em.

WILLMORE. I should have changed my eternal buff[37] too; but no matter, my little Gypsy would not have found me out then, for if she should change hers, it is impossible I should know her, unless I should hear her prattle. A pox on't, I cannot get her out of my head. Pray Heaven, if ever I do see her again, she prove damnably ugly, that I may fortify myself against her tongue.

BELVILE. Have a care of love, for o' my conscience, she was not of a quality to give thee any hopes.

WILLMORE. Pox on 'em, why do they draw a man in then? She has played with my heart so, that 'twill never lie still till I have met with some kind wench that will play the game out with me. Oh, for my arms full of soft, white, kind—woman! such as I fancy Angellica.

BELVILE. This is her house, if you were but in stock[38] to get admittance. They have not dined yet; I perceive the picture is not out.

---

35 geld] Behn (whose spelling is "gueld") puns on near homonyms: geld] to castrate; gild] to overlay with gold. The second is latent because Frederick has just referred to pieces of eight. There is a third possible pun in the archaic sense of gild] to make bloody. Both the second and third meanings seem picked up in Frederick's subsequent "beaten."

36 Paduana] woman from Padua.

37 buff] leather military coat.

38 in stock] supplied with funds.

Enter Blunt.

WILLMORE. I long to see the shadow of the fair
substance; a man may gaze on that for nothing.   25

BLUNT. Colonel, thy hand—and thine, Fred. I have
been an ass, a deluded fool, a very coxcomb from
my birth till this hour, and heartily repent my little
faith.

BELVILE. What the devil's the matter with thee,   30
Ned?

BLUNT. Oh such a mistress, Fred, such a girl!

WILLMORE. Ha! where?

FREDERICK. Ay, where!

BLUNT. So fond, so amorous, so toying and so fine!   35
and all for sheer love, ye rogue! Oh how she looked
and kissed! and soothed my heart from my bosom.
I cannot think I was awake, and yet methinks I
see and feel her charms still. Fred, try if she have
not left the taste of her balmy kisses upon my lips.   40
(*Kisses him.*)

BELVILE. Ha! Ha! Ha!

WILLMORE. Death, man, where is she?

BLUNT. What a dog was I to stay in dull England
so long. How have I laughed at the colonel when   45
he sighed for love! But now the little archer[39] has
revenged him! And by this one dart, I can guess
at all his joys, which then I took for fancies, mere
dreams and fables. Well, I'm resolved to sell all in
Essex, and plant here for ever.   50

BELVILE. What a blessing 'tis thou hast a mistress
thou dar'st boast of, for I know thy humour is
rather to have a proclaimed clap than a secret
amour.

WILLMORE. Dost know her name?   55

BLUNT. Her name? No, 'sheartlikins, what care I for
names? She's fair! young! brisk and kind! even to
ravishment! And what a pox care I for knowing her
by any other title?

WILLMORE. Didst give her anything?   60

BLUNT. Give her! Ha, ha, ha! Why she's a person
of quality. That's a good one, give her! 'Sheartlikins,
dost think such creatures are to be bought? Or are
we provided for such a purchase? Give her, quoth
ye? Why, she presented me with this bracelet for   65

---

39 little archer] Cupid.

---

the toy of a diamond I used to wear. No,
gentlemen, Ned Blunt is not everybody. She
expects me again tonight.

WILLMORE. Egad, that's well; we'll all go.

BLUNT. Not a soul. No, gentlemen, you are wits; I   70
am a dull country rogue, I.

FREDERICK. Well, sir, for all your person of
quality, I shall be very glad to understand your
purse be secure; 'tis our whole estate at present,
which we are loath to hazard in one bottom.   75
Come, sir, unlade.

BLUNT. Take the necessary trifle, useless now to me
that am beloved by such a gentlewoman.
'Sheartlikins, money! Here, take mine too.

FREDERICK. No, keep that to be cozened, that we   80
may laugh.

WILLMORE. Cozened! Death! Would I could meet
with one that would cozen me of all the love I
could spare tonight.

FREDERICK. Pox, 'tis some common whore, upon   85
my life.

BLUNT. A whore! Yes, with such clothes! such jewels!
such a house! such furniture, and so attended! A
whore!

BELVILE. Why yes, sir, they are whores, though   90
they'll neither entertain you with drinking,
swearing, or bawdry; are whores in all those gay
clothes and right jewels; are whores with those
great houses richly furnished with velvet beds, store
of plate, handsome attendance and fine coaches;   95
are whores, and arrant ones.

WILLMORE. Pox on't, where do these fine whores
live?

BELVILE. Where no rogues in office yclept[40]
constables dare give 'em laws, nor the wine-   100
inspired bullies of the town break their windows;
yet they are whores, though this Essex calf[41]
believe 'em persons of quality.

BLUNT. 'Sheartlikins, y'are all fools; there are things
about this Essex calf that shall take with the ladies,   105
beyond all your wit and parts. This shape and size,
gentlemen, are not to be despised—my waist too,

---

40 yclept] called, addressed as.
41 Essex calf] fool; a native of Essex. Blunt's home county
of Essex was famous for its calves.

tolerably long, with other inviting signs, that shall be nameless.

WILLMORE. Egad, I believe he may have met with some person of quality that may be kind to him. 110

BELVILE. Dost thou perceive any such tempting things about him that should make a fine woman, and of quality, pick him out from all mankind to throw away her youth and beauty upon, nay and 115 her dear heart too! No, no, Angellica has raised the price too high.

WILLMORE. May she languish for mankind till she die, and be damned for that one sin alone.

Enter two bravoes, and hang up a great picture of Angellica's against the balcony, and two little ones at each side of the door.

BELVILE. See there, the fair sign to the inn where a 120 man may lodge that's fool enough to give her price.

Willmore gazes on the picture.

BLUNT. 'Sheartlikins, gentlemen, what's this!

BELVILE. A famous courtesan, that's to be sold.

BLUNT. How? To be sold! Nay then, I have nothing to say to her. Sold! What impudence is practised 125 in this country? With what order and decency whoring's established here by virtue of the Inquisition. Come, let's be gone, I'm sure we're no chapmen for this commodity.

FREDERICK. Thou art none, I'm sure, unless thou 130 could'st have her in thy bed at a price of a coach in the street.

WILLMORE. How wondrous fair she is. A thousand crowns a month! By heaven, as many kingdoms were too little. A plague of this poverty—of which 135 I ne'er complain but when it hinders my approach to beauty which virtue ne'er could purchase. (*Turns from the picture.*)

BLUNT. What's this? (*Reads.*) "A thousand crowns a month"!—'Sheartlikins, here's a sum! Sure 'tis a 140 mistake.—Hark you friend, does she take or give so much by the month?

FREDERICK. A thousand crowns! Why 'tis a portion for the Infanta.[42]

BLUNT. Hark ye, friends, won't she trust? 145

---

42 Infanta] daughter of the king and queen of Spain.

BRAVO. This is a trade, sir, that cannot live by credit.

Enter Don Pedro in masquerade, followed by Stephano.

BELVILE. See, here's more company. Let's walk off a while.

Exeunt English. Pedro reads. Enter Angellica and Moretta in the balcony, and draw a silk curtain.

PEDRO. Fetch me a thousand crowns, I never wished 150 to buy this beauty at an easier rate. (*Passes off.*)

ANGELLICA. Prithee, what said those fellows to thee?

BRAVO. Madam, the first were admirers of beauty only, but no purchasers; they were merry with your 155 price and picture, laughed at the sum, and so passed off.

ANGELLICA. No matter, I'm not displeased with their rallying; their wonder feeds my vanity, and he that wishes but to buy gives me more 160 pride than he that gives my price can make my pleasure.

BRAVO. Madam, the last I knew through all his disguises to be Don Pedro, nephew to the general, and who was with him in Pamplona. 165

ANGELLICA. Don Pedro! My old gallant's nephew. When his uncle died he left him a vast sum of money; it is he who was so in love with me at Padua, and who used to make the general so jealous. 170

MORETTA. Is this he that used to prance before our window and take such care to show himself an amorous ass? If I am not mistaken, he is the likeliest man to give your price.

ANGELLICA. The man is brave and generous, but 175 of an humour so uneasy and inconstant, that the victory over his heart is as soon lost as won, a slave that can add little to the triumph of the conqueror. But inconstancy's the sin of all mankind; therefore, I'm resolved that nothing but gold shall charm my 180 heart.

MORETTA. I'm glad on't; 'tis only interest that women of our profession ought to consider, though I wonder what has kept you from that general disease of our sex so long, I mean that of 185 being in love.

ANGELLICA. A kind but sullen star under which I had the happiness to be born. Yet I have had no time for love; the bravest and noblest of mankind have purchased my favours at so dear a rate as if 190 no coin but gold were current with our trade.— But here's Don Pedro again, fetch me my lute, for 'tis for him or Don Antonio the viceroy's son that I have spread my nets.

Enter at one door Don Pedro, Stephano; Don Antonio and Diego [Page] at the other door, with people following him in masquerade, antically attired, some with music; they both go up to the picture.

ANTONIO. A thousand crowns! Had not the 195 painter flattered her, I should not think it dear.

PEDRO. Flattered her! By Heav'n, he cannot; I have seen the original, nor is there one charm here more than adorns her face and eyes; all this soft and sweet, with a certain languishing air, that no artist 200 can represent.

ANTONIO. What I heard of her beauty before had fired my soul, but this confirmation of it has blown it to a flame.

PEDRO. Hah! 205

PAGE. Sir, I have known you throw away a thousand crowns on a worse face, and though y'are near your marriage, you may venture a little love here. Florinda will not miss it.

PEDRO. (*Aside.*) Hah! Florinda! Sure 'tis Antonio. 210

ANTONIO. Florinda! Name not those distant joys; there's not one thought of her will check my passion here.

PEDRO. Florinda scorned! (*A noise of a lute above.*) and all my hopes defeated of the possession of 215 Angellica. (*Antonio gazes up.*) Her injuries, by Heaven, he shall not boast of.

Song (*to a lute above.*)
When Damon first began to love
He languished in a soft desire,
And knew not how the gods to move, 220
To lessen or increase his fire.
For Caelia in her charming eyes
Wore all love's sweets, and all his cruelties.

II.
But as beneath a shade he lay,
Weaving of flow'rs for Caelia's hair, 225
She chanced to lead her flock that way,
And saw the am'rous shepherd there.
She gazed around upon the place,
And saw the grove (resembling night)
To all the joys of love invite, 230
Whilst guilty smiles and blushes dressed her face.
At this the bashful youth all transport grew,
And with kind force he taught the virgin how
To yield what all his sighs could never do.

Angellica throws open the curtains and bows to Antonio, who pulls off his vizard and bows and blows up kisses. Pedro unseen looks in's face.

ANTONIO. By Heav'n, she's charming fair! 235

PEDRO. 'Tis he; the false Antonio!

ANTONIO. (*To the bravo.*) Friend, where must I pay my offering of love?
My thousand crowns I mean.

PEDRO. That offering I have designed to make.
And yours will come too late. 240

ANTONIO. Prithee, be gone, I shall grow angry else.
And then thou art not safe.

PEDRO. My anger may be fatal, sir, as yours,
And he that enters here may prove this truth.

ANTONIO. I know not who thou art, but I am sure 245 thou'rt worth my killing, for aiming at Angellica.

They draw and fight. Enter Willmore and Blunt who draw and part 'em.

BLUNT. 'Sheartlikins, here's fine doings.

WILLMORE. Tilting for the wench, I'm sure. Nay, gad, if that would win her, I have as good a sword as the best of ye. Put up—put up, and take another 250 time and place, for this is designed for lovers only.

They all put up.

PEDRO: We are prevented; dare you meet me tomorrow on the Molo?[43]
For I've a title to a better quarrel,

---

43 the Molo] pier; from French *môle*.

That of Florinda, in whose credulous heart 255
Thou'st made an int'rest and destroyed my hopes.
ANTONIO: Dare!
I'll meet thee there as early as the day.
PEDRO. We will come thus disguised that whosoever
chance to get the better, he may escape unknown. 260
ANTONIO. It shall be so.

Exeunt Pedro and Stephano.

Who should this rival be? unless the English
colonel, of whom I've often heard Don Pedro
speak; it must be he, and time he were removed,
who lays claim to all my happiness. 265

*Willmore having gazed all this while on the picture,
pulls down a little one.*

WILLMORE: This posture's loose and negligent,
The sight on't would beget a warm desire
In souls whom impotence and age had chilled.
—This must along with me.
BRAVO. What means this rudeness, sir? Restore the 270
picture.
ANTONIO. Hah! Rudeness committed to the fair
Angellica! Restore the picture, sir—
WILLMORE. Indeed I will not, sir.
ANTONIO. By Heaven, but you shall. 275
WILLMORE. Nay, do not show your sword; if you
do, by this dear beauty—I will show mine too.
ANTONIO. What right can you pretend to't?
WILLMORE. That of possession, which I will
maintain. You perhaps have a thousand crowns to 280
give for the original.
ANTONIO. No matter, sir, you shall restore the
picture.

Angellica and Moretta above.

ANGELLICA. Oh Moretta! What's the matter?
ANTONIO. Or leave your life behind. 285
WILLMORE. Death! You lie. I will do neither.

*They fight; the Spaniards join with Antonio; Blunt
laying on like mad.*

ANGELLICA. Hold, I command you, if for me you
fight.

They leave off and bow.

WILLMORE. How heavenly fair she is! Ah, plague
of her price. 290
ANGELLICA. You sir, in buff, you that appear a
soldier, that first began this insolence—
WILLMORE. 'Tis true, I did so, if you call it
insolence for a man to preserve himself. I saw your
charming picture and was wounded; quite through 295
my soul each pointed beauty ran, and wanting a
thousand crowns to procure my remedy, I laid this
little picture to my bosom—which if you cannot
allow me, I'll resign.
ANGELLICA. No, you may keep the trifle. 300
ANTONIO. You shall first ask me leave, and this.
(*Fight again as before.*)

Enter Belvile and Frederick who join with the English.

ANGELLICA. Hold! Will you ruin me? Biskey—
Sebastian—part 'em.

The Spaniards are beaten off.

MORETTA. Oh madam, we're undone. A pox upon 305
that rude fellow, he's set on to ruin us. We shall
never see good days till all these fighting poor
rogues are sent to the galleys.

*Enter Belvile, Blunt, Frederick, and Willmore with's
shirt bloody.*

BLUNT. 'Sheartlikins, beat me at this sport, and I'll
ne'er wear sword more. 310
BELVILE. The devil's in thee for a mad fellow; thou
art always one at an unlucky adventure. Come, let's
be gone whilst we're safe, and remember these are
Spaniards, a sort of people that know how to
revenge an affront. 315
FREDERICK. (*To Willmore.*) You bleed! I hope you
are not wounded.
WILLMORE. Not much. A plague on your dons;[44]
if they fight no better, they'll ne'er recover Flanders.
What the devil was't to them that I took down the 320
picture?
BLUNT. Took it! 'Sheartlikins, we'll have the great
one too; 'tis ours by conquest. Prithee, help me up
and I'll pull it down—

---

44 dons] Spaniards.

THE ROVER 517

ANGELLICA. Stay, sir, and ere you affront me   325
farther, let me know how you durst commit this
outrage. To you I speak, sir, for you appear a
gentleman.

WILLMORE. To me, madam?—Gentlemen, your
servant.   330

Belvile stays him.

BELVILE. Is the devil in thee? Dost know the danger
of entering the house of an incensed courtesan?

WILLMORE. I thank you for your care, but there
are other matters in hand, there are, though we
have no great temptation.—Death! Let me go.   335

FREDERICK. Yes, to your lodging if you will, but
not in here.—Damn these gay harlots. By this
hand I'll have as sound and handsome a whore for
a patacoon.[45]—Death, man, she'll murder thee.

WILLMORE. Oh! Fear me not. Shall I not venture   340
where a beauty calls? a lovely, charming beauty! for
fear of danger! when, by Heaven, there's none so
great as to long for her whilst I want money to
purchase her.

FREDERICK. Therefore, 'tis loss of time unless you   345
had the thousand crowns to pay.

WILLMORE. It may be she may give a favour; at
least I shall have the pleasure of saluting her when
I enter, and when I depart.

BELVILE. Pox, she'll as soon lie with thee as kiss   350
thee, and sooner stab than do either. You shall not
go.

ANGELLICA. Fear not, sir, all I have to wound with
is my eyes.

BLUNT. Let him go. 'Sheartlikins, I believe the   355
gentle-woman means well.

BELVILE. Well, take thy fortune; we'll expect you
in the next street. Farewell, fool—farewell—

WILLMORE. Bye, Colonel. (*Goes in.*)

FREDERICK. The rogue's stark mad for a wench.   360

Exeunt.

SCENE II. A FINE CHAMBER.

Enter Willmore, Angellica and Moretta.

ANGELLICA. Insolent sir, how durst you pull down
my picture?

WILLMORE. Rather, how durst you set it up, to
tempt poor amorous mortals with so much
excellence, which I find you have but too well   5
consulted by the unmerciful price you set upon't?
Is all this heaven of beauty shown to move despair
in those that cannot buy? And can you think
th'effects of that despair should be less extravagant
than I have shown?   10

ANGELLICA. I sent for you to ask my pardon, sir,
not to aggravate your crime. I thought I should
have seen you at my feet imploring it.

WILLMORE. You are deceived; I came to rail at you,
and rail such truths too, as shall let you see the   15
vanity of that pride which taught you how to set
such price on sin. For such it is, whilst that which
is love's due is meanly bartered for.

ANGELLICA. Ha! ha! ha! Alas, good captain, what
pity 'tis your edifying doctrine will do no good   20
upon me.—Moretta! Fetch the gentleman a glass,
and let him survey himself, to see what charms he
has—(*Aside in a soft tone.*) and guess my business.

MORETTA. He knows himself of old; I believe
those breeches and he have been acquainted ever   25
since he was beaten at Worcester.[46]

ANGELLICA. Nay, do not abuse the poor
creature—

MORETTA. Good weather-beaten corporal, will you
march off? We have no need of your doctrine,   30
though you have of our charity, but at present we
have no scraps, we can afford no kindness for
God's sake. In fine, sirrah, the price is too high
i'th'mouth[47] for you; therefore, troop, I say.

WILLMORE. Here, good forewoman of the shop,   35
serve me, and I'll be gone.

---

45 patacoon] Spanish coin, equivalent in the seventeenth
century to roughly one quarter of an English pound.

46 Worcester] The Battle of Worcester (1651) was the final
defeat of Charles II by the Parliamentary forces, after
which he fled to the continent.
47 high i'th'mouth] elevated.

MORETTA. Keep it to pay your laundress, your linen stinks of the gunroom, for here's no selling by retail.

WILLMORE. Thou hast sold plenty of thy stale ware at a cheap rate. 40

MORETTA. Ay, the more silly,[48] kind heart I, but this is an age wherein beauty is at higher rates. In fine, you know the price of this.

WILLMORE. I grant you 'tis here set down, a 45 thousand crowns a month. Pray, how much may come to my share for a pistole[49]? Bawd, take your black lead and sum it up, that I may have a pistole's worth of this vain gay thing, and I'll trouble you no more. 50

MORETTA. Pox on him, he'll fret me to death.— Abominable fellow, I tell thee, we only sell by the whole piece.

WILLMORE. 'Tis very hard, the whole cargo or nothing. Faith, madam, my stock will not reach 55 it; I cannot be your chapman. Yet I have country-men in town, merchants of love like me; I'll see if they'll put in for a share. We cannot lose much by it, and what we have no use for, we'll sell upon the Friday's mart at "Who gives more?"—I am study- 60 ing, madam, how to purchase you, though at present I am unprovided of money.

ANGELLICA. [*Aside.*] Sure, this from any other man would anger me, nor shall he know the conquest he has made.—Poor angry man, how I despise this 65 railing.

WILLMORE: Yes, I am poor—but I'm a gentleman,
And one that scorns this baseness which you practise;
Poor as I am, I would not sell myself,
No, not to gain your charming, high-prized person. 70
Though I admire you strangely for your beauty,
Yet I contemn your mind.—
And yet I would at any rate enjoy you
At your own rate—but cannot. See here
The only sum I can command on earth; 75
I know not where to eat when this is gone.
Yet such a slave I am to love and beauty
This last reserve I'll sacrifice to enjoy you.
—Nay, do not frown, I know you're to be bought,

And would be bought by me, by me, 80
For a mean trifling sum if I could pay it down;
Which happy knowledge I will still repeat,
And lay it to my heart; it has a virtue in't,
And soon will cure those wounds your eyes have made.
—And yet—there's something so divinely 85
powerful there—
Nay, I will gaze—to let you see my strength.

Holds her, looks on her, and pauses and sighs.

By Heav'n, bright creature—I would not for the world
Thy fame were half so fair as is thy face.

Turns her away from him.

ANGELLICA. (*Aside.*) His words go through me to the very soul.
—If you have nothing else to say to me— 90

WILLMORE. Yes, you shall hear how infamous you are—
For which I do not hate thee—
But that secures my heart, and all the flames it feels
Are but so many lusts—
I know it by their sudden bold intrusion. 95
The fire's impatient and betrays, 'tis false—
For had it been the purer flame of love,
I should have pined and languished at your feet,
Ere found the impudence to have discovered it.
I now dare stand your scorn, and your denial. 100

MORETTA. Sure she's bewitched, that she can stand thus tamely and hear his saucy railing.—Sirrah, will you be gone?

ANGELLICA. (*To Moretta.*) How dare you take this liberty? Withdraw.—Pray tell me, sir, are not you 105 guilty of the same mercenary crime? When a lady is proposed to you for a wife, you never ask how fair, discreet, or virtuous she is, but what's her fortune—which if but small, you cry, "She will not do my business" and basely leave her, though she 110 languish for you. Say, is not this as poor?

WILLMORE. It is a barbarous custom, which I will scorn to defend in our sex, and do despise in yours.

ANGELLICA. Thou'rt a brave fellow! Put up thy gold, and know,
That were thy fortune large as is thy soul, 115

---

48 silly] innocent, unsophisticated.
49 pistole] Spanish gold coin worth 18*s.* or a little less.

Thou should'st not buy my love.
Couldst thou forget those mean effects of vanity
Which set me out to sale, and, as a lover, prize my
    yielding joys?
Canst thou believe they'll be entirely thine,
Without considering they were mercenary?   120
WILLMORE. I cannot tell, I must bethink me first.
    (*Aside.*) Hah! Death, I'm going to believe her.
ANGELLICA. Prithee, confirm that faith—or if
    thou canst not—flatter me a little, 'twill please me
    from thy mouth.   125
WILLMORE. (*Aside.*) Curse on thy charming
        tongue!—Dost thou return
My feigned contempt with so much subtlety?
Thou'st found the easiest way into my heart,
Though I yet know that all thou say'st is false.

Turning from her in rage.

ANGELLICA. By all that's good, 'tis real;   130
I never loved before, though oft a mistress.
Shall my first vows be slighted?
WILLMORE. (*Aside.*) What can she mean?
ANGELLICA. (*In an angry tone.*) I find you cannot
    credit me.
WILLMORE. I know you take me for an arrant ass,   135
An ass that may be soothed into belief
And then be used at pleasure—
But madam, I have been so often cheated
By perjured, soft, deluding hypocrites,
That I've no faith left for the cozening sex;   140
Especially for women of your trade.
ANGELLICA. The low esteem you have of me,
    perhaps
May bring my heart again—
For I have pride that yet surmounts my love.

She turns with pride; he holds her.

WILLMORE. Throw off this pride, this enemy to   145
    bliss,
And show the pow'r of love; 'tis with those arms
I can be only vanquished, made a slave.
ANGELLICA. Is all my mighty expectation
    vanished?
—No, I will not hear thee talk. Thou hast a charm
In every word that draws my heart away.   150
And all the thousand trophies I designed

Thou hast undone—Why art thou soft?
Thy looks are bravely rough, and meant for war.
Could'st thou not storm on still?
I then perhaps had been as free as thou.   155
WILLMORE. (*Aside.*) Death, how she throws her
    fire about my soul!
—Take heed, fair creature, how you raise my hope,
Which, once assumed, pretends to all dominion.
There's not a joy thou hast in store,
I shall not then command—   160
For which I'll pay thee back my soul! my life!
—Come, let's begin th'account this happy minute!
ANGELLICA. And will you pay me then the price I
    ask?
WILLMORE. Oh, why dost thou draw me from an
    awful worship,
By showing thou art no divinity?   165
Conceal the fiend, and show me all the angel!
Keep me but ignorant, and I'll be devout
And pay my vows forever at this shrine.

Kneels and kisses her hand.

ANGELLICA. The pay I mean is but thy love for mine.
Can you give that?—   170
WILLMORE. Entirely. Come, let's withdraw! where
I'll renew my vows—and breathe 'em with such
ardour thou shalt not doubt my zeal.
ANGELLICA. Thou hast a pow'r too strong to be
    resisted.   175

Exeunt Willmore and Angellica.

MORETTA. Now my curse go with you. Is all our
    project fallen to this? to love the only enemy to
    our trade? Nay, to love such a shameroon,[50] a very
    beggar, nay a pirate beggar, whose business is to
    rifle, and be gone, a no-purchase, no-pay tatter-   180
    demalion[51] and English picaroon,[52] a rogue that
    fights for daily drink and takes a pride in being
    loyally lousy. Oh, I could curse now, if I durst. This
    is the fate of most whores.

---

[50] shameroon] one who deceives or uses false pretenses.
[51] tatterdemalion] person dressed in tattered clothes; a raga-
    muffin.
[52] picaroon] pirate.

Trophies, which from believing fops we win,   185
Are spoils to those who cozen us again.

ACT III, SCENE I. A STREET.

*Enter Florinda, Valeria, Hellena, in antic different
dresses from what they were in before. Callis attending.*

FLORINDA. I wonder what should make my
brother in so ill a humour? I hope he has not
found out our ramble this morning.

HELLENA. No, if he had, we should have heard on't
at both ears, and have been mewed up this   5
afternoon, which I would not for the world should
have happened.—Hey ho, I'm as sad as a lover's
lute.

VALERIA. Well, methinks we have learnt this trade
of gypsies as readily as if we have been bred upon   10
the road to Loretto,[53] and yet I did so fumble
when I told the stranger his fortune that I was
afraid I should have told my own and yours by
mistake. But methinks Hellena has been very
serious ever since.   15

FLORINDA. I would give my garters she were in
love to be revenged upon her for abusing me.—
How is't, Hellena?

HELLENA. Ah—would I had never seen my mad
monsieur—and yet for all your laughing, I am not   20
in love—and yet this small acquaintance, o'my
conscience, will never out of my head.

VALERIA. Ha, ha, ha! I laugh to think how thou
art fitted with a lover, a fellow that I warrant loves
every new face he sees.   25

HELLENA. Hum—he has not kept his word with
me here—and may be taken up. That thought is
not very pleasant to me. What the deuce should
this be, now, that I feel?

VALERIA. What is't like?   30

HELLENA. Nay, the lord knows. But if I should be
hanged, I cannot choose but be angry and afraid
when I think that mad fellow should be in love
with anybody but me. What to think of myself, I
know not. Would I could meet with some true   35
damned Gypsy, that I might know my fortune.

VALERIA. Know it! Why there's nothing so easy;

thou wilt love this wandering inconstant till thou
find'st thyself hanged about his neck, and then be
as mad to get free again.   40

FLORINDA. Yes, Valeria, we shall see her bestride
his baggage horse, and follow him to the campaign.

HELLENA. So, so, now you are provided for, there's
no care taken of poor me. But since you have set
my heart a-wishing, I am resolved to know for   45
what. I will not die of the pip,[54] so I will not.

FLORINDA. Art thou mad to talk so? Who will like
thee well enough to have thee that hears what a
mad wench thou art?

HELLENA. Like me! I don't intend every he that   50
likes me shall have me, but he that I like; I should
have stayed in the nunnery still, if I had liked my
lady Abbess as well as she liked me. No, I came
thence not (as my wise brother imagines) to take
an eternal farewell of the world, but to love and   55
to be beloved, and I will be beloved, or I'll get one
of your men, so I will.

VALERIA. Am I put into the number of lovers?

HELLENA. You? Why, coz, I know thou'rt too good-
natured to leave us in any design; thou wouldst   60
venture a cast, though thou comest off a loser,
especially with such a gamester. I observe your man
and your willing ear incline that way; and if you
are not a lover, 'tis an art soon learnt, that I find.
(*Sighs.*)   65

FLORINDA. I wonder how you learnt to love so
easily; I had a thousand charms to meet my eyes
and ears ere I could yield, and 'twas the knowledge
of Belvile's merit, not the surprising person, took
my soul. Thou art too rash to give a heart at first   70
sight.

HELLENA. Hang your considering lover; I never
thought beyond the fancy that 'twas a very pretty,
idle, silly kind of pleasure to pass one's time with,
to write little soft nonsensical billets, and with great   75
difficulty and danger receive answers in which I
shall have my beauty praised, my wit admired
(though little or none), and have the vanity and
power to know I am desirable; then I have the
more inclination that way, because I am to be a   80

---

[53] Loretto] a city in Italy famous as a place of pilgrimage.

[54] the pip] originally a poultry disease, but applied jokingly
to miscellaneous human ailments, such as depression.

nun, and so shall not be suspected to have any such earthly thoughts about me. But when I walk thus—and sigh thus—they'll think my mind's upon my monastery and cry how happy 'tis she's so resolved. But not a word of man. 85

FLORINDA. What a mad creature's this?

HELLENA. I'll warrant, if my brother hears either of you sigh, he cries (gravely), "I fear you have the indiscretion to be in love, but take heed of the honour of our house, and your own unspotted 90 fame," and so he conjures on till he has laid the soft-winged god in your hearts, or broke the bird's nest.—But see, here comes your lover, but where's my inconstant? Let's step aside, and we may learn something. (*Go aside.*) 95

Enter Belvile, Frederick and Blunt.

BELVILE. What means this! The picture's taken in.

BLUNT. It may be the wench is good-natured and will be kind gratis. Your friend's a proper handsome fellow.

BELVILE. I rather think she has cut his throat and 100 is fled: I am mad he should throw himself into dangers. Pox on't, I shall want him too at night. Let's knock and ask for him.

HELLENA. My heart goes a-pit a-pat, for fear 'tis my man they talk of. 105

Knock; Moretta above.

MORETTA. What would you have!

BELVILE. Tell the stranger that entered here about two hours ago that his friends stay here for him.

MORETTA. A curse upon him for Moretta; would he were at the devil. But he's coming to you. 110

Enter Willmore.

HELLENA. Aye, aye, 'tis he! Oh how this vexes me.

BELVILE. And how and how dear lad, has fortune smiled? Are we to break her windows? Or raise up altars to her, hah?

WILLMORE. Does not my fortune sit triumphant 115 on my brow? Dost not see the little wanton god there all gay and smiling? Have I not an air about my face and eyes that distinguish me from the crowd of common lovers? By Heaven, Cupid's quiver has not half so many darts as her eyes! Oh, 120

such a bona roba[55]! To sleep in her arms is lying in fresco,[56] all perfumed air about me.

HELLENA. (*Aside.*) Here's fine encouragement for me to fool on.

WILLMORE. Hark ye, where didst thou purchase 125 that rich canary[57] we drank today! Tell me, that I may adore the spigot and sacrifice to the butt! The juice was divine! into which I must dip my rosary and then bless all things that I would have bold or fortunate. 130

BELVILE. Well, sir, let's go take a bottle and hear the story of your success.

FREDERICK. Would not French wine do better?

WILLMORE. Damn the hungry balderdash,[58] cheerful sack has a generous virtue in't inspiring a 135 successful confidence, gives eloquence to the tongue, and vigour to the soul, and has in a few hours completed all my hopes and wishes! There's nothing left to raise a new desire in me. Come, let's be gay and wanton—and gentlemen, study, 140 study what you want, for here [*jingles a purse*] are friends that will supply, gentlemen. Hark! What a charming sound they make—'tis he and she gold whilst here, and shall beget new pleasures every moment. 145

BLUNT. But hark ye sir, you are not married, are you?

WILLMORE. All the honey of matrimony, but none of the sting, friend.

BLUNT. 'Sheartlikins, thou'rt a fortunate rogue! 150

WILLMORE. I am so, sir, let these [*jingles again*] inform you! Hah, how sweetly they chime! Pox of poverty, it makes a man a slave, makes wit and honour sneak. My soul grew lean and rusty for want of credit. 155

BLUNT. 'Sheartlikins, this I like well, it looks like my lucky bargain! Oh how I long for the approach of my squire that is to conduct me to her house again. Why, here's two provided for.

FREDERICK. By this light, y'are happy men. 160

---

55 bona roba] lit., "good gown," but meaning a compliant woman or courtesan.

56 in fresco] alfresco, outside.

57 canary] sweet wine from the Canary Islands.

58 balderdash] a mixture of alcoholic drinks.

BLUNT. Fortune is pleased to smile on us, gentle-men—to smile on us.

Enter Sancho and pulls down Blunt by the sleeve.

SANCHO. Sir, my lady expects you—(*They go aside.*) She has removed all that might oppose your will and pleasure—and is impatient till you come. 165

BLUNT. Sir, I'll attend you.—Oh, the happiest rogue! I'll take no leave, lest they either dog me, or stay me.

Exit with Sancho.

BELVILE. But then the little Gypsy is forgot?

WILLMORE. A mischief on thee for putting her 170 into my thoughts. I had quite forgot her else, and this night's debauch had drunk her quite down.

HELLENA. Had it so, good captain! (*Claps him on the back.*)

WILLMORE. (*Aside.*) Hah! I hope she did not hear 175 me.

HELLENA. What, afraid of such a champion?

WILLMORE. Oh! You're a fine lady of your word, are you not? To make a man languish a whole day—

HELLENA. In tedious search of me. 180

WILLMORE. Egad child, thou'rt in the right; had'st thou seen what a melancholy dog I have been ever since I was a lover, how I have walked the streets like a Capuchin with my hands in my sleeves, faith, sweetheart, thou wouldst pity me. 185

HELLENA. [*Aside.*] Now if I should be hanged I can't be angry with him, he dissembles so heartily.—Alas, good captain, what pains you have taken. Now were I ungrateful not to reward so true a servant. 190

WILLMORE. Poor soul! That's kindly said; I see thou bearest a conscience. Come then, for a beginning show me thy dear face.

HELLENA. I'm afraid, my small acquaintance, you have been staying that swingeing stomach you 195 boasted this morning; I then remember my little collation would have gone down with you, without the sauce of a handsome face. Is your stomach so queasy now?

WILLMORE. Faith, long fasting, child, spoils a 200 man's appetite—yet if you durst treat, I could so lay about me still—

HELLENA. And would you fall to, before a priest says grace?

WILLMORE. Oh fie, fie, what an old, out of 205 fashioned thing hast thou named? Thou couldst not dash me more out of countenance shouldst thou show me an ugly face.

Whilst he is seemingly courting Hellena, enter Angellica, Moretta, Biskey and Sebastian, all in masquerade; Angellica sees Willmore and stares.

ANGELLICA. Heavens, 'tis he! and passionately fond to see another woman. 210

MORETTA. What could you less expect from such a swaggerer?

ANGELLICA. Expect! As much as I paid him, a heart entire
Which I had pride enough to think when ere I gave,
It would have raised the man above the vulgar, 215
Made him all soul! and that all soft and constant.

HELLENA. You see, Captain, how willing I am to be friends with you, till time and ill luck make us lovers, and ask you the question first, rather than put your modesty to the blush by asking me (for 220 alas!) I know you captains are such strict men and such severe observers of your vows to chastity, that 'twill be hard to prevail with your tender con-science to marry a young willing maid.

WILLMORE. Do not abuse me, for fear I should 225 take thee at thy word, and marry thee indeed, which I'm sure will be revenge sufficient.

HELLENA. O' my conscience, that will be our destiny, because we are both of one humour; I am as inconstant as you, for I have considered, 230 Captain, that a handsome woman has a great deal to do whilst her face is good, for then is our harvest-time to gather friends; and should I in these days of my youth catch a fit of foolish constancy, I were undone; 'tis loitering by daylight 235 in our great journey. Therefore, I declare I'll allow but one year for love, one year for indifference, and one year for hate—and then—go hang yourself! For I profess myself the gay, the kind, and the inconstant. The devil's in't if this won't please you. 240

WILLMORE. Oh most damnably! I have a heart with a hole quite through it too: no prison mine to keep a mistress in.

ANGELLICA. (*Aside.*) Perjured man! How I believe thee now. 245

HELLENA. Well, I see our business as well as humours are alike; yours to cozen as many maids as will trust you, and I as many men as have faith. See if I have not as desperate a lying look as you can have for the heart of you. (*Pulls off her vizard:* 250 *he starts.*)

How do you like it, captain?

WILLMORE. Like it! By Heaven, I never saw so much beauty! Oh the charms of those sprightly black eyes! that strangely fair face, full of smiles and 255 dimples! those soft round melting cherry lips! and small even white teeth! not to be expressed, but silently adored! Oh, one look more! and strike me dumb, or I shall repeat nothing else till I'm mad.

He seems to court her to pull off her vizard: she refuses.

ANGELLICA. I can endure no more, nor is it fit to 260 interrupt him, for if I do, my jealousy has so destroyed my reason, I shall undo him; therefore, I'll retire. (*To one of her bravoes.*) And you, Sebastian, follow that woman and learn who 'tis, (*To the other bravo.*) while you tell the fugitive, I 265 would speak to him instantly.

Exit. This while Florinda is talking to Belvile, who stands sullenly. Frederick courting Valeria.

VALERIA. [*To Belvile.*] Prithee, dear stranger, be not so sullen, for though you have lost your love, you see my friend frankly offers you hers to play with in the meantime. 270

BELVILE. Faith, madam, I am sorry I can't play at her game.

FREDERICK. Pray, leave your intercession and mind your own affair. They'll better agree apart; he's a modest sigher in company, but alone no 275 woman scapes him.

FLORINDA. [*Aside.*] Sure he does but rally, yet if it should be true—I'll tempt him farther.—Believe me, noble stranger, I'm no common mistress, and for a little proof on't, wear this jewel—nay, take 280 it, sir, 'tis right, and bills of exchange may sometimes miscarry.

BELVILE. Madam, why am I chose out of all mankind to be the object of your bounty?

VALERIA. There's another civil question asked. 285

FREDERICK. Pox of's modesty, it spoils his own markets and hinders mine.

FLORINDA. Sir, from my window, I have often seen you, and women of my quality have so few opportunities for love that we ought to lose none. 290

FREDERICK. Aye, this is something! Here's a woman! When shall I be blessed with so much kindness from your fair mouth?

(*Aside to Belvile.*)—Take the jewel, fool.

BELVILE. You tempt me strangely, madam, every 295 way—

FLORINDA. (*Aside.*) So, if I find him false, my whole repose is gone.

BELVILE. And but for a vow I've made to a very fair lady, this goodness had subdued me. 300

FREDERICK. Pox on't, be kind, in pity to me be kind, for I am to thrive here but as you treat her friend.

HELLENA. Tell me what you did in yonder house, and I'll unmask. 305

WILLMORE. Yonder house—oh—I went to—a— to—why, there's a friend of mine lives there.

HELLENA. What, a she, or a he friend?

WILLMORE. A man, upon honour! a man. A she friend? No, no, madam, you have done my 310 business, I thank you.

HELLENA. And was't your man friend that had more darts in's eyes than Cupid carries in's whole budget of arrows?

WILLMORE. So— 315

HELLENA. Ah, such a bona roba! to be in her arms is lying alfresco, all perfumed air about me—was this your man friend too?

WILLMORE. So—

HELLENA. That gave you the he and the she gold 320 that begets young pleasures?

WILLMORE. Well, well, madam, then you see there are ladies in the world that will not be cruel—there are, madam, there are—

HELLENA. And there be men too, as fine, wild, 325 inconstant fellows as yourself, there be, Captain, there be, if you go to that now. Therefore, I'm resolved—

WILLMORE. Oh!

HELLENA. To see your face no more— 330

WILLMORE. Oh!

HELLENA. Till tomorrow.

WILLMORE. Egad, you frighted me.

HELLENA. Nor then neither, unless you'll swear never to see that lady more. 335

WILLMORE. See her! Why, never to think of womankind again.

HELLENA. Kneel—and swear—

Kneels, she gives him her hand.

WILLMORE. I do, never to think—to see—to love—nor lie—with any but thy self. 340

HELLENA. Kiss the book.

WILLMORE. Oh, most religiously. (*Kisses her hand.*)

HELLENA. Now what a wicked creature am I, to damn a proper fellow.

CALLIS. (*To Florinda.*) Madam, I'll stay no longer, 345 'tis e'en dark.

FLORINDA. However, sir, I'll leave this with you—that when I'm gone, you may repent the opportunity you have lost by your modesty.

Gives him the jewel which is her picture, and exits. He gazes after her.

WILLMORE. 'Twill be an age till tomorrow—and 350 till then I will most impatiently expect you. Adieu, my dear pretty angel.

Exeunt all the women.

BELVILE. Hah! Florinda's picture—'twas she herself—what a dull dog was I! I would have given the world for one minute's discourse with her. 355

FREDERICK. This comes of your modesty! Ah, pox o' your vow, 'twas ten to one, but we had lost the jewel by't.

BELVILE. Willmore! The blessed'st opportunity lost! Florinda! Friends! Florinda! 360

WILLMORE. Ah rogue! such black eyes! such a face! such a mouth! such teeth! and so much wit!

BELVILE. All, all, and a thousand charms besides.

WILLMORE. Why, dost thou know her?

BELVILE. Know her! Aye, aye, and a pox take me 365 with all my heart for being modest.

WILLMORE. But hark ye, friend of mine, are you my rival? And have I been only beating the bush all this while?

BELVILE. I understand thee not. I'm mad. See 370 here— (*Shows the picture.*)

WILLMORE. Hah! Whose picture's this? 'Tis a fine wench!

FREDERICK. The colonel's mistress, sir.

WILLMORE. Oh, oh, here—I thought't had been 375 another prize. Come, come, a bottle will set thee right again. (*Gives the picture back.*)

BELVILE. I am content to try, and by that time 'twill be late enough for our design.

WILLMORE. Agreed. 380
Love does all day the soul's great empire keep,
But wine at night lulls the soft god asleep.

Exeunt.

SCENE II. LUCETTA'S HOUSE.

Enter Blunt and Lucetta with a light.

LUCETTA. Now we are safe and free; no fears of the coming home of my old jealous husband, which made me a little thoughtful when you came in first. But now love is all the business of my soul. 5

BLUNT. (*Aside.*) I am transported! Pox on't, that I had but some fine things to say to her, such as lovers use. I was a fool not to learn of Frederick a little by heart before I came. Something I must say.—'Sheartlikins, sweet soul! I am not used to 10 compliment, but I'm an honest gentleman, and thy humble servant.

LUCETTA. I have nothing to pay for so great a favour, but such a love as cannot but be great, since at first sight of that sweet face and shape, it made 15 me your absolute captive.

BLUNT. Kind heart! (*Aside.*) How prettily she talks! Egad, I'll show her husband a Spanish trick: send him out of the world and marry her. She's damnably in love with me and will ne'er mind 20 settlements, and so there's that saved.

LUCETTA. Well, sir, I'll go and undress me and be with you instantly.

BLUNT. Make haste, then, for 'sheartlikins, dear soul, thou canst not guess at the pain of a longing 25 lover, when his joys are drawn within the compass of a few minutes.

LUCETTA. You speak my sense, and I'll make haste to prove it.

Exit.

BLUNT. 'Tis a rare girl! And this one night's enjoyment with her will be worth all the days I ever passed in Essex. Would she would go with me into England; though to say truth, there's plenty of whores already. But a pox on 'em, they are such mercenary, prodigal whores, that they want such a one as this that's free and generous to give 'em good examples. Why, what a house she has, how rich and fine! 30 35

Enter Sancho.

SANCHO. Sir, my lady has sent me to conduct you to her chamber. 40

BLUNT. Sir, I shall be proud to follow.—Here's one of her servants too! 'Sheartlikins, by this garb and gravity, he might be a justice of peace in Essex and is but a pimp here.

Exeunt.

SCENE III.

The scene changes to a chamber with an alcove bed in't, a table, etc. Lucetta in bed. Enter Sancho and Blunt, who takes the candle of Sancho at the door.

SANCHO. Sir, my commission reaches no farther.
BLUNT. Sir, I'll excuse your compliment.

[Exit Sancho.]

What, in bed my sweet mistress?
LUCETTA. You see, I still outdo you in kindness.
BLUNT. And thou shalt see what haste I'll make to quit scores. —Oh, the luckiest rogue! (*He undresses himself.*) 5
LUCETTA. Should you be false or cruel now!
BLUNT. False! 'Sheartlikins, what dost thou take me for? a Jew? an insensible heathen? A pox of thy old jealous husband; an he were dead, egad, sweet soul, it should be none of my fault if I did not marry thee. 10
LUCETTA. It never should be mine.
BLUNT. Good soul! [*Aside.*] I'm the fortunatest dog!
LUCETTA. Are you not undressed yet? 15

BLUNT. As much as my impatience will permit.

Goes toward the bed in his shirt, drawers, etc.

LUCETTA. Hold, sir, put out the light, it may betray us else.
BLUNT. Anything, I need no other light but that of thine eyes! —'Sheartlikins, there I think I had it. 20

Puts out the candle; the bed descends [presumably through a trap door]; he gropes about to find it.

Why—why—where am I got? What, not yet? Where are you sweetest? Ah, the rogue's silent now—a pretty love-trick this. How she'll laugh at me anon!—You need not, my dear rogue! You need not! I'm all on fire already. Come, come, now call me in pity.—Sure I'm enchanted! I have been round the chamber and can find neither woman nor bed. I locked the door. I'm sure she cannot go that way, or if she could, the bed could not.— Enough, enough, my pretty wanton, do not carry the jest too far— (*Lights on a trap and is let down.*) Hah, betrayed! Dogs! Rogues! Pimps! Help! Help! 25 30

Enter Lucetta, Phillippo, and Sancho with a light.

PHILLIPPO. Ha, ha, ha, he's dispatched finely.
LUCETTA. Now, sir, had I been coy, we had missed of this booty. 35
PHILLIPPO. Nay, when I saw't was a substantial fool, I was mollified; but when you dote upon a serenading coxcomb, upon a face, fine clothes, and a lute, it makes me rage. 40
LUCETTA. You know I was never guilty of that folly, my dear Phillippo, but with yourself. But come, let's see what we have got by this.
PHILLIPPO. A rich coat! Sword and hat—these breeches, too, are well lined. See here, a gold watch! a purse—hah! Gold! at least two hundred pistoles! a bunch of diamond rings! and one with the family arms! a gold box—with a medal of his king! and his lady mother's picture! These were sacred relics, believe me. See, the waistband of his breeches have a mine of gold! Old Queen Bess's,[59] we have a 45 50

---

59 Old Queen Bess] Queen Elizabeth I, who reigned from 1558 to 1603.

quarrel[60] to her ever since eighty-eight,[61] and may therefore justify the theft; the Inquisition might have committed it.

LUCETTA. See, a bracelet of bowed[62] gold! These his sisters tied about his arm at parting. But well—for all this, I fear his being a stranger may make a noise and hinder our trade with them hereafter.

PHILLIPPO. That's our security; he is not only a stranger to us, but to the country too. The common shore[63] into which he is descended, thou knowst conducts him into another street, which this light will hinder him from ever finding again. He knows neither your name, nor that of the street where your house is, nay, nor the way to his own lodgings.

LUCETTA. And art not thou an unmerciful rogue! not to afford him one night for all this? I should not have been such a Jew.

PHILLIPPO. Blame me not, Lucetta, to keep as much of thee as I can to myself. Come, that thought makes me wanton! Let's to bed!—Sancho, lock up these.
This is the fleece which fools do bear,
Designed for witty men to shear.

Exeunt.

SCENE IV.

The scene changes and discovers Blunt, creeping out of a common shore, his face, etc. all dirty.

BLUNT. Oh lord! (*Climbing up.*) I am got out at last, and (which is a miracle) without a clue—and now to damning and cursing—but if that would ease me, where shall I begin? With my fortune, myself, or the quean[64] that cozened me? What a dog was I to believe in woman! Oh coxcomb! Ignorant conceited coxcomb! To fancy she could be enamoured with my person! At first sight enamoured! Oh, I'm a cursed puppy! 'Tis plain, "fool" was writ upon my forehead! She perceived it—saw the Essex calf there—for what allurements could there be in this countenance, which I can endure, because I'm acquainted with it—oh, dull, silly dog! To be thus soothed into a cozening! Had I been drunk, I might fondly have credited the young quean! But as I was in my right wits, to be thus cheated confirms it I am a dull, believing, English country fop—but my comrades! Death and the devil! There's the worst of all—then a ballad will be sung tomorrow on the *prado*,[65] to a lousy tune of "The Enchanted 'Squire, and the Annihilated Damsel"—but Frederick, that rogue, and the colonel, will abuse me beyond all Christian patience—had she left me my clothes, I have a bill of exchange at home would have saved my credit—but now all hope is taken from me—well, I'll home (if I can find the way) with this consolation, that I am not the first kind, believing coxcomb; but there are, gallants, many such good natures amongst ye.
And though you've better arts to hide your follies,
Adsheartlikins y'are all as arrant cullies.

Exit.

SCENE V. THE GARDEN IN THE NIGHT.

Enter Florinda in an undress, with a key and a little box.

FLORINDA. Well, thus far I'm on my way to happiness. I have got myself free from Callis; my brother, too, I find by yonder light, is got into his cabinet and thinks not of me; I have by good fortune got the key of the garden back door. I'll open it to prevent Belvile's knocking—a little noise will now alarm my brother. Now am I as fearful as a young thief. (*Unlocks the door.*) Hark—what noise is that? Oh, 'twas the wind that played amongst the boughs.—Belvile stays long, methinks—it's time—stay—for fear of a surprise, I'll hide these jewels in yonder jessamine. (*She goes to lay down the box.*)

---

60 quarrel] a real physical fight (not a verbal disagreement).
61 eighty-eight] 1588, year of the defeat of the Spanish Armada.
62 bowed] bent, braided.
63 shore] open sewer.
64 quean] bad or bold woman, a jade or strumpet.

65 *prado*] field, lawn, meadow (Sp.).

Enter Willmore drunk.[66]

WILLMORE. What the devil is become of these fellows, Belvile and Frederick? They promised to stay at the next corner for me, but who the devil knows the corner of a full moon? Now, whereabouts am I? Hah—what have we here? a garden! a very convenient place to sleep in. Hah—what has God sent us here? a female! by this light, a woman! I'm a dog if it be not a very wench!   15

  20

FLORINDA. He's come! Hah—who's there?

WILLMORE. Sweet soul! Let me salute[67] thy shoestring.

FLORINDA. 'Tis not my Belvile. Good heavens! I know him not.—Who are you, and from whence come you?   25

WILLMORE. Prithee, prithee child—not so many questions. Let it suffice I am here, child. Come, come kiss me.   30

FLORINDA. Good gods! what luck is mine?

WILLMORE. Only good luck, child, parlous good luck. Come hither. —'Tis a delicate, shining wench—by this hand she's perfumed and smells like any nosegay.—Prithee, dear soul, let's not play the fool and lose time, precious time, for as Gad shall save me, I'm as honest a fellow as breathes, though I'm a little disguised[68] at present. Come, I say. Why, thou may'st be free with me, I'll be very secret. I'll not boast who 'twas obliged me, not I—for hang me if I know thy name.   35

  40

FLORINDA. Heavens! What a filthy beast is this?

WILLMORE. I am so, and thou ought'st the sooner to lie with me for that reason—for look you child, there will be no sin in't, because 'twas neither designed nor premeditated. 'Tis pure accident on both sides—that's a certain thing now. Indeed, should I make love to you, and to you vow fidelity—and swear and lie till you believed and yielded—that were to make it wilful fornication, the crying sin of the nation. Thou art therefore (as   45

  50

thou art a good Christian) obliged in conscience to deny me nothing. Now—come be kind without any more idle prating.

FLORINDA. Oh I am ruined.—Wicked man, unhand me.   55

WILLMORE. Wicked! Egad child, a judge, were he young and vigorous and saw those eyes of thine, would know 'twas they gave the first blow—the first provocation. Come prithee, let's lose no time, I say—this is a fine convenient place.   60

FLORINDA. Sir, let me go, I conjure you, or I'll call out.

WILLMORE. Aye, aye, you were best to call witness to see how finely you treat me—do—   65

FLORINDA. I'll cry murder! rape! or anything! if you do not instantly let me go.

WILLMORE. A rape! Come, come, you lie, you baggage, you lie. What, I'll warrant you would fain have the world believe now that you are not so forward as I. No, not you. Why, at this time of night, was your cobweb door set open, dear spider—but to catch flies? Hah—come—or I shall be damnably angry. Why, what a coil is here—   70

FLORINDA. Sir, can you think—   75

WILLMORE. That you would do't for nothing—oh, oh, I find what you would be at—look, here's a pistole for you—here's a work indeed—here—take it I say—

FLORINDA. For Heaven's sake, sir, as you're a gentleman—   80

WILLMORE. So—now—now—she would be wheedling me for more—what, you will not take it then—you are resolved you will not? Come, come take it or I'll put it up again—for look ye, I never give more. Why how now, mistress, are you so high i'th'mouth a pistole won't down with you? Hah—why, what a work's here—in good time—come, no struggling to be gone—but an y'are good at a dumb wrestle I'm for ye—look ye—I'm for ye— (*She struggles with him.*)   85

  90

Enter Belvile and Frederick.

BELVILE. The door is open. A pox of this mad fellow; I'm angry that we've lost him; I durst have sworn he had followed us.

FREDERICK. But you were so hasty, Colonel, to be gone.   95

---

66 drunk] Restoration standards were high; drunk suggests "*very* drunk."

67 salute] to greet with a kiss or embrace; no military connotations.

68 disguised] drunk.

FLORINDA. Help! Help! Murder! Help—oh, I am ruined.

BELVILE. Hah! Sure that's Florinda's voice. (*Comes up to them.*) A man!—Villain, let go that lady! 100

Willmore turns and draws, Frederick interposes.

FLORINDA. Belvile! (*A noise.*) Heavens! My brother too is coming, and 'twill be impossible to escape.— Belvile, I conjure you to walk under my chamber window, from whence I'll give you some instructions what to do. This rude man has undone us. 105

Exit.

WILLMORE. Belvile!

Enter Pedro, Stephano, and other servants with lights.

PEDRO. I'm betrayed! Run, Stephano, and see if Florinda be safe.

Exit Stephano.

So, whoe'er they be, all is not well. I'll to Florinda's chamber. 110

They fight and Pedro's party beats 'em out. Going out, meets Stephano.

STEPHANO. You need not, sir; the poor lady's fast asleep and thinks no harm. I would not awake her, sir, for fear of frighting her with your danger.

PEDRO. I'm glad she's there.—Rascals, how came the garden door open? 115

STEPHANO. That question comes too late, sir; some of my fellow servants masquerading, I'll warrant.

PEDRO. Masquerading! a lewd custom to debauch our youth. There's something more in this than I 120 imagine.

Exeunt.

SCENE VI. SCENE CHANGES TO THE STREET.

Enter Belvile in rage, Frederick holding him, and Willmore melancholy.

WILLMORE. Why, how the devil should I know Florinda?

BELVILE. A plague of your ignorance! If it had not been Florinda, must you be a beast? a brute? a senseless swine? 5

WILLMORE. Well, sir, you see I am endued with patience—I can bear—though egad, y'are very free with me, methinks. I was in good hopes the quarrel would have been on my side, for so uncivilly interrupting me. 10

BELVILE. Peace, brute! whilst thou'rt safe.—Oh, I'm distracted.

WILLMORE. Nay, nay, I'm an unlucky dog, that's certain.

BELVILE. Ah, curse upon the star that ruled my 15 birth! or whatsoever other influence that makes me still[69] so wretched.

WILLMORE. Thou break'st my heart with these complaints. There is no star in fault, no influence but sack, the cursed sack I drunk. 20

FREDERICK. Why, how the devil came you so drunk?

WILLMORE. Why, how the devil came you so sober?

BELVILE. A curse upon his thin skull, he was always 25 beforehand that way.

FREDERICK. Prithee, dear Colonel, forgive him, he's sorry for his fault.

BELVILE. He's always so after he has done a mischief—a plague on all such brutes. 30

WILLMORE. By this light, I took her for an arrant harlot.

BELVILE. Damn your debauched opinion! Tell me sot, had'st thou so much sense and light about thee to distinguish her woman, and could'st not see 35 something about her face and person to strike an awful reverence into thy soul?

WILLMORE. Faith no, I considered her as mere[70] a woman as I could wish.

BELVILE. 'Sdeath,[71] I have no patience.—Draw, or 40 I'll kill you.

WILLMORE. Let that alone till tomorrow, and if I set not all right again, use your pleasure.

---

69 still] always.

70 mere] no less than.

71 'sdeath] by God's death.

BELVILE. Tomorrow! Damn it.
The spiteful light will lead me to no happiness.   45
Tomorrow is Antonio's and perhaps
Guides him to my undoing. Oh, that I could meet
This rival! This pow'rful fortunate!

WILLMORE. What then?

BELVILE. Let thy own reason, or my rage, instruct   50
thee.

WILLMORE. I shall be finely informed, then, no
doubt. Hear me, Colonel—hear me—show me the
man and I'll do his business.

BELVILE. I know him no more than thou, or if I   55
did, I should not need thy aid.

WILLMORE. This, you say, is Angellica's house. I
promised the kind baggage to lie with her tonight.
(*Offers to go in.*)

*Enter Antonio and his page. Antonio knocks on the hilt
of's sword.*

ANTONIO. You paid the thousand crowns I   60
directed?

PAGE. To the lady's old woman, sir, I did.

WILLMORE. Who the devil have we here!

BELVILE. I'll now plant myself under Florinda's
window, and if I find no comfort there, I'll die.   65

Exeunt Belvile and Frederick. Enter Moretta.

MORETTA. Page!

PAGE. Here's my lord.

WILLMORE. How is this! a picaroon going to board
my frigate? Here's one chase gun[72] for you.

*Drawing his sword, jostles Antonio who turns and
draws. They fight, Antonio falls.*

MORETTA. Oh bless us! We're all undone! (*Runs   70
in and shuts the door.*)

PAGE. Help! Murder!

Belvile returns at the noise of the fighting.

BELVILE. Hah! The mad rogue's engaged in some
unlucky adventure again.

Enter two or three masqueraders.

MASQUERADERS. Hah! A man killed!   75

WILLMORE. How! a man killed! Then I'll go home
to sleep.

Puts up and reels out. Exeunt masqueraders another way.

BELVILE. Who should it be! Pray Heaven the rogue
is safe, for all my quarrel to him.

*As Belvile is groping about, enter an officer and six
soldiers.*

SOLDIER. Who's there?   80

OFFICER. So here's one dispatched.—Secure the
murderer.

Soldiers seize on Belvile.

BELVILE. Do not mistake my charity for murder!
I came to his assistance.

OFFICER. That shall be tried, sir.—St. Jago,[73]   85
swords drawn in Carnival time! (*Goes to Antonio.*)

ANTONIO. Thy hand, prithee.

OFFICER. Hah! Don Antonio!—Look well to the
villain there.—How is it, sir?

ANTONIO. I'm hurt.   90

BELVILE. Has my humanity made me a criminal?

OFFICER. Away with him.

BELVILE. What a cursed chance is this!

Exeunt soldiers with Belvile.

ANTONIO. This is the man that has set upon me
twice.—(*To the officer.*) Carry him to my apart-   95
ment, till you have farther orders from me.

Exit Antonio led.

ACT IV, SCENE I. A FINE ROOM.

Discovers Belvile as by dark alone.

BELVILE. When shall I be weary of railing on
Fortune, who is resolved never to turn with smiles
upon me? Two such defeats in one night none but
the devil and that mad rogue could have contrived
to have plagued me with. I am here a prisoner—   5
but where, Heaven knows—and if there be murder

---

72 chase gun] swivel gun on bow or stern used in pursuit.

73 St. Jago] Santiago (St. James the Apostle), patron saint
of Spain.

done, I can soon decide[74] the fate of a stranger in a nation without mercy. Yet this is nothing to the torture my soul bows with when I think of losing my fair, my dear, Florinda.—Hark, my door opens—a light—a man—and seems of quality— armed too! Now shall I die like a dog without defense.

Enter Antonio in a nightgown with a light; his arm in a scarf, and a sword under his arm. He sets the candle on the table.

ANTONIO. Sir, I come to know what injuries I have done you that could provoke you to so mean an action as to attack me basely, without allowing time for my defense?

BELVILE. Sir, for a man in my circumstances to plead innocence would look like fear, but view me well, and you will find no marks of coward on me, nor anything that betrays that brutality you accuse me with.

ANTONIO. In vain, sir, you impose upon my sense. You are not only he who drew on me last night, But yesterday before the same house, that of Angellica. Yet there is something in your face and mien That makes me wish I were mistaken.

BELVILE. I own I fought today in the defense of a friend of mine with whom you (if you're the same) and your party were first engaged. Perhaps you think this crime enough to kill me, But if you do, I cannot fear you'll do it basely.

ANTONIO. No, sir, I'll make you fit for a defense with this. (*Gives him the sword.*)

BELVILE. This gallantry surprises me—nor know I how to use this present, sir, against a man so brave.

ANTONIO. You shall not need. For know, I come to snatch you from a danger That is decreed against you: Perhaps your life or long imprisonment; And 'twas with so much courage you offended, I cannot see you punished.

BELVILE. How shall I pay this generosity?

ANTONIO. It had been safer to have killed another Than have attempted me.

To show your danger, sir, I'll let you know my quality; And 'tis the viceroy's son whom you have wounded.

BELVILE. The viceroy's son! (*Aside.*) Death and confusion! Was this plague reserved To complete all the rest? Obliged by him! The man of all the world I would destroy.

ANTONIO. You seem disordered, sir.

BELVILE. Yes, trust me, sir, I am, and 'tis with pain That man receives such bounties Who wants the pow'r to pay 'em back again.

ANTONIO. To gallant spirits 'tis indeed uneasy; But you may quickly overpay me, sir.

BELVILE. (*Aside.*) Then I am well.—Kind Heav'n, but set us even, That I may fight with him and keep my honour safe. —Oh, I'm impatient, sir, to be discounting The mighty debt I owe you. Command me quickly—

ANTONIO. I have a quarrel with a rival, sir, About the maid we love.

BELVILE. (*Aside.*) Death, 'tis Florinda he means— That thought destroys my reason, And I shall kill him—

ANTONIO. My rival, sir, Is one has all the virtues man can boast of.

BELVILE. (*Aside.*) Death! Who should this be?

ANTONIO. He challenged me to meet him on the Molo As soon as day appeared; but last night's quarrel Has made my arm unfit to guide a sword.

BELVILE. I apprehend you, sir; you'd have me kill the man That lays a claim to the maid you speak of. I'll do't—I'll fly to do't!

ANTONIO. Sir, do you know her?

BELVILE. No, sir, but 'tis enough she is admired by you.

ANTONIO. Sir, I shall rob you of the glory on't, For you must fight under my name and dress.

BELVILE. That opinion must be strangely obliging that makes You think I can personate the brave Antonio, Whom I can but strive to imitate.

ANTONIO. You say too much to my advantage.

74 decide] determine.

Come, sir, the day appears that calls you forth.
Within, sir, is the habit.   85

Exit Antonio.

BELVILE. Fantastic Fortune, thou deceitful light,
That cheats the wearied traveller by night,
Though on a precipice each step you tread,
I am resolved to follow where you lead.

Exit.

SCENE II. THE MOLO.

Enter Florinda and Callis in masks with Stephano.

FLORINDA. (*Aside.*) I'm dying with my fears;
Belvile's not coming as I expected under my
window makes me believe that all those fears are
true.—Canst thou not tell with whom my brother
fights?   5
STEPHANO. No, madam, they were both in
masquerade. I was by when they challenged one
another, and they had decided the quarrel then,
but were prevented by some cavaliers, which made
'em put it off till now—but I am sure 'tis about   10
you they fight.
FLORINDA. (*Aside.*) Nay, then 'tis with Belvile, for
what other lover have I that dares fight for me,
except Antonio? And he is too much in favour with
my brother. If it be he, for whom shall I direct my   15
prayers to heaven?
STEPHANO. Madam, I must leave you, for if my
master see me, I shall be hanged for being your
conductor. I escaped narrowly for the excuse I
made for you last night i'th'garden.   20
FLORINDA. And I'll reward thee for't. Prithee no
more.

*Exit Stephano. Enter Don Pedro in his masquing
habit.*

PEDRO. Antonio's late today; the place will fill, and
we may be prevented. (*Walks about.*)
FLORINDA. (*Aside.*) "Antonio"—sure I heard amiss.   25
PEDRO. But who will not excuse a happy lover
When soft fair arms confine the yielding neck,
And the kind whisper languishingly breathes,
"Must you be gone so soon?"

Sure I had dwelt for ever on her bosom.   30
But stay, he's here.

Enter Belvile dressed in Antonio's clothes.

FLORINDA. 'Tis not Belvile; half my fears are
vanished.
PEDRO. Antonio!
BELVILE. (*Aside.*) This must be he.—You're early,   35
sir. I do not use to be outdone this way.
PEDRO. The wretched, sir, are watchful, and 'tis
enough
You've the advantage of me in Angellica.
BELVILE. (*Aside.*) Angellica! Or I've mistook my
man or else Antonio.
Can he forget his int'rest in Florinda,   40
And fight for common prize?
PEDRO. Come, sir, you know our terms—
BELVILE. (*Aside.*) By Heav'n not I.—
No talking, I am ready, sir. (*Offers to fight,
Florinda runs in.*)
FLORINDA. (*To Belvile.*) Oh hold! Whoe'er you   45
be, I do conjure you hold!
If you strike here—I die.
PEDRO. Florinda!
BELVILE. [*Aside.*] Florinda imploring for my rival!
PEDRO. Away, this kindness is unseasonable.

*Puts her by; they fight; she runs in just as Belvile
disarms Pedro.*

FLORINDA. Who are you, sir, that dares deny my   50
prayers?
BELVILE. Thy prayers destroy him; if thou would'st
preserve him,
Do that thou'rt unacquainted with and curse him.

She holds him.

FLORINDA. By all you hold most dear, by her you
love,
I do conjure you, touch him not.
BELVILE. By her I love!   55
See—I obey—and at your feet resign
The useless trophy of my victory.

Lays his sword at her feet.

PEDRO. Antonio, you've done enough to prove you
love Florinda.

BELVILE. Love Florinda! Does Heav'n love adora- 60
tion, prayer or penitence! Love her! Here,
sir—your sword again. (*Snatches up the sword and
gives it him.*)
Upon this truth I'll fight my life away.
PEDRO. No, you've redeemed my sister, and my 65
friendship!

*He gives him Florinda and pulls off his vizard to show
his face and puts it on again.*

BELVILE. Don Pedro!
PEDRO. Can you resign your claims to other women,
And give your heart entirely to Florinda?
BELVILE. Entire! as dying saints' confessions are! 70
I can delay my happiness no longer.
This minute let me make Florinda mine!
PEDRO. This minute let it be—no time so proper.
This night my father will arrive from Rome
And possibly may hinder what we purpose! 75
FLORINDA. Oh heavens! this minute!

Enter masqueraders and pass over.

BELVILE. Oh, do not ruin me!
PEDRO. The place begins to fill, and that we may
not be observed, do you walk off to St. Peter's
Church, where I will meet you and conclude your 80
happiness.
BELVILE. I'll meet you there—(*Aside.*) if there be
no more saints' churches in Naples.
FLORINDA. Oh, stay sir, and recall your hasty doom!
Alas, I have not yet prepared my heart 85
To entertain[75] so strange a guest.
PEDRO. Away, this silly modesty is assumed too
late. (*Pedro talks to Callis this while.*)
BELVILE. Heaven, madam! What do you do?
FLORINDA. Do! Despise the man that lays a
tyrant's claim
To what he ought to conquer by submission. 90
BELVILE. You do not know me. Move a little this
way. (*Draws her aside.*)
FLORINDA. Yes, you may force me even to the
altar,
But not the holy man that offers there
Shall force me to be thine.

---

[75] entertain] receive.

BELVILE. Oh do not lose so blest an opportunity— 95
See—'tis your Belvile—not Antonio,
Whom your mistaken scorn and anger ruins.
(*Pulls off his vizard.*)
FLORINDA. Belvile!
Where was my soul it could not meet thy voice
And take this knowledge in? 100

*As they are talking, enter Willmore, finely dressed, and
Frederick.*

WILLMORE. No intelligence, no news of Belvile
yet! Well, I am the most unlucky rascal in nature.
Hah—am I deceived? or is it he? Look, Fred—'tis
he—my dear Belvile!

*Runs and embraces him. Belvile's vizard falls out on's
hand.*

BELVILE. Hell and confusion seize thee! 105
PEDRO. Hah! Belvile! I beg your pardon sir.

Takes Florinda from him.

BELVILE. Nay, touch her not. She's mine by conquest,
sir;
I won her by my sword.
WILLMORE. Didst thou so! And egad, child, we'll
keep her by the sword.

Draws on Pedro. Belvile goes between.

BELVILE. Stand off! 110
Thou'rt so profanely lewd, so curst by Heaven,
All quarrels thou espousest must be fatal.
WILLMORE. Nay, an you be so hot, my valor's coy,
and shall be courted when you want it next. (*Puts
up his sword.*) 115
BELVILE. (*To Pedro.*) You know I ought to claim a
victor's right.
But you're the brother to divine Florinda,
To whom I'm such a slave—to purchase her,
I durst not hurt the man she holds so dear.
PEDRO. 'Twas by Antonio's, not by Belvile's sword 120
This question should have been decided, sir.
I must confess, much to your bravery's due,
Both now, and when I met you last in arms.
But I am nicely punctual in my word,
As men of honour ought, and beg your pardon. 125
For this mistake another time shall clear.

(Aside to Florinda as they are going out.)

This was some plot between you and Belvile.
But I'll prevent you.

Belvile looks after her and begins to walk up and down in rage.

WILLMORE. Do not be modest now and lose the
    woman, but if we shall fetch her back so—   130
BELVILE. Do not speak to me—
WILLMORE. Not speak to you? Egad, I'll speak to
    you, and will be answered, too.
BELVILE. Will you, sir—
WILLMORE. I know I've done some mischief, but   135
    I'm so dull a puppy, that I'm the son of a whore if
    I know how, or where—prithee inform my
    understanding—
BELVILE. Leave me, I say, and leave me instantly.
WILLMORE. I will not leave you in this humour,   140
    nor till I know my crime.
BELVILE. Death, I'll tell you sir—

Draws and runs at Willmore. He runs out, Belvile after him; Frederick interposes. Enter Angellica, Moretta and Sebastian.

ANGELLICA. Hah—Sebastian—
    Is not that Willmore? Haste—haste and bring
      him back.
FREDERICK. The colonel's mad—I never saw him   145
    thus before. I'll after 'em lest he do some mischief,
    for I am sure Willmore will not draw on him.

Exit.

ANGELLICA. I am all rage! my first desires defeated!
    For one for aught he knows that has no
    Other merit than her quality,   150
    Her being Don Pedro's sister—he loves her!
    I know 'tis so—dull, dull, insensible—
    He will not see me now though oft invited,
    And broke his word last night—false perjured man!
    He that but yesterday fought for my favours   155
    And would have made his life a sacrifice
    To've gained one night with me
    Must now be hired and courted to my arms.
MORETTA. I told you what would come on't, but
    Moretta's an old doting fool. Why did you give   160

him five hundred crowns, but to set himself out
for other lovers! You should have kept him poor
if you had meant to have had any good from him.
ANGELLICA. Oh, name not such mean trifles; had
    I given him all
    My youth has earned from sin,   165
    I had not lost a thought, nor sigh upon't.
    But I have given him my eternal rest,
    My whole repose, my future joys, my heart!
    My virgin heart, Moretta! Oh, 'tis gone!
MORETTA. Curse on him, here he comes; how fine   170
    she has made him too.

Enter Willmore and Sebastian; Angellica turns and walks away.

WILLMORE. How now, turned shadow!
    Fly when I pursue and follow when I fly! *(Sings.)*
    Stay, gentle shadow of my dove
    And tell me ere I go,   175
    Whether the substance may not prove
    A fleeting thing like you.

As she turns she looks on him.

There's a soft kind look remaining yet.
ANGELLICA. Well sir, you may be gay; all
    happiness, all joys, pursue you still. Fortune's your   180
    slave and gives you every hour choice of new hearts
    and beauties, till you are cloyed with the repeated
    bliss which others vainly languish for. (*Turns away
    in rage.*) But know, false man, that I shall be
    revenged.   185
WILLMORE. So, gad, there are of those faint-
    hearted lovers whom such a sharp lesson next their
    hearts would make as impotent as fourscore. Pox
    o' this whining. My business is to laugh and love.
    A pox on't, I hate your sullen lover. A man shall   190
    lose as much time to put you in humour now, as
    would serve to gain a new woman.
ANGELLICA. I scorn to cool that fire I cannot raise,
    Or do the drudgery of your virtuous mistress.
WILLMORE. A virtuous mistress! Death, what a   195
    thing thou hast found out for me! Why, what the
    devil should I do with a virtuous woman? a sort
    of ill-natured creatures, that take a pride to
    torment a lover. Virtue is but an infirmity in
    woman, a disease that renders even the handsome   200

ungrateful; whilst the ill-favoured, for want of solicitations and address, only fancy themselves so. I have lain with a woman of quality, who has all the while been railing at whores.

ANGELLICA. I will not answer for your mistress's virtue, 205
Though she be young enough to know no guilt;
And I could wish you would persuade my heart
'Twas the two hundred thousand crowns you courted.

WILLMORE. Two hundred thousand crowns! What story's this? What trick? What woman? Hah! 210

ANGELLICA. How strange you make it; have you forgot the creature you entertained on the piazza last night?

WILLMORE. (*Aside.*) Hah! My Gypsy worth two hundred thousand crowns! Oh, how I long to be 215 with her. Pox, I knew she was of quality.

ANGELLICA. False man! I see my ruin in thy face.
How many vows you breathed upon my bosom,
Never to be unjust—have you forgot so soon?

WILLMORE. Faith no, I was just coming to repeat 220 'em—but here's a humour indeed would make a man a saint. (*Aside.*) Would she would be angry enough to leave me and command me not to wait on her.

Enter Hellena dressed in man's clothes.

HELLENA. This must be Angellica! I know it by her 225 mumping[76] matron here. Aye, aye, 'tis she! My mad captain's with her too, for all his swearing— how this unconstant humour makes me love him!—Pray, good grave gentlewoman, is not this Angellica? 230

MORETTA. My too young sir, it is.—I hope 'tis one from Don Antonio. (*Goes to Angellica.*)

HELLENA. (*Aside.*) Well, something I'll do to vex him for this.

ANGELLICA. I will not speak with him; am I in 235 humour to receive a lover?

WILLMORE. Not speak with him! Why, I'll be gone and wait your idler minutes. Can I show less obedience to the thing I love so fondly? (*Offers to go.*)

ANGELLICA. A fine excuse this! Stay— 240

WILLMORE. And hinder your advantage! Should I repay your bounties so ungratefully?

ANGELLICA. Come hither, boy—that I may let you see
How much above the advantages you name
I prize one minute's joy with you. 245

WILLMORE. Oh, you destroy me with this endearment. (*Impatient to be gone.*) Death! How shall I get away?—Madam, 'twill not be fit I should be seen with you; besides, it will not be convenient— and I've a friend—that's dangerously sick. 250

ANGELLICA. I see you're impatient—yet you shall stay.

WILLMORE. (*Aside, and walks about impatiently.*) And miss my assignation with my Gypsy.

Moretta brings Hellena, who addresses herself to Angellica.

HELLENA. Madam, you'll hardly pardon my intrusion
When you shall know my business, 255
And I'm too young to tell my tale with art;
But there must be a wondrous store of goodness,
Where so much beauty dwells.

ANGELLICA. A pretty advocate, whoever sent thee.
Prithee proceed—(*To Willmore, who is stealing 260 off.*) Nay, sir, you shall not go.

WILLMORE. (*Aside.*) Then I shall lose my dear Gypsy for ever. Pox on't, she stays me out of spite.

HELLENA. I am related to a lady, madam,
Young, rich, and nobly born, but has the fate
To be in love with a young English gentleman. 265
Strangely she loves him, at first sight she loved him,
But did adore him when she heard him speak;
For he, she said, had charms in every word,
That failed not to surprise, to wound and conquer.

WILLMORE. (*Aside.*) Hah! Egad, I hope this 270 concerns me.

ANGELLICA. [*Aside.*] 'Tis my false man, he means—would he were gone.
This praise will raise his pride and ruin me— (*To Willmore.*) Well
Since you are so impatient to be gone,
I will release you, sir.

WILLMORE. (*Aside.*) Nay, then, I'm sure 'twas me 275 he spoke of; this cannot be the effects of kindness

---

76 mumping] moving the mouth unpleasantly, gumming.

in her.—No, madam, I've considered better on't
and will not give you cause of jealousy.

ANGELLICA. But, sir, I've—business, that—

WILLMORE. This shall not do; I know 'tis but to   280
try me.

ANGELLICA. Well, to your story, boy— (*Aside.*)
though 'twill undo me.

HELLENA. With this addition to his other beauties,
He won her unresisting tender heart.
He vowed, and sighed, and swore he loved her dearly;
And she believed the cunning flatterer   285
And thought herself the happiest maid alive.
Today was the appointed time by both
To consummate their bliss,
The virgin, altar, and the priest were dressed
And whilst she languished for th'expected   290
bridegroom,
She heard he paid his broken vows to you.

WILLMORE. So, this is some dear rogue that's in love
with me and this way lets me know it, or if it be not
me, he means someone whose place I may supply.

ANGELLICA. Now I perceive   295
The cause of thy impatience to be gone
And all the business of this glorious dress.

WILLMORE. Damn the young prater, I know not
what he means.

HELLENA. Madam,
In your fair eyes I read too much concern   300
To tell my farther business.

ANGELLICA. Prithee, sweet youth, talk on, thou
mayest perhaps
Raise here a storm that may undo my passion,
And then I'll grant thee anything.

HELLENA. Madam, 'tis to entreat you (oh   305
unreasonable)
You would not see this stranger;
For if you do, she vows you are undone,
Though nature never made a man so excellent,
And sure he'd been a god, but for inconstancy.

WILLMORE. (*Aside.*) Ah, rogue, how finely he's   310
instructed! 'Tis plain; some woman that has seen
me *en passant.*

ANGELLICA. Oh, I shall burst with jealousy! Do
you know the man you speak of?

HELLENA. Yes, madam, he used to be in buff and   315
scarlet.

ANGELLICA. (*To Willmore.*) Thou, false as hell,
what canst thou say to this?

WILLMORE. By Heaven— (*He walks about, they
follow.*)

ANGELLICA. Hold, do not damn thyself—   320

HELLENA. Nor hope to be believed.

ANGELLICA. Oh perjured man!
Is't thus you pay my generous passion back?

HELLENA. Why would you, sir, abuse my lady's
faith?

ANGELLICA. And use me so unhumanely.   325

HELLENA. A maid so young, so innocent—

WILLMORE. Ah, young devil.

ANGELLICA. Dost thou know thy life is in my
power?

HELLENA. Or think my lady cannot be revenged?

WILLMORE. (*Aside.*) So, so, the storm comes   330
finely on.

ANGELLICA. Now thou art silent, guilt has struck
thee dumb.
Oh, hadst thou still been so, I'd lived in safety.
(*She turns away and weeps.*)

WILLMORE. (*Aside to Hellena; looks toward
Angellica to watch her turning and as she comes
towards them he meets her.*) Sweetheart, the lady's   335
name and house—quickly, I'm impatient to be
with her.

HELLENA. (*Aside.*) So, now is he for another woman.

WILLMORE. The impudent'st young thing in nature,
I cannot persuade him out of his error, madam.   340

ANGELLICA. I know he's in the right—yet thou'st
a tongue
That would persuade him to deny his faith. (*In
rage walks away.*)

WILLMORE. Her name, her name, dear boy—
(*Said softly to Hellena.*)

HELLENA. Have you forgot it, sir?

WILLMORE. (*Aside.*) Oh, I perceive he's not to   345
know I am a stranger to this lady.—Yes, yes, I do
know—but I have forgot the—

Angellica turns.

—By heaven such early confidence I never saw.

ANGELLICA. Did I not charge you with this
mistress, sir?
Which you denied, though I beheld your perjury.   350

This little generosity of thine has rendered back my heart. (*Walks away.*)

WILLMORE. So, you have made sweet work here, my little mischief; look your lady be kind and good-natured now, or I shall have but a cursed bargain on't. 355

Angellica turns toward them.

—The rogue's bred up to mischief;
Art thou so great a fool to credit him?

ANGELLICA. Yes, I do, and you in vain impose upon me.

—Come hither, boy. Is not this he you spake of?

HELLENA. I think—it is; I cannot swear, but I vow 360 he has just such another lying lover's look. (*Hellena looks in his face, he gazes on her.*)

WILLMORE. (*Aside.*) Hah! Do not I know that face? By Heaven, my little Gypsy! what a dull dog was I! Had I but looked that way I'd known her. 365 Are all my hopes of a new woman banished?— Egad, if I do not fit thee for this, hang me.— Madam, I have found out the plot.

HELLENA. [*Aside.*] Oh lord, what does he say? Am I discovered now? 370

WILLMORE. Do you see this young spark here?

HELLENA. [*Aside.*] He'll tell her who I am.

WILLMORE. Who do you think this is?

HELLENA. [*Aside.*] Aye, aye, he does know me.— Nay, dear Captain! I am undone if you discover 375 me.

WILLMORE. Nay, nay, no cogging; she shall know what a precious[77] mistress I have.

HELLENA. Will you be such a devil?

WILLMORE. Nay, nay, I'll teach you to spoil sport 380 you will not make.—This small ambassador comes not from a person of quality, as you imagine and he says, but from a very arrant Gypsy, the talkingest, pratingest, cantingest little animal thou ever saw'st. 385

ANGELLICA. What news you tell me, that's the thing I mean.

HELLENA. (*Aside.*) Would I were well off the place; if ever I go a captain-hunting again—

WILLMORE. Mean that thing? that Gypsy thing? 390 Thou may'st as well be jealous of thy monkey or parrot, as of her; a German motion[78] were worth a dozen of her, and a dream were a better enjoyment, a creature of a constitution fitter for heaven than man. 395

HELLENA. (*Aside.*) Though I'm sure he lies, yet this vexes me.

ANGELLICA. You are mistaken, she's a Spanish woman
Made up of no such dull materials.

WILLMORE. Materials, egad, an she be made of any that will either dispense or admit of love, I'll 400 be bound to continence.

HELLENA. (*Aside to him.*) Unreasonable man, do you think so?

WILLMORE. You may return, my little brazen head,[79] and tell your lady that till she be handsome 405 enough to be beloved, or I dull enough to be religious, there will be small hopes of me.

ANGELLICA. Did you not promise then to marry her?

WILLMORE. Not I, by Heaven. 410

ANGELLICA. You cannot undeceive my fears and torments till you have vowed you will not marry her.

HELLENA. (*Aside.*) If he swears that, he'll be revenged on me indeed for all my rogueries. 415

ANGELLICA. I know what arguments you'll bring up against me—fortune, and honour—

WILLMORE. Honour, I tell you, I hate it in your sex, and those that fancy themselves possessed of that foppery are the most impertinently trouble- 420 some of all womankind and will transgress nine commandments to keep one, and to satisfy your jealousy, I swear—

HELLENA. (*Aside to him.*) Oh, no swearing, dear Captain. 425

WILLMORE. If it were possible I should ever be inclined to marry, it should be some kind young sinner, one that has generosity enough to give a favour handsomely to one that can ask it discreetly,

---

77 precious] notorious.

78 motion] puppet.

79 brazen head] a brass head that speaks/delivers oracular wisdom.

one that has wit enough to manage an intrigue of 430
love—oh, how civil such a wench is, to a man that
does her the honour to marry her.

ANGELLICA. By Heaven, there's no faith in
anything he says.

Enter Sebastian.

SEBASTIAN. Madam, Don Antonio— 435
ANGELLICA. Come hither.
HELLENA. [*Aside.*] Hah! Antonio! He may be
coming hither, and he'll certainly discover me. I'll
therefore retire without a ceremony.

Exit Hellena.

ANGELLICA. I'll see him; get my coach ready. 440
SEBASTIAN. It waits you, madam.
WILLMORE. This is lucky.—What, madam, now
I may be gone and leave you to the enjoyment of
my rival?
ANGELLICA. Dull man, that canst not see how ill, 445
how poor,
That false dissimulation looks. Be gone,
And never let me see thy cozening face again,
Lest I relapse and kill thee.
WILLMORE. Yes, you can spare me now—Farewell,
till you're in better humour.—I'm glad of this re- 450
lease—
Now for my Gypsy:
For though to worse we change, yet still we find
New joys, new charms, in a new miss that's kind.

Exit Willmore.

ANGELLICA. He's gone, and in this ague of my soul, 455
The shivering fit returns;
Oh, with what willing haste he took his leave,
As if the longed-for minute were arrived
Of some blest assignation.
In vain I have consulted all my charms, 460
In vain this beauty prized, in vain believed
My eyes could kindle any lasting fires.
I had forgot my name, my infamy,
And the reproach that honour lays on those
That dare pretend a sober passion here. 465
Nice reputation, though it leave behind
More virtues than inhabit where that dwells,
Yet that once gone, those virtues shine no more.

Then since I am not fit to be beloved,
I am resolved to think on a revenge 470
On him that soothed me thus to my undoing.

Exeunt.

SCENE III. A STREET.

*Enter Florinda and Valeria in habits different from
what they have been seen in.*

FLORINDA. We're happily escaped, and yet I
tremble still.
VALERIA. A lover and fear! Why, I am but half an
one, and yet I have courage for any attempt.
Would Hellena were here, I would fain have had 5
her as deep in this mischief as we; she'll fare but
ill else, I doubt.
FLORINDA. She pretended a visit to the Augustine
nuns, but I believe some other design carried her
out. Pray Heaven we light on her. Prithee, what 10
didst do with Callis?
VALERIA. When I saw no reason would do good
on her, I followed her into the wardrobe, and as
she was looking for something in a great chest, I
toppled her in by the heels, snatched the key of 15
the apartment where you were confined, locked
her in, and left her bawling for help.
FLORINDA. 'Tis well you resolve to follow my
fortunes, for thou darest never appear at home
again after such an action. 20
VALERIA. That's according as the young stranger and
I shall agree. But to our business: I delivered your
letter, your note to Belvile, when I got out under
pretence of going to mass. I found him at his
lodging, and believe me it came seasonably, for never 25
was a man in so desperate a condition. I told him of
your resolution of making your escape today if your
brother would be absent long enough to permit you;
if not, to die rather than be Antonio's.
FLORINDA. Thou shouldst have told him I was 30
confined to my chamber upon my brother's
suspicion that the business on the Molo was a plot
laid between him and I.
VALERIA. I said all this, and told him your brother
was now gone to his devotion, and he resolves to 35
visit every church till he find him and not only

undeceive him in that, but caress him so as shall
delay his return home.

FLORINDA. Oh heavens! He's here, and Belvile
with him too.

*They put on their vizards. Enter Don Pedro, Belvile,
Willmore; Belvile and Don Pedro seeming in serious
discourse.*

VALERIA. Walk boldly by them, and I'll come at
distance, lest he suspect us. (*She walks by them, and
looks back on them.*)

WILLMORE. Hah! A woman, and of an excellent
mien.

PEDRO. She throws a kind look back on you.

WILLMORE. Death, 'tis a likely wench, and that
kind look shall not be cast away—I'll follow her.

BELVILE. Prithee do not.

WILLMORE. Do not? By heavens, to the antipodes
with such an invitation.

She goes out, and Willmore follows her.

BELVILE. 'Tis a mad fellow for a wench.

Enter Frederick.

FREDERICK. Oh Colonel, such news!

BELVILE. Prithee what?

FREDERICK. News that will make you laugh in
spite of Fortune.

BELVILE. What, Blunt has had some damned trick
put upon him: Cheated, banged or clapped?[80]

FREDERICK. Cheated sir, rarely cheated of all but
his shirt and drawers. The unconscionable whore,
too, turned him out before consummation, so that
traversing the streets at midnight, the watch found
him in this fresco, and conducted him home. By
Heaven, 'tis such a sight, and yet I durst as well
been hanged as laugh at him or pity him; he beats
all that do but ask him a question, and is in such
an humour.

PEDRO. Who is't has met with this ill usage, sir?

BELVILE. A friend of ours whom you must see for
mirth's sake. (*Aside.*) I'll employ him to give
Florinda time for an escape.

PEDRO. What is he?

BELVILE. A young countryman of ours, one that has
been educated at so plentiful a rate, he yet ne'er
knew the want of money, and 'twill be a great jest
to see how simply he'll look without it. For my
part, I'll lend him none, an the rogue know not
how to put on a borrowing face and ask first; I'll
let him see how good 'tis to play our parts whilst
I play his.—Prithee Frederick, do you go home
and keep him in that posture till we come.

*Exeunt. Enter Florinda from the farther end of the
scene, looking behind her.*

FLORINDA. I am followed still— Hah! my brother
too, advancing this way. Good heavens, defend me
from being seen by him.

*She goes off. Enter Willmore, and after him Valeria, at
a little distance.*

WILLMORE. Ah! There she sails; she looks back as
she were willing to be boarded. I'll warrant her
prize.[81]

*He goes out, Valeria following. Enter Hellena, just as
he goes out, with a page.*

HELLENA. Hah, is not that my captain that has a
woman in chase? 'Tis not Angellica. Boy, follow
those people at a distance, and bring me an
account where they go in.—I'll find his haunts and
plague him everywhere.—Hah, my brother—

*Exit page; Belvile, Willmore, Pedro cross the stage;
Hellena runs off.*

SCENE IV. SCENE CHANGES TO ANOTHER STREET.

Enter Florinda.

FLORINDA. What shall I do, my brother now
pursues me.
Will no kind pow'r protect me from his tyranny?

---

80 clapped] hit, struck; but also to be given a venereal disease.

81 sails ... boarded ... prize] In sea battles and piracy, captured ships, called prizes, were seized as the property of
those who boarded them.

Hah, here's a door open; I'll venture in, since nothing can be worse than to fall into his hands. My life and honour are at stake, and my necessity has no choice.

She goes in. Enter Valeria and Hellena's page peeping after Florinda.

PAGE. Here she went in; I shall remember this house.

Exit Boy.

VALERIA. This is Belvile's lodging; she's gone in as readily as if she knew it.—Hah! here's that mad fellow again. I dare not venture in. I'll watch my opportunity.

Goes aside. Enter Willmore, gazing about him.

WILLMORE. I have lost her hereabouts. Pox on't, she must not scape me so. (*Goes out.*)

SCENE V. BLUNT'S CHAMBER.

Blunt discovered sitting on a couch in his shirt and drawers, reading.

BLUNT. So, now my mind's a little at peace, since I have resolved revenge. A pox on this tailor though, for not bringing home the clothes I bespoke. And a pox of all poor cavaliers, a man can never keep a spare suit for 'em, and I shall have these rogues come in and find me naked. And then I'm undone. But I'm resolved to arm myself—the rascals shall not insult over me too much. (*Puts on an old rusty sword and buff belt.*) Now, how like a morris dancer I am equipped. A fine ladylike whore to cheat me thus, without affording me a kindness for my money. A pox light on her, I shall never be reconciled to the sex more; she has made me as faithless as a physician, as uncharitable as a churchman, and as ill-natured as a poet. Oh, how I'll use all womankind hereafter! What would I give to have one of 'em within my reach now! Any mortal thing in petticoats, kind Fortune, send me, and I'll forgive thy last night's malice. Here's a cursed book too (a warning to all young travellers) that can instruct me how to prevent such mischiefs

now 'tis too late; well, 'tis a rare convenient thing to read a little now and then, as well as hawk and hunt. (*Sits down again and reads.*)

Enter to him Florinda.

FLORINDA. This house is haunted sure; 'tis well furnished and no living thing inhabits it.—Hah, a man! Heavens, how he's attired! Sure 'tis some ropedancer or fencing master; I tremble now for fear, and yet I must venture now to speak to him.—Sir, if I may not interrupt your meditations—

He starts up and gazes.

BLUNT. Hah, what's here! Are my wishes granted? and is not that a she creature? 'Sheartlikins, 'tis! What wretched thing art thou—hah!

FLORINDA. Charitable sir, you've told yourself already what I am, a very wretched maid, forced by a strange unlucky accident to seek safety here, And must be ruined, if you do not grant it.

BLUNT. Ruined! Is there any ruin so inevitable as that which now threatens thee? Dost thou know, miserable woman, into what den of mischiefs thou art fallen? what abyss of confusion—hah! Dost not see something in my looks that frights thy guilty soul and makes thee wish to change that shape of woman for any humble animal or devil? For those were safer for thee, and less mischievous.

FLORINDA. Alas, what mean you, sir? I must confess, your looks have something in 'em makes me fear, but I beseech you, as you seem a gentleman, pity a harmless virgin that takes your house for sanctuary.

BLUNT. Talk on, talk on, and weep too, till my faith return. Do, flatter me out of my senses again—a harmless virgin with a pox, as much one as t'other, 'sheartlikins. Why, what the devil, can I not be safe in my house for you, not in my chamber, nay, even being naked too cannot secure me; this is an impudence greater than has invaded me yet. (*Pulls her rudely.*) Come, no resistance.

FLORINDA. Dare you be so cruel?

BLUNT. Cruel? 'Sheartlikins, as a galley slave, or a Spanish whore. Cruel? Yes, I will kiss and beat thee all over, kiss and see thee all over; thou shalt lie with me too, not that I care for the enjoyment, but to let thee see I have ta'en deliberated malice to thee and will be revenged on one whore for the sins of another. I will smile and deceive thee, flatter thee, and beat thee, kiss and swear and lie to thee, embrace thee and rob thee, as she did me; fawn on thee and strip thee stark naked; then hang thee out at my window by the heels, with a paper of scurvy verses fastened to thy breast, in praise of damnable women. Come, come along.

FLORINDA. Alas, sir, must I be sacrificed for the crimes of the most infamous of my sex? I never understood the sins you name.

BLUNT. Do, persuade the fool you love him, or that one of you can be just or honest; tell me I was not an easy coxcomb, or any strange impossible tale. It will be believed sooner than thy false showers or protestations. A generation of damned hypocrites to flatter my very clothes from my back! Dissembling witches! Are these the returns you make an honest gentleman, that trusts, believes, and loves you? But if I be not even with you— (*Pulls her again.*) Come along—or I shall—

Enter Frederick.

FREDERICK. Hah! What's here to do?

BLUNT. 'Sheartlikins, Fred. I am glad thou art come to be a witness of my dire revenge.

FREDERICK. What's this, a person of quality too, who is upon the ramble to supply the defects of some grave impotent husband?

BLUNT. No, this has another pretence; some very unfortunate accident brought her hither to save a life pursued by I know not who, or why, and forced to take sanctuary here at Fool's Haven. 'Sheartlikins, to me of all mankind for protection? Is the ass to be cajoled again, think ye? No, young one, no prayers or tears shall mitigate my rage; therefore, prepare for both my pleasures of enjoyment and revenge, for I am resolved to make up my loss here on thy body; I'll take it out in kindness and in beating.

FREDERICK. Now, mistress of mine, what do you think of this?

FLORINDA. I think he will not—dares not—be so barbarous.

FREDERICK. Have a care, Blunt, she fetched a deep sigh; she is enamored with thy shirt and drawers. She'll strip thee even of that. There are of her calling such unconscionable baggages, and such dextrous thieves, they'll flay a man and he shall ne'er miss his skin till he feels the cold. There was a countryman of ours robbed of a row of teeth whilst he was a-sleeping, which the jilt made him buy again when he waked. You see, lady, how little reason we have to trust you.

BLUNT. 'Sheartlikins, why this is most abominable.

FLORINDA. Some such devils there may be, but by all that's holy, I am none such; I entered here to save a life in danger.

BLUNT. For no goodness, I'll warrant her.

FREDERICK. Faith, damsel, you had e'en confessed the plain truth, for we are fellows not to be caught twice in the same trap. Look on that wreck, a tight vessel when he set out of haven, well trimmed and laden, and see how a female picaroon of this island of rogues has shattered him, and canst thou hope for any mercy?

BLUNT. No, no, gentlewoman, come along; 'sheartlikins, we must be better acquainted.—We'll both lie with her, and then let me alone to bang her.

FREDERICK. I'm ready to serve you in matters of revenge that has a double pleasure in't.

BLUNT. Well said. You hear, little one, how you are condemned by public vote to the bed within. (*Pulls her.*) There's no resisting your destiny, sweetheart.

FLORINDA. Stay, sir, I have seen you with Belvile, an English cavalier; for his sake use me kindly. You know him, sir.

BLUNT. Belvile, why yes, sweeting, we do know Belvile, and wish he were with us now; he's a cormorant at whore and bacon; he'd have a limb or two of thee, my virgin pullet, but 'tis no matter, we'll leave him the bones to pick.

FLORINDA. Sir, if you have any esteem for that Belvile, I conjure you to treat me with more gentleness; he'll thank you for the justice.

FREDERICK. Hark ye, Blunt, I doubt we are mistaken in this matter.

FLORINDA. Sir, if you find me not worth Belvile's care, use me as you please, and that you may think

I merit better treatment than you threaten—pray take this present— 155

Gives him a ring; he looks on it.

BLUNT. Hum—a diamond! Why, 'tis a wonderful virtue now that lies in this ring, a mollifying virtue; 'sheartlikins, there's more persuasive rhetoric in't than all her sex can utter.

FREDERICK. I begin to suspect something; and 'twould anger us vilely to be trussed up for a rape upon a maid of quality, when we only believe we ruffle a harlot. 160

BLUNT. Thou art a credulous fellow, but 'sheartlikins, I have no faith yet. Why, my saint prattled as parlously as this does, she gave me a bracelet too, a devil on her, but I sent my man to sell it today for necessaries, and it proved as counterfeit as her vows of love. 165

FREDERICK. However, let it reprieve her till we see Belvile. 170

BLUNT. That's hard, yet I will grant it.

Enter a servant.

SERVANT. Oh, sir, the colonel is just come in with his new friend and a Spaniard of quality, and talks of having you to dinner with 'em. 175

BLUNT. 'Sheartlikins, I'm undone—I would not see 'em for the world. Hark ye, Fred, lock up the wench in your chamber.

FREDERICK. Fear nothing, madam; whate'er he threatens, you are safe whilst in my hands. 180

Exeunt Frederick and Florinda.

BLUNT. And, sirrah, upon your life, say—I am not at home—or that I'm asleep—or—or anything—away—I'll prevent their coming this way.

Locks the door and exeunt.

ACT V, SCENE I. BLUNT'S CHAMBER.

After a great knocking as at his chamber door, enter Blunt softly crossing the stage, in his shirt and drawers as before.

[VOICES.] (*Call and knocking within.*) Ned, Ned Blunt, Ned Blunt.

BLUNT. The rogues are up in arms. 'Sheartlikins, this villainous Frederick has betrayed me; they have heard of my blessed fortune— 5

[VOICES.] Ned Blunt, Ned, Ned—

BELVILE. [*Within.*] Why, he's dead, sir, without dispute dead, he has not been seen today; let's break open the door—here—boy—

BLUNT. Hah, break open the door! 'Sheartlikins, that mad fellow will be as good as his word. 10

BELVILE. [*Within.*] Boy, bring something to force the door.

A great noise within, at the door again.

BLUNT. So, now must I speak in my own defense; I'll try what rhetoric will do.—Hold, hold, what do you mean gentlemen, what do you mean? 15

BELVILE. (*Within.*) Oh rogue, art alive? Prithee, open the door and convince us.

BLUNT. Yes, I am alive gentlemen—but at present a little busy. 20

BELVILE. (*Within.*) How, Blunt grown a man of business? Come, come, open and let's see this miracle.

BLUNT. No, no, no, no, gentlemen, 'tis no great business—but—I am—at—my devotion—'sheartlikins, will you not allow a man time to pray? 25

BELVILE. (*Within.*) Turned religious! a greater wonder than the first! Therefore, open quickly, or we shall unhinge, we shall.

BLUNT. This won't do—why hark ye, Colonel, to tell you the plain truth, I am about a necessary affair of life—I have a wench with me—you apprehend me?—The devil's in't if they be so uncivil as to disturb me now. 30

WILLMORE. [*Within.*] How, a wench! Nay then, we must enter and partake. No resistance—unless it be your lady of quality, and then we'll keep our distance. 35

BLUNT. So, the business is out.

WILLMORE. [*Within.*] Come, come, lend's more hands to the door—now heave altogether—so, well done, my boys— (*Breaks open the door.*) 40

Enter Belvile, Willmore, Frederick, Pedro [and Boy]. Blunt looks simply, they all laugh at him, he lays his hand on his sword, and comes up to Willmore.

BLUNT. Hark ye sir, laugh out your laugh quickly, d'ye hear, and be gone. I shall spoil your sport else, 'sheartlikins sir, I shall—the jest has been carried on too long. (*Aside.*) A plague upon my tailor. 45

WILLMORE. 'Sdeath, how the whore has dressed him. Faith, sir, I'm sorry.

BLUNT. Are you so, sir; keep't to yourself then, sir, I advise you, d'ye hear, for I can as little endure your pity as his mirth. (*Lays his hand on's sword.*) 50

BELVILE. Indeed, Willmore, thou wert a little too rough with Ned Blunt's mistress. Call a person of quality whore? and one so young, so handsome, and so eloquent—ha, ha, he— 55

BLUNT. Hark ye sir, you know me, and know I can be angry; have a care—for, 'sheartlikins, I can fight too—I can, sir—do you mark me? No more—

BELVILE. Why so peevish, good Ned? Some disappointments I'll warrant. What, did the jealous count her husband return just in the nick? 60

BLUNT. Or the devil, sir. (*They laugh.*) D'ye laugh? Look ye settle me a good sober countenance, and that quickly too, or you shall know Ned Blunt is not— 65

BELVILE. Not everybody, we know that.

BLUNT. Not an ass to be laughed at, sir.

WILLMORE. Unconscionable sinner, to bring a lover so near his happiness, a vigorous, passionate lover, and then not only cheat him of his movables, but his very desires too. 70

BELVILE. Ah! Sir, a mistress is a trifle with Blunt. He'll have a dozen the next time he looks abroad. His eyes have charms not to be resisted; there needs no more than to expose that taking person to the view of the fair, and he leads 'em all in triumph. 75

PEDRO. Sir, though I'm a stranger to you, I am ashamed at the rudeness of my nation and, could you learn who did it, would assist you to make an example of 'em. 80

BLUNT. Why, aye, there's one speaks sense now, and han'somely; and let me tell you, gentlemen, I should not have showed myself like a Jack Pudding,[82] thus to have made you mirth, but that I have revenge within my power. For know, I have got into my possession a female who had better have fallen under any curse than the ruin I design her; 'sheartlikins, she assaulted me here in my own lodgings, and had doubtless committed a rape upon me, had not this sword defended me. 85 90

FREDERICK. I know not that, but o' my conscience, thou had ravished her, had she not redeemed herself with a ring. Let's see't, Blunt. (*Blunt shows the ring.*)

BELVILE. [*Aside.*] Hah, the ring I gave Florinda, when we exchanged our vows!—Hark ye Blunt— (*Goes to whisper to him.*) 95

WILLMORE. No whispering, good Colonel, there's a woman in the case; no whispering.

BELVILE. Hark ye fool, be advised, and conceal both the ring and the story for your reputation's sake. Do not let people know what despised cullies we English are, to be cheated and abused by one whore, and another rather bribe thee than be kind to thee, is an infamy to our nation. 100 105

WILLMORE. Come, come, where's the wench? We'll see her, let her be what she will; we'll see her.

PEDRO. Aye, aye, let us see her. I can soon discover whether she be of quality, or for your diversion.

BLUNT. She's in Fred's custody. 110

WILLMORE. Come, come, the key. (*To Frederick who gives him the key; they are going.*)

BELVILE. Death, what shall I do?—Stay gentlemen.—Yet if I hinder 'em, I shall discover[83] all.—Hold, let's go at once. Give me the key. 115

WILLMORE. Nay, hold there, Colonel. I'll go first.

FREDERICK. Nay, no dispute, Ned and I have the propriety of her.

WILLMORE. Damn propriety. Then we'll draw cuts. (*Belvile goes to whisper Willmore.*) Nay, no corruption, good Colonel. Come, the longest sword carries her— 120

They all draw, forgetting Don Pedro, being as a Spaniard, had the longest.

BLUNT. I yield up my interest to you, gentlemen, and that will be revenge sufficient.

---

82 Jack Pudding] a clown or buffoon; clowning assistant to a mountebank or street performer.

---

83 discover] reveal.

WILLMORE. (*To Pedro.*) The wench is yours— 125
[*Aside.*] Pox of his Toledo,[84] I had forgot that.

FREDERICK. Come sir, I'll conduct you to the lady.

Exeunt Frederick and Pedro.

BELVILE. (*Aside.*) To hinder him will certainly
discover her.—Dost know, dull beast, what
mischief thou hast done? 130

Willmore walking up and down out of humour.

WILLMORE. Aye, aye, to trust our fortune to lots,
a devil on't; 'twas madness, that's the truth on't.

BELVILE. Oh intolerable sot—

*Enter Florinda running masked, Pedro after her;
Willmore gazing round her.*

FLORINDA. (*Aside.*) Good Heaven, defend me
from discovery. 135

PEDRO. 'Tis but in vain to fly me, you're fallen to
my lot.

BELVILE. Sure she's undiscovered yet, but now I fear
there is no way to bring her off.

WILLMORE. Why, what a pox; is not this my 140
woman, the same I followed but now?

Pedro talking to Florinda, who walks up and down.

PEDRO. As if I did not know ye, and your business
here.

FLORINDA. (*Aside.*) Good Heaven, I fear he does
indeed— 145

PEDRO. Come, pray be kind; I know you meant to
be so when you entered here, for these are proper
gentlemen.

WILLMORE. But sir—perhaps the lady will not be
imposed upon. She'll choose her man. 150

PEDRO. I am better bred, than not to leave her
choice free.

Enter Valeria, and is surprised at sight of Don Pedro.

VALERIA. (*Aside.*) Don Pedro here! There's no
avoiding him.

FLORINDA. (*Aside.*) Valeria! Then I'm undone— 155

---

84 Toledo] Spanish sword famous for its long blade and
good steel.

VALERIA. (*To Pedro, running to him.*) Oh! Have I
found you, sir. The strangest accident—if I had
breath—to tell it.

PEDRO. Speak: Is Florinda safe? Hellena well?

VALERIA. Aye, aye, sir—Florinda—is safe—from 160
any fears of you.

PEDRO. Why, where's Florinda? Speak—

VALERIA. Ay, where indeed, sir, I wish I could
inform you—but to hold you no longer in
doubt— 165

FLORINDA. (*Aside.*) Oh, what will she say—

VALERIA. She's fled away in the habit—of one of
her pages, sir—but Callis thinks you may retrieve
her yet. If you make haste away, she'll tell you, sir,
the rest— (*Aside.*) if you can find her out. 170

PEDRO. Dishonourable girl, she has undone my
aim.—Sir, you see my necessity of leaving you, and
I hope you'll pardon it; my sister, I know, will
make her flight to you; and if she do, I shall expect
she should be rendered back. 175

BELVILE. I shall consult my love and honour, sir.

Exit Pedro.

FLORINDA. (*To Valeria.*) My dear preserver, let me
embrace thee.

WILLMORE. What the devil's all this?

BLUNT. Mystery by this light. 180

VALERIA. Come, come, make haste and get
yourselves married quickly, for your brother will
return again.

BELVILE. I'm so surprised with fears and joys, so
amazed to find you here in safety, I can scarce 185
persuade my heart into a faith of what I see.

WILLMORE. Hark ye, Colonel, is this that mistress
who has cost you so many sighs, and me so many
quarrels with you?

BELVILE. It is— (*To Florinda.*) Pray give him the 190
honour of your hand.

WILLMORE. Thus it must be received then.
(*Kneels and kisses her hand.*)
And with it give your pardon, too.

FLORINDA. The friend to Belvile may command
me anything. 195

WILLMORE. (*Aside.*) Death, would I might; 'tis a
surprising beauty.

BELVILE. Boy, run and fetch a father instantly.

Exit Boy.

FREDERICK. So, now do I stand like a dog and have not a syllable to plead my own cause with. By this hand, madam, I was never thoroughly confounded before, nor shall I ever more dare look up with confidence, till you are pleased to pardon me.   200

FLORINDA. Sir, I'll be reconciled to you on one condition, that you'll follow the example of your friend, in marrying a maid that does not hate you and whose fortune (I believe) will not be unwelcome to you.   205

FREDERICK. Madam, had I no inclinations that way, I should obey your kind commands.   210

BELVILE. Who, Frederick marry? He has so few inclinations for womankind, that had he been possessed of paradise he might have continued there to this day, if no crime but love could have disinherited him.   215

FREDERICK. Oh, I do not use to boast of my intrigues.

BELVILE. Boast, why thou dost nothing but boast; and I dare swear, wert thou as innocent from the sin of the grape, as thou art from the apple, thou might'st yet claim that right in Eden which our first parents lost by too much loving.   220

FREDERICK. I wish this lady would think me so modest a man.

VALERIA. She would be sorry, then, and not like you half so well, and I should be loath to break my word with you, which was, that if your friend and mine agreed, it should be a match between you and I. (*She gives him her hand.*)   225

FREDERICK. Bear witness, Colonel, 'tis a bargain. (*Kisses her hand.*)   230

BLUNT. (*To Florinda.*) I have a pardon to beg too, but 'sheartlikins, I am so out of countenance that I'm a dog if I can say anything to purpose.

FLORINDA. Sir, I heartily forgive you all.   235

BLUNT. That's nobly said, sweet lady.—Belvile, prithee present her her ring again; for I find I have not courage to approach her myself.

Gives him the ring; he gives it to Florinda. Enter Boy.

BOY. Sir, I have brought the father that you sent for. [*Exit.*]   240

BELVILE. 'Tis well, and now my dear Florinda, let's fly to complete that mighty joy we have so long wished and sighed for.—Come, Fred—you'll follow?

FREDERICK. Your example, sir, 'twas ever my ambition in war, and must be so in love.   245

WILLMORE. And must not I see this juggling knot tied?

BELVILE. No, thou shalt do us better service, and be our guard, lest Don Pedro's sudden return interrupt the ceremony.   250

WILLMORE. Content. I'll secure this pass.

Exeunt Belvile, Florinda, Frederick and Valeria. Enter Boy.

BOY. (*To Willmore.*) Sir, there's a lady without would speak to you.

WILLMORE. Conduct her in, I dare not quit my post.   255

BOY. And sir, your tailor waits you in your chamber.

BLUNT. Some comfort yet, I shall not dance naked at the wedding.

Exeunt Blunt and Boy. Enter again the Boy, conducting in Angellica in a masquing habit and a vizard. Willmore runs to her.

WILLMORE. This can be none but my pretty Gypsy.—Oh, I see you can follow as well as fly. Come, confess thyself the most malicious devil in nature; you think you have done my business with Angellica—   260

ANGELLICA. Stand off, base villain— (*She draws a pistol, and holds it to his breast.*)   265

WILLMORE. Hah, 'tis not she.—Who art thou? and what's thy business?

ANGELLICA. One thou hast injured and who comes to kill thee for't.   270

WILLMORE. What the devil canst thou mean?

ANGELLICA. By all my hopes to kill thee— (*Holds still the pistol to his breast, he going back, she following still.*)

WILLMORE. Prithee, on what acquaintance? For I know thee not.   275

ANGELLICA. Behold this face—so lost to thy remembrance,

And then call all thy sins about thy soul, (*Pulls off her vizard.*)

And let 'em die with thee.

WILLMORE. Angellica! 280

ANGELLICA. Yes, traitor,

Does not thy guilty blood run shivering through thy veins?

Hast thou no horror at this sight that tells thee

Thou hast not long to boast thy shameful conquest?

WILLMORE. Faith, no, child, my blood keeps its 285 old ebbs and flows still and that usual heat too that could oblige thee with a kindness, had I but opportunity.

ANGELLICA. Devil! Dost wanton with my pain?

Have at thy heart. 290

WILLMORE. Hold, dear virago! Hold thy hand a little; I am not now at leisure to be killed—hold and hear me— (*Aside.*) Death, I think she's in earnest.

ANGELLICA. (*Aside, turning from him.*) Oh, if I 295 take not heed,

My coward heart will leave me to his mercy.

—What have you, sir, to say? But should I hear thee,

Thou'dst talk away all that is brave about me:

(*Follows him with the pistol to his breast.*)

And I have vowed thy death, by all that's sacred.

WILLMORE. Why, then there's an end of a proper 300 handsome fellow,

That might 'a lived to have done good service yet;

That's all I can say to't.

ANGELLICA. (*Pausingly.*) Yet—I would give thee—time for—penitence.

WILLMORE. Faith child, I thank God I have ever took

Care to lead a good, sober, hopeful life, and am of 305 a religion

That teaches me to believe I shall depart in peace.

ANGELLICA. So will the devil! Tell me,

How many poor believing fools thou hast undone?

How many hearts thou hast betrayed to ruin?

Yet these are little mischiefs to the ills 310

Thou'st taught mine to commit: thou'st taught it love.

WILLMORE. Egad, 'twas shrewdly hurt the while.

ANGELLICA. Love, that has robbed it of its unconcern,

Of all that pride that taught me how to value it.

And in its room 315

A mean submissive passion was conveyed,

That made me humbly bow, which I ne'er did

To any thing but Heaven.

Thou, perjured man, didst this, and with thy oaths,

Which on thy knees, thou didst devoutly make, 320

Softened my yielding heart—and then, I was a slave—

Yet still had been content to've worn my chains,

Worn 'em with vanity and joy forever,

Hadst thou not broke those vows that put them on.

'Twas then I was undone. (*All this while follows* 325 *him with the pistol to his breast.*)

WILLMORE. Broke my vows! Why, where hast thou lived?

Amongst the gods? For I never heard of mortal man

That has not broke a thousand vows.

ANGELLICA. Oh impudence!

WILLMORE. Angellica! That beauty has been too 330 long tempting

Not to have made a thousand lovers languish,

Who in the amorous fever no doubt have sworn

Like me. Did they all die in that faith? still adoring?

I do not think they did.

ANGELLICA. No, faithless man; had I repaid their 335 vows, as I did thine,

I would have killed the ingrateful that had abandoned me.

WILLMORE. This old general has quite spoiled thee; nothing makes a woman so vain as being flattered. Your old lover ever supplies the defects of age, with intolerable dotage, vast charge, and 340 that which you call constancy; and attributing this to your own merits, you domineer, and throw your favours in's teeth, upbraiding him still with the defects of age, and cuckold him as often as he deceives your expectations. But the gay, young, 345 brisk lover that brings his equal fires, and can give you dart for dart, will be as nice as you sometimes.

ANGELLICA. All this thou'st made me know, for which I hate thee.

Had I remained in innocent security,

I should have thought all men were born my slaves, 350

And worn my pow'r like lightning in my eyes,

To have destroyed at pleasure when offended.

But when love held the mirror, the undeceiving glass
Reflected all the weakness of my soul, and made
  me know
My richest treasure being lost, my honour,   355
All the remaining spoil could not be worth
The conqueror's care or value.
Oh how I fell, like a long worshipped idol
Discovering all the cheat.
Would not the incense and rich sacrifice,   360
Which blind devotion offered at my altars,
Have fall'n to thee?
Why wouldst thou then destroy my fancied pow'r?
WILLMORE. By Heaven, thou'rt brave, and I
  admire thee strangely.
I wish I were that dull, that constant thing   365
Which thou wouldst have and nature never meant
  me.
I must, like cheerful birds, sing in all groves
And perch on every bough,
Billing the next kind she that flies to meet me;
Yet after all could build my nest with thee,   370
Thither repairing when I'd loved my round,
And still reserve a tributary flame.
To gain your credit, I'll pay you back your charity
And be obliged for nothing but for love. (*Offers*
  her a purse of gold.)
ANGELLICA. Oh that thou wert in earnest!   375
So mean a thought of me
Would turn my rage to scorn, and I should pity thee
And give thee leave to live;
Which for the public safety of our sex
And my own private injuries I dare not do.   380
Prepare— (*Follows still, as before.*)
I will no more be tempted with replies.
WILLMORE. Sure—
ANGELLICA. Another word will damn thee! I've
  heard thee talk too long.

*She follows him with the pistol ready to shoot; he retires
still amazed. Enter Don Antonio, his arm in a scarf,
and lays hold on the pistol.*

ANTONIO. Hah! Angellica!   385
ANGELLICA. Antonio! What devil brought thee
  hither?
ANTONIO. Love and curiosity, seeing your coach
  at door.

Let me disarm you of this unbecoming instrument of
  death—
(*Takes away the pistol.*) Amongst the number of
your slaves, was there not one worthy the honour   390
to have fought your quarrel?
—Who are you, sir, that are so very wretched
To merit death from her?
WILLMORE. One, sir, that could have made a
better end of an amorous quarrel without you than   395
with you.
ANTONIO. Sure 'tis some rival. Hah, the very man
took down her picture yesterday, the very same that
set on me last night. Blest opportunity— (*Offers
to shoot him.*)   400
ANGELLICA. Hold, you're mistaken sir.
ANTONIO. By Heaven, the very same!
—Sir, what pretensions have you to this lady?
WILLMORE. Sir, I do not use to be examined and
am ill at all disputes but this— (*Draws; Antonio*   405
offers to shoot.)
ANGELLICA. (*To Willmore.*) Oh hold! You see he's
  armed with certain death.
—And you Antonio, I command you hold,
By all the passion you've so lately vowed me.

Enter Don Pedro, sees Antonio and stays.

PEDRO. (*Aside.*) Hah, Antonio! and Angellica!   410
ANTONIO. When I refuse obedience to your will,
May you destroy me with your mortal hate.
By all that's holy I adore you so,
That even my rival, who has charms enough
To make him fall a victim to my jealousy,   415
Shall live, nay and have leave to love on still.
PEDRO. (*Aside.*) What's this I hear?
ANGELLICA. (*Pointing to Willmore.*) Ah thus!
'Twas thus he talked, and I believed.
—Antonio, yesterday,
I'd not have sold my interest in his heart   420
For all the sword has won and lost in battle.
—But now to show my utmost of contempt,
I give thee life, which if thou wouldst preserve,
Live where my eyes may never see thee more,
Live to undo someone whose soul may prove   425
So bravely constant to revenge my love.

Goes out, Antonio follows, but Pedro pulls him back.

PEDRO. Antonio—stay.

ANTONIO. Don Pedro—

PEDRO. What coward fear was that prevented thee
From meeting me this morning on the Molo?   430

ANTONIO. Meet thee?

PEDRO. Yes me; I was the man that dared thee to't.

ANTONIO. Hast thou so often seen me fight in war
To find no better cause to excuse my absence?
I sent my sword and one to do thee right,   435
Finding myself uncapable to use a sword.

PEDRO. But 'twas Florinda's quarrel we fought,
And you, to show how little you esteemed her,
Sent me your rival, giving him your interest.
But I have found the cause of this affront,   440
And when I meet you fit for the dispute,
I'll tell you my resentment.

ANTONIO. I shall be ready, sir, ere long, to do you
reason.

Exit Antonio.

PEDRO. If I could find Florinda now whilst my
anger's high, I think I should be kind and give her   445
to Belvile in revenge.

WILLMORE. Faith, sir, I know not what you would
do, but I believe the priest within has been so kind.

PEDRO. How! My sister married?

WILLMORE. I hope by this time he is, and bedded   450
too, or he has not my longings about him.

PEDRO. Dares he do this! Does he not fear my
power?

WILLMORE. Faith, not at all. If you will go in, and
thank him for the favour he has done your sister,   455
so; if not, sir, my power's greater in this house than
yours. I have a damned surly crew here, that will
keep you till the next tide, and then clap you on
board for prize; my ship lies but a league off the
Molo, and we shall show your donship a damned   460
tramontane[85] rover's trick.

Enter Belvile.

BELVILE. This rogue's in some new mischief—hah,
Pedro returned!

---

85 tramontane] from beyond the mountains, esp. of Italy,
often with the connotation of barbarous or uncouth.

PEDRO. Colonel Belvile, I hear you have married
my sister?   465

BELVILE. You have heard the truth then, sir.

PEDRO. Have I so; then, sir, I wish you joy.

BELVILE. How!

PEDRO. By this embrace I do, and I am glad on't.

BELVILE. Are you in earnest?   470

PEDRO. By our long friendship and my obligations
to thee, I am,
The sudden change I'll give you reasons for anon.
Come lead me to my sister,
That she may know I now approve her choice.

*Exeunt Belvile with Pedro. Willmore goes to follow
them. Enter Hellena as before in boy's clothes, and pulls
him back.*

WILLMORE. Hah! My Gypsy!—Now a thousand   475
blessings on thee for this kindness. Egad child, I
was e'en in despair of ever seeing thee again; my
friends are all provided for within, each man his
kind woman.

HELLENA. Hah! I thought they had served me   480
some such trick!

WILLMORE. And I was e'en resolved to go aboard
and condemn myself to my lone cabin and the
thoughts of thee.

HELLENA. And could you have left me behind,   485
would you have been so ill natured?

WILLMORE. Why, 'twould have broke my heart,
child. But since we are met again, I defy foul
weather to part us.

HELLENA. And would you be a faithful friend now, 490
if a maid should trust you?

WILLMORE. For a friend I cannot promise; thou
art of a form so excellent, a face and humour too
good for cold dull friendship. I am parlously afraid
of being in love, child, and you have not forgot   495
how severely you have used me?

HELLENA. That's all one; such usage you must still
look for, to find out all your haunts, to rail at you
to all that love you, till I have made you love only
me in your own defense, because nobody else will   500
love you.

WILLMORE. But hast thou no better quality to
recommend thyself by?

HELLENA. Faith, none, Captain. Why, 'twill be the

greater charity to take me for thy mistress. I am a lone child, a kind of orphan lover, and why I should die a maid, and in a captain's hands too, I do not understand.

WILLMORE. Egad, I was never clawed away with broadsides from any female before. Thou hast one virtue I adore, good nature. I hate a coy, demure mistress, she's as troublesome as a colt; I'll break none. No, give me a mad mistress when mewed and, in flying, one I dare trust upon the wing, that whilst she's kind will come to the lure.

HELLENA. Nay, as kind as you will, good Captain, whilst it lasts, but let's lose no time.

WILLMORE. My time's as precious to me as thine can be; therefore, dear creature, since we are so well agreed, let's retire to my chamber, and if ever thou wert treated with such savory love—Come, my bed's prepared for such a guest, all clean and sweet as thy fair self. I love to steal a dish and a bottle with a friend, and hate long graces. Come let's retire and fall to.

HELLENA. 'Tis but getting my consent, and the business is soon done. Let but old gaffer Hymen and his priest say amen to't, and I dare lay my mother's daughter by as proper a fellow as your father's son, without fear or blushing.

WILLMORE. Hold, hold, no bug[86] words, child. Priest and Hymen! Prithee, add a hangman to 'em to make up the consort. No, no, we'll have no vows but love, child, nor witness but the lover; the kind deity enjoins naught but love and enjoy! Hymen and priest wait still upon portion and jointure; love and beauty have their own ceremonies. Marriage is as certain a bane to love as lending money is to friendship. I'll neither ask nor give a vow—though I could be content to turn Gypsy, and become a left-handed bridegroom[87] to have the pleasure of working that great miracle of making a maid a mother, if you durst venture; 'tis upse[88] Gypsy that, and if I miss, I'll lose my labour.

HELLENA. And if you do not lose, what shall I get? a cradle full of noise and mischief, with a pack of repentance at my back? Can you teach me to weave inkle[89] to pass my time with? 'Tis upse Gypsy that too.

WILLMORE. I can teach thee to weave a true love's knot better.

HELLENA. So can my dog.

WILLMORE. Well, I see we are both upon our guards, and I see there's no way to conquer good nature, but by yielding—here—give me thy hand—one kiss and I am thine—

HELLENA. One kiss! How like my page he speaks; I am resolved you shall have none, for asking such a sneaking sum. He that will be satisfied with one kiss, will never die of that longing. Good friend single kiss, is all your talking come to this? a kiss, a caudle! Farewell, captain single kiss. (*Going out; he stays her.*)

WILLMORE. Nay, if we part so, let me die like a bird upon a bough, at the sheriff's charge.[90] By Heaven, both the Indies shall not buy thee from me. I adore thy humour and will marry thee, and we are so of one humour, it must be a bargain. Give me thy hand— (*Kisses her hand.*) And now let the blind ones (Love and Fortune) do their worst.

HELLENA. Why, God-a-mercy, Captain!

WILLMORE. But hark ye, the bargain is now made, but is it not fit we should know each other's names, that when we have reason to curse one another hereafter (and people ask me who 'tis I give to the devil) I may at least be able to tell what family you came of.

HELLENA. Good reason, Captain; and where I have cause (as I doubt not but I shall have plentiful) that I may know at whom to throw my—blessings—I beseech ye your name.

WILLMORE. I am called Robert the Constant.

HELLENA. A very fine name; pray was it your falconer or butler that christened you? Do they not use to whistle when they call you?

---

86 bug] as in bugbear, or bogy, an imaginary terror or threat.
87 left-handed bridegroom] one whose marriage contract stipulates he will inherit neither money nor social standing.
88 upse] in the manner or fashion of.
89 inkle] a linen thread or yarn.
90 let me … at the sheriff's charge] let me be hanged (Spencer).

WILLMORE. I hope you have a better, that a man may name without crossing himself, you are so merry with mine.

HELLENA. I am called Hellena the Inconstant. 590

Enter Pedro, Belvile, Florinda, Frederick, Valeria.

PEDRO. [*Aside.*] Hah! Hellena!

FLORINDA. Hellena!

HELLENA. The very same.—Hah, my brother!— Now Captain, show your love and courage; stand to your arms, and defend me bravely, or I am lost 595 forever.

PEDRO. What's this I hear! False girl, how came you hither and what's your business? Speak. (*Goes roughly to her.*)

WILLMORE. Hold off, sir, you have leave to parley 600 only. (*Puts himself between.*)

HELLENA. I had e'en as good tell it, as you guess it; faith, brother, my business is the same with all living creatures of my age, to love, and be beloved, and here's the man. 605

PEDRO. Perfidious maid, hast thou deceived me too? deceived thyself and Heaven?

HELLENA. 'Tis time enough to make my peace with that.
Be you but kind; let me alone with Heaven.

PEDRO. Belvile, I did not expect this false play from 610 you. Was't not enough you'd gain Florinda (which I pardoned) but your lewd friends too must be enriched with the spoils of a noble family?

BELVILE. Faith, sir, I am as much surprised at this as you can be. Yet sir, my friends are gentlemen, 615 and ought to be esteemed for their misfortunes, since they have the glory to suffer with the best of men and kings; 'tis true, he's a rover of fortune, yet a prince aboard his little wooden world.

PEDRO. What's this to the maintenance of a woman 620 of her birth and quality?

WILLMORE. Faith, sir, I can boast of nothing but a sword which does me right where'er I come and has defended a worse cause than a woman's; and since I loved her before I either knew her birth 625 or name, I must pursue my resolution and marry her.

PEDRO. And is all your holy intent of becoming a nun debauched into a desire of man?

HELLENA. Why, I have considered the matter, 630 brother, and find the three hundred thousand crowns my uncle left me (and you cannot keep from me) will be better laid out in love than in religion, and turn to as good an account. Let most voices carry it, for Heaven or the captain? 635

ALL CRY. A captain! A captain!

HELLENA. Look ye, sir, 'tis a clear case.

PEDRO. (*Aside.*) Oh I am mad. If I refuse, my life's in danger.—Come. There's one motive induces me. Take her. I shall now be free from fears of her 640 honour. Guard it you now, if you can; I have been a slave to't long enough. (*Gives her to him.*)

WILLMORE. Faith, sir, I am of a nation that are of opinion a woman's honour is not worth guarding when she has a mind to part with it. 645

HELLENA. Well said, Captain.

PEDRO. (*To Valeria.*) This was your plot, mistress, but I hope you have married one that will revenge my quarrel to you—

VALERIA. There's no altering destiny, sir. 650

PEDRO. Sooner than a woman's will. Therefore, I forgive you all—and wish you may get my father's pardon as easily, which I fear.

Enter Blunt dressed in a Spanish habit, looking very ridiculously; his man adjusting his band.

MAN. 'Tis very well, sir—

BLUNT. Well sir, 'sheartlikins, I tell you 'tis 655 damnable ill, sir—a Spanish habit, good lord! Could the devil and my tailor devise no other punishment for me, but the mode of a nation I abominate?

BELVILE. What's the matter, Ned? 660

BLUNT. Pray view me round, and judge— (*Turns round.*)

BELVILE. I must confess thou art a kind of an odd figure.

BLUNT. In a Spanish habit with a vengeance! I had 665 rather be in the Inquisition for Judaism, than in this doublet and breeches; a pillory were an easy collar to this, three handfuls high; and these shoes too, are worse than the stocks, with the sole an inch shorter than my foot. In fine, gentlemen, 670 methinks I look altogether like a bag of bays[91] stuffed full of fool's flesh.

BELVILE. Methinks 'tis well, and makes thee look *en cavalier.* Come, sir, settle your face and salute our friends.—Lady— 675

BLUNT. Hah! Say'st thou so, my little rover— (*To Hellena.*) Lady (if you be one), give me leave to kiss your hand, and tell you, 'sheartlikins, for all I look so, I am your humble servant.—A pox of my Spanish habit. 680

Music is heard to play. Enter Boy.

WILLMORE. Hark—what's this?

BOY. Sir, as the custom is, the gay people in masquerade who make every man's house their own are coming up.

Enter several men and women in masquing habits with music; they put themselves in order and dance.

BLUNT. 'Sheartlikins, would 'twere lawful to pull off 685 their false faces, that I might see if my doxy were not among'st 'em.

BELVILE. (*To the masquers.*) Ladies and gentlemen, since you are come so apropos, you must take a small collation with us. 690

WILLMORE. Whilst we'll to the good man within, who stays to give us a cast of his office. (*To Hellena.*) Have you no trembling at the near approach?

HELLENA. No more than you have in an engage- 695 ment[92] or a tempest.

WILLMORE. Egad thou'rt a brave girl, and I admire thy love and courage.

Lead on, no other dangers they can dread,
Who venture in the storms o'th' marriage bed.

Exeunt.

THE END.

---

[91] bag of bays] the sachet of bay leaves used to infuse a soup or stew.

[92] engagement] i.e., a military engagement.

WILLIAM WYCHERLEY

The Country Wife[1]

Edited and introduced by Peggy Thompson[2]

W illiam Wycherley (1641–1715) was an aspiring courtier, occasional soldier, and Shropshire heir, whose long life was marred by illness, debt, litigation, and two controversial marriages. At the time he wrote *The Country Wife* (1675), however, he enjoyed the friendship of the Court wits, the admiration of the Court ladies, and the fondness of the king himself. The third of Wycherley's four comedies for the stage, *The Country Wife* was first performed by the King's Company at the Theatre Royal, Drury Lane, probably on January 12, 1675. It featured several original members of the company, including Charles Hart as the deceptive, self-serving Horner, a role that contrasted sharply with the many heroic and tragic parts Hart had played previously. Elizabeth Boutell created the part of Margery Pinchwife, one of the breeches roles for which she was famous and which, with the introduction of women to the acting profession after the Restoration, had assumed new significance by publicly exposing the shape of a woman's legs.

The importance of this play in the history of dramatic literature is suggested by both the extensive praise it received for its wit and the increasing censure it incurred for its licentiousness. It was moderately successful on the stage through to the middle of the eighteenth century. But it was controversial almost immediately, as evidenced by Wycherley's next play, *The Plain Dealer* (1676), which features a discussion of the offending "china scene." In 1753, *The Country Wife* disappeared from the stage, replaced a few years later by two radically expurgated adaptations which claimed to have excised the impropriety of the original: a two-act afterpiece by John Lee (1765), and a full-length play, *The Country Girl*, by David Garrick (1766). Both eliminated the vital centre of the play: the part of Horner and the Fidget-Squeamish subplot. Although *The Country Wife*, together with *The Plain Dealer*, eventually secured Wycherley's reputation as a powerful comedic and satiric dramatist, Wycherley's own comedy did not reappear on the English stage until 1924.

---

[1] Copytext is the first edition, a 1675 quarto (Q1). Also consulted: modern editions of 1924 (Summers), 1967 (Weales), 1975 (Cook and Swannell), 1979 (Friedman), 1981 (Holland), 1991 (Ogden), and 1996 (Dixon).

[2] The text and annotations are based on Thompson's edition as previously published in J. Douglas Canfield's *The Broadview Anthology of Restoration and Early Eighteenth-Century Drama* (2001), although I have added a number of notes of my own. [J.W.]

WILLIAM WYCHERLEY
The Country Wife

DRAMATIS PERSONAE
[MEN]
  MR. HORNER.
  MR. HARCOURT.
  MR. DORILANT.
  MR. PINCHWIFE.
  MR. SPARKISH.
  SIR JASPAR FIDGET.
  A BOY.
  [DR.] QUACK.
  [CLASP, a bookseller.]
  [A PARSON.]
  WAITERS, SERVANTS, AND ATTENDANTS.
[WOMEN]
  MRS.[1] MARGERY PINCHWIFE.
  MRS. ALITHEA.
  MY LADY FIDGET.
  MRS. DAINTY FIDGET.
  MRS. SQUEAMISH.
  OLD LADY SQUEAMISH.
  LUCY, Alithea's maid.

THE SCENE: LONDON.

Indignor quicquam reprehendi, non quia crasse
Compositum illepideve putetur, sed quia nuper,
Nec veniam antiquis, sed honorem et praemia posci.
    Horat.[2]

---

1 Mrs.] pronounced "Mistress," and used for married and unmarried women alike.
2 *Indignor ... Horat.*] Horace, *Epistles* II.i.76-78: "I am impatient that any work is censured, not because it is thought to be coarse or inelegant in style, but because it is modern, and that what is claimed for the ancients should be, not indulgence, but honour and rewards" (Loeb Classical Library Vol. 2; Harvard 1926).

ACT I, SCENE I. [HORNER'S LODGING.]

Enter Horner and Quack following him at a distance.

HORNER. (*Aside.*) A quack is as fit for a pimp as a midwife for a bawd; they are still but in their way both helpers of nature.[3]—Well my dear doctor, hast thou done what I desired?

QUACK. I have undone you forever with the women and reported you throughout the whole Town as bad as an eunuch[4] with as much trouble as if I had made you one in earnest.

HORNER. But have you told all the midwives you know, the orange wenches at the playhouses,[5] the City husbands,[6] and old fumbling keepers[7] of this end of the Town? For they'll be the readiest to report it.

QUACK. I have told all the chambermaids, waiting women, tirewomen,[8] and old women of my acquaintance, nay, and whispered it as a secret to 'em and to the whisperers of Whitehall,[9] so that you need not doubt 'twill spread, and you will be as odious to the handsome young women as—

HORNER. As the small pox. Well—

---

3 A quack ... a bawd] that is, their proximity to the body makes them both serviceable for sexual intrigues.
4 eunuch] literally a bed-chamber or harem attendant, but usually meaning a castrated male.
5 orange wenches] women who hawked oranges as snacks in the theatres, often doing double duty as bawds.
6 City husbands] men who frequent the financial centre of London as stock-market traders, etc.
7 keepers] rich men who keep mistresses by supporting them financially.
8 tirewomen] ladies' maids in charge of attire, especially in the green rooms, or "tiring rooms" backstage at the theatres.
9 Whitehall] royal palace in London and the area around it.

QUACK. And to the married women of this end of the Town as—

HORNER. As the great ones,[10] nay, as their own husbands.

QUACK. And to the City dames as Aniseed Robin[11] of filthy and contemptible memory, and they will frighten their children with your name, especially their females.

HORNER. And cry, "Horner's coming to carry you away!" I am only afraid 'twill not be believed. You told 'em 'twas by an English-French disaster and an English-French chirurgeon,[12] who has given me at once, not only a cure, but an antidote for the future against that damned malady and that worse distemper, love, and all other women's evils.

QUACK. Your late journey into France has made it the more credible, and your being here a fortnight before you appeared in public looks as if you apprehended the shame, which I wonder you do not. Well, I have been hired by young gallants to belie 'em t'other way,[13] but you are the first would be thought a man unfit for women.

HORNER. Dear Mr. Doctor, let vain rogues be contented only to be thought abler men than they are; generally 'tis all the pleasure they have, but mine lies another way.

QUACK. You take, methinks, a very preposterous way to it and as ridiculous as if we operators in physic should put forth bills to disparage our medicaments with hopes to gain customers.

HORNER. Doctor, there are quacks in love as well as physic who get but the fewer and worse patients for their boasting; a good name is seldom got by giving it one's self, and women no more than honour are compassed by bragging. Come, come, doctor, the wisest lawyer never discovers[14] the merits of his cause till the trial; the wealthiest man conceals his riches, and the cunning gamester his play; shy husbands and keepers, like old rooks,[15] are not to be cheated but by a new unpractised trick: false friendship will pass now no more than false dice upon 'em, no, not in the City.

Enter boy.

BOY. There are two ladies and a gentleman coming up.

HORNER. A pox! some unbelieving sisters of my former acquaintance, who, I am afraid, expect their sense should be satisfied of the falsity of the report.

Enter Sir Jaspar Fidget, Lady Fidget, and Dainty.

No—this formal fool and women!

QUACK. His wife and sister.

SIR JASPAR. My coach breaking just now before your door, sir, I look upon as an occasional[16] reprimand to me, sir, for not kissing your hands, sir, since your coming out of France, sir, and so my disaster, sir, has been my good fortune, sir, and this is my wife and sister, sir.

HORNER. What then, sir?

SIR JASPAR. My lady and sister, sir.—Wife, this is Master Horner.

LADY FIDGET. Master Horner, husband!

SIR JASPAR. My lady, my Lady Fidget, sir.

HORNER. So, sir.

SIR JASPAR. Won't you be acquainted with her, sir? (*Aside.*) So the report is true, I find by his coldness or aversion to the sex, but I'll play the wag with him.—Pray salute[17] my wife, my lady, sir.

HORNER. I will kiss no man's wife, sir, for him, sir; I have taken my eternal leave, sir, of the sex already, sir.

SIR JASPAR. (*Aside.*) Ha, ha, ha, I'll plague him yet.—Not know my wife, sir?

HORNER. I do know your wife, sir: she's a woman, sir, and consequently a monster, sir, a greater monster than a husband, sir.

SIR JASPAR. A husband! How, sir?

---

[10] the great ones] the great (or French) pox, i.e, syphilis.

[11] Aniseed Robin] a notorious hermaphrodite.

[12] English-French disaster … English-French chirurgeon] a French pox caught by an Englishman, treated by an English doctor practising in France.

[13] belie 'em t'other way] i.e., to exaggerate their masculinity.

[14] discovers] reveals.

[15] rooks] cheats, con men.

[16] occasional] timely, arising from the occasion.

[17] salute] kiss or embrace in greeting.

HORNER. (*Makes horns.*[18]) So, sir. But I make no more cuckolds, sir.[19] 95

SIR JASPAR. Ha, ha, ha, Mercury, Mercury.[20]

LADY FIDGET. Pray Sir Jaspar, let us be gone from this rude fellow.

DAINTY. Who, by his breeding, would think he had ever been in France? 100

LADY FIDGET. Faugh, he's but too much a French fellow, such as hate women of quality and virtue for their love to their husbands, Sir Jaspar; a woman is hated by 'em as much for loving her 105 husband as for loving their money. But pray, let's be gone.

HORNER. You do well, madam, for I have nothing that you came for. I have brought over not so much as a bawdy picture, new postures,[21] nor the 110 second part of the *Ecole des filles*,[22] nor—

QUACK. (*Apart to Horner.*) Hold for shame, sir. What d'ye mean? You'll ruin yourself forever with the sex.

SIR JASPAR. Ha, ha, ha, he hates women perfectly, 115 I find.

DAINTY. What pity 'tis he should.

LADY FIDGET. Aye, he's a base rude fellow for it, but affectation makes not a woman more odious to them than virtue. 120

HORNER. Because your virtue is your greatest affectation, madam.

LADY FIDGET. How, you saucy fellow, would you wrong my honour?

HORNER. If I could. 125

LADY FIDGET. How d'ye mean, sir?

SIR JASPAR. Ha, ha, ha, no, he can't wrong your ladyship's honour, upon my honour; he, poor man—hark you in your ear—a mere eunuch.

LADY FIDGET. Oh filthy French beast! Faugh, 130 faugh! Why do we stay? Let's be gone; I can't endure the sight of him.

SIR JASPAR. Stay but till the chairs[23] come; they'll be here presently.

LADY FIDGET. No, no. 135

SIR JASPAR. Nor can I stay longer: 'tis—let me see, a quarter and a half quarter of a minute past eleven; the Council[24] will be sat; I must away. Business must be preferred always before love and ceremony with the wise, Mr. Horner. 140

HORNER. And the impotent, Sir Jaspar.

SIR JASPAR. Aye, aye, the impotent Master Horner, ha, ha, ha!

LADY FIDGET. What, leave us with a filthy man alone in his lodgings? 145

SIR JASPAR. He's an innocent man now, you know. Pray stay, I'll hasten the chairs to you.—Mr. Horner, your servant. I should be glad to see you at my house. Pray, come and dine with me and play at cards with my wife after dinner; you are 150 fit for women at that game yet, ha, ha! (*Aside.*) 'Tis as much a husband's prudence to provide innocent diversion for a wife as to hinder her unlawful pleasures, and he had better employ her than let her employ herself.—Farewell. (*Exit.*) 155

HORNER. Your servant, Sir Jaspar.

LADY FIDGET. I will not stay with him, faugh!

HORNER. Nay madam, I beseech you stay, if it be but to see I can be as civil to ladies yet as they would desire. 160

LADY FIDGET. No, no, faugh, you cannot be civil to ladies.

DAINTY. You as civil as ladies would desire!

LADY FIDGET. No, no, no, faugh, faugh, faugh!

Exeunt Lady Fidget and Dainty.

QUACK. Now I think, I, or you yourself rather, have 165 done your business with the women.

---

18 horns] the horns that supposedly sprout from the forehead of a cuckold, a man whose wife has been unfaithful.

19 no more cuckolds] As Horner's name suggests, making cuckolds was his specialty.

20 Mercury] god associated with wit (who wears a hat with wings resembling cuckold's horns); also, substance used to treat venereal disease.

21 postures] erotic illustrations, esp. accompanying the "Lewd Sonnets" of Pietro Arentino (1492–1556).

22 *Ecole des filles*] notoriously bawdy dialogues by Michel Millot (1655).

---

23 chairs] portable sedan-chairs carried by hirelings through the streets.

24 Council] the Privy Council, the king's advisory body.

HORNER. Thou art an ass. Don't you see already upon the report and my carriage, this grave man of business leaves his wife in my lodgings, invites me to his house and wife, who before would not be acquainted with me out of jealousy? 170

QUACK. Nay, by this means you may be the more acquainted with the husbands, but the less with the wives.

HORNER. Let me alone; if I can but abuse the husbands, I'll soon disabuse the wives. Stay—I'll reckon you up the advantages I am like to have by my stratagem: first, I shall be rid of all my old acquaintances, the most insatiable sorts of duns that invade our lodgings in a morning. And next to the pleasure of making a new mistress is that of being rid of an old one and of all old debts: love, when it comes to be so, is paid the most unwillingly. 175 180

QUACK. Well, you may be so rid of your old acquaintances, but how will you get any new ones? 185

HORNER. Doctor, thou wilt never make a good chemist,[25] thou art so incredulous and impatient. Ask but all the young fellows of the Town if they do not lose more time, like huntsmen, in starting the game than in running it down; one knows not where to find 'em, who will or will not. Women of quality are so civil, you can hardly distinguish love from good breeding, and a man is often mistaken. But now I can be sure, she that shows an aversion to me loves the sport,[26] as those women that are gone, whom I warrant to be right. And then the next thing is, your women of honour, as you call 'em, are only chary of their reputations, not their persons, and 'tis scandal they would avoid, not men. Now may I have by the reputation of an eunuch the privileges of one and be seen in a lady's chamber in a morning as early as her husband, kiss virgins before their parents or lovers, and may be, in short, the passe-partout of the Town. Now, doctor. 190 195 200 205

QUACK. Nay, now you shall be the doctor, and your process is so new that we do not know but it may succeed.

HORNER. Not so new neither: *probatum est*,[27] doctor. 210

QUACK. Well, I wish you luck and many patients whilst I go to mine. (*Exit.*)

Enter Harcourt and Dorilant to Horner.

HARCOURT. Come, your appearance at the play yesterday has, I hope, hardened you for the future against the women's contempt and the men's raillery, and now you'll abroad as you were wont. 215

HORNER. Did I not bear it bravely?

DORILANT. With a most theatrical impudence, nay, more than the orange wenches show there or a drunken vizard mask[28] or a great bellied actress,[29] nay, or the most impudent of creatures, an ill poet, or what is yet more impudent, a second-hand critic. 220

HORNER. But what say the ladies? Have they no pity? 225

HARCOURT. What ladies? The vizard masks, you know, never pity a man when all's gone though in their service.

DORILANT. And for the women in the boxes,[30] you'd never pity them when 'twas in your power. 230

HARCOURT. They say 'tis pity, but all that deal with common women should be served so.

DORILANT. Nay I dare swear, they won't admit you to play at cards with them, go to plays with 'em, or do the little duties which other shadows of men are wont to do for 'em. 235

HORNER. Who do you call shadows of men?

DORILANT. Half men.

HORNER. What, boys?

---

25 chemist] alchemist, who needs both credulity and patience to see his projection through.

26 the sport] i.e., sex. Horner is saying that sexually active women used to be difficult to identify, but will now announce themselves instantly by shunning him, thinking him sexually useless.

27 *probatum est*] tried and tested, or lit., "it is approved," a Latin formula often written on prescription drugs.

28 vizard mask] a half-mask covering the eyes, often worn by prostitutes working the theatres; here, the woman wearing it.

29 great bellied actress] that is, pregnant, likely with the bastard child of a member of the audience.

30 boxes] theatre seats between the pit and the upper galleries where "respectable" wives, etc. sat.

DORILANT. Aye, your old boys, old *beaux garçons*,[31] who like superannuated stallions are suffered to run, feed, and whinny with the mares as long as they live, though they can do nothing else.

HORNER. Well, a pox on love and wenching; women serve but to keep a man from better company. Though I can't enjoy them, I shall you the more. Good fellowship and friendship are lasting, rational, and manly pleasures.

HARCOURT. For all that, give me some of those pleasures you call effeminate, too; they help to relish one another.

HORNER. They disturb one another.

HARCOURT. No, mistresses are like books: if you pore upon them too much, they doze you and make you unfit for company, but if used discreetly, you are the fitter for conversation by 'em.

DORILANT. A mistress should be like a little country retreat near the Town, not to dwell in constantly but only for a night and away, to taste the Town the better when a man returns.

HORNER. I tell you, 'tis as hard to be a good fellow, a good friend, and a lover of women as 'tis to be a good fellow, a good friend, and a lover of money. You cannot follow both; then choose your side. Wine gives you liberty; love takes it away.

DORILANT. Gad, he's in the right on't.

HORNER. Wine gives you joy; love, grief and tortures, besides the chirurgeon's. Wine makes us witty; love, only sots. Wine makes us sleep; love breaks it.

DORILANT. By the world, he has reason, Harcourt.

HORNER. Wine makes—

DORILANT. Aye, wine makes us—makes us princes; love makes us beggars, poor rogues, egad—and wine—

HORNER. So, there's one converted.—No, no, love and wine, oil and vinegar.

HARCOURT. I grant it: love will still[32] be uppermost.

HORNER. Come, for my part I will have only those glorious manly pleasures of being very drunk and very slovenly.

Enter boy.

BOY. Mr. Sparkish is below, sir.

HARCOURT. What, my dear friend! a rogue that is fond of me only, I think, for abusing him.

DORILANT. No, he can no more think the men laugh at him than that women jilt him, his opinion of himself is so good.

HORNER. Well, there's another pleasure by drinking, I thought not of: I shall lose his acquaintance because he cannot drink, and you know 'tis a very hard thing to be rid of him, for he's one of those nauseous offerers at wit who, like the worst fiddlers, run themselves into all companies.

HARCOURT. One that by being in the company of men of sense would pass for one.

HORNER. And may so to the short-sighted world, as a false jewel amongst true ones is not discerned at a distance; his company is as troublesome to us as a cuckold's when you have a mind to his wife's.

HARCOURT. No, the rogue will not let us enjoy one another, but ravishes our conversation, though he signifies no more to't than Sir Martin Mar-all's[33] gaping and awkward thrumming upon the lute does to his man's voice and music.

DORILANT. And to pass for a wit in Town shows himself a fool every night to us that are guilty of the plot.

HORNER. Such wits as he are, to a company of reasonable men, like rooks[34] to the gamesters, who only fill a room at the table but are so far from contributing to the play that they only serve to spoil the fancy of those that do.

DORILANT. Nay, they are used like rooks, too—snubbed, checked, and abused—yet the rogues will hang on.

---

31 *beaux garçons*] fops (literally, pretty boys [Fr.]).
32 still] always.

33 Sir Martin Mar-all] foolish hero of Dryden's play of that name (1667), who mimes a serenade to his mistress even after his hidden servant has stopped singing and playing the lute.
34 rooks] here gulls or foolish victims, rather than the more common meaning, tricksters or cheaters.

HORNER. A pox on 'em and all that force Nature and would be still what she forbids 'em; affectation is her greatest monster. 320

HARCOURT. Most men are the contraries to that they would seem: your bully, you see, is a coward with a long sword; the little humbly fawning physician with his ebony cane is he that destroys men. 325

DORILANT. The usurer, a poor rogue possessed of mouldy bonds and mortgages, and we they call spendthrifts are only wealthy who lay out his money upon daily new purchases of pleasure. 330

HORNER. Aye, your arrantest cheat is your trustee or executor; your jealous man, the greatest cuckold; your churchman, the greatest atheist; and your noisy pert rogue of a wit, the greatest fop, dullest ass, and worst company, as you shall see. For here he comes. 335

Enter Sparkish to them.

SPARKISH. How is't, sparks, how is't? Well faith, Harry, I must rally thee a little, ha, ha, ha, upon the report in Town of thee, ha, ha, ha. I can't hold i'faith. Shall I speak? 340

HORNER. Yes, but you'll be so bitter then.

SPARKISH. Honest Dick and Frank here shall answer for me; I will not be extreme bitter, by the universe.

HARCOURT. We will be bound in ten thousand pound bond, he shall not be bitter at all. 345

DORILANT. Nor sharp, nor sweet.

HORNER. What, not downright insipid?

SPARKISH. Nay then, since you are so brisk and provoke me, take what follows: you must know, I was discoursing and rallying with some ladies yesterday, and they happened to talk of the fine new signs in Town. 350

HORNER. Very fine ladies, I believe.

SPARKISH. Said I, "I know where the best new sign is." "Where?" says one of the ladies. "In Covent Garden,"[35] I replied. Said another, "In what street?" "In Russell Street," answered I. "Lord," says another, 355

"I'm sure there was ne'er a fine new sign there yesterday." "Yes, but there was," said I again, "and it came out of France and has been there a fortnight." 360

DORILANT. A pox, I can hear no more, prithee.

HORNER. No, hear him out; let him tune his crowd[36] a while.

HARCOURT. The worst music, the greatest preparation. 365

SPARKISH. Nay faith, I'll make you laugh. "It cannot be," says a third lady. "Yes, yes," quoth I again. Says a fourth lady—

HORNER. Look to't, we'll have no more ladies. 370

SPARKISH. No? Then mark, mark, now. Said I to the fourth, "Did you never see Mr. Horner? He lodges in Russell Street, and he's a sign of a man, you know, since he came out of France." He, ha, he! 375

HORNER. But the devil take me if thine be the sign of a jest.

SPARKISH. With that they all fell a-laughing till they bepissed themselves. What, but it does not move you, me-thinks? Well, I see one had as good go to law without a witness as break a jest without a laugher on one's side.—Come, come, sparks, but where do we dine? I have left at Whitehall an earl to dine with you. 380

DORILANT. Why, I thought thou hadst loved a man with a title better than a suit with a French trimming to't. 385

HARCOURT. Go, to him again.

SPARKISH. No sir, a wit to me is the greatest title in the world. 390

HORNER. But go dine with your earl, sir; he may be exceptious. We are your friends and will not take it ill to be left, I do assure you.

HARCOURT. Nay, faith he shall go to him.

SPARKISH. Nay, pray gentlemen. 395

DORILANT. We'll thrust you out if you wonnot. What, disappoint anybody for us?

SPARKISH. Nay, dear gentlemen, hear me.

HORNER. No, no, sir, by no means; pray go, sir.

SPARKISH. Why, dear rogues— 400

DORILANT. No, no.

---

35 Covent Garden] originally "Convent Garden," a fashionable residential neighbourhood during the Restoration (only later associated with prostitution and the theatre).

36 crowd] fiddle.

They all thrust him out of the room.

ALL. Ha, ha, ha.

Sparkish returns.

SPARKISH. But sparks, pray hear me. What, d'ye think I'll eat then with gay shallow fops and silent coxcombs? I think wit as necessary at dinner as a glass of good wine, and that's the reason I never have any stomach when I eat alone. Come, but where do we dine? 405

HORNER. Ev'n where you will.

SPARKISH. At Chateline's.37 410

DORILANT. Yes, if you will.

SPARKISH. Or at the Cock.38

DORILANT. Yes, if you please.

SPARKISH. Or at the Dog and Partridge.39

HORNER. Aye, if you have a mind to't, for we shall dine at neither. 415

SPARKISH. Pshaw, with your fooling we shall lose the new play, and I would no more miss seeing a new play the first day than I would miss sitting in the wits' row;40 therefore, I'll go fetch my mistress and away. (*Exit.*) 420

Enter Pinchwife.

HORNER. Who have we here, Pinchwife?

PINCHWIFE. Gentlemen, your humble servant.

HORNER. Well Jack, by thy long absence from the Town, the grumness41 of thy countenance, and the slovenliness of thy habit, I should give thee joy, should I not, of marriage? 425

PINCHWIFE. (*Aside.*) Death, does he know I'm married, too? I thought to have concealed it from him at least.—My long stay in the country will excuse my dress, and I have a suit of law that brings 430 me up to Town that puts me out of humour; besides, I must give Sparkish tomorrow five thousand pound to lie with my sister.

HORNER. Nay, you country gentlemen, rather than not purchase, will buy anything, and he is a cracked title,42 if we may quibble. Well, but am I to give thee joy? I heard thou wert married. 435

PINCHWIFE. What then?

HORNER. Why, the next thing that is to be heard is thou'rt a cuckold. 440

PINCHWIFE. (*Aside.*) Insupportable name.

HORNER. But I did not expect marriage from such a whoremaster as you: one that knew the Town so much and women so well. 445

PINCHWIFE. Why, I have married no London wife.

HORNER. Pshaw, that's all one: that grave circumspection in marrying a country wife is like refusing a deceitful pampered Smithfield43 jade to go and be cheated by a friend in the country. 450

PINCHWIFE. (*Aside.*) A pox on him and his simile.—At least we are a little surer of the breed there, know what her keeping has been, whether foiled44 or unsound.45 455

HORNER. Come, come, I have known a clap gotten in Wales, and there are cozens,46 justices, clerks, and chaplains in the country; I won't say coachmen. But she's handsome and young?

PINCHWIFE. (*Aside.*) I'll answer as I should do.— No, no, she has no beauty but her youth, no attraction but her modesty: wholesome, homely, and housewifely, that's all. 460

DORILANT. He talks as like a grazier47 as he looks.

PINCHWIFE. She's too awkward, ill-favoured, and silly48 to bring to Town. 465

---

37 Chateline's] fashionable French restaurant in Covent Garden.

38 the Cock] Out of many taverns by that name, this probably refers to a less fashionable one in Bow Street, Covent Garden, frequented by Wycherley.

39 the Dog and Partridge] an unfashionable tavern in Fleet Street.

40 wits' row] benches near the front of the pit, close to the orchestra and stage.

41 grumness] moroseness, gloominess.

42 cracked title] Either Sparkish's patrimony or his genealogy is questionable.

43 Smithfield] suburban market, known for crooked trade.

44 foiled] injured (when said of a horse); deflowered (when said of a woman).

45 unsound] unhealthy, particularly with a venereal disease.

46 cozens] either a variant of "cozeners" or an alternate spelling of "cousins."

47 grazier] one who fattens up cattle for market.

48 silly] innocent, unsophisticated.

HARCOURT. Then methinks you should bring her to be taught breeding.

PINCHWIFE. To be taught! No sir, I thank you, good wives and private soldiers should be ignorant. [Aside.] I'll keep her from your instructions, I warrant you. 470

HARCOURT. (Aside.) The rogue is as jealous as if his wife were not ignorant.

HORNER. Why, if she be ill-favored, there will be less danger here for you than by leaving her in the country: we have such variety of dainties that we are seldom hungry. 475

DORILANT. But they have always coarse, constant, swingeing stomachs in the country. 480

HARCOURT. Foul feeders indeed.

DORILANT. And your hospitality is great there.

HARCOURT. Open house, every man's welcome.

PINCHWIFE. So, so, gentlemen.

HORNER. But prithee, why wouldst thou marry her? If she be ugly, ill-bred, and silly, she must be rich then. 485

PINCHWIFE. As rich as if she brought me twenty thousand pound out of this Town, for she'll be as sure not to spend her moderate portion as a London baggage would be to spend hers, let it be what it would; so 'tis all one. Then because she's ugly, she's the likelier to be my own, and being ill-bred, she'll hate conversation and, since silly and innocent, will not know the difference betwixt a man of one-and-twenty and one of forty. 490 495

HORNER. Nine—to my knowledge. But if she be silly, she'll expect as much from a man of forty-nine as from him of one-and-twenty. But methinks wit is more necessary than beauty, and I think no young woman ugly that has it and no handsome woman agreeable without it. 500

PINCHWIFE. 'Tis my maxim: he's a fool that marries, but he's a greater that does not marry a fool. What is wit in a wife good for but to make a man a cuckold? 505

HORNER. Yes, to keep it from his knowledge.

PINCHWIFE. A fool cannot contrive to make her husband a cuckold.

HORNER. No, but she'll club with a man that can, and what is worse, if she cannot make her husband a cuckold, she'll make him jealous and pass for one, and then 'tis all one. 510

PINCHWIFE. Well, well, I'll take care for one: my wife shall make me no cuckold though she had your help, Mr. Horner. I understand the Town, sir. 515

DORILANT. (Aside.) His help!

HARCOURT. (Aside.) He's come newly to Town, it seems, and has not heard how things are with him.

HORNER. But tell me, has marriage cured thee of whoring, which it seldom does? 520

HARCOURT. 'Tis more than age can do.

HORNER. No, the word is, "I'll marry and live honest."[49] But a marriage vow is like a penitent gamester's oath and entering into bonds and penalties to stint himself to such a particular small sum at play for the future, which makes him but the more eager, and not being able to hold out, loses his money again and his forfeit to boot. 525

DORILANT. Aye, aye, a gamester will be a gamester whilst his money lasts, and a whoremaster, whilst his vigour. 530

HARCOURT. Nay, I have known 'em, when they are broke and can lose no more, keep a-fumbling with the box[50] in their hands to fool with only and hinder other gamesters. 535

DORILANT. That had wherewithal to make lusty stakes.

PINCHWIFE. Well gentlemen, you may laugh at me, but you shall never lie with my wife. I know the Town. 540

HORNER. But prithee, was not the way you were in better? Is not keeping better than marriage?

PINCHWIFE. A pox on't, the jades would jilt me; I could never keep a whore to myself. 545

HORNER. So then you only married to keep a whore to yourself. Well but let me tell you, women, as you say, are, like soldiers, made constant and loyal by good pay rather than by oaths and covenants. Therefore, I'd advise my friends to keep rather than marry since, too, I find by your example it does not serve one's turn, for I saw you yesterday in the eighteen-penny place[51] with a pretty country wench. 550

---

49 honest] chaste.

50 box] dice cup, with bawdy connotations.

51 eighteen-penny place] the middle gallery in the theatre, not frequented by the fashionable set.

PINCHWIFE. (*Aside.*) How the devil! Did he see my
wife then? I sat there that she might not be seen,
but she shall never go to a play again.

HORNER. What, dost thou blush at nine-and-forty
for having been seen with a wench?

DORILANT. No faith, I warrant 'twas his wife,
which he seated there out of sight, for he's a
cunning rogue and understands the Town.

HARCOURT. He blushes; then 'twas his wife, for
men are now more ashamed to be seen with them
in public than with a wench.

PINCHWIFE. (*Aside.*) Hell and damnation! I'm
undone since Horner has seen her and they know
'twas she.

HORNER. But prithee, was it thy wife? She was
exceedingly pretty. I was in love with her at that
distance.

PINCHWIFE. You are like never to be nearer to her.
Your servant, gentlemen. (*Offers to go.*)

HORNER. Nay, prithee stay.

PINCHWIFE. I cannot; I will not.

HORNER. Come, you shall dine with us.

PINCHWIFE. I have dined already.

HORNER. Come, I know thou hast not. I'll treat
thee, dear rogue; thou shalt spend none of thy
Hampshire money today.

PINCHWIFE. (*Aside.*) Treat me! So he uses me
already like his cuckold.

HORNER. Nay, you shall not go.

PINCHWIFE. I must. I have business at home.
(*Exit.*)

HARCOURT. To beat his wife: he's as jealous of her
as a Cheapside[52] husband of a Covent Garden
wife.

HORNER. Why, 'tis as hard to find an old
whoremaster without jealousy and the gout as a
young one without fear or the pox.
As gout in age from pox in youth proceeds,
So wenching past, then jealousy succeeds:
The worst disease that love and wenching breeds.

[*Exeunt.*]

---

52 Cheapside] business district in London, i.e., middle class.

ACT II, SCENE I. [PINCHWIFE'S LODGING.]

*Margery Pinchwife and Alithea, Pinchwife peeping
behind at the door.*

MARGERY. Pray sister, where are the best fields and
woods to walk in in London?

ALITHEA. A pretty question. Why sister, Mulberry
Garden[53] and St. James's Park[54] and, for close
walks, the New Exchange.[55]

MARGERY. Pray sister, tell me why my husband
looks so grum here in Town and keeps me up so
close and will not let me go a-walking nor let me
wear my best gown yesterday?

ALITHEA. Oh, he's jealous, sister.

MARGERY. Jealous, what's that?

ALITHEA. He's afraid you should love another man.

MARGERY. How should he be afraid of my loving
another man when he will not let me see any but
himself?

ALITHEA. Did he not carry you yesterday to a play?

MARGERY. Aye, but we sat amongst ugly people;
he would not let me come near the gentry, who
sat under us, so that I could not see 'em. He told
me none but naughty women sat there, whom they
toused and moused, but I would have ventured for
all that.

ALITHEA. But how did you like the play?

MARGERY. Indeed I was aweary of the play, but I
liked hugeously the actors; they are the goodliest,
properest men, sister.

ALITHEA. Oh, but you must not like the actors,
sister.

MARGERY. Ay, how should I help it, sister? Pray
sister, when my husband comes in, will you ask
leave for me to go a-walking?

ALITHEA. (*Aside.*) A-walking, ha, ha! Lord, a
country gentlewoman's leisure is the drudgery of
a foot post, and she requires as much airing as her
husband's horses.

---

53 Mulberry Garden] a promenade within St. James's Park
(see below) on the current site of Buckingham Palace.
54 St. James Park] very fashionable district at the western
end of Pall Mall, near Westminster.
55 New Exchange] stock exchange; meeting place for bank-
ers and traders; included a gallery of fashionable shops.

Enter Pinchwife.

But here comes your husband; I'll ask, though I'm sure he'll not grant it.

MARGERY. He says he won't let me go abroad for fear of catching the pox.

ALITHEA. Fie, the small pox you should say. 40

MARGERY. Oh my dear, dear bud, welcome home. Why dost thou look so froppish?[56] Who has nangered[57] thee?

PINCHWIFE. You're a fool.

Margery goes aside and cries.

ALITHEA. Faith so she is, for crying for no fault, 45 poor, tender creature!

PINCHWIFE. What, you would have her as impudent as yourself, as arrant a jill-flirt, a gadder, a magpie, and, to say all, a mere notorious Town woman? 50

ALITHEA. Brother, you are my only censurer, and the honour of your family shall sooner suffer in your wife there than in me, though I take the innocent liberty of the Town.

PINCHWIFE. Hark you, mistress, do not talk so 55 before my wife. The innocent liberty of the Town!

ALITHEA. Why pray, who boasts of any intrigue with me? What lampoon has made my name notorious? What ill women frequent my lodgings? I keep no company with any women of scandalous 60 reputations.

PINCHWIFE. No, you keep the men of scandalous reputations company.

ALITHEA. Where? Would you not have me civil? answer 'em in a box at the plays? in the Drawing 65 Room[58] at White-hall? in St. James's Park? Mulberry Garden? or—

PINCHWIFE. Hold, hold, do not teach my wife where the men are to be found; I believe she's the worse for your Town documents[59] already. I bid 70 you keep her in ignorance as I do.

MARGERY. Indeed, be not angry with her, bud; she will tell me nothing of the Town, though I ask her a thousand times a day.

PINCHWIFE. Then you are very inquisitive to 75 know, I find?

MARGERY. Not I, indeed, dear. I hate London. Our place-house[60] in the country is worth a thousand of't. Would I were there again!

PINCHWIFE. So you shall, I warrant, but were you 80 not talking of plays and players when I came in?— You are her encourager in such discourses.

MARGERY. No indeed, dear, she chid me just now for liking the playermen.

PINCHWIFE. (*Aside.*) Nay, if she be so innocent as 85 to own to me her liking them, there is no hurt in't.—Come my poor rogue, but thou lik'st none better than me?

MARGERY. Yes indeed, but I do: the playermen are finer folks. 90

PINCHWIFE. But you love none better then me?

MARGERY. You are mine own dear bud, and I know you; I hate a stranger.

PINCHWIFE. Aye my dear, you must love me only and not be like the naughty Town women, who 95 only hate their husbands and love every man else, love plays, visits, fine coaches, fine clothes, fiddles, balls, treats, and so lead a wicked Town life.

MARGERY. Nay, if to enjoy all these things be a Town life, London is not so bad a place, dear. 100

PINCHWIFE. How! If you love me, you must hate London.

ALITHEA. [*Aside.*] The fool has forbid me discovering to her the pleasures of the Town, and he is now setting her agog upon them himself. 105

MARGERY. But husband, do the Town women love the playermen, too?

PINCHWIFE. Yes, I warrant you.

MARGERY. Ay, I warrant you.

PINCHWIFE. Why, you do not, I hope? 110

MARGERY. No, no, bud, but why have we no playermen in the country?

PINCHWIFE. Hah! Mrs. Minx, ask me no more to go to a play.

---

56 froppish] fretful, peevish.

57 nangered] angered; Margery tacks on the *n* in her characteristic baby-talk with her "bud."

58 Drawing Room] reception room at the palace.

59 documents] lessons.

60 place-house] chief residence of an estate.

MARGERY. Nay, why, love? I did not care for going, but when you forbid me, you make me, as't were, desire it. 115

ALITHEA. (*Aside.*) So 'twill be in other things, I warrant.

MARGERY. Pray, let me go to a play, dear. 120

PINCHWIFE. Hold your peace; I wonnot.

MARGERY. Why, love?

PINCHWIFE. Why, I'll tell you.

ALITHEA. (*Aside.*) Nay, if he tell her, she'll give him more cause to forbid her that place. 125

MARGERY. Pray, why, dear?

PINCHWIFE. First, you like the actors, and the gallants may like you.

MARGERY. What, a homely country girl? No, bud, nobody will like me. 130

PINCHWIFE. I tell you, yes, they may.

MARGERY. No, no, you jest. I won't believe you; I will go.

PINCHWIFE. I tell you then that one of the lewdest fellows in Town, who saw you there, told me he was in love with you. 135

MARGERY. Indeed! Who, who, pray, who was't?

PINCHWIFE. (*Aside.*) I've gone too far and slipped before I was aware. How overjoyed she is!

MARGERY. Was it any Hampshire gallant, any of our neighbors? I promise you, I am beholding to him. 140

PINCHWIFE. I promise you, you lie, for he would but ruin you as he has done hundreds. He has no other love for women but that. Such as he look upon women like basilisks, but to destroy 'em. 145

MARGERY. Ay, but if he loves me, why should he ruin me? Answer me to that. Methinks he should not; I would do him no harm.

ALITHEA. Ha, ha, ha. 150

PINCHWIFE. 'Tis very well, but I'll keep him from doing you any harm, or me either.

Enter Sparkish and Harcourt.

But here comes company. Get you in, get you in.

MARGERY. But pray, husband, is he a pretty gentleman that loves me? 155

PINCHWIFE. In baggage, in. (*Thrusts her in; shuts the door.*) What, all the lewd libertines of the Town brought to my lodging by this easy coxcomb!

S'death,[61] I'll not suffer it.

SPARKISH. Here Harcourt, do you approve my choice?—Dear little rogue, I told you I'd bring you acquainted with all my friends, the wits, and— 160

Harcourt salutes her.

PINCHWIFE. Aye, they shall know her as well as you yourself will, I warrant you.

SPARKISH. This is one of those, my pretty rogue, that are to dance at your wedding tomorrow, and him you must bid welcome ever to what you and I have. 165

PINCHWIFE. (*Aside.*) Monstrous!

SPARKISH. Harcourt, how dost thou like her, faith?—Nay dear, do not look down; I should hate to have a wife of mine out of countenance at any thing. 170

PINCHWIFE. Wonderful!

SPARKISH. Tell me, I say, Harcourt, how dost thou like her? Thou hast stared upon her enough to resolve me. 175

HARCOURT. So infinitely well that I could wish I had a mistress, too, that might differ from her in nothing but her love and engagement to you. 180

ALITHEA. Sir, Master Sparkish has often told me that his acquaintance were all wits and railleurs,[62] and now I find it.

SPARKISH. No, by the universe, madam, he does not rally now; you may believe him. I do assure you, he is the honestest, worthiest, true-hearted gentleman—a man of such perfect honour, he would say nothing to a lady he does not mean. 185

PINCHWIFE. [*Aside.*] Praising another man to his mistress! 190

HARCOURT. Sir, you are so beyond expectation obliging, that—

SPARKISH. Nay, egad, I am sure you do admire her extremely; I see't in your eyes.—He does admire you, madam.—By the world, don't you? 195

HARCOURT. Yes, above the world or the most glorious part of it, her whole sex, and till now I never thought I should have envied you, or any

---

61 S'death] contraction of "God's death."

62 railleurs] those who banter or mock; a fashionable French word appealing to Sparkish.

man about to marry, but you have the best excuse for marriage I ever knew. 200

ALITHEA. Nay, now, sir, I'm satisfied you are of the society of the wits and railleurs since you cannot spare your friend, even when he is but too civil to you, but the surest sign is since you are an enemy to marriage, for that I hear you hate as much as 205 business or bad wine.

HARCOURT. Truly madam, I never was an enemy to marriage till now because marriage was never an enemy to me before.

ALITHEA. But why, sir, is marriage an enemy to you 210 now? because it robs you of your friend here? For you look upon a friend married as one gone into a monastery, that is, dead to the world.

HARCOURT. 'Tis indeed because you marry him. I see, madam, you can guess my meaning. I do 215 confess heartily and openly I wish it were in my power to break the match. By heavens, I would!

SPARKISH. Poor Frank!

ALITHEA. Would you be so unkind to me?

HARCOURT. No, no, 'tis not because I would be 220 unkind to you.

SPARKISH. Poor Frank! No, gad, 'tis only his kindness to me.

PINCHWIFE. (*Aside.*) Great kindness to you, indeed. Insensible fop, let a man make love[63] to 225 his wife to his face!

SPARKISH. Come, dear Frank, for all my wife there that shall be, thou shalt enjoy me sometimes, dear rogue. By my honour, we men of wit condole for our deceased brother in marriage as much as for 230 one dead in earnest. I think that was prettily said of me, hah, Harcourt? But come, Frank, be not melancholy for me.

HARCOURT. No, I assure you I am not melancholy for you. 235

SPARKISH. Prithee Frank, dost think my wife that shall be there a fine person?

HARCOURT. I could gaze upon her till I became as blind as you are.

SPARKISH. How, as I am! How? 240

HARCOURT. Because you are a lover, and true lovers are blind, stock-blind.[64]

SPARKISH. True, true, but by the world, she has wit, too, as well as beauty. Go, go with her into a corner and try if she has wit; talk to her anything; 245 she's bashful before me.

HARCOURT. Indeed, if a woman wants[65] wit in a corner, she has it nowhere.

ALITHEA. (*Aside to Sparkish.*) Sir, you dispose of me a little before your time. 250

SPARKISH. Nay, nay, madam, let me have an earnest of your obedience, or—Go, go, madam.

Harcourt courts Alithea aside.

PINCHWIFE. How, sir! if you are not concerned for the honour of a wife, I am for that of a sister. He shall not debauch her. Be a pander to your own 255 wife, bring men to her, let 'em make love before your face, thrust 'em into a corner together, then leave 'em in private! Is this your Town wit and conduct?

SPARKISH. Ha, ha, ha, a silly wise rogue would 260 make one laugh more than a stark fool, ha, ha! I shall burst. Nay, you shall not disturb 'em. I'll vex thee, by the world. (*Struggles with Pinchwife to keep him from Harcourt and Alithea.*)

ALITHEA. The writings are drawn, sir, settlements 265 made; 'tis too late, sir, and past all revocation.

HARCOURT. Then so is my death.

ALITHEA. I would not be unjust to him.

HARCOURT. Then why to me so?

ALITHEA. I have no obligation to you. 270

HARCOURT. My love.

ALITHEA. I had his before.

HARCOURT. You never had it: he wants, you see, jealousy, the only infallible sign of it.

ALITHEA. Love proceeds from esteem; he cannot 275 distrust my virtue. Besides, he loves me, or he would not marry me.

HARCOURT. Marrying you is no more sign of his love than bribing your woman, that he may marry you, is a sign of his generosity. Marriage is rather 280 a sign of interest than love, and he that marries a fortune, covets a mistress, not loves her. But if you take marriage for a sign of love, take it from me immediately.

---

63 make love] pay court, verbally.

64 stock-blind] blind as a stock, or log, as in "stock-still."

65 wants] here as elsewhere, "to want" means to lack.

ALITHEA. No, now you have put a scruple in my head. But in short, sir, to end our dispute, I must marry him: my reputation would suffer in the world else. 285

HARCOURT. No, if you do marry him, with your pardon, madam, your reputation suffers in the world, and you would be thought in necessity for a cloak. 290

ALITHEA. Nay, now you are rude, sir.—Mr. Sparkish, pray come hither; your friend here is very troublesome and very loving. 295

HARCOURT. (*Aside to Alithea.*) Hold, hold—

PINCHWIFE. D'ye hear that?

SPARKISH. Why, d'ye think I'll seem to be jealous, like a country bumpkin?

PINCHWIFE. No, rather be a cuckold, like a credulous cit.[66] 300

HARCOURT. Madam, you would not have been so little generous[67] as to have told him.

ALITHEA. Yes, since you could be so little generous as to wrong him. 305

HARCOURT. Wrong him! No man can do't; he's beneath an injury: a bubble,[68] a coward, a senseless idiot, a wretch so contemptible to all the world but you that—

ALITHEA. Hold, do not rail at him, for since he is like to be my husband, I am resolved to like him. Nay, I think I am obliged to tell him you are not his friend.—Master Sparkish, Master Sparkish. 310

SPARKISH. What, what? Now, dear rogue, has not she wit? 315

HARCOURT. (*Speaks surlily.*) Not so much as I thought and hoped she had.

ALITHEA. Mr. Sparkish, do you bring people to rail at you?

HARCOURT. Madam— 320

SPARKISH. How! No, but if he does rail at me, 'tis but in jest, I warrant, what we wits do for one another and never take any notice of it.

ALITHEA. He spoke so scurrilously of you I had no patience to hear him; besides, he has been making love to me. 325

HARCOURT. (*Aside.*) True, damned, tell-tale woman.

SPARKISH. Pshaw, to show his parts.[69] We wits rail and make love often but to show our parts; as we have no affections, so we have no malice, we— 330

ALITHEA. He said you were a wretch, below an injury.

SPARKISH. Pshaw.

HARCOURT. [*Aside.*] Damned, senseless, impudent, virtuous jade! Well, since she won't let me have her, she'll do as good: she'll make me hate her. 335

ALITHEA. A common bubble.

SPARKISH. Pshaw. 340

ALITHEA. A coward.

SPARKISH. Pshaw, pshaw.

ALITHEA. A senseless, driveling idiot.

SPARKISH. How! Did he disparage my parts? Nay, then my honour's concerned. I can't put up that, sir.—By the world, brother, help me to kill him. (*Aside.*) I may draw now, since we have the odds of him; 'tis a good occasion, too, before my mistress. (*Offers to draw.*) 345

ALITHEA. Hold, hold! 350

SPARKISH. What, what?

ALITHEA. (*Aside.*) I must not let 'em kill the gentleman neither, for his kindness[70] to me. I am so far from hating him that I wish my gallant had his person and understanding. Nay, if my honour— 355

SPARKISH. I'll be thy death.

ALITHEA. Hold, hold! Indeed, to tell the truth, the gentleman said after all that what he spoke was but out of friendship to you.

SPARKISH. How! Say I am, I am a fool, that is, no wit, out of friendship to me? 360

ALITHEA. Yes, to try whether I was concerned enough for you, and made love to me only to be satisfied of my virtue, for your sake.

HARCOURT. (*Aside.*) Kind however— 365

SPARKISH. Nay, if it were so, my dear rogue, I ask thee pardon, but why would not you tell me so, faith?

---

66 cit] citizen of the City of London, but in the derogatory sense of being engaged in trade and finance; a "yuppy."
67 generous] high-born, well-bred.
68 bubble] the victim of a swindle.

69 parts] wit, talent and other (non-physical) attributes and abilities.
70 kindness] affection, to the point of sexual interest.

HARCOURT. Because I did not think on't, faith.

SPARKISH. Come, Horner does not come, Harcourt, let's be gone to the new play.—Come, madam. 370

ALITHEA. I will not go if you intend to leave me alone in the box and run into the pit, as you use to do. 375

SPARKISH. Pshaw, I'll leave Harcourt with you in the box to entertain you, and that's as good. If I sat in the box, I should be thought no judge but of trimmings.[71]—Come away, Harcourt, lead her down. 380

Exeunt Sparkish, Harcourt, and Alithea.

PINCHWIFE. Well, go thy ways, for the flower of the true Town fops, such as spend their estates before they come to 'em and are cuckolds before they're married. But let me go look to my own freehold.—How— 385

Enter My Lady Fidget, Dainty, and Mistress Squeamish.

LADY FIDGET. Your servant, sir. Where is your lady? We are come to wait upon her to the new play.

PINCHWIFE. New play!

LADY FIDGET. And my husband will wait upon you presently. 390

PINCHWIFE. (*Aside.*) Damn your civility.— Madam, by no means, I will not see Sir Jaspar here till I have waited upon him at home, nor shall my wife see you till she has waited upon your ladyship at your lodgings. 395

LADY FIDGET. Now we are here, sir—

PINCHWIFE. No, madam.

DAINTY. Pray, let us see her.

MRS. SQUEAMISH. We will not stir till we see her. 400

PINCHWIFE. (*Aside.*) A pox on you all. (*Goes to the door and returns.*) She has locked the door and is gone abroad.

LADY FIDGET. No, you have locked the door, and she's within. 405

DAINTY. They told us below she was here.

PINCHWIFE. [*Aside.*] Will nothing do?—Well it must out then: to tell you the truth, ladies, which I was afraid to let you know before lest it might endanger your lives, my wife has just now the small pox come out upon her. Do not be frightened, but pray, be gone ladies. You shall not stay here in danger of your lives. Pray get you gone, ladies. 410

LADY FIDGET. No, no, we have all had 'em.

MRS. SQUEAMISH. Alack, alack. 415

DAINTY. Come, come, we must see how it goes with her. I understand the disease.

LADY FIDGET. Come.

PINCHWIFE. (*Aside.*) Well, there is no being too hard for women at their own weapon, lying; therefore, I'll quit the field. (*Exit.*) 420

MRS. SQUEAMISH. Here's an example of jealousy.

LADY FIDGET. Indeed, as the world goes, I wonder there are no more jealous, since wives are so neglected. 425

DAINTY. Pshaw, as the world goes, to what end should they be jealous?

LADY FIDGET. Faugh, 'tis a nasty world.

MRS. SQUEAMISH. That men of parts, great acquaintance, and quality should take up with and spend themselves and fortunes in keeping little playhouse creatures, faugh! 430

LADY FIDGET. Nay, that women of understanding, great acquaintance, and good quality should fall a-keeping, too, of little creatures, faugh! 435

MRS. SQUEAMISH. Why, 'tis the men of quality's fault: they never visit women of honour and reputation as they used to do and have not so much as common civility for ladies of our rank but use us with the same indifferency and ill breeding as if we were all married to 'em. 440

LADY FIDGET. She says true. 'Tis an arrant shame women of quality should be so slighted; methinks birth, birth, should go for something. I have known men admired, courted, and followed for their titles only. 445

MRS. SQUEAMISH. Aye, one would think men of honour should not love, no more than marry, out of their own rank.

DAINTY. Fie, fie upon 'em, they are come to think crossbreeding for themselves best, as well as for their dogs and horses. 450

---

71 trimmings] i.e., the ribbons and lace on women's clothes, whereas Sparkish desires to be thought a judge of plays.

LADY FIDGET. They are dogs and horses for't.

MRS. SQUEAMISH. One would think if not for love, for vanity a little. 455

DAINTY. Nay, they do satisfy their vanity upon us sometimes and are kind to us in their report, tell all the world they lie with us.

LADY FIDGET. Damned rascals, that we should be only wronged by 'em! To report a man has had a 460 person, when he has not had a person, is the greatest wrong in the whole world that can be done to a person.

MRS. SQUEAMISH. Well, 'tis an arrant shame noble persons should be so wronged and neglected. 465

LADY FIDGET. But still 'tis an arranter shame for a noble person to neglect her own honour and defame her own noble person with little inconsiderable fellows, faugh!

DAINTY. I suppose the crime against our honour 470 is the same with a man of quality as with another.

LADY FIDGET. How! No, sure the man of quality is likest one's husband, and therefore, the fault should be the less.

DAINTY. But then the pleasure should be the less. 475

LADY FIDGET. Fie, fie, fie, for shame sister! Whither shall we ramble? Be continent in your discourse, or I shall hate you.

DAINTY. Besides, an intrigue is so much the more notorious for the man's quality. 480

MRS. SQUEAMISH. 'Tis true, nobody takes notice of a private man, and therefore, with him 'tis more secret, and the crime's the less when 'tis not known.

LADY FIDGET. You say true. I'faith, I think you are in the right on't. 'Tis not an injury to a 485 husband till it be an injury to our honours, so that a woman of honour loses no honour with a private person, and to say truth—

DAINTY. (*Apart to Mrs. Squeamish.*) So the little fellow is grown a private person—with her— 490

LADY FIDGET. But still my dear, dear honour.

Enter Sir Jaspar, Horner, Dorilant.

SIR JASPAR. Aye, my dear, dear of honour, thou hast still so much honour in thy mouth—

HORNER. (*Aside.*) That she has none elsewhere—

LADY FIDGET. Oh, what d'ye mean to bring in 495 these upon us?

DAINTY. Faugh, these are as bad as wits!

MRS. SQUEAMISH. Faugh!

LADY FIDGET. Let us leave the room.

SIR JASPAR. Stay, stay, faith, to tell you the naked 500 truth.

LADY FIDGET. Fie, Sir Jaspar, do not use that word "naked."

SIR JASPAR. Well, well, in short, I have business at Whitehall and cannot go to the play with you; 505 therefore, would have you go—

LADY FIDGET. With those two to a play?

SIR JASPAR. No, not with t'other, but with Mr. Horner; there can be no more scandal to go with him than with Mr. Tattle or Master Limberham.[72] 510

LADY FIDGET. With that nasty fellow! No—no.

SIR JASPAR. Nay prithee dear, hear me. (*Whispers to Lady Fidget.*)

Horner, Dorilant drawing near Squeamish and Dainty.

HORNER. Ladies.

DAINTY. Stand off. 515

MRS. SQUEAMISH. Do not approach us.

DAINTY. You herd with the wits; you are obscenity all over.

MRS. SQUEAMISH. And I would as soon look upon a picture of Adam and Eve without fig leaves 520 as any of you, if I could help it; therefore, keep off and do not make us sick.

DORILANT. What a devil are these?

HORNER. Why, these are pretenders to honour, as critics to wit, only by censuring others, and as 525 every raw, peevish, out-of-humoured, affected, dull, tea-drinking, arithmetical[73] fop sets up for a wit by railing at men of sense, so these for honour, by railing at the Court and ladies of as great honour as quality. 530

SIR JASPAR. Come Mr. Horner, I must desire you to go with these ladies to the play, sir.

HORNER. I, sir!

---

72 Mr. Tattle or Master Limberham] reference is obscure, but presumably unthreatening companions: Tattle would tell all, and thus not be secretive; Limberham implies loose-limbed ("weak-kneed"?).

73 arithmetical] precise.

SIR JASPAR. Aye, aye, come, sir.

HORNER. I must beg your pardon, sir, and theirs. 535
I will not be seen in women's company in public
again for the world.

SIR JASPAR. Ha, ha, strange aversion!

MRS. SQUEAMISH. No, he's for women's company
in private. 540

SIR JASPAR. He—poor man—he! Ha, ha, ha.

DAINTY. 'Tis a greater shame amongst lewd fellows
to be seen in virtuous women's company than for
the women to be seen with them.

HORNER. Indeed madam, the time was I only 545
hated virtuous women, but now I hate the other,
too. I beg your pardon, ladies.

LADY FIDGET. You are very obliging, sir, because
we would not be troubled with you.

SIR JASPAR. In sober sadness he shall go. 550

DORILANT. Nay, if he wonnot, I am ready to wait
upon the ladies, and I think I am the fitter man.

SIR JASPAR. You, sir! no, I thank you for that.
Master Horner is a privileged man amongst the
virtuous ladies; 'twill be a great while before you 555
are so. He, he, he, he's my wife's gallant, he, he,
he. No, pray withdraw, sir, for as I take it, the
virtuous ladies have no business with you.

DORILANT. And I am sure, he can have none with
them. 'Tis strange a man can't come amongst 560
virtuous women now but upon the same terms as
men are admitted into the Great Turk's seraglio,
but heavens keep me from being an ombre[74]
player with 'em. But where is Pinchwife? (*Exit.*)

SIR JASPAR. Come, come, man. What, avoid the 565
sweet society of womankind? that sweet, soft,
gentle, tame, noble creature woman, made for
man's companion—

HORNER. So is that soft, gentle, tame, and more
noble creature a spaniel, and has all their tricks: 570
can fawn, lie down, suffer beating, and fawn the
more, barks at your friends when they come to see
you, makes your bed hard, gives you fleas and the
mange sometimes, and all the difference is, the
spaniel's the more faithful animal and fawns but 575
upon one master.

SIR JASPAR. He, he, he.

MRS. SQUEAMISH. Oh, the rude beast!

DAINTY. Insolent brute!

LADY FIDGET. Brute! Stinking, mortified, rotten 580
French wether, to dare—

SIR JASPAR. Hold, an't[75] please your ladyship.—
For shame, Master Horner, your mother was a
woman. (*Aside.*) Now shall I never reconcile
'em.—Hark you, madam, take my advice in your 585
anger: you know you often want one to make up
your drolling pack of ombre players, and you may
cheat him easily, for he's an ill gamester and
consequently loves play. Besides, you know, you
have but two old civil gentlemen (with stinking 590
breaths, too) to wait upon you abroad. Take in the
third into your service. The other are but crazy, and
a lady should have a supernumerary gentleman-
usher, as a supernumerary coach-horse, lest
sometimes you should be forced to stay at home. 595

LADY FIDGET. But are you sure he loves play and
has money?

SIR JASPAR. He loves play as much as you and has
money as much as I.

LADY FIDGET. Then I am contented to make him 600
pay for his scurrility; money makes up in a measure
all other wants in men. (*Aside.*) Those whom we
cannot make hold for gallants, we make fine.[76]

SIR JASPAR. (*Aside.*) So, so, now to mollify, to
wheedle him.—Master Horner, will you never 605
keep civil company? Methinks 'tis time now, since
you are only fit for them. Come, come, man, you
must e'en fall to visiting our wives, eating at our
tables, drinking tea with our virtuous relations after
dinner, dealing cards to 'em, reading plays and 610
gazettes to 'em, picking fleas out of their shocks[77]
for 'em, collecting receipts,[78] new songs, women,
pages, and footmen for 'em.

HORNER. I hope they'll afford me better employment, sir. 615

SIR JASPAR. He, he, he! 'Tis fit you know your
work before you come into your place, and since
you are unprovided of a lady to flatter and a good

---

[74] ombre] a popular card game, played by three persons.

[75] an't] if it.

[76] fine] pay a penalty.

[77] shocks] shaggy dogs.

[78] receipts] recipes.

house to eat at, pray frequent mine and call my wife "mistress," and she shall call you "gallant," according to the custom.

HORNER. Who, I?

SIR JASPAR. Faith, thou shalt for my sake; come, for my sake only.

HORNER. For your sake—

SIR JASPAR. Come, come, here's a gamester for you; let him be a little familiar sometimes. Nay, what if a little rude? Gamesters may be rude with ladies, you know.

LADY FIDGET. Yes, losing gamesters have a privilege with women.

HORNER. I always thought the contrary, that the winning gamester had most privilege with women, for when you have lost your money to a man, you'll lose anything you have, all you have, they say, and he may use you as he pleases.

SIR JASPAR. He, he, he! Well, win or lose, you shall have your liberty with her.

LADY FIDGET. As he behaves himself and for your sake, I'll give him admittance and freedom.

HORNER. All sorts of freedom, madam?

SIR JASPAR. Aye, aye, aye, all sorts of freedom thou canst take, and so go to her; begin thy new employment. Wheedle her, jest with her, and be better acquainted one with another.

HORNER. (*Aside.*) I think I know her already, therefore, may venture with her, my secret for hers.

Horner and Lady Fidget whisper.

SIR JASPAR. Sister, cuz, I have provided an innocent playfellow for you there.

DAINTY. Who, he!

MRS. SQUEAMISH. There's a playfellow indeed.

SIR JASPAR. Yes, sure. What, he is good enough to play at cards, blindman's buff, or the fool with sometimes.

MRS. SQUEAMISH. Faugh, we'll have no such playfellows.

DAINTY. No sir, you shan't choose playfellows for us, we thank you.

SIR JASPAR. Nay, pray hear me. (*Whispering to them.*)

LADY FIDGET. [*Aside to Horner.*] But poor gentleman, could you be so generous? so truly a man of honour, as for the sakes of us women of honour, to cause your self to be reported no man? no man! and to suffer your self the greatest shame that could fall upon a man, that none might fall upon us women by your conversation. But indeed, sir, [are you] as perfectly, perfectly the same man as before your going into France, sir, as perfectly, perfectly, sir?

HORNER. As perfectly, perfectly, madam. Nay, I scorn you should take my word; I desire to be tried only, madam.

LADY FIDGET. Well, that's spoken again like a man of honour; all men of honour desire to come to the test. But indeed, generally [when] you men report such things of yourselves one does not know how or whom to believe, and it is come to that pass, we dare not take your words, no more than your tailor's, without some staid servant of yours be bound with you. But I have so strong a faith in your honour, dear, dear, noble sir, that I'd forfeit mine for yours at any time, dear sir.

HORNER. No madam, you should not need to forfeit it for me: I have given you security already to save you harmless, my late reputation being so well known in the world, madam.

LADY FIDGET. But if upon any future falling out, or upon a suspicion of my taking the trust out of your hands to employ some other, you yourself should betray your trust, dear sir? I mean, if you'll give me leave to speak obscenely, you might tell, dear sir.

HORNER. If I did, nobody would believe me: the reputation of impotency is as hardly recovered again in the world as that of cowardice, dear madam.

LADY FIDGET. Nay then, as one may say, you may do your worst, dear, dear, sir.

SIR JASPAR. Come, is your ladyship reconciled to him yet? Have you agreed on matters? For I must be gone to Whitehall.

LADY FIDGET. Why indeed, Sir Jaspar, Master Horner is a thousand, thousand times a better man than I thought him.—Cousin Squeamish, Sister Dainty, I can name him now. Truly not long ago, you know, I thought his very name obscenity, and I would as soon have lain with him as have named him.

SIR JASPAR. Very likely, poor madam.

DAINTY. I believe it.   710

MRS. SQUEAMISH. No doubt on't.

SIR JASPAR. Well, well, that your ladyship is as virtuous as any she, I know, and him all the Town knows, he, he, he. Therefore, now you like him, get you gone to your business together. Go, go, to   715
your business, I say, pleasure, whilst I go to my pleasure, business.

LADY FIDGET. Come then, dear gallant.

HORNER. Come away, my dearest mistress.

SIR JASPAR. So, so, why 'tis as I'd have it. (*Exit*.)   720

HORNER. And as I'd have it.

LADY FIDGET. Who for his business from his wife
   will run
   Takes the best care to have her business done.

Exeunt.

ACT III, SCENE I. [PINCHWIFE'S LODGING.]

Alithea and Margery.

ALITHEA. Sister, what ails you, you are grown melancholy?

MARGERY. Would it not make anyone melancholy to see you go every day fluttering about abroad, whilst I must stay at home like a poor lonely, sullen   5
bird in a cage?

ALITHEA. Aye sister, but you came young and just from the nest to your cage, so that I thought you liked it and could be as cheerful in't as others that took their flight themselves early and are hopping   10
abroad in the open air.

MARGERY. Nay, I confess I was quiet enough till my husband told me what pure[79] lives the London ladies live abroad, with their dancing, meetings, and junketings, and dressed every day in their best   15
gowns, and I warrant you, play at ninepins every day of the week, so they do.

Enter Pinchwife.

PINCHWIFE. Come, what's here to do? You are putting the Town pleasures in her head and setting her a-longing.   20

_____

[79] pure] fine, wonderful; a ruralism.

ALITHEA. Yes, after ninepins! You suffer none to give her those longings, you mean, but yourself.

PINCHWIFE. I tell her of the vanities of the Town like a confessor.

ALITHEA. A confessor! just such a confessor as he   25
that by forbidding a silly ostler to grease the horses' teeth,[80] taught him to do't.

PINCHWIFE. Come Mistress Flippant, good precepts are lost when bad examples are still before us: the liberty you take abroad makes her hanker   30
after it and out of humour at home, poor wretch! She desired not to come to London; I would bring her.

ALITHEA. Very well.

PINCHWIFE. She has been this week in Town and   35
never desired, till this afternoon, to go abroad.

ALITHEA. Was she not at a play yesterday?

PINCHWIFE. Yes, but she ne'er asked me; I was myself the cause of her going.

ALITHEA. Then if she ask you again, you are the   40
cause of her asking, and not my example.

PINCHWIFE. Well, tomorrow night I shall be rid of you, and the next day before 'tis light, she and I'll be rid of the Town and my dreadful apprehensions.—Come, be not melancholy, for thou shalt   45
go into the country after tomorrow, dearest.

ALITHEA. Great comfort.

MARGERY. Pish, what d'ye tell me of the country for?

PINCHWIFE. How's this! What, pish at the   50
country?

MARGERY. Let me alone; I am not well.

PINCHWIFE. Oh, if that be all—what ails my dearest?

MARGERY. Truly I don't know, but I have not been   55
well since you told me there was a gallant at the play in love with me.

PINCHWIFE. Hah—

ALITHEA. That's by my example too.

PINCHWIFE. Nay, if you are not well but are so   60
concerned because a lewd fellow chanced to lie and say he liked you, you'll make me sick, too.

MARGERY. Of what sickness?

_____

[80] grease the horses' teeth] a ruse so that the horses cannot eat what the owner has paid for.

PINCHWIFE. Oh, of that which is worse than the plague, jealousy. 65

MARGERY. Pish, you jeer. I'm sure there's no such disease in our receipt-book[81] at home.

PINCHWIFE. No, thou never met'st with it, poor innocent. (*Aside.*) Well, if thou cuckold me, 'twill be my own fault, for cuckolds and bastards are generally makers of their own fortune. 70

MARGERY. Well but pray, bud, let's go to a play tonight.

PINCHWIFE. 'Tis just done; she comes from it.— But why are you so eager to see a play? 75

MARGERY. Faith dear, not that I care one pin for their talk there, but I like to look upon the playermen and would see, if I could, the gallant you say loves me; that's all, dear bud.

PINCHWIFE. Is that all, dear bud? 80

ALITHEA. This proceeds from my example.

MARGERY. But if the play be done, let's go abroad, however, dear bud.

PINCHWIFE. Come, have a little patience, and thou shalt go into the country on Friday. 85

MARGERY. Therefore, I would see first some sights to tell my neighbors of. Nay, I will go abroad, that's once.[82]

ALITHEA. I'm the cause of this desire, too.

PINCHWIFE. But now I think on't, who was the cause of Horner's coming to my lodging today? That was you. 90

ALITHEA. No, you, because you would not let him see your handsome wife out of your lodging.

MARGERY. Why, oh Lord! Did the gentleman come hither to see me indeed? 95

PINCHWIFE. No, no.—You are not cause of that damned question, too, Mistress Alithea? (*Aside.*) Well, she's in the right of it: he is in love with my wife—and comes after her. 'Tis so. But I'll nip his love in the bud, lest he should follow us into the country and break his chariot wheel near our house on purpose for an excuse to come to't. But I think I know the Town. 100

MARGERY. Come, pray bud, let's go abroad before 'tis late, for I will go, that's flat and plain. 105

PINCHWIFE. (*Aside.*) So! The obstinacy already of a Town wife, and I must, whilst she's here, humour her like one.—Sister, how shall we do, that she may not be seen or known? 110

ALITHEA. Let her put on her mask.

PINCHWIFE. Pshaw, a mask makes people but the more inquisitive and is as ridiculous a disguise as a stage beard; her shape, stature, habit will be known, and if we should meet with Horner, he would be sure to take acquaintance with us, must wish her joy, kiss her, talk to her, leer upon her, and the devil and all. No, I'll not use her to a mask; 'tis dangerous, for masks have made more cuckolds than the best faces that ever were known. 115 120

ALITHEA. How will you do then?

MARGERY. Nay, shall we go? The Exchange will be shut, and I have a mind to see that.

PINCHWIFE. So—I have it. I'll dress her up in the suit we are to carry down to her brother, little Sir James; nay, I understand the Town tricks. Come, let's go dress her. A mask! No—a woman masked, like a covered dish, gives a man curiosity and appetite, when, it may be, uncovered, 'twould turn his stomach. No, no. 125 130

ALITHEA. Indeed, your comparison is something a greasy one. But I had a gentle gallant used to say, a beauty masked, like the sun in eclipse, gathers together more gazers than if it shined out.

Exeunt.

ACT III, SCENE II. THE NEW EXCHANGE.

Enter Horner, Harcourt, Dorilant; [Clasp at his booth].

DORILANT. Engaged to women, and not sup with us?

HORNER. Aye, a pox on 'em all.

HARCOURT. You were much a more reasonable man in the morning and had as noble resolutions against 'em as a widower of a week's liberty. 5

DORILANT. Did I ever think to see you keep company with women in vain?

HORNER. In vain! No, 'tis since I can't love 'em, to be revenged on 'em. 10

HARCOURT. Now your sting is gone, you looked in the box amongst all those women like a drone

---

81 receipt-book] book of prescriptions for ailments.

82 that's once] that's final, or positive; once and for all.

in the hive: all upon you, shoved and ill-used by
'em all, and thrust from one side to t'other.

DORILANT. Yet he must be buzzing amongst 'em 15
still, like other old beetle-headed, lickerish drones.
Avoid 'em and hate 'em as they hate you.

HORNER. Because I do hate 'em and would hate
'em yet more, I'll frequent 'em. You may see by
marriage, nothing makes a man hate a woman 20
more than her constant conversation. In short, I
converse with 'em, as you do with rich fools, to
laugh at 'em and use 'em ill.

DORILANT. But I would no more sup with women
unless I could lie with 'em, than sup with a rich 25
coxcomb unless I could cheat him.

HORNER. Yes, I have known thee sup with a fool
for his drinking; if he could set out your hand[83]
that way only, you were satisfied, and if he were a
wine-swallowing mouth, 'twas enough. 30

HARCOURT. Yes, a man drinks often with a fool,
as he tosses with a marker, only to keep his hand
in ure.[84] But do the ladies drink?

HORNER. Yes sir, and I shall have the pleasure at
least of laying 'em flat with a bottle and bring as 35
much scandal that way upon 'em as formerly
t'other.

HARCOURT. Perhaps you may prove as weak a
brother amongst 'em that way as t'other.

DORILANT. Faugh, drinking with women is as 40
unnatural as scolding with 'em, but 'tis a pleasure
of decayed fornicators and the basest way of
quenching love.

HARCOURT. Nay, 'tis drowning love instead of
quenching it. But leave us for civil women, too! 45

DORILANT. Aye, when he can't be the better for
'em. We hardly pardon a man that leaves his friend
for a wench, and that's a pretty lawful call.

HORNER. Faith, I would not leave you for 'em if
they would not drink. 50

DORILANT. Who would disappoint his company
at Lewis's[85] for a gossiping?

---

83 set out your hand] furnish you with drink.
84 tosses … ure] throws dice with a scorekeeper (i.e., one
who doesn't play for money) only to keep in practice.
85 Lewis's] reference obscure; presumably a tavern or eating house.

HARCOURT. Faugh, wine and women good apart,
together as nauseous as sack[86] and sugar. But hark
you, sir, before you go, a little of your advice; an 55
old maimed general, when unfit for action, is fittest
for counsel. I have other designs upon women than
eating and drinking with them. I am in love with
Sparkish's mistress, whom he is to marry tomorrow.
Now how shall I get her? 60

Enter Sparkish, looking about.

HORNER. Why, here comes one will help you to
her.

HARCOURT. He! He, I tell you, is my rival and will
hinder my love.

HORNER. No, a foolish rival and a jealous husband 65
assist their rivals' designs, for they are sure to make
their women hate them, which is the first step to
their love for another man.

HARCOURT. But I cannot come near his mistress
but in his company. 70

HORNER. Still the better for you, for fools are most
easily cheated when they themselves are accessories,
and he is to be bubbled of his mistress, as of his
money, the common mistress, by keeping him
company. 75

SPARKISH. Who is that, that is to be bubbled?
Faith, let me snack;[87] I han't met with a bubble
since Christmas. Gad, I think bubbles are like their
brother woodcocks, go out with the cold weather.

HARCOURT. (*Apart to Horner.*) A pox! He did not 80
hear all, I hope.

SPARKISH. Come, you bubbling rogues, you.
Where do we sup?—Oh Harcourt, my mistress
tells me you have been making fierce love to her
all the play long, ha, ha—but I— 85

HARCOURT. I make love to her?

SPARKISH. Nay, I forgive thee, for I think I know
thee, and I know her, but I am sure I know myself.

HARCOURT. Did she tell you so? I see all women are
like these of the Exchange, who, to enhance the 90
price of their commodities, report to their fond[88]
customers offers which were never made 'em.

---

86 sack] wine.
87 snack] share, take part.
88 fond] foolish.

HORNER. Aye, women are as apt to tell before the intrigue as men after it and so show themselves the vainer sex. But hast thou a mistress, Sparkish? 'Tis as hard for me to believe it as that thou ever hadst a bubble, as you bragged just now.

SPARKISH. Oh your servant, sir. Are you at your raillery, sir? But we were some of us beforehand with you today at the play. The wits were something bold with you, sir. Did you not hear us laugh?

HARCOURT. Yes, but I thought you had gone to plays to laugh at the poet's wit, not at your own.

SPARKISH. Your servant, sir. No, I thank you. Gad, I go to a play as to a country treat: I carry my own wine to one and my own wit to t'other, or else I'm sure I should not be merry at either, and the reason why we are so often louder than the players is because we think we speak more wit and so become the poet's rivals in his audience. For to tell you the truth, we hate the silly rogues, nay, so much that we find fault even with their bawdy upon the stage whilst we talk nothing else in the pit as loud.

HORNER. But why shouldst thou hate the silly poets? Thou hast too much wit to be one, and they, like whores, are only hated by each other, and thou dost scorn writing, I'm sure.

SPARKISH. Yes, I'd have you to know, I scorn writing, but women, women, that make men do all foolish things, make 'em write songs, too; everybody does it. 'Tis e'en as common with lovers as playing with fans, and you can no more help rhyming to your Phyllis than drinking to your Phyllis.

HARCOURT. Nay, poetry in love is no more to be avoided than jealousy.

DORILANT. But the poets damned your songs, did they?

SPARKISH. Damn the poets! They turned 'em into burlesque, as they call it; that burlesque is a hocus-pocus trick they have got, which by the virtue of "hictius doctius,[89] topsey turvey," they make a wise and witty man in the world a fool upon the stage,

you know not how, and 'tis, therefore, I hate 'em too, for I know not but it may be my own case, for they'll put a man into a play for looking asquint. Their predecessors were contented to make serving men only their stage fools, but these rogues must have gentlemen, with a pox to 'em, nay, knights. And indeed, you shall hardly see a fool upon the stage but he's a knight, and to tell you the truth, they have kept me these six years from being a knight in earnest, for fear of being knighted in a play and dubbed a fool.

DORILANT. Blame 'em not; they must follow their copy, the age.

HARCOURT. But why shouldst thou be afraid of being in a play, who expose yourself everyday in the playhouses and as public places?

HORNER. 'Tis but being on the stage instead of standing on a bench in the pit.

DORILANT. Don't you give money to painters to draw your like[ness]? And are you afraid of your pictures at length in a playhouse where all your mistresses may see you?

SPARKISH. A pox! Painters don't draw the small pox or pimples in one's face. Come, damn all your silly authors whatever, all books and booksellers, by the world, and all readers, courteous or uncourteous.

HARCOURT. But who comes here, Sparkish?

Enter Pinchwife and his wife in man's clothes; Alithea; Lucy, her maid.

SPARKISH. Oh hide me! There's my mistress, too. (*Hides himself behind Harcourt.*)

HARCOURT. She sees you.

SPARKISH. But I will not see her; 'tis time to go to Whitehall, and I must not fail the Drawing Room.

HARCOURT. Pray, first carry me and reconcile me to her.

SPARKISH. Another time, faith, the King will have supped.

HARCOURT. Not with the worse stomach for thy absence. Thou art one of those fools that think their attendance at the King's meals as necessary as his physicians', when you are more troublesome to him than his doctors or his dogs.

SPARKISH. Pshaw, I know my interest, sir. Prithee hide me.

---

89 *hictius doctius*] standard part of a magician or juggler's performance; perhaps from the Latin *hicce est doctus* ("this is the doctor").

[III.ii]

HORNER. Your servant, Pinchwife.—What, he knows us not!

PINCHWIFE. (*To his wife aside.*) Come along. 180

MARGERY. Pray, have you any ballads? Give me six-penny worth.

CLASP. We have no ballads.

MARGERY. Then give me *Covent Garden Drollery*,[90] and a play or two.—Oh here's *Tarugo's Wiles* and *The Slighted Maiden*.[91] I'll have them. 185

PINCHWIFE. (*Apart to her.*) No, plays are not for your reading. Come along. Will you discover yourself?

HORNER. Who is that pretty youth with him, Sparkish? 190

SPARKISH. I believe his wife's brother, because he's something like her, but I never saw her but once.

HORNER. Extremely handsome. I have seen a face like it, too. Let us follow 'em. 195

Exeunt Pinchwife, Margery; Alithea, Lucy, Horner, Dorilant following them.

HARCOURT. Come Sparkish, your mistress saw you and will be angry you go not to her; besides, I would fain be reconciled to her, which none but you can do, dear friend.

SPARKISH. Well that's a better reason, dear friend. 200 I would not go near her now for hers or my own sake, but I can deny you nothing, for though I have known thee a great while, never go,[92] if I do not love thee as well as a new acquaintance.

HARCOURT. I am obliged to you indeed, dear 205 friend. I would be well with her only to be well with thee still, for these ties to wives usually dissolve all ties to friends. I would be contented she should enjoy you a-nights, but I would have you to my self a-days, as I have had, dear friend. 210

SPARKISH. And thou shalt enjoy me a-days, dear, dear friend, never stir, and I'll be divorced from her sooner than from thee. Come along.

HARCOURT. (*Aside.*) So we are hard put to't when we make our rival our procurer, but neither she nor 215 her brother would let me come near her now. When all's done, a rival is the best cloak to steal to a mistress under without suspicion, and when we have once got to her as we desire, we throw him off like other cloaks. 220

Exit Sparkish, Harcourt following him. Re-enter Pinchwife, Margery in man's clothes.

PINCHWIFE. (*To Alithea [offstage]*.) Sister, if you will not go, we must leave you. (*Aside.*) The fool, her gallant, and she will muster up all the young saunterers of this place, and they will leave their dear seamstresses to follow us. What a swarm of 225 cuckolds and cuckold-makers are here?—Come let's be gone, Mistress Margery.

MARGERY. Don't you believe that, I han't half my belly full of sights yet.

PINCHWIFE. Then walk this way. 230

MARGERY. Lord, what a power of brave signs are here! Stay—the Bull's Head, the Ram's Head, and the Stag's Head, dear—

PINCHWIFE. Nay, if every husband's proper sign here were visible, they would be all alike. 235

MARGERY. What d'ye mean by that, bud?

PINCHWIFE. 'Tis no matter—no matter, bud.

MARGERY. Pray tell me, nay, I will know.

PINCHWIFE. They would be all bulls', stags', and rams' heads.[93] 240

Exeunt Pinchwife, Margery. Re-enter Sparkish, Harcourt, Alithea, Lucy at t'other door.

SPARKISH. Come dear madam, for my sake, you shall be reconciled to him.

ALITHEA. For your sake, I hate him.

HARCOURT. That's something too cruel, madam, to hate me for his sake. 245

SPARKISH. Aye indeed, madam, too, too cruel to me to hate my friend for my sake.

90 *Covent Garden Drollery*] a miscellany of songs, poems, prologues and epilogues by various writers, including Wycherley, published in 1672.
91 *Tarugo's Wiles* and *The Slighted Maiden*] a comedy by Sir Thomas St. Serfe (1668) and a tragicomedy by Sir Robert Staplyton (1663).
92 never go] like "never stir" below, a phrase of reassurance meaning roughly "don't worry."
93 They would … heads] that is, they would all have horns (of cuckoldry).

ALITHEA. I hate him because he is your enemy, and you ought to hate him, too, for making love to me, if you love me. 250

SPARKISH. That's a good one! I hate a man for loving you! If he did love you, 'tis but what he can't help, and 'tis your fault not his, if he admires you. I hate a man for being of my opinion! I'll ne'er do't, by the world. 255

ALITHEA. Is it for your honour or mine to suffer a man to make love to me, who am to marry you tomorrow?

SPARKISH. Is it for your honour or mine to have me jealous? That he makes love to you is a sign 260 you are handsome, and that I am not jealous is a sign you are virtuous. That, I think, is for your honour.

ALITHEA. But 'tis your honour, too, I am concerned for. 265

HARCOURT. But why, dearest madam, will you be more concerned for his honour than he is himself? Let his honour alone for my sake and his. He, he, has no honour—

SPARKISH. How's that? 270

HARCOURT. But what my dear friend can guard himself.

SPARKISH. Oh ho—that's right again.

HARCOURT. Your care of his honour argues his neglect of it, which is no honour to my dear friend 275 here; therefore, once more, let his honour go which way it will, dear madam.

SPARKISH. Aye, aye, were it for my honour to marry a woman whose virtue I suspected and could not trust her in a friend's hands? 280

ALITHEA. Are you not afraid to lose me?

HARCOURT. He afraid to lose you, madam! No, no— you may see how the most estimable and most glorious creature in the world is valued by him. Will you not see it? 285

SPARKISH. Right, honest Frank, I have that noble value for her that I cannot be jealous of her.

ALITHEA. You mistake him: he means you care not for me nor who has me.

SPARKISH. Lord madam, I see you are jealous. Will 290 you wrest a poor man's meaning from his words?

ALITHEA. You astonish me, sir, with your want of jealousy.

SPARKISH. And you make me giddy, madam, with your jealousy and fears and virtue and honour; gad, 295 I see virtue makes a woman as troublesome as a little reading or learning.

ALITHEA. Monstrous!

LUCY. (*Behind.*) Well, to see what easy husbands these women of quality can meet with! A poor 300 chambermaid can never have such ladylike luck. Besides, he's thrown away upon her; she'll make no use of her fortune, her blessing. None to a gentleman for a pure cuckold, for it requires good breeding to be a cuckold. 305

ALITHEA. I tell you then plainly: he pursues me to marry me.

SPARKISH. Pshaw—

HARCOURT. Come madam, you see you strive in vain to make him jealous of me; my dear friend is 310 the kindest creature in the world to me.

SPARKISH. Poor fellow.

HARCOURT. But his kindness only is not enough for me, without your favour; your good opinion, dear madam, 'tis that must perfect my happiness. 315 Good gentleman, he believes all I say; would you would do so. Jealous of me! I would not wrong him nor you for the world.

Alithea walks carelessly to and fro.

SPARKISH. Look you there, hear him, hear him, and do not walk away so. 320

HARCOURT. I love you, madam, so—

SPARKISH. How's that! Nay—now you begin to go too far indeed.

HARCOURT. So much, I confess, I say I love you, that I would not have you miserable and cast your- 325 self away upon so unworthy and inconsiderable a thing as what you see here. (*Clapping his hand on his breast, points at Sparkish.*)

SPARKISH. No, faith, I believe thou wouldst not, now his meaning is plain. But I knew before thou 330 wouldst not wrong me nor her.

HARCOURT. No, no, heavens forbid the glory of her sex should fall so low as into the embraces of such a contemptible wretch, the last of mankind— my dear friend here—I injure him. (*Embracing* 335 *Sparkish.*)

ALITHEA. Very well.

SPARKISH. No, no, dear friend, I knew it.—
Madam, you see he will rather wrong himself than
me in giving himself such names.   340

ALITHEA. Do not you understand him yet?

SPARKISH. Yes, how modestly he speaks of himself,
poor fellow.

ALITHEA. Methinks he speaks impudently of yourself, since—before yourself, too, insomuch that I   345
can no longer suffer his scurrilous abusiveness to
you, no more than his love to me. (*Offers to go.*)

SPARKISH. Nay, nay, madam, pray stay. His love
to you! Lord madam, has he not spoke yet plain
enough?   350

ALITHEA. Yes indeed, I should think so.

SPARKISH. Well then, by the world, a man can't
speak civilly to a woman now but presently she
says he makes love to her. Nay madam, you shall
stay, with your pardon, since you have not yet un-   355
derstood him, till he has made an éclaircissement
of his love to you, that is, what kind of love it is.—
Answer to thy catechism. Friend, do you love my
mistress here?

HARCOURT. Yes, I wish she would not doubt it.   360

SPARKISH. But how do you love her?

HARCOURT. With all my soul.

ALITHEA. I thank him, methinks he speaks plain
enough now.

SPARKISH. (*To Alithea.*) You are out[94] still.—But   365
with what kind of love, Harcourt?

HARCOURT. With the best and truest love in the
world.

SPARKISH. Look you there then: that is with no
matrimonial love, I'm sure.   370

ALITHEA. How's that, do you say matrimonial love
is not best?

SPARKISH. [*Aside.*] Gad, I went too far ere I was
aware.—But speak for thyself, Harcourt: you said
you would not wrong me nor her.   375

HARCOURT. No, no, madam, e'en take him for
Heaven's sake—

SPARKISH. Look you there, madam.

HARCOURT. Who should in all justice be yours,
he that loves you most. (*Claps his hand on his*   380
breast.)

------

94 out] mistaken.

ALITHEA. Look you there, Mr. Sparkish. Who's
that?

SPARKISH. Who should it be? Go on, Harcourt.

HARCOURT. Who loves you more than women,   385
titles, or fortune fools. (*Points at Sparkish.*)

SPARKISH. Look you there: he means me still, for
he points at me.

ALITHEA. Ridiculous!

HARCOURT. Who can only match your faith and   390
constancy in love.

SPARKISH. Aye.

HARCOURT. Who knows, if it be possible, how to
value so much beauty and virtue.

SPARKISH. Aye.   395

HARCOURT. Whose love can no more be equalled
in the world than that heavenly form of yours.

SPARKISH. No—

HARCOURT. Who could no more suffer a rival
than your absence and yet could no more suspect   400
your virtue than his own constancy in his love to
you.

SPARKISH. No—

HARCOURT. Who, in fine, loves you better than
his eyes that first made him love you.   405

SPARKISH. Aye.—Nay madam, faith you shan't go
till—

ALITHEA. Have a care lest you make me stay too
long—

SPARKISH. But till he has saluted you, that I may   410
be assured you are friends after his honest advice
and declaration. Come pray, madam, be friends
with him.

Enter Pinchwife, Margery.

ALITHEA. You must pardon me, sir, that I am not
yet so obedient to you.   415

PINCHWIFE. What, invite your wife to kiss men?
Monstrous! Are you not ashamed? I will never
forgive you.

SPARKISH. Are you not ashamed that I should have
more confidence in the chastity of your family than 420
you have? You must not teach me: I am a man of
honour, sir, though I am frank and free. I am
frank, sir—

PINCHWIFE. Very frank, sir, to share your wife
with your friends.   425

SPARKISH. He is an humble, menial friend, such as reconciles the differences of the marriage bed. You know man and wife do not always agree. I design him for that use, therefore, would have him well with my wife. 430

PINCHWIFE. A menial friend—you will get a great many menial friends by showing your wife as you do.

SPARKISH. What then, it may be I have a pleasure in't, as I have to show fine clothes at a playhouse 435 the first day and count money before poor rogues.

PINCHWIFE. He that shows his wife or money will be in danger of having them borrowed sometimes.

SPARKISH. I love to be envied and would not marry a wife that I alone could love; loving alone is as 440 dull as eating alone. Is it not a frank age, and I am a frank person? And to tell you the truth, it may be I love to have rivals in a wife: they make her seem to a man still but as a kept mistress, and so good night, for I must to Whitehall.—Madam, 445 I hope you are now reconciled to my friend, and so I wish you a good night, madam, and sleep if you can, for tomorrow you know I must visit you early with a canonical gentleman.—Good night, dear Harcourt. (*Exit.*) 450

HARCOURT. Madam, I hope you will not refuse my visit tomorrow, if it should be earlier, with a canonical gentleman, than Mr. Sparkish's.

PINCHWIFE. (*Coming between Alithea and Harcourt.*) This gentlewoman is yet under my care; 455 therefore, you must yet forbear your freedom with her, sir.

HARCOURT. Must, sir—

PINCHWIFE. Yes, sir, she is my sister.

HARCOURT. 'Tis well she is, sir—for I must be her 460 servant, sir.—Madam—

PINCHWIFE. Come away, sister. We had been gone if it had not been for you and so avoided these lewd rakehells who seem to haunt us.

Enter Horner, Dorilant to them.

HORNER. How now, Pinchwife? 465

PINCHWIFE. Your servant.

HORNER. What, I see a little time in the country makes a man turn wild and unsociable and only fit to converse with his horses, dogs, and his herds.

PINCHWIFE. I have business, sir, and must mind 470 it. Your business is pleasure; therefore, you and I must go different ways.

HORNER. Well, you may go on, but this pretty young gentleman— (*Takes hold of Margery.*)

HARCOURT. The lady— 475

DORILANT. And the maid—

HORNER. Shall stay with us, for I suppose their business is the same with ours, pleasure.

PINCHWIFE. (*Aside.*) 'Sdeath, he knows her, she carries it so sillily, yet if he does not, I should be 480 more silly to discover it first.

ALITHEA. Pray let us go, sir.

PINCHWIFE. Come, come—

HORNER. (*To Margery.*) Had you not rather stay with us?—Prithee Pinchwife, who is this pretty 485 young gentleman?

PINCHWIFE. One to whom I'm a guardian. (*Aside.*) I wish I could keep her out of your hands—

HORNER. Who is he? I never saw any thing so pretty in all my life. 490

PINCHWIFE. Pshaw, do not look upon him so much. He's a poor bashful youth; you'll put him out of countenance. Come away, brother. (*Offers to take her away.*)

HORNER. Oh your brother! 495

PINCHWIFE. Yes, my wife's brother.—Come, come, she'll stay supper for us.

HORNER. I thought so, for he is very like her I saw you at the play with, whom I told you I was in love with. 500

MARGERY. (*Aside.*) Oh jiminy![95] Is this he that was in love with me? I am glad on't, I vow, for he's a curious fine gentleman, and I love him already, too. (*To Mr. Pinchwife.*) Is this he, bud?

PINCHWIFE. (*To his wife.*) Come away, come away. 505

HORNER. Why, what haste are you in? Why won't you let me talk with him?

PINCHWIFE. Because you'll debauch him. He's yet young and innocent, and I would not have him debauched for anything in the world. (*Aside.*) How 510 she gazes on him! The devil—

HORNER. Harcourt, Dorilant, look you here: this is the likeness of that dowdy he told us of, his wife.

---

[95] jiminy] a mild oath, possibly a corruption of *jesu domine*.

Did you ever see a lovelier creature? The rogue has reason to be jealous of his wife, since she is like him, for she would make all that see her in love with her. 515

HARCOURT. And as I remember now, she is as like him here as can be.

DORILANT. She is indeed very pretty, if she be like him. 520

HORNER. Very pretty? a very pretty commendation! She is a glorious creature, beautiful beyond all things I ever beheld.

PINCHWIFE. So, so. 525

HARCOURT. More beautiful than a poet's first mistress of imagination.

HORNER. Or another man's last mistress of flesh and blood.

MARGERY. Nay, now you jeer, sir. Pray don't jeer me— 530

PINCHWIFE. Come, come. (*Aside.*) By heavens, she'll discover herself!

HORNER. I speak of your sister, sir.

PINCHWIFE. Aye, but saying she was handsome, if like him, made him blush. (*Aside.*) I am upon a rack— 535

HORNER. Methinks he is so handsome, he should not be a man.

PINCHWIFE. [*Aside.*] Oh there 'tis out! He has discovered her! I am not able to suffer any longer. (*To his wife.*) Come, come away, I say— 540

HORNER. Nay by your leave, sir, he shall not go yet.—Harcourt, Dorilant, let us torment this jealous rogue a little. 545

HARCOURT AND DORILANT. How?

HORNER. I'll show you.

PINCHWIFE. Come, pray let him go. I cannot stay fooling any longer. I tell you his sister stays supper for us. 550

HORNER. Does she? Come then we'll all go sup with her and thee.

PINCHWIFE. No, now I think on't, having stayed so long for us, I warrant she's gone to bed. (*Aside.*) I wish she and I were well out of their hands.— 555 Come, I must rise early tomorrow, come.

HORNER. Well then, if she be gone to bed, I wish her and you a good night.—But pray, young gentleman, present my humble service to her.

MARGERY. Thank you heartily, sir. 560

PINCHWIFE. (*Aside.*) S'death, she will discover herself yet in spite of me.—He is something more civil to you, for your kindness to his sister, than I am, it seems.

HORNER. Tell her, dear sweet little gentleman, for all your brother there, that you have revived the love I had for her at first sight in the playhouse. 565

MARGERY. But did you love her indeed and indeed?

PINCHWIFE. (*Aside.*) So, so.—Away, I say.

HORNER. Nay, stay. Yes, indeed and indeed, pray do you tell her so and give her this kiss from me. (*Kisses her.*) 570

PINCHWIFE. (*Aside.*) Oh heavens! What do I suffer! Now 'tis too plain he knows her and yet—

HORNER. And this and this— (*Kisses her again.*) 575

MARGERY. What do you kiss me for? I am no woman.

PINCHWIFE. (*Aside.*) So—there 'tis out.—Come, I cannot, nor will stay any longer.

HORNER. Nay, they shall send your lady a kiss, too. Here Harcourt, Dorilant, will you not? 580

They kiss her.

PINCHWIFE. (*Aside.*) How! Do I suffer this? Was I not accusing another just now for this rascally patience in permitting his wife to be kissed before his face? Ten thousand ulcers gnaw away their lips.—Come, come. 585

HORNER. Good night, dear little gentleman.—Madam, good night.—Farewell, Pinchwife. (*Apart to Harcourt and Dorilant.*) Did not I tell you I would raise his jealous gall? 590

Exeunt Horner, Harcourt, and Dorilant.

PINCHWIFE. So they are gone at last.—Stay, let me see first if the coach be at this door. (*Exit.*)

Horner, Harcourt, Dorilant return.

HORNER. What, not gone yet? Will you be sure to do as I desired you, sweet sir?

MARGERY. Sweet sir, but what will you give me then? 595

HORNER. Anything. Come away into the next walk.

Exit Horner, haling away Margery.

ALITHEA. Hold, hold, what d'ye do?

LUCY. Stay, stay, hold—

Alithea, Lucy struggling with Harcourt and Dorilant.

HARCOURT. Hold, madam, hold. Let him present[96] 600
him; he'll come presently. Nay, I will never let you go
till you answer my question.

LUCY. For God's sake, sir, I must follow 'em.

DORILANT. No, I have something to present you
with, too. You shan't follow them. 605

Pinchwife returns.

PINCHWIFE. Where? how? what's become of—?
Gone! Whither?

LUCY. He's only gone with the gentleman, who will
give him something, an't please your worship.

PINCHWIFE. Something—give him something, 610
with a pox! Where are they?

ALITHEA. In the next walk only, brother.

PINCHWIFE. Only! Only! Where? Where? (*Exit
and returns presently, then goes out again.*)

HARCOURT. What's the matter with him? Why so 615
much concerned?—But dearest madam—

ALITHEA. Pray let me go, sir. I have said and
suffered enough already.

HARCOURT. Then you will not look upon nor pity
my sufferings? 620

ALITHEA. To look upon 'em, when I cannot help
'em, were cruelty, not pity; therefore, I will never
see you more.

HARCOURT. Let me then, madam, have my
privilege of a banished lover: complaining or 625
railing and giving you but a farewell reason why,
if you cannot condescend to marry me, you should
not take that wretch my rival.

ALITHEA. He only, not you, since my honour is
engaged so far to him, can give me a reason why I 630
should not marry him, but if he be true and what
I think him to me, I must be so to him. Your
servant, sir.

HARCOURT. Have women only constancy when
'tis a vice and, like Fortune, only true to fools? 635

DORILANT. (*To Lucy, who struggles to get from him.*)
Thou shalt not stir, thou robust creature. You see

---

[96] present] give him a present.

I can deal with you; therefore, you should stay the
rather and be kind.

Enter Pinchwife.

PINCHWIFE. Gone, gone, not to be found! quite 640
gone! Ten thousand plagues go with 'em! Which
way went they?

ALITHEA. But into t'other walk, brother.

LUCY. Their business will be done presently sure,
an't please your worship; it can't be long in doing, 645
I'm sure on't.

ALITHEA. Are they not there?

PINCHWIFE. No, you know where they are, you
infamous wretch, eternal shame of your family,
which you do not dishonour enough yourself, you 650
think, but you must help her to do it, too, thou
legion of bawds!

ALITHEA. Good brother!

PINCHWIFE. Damned, damned sister!

ALITHEA. Look you here, she's coming. 655

*Enter Margery in man's clothes, running with her hat
under her arm, full of oranges and dried fruit, Horner
following.*

MARGERY. Oh dear bud, look you here what I have
got! See.

PINCHWIFE. (*Aside, rubbing his forehead.*) And
what I have got here, too, which you can't see.

MARGERY. The fine gentleman has given me better 660
things yet.

PINCHWIFE. Has he so? (*Aside.*) Out of breath and
coloured—I must hold yet.

HORNER. I have only given your little brother an
orange, sir. 665

PINCHWIFE. (*To Horner.*) Thank you, sir. (*Aside.*)
You have only squeezed my orange, I suppose, and
given it me again, yet I must have a City patience.
(*To his wife.*) Come, come away.

MARGERY. Stay, till I have put up my fine things, 670
bud.

Enter Sir Jaspar Fidget.

SIR JASPAR. Oh, Master Horner, come, come, the
ladies stay for you. Your mistress, my wife, wonders
you make not more haste to her.

HORNER. I have stayed this half hour for you here, 675
and 'tis your fault I am not now with your wife.

SIR JASPAR. But pray, don't let her know so much; the truth on't is I was advancing a certain project to his Majesty about—I'll tell you.

HORNER. No, let's go and hear it at your house.— Good night, sweet little gentleman. One kiss more. (*Kisses her.*) You'll remember me now, I hope.

DORILANT. What, Sir Jaspar, will you separate friends? He promised to sup with us, and if you take him to your house, you'll be in danger of our company, too.

SIR JASPAR. Alas gentlemen, my house is not fit for you: there are none but civil women there, which are not for your turn. He, you know, can bear with the society of civil women, now, ha, ha, ha. Besides he's one of my family;[97] he's—he, he, he.

DORILANT. What is he?

SIR JASPAR. Faith my eunuch, since you'll have it, he, he, he.

Exit Sir Jaspar Fidget and Horner.

DORILANT. I rather wish thou wert his, or my cuckold.—Harcourt, what a good cuckold is lost there for want of a man to make him one; thee and I cannot have Horner's privilege, who can make use of it.

HARCOURT. Aye, to poor Horner 'tis like coming to an estate at threescore, when a man can't be the better for't.

PINCHWIFE. Come.

MARGERY. Presently, bud.

DORILANT. Come, let us go, too. (*To Alithea.*) Madam, your servant. (*To Lucy.*) Good night, strapper.

HARCOURT. Madam, though you will not let me have a good day or night, I wish you one, but dare not name the other half of my wish.

ALITHEA. Good night, sir, forever.

MARGERY. I don't know where to put this. Here, dear bud, you shall eat it. Nay, you shall have part of the fine gentleman's good things, or treat as you call it, when we come home.

PINCHWIFE. Indeed I deserve it, since I furnished the best part of it. (*Strikes away the orange.*)
The gallant treats, presents, and gives the ball,
But 'tis the absent cuckold pays for all.

---

97 family] entire household including servants.

ACT IV, SCENE I. PINCHWIFE'S HOUSE IN THE MORNING.

Lucy, Alithea dressed in new clothes.

LUCY. Well madam, now have I dressed you and set you out with so many ornaments and spent upon you ounces of essence and pulvillio,[98] and all this for no other purpose but as people adorn and perfume a corpse for a stinking second-hand grave, such or as bad I think Master Sparkish's bed.

ALITHEA. Hold your peace.

LUCY. Nay madam, I will ask you the reason why you would banish poor Master Harcourt forever from your sight? How could you be so hard-hearted?

ALITHEA. 'Twas because I was not hard-hearted.

LUCY. No, no, 'twas stark love and kindness, I warrant.

ALITHEA. It was so: I would see him no more because I love him.

LUCY. Hey day, a very pretty reason.

ALITHEA. You do not understand me.

LUCY. I wish you may yourself.

ALITHEA. I was engaged to marry, you see, another man, whom my justice will not suffer me to deceive or injure.

LUCY. Can there be a greater cheat or wrong done to a man than to give him your person without your heart? I should make a conscience of it.

ALITHEA. I'll retrieve it for him after I am married awhile.

LUCY. The woman that marries to love better will be as much mistaken as the wencher that marries to live better. No madam, marrying to increase love is like gaming to become rich: alas, you only lose what little stock you had before.

ALITHEA. I find by your rhetoric you have been bribed to betray me.

LUCY. Only by his merit that has bribed your heart, you see, against your word and rigid honour. But what a devil is this honour? 'Tis sure a disease in the head, like the megrim[99] or falling sickness,[100]

---

98 pulvillio] powdered perfume.
99 megrim] migraine.
100 falling sickness] epilepsy.

that always hurries people away to do themselves mischief. Men lose their lives by it; women, what's dearer to 'em, their love, the life of life. 40

ALITHEA. Come, pray talk you no more of honour nor Master Harcourt. I wish the other would come to secure my fidelity to him and his right in me.

LUCY. You will marry him then? 45

ALITHEA. Certainly, I have given him already my word and will my hand, too, to make it good when he comes.

LUCY. Well, I wish I may never stick pin more, if he be not an arrant natural[101] to t'other fine gentleman. 50

ALITHEA. I own he wants the wit of Harcourt, which I will dispense withal for another want he has, which is want of jealousy, which men of wit seldom want. 55

LUCY. Lord madam, what should you do with a fool to your husband? You intend to be honest,[102] don't you? Then that husbandly virtue, credulity, is thrown away upon you.

ALITHEA. He only that could suspect my virtue should have cause to do it; 'tis Sparkish's confidence in my truth that obliges me to be so faithful to him. 60

LUCY. You are not sure his opinion may last.

ALITHEA. I am satisfied 'tis impossible for him to be jealous after the proofs I have had of him. Jealousy in a husband, Heaven defend me from it! It begets a thousand plagues to a poor woman: the loss of her honour, her quiet, and her— 65

LUCY. And her pleasure. 70

ALITHEA. What d'ye mean, impertinent?

LUCY. Liberty is a great pleasure, madam.

ALITHEA. I say loss of her honour, her quiet, nay, her life sometimes, and what's as bad almost, the loss of this Town; that is, she is sent into the country, which is the last ill usage of a husband to a wife, I think. 75

LUCY. (Aside.) Oh does the wind lie there?—Then of necessity, madam, you think a man must carry his wife into the country if he be wise. The country is as terrible I find to our young English ladies as 80

a monastery to those abroad. And on my virginity, I think they would rather marry a London gaoler than a high sheriff of a county, since neither can stir from his employment. Formerly women of wit married fools for a great estate, a fine seat, or the like, but now 'tis for a pretty seat only in Lincoln's Inn Fields, St. James's Fields, or the Pall Mall.[103] 85

Enter to them Sparkish and Harcourt dressed like a parson.

SPARKISH. Madam, your humble servant, a happy day to you and to us all. 90

HARCOURT. Amen.

ALITHEA. Who have we here?

SPARKISH. My chaplain, faith. Oh madam, poor Harcourt remembers his humble service to you and, in obedience to your last commands, refrains coming into your sight. 95

ALITHEA. Is not that he?

SPARKISH. No, fie, no, but to show that he ne'er intended to hinder our match, has sent his brother here to join our hands. When I get me a wife, I must get her a chaplain, according to the custom; this is his brother and my chaplain. 100

ALITHEA. His brother?

LUCY. (Aside.) And your chaplain, to preach in your pulpit then. 105

ALITHEA. His brother!

SPARKISH. Nay, I knew you would not believe it.— I told you, sir, she would take you for your brother Frank.

ALITHEA. Believe it! 110

LUCY. (Aside.) His brother! Ha, ha, he, he has a trick left still it seems.

SPARKISH. Come my dearest, pray let us go to church before the canonical hour[104] is past.

ALITHEA. For shame! You are abused still. 115

SPARKISH. By the world, 'tis strange now you are so incredulous.

ALITHEA. 'Tis strange you are so credulous.

SPARKISH. Dearest of my life, hear me: I tell you this is Ned Harcourt of Cambridge; by the world, 120

101 natural] fool.
102 honest] chaste, faithful.
103 Lincoln's Inns Fields, St. James's Fields, … the Pall Mall] fashionable places to live in London.
104 canonical hour] before noon.

you see he has a sneaking college look. 'Tis true he's something like his brother Frank, and they differ from each other no more than in their age, for they were twins.

LUCY. Ha, ha, he. 125

ALITHEA. Your servant, sir. I cannot be so deceived, though you are. But come let's hear, how do you know what you affirm so confidently?

SPARKISH. Why, I'll tell you all. Frank Harcourt coming to me this morning to wish me joy and 130 present his service to you, I asked him if he could help me to a parson, whereupon he told me he had a brother in Town who was in orders, and he went straight away and sent him you see there to me.

ALITHEA. Yes, Frank goes, and puts on a black coat, 135 then tells you he is Ned; that's all you have for't.

SPARKISH. Pshaw, pshaw, I tell you by the same token, the midwife put her garter about Frank's neck to know 'em asunder, they were so like.

ALITHEA. Frank tells you this, too. 140

SPARKISH. Aye, and Ned there too; nay, they are both in a story.

ALITHEA. So, so, very foolish.

SPARKISH. Lord, if you won't believe one, you had best try him by your chambermaid there, for 145 chamber-maids must needs know chaplains from other men, they are so used to 'em.[105]

LUCY. Let's see: nay, I'll be sworn he has the canonical smirk and the filthy, clammy palm of a chaplain. 150

ALITHEA. Well, most reverend doctor, pray let us make an end of this fooling.

HARCOURT. With all my soul, divine, heavenly creature, when you please.

ALITHEA. He speaks like a chaplain indeed. 155

SPARKISH. Why, was there not, "soul," "divine," "heavenly," in what he said?

ALITHEA. Once more, most impertinent blackcoat, cease your persecution and let us have a conclusion of this ridiculous love. 160

HARCOURT. (Aside.) I had forgot, I must suit my style to my coat, or I wear it in vain.

ALITHEA. I have no more patience left; let us make once an end of this troublesome love, I say.

HARCOURT. So be it, seraphic lady, when your 165 honour shall think it meet and convenient so to do.

SPARKISH. Gad, I'm sure none but a chaplain could speak so, I think.

ALITHEA. Let me tell you, sir, this dull trick will not serve your turn. Though you delay our 170 marriage, you shall not hinder it.

HARCOURT. Far be it from me, munificent patroness, to delay your marriage. I desire nothing more than to marry you presently, which I might do, if you yourself would, for my noble, good- 175 natured, and thrice generous patron here would not hinder it.

SPARKISH. No, poor man, not I, faith.

HARCOURT. And now, madam, let me tell you plainly, nobody else shall marry you, by heavens. 180 I'll die first, for I'm sure I should die[106] after it.

LUCY. [Aside.] How his love has made him forget his function, as I have seen it in real parsons.

ALITHEA. That was spoken like a chaplain, too! Now you understand him, I hope. 185

SPARKISH. Poor man, he takes it heinously to be refused. I can't blame him; 'tis putting an indignity upon him not to be suffered. But you'll pardon me, madam, it shan't be; he shall marry us. Come away, pray madam. 190

LUCY. Ha, ha, he, more ado! 'Tis late.

ALITHEA. Invincible stupidity, I tell you he would marry me as your rival, not as your chaplain.

SPARKISH. (Pulling her away.) Come, come, madam. 195

LUCY. I pray, madam, do not refuse this reverend divine the honour and satisfaction of marrying you, for I dare say, he has set his heart upon't, good doctor.

ALITHEA. What can you hope or design by this? 200

HARCOURT. [Aside.] I could answer her, a reprieve for a day only often revokes a hasty doom; at worst, if she will not take mercy on me and let me marry her, I have at least the lover's second pleasure, hindering my rival's enjoyment, though 205 but for a time.

---

105 chambermaids … used to 'em] Alleged promiscuity between chambermaids and the clergy was a standard joke of the time.

106 die] suffer the "little death" of sexual orgasm.

SPARKISH. Come, madam, 'tis e'en twelve o'clock, and my mother charged me never to be married out of the canonical hours. Come, come. Lord, here's such a deal of modesty, I warrant, the first 210 day.

LUCY. Yes, an't please your worship, married women show all their modesty the first day, because married men show all their love the first day.

Exeunt.

SCENE [II]. A BEDCHAMBER.

Pinchwife, Margery.

PINCHWIFE. Come tell me, I say.

MARGERY. Lord, han't I told it an hundred times over?

PINCHWIFE. (*Aside.*) I would try, if in the repetition of the ungrateful tale, I could find her 5 altering it in the least circumstance, for if her story be false, she is so too.—Come how was't, baggage?

MARGERY. Lord, what pleasure you take to hear it, sure!

PINCHWIFE. No, you take more in telling it, I 10 find, but speak. How was't?

MARGERY. He carried me up into the house next to the Exchange.

PINCHWIFE. So, and you two were only in the room. 15

MARGERY. Yes, for he sent away a youth that was there, for some dried fruit and China oranges.

PINCHWIFE. Did he so? Damn him for it—and for—

MARGERY. But presently came up the gentlewoman 20 of the house.

PINCHWIFE. Oh 'twas well she did. But what did he do whilst the fruit came?

MARGERY. He kissed me an hundred times and told me he fancied he kissed my fine sister, 25 meaning me, you know, whom he said he loved with all his soul and bid me be sure to tell her so and to desire her to be at her window by eleven of the clock this morning, and he would walk under it at that time. 30

PINCHWIFE. (*Aside.*) And he was as good as his word, very punctual. A pox reward him for't.

MARGERY. Well, and he said if you were not within, he would come up to her, meaning me, you know, bud, still. 35

PINCHWIFE. (*Aside.*) So—he knew her certainly, but for this confession I am obliged to her simplicity.—But what, you stood very still when he kissed you?

MARGERY. Yes, I warrant you. Would you have had 40 me discovered myself?

PINCHWIFE. But you told me he did some beastliness to you, as you called it. What was't?

MARGERY. Why, he put—

PINCHWIFE. What? 45

MARGERY. Why he put the tip of his tongue between my lips and so muzzled me—and I said I'd bite it.

PINCHWIFE. An eternal canker seize it, for a dog!

MARGERY. Nay, you need not be so angry with him 50 neither, for to say truth, he has the sweetest breath I ever knew.

PINCHWIFE. The devil—you were satisfied with it then and would do it again.

MARGERY. Not unless he should force me. 55

PINCHWIFE. Force you, changeling! I tell you no woman can be forced.

MARGERY. Yes, but she may sure, by such a one as he, for he's a proper, goodly strong man; 'tis hard, let me tell you, to resist him. 60

PINCHWIFE. [*Aside.*] So, 'tis plain she loves him, yet she has not love enough to make her conceal it from me, but the sight of him will increase her aversion for me and love for him, and that love instruct her how to deceive me and satisfy him, 65 all idiot as she is. Love, 'twas he gave women first their craft, their art of deluding; out of Nature's hands they came plain, open, silly, and fit for slaves, as she and Heaven intended 'em, but damned Love—well—I must strangle that little 70 monster whilst I can deal with him.—Go fetch pen, ink, and paper out of the next room.

MARGERY. Yes bud. (*Exit.*)

PINCHWIFE. Why should women have more invention in love than men? It can only be because 75 they have more desires, more soliciting passions, more lust, and more of the Devil.

Margery returns.

Come minx, sit down and write.

MARGERY. Aye, dear bud, but I can't do't very well.

PINCHWIFE. I wish you could not at all.   80

MARGERY. But what should I write for?

PINCHWIFE. I'll have you write a letter to your lover.

MARGERY. Oh Lord, to the fine gentleman a letter!

PINCHWIFE. Yes, to the fine gentleman.   85

MARGERY. Lord, you do but jeer; sure you jest.

PINCHWIFE. I am not so merry. Come write as I bid you.

MARGERY. What, do you think I am a fool?

PINCHWIFE. [*Aside.*] She's afraid I would not   90
dictate any love to him; therefore, she's unwilling.
—But you had best begin.

MARGERY. Indeed and indeed, but I won't, so I won't.

PINCHWIFE. Why?   95

MARGERY. Because he's in Town; you may send for him if you will.

PINCHWIFE. Very well, you would have him brought to you. Is it come to this? I say take the pen and write, or you'll provoke me.   100

MARGERY. Lord, what d'ye make a fool of me for? Don't I know that letters are never writ but from the country to London and from London into the country? Now he's in Town, and I am in Town, too; therefore, I can't write to him, you know.   105

PINCHWIFE. (*Aside.*) So, I am glad it is no worse; she is innocent enough yet.—Yes, you may when your husband bids you write letters to people that are in Town.

MARGERY. Oh may I so! Then I'm satisfied.   110

PINCHWIFE. Come begin. (*Dictates.*) "Sir"—

MARGERY. Shan't I say, "Dear Sir"? You know one says always something more than bare "Sir."

PINCHWIFE. Write as I bid you, or I will write whore with this penknife in your face.   115

MARGERY. Nay, good bud. (*She writes.*) "Sir"—

PINCHWIFE. "Though I suffered last night your nauseous, loathed kisses and embraces"—Write.

MARGERY. Nay, why should I say so? You know I told you he had a sweet breath.   120

PINCHWIFE. Write!

MARGERY. Let me but put out "loathed."

PINCHWIFE. Write I say!

MARGERY. Well then. (*Writes.*)

PINCHWIFE. Let's see what have you writ. (*Takes   125
the paper and reads.*) "Though I suffered last night your kisses and embraces"—Thou impudent creature! Where is "nauseous" and "loathed"?

MARGERY. I can't abide to write such filthy words.

PINCHWIFE. (*Holds up penknife.*) Once more,   130
write as I'd have you and question it not, or I will spoil thy writing with this. I will stab out those eyes that cause my mischief.

MARGERY. Oh Lord, I will! [*Writes.*]

PINCHWIFE. So—so—let's see now! (*Reads.*)   135
"Though I suffered last night your nauseous, loathed kisses, and embraces." Go on: "Yet I would not have you presume that you shall ever repeat them." So—

She writes.

MARGERY. I have writ it.   140

PINCHWIFE. On then: "I then concealed myself from your knowledge to avoid your insolencies."

She writes.

MARGERY. So—

PINCHWIFE. "The same reason now I am out of your hands"—   145

She writes.

MARGERY. So—

PINCHWIFE. "Makes me own to you my unfortunate though innocent frolic of being in man's clothes"—

She writes.

MARGERY. So—   150

PINCHWIFE. "That you may forever more cease to pursue her who hates and detests you"—

She writes on.

MARGERY. So—h— (*Sighs.*)

PINCHWIFE. What, do you sigh?—"detests you—as much as she loves her husband and her honour."   155

MARGERY. I vow, husband, he'll ne'er believe I should write such a letter.

PINCHWIFE. What, he'd expect a kinder from you? Come now, your name only.

MARGERY. What, shan't I say "Your most faithful, humble servant till death"? 160

PINCHWIFE. No, tormenting fiend. (*Aside.*) Her style, I find, would be very soft.—Come wrap it up now whilst I go fetch wax and a candle and write on the back side "For Mr. Horner." (*Exit.*) 165

MARGERY. "For Mr. Horner." So, I am glad he has told me his name. Dear Mr. Horner, but why should I send thee such a letter that will vex thee and make thee angry with me?—Well, I will not send it.—Aye, but then my husband will kill me, 170 for I see plainly he won't let me love Mr. Horner.—But what care I for my husband?—I won't so, I won't send poor Mr. Horner such a letter.—But then my husband—But oh, what if I writ at bottom, "My husband made me write it"?—Aye, 175 but then my husband would see't.—Can one have no shift? Ah, a London woman would have had a hundred presently. Stay—what if I should write a letter and wrap it up like this and write upon't, too?—Aye, but then my husband would see't.—I 180 don't know what to do.—But yet y'vads[107] I'll try, so I will, for I will not send this letter to poor Mr. Horner, come what will on't. (*She writes and repeats what she hath writ.*) "Dear, sweet Mr. Horner"—so—"My husband would have me send you a base, 185 rude, unmannerly letter, but I won't,"—so—"and would have me forbid you loving me, but I won't,"—so—"and would have me say to you, I hate you, poor Mr. Horner, but I won't tell a lie for him,"—there—"for I'm sure if you and I were 190 in the country at cards together,"—so—"I could not help treading on your toe under the table"—so—"or rubbing knees with you and staring in your face till you saw me"—very well—"and then looking down and blushing for an hour 195 together."—so—"But I must make haste before my husband come, and now he has taught me to write letters, you shall have longer ones from me who am, dear, dear, poor dear Mr. Horner, your most humble friend and servant to command till 200 death, Margery Pinchwife." Stay, I must give him

a hint at bottom—so—now wrap it up just like t'other—so—now write "For Mr. Horner."—But oh now what shall I do with it? For here comes my husband. 205

Enter Pinchwife.

PINCHWIFE. (*Aside.*) I have been detained by a sparkish coxcomb who pretended a visit to me, but I fear 'twas to my wife.—What, have you done?

MARGERY. Aye, aye, bud, just now.

PINCHWIFE. Let's see't. What d'ye tremble for? 210 What, you would not have it go?

MARGERY. Here. (*Aside.*) No, I must not give him that; so I had been served if I had given him this.

He opens and reads the first letter.

PINCHWIFE. Come, where's the wax and seal?

MARGERY. (*Aside.*) Lord, what shall I do now? Nay, 215 then I have it.—Pray let me see't. Lord, you think me so arrant a fool, I cannot seal a letter? I will do't, so I will. (*Snatches the letter from him, changes it for the other, seals it, and delivers it to him.*)

PINCHWIFE. Nay, I believe you will learn that and 220 other things, too, which I would not have you.

MARGERY. So, han't I done it curiously?[108] (*Aside.*) I think I have: there's my letter going to Mr. Horner, since he'll needs have me send letters to folks. 225

PINCHWIFE. 'Tis very well, but I warrant, you would not have it go now?

MARGERY. Yes indeed, but I would, bud, now.

PINCHWIFE. Well, you are a good girl then. Come let me lock you up in your chamber till I come 230 back, and be sure you come not within three strides of the window when I am gone, for I have a spy in the street.

Exit Margery. Pinchwife locks the door.

At least 'tis fit she think so. If we do not cheat women, they'll cheat us, and fraud may be justly 235 used with secret enemies, of which a wife is the most dangerous. And he that has a handsome one to keep, and a frontier town, must provide against treachery rather than open force. Now I have

---

107 y'vads] in faith; a rustic expression.

108 curiously] skillfully.

secured all within, I'll deal with the foe without   240
with false intelligence.

Holds up the letter and exits.

SCENE [III]. HORNER'S LODGING.

Quack and Horner.

QUACK. Well sir, how fadges[109] the new design?
Have you not the luck of all your brother
projectors,[110] to deceive only yourself at last?

HORNER. No, good domine[111] doctor, I deceive
you, it seems, and others too, for the grave matrons   5
and old rigid husbands think me as unfit for love
as they are. But their wives, sisters, and daughters
know, some of 'em, better things already.

QUACK. Already!

HORNER. Already, I say. Last night I was drunk   10
with half a dozen of your civil persons, as you call
'em, and people of honour and so was made free
of their society and dressing rooms forever
hereafter and am already come to the privileges of
sleeping upon their pallets, warming smocks, tying   15
shoes and garters, and the like, doctor, already,
already, doctor.

QUACK. You have made use of your time, sir.

HORNER. I tell thee, I am now no more interruption to 'em when they sing or talk bawdy than a   20
little, squab, French page who speaks no English.

QUACK. But do civil persons and women of honour
drink and sing bawdy songs?

HORNER. Oh amongst friends, amongst friends.
For your bigots in honour are just like those in   25
religion: they fear the eye of the world more than
the eye of Heaven and think there is no virtue but
railing at vice and no sin but giving scandal. They
rail at a poor, little, kept player[112] and keep
themselves some young, modest pulpit comedian   30
to be privy to their sins in their closets,[113] not to
tell 'em of them in their chapels.

---

109 fadges] prospers.
110 projectors] schemers.
111 domine] master (of a profession).
112 kept player] an actor supported financially as a lover;
here a female actor is meant.
113 closets] inner rooms of one's lodgings.

QUACK. Nay, the truth on't is, priests amongst the
women now have quite got the better of us lay
confessors, physicians.   35

HORNER. And they are rather their patients, but—

Enter Lady Fidget, looking about her.

Now we talk of women of honour, here comes one.
Step behind the screen there and but observe if I
have not particular privileges with the women of
reputation already, doctor, already.   40

LADY FIDGET. Well Horner, am not I a woman
of honour? You see I'm as good as my word.

HORNER. And you shall see, madam, I'll not be
behindhand with you in honour, and I'll be as
good as my word, too, if you please but to   45
withdraw into the next room.

LADY FIDGET. But first, my dear sir, you must
promise to have a care of my dear honour.

HORNER. If you talk a word more of your honour,
you'll make me incapable to wrong it. To talk of   50
honour in the mysteries of love is like talking of
Heaven or the Deity in an operation of witchcraft:
just when you are employing the Devil, it makes
the charm impotent.

LADY FIDGET. Nay, fie, let us not be smutty! But   55
you talk of mysteries and bewitching to me; I don't
understand you.

HORNER. I tell you, madam, the word "money" in
a mistress's mouth at such a nick of time is not a
more disheartening sound to a younger brother   60
than that of "honour" to an eager lover like myself.

LADY FIDGET. But you can't blame a lady of my
reputation to be chary.

HORNER. Chary! I have been chary of it already
by the report I have caused of myself.   65

LADY FIDGET. Aye, but if you should ever let other
women know that dear secret, it would come out.
Nay, you must have a great care of your conduct,
for my acquaintance are so censorious (oh 'tis a
wicked censorious world, Mr. Horner), I say, are   70
so censorious and detracting that perhaps they'll
talk to the prejudice of my honour, though you
should not let them know the dear secret.

HORNER. Nay madam, rather than they shall
prejudice your honour, I'll prejudice theirs, and to   75
serve you, I'll lie with 'em all, make the secret their

own, and then they'll keep it. I am a Machiavel[114] in love, madam.

LADY FIDGET. Oh no, sir, not that way.

HORNER. Nay, the devil take me if censorious women are to be silenced any other way. 80

LADY FIDGET. A secret is better kept, I hope, by a single person than a multitude; therefore, pray do not trust anybody else with it, dear, dear Mr. Horner. (*Embracing him.*) 85

Enter Sir Jaspar Fidget.

SIR JASPAR. How now!

LADY FIDGET. (*Aside.*) Oh my husband— prevented—and what's almost as bad, found with my arms about another man. That will appear too much. What shall I say?— Sir Jaspar, come hither. 90 I am trying if Mr. Horner were ticklish, and he's as ticklish as can be. I love to torment the confounded toad. Let you and I tickle him.

SIR JASPAR. No, your ladyship will tickle him better without me, I suppose. But is this your buying 95 china? I thought you had been at the china house?

HORNER. (*Aside.*) China house, that's my cue; I must take it.—A pox, can't you keep your imper- tinent wives at home? Some men are troubled with the husbands, but I with the wives. But I'd have 100 you to know, since I cannot be your journeyman by night, I will not be your drudge by day, to squire your wife about and be your man of straw, or scarecrow, only to pies and jays that would be nibbling at your forbidden fruit. I shall be shortly 105 the hackney gentleman-usher of the Town.

SIR JASPAR. (*Aside.*) He, he, he, poor fellow, he's in the right on't, faith: to squire women about for other folks is as ungrateful an employment as to tell money for other folks.—He, he, he, ben't 110 angry, Horner—

LADY FIDGET. No, 'tis I have more reason to be angry, who am left by you to go abroad indecently alone or, what is more indecent, to pin myself upon such ill-bred people of your acquaintance, as 115 this is.

SIR JASPAR. Nay prithee, what has he done?

LADY FIDGET. Nay, he has done nothing.

SIR JASPAR. But what d'ye take ill if he has done nothing? 120

LADY FIDGET. Ha, ha, ha! Faith, I can't but laugh, however. Why, d'ye think, the unmannerly toad would not come down to me to the coach. I was fain to come up to fetch him or go without him, which I was resolved not to do, for he knows china 125 very well and has himself very good, but will not let me see it, lest I should beg some. But I will find it out and have what I came for yet.

Exit Lady Fidget, and locks the door, followed by Horner to the door.

HORNER. (*Apart to Lady Fidget.*) Lock the door, madam.— So, she has got into my chamber and 130 locked me out. Oh the impertinency of woman- kind! Well Sir Jaspar, plain dealing is a jewel: if ever you suffer your wife to trouble me again here, she shall carry you home a pair of horns, by my Lord Mayor she shall; though I cannot furnish you my- 135 self, you are sure yet I'll find a way.

SIR JASPAR. (*Aside.*) Ha, ha, he, at my first coming in and finding her arms about him, tickling him it seems, I was half jealous, but now I see my folly.—He, he, he, poor Horner. 140

HORNER. Nay, though you laugh now, 'twill be my turn ere long. Oh women, more impertinent, more cunning, and more mischievous than their monkeys and to me almost as ugly.—Now is she throwing my things about and rifling all I have, 145 but I'll get into her the back way and so rifle her[115] for it.

SIR JASPAR. Ha, ha, ha, poor angry Horner.

HORNER. Stay here a little. I'll ferret her out to you presently, I warrant. (*Exit at t'other door.*) 150

SIR JASPAR. Wife, my Lady Fidget, wife, he is coming into you the back way.

---

114 Machiavel] Renaissance writer Niccolò Machiavelli, thought to advocate unscrupulous, self-interested scheming.

115 throwing my things … back way … rifle her] Through- out the following scene, the double entendres come thick and fast, as do the sound effects. The noise referred to here is perhaps Lady Fidget undressing ; other sounds, including crashing china, will mount steadily as Horner enters "the back way."

Sir Jaspar calls through the door to his wife; she answers from within.

LADY FIDGET. Let him come, and welcome, which way he will.

SIR JASPAR. He'll catch you and use you roughly and be too strong for you. 155

LADY FIDGET. Don't you trouble yourself; let him if he can.

QUACK. (*Behind.*) This indeed I could not have believed from him nor any but my own eyes. 160

Enter Mistress Squeamish.

MRS. SQUEAMISH. Where's this woman-hater, this toad, this ugly, greasy, dirty sloven?

SIR JASPAR. [*Aside.*] So the women all will have him ugly. Methinks he is a comely person, but his wants make his form contemptible to 'em, and 'tis 165 e'en as my wife said yesterday, talking of him, that a proper handsome eunuch was as ridiculous a thing as a gigantic coward.

MRS. SQUEAMISH. Sir Jaspar, your servant. Where is the odious beast? 170

SIR JASPAR. He's within in his chamber with my wife; she's playing the wag with him.

MRS. SQUEAMISH. Is she so? And he's a clown-ish[116] beast: he'll give her no quarter; he'll play the wag with her again, let me tell you. Come, let's go 175 help her. What, the door's locked?

SIR JASPAR. Aye, my wife locked it.

MRS. SQUEAMISH. Did she so? Let us break it open then.

SIR JASPAR. No, no, he'll do her no hurt. 180

MRS. SQUEAMISH. No. (*Aside.*) But is there no other way to get into 'em? Whither goes this? I will disturb 'em.

Exit Squeamish at another door. Enter Old Lady Squeamish.

OLD LADY SQUEAMISH. Where is this harlotry, this impudent baggage, this rambling tomrig?[117]— 185 Oh Sir Jaspar, I'm glad to see you here. Did you not see my vild[118] grandchild come in hither just now?

SIR JASPAR. Yes.

OLD LADY SQUEAMISH. Aye, but where is she then? Where is she? Lord, Sir Jaspar, I have e'en 190 rattled myself to pieces in pursuit of her. But can you tell what she makes here? They say below, no woman lodges here.

SIR JASPAR. No.

OLD LADY SQUEAMISH. No—what does she 195 here then? Say if it be not a woman's lodging, what makes she here? But are you sure no woman lodges here?

SIR JASPAR. No, nor no man neither: this is Mr. Horner's lodging. 200

OLD LADY SQUEAMISH. Is it so? Are you sure?

SIR JASPAR. Yes, yes.

OLD LADY SQUEAMISH. So then there's no hurt in't, I hope. But where is he?

SIR JASPAR. He's in the next room with my wife. 205

OLD LADY SQUEAMISH. Nay, if you trust him with your wife, I may with my Biddy. They say he's a merry, harmless man now, e'en as harmless a man as ever came out of Italy with a good voice[119] and as pretty harmless company for a lady 210 as a snake without his teeth.

SIR JASPAR. Aye, aye, poor man.

Enter Mrs. Squeamish.

MRS. SQUEAMISH. I can't find 'em.—Oh are you here, Grandmother? I followed, you must know, my Lady Fidget hither; 'tis the prettiest lodging, 215 and I have been staring on the prettiest pictures.

Enter Lady Fidget with a piece of china in her hand and Horner following.

LADY FIDGET. And I have been toiling and moiling for the prettiest piece of china, my dear.

HORNER. Nay, she has been too hard for me, do what I could. 220

MRS. SQUEAMISH. Oh Lord, I'll have some china, too. Good Mr. Horner, don't think to give other people china and me none. Come in with me, too.

HORNER. Upon my honour I have none left now.

---

116 clownish] rustic, countrified.

117 tomrig] tomboy.

118 vild] archaic (as suits Old Lady Squeamish) form of "vile."

119 came out … Italy … good voice] i.e., as a *castrato*, a cas-trated male singer.

MRS. SQUEAMISH. Nay, nay, I have known you deny your china before now, but you shan't put me off so. Come— 225

HORNER. This lady had the last there.

LADY FIDGET. Yes indeed, madam, to my certain knowledge he has no more left. 230

MRS. SQUEAMISH. Oh but it may be he may have some you could not find.

LADY FIDGET. What, d'ye think if he had had any left, I would not have had it too? For we women of quality never think we have china enough. 235

HORNER. Do not take it ill. I cannot make china for you all, but I will have a roll-waggon[120] for you, too, another time.

MRS. SQUEAMISH. Thank you, dear toad.

LADY FIDGET. (To Horner, aside.) What do you mean by that promise? 240

HORNER. (Apart to Lady Fidget.) Alas, she has an innocent, literal understanding.

OLD LADY SQUEAMISH. Poor Mr. Horner. He has enough to do to please you all, I see. 245

HORNER. Aye madam, you see how they use me.

OLD LADY SQUEAMISH. Poor gentleman, I pity you.

HORNER. I thank you, madam. I could never find pity but from such reverend ladies as you are; the young ones will never spare a man. 250

MRS. SQUEAMISH. Come, come, beast, and go dine with us, for we shall want a man at ombre after dinner.

HORNER. That's all their use of me, madam, you see. 255

MRS. SQUEAMISH. Come sloven, I'll lead you to be sure of you. (Pulls him by the cravat.)

OLD LADY SQUEAMISH. Alas, poor man, how she tugs him. Kiss, kiss her! That's the way to make such nice[121] women quiet. 260

HORNER. No madam, that remedy is worse than the torment; they know I dare suffer anything rather than do it.

OLD LADY SQUEAMISH. Prithee, kiss her, and I'll give you her picture in little[122] that you admired so last night, prithee do. 265

HORNER. Well, nothing but that could bribe me. I love a woman only in effigy and good painting as much as I hate them. I'll do't, for I could adore the Devil well painted. (Kisses Mrs. Squeamish.) 270

MRS. SQUEAMISH. Faugh, you filthy toad! Nay, now I've done jesting.

OLD LADY SQUEAMISH. Ha, ha, ha, I told you so.

MRS. SQUEAMISH. Faugh, a kiss of his—

SIR JASPAR. Has no more hurt in't than one of my spaniel's. 275

MRS. SQUEAMISH. Nor no more good neither.

QUACK. (Behind.) I will now believe anything he tells me.

Enter Pinchwife.

LADY FIDGET. Oh Lord, here's a man, Sir Jaspar! My mask, my mask. I would not be seen here for the world. 280

SIR JASPAR. What, not when I am with you?

LADY FIDGET. No, no, my honour—let's be gone.

MRS. SQUEAMISH. Oh Grandmother, let us be gone. Make haste, make haste. I know not how he may censure us. 285

LADY FIDGET. Be found in the lodging of anything like a man? Away.

Exeunt Sir Jaspar, Lady Fidget, Old Lady Squeamish, Mrs. Squeamish.

QUACK. (Behind.) What's here, another cuckold? He looks like one, and none else sure have any business with him. 290

HORNER. Well, what brings my dear friend hither?

PINCHWIFE. Your impertinency.

HORNER. My impertinency! Why, you gentlemen that have got handsome wives think you have a privilege of saying anything to your friends and are as brutish as if you were our creditors. 295

PINCHWIFE. No sir, I'll ne'er trust you anyway.

HORNER. But why not, dear Jack? Why diffide in[123] me thou knowst so well? 300

PINCHWIFE. Because I do know you so well.

HORNER. Han't I been always thy friend, honest Jack, always ready to serve thee, in love or battle, before thou wert married and am so still? 305

---

120 roll-waggon] a cylindrically shaped Chinese vase.
121 nice] fastidious, picky.
122 picture in little] miniature.

123 diffide in] distrust.

PINCHWIFE. I believe so; you would be my second[124] now indeed.

HORNER. Well then, dear Jack, why so unkind, so grum, so strange to me? Come, prithee kiss me, dear rogue. Gad, I was always, I say, and am still as much thy servant as— 310

PINCHWIFE. As I am yours, sir. What, you would send a kiss to my wife, is that it?

HORNER. So there 'tis. A man can't show his friendship to a married man but presently he talks of his wife to you. Prithee, let thy wife alone and let thee and I be all one, as we were wont. What, thou art as shy of my kindness as a Lombard Street[125] alderman of a courtier's civility at Locket's.[126] 315

PINCHWIFE. But you are over-kind to me, as kind as if I were your cuckold already, yet I must confess you ought to be kind and civil to me since I am so kind, so civil to you as to bring you this. Look you there, sir. (*Delivers him a letter.*) 325

HORNER. What is't?

PINCHWIFE. Only a love letter, sir.

HORNER. From whom? (*Reads.*)
How, this is from your wife!—hum—and hum—

PINCHWIFE. Even from my wife, sir. Am I not 330 wondrous kind and civil to you now, too? (*Aside.*) But you'll not think her so.

HORNER. (*Aside.*) Hah, is this a trick of his or hers?

PINCHWIFE. The gentleman's surprised, I find. What, you expected a kinder letter? 335

HORNER. No faith, not I. How could I?

PINCHWIFE. Yes, yes, I'm sure you did. A man so well made as you are must needs be disappointed if the women declare not their passion at first sight or opportunity. 340

HORNER. [*Aside.*] But what should this mean? Stay, the postscript: "Be sure you love me whatsoever my husband says to the contrary, and let him not see this, lest he should come home and pinch me or kill my squirrel." It seems he knows not what the 345 letter contains.

PINCHWIFE. Come, ne'er wonder at it so much.

---

124 my second] his assistant were he challenged to a duel.
125 Lombard Street] in the City.
126 Locket's] a fashionable eating-house.

HORNER. Faith, I can't help it.

PINCHWIFE. Now I think I have deserved your infinite friendship and kindness and have showed 350 myself sufficiently an obliging kind friend and husband. Am I not so, to bring a letter from my wife to her gallant?

HORNER. Aye, the devil take me, art thou the most obliging, kind friend and husband in the world, 355 ha, ha.

PINCHWIFE. Well, you may be merry, sir, but in short I must tell you, sir, my honour will suffer no jesting.

HORNER. What dost thou mean? 360

PINCHWIFE. Does the letter want a comment? Then know, sir, though I have been so civil a husband as to bring you a letter from my wife, to let you kiss and court her to my face, I will not be a cuckold, sir, I will not. 365

HORNER. Thou art mad with jealousy. I never saw thy wife in my life but at the play yesterday, and I know not if it were she or no. I court her, kiss her!

PINCHWIFE. I will not be a cuckold, I say; there will be danger in making me a cuckold. 370

HORNER. Why, wert thou not well cured of thy last clap?

PINCHWIFE. I wear a sword.

HORNER. It should be taken from thee lest thou shouldst do thyself a mischief with it. Thou art 375 mad, man.

PINCHWIFE. As mad as I am and as merry as you are, I must have more reason from you ere we part, I say again, though you kissed and courted last night my wife in man's clothes, as she confesses in 380 her letter.

HORNER. (*Aside.*) Hah!

PINCHWIFE. Both she and I say you must not design it again, for you have mistaken your woman, as you have done your man. 385

HORNER. (*Aside.*) Oh I understand something now.—Was that thy wife? Why wouldst thou not tell me 'twas she? Faith, my freedom with her was your fault, not mine.

PINCHWIFE. (*Aside.*) Faith, so 'twas. 390

HORNER. Fie, I'd never do't to a woman before her husband's face, sure.

PINCHWIFE. But I had rather you should do't to

my wife before my face than behind my back, and
that you shall never do. 395

HORNER. No, you will hinder me.

PINCHWIFE. If I would not hinder you, you see
by her letter, she would.

HORNER. Well, I must e'en acquiesce then and be
contented with what she writes. 400

PINCHWIFE. I'll assure you 'twas voluntarily writ;
I had no hand in't, you may believe me.

HORNER. I do believe thee, faith.

PINCHWIFE. And believe her too, for she's an
innocent creature, has no dissembling in her, and 405
so fare you well, sir.

HORNER. Pray however, present my humble service
to her and tell her I will obey her letter to a tittle
and fulfill her desires be what they will or with
what difficulty soever I do't, and you shall be no 410
more jealous of me, I warrant her, and you—

PINCHWIFE. Well then, fare you well, and play
with any man's honour but mine, kiss any man's
wife but mine, and welcome. (*Exit.*)

HORNER. Ha, ha, ha, doctor. 415

QUACK. It seems he has not heard the report of you
or does not believe it.

HORNER. Ha, ha, now doctor, what think you?

QUACK. Pray let's see the letter. (*Reads.*) Hum—
"for"—"dear"—"love you"— 420

HORNER. I wonder how she could contrive it!
What say'st thou to't? 'Tis an original.

QUACK. So are your cuckolds, too, originals, for
they are like no other common cuckolds, and I will
henceforth believe it not impossible for you to 425
cuckold the Grand Signior[127] amidst his guards
of eunuchs, that I say.

HORNER. And I say for the letter, 'tis the first love
letter that ever was without flames, darts, fates,
destinies, lying, and dissembling in't. 430

Enter Sparkish pulling in Pinchwife.

SPARKISH. Come back! You are a pretty brother-
in-law, neither go to church nor to dinner with
your sister bride.

PINCHWIFE. My sister denies her marriage and
you see is gone away from you dissatisfied. 435

SPARKISH. Pshaw, upon a foolish scruple that our
parson was not in lawful orders and did not say
all the Common Prayer,[128] but 'tis her modesty
only, I believe. But let women be never so modest
the first day, they'll be sure to come to themselves 440
by night, and I shall have enough of her then. In
the meantime, Harry Horner, you must dine with
me; I keep my wedding at my aunt's in the
Piazza.[129]

HORNER. Thy wedding! What stale maid has lived 445
to despair of a husband, or what young one of a
gallant?

SPARKISH. Oh your servant, sir. This gentleman's
sister then—no stale maid.

HORNER. I'm sorry for't. 450

PINCHWIFE. (*Aside.*) How comes he so concerned
for her?

SPARKISH. You sorry for't! Why, do you know any
ill by her?

HORNER. No, I know none but by thee; 'tis for her 455
sake, not yours, and another man's sake that might
have hoped, I thought—

SPARKISH. Another man, another man, what is his
name?

HORNER. Nay, since 'tis past, he shall be nameless. 460
(*Aside.*) Poor Harcourt, I am sorry thou hast
missed her.

PINCHWIFE. (*Aside.*) He seems to be much
troubled at the match.

SPARKISH. Prithee, tell me.—Nay, you shan't go, 465
brother.

PINCHWIFE. I must of necessity, but I'll come to
you to dinner. (*Exit.*)

SPARKISH. But Harry, what, have I a rival in my
wife already? But with all my heart, for he may be 470
of use to me hereafter, for though my hunger is
now my sauce and I can fall on heartily without.
But the time will come, when a rival will be as
good sauce for a married man to a wife as an
orange to veal. 475

HORNER. Oh thou damned rogue, thou hast set
my teeth on edge with thy orange.

127 Grand Signior] the Sultan of Turkey.

128 Common Prayer] the marriage service within the An-
glican *Book of Common Prayer.*

129 Piazza] arcade around two sides of Covent Garden.

SPARKISH. Then let's to dinner. There I was with
 you again. Come.

HORNER. But who dines with thee? 480

SPARKISH. My friends and relations, my brother
 Pinchwife, you see, of your acquaintance.

HORNER. And his wife?

SPARKISH. No, gad, he'll ne'er let her come
 amongst us good fellows. Your stingy country 485
 coxcomb keeps his wife from his friends as he does
 his little firkin of ale for his own drinking, and a
 gentleman can't get a smack on't. But his servants,
 when his back is turned, broach it at their pleasure
 and dust it away, ha, ha, ha. Gad, I am witty, I 490
 think, considering I was married today, by the
 world, but come—

HORNER. No, I will not dine with you unless you
 can fetch her, too.

SPARKISH. Pshaw, what pleasure canst thou have 495
 with women now, Harry?

HORNER. My eyes are not gone. I love a good
 prospect yet and will not dine with you unless she
 does too. Go fetch her, therefore, but do not tell
 her husband 'tis for my sake. 500

SPARKISH. Well, I'll go try what I can do. In the
 meantime, come away to my aunt's lodging; 'tis in
 the way to Pinchwife's.

HORNER. [Apart to Quack.] The poor woman has
 called for aid and stretched forth her hand, doctor; 505
 I cannot but help her over the pale out of the
 briars.

Exeunt.

SCENE [IV]. PINCHWIFE'S HOUSE.

*Margery alone leaning on her elbow. A table, pen, ink,
and paper.*

MARGERY. Well 'tis e'en so: I have got the London
 disease they call love; I am sick of my husband and
 for my gallant. I have heard this distemper called
 a fever, but methinks 'tis liker an ague, for when I
 think of my husband, I tremble and am in a cold 5
 sweat and have inclinations to vomit, but when I
 think of my gallant, dear Mr. Horner, my hot fit
 comes, and I am all in a fever indeed, and as in
 other fevers, my own chamber is tedious to me,
 and I would fain be removed to his, and then 10
 methinks I should be well. Ah poor Mr. Horner!
 Well, I cannot, will not stay here; therefore, I'll
 make an end of my letter to him, which shall be a
 finer letter than my last, because I have studied it
 like anything. Oh sick! sick! (*Takes the pen and* 15
 writes.)

*Enter Mr. Pinchwife, who, seeing her writing, steals
softly behind her and looking over her shoulder,
snatches the paper from her.*

PINCHWIFE. What, writing more letters?

MARGERY. Oh Lord, bud, why d'ye fright me so?

She offers to run out; he stops her and reads.

PINCHWIFE. How's this! Nay, you shall not stir,
 madam. "Dear, dear, dear, Mr. Horner"—very 20
 well—I have taught you to write letters to good
 purpose, but let's see't. "First I am to beg your
 pardon for my boldness in writing to you, which
 I'd have you to know I would not have done, had
 not you said first you loved me so extremely, which 25
 if you do, you will never suffer me to lie in the
 arms of another man, whom I loathe, nauseate,
 and detest." Now you can write these filthy words!
 But what follows? "Therefore, I hope you will
 speedily find some way to free me from this 30
 unfortunate match, which was never, I assure you,
 of my choice, but I'm afraid 'tis already too far
 gone; however, if you love me, as I do you, you
 will try what you can do, but you must help me
 away before tomorrow, or else, alas, I shall be 35
 forever out of your reach for I can defer no longer
 our—" (*The letter concludes.*) "Our"? What is to
 follow "our"? Speak! What? Our journey into the
 country, I suppose. Oh woman, damned woman!
 And Love, damned Love, their old tempter! For 40
 this is one of his miracles: in a moment he can
 make those blind that could see and those see that
 were blind, those dumb that could speak and those
 prattle who were dumb before, nay, what is more
 than all, make these dough-baked,[130] senseless, 45
 indocile animals, women, too hard for us, their
 politic lords and rulers, in a moment. But make

---

130 dough-baked] half-baked, foolish.

an end of your letter, and then I'll make an end of you thus and all my plagues together. (*Draws his sword.*)

MARGERY. Oh Lord, oh Lord, you are such a passionate man, bud! 50

Enter Sparkish.

SPARKISH. How now, what's here to do?

PINCHWIFE. This fool here now!

SPARKISH. What, drawn upon your wife? You should never do that but at night in the dark when you can't hurt her. This is my sister-in-law, is it not? (*Pulls aside her handkerchief.*) Aye faith, e'en our country Margery, one may know her. Come, she and you must go dine with me; dinner's ready, come. But where's my wife? Is she not come home yet? Where is she? 55 60

PINCHWIFE. Making you a cuckold. 'Tis that they all do as soon as they can.

SPARKISH. What, the wedding day? No, a wife that designs to make a cully of her husband will be sure to let him win the first stake of love, by the world. But come, they stay dinner for us; come, I'll lead down, our Margery. 65

MARGERY. No sir, go, we'll follow you. 70

SPARKISH. I will not wag without you.

PINCHWIFE. This coxcomb is a sensible torment to me amidst the greatest in the world.

SPARKISH. Come, come, Madam Margery.

PINCHWIFE. No, I'll lead her my way. What, would you treat your friends with mine, for want of your own wife? (*Leads her to t'other door and locks her in and returns. Aside.*) I am contented my rage should take breath. 75

SPARKISH. I told Horner this. 80

PINCHWIFE. Come now.

SPARKISH. Lord, how shy you are of your wife, but let me tell you, brother, we men of wit have amongst us a saying that cuckolding, like the small pox, comes with a fear, and you may keep your wife as much as you will out of danger of infection, but if her constitution incline her to't, she'll have it sooner or later, by the world, say they. 85

PINCHWIFE. (*Aside.*) What a thing is a cuckold, that every fool can make him ridiculous.—Well sir, but let me advise you, now you are come to be 90 concerned because you suspect the danger, not to neglect the means to prevent it, especially when the greatest share of the malady will light upon your own head, for 95

Hows'e'er the kind wife's belly comes to swell,
The husband breeds[131] for her and first is ill.

ACT V, SCENE I. PINCHWIFE'S HOUSE.

Enter Pinchwife and Margery. A table and candle.

PINCHWIFE. Come, take the pen and make an end of the letter, just as you intended. If you are false in a tittle, I shall soon perceive it and punish you with this as you deserve. (*Lays his hand on his sword.*) 5

Write what was to follow. Let's see. "You must make haste and help me away before tomorrow, or else I shall be forever out of your reach, for I can defer no longer our—" What follows "our"?

MARGERY. Must all out then, bud? (*Margery takes the pen and writes.*) Look you there then. 10

PINCHWIFE. Let's see. "For I can defer no longer our—wedding. Your slighted Alithea." What's the meaning of this, my sister's name to't? Speak, unriddle! 15

MARGERY. Yes indeed, bud.

PINCHWIFE. But why her name to't? Speak—speak, I say!

MARGERY. Aye, but you'll tell her then again. If you would not tell her again— 20

PINCHWIFE. I will not. I am stunned; my head turns round. Speak.

MARGERY. Won't you tell her indeed and indeed?

PINCHWIFE. No. Speak, I say.

MARGERY. She'll be angry with me, but I had rather she should be angry with me than you, bud, and to tell you the truth, 'twas she made me write the letter and taught me what I should write. 25

PINCHWIFE. [*Aside.*] Hah! I thought the style was somewhat better than her own.—But how could she come to you to teach you, since I had locked you up alone? 30

MARGERY. Oh, through the keyhole, bud.

---

131 breeds] grows the cuckold's horns.

PINCHWIFE. But why should she make you write a letter for her to him, since she can write herself? 35

MARGERY. Why, she said because—for I was unwilling to do it.

PINCHWIFE. Because what? Because?

MARGERY. Because lest Mr. Horner should be cruel and refuse her, or vain afterwards and show the letter, she might disown it, the hand not being hers. 40

PINCHWIFE. (*Aside.*) How's this? Hah! Then I think I shall come to myself again. This changeling could not invent this lie. But if she could, why should she? She might think I should soon discover it. Stay—now I think on't, too, Horner said he was sorry she had married Sparkish, and her disowning her marriage to me makes me think she has evaded it for Horner's sake. Yet why should she take this course? But men in love are fools; women may well be so.—But hark you, madam, your sister went out in the morning and I have not seen her within since. 45 50

MARGERY. Alackaday, she has been crying all day above, it seems, in a corner. 55

PINCHWIFE. Where is she? Let me speak with her.

MARGERY. (*Aside.*) Oh Lord, then he'll discover all.—Pray hold, bud. What, d'ye mean to discover me? She'll know I have told you then. Pray bud, let me talk with her first. 60

PINCHWIFE. I must speak with her to know whether Horner ever made her any promise and whether she be married to Sparkish or no.

MARGERY. Pray dear bud, don't till I have spoken with her and told her that I have told you all, for she'll kill me else. 65

PINCHWIFE. Go then, and bid her come out to me.

MARGERY. Yes, yes, bud.

PINCHWIFE. Let me see—

MARGERY. [*Aside.*] I'll go, but she is not within to come to him. I have just got time to know of Lucy, her maid, who first set me on work, what lie I shall tell next, for I am e'en at my wit's end. (*Exit.*) 70

PINCHWIFE. Well, I resolve it: Horner shall have her. I'd rather give him my sister than lend him my wife, and such an alliance will prevent his pretensions to my wife, sure. I'll make him of kin to her, and then he won't care for her. 75

Margery returns.

MARGERY. Oh Lord, bud, I told you what anger you would make me with my sister. 80

PINCHWIFE. Won't she come hither?

MARGERY. No no, alackaday, she's ashamed to look you in the face, and she says if you go in to her, she'll run away downstairs and shamefully go herself to Mr. Horner, who has promised her marriage, she says, and she will have no other, so she won't— 85

PINCHWIFE. Did he so—promise her marriage? Then she shall have no other. Go tell her so, and if she will come and discourse with me a little concerning the means, I will about it immediately. Go. 90

Exit Margery.

His estate is equal to Sparkish's, and his extraction as much better than his as his parts are, but my chief reason is I'd rather be of kin to him by the name of brother-in-law than that of cuckold. 95

Enter Margery.

Well, what says she now?

MARGERY. Why, she says she would only have you lead her to Horner's lodging—with whom she first will discourse the matter before she talk with you, which yet she cannot do, for, alack poor creature, she says she can't so much as look you in the face; therefore, she'll come to you in a mask, and you must excuse her if she make you no answer to any question of yours till you have brought her to Mr. Horner, and if you will not chide her nor question her, she'll come out to you immediately. 100 105

PINCHWIFE. Let her come. I will not speak a word to her nor require a word from her.

MARGERY. Oh, I forgot: besides, she says, she cannot look you in the face though through a mask; therefore, would desire you to put out the candle. 110

PINCHWIFE. I agree to all; let her make haste.

Exit Margery; [Pinchwife] puts out the candle.

There, 'tis out. My case is something better: I'd rather fight with Horner for not lying with my sister than for lying with my wife, and of the two, I had rather find my sister too forward than my wife. I expected no other from her free education, 115 as she calls it, and her passion for the Town. Well, wife and sister are names which make us expect love and duty, pleasure and comfort, but we find 'em plagues and torments and are equally, though differently, troublesome to their keeper, for we have as much ado to get people to lie with our sisters as to keep 'em from lying with our wives.

Enter Margery masked and in hoods and scarves and a nightgown and petticoat of Alithea's, in the dark.

What, are you come, sister? Let us go then, but first let me lock up my wife. Mistress Margery, where are you?

MARGERY. Here, bud.

PINCHWIFE. Come hither, that I may lock you up.

Margery gives him her hand, but when he lets her go, she steals softly on t'other side of him.

Get you in. (*Locks the door.*) Come, sister, where are you now?

[*She*] *is led away by him for his sister Alithea.*

SCENE [II]. HORNER'S LODGING.

Quack, Horner.

QUACK. What, all alone, not so much as one of your cuckolds here nor one of their wives? They use to take their turns with you as if they were to watch you.

HORNER. Yes, it often happens that a cuckold is but his wife's spy and is more upon family duty when he is with her gallant abroad hindering his pleasure than when he is at home with her playing the gallant. But the hardest duty a married woman imposes upon a lover is keeping her husband company always.

QUACK. And his fondness wearies you almost as soon as hers.

HORNER. A pox, keeping a cuckold company after you have had his wife is as tiresome as the company of a country squire to a witty fellow of the Town when he has got all his money.

QUACK. And as at first a man makes a friend of the husband to get the wife, so at last you are fain to fall out with the wife to be rid of the husband.

HORNER. Aye, most cuckold-makers are true courtiers: when once a poor man has cracked his credit for 'em, they can't abide to come near him.

QUACK. But at first to draw him in, are so sweet, so kind, so dear, just as you are to Pinchwife. But what becomes of that intrigue with his wife?

HORNER. A pox, he's as surly as an alderman that has been bit,[132] and since he's so coy, his wife's kindness is in vain, for she's a silly innocent.

QUACK. Did she not send you a letter by him?

HORNER. Yes, but that's a riddle I have not yet solved. Allow the poor creature to be willing, she is silly, too, and he keeps her up so close—

QUACK. Yes, so close that he makes her but the more willing and adds but revenge to her love, which two, when met, seldom fail of satisfying each other one way or other.

HORNER. What, here's the man we are talking of, I think.

Enter Pinchwife leading in his wife masked, muffled, and in her sister's gown.

HORNER. Pshaw.

QUACK. Bringing his wife to you is the next thing to bringing a love letter from her.

HORNER. What means this?

PINCHWIFE. The last time, you know, sir, I brought you a love letter; now you see a mistress. I think you'll say I am a civil man to you.

HORNER. Aye, the devil take me, will I say thou art the civilest man I ever met with, and I have known some. I fancy I understand thee now better than I did the letter, but hark thee in thy ear—

PINCHWIFE. What?

HORNER. Nothing but the usual question, man. Is she sound, on thy word?

PINCHWIFE. What, you take her for a wench and me for a pimp?

HORNER. Pshaw, wench and pimp, paw[133] words. I know thou art an honest fellow and hast a great acquaintance among the ladies and perhaps hast made love for me rather than let me make love to thy wife—

---

132 bit] cheated.

133 paw] filthy, obscene.

PINCHWIFE. Come sir, in short, I am for no
fooling.

HORNER. Nor I neither. Therefore, prithee, let's see
her face presently; make her show, man. Art thou
sure I don't know her?   65

PINCHWIFE. I am sure you do know her.

HORNER. A pox, why dost thou bring her to me
then?

PINCHWIFE. Because she's a relation of mine.

HORNER. Is she, faith, man? Then thou art still   70
more civil and obliging, dear rogue.

PINCHWIFE. Who desired me to bring her to you.

HORNER. Then she is obliging, dear rogue.

PINCHWIFE. You'll make her welcome, for my
sake, I hope.   75

HORNER. I hope she is handsome enough to make
herself welcome. Prithee, let her unmask.

PINCHWIFE. Do you speak to her; she would never
be ruled by me.

HORNER. Madam—   80

Margery whispers to Horner.

She says she must speak with me in private.
Withdraw, prithee.

PINCHWIFE. (*Aside.*) She's unwilling, it seems, I
should know all her undecent conduct in this
business.—Well then, I'll leave you together and   85
hope when I am gone you'll agree; if not, you and
I shan't agree, sir.

HORNER. [*Aside.*] What means the fool?—If she
and I agree, 'tis no matter what you and I do.

*Whispers to Margery, who makes signs with her hand
for [Pinchwife] to be gone.*

PINCHWIFE. In the meantime, I'll fetch a parson   90
and find out Sparkish and disabuse him. You
would have me fetch a parson, would you not?
[*Aside.*] Well then, now I think I am rid of her and
shall have no more trouble with her. Our sisters
and daughters, like usurers' money, are safest when 95
put out, but our wives, like their writings, never
safe but in our closets under lock and key. (*Exit.*)

Enter Boy.

BOY. Sir Jaspar Fidget, sir, is coming up.

HORNER. [*Aside to Quack.*] Here's the trouble of a
cuckold now we are talking of. A pox on him! Has   100
he not enough to do to hinder his wife's sport, but
he must other women's, too?—Step in here,
madam.

Exit Margery. Enter Sir Jaspar.

SIR JASPAR. My best and dearest friend.

HORNER. [*Aside to Quack.*] The old style, doctor.— 105
Well, be short, for I am busy. What would your
impertinent wife have now?

SIR JASPAR. Well guessed i'faith, for I do come
from her.

HORNER. To invite me to supper. Tell her I can't   110
come. Go.

SIR JASPAR. Nay, now you are out, faith, for my
lady and the whole knot of the virtuous gang, as
they call themselves, are resolved upon a frolic of
coming to you tonight in a masquerade and are   115
all dressed already.

HORNER. I shan't be at home.

SIR JASPAR. Lord, how churlish he is to women!
Nay, prithee don't disappoint 'em; they'll think 'tis
my fault. Prithee, don't. I'll send in the banquet   120
and the fiddles, but make no noise on't, for the
poor virtuous rogues would not have it known for
the world that they go a-masquerading, and they
would come to no man's ball but yours.

HORNER. Well, well—get you gone and tell 'em if   125
they come, 'twill be at the peril of their honour
and yours.

SIR JASPAR. He, he, he—we'll trust you for that.
Farewell. (*Exit.*)

HORNER. Doctor, anon you too shall be my guest,   130
But now I'm going to a private feast.

[*Exeunt.*]

SCENE [III]. THE PIAZZA OF
COVENT GARDEN.

Sparkish, Pinchwife.

SPARKISH. (*The letter in his hand.*) But who would
have thought a woman could have been false to
me? By the world, I could not have thought it.

PINCHWIFE. You were for giving and taking
liberty; she has taken it only, sir, now you find in   5

that letter. You are a frank person, and so is she, you see there.

SPARKISH. Nay, if this be her hand, for I never saw it.

PINCHWIFE. 'Tis no matter whether that be her hand or no. I am sure this hand, at her desire, led her to Mr. Horner, with whom I left her just now to go fetch a parson to 'em at their desire, too, to deprive you of her forever, for it seems yours was but a mock marriage.

SPARKISH. Indeed, she would needs have it that 'twas Harcourt himself in a parson's habit that married us, but I'm sure he told me 'twas his brother Ned.

PINCHWIFE. Oh there 'tis out, and you were deceived, not she, for you are such a frank person. But I must be gone. You'll find her at Mr. Horner's; go and believe your eyes. (*Exit.*)

SPARKISH. Nay, I'll to her and call her as many crocodiles, sirens, harpies, and other heathenish names as a poet would do a mistress who had refused to hear his suit, nay more, his verses on her. But stay, is not that she following a torch at t'other end of the Piazza, and from Horner's certainly? 'Tis so.

Enter Alithea following a torch and Lucy behind.

You are well met, madam, though you don't think so. What, you have made a short visit to Mr. Horner, but I suppose you'll return to him presently; by that time the parson can be with him.

ALITHEA. Mr. Horner and the parson, sir!

SPARKISH. Come madam, no more dissembling, no more jilting, for I am no more a frank person.

ALITHEA. How's this?

LUCY. (*Aside.*) So 'twill work, I see.

SPARKISH. Could you find out no easy country fool to abuse? None but me, a gentleman of wit and pleasure about the Town? But it was your pride to be too hard for a man of parts, unworthy, false woman, false as a friend that lends a man money to lose, false as dice, who undo those that trust all they have to 'em.

LUCY. (*Aside.*) He has been a great bubble by his similes, as they say.

ALITHEA. You have been too merry, sir, at your wedding dinner, sure.

SPARKISH. What, d'ye mock me too?

ALITHEA. Or you have been deluded.

SPARKISH. By you.

ALITHEA. Let me understand you.

SPARKISH. Have you the confidence—I should call it something else, since you know your guilt—to stand my just reproaches? You did not write an impudent letter to Mr. Horner, who I find now has clubbed with you in deluding me with his aversion for women, that I might not, forsooth, suspect him for my rival?

LUCY. (*Aside.*) D'ye think the gentleman can be jealous now, madam?

ALITHEA. I write a letter to Mr. Horner!

SPARKISH. Nay madam, do not deny it; your brother showed it me just now and told me likewise he left you at Horner's lodging to fetch a parson to marry you to him, and I wish you joy, madam, joy, joy, and to him, too, much joy and to myself, more joy for not marrying you.

ALITHEA. (*Aside.*) So I find my brother would break off the match, and I can consent to't, since I see this gentleman can be made jealous.—Oh Lucy, by his rude usage and jealousy, he makes me almost afraid I am married to him. Art thou sure 'twas Harcourt himself and no parson that married us?

SPARKISH. No madam, I thank you. I suppose that was a contrivance too of Mr. Horner's and yours to make Harcourt play the parson, but I would as little as you have him one now, no, not for the world, for shall I tell you another truth? I never had any passion for you till now, for now I hate you. 'Tis true I might have married your portion, as other men of parts of the Town do sometimes, and so, your servant, and to show my unconcernedness, I'll come to your wedding and resign you with as much joy as I would a stale wench to a new cully, nay, with as much joy as I would after the first night, if I had been married to you. There's for you, and so, your servant, servant. (*Exit.*)

ALITHEA. How was I deceived in a man!

LUCY. You'll believe, then, a fool may be made jealous now? For that easiness in him that suffers him to be led by a wife will likewise permit him to be persuaded against her by others.

ALITHEA. But marry Mr. Horner? My brother does not intend it, sure. If I thought he did, I would take thy advice and Mr. Harcourt for my husband, and now I wish that if there be any over-wise woman of the Town, who, like me, would marry 100 a fool for fortune, liberty, or title: first, that her husband may love play and be a cully to all the Town but her and suffer none but Fortune to be mistress of his purse; then, if for liberty, that he may send her into the country under the conduct 105 of some housewifely mother-in-law; and if for title, may the world give 'em none but that of cuckold.

LUCY. And for her greater curse, madam, may he not deserve it.

ALITHEA. Away, impertinent!—Is not this my old 110 Lady Lanterlu's?[134]

LUCY. Yes, madam. (*Aside.*) And here I hope we shall find Mr. Harcourt.

Exeunt.

SCENE [IV]. HORNER'S LODGING.

Horner, Lady Fidget, Dainty, Mrs. Squeamish.
A table, banquet, and bottles.

HORNER. (*Aside.*) A pox, they are come too soon— before I have sent back my new mistress! All I have now to do is to lock her in that they may not see her.

LADY FIDGET. That we may be sure of our 5 welcome, we have brought our entertainment with us and are resolved to treat thee, dear toad—

DAINTY. And that we may be merry to purpose, have left Sir Jaspar and my old Lady Squeamish quarreling at home at backgammon. 10

MRS. SQUEAMISH. Therefore, let us make use of our time, lest they should chance to interrupt us.

LADY FIDGET. Let us sit then.

HORNER. First that you may be private, let me lock this door and that, and I'll wait upon you 15 presently.

LADY FIDGET. No sir, shut 'em only and your lips forever, for we must trust you as much as our women.[135]

HORNER. You know all vanity's killed in me; I have 20 no occasion for talking.

LADY FIDGET. Now ladies, supposing we had drank each of us our two bottles, let us speak the truth of our hearts.

DAINTY AND MRS. SQUEAMISH. Agreed. 25

LADY FIDGET. By this brimmer, for truth is nowhere else to be found. (*Aside to Horner.*) Not in thy heart, false man.

HORNER. (*Aside to Lady Fidget.*) You have found me a true man, I'm sure. 30

LADY FIDGET. (*Aside to Horner.*) Not every way.— But let us sit and be merry. (*Sings.*)

I.

Why should our damned tyrants oblige us to live
On the pittance of pleasure which they only give?
We must not rejoice 35
With wine and with noise.
In vain we must wake in a dull bed alone,
Whilst to our warm rival the bottle they're gone.
Then lay aside charms
And take up these arms.[136] 40

II.

'Tis wine only gives 'em their courage and wit;
Because we live sober to men, we submit.
If for beauties you'd pass,
Take a lick of the glass;
'Twill mend your complexions, and when they are 45
gone,
The best red we have is the red of the grape.
Then sisters lay't on
And damn a good shape.

DAINTY. Dear brimmer! Well, in token of our openness and plain dealing, let us throw our masks 50 over our heads.

HORNER. So 'twill come to the glasses anon.

MRS. SQUEAMISH. Lovely brimmer! Let me enjoy him first.

---

134 Lady Lanterlu's] Horner's landlady. Lanterloo, or loo, was a popular card game; from *lanturelu*, French for twaddle.

135 women] waiting-women, usually of similar social status.
136 arms] their wine glasses.

LADY FIDGET. No, I never part with a gallant till I've tried him. Dear brimmer that mak'st our husbands short-sighted— 55

DAINTY. And our bashful gallants bold—

MRS. SQUEAMISH. And for want of a gallant, the butler lovely in our eyes. Drink, eunuch. 60

LADY FIDGET. Drink, thou representative of a husband. Damn a husband—

DAINTY. And as it were a husband, an old keeper—

MRS. SQUEAMISH. And an old grandmother—

HORNER. And an English bawd and a French chirurgeon. 65

LADY FIDGET. Aye, we have all reason to curse 'em.

HORNER. For my sake, ladies.

LADY FIDGET. No, for our own, for the first spoils all young gallant's industry— 70

DAINTY. And the other's art makes 'em bold only with common women—

MRS. SQUEAMISH. And rather run the hazard of the vile distemper amongst them than of a denial amongst us. 75

DAINTY. The filthy toads choose mistresses now as they do stuffs,[137] for having been fancied and worn by others—

MRS. SQUEAMISH. For being common and cheap— 80

LADY FIDGET. Whilst women of quality, like the richest stuffs, lie untumbled and unasked for.

HORNER. Aye, neat and cheap and new often they think best. 85

DAINTY. No sir, the beasts will be known by a mistress longer than by a suit—

MRS. SQUEAMISH. And 'tis not for cheapness neither—

LADY FIDGET. No, for the vain fops will take up druggets[138] and embroider 'em. But I wonder at the depraved appetites of witty men; they used to be out of the common road and hate imitation. Pray tell me, beast, when you were a man, why you rather chose to club with a multitude in a common house for an entertainment than to be the only guest at a good table. 90 95

HORNER. Why faith, ceremony and expectation are unsufferable to those that are sharp bent;[139] people always eat with the best stomach at an ordinary, where every man is snatching for the best bit— 100

LADY FIDGET. Though he get a cut over the fingers. But I have heard people eat most heartily of another man's meat, that is, what they do not pay for. 105

HORNER. When they are sure of their welcome and freedom, for ceremony in love and eating is as ridiculous as in fighting: falling on briskly is all should be done in those occasions.

LADY FIDGET. Well then, let me tell you, sir, there is nowhere more freedom than in our houses, and we take freedom from a young person as a sign of good breeding, and a person may be as free as he pleases with us, as frolic, as gamesome, as wild as he will. 110 115

HORNER. Han't I heard you all declaim against wild men?

LADY FIDGET. Yes, but for all that, we think wildness in a man as desirable a quality as in a duck or rabbit. A tame man, faugh! 120

HORNER. I know not, but your reputations frightened me as much as your faces invited me.

LADY FIDGET. Our reputation! Lord, why should you not think that we women make use of our reputation as you men of yours, only to deceive the world with less suspicion? Our virtue is like the stateman's religion, the Quaker's word,[140] the gamester's oath, and the great man's honour: but to cheat those that trust us. 125

MRS. SQUEAMISH. And that demureness, coyness, and modesty that you see in our faces in the boxes at plays is as much a sign of a kind woman as a vizard-mask in the pit. 130

DAINTY. For I assure you, women are least masked when they have the velvet vizard on. 135

LADY FIDGET. You would have found us modest women in our denials only—

MRS. SQUEAMISH. Our bashfulness is only the reflection of the men's—

DAINTY. We blush when they are shame-faced. 140

---

[137] stuffs] textiles, material for making clothes.
[138] druggets] rough fabric used for floor coverings.
[139] sharp bent] hungry.
[140] Quaker's word] Quakers do not take oaths.

HORNER. I beg your pardon, ladies, I was deceived in you devilishly. But why that mighty pretense to honour?

LADY FIDGET. We have told you, but sometimes 'twas for the same reason you men pretend business often: to avoid ill company, to enjoy the better and more privately those you love. 145

HORNER. But why would you ne'er give a friend a wink then?

LADY FIDGET. Faith, your reputation frightened us as much as ours did you, you were so notoriously lewd— 150

HORNER. And you so seemingly honest.

LADY FIDGET. Was that all that deterred you?

HORNER. And so expensive— (You allow freedom, you say?) 155

LADY FIDGET. Aye, aye.

HORNER. That I was afraid of losing my little money, as well as my little time, both which my other pleasures required. 160

LADY FIDGET. Money, faugh! You talk like a little fellow now. Do such as we expect money?

HORNER. I beg your pardon, madam, I must confess I have heard that great ladies, like great merchants, set but the higher prices upon what they have because they are not in necessity of taking the first offer. 165

DAINTY. Such as we make sale of our hearts?

MRS. SQUEAMISH. We bribed for our love? Faugh! 170

HORNER. With your pardon, ladies, I know, like great men in offices, you seem to exact flattery and attendance only from your followers, but you have receivers[141] about you and such fees to pay, a man is afraid to pass your grants;[142] besides, we must let you win at cards, or we lose your hearts, and if you make an assignation, 'tis at a goldsmith's, jeweller's, or china house, where for your honour you deposit to him, he must pawn his to the punctual cit, and so paying for what you take up, pays for what he takes up. 175 180

DAINTY. Would you not have us assured of our gallant's love?

MRS. SQUEAMISH. For love is better known by liberality than by jealousy— 185

LADY FIDGET. For one may be dissembled, the other not. (*Aside.*) But my jealousy can be no longer dissembled, and they are telling-ripe.— Come, here's to our gallants in waiting, whom we must name, and I'll begin: this is my false rogue. (*Claps him on the back.*) 190

MRS. SQUEAMISH. How!

HORNER. So all will out now—

MRS. SQUEAMISH. (*Aside to Horner.*)

Did you not tell me 'twas for my sake only you reported yourself no man? 195

DAINTY. (*Aside.*) Oh wretch! Did you not swear to me 'twas for my love and honour you passed for that thing you do?

HORNER. So, so. 200

LADY FIDGET. Come, speak ladies. This is my false villain.

MRS. SQUEAMISH. And mine too.

DAINTY. And mine.

HORNER. Well then, you are all three my false rogues too, and there's an end on't. 205

LADY FIDGET. Well then, there's no remedy, sister sharers. Let us not fall out but have a care of our honour. Though we get no presents, no jewels of him, we are savers of our honour, the jewel of most value and use, which shines yet to the world unsuspected, though it be counterfeit. 210

HORNER. Nay and is e'en as good as if it were true, provided the world think so, for honour, like beauty now, only depends on the opinion of others. 215

LADY FIDGET. Well Harry Common, I hope you can be true to three. Swear. But 'tis no purpose to require your oath, for you are as often forsworn as you swear to new women. 220

HORNER. Come, faith madam, let us e'en pardon one another, for all the difference I find betwixt we men and you women, we forswear ourselves at the beginning of an amour, you, as long as it lasts. 225

Enter Sir Jaspar Fidget and Old Lady Squeamish.

---

141 receivers] servants who must be paid for cooperation and silence.

142 pass your grants] accept your favours.

SIR JASPAR. Oh my Lady Fidget, was this your cunning, to come to Mr. Horner without me? But you have been no where else, I hope?

LADY FIDGET. No, Sir Jaspar.

OLD LADY SQUEAMISH. And you came straight hither, Biddy? 230

MRS. SQUEAMISH. Yes indeed, Lady Grandmother.

SIR JASPAR. 'Tis well, 'tis well. I knew when once they were thoroughly acquainted with poor Horner, they'd ne'er be from him. You may let her 235 masquerade it with my wife and Horner, and I warrant her reputation safe.

Enter boy.

BOY. Oh sir, here's the gentleman come whom you bid me not suffer to come up without giving you notice, with a lady, too, and other gentlemen. 240

HORNER. Do you all go in there, whilst I send 'em away.—And boy, do you desire 'em to stay below till I come, which shall be immediately.

Exeunt Sir Jaspar, [Old] Lady Squeamish, Lady Fidget, Dainty, Mrs. Squeamish.

BOY. Yes sir. (*Exit.*)

Exit Horner at t'other door, and returns with Margery.

HORNER. You would not take my advice to be 245 gone home before your husband came back. He'll now discover all, yet pray, my dearest, be persuaded to go home and leave the rest to my management; I'll let you down the back way.

MARGERY. I don't know the way home, so I don't. 250

HORNER. My man shall wait upon you.

MARGERY. No, don't you believe that I'll go at all. What, are you weary of me already?

HORNER. No my life, 'tis that I may love you long, 'tis to secure my love and your reputation with 255 your husband; he'll never receive you again else.

MARGERY. What care I? D'ye think to frighten me with that? I don't intend to go to him again; you shall be my husband now.

HORNER. I cannot be your husband, dearest, since 260 you are married to him.

MARGERY. Oh, would you make me believe that? Don't I see every day at London here, women leave their first husbands and go and live with other men

as their wives? Pish, pshaw, you'd make me angry, 265 but that I love you so mainly.

HORNER. So, they are coming up. In again, in, I hear 'em.

Exit Margery.

Well, a silly mistress is like a weak place, soon got, soon lost; a man has scarce time for plunder. She 270 betrays her husband first to her gallant and then her gallant to her husband.

Enter Pinchwife, Alithea, Harcourt, Sparkish, Lucy, and a parson.

PINCHWIFE. Come madam, 'tis not the sudden change of your dress, the confidence of your asseverations, and your false witness there shall 275 persuade me I did not bring you hither just now; here's my witness, who cannot deny it, since you must be confronted.—Mr. Horner, did not I bring this lady to you just now?

HORNER. (*Aside.*) Now must I wrong one woman 280 for another's sake, but that's no new thing with me, for in these cases I am still on the criminal's side against the innocent.

ALITHEA. Pray speak, sir.

HORNER. (*Aside.*) It must be so. I must be 285 impudent and try my luck; impudence uses to be too hard for truth.

PINCHWIFE. What, you are studying an evasion or excuse for her. Speak, sir.

HORNER. No, faith, I am something backward 290 only to speak in women's affairs or disputes.

PINCHWIFE. She bids you speak.

ALITHEA. Aye, pray sir, do, pray satisfy him.

HORNER. Then truly, you did bring that lady to me just now. 295

PINCHWIFE. Oh ho!

ALITHEA. How, sir!

HARCOURT. How, Horner!

ALITHEA. What mean you, sir? I always took you for a man of honour. 300

HORNER. (*Aside.*) Aye, so much a man of honour that I must save my mistress, I thank you, come what will on't.

SPARKISH. So if I had had her, she'd have made me believe, the moon had been made of a Christmas pie. 305

LUCY. (*Aside.*) Now could I speak, if I durst, and solve the riddle, who am the author of it.

ALITHEA. Oh unfortunate woman! [*To Harcourt.*] A combination against my honour, which most concerns me now, because you share in my disgrace, sir, and it is your censure, which I must now suffer, that troubles me, not theirs. 310

HARCOURT. Madam, then have no trouble; you shall now see 'tis possible for me to love, too, without being jealous. I will not only believe your innocence myself, but make all the world believe it. (*Apart to Horner.*) Horner, I must now be concerned for this lady's honour. 315

HORNER. And I must be concerned for a lady's honour, too. 320

HARCOURT. This lady has her honour, and I will protect it.

HORNER. My lady has not her honour, but has given it me to keep, and I will preserve it.

HARCOURT. I understand you not. 325

HORNER. I would not have you.

MARGERY. (*Peeping in behind.*) What's the matter with 'em all?

PINCHWIFE. Come, come, Mr. Horner, no more disputing. Here's the parson; I brought him not in vain. 330

HARCOURT. No sir, I'll employ him, if this lady please.

PINCHWIFE. How, what d'ye mean?

SPARKISH. Aye, what does he mean? 335

HORNER. Why, I have resigned your sister to him; he has my consent.

PINCHWIFE. But he has not mine, sir. A woman's injured honour, no more than a man's, can be repaired or satisfied by any but him that first wronged it, and you shall marry her presently, or— (*Lays his hand on his sword.*) 340

Enter Margery.

MARGERY. Oh Lord, they'll kill poor Mr. Horner! Besides, he shan't marry her whilst I stand by and look on; I'll not lose my second husband so. 345

PINCHWIFE. What do I see?

ALITHEA. My sister in my clothes!

SPARKISH. Hah!

MARGERY. (*To Pinchwife.*) Nay, pray now don't quarrel[143] about finding work for the parson; he shall marry me to Mr. Horner, for now I believe you have enough of me. 350

HORNER. Damned, damned, loving changeling.

MARGERY. Pray sister, pardon me for telling so many lies of you. 355

HARCOURT. I suppose the riddle is plain now.

LUCY. No, that must be my work, good sir, hear me. (*Kneels to Pinchwife, who stands doggedly, with his hat over his eyes.*)

PINCHWIFE. I will never hear woman again, but make 'em all silent thus— (*Offers to draw upon his wife.*) 360

HORNER. No, that must not be.

PINCHWIFE. You then shall go first; 'tis all one to me. (*Offers to draw on Horner, stopped by Harcourt.*) 365

HARCOURT. Hold—

Enter Sir Jaspar Fidget, Lady Fidget, Old Lady Squeamish, Dainty, Mrs. Squeamish.

SIR JASPAR. What's the matter, what's the matter, pray what's the matter, sir? I beseech you communicate, sir.

PINCHWIFE. Why, my wife has communicated, sir, as your wife may have done, too, sir, if she knows him, sir. 370

SIR JASPAR. Pshaw, with him, ha, ha, he!

PINCHWIFE. D'ye mock me, sir? A cuckold is a kind of wild beast, have a care, sir. 375

SIR JASPAR. No, sure you mock me, sir. He cuckold you! It can't be, ha, ha, he. Why, I'll tell you, sir. (*Offers to whisper.*)

PINCHWIFE. I tell you again, he has whored my wife and yours, too, if he knows her, and all the women he comes near. 'Tis not his dissembling, his hypocrisy can wheedle me. 380

SIR JASPAR. How! Does he dissemble? Is he a hypocrite? Nay, then—how—wife—sister, is he a hypocrite? 385

OLD LADY SQUEAMISH. A hypocrite! A dissembler! Speak, young harlotry, speak. How!

SIR JASPAR. Nay, then—oh my head too—oh thou libidinous lady!

---

143 quarrel] engage in a physical fight.

OLD LADY SQUEAMISH. Oh thou harloting 390
harlotry, hast thou done't then?

SIR JASPAR. Speak, good Horner. Art thou a
dissembler, a rogue? Hast thou—

HORNER. Soh—

LUCY. (*Apart to Horner.*) I'll fetch you off and her 395
too, if she will but hold her tongue.

HORNER. (*Apart to Lucy.*) Canst thou? I'll give
thee—

LUCY. (*To Mr. Pinchwife.*) Pray have but patience
to hear me, sir, who am the unfortunate cause of 400
all this confusion. Your wife is innocent, I only
culpable, for I put her upon telling you all these
lies concerning my mistress in order to the
breaking off the match between Mr. Sparkish and
her to make way for Mr. Harcourt. 405

SPARKISH. Did you so, eternal rotten tooth? Then
it seems my mistress was not false to me; I was only
deceived by you.—Brother that should have been,
now, man of conduct, who is a frank person now?
To bring your wife to her lover—hah! 410

LUCY. I assure you, sir, she came not to Mr. Horner
out of love, for she loves him no more—

MARGERY. Hold! I told lies for you, but you shall
tell none for me, for I do love Mr. Horner with
all my soul, and nobody shall say me nay. Pray 415
don't you go to make poor Mr. Horner believe to
the contrary. 'Tis spitefully done of you, I'm sure.

HORNER. (*Aside to Margery.*) Peace, dear idiot.

MARGERY. Nay, I will not peace.

PINCHWIFE. Not till I make you. 420

Enter Dorilant, Quack.

DORILANT. Horner, your servant. I am the doctor's
guest; he must excuse our intrusion.

QUACK. But what's the matter, gentlemen? For
Heaven's sake, what's the matter?

HORNER. Oh 'tis well you are come. 'Tis a 425
censorious world we live in. You may have brought
me a reprieve, or else I had died for a crime I never
committed, and these innocent ladies had suffered
with me; therefore, pray satisfy these worthy,
honourable, jealous gentlemen that—(*Whispers.*) 430

QUACK. Oh I understand you. Is that all?—Sir
Jasper, by heavens and upon the word of a
physician, sir,— (*Whispers to Sir Jaspar.*)

SIR JASPAR. Nay, I do believe you truly.—Pardon
me, my virtuous lady and dear of honour. 435

OLD LADY SQUEAMISH. What, then all's right
again.

SIR JASPAR. Aye, aye, and now let us satisfy him,
too.

They whisper with Pinchwife.

PINCHWIFE. An eunuch! Pray no fooling with me. 440

QUACK. I'll bring half the chirurgeons in Town to
swear it.

PINCHWIFE. They! They'll swear a man that bled
to death through his wounds died of an apoplexy.

QUACK. Pray hear me, sir. Why, all the Town has 445
heard the report of him.

PINCHWIFE. But does all the Town believe it?

QUACK. Pray inquire a little and first of all these.

PINCHWIFE. I'm sure when I left the Town he was
the lewdest fellow in't. 450

QUACK. I tell you, sir, he has been in France since.
Pray ask but these ladies and gentlemen, your
friend Mr. Dorilant.—Gentlemen and ladies, han't
you all heard the late sad report of poor Mr.
Horner? 455

ALL LADIES. Aye, aye, aye.

DORILANT. Why, thou jealous fool, dost thou
doubt it? He's an arrant French capon.

MARGERY. 'Tis false, sir, you shall not disparage
poor Mr. Horner, for to my certain knowledge— 460

LUCY. Oh hold!

MRS.SQUEAMISH. (*Aside to Lucy.*) Stop her
mouth!

LADY FIDGET. (*To Pinchwife.*) Upon my honour,
sir, 'tis as true— 465

DAINTY. D'ye think we would have been seen in
his company—

MRS. SQUEAMISH. Trust our unspotted reputations with him?

LADY FIDGET. (*Aside to Horner.*) This you get and 470
we, too, by trusting your secret to a fool.

HORNER. Peace, madam. (*Aside to Quack.*) Well
Doctor, is not this a good design that carries a man
on unsuspected and brings him off safe?

PINCHWIFE. (*Aside.*) Well, if this were true, but 475
my wife—

Dorilant whispers with Margery.

ALITHEA. Come brother, your wife is yet innocent, you see, but have a care of too strong an imagination, lest like an over-concerned, timorous gamester, by fancying an unlucky cast, it should come. Women and Fortune are truest still to those that trust 'em. 480

LUCY. And any wild thing grows but the more fierce and hungry for being kept up and more dangerous to the keeper. 485

ALITHEA. There's doctrine for all husbands, Mr. Harcourt.

HARCOURT. And I edify, madam, so much that I am impatient till I am one.

DORILANT. And I edify so much by example I will never be one. 490

SPARKISH. And because I will not disparage my parts, I'll ne'er be one.

HORNER. And I, alas, can't be one.

PINCHWIFE. But I must be one against my will, to a country wife, with a country murrain[144] to me. 495

MARGERY. (*Aside.*) And I must be a country wife still, too, I find, for I can't, like a City one, be rid of my musty husband and do what I list. 500

HORNER. Now sir, I must pronounce your wife innocent, though I blush whilst I do it, and I am the only man by her now exposed to shame, which I will straight drown in wine, as you shall your suspicion, and the ladies' troubles we'll divert with a ballet.—Doctor, where are your maskers? 505

LUCY. Indeed, she's innocent, sir. I am her witness, and her end of coming out was but to see her sister's wedding, and what she has said to your face of her love to Mr. Horner was but the usual innocent revenge on a husband's jealousy, was it not? Madam, speak. 510

MARGERY. (*Aside to Lucy and Horner.*) Since you'll have me tell more lies.—Yes indeed, bud.

PINCHWIFE. For my own sake, fain I would all believe: 515
Cuckolds, like lovers, should themselves deceive.
But— (*Sighs.*)
His honour is least safe (too late I find)
Who trusts it with a foolish wife or friend.

A dance of cuckolds.

HORNER. Vain fops but court and dress and keep a pother 520
To pass for women's men with one another,
But he who aims by women to be prized,
First by the men, you see, must be despised.

[*Exeunt.*]

FINIS.

---

144 murrain] contagious cattle disease, with overtones of death (related to Fr. *mourire and* Latin *mori*, to die).

WILLIAM CONGREVE

The Way of the World[1]

Edited and introduced by Richard Kroll[2]

A lthough William Congreve (1670–1729) was to remain active into the eighteenth century, *The Way of the World*, performed in 1700 and considered in subsequent theatre history to be a jewel of great comedy, marked the end of a brief but brilliant stage career. The commonly held view that *The Way of the World* was a flop is mistaken, though that may reflect the notorious difficulty—for critics and audiences alike—of disentangling the complex web of social relations in the play. The central action of the play, however, can be understood by the following question: How can Mirabell successfully court Millamant, a vastly rich heiress, yet secure her entire fortune of twelve thousand pounds, which depends on her marrying with the consent of her aunt and guardian Lady Wishfort?

The play is often thought of as one of the last true Restoration comedies, bearing close affinities in theme and style to some of the great comedies of the 1670s. It is important to see how this play both follows and differs from plays like Etherege's *The Man of Mode* (1676). Both plays bring witty rakes into proximate union with heiresses. Yet Congreve was writing in a new social atmosphere that seems to have emerged after 1688. This change of opinion is epitomized, both in theatre histories and in Congreve's own references in the play itself, by Jeremy Collier's misleadingly titled *A Short View of the Immorality and Profaneness of the English Stage, Together with the Sense of Antiquity upon this Argument* (1698). In this tract, which follows a long line of seventeenth-century attacks on the stage (and which Congreve also places satirically as reading matter in Lady Wishfort's closet), Collier vents his fury against what he sees as the excesses of comedies of the 1670s, in particular plays like Wycherley's *The Country Wife* (1675). At one level Congreve rebuffs Collier by writing a play that, in its broad outline and in its language, echoes those of his distinguished forerunners; at another level, Congreve massages the plot in such a way as to avoid any further attacks like Collier's. It is true that Dorimant (Etherege's hero) and Mirabell (Congreve's) are cousins, but there are important differences. Whereas we are allowed to witness the messy consequences of Dorimant's various affairs in *The Man of Mode*, the entire plot of *The Way of the World* hinges on the fact that Mirabell is a reformed rake, having arranged that his former lover marry Fainall, while at the same time holding her money in trust for her future security, so that Fainall cannot succeed in his attempt to seize her assets for his own purposes.

---

[1] Copytext is the first edition, a 1700 quarto (Q1). Also consulted, the second quarto of 1706 (Q2) and editions of the collected works in 1710 (W1) and 1719 (W2); the definitive modern edition of 1967 (Davis).

[2] The text and annotations are based on Kroll's edition as published in J. Douglas Canfield's *Broadview Anthology of Restoration and Early Eighteenth-Century Drama* (2001), with some additional notes of my own. [J.W.]

Finally, the play echoes its era by concerning itself with the difficulties and dangers of women in the sexual marketplace. Millamant is a splendid creation who lives with the consciousness that she will grow older and perhaps as desperate as Lady Wishfort, who will not commit Mrs. Fainall's mistake, and who cannot allow herself to be governed by vengeful jealousies like Mrs. Marwood. Surrounded by warnings of the dangers of her situation, she must delay marriage so that she can choose well, while marriage itself remains inescapable. The inevitability of marriage for a woman, with the hope that some of its otherwise draconian consequences can be mitigated by negotiation, is the moral framework of the proviso scene, in which Mirabell and Millamant debate the circumstances of their intended union. Some critics have pointed out that this scene—the most famous in Restoration comedy after the china scene in *The Country Wife*—shows Congreve's approval of the Glorious Revolution because Mirabell and Millamant's compact echoes the terms of John Locke's second *Treatise of Government*, which had been published five years earlier. For Congreve, apparently, the "way of the world" involves the need to forge workable political compromises.

WILLIAM CONGREVE
The Way of the World

DRAMATIS PERSONAE

MEN

FAINALL, in love with Mrs.[1] Marwood.
MIRABELL, in love with Mrs. Millamant.
WITWOUD,]
PETULANT,] followers of Mrs. Millamant.
SIR WILFULL WITWOUD, half–brother to Witwoud and nephew to Lady Wishfort.
WAITWELL, servant to Mirabell.

WOMEN

LADY WISHFORT, enemy to Mirabell for having falsely pretended love to her.
MRS. MILLAMANT, a fine lady, niece to Lady Wishfort and loves Mirabell.
MRS. MARWOOD, friend to Mr. Fainall, and likes Mirabell.
MRS. FAINALL, daughter to Lady Wishfort and wife to Fainall, formerly friend to Mirabell.
FOIBLE, woman to Lady Wishfort.

MINCING, woman to Mrs. Millamant.
DANCERS, FOOTMEN, AND ATTENDANTS.

SCENE: LONDON. THE TIME EQUAL TO THAT OF THE PRESENT ACTION.

THE WAY OF THE WORLD.

Audire est Operae pretium, procedere recte
Qui moechis non voltis ... Hor. Sat. 2.1.1

... *Metuat, doti deprensa.* ... Ibid.[2]

---

[1] Mrs.] pronounced 'mistress' and used by married and unmarried women alike.

[2] *Audire* ... Ibid.] Horace, *Satire* 1.2.37 ff, 131. Congreve expects his audience to remember the rest of the opening sentence: "*ut omni parte laborent, / utque illis multo corrupta dolore voluptas / atque haec rara cadat dura inter saepe pericla*": "It is worth your while, ye who would have disaster wait on adulterers, to hear how on every side they fare ill, and how for them pleasure is marred by much pain, and, rare as it is, comes oft amid cruel perils" (Loeb Classical Library Vol. 2; Harvard, 1926); "She fears being deprived of her dowry."

ACT I. A CHOCOLATE HOUSE.

Mirabell and Fainall rising from cards, Betty waiting.

MIRABELL. You are a fortunate man, Mr. Fainall.

FAINALL. Have we done?

MIRABELL. What you please. I'll play on to entertain you.

FAINALL. No, I'll give you your revenge another time, when you are not so indifferent; you are thinking of something else now, and play too negligently. The coldness of a losing gamester lessens the pleasure of the winner. I'd no more play with a man that slighted his ill fortune, than I'd make love³ to a woman who undervalued the loss of her reputation.

MIRABELL. You have a taste extremely delicate and are for refining on your pleasures.

FAINALL. Prithee, why so reserved? Something has put you out of humour.

MIRABELL. Not at all. I happen to be grave today, and you are gay. That's all.

FAINALL. Confess, Millamant and you quarrelled last night after I left you. My fair cousin has some humours that would tempt the patience of a Stoic. What, some coxcomb came in and was well received by her while you were by.

MIRABELL. Witwoud and Petulant. And what was worse, her aunt, your wife's mother, my evil genius, or to sum up all in her own name, my old Lady Wishfort came in.

FAINALL. Oh there it is then. She has a lasting passion for you, and with reason. What, then my wife was there?

MIRABELL. Yes, and Mrs. Marwood and three or four more, whom I never saw before. Seeing me, they all put on their grave faces, whispered one another, then complained aloud of the vapours, and after fell into a profound silence.

FAINALL. They had a mind to be rid of you.

MIRABELL. For which reason I resolved not to stir. At last the good old lady broke through her painful taciturnity with an invective against long visits. I would not have understood her, but Millamant joining in the argument, I rose and with a constrained smile told her I thought nothing was so easy as to know when a visit began to be troublesome; she reddened and I withdrew, without expecting her reply.

FAINALL. You were to blame to resent what she spoke only in compliance with her aunt.

MIRABELL. She is more mistress of herself than to be under the necessity of such a resignation.

FAINALL. What? Though half her fortune depends upon her marrying with my lady's approbation?

MIRABELL. I was then in such a humour that I should have been better pleased if she had been less discreet.

FAINALL. Now I remember, I wonder not that they were weary of you. Last night was one of their cabal nights; they have 'em three times a week and meet by turns at one another's apartments, where they come together like the coroner's inquest, to sit upon the murdered reputations of the week. You and I are excluded, and it was once proposed that all the male sex should be excepted, but somebody moved that to avoid scandal there might be one man of the community, upon which motion Witwoud and Petulant were enrolled members.

MIRABELL. And who may have been the foundress of this sect? My Lady Wishfort, I warrant, who publishes her detestation of mankind and, full of the vigour of fifty-five, declares for a friend and ratafia,⁴ and let posterity shift for itself, she'll breed no more.

FAINALL. The discovery of your sham addresses to her, to conceal your love to her niece, has provoked this separation. Had you dissembled better, things might have continued in the state of nature.

MIRABELL. I did as much as man could with any reasonable conscience: I proceeded to the very last act of flattery with her and was guilty of a song in her commendation. Nay, I got a friend to put her into a lampoon and complement her with the imputation of an affair with a young fellow, which I carried so far that I told her the malicious Town took notice that she was grown fat of a sudden and, when she lay in of a dropsy, persuaded her she was reported to be in labour. The devil's in't if

³ make love] pay court, verbally.

⁴ ratafia] fruit-flavored liqueur.

an old woman is to be flattered further, unless a man should endeavour downright personally to debauch her, and that my virtue forbade me. But for the discovery of that amour, I am indebted to your friend, or your wife's friend, Mrs. Marwood.   85

FAINALL. What should provoke her to be your enemy, without she has made you advances which you have slighted? Women do not easily forgive omissions of that nature.   90

MIRABELL. She was always civil to me, till of late. I confess I am not one of those coxcombs who are apt to interpret a woman's good manners to her prejudice and think that she who does not refuse 'em everything can refuse 'em nothing.   95

FAINALL. You are a gallant man, Mirabell, and though you may have cruelty enough not to satisfy a lady's longing, you have too much generosity not to be tender of her honour. Yet you speak with an indifference which seems to be affected and confesses you are conscious of a negligence.   100

MIRABELL. You pursue the argument with a distrust that seems to be unaffected and confesses you are conscious of a concern for which the lady is more indebted to you than your wife.   105

FAINALL. Fie, fie, friend, if you grow censorious, I must leave you; I'll look upon the gamesters in the next room.   110

MIRABELL. Who are they?

FAINALL. Petulant and Witwoud. [*To Betty.*] Bring me some chocolate. (*Exit.*)

MIRABELL. Betty, what says your clock?   115

BETTY. Turned of the last canonical hour,[5] sir. (*Exit.*)

MIRABELL. How pertinently the jade answers me! (*Looking on his watch.*) Hah? Almost one o'clock!

Enter a servant.

Oh, you are come. Well, is the grand affair over? You have been something tedious.   120

SERVANT. Sir, there's such coupling at Pancras[6] that they stand behind one another as 'twere in a country dance. Ours was the last couple to lead up, and no hopes appearing of despatch; besides, the parson growing hoarse, we were afraid his lungs would have failed before it came to our turn, so we drove round to Duke's Place,[7] and there they were rivetted in a trice.   125

MIRABELL. So, so, you are sure they are married.   130

SERVANT. Married and bedded, sir, I am witness.

MIRABELL. Have you the certificate?

SERVANT. Here it is, sir.

MIRABELL. Has the tailor brought Waitwell's clothes home and the new liveries?   135

SERVANT. Yes sir.

MIRABELL. That's well. Do you go home again, d'ye hear, and adjourn the consummation till farther order. Bid Waitwell shake his ears and Dame Partlet[8] rustle up her feathers and meet me at one o'clock by Rosamond's Pond[9] that I may see her before she returns to her lady. And as you tender your ears, be secret.   140

Exit servant. Reenter Fainall [and Betty].

FAINALL. Joy of your success, Mirabell; you look pleased.   145

MIRABELL. Aye, I have been engaged in a matter of some sort of mirth, which is not ripe for discovery. I am glad this is not a cabal night. I wonder, Fainall, that you who are married, and of consequence should be discreet, will suffer your wife to be of such a party.   150

FAINALL. Faith, I am not jealous. Besides, most who are engaged are women and relations, and for the men, they are of a kind too contemptible to give scandal.   155

MIRABELL. I am of another opinion. The greater the coxcomb, always the more the scandal: for a woman who is not a fool can have but one reason for associating with a man that is.

---

5 last canonical hour] noon, after which time marriages could not legally be performed.

6 Pancras] At the time, St. Pancras was outside City jurisdiction and so marriages could be performed for a fee on demand.

7 Duke's Place] St. James's church, Duke's Place, Aldgate, notorious for irregular marriages.

8 Dame Partlet] wife of Chanticleer in Chaucer's fable (the *Nun's Priest's Tale*).

9 Rosamond's Pond] popular spot for amorous meetings in St. James's Park, named after a mistress of Henry II.

FAINALL. Are you jealous as often as you see Witwoud entertained by Millamant? 160

MIRABELL. Of her understanding I am, if not of her person.

FAINALL. You do her wrong, for to give her her due, she has wit. 165

MIRABELL. She has beauty enough to make any man think so and complaisance enough not to contradict him who shall tell her so.

FAINALL. For a passionate lover, methinks you are a man somewhat too discerning in the failings of 170 your mistress.

MIRABELL. And for a discerning man, somewhat too passionate a lover, for I like her with all her faults, nay, like her for her faults. Her follies are so natural or so artful that they become her, and 175 those affectations which in another woman would be odious serve but to make her more agreeable. I'll tell thee, Fainall, she once used me with that insolence, that in revenge I took her to pieces, sifted her and separated her failings; I studied 'em 180 and got 'em by rote. The catalogue was so large, that I was not without hopes one day or other to hate her heartily: to which end I so used myself to think of 'em, that at length, contrary to my design and expectation, they gave me every hour 185 less and less disturbance, till in a few days it became habitual to me to remember 'em without being displeased. They are now grown as familiar to me as my own frailties, and in all probability in a little time longer I shall like 'em as well. 190

FAINALL. Marry her, marry her. Be half as well acquainted with her charms as you are with her defects, and my life on't, you are your own man again.

MIRABELL. Say you so? 195

FAINALL. Aye, aye, I have experience: I have a wife, and so forth.

Enter messenger.

MESSENGER. Is one Squire Witwoud here?

BETTY. Yes, what's your business?

MESSENGER. I have a letter for him, from his 200 brother Sir Wilfull, which I am charged to deliver into his own hands.

BETTY. He's in the next room, friend—that way.

Exit messenger.

MIRABELL. What, is the chief of that noble family in Town, Sir Wilfull Witwoud? 205

FAINALL. He is expected today. Do you know him?

MIRABELL. I have seen him. He promises to be an extraordinary person. I think you have the honour to be related to him.

FAINALL. Yes, he is half-brother to this Witwoud 210 by a former wife, who was sister to my Lady Wishfort, my wife's mother. If you marry Millamant, you must call cousins too.

MIRABELL. I had rather be his relation than his acquaintance. 215

FAINALL. He comes to Town in order to equip himself for travel.

MIRABELL. For travel? Why the man that I mean is above forty.

FAINALL. No matter for that; 'tis for the honour 220 of England that all Europe should know that we have blockheads of all ages.

MIRABELL. I wonder there is not an act of Parliament to save the credit of the Nation and prohibit the exportation of fools. 225

FAINALL. By no means, 'tis better as 'tis; 'tis better to trade with a little loss than to be quite eaten up with being overstocked.

MIRABELL. Pray, are the follies of this knight-errant, and those of the squire his brother, 230 anything related?

FAINALL. Not at all. Witwoud grows by the knight, like a medlar grafted on a crab. One will melt in your mouth, and t'other set your teeth on edge; one is all pulp, and the other all core. 235

MIRABELL. So one will be rotten before he be ripe, and the other will be rotten without ever being ripe at all.

FAINALL. Sir Wilfull is an odd mixture of bashfulness and obstinacy. But when he's drunk, he's as 240 loving as the monster in *The Tempest*[10] and after much the same manner. To give t'other his due, he has something of good nature and does not always want[11] wit.

---

10 *Tempest*] an allusion to Caliban in Dryden and Davenant's version of Shakespeare's play.

11 want] lack.

MIRABELL. Not always, but as often as his memory 245
fails him and his commonplace of comparisons.
He is a fool with a good memory and some few
scraps of other folks' wit. He is one whose
conversation can never be approved, yet it is now
and then to be endured. He has indeed one good 250
quality: he is not exceptious, for he so passionately
affects the reputation of understanding raillery that
he will construe an affront into a jest and call
downright rudeness and ill language satire and fire.

FAINALL. If you have a mind to finish his picture, 255
you have an opportunity to do it at full length.
Behold the original.

Enter Witwoud.

WITWOUD. Afford me your compassion, my dears,
pity me, Fainall, Mirabell, pity me.

MIRABELL. I do from my soul. 260

FAINALL. Why, what's the matter?

WITWOUD. No letters for me, Betty?

BETTY. Did not the messenger bring you one but
now, sir?

WITWOUD. Aye, but no other? 265

BETTY. No sir.

WITWOUD. That's hard, that's very hard. A
messenger, a mule, a beast of burden, he has
brought me a letter from the fool my brother as
heavy as a panegyric in a funeral sermon or a copy 270
of commendatory verses from one poet to another.
And what's worse, 'tis as sure a forerunner of the
author as an epistle dedicatory.

MIRABELL. A fool, and your brother, Witwoud!

WITWOUD. Aye, aye, my half-brother. My half- 275
brother he is, no nearer, upon honour.

MIRABELL. Then 'tis possible he may be but half a
fool.

WITWOUD. Good, good Mirabell, *le drôle!* Good,
good, hang him, don't let's talk of him.—Fainall, 280
how does your lady? Gad, I say anything in the
world to get this fellow out of my head. I beg
pardon that I should ask a man of pleasure and
the Town a question at once so foreign and
domestic. But I talk like an old maid at a marriage, 285
I don't know what I say, but she's the best woman
in the world.

FAINALL. 'Tis well you don't know what you say,

or else your commendation would go near to make
me either vain or jealous. 290

WITWOUD. No man in Town lives well with a wife
but Fainall.—Your judgment, Mirabell?

MIRABELL. You had better step and ask his wife if
you would be credibly informed.

WITWOUD. Mirabell. 295

MIRABELL. Aye.

WITWOUD. My dear, I ask ten thousand pardons—
Gad I have forgot what I was going to say to you.

MIRABELL. I thank you heartily, heartily.

WITWOUD. No, but prithee excuse me—my 300
memory is such a memory.

MIRABELL. Have a care of such apologies, Witwoud, for I never knew a fool but he affected to
complain either of the spleen or his memory.

FAINALL. What have you done with Petulant? 305

WITWOUD. He's reckoning his money—my
money it was. I have no luck today.

FAINALL. You may allow him to win of you at play,
for you are sure to be too hard for him at repartee.
Since you monopolize the wit that is between you, 310
the fortune must be his of course.

MIRABELL. I don't find that Petulant confesses the
superiority of wit to be your talent, Witwoud.

WITWOUD. Come, come, you are malicious now
and would breed debates. Petulant's my friend and 315
a very honest fellow and a very pretty fellow and
has a smattering, faith and troth, a pretty deal of
an odd sort of a small wit. Nay, I'll do him justice.
I'm his friend, I won't wrong him neither. And if
he had but any judgment in the world, he would 320
not be altogether contemptible. Come, come, don't
detract from the merits of my friend.

FAINALL. You don't take your friend to be over-
nicely bred.

WITWOUD. No, no, hang him, the rogue has no 325
manners at all, that I must own. No more breeding
than a bum-baily,[12] that I grant you. 'Tis pity,
faith, the fellow has fire and life.

MIRABELL. What, courage?

WITWOUD. Hum, faith I don't know as to that— 330

---

12 bum-baily] the lowest kind of bailiff, involved in enforc-
ing arrests.

I can't say as to that—Yes faith, in a controversy he'll contradict anybody.

MIRABELL. Though 'twere a man whom he feared or a woman whom he loved?

WITWOUD. Well, well, he does not always think 335 before he speaks. We have all our failings. You're too hard upon him, you are faith. Let me excuse him. I can defend most of his faults except one or two; one he has, that's the truth on't, if he were my brother, I could not acquit him, that indeed I 340 could wish were otherwise.

MIRABELL. Aye marry,[13] what's that, Witwoud?

WITWOUD. Oh pardon me—expose the infirmities of my friend—no, my dear, excuse me there.

FAINALL. What, I warrant he's unsincere, or 'tis 345 some such trifle.

WITWOUD. No, no, what if he be? 'Tis no matter for that, his wit will excuse that: a wit should no more be sincere than a woman constant; one argues a decay of parts,[14] as t'other of beauty. 350

MIRABELL. Maybe you think him too positive?

WITWOUD. No, no, his being positive is an incentive to argument and keeps up conversation.

FAINALL. Too illiterate!

WITWOUD. That! That's his happiness. His want 355 of learning gives him more opportunities to show his natural parts.

MIRABELL. He wants words?

WITWOUD. Aye, but I like him for that now, for his want of words gives me the pleasure very often 360 to explain his meaning.

FAINALL. He's impudent?

WITWOUD. No, that's not it.

MIRABELL. Vain?

WITWOUD. No. 365

MIRABELL. What! He speaks unseasonable truths sometimes, because he has not wit enough to invent an evasion.

WITWOUD. Truths! Ha, ha, ha! No, no, since you will have it—I mean he never speaks truth at all, 370 that's all. He will lie like a chambermaid or a woman of quality's porter. Now that is a fault.

Enter coachman.

COACHMAN. Is Master Petulant here, mistress?

BETTY. Yes.

COACHMAN. Three gentlewomen in the coach 375 would speak with him.

FAINALL. Oh brave[15] Petulant, three!

BETTY. I'll tell him.

COACHMAN. You must bring two dishes of chocolate and a glass of cinnamon-water. 380

Exeunt Coachman [and Betty].

WITWOUD. That should be for two fasting strumpets and a bawd troubled with wind. Now you may know what the three are.

MIRABELL. You are very free with your friend's acquaintance. 385

WITWOUD. Aye, aye, friendship without freedom is as dull as love without enjoyment or wine without toasting. But to tell you a secret, these are trulls[16] that he allows coach-hire, and something more by the week, to call on him once a day at 390 public places.

MIRABELL. How!

WITWOUD. You shall see that he won't go to 'em because there's no more company here to take notice of him. Why, this is nothing to what he 395 used to do. Before he found out this way, I have known him call for himself.

FAINALL. Call for himself? What dost thou mean?

WITWOUD. Mean? Why he would slip you out of this chocolate house, just when you had been 400 talking to him. As soon as your back was turned, whip he was gone, then trip to his lodging, clap on a hood and scarf and mask, slap into a hackney-coach, and drive hither to the door again in a trice, where he would send in for himself, that I mean, 405 call for himself, wait for himself, nay and what's more, not finding himself, sometimes leave a letter for himself.

MIRABELL. I confess this is something extraordinary. I believe he waits for himself now, he is 410 so long a-coming. Oh, I ask his pardon.

---

13 marry] by St. Mary, a gentle oath.
14 parts] talents, abilities.

15 brave] excellent.
16 trulls] prostitutes.

Enter Petulant.

BETTY. Sir, the coach stays.

PETULANT. Well, well, I come. 'Sbud,[17] a man had as good be a professed midwife as a professed whoremaster, at this rate: to be knocked up and raised at all hours and in all places. Pox on 'em, I won't come, d'ye hear, tell 'em I won't come. Let 'em snivel and cry their hearts out. 415

FAINALL. You are very cruel, Petulant.

PETULANT. All's one, let it pass. I have a humour to be cruel. 420

MIRABELL. I hope they are not persons of condition that you use at this rate.

PETULANT. Condition! Condition's a dried fig, if I am not in humour. By this hand, if they were your—a—a—your what-d'ye-call-'ems themselves, they must wait or rub off, if I want appetite. 425

MIRABELL. What-d'ye-call-'ems! What are they, Witwoud?

WITWOUD. Empresses, my dear, by your what-d'ye-call-'ems he means sultana queens. 430

PETULANT. Aye, Roxolanas.[18]

MIRABELL. Cry you mercy.

FAINALL. Witwoud says they are—

PETULANT. What does he say th'are? 435

WITWOUD. I? Fine ladies, I say.

PETULANT. Pass on Witwoud.—Harkee by this light, his relations: two co-heiresses, his cousins, and an old aunt that loves caterwauling better than a conventicle.[19] 440

WITWOUD. Ha, ha, ha, I had a mind to see how the rogue would come off. Ha, ha, ha, Gad, I can't be angry with him if he said they were my mother and my sisters.

MIRABELL. No! 445

WITWOUD. No, the rogue's wit and readiness of invention charm me. Dear Petulant.

BETTY. They are gone, sir, in great anger.

PETULANT. Enough, let 'em trundle. Anger helps complexion, saves paint. 450

---

17 'Sbud] God's blood.

18 Roxolanas] ironically named after the Sultana in Davenant's *Siege of Rhodes*.

19 conventicle] clandestine or illegal political or religious meeting.

FAINALL. This continence is all dissembled; this is in order to have something to brag of the next time he makes court to Millamant and swear he has abandoned the whole sex for her sake.

MIRABELL. Have you not left off your impudent pretensions there yet? I shall cut your throat sometime or other, Petulant, about that business. 455

PETULANT. Aye, aye, let that pass, there are other throats to be cut—

MIRABELL. Meaning mine, sir? 460

PETULANT. Not I—I mean nobody—I know nothing—but there are uncles and nephews in the world—and they may be rivals—what then? All's one for that—

MIRABELL. How! Harkee Petulant, come hither. Explain, or I shall call your interpreter. 465

PETULANT. Explain? I know nothing. Why you have an uncle, have you not, lately come to Town and lodges by my Lady Wishfort's?

MIRABELL. True. 470

PETULANT. Why that's enough. You and he are not friends, and if he should marry and have a child, you may be disinherited, hah?

MIRABELL. Where hast thou stumbled upon all this truth? 475

PETULANT. All's one for that. Why, then say I know something.

MIRABELL. Come, thou art an honest fellow, Petulant, and shalt make love to my mistress, thou sha't, faith. What hast thou heard of my uncle? 480

PETULANT. I? Nothing I. If throats are to be cut, let swords clash. Snug's the word, I shrug and am silent.

MIRABELL. Oh raillery, raillery. Come, I know thou art in the women's secrets. What, you're a cabalist. I know you stayed at Millamant's last night after I went. Was there any mention made of my uncle or me? Tell me. If thou hadst but good nature equal to thy wit, Petulant, Tony Witwoud, who is now thy competitor in fame, would show as dim by thee as a dead whiting's eye by a pearl of orient; he would no more be seen by thee than Mercury is by the sun. Come, I'm sure thou wouldst tell me. 485 490

PETULANT. If I do, will you grant me common sense, then, for the future? 495

MIRABELL. Faith, I'll do what I can for thee, and I'll pray that Heaven may grant it thee in the meantime.

PETULANT. Well, harkee. 500

FAINALL. Petulant and you both will find Mirabell as warm a rival as a lover.

WITWOUD. Pshaw, pshaw, that she laughs at Petulant is plain. And for my part, but that it is almost a fashion to admire her, I should—Harkee, 505 to tell you a secret, but let it go no further, between friends, I shall never break my heart for her.

FAINALL. How!

WITWOUD. She's handsome, but she's sort of an uncertain woman. 510

FAINALL. I thought you had died for her.

WITWOUD. Umh—no—

FAINALL. She has wit.

WITWOUD. 'Tis what she will hardly allow anybody else. Now demme, I should hate that if 515 she were as handsome as Cleopatra. Mirabell is not so sure of her as he thinks for.

FAINALL. Why do you think so?

WITWOUD. We stayed pretty late there last night and heard something of an uncle to Mirabell who 520 is lately come to Town and is between him and the best part of his estate. Mirabell and he are at some distance, as my Lady Wishfort has been told, and you know she hates Mirabell worse than a Quaker hates a parrot or than a fishmonger hates a hard 525 frost. Whether this uncle has seen Mrs. Millamant or not I cannot say, but there were items of such a treaty being in embryo, and if it should come to life, poor Mirabell would be in some sort unfortunately fobbed, i'faith. 530

FAINALL. 'Tis impossible Millamant should hearken to it.

WITWOUD. Faith my dear, I can't tell; she's a woman and a kind of humourist.

MIRABELL. And this is the sum of what you could 535 collect last night?

PETULANT. The quintessence. Maybe Witwoud knows more: he stayed longer. Besides, they never mind him; they say anything before him.

MIRABELL. I thought you had been the greatest 540 favourite.

PETULANT. Aye, tête-a-tête, but not in public, because I make remarks.

MIRABELL. Do you?

PETULANT. Aye, aye, pox I'm malicious, man. 545 Now he's soft you know, they are not in awe of him. The fellow's well bred, he's what you call a—what-d'ye-call-'em, a fine gentleman, but he's silly withal.

MIRABELL. I thank you, I know as much as my 550 curiosity requires.—Fainall, are you for the Mall?[20]

FAINALL. Aye, I'll take a turn before dinner.

WITWOUD. Aye, we'll all walk in the Park.[21] The ladies talked of being there.

MIRABELL. I thought you were obliged to watch 555 for your brother Sir Wilfull's arrival.

WITWOUD. No, no, he comes to his aunt's, my Lady Wishfort. Pox on him, I shall be troubled with him too. What shall I do with the fool?

PETULANT. Beg him for his estate, that I may beg 560 you afterwards and so have but one trouble with you both.

WITWOUD. Oh rare Petulant, thou art as quick as a fire in a frosty morning; thou shalt to the Mall with us, and we'll be very severe. 565

PETULANT. Enough, I'm in a humour to be severe.

MIRABELL. Are you? Pray then walk by yourselves. Let us not be accessory to your putting the ladies out of countenance with your senseless ribaldry, which you roar out aloud as often as they pass by 570 you, and when you have made a handsome woman blush, then you think you have been severe.

PETULANT. What, what? Then let 'em either show their innocence by not understanding what they hear or else show their discretion by not hearing 575 what they would not be thought to understand.

MIRABELL. But hast not thou then sense enough to know that thou ought'st to be most ashamed of thyself when thou hast put another out of countenance. 580

PETULANT. Not I, by this hand, I always take blushing either for a sign of guilt or ill breeding.

---

20 Mall] Pall Mall, a fashionable promenade.
21 Park] St. James's, the royal park of St. James's Palace, and a fashionable place to stroll.

MIRABELL. I confess you ought to think so. You are in the right, that you may plead the error of your judgment in defence of your practice. Where modesty's ill manners, 'tis but fit That impudence and malice pass for wit. 585

Exeunt.

ACT II. ST. JAMES'S PARK.

Enter Mrs. Fainall and Mrs. Marwood.

MRS. FAINALL. Aye, aye, dear Marwood, if we will be happy, we must find the means in ourselves and among ourselves. Men are ever in extremes, either doting or averse. While they are lovers, if they have fire and sense, their jealousies are insupportable. 5 And when they cease to love (we ought to think at least), they loathe; they look upon us with horror and distaste; they meet us like the ghosts of what we were and as such fly from us.

MRS. MARWOOD. True, 'tis an unhappy circum- 10 stance of life that love should ever die before us and that the man so often should outlive the lover. But say what you will, 'tis better to be left than never to have been loved. To pass our youth in dull indifference, to refuse the sweets of life because 15 they once must leave us, is as preposterous as to wish to have been born old because we one day must be old. For my part, my youth may wear and waste, but it shall never rust in my possession.

MRS. FAINALL. Then it seems you dissemble an 20 aversion to mankind only in compliance with my mother's humour.

MRS. MARWOOD. Certainly. To be free, I have no taste of those insipid dry discourses with which our sex of force must entertain themselves apart from 25 men. We may affect endearments to each other, profess eternal friendships, and seem to dote like lovers, but 'tis not in our natures long to persevere. Love will resume his empire in our breasts, and every heart, or soon or late, receive and readmit 30 him as its lawful tyrant.

MRS. FAINALL. Bless me, how have I been deceived! Why you profess a libertine.

MRS. MARWOOD. You see my friendship by my freedom. Come, be as sincere, acknowledge that 35 your sentiments agree with mine.

MRS. FAINALL. Never.

MRS. MARWOOD. You hate mankind.

MRS. FAINALL. Heartily, inveterately.

MRS. MARWOOD. Your husband? 40

MRS. FAINALL. Most transcendently, aye, though I say it, meritoriously.

MRS. MARWOOD. Give me your hand upon it.

MRS. FAINALL. There.

MRS. MARWOOD. I join with you. What I have 45 said has been to try you.

MRS. FAINALL. Is it possible? Dost thou hate those vipers, men?

MRS. MARWOOD. I have done hating 'em and am now come to despise 'em; the next thing I have to 50 do is eternally to forget 'em.

MRS. FAINALL. There spoke the spirit of an Amazon, a Penthesilea.[22]

MRS. MARWOOD. And yet I am thinking some-times to carry my aversion further. 55

MRS. FAINALL. How?

MRS. MARWOOD. Faith, by marrying. If I could but find one that loved me very well and would be thoroughly sensible of ill usage, I think I should do myself the violence of undergoing the ceremony. 60

MRS. FAINALL. You would not make him a cuckold?

MRS. MARWOOD. No, but I'd make him believe I did, and that's as bad.

MRS. FAINALL. Why, had you as good do it? 65

MRS. MARWOOD. Oh if he should ever discover it, he would then know the worst and be out of his pain, but I would have him ever to continue upon the rack of fear and jealousy.

MRS. FAINALL. Ingenious mischief! Would thou 70 wert married to Mirabell.

MRS. MARWOOD. Would I were.

MRS. FAINALL. You change colour.

MRS. MARWOOD. Because I hate him.

MRS. FAINALL. So do I, but I can hear him named. 75 But what reason have you to hate him in particular?

MRS. MARWOOD. I never loved him. He is and always was insufferably proud.

MRS. FAINALL. By the reason you gave for your

---

22 Penthesilea] a queen of the Amazons.

aversion, one would think it dissembled, for you have laid a fault to his charge of which his enemies must acquit him. 80

MRS. MARWOOD. Oh, then it seems you are one of his favourable enemies. Methinks you look a little pale, and now you flush again. 85

MRS. FAINALL. Do I? I think I am a little sick o'the sudden.

MRS. MARWOOD. What ails you?

MRS. FAINALL. My husband. Don't you see him? He turned short upon me unawares and has almost overcome me. 90

Enter Fainall and Mirabell.

MRS. MARWOOD. Ha, ha, ha, he comes opportunely for you.

MRS. FAINALL. For you, for he has brought Mirabell with him. 95

FAINALL. My dear.

MRS. FAINALL. My soul.

FAINALL. You don't look well today, child.

MRS. FAINALL. D'ye think so?

MIRABELL. He is the only man that does, madam. 100

MRS. FAINALL. The only man that would tell me so at least, and the only man from whom I could hear it without mortification.

FAINALL. Oh my dear, I am satisfied of your tenderness; I know you cannot resent anything from me, especially what is an effect of my concern. 105

MRS. FAINALL. Mr. Mirabell, my mother interrupted you in a pleasant relation last night. I would fain hear it out.

MIRABELL. The persons concerned in that affair have yet a tolerable reputation. I am afraid Mr. Fainall will be censorious. 110

MRS. FAINALL. He has a humour more prevailing than his curiosity and will willingly dispense with the hearing of one scandalous story to avoid giving an occasion to make another by being seen to walk with his wife. This way, Mr. Mirabell, and I dare promise you will oblige us both. 115

Exeunt Mrs. Fainall and Mirabell.

FAINALL. Excellent creature! Well, sure if I should live to be rid of my wife, I should be a miserable man. 120

MRS. MARWOOD. Aye!

FAINALL. For having only that one hope, the accomplishment of it of consequence must put an end to all my hopes. And what a wretch is he who must survive his hopes! Nothing remains when that day comes but to sit down and weep like Alexander[23] when he wanted other worlds to conquer. 125

MRS. MARWOOD. Will you not follow 'em? 130

FAINALL. Faith, I think not.

MRS. MARWOOD. Pray let us; I have a reason.

FAINALL. You are not jealous?

MRS. MARWOOD. Of whom?

FAINALL. Of Mirabell. 135

MRS. MARWOOD. If I am, is it inconsistent with my love to you that I am tender of your honour?

FAINALL. You would intimate, then, as if there were a fellow-feeling between my wife and him.

MRS. MARWOOD. I think she does not hate him to that degree she would be thought. 140

FAINALL. But he, I fear, is too insensible.

MRS. MARWOOD. It may be you are deceived.

FAINALL. It may be so. I do now begin to apprehend it. 145

MRS. MARWOOD. What?

FAINALL. That I have been deceived madam, and you are false.

MRS. MARWOOD. That I am false! What mean you? 150

FAINALL. To let you know I see through all your little arts. Come, you both love him, and both have equally dissembled your aversion. Your mutual jealousies of one another have made you clash till you have both struck fire. I have seen the warm confession reddening on your cheeks and sparkling from your eyes. 155

MRS. MARWOOD. You do me wrong.

FAINALL. I do not. 'Twas for my ease to oversee and wilfully neglect the gross advances made him by my wife, that by permitting her to be engaged, I might continue unsuspected in my pleasures and take you oftener to my arms in full security. But could you think because the nodding husband would not wake, that e'er the watchful lover slept? 160 165

---

23 Alexander] the Great.

MRS. MARWOOD. And wherewithal can you reproach me?

FAINALL. With infidelity, with loving of another, with love of Mirabell.

MRS. MARWOOD. 'Tis false. I challenge you to 170 show an instance that can confirm your groundless accusation. I hate him.

FAINALL. And wherefore do you hate him? He is insensible, and your resentment follows his neglect. An instance? The injuries you have done him are 175 a proof: your interposing in his love. What cause had you to make discoveries of his pretended passion? To undeceive the credulous aunt and be the officious obstacle of his match with Millamant.

MRS. MARWOOD. My obligations to my lady 180 urged me. I had professed a friendship to her and could not see her easy nature so abused by that dissembler.

FAINALL. What, was it conscience then? Professed a friendship! Oh the pious friendships of the 185 female sex!

MRS. MARWOOD. More tender, more sincere, and more enduring than all the vain and empty vows of men, whether professing love to us or mutual faith to one another. 190

FAINALL. Ha, ha, ha, you are my wife's friend too.

MRS. MARWOOD. Shame and ingratitude! Do you reproach me? You, you upbraid me! Have I been false to her through strict fidelity to you and sacrificed my friendship to keep my love inviolate, 195 and have you the baseness to charge me with the guilt, unmindful of the merit? To you it should be meritorious that I have been vicious. And do you reflect that guilt upon me which should lie buried in your bosom? 200

FAINALL. You misinterpret my reproof. I meant but to remind you of the slight account you once could make of strictest ties when set in competition with your love to me.

MRS. MARWOOD. 'Tis false, you urged it with 205 deliberate malice. 'Twas spoke in scorn, and I never will forgive it.

FAINALL. Your guilt, not your resentment, begets your rage. If yet you loved, you could forgive a jealousy, but you are stung to find you are 210 discovered.

MRS. MARWOOD. It shall be all discovered. You too shall be discovered, be sure you shall. I can but be exposed. If I do it myself, I shall prevent[24] your baseness. 215

FAINALL. Why, what will you do?

MRS. MARWOOD. Disclose it to your wife, own what has passed between us.

FAINALL. Frenzy!

MRS. MARWOOD. By all my wrongs, I'll do't, I'll 220 publish to the world the injuries you have done me both in my fame and fortune. With both I trusted you, you bankrupt in honour as indigent of wealth.

FAINALL. Your fame I have preserved. Your fortune has been bestowed as the prodigality of your love 225 would have it, in pleasures which we both have shared. Yet had not you been false, I had ere this repaid it. 'Tis true, had you permitted Mirabell with Millamant to have stolen their marriage, my lady had been incensed beyond all means of 230 reconcilement: Millamant had forfeited the moiety of her fortune, which then would have descended to my wife. And wherefore did I marry but to make lawful prize of a rich widow's wealth and squander it on love and you? 235

MRS. MARWOOD. Deceit and frivolous pretence.

FAINALL. Death, am I not married? What's pretence? Am I not imprisoned, fettered? Have I not a wife? Nay a wife that was a widow, a young widow, a handsome widow, and would be again a 240 widow but that I have a heart of proof and something of a constitution to bustle through the ways of wedlock and this world. Will you yet be reconciled to truth and me?

MRS. MARWOOD. Impossible. Truth and you are 245 inconsistent. I hate you, and shall forever.

FAINALL. For loving you?

MRS. MARWOOD. I loathe the name of love after such usage, and next to the guilt with which you would asperse me, I scorn you most. Farewell. 250

FAINALL. Nay, we must not part thus.

MRS. MARWOOD. Let me go.

FAINALL. Come, I'm sorry.

MRS. MARWOOD. I care not. Let me go. Break my hands, do, I'd leave 'em to get loose. 255

---

24 prevent] to come before, anticipate.

FAINALL. I would not hurt you for the world. Have I no other hold to keep you here?

MRS. MARWOOD. Well, I have deserved it all.

FAINALL. You know I love you.

MRS. MARWOOD. Poor dissembling! Oh that— 260
Well, it is not yet—

FAINALL. What? What is it not? What is it not yet? It is not yet too late?

MRS. MARWOOD. No, it is not yet too late, I have that comfort. 265

FAINALL. It is to love another.

MRS. MARWOOD. But not to loathe, detest, abhor mankind, myself, and the whole treacherous world.

FAINALL. Nay, this is extravagance. Come, I ask your pardon. No tears. I was to blame. I could not 270
love you and be easy in my doubts. Pray forbear. I believe you. I'm convinced I've done you wrong and any way, every way will make amends. I'll hate my wife yet more. Damn her, I'll part with her, rob her of all she's worth, and will retire some- 275
where, anywhere to another world. I'll marry thee. Be pacified.—'Sdeath,[25] they come. Hide your face, your tears. You have a mask, wear it a mo- ment. This way, this way, be persuaded.

Exeunt. Enter Mirabell and Mrs. Fainall.

MRS. FAINALL. They are here yet. 280

MIRABELL. They are turning into the other walk.

MRS. FAINALL. While I only hated my husband, I could bear to see him, but since I have despised him, he's too offensive.

MIRABELL. Oh, you should hate with prudence. 285

MRS. FAINALL. Yes, for I have loved with indis- cretion.

MIRABELL. You should have just so much disgust for your husband as may be sufficient to make you relish your lover. 290

MRS. FAINALL. You have been the cause that I have loved without bounds, and would you set limits to that aversion of which you have been the occasion? Why did you make me marry this man?

MIRABELL. Why do we daily commit disagreeable 295
and dangerous actions? To save that idol reputa- tion. If the familiarities of our loves had produced that consequence of which you were apprehensive, where could you have fixed a father's name with credit but on a husband? I knew Fainall to be a 300
man lavish of his morals, an interested and pro- fessing friend, a false and designing lover, yet one whose wit and outward fair behaviour have gained a reputation with the Town, enough to make that woman stand excused who has suffered herself to 305
be won by his addresses. A better man ought not to have been sacrificed to the occasion; a worse had not answered to the purpose. When you are weary of him, you know your remedy.

MRS. FAINALL. I ought to stand in some degree 310
of credit with you, Mirabell.

MIRABELL. In justice to you I have made you privy to my whole design and put it in your power to ruin or advance my fortune.

MRS. FAINALL. Whom have you instructed to 315
represent your pretended uncle?

MIRABELL. Waitwell, my servant.

MRS. FAINALL. He is an humble servant to Foible my mother's woman and may win her to your interest. 320

MIRABELL. Care is taken for that: she is won and worn by this time. They were married this morning.

MRS. FAINALL. Who?

MIRABELL. Waitwell and Foible. I would not tempt my servant to betray me by trusting him too far. 325
If your mother, in hopes to ruin me, should consent to marry my pretended uncle, he might, like Mosca in *The Fox*,[26] stand upon terms; so I made him sure beforehand.

MRS. FAINALL. So, if my poor mother is caught 330
in a contract, you will discover[27] the imposture betimes and release her by producing a certificate of her gallant's former marriage.

MIRABELL. Yes, upon condition she consent to my marriage with her niece and surrender the moiety 335
of her fortune in her possession.

---

25 'Sdeath] God's death.

26 Mosca in *The Fox*] the tricky servant who betrays his master, the title character in Ben Jonson's Jacobean com- edy, *Volpone*.

27 discover] reveal.

MRS. FAINALL. She talked last night of endeavouring at a match between Millamant and your uncle.

MIRABELL. That was by Foible's direction and my instruction, that she might seem to carry it more privately. 340

MRS. FAINALL. Well, I have an opinion of your success, for I believe my lady will do anything to get a husband, and when she has this, which you have provided for her, I suppose she will submit to anything to get rid of him. 345

MIRABELL. Yes, I think the good lady would marry anything that resembled a man, though 'twere no more than what a butler could pinch out of a napkin. 350

MRS. FAINALL. Female frailty! We must all come to it if we live to be old and feel the craving of a false appetite when the true is decayed.

MIRABELL. An old woman's appetite is depraved like that of a girl: 'tis the green sickness of a second childhood and, like the faint offer of a latter spring, serves but to usher in the fall and withers in an affected bloom. 355

MRS. FAINALL. Here's your mistress.

Enter Mrs. Millamant, Witwoud, and Mincing.

MIRABELL. Here she comes i'faith full sail, with her fan spread and her streamers out and a shoal of fools for tenders. Hah, no, I cry her mercy. 360

MRS. FAINALL. I see but one poor empty sculler, and he tows her woman after him.

MIRABELL. You seem to be unattended, madam. You used to have the beau monde throng after you, and a flock of gay fine perrukes hovering round you. 365

WITWOUD. Like moths about a candle. I had like to have lost my comparison for want of breath. 370

MILLAMANT. Oh I have denied myself airs today. I have walked as fast through the crowd—

WITWOUD. As a favourite in disgrace, and with as few followers.

MILLAMANT. Dear Mr. Witwoud, truce with your similitudes, for I am as sick of 'em— 375

WITWOUD. As a physician of a good air. I cannot help it madam, though 'tis against myself.

MILLAMANT. Yet again! Mincing, stand between me and his wit. 380

WITWOUD. Do Mrs. Mincing, like a screen before a great fire. I confess I do blaze today, I am too bright.

MRS. FAINALL. But dear Millamant, why were you so long? 385

MILLAMANT. Long! Lord, have I not made violent haste? I have asked every living thing I met for you; I have enquired after you as after a new fashion.

WITWOUD. Madam, truce with your similitudes. No, you met her husband and did not ask him for her. 390

MIRABELL. By your leave, Witwoud, that were like enquiring after an old fashion, to ask a husband for his wife.

WITWOUD. Hum, a hit, a hit, a palpable hit, I confess it. 395

MRS. FAINALL. You were dressed before I came abroad.

MILLAMANT. Aye, that's true. Oh, but then I had—Mincing, what had I? Why was I so long? 400

MINCING. Oh mem, your la'ship stayed to peruse a packet of letters.

MILLAMANT. Oh aye, letters—I had letters—I am persecuted with letters—I hate letters—nobody knows how to write letters, and yet one has 'em, one does not know why. They serve one to pin up one's hair. 405

WITWOUD. Is that the way? Pray madam, do you pin up your hair with all your letters? I find I must keep copies. 410

MILLAMANT. Only with those in verse, Mr. Witwoud. I never pin up my hair with prose. I fancy one's hair would not curl if it were pinned up with prose. I think I tried once, Mincing.

MINCING. Oh mem, I shall never forget it. 415

MILLAMANT. Aye, poor Mincing tiffed[28] and tiffed all the morning.

MINCING. 'Till I had the cremp in my fingers, I'll vow mem. And all to no purpose. But when your la'ship pins it up with poetry, it sits so pleasant the next day as anything, and is so pure and so crips. 420

WITWOUD. Indeed, so crips?

MINCING. You are such a critic, Mr. Witwoud.

MILLAMANT. Mirabell, did not you take excep-

---

28 tiffed] arranged, decked out.

tions last night? Oh aye, and went away. Now I think on't, I'm angry—No, now I think on't, I'm pleased. For I believe I gave you some pain.

MIRABELL. Does that please you?

MILLAMANT. Infinitely. I love to give pain.

MIRABELL. You would affect a cruelty which is not in your nature; your true vanity is in the power of pleasing.

MILLAMANT. Oh I ask your pardon for that. One's cruelty is one's power, and when one parts with one's cruelty, one parts with one's power, and when one has parted with that, I fancy one's old and ugly.

MIRABELL. Aye, aye, suffer your cruelty to ruin the object of your power, to destroy your lover. And then how vain, how lost a thing you'll be! Nay, 'tis true: you are no longer handsome when you've lost your lover; your beauty dies upon the instant, for beauty is the lover's gift. 'Tis he bestows your charms; your glass is all a cheat. The ugly and the old, whom the looking glass mortifies, yet after commendation can be flattered by it and discover beauties in it, for that reflects our praises rather than your face.

MILLAMANT. Oh the vanity of these men! Fainall, d'ye hear him? If they did not commend us, we were not handsome! Now you must know they could not commend one if one was not handsome. Beauty the lover's gift! Lord, what is a lover, that it can give? Why, one makes lovers as fast as one pleases, and they live as long as one pleases, and they die as soon as one pleases, and then if one pleases, one makes more.

WITWOUD. Very pretty. Why, you make no more of making of lovers, madam, than of making so many card-matches.[29]

MILLAMANT. One no more owes one's beauty to a lover than one's wit to an echo. They can but reflect what we look and say: vain empty things if we are silent or unseen, and want a being.

MIRABELL. Yet to those two vain empty things, you owe two the greatest pleasures of your life.

MILLAMANT. How so?

MIRABELL. To your lover you owe the pleasure of hearing yourselves praised, and to an echo the pleasure of hearing yourselves talk.

WITWOUD. But I know a lady that loves talking so incessantly she won't give an echo fair play; she has that everlasting rotation of tongue, that an echo must wait till she dies before it can catch her last words.

MILLAMANT. Oh fiction. Fainall, let us leave these men.

MIRABELL. (*Aside to Mrs. Fainall.*) Draw off Witwoud.

MRS. FAINALL. Immediately.—I have a word or two for Mr. Witwoud.

MIRABELL. I would beg a little private audience too.

Exeunt Witwoud and Mrs. Fainall.

You had the tyranny to deny me last night, though you knew I came to impart a secret to you that concerned my love.

MILLAMANT. You saw I was engaged.

MIRABELL. Unkind. You had the leisure to entertain a herd of fools, things who visit you from their excessive idleness, bestowing on your easiness that time which is the encumbrance of their lives. How can you find delight in such society? It is impossible they should admire you; they are not capable, or if they were, it should be to you as a mortification, for sure to please a fool is some degree of folly.

MILLAMANT. I please myself. Besides, sometimes to converse with fools is for my health.

MIRABELL. Your health? Is there a worse disease than the conversation of fools?

MILLAMANT. Yes, the vapours; fools are physic for it, next to asafoetida.[30]

MIRABELL. You are not in a course of fools?

MILLAMANT. Mirabell, if you persist in this offensive freedom, you'll displease me. I think I must resolve after all not to have you. We shan't agree.

MIRABELL. Not in our physic it may be.

---

29 card-matches] matches made of cardboard.

30 asafoetida] "stinking asa," a medicinal plant used as an antispasmodic.

MILLAMANT. And yet our distemper in all likelihood will be the same, for we shall be sick of one another. I shan't endure to be reprimanded nor instructed. 'Tis so dull to act always by advice and so tedious to be told of one's faults. I can't bear it. Well, I won't have you Mirabell—I'm resolved—I think—you may go—ha, ha, ha. What would you give that you could help loving me? 510 515

MIRABELL. I would give something that you did not know I could not help it.

MILLAMANT. Come, don't look grave then. Well, what do you say to me? 520

MIRABELL. I say that a man may as soon make a friend by his wit or a fortune by his honesty as win a woman with plain dealing and sincerity.

MILLAMANT. Sententious Mirabell! Prithee don't look with that violent and inflexible wise face, like Solomon at the dividing of the child in an old tapestry-hanging.[31] 525

MIRABELL. You are merry, madam, but I would persuade you for one moment to be serious.

MILLAMANT. What, with that face? No, if you keep your countenance, 'tis impossible I should hold mine. Well, after all, there is something very moving in a love-sick face. Ha, ha, ha! Well I won't laugh, don't be peevish. Heigho! Now I'll be melancholy, as melancholy as a watch-light.[32] Well Mirabell, if ever you will win me, woo me now. Nay, if you are so tedious, fare you well.—I see they are walking away. 530 535

MIRABELL. Can you not find in the variety of your disposition one moment— 540

MILLAMANT. To hear you tell me that Foible's married and your plot like to speed? No.

MIRABELL. But how you came to know it—

MILLAMANT. Unless by the help of the devil, you can't imagine. Unless she should tell me herself. Which of the two it may have been, I will leave you to consider, and when you have done thinking of that, think of me. (*Exit.*) 545

MIRABELL. I have something more— Gone. Think of you! To think of a whirlwind, though 'twere in 550 a whirlwind, were a case of more steady contemplation, a very tranquility of mind and mansion. A fellow that lives in a windmill has not a more whimsical dwelling than the heart of a man that is lodged in a woman. There is no point of the compass to which they cannot turn and by which they are not turned and by one as well as another, for motion not method is their occupation. To know this and yet continue to be in love is to be made wise from the dictates of reason and yet persevere to play the fool by the force of instinct.— Oh, here come my pair of turtles.[33] 555 560

Enter Waitwell and Foible.

What, billing so sweetly! Is not Valentine's Day over with you yet? Sirrah Waitwell, why sure you think you were married for your own recreation and not for my conveniency. 565

WAITWELL. Your pardon, sir. With submission, we have indeed been solacing in lawful delights, but still with an eye to business, sir. I have instructed her as well as I could. If she can take your directions as readily as my instructions, sir, your affairs are in a prosperous way. 570

MIRABELL. Give you joy, Mrs. Foible.

FOIBLE. Oh las sir, I am so ashamed. I'm afraid my lady has been in a thousand inquietudes for me. But I protest, sir, I made as much haste as I could. 575

WAITWELL. That she did indeed, sir. It was my fault that she did not make more.

MIRABELL. That I believe.

FOIBLE. But I told my lady as you instructed me, sir: that I had a prospect of seeing Sir Rowland, your uncle, and that I would put her ladyship's picture in my pocket to show him, which I'll be sure to say has made him so enamoured of her beauty that he burns with impatience to lie at her ladyship's feet and worship the original. 580 585

MIRABELL. Excellent Foible! Matrimony has made you eloquent in love.

WAITWELL. I think she has profited, sir. I think so. 590

FOIBLE. You have seen madam Millamant, sir?

MIRABELL. Yes.

---

31 Solomon … tapestry-hanging] a portrayal of Solomon's famous judgement; see 1 Kings 3:16–28.
32 watch-light] night-light, hence dim, dark.

---

33 turtles] i.e., turtle-doves.

FOIBLE. I told her, sir, because I did not know that you might find an opportunity. She had so much company last night. 595

MIRABELL. (*Gives money.*) Your diligence will merit more. In the meantime—

FOIBLE. Oh dear sir, your humble servant.

WAITWELL. Spouse.

MIRABELL. Stand off sir, not a penny.—Go on and prosper, Foible. The lease shall be made good and the farm stocked, if we succeed. 600

FOIBLE. I don't question your generosity, sir, and you need not doubt of success. If you have no more commands, sir, I'll be gone. I'm sure my lady is at her toilet[34] and can't dress till I come. (*Looking out.*) Oh dear, I'm sure that was Mrs. Marwood that went by in a mask. If she has seen me with you, I'm sure she'll tell my lady. I'll make haste home and prevent her. Your servant, sir. B'w'y,[35] Waitwell. (*Exit.*) 605 610

WAITWELL. Sir Rowland, if you please.—The jade's so pert upon her preferment, she forgets herself.

MIRABELL. Come sir, will you endeavour to forget yourself and transform into Sir Rowland? 615

WAITWELL. Why sir, it will be impossible I should remember myself: married, knighted, and attended all in one day! 'Tis enough to make any man forget himself. The difficulty will be how to recover my acquaintance and familiarity with my former self and fall from my transformation to a reformation into Waitwell. Nay, I shan't be quite the same Waitwell neither. For now I remember me, I am married and can't be my own man again. 620

Aye, there's the grief; that's the sad change of life: To lose my title and yet keep my wife. 625

Exeunt.

ACT III. A ROOM IN LADY WISHFORT'S HOUSE.

Lady Wishfort at her toilet, Peg waiting.

LADY WISHFORT. Merciful, no news of Foible yet?

PEG. No madam.

LADY WISHFORT. I have no more patience. If I have not fretted myself till I am pale again, there's no veracity in me. Fetch me the red. The red, do you hear, sweetheart? An arrant ash colour, as I'm a person. Look you how this wench stirs! Why dost thou not fetch me a little red? Didst thou not hear me, Mopus?[36] 5

PEG. The red ratafia does your ladyship mean or the cherry brandy? 10

LADY WISHFORT. Ratafia, fool? No, fool. Not the ratafia, fool. Grant me patience! I mean the Spanish paper,[37] idiot. Complexion darling. Paint, paint, paint, dost thou understand that, change-ling, dangling thy hands like bobbins before thee. Why dost thou not stir, puppet? Thou wooden thing upon wires. 15

PEG. Lord madam, your ladyship is so impatient. I cannot come at the paint, madam; Mrs. Foible has locked it up and carried the key with her. 20

LADY WISHFORT. A pox take you both. Fetch me the cherry brandy then.

Exit Peg.

I'm as pale and as faint, I look like Mrs. Qualmsick the curate's wife that's always breeding.—Wench, come, come, wench. What art thou doing? Sipping? Tasting? Save thee, dost thou not know the bottle? 25

Enter Peg with a bottle and china cup.

PEG. Madam, I was looking for a cup.

LADY WISHFORT. A cup, save thee, and what a cup hast thou brought! Dost thou take me for a fairy, to drink out of an acorn? Why didst thou not bring thy thimble? Hast thou ne'er a brass thimble clinking in thy pocket with a bit of nutmeg?[38] I warrant thee. Come, fill, fill. So. Again. 30 35

One knocks.

See who that is. Set down the bottle first. Here, here, under the table. What, wouldst thou go with

---

34 at her toilet] in the act of dressing.
35 B'w'y] (God) be with you.

36 Mopus] a stupid person.
37 Spanish paper] a kind of rouge, presumably.
38 thimble … nutmeg] used as good-luck charms.

the bottle in thy hand like a tapster? As I'm a person, this wench has lived in an inn upon the road before she came to me, like Maritornes the Asturian in *Don Quixote*. No Foible yet? 40

PEG. No madam, Mrs. Marwood.

LADY WISHFORT. Oh Marwood, let her come in. Come in good Marwood. 45

Enter Mrs. Marwood.

MRS. MARWOOD. I'm surprised to find your Ladyship in deshabille at this time of day.

LADY WISHFORT. Foible's a lost thing, has been abroad since morning and never heard of since.

MRS. MARWOOD. I saw her but now as I came 50 masked through the Park, in conference with Mirabell.

LADY WISHFORT. With Mirabell! You call my blood into my face with mentioning that traitor. She durst not have the confidence. I sent her to 55 negotiate an affair, in which if I'm detected I'm undone. If that wheedling villain has wrought upon Foible to detect me, I'm ruined. Oh my dear friend, I'm a wretch of wretches if I'm detected.

MRS. MARWOOD. Oh madam, you cannot 60 suspect Mrs. Foible's integrity.

LADY WISHFORT. Oh, he carries poison in his tongue that would corrupt integrity itself. If she has given him an opportunity, she has as good put her integrity into his hands. Ah dear Marwood, 65 what's integrity to an opportunity? Hark! I hear her.—Go, you thing, and send her in.

Exit Peg.

Dear friend, retire into my closet[39] that I may examine her with more freedom. You'll pardon me, dear friend, I can make bold with you. There are 70 books over the chimney—Quarles and Prynne, and the *Short View of the Stage*, with Bunyan's works—to entertain you.[40]

Exit Marwood. Enter Foible.

_____

39 closet] inner room of her suite.
40 Quarles ... Bunyan] Francis Quarles and John Bunyan wrote devotional works; William Prynne and Jeremy Collier, author of the *Short View*, wrote tracts against the theatre.

Oh Foible, where hast thou been? What hast thou been doing? 75

FOIBLE. Madam, I have seen the party.

LADY WISHFORT. But what hast thou done?

FOIBLE. Nay, 'tis your ladyship has done, and are to do; I have only promised. But a man so enamoured, so transported! Well, here it is, all that 80 is left, all that is not kissed away. Well, if worshipping of pictures be a sin, poor Sir Rowland, I say.

LADY WISHFORT. The miniature has been counted like. But hast thou not betrayed me, 85 Foible? Hast thou not detected me to that faithless Mirabell? What hadst thou to do with him in the Park? Answer me, has he got nothing out of thee?

FOIBLE. [*Aside.*] So, the devil has been beforehand with me. What shall I say?—Alas madam, could I 90 help it if I met that confident thing? Was I in fault? If you had heard how he used me, and all upon your ladyship's account, I'm sure you would not suspect my fidelity. Nay, if that had been the worst, I could have borne, but he had a fling at your 95 Ladyship too, and then I could not hold. But i'faith, I gave him his own.

LADY WISHFORT. Me? What did the filthy fellow say?

FOIBLE. Oh madam, 'tis a shame to say what he said, 100 with his taunts and his fleers, tossing up his nose. "Humph," says he, "what, you are a-hatching some plot," says he, "you are so early abroad, or catering," says he, "ferreting for some disbanded officer, I warrant. Half pay is but thin subsistence," says he, 105 "well, what pension does your lady propose? Let me see," says he, "what, she must come down pretty deep now she's superannuated," says he, "and"—

LADY WISHFORT. 'Odds my life, I'll have him, I'll have him murdered. I'll have him poisoned. Where 110 does he eat? I'll marry a drawer to have him poisoned in his wine. I'll send for Robin from Locket's[41] immediately.

FOIBLE. Poison him? Poisoning's too good for him. Starve him, madam, starve him: marry Sir 115 Rowland and get him disinherited. Oh you would bless yourself to hear what he said.

_____

41 Locket's] fashionable eating-place.

LADY WISHFORT. A villain. Superannuated!

FOIBLE. "Humph," says he, "I hear you are laying designs against me too," says he, "and Mrs. Millamant is to marry my uncle." (He does not suspect a word of your ladyship.) "But," says he, "I'll fit you for that, I warrant you," says he, "I'll hamper you for that," says he, "you and your old frippery too," says he, "I'll handle you"— 120 125

LADY WISHFORT. Audacious villain! Handle me, would he durst. Frippery? Old frippery! Was there ever such a foul-mouthed fellow? I'll be married tomorrow; I'll be contracted tonight.

FOIBLE. The sooner the better, madam. 130

LADY WISHFORT. Will Sir Rowland be here, say'st thou? When, Foible?

FOIBLE. Incontinently, madam. No new sheriff's wife expects the return of her husband after knighthood with that impatience in which Sir Rowland burns for the dear hour of kissing your ladyship's hands after dinner. 135

LADY WISHFORT. Frippery? Superannuated frippery! I'll frippery the villain; I'll reduce him to frippery and rags. A tatterdemalion! I hope to see him hung with tatters, like a Long Lane penthouse[42] or a gibbet-thief. A slander-mouthed railer. I warrant the spendthrift prodigal's in debt as much as the million lottery[43] or the whole court upon a birthday. I'll spoil his credit with his tailor. Yes, he shall have my niece with her fortune, he shall. 140 145

FOIBLE. He! I hope to see him lodge in Ludgate[44] first and angle into Blackfriars[45] for brass farthings with an old mitten.

LADY WISHFORT. Aye, dear Foible. Thank thee for that, dear Foible. He has put me out of all patience. I shall never recompose my features to receive Sir Rowland with any economy of face. This wretch has fretted me that I am absolutely decayed. Look Foible. 150 155

FOIBLE. Your ladyship has frowned a little too rashly, indeed, madam. There are some cracks discernible in the white varnish.

LADY WISHFORT. Let me see the glass. Cracks, say'st thou? Why, I'm arrantly flayed; I look like an old peeled wall. Thou must repair me, Foible, before Sir Rowland comes, or I shall never keep up to my picture. 160

FOIBLE. I warrant you, madam, a little art once made your picture like you, and now a little of the same art must make you like your picture. Your picture must sit for you, madam. 165

LADY WISHFORT. But art thou sure Sir Rowland will not fail to come? Or will a[46] not fail when he does come? Will he be importunate, Foible, and push? For if he should not be importunate, I shall never break decorums. I shall die with confusion if I am forced to advance. Oh no, I can never advance; I shall swoon if he should expect advances. No, I hope Sir Rowland is better bred than to put a lady to the necessity of breaking her forms. I won't be too coy neither. I won't give him despair. But a little disdain is not amiss; a little scorn is alluring. 170 175

FOIBLE. A little scorn becomes your ladyship. 180

LADY WISHFORT. Yes, but tenderness becomes me best, a sort of a-dyingness. You see that picture has a sort of a—hah, Foible? A swimmingness in the eyes. Yes, I'll look so. My niece affects it, but she wants features. Is Sir Rowland handsome? Let my toilet be removed. I'll dress above. I'll receive Sir Rowland here. Is he handsome? Don't answer me. I won't know; I'll be surprised. I'll be taken by surprise. 185

FOIBLE. By storm, madam. Sir Rowland's a brisk man. 190

LADY WISHFORT. Is he? Oh then he'll importune, if he's a brisk man. I shall save decorums if Sir Rowland importunes. I have a mortal terror at the apprehension of offending against decorums. Nothing but importunity can surmount decorums. Oh I'm glad he's a brisk man. Let my things be removed, good Foible. (*Exit.*) 195

---

42 Long Lane penthouse] Long Lane is where the rag trade flourished.

43 million lottery] possibly referring to the government lottery of 1694, which attempted to raise £1,000,000.

44 Ludgate] prison near the west gate of the City of London.

45 Blackfriars] residential district of the City.

---

46 a] he.

Enter Mrs. Fainall.

MRS. FAINALL. Oh Foible, I have been in a fright lest I should come too late. That devil Marwood saw you in the Park with Mirabell, and I'm afraid will discover it to my lady.   200

FOIBLE. Discover what, madam?

MRS. FAINALL. Nay, nay, put not on that strange face. I am privy to the whole design and know what Waitwell, to whom thou wert this morning married, is to personate Mirabell's uncle, and as such winning my lady, to involve her in those difficulties from which Mirabell only must release her by his making his conditions to have my cousin and her fortune left to her own disposal.   205   210

FOIBLE. Oh dear madam, I beg your pardon. It was not my confidence in your ladyship that was deficient, but I thought the former good correspondence between your ladyship and Mr. Mirabell might have hindered his communicating this secret.   215

MRS. FAINALL. Dear Foible, forget that.

FOIBLE. Oh dear madam, Mr. Mirabell is such a sweet winning gentleman—but your ladyship is the pattern of generosity, sweet lady, to be so good! Mr. Mirabell cannot choose but be grateful. I find your ladyship has his heart still. Now madam, I can safely tell your ladyship our success. Mrs. Marwood had told my lady, but I warrant, I managed myself. I turned it all for the better. I told my lady that Mr. Mirabell railed at her. I laid horrid things to his charge, I'll vow, and my lady is so incensed that she'll be contracted to Sir Rowland tonight, she says. I warrant, I worked her up, that he may have her for asking for, as they say of a Welsh maidenhead.   220   225   230

MRS. FAINALL. Oh rare Foible!

FOIBLE. Madam, I beg your ladyship to acquaint Mr. Mirabell of his success. I would be seen as little as possible to speak to him; besides, I believe Madam Marwood watches me. She has a month's mind,[47] but I know Mr. Mirabell can't abide her.   235

Enter Footman.

John, remove my lady's toilet.—Madam, your servant. My lady is so impatient, I fear she'll come for me if I stay.   240

MRS. FAINALL. I'll go with you up the back stairs, lest I should meet her.

Exeunt. Enter Mrs. Marwood.

MRS. MARWOOD. Indeed Mrs. Engine,[48] is it thus with you? Are you become a go-between of this importance? Yes, I shall watch you. Why, this wench is the passe-partout, a very master-key to everybody's strongbox. My friend Fainall, have you carried it so swimmingly? I thought there was something in it, but it seems it's over with you. Your loathing is not from a want of appetite, then, but from a surfeit. Else you could never be so cool to fall from a principal to be an assistant, to procure for him! A pattern of generosity, that I confess. Well, Mr. Fainall, you have met with your match. Oh man, man! Woman, woman! The devil's an ass. If I were a painter, I would draw him like an idiot, a driveler, with a bib and bells. Man should have his head and horns,[49] and woman the rest of him. Poor simple fiend! Madam Marwood has a month's mind, but he can't abide her. 'Twere better for him you had not been his confessor in that affair without you had kept his counsel closer. I shall not prove another pattern of generosity and stalk for him till he takes his stand to aim at a fortune. He has not obliged me to that with those excesses of himself. And now I'll have none of him.—Here comes the good lady, panting ripe, with a heart full of hope and a head full of care, like any chemist upon the day of projection.   245   250   255   260   265   270

Enter Lady Wishfort.

LADY WISHFORT. Oh dear Marwood, what shall I say for this rude forgetfulness? But my dear friend is all goodness.

MRS. MARWOOD. No apologies, dear madam. I have been very well entertained.   275

LADY WISHFORT. As I'm a person, I am in a very

---

47 month's mind] long-held and intense desire or inclination.

48 Engine] artificial or human tool, device.

49 horns] that supposedly sprout from a man's forehead when he has been cuckolded (cheated on).

chaos to think I should so forget myself. But I have such an olio[50] of affairs, really I know not what to do. (*Calls.*) Foible—I expect my nephew Sir Wilfull every moment too.—Why Foible.—He means to travel for improvement.

MRS. MARWOOD. Methinks Sir Wilfull should rather think of marrying than travelling at his years. I hear he is turned of forty.

LADY WISHFORT. Oh he's in less danger of being spoiled by his travels. I am against my nephew's marrying too young. It will be time enough when he comes back and has acquired discretion to choose for himself.

MRS. MARWOOD. Methinks Mrs. Millamant and he would make a very fit match. He may travel afterwards. 'Tis a thing very usual with young gentlemen.

LADY WISHFORT. I promise you I have thought on't. And since 'tis your judgment, I'll think on't again. I assure you I will; I value your judgment extremely. On my word I'll propose it.

Enter Foible.

Come, come Foible, I had forgot my nephew will be here before dinner. I must make haste.

FOIBLE. Mr. Witwoud and Mr. Petulant are come to dine with your ladyship.

LADY WISHFORT. Oh dear, I can't appear till I'm dressed. Dear Marwood, shall I be free with you again and beg you to entertain 'em? I'll make all imaginable haste. Dear friend excuse me.

Exeunt Lady Wishfort and Foible. Enter Mrs. Millamant and Mincing.

MILLAMANT. Sure never anything was so unbred as that odious man.—Marwood, your servant.

MRS. MARWOOD. You have a colour. What's the matter?

MILLAMANT. That horrid fellow Petulant has provoked me into a flame. I have broke my fan.—Mincing, lend me yours.—Is not all the powder out of my hair?

MRS. MARWOOD. No. What has he done?

MILLAMANT. Nay, he has done nothing; he has only talked. Nay, he has said nothing neither, but he has contradicted everything that has been said. For my part, I thought Witwoud and he would have quarrelled.[51]

MINCING. I vow mem, I thought once they would have fit.

MILLAMANT. Well, 'tis a lamentable thing, I'll swear, that one has not the liberty of choosing one's acquaintance as one does one's clothes.

MRS. MARWOOD. If we had the liberty, we should be as weary of one set of acquaintance, though never so good, as we are of one suit, though never so fine. A fool and a doily stuff[52] would now and then find days of grace and be worn for variety.

MILLAMANT. I could consent to wear 'em if they would wear alike, but fools never wear out. They are such drap-du-Berry[53] things without one could give 'em to one's chambermaid after a day or two.

MRS. MARWOOD. 'Twere better so indeed. Or what think you of the playhouse? A fine, gay, glossy fool should be given there, like a new masking habit after the masquerade is over and we have done with the disguise. For a fool's visit is always a disguise and never admitted by a woman of wit but to blind her affair with a lover of sense. If you would but appear bare-faced now and own Mirabell, you might as easily put off Petulant and Witwoud as your hood and scarf. And indeed 'tis time, for the Town has found it: the secret is grown too big for the pretence. 'Tis like Mrs. Primly's great belly: she may lace it down before, but it burnishes on her hips. Indeed Millamant, you can no more conceal it than my Lady Strammel can her face, that goodly face, which, in defiance of her Rhenish-wine tea,[54] will not be comprehended in a mask.

MILLAMANT. I'll take my death, Marwood, you are more censorious than a decayed beauty or a discarded toast.—Mincing, tell the men they may come up. My aunt is not dressing.

---

50 olio] dish of various mixed ingredients, hence, a hotch-potch.

51 quarrelled] fought, physically.

52 doily stuff] light, cheap, woollen material.

53 Drap-du-Berry] woollen cloth from Berry, France.

54 Rhenish-wine-tea] Rhine wines were thought to be slimming.

Exit Mincing.

Their folly is less provoking than your malice; the   355
Town has found it. What has it found? That
Mirabell loves me is no more a secret than it is a
secret that you discovered it to my aunt or than
the reason why you discovered it is a secret.

MRS. MARWOOD. You are nettled.   360

MILLAMANT. You're mistaken. Ridiculous!

MRS. MARWOOD. Indeed my dear, you'll tear
another fan if you don't mitigate those violent airs.

MILLAMANT. Oh silly! Ha, ha, ha. I could laugh
immoderately. Poor Mirabell! His constancy to me   365
has quite destroyed his complaisance for all the
world beside. I swear, I never enjoined it him to
be so coy. If I had the vanity to think he would
obey me, I would command him to show more
gallantry. 'Tis hardly well bred to be so particular   370
on one hand and so insensible on the other. But I
despair to prevail and so let him follow his own
way. Ha, ha, ha. Pardon me, dear creature, I must
laugh, ha, ha, ha, though I grant you 'tis a little
barbarous, ha, ha, ha.   375

MRS. MARWOOD. What pity 'tis, so much fine
raillery, and delivered with so significant gesture,
should be so unhappily directed to miscarry.

MILLAMANT. Hah? Dear creature, I ask your
pardon. I swear, I did not mind you.   380

MRS. MARWOOD. Mr. Mirabell and you both
may think it a thing impossible, when I shall tell
him, by telling you—

MILLAMANT. Oh dear, what? For it is the same
thing, if I hear it—ha, ha, ha.   385

MRS. MARWOOD. That I detest him, hate him,
madam.

MILLAMANT. Oh madam, why so do I. And yet
the creature loves me, ha, ha, ha. How can one
forbear laughing to think of it. I am a sibyl if I   390
am not amazed to think what he can see in me.
I'll take my death, I think you are handsomer. And
within a year or two as young. If you could but
stay for me, I should overtake you. But that cannot
be. Well, that thought makes me melancholy. Now   395
I'll be sad.

MRS. MARWOOD. Your merry note may be
changed sooner than you think.

MILLAMANT. D'ye say so? Then I'm resolved I'll
have a song to keep up my spirits.   400

Enter Mincing.

MINCING. The gentlemen stay but to comb,
madam, and will wait on you.

MILLAMANT. Desire Mrs. ____[55] that is in the
next room to sing the song I would have learned
yesterday.—You shall hear it madam. Not that   405
there's any great matter in it. But 'tis agreeable to
my humour.
Song.[56]

I.

Love's but the frailty of the mind
When 'tis not with ambition joined,
A sickly flame, which if not fed expires,   410
And feeding, wastes in self-consuming fires.

II.

'Tis not to wound a wanton boy
Or am'rous youth that gives the joy,
But 'tis the glory to have pierced a swain,
For whom inferior beauties sighed in vain.   415

III.

Then I alone the conquest prize
When I insult a rival's eyes;
If there's delight in love, 'tis when I see
The heart which others bleed for, bleed for me.

Enter Petulant and Witwoud.

MILLAMANT. Is your animosity composed,   420
gentlemen?

WITWOUD. Raillery, raillery, madam. We have no
animosity. We hit off a little wit now and then,
but no animosity. The falling out of wits is like the
falling out of lovers. We agree in the main,[57] like   425
treble and bass. Hah, Petulant?

PETULANT. Aye in the main, but when I have a
humour to contradict—

WITWOUD. Aye, when he has a humour to
contradict, then I contradict too. What, I know   430
my cue. Then we contradict one another like two

---

55 ____] to be filled in by the actor; see below.
56 Song] composed by John Eccles and sung by a "Mrs.
    Hodgson."
57 main] the middle or tenor part.

battledores, for contradictions beget one another like Jews.

PETULANT. If he says black's black—if I have a humour to say 'tis blue—let that pass—all's one for that. If I have a humour to prove it, it must be granted. 435

WITWOUD. Not positively must, but it may, it may.

PETULANT. Yes, it positively must, upon proof positive. 440

WITWOUD. Aye, upon proof positive it must, but upon proof presumptive it only may. That's a logical distinction now, madam.

MRS. MARWOOD. I perceive your debates are of importance and very learnedly handled. 445

PETULANT. Importance is one thing, and learning's another, but a debate's a debate, that I assert.

WITWOUD. Petulant's an enemy to learning; he relies altogether on his parts. 450

PETULANT. No, I'm no enemy to learning; it hurts not me.

MRS. MARWOOD. That's a sign indeed it's no enemy to you.

PETULANT. No, no, it's no enemy to anybody but them that have it. 455

MILLAMANT. Well, an illiterate man's my aversion. I wonder at the impudence of any illiterate man to offer to make love.

WITWOUD. That I confess I wonder at too. 460

MILLAMANT. Ah! To marry an ignorant that can hardly read or write!

PETULANT. Why should a man be ever the further from being married though he can't read any more than he is from being hanged? The ordinary's[58] paid for setting the psalm, and the parish priest for reading the ceremony. And for the rest which is to follow in both cases, a man may do it without book. So all's one for that. 465

MILLAMANT. D'ye hear that creature? Lord, here's company. I'll be gone. 470

Exeunt Millamant and Mincing.

WITWOUD. In the name of Bartlemew and his fair,[59] what have we here?

MRS. MARWOOD. 'Tis your brother, I fancy. Don't you know him? 475

WITWOUD. Not I—yes, I think it is he—I've almost forgotten him; I have not seen him since the Revolution.[60]

Enter Sir Wilfull Witwoud in a country riding habit, and servant to Lady Wishfort.

SERVANT. Sir, my lady's dressing. Here's company, if you please to walk in, in the mean time. 480

SIR WILFULL. Dressing! What, it's but morning here I warrant with you in London; we should count it towards afternoon in our parts, down in Shropshire. Why then belike my aunt han't dined yet, hah friend? 485

SERVANT. Your aunt, sir?

SIR WILFULL. My aunt sir, yes my aunt sir, and your lady sir. Your lady is my aunt, sir. Why, what, dost thou not know me, friend? Why then send somebody here that does. How long hast thou lived with thy lady, fellow, hah? 490

SERVANT. A week, sir, longer than anybody in the house, except my lady's woman.

SIR WILFULL. Why then belike thou dost not know thy lady if thou see'st her, hah friend? 495

SERVANT. Why truly sir, I cannot safely swear to her face in a morning before she is dressed. 'Tis like I may give a shrewd guess at her by this time.

SIR WILFULL. Well prithee try what thou canst do. If thou canst not guess, enquire her out, dost hear fellow? And tell her, her nephew Sir Wilfull Witwoud is in the house. 500

SERVANT. I shall, sir.

SIR WILFULL. Hold ye, hear me friend. A word with you in your ear. Prithee who are these gallants? 505

SERVANT. Really sir, I can't tell; here come so many here, 'tis hard to know 'em all. (*Exit.*)

---

58 being hanged … ordinary] Prisoners who could read (usually a psalm chosen by the ordinary or prison chaplain) were saved from being hanged "by benefit of clergy."

59 Bartlemew] Bartholemew Fair was held at Smithfield every August 24 (St. Bartholemew's Day); it was the site of many curiosities.

60 Revolution] the "Glorious" Revolution of 1688, hence, twelve years.

SIR WILFULL. 'Oons,[61] this fellow knows less than a starling; I don't think a knows his own name. 510

MRS. MARWOOD. Mr. Witwoud, your brother is not behindhand in forgetfulness. I fancy he has forgot you too.

WITWOUD. I hope so. The devil take him that remembers first, I say. 515

SIR WILFULL. Save you gentlemen and lady.

MRS. MARWOOD. For shame Mr. Witwoud. Why won't you speak to him?—And you, sir.

WITWOUD. Petulant, speak.

PETULANT. And you, sir. 520

SIR WILFULL. No offence, I hope. (Salutes[62] Marwood.)

MRS. MARWOOD. No sure, sir.

WITWOUD. This is a vile dog, I see that already. No offence! Ha, ha, ha, to him, to him Petulant. 525 Smoke him.

PETULANT. (Surveying him round.) It seems as if you had come a journey, sir, hem, hem.

SIR WILFULL. Very likely, sir, that it may seem so.

PETULANT. No offence, I hope, sir. 530

WITWOUD. Smoke the boots, the boots, Petulant, the boots, ha, ha, ha.

SIR WILFULL. Maybe not, sir; thereafter as 'tis meant, sir.

PETULANT. Sir, I presume upon the information 535 of your boots.

SIR WILFULL. Why 'tis like you may, sir. If you are not satisfied with the information of my boots, sir, if you will step to the stable, you may enquire further of my horse, sir. 540

PETULANT. Your horse, sir! Your horse is an ass, sir!

SIR WILFULL. Do you speak by way of offence, sir?

MRS. MARWOOD. The gentleman's merry, that's all, sir.—S'life, we shall have a quarrel betwixt an 545 horse and an ass before they find one another out.—You must not take anything amiss from your friends, sir. You are among your friends here, though it may be you don't know it. If I am not mistaken, you are Sir Wilfull Witwoud. 550

SIR WILFULL. Right lady, I am Sir Wilfull Witwoud, so I write myself—no offence to anybody, I hope—and nephew to the Lady Wishfort of this mansion.

MRS. MARWOOD. Don't you know this gentle- 555 man, sir?

SIR WILFULL. Hum! What, sure 'tis not—yea by'r lady, but 'tis—'sheart I know not whether 'tis or no—yea but 'tis, by the Wrekin.[63] Brother Anthony! What, Tony i'faith! What, dost thou not 560 know me? By'r lady, nor I thee, thou art so becravatted and beperriwigged. 'Sheart, why dost not speak? Art thou o'erjoyed?

WITWOUD. 'Odso brother, is it you? Your servant, brother. 565

SIR WILFULL. Your servant! Why yours, sir. Your servant again. 'Sheart, and your friend and servant to that—and a—(Puff.) and a flap-dragon[64] for your service, sir. And a hare's foot and a hare's scut for your service, sir, an[65] you be so cold and so 570 courtly!

WITWOUD. No offence, I hope, brother.

SIR WILFULL. 'Sheart, sir, but there is, and much offence. A pox, is this your Inns o'Court[66] breeding not to know your friends and your 575 relations, your elders and your betters.

WITWOUD. Why, brother Wilfull of Salop, you may be as short as a Shrewsbury cake,[67] if you please. But I tell you, 'tis not modish to know relations in Town. You think you're in the country, 580 where great lubberly brothers slabber and kiss one another when they meet, like a call of serjeants.[68] 'Tis not the fashion here, 'tis not indeed, dear brother.

SIR WILFULL. The fashion's a fool, and you're a fop, 585 dear brother. 'Sheart, I've suspected this. By'r lady,

---

61 'Oons] God's wounds; also, in what follows, God's life (s'life, 'slife), heart, etc.

62 Salutes] greets with a kiss or embrace.

63 Wrekin] an important hill in Shropshire.

64 flap-dragon] raisin snatched from burning brandy and popped in the mouth, hence insignificant thing.

65 an] if.

66 Inns o' Court] residences of law students.

67 Shrewsbury cake] a flat cake associated with the chief market town in Shropshire.

68 call of serjeants] a group called to the bar at the same time.

I conjectured you were a fop since you began to change the style of your letters and write in a scrap of paper gilt round the edges no broader than a subpoena. I might expect this, when you left off 590 "honoured brother" and "hoping you are in good health," and so forth, to begin with a "Rat me, knight, I am so sick of last night's debauch," 'Od's heart, and then tell a familiar tale of a cock and a bull and a whore and a bottle and so conclude. You 595 could write news before you were out of your time,[69] when you lived with honest Pimple Nose the attorney of Furnival's Inn.[70] You could entreat to be remembered then to your friends round the Wrekin. We could have gazettes then, and *Dawks's* 600 *Letter*,[71] and the weekly bill,[72] till of late days.

PETULANT. 'Slife, Witwoud, were you ever an attorney's clerk? Of the family of the Furnivals? Ha, ha, ha.

WITWOUD. Aye, aye, but that was for a while. Not 605 long, not long. Pshaw, I was not in my own power then. An orphan, and this fellow was my guardian. Aye, aye, I was glad to consent to that man to come to London. He had the disposal of me then. If I had not agreed to that, I might have been 610 bound prentice to a felt-maker in Shrewsbury. This fellow would have bound me to a maker of felts.

SIR WILFULL. 'Sheart, and better than to be bound to a maker of fops, where, I suppose, you have served your time, and now you may set up for 615 yourself.

MRS. MARWOOD. You intend to travel, sir, as I'm informed.

SIR WILFULL. Belike I may, madam. I may chance to sail upon the salt seas, if my mind hold. 620

PETULANT. And the wind serve.

SIR WILFULL. Serve or not serve, I shan't ask licence of you, sir, nor the weathercock your companion. I direct my discourse to the lady, sir.— 'Tis like my aunt may have told you, madam. Yes, 625 I have settled my concerns, I may say now, and

am minded to see foreign parts. If and how that the peace[73] holds, whereby, that is, taxes abate.

MRS. MARWOOD. I thought you had designed for France at all adventures. 630

SIR WILFULL. I can't tell that. 'Tis like I may, and 'tis like I may not. I am somewhat dainty in making a resolution, because when I make it, I keep it. I don't stand shilly-shally, then. If I say't, I'll do't. But I have thoughts to tarry a small matter 635 in Town, to learn somewhat of your lingo first before I cross the seas. I'd gladly have a spice of your French, as they say, whereby to hold discourse in foreign countries.

MRS. MARWOOD. Here is an academy in Town 640 for that use.

SIR WILFULL. There is? 'Tis like there may.

MRS. MARWOOD. No doubt you will return very much improved.

WITWOUD. Yes, refined, like a Dutch skipper from 645 a whale-fishing.

Enter Lady Wishfort and Fainall.

LADY WISHFORT. Nephew, you are welcome.

SIR WILFULL. Aunt, your servant.

FAINALL. Sir Wilfull, your most faithful servant.

SIR WILFULL. Cousin Fainall, give me your hand. 650

LADY WISHFORT. Cousin Witwoud, your servant. Mr. Petulant, your servant. Nephew, you are welcome again. Will you drink anything after your journey, Nephew, before you eat? Dinner's almost ready. 655

SIR WILFULL. I'm very well, I thank you, Aunt. However, I thank you for your courteous offer. 'Sheart, I was afraid you would have been in the fashion too and have remembered to have forgot your relations. Here's your cousin Tony. Belike I 660 mayn't call him brother for fear of offence.

LADY WISHFORT. Oh, he's a railer, Nephew. My cousin's a wit. And your wits always rally their best friends to choose. When you have been abroad, Nephew, you'll understand raillery better. 665

Fainall and Mrs. Marwood talk apart.

---

69 out of your time] while you were still clerking for a lawyer.
70 Furnival's Inn] associated with the major Inns of Court.
71 Dawks's Letter] a contemporary newspaper.
72 bill] weekly published list of births, deaths, etc.

---

73 peace] the Peace of Ryswick (1697), creating a lull in William III's wars with France.

SIR WILFULL. Why then, let him hold his tongue in the meantime and rail when that day comes.

Enter Mincing.

MINCING. Mem, I come to acquaint your la'ship that dinner is impatient.

SIR WILFULL. Impatient? Why then belike it won't 670 stay till I pull off my boots. Sweetheart, can you help me to a pair of slippers? My man's with his horses, I warrant.

LADY WISHFORT. Fie, fie, Nephew, you would not pull off your boots here. Go down into the 675 hall. Dinner shall stay for you.—My nephew's a little unbred; you'll pardon him, madam. Gentlemen will you walk? Marwood—

MRS. MARWOOD. I'll follow you, madam, before Sir Wilfull is ready. 680

[Exeunt all but] Mrs. Marwood and Fainall.

FAINALL. Why then, Foible's a bawd, an arrant, rank, match-making bawd. And I it seems am a husband, a rank husband, and my wife a very arrant, rank wife—all in the way of the world. 'Sdeath, to be an anticipated cuckold, a cuckold 685 in embryo! Sure I was born with budding antlers like a young satyr or a citizen's child.[74] 'Sdeath, to be outwitted, to be out-jilted, out-matrimonied. If I had kept my speed like a stag, 'twere somewhat, but to crawl after with my horns like a snail and 690 outstripped by my wife, 'tis scurvy wedlock.

MRS. MARWOOD. Then shake it off. You have often wished for an opportunity to part, and now you have it. But first, prevent their plot. The half of Millamant's fortune is too considerable to be 695 parted with to a foe, to Mirabell.

FAINALL. Damn him, that had been mine, had you not made that fond[75] discovery. That had been forfeited, had they been married. My wife had added luster to my horns by that increase of 700 fortune: I could have worn 'em tipped with gold, though my forehead had been furnished like a deputy-lieutenant's hall.

MRS. MARWOOD. They may prove a cap of maintenance[76] to you still, if you can away with 705 your wife. And she's no worse than when you had her. I dare swear she had given up her game before she was married.

FAINALL. Hum! That may be. She might throw up her cards, but I'll be hanged if she did not put 710 Pam[77] in her pocket.

MRS. MARWOOD. You married her to keep you, and if you can contrive to have her keep you better than you expected, why should you not keep her longer than you intended? 715

FAINALL. The means, the means?

MRS. MARWOOD. Discover to my lady your wife's conduct. Threaten to part with her. My lady loves her and will come to any composition to save her reputation. Take the opportunity of breaking it just 720 upon the discovery of this imposture. My lady will be enraged beyond bounds and sacrifice niece and fortune and all at that conjuncture. And let me alone to keep her warm. If she should flag in her part, I will not fail to prompt her. 725

FAINALL. Faith, this has an appearance.

MRS. MARWOOD. I'm sorry I hinted to my lady to endeavour a match between Millamant and Sir Wilfull. That may be an obstacle.

FAINALL. Oh for that matter, leave me to manage 730 him. I'll disable him for that; he will drink like a Dane. After dinner, I'll set his hand in.

MRS. MARWOOD. Well, how do you stand affected towards your lady?

FAINALL. Why faith, I'm thinking of it. Let me see. 735 I am married already, so that's over. My wife has played the jade with me. Well, that's over too. I never loved her, or if I had, why, that would have been over too by this time. Jealous of her I cannot be, for I am certain; so there's an end of jealousy. 740 Weary of her I am and shall be. No, there's no end of that; no, no, that were too much to hope. Thus far concerning my repose. Now for my reputation. As to my own, I married not for it, so that's out

---

74 citizen's child] Citizens or burghers were conventionally cuckolded by fine gentlemen or courtiers.

75 fond] foolish.

---

76 cap of maintenance] cap with two points like horns behind, featured in some families' coats of arms.

77 Pam] the Jack of Clubs, highest trumps in the game of loo.

of the question. And as to my part in my wife's, why, she had parted with hers before. So, bringing none to me, she can take none from me. 'Tis against all rule of play that I should lose to one who has not wherewithal to stake. 745

MRS. MARWOOD. Besides, you forget, marriage is honourable. 750

FAINALL. Hum! Faith, and that's well thought on. Marriage is honourable, as you say, and if so, wherefore should cuckoldom be a discredit, being derived from so honourable a root? 755

MRS. MARWOOD. Nay, I know not. If the root be honourable, why not the branches?

FAINALL. So, so, why this point's clear. Well, how do we proceed?

MRS. MARWOOD. I will contrive a letter which shall be delivered to my lady at the time when the rascal who is to act Sir Rowland is with her. It shall come as from an unknown hand, for the less I appear to know of the truth, the better I can play the incendiary. Besides, I would not have Foible provoked if I could help it, because, you know, she knows some passages. Nay, I expect all will come out, but let the mine be sprung first, and then I care not if I'm discovered. 760 765

FAINALL. If the worst come to the worst, I'll turn my wife to grass. I have already a deed of settlement of the best part of her estate, which I wheedled out of her, and that you shall partake at least. 770

MRS. MARWOOD. I hope you are convinced that I hate Mirabell. Now you'll be no more jealous. 775

FAINALL. Jealous, no, by this kiss. Let husbands be jealous, but let the lover still believe. Or if he doubt, let it be only to endear his pleasure and prepare the joy that follows when he proves his mistress true. But let husbands' doubts convert to endless jealousy, or if they have belief, let it corrupt to superstition and blind credulity. I am single and will herd no more with 'em. True, I wear the badge, but I'll disown the order. And since I take my leave of 'em, I care not if I leave 'em a common motto, to their common crest: 780 785

All husbands must or pain or shame endure;
The wise too jealous are, fools too secure.

Exeunt.

ACT IV. [SCENE CONTINUES.]

Enter Lady Wishfort and Foible.

LADY WISHFORT. Is Sir Rowland coming, say'st thou, Foible? And are things in order?

FOIBLE. Yes, madam. I have put wax lights in the sconces and placed the footmen in a row in the hall in their best liveries, with the coachman and postilion to fill up the equipage. 5

LADY WISHFORT. Have you pulvilled[78] the coachman and postilion that they may not stink of the stable when Sir Rowland comes by?

FOIBLE. Yes, madam. 10

LADY WISHFORT. And are the dancers and the music ready, that he may be entertained in all points with correspondence to his passion?

FOIBLE. All is ready, madam.

LADY WISHFORT. And—well—and how do I look, Foible? 15

FOIBLE. Most killing well, madam.

LADY WISHFORT. Well, and how shall I receive him? In what figure shall I give his heart the first impression? There is a great deal in the first impression. Shall I sit? No I won't sit. I'll walk. Aye, I'll walk from the door upon his entrance, and then turn full upon him. No, that will be too sudden. I'll lie—aye, I'll lie down. I'll receive him in my little dressing room: there's a couch. Yes, yes, I'll give the first impression on a couch. I won't lie neither but loll and lean upon one elbow with one foot a little dangling off, jogging in a thoughtful way. Yes. And then as soon as he appears, start, aye, start and be surprised, and rise to meet him in a pretty disorder. Yes. Oh, nothing is more alluring than a levee from a couch in some confusion. It shows the foot to advantage and furnishes with blushes and recomposing airs beyond comparison. Hark! There's a coach. 20 25 30 35

FOIBLE. 'Tis he, madam.

LADY WISHFORT. Oh dear, has my nephew made his addresses to Millamant? I ordered him.

FOIBLE. Sir Wilfull is set into drinking, madam, in the parlour. 40

---

78 pulvilled] to perfume with powder.

LADY WISHFORT. 'Od's my life, I'll send him to her. Call her down, Foible, bring her hither. I'll send him as I go. When they are together, then come to me, Foible, that I may not be too long alone with Sir Rowland. (*Exit.*) 45

Enter Mrs. Millamant and Mrs. Fainall.

FOIBLE. Madam, I stayed here to tell your ladyship that Mr. Mirabell has waited this half hour for an opportunity to talk with you, though my lady's orders were to leave you and Sir Wilfull together. Shall I tell Mr. Mirabell that you are at leisure? 50

MILLAMANT. No. What would the dear man have? I am thoughtful and would amuse myself. Bid him come another time. (*Repeating and walking about.*) "There never yet was woman made
Nor shall but to be cursed."[79] 55
That's hard!

MRS. FAINALL. You are very fond of Sir John Suckling today, Millamant, and the poets.

MILLAMANT. He? Aye, and filthy verses. So I am.

FOIBLE. Sir Wilfull is coming, madam. Shall I send 60
Mr. Mirabell away?

MILLAMANT. Aye, if you please, Foible, send him away, or send him hither. Just as you will, dear Foible. I think I'll see him. Shall I? Aye, let the wretch come. (*Repeating.*) 65
"Thyrsis a youth of the inspired train"—[80]
Dear Fainall, entertain Sir Wilfull. Thou hast philosophy to undergo a fool; thou art married and hast patience. I would confer with my own thoughts.

MRS. FAINALL. I am obliged to you that you 70
would make me your proxy in this affair, but I have business of my own.

Enter Sir Wilfull.

Oh Sir Wilfull, you are come at the critical instant. There's your mistress up to the ears in love and contemplation. Pursue your point, now or never. 75

SIR WILFULL. (*This while Millamant walks about repeating to herself.*) Yes, my aunt would have it so.

---

79 "There ... cursed"] the opening lines of a lyric by Sir John Suckling (1609–42).
80 "Thyrsis ... train"] opening line of "The Story of Phoebus and Daphne, Applied," by Edmund Waller (1606–87).

I would gladly have been encouraged with a bottle or two, because I'm somewhat wary at first before I am acquainted. But I hope after a time I shall break my mind, that is, upon further acquaintance. 80
So for the present, cousin, I'll take my leave. If so be you'll be so kind to make my excuse, I'll return to my company.

MRS. FAINALL. Oh fie, Sir Wilfull! What, you 85
must not be daunted.

SIR WILFULL. Daunted? No, that's not it; it is not so much for that, for if so be that I set on't, I'll do't. But only for the present. 'Tis sufficient till further acquaintance. That's all. Your servant. 90

MRS. FAINALL. Nay, I'll swear you shall never lose so favourable an opportunity, if I can help it. I'll leave you together and lock the door. (*Exit.*)

SIR WILFULL. Nay, nay, cousin, I have forgot my gloves. What d'ye do? 'Sheart, a has locked the 95
door indeed, I think. Nay, cousin Fainall, open the door. Pshaw, what a vixen trick is this? Nay, now a has seen me too.—Cousin, I made bold to pass through as it were. I think this door's enchanted.

MILLAMANT. (*Repeating.*) "I prithee spare me 100
gentle boy,
Press me no more for that slight toy."[81]

SIR WILFULL. Anon? Cousin, your servant.

MILLAMANT. "That foolish trifle of a heart."—Sir Wilfull!

SIR WILFULL. Yes, your servant. No offence I hope, 105
cousin.

MILLAMANT. (*Repeating.*) "I swear it will not do its part,
Though thou dost thine, employ'st thy power and art."
Natural, easy Suckling!

SIR WILFULL. Anon? Suckling! No such suckling 110
neither, cousin, nor stripling. I thank heaven, I'm no minor.

MILLAMANT. Ah rustic! Ruder than Gothic.

SIR WILFULL. Well, well, I shall understand your lingo one of these days, cousin. In the meanwhile, 115
I must answer in plain English.

MILLAMANT. Have you any business with me, Sir Wilfull?

---

81 "I ... toy"] Millamant continues to quote Suckling.

SIR WILFULL. Not at present, cousin. Yes, I made
bold to see, to come and know if that how you 120
were disposed to fetch a walk this evening. If so
be that I might not be troublesome, I would have
sought a walk with you.

MILLAMANT. A walk? What then?

SIR WILFULL. Nay, nothing. Only for the walk's 125
sake, that's all.

MILLAMANT. I nauseate walking. 'Tis a country
diversion. I loathe the country and everything that
relates to it.

SIR WILFULL. Indeed! Hah! Look ye, look ye, you 130
do? Nay, 'tis like you may. Here are choice of
pastimes here in Town, as plays and the like; that
must be confessed indeed.

MILLAMANT. Ah *l'etourdi*!82 I hate the Town too.

SIR WILFULL. Dear heart, that's much. Hah! That 135
you should hate 'em both! Hah! 'Tis like you may.
There are some can't relish the Town, and others
can't away with the country. 'Tis like you may be
one of those, cousin.

MILLAMANT. Ha, ha, ha. Yes, 'tis like I may. You 140
have nothing further to say to me?

SIR WILFULL. Not at present, cousin. 'Tis like
when I have an opportunity to be more private, I
may break my mind in some measure. I conjecture
you partly guess. However that's as time shall try, 145
but spare to speak and spare to speed, as they say.

MILLAMANT. If it is of no great importance, Sir
Wilfull, you will oblige me to leave me. I have just
now a little business.

SIR WILFULL. Enough, enough, cousin. Yes, yes, 150
all a case. When you're disposed, when you're
disposed. Now's as well as another time, and
another time as well as now. All's one for that. Yes,
yes, if your concerns call you, there's no haste. It
will keep cold as they say. Cousin, your servant. I 155
think this door's locked.

MILLAMANT. You may go this way, sir.

SIR WILFULL. Your servant, then. With your leave,
I'll return to my company. (*Exit.*)

MILLAMANT. Aye, aye, ha, ha, ha. 160
"Like Phoebus sung the no less am'rous boy"—

---

82 *l'etourdi*] scatterbrain.

Enter Mirabell.

MIRABELL. "Like Daphne she as lovely and as
coy."83
Do you lock your self up from me to make my
search more curious? Or is this pretty artifice
contrived to signify that here the chase must end 165
and my pursuit be crowned, for you can fly no
further.

MILLAMANT. Vanity! No. I'll fly and be followed
to the last moment, though I am upon the very
verge of matrimony. I expect you should solicit me 170
as much as if I were wavering at the grate of a
monastery with one foot over the threshold. I'll be
solicited to the very last, nay and afterwards.

MIRABELL. What, after the last?

MILLAMANT. Oh, I should think I was poor and 175
had nothing to bestow if I were reduced to an
inglorious ease and freed from the agreeable
fatigues of solicitation.

MIRABELL. But do not you know that, when
favours are conferred upon instant and tedious 180
solicitation, that they diminish in their value, and
that both the giver loses the grace and the receiver
lessens his pleasure?

MILLAMANT. It may be in things of common
application, but never sure in love. Oh, I hate a 185
lover that can dare to think he draws a moment's
air independent on the bounty of his mistress.
There is not so impudent thing in nature as the
saucy look of an assured man, confident of success.
The pedantic arrogance of a very84 husband has 190
not so pragmatical an air. Ah! I'll never marry
unless I am first made sure of my will and pleasure.

MIRABELL. Would you have 'em both before
marriage? Or will you be contented with the first
now and stay for the other till after grace?85 195

MILLAMANT. Ah, don't be impertinent.—My dear
liberty, shall I leave thee? My faithful solitude, my
darling contemplation, must I bid you then adieu?
Ay, adieu my morning thoughts, agreeable

---

83 Like Phoebus … coy] a couplet from Waller's "Story of
Phoebus and Daphne."

84 very] genuine, veritable.

85 grace] the prayer concluding the marriage ceremony.

wakings, indolent slumbers, all ye *douceurs*, ye *sommeils du matin*,[86] adieu. I can't do't. 'Tis more than impossible. Positively, Mirabell, I'll lie a bed in a morning as long as I please.

MIRABELL. Then I'll get up in a morning as early as I please.

MILLAMANT. Ah! Idle creature, get up when you will. And d'ye hear, I won't be called names after I'm married. Positively, I won't be called names.

MIRABELL. Names?

MILLAMANT. Aye, as wife, spouse, my dear, joy, jewel, love, sweetheart and the rest of that nauseous cant in which men and their wives are so fulsomely familiar. I shall never bear that. Good Mirabell, don't let us be familiar or fond nor kiss before folks, like my Lady Fadler[87] and Sir Francis, nor go to Hyde Park together the first Sunday in a new chariot to provoke eyes and whispers and then never to be seen there together again, as if we were proud of one another the first week and ashamed of one another forever after. Let us never visit together nor go to a play together, but let us be very strange and well bred. Let us be as strange as if we had been married a great while and as well bred as if we were not married at all.

MIRABELL. Have you any more conditions to offer? Hitherto your demands are pretty reasonable.

MILLAMANT. Trifles: as liberty to pay and receive visits to and from whom I please; to write and receive letters without interrogatories or wry faces on your part; to wear what I please and choose conversation with regard only to my own taste; to have no obligation upon me to converse with wits that I don't like because they are your acquaintance or to be intimate with fools because they may be your relations. Come to dinner when I please. Dine in my dressing room when I'm out of humour without giving a reason. To have my closet inviolate. To be sole empress of my tea table, which you must never presume to approach without first asking leave. And lastly, wherever I am, you shall always knock at the door before you come in. These articles subscribed, if I continue to endure you a little longer, I may by degrees dwindle into a wife.

MIRABELL. Your bill of fare is something advanced in this latter account. Well, have I liberty to offer conditions, that when you are dwindled into a wife, I may not be beyond measure enlarged into a husband?

MILLAMANT. You have free leave. Propose your utmost. Speak and spare not.

MIRABELL. I thank you. Imprimis, then, I covenant that your acquaintance be general; that you admit no sworn confidante or intimate of your own sex; no she friend to screen her affairs under your countenance and tempt you to make trial of a mutual secrecy. No decoy-duck to wheedle you a fop, scrambling to the play in a mask, then bring you home in a pretended fright, when you think you shall be found out, and rail at me for missing the play and disappointing the frolic which you had, to pick me up and prove my constancy.

MILLAMANT. Detestable imprimis! I go to the play in a mask!

MIRABELL. Item, I article that you continue to like your own face as long as I shall and, while it passes current with me, that you endeavor not to new coin it. To which end, together with all vizards for the day, I prohibit all masks for the night made of oiled skins and I know not what: hog's bones, hare's gall, pig water, and the marrow of a roasted cat. In short, I forbid all commerce with the gentlewoman in what-d'ye-call-it court. Item, I shut my doors against all bawds with baskets and pennyworths of muslin, china, fans, atlases,[88] etcetera. Item, when you shall be breeding—

MILLAMANT. Ah! Name it not.

MIRABELL. Which may be presumed, with a blessing on our endeavors—

MILLAMANT. Odious endeavors!

MIRABELL. I denounce against all strait-lacing, squeezing for a shape, till you mold my boy's head like a sugarloaf and, instead of a man-child, make me the father to a crooked billet. Lastly, to the dominion of the tea table I submit. But with proviso that you exceed not in your province but

---

86 *douceurs ... matin*] sweetnesses ... morning slumbers.
87 Fadler] To "faddle" is to fondle.

88 atlas] silk-satin manufactured in the Far East.

restrain yourself to native and simple tea-table drinks, as tea, chocolate, and coffee. As likewise to genuine and authorized tea-table talk, such as mending of fashions, spoiling reputations, railing at absent friends, and so forth, but that on no account you encroach upon the men's prerogative and presume to drink healths or toast fellows. For prevention of which, I banish all foreign forces, all auxiliaries to the tea table, as orange-brandy, all aniseed, cinnamon, citron, and Barbados-Waters, together with ratafia and the most noble spirit of clary.[89] But for cowslip-wine, poppy-water, and all dormatives,[90] those I allow. These provisos admitted, in other things I may prove a tractable and complying husband. 290 295 300

MILLAMANT. Oh horrid provisos! Filthy strong waters! I toast fellows, odious men! I hate your odious provisos.

MIRABELL. Then we're agreed. Shall I kiss your hand upon the contract? And here comes one to be a witness to the sealing of the deed. 305

Enter Mrs. Fainall.

MILLAMANT. Fainall, what shall I do? Shall I have him? I think I must have him.

MRS. FAINALL. Aye, aye, take him, take him. What should you do? 310

MILLAMANT. Well then. I'll take my death: I'm in a horrid fright. Fainall, I shall never say it. Well— I think—I'll endure you.

MRS. FAINALL. Fie, fie, have him, have him, and tell him so in plain terms, for I am sure you have a mind to him. 315

MILLAMANT. Are you? I think I have—and the horrid man looks as if he thought so too.—Well, you ridiculous thing you, I'll have you. I won't be kissed, nor I won't be thanked. Here, kiss my hand though. So, hold your tongue now, and don't say a word. 320

MRS. FAINALL. Mirabell, there's a necessity for your obedience. You have neither time to talk nor stay. My mother is coming and, in my conscience, if she should see you, would fall into fits and 325

maybe not recover time enough to return to Sir Rowland, who as Foible tells me is in a fair way to succeed. Therefore, spare your extasies for another occasion and slip down the back stairs, where Foible waits to consult you. 330

MILLAMANT. Aye, go, go. In the meantime, I suppose you have said something to please me.

MIRABELL. I am all obedience. (*Exit.*) 335

MRS. FAINALL. Yonder Sir Wilfull's drunk and so noisy that my mother has been forced to leave Sir Rowland to appease him, but he answers her only with singing and drinking. What they have done by this time, I know not. But Petulant and he were upon quarrelling as I came by. 340

MILLAMANT. Well, if Mirabell should not make a good husband, I am a lost thing, for I find I love him violently.

MRS. FAINALL. So it seems, when you mind not what's said to you. If you doubt him, you had best take up with Sir Wilfull. 345

MILLAMANT. How can you name that super-annuated lubber? Faugh!

Enter Witwoud from drinking.

MRS. FAINALL. So, is the fray made up, that you have left 'em? 350

WITWOUD. Left 'em? I could stay no longer. I have laughed like ten christenings—I am tipsy with laughing. If I had stayed any longer I should have burst; I must have been let out and pieced in the sides like an unsized camlet.[91] Yes, yes, the fray is composed. My lady came in like a nolle prosequi[92] and stopped their proceedings. 355

MILLAMANT. What was the dispute?

WITWOUD. That's the jest. There was no dispute. They could neither of 'em speak for rage and so fell a-sputtering at one another like two roasting apples. 360

Enter Petulant drunk.

---

89 orange-brandy … clary] strong fortified drinks.
90 dormatives] sleeping-draughts.

---

91 camlet] garment made from expensive Asian material such as Angora hair, silk and the like.
92 nolle prosequi] Latin legal phrase, "to be unwilling to pursue," signalling an end to the prosecution of a case.

Now Petulant, all's over, all's well. Gad, my head begins to whim it about. Why dost thou not speak? Thou art both as drunk and as mute as a fish. 365

PETULANT. Look you, Mrs. Millamant, if you can love me, dear nymph, say it, and that's the conclusion. Pass on or pass off. That's all. 370

WITWOUD. Thou hast uttered volumes, folios, in less than *decimo sexto*,[93] my dear Lacedae-monian.[94] Sirrah Petulant, thou art an epitomizer of words.

PETULANT. Witwoud, you are an annihilator of sense. 375

WITWOUD. Thou art a retailer of phrases and dost deal in remnants of remnants, like a maker of pincushions. Thou art in truth (metaphorically speaking) a speaker of shorthand. 380

PETULANT. Thou art (without a figure) just one half of an ass, and Baldwin[95] yonder, thy half-brother, is the rest. A gemini of asses split would make just four of you.

WITWOUD. Thou dost bite, my dear mustard seed. 385
Kiss me for that.

PETULANT. Stand off. I'll kiss no more males. I have kissed your twin yonder in a humour of reconciliation till he (*Hiccup.*) rises upon my stomach like a radish. 390

MILLAMANT. Eh! Filthy creature. What was the quarrel?

PETULANT. There was no quarrel. There might have been a quarrel.

WITWOUD. If there had been words enow between 395
'em to have expressed provocation, they had gone together by the ears like a pair of castanets.

PETULANT. You were the quarrel.

WITWOUD. Me?

PETULANT. If I had a humour to quarrel, I can 400
make less matters conclude premises. If you are not handsome, what then, if I have a humour to prove it? If I shall have my reward, say so; if not, fight for your face the next time yourself. I'll go sleep.

---

93 *decimo sexto*] a very small book, about 1/8 the size of a folio (a large book).

94 Lacedaemonian] Spartan, or, as here, laconic.

95 Baldwin] an ass in the beast epic, *Reynard the Fox.*

WITWOUD. Do, wrap thyself up like a wood louse 405
and dream revenge. And hear me, if thou canst learn to write by tomorrow morning, pen me a challenge. I'll carry it for thee.

PETULANT. Carry your mistress's monkey a spider. Go flay dogs and read romances. I'll go to bed to 410
my maid. (*Exit.*)

MRS. FAINALL. He's horridly drunk. How came you all in this pickle?

WITWOUD. A plot, a plot to get rid of the knight. Your husband's advice, but he sneaked off. 415

Enter Lady Wishfort and Sir Wilfull drunk.

LADY WISHFORT. Out upon't, out upon't, at years of discretion and comport yourself at this rantipole[96] rate.

SIR WILFULL. No offence, Aunt.

LADY WISHFORT. Offence? As I'm a person, I'm 420
ashamed of you. Faugh! How you stink of wine! D'ye think my niece will ever endure such a borachio?[97] You're an absolute borachio.

SIR WILFULL. Borachio?

LADY WISHFORT. At a time when you should 425
commence an amour and put your best foot foremost.

SIR WILFULL. 'Sheart, an you grudge me your liquor, make a bill. Give me more drink and take my purse. (*Sings.*) 430

    Prithee fill me the glass
    Till it laugh in my face,
With ale that is potent and mellow;
    He that whines for a lass
    Is an ignorant ass, 435
For a bumper has not its fellow.

But if you would have me marry my cousin, say the word, and I'll do't. Wilfull will do't, that's the word. Wilfull will do't, that's my crest. My motto I have forgot. 440

LADY WISHFORT. My nephew's a little overtaken, cousin. But 'tis with drinking your health. O'my word, you are obliged to him.

SIR WILFULL. In vino veritas, Aunt.—If I drunk your health today, cousin, I am a borachio. But if 445

---

96 rantipole] unmannerly.

97 borachio] drunkard.

you have a mind to be married, say the word and send for the piper: Wilfull will do't. If not, dust it away, and let's have t'other round.—Tony, 'Odd's heart, where's Tony? Tony's an honest fellow, but he spits after a bumper, and that's a fault. (*Sings.*) 450

We'll drink and we'll never have done, boys,
Put the glass then around with the sun, boys.
Let Apollo's example invite us;
For he's drunk every night,
And that makes him so bright, 455
That he's able next morning to light us.

The sun's a good pimple,[98] an honest soaker: he has a cellar at your antipodes. If I travel, Aunt, I touch at your[99] antipodes. Your antipodes are a good rascally sort of topsy-turvy fellows. If I had 460 a bumper, I'd stand upon my head and drink a health to 'em.—A match or no match, cousin with the hard name.—Aunt, Wilfull will do't. If she has her maidenhead, let her look to't. If she has not, let her keep her own counsel in the meantime and 465 cry out at the nine months' end.

MILLAMANT. Your pardon madam, I can stay no longer. Sir Wilfull grows very powerful. Egh! How he smells! I shall be overcome if I stay.—Come, cousin. 470

Exeunt Millamant and Mrs. Fainall.

LADY WISHFORT. Smells! He would poison a tallow chandler and his family. Beastly creature, I know not what to do with him. Travel, quotha. Aye travel, travel. Get thee gone, get thee but far enough, to the Saracens or the Tartars or the Turks, 475 for thou art not fit to live in a Christian commonwealth, thou beastly pagan.

SIR WILFULL. Turks, no. No Turks, Aunt. Your Turks are infidels and believe not in the grape. Your Mahometan, your Mussulman is a dry stinkard. 480 No offence, Aunt. My map says that your Turk is not so honest a man as your Christian. I cannot find by the map that your mufti is orthodox, whereby it is a plain case, that orthodox is a hard word, Aunt, and (*Hiccup.*) Greek for claret. (*Sings.*) 485

To drink is a Christian diversion,
Unknown to the Turk and the Persian:
    Let Mahometan fools
    Live by heathenish rules,
And be damned over teacups and coffee. 490
    But let British lads sing,
    Crown a health to the King,
And a fig for your sultan and sophy.[100]

Ah, Tony!

Enter Foible and whispers Lady Wishfort.

LADY WISHFORT. Sir Rowland impatient? Good 495 lack! What shall I do with this beastly tumbrel?— Go lie down and sleep, you sot, or, as I'm a person, I'll have you bastinadoed with broomsticks.—Call up the wenches.

Exit Foible.

SIR WILFULL. Ahey! Wenches, where are the 500 wenches?

LADY WISHFORT. Dear cousin Witwoud, get him away and you will bind me to you inviolably. I have an affair of moment that invades me with some precipitation. You will oblige me to all 505 futurity.

WITWOUD. Come, knight.—Pox on him, I don't know what to say to him.—Will you go to a cockmatch?

SIR WILFULL. With a wench, Tony? Is she a shake- 510 bag,[101] sirrah? Let me bite your cheek for that.

WITWOUD. Horrible! He has a breath like a bagpipe.—Aye, aye, come, will you march, my Salopian?[102]

SIR WILFULL. Lead on, little Tony. I'll follow thee, 515 my Anthony, my Tantony. Sirrah, thou shalt be my Tantony, and I'll be thy pig.[103]

And a fig for your sultan and sophy. (*Exit singing with Witwoud.*)

LADY WISHFORT. This will never do. It will never 520 make a match at least before he has been abroad.

---

[98] pimple] boon companion.
[99] your] the.

[100] sophy] the Shah, or Persian monarch.
[101] shake-bag] a large fowl.
[102] Salopian] person from Shropshire.
[103] Anthony … pig] St. Anthony was often depicted accompanied by a pig.

Enter Waitwell, disguised as Sir Rowland.

Dear Sir Rowland, I am confounded with confusion at the retrospection of my own rudeness. I have more pardons to ask than the Pope distributes in the year of jubilee. But I hope where there is likely to be so near an alliance, we may unbend the severity of decorum and dispense with a little ceremony. 525

WAITWELL. My impatience, madam, is the effect of my transport, and till I have possession of your adorable person, I am tantalized on a rack and do but hang, madam, on the tenter of expectation. 530

LADY WISHFORT. You have excess of gallantry, Sir Rowland, and press things to a conclusion with the most prevailing vehemence. But a day or two for decency of marriage— 535

WAITWELL. For decency of funeral, madam. The delay will break my heart, or if that should fail, I shall be poisoned. My nephew will get an inkling of my designs and poison me, and I would willingly starve him before I die. I would gladly go out of the world with that satisfaction. That would be some comfort to me, if I could but live so long as to be revenged on that unnatural viper. 540

LADY WISHFORT. Is he so unnatural, say you? Truly, I would contribute much both to the saving of your life and the accomplishment of your revenge. Not that I respect myself, though he has been a perfidious wretch to me. 545

WAITWELL. Perfidious to you! 550

LADY WISHFORT. Oh Sir Rowland, the hours that he has died away at my feet, the tears that he has shed, the oaths that he has sworn, the palpitations that he has felt. The trances and the tremblings, the ardours and the extacies, the keelings and the risings, the heart-heavings and the hand-grippings, the pangs and the pathetic regards of his protesting eyes! Oh no memory can register. 555

WAITWELL. What, my rival? Is the rebel my rival? A dies. 560

LADY WISHFORT. No, don't kill him at once, Sir Rowland; starve him gradually inch by inch.

WAITWELL. I'll do't. In three weeks he shall be barefoot, in a month out at knees with begging an alms. He shall starve upward and upward, till he 565 has nothing living but his head and then go out in a stink like a candle's end upon a save-all.

LADY WISHFORT. Well Sir Rowland, you have the way. You are no novice in the labyrinth of love: you have the clue. But as I am a person, Sir 570 Rowland, you must not attribute my yielding to any sinister appetite or indigestion of widowhood nor impute my complacency to any lethargy of continence. I hope you do not think me prone to any iteration of nuptials. 575

WAITWELL. Far be it from me—

LADY WISHFORT. If you do, I protest I must recede—or think that I have made a prostitution of decorums, but in the vehemence of compassion and to save the life of a person of so much 580 importance.

WAITWELL. I esteem it so.

LADY WISHFORT. Or else you wrong my conde-scension—

WAITWELL. I do not, I do not— 585

LADY WISHFORT. Indeed you do.

WAITWELL. I do not, fair shrine of virtue.

LADY WISHFORT. If you think the least scruple of carnality was an ingredient—

WAITWELL. Dear madam, no. You are all cam- 590 phor[104] and frankincense, all chastity and odour.

LADY WISHFORT. Or that—

Enter Foible.

FOIBLE. Madam, the dancers are ready, and there's one with a letter, who must deliver it into your own hands. 595

LADY WISHFORT. Sir Rowland, will you give me leave? Think favourably, judge candidly, and conclude you have found a person who would suffer racks in honour's cause, dear Sir Rowland, and will wait on you incessantly. (*Exit.*) 600

WAITWELL. Fie, fie! What a slavery have I undergone. Spouse, hast thou any cordial? I want spirits.

FOIBLE. What a washy rogue art thou to pant thus for a quarter of an hour's lying and swearing to a 605 fine lady.

---

[104] camphor] distilled plant extract, thought to modify sexual desire.

WAITWELL. Oh, she is the antidote to desire. Spouse, thou wilt fare the worse for't. I shall have no appetite to iteration of nuptials this eight and forty hours. By this hand I had rather be a chairman[105] in the dog days than act Sir Rowland till this time tomorrow. 610

Enter Lady Wishfort with a letter.

LADY WISHFORT. Call in the dancers.—Sir Rowland, we'll sit if you please, and see the entertainment. 615

Dance.

Now with your permission, Sir Rowland, I will peruse my letter. I would open it in your presence, because I would not make you uneasy. If it should make you uneasy, I would burn it. Speak if it does. But you may see by the superscription it is like a woman's hand. 620

FOIBLE. [*Aside.*] By Heaven! Mrs. Marwood's. I know it. My heart aches. (*To Waitwell.*) Get it from her.

WAITWELL. A woman's hand? No madam, that's no woman's hand. I see that already. That's somebody whose throat must be cut. 625

LADY WISHFORT. Nay Sir Rowland, since you give me a proof of your passion by your jealousy, I'll promise you I'll make you a return by a frank communication. You shall see it. We'll open it together. Look you here. (*Reads.*) "Madam, though unknown to you"— Look you there, 'tis from nobody that I know. "I have that honour for your character, that I think myself obliged to let you know you are abused. He who pretends to be Sir Rowland is a cheat and a rascal"— Oh heavens! What's this? 630 635

FOIBLE. [*Aside.*] Unfortunate, all's ruined.

WAITWELL. How, how, let me see, let me see. (*Reading.*) "A rascal, and disguised and suborned for that imposture"— Oh villainy, oh villainy! "by the contrivance of"— 640

LADY WISHFORT. I shall faint, I shall die, I shall die, oh! 645

---

105 chairman] hireling who carries gentry through the streets on a portable chair.

FOIBLE. (*To Waitwell.*) Say 'tis your nephew's hand. Quickly, his plot, swear, swear it.

WAITWELL. Here's a villain! Madam, don't you perceive it, don't you see it?

LADY WISHFORT. Too well, too well. I have seen too much. 650

WAITWELL. I told you at first I knew the hand. A woman's hand? The rascal writes a sort of a large hand, your Roman[106] hand. I saw there was a throat to be cut presently. If he were my son as he is my nephew, I'd pistol him. 655

FOIBLE. Oh treachery! But are you sure, Sir Rowland, it is his writing?

WAITWELL. Sure? Am I here? Do I live? Do I love this pearl of India? I have twenty letters in my pocket from him in the same character. 660

LADY WISHFORT. How!

FOIBLE. Oh what luck it is, Sir Rowland, that you were present at this juncture! This was the business that brought Mr. Mirabell disguised to Madam Millamant this afternoon. I thought something was contriving when he stole by me and would have hid his face. 665

LADY WISHFORT. How, how! I heard the villain was in the house indeed, and now I remember, my niece went away abruptly when Sir Wilfull was to have made his addresses. 670

FOIBLE. Then, then madam, Mr. Mirabell waited for her in her chamber, but I would not tell your ladyship to discompose you when you were to receive Sir Rowland. 675

WAITWELL. Enough, his date is short.

FOIBLE. No, good Sir Rowland, don't incur the law.

WAITWELL. Law? I care not for law. I can but die, and 'tis in a good cause. My lady shall be satisfied of my truth and innocence, though it cost me my life. 680

LADY WISHFORT. No, dear Sir Rowland, don't fight. If you should be killed, I must never show my face—or hanged. Oh consider my reputation, Sir Rowland. No, you shan't fight. I'll go in and examine my niece. I'll make her confess. I conjure you, Sir Rowland, by all your love not to fight. 685

WAITWELL. I am charmed madam, I obey. But some proof you must let me give you. I'll go for a

---

106 Roman] round and bold.

black box, which contains the writings of my whole estate, and deliver that into your hands. 690

LADY WISHFORT. Aye, dear Sir Rowland, that will be some comfort. Bring the black box.

WAITWELL. And may I presume to bring a contract to be signed this night? May I hope so far? 695

LADY WISHFORT. Bring what you will but come alive, pray come alive. Oh this is a happy discovery.

WAITWELL. Dead or alive, I'll come, and married we will be in spite of treachery, aye, and get an heir 700 that shall defeat the last remaining glimpse of hope in my abandoned nephew. Come, my buxom widow.

Ere long you shall substantial proof receive

That I'm an errant knight— 705

FOIBLE. Or arrant knave.

Exeunt.

ACT V. SCENE CONTINUES.

Lady Wishfort and Foible.

LADY WISHFORT. Out of my house, out of my house, thou viper, thou serpent that I have fostered, thou bosom traitress that I raised from nothing. Be gone, be gone, be gone, go, go, that I took from washing of old gauze and weaving of 5 dead hair, with a bleak, blue nose, over a chafing dish of starved embers and dining behind a traverse rag in a shop no bigger than a bird cage. Go, go, starve again, do, do.

FOIBLE. Dear madam, I'll beg pardon on my knees. 10

LADY WISHFORT. Away, out, out, go set up for yourself again. Do, drive a trade, do, with your threepenny-worth of small ware, flaunting upon a packthread, under a brandy-seller's bulk,[107] or against a dead wall by a ballad-monger. Go hang 15 out an old frisoneer-gorget,[108] with a yard of yellow colberteen[109] again, do, an old gnawed mask, two rows of pins and a child's fiddle, a glass necklace with the beads broken, and a quilted

nightcap with one ear. Go, go, drive a trade: these 20 were your commodities, you treacherous trull, this was your merchandise you dealt in when I took you into my house, placed you next myself, and made you governante of my whole family. You have forgot this, have you? Now you have feathered 25 your nest.

FOIBLE. No, no, dear madam. Do but hear me, have but a moment's patience. I'll confess all. Mr. Mirabell seduced me. I am not the first that he has wheedled with his dissembling tongue. Your 30 ladyship's own wisdom has been deluded by him. Then how should I, a poor ignorant, defend myself? Oh madam, if you knew but what he promised me and how he assured me your Ladyship should come to no damage, or else the 35 wealth of the Indies should not have bribed me to conspire against so good, so sweet, so kind a lady as you have been to me.

LADY WISHFORT. No damage? What, to betray me, to marry me to a cast[110] serving man, to make 40 me a receptacle and hospital for a decayed pimp? No damage? Oh thou frontless impudence, more than a big-bellied actress.

FOIBLE. Pray, do but hear me, madam: he could not marry your ladyship, madam. No indeed, his 45 marriage was to have been void in law, for he was married to me first to secure your ladyship. He could not have bedded your ladyship, for if he had consummated with your ladyship, he must have run the risk of the law and been put upon his 50 clergy.[111] Yes indeed, I enquired of the law in that case before I would meddle or make.

LADY WISHFORT. What, then I have been your property, have I? I have been convenient to you it seems. While you were catering for Mirabell, I have 55 been broker for you? What, have you made a passive bawd of me? This exceeds all precedent. I am brought to fine uses, to become a botcher of second-hand marriages between Abigails and Andrews! I'll couple you. Yes, I'll baste you 60

---

107 bulk] stall.
108 frisoneer-gorget] woollen covering for the neck.
109 colberteen] cheap lace.

110 cast] discarded.
111 risk … clergy] risk of being potentially hanged for bigamy, from which he could escape through benefit of clergy.

together, you and your Philander. I'll Duke's Place you, as I'm a person. Your turtle is in custody already; you shall coo in the same cage, if there be constable or warrant in the parish. (*Exit.*)

FOIBLE. Oh that ever I was born. Oh that I was ever married. A bride, aye I shall be a Bridewell[112] bride. Oh! 65

Enter Mrs. Fainall.

MRS. FAINALL. Poor Foible, what's the matter?

FOIBLE. Oh madam, my lady's gone for a constable. I shall be had to a justice and put to Bridewell to beat hemp. Poor Waitwell's gone to prison already. 70

MRS. FAINALL. Have a good heart, Foible, Mirabell's gone to give security for him. This is all Marwood's and my husband's doing.

FOIBLE. Yes, yes, I know it madam. She was in my lady's closet and overheard all that you said to me before dinner. She sent the letter to my lady, and that missing effect, Mr. Fainall laid this plot to arrest Waitwell, when he pretended to go for the papers, and in the meantime, Mrs. Marwood declared all to my lady. 75 80

MRS. FAINALL. Was there no mention made of me in the letter? My mother does not suspect my being in the confederacy? I fancy Marwood has not told her, though she has told my husband. 85

FOIBLE. Yes madam, but my lady did not see that part: we stifled the letter before she read so far. Has that mischievous devil told Mr. Fainall of your ladyship then?

MRS. FAINALL. Aye, all's out: my affair with Mirabell, everything discovered. This is the last day of our living together, that's my comfort. 90

FOIBLE. Indeed madam, and so 'tis a comfort if you knew all. He has been even with your ladyship, which I could have told you long enough since, but I love to keep peace and quietness by my goodwill. I had rather bring friends together than set 'em at distance. But Mrs. Marwood and he are nearer related than ever their parents thought for. 95

MRS. FAINALL. Say'st thou so, Foible? Canst thou prove this? 100

FOIBLE. I can take my oath of it, madam. So can Mrs. Mincing. We have had many a fair word from Madam Marwood to conceal something that passed in our chamber one evening when you were at Hyde Park and we were thought to have gone a-walking. But we went up unawares, though we were sworn to secrecy too. Madam Marwood took a book and swore us upon it, but it was but a book of verses and poems. So long as it was not a Bible oath, we may break it with a safe conscience. 105 110

MRS. FAINALL. This discovery is the most opportune thing I could wish.—Now Mincing?

Enter Mincing.

MINCING. My lady would speak with Mrs. Foible, mem. Mr. Mirabell is with her. He has set your spouse at liberty, Mrs. Foible, and would have you hide yourself in my lady's closet, till my old lady's anger is abated. Oh, my old lady is in a perilous passion at something Mr. Fainall has said. He swears, and my old Lady cries. There's a fearful hurricane, I vow. He says, mem, how that he'll have my lady's fortune made over to him or he'll be divorced. 115 120

MRS. FAINALL. Does your lady and Mirabell know that? 125

MINCING. Yes mem, they have sent me to see if Sir Wilfull be sober and to bring him to them. My lady is resolved to have him, I think, rather than lose such a vast sum as six thousand pound.—Oh come, Mrs. Foible, I hear my old lady. 130

MRS. FAINALL. Foible, you must tell Mincing that she must prepare to vouch when I call her.

FOIBLE. Yes, yes madam.

MINCING. Oh yes, mem, I'll vouch anything for your ladyship's service, be what it will. 135

Exeunt Mincing and Foible. Enter Lady Wishfort and Marwood.

LADY WISHFORT. Oh my dear friend, how can I enumerate the benefits that I have received from your goodness? To you I owe the timely discovery of the false vows of Mirabell, to you the detection of the impostor Sir Rowland. And now you are become an intercessor with my son-in-law to save the honour of my house and compound for the 140

---

112 Bridewell] a London jail.

frailties of my daughter. Well friend, you are enough to reconcile me to the bad world, or else I would retire to deserts and solitudes and feed harmless sheep by groves and purling streams. Dear Marwood, let us leave the world and retire by ourselves and be shepherdesses.

MRS. MARWOOD. Let us first despatch the affair in hand, madam. We shall have leisure to think of retirement afterwards. Here is one who is concerned in the treaty.

LADY WISHFORT. Oh daughter, daughter, is it possible thou shouldst be my child, bone of my bone and flesh of my flesh, and as I may say, another me, and yet transgress the most minute particle of severe virtue? Is it possible you should lean aside to iniquity who have been cast in the direct mould of virtue? I have not only been a mould but a pattern for you and a model for you after you were brought into the world.

MRS. FAINALL. I don't understand your ladyship.

LADY WISHFORT. Not understand? Why, have you not been naught?[113] Have you not been sophisticated?[114] Not understand? Here I am ruined to compound for your caprices and your cuckoldoms. I must pawn my plate and my jewels and ruin my niece, and all little enough—

MRS. FAINALL. I am wronged and abused, and so are you. 'Tis a false accusation, as false as hell, as false as your friend there, aye, or your friend's friend, my false husband.

MRS. MARWOOD. My friend, Mrs. Fainall? Your husband my friend? What do you mean?

MRS. FAINALL. I know what I mean, madam, and so do you, and so shall the world at a time convenient.

MRS. MARWOOD. I am sorry to see you so passionate, madam. More temper would look more like innocence. But I have done.—I am sorry my zeal to serve your ladyship and family should admit of misconstruction or make me liable to affronts. You will pardon me, madam, if I meddle no more with an affair in which I am not personally concerned.

LADY WISHFORT. Oh dear friend, I am so ashamed that you should meet with such returns.—You ought to ask pardon on your knees, ungrateful creature: she deserves more from you than all your life can accomplish.—Oh don't leave me destitute in this perplexity. No, stick to me, my good genius.

MRS. FAINALL. I tell you, madam, you're abused. Stick to you? Aye, like a leech, to suck your best blood. She'll drop off when she's full. Madam, you shan't pawn a bodkin nor part with a brass counter in composition for me. I defy 'em all. Let 'em prove their aspersions. I know my own innocence and dare stand a trial. (*Exit.*)

LADY WISHFORT. Why, if she should be innocent, if she should be wronged after all, hah? I don't know what to think, and I promise you, her education has been unexceptionable. I may say it, for I chiefly made it my own care to initiate her very infancy in the rudiments of virtue and to impress upon her tender years a young odium and aversion to the very sight of men. Aye friend, she would ha' shrieked if she had but seen a man till she was in her teens. As I am a person, 'tis true. She was never suffered to play with a male child, though but in coats;[115] nay, her very babies[116] were of the feminine gender. Oh, she never looked a man in the face but her own father or the chaplain, and him we made a shift to put upon her for a woman by the help of his long garments and his sleek face till she was going in her fifteen.

MRS. MARWOOD. 'Twas much she should be deceived so long.

LADY WISHFORT. I warrant you, or she would never have borne to have been catechised by him and have heard his long lectures against singing and dancing and such debaucheries and going to filthy plays and profane music-meetings, where the lewd trebles squeak nothing but bawdy and the basses roar blasphemy. Oh, she would have swooned at the sight or name of an obscene playbook. And can I think after all this that my

---

113 naught] naughty.
114 sophisticated] false.

---

115 male ... coats] Boys were dressed in (petti)coats, not breeches.
116 babies] dolls.

daughter can be naught? What, a whore? And thought it excommunication to set her foot within the door of a playhouse. Oh my dear friend, I can't believe it. No, no, as she says, let him prove it, let him prove it. 230

MRS. MARWOOD. Prove it, madam? What, and have your name prostituted in a public court, yours and your daughter's reputation worried at the bar by a pack of bawling lawyers? To be ushered in by an oyez of scandal and have your case opened by an old fumbling lecher in a coif like a man midwife to bring your daughter's infamy to light, to be a theme for legal punsters and quibblers by the statute and become a jest, against a rule of court, where there is no precedent for a jest in any record, not even in Domesday Book. To discompose the gravity of the bench and provoke naughty interrogatories in more naughty law-Latin, while the good judge, tickled with the proceeding, simpers under a gray beard and fidges off and on his cushion as if he had swallowed cantharides,[117] or sat upon cow-itch.[118] 235 240 245

LADY WISHFORT. Oh, 'tis very hard. 250

MRS. MARWOOD. And then to have my young revellers of the Temple[119] take notes like prentices at a conventicle and, after, talk it all over again in commons or before drawers in an eating house.

LADY WISHFORT. Worse and worse. 255

MRS. MARWOOD. Nay, this is nothing; if it would end here, 'twere well. But it must after this be consigned by the shorthand writers to the public press and from thence be transferred to the hands, nay, into the throats and lungs of hawkers with voices more licentious than the loud flounder-man's or the woman that cries "gray peas." And this you must hear till you are stunned; nay, you must hear nothing else for some days. 260

LADY WISHFORT. Oh, 'tis insupportable. No, no, dear friend, make it up, make it up. Aye, aye, I'll compound. I'll give up all, myself and my all, my niece and her all—anything, everything for composition. 265

MRS. MARWOOD. Nay madam, I advise nothing. I only lay before you as a friend the inconveniencies which perhaps you have overseen. Here comes Mr. Fainall. If he will be satisfied to huddle up all in silence, I shall be glad. You must think I would rather congratulate than condole with you. 270 275

Enter Fainall.

LADY WISHFORT. Aye, aye, I do not doubt it, dear Marwood. No, no, I do not doubt it.

FAINALL. Well madam, I have suffered myself to be overcome by the importunity of this lady your friend and am content you shall enjoy your own proper estate during life, on condition you oblige yourself never to marry, under such penalty as I think convenient. 280

LADY WISHFORT. Never to marry?

FAINALL. No more Sir Rowlands. The next imposture may not be so timely detected. 285

MRS. MARWOOD. That condition, I dare answer, my lady will consent to without difficulty. She has already but too much experienced the perfidiousness of men. Besides, madam, when we retire to our pastoral solitude, we shall bid adieu to all other thoughts. 290

LADY WISHFORT. Aye, that's true, but in case of necessity, as of health or some such emergency—

FAINALL. Oh, if you are prescribed marriage, you shall be considered. I will only reserve to myself the power to choose for you. If your physic be wholesome, it matters not who is your apothecary. Next, my wife shall settle on me the remainder of her fortune not made over already and for her maintenance depend entirely on my discretion. 295 300

LADY WISHFORT. This is most inhumanly savage, exceeding the barbarity of a Muscovite husband.

FAINALL. I learned it from his Czarish majesty's retinue[120] in a winter evening's conference over brandy and pepper, amongst other secrets of matrimony and policy as they are at present practised in the northern hemisphere. But this must be agreed unto and that positively. Lastly, I will be endowed in right of my wife with that six 305 310

---

117 cantharides] taken as a diuretic.
118 cow-itch] stinging plant.
119 Temple] one of the Inns of Court, hence, law students.

120 Czarish … retinue] Peter the Great had visited London in the mid 1690s.

thousand pound which is the moiety of Mrs. Millamant's fortune in your possession and which she has forfeited (as will appear by the last will and testament of your deceased husband, Sir Jonathan Wishfort) by her disobedience in contracting herself against your consent or knowledge and by refusing the offered match with Sir Wilfull Witwoud, which you like a careful aunt had provided for her. 315

LADY WISHFORT. My nephew was *non compos*[121] and could not make his addresses. 320

FAINALL. I come to make demands. I'll hear no objections.

LADY WISHFORT. You will grant me time to consider. 325

FAINALL. Yes, while the instrument is drawing, to which you must set your hand till more sufficient deeds can be perfected, which I will take care shall be done with all possible speed. In the meanwhile, I will go for the said instrument, and till my return you may balance this matter in your own discretion. (*Exit.*) 330

LADY WISHFORT. This insolence is beyond all precedent, all parallel. Must I be subject to this merciless villain? 335

MRS. MARWOOD. 'Tis severe indeed, madam, that you should smart for your daughter's wantonness.

LADY WISHFORT. 'Twas against my consent that she married this barbarian, but she would have him, though her year[122] was not out. Ah! Her first husband, my son Languish, would not have carried it thus. Well, that was my choice; this is hers. She is matched now, with a witness. I shall be mad, dear friend. Is there no comfort for me? Must I live to be confiscated at this rebel-rate? Here come two more of my Egyptian plagues[123] too. 340 345

Enter Millamant and Sir Wilfull.

SIR WILFULL. Aunt, your servant.

LADY WISHFORT. Out caterpillar, call not me aunt. I know thee not. 350

WILFULL. I confess I have been a little in disguise[124] as they say. S'heart! And I am sorry for't. What would you have? I hope I committed no offence, Aunt, and if I did, I am willing to make satisfaction. And what can a man say fairer? If I have broke anything, I'll pay for't, an it cost a pound. And so let that content for what's past, and make no more words. For what's to come, to pleasure you I'm willing to marry my cousin. So pray, let's all be friends. She and I are agreed on the matter before a witness. 355 360

LADY WISHFORT. How's this, dear niece? Have I any comfort? Can this be true?

MILLAMANT. I am content to be a sacrifice to your repose, madam, and to convince you that I had no hand in the plot, as you were misinformed, I have laid my commands on Mirabell to come in person and be a witness that I give my hand to this flower of knighthood. And for the contract that passed between Mirabell and me, I have obliged him to make a resignation of it in your ladyship's presence. He is without and waits your leave for admittance. 365 370

LADY WISHFORT. Well, I'll swear I am something revived at this testimony of your obedience, but I cannot admit that traitor. I fear I cannot fortify myself to support his apprearance. He is as terrible to me as a Gorgon; if I see him, I fear I shall turn to stone, petrify incessantly.[125] 375

MILLAMANT. If you disoblige him, he may resent your refusal and insist upon the contract still. Then, 'tis the last time he will be offensive to you. 380

LADY WISHFORT. Are you sure it will be the last time? If I were sure of that—shall I never see him again? 385

MILLAMANT. Sir Wilfull, you and he are to travel together, are you not?

SIR WILFULL. 'Sheart, the gentleman's a civil gentleman. Aunt, let him come in. Why, we are sworn brothers and fellow travellers. We are to be 390

---

121 *non compos*] not in his right mind.
122 her year] conventional period of mourning after the death of a husband.
123 Egyptian plagues] those visited on Egypt by Moses (Exodus 7–11).

124 disguise] drunk.
125 incessantly] immediately.

Pylades and Orestes,[126] he and I; he is to be my interpreter in foreign parts. He has been overseas once already and, with proviso that I marry my cousin, will cross 'em once again only to bear me company. 'Sheart, I'll call him in. An I set on't once, he shall come in, and see who'll hinder him. (*Exit.*)

MRS. MARWOOD. [*Aside.*] This is precious fooling, if it would pass, but I'll know the bottom of it.

LADY WISHFORT. Oh dear Marwood, you are not going?

MRS. MARWOOD. Not far madam; I'll return immediately. (*Exit.*)

Reenter Sir Wilfull and Mirabell.

SIR WILFULL. Look up man, I'll stand by you; 'sbud, an she do frown, she can't kill you. Besides, hearkee, she dare not frown desperately, because her face is none of her own. 'Sheart, an she should, her forehead would wrinkle like the coat of a cream cheese, but mum for that, fellow traveller.

MIRABELL. If a deep sense of the many injuries I have offered to so good a lady, with a sincere remorse and a hearty contrition, can but obtain the least glance of compassion, I am too happy. Ah madam, there was a time—but let it be forgotten. I confess I have deservedly forfeited the high place I once held of sighing at your feet. Nay, kill me not by turning from me in disdain. I come not to plead for favour, nay not for pardon; I am a suppliant only for your pity. I am going where I never shall behold you more—

SIR WILFULL. How, fellow traveller! You shall go by yourself, then.

MIRABELL. Let me be pitied first and afterwards forgotten. I ask no more.

SIR WILFULL. By'r lady, a very reasonable request and will cost you nothing, Aunt. Come, come, forgive and forget, Aunt. Why, you must an you are a Christian.

MIRABELL. Consider madam, in reality you could not receive much prejudice. It was an innocent device; though I confess it had a face of guiltiness, it was at most an artifice which love contrived, and errors which love produces have ever been accounted venial. At least think it is punishment enough that I have lost what in my heart I hold most dear; that to your cruel indignation I have offered up this beauty and with her my peace and quiet, nay, all my hopes of future comfort.

SIR WILFULL. An he does not move me, would I might never be o'the quorum.[127] An it were not as good a deed as to drink to give her to him again, I would I might never take shipping. Aunt, if you don't forgive quickly, I shall melt, I can tell you that. My contract went no further than a little mouth glue, and that's hardly dry. One doleful sigh more from my fellow traveller and 'tis dissolved.

LADY WISHFORT. Well Nephew, upon your account—ah, he has a false insinuating tongue.— Well sir, I will stifle my just resentment at my nephew's request. I will endeavour what I can to forget but on proviso that you resign the contract with my niece immediately.

MIRABELL. It is in writing and with papers of concern, but I have sent my servant for it, and will deliver it to you with all acknowledgments for your transcendent goodness.

LADY WISHFORT. (*Apart.*) Oh, he has witchcraft in his eyes and tongue. When I did not see him, I could have bribed a villain to his assassination, but his appearance rakes the embers which have so long lain smothered in my breast.

Enter Fainall and Mrs. Marwood.

FAINALL. Your date of deliberation, madam, is expired. Here is the instrument. Are you prepared to sign?

LADY WISHFORT. If I were prepared, I am not empowered. My niece exerts a lawful claim, having matched herself by my direction to Sir Wilfull.

FAINALL. That sham is too gross to pass on me, though 'tis imposed on you, madam.

MILLAMANT. Sir, I have given my consent.

MIRABELL. And sir, I have resigned my pretensions.

---

126 Pylades and Orestes] classical emblem of friendship in foreign exile; see Aeschylus's *Oresteia*.

127 o'the quorum] a justice of the peace or county magistrate.

SIR WILFULL. And sir, I assert my right and will maintain it in defiance of you, sir, and of your instrument. S'heart, an you talk of an instrument, sir, I have an old fox by my thigh shall hack your instrument of ram vellum to shreds, sir. It shall not be sufficient for a mittimus[128] or a tailor's measure.[129] Therefore, withdraw your instrument, sir, or by'r lady, I shall draw mine. 475 480

LADY WISHFORT. Hold, Nephew, hold.

MILLAMANT. Good Sir Wilfull, respite your valour.

FAINALL. Indeed? Are you provided of a guard, with your single beefeater there? But I'm prepared for you and insist on my first proposal. You shall submit your own estate to my management and absolutely make over my wife's to my sole use, as pursuant to the purport and tenor of this other covenant.—I suppose, madam, your consent is not requisite in this case, nor, Mr. Mirabell, your resignation, nor, Sir Wilfull, your right. You may draw your fox if you please, sir, and make a Bear Garden[130] flourish somewhere else, for here it will not avail. This, my Lady Wishfort, must be subscribed, or your darling daughter's turned adrift like a leaky hulk to sink or swim as she and the current of this lewd Town can agree. 485 490 495

LADY WISHFORT. Is there no means, no remedy, to stop my ruin? Ungrateful wretch! Dost thou not owe thy being, thy subsistence to my daughter's fortune? 500

FAINALL. I'll answer you when I have the rest of it in my possession.

MIRABELL. But that you would not accept of a remedy from my hands—I own I have not deserved you should owe any obligation to me, or else perhaps I could advise— 505

LADY WISHFORT. Oh what? What? To save me and my child from ruin, from want, I'll forgive all that's past. Nay, I'll consent to anything to come, to be delivered from this tyranny. 510

MIRABELL. Aye madam, but that is too late: my reward is intercepted. You have disposed of her who only could have made me a compensation for all my services. But be it as it may, I am resolved I'll serve you. You shall not be wronged in this savage manner. 515

LADY WISHFORT. How! Dear Mr. Mirabell, can you be so generous at last? But it is not possible. Hearkee, I'll break my nephew's match: you shall have my niece yet and all her fortune, if you can but save me from this imminent danger. 520

MIRABELL. Will you? I take you at your word. I ask no more. I must have leave for two criminals to appear. 525

LADY WISHFORT. Aye, aye, anybody, anybody.

MIRABELL. Foible is one, and a penitent.

Enter Mrs. Fainall, Foible, and Mincing. Mirabell and Lady Wishfort go to Mrs. Fainall and Foible.

MRS. MARWOOD. (*To Fainall.*) Oh my shame! These corrupt things are bought and brought hither to expose me. 530

FAINALL. If it must all come out, why, let 'em know it. 'Tis but the way of the world. That shall not urge me to relinquish or abate one tittle of my terms. No, I will insist the more.

FOIBLE. Yes indeed madam, I'll take my Bible oath of it. 535

MINCING. And so will I, mem.

LADY WISHFORT. Oh Marwood, Marwood, art thou false? My friend deceive me? Hast thou been a wicked accomplice with that profligate man? 540

MRS. MARWOOD. Have you so much ingratitude and injustice to give credit against your friend to the aspersions of two such mercenary trulls?

MINCING. Mercenary, mem? I scorn your words. 'Tis true we found you and Mr. Fainall in the blue garret. By the same token, you swore us to secrecy upon Messalina's poems. Mercenary? No, if we would have been mercenary, we should have held our tongues. You would have bribed us sufficiently. 545 550

FAINALL. Go, you are an insignificant thing. Well, what are you the better for this? Is this Mr. Mirabell's expedient? I'll be put off no longer. You thing that was a wife shall smart for this. I will not

---

128 mittimus] legal document, writ.

129 tailor's measure] tape measure, often made from a strip of parchment.

130 Bear Garden] outdoor theatre housing the spectator sport of bear-baiting, here connoting cheap, sensational violence.

leave thee wherewithal to hide thy shame; your body shall be naked as your reputation. 555

MRS. FAINALL. I despise you and defy your malice. You have aspersed me wrongfully. I have proved your falsehood. Go you and your treacherous—I will not name it—but starve together, perish. 560

FAINALL. Not while you are worth a groat, indeed, my dear.—Madam, I'll be fooled no longer.

LADY WISHFORT. Ah Mr. Mirabell, this is small comfort, the detection of this affair.

MIRABELL. Oh in good time. Your leave for the 565 other offender and penitent to appear, madam.

Enter Waitwell with a box of writings.

LADY WISHFORT. Oh Sir Rowland—Well, rascal?

WAITWELL. What your ladyship pleases. I have brought the black box at last, madam.

MIRABELL. Give it me.—Madam, you remember 570 your promise?

LADY WISHFORT. Aye, dear sir!

MIRABELL. Where are the gentlemen?

WAITWELL. At hand, sir, rubbing their eyes, just risen from sleep. 575

FAINALL. S'death, what's this to me? I'll not wait your private concerns.

Enter Petulant and Witwoud.

PETULANT. How now? What's the matter? Whose hand's out?

WITWOUD. Hey day! What, are you all got 580 together like players at the end of the last act?

MIRABELL. You may remember, gentlemen, I once requested your hands as witnesses to a certain parchment.

WITWOUD. Aye, I do, my hand I remember. 585 Petulant set his mark.

MIRABELL. You wrong him; his name is fairly written, as shall appear. (*Undoing the box.*) You do not remember, gentlemen, anything of what that parchment contained? 590

WITWOUD. No.

PETULANT. Not I. I writ. I read nothing.

MIRABELL. Very well, now you shall know.— Madam, your promise.

LADY WISHFORT. Aye, aye, sir, upon my honour. 595

MIRABELL. Mr. Fainall, it is now time that you should know that your lady, while she was at her own disposal and before you had by your insinuations wheedled her out of a pretended settlement of the greatest part of her fortune— 600

FAINALL. Sir! Pretended?

MIRABELL. Yes sir. I say that this lady, while a widow, having, it seems, received some cautions respecting your inconstancy and tyranny of temper, which from her own partial opinion and fondness of you 605 she could never have suspected, she did, I say, by the wholesome advice of friends and of sages learned in the laws of this land, deliver this same as her act and deed to me in trust and to the uses within mentioned. (*Holding out the parchment.*) You may read if 610 you please, though perhaps what is inscribed on the back may serve your occasions.

FAINALL. Very likely sir. What's here? Damnation! (*Reads.*) "A deed of conveyance of the whole estate real of Arabella Languish, widow, in trust to 615 Edward Mirabell." Confusion!

MIRABELL. Even so, sir, 'tis the way of the world, sir, of the widows of the world. I suppose this deed may bear an elder date than what you have obtained from your lady. 620

FAINALL. Perfidious fiend! Then thus I'll be revenged— (*Offers to run at Mrs. Fainall.*)

SIR WILFULL. Hold sir. Now you may make your Bear Garden flourish somewhere else, sir.

FAINALL. Mirabell, you shall hear of this, sir, be 625 sure you shall.—Let me pass, oaf. (*Exit.*)

MRS. FAINALL. Madam, you seem to stifle your resentment. You had better give it vent.

MRS. MARWOOD. Yes, it shall have vent—and to your confusion, or I'll perish in the attempt. (*Exit.*) 630

LADY WISHFORT. Oh daughter, daughter, 'tis plain thou hast inherited thy mother's prudence.

MRS. FAINALL. Thank Mr. Mirabell, a cautious friend, to whose advice all is owing.

LADY WISHFORT. Well Mr. Mirabell, you have 635 kept your promise, and I must perform mine. First, I pardon for your sake Sir Rowland there and Foible. The next thing is to break the matter to my nephew. And how to do that—

MIRABELL. For that, madam, give yourself no 640 trouble. Let me have your consent. Sir Wilfull is my friend; he has had compassion upon lovers and generously engaged a volunteer in this action for our service and now designs to prosecute his travels.

SIR WILFULL. S'heart, Aunt, I have no mind to marry. My cousin's a fine lady, and the gentleman loves her and she loves him, and they deserve one another. My resolution is to see foreign parts. I have set on't, and when I'm set on't, I must do't. And if these two gentlemen would travel too, I think they may be spared.

PETULANT. For my part, I say little. I think things are best off or on.

WITWOUD. Egad, I understand nothing of the matter. I'm in a maze yet, like a dog in a dancing school.

LADY WISHFORT. Well sir, take her, and with her all the joy I can give you.

MILLAMANT. Why does not the man take me? Would you have me give myself to you over again?

MIRABELL. (*Kisses her hand.*) Aye, and over and over again, for I would have you as often as possibly I can. Well, Heaven grant I love you not too well; that's all my fear.

SIR WILFULL. S'heart, you'll have him time enough to toy after you're married, or if you will, toy now. Let us have a dance in the meantime, that we who are not lovers may have some other employment besides looking on.

MIRABELL. With all my heart, dear Sir Wilfull. What shall we do for music?

FOIBLE. Oh sir, some that were provided for Sir Rowland's entertainment are yet within call.

A dance.

LADY WISHFORT. As I am a person, I can hold out no longer. I have wasted my spirits so today already, that I am ready to sink under the fatigue, and I cannot but have some fears upon me yet that my son Fainall will pursue some desperate course.

MIRABELL. Madam, disquiet not yourself on that account. To my knowledge his circumstances are such he must of force comply. For my part, I will contribute all that in me lies to a reunion. (*To Mrs. Fainall.*) In the meantime, madam, let me before these witnesses restore to you this deed of trust. It may be a means, well managed, to make you live easily together.

From hence let those be warned who mean to
    wed,
Lest mutual falsehood stain the bridal bed,
For each deceiver to his cost may find
That marriage frauds too oft are paid in kind.

Exeunt omnes.

FINIS.

SUSANNAH CENTLIVRE

A Bold Stroke for a Wife[1]

Edited and introduced by Nancy Copeland[2]

S usannah Centlivre (1669?–1723) was one of the most important English comic playwrights of the first half of the eighteenth century. She was also the most successful female dramatist in London between 1660 and 1800, in terms of the number of her plays that were produced and the number of years some of them, including *A Bold Stroke for a Wife*, remained in the repertoire. *A Bold Stroke* typifies her comic style in its combination of an intricate love intrigue, humourous comedy (in the characterization of the guardians), and the outrageous situations and physical comedy of farce. In its emphasis on action and situation rather than wit, its mild satire, and the honest, straightforward relationship of its lovers, it exemplifies the kind of play that Shirley Strum Kenney terms "humane comedy."

First performed on February 3, 1718 at Lincoln's Inn Fields, *A Bold Stroke* was well suited to the resources of the company, which featured established comic performers such as William Bullock (Tradelove) and George Pack (Prim). Fainwell was a vehicle for Christopher Bullock (William's son), who was also co-manager of the theatre during this season, while his wife, Jane, played Anne Lovely. Some of the play's features recall the harlequinades that were then a mainstay of the company's repertoire. Such entertainments, not yet called pantomimes, are particularly evoked by the play's fairy-tale plot, by the centrality of transformation, and by some of the more extravagant farce, notably in the scene in Act III in which Fainwell convinces Periwinkle that he can make himself invisible by sinking through the stage's trapdoor.

The play portrays the mercantile culture of early Georgian London, most explicitly in the scene inside Jonathan's Coffee-house (IV.i), but also through its characters. The guardians represent a range of propertied urban types, and Fainwell's plotting is well suited to his capitalist milieu. Like a tradesman who suits his manner to his customers, Fainwell adopts characters that flatter the prejudices of each of the guardians to get the better of them in a bargain for Anne Lovely, a bargain that is confirmed by a written contract. Anne's position within these transactions is that of a commodity, coveted by Fainwell and traded by her guardians. Her largely passive role is characteristic of the developing position of the genteel middle-class woman within capitalism, and she struggles against the Prims

---

[1] The copytext is the 1718 duodecimo, which exists in two states, with a copy in the British Library containing three press variants. This issue is designated D1a, the others D1b. When all three copies of the first edition agree, they are referred to as D1. There was another duodecimo edition (D2) in 1724, of doubtful authority. Also consulted are modern editions by Stathis (1968) and Rogers (1994).

[2] The text and annotations are based on Copeland's edition as published in J. Douglas Canfield's *Broadview Anthology of Restoration and Early Eighteenth-Century Drama* (2001), with some additional notes of my own. [J.W.]

to exercise her right to be an idle consumer of luxury goods. The guardians too, despite their differences, all participate in the pervasive commercial culture, either as producers or consumers.

Centlivre was unequivocally Whig in her politics, and *A Bold Stroke* is permeated by Whig principles. The play constructs an implicit, Whiggish argument that the propertied interests represented by the guardians, both "trading" and "landed," should cooperate with one another and unite behind the army through supporting Colonel Fainwell, one of Centlivre's many soldier heroes. The concept of liberty, fundamental to Whig ideology, connects Centlivre's political views to her feminism: Anne Lovely, for example, speaks of the "tyranny" of her guardians in the language of political liberty.

The play was successful from its first production and became one of Centlivre's most-performed plays. Thanks to the opportunities Fainwell offers to the virtuoso comic actor, the play continued to be frequently performed throughout the eighteenth century and well into the nineteenth.

SUSANNAH CENTLIVRE
A Bold Stroke for a Wife

DRAMATIS PERSONAE

MEN

SIR PHILIP MODELOVE, an old beau.

PERIWINKLE, a kind of a silly virtuoso.[1]

TRADELOVE, a changebroker.[2]

OBADIAH PRIM, a Quaker.

COLONEL FAINWELL, in love with Mrs.[3] Lovely.

FREEMAN, his friend, a merchant.

SIMON PURE, a Quaking preacher.

MR. SACKBUT,[4] a tavern-keeper.

WOMEN

MRS. LOVELY, a fortune of thirty thousand pound.

MRS. PRIM, wife to Prim the hosier.[5]

BETTY, servant to Mrs. Lovely.

FOOTMEN, DRAWERS, ETC.

A BOLD STROKE FOR A WIFE.

Omnia vincit amor.[6]

ACT I, SCENE I. A TAVERN.

Colonel Fainwell and Freeman over a bottle.

FREEMAN. Come, Colonel, His Majesty's health. You are as melancholy as if you were in love; I wish some of the beauties at Bath[7] ha'n't snapped your heart.

---

[1] virtuoso] a collector of antiquities and natural curiosities.

[2] changebroker] an exchange broker, a middleman in the exchange of bills of credit.

[3] Mrs.] pronounced "Mistress," and used by married and unmarried women alike.

[4] Sackbut] a compound: sack, white wine imported from Spain or the Canary Islands; butt, a wine cask.

[5] hosier] a dealer in stockings and knitted underclothes.

[6] *Omnia … amor.*] Virgil, *Eclogues* X: Love conquers all (Lat.).

[7] Bath] In the eighteenth century Bath, with its medicinal springs and baths, became a fashionable summer resort for the titled and the wealthy.

COLONEL. Why, faith, Freeman, there is something in't; I have seen a lady at Bath who has kindled such a flame in me that all the waters there can't quench.

FREEMAN. Women, like some poisonous animals, carry their antidote about 'em. Is she not to be had, Colonel?

COLONEL. That's a difficult question to answer; however, I resolve to try. Perhaps you may be able to serve me; you merchants know one another. The lady told me herself she was under the charge of four persons.

FREEMAN. Odso! 'Tis Mrs. Anne Lovely.

COLONEL. The same. Do you know her?

FREEMAN. Know her! Aye—Faith, Colonel, your condition is more desperate than you imagine; why she is the talk and pity of the whole town; and it is the opinion of the learned that she must die a maid.

COLONEL. Say you so? That's somewhat odd, in this charitable city. She's a woman, I hope.

FREEMAN. For aught I know; but it had been as well for her had nature made her any other part of the creation. The man which keeps this house served her father; he is a very honest fellow and may be of use to you; we'll send for him to take a glass with us; he'll give you the whole history, and 'tis worth your hearing.

COLONEL. But may one trust him?

FREEMAN. With your life; I have obligations enough upon him to make him do anything; I serve him with wine. (*Knocks.*)

COLONEL. Nay, I know him pretty well myself; I once used to frequent a club that was kept here.

Enter drawer.

DRAWER. Gentlemen, d'you call?

FREEMAN. Aye, send up your master.

DRAWER. Yes, sir. (*Exit.*)

COLONEL. Do you know any of this lady's guardians, Freeman?

FREEMAN. Yes, I know two of them very well.

COLONEL. What are they?

Enter Sackbut.

FREEMAN. Here comes one will give you an account of them all.—Mr. Sackbut, we sent for you to take a glass with us. 'Tis a maxim among the friends of the bottle, that as long as the master is in company one may be sure of good wine.

SACKBUT. Sir, you shall be sure to have as good wine as you send in.—Colonel, your most humble servant; you are welcome to town.

COLONEL. I thank you, Mr. Sackbut.

SACKBUT. I am as glad to see you as I should a hundred tun of French claret custom-free. My service to you, sir. (*Drinks.*) You don't look so merry as you used to do. Are you not well, Colonel?

FREEMAN. He has got a woman in his head, landlord, can you help him?

SACKBUT. If 'tis in my power, I shan't scruple to serve my friend.

COLONEL. 'Tis one perquisite of your calling.

SACKBUT. Aye, at t'other end of the town,[8] where you officers use, women are good forcers of trade; a well-customed house, a handsome bar-keeper, with clean, obliging drawers, soon gets the master an estate; but our citizens[9] seldom do anything but cheat within the walls. But as to the lady, Colonel: Point you at particulars, or have you a good champagne[10] stomach? Are you in full pay or reduced, Colonel?

COLONEL. Reduced, reduced, landlord.

FREEMAN. To the miserable condition of a lover!

SACKBUT. Pish! That's preferable to half pay; a woman's resolution may break before the peace;[11] push her home, Colonel, there's no parleying with that sex.

---

8 t'other … town] the West End, the fashionable part of London, which Sackbut contrasts with the City, the old part of London proper, which housed the financial district. Women in West End establishments would draw in customers with the prospect of sex, to the profit of the tavern owners; city cheaters were not, according to Sackbut, so enterprising.

9 citizens] used here as often in the derogatory sense of men of business.

10 champagne] probably in two senses: an open field and a military campaign.

11 the peace] The Peace of Utrecht (1713) led to officers being reduced to half pay; it was unpopular with many Whigs, including Centlivre.

COLONEL. Were the lady her own mistress, I have some reasons to believe I should soon command in chief. 80

FREEMAN. You know Mrs. Lovely, Mr. Sackbut.

SACKBUT. Know her! Aye, poor Nancy;[12] I have carried her to school many a frosty morning. Alas! If she's the woman, I pity you, Colonel. Her father, my old master, was the most whimsical, out-of-the-way tempered man I ever heard of, as you will guess by his last will and testament. This was his only child: I have heard him wish her dead a thousand times. 85

COLONEL. Why so? 90

SACKBUT. He hated posterity, you must know, and wished the world were to expire with himself. He used to swear if she had been a boy, he would have qualified him for the opera.[13]

FREEMAN. 'Tis a very unnatural resolution in a father. 95

SACKBUT. He died worth thirty thousand pounds, which he left to this daughter, provided she married with the consent of her guardians. But that she might be sure never to do so, he left her in the care of four men as opposite to each other as light and darkness. Each has his quarterly rule, and three months in a year she is obliged to be subject to each of their humours, and they are pretty different, I assure you. She is just come from Bath. 100 105

COLONEL. 'Twas there I saw her.

SACKBUT. Aye, sir, the last quarter was her beau-guardian's. She appears in all public places during his reign. 110

COLONEL. She visited a lady who boarded in the same house with me. I liked her person,[14] and found an opportunity to tell her so. She replied, she had no objection to mine; but if I could not reconcile contradictions, I must not think of her, for that she was condemned to the caprice of four persons who never yet agreed in any one thing, and she was obliged to please them all. 115

SACKBUT. 'Tis most true, sir; I'll give you a short description of the men and leave you to judge of the poor lady's condition. One is a kind of a virtuoso, a silly, half-witted fellow, but positive and surly; fond of nothing but what is antique and foreign, and wears his clothes of the fashion of the last century; dotes upon travellers and believes Sir John Mandeville[15] more than the Bible. 120 125

COLONEL. That must be a rare old fellow!

SACKBUT. Another is a changebroker; a fellow that will out-lie the devil for the advantage of stock and cheat his father that got him in a bargain. He is a great stickler for trade and hates everything that wears a sword. 130

FREEMAN. He is a great admirer of the Dutch management[16] and swears they understand trade better than any nation under the sun. 135

SACKBUT. The third is an old beau that has May in his fancy and dress, but December in his face and his heels; he admires nothing but new fashions, and those must be French; loves operas, balls, masquerades, and is always the most tawdry of the whole company on a birthday.[17] 140

COLONEL. These are pretty opposite to one another, truly! And the fourth, what is he, landlord?

SACKBUT. A very rigid Quaker, whose quarter begun this day. I saw Mrs. Lovely go in not above two hours ago. Sir Philip set her down. What think you now, Colonel, is not the poor lady to be pitied? 145

COLONEL. Aye, and rescued too, landlord.

FREEMAN. In my opinion, that's impossible. 150

COLONEL. There is nothing impossible to a lover. What would not a man attempt for a fine woman and thirty thousand pounds? Besides, my honour is at stake; I promised to deliver her—and she bade me win her and take her. 155

---

12 Nancy] diminutive of Anne.

13 qualified ... opera] castrated him, as were the *castrati* who sang male soprano roles in Italian opera.

14 person] appearance.

---

15 Sir John Mandeville] (fl. 1356) the ostensible author of a collection of travellers' tales, who by the eighteenth century was regarded as a great liar.

16 Dutch management] The Dutch provided the English with models for advanced trade and financial practices, including the national debt and the stock market.

17 birthday] that is, the monarch's birthday, to the party for which the gentry wore fancy new clothes.

SACKBUT. That's fair, faith.

FREEMAN. If it depended upon knight-errantry, I should not doubt your setting free the damsel; but to have avarice, impertinence, hypocrisy, and pride at once to deal with, requires more cunning than generally attends a man of honour. 160

COLONEL. My fancy tells me I shall come off with glory; I resolve to try, however.—Do you know all the guardians, Mr. Sackbut?

SACKBUT. Very well, sir, they all use my house. 165

COLONEL. And will you assist me, if occasion be?

SACKBUT. In everything I can, Colonel.

FREEMAN. I'll answer for him; and whatever I can serve you in, you may depend on. I know Mr. Periwinkle and Mr. Tradelove; the latter has a very great opinion of my interest abroad. I happened to have a letter from a correspondent two hours before the news arrived of the French king's death;[18] I communicated it to him; upon which he bought up all the stock he could, and what with that and some wagers he laid, he told me, he had got to the tune of five hundred pounds; so that I am much in his good graces. 170 175

COLONEL. I don't know but you may be of service to me, Freeman. 180

FREEMAN. If I can, command me, Colonel.

COLONEL. Is it not possible to find a suit of clothes ready-made at some of these sale shops,[19] fit to rig out a beau, think you, Mr. Sackbut?

SACKBUT. Oh, hang 'em. No, Colonel, they keep nothing ready-made that a gentleman would be seen in. But I can fit you with a suit of clothes, if you'd make a figure—velvet and gold brocade— they were pawned to me by a French Count, who had been stripped at play and wanted money to carry him home; he promised to send for them, but I have heard nothing from him. 185 190

FREEMAN. He has not fed upon frogs long enough yet to recover his loss! Ha, ha.

COLONEL. Ha, ha. Well, those clothes will do, Mr. Sackbut—though we must have three or four fellows in tawdry liveries; those can be procured, I hope. 195

FREEMAN. Egad, I have a brother come from the West Indies that can match you; and, for expedition sake, you shall have his servants; there's a black, a tawny-moor,[20] and a Frenchman; they don't speak one word of English, so can make no mistake. 200

COLONEL. Excellent. Egad, I shall look like an Indian prince. First I'll attack my beau-guardian. Where lives he? 205

SACKBUT. Faith, somewhere about St. James's; though to say in what street, I cannot; but any chairman[21] will tell you where Sir Philip Modelove lives. 210

FREEMAN. Oh! You'll find him in the Park[22] at eleven every day; at least I never passed through at that hour without seeing him there. But what do you intend? 215

COLONEL. To address him in his own way, and find what he designs to do with the lady.

FREEMAN. And what then?

COLONEL. Nay, that I can't tell, but I shall take my measures accordingly. 220

SACKBUT. Well, 'tis a mad undertaking, in my mind; but here's to your success, Colonel. (*Drinks.*)

COLONEL. 'Tis something out of the way, I confess; but Fortune may chance to smile, and I succeed. Come, landlord, let me see those clothes. Freeman, I shall expect you'll leave word with Mr. Sackbut where one may find you upon occasion; and send my equipage of India immediately, do you hear? 225

FREEMAN. Immediately. (*Exit.*) 230

COLONEL. Bold was the man who ventured first
    to sea,
But the first vent'ring lovers bolder were:

---

18 French king's death] Louis XIV died September 1, 1715; this prevented France from carrying out plans to support the Jacobite rebellion in England and was therefore good for trade.

19 sale shops] shops specializing in inferior, ready-made clothing.

20 tawny-moor] brown-skinned foreigner, originally referring to North Africans.

21 chairman] hireling who transported gentry through the streets on portable chairs.

22 park] St. James's, connected to the royal palace and a fashionable promenade.

The path of love's a dark and dangerous way,
Without a landmark, or one friendly star,
And he that runs the risk, deserves the fair. (*Exit.*) 235

SCENE II. PRIM'S HOUSE.

Enter Mrs. Lovely and her maid Betty.

BETTY. Bless me, madam! Why do you fret and tease yourself so? This is giving them the advantage with a witness.

MRS. LOVELY. Must I be condemned all my life to the preposterous humours of other people and pointed at by every boy in town? Oh! I could tear my flesh and curse the hour I was born. Is it not monstrously ridiculous that they should desire to impose their Quaking dress[23] upon me at these years? When I was a child, no matter what they made me wear; but now— 5 ... 10

BETTY. I would resolve against it, madam; I'd see 'em hanged before I'd put on the pinched[24] cap again.

MRS. LOVELY. Then I must never expect one moment's ease; she has rung such a peal in my ears already that I shan't have the right use of them this month. What can I do? 15

BETTY. What can you not do, if you will but give your mind to it? Marry, madam. 20

MRS. LOVELY. What! and have my fortune go to build churches and hospitals?

BETTY. Why, let it go. If the Colonel loves you, as he pretends, he'll marry you without a fortune, madam; and I assure you, a colonel's lady is no despicable thing; a colonel's post will maintain you like a gentlewoman, madam. 25

MRS. LOVELY. So you would advise me to give up my own fortune and throw myself upon the colonel's. 30

BETTY. I would advise you to make yourself easy, madam.

MRS. LOVELY. That's not the way, I am sure. No, no, girl, there are certain ingredients to be mingled with matrimony without which I may as well 35

change for the worse as for the better. When the woman has fortune enough to make the man happy, if he has either honour or good manners, he'll make her easy. Love makes but a slovenly figure in that house where poverty keeps the door. 40

BETTY. And so you resolve to die a maid, do you, madam?

MRS. LOVELY. Or have it in my power to make the man I love master of my fortune.

BETTY. Then you don't like the colonel so well as I thought you did, madam, or you would not take such a resolution. 45

MRS. LOVELY. It is because I do like him, Betty, that I take such a resolution.

BETTY. Why, do you expect, madam, the colonel can work miracles? Is it possible for him to marry you with the consent of all your guardians? 50

MRS. LOVELY. Or he must not marry me at all, and so I told him; and he did not seem displeased with the news. He promised to set me free, and I, on that condition, promised to make him master of that freedom. 55

BETTY. Well! I have read of enchanted castles, ladies delivered from the chains of magic, giants killed, and monsters overcome; so that I shall be the less surprised if the colonel should conjure you out of the power of your guardians. If he does, I am sure he deserves your fortune. 60

MRS. LOVELY. And shall have it, girl, if it were ten times as much. For I'll ingenuously confess to thee, that I do like the colonel above all men I ever saw. There's something so *jantée*[25] in a soldier, a kind of a je ne sais quoi air that makes 'em more agreeable than the rest of mankind. They command regard, as who should say, "We are your defenders, we preserve your beauties from the insults of rude, unpolished foes," and ought to be preferred before those lazy, indolent mortals, who, by dropping into their father's estate, set up their coaches and think to rattle themselves into our affections. 65 ... 70 ... 75

BETTY. Nay, madam, I confess that the army has engrossed all the prettiest fellows. A laced coat and feather have irresistible charms.

---

23 Quaking dress] the very plain, old-fashioned, and concealing style of dress worn by Quaker women.
24 pinched] pleated.

---

25 *jantée*] dashing (Fr.).

MRS. LOVELY. But the colonel has all the beauties of the mind, as well as person. Oh all ye powers that favour happy lovers, grant he may be mine! Thou God of Love, if thou be'st ought but name, assist my Fainwell. 80
Point all thy darts to aid my love's design,
And make his plots as prevalent as thine. 85

ACT II, SCENE I. THE PARK.

Enter Colonel finely dressed, three footmen after him.

COLONEL. So, now if I can but meet this beau. Egad, methinks I cut a smart figure, and have as much of the tawdry air as any Italian count or French marquis of 'em all. Sure I shall know this knight again.—Hah! Yonder he sits, making love[26] to a mask,[27] i'faith. I'll walk up the Mall,[28] and come down by him. (*Exit.*) 5

Scene draws and discovers[29] Sir Philip upon a bench with a woman, masked.

SIR PHILIP. Well, but, my dear, are you really constant to your keeper?[30]
WOMAN. Yes, really, sir.—Hey day! Who comes yonder? He cuts a mighty figure. 10
SIR PHILIP. Hah! A stranger, by his equipage keeping so close at his heels. He has the appearance of a man of quality. Positively French by his dancing air. 15
WOMAN. He crosses, as if he meant to sit down here.
SIR PHILIP. He has a mind to make love to thee, child.

Enter Colonel and seats himself upon the bench by Sir Philip.

WOMAN. It will be to no purpose if he does. 20
SIR PHILIP. Are you resolved to be cruel then?

---

26 making love] paying court, verbally.
27 mask] woman wearing a half-mask over the eyes, often a prostitute.
28 Mall] Pall Mall.
29 discovers] reveals.
30 keeper] financial supporter and lover.

COLONEL. You must be very cruel, indeed, if you can deny anything to so fine a gentleman, madam. (*Takes out his watch.*)
WOMAN. I never mind the outside of a man. 25
COLONEL. And I'm afraid thou art no judge of the inside.
SIR PHILIP. I am, positively, of your mind, sir. For creatures of her function seldom penetrate beyond the pocket. 30
WOMAN. (*Aside.*) Creatures of your composition have, indeed, generally more in their pockets than in their heads.
SIR PHILIP. Pray what says your watch? Mine is down. (*Pulling out his watch.*) 35
COLONEL. I want[31] thirty-six minutes of twelve, sir. (*Puts up his watch and takes out his snuffbox.*)
SIR PHILIP. May I presume, sir?
COLONEL. Sir, you honour me. (*Presenting the box.*) 40
SIR PHILIP. [*Aside.*] He speaks good English, though he must be a foreigner.—This snuff is extremely good and the box prodigious fine; the work is French, I presume, sir.
COLONEL. I bought it in Paris, sir. I do think the workman-ship pretty neat. 45
SIR PHILIP. Neat, 'tis exquisitely fine, sir; pray, sir, if I may take the liberty of inquiring—what country is so happy to claim the birth of the finest gentleman in the universe? France, I presume. 50
COLONEL. Then you don't think me an English-man?
SIR PHILIP. No, upon my soul don't I.
COLONEL. I am sorry for't.
SIR PHILIP. Impossible you should wish to be an Englishman. Pardon me, sir, this island could not produce a person of such alertness. 55
COLONEL. As this mirror shows you, sir. (*Puts up a pocket-glass to Sir Philip's face.*)
WOMAN. [*Aside.*] Coxcombs, I'm sick to hear 'em praise one another; one seldom gets anything by such animals, not even a dinner, unless one can dine upon soup and celery. (*Exit.*) 60
SIR PHILIP. Oh Ged, sir!—Will you leave us, madam? Ha, ha. 65

---

31 want] lack.

COLONEL. She fears 'twill be only losing time to stay here, ha, ha. I know not how to distinguish you, sir, but your mien and address speak you Right Honourable.[32]

SIR PHILIP. Thus great souls judge of others by themselves. I am only adorned with knighthood, that's all, I assure you, sir; my name is Sir Philip Modelove.

COLONEL. Of French extraction?

SIR PHILIP. My father was French.

COLONEL. One may plainly perceive it—there is a certain gaiety peculiar to my nation (for I will own myself a Frenchman), which distinguishes us everywhere. A person of your figure would be a vast addition to a coronet.

SIR PHILIP. I must own, I had the offer of a barony about five years ago,[33] but I abhorred the fatigue which must have attended it. I could never yet bring myself to join with either party.

COLONEL. You are perfectly in the right, Sir Philip. A fine person should not embark himself in the slovenly concern of politics; dress and pleasure are objects proper for the soul of a fine gentleman.

SIR PHILIP. And love—

COLONEL. Oh! That's included under the article of pleasure.

SIR PHILIP. *Parbleu, il est un homme d'esprit.*[34]—I must embrace you. (*Rises and embraces.*) Your sentiments are so agreeable to mine that we appear to have but one soul, for our ideas and conceptions are the same.

COLONEL. (*Aside.*) I should be sorry for that.— You do me too much honour, Sir Philip.

SIR PHILIP. Your vivacity and *jantée* mien assured me at first sight there was nothing of this foggy island in your composition. May I crave your name, sir?

COLONEL. My name is La Fainwell, sir, at your service.

SIR PHILIP. The La Fainwells are French, I know; though the name is become very numerous in Great Britain of late years. I was sure you was French the moment I laid my eyes upon you; I could not come into the supposition of your being an Englishman; this island produces few such ornaments.

COLONEL. Pardon me, Sir Philip, this island has two things superior to all nations under the sun.

SIR PHILIP. Aye! What are they?

COLONEL. The ladies and the laws.

SIR PHILIP. The laws indeed do claim a preference of other nations, but by my soul there are fine women everywhere. I must own I have felt their power in all countries.

COLONEL. There are some finished beauties, I confess, in France, Italy, Germany, nay, even in Holland; *mais sont bien rares.*[35] But *les belles Anglaises!*[36] Oh, Sir Philip, where find we such women! such symmetry of shape! such elegancy of dress! such regularity of features! such sweetness of temper! such commanding eyes! and such bewitching smiles?

SIR PHILIP. Ah! *Parbleu, vous êtes attrapé.*[37]

COLONEL. *Non, je vous assure, chevalier*[38]—but I declare there is no amusement so agreeable to my *goût*,[39] as the conversation of a fine woman. I could never be prevailed upon to enter into what the vulgar calls the pleasure of the bottle.

SIR PHILIP. My own taste, *positivement*. A ball or a masquerade is certainly preferable to all the productions of the vineyard.

COLONEL. Infinitely! I hope the people of quality in England will support that branch of pleasure which was imported with their peace[40] and since naturalized by the ingenious Mr. Heidegger.[41]

---

32 Right Honorable] i.e., a member of the nobility.

33 offer ... ago] a reference to Queen Anne's creation of twelve new Tory peers in 1712 to ensure that the Treaty of Utrecht would pass the House of Lords.

34 *Parbleu ... d'esprit*] Good Lord, he is a man of wit. (Fr.).

35 *mais ... rares*] but they are very rare (Fr.).

36 *les ... Anglaises*] the English beauties (Fr.).

37 *Parbleu ... attrapé*] Good Lord, you are caught (Fr.).

38 *Non ... chevalier*] No, I assure you, knight (Fr.).

39 *goût*] taste (Fr.).

40 branch ... peace] The French ambassador to England, the Duc D'Aumont, held some of the earliest masked balls in London in 1713, after the Peace of Utrecht.

41 Mr. Heidegger] John James ("Count") Heidegger (1659?–1749), the manager of the Haymarket Theater, who began presenting public masquerades there in 1717.

SIR PHILIP. The ladies assure me it will become part of the constitution, upon which I subscribed an hundred guineas. It will be of great service to the public, at least to the Company of Surgeons[42] and the City in general.

COLONEL. Ha, ha, it may help to ennoble the blood of the City.[43] Are you married, Sir Philip?

SIR PHILIP. No, nor do I believe I ever shall enter into that honourable state; I have an absolute tender for the whole sex.

COLONEL. (*Aside.*) That's more than they have for you I dare swear.

SIR PHILIP. And I have the honour to be very well with the ladies, I can assure you, sir, and I won't affront a million of fine women to make one happy.

COLONEL. Nay, marriage is really reducing a man's taste to a kind of half-pleasure, but then it carries the blessing of peace along with it; one goes to sleep without fear and wakes without pain.

SIR PHILIP. There is something of that in't; a wife is a very good dish for an English stomach, but gross feeding for nicer[44] palates, ha, ha, ha!

COLONEL. I find I was very much mistaken—I imagined you had been married to that young lady which I saw in the chariot with you this morning in Gracechurch Street.[45]

SIR PHILIP. Who, Nancy Lovely? I am a piece of a guardian to that lady, you must know; her father, I thank him, joined me with three of the most preposterous old fellows—that upon my soul I'm in pain for the poor girl—she must certainly lead apes,[46] as the saying is, ha, ha.

COLONEL. That's pity. Sir Philip, if the lady would give me leave, I would endeavor to avert that curse.

SIR PHILIP. As to the lady, she'd gladly be rid of us at any rate, I believe; but here's the mischief, he who marries Miss Lovely, must have the consent of us all four, or not a penny of her portion. For my part, I shall never approve of any but a man of figure, and the rest are not only averse to cleanliness, but have each a peculiar taste to gratify. For my part, I declare, I would prefer you to all men I ever saw—

COLONEL. And I her to all women—

SIR PHILIP. I assure you, Mr. Fainwell, I am for marrying her, for I hate the trouble of a guardian, especially among such wretches; but resolve never to agree to the choice of any one of them, and I fancy they'll be even with me, for they never came into any proposal of mine yet.

COLONEL. I wish I had your leave to try them, Sir Philip.

SIR PHILIP. With all my soul, sir, I can refuse a person of your appearance nothing.

COLONEL. Sir, I am infinitely obliged to you.

SIR PHILIP. But do you really like matrimony?

COLONEL. I believe I could with that lady, sir.

SIR PHILIP. The only point in which we differ— but you are master of so many qualifications that I can excuse one fault, for I must think it a fault in a fine gentleman; and that you are such, I'll give it under my hand.

COLONEL. I wish you'd give me your consent to marry Mrs. Lovely under your hand, Sir Philip.

SIR PHILIP. I'll do't, if you'll step into St. James's Coffee-house,[47] where we may have pen and ink. Though I can't forsee what advantage my consent will be to you without you could find a way to get the rest of the guardians'. But I'll introduce you, however; she is now at a Quaker's, where I carried her this morning, when you saw us in Gracechurch Street. I assure you she has an odd *ragoût* of guardians, as you will find when you hear the characters, which I'll endeavor to give you as we go along.— Hey! Pierre, Jacques, Renault—where

---

42 Company of Surgeons] the doctors' guild, the members of which will be paid for cures for venereal disease.

43 ennoble … City] Masquerades were condemned for promoting immorality and the indiscriminate mingling of classes (thanks to the leveling anonymity of masquerade costume which fostered sexual liaisons across class boundaries).

44 nicer] more discriminating.

45 Gracechurch Street] in the City, running from London Bridge and the Monument to Cornhill; nearby was the oldest Quaker meeting-house in London.

46 lead apes] proverbial: old maids lead apes in hell as punishment for not marrying while they could.

47 St. James's Coffee-house] on St. James's Street, a Whig establishment, patronized by Steele and Addison.

are you all, scoundrels? Order the chariot to St. James's Coffee-house.

COLONEL. *Le noir, le brun, le blanc—mortbleu, où sont ces coquins-là? Allons, monsieur le chevalier.*[48]

SIR PHILIP. Ah! *Pardonnez moi, monsieur.*   220

COLONEL. Not one step, upon my soul, Sir Philip.

SIR PHILIP. The best-bred man in Europe, positively.

Exeunt.

SCENE II. OBADIAH PRIM'S HOUSE.

Enter Mrs. Lovely followed by Mrs. Prim.

MRS. PRIM. Then thou[49] wilt not obey me; and thou dost really think those fal-lals[50] becometh thee?

MRS. LOVELY. I do, indeed.

MRS. PRIM. Now will I be judged by all sober people, if I don't look more like a modest woman   5
than thou dost, Anne.

MRS. LOVELY. More like a hypocrite, you mean, Mrs. Prim.

MRS. PRIM. Ah! Anne, Anne, that wicked Philip Modelove will undo thee. Satan so fills thy heart   10
with pride during the three months of his guardianship, that thou becomest a stumbling block to the upright.

MRS. LOVELY. Pray, who are they? Are the pinched cap and formal hood the emblems of sanctity?   15
Does your virtue consist in your dress, Mrs. Prim?

MRS. PRIM. It doth not consist in cut hair, spotted face,[51] and bare necks. Oh, the wickedness of this generation! The primitive women[52] knew not the abomination of hooped petticoats.   20

MRS. LOVELY. No, nor the abomination of cant neither. Don't tell me, Mrs. Prim, don't. I know you have as much pride, vanity, self-conceit, and ambition among you, couched under that formal habit and sanctified countenance, as the proudest   25
of us all; but the world begins to see your prudery.

MRS. PRIM. Prudery! What! Do they invent new words[53] as well as new fashions? Ah! Poor, fantastic age, I pity thee. Poor deluded Anne, which dost thou think most resemblest the saint and which   30
the sinner, thy dress or mine? Thy naked bosom allureth the eye of the bystander, encourageth the frailty of human nature, and corrupteth the soul with evil longings.

MRS. LOVELY. And pray who corrupted your son   35
Tobias with evil longings? Your maid Tabitha wore a handkerchief,[54] and yet he made the Saint a sinner.

MRS. PRIM. Well, well, spit thy malice. I confess Satan did buffet my son Tobias and my servant   40
Tabitha; the evil spirit was at that time too strong and they both became subject to its workings— not from any outward provocation—but from an inward call; he was not tainted with the rottenness of the fashions, nor did his eyes take in the   45
drunkenness of beauty.

MRS. LOVELY. No! That's plainly to be seen.

MRS. PRIM. Tabitha is one of the faithful, he fell not with a stranger.

MRS. LOVELY. So! Then you hold wenching no   50
crime, provided it be within the pale of your own tribe. You are an excellent casuist, truly.

Enter Obadiah Prim.

OBADIAH PRIM. Not stripped of thy vanity yet, Anne? Why dost not thou make her put it off, Sarah?   55

MRS. PRIM. She will not do it.

OBADIAH PRIM. Verily, thy naked breasts

---

48 *Le noir ... chevalier*] The black, the brown, the white— zounds, where are these rascals? Let us go, sir knight (Fr.).

49 thou] The use of "thee" and "thou" was one of the Quaker "public testimonies" of conversion; it was intended to reproduce biblical language and to eliminate one of the designations of rank, since inferiors were expected to use "you" to their superiors.

50 fal-lals] decorative items of dress, fripperies.

51 cut hair, spotted face] hair trimmed to frame the face, rather than being pulled straight back; face fashionably decorated with patches made of silk or velvet.

52 primitive women] women of the earliest Christian church.

53 Prudery ... new words] originally French; the first recorded English usage occurs in *The Tatler*, No. 126 (1709).

54 handkerchief] scarf draped around the neck to conceal the area above the breast.

troubleth my outward man; I pray thee hide 'em, Anne; put on a hand-kerchief, Anne Lovely.

MRS. LOVELY. I hate handkerchiefs when 'tis not cold weather, Mr. Prim. 60

MRS. PRIM. I have seen thee wear a handkerchief; nay, and a mask to boot, in the middle of July.

MRS. LOVELY. Aye, to keep the sun from scorching me. 65

OBADIAH PRIM. If thou couldst not bear the sunbeams, how dost thou think man should bear thy beams? Those breasts inflame desire; let them be hid, I say.

MRS. LOVELY. Let me be quiet, I say. Must I be 70 tormented thus forever? Sure no woman's condition ever equalled mine; foppery, folly, avarice, and hypocrisy are by turns my constant companions, and I must vary shapes as often as a player. I cannot think my father meant this tyranny! No; you 75 usurp an authority which he never intended you should take.

OBADIAH PRIM. Hark thee, dost thou call good counsel tyranny? Do I, or my wife, tyrannize when we desire thee in all love to put off thy tempting 80 attire and veil thy provokers to sin?

MRS. LOVELY. Deliver me, good Heaven! Or I shall go distracted. (*Walks about.*)

MRS. PRIM. So! Now thy pinners are tossed and thy breasts pulled up; verily they were seen enough 85 before; fie upon the filthy tailor who made them stays.

MRS. LOVELY. I wish I were in my grave! Kill me rather than treat me thus.

OBADIAH PRIM. Kill thee! Ha, ha; thou think'st 90 thou art acting some lewd play sure; kill thee! Art thou prepared for death, Anne Lovely? No, no, thou wouldst rather have a husband, Anne. Thou wantest a gilt coach with six lazy fellows behind to flaunt it in the ring of vanity among the princes 95 and rulers of the land, who pamper themselves with the fatness thereof; but I will take care that none shall squander away thy father's estate; thou shalt marry none such, Anne.

MRS. LOVELY. Would you marry me to one of your 100 own canting sect?

OBADIAH PRIM. Yea, verily, none else shall ever get my consent, I do assure thee, Anne.

MRS. LOVELY. And I do assure thee, Obadiah, that I will as soon turn papist and die in a convent. 105

MRS. PRIM. Oh wickedness!

MRS. LOVELY. Oh stupidity!

OBADIAH PRIM. Oh blindness of heart!

MRS. LOVELY. [*Aside to Prim.*] Thou blinder of the world, don't provoke me, lest I betray your sanctity 110 and leave your wife to judge of your purity. What were the emotions of your spirit when you squeezed Mary by the hand last night in the pantry, when she told you, you bussed so filthily? Ah! You had no aversion to naked bosoms when you begged her to 115 show you a little, little, little bit of her delicious bubby. Don't you remember those words, Mr. Prim?

MRS. PRIM. What does she say, Obadiah?

OBADIAH PRIM. She talketh unintelligibly, Sarah. (*Aside.*) Which way did she hear this? This should 120 not have reached the ears of the wicked ones; verily, it troubleth me.

Enter servant.

SERVANT. Philip Modelove, whom they call Sir Philip,[55] is below, and such another with him; shall I send them up? 125

OBADIAH PRIM. Yea. (*Exit* [*servant*].)

Enter Sir Philip and Colonel.

SIR PHILIP. How dost thou do, Friend Prim. Odso! My she-Friend here too! What, you are documenting[56] Miss Nancy, reading her a lecture upon the pinched coif, I warrant ye. 130

MRS. PRIM. I am sure thou never readest her any lecture that was good.—My flesh riseth so at these wicked ones that prudence adviseth me to withdraw from their sight. (*Exit.*)

COLONEL. (*Aside.*) Oh! That I could find means 135 to speak to her! How charming she appears! I wish I could get this letter into her hand.

SIR PHILIP. Well, Miss Cocky,[57] I hope thou hast got the better of them.

---

55 Philip … Sir Philip] The refusal to use honorific titles was another Quaker public testimony.

56 documenting] admonishing in an authoritative or imperious manner.

57 Miss Cocky] a term of endearment.

MRS. LOVELY. The difficulties of my life are not to be surmounted, Sir Philip. (*Aside.*) I hate the impertinence of him as much as the stupidity of the other. 140

OBADIAH PRIM. Verily, Philip, thou wilt spoil this maiden. 145

SIR PHILIP. I find we still differ in opinion; but that we may none of us spoil her, prithee, Prim, let us consent to marry her. I have sent for our brother guardians to meet me here about that very thing.—Madam, will you give me leave to recommend a husband to you? Here's a gentleman which, in my mind, you can have no objection to. (*Presents the Colonel to her; she looks another way.*) 150

MRS. LOVELY. (*Aside.*) Heaven deliver me from the formal and the fantastic fool. 155

COLONEL. A fine woman, a fine horse, and fine equipage are the finest things in the universe. And if I am so happy to possess you, madam, I shall become the envy of mankind, as much as you outshine your whole sex. (*As he takes her hand to kiss it, he endeavours to put a letter into it; she lets it drop; Prim takes it up.*) 160

MRS. LOVELY. (*Turning from him.*) I have no ambition to appear conspicuously ridiculous, sir.

COLONEL. So fall the hopes of Fainwell. 165

MRS. LOVELY. (*Aside.*) Hah! Fainwell! 'Tis he! What have I done? Prim has the letter and all will be discovered.

OBADIAH PRIM. Friend, I know not thy name, so cannot call thee by it, but thou seest thy letter is unwelcome to the maiden; she will not read it. 170

MRS. LOVELY. Nor shall you. (*Snatches the letter.*) I'll tear it in a thousand pieces and scatter it, as I will the hopes of all those that any of you shall recommend to me. (*Tears the letter.*) 175

SIR PHILIP. Hah! Right woman, faith!

COLONEL. (*Aside.*) Excellent woman.

OBADIAH PRIM. Friend, thy garb favoureth too much of the vanity of the age for my approbation; nothing that resembleth Philip Modelove shall I love, mark that; therefore, Friend Philip, bring no more of thy own apes under my roof. 180

SIR PHILIP. I am so entirely a stranger to the monsters of thy breed that I shall bring none of them, I am sure. 185

COLONEL. (*Aside.*) I am likely to have a pretty task by that time I have gone through them all; but she's a city worth taking and egad I'll carry on the siege. If I can but blow up the outworks, I fancy I am pretty secure of the town. 190

Enter servant.

SERVANT. (*To Sir Philip.*) Toby Periwinkle and Thomas Tradelove demandeth to see thee.

SIR PHILIP. Bid them come up.

MRS. LOVELY. Deliver me from such an inundation of noise and nonsense. [*Aside.*] Oh Fainwell! Whatever thy contrivance is, prosper it Heaven; but oh, I fear thou never canst redeem me. (*Exit.*) 195

SIR PHILIP. Sic transit gloria mundi.

Enter Mr. Periwinkle and Tradelove.

(*Aside to the Colonel.*) These are my brother guardians, Mr. Fainwell; prithee observe the creatures. 200

TRADELOVE. Well, Sir Philip, I obey your summons.

PERIWINKLE. Pray, what have you to offer for the good of Mrs. Lovely, Sir Philip? 205

SIR PHILIP. First, I desire to know what you intend to do with that lady. Must she be sent to the Indies for a venture,[58] or live to be an old maid and then entered amongst your curiosities and shown for a monster,[59] Mr. Periwinkle? 210

COLONEL. (*Aside.*) Humph, curiosities! That must be the virtuoso.

PERIWINKLE. Why, what would you do with her?

SIR PHILIP. I would recommend this gentleman to her for a husband, sir—a person whom I have picked out from the whole race of mankind. 215

OBADIAH PRIM. I would advise thee to shuffle him again with the rest of mankind, for I like him not.

---

58 sent … venture] sent to the colonies in one of Tradelove's enterprises, here perhaps securing a marriage to a wealthy planter.

59 live … monster] Old maids were considered unnatural in the sense that their reproductive capacities were not turned to account; as a virtuoso, Periwinkle collects such oddities ("curiosities").

COLONEL. Pray, sir, without offence to your formality, what may be your objections? 220

OBADIAH PRIM. Thy person; thy manners; thy dress; thy acquaintance; thy everything, Friend.

SIR PHILIP. You are most particulary obliging, Friend, ha, ha. 225

TRADELOVE. What business do you follow, pray, sir?

COLONEL. (*Aside.*) Humph, by that question he must be the broker.—Business, sir! The business of a gentleman. 230

TRADELOVE. That is as much to say, you dress fine, feed high, lie with every woman you like, and pay your surgeon's bills[60] better than your tailor's or your butcher's.

COLONEL. The Court is much obliged to you, sir, for your character[61] of a gentleman. 235

TRADELOVE. The Court, sir! What would the Court do without us citizens?

SIR PHILIP. Without your wives and daughters, you mean, Mr. Tradelove? 240

PERIWINKLE. Have you ever travelled, sir?

COLONEL. [*Aside.*] That question must not be answered now.—In books I have, sir.

PERIWINKLE. In books? That's fine travelling indeed!—Sir Philip, when you present a person I like, he shall have my consent to marry Mrs. Lovely—till when, your servant. (*Exit.*) 245

COLONEL. (*Aside.*) I'll make you like me before I have done with you, or I am mistaken.

TRADELOVE. And when you can convince me that a beau is more useful to my country than a merchant, you shall have mine—till then, you must excuse me. (*Exit.*) 250

COLONEL. (*Aside.*) So much for trade. I'll fit you too. 255

SIR PHILIP. In my opinion, this is very inhumane treatment as to the lady, Mr. Prim.

OBADIAH PRIM. Thy opinion and mine happens to differ as much as our occupations, Friend; business requireth my presence and folly thine, and so I must bid thee farewell. (*Exit.*) 260

SIR PHILIP. Here's breeding for you, Mr. Fainwell!

Gad take me, I'd give half my estate to see these rascals bit.[62]

COLONEL. (*Aside.*) I hope to bite you all, if my plots hit. 265

ACT III, SCENE I. THE TAVERN.

Sackbut and the Colonel in an Egyptian dress.[63]

SACKBUT. A lucky beginning, Colonel—you have got the old beau's consent.

COLONEL. Aye, he's a reasonable creature, but the other three will require some pains. Shall I pass upon him, think you? Egad, in my mind, I look as antique as if I had been preserved in the ark. 5

SACKBUT. Pass upon him! Aye, aye, as roundly as white wine dashed with sack does for mountain[64] and sherry, if you have but assurance enough.

COLONEL. I have no apprehension from that quarter; assurance is the cockade of a soldier. 10

SACKBUT. Aye, but the assurance of a soldier differs much from that of a traveller. Can you lie with a good grace?

COLONEL. As heartily, when my mistress is the prize, as I would meet the foe when my country called and king commanded; so don't you fear that part; if he don't know me again, I'm safe. I hope he'll come. 15

SACKBUT. I wish all my debts would come as sure. I told him you had been a great traveller, had many valuable curiosities, and was a person of a most singular taste; he seemed transported and begged me to keep you till he came. 20

COLONEL. Aye, aye, he need not fear my running away. Let's have a bottle of sack, landlord, our ancestors drank sack. 25

SACKBUT. You shall have it.

COLONEL. And whereabouts is the trap door you mentioned? 30

SACKBUT. There's the conveyance, sir. (*Exit.*)

COLONEL. Now if I should cheat all these roguish guardians and carry off my mistress in triumph, it would be what the French call a *grand coup d'éclat*.[65] Odso! Here comes Periwinkle. Ah! Deuce take this beard; pray Jupiter it does not give me the slip and spoil all. 35

Enter Sackbut with wine and Periwinkle following.

SACKBUT. Sir, this gentleman, hearing you have been a great traveller and a person of fine speculation,[66] begs leave to take a glass with you; he is a man of curious taste himself. 40

COLONEL. The gentleman has it in his face and garb: sir, you are welcome.

PERIWINKLE. Sir, I honour a traveller and men of your inquiring disposition. The oddness of your habit pleases me extremely; 'tis very antique, and for that I like it. 45

COLONEL. It is very antique, sir. This habit once belonged to the famous Claudius Ptolemeus,[67] who lived in the year a hundred and thirty five. 50

SACKBUT. (*Aside.*) If he keeps up to the sample, he shall lie with the devil for a bean-stack and win it every straw.[68]

PERIWINKLE. A hundred and thirty-five! Why, that's prodigious now. Well, certainly 'tis the finest thing in the world to be a traveller. 55

COLONEL. For my part, I value none of the modern fashions of[69] a fig-leaf.

PERIWINKLE. No more do I, sir; I had rather be the jest of a fool, than his favourite. I am laughed at here for my singularity. This coat, you must know, sir, was formerly worn by that ingenious and very learned person, John Tradescant.[70] 60

---

65 *grand ... d'éclat*] great, dazzling feat (Fr.).
66 speculation] profound, conjectural reasoning.
67 Claudius Ptolemeus] famous Greek astronomer, mathematician, and geographer of Alexandria, also known as Ptolemy.
68 lie ... straw] In a lying contest with the devil for a stack of recently harvested beans, the Colonel would win it down to the last straw.
69 of] at.
70 John Tradescant] (1608–1662) traveller, naturalist, and gardener; his collection of natural curiosities was famous and became the basis of the Ashmolean Museum.

COLONEL. John Tradescant! Let me embrace you, sir. John Tradescant was my uncle, by mother-side; and I thank you for the honour you do his memory; he was a very curious man indeed. 65

PERIWINKLE. Your uncle, sir! Nay then, 'tis no wonder that your taste is so refined; why, you have it in your blood. My humble service to you, sir, to the immortal memory of John Tradescant, your never-to-be-forgotten uncle. (*Drinks.*) 70

COLONEL. Give me a glass, landlord.

PERIWINKLE. I find you are primitive even in your wine; canary was the drink of our wise forefathers; 'tis balsamic and saves the charge of apothecaries' cordials. Oh! that I had lived in your uncle's days! Or rather, that he were now alive. Oh! How proud he'd be of such a nephew! 75

SACKBUT. (*Aside.*) Oh pox! That would have spoiled the jest. 80

PERIWINKLE. A person of your curiosity must have collected many rarities.

COLONEL. I have some, sir, which are not yet come ashore, as an Egyptian's idol. 85

PERIWINKLE. Pray, what might that be?

COLONEL. It is, sir, a kind of an ape, which they formerly worshipped in that country; I took it from the breast of a female mummy.

PERIWINKLE. Ha, ha! Our women retain part of their idolatry to this day, for many an ape lies on a lady's breast, ha, ha— 90

SACKBUT. (*Aside.*) A smart old thief.

COLONEL. Two tusks of an hippopotamus, two pair of Chinese nutcrackers, and one Egyptian mummy. 95

PERIWINKLE. Pray, sir, have you never a crocodile?

COLONEL. Humph! The boatswain brought one with design to show it, but touching at Rotterdam and hearing it was no rarity in England, he sold it to a Dutch poet. 100

SACKBUT. The devil's in that nation, it rivals us in everything.

PERIWINKLE. I should have been very glad to have seen a living crocodile. 105

COLONEL. My genius led me to things more worthy of my regard. Sir, I have seen the utmost limits of this globular world; I have seen the sun rise and set; know in what degree of heat he is at noon to the breadth of a hair and what quantity of combustibles he burns in a day, how much of it turns to ashes and how much to cinders. 110

PERIWINKLE. To cinders? You amaze me, sir; I never heard that the sun consumed anything. Descartes[71] tells us— 115

COLONEL. Descartes, with the rest of his brethren both ancient and modern, knew nothing of the matter. I tell you, sir, that nature admits an annual decay, though imperceptible to vulgar eyes. Sometimes his rays destroy below, sometimes above. You 120 have heard of blazing comets, I suppose?

PERIWINKLE. Yes, yes, I remember to have seen one and our astrologers tell us of another which shall happen very quickly.[72]

COLONEL. Those comets are little islands border- 125 ing on the sun, which at certain times are set on fire by that luminous body's moving over them perpendicular, which will one day occasion a general conflagration.

SACKBUT. (*Aside.*) One need not scruple the 130 colonel's capacity, faith.

PERIWINKLE. This is marvellous strange! These cinders are what I never read of in any of our learned dissertations.

COLONEL. (*Aside.*) I don't know how the devil you 135 should.

SACKBUT. (*Aside.*) He has it at his fingers' ends; one would swear he had learned to lie at school, he does it so cleverly.

PERIWINKLE. Well, you travellers see strange 140 things! Pray, sir, have you any of those cinders?

COLONEL. I have, among my other curiosities.

PERIWINKLE. Oh, what have I lost for want of travelling! Pray, what have you else?

COLONEL. Several things worth your attention. I 145 have a muff made of the feathers of those geese that saved the Roman Capitol.[73]

PERIWINKLE. Is't possible?

SACKBUT. (*Aside.*) Yes, if you are such a goose to believe him. 150

COLONEL. I have an Indian leaf, which open will cover an acre of land, yet folds up into so little a compass, you may put it into your snuffbox.

SACKBUT. (*Aside.*) Humph! That's a thunderer.

PERIWINKLE. Amazing! 155

COLONEL. Ah! Mine is but a little one; I have seen some of them that would cover one of the Caribbean islands.

PERIWINKLE. Well, if I don't travel before I die, I shan't rest in my grave. Pray, what do the Indians 160 with them?

COLONEL. Sir, they use them in their wars for tents, the old women for riding hoods, the young for fans and umbrellas.

SACKBUT. (*Aside.*) He has a fruitful invention. 165

PERIWINKLE. I admire our East India Company[74] imports none of them; they would certainly find their account in them.

COLONEL. (*Aside.*) Right, if they could find the leaves.—Look ye, sir, do you see this little vial? 170

PERIWINKLE. Pray you, what is it?

COLONEL. This is called *poluflosboio*.[75]

PERIWINKLE. *Poluflosboio*! It has a rumbling sound.

COLONEL. Right, sir, it proceeds from a rumbling 175 nature. This water was part of those waves which bore Cleopatra's vessel when she sailed to meet Anthony.

PERIWINKLE. Well, of all that ever travelled, none had a taste like you. 180

COLONEL. But here's the wonder of the world. This, sir, is called, *zona*[76] or *moros musphonon*,[77] the virtues of this is inestimable.

---

71 Descartes] René Descartes (1596–1650) wrote about sun spots in his unfinished scientific work, *The World*.

72 astrologers … quickly] astronomers; in 1705 Edmund Halley predicted the return of the comet he had observed in 1682.

73 geese … Capitol] According to Roman legend, the cackling of geese in Juno's temple warned the guards of an invasion.

---

74 East India Company] joint-stock trading company with the monopoly on trade with India and Asia.

75 *poluflosboio*] loud-roaring (as of the sea—Gr.).

76 *zona*] Latin form of the Greek word *zone*, a sash wrapped about the waist, usually having magical properties, sometimes called a girdle.

77 *moros musphonon*] fanciful Greek: "mousetrap for a fool" (Stathas).

PERIWINKLE. *Moros musphonon*! What in the name of wisdom can that be? To me it seems a plain belt. 185

COLONEL. This girdle has carried me all the world over.

PERIWINKLE. You have carried it, you mean.

COLONEL. I mean as I say, sir. Whenever I am girded with this, I am invisible; and by turning this little screw can be in the court of the Great Mogul, the Grand Seignior,[78] and King George in as little time as your cook can poach an egg. 190

PERIWINKLE. You must pardon me, sir, I can't believe it. 195

COLONEL. If my landlord pleases, he shall try the experiment immediately.

SACKBUT. I thank you kindly, sir, but I have no inclination to ride post to the devil. 200

COLONEL. No, no, you shan't stir a foot; I'll only make you invisible.

SACKBUT. But if you could not make me visible again?

PERIWINKLE. Come try it upon me, sir, I am not afraid of the devil nor all his tricks. 'Zbud, I'll stand 'em all. 205

COLONEL. There, sir, put it on. Come, landlord, you and I must face the east. (*They turn about.*) Is it on, sir? 210

PERIWINKLE. 'Tis on. (*They turn about again.*)

SACKBUT. Heaven protect me! Where is he?

PERIWINKLE. Why here, just where I was.

SACKBUT. Where, where, in the name of virtue? Ah, poor Mr. Periwinkle! Egad, look to't, you had best, sir, and let him be seen again, or I shall have you burnt for a wizard. 215

COLONEL. Have patience, good landlord.

PERIWINKLE. But really, don't you see me now?

SACKBUT. No more than I see my grandmother that died forty years ago. 220

PERIWINKLE. Are you sure you don't lie? Methinks I stand just where I did and see you as plain as I did before.

SACKBUT. Ah! I wish I could see you once again. 225

COLONEL. Take off the girdle, sir. (*He takes it off.*)

SACKBUT. Ah, sir, I am glad to see you with all my heart. (*Embraces him.*)

PERIWINKLE. This is very odd; certainly, there must be some trick in't.—Pray, sir, will you do me the favour to put it on yourself? 230

COLONEL. With all my heart.

PERIWINKLE. But first I'll secure the door.

COLONEL. You know how to turn the screw, Mr. Sackbut. 235

SACKBUT. Yes, yes.—Come, Mr. Periwinkle, we must turn full east.

They turn; the Colonel sinks down a trapdoor.

COLONEL. 'Tis done; now turn.

They turn.

PERIWINKLE. Hah! Mercy upon me! My flesh creeps upon my bones.—This must be a conjurer, Mr. Sackbut. 240

SACKBUT. He is the devil, I think.

PERIWINKLE. Oh! Mr. Sackbut, why do you name the devil when perhaps he may be at your elbow.

SACKBUT. At my elbow! Marry, Heaven forbid. 245

COLONEL. (*Below.*) Are you satisfied, sir?

PERIWINKLE. Yes, sir, yes.—How hollow his voice sounds!

SACKBUT. Yours seemed just the same. Faith, I wish this girdle were mine, I'd sell wine no more. Hark ye, Mr. Periwinkle (*takes him aside till the Colonel rises again*), if he would sell this girdle, you might travel with great expedition. 250

COLONEL. But it is not to be parted with for money. 255

PERIWINKLE. I am sorry for't, sir, because I think it the greatest curiosity I ever heard of.

COLONEL. By the advice of a learned physiognomist in Grand Cairo, who consulted the lines in my face, I returned to England, where he told me I should find a rarity in the keeping of four men, which I was born to possess for the benefit of mankind, and the first of the four that gave me his consent, I should present him with this girdle. Till I have found this jewel, I shall not part with the girdle. 260 265

PERIWINKLE. What can that rarity be? Did he not name it to you?

---

78 Grand Seignior] the Sultan of Turkey.

COLONEL. Yes, sir; he called it a chaste, beautiful, unaffected woman. 270

PERIWINKLE. Pish! Women are no rarities. I never had any great taste that way. I married, indeed, to please a father and I got a girl to please my wife; but she and the child (thank Heaven) died together. Women are the very gewgaws of the creation; playthings for boys, which, when they write man, they ought to throw aside. 275

SACKBUT. (*Aside.*) A fine lecture to be read to a circle of ladies!

PERIWINKLE. What woman is there, dressed in all the pride and foppery of the times, can boast of such a foretop[79] as the cockatoo? 280

COLONEL. (*Aside.*) I must humour him.—Such a skin as the lizard?

PERIWINKLE. Such a shining breast as the hummingbird? 285

COLONEL. Such a shape as the antelope?

PERIWINKLE. Or, in all the artful mixture of their various dresses, have they half the beauty of one box of butterflies? 290

COLONEL. No, that must be allowed. For my part, if it were not for the benefit of mankind, I'd have nothing to do with them, for they are as indifferent to me as a sparrow or a flesh fly.

PERIWINKLE. Pray, sir, what benefit is the world to reap from this lady? 295

COLONEL. Why, sir, she is to bear me a son, who shall restore the art of embalming and the old Roman manner of burying their dead, and, for the benefit of posterity, he is to discover the longitude,[80] so long sought for in vain. 300

PERIWINKLE. Od! These are very valuable things, Mr. Sackbut.

SACKBUT. (*Aside.*) He hits it off admirably and t'other swallows it like sack and sugar.—Certainly this lady must be your ward, Mr. Periwinkle, by her being under the care of four persons. 305

PERIWINKLE. By the description it should. (*Aside.*)

Egad, if I could get that girdle, I'd ride with the sun and make the tour of the whole world in four-and-twenty hours.—And are you to give that girdle to the first of the four guardians that shall give his consent to marry that lady, say you, sir? 310

COLONEL. I am so ordered, when I can find him.

PERIWINKLE. I fancy I know the very woman—her name is Anne Lovely. 315

COLONEL. Excellent! He said, indeed, that the first letter of her name was *L*.

PERIWINKLE. Did he really? Well, that's prodigiously amazing, that a person in Grand Cairo should know anything of my ward. 320

COLONEL. Your ward?

PERIWINKLE. To be plain with you, sir, I am one of those four guardians.

COLONEL. Are you indeed, sir? I am transported to find the man who is to possess this *moros musphonon* is a person of so curious a taste. Here is a writing drawn up by that famous Egyptian, which, if you will please to sign, you must turn your face full north, and the girdle is yours. 325 330

PERIWINKLE. If I live till this boy is born, I'll be embalmed and sent to the Royal Society[81] when I die.

COLONEL. That you shall most certainly.

Enter drawer.

DRAWER. Here's Mr. Staytape the tailor, inquires for you, Colonel. 335

SACKBUT. Who do you speak to, you son of a whore?

PERIWINKLE. (*Aside.*) Hah! Colonel!

COLONEL. (*Aside.*) Confound the blundering dog! 340

DRAWER. Why, to Colonel—

SACKBUT. Get you out, you rascal. (*Kicks him out and exit after him.*)

DRAWER. [*As he exits.*] What the devil is the matter?

COLONEL. (*Aside.*) This dog has ruined all my scheme, I see by Periwinkle's looks. 345

PERIWINKLE. How finely I should have been choused.—Colonel, you'll pardon me that I did not give you your title before; it was pure

---

79 foretop] a nautical term, applied to hair arranged on the forehead; by analogy, the cockatoo's crest.

80 discover the longitude] Parliament had passed a bill in 1714 offering a prize of £20,000 for the first person to develop an accurate way of finding the longitude at sea.

81 Royal Society] scientific society founded by Royal Charter in 1662; by 1718 it was the butt of many a joke.

ignorance, faith it was. Pray—hem, hem—pray, 350
Colonel, what post had this learned Egyptian in
your regiment?

COLONEL. (*Aside.*) A pox of your sneer.—I don't
understand you, sir.

PERIWINKLE. No? That's strange! I understand 355
you, Colonel. An Egyptian of Grand Cairo! Ha,
ha, ha. I am sorry such a well-invented tale should
do you no more service. We old fellows can see as
far into a millstone[82] as him that picks it. I am
not to be tricked out of my trust, mark that. 360

COLONEL. (*Aside.*) The devil! I must carry it off; I
wish I were fairly out.—Look ye, sir, you may
make what jest you please, but the stars will be
obeyed, sir, and, depend upon it, I shall have the
lady and you none of the girdle. (*Aside.*) Now for 365
Freeman's part of the plot. (*Exit.*)

PERIWINKLE. The stars! Ha, ha. No star has
favoured you, it seems. The girdle! Ha, ha, ha,
none of your legerdemain tricks can pass upon me.
Why, what a pack of trumpery has this rogue 370
picked up? His *pagod*,[83] *poluflosboios*, his *zonas*,
moros musphonons, and the devil knows what. But
I'll take care— Hah! Gone? Aye, 'twas time to
sneak off.—Soho! the house! (*Enter Sackbut.*)
Where is this trickster? Send for a constable, I'll 375
have this rascal before the Lord Mayor; I'll Grand
Cairo him, with a pox to him. I believe you had a
hand in putting this imposture upon me, Sackbut.

SACKBUT. Who, I, Mr. Periwinkle? I scorn it; I
perceived he was a cheat and left the room on 380
purpose to send for a constable to apprehend him,
and endeavoured to stop him when he went out,
but the rogue made but one step from the stairs
to the door, called a coach, leapt into it, and drove
away like the devil, as Mr. Freeman can witness, 385
who is at the bar and desires to speak with you;
he is this minute come to town.

PERIWINKLE. Send him in. (*Exit Sackbut.*) What
a scheme this rogue had laid! How I should have
been laughed at, had it succeeded! (*Enter Freeman* 390
booted and spurred.) Mr. Freeman, your dress
commands your welcome to town. What will you
drink? I had like to have been imposed upon here
by the veriest rascal—

FREEMAN. I am sorry to hear it. The dog flew 395
for't—he had not 'scaped me if I had been aware
of him; Sackbut struck at him, but missed his
blow, or he had done his business for him.

PERIWINKLE. I believe you never heard of such a
contrivance, Mr. Freeman, as this fellow had found 400
out.

FREEMAN. Mr. Sackbut has told me the whole
story, Mr. Periwinkle, but now I have something
to tell you of much more importance to yourself.
I happened to lie one night at Coventry, and 405
knowing your uncle, Sir Toby Periwinkle, I paid
him a visit and to my great surprise found him
dying.

PERIWINKLE. Dying!

FREEMAN. Dying, in all appearance; the servants 410
weeping, the room in darkness; the apothecary,
shaking his head, told me the doctors had given
him over, and then there is small hopes, you know.

PERIWINKLE. I hope he has made his will. He
always told me he would make me his heir. 415

FREEMAN. I have heard you say as much and
therefore resolved to give you notice. I should
think it would not be amiss if you went down
tomorrow morning.

PERIWINKLE. It is a long journey, and the roads 420
very bad.

FREEMAN. But he has a great estate, and the land
very good. Think upon that.

PERIWINKLE. Why, that's true, as you say; I'll
think upon it. In the meantime, I give you many 425
thanks for your civility, Mr. Freeman, and should
be glad of your company to dine with me.

FREEMAN. I am obliged to be at Jonathan's Coffee-
house[84] at two, and it is now half-an-hour after
one; if I dispatch my business, I'll wait on you; I 430
know your hour.

PERIWINKLE. You shall be very welcome, Mr.
Freeman; and so, your humble servant. (*Exit.*)

---

82 see ... millstone] proverbial for acute vision.
83 *pagod*] an Eastern idol.

84 Jonathan's Coffee-house] in Exchange Alley near the
Royal Exchange; centre for speculators; the forerunner
of the Stock Exchange.

Re-enter Colonel and Sackbut.

FREEMAN. Ha, ha, ha! I have done your business, Colonel; he has swallowed the bait. 435

COLONEL. I overheard all, though I am a little in the dark. I am to personate a highwayman, I suppose. That's a project I am not fond of; for though I may fright him out of his consent, he may fright me out of my life[85] when he discovers 440 me, as he certainly must in the end.

FREEMAN. No, no, I have a plot for you without danger, but first we must manage Tradelove. Has the tailor brought your clothes?

SACKBUT. Yes, pox take the thief. 445

COLONEL. Pox take your drawer for a jolt-headed rogue.

FREEMAN. Well, well, no matter, I warrant we have him yet. But now you must put on the Dutch merchant. 450

COLONEL. The deuce of this trading-plot. I wish he had been an old soldier, that I might have attacked him in my own way, heard him fight over all the battles of the Civil War—but for trade, by Jupiter, I shall never do it. 455

SACKBUT. Never fear, Colonel, Mr. Freeman will instruct you.

FREEMAN. You'll see what others do, the coffee-house will instruct you.

COLONEL. I must venture, however. But I have a 460 farther plot in my head upon Tradelove, which you must assist me in, Freeman; you are in credit with him, I heard you say.

FREEMAN. I am, and will scruple nothing to serve you, Colonel. 465

COLONEL. Come along then. Now for the Dutchman. Honest Ptolemy, by your leave, Now must bob wig[86] and business come in play, And a fair thirty-thousand-pounder leads the way.

---

85 *fright … life*] because highway robbery was punishable by death.

86 bob wig] a simple, informal wig.

ACT IV, SCENE I. JONATHAN'S COFFEE-HOUSE IN EXCHANGE ALLEY.

Crowd of people with rolls of paper and parchment[87] *in their hands; a bar, and coffee-boys waiting. Enter Tradelove and stockjobbers with rolls of paper and parchment.*

FIRST STOCKJOBBER. South Sea at seven-eighths![88] Who buys?

SECOND STOCKJOBBER. South Sea bonds due at Michaelmas,[89] 1718. Class lottery tickets.[90]

THIRD STOCKJOBBER. East India bonds? 5

FOURTH STOCKJOBBER. What, all sellers and no buyers? Gentlemen, I'll buy a thousand pound for Tuesday next at three-fourths.

COFFEE-BOY. Fresh coffee, gentlemen, fresh coffee?

TRADELOVE. Hark ye, Gabriel, you'll pay the 10 difference of that stock we transacted for t'other day.

GABRIEL. Aye, Mr. Tradelove, here's a note for the money upon the Sword Blade Company.[91] (*Gives him a note.*)

COFFEE-BOY. Bohea tea, gentlemen? 15

Enter a Man.

MAN. Is Mr. Smuggle here?

FIRST COFFEE-BOY. Mr. Smuggle's not here, sir, you'll find him at the books.

SECOND STOCKJOBBER. Ho! Here come two sparks from the other end of the town. What news 20 bring they?

---

87 *rolls … parchment*] for recording stock transactions.

88 South Sea at seven-eighths] stock in the South Sea Company, a chartered joint-stock trading company, with the monopoly on English trade with South America and the Pacific; founded in 1711, mainly to fund the national debt. Stock prices were conventionally quoted in eighths; only the final fraction is quoted.

89 Michaelmas] Feast of St. Michael, September 29; one of the four quarter days of the business year, on which financial transactions were completed.

90 Class lottery tickets] one of the lotteries run by the government to fund the national debt; tickets were divided into classes with different prizes for each.

91 Sword Blade Company] the major stock brokerage firm of the time and banker for the South Sea Company.

Enter Two Gentlemen.

TRADELOVE. I would fain bite that spark in the brown coat: he comes very often into the Alley, but never employs a broker.

Enter Colonel and Freeman.

SECOND STOCKJOBBER. Who does anything in the Civil List lottery?[92] Or cacao? Zounds, where are all the Jews[93] this afternoon? Are you a bull or a bear today, Abraham? 25

THIRD STOCKJOBBER. A bull, faith, but I have a good put[94] for next week. 30

TRADELOVE. Mr. Freeman, your servant! Who is that gentleman?

FREEMAN. A Dutch merchant, just come to England. But hark ye, Mr. Tradelove, I have a piece of news will get you as much as the French king's death did, if you are expeditious. 35

TRADELOVE. Say you so, sir! Pray, what is it?

FREEMAN. (*Showing him a letter.*) Read there, I received it just now from one that belongs to the Emperor's[95] minister. 40

TRADELOVE. (*Reads.*) "Sir, As I have many obligations to you, I cannot miss any opportunity to show my gratitude; this moment my lord has received a private express that the Spaniards have raised their siege from before Cagliari;[96] if this prove any advantage to you, it will answer both the ends and wishes of, sir, your most obliged humble servant, Henricus Dusseldorp. Postscript, In two or three hours the news will be public." (*Aside to Freeman.*) May one depend upon this, Mr. Freeman? 45 50

FREEMAN. You may. I never knew this person send me a false piece of news in my life.

TRADELOVE. Sir, I am much obliged to you. Egad, 'tis rare news.—Who sells South Sea[97] for next week? 55

STOCKJOBBERS. (*All together.*) I sell; I, I, I, I, I sell.

FIRST STOCKJOBBER. I'll sell five thousand pounds for next week at five-eighths. 60

SECOND STOCKJOBBER. I'll sell ten thousand at five-eighths for the same time.

TRADELOVE. Nay, nay, hold, hold, not all together, gentlemen, I'll be no bull, I'll buy no more than I can take. Will you sell ten thousand pound at a half for any day next week, except Saturday? 65

FIRST STOCKJOBBER. I'll sell it you, Mr. Tradelove.

Freeman whispers to one of the gentlemen.

GENTLEMAN. (*Aloud.*) The Spaniards raised the siege of Cagliari! I don't believe one word of it. 70

SECOND GENTLEMAN. Raised the siege! As much as you have raised the Monument.[98]

FREEMAN. 'Tis raised, I assure you, sir.

SECOND GENTLEMAN. What will you lay on't? 75

FREEMAN. What you please.

FIRST GENTLEMAN. Why, I have a brother upon the spot in the Emperor's service; I am certain if there were any such thing, I should have had a letter. 80

A STOCKJOBBER. How's this? The siege of Cagliari raised; I wish it may be true, 'twill make business stir and stocks rise.

FIRST STOCKJOBBER. Tradelove's a cunning fat bear; if this news proves true, I shall repent I sold him the five thousand pounds.[99]—Pray, sir, what assurance have you that the siege is raised? 85

---

92 Civil … lottery] a government lottery (1713) to discharge the debts of the royal household.

93 Jews] for perhaps the first time in English literature, meant in a positive sense, of keeping the stock market going. [J.W.]

94 put] stockjobber talk; an option on a stock for a period of time at a guaranteed price.

95 Emperor's] Charles VI, Emperor of Austria.

96 siege … Cagliari] Cagliari is the capital of Sardinia, at this time part of the Austrian empire; Spain had invaded Sardinia in August 1717, provoking a crisis in the Mediterranean.

---

97 South Sea] The South Sea Company traded with the Spanish empire, whose military fortunes would affect stock prices.

98 Monument] a column designed by Christopher Wren commemorating London's Great Fire of 1666.

99 five thousand pounds] ten thousand according to the first stockjobber's revised offer to Tradelove.

FREEMAN. There is come an express to the Emperor's minister.

SECOND STOCKJOBBER. I'll know that pres- 90
ently. (*Exit.*)

FIRST GENTLEMAN. Let it come where it will, I'll hold you fifty pounds 'tis false.

FREEMAN. 'Tis done.

SECOND GENTLEMAN. I'll lay you a brace of 95
hundreds upon the same.

FREEMAN. I'll take you.

FOURTH STOCKJOBBER. Egad, I'll hold twenty pieces 'tis not raised, sir.

FREEMAN. Done with you too. 100

TRADELOVE. I'll lay any man a brace of thousands the siege is raised.

FREEMAN. (*Aside to Tradelove.*) The Dutch merchant is your man to take in.

TRADELOVE. Does not he know the news? 105

FREEMAN. (*To Tradelove.*) Not a syllable; if he did, he would bet a hundred thousand pound as soon as one penny; he's plaguy rich, and a mighty man at wagers.

TRADELOVE. Say you so.—Egad, I'll bite him if 110
possible.—Are you from Holland, sir?

COLONEL. Ya, mynheer.

TRADELOVE. Had you the news before you came away?

COLONEL. Wat believe you, mynheer? 115

TRADELOVE. What do I believe? Why, I believe that the Spaniards have actually raised the siege of Cagliari.

COLONEL. Wat duyvels niews is dat? 'Tis niet waer, mynheer,—'tis no true, sir. 120

TRADELOVE. 'Tis so true, mynheer, that I'll lay you two thousand pounds upon it.—You are sure the letter may be depended upon, Mr. Freeman?

FREEMAN. (*Aside to Tradelove.*) Do you think I would venture my money if I were not sure of the 125
truth of it?

COLONEL. Two duysend pond, mynheer, 'tis gedaen—dis gentleman sal hold de gelt. (*Gives Freeman money.*)

TRADELOVE. With all my heart—this binds the 130
wager. You have certainly lost, mynheer, the siege is raised indeed.

COLONEL. Ik gelove't niet, Mynheer Freeman, ik sal ye dubbled houden, if you please.

FREEMAN. I am let into the secret, therefore won't 135
win your money.

TRADELOVE. Ha, ha, ha! I have snapped the Dutchman, faith, ha, ha! This is no ill day's work.—Pray, may I crave your name, mynheer?

COLONEL. Myn naem, mynheer! Myn naem is Jan 140
Van Timtamtirelireletta Heer Van Fainwell.

TRADELOVE. Zounds, 'tis a damned long name, I shall never remember it: Mynheer Van Tim, Tim, Tim— What the devil is it?

FREEMAN. Oh! Never heed, I know the gentleman 145
and will pass my word for twice the sum.

TRADELOVE. That's enough.

COLONEL. (*Aside.*) You'll hear of me sooner than you'll wish, old gentleman, I fancy.—You'll come to Sackbut's, Freeman? (*Exit.*) 150

FREEMAN. (*Aside to the Colonel.*) Immediately.

FIRST MAN. Humphrey Hump here?

SECOND COFFEE-BOY. Mr. Humphrey Hump is not here; you'll find him upon the Dutch walk.[100]

TRADELOVE. Mr. Freeman, I give you many 155
thanks for your kindness.

FREEMAN. (*Aside.*) I fear you'll repent when you know all.

TRADELOVE. Will you dine with me?

FREEMAN. I am engaged at Sackbut's; adieu. (*Exit.*) 160

TRADELOVE. Sir, your humble servant. Now I'll see what I can do upon Change with my news. (*Exit.*)

SCENE II. THE TAVERN.

Enter Freeman and Colonel.

FREEMAN. Ha, ha, ha! The old fellow swallowed the bait as greedily as a gudgeon.

COLONEL. I have him, faith, ha, ha, ha. His two thousand pound's secure—if he would keep his money, he must part with the lady, ha, ha. What 5
came of your two friends? They performed their part very well; you should have brought 'em to take a glass with us.

FREEMAN. No matter, we'll drink a bottle together another time. I did not care to bring them hither; 10

---

100 Dutch walk] meeting place for Dutch merchants in the courtyard of the Royal Exchange.

there's no necessity to trust them with the main secret, you know, Colonel.

COLONEL. Nay, that's right, Freeman.

Enter Sackbut.

SACKBUT. Joy, joy, Colonel, the luckiest accident in the world! 15

COLONEL. What say'st thou?

SACKBUT. This letter does your business.

COLONEL. (*Reads.*) "To Obadiah Prim, hosier, near the building called the Monument, in London."

FREEMAN. A letter to Prim; how came you by it? 20

SACKBUT. Looking over the letters our post-woman brought, as I always do, to see what letters are directed to my house (for she can't read, you must know), I spied this to Prim, so paid for't[101] among the rest; I have given the old jade a pint of wine 25 on purpose to delay time, till you see if the letter will be of any service; then I'll seal it up again and tell her I took it by mistake; I have read it and fancy you'll like the project—read, read, Colonel.

COLONEL. (*Reads.*) "Friend Prim, There is arrived 30 from Pennsylvania one Simon Pure, a leader of the faithful, who hath sojourned with us eleven days and hath been of great comfort to the brethren. He intendeth for the quarterly meeting in London; I have recommended him to thy house; I pray thee 35 entreat him kindly and let thy wife cherish him, for he's of weakly constitution. He will depart from us the third day;[102] which is all from thy Friend in the faith, Aminidab Holdfast." Ha, ha! Excellent! I understand you, landlord, I am to 40 personate this Simon Pure, am I not?

SACKBUT. Don't you like the hint?

COLONEL. Admirably well!

FREEMAN. 'Tis the best contrivance in the world, if the right Simon gets not there before you. 45

COLONEL. No, no, the Quakers never ride post; he can't be here before tomorrow at soonest. Do you send and buy me a Quaker's dress, Mr.

Sackbut; and suppose, Freeman, you should wait at the Bristol coach, that if you see any such 50 person, you might contrive to give me notice.

FREEMAN. I will.—The country dress and boots, are they ready?

SACKBUT. Yes, yes, everything, sir.

FREEMAN. Bring 'em in then. (*Exit Sackbut.*) Thou 55 must dispatch Periwinkle first. Remember his uncle, Sir Toby Periwinkle, is an old bachelor of seventy-five; that he has seven hundred a year, most in abbey land;[103] that he was once in love with your mother, and shrewdly suspected by some to 60 be your father; that you have been thirty years his steward, and ten years his gentleman—remember to improve these hints.

COLONEL. Never fear, let me alone for that—but what's the steward's name? 65

FREEMAN. His name is Pillage.

COLONEL. Enough. (*Enter Sackbut with clothes.*) Now for the country put.[104] (*Dresses.*)

FREEMAN. Egad, landlord, thou deservest to have the first night's lodging with the lady for thy 70 fidelity. What say you, Colonel, shall we settle a club here, you'll make one?

COLONEL. Make one? I'll bring a set of honest officers that will spend their money as freely to their King's health as they would their blood in his 75 service.

SACKBUT. I thank you, Colonel. (*Bell rings.*) Here, here. (*Exit Sackbut.*)

COLONEL. So now for my boots. (*Puts on boots.*) Shall I find you here, Freeman, when I come back? 80

FREEMAN. Yes, or I'll leave word with Sackbut where he may send for me. Have you the writings? the will, and everything?

COLONEL. All, all!

Enter Sackbut.

SACKBUT. Zounds! Mr. Freeman! Yonder is 85 Tradelove in the damnedest passion in the world. He swears you are in the house—he says you told him you was to dine here.

---

101 paid for't] Postage at the time was paid by the recipient.

102 third day] Tuesday; Quakers designated the days of the week in this way to avoid the conventional designations derived from the names of the pagan gods.

103 abbey land] part of the estate of an abbey before the dissolution of the monasteries at the Reformation.

104 country put] bumpkin.

FREEMAN. I did so. Ha, ha, ha! He has found himself bit already.

COLONEL. The devil! He must not see me in this dress.

SACKBUT. I told him I expected you here, but you were not come yet.

FREEMAN. Very well.—Make you haste out, Colonel, and let me alone to deal with him. Where is he?

SACKBUT. In the King's Head.

COLONEL. You remember what I told you?

FREEMAN. Aye, aye, very well.—Landlord, let him know I am come in.—And now, Mr. Pillage, success attend you.

Exit Sackbut.

COLONEL. Mr. Proteus, rather.
From changing shape and imitating Jove,
I draw the happy omens of my love.
I'm not the first young brother of the blade
Who made his fortune in a masquerade. (*Exit Colonel.*)

Enter Tradelove.

FREEMAN. Zounds! Mr. Tradelove, we're bit it seems.

TRADELOVE. Bit do you call it, Mr. Freeman, I am ruined. Pox on your news.

FREEMAN. Pox on the rascal that sent it me.

TRADELOVE. Sent it you! Why Gabriel Skinflint has been at the minister's and spoke with him, and he has assured him 'tis every syllable false; he received no such express.

FREEMAN. I know it. I this minute parted with my friend, who protested he never sent me any such letter. Some roguish stockjobber has done it on purpose to make me lose my money, that's certain. I wish I knew who he was, I'd make him repent it—I have lost three hundred pounds by it.

TRADELOVE. What signifies your three hundred pounds to what I have lost? There's two thousand pounds to that Dutchman with the cursed long name, besides the stock I bought. The devil! I could tear my flesh. I must never show my face upon Change more, for, by my soul, I can't pay it.

FREEMAN. I am heartily sorry for't! What can I serve you in? Shall I speak to the Dutch merchant and try to get you time for the payment?

TRADELOVE. Time! Adsheart! I shall never be able to look up again.

FREEMAN. I am very much concerned that I was the occasion and wish I could be an instrument of retrieving your misfortune; for my own, I value it not.—Adso! A thought comes into my head, that well improved, may be of service.

TRADELOVE. Ah! There's no thought can be of any service to me, without paying the money or running away.

FREEMAN. How do you know? What do you think of my proposing Mrs. Lovely to him? He is a single man, and I heard him say he had a mind to marry an English woman. Nay, more than that, he said somebody told him, you had a pretty ward. He wished you had bet her instead of your money.

TRADELOVE. Aye, but he'd be hanged before he'd take her instead of the money: the Dutch are too covetous for that. Besides, he did not know that there were three more of us, I suppose.

FREEMAN. So much the better; you may venture to give him your consent, if he'll but forgive you the wager. It is not your business to tell him that your consent will signify nothing.

TRADELOVE. That's right, as you say, but will he do it, think you?

FREEMAN. I can't tell that, but I'll try what I can do with him. He has promised me to meet me here an hour hence; I'll feel his pulse and let you know. If I find it feasible, I'll send for you; if not, you are at liberty to take what measures you please.

TRADELOVE. You must extol her beauty, double her portion, and tell him I have the entire disposal of her and that she can't marry without my consent and that I am a covetous rogue and will never part with her without a valuable consideration.

FREEMAN. Aye, aye, let me alone for a lie at a pinch.

TRADELOVE. Egad, if you can bring this to bear, Mr. Freeman, I'll make you whole again; I'll pay the three hundred pounds you lost, with all my soul.

FREEMAN. Well, I'll use my best endeavours. Where will you be?

TRADELOVE. At home. Pray Heaven you prosper.
 If I were but the sole trustee now, I should not fear
 it. Who the devil would be a guardian,
 If when cash runs low, our coffers t'enlarge,
 We can't, like other stocks, transfer our charge? 180
  (*Exit.*)
FREEMAN. Ha, ha, ha! He has it. (*Exit.*)

SCENE III. PERIWINKLE'S HOUSE.

Enter Periwinkle on one side and footman on the other.

FOOTMAN. A gentleman from Coventry inquires
 for you, sir.
PERIWINKLE. From my uncle, I warrant you,
 bring him up. [*Exit footman.*] This will save me the
 trouble, as well as the expenses of a journey. 5

Enter Colonel.

COLONEL. Is your name Periwinkle, sir?
PERIWINKLE. It is, sir.
COLONEL. I am sorry for the message I bring. My
 old master, whom I served these forty years, claims
 the sorrow due from a faithful servant to an 10
 indulgent master. (*Weeps.*)
PERIWINKLE. By this I understand, sir, my uncle,
 Sir Toby Periwinkle, is dead.
COLONEL. He is, sir, and he has left you heir to
 seven hundred a year in as good abbey land as ever 15
 paid Peter's pence to Rome. I wish you long to
 enjoy it, but my tears will flow when I think of
 my benefactor. (*Weeps.*) Ah! He was a good man—
 he has not left many of his fellows—the poor
 laments him sorely. 20
PERIWINKLE. I pray, sir, what office bore you?
COLONEL. I was his steward, sir.
PERIWINKLE. I have heard him mention you with
 much respect; your name is—
COLONEL. Pillage, sir. 25
PERIWINKLE. Aye, Pillage! I do remember he
 called you Pillage. Pray, Mr. Pillage, when did my
 uncle die?
COLONEL. Monday last, at four in the morning.
 About two he signed this will and gave it into my 30
 hands and strictly charged me to leave Coventry
 the moment he expired and deliver it to you with
 what speed I could. I have obeyed him, sir, and
 there is the will. (*Gives it to Periwinkle.*)

PERIWINKLE. 'Tis very well, I'll lodge it in the 35
 Commons.[105]
COLONEL. There are two things which he forgot
 to insert, but charged me to tell you that he desired
 you'd perform them as readily as if you had found
 them written in the will, which is to remove his 40
 corpse and bury him by his father in St. Paul,
 Covent Garden, and to give all his servants
 mourning.
PERIWINKLE. (*Aside.*) That will be a considerable
 charge; a pox of all modern fashions.—Well! It 45
 shall be done, Mr. Pillage; I will agree with one of
 death's fashion-mongers, called an undertaker, to
 go down and bring up the body.
COLONEL. I hope, sir, I shall have the honour to
 serve you in the same station I did your worthy 50
 uncle; I have not many years to stay behind him
 and would gladly spend them in the family where
 I was brought up. (*Weeps.*) He was a kind and
 tender master to me.
PERIWINKLE. Pray don't grieve, Mr. Pillage; you 55
 shall hold your place and everything else which you
 held under my uncle. You make me weep to see
 you so concerned. (*Weeps.*) He lived to a good old
 age—and we are all mortal.
COLONEL. We are so, sir, and therefore I must beg 60
 you to sign this lease. You'll find Sir Toby has ta'en
 particular notice of it in his will. I could not get
 it time enough from the lawyer, or he had signed
 it before he died. (*Gives him a paper.*)
PERIWINKLE. A lease for what? 65
COLONEL. I rented a hundred a year of Sir Toby
 upon lease, which lease expires at Lady Day next,
 and I desire to renew it for twenty years—that's
 all, sir.
PERIWINKLE. Let me see. (*Looks over the lease.*) 70
COLONEL. (*Aside.*) Matters go swimmingly, if
 nothing intervene.
PERIWINKLE. Very well. Let's see what he says in
 his will about it. (*Lays the lease upon the table and
 looks on the will.*) 75
COLONEL. (*Aside.*) He's very wary, yet I fancy I
 shall be too cunning for him.

---

105 lodge … Commons] register it with the College of Doctors of Civil Law (the appropriate legal office).

PERIWINKLE. Ho, here it is. "—The farm lying—now in possession of Samuel Pillage—suffer him to renew his lease—at the same rent."—Very well, Mr. Pillage, I see my uncle does mention it, and I'll perform his will. Give me the lease. (*Colonel gives it him; he looks upon it and lays it upon the table.*) Pray you step to the door and call for a pen and ink, Mr. Pillage. 85

COLONEL. I have pen and ink in my pocket, sir. (*Pulls out an inkhorn.*) I never go without that.

PERIWINKLE. I think it belongs to your profession. (*He looks upon the pen while the Colonel changes the lease and lays down the contract.*) I doubt this is but 90 a sorry pen, though it may serve to write my name. (*Writes.*)

COLONEL. (*Aside.*) Little does he think what he signs.

PERIWINKLE. There is your lease, Mr. Pillage. 95 (*Gives him the paper.*) Now I must desire you to make what haste you can down to Coventry and take care of everything, and I'll send down the undertaker for the body; do you attend it up, and whatever charge you are at, I will repay you. 100

COLONEL. (*Aside.*) You have paid me already, I thank you, sir.

PERIWINKLE. Will you dine with me?

COLONEL. I would rather not; there are some of my neighbours which I met as I came along, who 105 leaves the town this afternoon, they told me, and I should be glad of their company down.

PERIWINKLE. Well, well, I won't detain you.

COLONEL. (*Aside.*) I don't care how soon I am out.

PERIWINKLE. I will give orders about mourning. 110

COLONEL. [*Aside.*] You will have cause to mourn, when you know your estate imaginary only.
You'll find your hopes and cares alike are vain,
In spite of all the caution you have ta'en,
Fortune rewards the faithful lover's pain. (*Exit.*) 115

PERIWINKLE. Seven hundred a year! I wish he had died seventeen years ago. What a valuable collection of rarities might I have had by this time? I might have travelled over all the known parts of the globe and made my own closet rival the 120 Vatican at Rome. Odso, I have a good mind to begin my travels now—let me see—I am but sixty! My father, grandfather, and great-grandfather reached ninety-odd; I have almost forty years good. Let me consider! What will seven hundred a year 125 amount to—in—aye! in thirty years, I'll say but thirty—thirty times seven, is seven times thirty—that is—just twenty-one thousand pound—'tis a great deal of money—I may very well reserve sixteen hundred of it for a collection of such 130 rarities as will make my name famous to posterity. I would not die like other mortals, forgotten in a year or two, as my uncle will be. No.
With nature's curious works I'll raise my fame,
That men, till doomsday, may repeat my name. 135
(*Exit.*)

SCENE IV. A TAVERN.

Freeman and Tradelove over a bottle.

TRADELOVE. Come, Mr. Freeman, here's Mynheer Jan Van Tim, Tam, Tam—I shall never think of that Dutchman's name.

FREEMAN. Mynheer Jan Van Timtamtirelireletta Heer Van Fainwell. 5

TRADELOVE. Aye, Heer Van Fainwell, I never heard such a confounded name in life—here's his health, I say. (*Drinks.*)

FREEMAN. With all my heart.

TRADELOVE. Faith, I never expected to have found 10 so generous a thing in a Dutchman.

FREEMAN. Oh, he has nothing of the Hollander in his temper—except an antipathy to monarchy.[106] As soon as I told him your circumstances, he replied he would not be the ruin of any 15 man for the world and immediately made this proposal himself. Let him take what time he will for the payment, said he, or if he'll give me his ward, I'll forgive him the debt.

TRADELOVE. Well, Mr. Freeman, I can but thank 20 you. Egad, you have made a man of me again, and if ever I lay a wager more, may I rot in a gaol.

FREEMAN. I assure you, Mr. Tradelove, I was very much concerned because I was the occasion—though very innocently, I protest. 25

TRADELOVE. I dare swear you was, Mr. Freeman.

---

106 antipathy to monarchy] Holland was a republic.

Enter a fiddler.

FIDDLER. Please to have a lesson of music or a song, gentlemen?

FREEMAN. A song, aye, with all our hearts. Have you ever a merry one? 30

FIDDLER. Yes, sir, my wife and I can give you a merry dialogue.

Here is the song.

TRADELOVE. 'Tis very pretty, faith.

FREEMAN. There's something for you to drink, friend; go, lose no time. 35

FIDDLER. I thank you, sir. (*Exit.*)

Enter drawer and Colonel, dressed for the Dutch merchant.

COLONEL. Hah, Mynheer Tradelove, Ik ben sorry voor your troubles, maer Ik sal you easie maeken, Ik wil de gelt niet hebben.

TRADELOVE. I shall forever acknowledge the obligation, sir. 40

FREEMAN. But you understand upon what condition, Mr. Tradelove: Mrs. Lovely.

COLONEL. Ya, de juffrow sal al te regt setten, mynheer. 45

TRADELOVE. With all my heart, mynheer, you shall have my consent to marry her freely.

FREEMAN. Well then, as I am a party concerned between you, Mynheer Jan Van Timtamtirelireletta Heer Van Fainwell shall give you a discharge of 50 your wager under his own hand, and you shall give him your consent to marry Mrs. Lovely under yours; that is the way to avoid all manner of disputes hereafter.

COLONEL. Ya, waeragtig. 55

TRADELOVE. Aye, aye, so it is, Mr. Freeman, I'll give it under mine this minute. (*Sits down to write.*)

COLONEL. And so sal Ik. (*Sits down to write.*)

FREEMAN. So, ho, the house. (*Enter drawer.*) Bid your master come up. [*Exit drawer.*] (*Aside.*) I'll see 60 there be witnesses enough to the bargain.

Enter Sackbut.

SACKBUT. Do you call, gentlemen?

FREEMAN. Aye, Mr. Sackbut, we shall want your hand here.

TRADELOVE. There, mynheer, there's my consent 65 as amply as you can desire, but you must insert your own name, for I know not how to spell it; I have left a blank for it. (*Gives the Colonel a paper.*)

COLONEL. Ya, Ik sal dat well doen.

FREEMAN. Now, Mr. Sackbut, you and I will 70 witness it. (*They write.*)

COLONEL. Daer, Mynheer Tradelove, is your discharge. (*Gives him a paper.*)

TRADELOVE. Be pleased to witness this receipt too, gentlemen. 75

Freeman and Sackbut put their hands.

FREEMAN. Aye, aye, that we will.

COLONEL. Well, mynheer, ye most meer doen, ye most myn voorspraek to de juffrow syn.

FREEMAN. He means you must recommend him to the lady. 80

TRADELOVE. That I will, and to the rest of my brother guardians.

COLONEL. Wat, voor den duyvel, heb you meer guardians?

TRADELOVE. Only three, mynheer. 85

COLONEL. Wat donder heb ye myn betrocken, mynheer? Had Ik that gewoeten, Ik soude eaven met you geweest syn.

SACKBUT. But Mr. Tradelove is the principal, and he can do a great deal with the rest, sir. 90

FREEMAN. And he shall use his interest I promise you, mynheer.

TRADELOVE. I will say all that ever I can think on to recommend you, mynheer, and if you please, I'll introduce you to the lady. 95

COLONEL. Well, dat is waer. Maer ye must first spreken of myn to de juffrow and to de oudere gentlemen.

FREEMAN. Aye, that's the best way, and then I and the Heer Van Fainwell will meet you there. 100

TRADELOVE. I will go this moment, upon honor. Your most obedient humble servant.—My speaking will do you little good, mynheer, ha, ha. We have bit you, faith, ha, ha. My debt's discharged, and for the man, 105
He's my consent—to get her if he can. (*Exit.*)

COLONEL. Ha, ha, ha, this was a masterpiece of contrivance, Freeman.

FREEMAN. He hugs himself with his supposed good fortune and little thinks the luck's of our side, but come, pursue the fickle goddess while she's in the mood. Now for the Quaker. 110

COLONEL. That's the hardest task.
Of all the counterfeits performed by man,
A soldier makes the simplest Puritan. (*Exit.*) 115

ACT V, SCENE I. PRIM'S HOUSE.

Enter Mrs. Prim and Mrs. Lovely in Quaker's dress, meeting.

MRS. PRIM. So, now I like thee, Anne. Art thou not better without thy monstrous hoop coat[107] and patches! If Heaven should make thee so many black spots upon thy face, would it not fright thee, Anne? 5

MRS. LOVELY. If it should turn your inside outward and show all the spots of your hypocrisy, 'twould fright me worse.

MRS. PRIM. My hypocrisy! I scorn thy words, Anne. I lay no baits. 10

MRS. LOVELY. If you did, you'd catch no fish.

MRS. PRIM. Well, well, make thy jests, but I'd have thee to know, Anne, that I could have catched as many fish (as thou call'st them) in my time, as ever thou didst with all thy fool-traps about thee. If 15 admirers be thy aim, thou wilt have more of them in this dress than thy other. The men, take my word for't, are most desirous to see what we are most careful to conceal.

MRS. LOVELY. Is that the reason for your formality, 20 Mrs. Prim? Truth will out. I ever thought, indeed, there was more design than godliness in the pinched cap.

MRS. PRIM. Go, thou art corrupted with reading lewd plays and filthy romances, good for nothing 25 but to lead youth into the high road of fornication. Ah! I wish thou art not already too familiar with the wicked ones.

MRS. LOVELY. Too familiar with the wicked ones! Pray, no more of those freedoms, madam. I am 30 familiar with none so wicked as yourself. How dare

you talk thus to me! You, you, you unworthy woman you. (*Bursts into tears.*)

Enter Tradelove.

TRADELOVE. What, in tears, Nancy? What have you done to her, Mrs. Prim, to make her weep? 35

MRS. LOVELY. Done to me! I admire I keep my senses among you. But I will rid myself of your tyranny, if there be either law or justice to be had; I'll force you to give me up my liberty.

MRS. PRIM. Thou hast more need to weep for thy 40 sins, Anne—yea, for thy manifold sins.

MRS. LOVELY. Don't think that I'll be still the fool which you have made me. No, I'll wear what I please, go when and where I please, and keep what company I think fit and not what you shall 45 direct—I will.

TRADELOVE. For my part, I do think all this very reasonable, Mrs. Lovely—'tis fit you should have your liberty, and for that very purpose I am come.

Enter Mr. Periwinkle and Obadiah Prim, with a letter in his hand.

PERIWINKLE. I have bought some black stockings 50 of your husband, Mrs. Prim, but he tells me the glover's trade belongs to you; therefore, I pray you look me out five or six dozen of mourning gloves, such as are given at funerals, and send them to my house. 55

OBADIAH PRIM. My friend Periwinkle has got a good windfall today—seven hundred a year.

MRS. PRIM. I wish thee joy of it, neighbour.

TRADELOVE. What, is Sir Toby dead then?

PERIWINKLE. He is!—You'll take care, Mrs. Prim? 60

MRS. PRIM. Yea, I will, neighbour.

OBADIAH PRIM. This letter recommendeth a speaker,[108] 'tis from Aminidab Holdfast of Bristol. Peradventure, he will be here this night; therefore, Sarah, do thou take care for his reception. (*Gives 65 her the letter.*)

MRS. PRIM. I will obey thee. (*Exit.*)

OBADIAH PRIM. What art thou in the dumps for, Anne?

---

107 hoop coat] hooped petticoat.

108 speaker] minister.

TRADELOVE. We must marry her, Mr. Prim. 70

OBADIAH PRIM. Why truly, if we could find a husband worth having, I should be as glad to see her married as thou wouldst, neighbour.

PERIWINKLE. Well said, there are but few worth having. 75

TRADELOVE. I can recommend you a man now, that I think you can none of you have an objection to!

Enter Sir Philip Modelove.

PERIWINKLE. You recommend! Nay, whenever she marries, I'll recommend the husband. 80

SIR PHILIP. What, must it be a whale or a rhinoceros, Mr. Periwinkle? Ha, ha, ha!—Mr. Tradelove, I have a bill upon you (*Gives him a paper.*) and have been seeking for you all over the town.

TRADELOVE. I'll accept it, Sir Philip, and pay it when due. 85

PERIWINKLE. He shall be none of the fops at your end of the town, with full perukes and empty skulls, nor yet none of your trading gentry, who puzzle the heralds to find arms for their coaches. No, he shall be a man famous for travels, solidity, and curiosity, one who has searched into the profundity of nature. When Heaven shall direct such a one, he shall have my consent, because it may turn to the benefit of mankind. 90 95

MRS. LOVELY. The benefit of mankind! What, would you anatomize me?

SIR PHILIP. Aye, aye, madam, he would dissect you.

TRADELOVE. Or pore over you through a microscope to see how your blood circulates from the crown of your head to the sole of your foot, ha, ha! But I have a husband for you, a man that knows how to improve your fortune, one that trades to the four corners of the globe. 100

MRS. LOVELY. And would send me for a venture perhaps. 105

TRADELOVE. One that will dress you in all the pride of Europe, Asia, Africa, and America—a Dutch merchant, my girl!

SIR PHILIP. A Dutchman! Ha, ha, there's a husband for a fine lady—Ya, juffrow, will you met myn slapen? Ha, ha! He'll learn you to talk the language of the hogs, madam, ha, ha. 110

TRADELOVE. He'll learn you that one merchant is of more service to a nation than fifty coxcombs. The Dutch know the trading interest to be of more benefit to the state than the landed. 115

SIR PHILIP. But what is either interest to a lady?

TRADELOVE. 'Tis the merchant makes the belle. How would the ladies sparkle in the box without the merchant? The Indian diamonds! The French brocade! The Italian fan! The Flanders lace! The fine Dutch holland! How would they vent their scandal over their tea tables? And where would you beaus have champagne to toast your mistresses, were it not for the merchant? 120 125

OBADIAH PRIM. Verily, neighbour Tradelove, thou dost waste thy breath about nothing. All that thou hast said tendeth only to debauch youth and fill their heads with the pride and luxury of this world. The merchant is a very great friend to Satan and sendeth as many to his dominions as the pope. 130

PERIWINKLE. Right, I say knowledge makes the man.

OBADIAH PRIM. Yea, but not thy kind of knowledge—it is the knowledge of Truth. Search thou for the light within and not for baubles, Friend. 135

MRS. LOVELY. Ah, study your country's good, Mr. Periwinkle, and not her insects. Rid you of your home-bred monsters before you fetch any from abroad. I dare swear you have maggots enough in your own brain to stock all the virtuosos in Europe with butterflies. 140

SIR PHILIP. By my soul, Miss Nancy's a wit. 145

OBADIAH PRIM. That is more than she can say by thee, Friend. Look ye, it is in vain to talk; when I meet a man worthy of her, she shall have my leave to marry him.

MRS. LOVELY. Provided he be one of the faithful. (*Aside.*) Was there ever such a swarm of caterpillars to blast the hopes of a woman!—Know this, that you contend in vain: I'll have no husband of your choosing, nor shall you lord it over me long. I'll try the power of an English senate. Orphans have been redressed and wills set aside, and none did ever deserve their pity more.—Oh Fainwell! Where are thy promises to free me from these vermin? Alas! The task was more difficult than he imagined! 150 155

A harder task than what the poets tell 160
Of yore, the fair Andromeda[109] befell;
She but one monster feared; I've four to fear,
And see no Perseus, no deliv'rer near. (*Exit.*)

Enter servant and whispers to Prim.

SERVANT. One Simon Pure inquireth for thee.
PERIWINKLE. The woman is mad. (*Exit.*) 165
SIR PHILIP. So are you all, in my opinion. (*Exit.*)
OBADIAH PRIM. Friend Tradelove, business requireth my presence.
TRADELOVE. Oh, I shan't trouble you.—Pox take him for an unmannerly dog.—However, I have 170 kept my word with my Dutchman, and will introduce him too for all you. (*Exit.*)

Enter Colonel in a Quaker's habit.

OBADIAH PRIM. Friend Pure, thou art welcome. How is it with Friend Holdfast and all Friends in Bristol? Timothy Littlewit, John Slenderbrain, and 175 Christopher Keepfaith?
COLONEL. (*Aside.*) A goodly company!—They are all in health, I thank thee for them.
OBADIAH PRIM. Friend Holdfast writes me word that thou camest lately from Pennsylvania. How 180 do all Friends there?
COLONEL. (*Aside.*) What the devil shall I say? I know just as much of Pennsylvania as I do of Bristol.
OBADIAH PRIM. Do they thrive? 185
COLONEL. Yea, Friend, the blessing of their good works fall upon them.

Enter Mrs. Prim and Mrs. Lovely.

OBADIAH PRIM. Sarah, know our Friend Pure.
MRS. PRIM. Thou art welcome.

He salutes[110] *her.*

COLONEL. (*Aside.*) Here comes the sum of all my 190 wishes. How charming she appears, even in that disguise.
OBADIAH PRIM. Why dost thou consider the maiden so intentively,[111] Friend?
COLONEL. I will tell thee. About four days ago I 195 saw a vision—this very maiden, but in vain attire, standing on a precipice—and heard a voice, which called me by my name and bade me put forth my hand and save her from the pit. I did so, and methought the damsel grew to my side. 200
MRS. PRIM. What can that portend?
OBADIAH PRIM. The damsel's conversion, I am persuaded.
MRS. LOVELY. (*Aside.*) That's false, I'm sure.
OBADIAH PRIM. Wilt thou use the means, Friend 205 Pure?
COLONEL. Means! What means? Is she not thy daughter and already one of the faithful?
MRS. PRIM. No, alas! She's one of the ungodly.
OBADIAH PRIM. Pray thee mind what this good 210 man will say unto thee; he will teach thee the way that thou shouldst walk, Anne.
MRS. LOVELY. I know my way without his instructions. I hoped to have been quiet, when once I had put on your odious formality here. 215
COLONEL. Then thou wearest it out of compulsion, not choice, Friend?
MRS. LOVELY. Thou art in the right of it, Friend.
MRS. PRIM. Art not thou ashamed to mimic the good man? Ah! Thou art a stubborn girl. 220
COLONEL. Mind her not; she hurteth not me. If thou wilt leave her alone with me, I will discuss some few points with her that may, perchance, soften her stubborness and melt her into compliance.
OBADIAH PRIM. Content, I pray thee put it home 225 to her. Come, Sarah, let us leave the good man with her.
MRS. LOVELY. (*Catching hold of Prim; he breaks loose and exits* [*with Mrs. Prim*].) What do you mean—to leave me with this old enthusiastical[112] canter? 230 Don't think, because I complied with your formality, to impose your ridiculous doctrine upon me.

---

[109] Andromeda] In Greek myth, this daughter of the Ethiopian King was chained to a rock as a sacrificial offering to Poseidon, who had unleashed a monster upon the country. Perseus saved and eventually married her by turning the monster to stone and then defeating her wicked uncle.
[110] salutes] greets with a kiss or embrace.

[111] intentively] earnestly, intently.
[112] enthusiastical] having the quality of religious fanaticism.

COLONEL. I pray thee, young woman, moderate thy passion.

MRS. LOVELY. I pray thee, walk after thy leader; you will but lose your labour upon me.—These wretches will certainly make me mad. 235

COLONEL. I am of another opinion; the spirit telleth me that I shall convert thee, Anne.

MRS. LOVELY. 'Tis a lying spirit; don't believe it. 240

COLONEL. Say'st thou so? Why then thou shalt convert me, my angel. (*Catching her in his arms.*)

MRS. LOVELY. (*Shrieks.*) Ah! Monster, hold off, or I'll tear thy eyes out.

COLONEL. Hush! For Heaven's sake—dost thou know me? I am Fainwell. 245

MRS. LOVELY. Fainwell! (*Enter old Prim. [Mrs. Lovely says] aside.*) Oh I'm undone, Prim here. I wish with all my soul I had been dumb.

OBADIAH PRIM. What is the matter? Why didst thou shriek out, Anne? 250

MRS. LOVELY. Shriek out! I'll shriek and shriek again, cry murder, thieves, or anything to drown the noise of that eternal babbler, if you leave me with him any longer. 255

OBADIAH PRIM. Was that all? Fie, fie, Anne.

COLONEL. No matter, I'll bring down her stomach, I'll warrant thee—leave us, I pray thee.

OBADIAH PRIM. Fare thee well. (*Exit.*)

COLONEL. (*Embraces her.*) My charming, lovely woman. 260

MRS. LOVELY. What means thou by this disguise, Fainwell?

COLONEL. To set thee free, if thou wilt perform thy promise. 265

MRS. LOVELY. Make me mistress of my fortune and make thy own conditions.

COLONEL. This night shall answer all thy wishes. See here, I have the consent of three of thy guardians already and doubt not but Prim shall make the fourth. 270

Prim listening.

OBADIAH PRIM. (*Aside.*) I would gladly hear what argument the good man useth to bend her.

MRS. LOVELY. Thy words give me new life, methinks. 275

OBADIAH PRIM. What do I hear?

MRS. LOVELY. Thou best of men, Heaven meant to bless me sure, when first I saw thee.

OBADIAH PRIM. He hath mollified her. Oh wonderful conversion! 280

COLONEL. Hah! Prim listening.—No more, my love, we are observed; seem to be edified and give 'em hopes that thou wilt turn Quaker, and leave the rest to me. (*Aloud.*) I am glad to find that thou art touched with what I said unto thee, Anne; 285 another time I will explain the other article to thee; in the meanwhile, be thou dutiful to our Friend Prim.

MRS. LOVELY. I shall obey thee in everything.

Enter old Prim.

OBADIAH PRIM. Oh what a prodigious change is 290 here! Thou hast wrought a miracle, Friend! Anne, how dost thou like the doctrine he hath preached?

MRS. LOVELY. So well, that I could talk to him forever, methinks. I am ashamed of my former folly and ask your pardon, Mr. Prim. 295

COLONEL. Enough, enough that thou art sorry; he is no pope, Anne.

OBADIAH PRIM. Verily, thou dost rejoice me exceedingly, Friend. Will it please thee to walk into the next room and refresh thyself? Come, take the 300 maiden by the hand.

COLONEL. We will follow thee.

Enter servant.

SERVANT. There is another Simon Pure inquireth for thee, master.

COLONEL. (*Aside.*) The devil there is. 305

OBADIAH PRIM. Another Simon Pure? I do not know him. Is he any relation of thine?

COLONEL. No, Friend, I know him not. (*Aside.*) Pox take him, I wish he were in Pennsylvania again, with all my blood. 310

MRS. LOVELY. (*Aside.*) What shall I do?

OBADIAH PRIM. Bring him up.

COLONEL. [*Aside.*] Humph! Then one of us must go down, that's certain. Now Impudence assist me.

Enter Simon Pure.

OBADIAH PRIM. What is thy will with me, 315 Friend?

SIMON PURE. Didst thou not receive a letter from Aminidab Holdfast of Bristol concerning one Simon Pure?

OBADIAH PRIM. Yea, and Simon Pure is already here, Friend. 320

COLONEL. (*Aside.*) And Simon Pure will stay here, Friend, if possible.

SIMON PURE. That's an untruth, for I am he.

COLONEL. Take thou heed, Friend, what thou dost say; I do affirm that I am Simon Pure. 325

SIMON PURE. Thy name may be Pure, Friend, but not that Pure.

COLONEL. Yea, that Pure which my good Friend Aminidab Holdfast wrote to my Friend Prim about, the same Simon Pure that came from Pennsylvania and sojourned in Bristol eleven days. Thou wouldst not take my name from me, wouldst thou? (*Aside.*) Till I have done with it. 330

SIMON PURE. Thy name! I am astonished. 335

COLONEL. At what? at thy own assurance? (*Going up to him; Simon Pure starts back.*)

SIMON PURE. *Avaunt, Sathan*, approach me not; I defy thee and all thy works.[113]

MRS. LOVELY. (*Aside.*) Oh, he'll outcant him. Undone, undone forever. 340

COLONEL. Hark thee, Friend, thy sham will not take. Don't exert thy voice; thou art too well acquainted with Sathan to start at him, thou wicked reprobate. What can thy design be here? 345

Enter servant and gives Prim a letter.

OBADIAH PRIM. One of these must be a counterfeit, but which I cannot say.

COLONEL. (*Aside.*) What can that letter be?

SIMON PURE. Thou must be the devil, Friend, that's certain, for no human power can stock so great a falsehood. 350

OBADIAH PRIM. This letter sayeth that thou art better acquainted with that prince of darkness than any here. Read that, I pray thee, Simon. (*Gives it the Colonel.*) 355

COLONEL. [*Aside.*] 'Tis Freeman's hand. (*Reads.*) "There is a design formed to rob your house this

night and cut your throat, and for that purpose there is a man disguised like a Quaker, who is to pass for one Simon Pure; the gang whereof I am one, though now resolved to rob no more, has been at Bristol; one of them came up in the coach with the Quaker, whose name he hath taken, and from what he gathered from him, formed that design, and did not doubt but he should impose so far upon you as to make you turn out the real Simon Pure and keep him with you. Make the right use of this. Adieu." (*Aside.*) Excellent well! 360 365

OBADIAH PRIM. (*To Simon Pure.*) Dost thou hear this? 370

SIMON PURE. Yea, but it moveth me not; that, doubtless, is the impostor. (*Pointing at the Colonel.*)

COLONEL. Ah! Thou wicked one—now I consider thy face I remember thou didst come up in the leathern convenience[114] with me—thou hadst a black bob wig on, and a brown camblet[115] coat with brass buttons. Canst thou deny it, hah? 375

SIMON PURE. Yea, I can, and with a safe conscience too, Friend.

OBADIAH PRIM. Verily, Friend, thou art the most impudent villain I ever saw. 380

MRS. LOVELY. (*Aside.*) Nay then, I'll have a fling at him too.—I remember the face of this fellow at Bath. Aye, this is he that picked my Lady Raffle's pocket upon the Grove.[116] Don't you remember that the mob pumped[117] you, Friend? This is the most notorious rogue. 385

SIMON PURE. What doth provoke thee to seek my life? Thou wilt not hang me, wilt thou, wrongfully?

OBADIAH PRIM. She will do thee no hurt, nor thou shalt do me none; therefore, get thee about thy business, Friend, and leave thy wicked course of life, or thou may'st not come off so favourably everywhere. 390

---

113 *Sathan ... works*] formulaic rejection of Satan, using an archaic pronunciation.

114 leathern convenience] Quaker for coach.

115 camblet] a light cloth of mixed silk and wool.

116 the Grove] the Orange Grove, a public walk planted with trees named for a column honouring William of Orange.

117 pumped] put under a stream of water from a pump, for punishment.

COLONEL. Go, Friend, I would advise thee, and 395
tempt thy fate no more.

SIMON PURE. Yea, I will go, but it shall be to thy
confusion; for I shall clear myself. I will return with
some proofs that shall convince thee, Obadiah,
that thou art highly imposed upon. (*Exit.*) 400

COLONEL. (*Aside.*) Then here will be no staying
for me, that's certain. What the devil shall I do?

OBADIAH PRIM. What monstrous works of
iniquity are there in this world, Simon!

COLONEL. Yea, the age is full of vice. (*Aside.*) 405
Z'death, I am so confounded, I know not what to
say.

OBADIAH PRIM. Thou art disordered, Friend—
art thou not well?

COLONEL. My spirit is greatly troubled, and 410
something telleth me, that though I have wrought
a good work in converting this maiden, this tender
maiden, yet my labour will be in vain; for the evil
spirit fighteth against her, and I see, yea I see with
the eyes of my inward man, that Sathan will 415
rebuffet her again, whenever I withdraw myself
from her, and she will, yea this very damsel will
return again to that abomination from whence I
have retrieved her, as if it were, yea, as if it were
out of the jaws of the Fiend—hum— 420

OBADIAH PRIM. Good lack! Thinkest thou so?

MRS. LOVELY. (*Aside.*) I must second him.—What
meaneth this struggling within me? I feel the spirit
resisting the vanities of this world, but the flesh is
rebellious, yea the flesh—I greatly fear the flesh 425
and the weakness thereof—hum—

OBADIAH PRIM. The maid is inspired.

COLONEL. Behold, her light begins to shine forth.
(*Aside.*) Excellent woman!

MRS. LOVELY. This good man hath spoken 430
comfort unto me, yea comfort, I say; because the
words which he hath breathed into my outward
ears are gone through and fixed in mine heart, yea
verily in mine heart, I say—and I feel the spirit
doth love him exceedingly, hum— 435

COLONEL. (*Aside.*) She acts it to the life.

OBADIAH PRIM. Prodigious! The damsel is filled
with the spirit, Sarah!

Enter Mrs. Prim.

MRS. PRIM. I am greatly rejoiced to see such a
change in our beloved Anne. I came to tell thee 440
that supper stayeth for thee.

COLONEL. I am not disposed for thy food—my
spirit longeth for more delicious meat; fain would
I redeem this maiden from the tribe of sinners and
break those cords asunder wherewith she is 445
bound—hum—

MRS. LOVELY. Something whispers in my ears,
methinks, that I must be subject to the will of this
good man and from him only must hope for
consolation—hum—it also telleth me that I am a 450
chosen vessel to raise up seed to the faithful and
that thou must consent that we two be one flesh
according to the Word—hum—

OBADIAH PRIM. What a Revelation is here? This
is certainly part of thy vision, Friend, this is the 455
maiden's growing to thy side. Ah! With what
willingness should I give thee my consent, could I
give thee her fortune too, but thou wilt never get
the consent of the wicked ones.

COLONEL. (*Aside.*) I wish I was as sure of yours. 460

OBADIAH PRIM. My soul rejoiceth, yea, it
rejoiceth, I say, to find the spirit within thee; for
lo, it moveth thee with natural agitation—yea,
with natural agitation, I say again, and stirreth up
the seeds of thy virgin inclination towards this 465
good man—yea, it stirreth, as one may say—yea
verily, I say it stirreth up thy inclination—yea, as
one would stir a pudding.

MRS. LOVELY. I see, I see! The spirit guiding of thy
hand, good Obadiah Prim, and now behold thou 470
art signing thy consent, and now I see myself
within thy arms, my Friend and Brother, yea, I am
become bone of thy bone and flesh of thy flesh.
(*Embraces him.*) Hum—

COLONEL. (*Aside.*) Admirably performed.—And I 475
will take thee in all spiritual love for an helpmeet,
yea, for the wife of my bosom—and now,
methinks—I feel a longing—yea, a longing, I say,
for the consummation of thy love, hum—yea, I
do long exceedingly. 480

MRS. LOVELY. And verily, verily my spirit feeleth
the same longing.

MRS. PRIM. The spirit hath greatly moved them
both. Friend Prim, thou must consent; there is no
resisting of the spirit. 485

OBADIAH PRIM. Yea, the light within showeth me that I shall fight a good fight—and wrestle through those reprobate fiends, thy other guardians—yea, I perceive the spirit will hedge thee into the flock of the righteous—Thou art a chosen Lamb—yea, a chosen Lamb, and I will not push thee back— no, I will not, I say—no, thou shalt leap-a, and frisk-a, and skip-a, and bound, and bound, I say— yea, bound within the fold of the righteous—yea, even within thy fold, my Brother. Fetch me the pen and ink, Sarah—and my hand shall confess its obedience to the spirit. [*Exit Mrs. Prim.*] 490

495

COLONEL. [*Aside.*] I wish it were over.

Enter Mrs. Prim with pen and ink.

MRS. LOVELY. (*Aside.*) I tremble lest this quaking rogue should return and spoil all. 500

OBADIAH PRIM. Here, Friend, do thou write what the spirit prompteth, and I will sign it.

Colonel sits down [and writes].

MRS. PRIM. Verily, Anne, it greatly rejoiceth me, to see thee reformed from that original wickedness wherein I found thee. 505

MRS. LOVELY. I do believe thou art, and I thank thee.

COLONEL. (*Reads.*) "This is to certify all whom it may concern, that I do freely give up all my right and title in Anne Lovely to Simon Pure, and my full consent that she shall become his wife according to the form of marriage. Witness my hand." 510

OBADIAH PRIM. That is enough—give me the pen. (*Signs it.*)

Enter Betty running to Mrs. Lovely.

BETTY. Oh! Madam, madam, here's the Quaking man again; he has brought a coachman and two or three more. 515

MRS. LOVELY. (*Aside to Colonel.*) Ruined past redemption.

COLONEL. [*Aside to her.*] No, no, one minute sooner had spoiled all, but now—(*Going up to Prim hastily.*) Here is company coming, Friend, give me the paper. 520

OBADIAH PRIM. Here it is, Simon, and I wish thee happy with the maiden. 525

MRS. LOVELY. 'Tis done, and now, devil do thy worst.

Enter Simon Pure and coachman, etc.

SIMON PURE. Look thee, Friend, I have brought these people to satisfy thee that I am not that impostor which thou didst take me for; this is the man which did drive the leathern conveniency that brought me from Bristol, and this is— 530

COLONEL. Look ye, Friend, to save the Court the trouble of examining witnesses, I plead guilty, ha, ha!

OBADIAH PRIM. How's this? Is not thy name Pure, then? 535

COLONEL. No really, sir, I only made bold with this gentleman's name, but I here give it up safe and sound; it has done the business which I had occasion for, and now I intend to wear my own, which shall be at his service upon the same occasion at any time, ha, ha, ha! 540

SIMON PURE. Oh! The wickedness of this age.

COACHMAN. Then you have no farther need of us, sir. (*Exit.*) 545

COLONEL. No, honest man, you may go about your business.

OBADIAH PRIM. I am struck dumb with thy impudence, Anne; thou hast deceived me and perchance undone thyself. 550

MRS. PRIM. Thou art a dissembling baggage, and shame will overtake thee. (*Exit.*)

SIMON PURE. I am grieved to see thy wife so much troubled; I will follow and console her. (*Exit.*)

Enter servant.

SERVANT. Thy brother guardians inquireth for thee; there is another man with them. 555

MRS. LOVELY. (*To the Colonel.*) Who can that other man be?

COLONEL. 'Tis one Freeman, a friend of mine, whom I ordered to bring the rest of thy guardians here. 560

Enter Sir Philip, Tradelove, Periwinkle, and Freeman.

FREEMAN. (*To the Colonel.*) Is all safe? Did my letter do you service?

COLONEL. (*Aside [to Freeman].*) All! All's safe; ample service. 565

SIR PHILIP. Miss Nancy, how dost do, child?

MRS. LOVELY. Don't call me miss, Friend Philip, my name is Anne, thou knowest.

SIR PHILIP. What, is the girl metamorphosed?

MRS. LOVELY. I wish thou wert so metamor- 570
phosed. Ah! Philip, throw off that gaudy attire and wear the clothes becoming of thy age.

OBADIAH PRIM. (*Aside.*) I am ashamed to see these men.

SIR PHILIP. My age! The woman is possessed. 575

COLONEL. No, thou art possessed rather, friend.

TRADELOVE. Hark ye, Mrs. Lovely, one word with you. (*Takes hold of her hand.*)

COLONEL. This maiden is my wife, thanks to Friend Prim, and thou hast no business with her. 580
(*Takes her from him.*)

TRADELOVE. His wife! Hark ye, Mr. Freeman—

PERIWINKLE. Why, you have made a very fine piece of work of it, Mr. Prim.

SIR PHILIP. Married to a Quaker! Thou art a fine 585
fellow to be left guardian to an orphan, truly— there's a husband for a young lady!

COLONEL. When I have put on my beau clothes, Sir Philip, you'll like me better.

SIR PHILIP. Thou wilt make a very scurvy beau, 590
Friend.

COLONEL. I believe I can prove it under your hand that you thought me a very fine gentleman in the park today, about thirty-six minutes after eleven; will you take a pinch, Sir Philip—out of the finest 595
snuffbox you ever saw. (*Offers him snuff.*)

SIR PHILIP. Ha, ha, ha! I am overjoyed, faith I am, if thou be'st that gentleman. I own I did give my consent to the gentleman I brought here today, but if this is he I can't be positive. 600

OBADIAH PRIM. Canst thou not. Now I think thou art a fine fellow to be left guardian to an orphan. Thou shallow-brained shuttlecock, he may be a pickpocket for aught thou dost know.

PERIWINKLE. You would have been two rare 605
fellows to have been trusted with the sole management of her fortune, would ye not, think ye? But Mr. Tradelove and myself shall take care of her portion.

TRADELOVE. Aye, aye, so we will. Did not you tell 610
me the Dutch merchant desired me to meet him here, Mr. Freeman?

FREEMAN. I did so, and I am sure he will be here, if you have a little patience.

COLONEL. What, is Mr. Tradelove impatient? Nay 615
then, ik ben gereet veor you, heb ye Jan Van Timtamtirelireletta Heer Van Fainwell vergeeten?

TRADELOVE. Oh! Pox of the name! What, have you tricked me too, Mr. Freeman?

COLONEL. Tricked, Mr. Tradelove! Did I not give 620
you two thousand pound for your consent fairly? And now do you tell a gentleman that he has tricked you?

PERIWINKLE. So, so, you are a pretty guardian, faith, sell your charge. What, did you look upon 625
her as part of your stock?

OBADIAH PRIM. Ha, ha, ha! I am glad thy knavery is found out however. I confess the maiden overreached me, and no sinister end at all.

PERIWINKLE. Aye, aye, one thing or another 630
overreached you all, but I'll take care he shall never finger a penny of her money, I warrant you. Overreached, quoth'a? Why I might have been overreached too, if I had had no more wit. I don't know but this very fellow may be him that was 635
directed to me from Grand Cairo today. Ha, ha, ha.

COLONEL. The very same, sir.

PERIWINKLE. Are you so, sir, but your trick would not pass upon me. 640

COLONEL. No, as you say, at that time it did not, that was not my lucky hour, but hark ye, sir, I must let you into one secret—you may keep honest John Tradescant's coat on, for your uncle, Sir Toby Peri-winkle, is not dead—so the charge of mourning 645
will be saved, ha, ha! Don't you remember Mr. Pil-lage, your uncle's steward, ha, ha, ha?

PERIWINKLE. Not dead! I begin to fear I am tricked too.

COLONEL. Don't you remember the signing of a 650
lease, Mr. Periwinkle?

PERIWINKLE. Well, and what signifies that lease, if my uncle is not dead? Hah! I am sure it was a lease I signed.

COLONEL. Aye, but it was a lease for life, sir, and 655
of this beautiful tenement, I thank you. (*Taking hold of Mrs. Lovely.*)

OMNES. Ha, ha, ha, neighbour's fare![118]

FREEMAN. So then, I find you are all tricked, ha, ha! 660

PERIWINKLE. I am certain I read as plain a lease as ever I read in my life.

COLONEL. You read a lease I grant you, but you signed this contract. (*Showing a paper.*)

PERIWINKLE. How durst you put this trick upon 665 me, Mr. Freeman, did not you tell me my uncle was dying?

FREEMAN. And would tell you twice as much to serve my friend, ha, ha.

SIR PHILIP. What, the learned, famous Mr. 670 Periwinkle choused[119] too? Ha, ha, ha! I shall die with laughing, ha, ha, ha.

OBADIAH PRIM. It had been well if her father had left her to wiser heads than thine and mine, Friend, ha, ha. 675

TRADELOVE. Well, since you have outwitted us all, pray you, what and who are you, sir?

SIR PHILIP. Sir, the gentleman is a fine gentleman. I am glad you have got a person, madam, who understands dress and good breeding. I was 680 resolved she should have a husband of my choosing.

OBADIAH PRIM. I am sorry the maiden is fallen into such hands.

TRADELOVE. A beau! Nay then, she is finely 685 helped up.

MRS. LOVELY. Why, beaus are great encouragers of trade, sir, ha, ha!

COLONEL. Look ye, gentlemen, I am the person who can give the best account of myself, and I 690 must beg Sir Philip's pardon, when I tell him that I have as much aversion to what he calls dress and breeding as I have to the enemies of my religion. I have had the honour to serve his Majesty and headed a regiment of the bravest fellows that ever 695 pushed bayonet in the throat of a Frenchman, and notwithstanding the fortune this lady brings me, whenever my country wants my aid, this sword and arm are at her service.

And now, my fair, if you'll but deign to smile, 700
I meet a recompense for all my toil:
Love and religion ne'er admit restraint,
Force makes many a sinner, not one saint;
Still free as air the active mind does rove,
And searches proper objects for its love, 705
But that once fixed, 'tis past the power of art
To chase the dear ideas from the heart:
'Tis liberty of choice that sweetens life,
Makes the glad husband and the happy wife.

FINIS.

---

[118] neighbour's fare] the same fate or luck.
[119] choused] cheated, tricked.

CARLO GOZZI

Turandot

urandot is one of ten fables written for Venetian audiences by Carlo Gozzi (1720–1806)
as part of his crusade against realism, feminism, and what he saw as the baneful influence
of the middle class. In 1761, when this fairytale was first performed by the acting company of Antonio Sacchi, the Enlightenment was in full swing across Europe. Middle-class drama
had triumphed in England, as had bourgeois drama in France. In Germany, too, under the influence of reformers like G.E. Lessing, the aesthetics and ideology of the old aristocratic order were
giving way, at least on stage, to egalitarian, liberty-loving depictions of everyday middle-class life.
But for "Count" Carlo Gozzi, an impoverished aristocrat, these commercially driven developments
were anathema to true art. He spent his life waging war on all of them, vilifying them as corrupting
"foreign" influences, and using the stage as a pulpit from which to attack their chief proponent in
Venice, playwright and reformer Carlo Goldoni (1707–1793).[1]

Unlike Goldoni, Gozzi wished to uphold the old traditions of *commedia dell'arte*, a once-be-
loved, but at that time somewhat moribund genre of masked, improvised comedy. Accordingly,
Turandot features such venerable stock characters as Truffaldino, Pantalone, and Brighella; the script
also indicates the actors' *lazzi*—the slapstick, acrobatic, and often obscene stage business typical of
the *commedia* style. Gozzi retains traditional *commedia* dialects as well: coarse Venetian for the comic
characters, literary Tuscan for the serious. But above all, he has preserved the element of fantasy, a
mainstay of *commedia dell'arte* since the Renaissance but banished from Italian comedy by progressive realists like Goldoni.

An exotic Peking, a magic portrait, a beautiful Princess, a parade of suitors, and three life-or-
death riddles—all these elements place *Turandot* within the realm of the fairytale. Based on a Persian fable, *Turandot* represents no ordinary, waking reality: the profundity of fairytales lies in their
ability to express powerful subconscious fears and wishes in a disguised, socially acceptable form.
Turandot fears that, by feeling love and marrying, she will become subservient to a selfish and unfaithful man, and lose her independence and self-respect as a result; Calaf faces the prospect of getting his head chopped off by a castrating harridan who demands that he satisfy her riddling
disposition—three times in a row!—yet who would sooner betray him than suffer humiliation herself. Both lovers harbour deep-seated anxieties about the other gender that seem to transcend the
social conditions of any particular time and place. For this reason, and despite Gozzi's clear intention to ridicule the feminists of his era, *Turandot* remains a durable psychological parable about the
power struggles of love and trust, and one that may say more about our dreams and nightmares of
desire than do the more "politically correct" plays of Gozzi's contemporaries.

---

[1] Although not necessarily as a result, Goldoni eventually decamped to Paris to write for the Italian actors at
the *Théâtre Italien*, and Gozzi claimed victory in the "War of the Carlos."

In fact, although successful in its time, *Turandot*, like Gozzi's other works, has seemed to grow ever more up-to-date. For the Romantics, *Turandot* was a revelation. Schiller, Goethe, the Schlegels, Mme. de Staël, Schopenhauer, and Wagner all admired or adapted it. Operatic versions of the 1920s—Prokofiev's *Love of Three Oranges* (1921) is based on another Gozzi play, and Puccini's *Turandot* (1926) remains one of the best-loved operas in the repertory—revealed Gozzi's surprisingly *avant garde* theatricality. His fairytales have been championed by Russian directors such as Meyerhold and Vakhtangov, and by postmodern artists such as Julie Taymor, whose inventive stagings of *The Green Bird* and *King Stag* have demonstrated the enduring theatrical power of these fables, especially for audiences weary of the literal, quotidian kitchen-sink details of realism and naturalism.

[J.W.]

CARLO GOZZI

Turandot

A Tragicomic Tale of China for the Theatre in Five Acts

Translated by Albert Bermel and Ted Emery

PREFACE[1]

A great many people confessed that *The Raven*[2] was an intrinsically powerful play. Many others, however moved they had been by it, and although they had seen it more than once with pleasure, refused to say that it had any real worth. They chattered on about it without any convincing proof, insisting that the play's successful run was due only to the skill of the comic actors (though the masks[3] had in fact had quite small parts), to the wonderful scenery, and to the transformations of a man into a statue, and a statue into a man.

In reality, the puerile title and unrealistic plot were the sole reasons why these people wouldn't give any credit to the poor *Raven*.

It was because of these ungrateful people that I based my next play on a Persian tale, the ridiculous story of Turandot. I used the commedia dell'arte characters very little, just enough to continue my support of them, and the play was almost entirely devoid of magic and miracles.

I wanted the three riddles of the Chinese princess, artfully situated in a tragic context, to give me material for two acts of the play. The difficulty of guessing two names, and the important consequences of success or failure, provided me with the theme for more, to create a seriocomic work in five acts.

Three riddles and two names are truly a large foundation on which to construct a play that must hold a cultured audience's attention for three hours, and keep them in a serious frame of mind at odds with the plot. If my critics, with their rare talents, had had such a beautiful plot on their hands, they would have created a famous and fabulously successful piece of work, and one far better than mine. I concede it.

The simplicity of this nonsensical tale, lacking

---

[1] From the first published edition of his plays (1772).
[2] First performed in Venice in 1761.
[3] Commedia dell'arte characters, who were associated with the masks they wore.

magic and transformations, allowed me to counter what my critics said about the worth of such transformations, although I knew from the outset that their objections had no basis in fact.

The transformations I used in my tales for the theatre were for the most part painful afflictions and consisted of nothing more than the final outcome of dramatic circumstances prepared and developed long before the physical changes occurred. They always had the power of holding the audience's attention for as long as I wished, and of maintaining a convincing and varied illusion, even during the transformation itself.

This artistic aim, for which I strove with all the strength of my weak intellect, was well understood by perceptive people. And if my stupid critics had observed that, after my foolish tales, the old-fashioned "magical" scenes of the commedia dell'arte fell entirely out of use, that objective fact would have convinced them of the truth, without requiring them to use the intelligence that they either do not have, or else use only for cheap malicious remarks.

The tale of Turandot, constructed around the impossible occurrences that you will see, with sparing use of the commedia dell'arte characters, and without showy magic effects or transformations, was brought onto the stage of the San Samuele Theatre of Venice by Sacchi's company on the twenty-second of January, 1761. It was repeated for seven nights to the applause of full houses, which somewhat reduced the previous criticism.

This work of theatrical fantasy did not die after its birth. It is still performed every year, and its success is the only reason for the anger of its enemies.

40

45

50

55

60

65

CHARACTERS
TURANDOT (TOO-rahn-DOHT), princess of
  China, daughter of
ALTOUM (ahl-TOOM), emperor of China
ADELMA (ah-DEL-mah), princess of Tartary,
  Turandot's favourite slave
ZELIMA (zay-LEE-mah), Turandot's servant

SCHIRINA (skee-REE-nah), Zelima's mother,
  wife of
BARACH (bah-RACK), under the name of
  Hassan, former tutor of
CALAF (kah-LAHF), prince of the Tartars, son of
TIMUR (tee-MOOR) king of Astrakhan
ISHMAEL, former tutor of the prince of
  Samarkand
PANTALONE, Altoum's secretary
TARTAGLIA, lord high chancellor
BRIGHELLA, master of the pages
TRUFFALDINO, chief eunuch of Turandot's
  seraglio
Eight SAGES of the Chinese high council
SLAVEWOMEN, EUNUCHS, SOLDIERS, PRIESTS,
  and an EXECUTIONER

The scene is in Peking and nearby. All characters wear Chinese garb, except for Adelma, Calaf, and Timur, who are dressed as Tartars.

ACT ONE

A view of the city gate of Peking. Above the gate are many iron spears. On each, a severed head is impaled.

SCENE 1

Calaf, then Barach

CALAF. (*Entering from the side*) I knew I could find one good-hearted person, even in Peking.
BARACH. (*Entering from the city*) No! Can it be...?
CALAF. (*Surprised*) Barach!
BARACH. Your Highness... 5
CALAF. You, in Peking?
BARACH. You alive? Here?
CALAF. Hush! For heaven's sake don't give me away. How did you come here?
BARACH. When King Carizmo destroyed your army 10 under the walls of Astrakhan, I saw the defeated Turks flee and the barbarous sultan Carizmo usurp your throne and overrun the realm. I went back, wounded, into the city. There I heard that you and your father, King Timur, had died in the battle, 15 and I wept. I ran to the palace to save your poor mother, Elmaze, but I could not find her. The enemy and his troops were already entering

Astrakhan unopposed. I had to escape. Months later, my wanderings brought me to Peking. I changed my name to Hassan, and pretended to be Persian. I met a poor widow who was down on her luck. With good advice and some gems I sold for her, I soon improved my fortune. I liked her, and she was grateful. In the end she became my wife, and to this day she thinks I'm Persian and calls me Hassan, not Barach. I am a poor man now, but at this moment I am wealthy beyond all imagination at seeing my dear Prince Calaf, whom I raised almost like a son and had mourned for dead. How do you come to be alive, and here in Peking?

CALAF. Don't mention my name. After that terrible battle, my father and I ran to the palace. We quickly packed up the best of the jewels, and with my mother we fled, disguised as peasants. Oh, God, Barach! What sufferings and hardships! At the foot of Mount Caucasus thieves stripped us of everything save our lives. Hunger and thirst were our constant companions. On we went. I carried my old father and mother on my back by turns, first one, then the other. Time and again I had to prevent my father from killing himself in desperation. I had to keep reviving my mother when she fainted from weariness and sorrow. One day we reached the city of Jaich. At the mosques and in the bazaar I begged for coins and crusts of bread. The shame! But that was not all. The savage tyrant Carizmo had not found our bodies and was not satisfied with the rumour of our deaths. He promised fat rewards to anyone who brought him our heads. You know how much people fear that ferocious man, and fallen kings have little influence when it comes to diplomacy. By chance, I discovered that the king of Jaich was secretly searching for us through the city. I ran to my parents, urged them to flee. They wept, they wanted to die. At last I calmed them, reminding them of heaven's secrets and its decrees, and we ran away— to undergo new hardships…

BARACH. (*Weeping*) Stop, Your Highness, my heart is breaking. The bravest, most merciful, the wisest of royal families reduced to beggars! Please answer me now: is my king still alive, and his wife?

CALAF. Yes, Barach, both he and my mother are living….But let me tell you the trials a man may be subjected to, although he is born to high station. A strong soul must bear good and harm alike. Compared to the gods, a king is nothing: only obedience to heaven's decrees gives a man his true worth. We found ourselves at the court of Cheicobad, the king of Carazani. I took on the most menial jobs to support my parents. The king's daughter, Adelma, took pity on me—and I think she felt something beyond mere pity. Her penetrating glances told me that she suspected I was more than a servant. But her father declared war on Altoum, the emperor of China—I don't know why, and I never believed the stupid stories told by the rabble. All I know is that the emperor defeated him, sacked his city, and put his entire family to the sword, except for Adelma, whom they drowned in a river. Or so the story goes. We took off again, to escape the slaughter and the raging war. After a long and painful journey, we came, ragged and barefoot, to Berlas. And there I provided for my poor parents for four years by working as—don't be shocked—a humble porter. Yes, I bore burdens on my back like a peasant.

BARACH. No more, Your Highness, say no more. Since I see you now in royal dress, please put this unhappiness aside, and tell me how fortune smiled upon you at last.

CALAF. Smiled? Wait. One day Alinguer, the emperor of Berlas, lost a precious falcon. I caught it and returned it to him. He asked me who I was. I told him only that I was a poor man and provided for my parents by carrying burdens. The emperor commanded that my mother and father be brought to the poorhouse, and that they be well served and looked after there. (*Weeping*) Barach, that is where your king and queen are…My mother and father live in constant fear that they will be discovered and beheaded.

BARACH. (*Weeping*) Oh, God! Such an unfair punishment!

CALAF. The emperor gave me this gold (*drawing a purse from his robes*), a good horse, and these fine clothes. In desperation, I embraced my parents, and told them I was going to seek my fortune. Either I'd lose my life or they could expect great things from me, for I could not bear to see them in such poverty. They wanted to stop me, follow me. Heaven keep them from doing so. I changed my name and came to Peking to join the emperor's army. If I can raise myself to a higher rank, Barach, if fortune favours me, I will take my revenge. But I don't understand why the city is so full of foreigners. I couldn't find lodgings. A kind woman in that house took me in and stabled my horse... 115

BARACH. Your Highness, she is my wife.

CALAF. Your wife! You are fortunate to possess such a gracious woman. (*Ready to leave*) I will return, Barach. I want to see this ceremony, which has drawn so many people to Peking. Then I will present myself to the emperor, and ask to be accepted as a soldier. (*He goes toward the city gate.*) 120 125

BARACH. Stop, Calaf! Don't be drawn into this grisly spectacle. Peking is a theatre of atrocities.

CALAF. What do you mean?

BARACH. Haven't you heard of Turandot, the emperor's only daughter? She is as cruel as she is beautiful. She brings us slaughter, tears, and mourning. 130

CALAF. I do remember hearing some foolish stories about her among some of the Carazani. They even said that King Cheicobad's son died in some horrible way here in Peking, and that was why the king declared war on China. But the ignorant common folk make these things up. They think they know their master's business, but the sensible man listens to them and laughs. 135 140

BARACH. Turandot is as wise as a sage, and so lovely that no painter can do her justice. Portraits of her have passed from hand to hand in foreign courts, and great princes have asked to marry her—all in vain, for the heartless creature hates men. 145

CALAF. Yes, that's the tale I heard. I laughed at it. Go on, Barach.

BARACH. It's not a tale. Her father tried to marry her many times. She will inherit the empire, and he wished to find a royal husband who'd be capable of governing it. The obstinate woman refused, and her loving father would not force her. He has had to fight wars because of her, and though he is powerful and has always won, he is growing old. Finally, he spoke to her firmly, trying to reason with her: "I am an old man," he said, "and I have angered too many 150 155

monarchs by promising your hand in marriage, only to find you opposed. Either take a husband, or tell me how to avoid these wars you have caused by your unjust refusals. Then you may live and die as you wish. My request is fair, and my love for you has never faltered." The proud Turandot begged him over and over to change his mind, but he would not. Finally the viper fell ill from sheer rage. On the point of death, she asked her saddened but steadfast father to grant her one diabolical request— 160 165

CALAF. Yes, that's the story I heard before. I know what you are about to say. She wanted her father to issue and edict that any prince could ask for her hand, but on this condition: that in the imperial council, before the sages, she would present the candidate with three riddles. If he solved them, she would accept him as a husband and heir to her empire. If he failed, the emperor Altoum, by solemn vow, would have him beheaded. Isn't that the same fairy tale, Barach? Tell me the rest, because I bore myself reciting it. 170 175

BARACH. Fairy tale? If only it were! The emperor rebelled when he heard that, but the tigerish woman drove the poor weak man nearly out of his mind. Sometimes she stormed at him, sometimes she pretended to be dying, and at last the emperor agreed. "No men will dare attempt it, and I will live in peace," she told her father. "And if any try, my father will not be blamed for carrying out a sworn public edict." This cruel law was sworn and publicly proclaimed, and I wish I could say it was a fairy tale, whose effects are no more than a dream. 180 185

CALAF. I believe it, since you are the one who is telling me. But certainly no prince can have been fool enough to take up the challenge. 190

BARACH. No? Look. (*He points to the skulls above the gate.*) Those are the heads of the young princes who have tried to solve Turandot's riddles.

CALAF. (*Shocked*) Monstrous! How can they have been so stupid? Throwing away their lives for such a bloodthirsty woman! 195

BARACH. You wouldn't say that, Calaf, if you had seen her portrait. It has such power of fascination that young men who glimpse it rush blindly to their death. 200

CALAF. A madman might do that.

BARACH. Even a wise man would. The crowds are here in Peking today to watch the beheading of the prince of Samarkand, the most handsome, intelligent, and gracious young man this city has ever seen. Altoum regrets his vow and weeps, while his prideful, inhuman daughter gloats in triumph. I left the city so as not to see it. (*The sorrowful sound of a drumroll is heard.*) Listen! That dreary sound is the signal for the ax to fall.

CALAF. These are strange events you've described, Barach. How could nature give birth to such a woman incapable of loving, so stripped of compassion?

BARACH. My wife's daughter is one of Turandot's servants. Now and then she tells my wife things. Turandot is a tigress, Your Highness, and her greatest sin is her unrelenting pride.

CALAF. To the devil with that inhuman abomination! If I were her father, I would burn her at the stake.

BARACH. (*Looking toward the city*) There is Ishmael, the tutor of the prince they have just executed. Oh, my poor friend—he's weeping!

SCENE 2

Ishmael, Calaf, and Barach

ISHMAEL. (*Enters weeping*) My prince is dead, Barach. Why didn't they behead me instead?

BARACH. But how could you let him take the chance of solving the riddles?

ISHMAEL. Don't add insult to my injuries. I did my duty, Barach. If I'd had time, I'd have told his father. But I had no time, and the boy wouldn't listen to reason. A tutor is only a servant, and cannot command his prince.

BARACH. Don't grieve for him, Ishmael. Try to take this calmly, like a philosopher.

ISHMAEL. Don't grieve for him! I loved him, Barach, and he wanted me by his side until his final moments. The memory of his last words will be a knife in my heart as long as I live. "Don't weep for me," he said, "I die willingly, since the cruel woman cannot be mine. Tell my royal father I beg his pardon for leaving his court without saying good-bye. I disobeyed him because I was afraid he would not let me go. Show him this portrait. (*He draws a portrait from his robes.*) When he sees her

beauty, he will forgive me, and pity my fate." After that, he kissed this loathsome portrait a hundred times, and drew his robes back from his neck. Then—ghastly sight!—I saw his blood spurt, and his body fall to the ground as the executioner clutched my dear master's severed head. I fled, blind with grief and horror. (*He throws the portrait to the ground and stamps on it.*) A curse on the foul, hellish portrait. If I could only trample on Turandot like this. (*To the portrait*) Take you back to my king? No, I'll never return to Samarkand. I'll go to the desert and weep away my life. (*Exits*)

SCENE 3

Calaf and Barach

BARACH. You heard that, Your Highness?

CALAF. Yes, and I pity him. But how can this painting have such unheard-of power? (*He is about to pick up the portrait; Barach stops him.*)

BARACH. Your Highness! What are you doing?

CALAF. (*Smiling*) Picking up the portrait. I want to see this enchanting beauty. (*Again he goes to pick up the portrait, and Barach holds his arm.*)

BARACH. It would be like looking at the Medusa.[4] I won't let you.

CALAF. Don't talk rubbish. (*He shakes off Barach and picks up the portrait.*) You may believe that foolishness, but I don't. I have never come across a woman who could make me look twice at her, much less one who could cut me to the heart. And I mean a living woman, Barach. Let's see if a few signs daubed by a painter can have such a dramatic effect. What a silly story. (*Sighing*) I have gloomier things to think about than love. (*He is about to look at the portrait, when Barach puts his hand in front of Calaf's eyes.*)

BARACH. Close your eyes, for pity's sake!

CALAF. (*Pushing him away*) Show some respect, you blockhead!

---

4 One of the earliest *femmes fatales* in the Western literary tradition, Medusa was queen of the gorgons, the snake-haired female monsters of Greek mythology. She was so hideous that men who looked at her were turned to stone.

(*He looks at the portrait, is visibly startled, and gradually, with a sequence of serious and dignified lazzi, shows that he has fallen under its spell.*)

BARACH. (*Brokenly*) I foresaw this disaster! 25

CALAF. (*Amazed*) Look, Barach! This sweet image, these gentle eyes, this soft breast—they could never conceal the stony, tyrannical heart you described.

BARACH. How do you mean, Your Highness? Turandot is even more lovely than her portrait. No 30 painter has captured all her beauty. I won't hide the truth. But neither could the highest eloquence of the finest speaker succeed in describing her pride, her ambition, the rancour and perversity in her heart. I beg you, my lord, throw that poisonous 35 image away, far from you. Its beauty is deadly, a plague.

CALAF. (*Still contemplating the portrait*) Don't try to frighten me. The curve of those blushing cheeks, the smiling lips and eyes! How blessed a man would be 40 to possess such harmony, perfection, here on earth, in a living, speaking form. (*Resolutely*) Barach, do not reveal my identity to anyone. I must grasp at my destiny. I will solve the riddles. I will win the most beautiful woman alive, together with her empire, or 45 else give up a life I could not endure without her. (*To the portrait*) Most dear one, I will unravel your enigmas or become your victim. Have mercy on me. (*To Barach*) If I fail, Barach, will they let me see her living beauty before I die? 50

(*A harsh drumroll is heard offstage, nearer than before. A Chinese Executioner, with bare, bloody arms, is seen above the gate, carrying a severed head. Calaf watches attentively as he affixes the head to a pike above the battlements and goes off.*)

BARACH. Look at that before you try the riddles. The prince of Samarkand's blood-soaked skull is still warm with his blood and steaming in this cold air. That man is his executioner, and will be yours as well. Your death is certain. The riddles cannot be 55 solved. Tomorrow your head will sit on a pike, with your face frozen and contorted, up there next to his, as an example to other brave fools.

CALAF. (*To the prince's head*) Unfortunate boy, what destiny drives me to become your companion? 60 Barach, you have mourned my death once; why

mourn again? I must take the chance. Don't tell anyone my name. Perhaps heaven is tired of inflicting misfortune on me, and will now make me happy. Perhaps I will save my parents. If I solve 65 the riddles, I will reward your concern for me. Farewell. (*He tries to leave. Barach restrains him.*)

BARACH. I can't let you…For pity's sake…My dear boy…Wife, come here, my friend hopes to solve Turandot's riddles! 70

SCENE 4

Enter Schirina.

SCHIRINA. What do you mean? Who? My guest? Who has persuaded you to go to your death?

CALAF. (*Showing her the portrait*) This beautiful face. She summons me.

SCHIRINA. (*Shocked, weeping*) Who gave you that 5 damnable painting?

BARACH. (*Weeping*) A chance encounter.

CALAF. Good woman, and you, Hassan, I leave my horse with you, and this purse … (*He takes the pouch out of his robes and gives it to Schirina.*) a 10 mere token of gratitude. If you are willing, use some of the gold for sacrifices—ask the gods to help me. Give some to the poor. Let everyone pray for this unfortunate man. Farewell. (*Exit, into the city.*) 15

BARACH. My lord…

SCHIRINA. Stop, boy…He won't listen. The poor, generous man! He's hurrying off to his death. Who is he, Hassan?

BARACH. Don't be so inquisitive. He has a sharp 20 mind. Perhaps there is hope for him. Wife, we must give every scrap of this gold to the poor and the priests. They'll pray for him. But we will have to mourn his death. (*He hurries off, grief-stricken.*)

SCHIRINA. I'll give all this gold to charity for him, 25 and all the money of my own I can scrape together. His handsome face, his elegant manners mark him as a noble-hearted soul. And he is a friend of my dear husband. We'll do all we can. We'll sacrifice three hundred chickens to mighty Berginguzino, 30 and three hundred fish from the river, and huge quantities of beans and rice. May Confucius listen to our prayers!

ACT TWO

*The hall of the high council. There are two large doors
on opposite sides of the stage. One leads to the quarters
of Turandot, the other to the emperor's apartments.*

SCENE 1

*Truffaldino and Eunuchs, later Brighella, all dressed in
Chinese style*

TRUFFALDINO. (*Enters running, sweeping the
Eunuchs before him with a gigantic broom*) Sweep!
Swash! Swish!…No, just sweep. I don't want you
eunuchs to start swishing on me. Get this council
room cleaned up! It's got to be spic and span before   5
the crowd gets here. Look at these cobwebs. (*He
swings the broom around in a huge arc to point at
them, accidentally decking a Eunuch.*) And the dust
in that corner!

(*Some business. Other improvised* lazzi *as desired. As
the scene continues, the Eunuchs set up two Chinese-
style thrones on opposite sides of the stage, and eight
chairs for the Sages.*)

BRIGHELLA. Hey, you! Head eunuch! What's all this?   10
TRUFFALDINO. Emergency meeting of the imperial
council in five minutes: the emperor, the judges,
my darling little princess, the whole gang. Business
is booming! Another prince begging to be
barbered—down to the collarbone.   15
BRIGHELLA. You beheaded one an hour ago! What
is this, two heads are better than one? What are
you tickled about?
TRUFFALDINO. Nobody makes these princes take
the risk. But when they see my cute little mistress,   20
they…lose their heads. Fine by me. Whenever a
new one gets it in the neck, the princess gives me
a healthy tip.
BRIGHELLA. Parasite! Sucker-up! If you love your
princess so much, why don't you marry her   25
yourself?
TRUFFALDINO. Don't make me sick. A wife?
Women! Every one of them's a pain in the acid.
And princesses are the worst.
BRIGHELLA. Of course! You're the number one   30
eunuch. You gave up the equipment. That was

reckless. Left you rockless. You'll never know what
you're missing.
TRUFFALDINO. (*Getting angry*) I'm not missing a
thing! Marriage is disgusting! You know why?   35
Because it produces little Brighellas like you, who
grow up to spurt out more little Brighellas.
BRIGHELLA. You don't realize what you're saying. If
your mother hadn't married, you'd never have been
born.   40
TRUFFALDINO. (*Shouting*) That's a stinking lie! My
mother was never married a day in her life, and I
did get born. Didn't I?
BRIGHELLA. Sure, you got born—against the rules.
TRUFFALDINO. Don't tell *me* rules, lover-boy—or   45
should I say boy-lover? I've heard you teach your
pages all there is to know about marriage.
BRIGHELLA. Why you dirty…I'll scar your cheeks
for you—all four of them!

(*They begin to fight, but the squabble is interrupted by
a blast of brassy music from offstage.*)

TRUFFALDINO. Watch it! The emperor's processional.   50
BRIGHELLA. Let's get out of here! Back to the
servants' quarters.
TRUFFALDINO. Back to the harem. (*Exeunt.*)

SCENE 2

*To the sounds of a march, enter Soldiers armed in
oriental fashion. They are followed by eight Sages, then
Pantalone and Tartaglia and finally Altoum. The
emperor is a venerable old man, richly attired. When
he appears, the others prostrate themselves, foreheads to
the ground. Altoum climbs the stairs and sits on one of
the thrones. Pantalone and Tartaglia flank him. The
Sages sit on their chairs, as the march ends.*

ALTOUM. My faithful subjects, how long must I put
up with this vile responsibility? One funeral is barely
over, I have hardly finished weeping over the death
of one unlucky prince when another appears to
renew my anguish. Cruel daughter, you were born   5
to torture me! I curse the day I swore to that solemn
vow to sacred Confucius. Ah, what good does
cursing do me? My daughter will not yield. And this
stream of insensate wooers never ceases. Who can
advise me how to break this desperate stalemate?   10

PANTALONE. My dear Majesty, I don't know what to say. In my country, there aren't any laws like that. Princes don't fall in love with portraits of girls—at least not enough to lose their heads over them. And we don't have girls like your daughter Turandot, who hate men. Not on your life! Before my bad luck made me leave my country, and good fortune rewarded me more than I deserve by making me your secretary, I didn't know a thing about China. I thought it was one of those powders you take for tertian fever.[5] I still can't believe all those vows and beheadings. If I told them about it back in Venice, they'd say, "Come off it, you old line spinner, you windbag, what are you trying to put over on us? Go tell your fairy tales to the kids." Then they'd laugh in my face and turn their backsides on me.

ALTOUM. Tartaglia, did you speak with the new candidate?

TARTAGLIA. Yes, Your Majesty. He's here in the palace, in the rooms we give the foreign princes. He is so handsome and has such a noble way of speaking—I could hardly believe it. I never saw a worthier man. I liked him right away. It breaks my heart—an attractive youngster like that, come to be slain like a lamb…(*He weeps.*)

ALTOUM. The misery of it! Have the sacrifices been performed? Perhaps this time the heavens will help a prince solve my daughter's riddles. A vain hope.

PANTALONE. We sacrificed all right: a hundred bulls to the sky, a hundred horses to the sun, and a hundred pigs to the moon. (*Aside*) But I don't see the good of all that imperial slaughter.

TARTAGLIA. (*Aside*) They should have sacrificed that virginal vixen of a Turandot. That would solve *our* riddles.

ALTOUM. Very well. Bring in the new prince. (*One of the Soldiers leaves.*) We will try to dissuade him. You, my faithful ministers, and you judges, help me convince him if words fail me in my sorrow.

PANTALONE. We've been through plenty of experience, Your Majesty. We'll wear out our lungs talking, then he'll go off and get his throat cut like a turkey.

---

5 In Italian, the word for a common fever-medicine, quinquina, is *china*, thus making a pun.

TARTAGLIA. Listen, Pantalone, he seemed bright. Don't give up hope yet.

PANTALONE. You think he can handle that bitch's riddles? Not a chance.

SCENE 3

Enter Calaf, with a Soldier.

CALAF (*Kneels and touches a hand to his forehead.*)
ALTOUM. Rise, you rash young man.

(*Calaf rises and goes to stand proudly in the middle of the council hall between the two thrones, facing the audience. Altoum looks closely at him, then continues in an aside.*)

What a noble bearing! It makes me pity him all the more. (*To Calaf*) Where are you from, you misguided man? What king is your father?

CALAF. (*A little surprised; then with a dignified bow*) My lord, may it please you to let my name remain unknown.

ALTOUM. You dare aspire to my daughter's hand without telling me who you are?

CALAF. (*Grandly*) I am a prince. If heaven wishes me to die, before the executioner's ax falls I will reveal my name and my nation. Then you will know that I did not aspire to the princess's hand without having royal blood in my own veins. (*He bows.*) But for now, may it please you to let my name remain unknown.

ALTOUM. (*Aside*) Nobly spoken! I pity him more than ever. (*Aloud*) But if you solve the riddles and I find you are not of noble birth, how…

CALAF. (*Boldly interrupting him*) The law applies only to princes! My lord, if I solve the riddles and cannot prove my blood noble, then strike my head from my shoulders and throw my body to the dogs and crows. There is someone in Peking who knows me and can tell you who I am. (*He bows.*) But for now, may it please you to let my name remain unknown.

ALTOUM. I will permit it. I can deny nothing to such a fine-looking young man, who speaks so exaltedly. If only you were as eager to grant the wish of an emperor…Draw back, young man, draw back from this frightful trial. You have made such a strong impression on me that I will offer you anything within my power. Join me now in ruling my empire, and after my death you will be royally rewarded. If you have any pity, brave man, do not force me to be a murderer against my will and to weep over your corpse. My subjects call me a weakling for having sworn such an unwise vow. They despise my daughter's vain, cruel obstinacy. And I despise myself for having given birth to her. Draw back from this trial, prince. Do not increase my misery. (*He weeps.*)

CALAF. Sire, the gods know how much I pity you. Your daughter could not have learned cruelty from such a father. Your only faults—if they *are* faults— were to bring into the world a woman whose beauty enthrals men, and to love your only child. I thank you for your generous offer, but I cannot accept. Heaven will make the empire mine by allowing me to possess your daughter, or I will die, unable to survive her loss. This is my choice: death or Turandot.

PANTALONE. But my dear young prince, you must have seen all the skulls posted above the city gates. Do I have to say more? I don't know why you want yourself slaughtered like a goat, without a hope of winning. Why make us weep? Listen, that princess will whip up three riddles even the astrologer Cingarello couldn't deal with. These judges here have studied for years, worn out their eyes poring over riddle books, and even they have a hard time figuring them out. They're tricky, not easy, not like "Why did the chicken swim the Grand Canal?" They're brand-new ones, and damned hard. And if the judges weren't given the right answer in sealed scrolls, even they wouldn't know what was going on. My dear boy, pull out of this mess while you can. Watching you there as handsome as a painting, I feel sorry for you. I like you, boy, but if you insist on going through with this trial, I'd give no more for your head than for a radish from the imperial gardens.

CALAF. You're wasting your time, old man. Your advice does not disconcert me. This is my choice: death or Turandot.

TARTAGLIA. Turandot! Turandot! My dear young fellow, you're as stubborn as the devil. Now, listen.

You're not betting a cup of hot chocolate or a coffee and cake on this, you know: we're talking about your brain-box, boy. Isn't that enough for you? His Majesty is practically on his royal knees; he's gone and sacrificed a hundred horses to the sun, a hundred pigs to the moon, and a hundred bulls to the sky to bring you luck. But you, you lump of ingratitude, you're going through with this no matter how much pain you cause him. Even if Turandot were the only woman on earth, your stubbornness would make no sense. Excuse me, my dear prince. It's my affection for you talking. Don't you understand—you'll lose your top! I can't believe this.

CALAF. You speak disrespectfully. I will not listen. This is my choice: death or Turandot.

ALTOUM. Then your cruelty shall be satisfied. Go forward to the death you desire, and leave me to my grief. (*To the Soldiers*) Bring the princess to the council hall to meet her new victim. (*A Soldier leaves.*)

CALAF. (*Aside, passionately*) Heavenly gods, inspire me! Don't let me be overwhelmed by her beauty. My mind falters, my heart is racing. (*To the whole assembly*) Members of the high council, sages, wise judges of my answers and my life, I beg you to pardon my daring. Have mercy on a man who is blinded by love, doesn't know where he is or what he's doing, and abandons himself to his destiny.

SCENE 4

March music, with tambourines. Enter Truffaldino, his scimitar at his shoulder, followed by a file of Eunuchs. After them, a file of Slave Women playing tambourines. Next, two slaves, veiled. One is dressed richly, after the fashion of the Tartars: this is Adelma. The other is dressed less richly, in Chinese style: this is Zelima. She also carries a small tray on which are scrolls, sealed: the answers to the riddles. As they pass the emperor's throne, Truffaldino and his Eunuchs prostrate themselves. The Slave Women kneel and place a hand to their foreheads. Enter Turandot, richly dressed in Chinese fashion; her manner is grave, but confident. The Sages and ministers prostrate themselves. Altoum stands. Turandot bows to her father, placing one hand to her forehead, then climbs to her throne and sits. She is flanked by Adelma and Zelima. Calaf, who has knelt at Turandot's entrance, rises and stares at her as if enchanted. When everyone is in place, Truffaldino takes the tray from Zelima and, after a few improvised lazzi, *gives the sealed answers to the Sages. After many bows, he retires. During all of this pantomimed ceremony, the march music is played. At Truffaldino's exit, the council chamber remains in silence.*

SCENE 5

Altoum, Turandot, Calaf, Zelima, Adelma, Pantalone, Tartaglia, Sages, and Soldiers

TURANDOT. (*Scornfully*) Who dares the secret of my riddles, after so many others have failed? Who wishes to throw away his life?

ALTOUM. Here, Daughter. (*He points to Calaf, who is standing as if enchanted in the center of the council hall.*) This man is worthy to be your husband. Take him, end these trials, and stop tormenting your father.

TURANDOT. (*To Zelima, softly, after having looked at Calaf for some time*) Zelima, this is the first time a prince has made me feel sorry for him.

ZELIMA. (*Softly*) Then give him easy riddles, Your Highness, and end your cruelty.

TURANDOT. (*Softly, but with arrogance*) What? And lose my reputation? How dare you suggest it?

ADELMA. (*Aside*) God in heaven! I can't believe this: the man who was servant in my father's court. And a prince? I knew it in my heart. I was sure of it.

TURANDOT. Prince, do not attempt this fatal trial. Whatever lies you have heard about me, the gods know that I am not heartless. But I abhor your sex, and I defend myself the only way I know, so that I may remain free from men. Why should I not be as free as you are? Who forced you to come here, to make me be cruel against my will? If prayers can convince you, I will beg you humbly to withdraw. Do not try to pit your skill against mine. My skill is the only thing I am proud of. God gave me intelligence and ability. If my ingenuity were beaten in this contest, I would die of shame. Go! Do not oblige me to put the riddles to you, or you will die.

CALAF. All this beauty of voice and face…all this spirit and discernment in a woman! How could a man be at fault in risking his life to possess you? Turandot, you boast of your intelligence—and yet you do not see that the greater your merits, the more men will yearn for you. If I had a thousand lives in this poor body, cruel princess, I would risk them all for you.

ZELIMA. (*Softly, to Turandot*) For pity's sake, make your riddles easy. He is worthy of you.

ADELMA. (*Aside*) How sweetly he speaks! If only he could be mine! Why didn't I realize he was a prince, before my fate turned me from a princess into a slave? My heart is alight with love, now that I know he is of noble birth. That love will give me courage. (*Softly, to Turandot*) Turandot, don't forsake your glory.

TURANDOT. (*Aside, perplexed*) How does this man weaken me with compassion? No! I must be strong. (*To Calaf, vehemently*) Foolhardy prince, prepare yourself for the contest.

ALTOUM. Prince, do you still insist?

CALAF. My lord, I do. This is my choice: death or Turandot.

ALTOUM. Let the fatal decree be read aloud. Listen, and tremble.

(*Pantalone takes the Book of Law from his robes, kisses it, and presses it first into his breast, then to his forehead. He presents it to Tartaglia, who prostrates himself, then accepts the book, and reads.*)

TARTAGLIA. It is written: "Any man of royal blood may vie for the hand of Turandot. Before the sages of the high council, she will ask three riddles. If he can answer them, she will become his wife. If he fails, let him be bound over to the executioner, his head to be struck from his body. To holy Confucius, Altoum, emperor of China, so solemnly swears."

(*When he has finished reading, he kisses the book, presses it to his breast and his forehead, and presents it to Pantalone, who receives it after prostrating himself, and then presents it to Altoum, who raises a hand and places it on the cover.*)

ALTOUM. (*Sighing*) This tormenting law…I swear that I will faithfully execute my vow. So be it.

(*Pantalone returns the book to his robes. The council hall is silent as Turandot rises to her feet.*)

TURANDOT. (*Solemnly*) Listen well, stranger.
We notice her presence in lands high and low,
In cities, the country—wherever we go… 70
In war, as in peace, she is safe in her place
And everyone living has looked on her face.
She is friendly to all and she strives for our gain,
Yet her unequalled splendour can drive men insane.
You know who she is, but don't know that you do— 75
Now answer me, stranger—my riddle is through.

(*She sits.*)

CALAF. (*He looks heavenward for a moment, lost in
thought, then bows to the princess with a hand on
his forehead and responds*) I shall be a happy man,
princess, if none of your riddles is more obscure 80
than this.
That presence we notice in lands high and low,
In cities, the country—wherever we go;
Who in war, as in peace, remains safe in her place
And whom everyone living has seen face to face; 85
That friend of all creatures, who strives for our gain
But whose unequalled splendour can drive men
insane
Has a name that I know, and your riddle's undone,
My princess. I give you my answer: the sun.
PANTALONE. (*Overjoyed*) Tartaglia, he got it! 90
TARTAGLIA. Bulls-eye!
SAGES. (*Opening the first riddle, then in unison*)
Correct. It is the sun, it is the sun, it is the sun.
ALTOUM. (*Ecstatic*) My boy, heaven help you with
the remaining riddles. 95
ZELIMA. (*Aside*) O gods, give him the correct
answers.
ADELMA. (*Aside, agitated*) Heaven forbid! He must
not become Turandot's husband! I feel faint.
TURANDOT. (*Aside, arrogantly*) Could he outwit and 100
defeat me? Never! (*Aloud, rising to her feet*) Listen
well, and riddle me this.
The tree in which the hours
Of human life are told
Is as young as a newborn infant, 105
Yet infinitely old.
Its leaves are white on one side,
On the other, black as sable.
Tell me what this tree is,
Prince, if you are able. 110

(*She sits*)

CALAF. (*After a moment's thought, he bows and
answers*) Do not be distressed princess, if I succeed
in solving your riddles.
The tree in which the hours
Of human life are told, 115
As young as a newborn infant,
Yet infinitely old,
Whose leaves, like days, are white,
And make your riddle clear
By being black as night below, 120
This tree must be: the year!
PANTALONE. (*Overjoyed*) Tartaglia, that's it!
TARTAGLIA. Another one, smack on target.
SAGES. (*In unison*) Correct. It is the year, it is the
year, it is the year. 125
ALTOUM. How happy this makes me! Great gods,
help him with the last riddle.
ZELIMA. (*Aside*) If only that had been the last one!
ADELMA. (*Aside*) Must I lose him? (*Softly, to
Turandot*) One more riddle, Your Highness, and 130
you will be shamed before the assembled high
council. He will defeat you.
TURANDOT. (*Aside, angrily*) Never! The heavens will
fall and the human race perish first. (*Aloud*) Fool!
Can't you see that I hate you more, the more you 135
hope to defeat me? Leave this council, escape this
last riddle, and save your life.
CALAF. Princess, your hatred saddens me. If I am not
worth your compassion, then let them strike my
head from my shoulders. 140
ALTOUM. Stop, my dear son. Stop, Daughter. We
have no need for a final riddle. He is worthy to
be your husband: accept him.
TURANDOT. Never! The law must take its course.
CALAF. My lord, don't be distressed. This is my 145
choice: death or Turandot.
TURANDOT. (*Scornfully*) Then take death! (*She rises
to her feet and solemnly intones the last riddle.*)
Tell me the name of the kingly beast
Who makes the world tremble and ruins his foes, 150
Still mighty today as he was in the past,
Winged and four-footed, in active repose.
His hindquarters rest on the restless seas,
His breast and his forepaws cover the sand.

His untiring wings will never cease 155
To cast their protection over the land.

(*After reciting the riddle, Turandot rips the veil from her face to dazzle Calaf.*)

Look at my face, and try not to tremble. Who is the beast, prince? Answer, or die.

CALAF. That beauty! Radiant! (*He hesitates, standing with his hands to his eyes.*) 160

ALTOUM. (*Agitated*) No! His mind is wandering. My son, don't be afraid. Come back to your senses.

ZELIMA. (*Aside, breathlessly*) I feel faint.

ADELMA. (*Aside*) Stranger, you're mine! Love will show me how to rescue you. 165

PANTALONE. (*Agitated*) Come on, boy, come on! Oh, if I could only help him! I'm so afraid for him, my guts are quivering.

TARTAGLIA. If I weren't in the royal presence, I'd run for the smelling salts. 170

TURANDOT. You have lost, prince! You shall have the death you asked for.

CALAF. (*Coming to his senses*) Turandot, the sight of your beauty stunned and confused me. But I have not lost. (*To the audience*) 175

The four-footed beast endowed with wings,
Who lives on land and sea, and brings
Protection to a lucky nation,
The mightiest power in all creation,
Who wards off every harm and menace: 180
I know his name, the lion of Venice![6]

PANTALONE. (*Jumping for joy*) Oh, bless you, boy, I'm bursting with happiness.

TARTAGLIA. Your Majesty, he made it all the way!

SAGES. (*They open the third riddle, then in unison*) 185
The lion of Venice. He's right! He's right!

(*Cheers from the assembled populace, and a noisy burst of music. Turandot faints and is assisted by Zelima and Adelma.*)

ZELIMA. He has won, princess. It's over.

ADELMA. (*Aside*) I've lost you, my love…But I can't give up yet.

---

6 For Gozzi's audience, the winged lion of St. Mark was a familiar and beloved symbol of their home town; what it is doing in a Chinese riddle is left mysterious.

(*Joyfully, Altoum descends from the throne, assisted by Pantalone and Tartaglia. The sages retire upstage in single file.*)

ALTOUM. Daughter, you can no longer rule me with 190
your whims. Come to me, prince.

(*He embraces Calaf. Turandot, who has regained consciousness, sweeps down from her throne.*)

TURANDOT. Stop this! He is not my husband yet—nor will he be. I must ask him three more riddles tomorrow. I demand it. I did not have time to prepare or time to think. Stop… 195

ALTOUM. (*Interrupting*) Senseless, cold-hearted woman! No more tolerance from me! The brutal law has been followed to the letter. My ministers will now pronounce your sentence.

PANTALONE. Pardon me, princess. We don't need 200
any more riddles, or any more heads chopped off like pumpkins. This boy came up with the answers, the law was followed, and by God we're going to enjoy your wedding cake. What do you say there, chancellor? 205

TARTAGLIA. It's an open and shut case: I sentence her to marriage. What do you say, judges?

SAGES. (*In unison*) The law is clear: the vow to Confucius has been fulfilled.

ALTOUM. Let us go to the temple. The stranger will 210
tell us who he is, and the priests—

TURANDOT. Father, have mercy, postpone—

ALTOUM. Mo more delays. I will not give way.

TURANDOT. (*Falling to her knees*) Father, if you love me, if you value my life, let me pose new questions. 215
I could not endure the shame. I'll die before you can subject me to this arrogant man and before I consent to become a wife. The thought of it, the very word "wife" is enough to kill me.

ALTOUM. I refuse to heed your stubborn, fanatical 220
brutality. Ministers, precede us to the temple.

CALAF. Rise, Turandot, my beloved tyrant. My lord, I beg you to revoke your orders. I cannot be happy so long as she hates me. I love her too much ever to cause her pain. What is my affection worth, if 225
it receives in return only hatred? Ruthless woman, if I cannot soften your heart, then you shall remain free. I will not be her husband. But, Turandot, if you felt my pain, you would feel for me. Do you

want me to die? If so, my lord, I agree to a new 230
contest because I no longer value my life.

ALTOUM. No. No more concessions. No more
contests. To the temple!

TURANDOT. (*Violently*) To the temple then…and
your daughter will die at the altar. 235

CALAF. Die? My lord, my princess, I beg of you to
grant me this much. Tomorrow, here in the council
hall, I will ask Turandot a riddle.

    Who is the prince who fed his father
    By carrying burdens and begging his bread? 240
    Who is the prince who loved a princess,
    And answered her riddles while risking his head?
    The prince whose bad fortune gave way to his
      fame,
    Yet still is unfortunate—what is his name?

Tomorrow, in the council hall, you must tell me 245
the name of that unlucky prince and of his father.
If you fail, torture me no longer! Give me your
hand: become my devoted wife. If you succeed, let
me die. Be satisfied with my blood.

TURANDOT. I accept your offer, stranger. 250

ZELIMA. (*Aside*) A new danger.

ADELMA. (*Aside*) I can hope again.

ALTOUM. I do *not* accept this offer. The law must
take its course.

CALAF. (*Kneeling*) Your Majesty, if I deserve anything 255
from you, if you have any mercy, concede this
favour to your daughter and to me. I do not wish
her to be dissatisfied. She is intelligent: let her
answer my riddle tomorrow in the council hall.

TURANDOT. (*Aside*) I'm suffocating with anger. He 260
is mocking me!

ALTOUM. How can you make that request, you
impudent man? You don't appreciate this woman's
cunning…But as you insist, I will agree to another
contest. If she answers your riddle, she need not 265
become your wife. But I will not allow her to put
you to death. Altoum will never again weep over
a murdered prince. (*Aside, to Calaf*) Follow me.
You fool, why did you do that?

(*The processional march begins again. Altoum and the soldiers, the sages, Pantalone, and Tartaglia leave through the
door leading to the emperor's quarters. Turandot, Adelma,
Zelima, eunuchs, and slave women leave through the door
leading to the princess's apartments.*)

ACT THREE

A room in Turandot's seraglio

SCENE 1

Adelma and a Slave Woman

ADELMA. I forbid you to say another word. I can't
follow your advice. Too much is weighing on my
heart. I love this nameless prince, and hate the evil
princess and my condition as a slave. For five years
I have kept my hatred a secret and have pretended 5
to be devoted to her and resigned to my own
slavery. But I too am of royal blood, at least her
equal. How long must I serve her? I'm withering
away with hatred I dare not express. I must strike
back and throw off my slavery or die. 10

SLAVE. No, my lady. It's too soon…

ADELMA. (*Angrily*) Don't ask me to bear it any longer.
Not another word! (*The Slave Woman bows her hand
to her forehead, and leaves the room*). She is coming—
my enemy, her heart overflowing with anger and 15
shame, almost demented. Time to risk everything or
die. I must listen to her. (*She hides.*)

SCENE 2

Turandot, Zelima, later Adelma

TURANDOT. Zelima, I can't bear it. My shame
scorches my heart.

ZELIMA. But my lady, how can such a handsome,
generous man provoke your hatred? He loves you
so much! 5

TURANDOT. Stop tormenting me! I am ashamed to
admit…he made me feel…as I've never felt before.
Feverish…ice-cold…It can't be true! Zelima, I hate
him, I wish him dead. He humiliated me in front
of the high council. Soon everyone in the empire 10
will know how I was overcome. They'll laugh at
me. Laugh! At my ignorance. Help me, Zelima. I
must not give the wrong answer tomorrow and be
forced to marry him.

    Who is the prince who fed his father
    By carrying burdens and begging his bread? 15
    Who is the prince who loved a princess,

And answered her riddles while risking his head?
The prince whose bad fortune gave way to his
    fame,
Yet still is unfortunate—what is his name? 20
He means himself, but who on earth can tell me
his name? The emperor says he may keep it a secret
until the moment of the trial. I accepted the
challenge only to gain time. I will never be able
to guess it. What can I do, Zelima? 25

ZELIMA. Aren't there magicians here in Peking or a
soothsayer to consult?

TURANDOT. You may be credulous, Zelima, but I
am not. Only the ignorant rabble believes in those
frauds. Have you no better suggestion? 30

ZELIMA. Do you remember how he sighed, how
much pain there was in his voice when he spoke
to you? When he went to his knees and begged
your father to let you ask more riddles?

TURANDOT. Stop! I feel…No! I won't give in. I wish 35
he were dead. Men are liars, cheats, incapable of
loving any woman. They pretend to love only in
order to seduce us. And when they have us, not
only do they not love us, but they also disregard
their marriage vows and skip from woman to 40
woman. They lust shamelessly after the vilest
woman, a slave or prostitute will do. Don't speak
in his favour, Zelima. If he wins tomorrow, I will
hate him more bitterly than death itself. If I let
myself think of it, if I see myself as a wife, 45
subjected to a man, if I imagine how I can be
defeated…I will go insane!

ZELIMA. You are young and proud, my lady. But an
unhappy time will come: there will be no more
suitors. Your regrets will then be unavailing. What 50
do you lose by being defeated? What fanatical
glory, what honour?

ADELMA. (*Little by little she has crept up on them, listen-*
ing. She interrupts) Those are the questions of a
lowborn woman. Zelima, you have no conception 55
of what a princess feels—the agonizing shame in
being publicly debased after so many victories. I saw
the eyes of those men—more than a hundred of
them—shining in triumph. They sneered, they
laughed at her riddles, as if an idiot child had asked 60
them. How can you feel for what she feels when she
may become a wife against her will and her instincts?

TURANDOT. Stop! I don't need to hear…

ZELIMA. In what way does it hurt to become a wife?

ADELMA. Please! How can you understand a noble 65
heart? I am no flatterer. Do you think it is easy to
accept the challenge, guess the prince's name, and
stand up before the high council tomorrow, in
front of the nobles and the rabble? And if she
answers incorrectly, or if she can't answer at all…I 70
seem to hear a thousand men laughing, and
making rude remarks, as if she weren't a princess,
but some poor actress who muffed her lines.

TURANDOT. (*Wildly*) Adelma, if I cannot announce
his name tomorrow in the council hall, I will stab 75
myself.

ADELMA. No, princess. You will solve the riddle, by
wit or by slyness.

ZELIMA. Very well, you understand the princess
better than I do. You help her. 80

TURANDOT. Yes, my dear Adelma. How will I learn
his name, and his father's name too, if I don't know
where he comes from?

ADLEMA. He said in the council hall that someone
in Peking can identify him. Search every corner of 85
the city, offer gems and gold…

TURANDOT. Take gold and gems. Spend them as
you will. Take all my treasure, but I *must* know that
name!

ZELIMA. How will you spend her treasure? Whom will 90
you search for? And how will you disguise her cheating? How will you hide the fact that she has discovered his name not by her own wits, but by fraud?

ADELMA. Who would know, unless *you* betrayed
her… 95

ZELIMA. You go too far. Princess, keep your treasure.
I hoped to calm you and reconcile you to a worthy
husband. But since I cannot, I will be ruled by my
duty to my mistress. My mother, Schirina, told me
she was delighted that the riddles had been solved. 100
She did not know about the new trial, but she said
the prince was staying at her house, and that my
stepfather Hassan knows him. I asked her his
name, but Hassan will not tell her. She promised
she would try to find out. Now, princess, you 105
cannot doubt my love for you, or my obedience.
(*Exit, angrily.*)

TURANDOT. Stay with me Zelima, don't go…

ADELMA. Turandot, Zelima may have given you a lead, but she is only a silly girl. It is senseless to think her stepfather will reveal the name, now that he has heard about the new trial. There is not time to lose. Let us retire, and I will give you my advice in secret. 110

TURANDOT. Yes, my friend, come. I will do anything to keep the stranger from winning. (*Exit.*) 115

ADELMA. Gods of love, help me to throw off this slavery. My enemy's pride will become my ally. (*Exit.*)

SCENE 3

A room in the palace. Calaf and Barach.

CALAF. But you are the only man in Peking who knows my name. Our kingdom is far from here, and it fell to the invader over eight years ago. We hid our identities, and there were rumours that we had died. A man who falls into poverty is quickly forgotten, Barach. 5

BARACH. Forgive me, my lord. You were unwise. Men who have been ill-used must learn to fear even the impossible. Walls, trees, inanimate objects denounce them, everyone is against them. I can't understand it. You were lucky enough to outdo that supremely beautiful woman; you won an empire at the risk of your life. And then suddenly, out of pity for her, you threw it all away. 10

CALAF. Barach, my love for her cannot be measured by material gain or loss. You didn't see my Turandot's anger, there in the council chamber, her desperation. 15

BARACH. As a son, you should have thought first of your parents' poverty, not of a beaten woman's anger. 20

CALAF. Do not scold me, Barach. I wanted to please her. I am trying to soften her heart. Perhaps she feels a spark of gratitude for what I did.

BARACH. Who? Turandot? You are dreaming. 25

CALAF. I cannot lose her now. Barach, did you reveal my name? Did you tell your wife?

BARACH. No, my lord. I know my duty toward you. And yet...this disturbing presentiment...I don't know why I'm trembling. 30

SCENE 4

Enter Pantalone, Tartaglia, Brighella, and Soldiers.

PANTALONE. (*Bustles in*) Here he is, here he is, by jingo.

TARTAGLIA. (*To Calaf*) Your Highness, who is this man?

PANTALONE. (*To Calaf*) Where did you run off to? Who's this fellow? 5

BARACH. (*Aside*) More trouble! What are they after?

CALAF. I don't know him. I met him just this minute. I was asking him about...ah...the city, the people...

TARTAGLIA. Excuse me, my lord, but you've got a screw loose under your turban. You're too trustful, I saw that in the council hall. How the devil could you do such a dumb thing? 10

PANTALONE. Come on, what's done is done. Your Highness, you may not know it but you're in way over your head. If we weren't here to watch out for you, you'd pull some stupid stunt and let that girl string you up like a salami. (*To Barach*) Hey, soup strainer, you there with the moustache, you can run along now. Your Highness, please go back to your room. Brighella, the emperor has mobilized two thousand soldiers, and you are to take all your pages and guard the prince's door. Nobody gets in, you hear that? Emperor's orders. He likes you, Your Highness, he wants you for a son-in-law, and he'll die of heartbreak if anything goes wrong. But listen, Your Highness, that was a crazy giveaway in the council hall. (*Softly, to Calaf*) For heaven's sake, don't let your name slip—unless maybe you want to whisper it to me, you know, as a special favour? 15 20 25 30

CALAF. Is that how you obey your emperor, old man?

PANTALONE. Bravo! All right, Brighella, he's all yours.

BRIGHELLA. I've been ready for half an hour. Sure you're finished talking?

TARTAGLIA. Guard him well, Brighella, if you're fond of your head. 35

BRIGHELLA. Don't worry about my head. I'm very attached to it.

TARTAGLIA. (*Softly, to Calaf*) I'm dying to know who you are, Your Highness. You can tell me. I know how to keep a secret. 40

CALAF. Don't try to wheedle me. You'll know my name tomorrow—not before.

[III.iv]

TARTAGLIA. Excellent. That's the ticket, don't tell a soul. 45

PANTALONE. Farewell, Your Highness. (*To Barach*) And you, mustache-face, why don't you get out of the palace? Go smoke a pipe in the square, and mind your own business (*Exit.*)

TARTAGLIA. And keep your mind on minding it. I don't like your looks, fellow. (*Exit.*) 50

BRIGHELLA. Excuse me, Your Highness. Emperor's orders. Shall I show you to your room?

CALAF. Yes, I'll come with you. Farewell, my friend, we'll meet again when all this is resolved for the best. 55

BARACH. Good-bye, my lord.

BRIGHELLA. Come on, that's enough. Haven't you finished yet?

(*He orders the Soldiers to surround Calaf, and they march off.*)

SCENE 5

Barach, then Timur. Timur is a feeble old man dressed in rags.

BARACH. (*After the departing Calaf*) Heaven help you to guard your tongue, my foolhardy prince. I will certainly guard mine.

TIMUR. (*Seeing his son surrounded by guards*) Can it be? My son, surrounded by soldiers. Have the troops of Carizmo, that tyrant who stole my kingdom, arrived in Peking as well? At least I can die with him. (*Trying to follow him*) Calaf! Calaf! 5

BARACH. (*Surprised, he draws his sword and grabs Timur by the arm*) Stop, old man. Keep silent or I'll kill you. Who are you? Where have you come from? And how do you know that name? 10

TIMUR. Barach! Alive, and here in Peking? And with your sword drawn against your sovereign!

BARACH. (*Amazed*) Timur! 15

TIMUR. Yes, you traitor. Go on, kill me—I'm weary of life. If my most trusted minister has turned his coat, if foul Carizmo has captured my son, then I have no reason to live. (*He weeps.*)

BARACH. Your Majesty...I recognize you. (*He kneels.*) Pardon, sire, my anger sprang from my affection for you and your son. I beg you, my lord, if you love him do not let his name or your own pass your lips. Here I am called Hassan, not 20

BARACH. (*Rising and looking anxiously around*) I hope we have not been overheard. Tell me, sire...Is the queen with you? 25

TIMUR. (*Weeping*) Must you remind me of my dear wife? There, in our poor refuge in Berlas, tormented by past troubles and present anguish, clasped in these weary arms, with my son's name the last word on her lips—she died. 30

BARACH. Oh, my poor queen!

TIMUR. In desperation, I came to Peking seeking my son, and my death too. This past moment, as I arrived, I saw him surrounded by soldiers—captured! 35

BARACH. We must not dawdle here, Your Majesty. Do not fear for your son. Perhaps tomorrow he will be a happy man, and you will be happy too—so long as you tell no one his name or yours. 40

TIMUR. What is this mystery?

BARACH. Come. When we are far from the palace, I will explain it all. (*He looks around suspiciously.*) What's this? Schirina, coming out of Turandot's rooms? We're lost! Where have you been? What were you doing? 45

SCENE 6

Enter Schirina

SCHIRINA. I was glad that the stranger had solved the riddles, and I wanted to find out whether that tiger of a Turandot could stand to become a wife. So I went to see Zelima.

BARACH. (*Angrily*) Foolish woman, before taking note of dangers, you run to your daughter and gossip! I was looking for you to forbid what you have just done—but the stupidity of women outruns the wise man's caution. Now I am too late. What did you tell her? I can almost hear it—you told her the stranger, the prince, is our guest, and I know who he is. Didn't you? 5, 10

SCHIRINA. (*Mortified*) But...would it be bad if I had said that?

BARACH. Did you say it? 15

SCHIRINA. Yes. And afterward she wanted to know his name. I didn't know, and to tell you the truth I promised—

BARACH. Idiot! Quickly, we must escape!

TIMUR. I don't understand this mystery. 20

700   THE ENLIGHTENMENT STAGE

BARACH. We must leave the palace and the city. Now! (*He looks off.*) No! It's too late. Here come Turandot's eunuchs. (*To Schirina*) Chatterbox! Thoughtless creature! They're after me—quickly, run, hide. Take this old man with you.

TIMUR. But can't you tell me…

BARACH. (*Softly, to Timur*) Be silent. Don't let your name cross your lips. (*Hurriedly, to Schirina*) Wife, if you are grateful for all I have done for you, if you want to make up for the tragedy you have set in motion, run now and hide until tomorrow.

SCHIRINA. Husband…

TIMUR. Can't you come with us? I don't understand…

BARACH. Don't talk back to me, Schirina. They've found me out, I have to stay. Now hurry. Go, hide!

TIMUR. But why…

BARACH. (*Uneasy*) God, what agony. (*Looks off.*)

SCHIRINA. What did I do wrong?

BARACH. (*Pushing them off*) Go! Tell no one your name. Stupid wife! Poor old man! Very well, then we will flee together. (*Looks off.*) No! Too late.

SCENE 7

Enter Truffaldino and Eunuchs, armed. Truffaldino and the Eunuchs surround them, hedging them in with their weapons.

BARACH. You are looking for Hassan. I am he.

TRUFFALDINO. Shut your trap. I've come to do you a favour. A big favour.

BARACH. Yes, I know. Come, take me away.

TRUFFALDINO. A favour like you never dreamed of. Nobody gets into the harem, into Turandot's rooms. Why, if even a fly tries to buzz in there, we check to see if it's male or female. And you, you lucky dog…Hey, who's the old geezer?

BARACH. A beggar. I don't know him. Shall we go?

TRUFFALDINO. Well, I'm in a generous mood. I'll do him a favour too, and bring him along. Who's the woman?

BARACH. Your mistress is searching for me, no one else. Leave the poor woman alone—I've never seen her before.

TRUFFALDINO. What are you, blind? I know who she is. Your wife—though you never saw her before. I'm not stupid. You crooked-mouth…I

ought to give you a fat lip. (*To his Eunuchs*) Grab them, boys, and let's move.

TIMUR. What do you want with me?

SCHIRINA. What's going on?

BARACH. What will they do with us? Whatever it is, we will have to be strong. (*To Timur*) Remember what I told you. (*To Schirina*) Now, woman, you'll pay for your flapping lounge.

TRUFFALDINO. All right, all right, shut your faces and get the lead out. *Hup*, two, three, four…

(*The eunuchs frog-march them off. Truffaldino supervises officiously.*)

ACT FOUR

A vestibule with columns. On a table there is a huge bowl full of gold coins. It is night.

SCENE 1

Turandot, Barach, Timur, Schirina, Zelima, and Eunuchs. The Eunuchs tie Barach and Timur to different columns. They have been stripped to the waist. Zelima and Schirina stand to one side, weeping. On the other side is Turandot.

TURANDOT. (*Fiercely*) You still have time to save yourselves. I repeat my offer: that pile of gold is yours. But I tell you again, if you refuse to confess the name of the prince and his father, my servants will whip you to death. Slaves!

(*The Eunuchs make a deep bow, then pick up whips and clubs.*)

BARACH. Are you satisfied, Schirina? Do you understand your mistake? (*Crying out*) Kill me or torture me, Turandot. I am ready to die. I know the names of the prince and his father, but I will suffer torment and death sooner than tell you. To me, your gold is less than dirt. Don't grieve for me, wife. Save your tears for this poor old man; beg the princess to spare his life, not mine. (*Weeping*) His only fault is that he is my friend.

SCHIRINA. (*Pleading*) Have mercy…

TIMUR. Stop. Do not beg for the life of an old man who wishes for death to ease his misery. My friend, I will die, but you must live. I will tell you, tyrant…

BARACH. No, for pity's sake! Don't let the stranger's name pass your lips or he will be lost. 20

TURANDOT. So you know his name, old man?

TIMUR. Do I know it? You cruel woman! (*To Barach*) Explain this mystery, my friend. Why can I not tell her?

BARACH. Because you would seal his death. And ours. 25

TURANDOT. Old man, he hopes to frighten you. Whip him, slaves!

(*The eunuchs make ready to whip Barach.*)

SCHIRINA. Husband! My husband!

TIMUR. Stop! This is torture! Princess, swear that his life and the prince's will be safe, and I will tell you the name. Let the punishment fall on me, I won't seek to escape it. 30

TURANDOT. I swear upon my head to dread Confucius that I will spare your lives and that of the unknown prince. (*She places a hand to her forehead in token of sincerity.*) 35

BARACH. (*Shouting*) Liar! Say nothing, old man. There is poison hidden in that oath. Turandot, swear that when you know the two names, you will marry the stranger, and not let him die of heartbreak. Swear that we will be safe, that you will spare our lives and not keep us in a dungeon to rot forever, so that no one will ever know that you cheated in the contest. If you swear all that, Turandot, I will gladly tell you the prince's name. 40 45

TIMUR. (*Astonished*) What mysteries are these? Heaven, enlighten me.

TURANDOT. I am tired of this resistance. Slaves! Kill them both.

(*The eunuchs step forward.*)

SCHIRINA. Mercy, Your Highness. 50

BARACH. (*To Timur*) Now you see what she is like.

TIMUR. My son, I surrender my life for you. Your mother is dead, and now I follow her. (*He weeps.*)

TURANDOT. Your son! Stop, slaves. You are a king? You are the prince's father? 55

TIMUR. Yes, I am a king…a father…a pauper.

SCHIRINA. A king! Reduced to this?

TURANDOT. (*Aside, moved*) A king, so abject, in such poverty! The father of the prince I am trying to hate, although…in my heart…(*Resolutely*) No, 60

what am I thinking? The father of the man who put me to shame, who tainted my glory. There is not much time left. (*Aloud*) Tell me more, old man. At once!

TIMUR. What should I do, my friend? 65

BARACH. Suffer, and remain silent. Turandot, he is a king. If you harm him, you disgrace your own nobility. Take your inhumanity out on me. But you will never know the prince's name.

TURANDOT. (*Furiously*) Yes, I will respect the old king, but you—you will feel the brunt of my anger. You prevented him from answering me, and now you'll pay for your folly. (*She gestures to the eunuchs, who pick up their whips and make ready to strike him.*) 70 75

SCHIRINA. My husband! Oh, gods, my husband!

SCENE 2

Enter Adelma.

ADELMA. Stop, my lady. I overheard what was said here. Quickly, have your slaves hide these two prisoners. Altoum will be here in a moment. Schirina, give me that gold. I have bribed the prince's guards, and we may enter his rooms and speak with him. It is my doing. If you all follow my advice, Turandot will be free, happy, and victorious again. Schirina, if you love your husband, and you Zelima, if your mother is dear to you, do exactly as I say. Carry out my plan, and you will be rich. Quickly—and before long we will all rejoice. 5 10

TURANDOT. My friend, do as you see fit. Take the gold. Schirina and Zelima will go with you. You three are my only hope. 15

ADELMA. Schirina, Zelima, follow me. (*Aside*) If only I can find out his name! Turandot will reject him. And then perhaps he will be mine—if I can convince him to leave this land, and take me with him. 20

(*Exeunt Adelma, Schirina, Zelima, and a eunuch with the gold.*)

BARACH. (*Calling after them*) Wife, Daughter, do not betray me. Do not obey these evil women. (*To Timur*) My lord, now the worst can happen to us.

TURANDOT. Slaves, put these prisoners under lock and key. Quickly. 25

TIMUR. Turandot, do what you like with me, but spare my son.

BARACH. This savage creature spare him? Your son will be betrayed, and we shall rot in the perpetual night of her dungeons so that no one knows of her 30 deception. Vile woman! Heaven will avenge us.

(*The eunuchs drag them off.*)

SCENE 3

TURANDOT. What will Adelma do? If this venture succeeds, no woman's name will be more celebrated than mine. No fool will ever again dare the riddles. I will revel in telling him his name, there in the council hall before the sages. I'll shame him, 5 and reject him. (*Hesitating*) And yet, am I sure that I will enjoy it?…I can almost see his sadness. It distresses me, I don't know why. Ah, Turandot! What are you thinking? Did he care how sad he made *me* when he solved the riddles? Heaven, 10 please help Adelma. Let me defeat the prince and remain a free woman—free to despise marriage, and men, who want to keep women weak and useless.

SCENE 4

Altoum, Pantalone, Tartaglia, soldiers, and Turandot

ALTOUM. (*Aside, thoughtfully*) So, the usurper Carizmo was fated to die. And Calaf, Timur's son, was meant to come to Peking and make his fortune in the contest. Heaven, your ways are unaccountable. Who can penetrate your mysteries? 5 Who dares ignore your will?

PANTALONE. (*Softly, to Tartaglia*) What the devil is wrong with the emperor? Look at him muttering to himself.

TARTAGLIA. (*Softly, to Pantalone*) He just received a 10 secret message. Something's in the wind, for sure.

ALTOUM. Daughter, dawn is near, and here you are: still awake, nervously pacing your room, trying to guess the unknowable. And while you rack your brains, chance has brought me the names you seek. 15

(*He takes a slip of paper, folded, from his robes.*) They are here. A secret messenger from a far land has just arrived. He spoke to me, then I had him put under guard until the morning. He gave me proof that the stranger is a king, the son of a king. You 20 cannot dream who they are, for their realm is very distant. I have come here out of pity for you. What satisfaction can you take in becoming a mockery for the second time in the council hall, before the people? The rabble will howl and whistle at the 25 merciless princess they hate, happy to see her pride humbled. The people cannot be controlled when they are angry. (*He makes a dignified gesture to Pantalone, Tartaglia, and the Soldiers. They bow low and leave.*) Daughter, I can protect your honour. 30

TURANDOT. My honour? What do you mean? Thank you, Father, but I need no help or protection. I will protect myself tomorrow in the council hall.

ALTOUM. No, Daughter. Believe me, this riddle is 35 beyond you. I can see the desperation on your face. Come, I am your father. You know I love you. There is no one here to listen. Tell me now—do you know those two names?

TURANDOT. You will hear them tomorrow, in the 40 council hall.

ALTOUM. No, Turandot, you can't know them. If you do, I entreat you to tell me. I ask it as a favour. If you know who he is, I will tell him he is defeated and allow him to leave the empire a free man. I will make 45 it known that you won, and that, in your mercy, you spared him a public defeat. That will save you from my subjects' hatred, and it will please your father. I have been a loving parent, Turandot. This is so little to ask. Can you refuse it? 50

TURANDOT. I know the names…That is, I don't but…Father, the prince thought nothing of how I felt when he triumphed over me in public. He deserves to suffer in the same way. Tomorrow you will see if I know the names. 55

ALTOUM. (*Impatient, he tries to force a reasonable tone*) He made you suffer because he loves you, and because his life was at stake. Conquer your anger for at least one moment, Turandot. I want you to realize how much your father cares for you. I 60 would wager my head that you do not know those names. I do know them, and I will tell them to you. Tomorrow, I will summon the council. The stranger will appear before it, and will suffer when you defeat him in public. Let him feel shame and anguish. Let him weep and despair because he has lost you, whom he loves more than his own life. All I ask is that, after his torment, you give him your hand in marriage. Daughter, swear to this, and I will tell you the names. No one else will know, and your reputation will remain unblemished. My subjects will begin to love you. You will have as your husband the most worthy man alive, and you will please your aged father after causing so much suffering.

TURANDOT. (*Aside, hesitant*) How persuasive he is! Should I trust Adelma, and hope to win by myself? Or ask my father the names, and consent to the repugnant bonds of marriage? If the prince were to win…it would be less shameful to give in to my father's request. But Adelma was sure of herself. What if she discovers the names, after I have promised…?

ALTOUM. What are you thinking, Daughter? What makes you hesitate? I can't believe that you have really learned those names. Come, give your father his wish.

TURANDOT. (*Aside*) No, wait. See what Adelma can manage. My father is too anxious. He must be afraid that I can come by the names on my own. He likes this stranger. Perhaps the prince himself gave him the names. Perhaps they planned this offer together, as a temptation.

ALTOUM. Come, Turandot, you must make up your mind. Calm your rebellious spirit. Stop tormenting yourself.

TURANDOT. I have decided. Let the sages be assembled tomorrow in the council hall.

ALTOUM. So, you are determined to be mocked in public? To yield to force rather than to a father's prayers?

TURANDOT. I insist. The trial shall be held.

ALTOUM. (*Angrily*) Fool! Most ignorant of women! You will be a laughingstock, I assure you. You will never guess the names. Hear me now: the council hall will be prepared for tomorrow's trial. When you have lost, you will be married there, immedi-

ately, against you will, while everyone mocks you. I will not forget that you refused to make your father happy. (*Exit, angrily.*)

TURANDOT. Adelma, my loving friend, my father is angry with me. You are now my only hope. (*Exit.*)

SCENE 5

The scene changes to a magnificent room with several doors and an oriental sofa, center. It is the middle of the night. Enter Brighella, carrying a torch, and Calaf.

BRIGHELLA. Your Highness, it's three o'clock in the morning. You've paced the room exactly three hundred and sixteen times. To tell you the truth, I'm bushed. If you want to get some sleep, don't worry, you're safe here.

CALAF. (*Preoccupied*) I'm restless, too nervous to sleep. But you may go, if you like.

BRIGHELLA. My dear Highness, can I ask a favour of you? If, ah…a ghost or two strolls by, don't lose your temper.

CALAF. Ghost? What do you mean?

BRIGHELLA. It's like this, Your Highness. We have orders to keep everyone out of your rooms, on pain of death. But…poor ministers…! The emperor is the emperor, but the princess, you might say she's the empress. You know what she's like. Poor ministers! It's tough to decide between them…If you only knew…We're between the devil and the deep blue sea. I wouldn't like anyone to get upset, if you know what I mean. Poor slobs! If we want to put anything aside for old age…well, we're in a hell of a fix.

CALAF. (*Surprised*) What do you mean? My life is not safe here?

BRIGHELLA. Well, I wouldn't say that. But you know how curious everybody is to know your name. Some little imp could slip through the keyhole to tempt you. All you have to do is keep your wits about you. Don't give anything away. You know what I mean? Poor ministers! Poor beggars!

CALAF. No need to worry, I'll be careful.

BRIGHELLA. Good. And please…don't give me away. I'm counting on you, Your Highness. (*Aside*) Could I refuse a bag of gold coins? I tried, but no luck. It's like being tickled—some people feel it, some don't. (*Exit.*) 35

CALAF. This is very suspicious. Who did he mean by "imps"? Well, let the whole of hell pour in. They'll never get me to tell my name. Winning Turandot matters too much to me. But dawn is near, and my anxiety and waiting are almost over. Will she still despise me? I must try to rest if I can. (*He is about to lie down on the couch.*) 40

SCENE 6

Enter Schirina, dressed as a soldier.

SCHIRINA. Boy…(*She looks around*) My lord— (*Looking around again*). My heart is racing.

CALAF. Who are you? What do you want?

SCHIRINA. I'm Schirina, the wife of Hassan—poor Hassan! I disguised myself as a soldier and mingled with your guards. When I saw my chance I slipped into your room. I have terrible things to tell you, Your Highness, but fear…doubts…sorrow clog my throat. 5

CALAF. What is wrong, Schirina? 10

SCHIRINA. My poor husband has gone into hiding. Someone told Turandot he knew you, and she ordered her men to search for him in secret. He is in danger, if they catch him he'll be tortured, and he has sworn to let them kill him before he reveals your name. 15

CALAF. My poor servant! Turandot is ruthless…

SCHIRINA. But there is more. Your father is at my house. He says your mother is dead…

CALAF. What are you saying? My God! 20

SCHIRINA. That isn't all. He knows that they are looking for Hassan, and that you are surrounded by soldiers. He is worried, afraid, tearful. He wants to come to the palace and tell them who he is. He keeps crying, "I want to die with my son!" I tried to stop him by telling him what you did today. He thinks I'm making it all up to keep him calm. The only thing that will stop him is a note from you, in your handwriting and signed with your name, telling him you are safe. That is why I took the frightful risk of coming here—for that note. 25 30

CALAF. My father, here in Peking! My mother, dead! Schirina, you are lying.

SCHIRINA. May Berginguzino blast me if I lie!

CALAF. My poor mother! Father, I am so sorry for you… 35

SCHIRINA. There is no time. Send the letter right away, or there will be worse trouble. Here, I brought a pen and ink with me. (*She takes the pen, paper, and inkwell out of her robes.*) Let your poor father see a few words from you, and he'll be happy. If not, he'll come to the palace and your name will soon be known. 40

CALAF. Yes, hand me that paper. (*He begins to write.*) No, what am I doing? (*He thinks for a moment, then throws the letter to the floor.*) Schirina, tell my father that I said he should go to the emperor and ask for a private audience. Altoum will tell him enough to set his mind at ease. That's the best way. 45

SCHIRINA. (*Confused*) You don't want to write? A line or two should be enough… 50

CALAF. No, Schirina, I will not write. No one will know my name until tomorrow. I am amazed that Hassan's wife would try to betray me.

SCHIRINA. (*Still more confused*) Betray you? What do you mean? (*Aside*) I pray Adelma's other plans don't go awry like this. (*Aloud*) Very well, Your Highness, I will tell your father what you have said. But I never expected to be called a traitor after all my efforts and risks on your behalf. (*Aside*) Adelma is smart, but this prince is no idiot either. (*Exit.*) 55 60

CALAF. Brighella was right. A ghost did appear. But Schirina swore a sacred oath that my father is in Peking, and my mother is dead. It must be true, alas. The blows of misfortune fall on me like hail…(*He looks toward another door.*) Another ghost. 65

SCENE 7

Enter Zelima.

ZELIMA. Prince, I am one of the slaves of Turandot. Her influence has made it possible for me to enter your room. I have good news.

CALAF. I wish that could be true, but I doubt it. Your princess is still angry, and her heart is hard. 5

ZELIMA. That is so, I can't deny it. But Your Highness, you are the first to make an impression on that heart. It seems impossible, and I know you will call me a liar, but though she says she hates you, I can tell that she's really in love. May the earth open and swallow me if I lie. 10

CALAF. Very well, I believe you. That is indeed good news. Do you have anything more to tell me?

ZELIMA. My lord, she is still desperately miserable. Her ambition makes her so. She knows she will 15 be unable to reveal your name tomorrow in the council hall. She fears that after so many ugly victories, the people will mock her unmercifully when she loses. May hell open and swallow this slave if she lies. 20

CALAF. There is no need to take such a heavy oath, slave. I believe you. Tell Turandot that the trial can be cancelled. The people will hate and mock her less if, instead of riddling, she knows herself capable of mercy, and takes pity on a lover's pain 25 and a father's anguish by agreeing to become my wife. Is that what you were sent to tell me?

ZELIMA. No, Your Highness. You must excuse the weakness of women. The princess begs a favour of you. She wants to save appearances, and to be able 30 to announce the names. After she does, she will descend from her throne and offer you her hand in marriage. We are alone here. It will cost you so little. A few words will win her heart, and make her your loving bride—not a wife by force. 35

CALAF. (Smiling) You left out a few words at the end of that speech, didn't you, slave?

ZELIMA. What words, Your Highness?

CALAF. "May hell open and swallow this slave if she lies." 40

ZELIMA. Do you think I'm not telling the truth?

CALAF. Perhaps not the whole truth. And my doubt is so strong that I will not do what you ask. Go back to Turandot and tell her to love me. Say that I refuse to reveal my name, not to cause her pain, 45 but because I love her so much.

ZELIMA. (Angrily) Foolish man, you have no idea what your defiance will cost you.

CALAF. I do not care if it costs me my life.

ZELIMA. (Fiercely) Good. Then you may get what 50 you ask for. (Aside) Useless! (Exit, infuriated.)

CALAF. Go, foolish ghosts. And yet somehow Schirina's words—they unsettle me. I wish my poor mother...my father...No! Be strong. Only a few hours, and you will know whether what she 55

told is the truth. I must rest, if I can. (He sits on the sofa.) My churning mind...it needs some respite. Perhaps I'll sleep. (He falls asleep.)

SCENE 8

Truffaldino enters on tiptoe, virtually on point, and cases the room fearfully, exploring its perimeter until he stumbles into the sleeping Calaf.

TRUFFALDINO. Great, he's snoring. (*In a whisper*) Or pretending? (*He retreats rapidly, trips, falls.*) No damage, luckily. I only hit my head. Where did I put that magic mandrake? (*He frantically searches his pockets.*) Truffaldino, don't say you lost it! Af- 5 ter you paid cash! Did I leave it somewhere? If one of my eunuchs picks it up, puts it under my pillow...disaster! I'll lose the reward: two bags of gold for his name. Think back, Truffaldino! You took it in your left hand for safety. It was clammy. 10 Why didn't you keep it there? I did! It's here! Still clammy. Magic mandrake, the root of truth. Now...I slide it under his pillow, like so. (*Calaf grunts. Truffaldino goes into a swift crouch. A bang*) Only my head again. Did he wake? Where's the 15 mandrake? Truffaldino, you didn't drop it? I did. (*He scrabbles around on his hands and knees.*) There you are, you rotten little root. Get under that pillow! Now...Give it about a minute to work. The mandrake dealer said you could ask questions and 20 it makes a person reply in his sleep. A general told an enemy spy a load of military secrets. A merchant told his son where he'd stashed away his savings. A minister told his wife about an affair he was having with her sister, the bastard. Talk about 25 the immorality of our times! Times? Time's up: put the question. Stranger, for two bags crammed with gold, what's your name? I want the straight answer. (*Calaf moves restlessly.*) That was a signal. He's spelling it out, letter by letter. I wish I could spell. That 30 looked like a T. (*Calaf continues to turn over, roll his head, stretch his arms, change his sleeping position, as Truffaldino counts off his interpretation letter by letter.*) So T—an R—a U—an F—another F— an A—an L—D—I—N—O...Who'd have 35 believed it? He has the only name I can spell. Race away, tell the princess, collect two bags of gold.

Wait, Truffaldino! Don't forget your mandrake. (*He recovers the mandrake gingerly from under Calaf's pillow.*) You clever little, clammy little root! You'll make me rich. Tonight I'll tickle you under the king's pillow…You're the best thing that ever hap—(*As he kisses the root he bangs into the door.*) No damage. Only my head again. (*Exit.*) 40

SCENE 9

Enter Adelma, veiled and carrying a small torch.

ADELMA. (*Aside*) My first plans failed and I could not discover the names, but perhaps I can now induce him to love me and take me away from the city. This is the moment. Gods of love, lend me strength and ingenuity. Fortune, make my plot succeed, and break the chains of my slavery. (*She holds her lamp over Calaf.*) My beloved is sleeping; he is so handsome. I wish I didn't have to wake him. But there is not a moment to lose. (*She puts the lamp down, and speaks aloud.*) Stranger, wake up. 5 10

CALAF. (*Startled awake, he rises*) Who woke me? Another ghost? What do you want? Won't you leave me alone?

ADELMA. Angry? How can an unhappy woman harm you? I have not come to fish for your name. Do you want to know what brings me here? Listen. 15

CALAF. What are you doing in this room, woman? I warn you, don't try to betray me.

ADELMA. (*Gently*) I, betray you? Ungrateful man! Tell me, stranger, didn't Schirina come? Didn't she try to convince you to write a letter? 20

CALAF. She did.

ADELMA. (*Anxiously*) You didn't write it?

CALAF. I am not a fool. No. 25

ADELMA. Thank heaven. Didn't a slave come with another story to find out your identity?

CALAF. Yes, but she went away without discovering it, exactly as you will.

ADELMA. If you knew me, my lord, you would not have such suspicions. First sit and listen to me. Then, if you think I'm betraying you, condemn me. (*She sits: Calaf sits next to her.*) 30

CALAF. Very well, tell me what you want.

ADELMA. Look at me first. Do you recognize me? 35

CALAF. (*Examining her*) There is an air about you, woman…your bearing, your behaviour are noble. From your dress, you seem to be a slave. Didn't I see you before in the council hall? I felt sorry for you. 40

ADELMA. As I felt sorry for you five years ago, when I saw you as a humble servant, and even more when I saw you today in the council hall. I knew in my heart that you were not of low birth. I did all I could for you then. You must have known, from the way I looked at you, how I felt. (*She removes her veil.*) Haven't you seen this face before? 45

CALAF. (*Surprised*) Adelma, the princess of Carazani? I thought you were dead. 50

ADELMA. Yes, Adelma, daughter of the king of Carazani—born to a throne—and now a miserable slave. (*She weeps.*)

CALAF. Everyone thought you were dead. Poor princess! A slave! 55

ADELMA. Let me describe my sad plight. I had a brother who was as mad with love for Turandot as you are now. He attempted the riddles. (*Weeping*) You have seen his skull, there with all the others above the city gates. 60

CALAF. Poor woman! I heard this once before, and I thought it was a story, a lying fairy tale. Now I know better.

ADELMA. My father was a brave man, who raged at the death of his son, and sought revenge. He led his army against Altoum's empire—but fate frowned on him. He lost the battle and was killed. One of Altoum's ministers, a pitiless man jealous of our royal titles, attempted to wipe out every member of my family. He slew my three remaining brothers, then threw my mother, my sisters, and myself into a river to drown. Just then the merciful Emperor Altoum arrived at the riverbank. He was angry at his minister's cruelty, and had his soldiers pull us out of the water. Too late! My mother and sisters were already dead. I was less fortunate. I lived, and the emperor gave me as a slave to his daughter. Prince, if you have human feelings, you will pity me. Think of how it feels to be a slave to the cruel Turandot: the cause of all my troubles, the fountain of my misfortune. (*She weeps.*) 65 70 75 80

CALAF. (*Moved*) I do pity you, princess. But your brother was the first cause of your misfortunes, and after that your father's rashness. What can I do for you now? I am helpless. If tomorrow I reach the pinnacle of happiness, I can give you your freedom. Until then, your story can only make my own sorrows harder to confront. 85

ADELMA. I revealed my identity by showing you my face. You know my lineage and my wretched history. I hope you will believe a princess's word when her compassion—I dare not say "her love"—forces her to tell you a secret. You are blindly in love with Turandot. May heaven help you to believe what I must tell you about her. 90 95

CALAF. Come, Adelma, what is it you want to say?

ADELMA. I want to say…But you will tell me that I came here to deceive you, you will think that I am like those lowborn women. (*She weeps.*)

CALAF. Adelma, don't keep me in suspense. What do you want to tell me about my beloved? 100

ADELMA. (*Aside*) Heaven, make him believe my lie. (*Aloud, forcefully*) My lord, Turandot—depraved vicious, infamous Turandot—has given orders to have you murdered at dawn. That is how the woman you love will treat you. 105

CALAF. (*Surprised, jumping to his feet*) Orders to kill me!

ADELMA. (*Rising*) Yes, to kill you. When you leave this room tomorrow, twenty swords will plunge into your body. 110

CALAF. (*Agitated*) I must call the guards (*Heading for the door*).

ADELMA. (*Holding him back*) No! What are you doing? If you hope to save yourself by warning the guards…Poor man, you have no idea how influential the princess is, how far her power extends. 115

CALAF. (*Desperate, he is raving*) Oh, poor Calaf! And Timur, Father! Is this how I have helped you? (*He buries his face in his hands.*) 120

ADELMA. (*Aside, surprised*) Calaf, the son of Timur! My lie brought me luck! He told me his name without meaning to. Now, gods of love, help me convince him to hate Turandot. 125

CALAF. (*Continues, desperately*) Fortune, what more can you do to a desperate, forsaken man—to an innocent and devoted prince? After so much misery, you add this final blow, that Turandot could commit such a murder? No, unthinkable. So lovely a face cannot mask a heart so evil. (*Scornfully*) Princess, you are lying. 130

ADELMA. That is an insult, but I will not be offended. I knew you would not believe me. Stranger, the riddle of your name has driven Turandot nearly mad. She knows that she will never solve it. (*Mockingly*) She paces back and forth like a madwoman, she shakes herself like a dog, and howls, and grimaces. Her face is pale and sickly green with fear, her eyes red and swollen, her expression clouded. She would look horrible to you now, not like the beauty you saw in the council hall. I told her how handsome you are, described you in the most convincing words, and argued that she should accept you as a husband. I failed. She gave her eunuchs orders to kill you secretly. A more infernal woman was never born. She repays your love with death. I know you don't believe me, and your distrust does not wound me—but I weep for the fate that hangs over you. (*She weeps.*) 135 140 145 150

CALAF. I am surrounded by an emperor's army, put there to protect me, and I am in danger of betrayal? That foul minister was right to say that self-interest and fear can make any man unfaithful. Ah, Turandot! Is this how you repay a lover who in his mad passion for you tries to be generous to the limit and give you all you desire? I do not wish to live. Let my callous destiny overtake me. 155 160

ADELMA. Stranger, Adelma will find a way for you to flee your fate. I pitied you, and so I bribed your guards with Turandot's gold. In a cave in my former kingdom an immense treasure is buried. Alinguer, the king of Berlas, is linked to me by both blood and friendship. Some of the guards will be our escort. Horses are ready for us. Let us escape from this ugly city. Together with Alinguer, we will have the strength to regain my kingdom, which will be yours, along with my gratitude, my love, and if you wish, myself. If you do not want me as your wife, there are many other princesses more beautiful that I among the Tartars. You may 165 170 have my kingdom, I wish only to save you from death and myself from slavery. If that could come to pass, I could even suppress my love for you— a love that is tearing me apart, a love I am embarrassed to confess so openly. But if my love means nothing to you, at least think of your life. Daybreak is near...Come, stranger, we must hasten away. 180

CALAF. You are a generous woman, Adelma. I am deeply sorry that I cannot free you from your slavery and escort you to Berlas. What would Altoum say about my flight? He would call me a traitor, and he would be right, since in freeing you I would violate the sacred laws of hospitality. 185

ADELMA. Say rather that his daughter violates them.

CALAF. She will never be my wife now, Adelma. I have lost hope of that. Yet I will be happy to die at the hands of a woman I adore. Escape if you wish: I will remain here. Without her, my life is worthless, no better than a living death. Let her murder me. 190

ADELMA. You're serious? Has love driven you into delirium? 195

CALAF. Love or death: my only choice.

ADELMA. Stranger, I know very well that she is more beautiful that I am, but I hoped you would at least be grateful to me. I can bear the shame of this rejection. It is your life that matters to me. Let us go together. Save your life, I beg you. 200

CALAF. Adelma, I have made up my mind. I will die.

ADELMA. Thankless man! If you will not escape, neither will I. I will remain a slave, but not for long. We shall see which of us can give up life, and scorn the punishment of adverse fortune more heroically. (*Aside*) Perseverance is often successful in love, Calaf, son of Timur. (*Aloud*) Stranger, farewell. (*Exit*.) 205 210

CALAF. Has any man ever passed a night of more torment? In love with a woman who hates me, surrounded by plots, my mother reported dead and my father fearful for me. And just when I hope that I am about to reach true happiness, I find that Turandot wants to murder me. Merciless woman! Her slave told me it would cost me dear when I refused to tell her my name. She was right. There, the sun is rising. (*The room lightens*.) It is time. Let 215

the serpent drink my blood, if she thirsts for it so badly, and end my misery. 220

SCENE 10

Enter Brighella and soldiers.

BRIGHELLA. Your Highness, it's time for the trial.

CALAF. (*Agitated*) So, minister, are you the one? Carry out your orders. Kill me if you will. I don't care.

BRIGHELLA. (*Thunderstruck*) Orders? My only orders are to bring you to the council hall, because the emperor is almost ready. 5

CALAF. Good, we'll make for the council hall, though I know I'll never arrive there. You will see that I can die with dignity. (*He throws down his sword*.) I will not defend myself. That spiteful woman will hear that I die for her of my own will. (*Exit, angrily*.) 10

BRIGHELLA. (*Amazed*) What the hell's got into him? Damned women! They wouldn't let him sleep, and he's gone off his rocker. All right, boys, we'll follow and make sure he's safe. Present arms! *Hup* two, three, four... 15

ACT FIVE

The scene returns to the council hall. Upstage, behind a curtain, an altar with a Chinese idol and two Priests. As the scene opens, Altoum is seated on his throne and the sages are in place. Pantalone and Tartaglia flank Altoum, and the soldiers are placed as in Act Two.

SCENE 1

Altoum, Pantalone, Tartaglia, sages, soldiers, then Calaf. Calaf enters as if agitated, looking around suspiciously. He comes center and bows to Altoum.

CALAF. (*Aside*) What is going on? All the way here I imagined that I was about to be attacked, but no one bothered me. Either Adelma was deceiving me, or Turandot had discovered the names and countermanded her orders to kill me. Is she lost to me, then? If that is true, I would rather die. (*He remains preoccupied*.) 5

ALTOUM. My son, you seem upset. You should be

happy. There is nothing to worry about. Today your misfortunes come to an end. What I have learned will give you great joy. My daughter will be your wife. Three times she has sent me messages, begging me to delay the trial and prevent the marriage. Do you see? Your victory is sure.

PANTALONE. It's a safe bet, Your Highness. Twice I was called to the door of the harem to receive her commands. I dressed in a hurry and ran to obey. It was so cold my beard is still shivering. But I didn't care—I got a kick out of seeing her so desperate. It warmed my heart just to think of all the happiness in store for us.

TARTAGLIA. I was there at six o'clock. The dawn was breaking. She kept me there for half an hour, begging. Between the cold and her anger, I lost my patience. I may have let a bad word slip. (*Aside*) I could have spanked her pretty behind.

ALTOUM. Do you see how late she is? I have sent strict orders for her to come; if she refuses I will have her dragged here by force. I have reason to be angry with her. Here she comes, with a sadder face than she has ever worn. Let her be sad, since she wouldn't let me help her. My son, rejoice.

CALAF. Pardon me, my lord. I thank you for your kind words, but certain fears are tormenting me, and I am distressed to cause her pain. I would rather…No, I cannot say that. I could never live without her. In time, my tenderness will make her forget her hatred of me. My whole heart will be dedicated to her. I will desire what she desires. When I am king, anyone who needs a royal favour will not need to seek out flatterers and court cronies. I will favour only those for whom my wife intercedes. I will always be faithful to her, and will never give her cause to distrust me. Before long, I hope, she will requite my love and regret her former hatred.

ALTOUM. Ministers! We are ready. Open the curtain and let her see that all is prepared for her to be married immediately, here in the council hall. She will see that I mean what I say. Let the people enter. It is time for my ungrateful daughter to pay in some small measure for what she made her father undergo. Let everyone rejoice. Let the wedding take place. Prepare the altar.

(*The upstage curtain opens, revealing altar and Priests.*)

PANTALONE. Here she comes, chancellor. Seems to me she's crying.

TARTAGLIA. Her escort is pretty melancholy. This wedding looks more like a funeral.

SCENE 2

Enter Adelma, Zelima, Truffaldino, eunuchs, slave women, and Turandot. The sound of a funeral march announces Turandot's entrance. She is preceded on stage by her usual escort, dressed in mourning. The ceremonies of Act Two are repeated. As she ascends her throne, Turandot is clearly surprised to see the altar and priests. All characters are placed as they were in Act Two.

TURANDOT. Stranger, I know that in your heart you are glad to see my servants' mourning clothes and their sad expressions. I see the altar prepared for my wedding, and I too am sad. I used all my skill to avenge the shame you put upon me by defeating me. But in the end, I had to yield to my destiny.

CALAF. Princess, I wish I could show you my heart, so that you could see how my joy is made bitter by your unhappiness. How can you regret making me happy when I adore you? Let us be united by mutual love. I beg to be forgiven, if a lover need ask forgiveness for loving.

ALTOUM. My son, she does not deserve such consideration. It is at last time for her to be humiliated. Let the music play, and the wedding proceed.

TURANDOT. No, it is not yet time for that. I could have no greater revenge than this: after lulling you into happiness with the appearance of sadness and defeat, I now shrivel you from joy to anguish. (*She rises.*) Calaf, son of Timur, leave this hall. Those are the two names you challenged me to guess. Look for another bride, and learn how easily Turandot unravels your feeble mysteries.

CALAF. (*Astonished and dismayed*) I have lost her.

ALTOUM. (*Surprised*) Gods, is it possible?

PANTALONE. By the blood and bones of Bacchus, she's given it to us. In the nose.

TARTAGLIA. Oh, Berginguzino! This is a knife in my heart.

CALAF. (*Desperately*) I have lost everything. Who can help me now? No one. I am my own murderer. I have lost my beloved by loving her too much. If I had not solved the riddles yesterday, my head would now be cut off, and I would have avoided this pain, which is worse that death. Altoum, why did you not agree to let her kill me if she revealed my name? If you had, I would now be more fortunate. (*He weeps.*) 35

ALTOUM. Calaf, I'm overcome…This unforeseen stroke grieves me deeply. 40

TURANDOT. (*Softly, to Zelima*) I'm sorry for the poor man. I can no longer defend my heart from him.

ZELIMA. (*Softly*) Then yield to your heart, Your Highness. Listen, the people are murmuring against you. 45

ADELMA. (*Aside*) What she decides now means life or death for me.

CALAF. (*Raving*) Is this a nightmare? Am I losing my mind? (*Angrily*) Tell me, you tyrant, are you unhappy that the man who adores you is still living? Then let your triumph include my death. (*Furious, he approaches Turandot's throne.*) Here is your victim at your feet: Calaf, whose name you know and curse. And I, Calaf, curse heaven, and earth, and my own destiny. Here, in your presence, I die. (*He draws a stiletto and is about to stab himself. Turandot rushes down from the throne and prevents him.*) 50 55

TURANDOT. (*Tenderly*) No, Calaf, I will not let you.

ALTOUM. What is this miracle? 60

CALAF. (*Surprised*) Turandot—why have you prevented my death? Are you capable of mercy? No, you woman of marble, you want to force me to suffer more by living without you. Do not carry your revenge so far. At least, let me escape my misery. If you wish to be truly merciful, help my father Timur who is here in Peking, poor, ragged, and persecuted. But let me die. (*He tries to stab himself. Turandot prevents him.*) 65

TURANDOT. No, Calaf. You must live for me. You have won. Listen…Zelima, run and give this happy news to the poor old man and his faithful minister. Go, and comfort your mother. 70

ZELIMA. Yes, Your Highness, I'll do so with pleasure.

ADELMA. (*Aside*) There is no more hope. Her choice is my death. 75

TURANDOT. I won the trial unfairly, Calaf. You revealed the names to Adelma last night, carried away by I don't know what outpouring of grief. She told them to me. Let the world know that I am incapable of a dishonest act. And let them know as well that your own merits, your generosity, and your handsome features have softened my heart. Live, Calaf! Turandot is your bride. 80

ADELMA. (*Aside, softly*) Oh, my misery! 85

CALAF. (*Throwing down the knife*) You are mine! I could die of joy!

ALTOUM. (*Descending from his throne*) Daughter…my dear daughter. I forgive all the pain you gave me, all your former cruelty. 90

PANTALONE. Time for the wedding! Time for the wedding! Make way there, sages.

TARTAGLIA. Withdraw to the rear of the hall.

(*The sages move to the rear.*)

ADELMA. (*Coming forward angrily*) Live then, you stubborn man, live with my enemy. Princess, I hate you. All my plots were aimed at winning this man, whom I have loved since I first saw him, five years ago, at my father's court. I pretended to help you while I was telling him you were wicked and asking him to flee with me. He accidentally revealed the names you sought. I told you, hoping you would reject him. I thought I could then convince him to escape with me, but he loves you too much. All my plotting was useless. My hopes have died. I have one choice left. I was born to royalty, and am ashamed to have lived as your slave. I abhor you and your wickedness. You took my family from me—my father, my brothers, my mother and sisters. You have taken my kingdom and the man I love. I am the last of my family—now slay me, too, if you wish. My blood will wash away that shame from the past. (*She picks up Calaf's knife.*) You drew this knife back from you lover's heart. Now it will pierce mine. Let the people see how I free myself from slavery. (*She tries to stab herself. Calaf prevents her.*) 95 100 105 110 115

CALAF. Stop, Adelma!

ADELMA. Let me go, oppressor! (*Weeping*) Let me go, thankless man. I want to die. (*She tries again to stab herself. Calaf takes the knife away from her.*) 120

CALAF. I will not let you. I received nothing but good from you. Your betrayal made me a happy man. The torment it aroused in me moved a woman who hated me but is now in love. Pardon me if my love for her was too great to overcome. I am not thankless. I swear to the gods that if I could love any other woman, it would be you. 125

ADELMA. (*Breaking into tears*) No, I am unworthy of you.

TURANDOT. Adelma, what is this madness? 130

ADELMA. (*To Turandot*) Princess, you have heard my grim story. Now you are stealing the man I love. I became a traitor for his sake, and now he robs me of my revenge. But give me my liberty, at least! Let me leave the city as a wandering beggar. Do not 135 make me stay to see Calaf in your arms: that would be too cruel. Remember, a jealous heart dares anything for revenge. You will always be in danger if Adelma is near. (*She weeps.*)

ALTOUM. (*Aside*) Poor princess, I pity you. 140

CALAF. Adelma, do not weep. I can now repay you in part for all you have inadvertently done for me. Wife, Altoum, if a request from me has any influence on you, give this princess her freedom.

TURANDOT. I ask it too, Father. I know she sees me 145 as a bitter reminder of her misfortunes. My love and complete trust in her were misplaced. She hated me secretly all along, and will never believe that I could wish to be more her friend than her superior. Let her go free. And if the prayers of 150 Calaf and your daughter can sway you, then we beg you to be still more generous.

ALTOUM. On such a glad day as this I cannot stint in my generosity. Adelma must be happy too. The princess shall have her kingdom back and choose 155 a husband who will rule more prudently than her rash father.

ADELMA. My lord…remorse…love…my emotions oppress me, and I cannot appreciate your liberality. Time will clear my mind. But for now I can only 160 feel sad and not hold back my tears.

CALAF. Is my father in Peking? Where can I find him and embrace him?

TURANDOT. He is in my care, and by now he has heard the joyful news. Please do not force me to 165 confess my folly in public. I am too ashamed. I will tell you everything when we are alone.

ALTOUM. Timur in your care! Rejoice, Calaf. My empire is yours already. And let Timur rejoice as well, for his kingdom is freed. The tyrant Carizmo, 170 whose savagery made him hated, has been assassinated by your subjects. A faithful minister holds the sceptre, awaiting your return, and has sent secret messages to kings and emperors describing you and your father, and recalling you 175 to the throne, if either one of you remains alive. This message will inform you of the usurper's death. (*He gives Calaf a message.*)

CALAF (*After reading it*). Gods in heaven, can it possibly be true? Turandot…My lord…But my 180 thanks should go to heaven, not to mortals. Gods, I raise my hands to bless and thank you, asking you to visit even greater misfortunes on me, to prove that your power to redeem us goes beyond all human expectation and understanding. I 185 humbly beg your pardon for my complaints, and if my desperation made me give up all hope of aid from an omnipotent hand, I ask your forgiveness, and repent my error.

(*The onlookers are visibly moved.*)

TURANDOT. Let no one else trouble my wedding 190 day. (*Thoughtfully*) Calaf risks his life out of love for me. A faithful minister scorns death to make his lord happy. Another minister, who could proclaim himself king, holds the throne for his rightful monarch. I saw an old man ready to die 195 for his son, and a woman I regarded more as a friend than a servant betrayed me. Heaven, I have indeed been brutal and stubborn in my hatred of men, and now I ask your pardon. (*She advances and addresses the audience.*) Gentlemen, I once 200 hated your sex, but I have repented. Pray, give me a sign of your forgiveness. (*She mimes applause.*)

THE END OF
TURANDOT

BEAUMARCHAIS

The Marriage of Figaro

W hen it was finally performed publicly without police interference in 1784, after six years of suppression, harassment, clandestine readings and underground popularity, *The Marriage of Figaro* broke all box-office records at Paris's Comédie-Française, playing for 73 nights in its first year. Despite the hundreds of casualties incurred during the crazed stampede for admission to the theatre that afternoon, *Figaro*'s long-awaited premiere is still remembered as perhaps the most glorious four-and-a-half hours in all of French theatre history.

Like Molière's *Tartuffe* a century before, *The Marriage of Figaro* achieved blockbuster status partly because of the elaborate measures taken to suppress it. After reading it in 1781, the King pronounced the play "detestable" and ordered that it "never" be performed. "It would be necessary," he facetiously suggested, "to destroy the Bastille" first—that is, dismantle the entire French police-state—for such a mocking, inflammatory work ever to be allowed on the stage. But *Figaro* was finally performed, and four years later, the Bastille was indeed destroyed, in the first act of the French Revolution, by a populace fed up, like Beaumarchais and his alter-ego Figaro, with all the tyrannical abuses this fortress represented. (Beaumarchais himself had suffered repeated imprisonment, censorship, and endless, impoverishing litigation.) Although the play's role in the Revolution shouldn't be exaggerated, the King's repeated banning of it did have tangible consequences, appalling aristocrats and shattering any illusions they might have had about the existence of civil rights in France. In portraying the Count as a profligate, comically stupid, and impotent despot who is easily defeated by his powerless subjects—women, children, and servants—working together, Beaumarchais proved remarkably prescient of the upheavals to come.

Figaro also harks back to the most ancient tradition of master/servant comedy. Its many Roman and *commedia dell'arte* elements include crafty servants, cunning plans, masters lusting after young lovers and trying to prevent their marriage; disguise and mistaken identity; the use of closets, doors, and furniture for concealment and surprise; long-lost parents; and a conventional happy ending. But because these theatrical devices are set within a teeming network of autobiographical and topical references—particularly in Figaro's and Marceline's big monologues, and throughout the courtroom scene—the play leans more toward satire than sitcom. And although he has taken up Diderot's proposals for the reform of the stage through visual and psychological realism—in his use of painterly tableaux and detailed costume, character, and stage directions—Beaumarchais has a tendency to satirize even these. He includes, for example, a "tearful recognition scene," a mainstay of middle-class drama of the period, but parodies its sentimentality with exaggeration and absurd juxtapositions: the foundling in *Figaro* is identified thanks to his mother having tattooed his arm at birth with a picture of a kitchen utensil.

Born Pierre-Augustin Caron, the son of a Parisian watchmaker, Beaumarchais (1732–1799) was as ebullient and multi-talented as his fictionalized self-portrait, Figaro. He revolutionized the mechanics of time-keeping, making clocks so tiny and accurate that they could be worn as pinky-rings. He was a brilliant harpist, the music master to Louis XV's daughters; later, he experimented with the first viable flying machines (hot-air balloons). He transformed the financial practices of the theatre and improved the lives of writers for all time by establishing the first copyright watchdog organization, the Society of Authors. He published the first complete works of Voltaire. He wrote the plays for operatic masterworks by Mozart, Salieri, and Rossini. He also lobbied for, arranged, and personally financed shipments of weapons to the American revolutionaries, helping to ensure the birth of the United States. Having poured all his outrage, charm, wit, love of civil liberty, and passion for equality into *The Marriage of Figaro,* he is also regarded by many critics as the creator of the single most important play of the eighteenth century.

[J.W.]

BEAUMARCHAIS
The Marriage of Figaro
Translated by John Van Burek and Jennifer Wise[1]

CHARACTERS AND COSTUMES

COUNT ALMAVIVA, *chief magistrate of Andalusia, must be acted with great nobility, but with grace and ease as well. The corruption of his heart mustn't detract from the elegance of his manners. It was customary for great men of his time period to view all their affairs with women as insignificant larks. The role is all the more difficult to play well because the character is the butt of everyone's jokes. But played by an excellent comedian (M. Molé), he brought the other characters into sharp relief and assured the success of the play. He is dressed in the first and second acts in a hunting outfit, with thigh-high boots of the old Spanish style. From the third act to the end, a superb suit in the same style.*

THE COUNTESS, *his wife Rosine. Torn between two opposing emotions, she should show neither in such a way as to degrade her lovable and virtuous character in the eyes of the audience: her hurt feelings must be restrained, and her anger only very moderate. This role, one of the most difficult in the play, displayed to perfection the tremendous talent of Mlle. Saint-Val the younger. Her clothing in the first, second, and fourth acts is a flowing dressing-gown, with no ornament on her head; she is keeping to her own rooms, supposedly indisposed. In the fifth act, she wears the wedding outfit and high feathered head-dress of Suzanne.*

FIGARO, *the Count's valet and concierge of the chateau. One cannot stress highly enough to the actor of this part how deeply he must penetrate into its spirit, as did M. d'Azincourt. Had he seen anything in it other than reason leavened with gaiety and witticisms, above all if he'd caricatured it even slightly, he would have degraded a role that the greatest comedian on the stage, M. Préville, judged worthy of the talent of whoever can grasp its multiplicity of nuances*

---

[1] The text is mainly the performance version of April, 1784, as edited by Jean-Pierre de Beaumarchais (Paris: Éditions Garnier Frères, 1980). For Figaro's long monologue in Act V, I have used parts of an earlier variant, from the Beaumarchais family archives, as reproduced in the Gallimard edition (Paris, 1988), edited by Pierre and Jacqueline Larthomas. [J.W.]

and rise to a conception of the whole. His costume is the same as in *The Barber of Seville.*

SUZANNE, *first chambermaid to the* Countess, *and* Figaro's *fiancée. A skillful, witty, and cheerful young person, but whose gaiety has nothing of the almost forced impudence typical of our scheming flirts today. Her lovely character is described in the Preface; an actress who hasn't seen Mlle. Contat must study that description to play the part well. For the first four acts she wears a tight white embroidered peasant bodice, very elegant, and a skirt to match, with the kind of little round hat that all milliners now call a hat "à la Suzanne." During the festivities of the fourth act, the* Count *places on her head a head-piece with a long veil, high plumes, and white ribbons. In the fifth act she wears the Countess's dressing-gown and no ornaments on her head.*

MARCELINE, *housekeeper to* Doctor Bartholo, *is a spirited woman, a bit wild in her youth but whose character has been improved by her mistakes and experience. If the actress who plays her can rise with fitting dignity to the moral grandeur that follows the recognition scene of the third act, she will add a great deal to the play's overall interest. Her dress is that of Spanish duennas, of a modest color, a black bonnet on her head.*

ANTONIO, *gardener of the chateau, uncle of* Suzanne, *and father of* Fanchette. *He should show only a half-drunkenness, and one that dissipates by degrees, so that by the fifth act it's scarcely noticeable. His clothing is that of a Spanish peasant, with sleeves hanging down behind, a hat and white shoes.*

FANCHETTE, Antonio's *daughter, is a child of twelve, very innocent. Her little outfit is a tight brown bodice with silver knots and buttons, a brightly-coloured skirt, and a black plumed hat. She will resemble the other peasants at the wedding.*

CHERUBIN, *the* Count's *first page. This role can only be played, as it was, by a young and very pretty girl; in our theatres today we simply have no very young men who are well-enough trained to convey its subtleties. Excessively shy before the* Countess, *otherwise a charming scamp; a vague and troubled longing is the basis of his character. He is hurtling toward puberty, but without any conscious plans, without understanding, and entirely at the mercy of each passing moment. In fact, he's exactly what every mother, deep down, wishes her son could be like, however much she may suffer for it. His rich clothing, in the first and second acts, is that of a page at the Spanish court, white and embroidered in silver, a light blue cape on his shoulder and a plumed hat. In the fourth act he wears the same bodice, skirt, and hat as the young peasants who lead him in. In the fifth act, an officer's uniform, a cockade, and a sword.*

BARTHOLO, *Doctor of Seville. Character and costume as in* The Barber of Seville. *In this play he has only a secondary role.*

BAZILE, *Music Master. Character and costume as in* The Barber of Seville. *In this play he has only a secondary role.*

DON GUSMAN BRID'OISON, *Judge. Must have the simple, frank assurance of animals that have lost their timidity. His slight speech impediment is just another trait and should hardly even be noticeable; the actor who exploits it for humour will make a serious mistake and defeat the purpose of the role. It is entirely in the contrast between the gravity of his function and the ridiculousness of his personality that the humour resides; the less the actor caricatures him, the more he shows true talent. He wears the robe of a Spanish judge, simpler than those of our French magistrates, almost a cassock; a large wig, Spanish neck band, and a long white stick in his hand.*

DOUBLE-MAIN, *clerk, secretary to Don Gusman. Dressed like the judge, but with a shorter white stick.*

THE BAILIFF, *or* ALGUAZIL. *Dress, cape, and sword of* Crispin,[2] *but carried at his side without a leather belt. Black shoes (not boots), a long white formal wig with many ringlets, and a short white stick.*

---

2 Crispin] a stock valet character of the *commedia dell'arte.*

GRIPPE-SOLEIL, *a young shepherd. Peasant outfit with hanging sleeves; brightly-coloured jacket and white hat.*

A YOUNG SHEPHERDESS. *Her costume is like* Fanchette's.

PÉDRILLE, *groom to* the Count. *In the jacket, waistcoat, belt, whip, and boots of a post-horse rider, a net on his head, and a courier's hat.*

NON-SPEAKING CHARACTERS. *Some dressed as judges, others as peasants, others in livery as servants.*

SCENE: THE CHATEAU D'AGUAS-FRESCAS, THREE LEAGUES FROM SEVILLE

ACT 1

A half-furnished bedroom; a large straight-backed armchair is in the middle of the room. Figaro is using a measuring stick to determine the floor space. In front of a mirror, Suzanne is tying a small bouquet of orange flowers, known as a bride's cap, in her hair.

SCENE 1

Figaro, Suzanne

FIGARO: Nineteen by twenty-six.

SUZANNE: Here, look Figaro, my little cap; do you like it better this way?

FIGARO: *(taking her hands)* No comparison, my darling. Oh how sweet, to a groom's adoring eye, is a pretty bridal bouquet on the head of a beautiful girl on the morning of her wedding— 5

SUZANNE: *(pulling away)* What are you measuring there, young man?

FIGARO: I'm checking, my little Suzanne, to see if 10 the handsome bed the Count is giving us will fit in here.

SUZANNE: In this room?

FIGARO: He's given it to us.

SUZANNE: I don't want it. 15

FIGARO: Why not?

SUZANNE: I just don't.

FIGARO: But why?

SUZANNE: I don't like it.

FIGARO: You need a reason. 20

SUZANNE: And if I don't want to tell you?

FIGARO: Oh! Once they're sure they've got us...!

SUZANNE: Proving that I'm right involves admitting that I could be wrong. Are my wishes your commands or not? 25

FIGARO: But you're turning your nose up at the handiest room in the whole chateau, right between their two apartments. At night, if Madame is indisposed, she'll give a little ring and Zing! Two steps and you're there. Monseigneur wants 30 something? he just gives a little dingle on his side and Zip! Three hops; there I am.

SUZANNE: That's just fine; but once he's given his little "dingle" in the morning and sent you off on some good long errand, Zing! in two steps he's at 35 my door, and Zip! In three hops—

FIGARO: What's that supposed to mean?

SUZANNE: Now listen to me calmly.

FIGARO: My god, what is it?

SUZANNE: You see, my friend, tired of chasing 40 women all over the neighbourhood, Count Alma-viva is ready to come home—but not to his wife; it's *your* wife, you see, that he's got his eye on, imagining that this room won't exactly get in the way. At least that's what Bazile, faithful agent of Monsieur's 45 pleasures and my esteemed music master, harps on every day throughout my singing lesson.

FIGARO: Bazile! Oh, my darling! If ever a backside required the application of a good hard thrashing with a long green switch— 50

SUZANNE: Well surely you don't imagine I was given that dowry just because of *your* stellar service, lovely boy?

FIGARO: I've done enough to hope so.

SUZANNE: Intelligent people can be such dunces! 55

FIGARO: So they say.

SUZANNE: But no one wants to believe it.

FIGARO: And they should.

SUZANNE: Understand, then, that he's earmarked this room to take from me, in private, in some 60 quick quarter-of-an-hour, one-on-one, what a former *droit du seigneur*[3]......Well, *you* know how miserable it was!

---

3 *Droit du seigneur*] lit. "right of the lord" to bed, on her wedding night, the bride of any of his vassals. Although scholars have argued that such a right never actually

FIGARO: I know it so well that if the Count had not abolished that outrageous privilege when he got married himself, I would never have consented to marrying you here at all. 65

SUZANNE: Well, if he abolished it, he wishes he hadn't; and it's from your fiancée that he wants to buy it back today. 70

FIGARO: (*rubbing his head*) My head is spinning from the shock—my fertile imagination—

SUZANNE: No, don't rub it!

FIGARO: Why not?

SUZANNE: (*laughing*) If a little bump were to appear,⁴ superstitious people— 75

FIGARO: Oh, you laugh, you cheeky devil! Ah! If only there was some way to trip this villain up, catch him in a clever trap, and pocket his gold!

SUZANNE: Intrigue and money—you're in your element now. 80

FIGARO: It's not shame that holds me back.....

SUZANNE: Fear?

FIGARO: Not of taking on a dangerous job, no, but of coming through unscathed and succeeding— because nothing's easier than to sneak into a man's house at night to steal his wife, and get a hundred lashes for your pains instead; a thousand foolish rascals do that every day. But— (*Someone rings from another room.*) 85

90

SUZANNE: Madame is awake; she begged me to be the first person to speak to her on the morning of my wedding.

FIGARO: Is that also supposed to mean something?

SUZANNE: The shepherd says it brings good luck to neglected wives. Bye-bye, my little Fi, Fi, Figaro; dream about our love. 95

FIGARO: To get me started, give me a little kiss.

SUZANNE: Kiss my lover, today? No chance! What would my husband say, tomorrow? 100

(*Figaro kisses her.*)

SUZANNE: Okay, enough, enough.

FIGARO: Is it? Then you obviously have no idea how much I love you.

SUZANNE: (*straightening herself*) You're such a pest—when will you stop telling me that from morning to night? 105

FIGARO: (*deviously*) When I can prove it to you from night until morning. (*Another ring.*)

SUZANNE: (*from across the room, fingers to her lips*) There's your kiss, Monsieur; that's all you'll get from me. 110

FIGARO: (*running after her*) Hey, I gave you a lot more than that!

SCENE 2

Figaro, alone

FIGARO: Such a charming girl! Always laughing, blooming, full of joy, high spirits, love and delight! But smart too! (*He walks about briskly, rubbing his hands.*) Ah! Monseigneur! My dear Monseigneur! So, you want to put one over on me, do you? Yes, I was wondering why, having made me head porter here, he suddenly decides to take me with him on his posting to London as his courier. I get it, Monsieur Count—three promotions at once: you, to deputy ambassador; me, to diplomatic desperado, and Suzanne, the lady of the place, to secret cabinet minister-ess! And then it's "high-ho, courier"! While I'm galloping off in one direction, you'll be heading in the other, wending your merry way to my beautiful wife! Me, covered in mud, knocking myself out for the glory of your family, while you condescend to assist with the increase of mine! What lovely reciprocity! But, Monseigneur, there's a conflict of interest here. To have to concern yourself in London, simultaneously, with the affairs of both your master and your valet—to represent both the King and me in foreign courts, that's too much by half, too much. As for you, Bazile, you little rat—oh how I'd love to teach you a lesson or two.....I'm going to—No, let's string them along, get them to tie each *other* up in knots. Figaro, this will be a day to remember! First, we'll have to reset the hour for our little fête⁵ a bit earlier, to get us safely married; and we'll have

5

10

15

20

25

---

existed, the notion was nevertheless a powerful symbol of the oppression of the people by the nobility.

⁴ bump ... appear] the horns of a cuckold.

---

⁵ fête] that is, his wedding reception, but with associations of an entertainment, feast, or public festival.

to dispose of Marceline, who's disturbingly fond
of me; and then we'll pocket the gold and all the
presents; and give the slip to the Count's little passions; and roundly thrash Monsieur Bazile, and— 30

SCENE 3

Marceline, Bartholo, Figaro

FIGARO: Hee hee hee, here comes the fat doctor,
so the party's complete. Well good day to you, dear
Doctor so near to my heart! Is it my wedding that
brings you to the chateau?

BARTHOLO: *(with disdain)* Ah! Not in the least, 5
my dear Monsieur!

FIGARO: That would be very generous of you
indeed.

BARTHOLO: Yes it would, and awfully foolish.

FIGARO: Especially since I had the misfortune of 10
upsetting yours.[6]

BARTHOLO: Do you have anything else to say to
us?

FIGARO: I trust someone's taken good care of your
mule? 15

BARTHOLO: *(furious)* You raving madman! Get
away.

FIGARO: Are you angry, Doctor? People of your profession are so hard! No more pity for poor animals,
truth be told, than if they were human! Goodbye, 20
Marceline—still, as always, bent on prosecuting me
in court? "If we're not to love, does that mean we
must hate?" I'll refer you to the doctor.

BARTHOLO: What's this about?

FIGARO: She'll explain the rest. *(He goes out.)* 25

SCENE 4

Marceline, Bartholo

BARTHOLO: *(watching him leave)* That clown will
never change! I bet he dies with an insolent smirk

---

6 misfortune … upsetting yours] refers to events in
Beaumarchais's earlier play, *The Barber of Seville* (1775).
In it, Figaro foiled Bartholo's plot to marry his own ward,
Rosine, who loved and, thanks to Figaro, succeeded in
marrying Count Almaviva instead and becoming the
Countess of this play.

on his face—unless of course somebody flays him
alive first.

MARCELINE *(turning to him)*: And you, you 5
everlasting doctor! Always so stuffy and plodding
that one could die awaiting your help, just as
someone was once married anyway, despite all your
precautions.[7]

BARTHOLO: Always so bitter and antagonistic! 10
So?—what makes my presence here so necessary
then? Has the Count had some kind of accident?

MARCELINE: No, Doctor.

BARTHOLO: Has his false little Countess Rosine
fallen ill, pray heaven? 15

MARCELINE: She's languishing.

BARTHOLO: From what?

MARCELINE: Her husband neglects her.

BARTHOLO: *(joyfully)* Ah! the worthy husband
exacts my revenge! 20

MARCELINE: He's impossible to describe, that
Count; he's jealous, *and* unfaithful.

BARTHOLO: Unfaithful out of boredom, jealous
out of vanity; it goes without saying.

MARCELINE: Today, for instance, he's marrying our 25
Suzanne to his valet, Figaro, whom he's showering
with gifts in honour of their union—

BARTHOLO: —which His Excellency has rendered
necessary!

MARCELINE: Not exactly; but which His Excel- 30
lency would love to celebrate privately with the
bride-to-be—

BARTHOLO: Of Monsieur Figaro? Surely that's a
bargain she'll accept.

MARCELINE: Not according to Bazille. 35

BARTHOLO: Does that lowlife live here, too? What
a nest of vipers! Ugh! So what's he doing here?

MARCELINE: All the evil he's capable of. But the
worst is the tedious passion he's had for me
since....*forever.* 40

BARTHOLO: You could have put an end to his
advances a long time ago.

MARCELINE: How?

BARTHOLO: By marrying him.

MARCELINE: You think that cruel, pathetic joke 45

---

7 married … precautions] again, a reference to Bartholo's
failed marriage plans in *The Barber of Seville*.

is so clever? Then why won't you put an end to my advances in the same way? Aren't you obliged to? What happened to all your promises? To your memory of our little Emmanuel, fruit of a forgotten love, who should have led us down the 50 isle of matrimony?

BARTHOLO: *(taking off his hat)* Did you make me come all the way from Seville just to listen to this nonsense? And this sudden fit of marriage-fever that seems to have flared up out of nowhere— 55

MARCELINE: Well, fine. We'll say no more about it. But since nothing will induce you to do me the justice of marrying me, then the least you can do is help me to get married to somebody else.

BARTHOLO: Oh, gladly: let's talk about this. But 60 what conceivable mortal, forsaken by God and all womankind—?

MARCELINE: Eh! Who else could it be, Doctor, but the handsome, the lively, the loveable Figaro?

BARTHOLO: That scoundrel? 65

MARCELINE: Never angry, always cheerful; lives joyfully in the moment, caring as little about the future as the past, vivacious, generous! generous as—

BARTHOLO: —as a thief.

MARCELINE: —as a lord. In a word, charming— 70 but he's an absolute brute!

BARTHOLO: And his Suzanne?

MARCELINE: That little sneak! She won't get him— *if* you'll be so kind as to help me, my dear Doctor, to make him honour his commitment to me. 75

BARTHOLO: On the day of his wedding?

MARCELINE: Ah, they can be broken off up to the last minute; and if I weren't afraid of revealing a certain little secret we women have—

BARTHOLO: Have they any secrets from their 80 doctors?

MARCELINE: Ah! You know that I have none from you. Our sex is ardent, but shy; though temptation may attract us to pleasure, even the most reckless of women has a voice inside her which 85 says: be beautiful if you can, wise if you wish; but be respected, that's a must. So, as we need to be, at the very least, respected, and since every woman knows the importance of preserving her reputation, let's frighten Suzanne, to begin with, by 90 threatening to divulge the Count's offers.

BARTHOLO: Where will that lead us?

MARCELINE: Seized by the collar with shame, she'll continue to refuse him—to avenge himself for which, the Count will support my opposition to 95 her marriage, thus ensuring my own.

BARTHOLO: She's right. By god, what a good trick that is—to marry off my old housekeeper to the devil who helped carry off my ward.

MARCELINE: *(quickly)* And who thinks he'll add 100 to his pleasures by dashing my hopes.

BARTHOLO: *(quickly)* And who once stole from me one hundred écus, which I haven't forgotten.

MARCELINE: Oh! how exquisite—

BARTHOLO: —to punish a villain! 105

MARCELINE: —to marry him, Doctor, to marry him!

SCENE 5

Suzanne, Marceline, Bartholo

SUZANNE: *(in her hand, a woman's bonnet with a large ribbon, on her arm, a woman's dress)* To marry him, to marry him! Who's he? My Figaro?

MARCELINE: *(bitterly)* Why not? *You* seem to want to. 5

BARTHOLO: *(laughing)* An angry woman's idea of effective argument! We were speaking, my beautiful Suzanne, of the happiness he'll have in possessing you.

MARCELINE: To say nothing of the happiness 10 of His Lordship, about whom the less said the better.

SUZANNE: *(with a curtsy)* Your servant, Madame; there's always something bitter in your remarks.

MARCELINE: *(with a curtsy)* And yours, Madame; 15 but where's the bitterness? Isn't it only fair that a generous lord should share a little of the joy he bestows upon his staff?

SUZANNE: That *he* bestows?

MARCELINE: Yes, Madame. 20

SUZANNE: Fortunately, while Madame's jealousy is legendary, her claim to Figaro is feeble.

MARCELINE: I might easily have strengthened it, had I resorted to your tactics.

SUZANNE: Oh, such tactics, Madame, are only for 25 the most experienced women.

MARCELINE: Which you, my child, are not at all! Innocent as an old judge!

BARTHOLO: *(pulling Marceline away)* Goodbye now, Figaro's pretty fiancée— 30

MARCELINE: *(with a curtsy)* —and the Count's secret present.

SUZANNE: *(with a curtsy)* —who highly esteems you, Madame.

MARCELINE: *(with a curtsy)* —and who will also 35 do me the honour of thinking kindly of me, Madame?

SUZANNE: *(with a curtsy)* —on which count, Madame has nothing left to desire.

MARCELINE: *(with a curtsy)* Madame is such a 40 pretty creature!

SUZANNE: *(with a curtsy)* Oh no, only enough to upset Madame.

MARCELINE: *(with a curtsy)* And so very respect- able! 45

SUZANNE: *(with a curtsy)* Oh, I leave respectability to the spinsters.

MARCELINE: *(incensed)* To the spinsters! To the spinsters!

BARTHOLO: *(stopping her)* Marceline! 50

MARCELINE: Let's go, Doctor; I can't take this. Goodbye, Madame. *(A curtsy.)*

SCENE 6

Suzanne, alone

SUZANNE: Go on, Madame; go on, you pedant! I'm as little afraid of your schemes as I am hurt by your insults. Will you look at that old Sybil![8] Just because she's had some education, and used it to torment Madame in her youth, she thinks she 5 can boss everyone around. *(She throws the dress she's been holding onto a chair.)* Now I've forgotten why I came in here.

---

8 Sibyl] ancient Greek and Roman name for female ora- cles, who often lived in caves and prophesied in an ec- static state; one of them was said to have lived a thousand years. It is used here to suggest a crazy old blathering hag.

SCENE 7

Chérubin, Suzanne

CHÉRUBIN: *(running in)* Ah! Suzanne, I've been waiting two hours for a chance to find you alone. Alas! you're getting married, and I have to leave.

SUZANNE: And why should my marriage send Monseigneur's number one page away? 5

CHÉRUBIN: *(pitifully)* Suzanne, *he's* sending me away.

SUZANNE: *(mimicking him)* Chérubin, you've been naughty.

CHÉRUBIN: He caught me last night at your cousin 10 Fanchette's, as I was innocently rehearsing her in her part in the fête tonight; and he flew into a rage when he saw me! "Get out," he says, "you little—!" I don't dare repeat the vulgar word he used, in front of a woman. "Get out; and this will be the last night you 15 sleep in this chateau." If my beautiful godmother, if the Countess can't calm him down, that's *it*, Suzanne; I'll be denied forever the joy of seeing you.

SUZANNE: Of seeing me? So now it's my turn? You're no longer sighing in secret for my mistress? 20

CHÉRUBIN: Ah! Suzanne, she's so beautiful and noble—but so intimidating!

SUZANNE: Which means that I'm not, so with me you can dare—

CHÉRUBIN: You know perfectly well, meany, that 25 I wouldn't dare to dare. But you're so lucky—you can see her whenever you want, talk to her, dress her in the morning, undress her at night, pin by pin! Ah! Suzanne! I would give—What's that you've got there? 30

SUZANNE: *(mockingly)* Alas, the lucky bonnet and the fortunate ribbon that tie up the hair of that beautiful godmother at night...

CHÉRUBIN: *(excitedly)* Her night ribbon! Oh, sweetheart, give it to me! 35

SUZANNE: *(pulling it away)* Hey, I will not! "Sweetheart!" Isn't he getting familiar! If you weren't such an inconsequential little snot— *(Chérubin snatches the ribbon away.)* Hey, the ribbon! 40

CHÉRUBIN: *(running around the big armchair)* Say that it was misplaced, got dirty, just disappeared! Say whatever you like.

SUZANNE: *(running after him)* Oh! In three or four years from now you're going to be the biggest little good-for-nothing, I can see that!...Will you give me back that ribbon? *(She tries to grab it.)* 45

CHÉRUBIN: *(pulling a love-song out of his pocket)* Oh, please, Suzanne, let me keep it; I'll give you my love-song; and while the memory of your beautiful mistress will sadden my every hour, my memory of you will cast the single ray of joy capable of gladdening my heart. 50

SUZANNE: *(grabbing the love-song)* "Gladden your heart"—you little rascal! Do you think you're talking to your Fanchette? You get caught with her, you sigh for Madame, and you talk nonsense to me into the bargain! 55

CHÉRUBIN: *(in exaltation)* But it's true, I swear! I don't know what's happening to me; but for some time now, I've felt this turmoil in my chest—my heart pounds at the mere sight of a woman; words like "love" and "sensual" thrill and disturb me. It's come to the point where the need to tell someone "I love you" is so urgent, that I say it even when I'm alone, when running around the grounds, to your mistress, to you, to the trees, the clouds, to the wind that blows them away with my lost words. Yesterday, I ran into Marceline... *(Suzanne bursts into laughter.)* Why not? She's a woman—a girl—a girl!—A woman! ah! how sweet those words are! how interesting, too! 60 65 70

SUZANNE: He's out of his mind!

CHÉRUBIN: Fanchette is sweet; at least she listens to me—more than I can say for you! 75

SUZANNE: That's just too bad—will you listen to this little man! *(She tries to get the ribbon.)*

CHÉRUBIN: *(running away)* Oh, no way! No one shall have it, you hear me, except with my life. And if that price doesn't satisfy you, I'll add a thousand kisses. *(He turns and chases her.)* 80

SUZANNE: *(running away from him)* A thousand slaps, if you come near me. I'm going to complain to my mistress about you, and far from interceding on your behalf with Monseigneur, I'll say: "Well done, Monseigneur; do relieve us of this little thief; yes, send him back to his parents, this wicked subject who has the presumption to love Madame and the nerve to try to kiss me in compensation! 85

(Chérubin sees the Count come in and throws himself behind the chair in terror.)

CHÉRUBIN: I'm done for! 90
SUZANNE: What a scaredy-cat!

SCENE 8

The Count, Suzanne, Chérubin (in hiding)

SUZANNE: *(seeing the Count)* Ah! *(She goes over to the armchair to mask Chérubin.)*

THE COUNT: *(coming toward her)* You're jumpy, Suzanne! You were talking to yourself and your little heart seems quite agitated...perfectly understandable, of course, on a day like today. 5

SUZANNE: *(wary)* Monseigneur, what can I do for you? If anyone were to see you with me—

THE COUNT: I'd be quite upset if anyone caught me here; but you know that I'm greatly interested in you. Bazile has left you with no doubts about my love. I've only a moment to describe my plans; listen. *(He sits in the armchair.)* 10

SUZANNE: *(intensely)* I'll listen to nothing.

THE COUNT: *(taking her hand)* Just one word. You know that the King has made me ambassador to London. I'm taking Figaro with me. I'm giving him an excellent position; and, since a wife's duty is to follow her husband— 15

SUZANNE: Oh! if I dared speak!

THE COUNT: *(draws her nearer)* Speak, speak, my dear; use today a right that you could wield for life. 20

SUZANNE: *(frightened)* I don't want to, Monseigneur; I don't want to. Please leave, I beg you.

THE COUNT: Finish what you were saying first. 25

SUZANNE: *(angry)* I forget what I was saying.

THE COUNT: About a wife's duty...?

SUZANNE: Alright then...When Monseigneur eloped with his, from the Doctor's house, and married her for love, for her sake he abolished a certain dreadful seigneurial privilege— 30

THE COUNT: *(gaily)* —which was a terrible blow to all the girls. Ah! Suzette! A *charming* privilege! If you were to come and have a little chat about it, in the garden, at dusk, I'd put such a price on that modest favour— 35

BAZILE: *(off stage)* Monseigneur's not in his rooms.

THE COUNT: *(getting up)* Whose voice is that?

SUZANNE: Oh, I'm so miserable!

THE COUNT: Go out there, so they don't come in. 40

SUZANNE: *(worried)* And leave you here?

BAZILE: *(from offstage)* Monseigneur was in Madame's rooms, but he's left; I'll go look.

THE COUNT: And nowhere to hide! Ah—behind this armchair...fairly hopeless; get rid of him 45 quickly.

(Suzanne blocks his way; he pushes her gently, she backs up, keeping herself between him and the little page; but, as the Count stoops down to assume the hiding place, Chérubin throws himself, terrified, into the chair on his knees and curls up there. Suzanne takes the dress she was carrying, throws it over the page, then stands in front of the chair.)

SCENE 9

Bazile, The Count and Chérubin hiding, Suzanne

BAZILE: Mademoiselle, have you seen Monseigneur?

SUZANNE: *(sharply)* Ha! Why should I have seen him? Get out.

BAZILE: *(coming nearer)* If you weren't so unreasonable, there would be nothing surprising about my 5 question. Figaro's looking for him.

SUZANNE: So he's looking for the one man who seeks to do him even more harm than you do?

THE COUNT: *(aside)* Let's see how well he carries out his orders. 10

BAZILE: Wanting to do some good for the wife— is that wishing to harm the husband?

SUZANNE: Not according to your vile principles, you agent of corruption.

BAZILE: Is anything being asked of you that you 15 won't soon be frittering away on someone else? Thanks to one sweet little ceremony, that which was forbidden to you yesterday will be required of you tomorrow.

SUZANNE: You're despicable! 20

BAZILE: Of all serious things, marriage is the most ridiculous, and I would have thought—

SUZANNE: *(outraged)* —some horrible thing or other! Who let you in here?

BAZILE: There, there, naughty girl; calm yourself 25

down for God's sake. Nothing's going to happen unless you wish it; but understand that I no longer regard Figaro as the main obstacle to Monseigneur's designs; if it weren't for that little page—

SUZANNE: *(timidly)* Don Chérubin? 30

BAZILE: *(mimicking her)* Cherubino di amore,[9] who's always hovering around you, and who only this morning, just after I left you, was already lurking in wait for a chance to come in. Are you going to tell me that's not true? 35

SUZANNE: What rubbish! Go away, you wicked man.

BAZILE: One is wicked because one sees clearly? And this love-song he's so secretive about—isn't it for you? 40

SUZANNE: *(angry)* Oh, sure—for me!

BAZILE: Unless, even worse, he composed it for the Countess. In fact, they say that when he serves her at table, he can't keep his eyes off her!....Whew— he'd better not try to play that game. Monseigneur 45 is *brutal* on that score.

SUZANNE: *(outraged)* And you, sufficiently evil to go around spreading rumours that could destroy a poor child who's already fallen into disgrace with his master. 50

BAZILE: Did I invent it? I only mention it because it's what everybody says.

THE COUNT: *(getting up)* Really? What everybody says?

SUZANNE: Oh, God! 55

BAZILE: Ah! Ah!

THE COUNT: Run, Bazile, and drive him out.

BAZILE: Ah! What a mistake it was ever to come in here!

SUZANNE: *(worried)* Dear God! Dear God! 60

THE COUNT: She's fainting. Help sit her in this chair.

SUZANNE: *(resisting him violently)* I don't want to sit. Just barging in here like that—it's outrageous!

THE COUNT: There are two of us with you, my 65 dear. There's no longer the slightest danger.

BAZILE: I'm sorry I made fun of the page like that, since you overheard me. I only said it to discover her true feelings, because deep down—

---

9 *Cherubino di amore*] cherub, or angel, of love (Ital.).

THE COUNT: Fifty pistoles, a horse, and we send him back to his parents. 70

BAZILE: Monseigneur, just because of a little joke?

THE COUNT: Because I already caught that little libertine yesterday, with the gardener's daughter.

BAZILE: With Fanchette? 75

THE COUNT: And in her room.

SUZANNE: (outraged) Where Monseigneur had business too, no doubt!

THE COUNT: (gaily) How sweet of you to think so. 80

BAZILE: It augers well.

THE COUNT: (gaily) No, no; I'd gone there to look for her uncle Antonio, my drunken gardener, to give him his orders. I knock; the door doesn't open for a long time; your cousin looks embarrassed; I 85 get suspicious. As I'm talking to her, I look around. Behind the door there was some kind of curtain, a garment-bag or something, covering some clothes. Without letting on, I move slowly, slowly, to lift the curtain (to illustrate, he lifts the dress on 90 the armchair) and what do I see—(he sees the page.) Ah!

BAZILE: Ha ha!

THE COUNT: The identical trick.

BAZILE: Even better. 95

THE COUNT (to Suzanne): You really are something, Mademoiselle; hardly even married yet, and you're already planning your affairs. Is that why you wished to be alone—to receive my page? [To Chérubin] And you, Monsieur, whose methods 100 never change—the one thing missing was to lose all respect for your godmother and try your luck with her first lady-in-waiting—your friend's wife! But I will not allow Figaro, a man I esteem and love, to be victimized by such trickery. Did he 105 come in with you, Bazile?

SUZANNE: (outraged) There's neither trickery nor victim; he was here the whole time you were talking to me.

THE COUNT: (beside himself) I hope you're lying! 110 His worst enemy couldn't wish that misfortune upon him.

SUZANNE: He was soliciting me to convince Madame to help win him your pardon. Your arrival so alarmed him that he hid in this chair. 115

THE COUNT: (angrily) A diabolical lie! I sat down there when I came in!

CHÉRUBIN: Alas! At that point, Monseigneur, I was trembling behind it.

THE COUNT: Another falsehood! I just hid there 120 myself!

CHÉRUBIN: Forgive me, but that's when I hid in the chair.

THE COUNT: (more and more beside himself) So this snake-in-the-grass, this little—serpent! He was 125 listening to everything!

CHÉRUBIN: On the contrary, Monseigneur, I did my best to hear nothing.

THE COUNT: What treachery! (To Suzanne.) You will not be marrying Figaro! 130

BAZILE: Control yourself; someone's coming.

THE COUNT: (pulling Chérubin out of the chair and onto his feet) There he'll stand, in front of the whole world.

SCENE 10

(The Countess, Figaro, Fanchette, Chérubin, Suzanne, The Count, Bazile, many valets, peasants dressed in white. Figaro is holding a woman's headdress, adorned with white ribbons and feathers.)

FIGARO: No one but you, Madame, can obtain this favour for us.

THE COUNTESS: You see, Monsieur Count, they credit me with powers I don't possess; but since their request isn't unreasonable... 5

THE COUNT: (with embarrassment) Even if it was much more so...

FIGARO: (aside to Suzanne) Help me out here.

SUZANNE: (aside to Figaro) It won't do any good.

FIGARO: (aside to Suzanne) Try anyway. 10

THE COUNT: (to Figaro) What do you want?

FIGARO: Monseigneur, your vassals, touched by your abolition of a certain disgraceful privilege, out of love for Madame—

THE COUNT: Fine, the privilege no longer exits; 15 your point being.....?

FIGARO: (maliciously) That it's high time that the goodness of such an excellent master be acknowledged; it has benefited me so greatly today that I'd like to be the first to celebrate it at my wedding. 20

THE COUNT: *(ever more embarrassed)* My friend, you must be joking—to abolish such a shameful privilege is merely to settle a debt with honesty. A Spaniard might well endeavour to conquer beauty with kindness; but to demand the first, the sweetest enjoyment of it as a servile duty—ah! that's the tyranny of a Vandal,[10] not the sworn right of a noble Castillian. ²⁵

FIGARO: *(holding Suzanne by the hand)* Then allow this young creature, whose honour has been preserved thanks to your wisdom, to receive this bride's cap publicly from your hands; adorned with feathers and white ribbons, it will symbolise the purity of your intentions. Adopt this ceremony for all marriages, and let a quatrain, sung in chorus, recall this moment forever— ³⁰ ³⁵

THE COUNT: *(embarrassed)* If I didn't know that lover, poet and musician are three titles that excuse all follies—

FIGARO: Join with me, my friends! ⁴⁰

EVERYONE: Monseigneur! Monseigneur!

SUZANNE: *(to the Count)* Why shy away from praise that's so well deserved?

THE COUNT: *(aside)* Perfidious woman!

FIGARO: Look at her, Monseigneur; never will a more beautiful bride demonstrate the grandeur of your sacrifice. ⁴⁵

SUZANNE: Never mind my looks; just praise his virtue.

THE COUNT: *(aside)* This is all a set-up. ⁵⁰

THE COUNTESS: I add my voice to theirs, Monsieur; this ceremony will always be dear to me, because it was inspired by the love you once had for me.

THE COUNT: Which I'll have forever, Madame; and on that account alone, I do consent. ⁵⁵

EVERYONE: *Vivat!*

THE COUNT: *(aside)* I'm trapped. *(aloud)* However, to add a little more splendour to the ceremony, I'd just like to delay it for a little while. *(aside)* Quick, I must find Marceline. ⁶⁰

FIGARO: *(to Chérubin)* So, mister monkey-business? You're not applauding?

---

10 Vandal] Germanic ("barbarian") tribe that invaded Western Europe in the fourth and fifth centuries.

SUZANNE: He's in despair; Monseigneur has sent him packing. ⁶⁵

THE COUNTESS: Ah! Monsieur, I beg you to forgive him.

THE COUNT: He doesn't deserve it.

THE COUNTESS: Alas—but he's so young!

THE COUNT: Not as young as you think. ⁷⁰

CHÉRUBIN: *(trembling)* To pardon generously—that's not a seigneurial privilege that you renounced when you married Madame.

THE COUNTESS: He only renounced the one that so distressed you all. ⁷⁵

SUZANNE: Had Monseigneur given up the right to grant pardons, surely that would be the first thing he'd want secretly to buy back.

THE COUNT: *(embarrassed)* No doubt.

THE COUNTESS: But why *buy* it back? ⁸⁰

CHÉRUBIN: *(to the Count)* It's true, Monseigneur, I behaved badly; but there was never the slightest falsehood in what I said—

THE COUNT: *(embarrassed)* All right, that's enough! ⁸⁵

FIGARO: What does he mean by that?

THE COUNT: *(with gusto)* That's enough, that's enough. Everyone sues for forgiveness; I grant it. And I'll go even further: I'll give him a company in my regiment. ⁹⁰

EVERYONE: *Vivat!*

THE COUNT: But only on condition that he leaves immediately to join up with it in Catalonia.

FIGARO: Ah! Monseigneur, tomorrow.

THE COUNT: *(insisting)* That's my wish. ⁹⁵

CHÉRUBIN: I'll obey.

THE COUNT: Say goodbye to your godmother and ask her blessing. *(Chérubin kneels before the Countess, but cannot speak.)*

THE COUNTESS: *(moved)* Since we cannot keep you beyond today—go, young man. A new life is calling; go and take it up with dignity, and make your benefactor proud. Remember this house, where you were treated so indulgently in your youth. Be obedient, honest and brave; we will all rejoice in your success. *(Chérubin gets up and returns to his place.)* ¹⁰⁰ ¹⁰⁵

THE COUNT: You seem quite moved, Madame.

THE COUNTESS: I don't deny it. Who knows

what might happen to a child thrown into such a dangerous career. He's related to my family, by marriage; and what's more, he's my godson.

THE COUNT: *(aside)* I see that Bazile was right. *(aloud)* Young man, embrace Suzanne... for the last time.

FIGARO: Why say that, Monseigneur? He'll be back for the winter. Kiss me too, captain! *(He embraces him)* Goodbye, my little Chérubin. You're in for quite a different life, my boy! No more whole days spent hanging around the ladies' quarters, no more hot teas and cream pies, no more hide-and-seek[11] or blindman's-bluff. Hearty soldiers, by golly, sunburned and ragged; a big musket, good and heavy: right face, left face, forward, march to glory; and never stumble along the way, unless of course some nice burst of gunfire—

SUZANNE: Stop, you're pitiless!

THE COUNTESS: What a prognosis!

THE COUNT: But where's Marceline? How strange that she's not with you.

FANCHETTE: Monseigneur, she's on her way to town, by the little farm path.

THE COUNT: And when will she be back?

BAZILE: When it shall please God.

FIGARO: May it please Him *never* to be thus pleased—

FANCHETTE: Monsieur the doctor was escorting her.

THE COUNT: *(sharply)* The doctor's here?

BAZILE: She commandeered him the second he got here.

THE COUNT: *(aside)* He couldn't have come at a better time.

FANCHETTE: She seemed quite worked up; she was talking very loudly as she walked, and then she stopped, and went like this, with her arms all hoity-toity...and the doctor went like this, with his hand, to calm her down. She was clearly so incensed, and she seemed to be talking about my cousin Figaro.

THE COUNT: *(taking her by the chin)* Cousin...to be.

FANCHETTE *(referring to Chérubin)*: Monseigneur, have you forgiven us for yesterday—?

THE COUNT: *(interrupting her)* Goodbye, goodbye, little one.

FIGARO: Marceline's puppy-love is filling her with delusions: she'd spoil my wedding if she could.

THE COUNT: *(aside)* Oh, she'll spoil it all right, I promise you. *(aloud)* Come, Madame; let's go in. Bazile, I'd like to see you for a moment in my room.

SUZANNE: *(to Figaro)* Will you be joining me later, young man?

FIGARO: *(aside to Suzanne)* Is he nicely snared?

SUZANNE: *(softly to Figaro)* You lovely boy!

(As the others all file out, Figaro stops Chérubin and Bazile.)

SCENE 11

Chérubin, Figaro, Bazile

FIGARO: Okay, lads. The ceremony's accepted and my fête tonight will follow next. We must be well rehearsed; we can't be like those actors whose performance is never worse than on the night when the critics are most alert. We don't have a performance tomorrow to make up for it; we must be letter-perfect in our parts today.

BAZILE: *(maliciously)* Mine's more difficult than you think.

FIGARO: *(mimes beating him behind his back)* But you have no idea how much you'll be applauded for it!

CHÉRUBIN: My friend, you forget that I'm leaving.

FIGARO: What, you'd rather stay?

CHÉRUBIN: Oh! If I could!

FIGARO: Here's how we'll work it. No grumbling about your departure; with your travel-cloak over your shoulders, pack your bags in plain sight, and let your horse be seen at the gate; gallop away for a while, as far as the farm, and then come back on foot by the back entrance; Monseigneur will think you've left. Just keep yourself out of his sight; I'll take care of calming him down after the fête.

CHÉRUBIN: But Fanchette won't know how to play her part!

---

[11] hide-and-seek] lit., "hot-hand," a popular game of the period.

BAZILE: Then what the devil have you been teaching her for the last eight days straight?

FIGARO: You've nothing to do today; give her a few lessons for goodness sake.

BAZILE: Watch out, young man, watch out! Her father is not pleased; she's already been slapped once; you're not her tutor. Chérubin! Chérubin! You'll bring her unhappiness. "If the jug goes too often to the well..." 30

FIGARO: Ah! Here goes our dimwit with his old proverbs! All right, pedant, what says the wisdom of the ages this time? "If the jug goes too often to the well, sooner or later—?"[12] 35

BAZILE: It fills up.[13]

FIGARO: (walking off) That's not bad, not bad at all! 40

ACT II, SCENE 1

(A magnificent bedroom, a large bed in an alcove, a riser in front of it. The main door into it opens and closes in the third wing, upstage right; a door into a dressing room is in the first wing, downstage left. A door on one side of the upstage wall goes toward the women's quarters. On the other side, a functional window. Suzanne and The Countess come in by the right-hand door.)

THE COUNTESS: (throws herself onto a divan) Close the door, Suzanne, and tell me everything in the greatest possible detail.

SUZANNE: I haven't hidden a thing, Madame.

THE COUNTESS: So, Suzanne, he tried to seduce you? 5

SUZANNE: Oh, no! Monseigneur didn't do anything so well-mannered with his servant: he tried to buy me.

THE COUNTESS: And the little page was right there? 10

SUZANNE: Well, in a way, hidden behind the big armchair. He'd come to ask me to convince you to help win him a pardon.

THE COUNTESS: But why not ask me directly? Would I have refused him, Suzanne? 15

SUZANNE: That's what I said. But he was so devastated by having to go away, above all by leaving you, Madame—"Ah, Suzanne, she's so noble and beautiful! but so intimidating!" 20

THE COUNTESS: Is that how I seem, Suzanne? I've always protected him.

SUZANNE: When he saw I had your night-ribbon in my hand, he threw himself on it—

THE COUNTESS: (smiling) My ribbon?...what childishness! 25

SUZANNE: I tried to get it back; Madame, he was like a lion, his eyes burning: "You shall not have it, except with my life," he said, trying to force down his sweet little pip-squeak voice. 30

THE COUNTESS: (dreamily) Really, Suzanne?

SUZANNE: Really, Madame; how do you get such a little devil to stop? "My godmother" this, "Oh how I wish" that; and since he wouldn't dare kiss even the hem of your gown, he's always trying to kiss me. 35

THE COUNTESS: (still dreamy) Well, we can forget....forget that silliness...So tell me, my poor Suzanne, my husband left off by saying—?

SUZANNE: —that if I didn't agree, he'd support Marceline. 40

THE COUNTESS: (rising, pacing about, and fanning herself vigorously) He doesn't love me at all anymore.

SUZANNE: Then why's he so jealous? 45

THE COUNTESS: Like all husbands, my dear, simply from pride. Ah! I've loved him too much! I've tired him with my affections and bored him with my love; that's my only offence against him; but I will not allow your honesty to bring any harm to you; you will marry Figaro. He's the only one who can help us—is he coming? 50

SUZANNE: As soon as he's sent off the hunt.

THE COUNTESS: (fanning herself) Open the garden window a little. It's so hot in here... 55

SUZANNE: It's because Madame is so agitated. (She goes to open the window at the back.)

THE COUNTESS: (having paused long and dreamily) If it weren't for his constancy in refusing me...Men are always to blame! 60

SUZANNE: (calling from the window) Ah! there goes Monseigneur now, crossing the kitchen-garden on

---

12 sooner or later] One expects, "... it will get broken."
13 fills up] i.e., with a baby.

horseback, followed by Pédrille and two, three, four greyhounds.

THE COUNTESS: That means some time to ourselves. *(She sits down.)* Is someone knocking, Suzanne? 65

SUZANNE: *(running to open the door and singing)* Oh, it's my Figaro! It's my Figaro!

SCENE 2

Figaro, Suzanne, The Countess (sitting)

SUZANNE: My dear friend, come in, come in! Madame is getting awfully impatient...

FIGARO: And what about you, my darling Suzanne? Madame, at least, has no reason to be. What's actually happened? The merest trifle. The Count finds our young lady attractive, he'd like to make her his mistress; it's only natural. 5

SUZANNE: Natural?

FIGARO: So he made me his courier and Suzanne a member of his cabinet. There's nothing surprising in that. 10

SUZANNE: Will you stop?

FIGARO: And because Suzanne, my fiancée, declines the appointment, he's going to support the claims of Marceline. Again, what could be simpler? Revenge yourself on whoever ruins your plans by ruining theirs; that's what everybody does, and we're going to do it ourselves. So, there you have it—simple. 15

THE COUNTESS: Figaro, how can you be so cavalier about something that makes us all so miserable? 20

FIGARO: Who says I am, Madame?

SUZANNE: Instead of being distressed by our problems—

FIGARO: Isn't it enough that I'm working on them? So, operating as methodically as he does, for a start we'll temper his ardour for our possession by making him worry about his own. 25

THE COUNTESS: That sounds good, but how?

FIGARO: It's already done, Madame; a false report, given out about you— 30

THE COUNTESS: About me? Have you lost your mind?

FIGARO: No, but he's losing his.

THE COUNTESS: A man that jealous— 35

FIGARO: All the better: to get to people like that, all you have to do is heat up their blood a little—something that women understand so well! Then, you keep them in a red-hot rage, and with a hint of intrigue you can lead them wherever you want—by the nose, right up the river.[14] I gave Bazile an anonymous note warning the Count that a gallant will attempt to see you this evening during the ball. 40

THE COUNTESS: And you can just toy with the truth like that, about a woman of honour! 45

FIGARO: There are few, Madame, with whom I would dare it, for fear I'd be proven right.

THE COUNTESS: I must remember to thank you!

FIGARO: But tell me it isn't amusing to manipulate his schedule like this, so that, prowling around, he'll spend all the time cursing his wife that he'd intended to spend enjoying himself with mine! He's already completely disoriented: should he chase after this one? keep a close watch on that one? In all his confusion, look, look, how he charges across the field, just to flush out some harmless little rabbit. Our wedding hour is arriving fast; he won't have time to head it off himself, and he'd never dare oppose it in your presence, Madame. 50 55 60

SUZANNE: No, but you can be sure that tender-hearted old Marceline will.

FIGARO: Brrrr! That one does worry me, no question. Send word to Monseigneur that you will meet him at dusk in the garden. 65

SUZANNE: You're counting on that?

FIGARO: Oh, come on—listen, people who'll have nothing to do with anything get nowhere and are good for nothing. That's my motto.

SUZANNE: How charming. 70

THE COUNTESS: Like his idea—you really want her to meet him there?

FIGARO: Not in the least. I'll have somebody wear one of Suzanne's dresses: and when we surprise him at the rendezvous, the Count won't be able to deny a thing, will he? 75

SUZANNE: And who's to wear my clothes?

FIGARO: Chérubin.

THE COUNTESS: He's gone.

---

[14] the river] lit., the Guadalquivir.

FIGARO: Not from me he isn't. Will you let me do it? 80

SUZANNE: We know we can always depend on you when it comes to intrigues.

FIGARO: Two, three, four at a time, all tangled up and over-lapping. I was born to be a courtier.

SUZANNE: They say it's a tough line of work. 85

FIGARO: Receiving, taking, and demanding; that's the secret, in three words.

THE COUNTESS: He's so sure of himself that he ends up persuading me.

FIGARO: That was the plan. 90

SUZANNE: So, you were saying.....?

FIGARO: That while Monseigneur is away, I'm going to send Chérubin to you; do his hair and dress him up; then, I'll take him in hand and rehearse him; and then, Monseigneur, you will 95 dance! (*He goes out.*)

SCENE 3

Suzanne, The Countess (sitting)

THE COUNTESS: (*holding her box of beauty-spots*) My God, Suzanne, look at the state I'm in! That young man's coming here—

SUZANNE: Doesn't Madame want him to be cured of his infatuation? 5

THE COUNTESS: (*dreaming before her make-up mirror*) Me?...Just wait; you'll see how I'll scold him.

SUZANNE: Let's make him sing us his love-song (*She gives it to the Countess.*) 10

THE COUNTESS: Well, I'll tell you one thing for sure: my hair is a mess...

SUZANNE: (*laughing*) I'll just pin up these two curls, and Madame will be able to scold him so much better. 15

THE COUNTESS: (*returning to herself*) What did you say, Mademoiselle?

SCENE 4

Chérubin, looking ashamed; Suzanne; The Countess, seated

SUZANNE: Come in, officer, Madame is receiving.

CHÉRUBIN: (*comes in, trembling*) Oh! How the name of officer depresses me, Madame! It reminds

me that I must leave this place...and a godmother who is so...good!... 5

SUZANNE: And so beautiful!

CHÉRUBIN: (*with a sigh*) Ah! yes.

SUZANNE: "Ah! yes." Oh, the fine young man, with his long hypocritical eyelashes. Come on, pretty bluebird, sing the love-song to Madame. 10

THE COUNTESS: (*unfolding it*) Who...did you say it was by?

SUZANNE: Look how the guilty one blushes! Has he got rouge on his cheeks?

CHÉRUBIN: Is it forbidden—to adore? 15

SUZANNE: (*brandishing her fist under his nose*) I'll tell her everything, you good-for-nothing!

THE COUNTESS: So. Is he singing or not?

CHÉRUBIN: Oh! Madame, I'm trembling!...

SUZANNE: (*laughing*) But "nyah, nyah, nyah, nyah, 20 nyah, nyah, nyah, since Madame insists...." The modest author! I'll accompany him.

THE COUNTESS: Take my guitar. (*Sitting, the Countess holds the paper to follow the words. Suzanne is behind the chair, and strums an introduction as 25 she reads the music over her mistress's shoulder. The young page is in front of her, eyes lowered. This tableau is a copy of the painting titled "la Conversation espagnole" by Vanloo.*[15])

ROMANCE
To the tune of "Malbrough s'en va-t-en guerre"[16]

My charger loose on the rein, 30
(Oh, my heart, my heart full of pain!)
I wandered over the plain
Wherever the steed did stray.

Wherever the steed did stray;
My squire was far away. 35
Where a fountain fell in rain
(Oh, my heart, my heart full of pain!)
My godmother filled my brain;
I found myself in tears.

---

15 Vanloo] Charles-André Vanloo (1705–1765), French painter, and one of Louis XV's favourites.

16 *To the tune of … guerre*] better known as "For He's a Jolly Good Fellow." English translation of the song by B.P. Ellis, "A mad day's work; or, The marriage of Figaro" (New York: Appleton-Century-Crofts, 1966), pp. 30–31).

I found myself in tears,   40
Desolate all my years.
On a tree I carved amain
(Oh, my heart, my heart full of pain!)
The letters of her name.
The King came passing by.   45

The King came passing by;
The Queen and all were nigh.
"Fair page, what makes this bane,"
(Oh, my heart, my heart full of pain!)
The Queen said, "Please explain   50
For whom do these tears fall?

For whom do these tears fall?
Now tell your sorrows all."
"My Queen, my Sovereign,
(Oh, my heart, my heart full of pain!)   55
My godmother all in vain
I always have adored.

I always have adored;
I'll die now on my sword."
"A godmother to gain,"   60
(Oh, my heart, my heart full of pain!)
Said the Queen, "if you are fain,
I shall be one to you.

I shall be one to you.
As my page you'll renew   65
Your hope with young Elaine;
(Oh, my heart, my heart full of pain!)
If her love you attain,
Then you shall married be.

Then you shall married be."   70
"No, that I'll never see;
I wish to drag my chain
(Oh, my heart, my heart full of pain!)
And rather die of pain
Than ever be consoled."   75

THE COUNTESS: It has a certain naiveté...and
feeling, too.

SUZANNE: (setting the guitar down on a chair) Oh,
as far as feeling is concerned, this young man is—
Oh! Mister Officer, have we told you? To liven up   80

the evening a bit, we want to see if you could fit
into one of my dresses.

THE COUNTESS: I'm afraid he won't.

SUZANNE: (measuring herself against him) He's
about my height. Let's remove the cloak first. (She   85
undoes it.)

THE COUNTESS: What if someone comes in?

SUZANNE: Are we doing anything wrong? I'll lock
the door (she does so, running); but it's the hairdo
that I want to see.   90

THE COUNTESS: On my dressing table, there's a
bathing bonnet. (Suzanne goes into the dressing-
room downstage left.)

SCENE 5

The Countess, Chérubin

THE COUNTESS: Right up until the ball begins,
the Count won't know you're here. Afterwards,
we'll tell him we got the idea while waiting for your
commission to be drawn up...

CHÉRUBIN: (showing it to her) Alas! Here it is,   5
Madame; he had Bazile deliver it to me.

THE COUNTESS: Already? They're afraid to lose a
minute. (She reads it.) They were in such a rush, they
forgot to put the seal on it. (She gives it back to him.)

SCENE 6

Suzanne, Chérubin, the Countess

SUZANNE: (coming in with a large bonnet) The seal?
For what?

THE COUNTESS: His commission.

SUZANNE: Already?

THE COUNTESS: That's what I thought. Is that   5
my bonnet?

SUZANNE: (sitting next to the Countess) And the
most beautiful one of all. (She sings with pins in
her mouth.)
    Turn this way, and that way bend,   10
    Jean of Lyra, my good friend.

(Chérubin kneels down. She puts the bonnet on his head.)

    Oh, Madame, he's adorable!

THE COUNTESS: Fix his collar—make it a little
more feminine.

SUZANNE: *(doing so)* There...Will you take a look at this little snot—he's so pretty as a girl! I'm actually jealous! *(She takes him by the chin.)* Will you please not be so pretty? 15

THE COUNTESS: She's crazy! We need to raise his sleeves or the dress won't hang properly...*(She rolls them up.)* What's this on his arm? A ribbon! 20

SUZANNE: And a ribbon of yours. I'm so glad Madame has seen it. I already told him I was going to tell you! Oh! if Monseigneur hadn't come in, I'd have gotten it back easily, because I'm almost as strong as he is. 25

THE COUNTESS: There's blood on it! *(She undoes the ribbon.)*

CHÉRUBIN: *(shame-faced)* This morning, figuring I was leaving, I was attaching the curb-chain to my horse; he tossed his head and a link slashed my arm. 30

THE COUNTESS: But one never uses ribbons for—

SUZANNE: Especially not *stolen* ribbons. Let's see what this curb-chain—superb-chain—disturb-chain did—I don't understand these horsey terms. Ah! What a white arm he has! It's like a woman's—whiter than mine! Look at that, Madame! *(She compares their arms.)* 35

THE COUNTESS: *(in an icy voice)* You just fetch me some sticking plaster from my dressing room. *(Suzanne pushes him on his head, laughing, and he falls forward onto his hands and knees. She exits into the dressing room.)* 40

SCENE 7

Chérubin, on his knees; The Countess sitting

THE COUNTESS: *(she waits for a moment before speaking, her eyes fixed on the ribbon. Chérubin devours her with his eyes.)* As for my ribbon, Monsieur... since it happens to be my favourite colour... I was extremely vexed to have lost it. 5

SCENE 8

Suzanne, Chérubin, The Countess

SUZANNE: *(coming back in)* And what will we use to bandage up his arm? *(She hands the Countess the sticking plaster and scissors.)*

THE COUNTESS: When you go to get your clothes for him, take the ribbon from another bonnet. *(Suzanne goes out by the upstage door, taking the page's cloak with her.)* 5

SCENE 9

Chérubin, still on his knees; The Countess sitting

CHÉRUBIN: *(eyes downcast)* The one you took away from me would have healed me in less than no time.

THE COUNTESS: And how is that? *(Showing him the sticking plaster.)* This will do better. 5

CHÉRUBIN: *(hesitantly)* When a ribbon...has encircled the head...or touched the skin of someone—

THE COUNTESS: —other than yourself, this makes it good for wounds? I had no idea it had such healing properties. To test it myself, I'll keep this one that bound your arm. At the first scratch...on one of my women, I'll give it a try. 10

CHÉRUBIN: *(touchingly)* You're keeping it, though I must go. 15

THE COUNTESS: Not for always.

CHÉRUBIN: I'm so unhappy.

THE COUNTESS: *(moved)* Now he's crying. It's all that villain Figaro's fault, with his cruel predictions!

CHÉRUBIN: *(transported)* Ah! How I wish his prediction would come true! If I was sure my death was imminent, then maybe my lips would dare to tell you— 20

THE COUNTESS: *(interrupting him and wiping his eyes with her handkerchief)* Hush, hush, child! There isn't an ounce of sense in anything you're saying. *(There's a knock at the door; she raises her voice.)* Who's knocking like that at my door? 25

SCENE 10

The Count, outside; Chérubin, The Countess

THE COUNT: Why is this locked?

THE COUNTESS: *(worried, rising)* It's my husband! Great Heavens! *(To Chérubin, who has also risen.)* You without your cloak, neck and arms bare, alone with me! This messy room, that note he received, his jealousy....! 5

THE COUNT: Are you opening or not?

THE COUNTESS: It's just that...I'm alone.

THE COUNT: Alone? Then who are you talking to?

THE COUNTESS: *(looking around)* ...To you, I guess.

CHÉRUBIN: *(aside)* After what happened yesterday and this morning, he'll kill me on the spot! *(He runs to the dressing room, closing the door behind him.)*

SCENE 11

The Countess, alone, removes the key and runs to open for the Count.

THE COUNTESS: Oh! What a mistake! What a mistake!

SCENE 12

The Count, The Countess

THE COUNT: *(a little severely)* You're not in the habit of locking yourself in.

THE COUNTESS: I—I was...worried that....that some clothes needed ironing, yes, Suzanne's been helping me; she's just gone off to her room for a minute.

THE COUNT: *(examining her)* You seem agitated...you sound strange.

THE COUNTESS: That's not surprising....not surprising at all...believe me...we were talking about you...as I said, she just left...

THE COUNT: Talking about me! I came back because I was quite distraught—as I was mounting my horse, someone handed me a note. I didn't believe a word of it, but it's......unnerved me.

THE COUNTESS: What, Monsieur?...what note?

THE COUNT: Madame, we're going to have to accept that one of us is surrounded by some pretty....nasty people. I've been told that, at some point today, someone I thought absent will try to meet with you.

THE COUNTESS: Well, whoever this reckless person might be, he'll have to get in here, because I don't intend to leave my room all day.

THE COUNT: And this evening, for Suzanne's wedding?

THE COUNTESS: For nothing on earth; I'm utterly indisposed.

THE COUNT: Luckily the doctor's here. *(The page knocks over a chair in the closet.)* What was that noise?

THE COUNTESS: What noise?

THE COUNT: Someone knocked over a piece of furniture.

THE COUNTESS: I...I....didn't hear anything, no....

THE COUNT: You must be extremely preoccupied.

THE COUNTESS: Preoccupied! With what?

THE COUNT: There's someone in that closet, Madame.

THE COUNTESS: Well, well—who do you think it could be, Monsieur?

THE COUNT: That's what I'm asking you; I just got here.

THE COUNTESS: Well...it's...probably Suzanne, tidying up.

THE COUNT: You said she'd gone to her room.

THE COUNTESS: Gone there...or in *there*...I don't know....whichever...

THE COUNT: If it's just Suzanne, why are you so agitated?

THE COUNTESS: Agitated, by my chambermaid?

THE COUNT: I don't know about the chambermaid part, but I've no doubt about the agitation.

THE COUNTESS: And I've no doubt, Monsieur, that that girl agitates *and* preoccupies you a lot more than she does me.

THE COUNT: *(angrily)* She preoccupies me so much, Madame, that I want to see her this instant.

THE COUNTESS: In fact I'd say you want that quite often. But listen to me; these suspicions are founded on nothing—

SCENE 13

The Count, the Countess, Suzanne (who comes in through the upstage door, carrying clothes)

THE COUNT: Fine, they'll be that much easier to dispel. *(He shouts toward the closet.)* Suzanne, I order you to come out of there! *(Suzanne stops next to the alcove, upstage.)*

THE COUNTESS: She's half naked, Monsieur; who ever barges in on women like this, in their own rooms! She's trying on clothes that I gave her for her wedding; she ran to hide when she heard you coming.

THE COUNT: If she's so afraid of showing herself, at least she can speak. *(Turning toward the door.)* Suzanne, answer me; are you in that closet? *(Suzanne, still upstage, ducks into the alcove and hides there.)* 10

THE COUNTESS: *(sharply, turning toward the door)* Suzanne, I forbid you to answer. *(To the Count.)* Never has tyranny been pushed so far! 15

THE COUNT: *(advancing on the door)* All right, since she can't speak, whether she's dressed or not, I'm going to see her. 20

THE COUNTESS: *(throwing herself in front of the door)* Anywhere else, I couldn't prevent this, but I hope that at least here, in my own rooms—

THE COUNT: And I hope to know, this instant, just who this mysterious Suzanne is. I see it would be futile to ask you for the key; but it won't take much to knock that flimsy door right in. Ho! Someone! 25

THE COUNTESS: What—you're going to call your people here and make a public scandal over a suspicion that will make us the laughing stock of the whole chateau? 30

THE COUNT: Very well, Madame; I'll take care of it myself. I'll go to my rooms right now to get what I need...*(He goes to leave but comes back.)* But, to ensure that everything stays just as it is, would you be so kind as to accompany me, quietly and without any fuss, since that kind of thing upsets you so much?...Such a simple thing, surely, you can't refuse me. 35

THE COUNTESS: *(troubled)* Ah, Monsieur, who would ever dream of contradicting you? 40

THE COUNT: Ah, I forgot the door to your servants' quarters; this should be locked as well, to insure your complete exoneration. *(He goes and locks the upstage door, taking the key.)* 45

THE COUNTESS: *(aside)* Oh, God, my fatal stupidity !

THE COUNT: *(coming back to her)* Now that room is safe; if you please, Madame, my arm; *(raising his voice)* and as for Suzanne of the closet, she must be kind enough to wait for me; and the slightest harm that may come to her when I get back— 50

THE COUNTESS: Really, Monsieur, this is the most disagreeable experience— *(The Count leads her out and locks the door.)* 55

SCENE 14

Suzanne, Chérubin

SUZANNE *(comes out of the alcove, runs to the closet door, and speaks though the keyhole)*: Open up, Chérubin, quick, open up—it's Suzanne; open up and get out.

CHÉRUBIN: *(coming out of the closet)* Ah! Suzanne, what a horrible scene! 5

SUZANNE: Get out of here, you don't have a second.

CHÉRUBIN: *(terrified)* Out!—but how? where?

SUZANNE: I don't know, just go. 10

CHÉRUBIN: But if there's no way out?

SUZANNE: After your last encounter, he'll kill you, and we'll all be lost...Run and tell Figaro—

CHÉRUBIN: Maybe the garden window isn't too high. *(He runs to look out.)* 15

SUZANNE: *(frightened)* It's a whole floor up! Impossible! Ah! My poor mistress! And my marriage! Oh, God!

CHÉRUBIN: It's right over the melons; I'll only spoil a row or two. 20

SUZANNE: *(holding him back)* You'll kill yourself!

CHÉRUBIN: *(exalted)* Into a fiery abyss, Suzanne— yes, I'd sooner throw myself there than let any harm come to her...And this kiss will bring me luck. *(He kisses Suzanne and, running, jumps out the window.)* 25

SCENE 15

Suzanne, alone, lets out a cry of horror.

SUZANNE: Ah!...*(She falls into a chair. She forces herself to go look out of the window, then comes back.)* He's already far away. Oh! The little scamp. As nimble as he is pretty. If that one's ever short of women....Let's take his place right away. *(As she goes into the closet.)* Now, Monsieur Count, you can break down the entire wall if that amuses you, and the devil I'll say a word. *(She shuts herself in.)* 5

SCENE 16

The Count, The Countess, coming back into the room.

THE COUNT: *(a crowbar in hand, which he tosses onto the chair.)* Everything's as I left it. Madame, before you force me to break open this door, think of the consequences. For the last time, will you open it?   5

THE COUNTESS: Ah! Monsieur, what terrible affliction is capable of destroying the bond between man and wife in this way? If it was love that drove you into such fits of rage, I'd excuse them no matter how unreasonable. Were that your motive, I might even be able to forgive the insult done to my innocence. But can mere vanity drive a courtly man like you to such wild extremes?   10

THE COUNT: Love or vanity, you will open that door regardless, or this instant I'm going to—   15

THE COUNTESS: *(in front of him)* Stop, Monsieur, I beg you! Do you really think me capable of forgetting my duty?

THE COUNT: Say what you like, Madame, but I *will* know who's in that closet.   20

THE COUNTESS: *(frightened)* Very well, Monsieur, then you will. Listen to me...calmly.

THE COUNT: So it's not Suzanne?

THE COUNTESS: *(timidly)* At least it's not someone...from whom you have anything to fear...We were planning a little joke for tonight— perfectly innocent, to tell you the truth...and I swear to you—   25

THE COUNT: And you swear to me?

THE COUNTESS: That neither he nor I had any wish to offend you.   30

THE COUNT: He? So it's a man?

THE COUNTESS: A child, Monsieur.

THE COUNT: Well then, who?

THE COUNTESS: I hardly dare name him.   35

THE COUNT: *(furious)* I'll kill him.

THE COUNTESS: Dear God!

THE COUNT: Out with it!

THE COUNTESS: The young....Chérubin—

THE COUNT: Chérubin! The insolent brat! That explains my suspicions, and the note.   40

THE COUNTESS: *(hands clasped)* Ah! Monsieur, you mustn't think—

THE COUNT: *(stamping his foot, aside)* Must I find this damned page everywhere? *(Aloud)* Come on, Madame, open up; I understand everything now. You wouldn't have been so upset at sending him away this morning; he would have left as I ordered; you wouldn't have fabricated all these lies about Suzanne; he wouldn't be so carefully hidden, if there was nothing improper going on.   45   50

THE COUNTESS: He was only afraid it would annoy you to see him.

THE COUNT: *(beside himself, yelling at the closet door)* Come out of there, you little wretch!   55

THE COUNTESS: *(throwing her arms around him to pull him away)* Ah! Monsieur, Monsieur, your anger makes me tremble for him. Don't believe an unjust suspicion, please, or that the disorder in which you find him—   60

THE COUNT: Disorder!

THE COUNTESS: Alas, yes; preparing to dress as a woman, with one of my bonnets on his head, in his shirt-sleeves, without his coat, his collar open, his arms bare. He was going to try—   65

THE COUNT: And you wanted to stay in your room! You disgraceful wife! Oh! You'll stay here, all right, for a long time; but first, I'm going flush this insolent wretch out of here—this time for good.

THE COUNTESS: *(throwing herself on her knees, pleading)* Monsieur, my Lord, spare the child; I'll never be able to forgive myself for causing—   70

THE COUNT: Your fearfulness only makes him guiltier.

THE COUNTESS: He's not guilty at all, he was leaving: it was I who called him back.   75

THE COUNT: *(furious)* Get up. Get out of the way...You're not in a position to speak on someone else's behalf!

THE COUNTESS: Very well, I'll get out of the way, Monsieur, and I'll get up; I'll even give you the key to my closet; but in the name of your love—   80

THE COUNT: Of my love! You perfidious woman!

THE COUNTESS: *(gets up and hands him the key)* Promise me you'll let the child go without harming him; afterwards you may vent all your wrath on me, if I can't convince you—   85

THE COUNT: *(taking the key)* I won't hear another word.

THE COUNTESS: *(throwing herself onto a divan, handkerchief at her eyes)* Oh, God in heaven; he's going to die.   90

THE COUNT: *(opening the door and recoiling)* It's Suzanne!

SCENE 17

The Countess, The Count, Suzanne

SUZANNE: *(coming out laughing)* "I'll kill him, I'll kill him!" Go ahead and kill him then, the wicked page!

THE COUNT: *(aside)* Ah! What a fiasco! *(Looking at The Countess, who is dumbfounded.)* Oh, you too? You feign astonishment?...But maybe she wasn't alone in there. *(He goes in.)*   5

SCENE 18

The Countess, Suzanne

SUZANNE: *(running to her)* Madame, pull yourself together; he's long gone; he jumped—

THE COUNTESS: Ah! Suzanne, I'm dead—

SCENE 19

The Count, The Countess, Suzanne

THE COUNT: *(emerging from the closet, looking confused; after a short silence)* There's no one there; for once, I was wrong. Madame? You're quite the actor.

SUZANNE: *(brightly)* And me, Monseigneur? *(The Countess, handkerchief over her mouth to recover, says nothing.)*   5

THE COUNT: *(approaching)* What, Madame—you were joking?

THE COUNTESS: *(finding a bit of strength)* And why not, Monsieur?   10

THE COUNT: What an appalling prank! And may one ask why?...

THE COUNTESS: Perhaps your folly deserves... pity?

THE COUNT: You call a matter of honour "folly"?   15

THE COUNTESS: *(vocally stronger by degrees)* Did I marry you to be eternally shackled to neglect *and* jealousy, two things only you would dare to combine?

THE COUNT: Ah, Madame, you're being cruel.   20

SUZANNE: Madame had only to let you call in your people.

THE COUNT: You're right. I'm the one who should be asking for forgiveness. Pardon me, please. I'm really confused!...   25

SUZANNE: You must admit, Monsieur, you deserved it a little!

THE COUNT: But why didn't you come out when I called you, you naughty girl?

SUZANNE: I was trying to put myself together as best I could, with a thousand pins....and Madame ordered me to stay put; she must have had her reasons.   30

THE COUNT: Instead of reminding me of my mistakes, help me to mollify her.   35

THE COUNTESS: No, Monsieur; such an outrage cannot be brushed aside. I'm going to retire to the Ursuline convent, which I see I should have done a long time ago.

THE COUNT: Could you do that, with no regrets?   40

SUZANNE: Oh, the day of her departure would be full of tears, that's for sure....

THE COUNTESS: Well, Suzanne may be right; but nevertheless I'd rather regret my decision than be so base as to pardon him; he's hurt me too deeply.   45

THE COUNT: Rosine!...

THE COUNTESS: I'm no longer the Rosine you pursued so ardently! I'm the poor Countess Almaviva, the sad abandoned wife you no longer love.   50

SUZANNE: Madame.

THE COUNT: *(pleading)* Have mercy.

THE COUNTESS: You had none for me.

THE COUNT: But there was also that note—it made my blood—   55

THE COUNTESS: It wasn't written with my consent.

THE COUNT: You knew about it?

THE COUNTESS: It's that numbskull Figaro—

THE COUNT: He was involved?   60

THE COUNTESS: —who gave it to Bazile.

THE COUNT: —who told me he got it from some peasant. Oh, the treacherous, two-faced crooner! He's going to pay for all of this!

THE COUNTESS: You ask for yourself a pardon   65

that you refuse others: that's men for you! Ah! If ever I consent to forgive the errors into which that letter led you, I'll demand that the amnesty be universal.

THE COUNT: Well then, Countess, with all my heart. But how can I make amends for such a humiliating mistake?   70

THE COUNTESS: (getting up) It was that for us both.

THE COUNT: Ah, no; for me alone. But I still can't fathom how it is that women can take on so quickly and so accurately the right tone and behaviour for a given situation. You flushed red, you cried, your face looked ashen—I'd swear it still does.   80

THE COUNTESS: (forcing herself to smile) I flushed....because I resented your suspicions. But aren't men refined enough to distinguish between the indignation of an honest, outraged soul, and the confusion of a truly guilty one?   85

THE COUNT: (smiling) And the page—dishevelled, in shirtsleeves, half naked—

THE COUNTESS: (pointing to Suzanne) There, you see him before you. Aren't you happier to have found her than him? In general you don't usually object to running into this one....   90

THE COUNT: (laughing harder) And those prayers, those sham tears—

THE COUNTESS: You're making me laugh, and I'm really not up to it.   95

THE COUNT: We like to believe we know something about politics, but we're only children. It's you, Madame, it's you the King should send as ambassador to London! You women must have made a very thorough study of the art of dissem-   100 bling in order to succeed to that degree!

THE COUNTESS: Yes, because you men always force us to.

SUZANNE: Leave us as prisoners on parole, and you'll see that we're people of honour.   105

THE COUNTESS: Let's drop all this, Monsieur. I may have gone too far, but my indulgence in such a serious matter ought at least to earn me yours.

THE COUNT: But tell me again that you pardon me?   110

THE COUNTESS: Is that what I said, Suzanne?

SUZANNE: I didn't hear it, Madame.

THE COUNT: Well—does the word escape you....?

THE COUNTESS: Do you deserve it, ingrate?

THE COUNT: Yes, because of my repentance.   115

SUZANNE: To suspect that Madame had a man in her closet!

THE COUNT: She has punished me most severely for it!

SUZANNE: And not believing her, when she said   120 was her chambermaid!

THE COUNT: Rosine, will you be merciless?

THE COUNTESS: Ah, Suzanne, I'm so weak! Some example I set for you! (Putting out her hand to the Count.) No one is going to believe in a woman's   125 anger ever again.

SUZANNE: Alas, Madame, with men, it always seems to come to this. (The Count ardently kisses his wife's hand.)

SCENE 20

Suzanne, Figaro, The Countess, The Count

FIGARO: (arriving all out of breath) They said— Madame indisposed. I ran quickly—happy to see she looks fine.

THE COUNT: (drily) You're so attentive.

FIGARO: It's just my duty. But since it's nothing,   5 Monseigneur, all your young vassals are waiting below with fiddles and bagpipes, to accompany me, the moment you will allow me to bring my fiancée—

THE COUNT: And who will watch over the   10 Countess, here in the chateau?

FIGARO: Watch over her! She's not ill.

THE COUNT: No; but that absent man who's going to try to meet her?

FIGARO: What absent man?   15

THE COUNT: The man in the note that you gave to Bazile.

FIGARO: Who said that?

THE COUNT: Even if I didn't already know it from elsewhere, scoundrel, your own face indicts you   20 and proves you're lying.

FIGARO: In that case, it's not me who's lying—it's my face.

SUZANNE: There, there, my poor Figaro; don't

waste your eloquence on a lost battle; we've told 25
him everything.

FIGARO: What have you told him? You treat me like
a Bazile!

SUZANNE: That you wrote that note to make
Monseigneur think, when he came in, that the 30
little page was in the closet rather than me.

THE COUNT: What do you say to that?

THE COUNTESS: There's nothing left to hide,
Figaro; the joke is consummated.

FIGARO: (trying to understand) The joke...is.... 35
consummated?

THE COUNT: Yes, consummated. What do you say
to that?

FIGARO: Me? I say...that I really wish I could say
the same about my marriage, so if you'll instruct— 40

THE COUNT: Then you do admit to that note?

FIGARO: Since Madame wants it, and Suzanne wants
it, and you want it yourself, apparently I'd better
want it too: but the truth is, Monseigneur, if I were
you, I wouldn't believe a word we're saying. 45

THE COUNT: Always lying, against all the
evidence! That really does irritate me.

THE COUNTESS: (laughing) Ah! The poor boy!
Why then, Monsieur, should you want him to tell
the truth even once? 50

FIGARO: (aside, to Suzanne) I've warned him of the
danger; that's all an honest man can do.

SUZANNE: (aside) Have you seen the little page?

FIGARO: (aside) Still pretty frazzled.

SUZANNE: (aside) Poor creature! 55

THE COUNTESS: Come, Monsieur; they're dying
to be married and their impatience is natural. Let's
go down for the ceremony.

THE COUNT: (aside) Yet, Marceline, Marceline...
(aloud) I should be...at least properly dressed. 60

THE COUNTESS: For our people?—look what I'm
wearing!

SCENE 21

Antonio, Figaro, Suzanne, The Countess, The Count

ANTONIO: (half-drunk, carrying a pot of crushed
peonies[17]) Monseigneur! Monseigneur!

---

17 peonies] lit., *giroflées*, or pinks.

THE COUNT: What is it you want, Antonio?

ANTONIO: Could you please put grates on the
windows above my flower-beds? They throw all 5
kinds of things out of those windows; just now
they even threw a man out of one.

THE COUNT: Out the window?

ANTONIO: Look what they did to my peonies!

SUZANNE: (softly to Figaro) Alarm, Figaro, alarm! 10

FIGARO: Monseigneur, he's been drinking all
morning.

ANTONIO: There you're wrong. This is just a little
left-over from yesterday. See, that's how people
jump to false...confusions. 15

THE COUNT: (flaming mad) That man! That man!
Where is he?

ANTONIO: Where is he?

THE COUNT: Yes.

ANTONIO: That's what I said. I got to find him 20
already. I work for you; it's me takes care of yer
garden; a man falls into it, and there you are: my
reputation's soiled.

SUZANNE: (softly to Figaro) Change the subject,
quickly. 25

FIGARO: So, you drink all the time, eh?

ANTONIO: If I didn't, I'd go insane.

THE COUNTESS: But to drink when you're not
even thirsty...

ANTONIO: Madame, to drink without thirst and 30
make love all year round, that's all that distinguishes us from the other animals.

THE COUNT: (impatiently) Answer me, or I'm
going to send you packing.

ANTONIO: And you think I'd leave, just for that? 35

THE COUNT: What?

ANTONIO: (touching his own forehead) Maybe you
don't got enough up here to hold on to a good
servant, but I ain't dumb enough to get rid of such
a good master. 40

THE COUNT: (shaking him angrily) Did you say
that someone threw a man out that window?

ANTONIO: Yes, My Excellency, just before, in a
white shirt, and he took off, dammit, running—

THE COUNT: (impatiently) And then—? 45

ANTONIO: I sure did try to run after him; but I
smashed my hand so hard against the gate that I
couldn't barely move hide nor hair of this here
finger. (Lifts his finger.)

THE COUNT: But you'd recognise the man wouldn't you? 50

ANTONIO: Oh, of course I would!—if I'd seen him.

SUZANNE: *(softly to Figaro)* He didn't see him.

FIGARO: What a lot of fuss about a pot of flowers! 55 Okay, crybaby, how much do you want for your peonies? You needn't look any further, Monseigneur; it's me who jumped.

THE COUNT: What, you?

ANTONIO: "Okay crybaby, how much do you 60 want?" So, your body's grown a lot bigger since then? Because you were a lot more punier and more skinnier last time I saw you!

FIGARO: Obviously. When you jump, you curl up...

ANTONIO: Y'ask me, it was...so to speak, that runt 65 of a page.

THE COUNT: You mean Chérubin?

FIGARO: Oh, sure—come back, expressly for that purpose on his horse, all the way from the gates of Seville, which is where no doubt he is right 70 now—

ANTONIO: Oh, no, I didn't say that, I didn't say that; I didn't see no horse jump, or I would have said so.

THE COUNT: Give me patience! 75

FIGARO: I was in the women's quarters in my white shirt—it was so hot!—and I was waiting for my little Suzanne when all of a sudden I heard Monseigneur's voice and some great noise being made! I don't know what fear possessed me, on 80 account of that note; but, since I must admit to my stupidity, I just jumped, without thinking, into the flowerbeds, where I even hurt my right foot a little. *(He rubs his foot.)*

ANTONIO: Since it's you, it's only right that you 85 get this bauble of paper that flowed out of your pocket when you fell.

THE COUNT: *(leaping forward)* Give me that. *(He unfolds the paper, then folds it up again.)*

FIGARO: *(aside)* I'm caught. 90

THE COUNT: *(to Figaro)* Your fear wouldn't have made you forget the contents of this paper, or how it came to be in your pocket?

FIGARO: *(rummaging with embarrassment in his pockets, pulling out papers)* Oh, absolutely not...But 95

I've got so many; everyone wants answers. *(He looks at one of the papers.)* What's this? Ah! A letter from Marceline, four pages long, so beautiful!...Would this be the petition from that poor jailed poacher? ...No, that's here...I had the furniture list for the 100 summer-house in the other pocket—

(The Count opens the paper he's holding.)

THE COUNTESS: *(softly to Suzanne)* Oh, God! Suzanne, it's the officer's commission.

SUZANNE: *(softly to Figaro)* All is lost—it's the commission. 105

THE COUNT: *(refolding the paper)* Well? Mister know-it-all, can't you guess?

ANTONIO: *(approaching Figaro)* Monseigneur asked if you can guess.

FIGARO: *(pushing him away)* Pouah! Villain, do you 110 have to speak right into my nose?

THE COUNT: You don't recall what this might be?

FIGARO: A—a—a—ah! *Povero!*[18] It must be that poor child's commission, which he gave me, and I forgot to give back. O—o—o—oh! Scatterbrain 115 that I am! What will he do without his commission? I'd better run—

THE COUNT: And why would he give it to you?

FIGARO: *(embarrassed)* He...he wanted me to do something to it. 120

THE COUNT: *(looking at the paper)* It doesn't need anything.

THE COUNTESS: *(softly to Suzanne)* The seal.

SUZANNE: *(softly to Figaro)* The seal is missing.

THE COUNT: *(to Figaro)* You don't answer? 125

FIGARO: Well...actually, there is one small thing missing. He said it is customary......

THE COUNT: Customary? Customary? What's customary?

FIGARO: To stamp it with your personal seal. But 130 perhaps you couldn't be bothered with such a trivial detail.

THE COUNT: *(opens the paper, then angrily crumples it)* So, I'm condemned to ignorance once again! *(Aside.)* It's Figaro who's behind all of it—oh, but 135 will I ever get my revenge! *(Greatly vexed, he starts to leave.)*

---

18 *Povero*] poor thing (Italian).

FIGARO: *(stopping him)* Are you leaving without giving orders for my wedding?

SCENE 22

Bazile, Bartholo, Marceline, Figaro, The Count, Grippe-Soleil, The Countess, Suzanne, Antonio; the Count's valets and vassals

MARCELINE: *(to the Count)* Don't give the orders, Monseigneur! Before doing him that honour, you owe us justice. He has commitments to me.

THE COUNT: *(aside)* At last; my revenge arrives.

FIGARO: Commitments! Of what kind? Explain yourself.

MARCELINE: Yes, I certainly will, you dishonest man! *(The Countess sits in an armchair. Suzanne stands behind her.)*

THE COUNT: What's this about, Marceline?

MARCELINE: A promise of marriage.

FIGARO: A promissory note, that's all, for money I borrowed.

MARCELINE: *(to the Count)* On condition that he marry me. You are a grand seigneur, the highest judge in the province—

THE COUNT: Present yourselves in court and I'll grant justice to everyone.

BAZILE: *(indicating Marceline)* In that case, will Your Highness also allow me to state my claims on Marceline?

THE COUNT: *(aside)* Ah, it's that scoundrel of a mailman.

FIGARO: Another nutcase!

THE COUNT: *(angrily, to Bazile)* Your rights! Your rights! You're in no position to demand anything from me, maestro moron!

ANTONIO: *(clapping his hands)* He hit it right on the head first time: that's his name alright!

THE COUNT: Marceline, we'll suspend everything until your claims have been duly examined, publically, in the great hall. Honest Bazile, my good and faithful agent, go into town and collect the magistrates.

BAZILE: For her case?

THE COUNT: And bring me the peasant who gave you that note.

BAZILE: How am I supposed to know who he is?

THE COUNT: Are you resisting me?

BAZILE: I didn't come to this chateau to run errands.

THE COUNT: Then why did you?

BAZILE: As the highly regarded organist of the village, I teach the harpsichord to Madame, singing to her ladies, the mandolin to the pages; but my main duty is to amuse your entourage with my guitar, when it pleases you so to command me.

GRIPPE-SOLEIL: *(comes forward)* I'll go, Monseigneur, if it please you.

THE COUNT: What's your name and your function?

GRIPPE-SOLEIL: I'm Grippe-Soleil, my good lord, the little goatherd, here today to work on the fireworks. There's a feast for them flock of lawyers today, so I know where to find the whole hopping lot of them.

THE COUNT: Ah, your zeal pleases me; go ahead then; but you: *(to Bazile)* accompany Monsieur by playing the guitar and singing for his amusement along the way. He's part of my entourage.

GRIPPE-SOLEIL: *(joyously)* Oh! Me? I'm part of your—? *(Suzanne calms him with her hand, indicating the Countess.)*

BAZILE: *(surprised)* I'm to accompany Grippe-Soleil, playing—?

THE COUNT: That's your job. Now go, or I'll have you removed.

(He leaves.)

SCENE 23

The previous actors, except The Count.

BAZILE: *(to himself)* Hah! I'm not going to sing my brains out, not me, who's—

FIGARO: —brainless already.

BAZILE: *(aside)* Instead of helping their marriage, I'm going to ensure my own with Marceline. *(To Figaro.)* Don't settle anything, you hear me, till I get back. *(He picks up the guitar from the armchair at the back.)*

FIGARO: *(following him)* Settle? Oh—go on, I've got nothing to fear, even if you do come back. You don't seem to be singing....? Do you want me to start you off? Come on—happy, happy! Let's have a big do-re-mi for my fiancée. *(He starts to leave, walking backwards, dancing and singing the following seguidilla; Bazile accompanies him; everyone follows except Suzanne and The Countess.)* 15

SEGUIDILLA:[19]

To all gems I prefer
The sparkling wit
Of my Suzanne,
Zan, zan, zan, Zan, zan, zan, 20
Zan, zan, zan, Zan, zan, zan!

Of her sweet gentleness
I'm a slave
And a fan,
Zan, zan, zan, Zan, zan, zan,
Zan, zan, zan, Zan, zan, zan! 25

(The singing fades as they leave.)

SCENE 24

Suzanne, The Countess

THE COUNTESS: *(in her armchair)* You see, Suzanne, the lovely scene your numbskull got me into with his note.

SUZANNE: Oh, Madame, when I came out of the closet, if you could have seen your face! First, it drained completely, but only as if whitened by a passing cloud—you then went red, and redder, and redder! 5

THE COUNTESS: He really jumped out the window? 10

SUZANNE: Without the slightest hesitation, the charming child! Light....as a bee!

THE COUNTESS: Ah! That ruinous gardener! I was so rattled by the whole thing—I couldn't put two thoughts together. 15

SUZANNE: Oh, Madame, on the contrary; I've always noticed how great ladies like yourself, used to life in fashionable society, are highly skilled in telling lies without anyone knowing.

THE COUNTESS: Do you think the Count was 20

fooled? If he should find that child in the chateau—!

SUZANNE: I'll make sure he's so well hidden—

THE COUNTESS: No, he must leave. After what's just happened, you can understand that I'm no longer tempted to send him to the garden in your place. 25

SUZANNE: And obviously I'm not going to go either. So, once again, there goes my marriage...

THE COUNTESS: *(getting up)* Wait. Instead of someone else, or you, what if I went myself? 30

SUZANNE: You, Madame?

THE COUNTESS: No one would run any risk... Then, the Count could hardly deny— To punish his jealousy, and prove his unfaithfulness! That would be— Let's do it. Succeeding in one adventure makes me want to try a second. Let him know immediately that you will meet him in the garden. But, above all, let nobody— 35

SUZANNE: Well, Figaro. 40

THE COUNTESS: No, no. He'll want to get involved. Get my velvet mask and my walking-stick....I'm going out on the terrace to think about this. *(Suzanne goes back into the dressing room.)*

SCENE 25

The Countess

THE COUNTESS: It's pretty disgraceful, my little plan! *(She turns around.)* Oh! the ribbon! My pretty ribbon, I almost forgot you. *(She retrieves it from the chair and rolls it up.)* You mustn't leave me ever again..You'll always remind me of the scene with that poor child—ah! Monsieur Count, what have you done? And me, what am I doing at this moment? 5

SCENE 26

Suzanne, The Countess, secretly hiding the ribbon in her bodice.

SUZANNE: Here's the stick and your mask.[20]

THE COUNTESS: Remember, I forbid you to say a word to Figaro.

---

[19] séguedilla] Spanish popular song in three-quarter time.

[20] mask] a half-mask that covers the eyes only.

SUZANNE: *(joyfully)* Madame, your plan is wonderful. I was just thinking about it. It brings everything together, settles everything, and wraps everything up; and, whatever happens, my marriage is now certain. *(She kisses her mistress's hand. They go out.)*

During the intermission, the valets set up the hall for the court: they bring in the two chair-benches for the lawyers, and place them on either side of the stage, leaving room to walk behind them. They set up a riser with two steps in the centre of the stage, toward the back, upon which they place the Count's armchair. On one side of this they set the clerk's table and stool off to the side, toward the front; on the other they place chairs for Brid'oison and the other judges.

ACT III

The stage represents a room in the chateau, known as the Throne Room, which serves as a public hearing room; on one side a raised, canopy-covered bench, beneath which hangs a portrait of the King.

SCENE 1

The Count, Pédrille (in a vest, wearing boots, holding a sealed package.)

THE COUNT: *(quickly)* Did you hear me?
PÉDRILLE: Yes, Your Excellency. *(He goes out.)*

SCENE 2

The Count, alone, calls out.

THE COUNT: Pédrille?

SCENE 3

Pédrille, coming back in, The Count

PÉDRILLE: Excellency?
THE COUNT: No one saw you?
PÉDRILLE: Not a soul.
THE COUNT: Take the barbary horse.
PÉDRILLE: He's at the garden gate, all saddled up.
THE COUNT: Head straight for Seville, no stops.
PÉDRILLE: It's only three leagues and the roads are good.

THE COUNT: When you get there, see if the page has arrived.
PÉDRILLE: At the ministry?
THE COUNT: Yes, and above all, find out when he got there.
PÉDRILLE: I understand.
THE COUNT: Give him his commission, then come right back.
PÉDRILLE: And if he's not there?
THE COUNT: Come back even faster and let me know. Go.

SCENE 4

The Count, alone, pacing about

THE COUNT: I made a mistake in alienating Bazile like that—anger only makes things worse. But that note he gave me, warning me of an advance on the Countess. The chambermaid locked in the closet when I arrive. Her mistress stricken with a panic that's either false or true; one man jumps out a window, and another admits to it—or pretends to admit to it...The connection escapes me, but there's something shady here... Liberties taken by my vassals—what do they matter among people of their kind? But the Countess! If any insolent devil ever tries—But what am I thinking? It's true—once you get all worked up, even the sanest imagination can go as crazy as a dream! No, she was just amusing herself: she stifled her laugh, but her pleasure was evident! She respects herself, and my honour—wherever the hell that is. On which subject, where am I? Has that little devil of a Suzanne betrayed my secret—since it's not yet hers as well?...And what's forcing me to keep pursuing her? Twenty times I've wanted to stop—How strange, the effect of indecisiveness! If I wanted her without question, she'd be a thousand times less desirable. That Figaro is certainly taking his time. I'll have to sound him out discretely—*(Figaro appears upstage; he stops.)*—and try to figure out whether or not he's wise to my love for Suzanne.

SCENE 5

Figaro, The Count

FIGARO: *(aside)* And here we are....

THE COUNT: ...If she's spoken a single word to him about it—

FIGARO: *(aside)* So, I was right.

THE COUNT: —I'll make him marry the old woman.

FIGARO: *(aside)* Monsieur Bazile's heart-throb?

THE COUNT: And then we'll see what to do with the young one.

FIGARO: *(aside)* Um, my *wife,* if you please.

THE COUNT: *(turning around)* Hm? What? Who's there?

FIGARO: *(stepping forward)* It's me, as you commanded.

THE COUNT: And what were you saying?

FIGARO: I didn't say anything.

THE COUNT: "My wife, if you please?"

FIGARO: That! Oh, that was just the end of an answer I was giving: "...go and tell my wife, if you please."

THE COUNT: *(pacing about)* "His wife!..." I'd really like to know what matter could delay Monsieur when I call for him?

FIGARO: *(pretending to fix his clothes)* I got dirty when I fell into the flowerbeds, so I changed.

THE COUNT: And that took an hour?

FIGARO: It took some time.

THE COUNT: The servants around here take longer to dress than their masters!

FIGARO: That's because they don't have valets to help them.

THE COUNT: I didn't fully understand, earlier, what forced you to take the unnecessary risk of jumping—

FIGARO: Risk! You could say I was swallowed alive—

THE COUNT: Don't try to give me the slip by pretending you don't understand, you insidious valet! You know perfectly well it's not the danger I care about, but the motive.

FIGARO: On false information you arrive, furious, knocking everything over like a raging river on the Morena;[21] you're looking for some man, and you want to catch him so badly that you'll break the locks, you'll knock down the door! I happen to be there; who knows if, in your fury—

THE COUNT: *(interrupting)* You could have escaped by the staircase.

FIGARO: And have you catch me in the hallway?

THE COUNT: *(angrily)* In the hallway! *(Aside.)* I'm getting angry and that keeps me from finding what I'm after.

FIGARO: *(aside)* Let's see where he goes, and play for keeps.

THE COUNT: *(softening up)* That's not what I meant to say; never mind all that. I'd been....Oh, yes, I'd been thinking I'd take you with me to London, as a dispatch courier...but, on second thought...

FIGARO: Monseigneur has changed his mind?

THE COUNT: In the first place, you don't speak English.

FIGARO: I can say god-damn.

THE COUNT: I don't understand.

FIGARO: I said, I can say god-damn.

THE COUNT: So?

FIGARO: The devil! What a beautiful language English is—you need so little to go so far. In England, with a "god-damn," you'll never lack for anything, anywhere. You're hungry for a good fat chicken? Go into the tavern and just make this gesture to the waiter *(He turns the spit.),* say "God-damn!" and they bring you a whole side of corned beef, no bread. It's amazing! You want a good bottle of Burgundy, or claret? All you need is this *(miming opening a bottle),* "God-damn!" and they serve you a mug of beer, in their best pewter, froth dripping over the edge. What satisfaction! You meet one of those lovely creatures who go trotting down the street, eyes lowered, elbows back, wiggling their hips a little? Just put your fingers daintily to your mouth. "Ah! God-damn!" and she'll slug you like a bricklayer, just to prove she understood. Sure, it's true that now and then the English do add a few other words in conversation; but it's not hard to see that "God-damn" is the basis of the language; and unless Monseigneur has no other reason to leave me here in Spain...

---

21 Morena] mountain range in Spain.

THE COUNT: *(aside)* He wants to come to London; she hasn't told him.

FIGARO: *(aside)* He thinks I don't know; let's just work him a bit at his own game. 90

THE COUNT: What motive could the Countess have to play a trick like that on me?

FIGARO: Believe me, Monseigneur, you know that better than I do. 95

THE COUNT: I anticipate her every wish and shower her with presents.

FIGARO: You give her plenty, but you're unfaithful. Who is grateful for superfluity when they're denied what's essential? 100

THE COUNT: You used to tell me everything.

FIGARO: And I'm hiding nothing from you now.

THE COUNT: How much did the Countess pay you for that little favour?

FIGARO: How much did you pay me to pluck her 105 from the hands of the Doctor? With all due respect, Monseigneur, we should not humiliate the man who serves us well, for fear of turning him into a bad valet.

THE COUNT: Why is there always something 110 slightly sleazy about everything you do?

FIGARO: If we look for faults, we'll find them everywhere.

THE COUNT: Your reputation is detestable!

FIGARO: But maybe I deserve a better one. How 115 many Seigneurs can say that?

THE COUNT: A hundred times I've seen you approach success—but you always veer off the path.

FIGARO: What do you expect? The whole mob's 120 already there, each one trying to run, push, elbow, knock you down, it's every man for himself and the rest get trampled. That's the way it is; me, I wash my hands of it.

THE COUNT: Of being successful? *(aside)* That's a 125 new one.

FIGARO: *(aside)* Now it's my turn. *(aloud)* Your Excellency rewarded me by making me Concierge for the chateau, a very nice fate. Of course, I won't be a courier, getting first crack at all the 130 interesting news; but on the other hand, happily ensconced with my wife in the backwaters of Andalusia—

THE COUNT: What would prevent you from taking her to London? 135

FIGARO: I'd have to leave her so often that I'd soon be fed up with marriage.

THE COUNT: With character and brains, you might even get somewhere at the embassy one day.

FIGARO: Brains, to get somewhere? Ha! Mon- 140 seigneur must think mine laughably small. Mediocrity and grovelling, ah yes—that's what gets us everywhere.

THE COUNT: ...You'd only need to study politics a bit, with me. 145

FIGARO: Politics? I already have.

THE COUNT: Like English, inside out!

FIGARO: Yes, if that's anything to brag about. Pretending to be ignorant about what you know and knowledgeable about what you don't; feigning 150 understanding of what you can't fathom and deafness to what you just heard; above all appearing capable of much more than you can really do, and always surrounding with great mystery things that don't even exist; being 155 "unavailable" when you're really just sharpening pencils, and appearing deep when in fact you're just empty and hollow; play-acting, either badly or well; planting spies and cultivating traitors; melting seals, intercepting letters, and always 160 whitewashing the shabbiness of the means with the loftiness of the ends—I'll be damned if that's not politics in a nutshell!

THE COUNT: But that's intrigue you're describing!

FIGARO: Politics, intrigue, whatever; in any case, 165 you can have them both. As the old songs says, "I'd rather have my beloved, any day."

THE COUNT: *(aside)* He wants to stay. I see... Suzanne has betrayed me.

FIGARO: *(aside)* I'm stringing him along, giving him 170 a taste of his own medicine.

THE COUNT: So, you expect to win your case against Marceline?

FIGARO: Would you make it a crime to refuse old maids, when Your Excellency reserves the right to 175 steal all the young ones?

THE COUNT: *(bandying)* In court, the magistrate forgets himself and sees only the law.

FIGARO: Easy on the great, hard on the little man....

THE COUNT: You think I'm joking? 180

FIGARO: Ah! Who knows, Monseigneur? As the Italians put it, *Tempo è galant'uomo*, time always tells the truth: it will show who wishes me well or ill.

THE COUNT: *(aside)* I see he knows everything; 185 he will marry the duenna.

FIGARO: *(aside)* He sparred with me; and what has he learned?

SCENE 6

A Lackey, The Count, Figaro

THE LACKEY: Don Gusman Brid'oison.

THE COUNT: Brid'oison?

FIGARO: But of course. He's the common-law judge, the local magistrate, your appointed councillor. 5

THE COUNT: Tell him to wait. *(The lackey goes out.)*

SCENE 7

The Count, Figaro

FIGARO: *(after a moment, observing the Count, who is preoccupied)* Did Monseigneur want anything else?

THE COUNT: *(still in his thoughts)* Me?...I said to get the hall set up for the hearing. 5

FIGARO: Oh; but what's missing? Your big armchair, good chairs for your councillors, the stool for the clerk, two benches for the lawyers, the floor for the quality and the rabble to the back. I'll send the cleaners away. *(He exits.)* 10

SCENE 8

The Count

THE COUNT: That scoundrel makes me squirm! He argues, he takes advantage, sets you up, corners you...Ah! You pair of hustlers! What have you got up your sleeves? You can be friends, you can be lovers, you can be whatever you want, but I'll be hanged if you'll be married— 5

SCENE 9

Suzanne, the Count

SUZANNE: *(out of breath)* Monseigneur... forgive me, Monseigneur.

THE COUNT: *(not pleased)* What can I do for you, Mademoiselle?

SUZANNE: You're angry. 5

THE COUNT: I assume you want something?

SUZANNE: *(timidly)* It's just that my mistress has the vapours. I ran to ask if we could borrow your bottle of ether. I'll bring it right back.

THE COUNT: *(giving it to her)* No, no, keep it. You 10 may need it again before long.

SUZANNE: You think women of my station get the vapours? It's an affliction of status; you catch it only in fancy boudoirs.

THE COUNT: A fiancée, head over heels in love, 15 who loses her intended—

SUZANNE: But when Marceline gets paid with the dowry you promised me—

THE COUNT: That *I* promised you? Me?

SUZANNE: *(lowering her eyes)* Monseigneur, I 20 believe you did.

THE COUNT: Yes—if you consented to hear me.[22]

SUZANNE: *(eyes lowered)* And is it not my duty to listen to His Excellency?

THE COUNT: Then why, cruel girl, didn't you say 25 so earlier?

SUZANNE: Is it ever too late to tell the truth?

THE COUNT: Will you go at sundown to the garden?

SUZANNE: Don't I walk there every evening? 30

THE COUNT: This morning you were so harsh with me.

SUZANNE: This morning?—with the page behind the chair?

THE COUNT: You're right; I forgot. But why that 35 obstinate refusal when Bazile, on my behalf—?

SUZANNE: Who needs a Bazile?...

THE COUNT: She's always right. However, there is a certain Figaro to whom I'm very much afraid you've told everything! 40

---

22 hear me] i.e., entertain his sexual proposal.

SUZANNE: Oh, yes! Of course I tell him every-thing—except what he mustn't know.

THE COUNT: *(laughing)* Ah! Charming! And you promise me? If you don't keep your word, let's get this straight, my little sweetheart: no rendezvous, no dowry, no marriage. 45

SUZANNE: *(making a curtsey)* By the same token, no marriage, no *droit du seigneur*, Monseigneur.

THE COUNT: Where does she get these ideas? She's going to drive me wild, I can see. But your mistress is waiting for that flask... 50

SUZANNE: *(returning it to him)* Could I have spoken to you without a pretext?

THE COUNT: *(going to kiss her)* Delicious creature!

SUZANNE: *(escaping)* Someone's coming. 55

THE COUNT: *(aside)* She's mine! *(He runs out.)*

SUZANNE: I must go quick and tell Madame.

SCENE 10

Figaro, Suzanne

FIGARO: Suzanne, Suzanne! Why are you running so fast in leaving Monseigneur?

SUZANNE: Go ahead, plead all you want; you've just won your case. *(She runs out.)*

FIGARO: *(following her)* Ah, but tell me what— 5

SCENE 11

The Count, coming back in

THE COUNT: "You've just won your case!" A nice little trap I was stepping into! Oh, my insolent darlings! You'll be punished for this...justly drawn and legally quartered...But if he actually pays the old bag—with what? But if he does pay... Ahhh! 5 Don't I still have the arrogant Antonio, whose bloated pride disdains a nobody like Figaro for his niece? I'll just encourage him in that folly...Why not? In the vast fields of intrigue, one must know how to cultivate everything, even the vanity of an 10 idiot. *(He calls out.)* Anto—*(He sees Marceline and the others coming. He leaves.)*

SCENE 12

Bartholo, Marceline, Brid'oison

MARCELINE: *(to Brid'oison)* Monsieur, listen to my case.

BRID'OISON: *(in his robes, stammering a bit)* V-v-very well, let's have it verbally.

BARTHOLO: It's a promise of marriage. 5

MARCELINE: Accompanied by a loan of money.

BRID'OISON: I understand, et cetera, and so on.

MARCELINE: No, Monsieur, there's no "et cetera."

BRID'OISON: I understand. You have the money?

MARCELINE: No, Monsieur; it's me who loaned it. 10

BRID'OISON: I understand perfectly. Y-y-you've asked for the money back?

MARCELINE: No, Monsieur; I ask that he marry me.

BRID'OISON: Ah, then I u-u-understand just fine. And him, d-does he agree to marry you? 15

MARCELINE: No, Monsieur; that's what this case is all about.

BRID'OISON: You think I don't understand this case?

MARCELINE: No, Monsieur. *(To Bartholo.)* Where 20 are we? *(To Brid'oison.[23])* What! Are you going to be judging?

BRID'OISON: For what other purpose do you think I b-b-bought my position?

MARCELINE: *(sighing)* It's a terrible thing that 25 they're up for sale.

BRID'OISON: Quite right—we really should be given them for free. Who are you pleading against?

SCENE 13

Bartholo, Marceline, Brid'oison; Figaro coming back in, rubbing his hands

MARCELINE: *(indicating Figaro)* Monsieur, against that dishonest man.

FIGARO: *(very gaily, to Marceline)* Am I bothering you in any way? Monseigneur will be right back, Councillor. 5

BRID'OISON: Where have I seen this b-b-boy before?

---

23 Brid'oison] who has presumably done something (like take his seat) to suggest that he is the judge.

FIGARO: At your wife's house, in Seville, when I was in Madame's service, Councillor.

BRID'OISON: When was th-that?

FIGARO: Nearly a year before the birth of your youngest son—a beautiful child, I'm proud to say.

BRID'OISON: Yes, the m-most beautiful of them all. I take it you've been up to your u-usual stunts here as well?

FIGARO: Monsieur is too kind. This is really nothing.

BRID'OISON: A promise of marriage! Ah, the poor fool.

FIGARO: Monsieur—

BRID'OISON: Have you seen that good lad my secretary?

FIGARO: Isn't that Double-Main,[24] the clerk?

BRID'OISON: Yes; because he eats at two troughs.

FIGARO: Eats! Trust me, he gorges. Oh yes, I saw him, for both the brief and the supplement to the brief, all according to usual practice, don't you know.

BRID'OISON: One must observe the proper forms.

FIGARO: Absolutely, Monsieur; if the essence of the legal process belongs to the litigants, we can be sure that the forms are the patrimony of the courts.

BRID'OISON: This boy isn't as stupid as I thought. Well, my friend, since you know so much about it, we'll be sure to pay special attention to your case.

FIGARO: Monsieur, I will depend upon your fairness, despite your position in our court.

BRID'OISON: Huh?... Yes, I am p-part of the court. But if you owe, and don't pay?...

FIGARO: Then, as Monsieur sees clearly, it's the same as if I owed nothing.

BRID'OISON: N-no doubt. —Huh? but what's he saying?

SCENE 14

The Count, a Bailiff, Bartholo, Marceline, Brid'oison, Figaro

BAILIFF: *(leading the Count in and announcing)* My Lords, Monseigneur His Excellency the Count.

THE COUNT: In your robes, my Lord Brid'oison? This is only a domestic matter; even city clothes are too good.

BRID'OISON: It's you who are too good, Monsieur. But I never go anywhere without my robes, on account of the forms, you see, the forms! Many a man who'd laugh at a judge in a suit will tremble at the sight of a humble solicitor in a robe. The forms, the forms!

THE COUNT: *(to the Bailiff)* Bring in the court.

BAILIFF: *(opening the doors, clapping his hands)* The court!

SCENE 15

The previous actors, Antonio, the valets of the chateau, the peasant men and women in their festive dress. The Count sits in the large armchair, Brid'oison in a chair beside him, the Clerk on the stool behind the table, the Judges and Lawyers on the benches, Marceline next to Bartholo, and Figaro on the other bench; the Peasants and the Valets stand behind, at the back.

BRID'OISON: Double-Main, read the cases.

DOUBLE-MAIN: *(reads a paper)* "Noble, very noble, infinitely noble, Don Pedro George, Hidalgo, Baron de Los Altos, y Montes Fieros, y otros montes; against Alonzo Calderon, young dramatist." It concerns a play that died on opening night, which each disowns and attributes to the other.

THE COUNT: They're both right. Case dismissed. If they collaborate on another work, in order for it to make some impression on the world, it is hereby decreed that the noble apply his name, the poet his talent.

DOUBLE-MAIN: *(reading another paper)* "André Petrutchio, labourer, against the Receiver General of the Province." It's a case of arbitrary enforcement of the tax-law.

THE COUNT: This case exceeds my jurisdiction. I serve my vassals better by protecting them from the King. Next.

DOUBLE-MAIN: *(takes a third paper; Bartholo and Figaro stand)* "Barbe-Agar-Raab-Madeleine-Nicole-Marceline de Verte-Allure, unmarried woman

---

24 Double-Main] "two-handed."

(Marceline stands and bows), against Figaro"— Christian name blank? 25

FIGARO: Anonymous.

BRID'OISON: Anonymous! Which saint is that?

FIGARO: Mine.

DOUBLE-MAIN: *(writes)* "Against Anonymous Figaro." Rank and title? 30

FIGARO: Gentleman.

THE COUNT: You're a gentleman? *(The clerk writes.)*

FIGARO: If heaven had wished it, I'd have been the son of a prince. 35

THE COUNT: *(to the clerk)* Carry on.

BAILIFF: *(clapping his hands)* Silence! Messieurs.

DOUBLE-MAIN: *(reading)* "...the cause being opposition made to the marriage of the said Figaro by the said Verte-Allure. Doctor Bartholo pleading 40 for the plaintiff, and the said Figaro for himself, if the Court will so permit, in defiance of the customary practice and jurisprudence of this bench."

FIGARO: Custom, Master Double-Main, is often 45 unjust. Even a half-ignorant client knows more about his case than a lot of lawyers—the kind who drip cold sweat, shout their heads off, know everything except the facts, and worry as little about about ruining the plaintiff as about boring 50 the audience and putting the judges to sleep: afterwards they're more puffed up than if they'd composed Cicero's defence of Murena.[25] As for me, I'll state the facts in few words. My Lords—

DOUBLE-MAIN: All utterly pointless, for you're 55 not the plaintiff; you're to defend yourself only. Approach, Doctor, and read the promise.

FIGARO: Yes, the promise!

BARTHOLO: *(putting on his glasses)* It's very precise.

BRID'OISON: We shall see. 60

DOUBLE-MAIN: Silence please, Messieurs.

BAILIFF: *(clapping his hands)* Silence!

BARTHOLO: *(reading)* "I the undersigned acknowledge receipt from Mademoiselle etc., etc.... Marceline de Verte-Allure, in the chateau of Aguas- 65

Frescas, the sum of two thousand piastres, milledged and unaltered, which sum I will repay her upon demand, in this chateau; and will marry her, in formal recognition of, etc. etc.. Signed, Figaro, for short." My terms are for the payment of the 70 loan and the execution of the promise, with costs. *(He pleads.)* My Lords...never has a more compelling case been submitted to the judgement of this Court. Not since Alexander the Great, who promised marriage to the beautiful Thalestris— 75

THE COUNT: *(interrupting)* Before we go any further, Councillor, do all agree to the accuracy of this account?

BRID'OISON: *(to Figaro)* Have y-you any obj-j-jection to this r-reading? 80

FIGARO: Only the fact, my lords, that there was malice, mistake or carelessness in the manner in which the document was read; because it does not say: "which sum I will repay her *and* I will marry her," but "which sum I will repay her *or* I will 85 marry her," which is quite different.

THE COUNT: What's written on the contract, "and" or "or"?

BARTHOLO: It says "and."

FIGARO: It says "or." 90

BRID'OISON: Double-Main, you read it for us.

DOUBLE-MAIN: *(taking the paper)* Yes, that's safest, because the parties themselves often disguise things when reading. *(He reads.)* Bla, bla, bla, bla, Mademoiselle bla, bla, bla de Verte-Allure, bla, bla, 95 bla, bla. Ah! here we are: "which sum I will repay her upon demand, in this chateau, and—or— and—or—." The word is so badly written...there's a...blob.

BRID'OISON: A blob? I know what that is. 100

BARTHOLO: *(pleading)* But I maintain it is the copulative conjunction "and" that joins the correlative parts of the phrase; I will repay the lady *and* I will marry her.

FIGARO: *(pleading)* And I maintain it is the alter- 105 native conjunction "or" that separates the said parts; I will repay madame *or* I will marry her. Once a pedant, always a pedant. If he wants to fiddle with Latin, I'll play the Greek and exterminate him. 110

THE COUNT: How do we judge such a question?

---

25 defence of Murena] delivered in 63 B.C.E. by Cicero (106–43), Roman orator and statesman. His trial speeches have since been synonymous with forensic eloquence.

[III.xv]

BARTHOLO: To simplify, my lords, and to cease quibbling over one word, we will concede that it reads "ou."[26]

FIGARO: In the court transcripts, please. 115

BARTHOLO: And we will stand by that. Such a flimsy refuge can hardly save the guilty. Let us examine the matter more closely. *(He reads.)* "...which sum I will repay her in this chateau, *où je l'épouserai.*"[27] Thus, we would say, my lords, 120 "You will be bled in this bed, *where* you shall remain"—in other words, "in which." Or indeed, "You will take two portions of rhubarb, *where* you will mix a pinch of tamarind;" that is "into which." Thus: "this chateau, *where* I will marry her, my 125 lords, is "this chateau *in which* I will marry her...""

FIGARO: Not at all. The phrase is meant in the sense of [*ou* without an accent, meaning "or"]: "either the disease will kill you *or* your doctor will;" it's clear. Another example: "either you write 130 nothing that people want to read, *or* every idiot becomes your critic;" meaning "the stupid and mean will attack you;" the sense is clear in that "the stupid and mean" are the substantives which govern. Does Master Bartholo think I have 135 forgotten my syntax? So it's "I will repay her in this chateau, comma, *or* I will marry her...""

BARTHOLO: *(quickly)* No comma.

FIGARO: *(quickly)* Yes, comma. It's "comma," my lords, "or I will marry her." 140

BARTHOLO: *(glancing sharply at the document)* No comma, my lords.

FIGARO: *(quickly)* There was one, my lords. Anyway, would the man who marries be required to pay the debt? 145

BARTHOLO: *(quickly)* Yes, we marry separately from our property rights.

---

26 The following section depends upon the fact that in French, the word for "or" (*ou*) sounds exactly the same as the word for "where" (*où*). The only difference is the accent, which is of course inaudible. In order to make the joke clear in English, a few words of the original French have been retained in what follows. Words in square brackets have been added for clarity.

27 *où je l'épouserai*] where I will marry her.

FIGARO: *(quickly)* And from our bodily rights, too, since marriage doesn't discharge them.

(The judges rise and quietly confer.)

BARTHOLO: A ridiculous idea! 150

DOUBLE-MAIN: Silence, Messieurs!

BAILIFF: *(clapping his hands)* Silence!

BARTHOLO: What cheek, to call that paying his debts!

FIGARO: Is it your *own* case that you're pleading 155 here, *advocate*?

BARTHOLO: I'm defending this young woman.

FIGARO: Fine, continue your lunacy, but stop insulting people. When the Courts allowed third parties to appear for fear that the plaintiffs 160 themselves might lose control, they did not intend that reasonable lawyers should have licence to be insolent with impunity. It would degrade the most noble of institutions.

(The judges continue to deliberate amongst themselves.)

ANTONIO: *(to Marceline, referring to the judges)* 165 What are they yacketty-yacking about?

MARCELINE: The chief justice has been bribed, now he's bribing the others, and I'm losing my case.

BARTHOLO: *(under his breath, in a dark tone)* 170 That's what I'm afraid of.

FIGARO: *(gaily)* Courage, Marceline!

DOUBLE-MAIN: *(standing, to Marceline)* That's the last straw! I hold you in contempt; and for the honour of the Court, I demand that before 175 pronouncing on the other matter, a ruling be made on this one.

THE COUNT: *(sitting back down)* No, clerk, I will not pass judgement on a personal affront to me; no judge in Spain shall blush over the kind of 180 tyranny typical of an Asiatic court; we've got enough abuses here as it is! But I shall redress one of them by explaining my decision to you: any judge who would refuse to do so is an enemy of the law. What can the plaintiff demand? Marriage 185 in default of payment; both together would be a contradiction.

DOUBLE-MAIN: Silence, Messieurs!

BAILIFF: *(clapping his hands)* Silence!

THE MARRIAGE OF FIGARO 747

THE COUNT: What does the defendant have to say? That he wants to retain his independence? It is granted. 190

FIGARO: *(joyously)* I've won!

THE COUNT: But, since the text says "which sum I will repay her upon demand, in this chateau; or else I will marry her, etcetera," the Court orders the defendant to pay two thousand piastres to the plaintiff, or else marry her this very day. *(He rises.)* 195

FIGARO: *(dumbfounded)* I've lost! 200

ANTONIO: *(joyfully)* Brilliant decision!

FIGARO: In what way?

ANTONIO: In that you ain't my nephew no more. A million thanks, Monseigneur.

BAILIFF: *(clapping his hands)* Please withdraw, Messieurs. *(The people leave.)* 205

ANTONIO: I've got to tell my niece all about this. *(He leaves.)*

SCENE 16

The Count, pacing back and forth; Marceline, Bartholo, Figaro, Brid'oison

MARCELINE: *(sitting down)* Ah! I can breathe!

FIGARO: And I'm suffocating.

THE COUNT: *(aside)* At least I get my revenge; that's some comfort.

FIGARO: *(aside)* And this Bazile, who was supposed to argue against the marriage to Marceline; let's see whether he returns. *(To the Count, who's leaving.)* Are you leaving us, Monseigneur? 5

THE COUNT: It's all settled.

FIGARO: *(to Brid'oison)* Thanks to this pompous boob of a councillor... 10

BRID'OISON: Me, a p-p-pompous b-b-boob!

FIGARO: No doubt. And I won't marry her: I'm a gentleman, after all. *(The Count stops.)*

BARTHOLO: You will marry her. 15

FIGARO: Without the blessing of my noble parents?

BARTHOLO: Name them; let's see them.

FIGARO: Give me a little time: I know I'll find them soon; I've been looking for them for fifteen years.

BARTHOLO: The conceited ass! A mere foundling! 20

FIGARO: A lost child, Doctor—or rather a stolen one.

THE COUNT: *(coming back)* Stolen, lost?—fine; prove it. If we don't let him try, he'll say his rights were violated. 25

FIGARO: Monseigneur, if the lace swaddling clothes, the embroidered blankets, the gold jewellery found about me by the brigands don't suffice to prove my high birth, then surely the care that was taken to tattoo my arm with distinctive signs clearly demonstrates that I was a precious child: this hieroglyph—*(He starts to roll up his sleeve.)* 30

MARCELINE: *(jumping to her feet)* —in the shape of a spatula, on your right arm?

FIGARO: How do you know what it is? 35

MARCELINE: Dear God! It's him!

FIGARO: Yes, it's me.

BARTHOLO: *(to Marceline)* Who? Him!

MARCELINE: *(excitedly)* It's Emmanuel!

BARTHOLO: *(to Figaro)* Were you stolen by gypsies? 40

FIGARO: *(excitedly)* Right near a chateau. My good Doctor, if you can return me to my family, you can name your price—piles of gold won't make my illustrious parents bat an eyelash. 45

BARTHOLO: *(indicating Marceline)* There's your mother.

FIGARO: ...Nurse?

BARTHOLO: Your own mother.

THE COUNT: His mother! 50

FIGARO: Explain...?

MARCELINE: *(indicating Bartholo)* That's your father.

FIGARO: *(crushed)* O-o-oh! My...god.......!

MARCELINE: Surely nature must have told you so a thousand times? 55

FIGARO: Not once.

THE COUNT: *(aside)* His mother!

BRID'OISON: Obviously he's not going to marry her. 60

BARTHOLO: Nor will I.

MARCELINE: Nor will you! And your son? You swore to me—

BARTHOLO: I wasn't in my right mind. If all such incidents were binding, we'd be forced to marry everyone. 65

BRID'OISON: And if we all examined things as closely as this, no one would marry anybody.

BARTHOLO: The shame, revealed for all to see! A deplorable youth. 70

MARCELINE: *(getting angrier by degrees)* Oh, yes, deplorable, and more so than you think! I don't deny my mistakes; they've been revealed all too clearly today. Oh, but how hard it is to expiate them after living modestly for thirty years! I was 75 born to behave well, and I started doing so the minute I was allowed to use my reason. But while still in her years of illusion, of inexperience and need, when she's besieged by seducers, and threatened by poverty, how can a child resist such 80 a horde of enemies? Among those who judge us so harshly now, there are men who, in their own lives, have ruined ten unfortunate girls themselves!

FIGARO: The guiltier they are, the less willing they are to forgive—that's the rule. 85

MARCELINE: *(heatedly)* Worse than ungrateful, you men blacken the toys of your passions, your victims, with contempt! It's you who should be punished for the errors of our youth; you and your magistrates, so proud of your right to judge us—you, who through 90 criminal negligence have left us without any honest way to make a living. Is there even a single profession available for ruined girls? They once had a natural right to the whole field of women's apparel; but no, a thousand workers of the opposite sex are now 95 being trained for that job!

FIGARO: *(angrily)* They're even forcing soldiers to do their own embroidery!

MARCELINE: *(on a roll)* Even in the highest ranks of society, we receive nothing from you but the 100 most patronizing attention; we are lured, by an apparent respect, into an actual servitude; we're treated like children when it comes to our property, but punished as adults for our faults! Ah! In all these ways, your behaviour toward us is either 105 horrible, or pathetic.

FIGARO: She's right!

THE COUNT: *(aside)* Much too right!

BRID'OISON: My God, is she right!

MARCELINE: But what can we do, my son, we vic- 110 tims of an unjust man? Forget where you've come from—look where you're going instead: that's all that matters for anyone. In a few months, your fiancée will be legally dependent on nobody; she'll accept you, take my word for it. Live, then, between a wife 115 and a tender mother who'll vie with one another in loving you. Be indulgent to them, and happy for yourself, my son; be cheerful, giving, and good to everyone, and your mother will lack for nothing.

FIGARO: Your words are golden, mother, and I agree. 120 What dolts we are—it's true. The world's been turning for millions of years, and in all that ocean of time, where I by chance picked up a measly, fleeting thirty years, I must go on tormenting myself about who it is I owe them to? Too bad for them, if people 125 want to torment themselves—to spend our lives squabbling like that is to be yanking forever against an iron yoke, like those miserable horses that draw up-river, who never rest, even when they stop, who're always pulling, even when they're standing 130 still. Let's look ahead.

THE COUNT: What an idiotic outcome.

BRID'OISON: *(to Figaro)*: What about your nob-b-bility, and that chateau? You've been obstructing justice! 135

FIGARO: Well, justice was about to make me do something pretty stupid! I almost knocked Monsieur senseless for a miserable hundred crowns, and now he turns out to be my father! But since Heaven has saved my virtue from these evils, 140 please, father, accept my apologies. And you, mother, embrace me—as maternally as you can.

(Marceline throws her arms around him.)

SCENE 17

Suzanne, Antonio, Bartholo, Figaro, Marceline, Brid'oison, The Count

SUZANNE: *(running in, a purse in her hand)* Monseigneur, wait; stop the marriage: I can pay Madame—with the dowry my mistress gave me.

THE COUNT: *(aside)* The devil take your mistress. It seems everything's conspiring.... *(He leaves.)* 5

SCENE 18

Bartholo, Antonio, Suzanne, Figaro, Marceline, Brid'oison

ANTONIO: *(seeing Figaro embrace his mother, addressing Suzanne)* Oh, sure, pay! Take a look at this.

SUZANNE: *(turning away)* I've seen enough: uncle, let's go.

FIGARO: *(stopping her)* No, please. What do you see? 5

SUZANNE: My stupidity and your depravity.

FIGARO: As little of one as the other.

SUZANNE: *(angrily)* And that you're marrying her by choice, since you're caressing her. 10

FIGARO: *(laughingly)* I'm caressing her, but I'm not marrying her. *(Suzanne tries to leave but Figaro stops her.)*

SUZANNE: *(giving him a slap)* How dare you try to stop me—the nerve of you! 15

FIGARO: *(to all assembled)* Is that love, or what? Before you go, I beg you—take a good look at this dear woman.

SUZANNE: I see her.

FIGARO: And she looks...? 20

SUZANNE: Hideous.

FIGARO: And *vive la jalousie!*[28] She's not holding back.

MARCELINE: *(arms wide open)* Kiss your mother, my pretty little Suzanne. That monster who's 25 tormenting you is my son.

SUZANNE: *(running to her)* You, his mother! *(They stay in each other's arms.)*

ANTONIO: Has this just happened?

FIGARO: —knowing about it, yes. 30

MARCELINE: *(exalted)* No; my heart, drawn inexorably to him, was only mistaken in its motive; it was blood that spoke to me.

FIGARO: And it was good sense, Mother, that instinctively told me to refuse you; because I 35 certainly didn't hate you; this contract is proof—

MARCELINE: *(handing him the paper)* It's yours: take back your note; it's your dowry.

SUZANNE: *(tossing him the purse)* And this too.

FIGARO: Many thanks. 40

MARCELINE: Unhappy as a girl, I was about to become the most miserable of women, and here I am, the most fortunate of mothers! Kiss me, my two children; I unite in you all my affection. As happy as I could ever be—ah! my children, how I 45 will love you!

---

28 *vive la jalousie*] long live jealousy.

FIGARO: *(touched, vivaciously)* Stop, dear Mother, stop it! Do you want to see my eyes dissolve in water, drown in the first tears they've ever shed? At least they're tears of joy. But what a dunce I 50 am—I was nearly ashamed of them! I felt them seeping through my fingers—look *(he shows his spread fingers)*, and I was holding them back! Shame, get you gone! I want to laugh and cry all at once: you don't get to feel twice what I'm feeling 55 now. *(He kisses his mother to one side of him, then Suzanne to the other.)*

MARCELINE: Oh, my darling!

SUZANNE: My dearest darling!

BRID'OISON: *(wiping his eyes with a handkerchief)* 60 Well, I guess I'm a dunce then too.

FIGARO: Sorrow, I defy you now! Try to get me, if you dare, between these two beloved women!

ANTONIO: *(to Figaro)* Spare us the slobbering, will you? When there's a marriage in the family, the 65 parents are supposed to go first, you know. Will yours join hands?

BARTHOLO: My hand will sooner wither and fall off than be joined to the mother of a dolt like him!

ANTONIO: *(to Bartholo)* So you're only an 70 illegitimate father? *(To Figaro)* In that case, Romeo, nothing's settled.

SUZANNE: Ah! Uncle—!

ANTONIO: I'm supposed to give my sister's child to the son of nobody? 75

BRID'OISON: How's that possible, you imbecile? Everyone's the child of somebody.

ANTONIO: Fooey! He'll never have her! *(He goes out.)*

SCENE 19

Bartholo, Suzanne, Figaro, Marceline, Brid'oison.

BARTHOLO: *(to Figaro)* Try finding someone to adopt you. *(He starts to go.)*

MARCELINE: *(running and throwing her arms around him and bringing him back)* Hold it, Doctor; don't go. 5

FIGARO: *(aside)* It seems that every numbskull in Andalusia has been unleashed to block my marriage.

SUZANNE: *(to Bartholo)* Dear little papa, he's your son. 10

MARCELINE: *(to Bartholo)*: In brains, in talent, and in looks.

FIGARO: *(to Bartholo)* And who hasn't cost you a dime.

BARTHOLO: And the hundred crowns he took from me? 15

MARCELINE: *(caressing him)* We'll take such good care of you, Papa!

SUZANNE: *(caressing him)* We'll love you so much, sweet Papa! 20

BARTHOLO: *(giving in)* Papa! Good papa! Sweet papa! Look, now I'm an even bigger dunce than Monsieur *(indicating Brid'oison)*. I'm letting myself go like a child. *(Marceline and Suzanne kiss him.)* Oh! no! I haven't said yes. *(He recollects himself.)* 25 What's happened to Monseigneur?

FIGARO: We'd better run and catch him, and get a commitment out of him. If we let him plot another intrigue, we'll have to start all over again.

ALL TOGETHER: Run, run, run, run. *(They drag* 30 *Bartholo off.)*

SCENE 20

Brid'oison

BRID'OISON: "An even b-bigger d-d-dunce than Monsieur!" That's the kind of thing one can say about oneself, but... They're not very polite around here.... *(He goes out.)*

ACT IV

A large, brightly-lit gallery with candelabras and chandeliers, flowers and garlands—in other words, all prepared for a big party. Downstage left, a table with an écritoire,[29] *and an armchair behind it.*

SCENE 1

Figaro, Suzanne

FIGARO: *(his arms around Suzanne)* So, my love, are you happy? That silver-tongued mother of mine has converted her doctor! He's going to marry her despite his reluctance, and your ass of an uncle has been bridled, too; there's only Monseigneur who's 5

---

29 écritoire] writing case.

still raging, because after all, our marriage will follow hard on the heels of theirs. What perfect results.

SUZANNE: Have you ever heard of anything so bizarre?

FIGARO: You mean anything so delightful? All we 10 wanted was to squeeze one dowry out of His Excellency; here we are with two in our hands, neither of which is from him. A crazed rival was hounding you; I was tormented by a fury; and both of them have been changed into the most 15 devoted of mothers. Yesterday, I was all alone in the world, and here I am, with both my parents— true, they're not as magnificent as I'd portrayed them, but they're good enough for us, who aren't fooled by riches. 20

SUZANNE: And yet, not a single thing that you'd planned for, that you arranged, actually happened.

FIGARO: Chance did a better job than we did, my little one! So goes the world: you work, you plan, you arrange for this and that—and luck accom- 25 plishes something else entirely. From the ravenous conqueror, who tries to swallow the earth, right down to the peaceful blindman who lets himself be led by his dog, we're all but playthings in the hands of chance—although the blindman's prob- 30 ably better led and less often cheated by his dog than an ambition-blinded leader is by his advisors. As for that adorable blindman we call Love... *(He wraps his arms tenderly around her once more.)*

SUZANNE: Ah! he's the only one who interests me! 35

FIGARO: Allow me, then, in assuming the function of folly, to be the good guide dog who'll lead Love to your darling door; and there we'll stay lodged for life.

SUZANNE: What, just you and little Cupid? 40

FIGARO: Cupid and me.

SUZANNE: And you won't go looking for other lodgings?

FIGARO: If you ever catch me, may a thousand million seducers— 45

SUZANNE: Don't overdo it: just tell the honest truth.

FIGARO: My truest truth!

SUZANNE: You naughty boy—is there more than one kind? 50

FIGARO: Of course! Once we realised that time

turns follies into wisdom eventually, and that even pathetic little lies, rooted in barely anything, can grow glorious truths in the end, we've had thousands of kinds. There are the truths we know, 55 though we dare not speak them—for not all truths are fit to be told; there are those we extol, even though we doubt them—for not all truths deserve our belief. There are oaths of passion, and threats of mothers; the drunkard's vow, the politician's 60 promise, the merchant's final offer—there's no end to them. But as for truth of the highest kind— there's only my love for Suzanne.

SUZANNE: I love your joy, because it's so insane; it tells me you're happy. But let's talk about this 65 rendezvous with the Count.

FIGARO: Rather, let's never talk about it; it almost cost me Suzanne.

SUZANNE: You no longer want to do it?

FIGARO: If you love me, Suzanne, your word of 70 honour on this; just let him squirm there by himself; that'll be his punishment.

SUZANNE: Compared to what it cost me to agree, it'll be easy to decline: so that's the end of it.

FIGARO: Your highest truth? 75

SUZANNE: Unlike all you clever people, I've only got one.

FIGARO: So you'll love me a little?

SUZANNE: A lot.

FIGARO: That's not very much. 80

SUZANNE: Why not?

FIGARO: Because when it comes to love, even too much isn't enough.

SUZANNE: Your subtleties are lost on me; but my husband will get all the love that I have. 85

FIGARO: Keep your word and you'll be a beautiful exception to the rule. *(He goes to kiss her.)*

SCENE 2

The Countess, Figaro, Suzanne

THE COUNTESS: Ah! Just as I thought: wherever they are, you can bet they're together. Come on now, Figaro; you're cheating the future, your marriage and yourself by stealing these moments together now. They're waiting for you, and getting 5 impatient.

FIGARO: You're right, Madame; I'm forgetting myself. I'd better offer them my excuse.... *(He tries to take Suzanne with him.)*

THE COUNTESS: *(holding her back)* She'll follow 10 in a minute.

SCENE 3

Suzanne, The Countess

THE COUNTESS: Do you have everything we need to exchange clothes?

SUZANNE: We don't need anything, Madame; the rendezvous is cancelled.

THE COUNTESS: Ah? You've changed your mind? 5

SUZANNE: It's Figaro.

THE COUNTESS: You're lying to me.

SUZANNE: Goodness gracious!

THE COUNTESS: Figaro's not one to let a dowry slip through his fingers. 10

SUZANNE: Madame! What are you suggesting!

THE COUNTESS: That you're in league with Count and regret having confided his plans in me. I can read you like a book. Leave me. *(She goes to leave.)* 15

SUZANNE: *(throwing herself on her knees)* Merciful god in Heaven! You've no idea, Madame, how much you wrong your Suzanne! After all your boundless kindness and the dowry you've given me...! 20

THE COUNTESS: *(lifting her back up)* Ah, me...I don't know what I'm saying! Let me have your place in the garden, and you won't have to go, my dear; you'll keep your word to your husband and help me to regain mine. 25

SUZANNE: How you hurt me!

THE COUNTESS: It's only because I'm not thinking straight. *(She kisses her on the brow.)* Where's your rendezvous?

SUZANNE: *(kisses her hand)* All I got was the word 30 garden.

THE COUNTESS: *(indicating the table)* Take that pen, and we'll choose a spot.

SUZANNE: Write to him!

THE COUNTESS: You must. 35

SUZANNE: Madame! At least if you—

THE COUNTESS: I'll take responsibility for

everything. *(Suzanne sits down; the Countess dictates.)* "A new song, to the tune of...How lovely it will be tonight, beneath the chestnut-trees...How lovely it will be tonight..." 40

SUZANNE: *(writes)* "How lovely it will be tonight..." What next?

THE COUNTESS: You don't think he'll understand? 45

SUZANNE: *(reading it over)* It's good. *(She folds the letter.)* How do we seal it?

THE COUNTESS: A pin, hurry! It'll do for the answer, too. Write on the back: "Return the cachet."30 50

SUZANNE: *(laughing as she writes)* Ha! "...the cachet." This seal's even more fun than the one on Chérubin's commission, Madame.

THE COUNTESS: *(with a painful memory)* Ah!

SUZANNE: *(searching on herself)* I don't have a pin at the moment. 55

THE COUNTESS: *(undoing her dressing gown)* Take this one. *(The page's ribbon falls from her bodice.)* Ah! My ribbon!

SUZANNE: *(picking it up)* It's the one that little thief stole! You had the cruelty—? 60

THE COUNTESS: Could I have left it on his arm? That would have been lovely. Give it back!

SUZANNE: Madame, you can't wear this anymore—it's stained with that young man's blood! 65

THE COUNTESS: *(taking it back)* Perfect for Fanchette. The first bouquet she brings me—

SCENE 4

A young shepherdess, Chérubin dressed as a girl, Fanchette with lots of young girls dressed as she is, all holding bouquets; The Countess, Suzanne

FANCHETTE: Madame, the girls from town have come to give you flowers.

THE COUNTESS: *(quickly hiding her ribbon)* Aren't they charming: forgive me, dear girls, for not knowing you all personally. *(Referring to Chérubin.)* And who is this lovely child, who seems so shy? 5

A SHEPHERDESS: One of my cousins, Madame, who's just here for the wedding.

THE COUNTESS: She's very pretty. Since I won't be able to carry all twenty bouquets, let's honour the visitor. *(She takes Chérubin's bouquet and kisses him on the forehead.)* She's blushing! *(To Suzanne.)* Suzanne, doesn't she... remind you of someone? 10

SUZANNE: Amazing resemblance!

CHÉRUBIN: *(aside, his hands on his heart)* Ah! That kiss—so close, and yet.....! 15

SCENE 5

The young girls, Chérubin in the midst of them, Fanchette, Antonio, The Count, The Countess, Suzanne

ANTONIO: I'm telling you, Monseigneur, he's here; they dressed him in my daughter's room; all his clothes are still there, and here's his officer's hat, which I pulled from the pile. *(He wades into the pack of young girls, recognizes Chérubin, and lifts off his woman's hat, allowing his long "cadenette"31 tresses to fall. He puts the soldier's hat on his head and says:)* Yessirree by golly—there's your officer! 5

THE COUNTESS: Oh, heavens!

SUZANNE: The little brat! 10

ANTONIO: Didn't I say up there that it was him?

THE COUNT: *(angrily)* Well, Madame?

THE COUNTESS: Well, Monsieur, I'm even more surprised than you, and, I might add, just as angry.

THE COUNT: Yes; but earlier, this morning? 15

THE COUNTESS: I would be guilty, indeed, if I were to pretend any longer. He came down to my rooms. We hit upon the prank that these children have just carried out; you surprised us as we were dressing him—but your first response is always so 20 hot! He saved himself; I was flustered; and the general panic took care of the rest.

---

30 cachet] literally, the seal, but the word also has satirical resonance insofar as the "lettre de cachet" was a loathed symbol of the arbitrary tyanny of the French monarchy. Such letters, sometimes pre-signed by the King and left otherwise blank, could be used by government officials to arrest and imprison anyone on the spot without recourse to law.

31 *cadenette*] long strands of hair on either side of the head; a style worn by soldiers in the infantry, named after Honoré d'Albert de Cadenet.

THE COUNT: (greatly frustrated, to Chérubin) Why haven't you left?

CHÉRUBIN: (hastily removing his hat) Mon- 25
seigneur—

THE COUNT: I will punish you for this disobedience.

FANCHETTE: (innocently) Ah, Monseigneur, listen
to me. You know how, whenever you come to kiss 30
me, you always say, "if you'll love me little
Fanchette, I'll give you anything you want"?

THE COUNT: (blushing) Me? I said that?

FANCHETTE: Yes, Monseigneur. Instead of
punishing Chérubin, give him to me in marriage, 35
and I'll love you like crazy.

THE COUNT: (aside) To be hexed by a page!

THE COUNTESS: Well, Monsieur, it's your turn.
The child's confession, as naïve as mine, reveals
two truths: that whenever I'm the cause of your 40
grief, it's always inadvertently, whereas you go out
of your way to increase and justify mine.

ANTONIO: You too, Monseigneur? Man, I'll have
to straighten her out, just like I did her late mother
who's dead...She may just be talking nonsense now; 45
but as Madame knows, little girls, when they grow
big—

THE COUNT: (disconcerted, aside) There's an evil
spirit that's turning everything against me!

SCENE 6

*Figaro, the young girls, Chérubin, Antonio, The
Count, The Countess, Suzanne*

FIGARO: Monseigneur, if you keep these girls any
longer, we won't be able to start the festivities, or
the dance.

THE COUNT: You, dance? I don't think so—after
your fall this morning, when you sprained your 5
right foot!

FIGARO: (wiggling his leg) It still hurts a bit, but not
too bad. (To the girls) Let's go, my beauties, come on.

THE COUNT: (turning him around) You certainly
were lucky that those flowerbeds had just been 10
covered in nice soft compost.

FIGARO: Very lucky, indeed; otherwise—

ANTONIO: (turning him around) And he stayed
scrunched in half, all the way to the bottom.

FIGARO: I suppose a more skilful person would 15
have stayed up in the air... (To the girls.) Are you
coming, girls?

ANTONIO: (turning him back around) And all this
time, the little page was galloping off on his horse
to Seville? 20

FIGARO: Galloping, cantering, who knows...

THE COUNT: (facing him) And you had his
commission in your pocket?

FIGARO: (a little surprised) Absolutely; but why the
inquest? (To the girls.) Let's go, young ladies! 25

ANTONIO: (taking Chérubin by the arm) Well,
here's someone who says that my future nephew
is nothing but a liar.

FIGARO: (surprised) Chérubin!... (Aside.) Damn that
little snot! 30

ANTONIO: You get it now?

FIGARO: (looking about) I get it... I get it... So,
what's he chirping about?

THE COUNT: (sharply) Oh, he's not chirping; he
simply says he's the one who jumped into the 35
peonies.

FIGARO: (dreamily) Ah! If he says so... he may be
right. I won't argue over what I don't know.

THE COUNT: You mean that both you and he?...

FIGARO: Why not? Maybe the urge to jump is 40
contagious—witness, for example, Panurge's
sheep;[32] and when you're angry, believe me,
anyone would rather risk—

THE COUNT: What, the two of them at once...!?

FIGARO: There could have been two dozen; but 45
what difference does it make, Monseigneur, since
nobody was hurt? (To the girls.) Aw, come on—
are you coming or not?

THE COUNT: (infuriated) Are we acting in a
comedy here? (A fanfare is heard striking up.) 50

FIGARO: That's the signal for the march. To your
places, my beauties, to your places! Here we go,
Suzanne, give me your arm. (They all run off;
Chérubin stays behind, head bowed.)

---

32 Panurge's sheep] a famous episode from the Renaissance
novelist François Rabelais (1494?–c.1553), in which the
crafty Jack-of-all-trades Panurge, a rather Figaro-like character, causes a whole shipload of sheep to leap into the sea,
one after another, by throwing one ram overboard.

SCENE 7

Chérubin, The Count, The Countess

THE COUNT: *(watching Figaro leave)* Have you ever seen such audacity? *(To the page.)* As for you, mister sneaky, who pretends to be ashamed, go and get changed this instant, and don't let me catch sight of you again this evening. 5

THE COUNTESS: He'll be awfully bored.

CHÉRUBIN: *(stupid with happiness)* Bored! I carry on my brow sufficient joy to last me a hundred years in prison. *(He puts on his hat and runs out.)*

SCENE 8

The Count, The Countess, vigorously fanning herself

THE COUNT: Why?—what's he got on his brow?

THE COUNTESS: *(embarrassed)* His...first officer's hat, no doubt; children dote on the silliest things. *(She goes to leave.)*

THE COUNT: You're not staying, Countess? 5

THE COUNTESS: You know I'm not feeling well.

THE COUNT: Surely a moment, for your protégé, or I'll think you're angry.

THE COUNTESS: Here come the two wedding parties; let's sit, then, and receive them. 10

THE COUNT: *(aside)* The wedding! One must endure what one cannot prevent. *(The Count and the Countess sit to one side of the gallery.)*

SCENE 9

The Count, the Countess, sitting; "Les folies d'Espagne"33 is played as a march.

THE PROCESSION: GAME-KEEPERS, guns on their shoulder; BAILIFF, JUDGES, BRID'OISON; PEASANTS, in festive dress; TWO YOUNG GIRLS carrying the bridal wreath with white feathers; TWO OTHERS, carrying the white veil; ANOTHER TWO, carrying gloves and the bridal bouquet; ANTONIO takes SUZANNE by the hand, as he is the one giving her to FIGARO. MORE YOUNG GIRLS carry another bridal

wreath, another veil, another white bouquet, similar to the first, for MARCELINE. FIGARO gives his hand to MARCELINE, to give her to the DOCTOR, who is bringing up the rear and wearing a large spray of flowers. The young girls, as they pass before THE COUNT, give his valets all the trimmings destined for SUZANNE and MARCELINE. THE PEASANTS, having formed two lines, dance one reprise of the fandango, accompanied by castanets. Then an introduction to the duet is played, while ANTONIO leads SUZANNE to THE COUNT; she kneels before him. While THE COUNT adorns her with the wreath, veil and bouquet, TWO YOUNG GIRLS sing the following duet:

> Pretty bride, sing the goodness and the glory
> Of a master who's renounced his right;
> Choosing pleasure of the noblest victory,
> He delivers you to your husband, chaste and pure
> and clad in white.

SUZANNE is on her knees and, during the last lines of the duet, she tugs on THE COUNT'S sleeve and shows him the note that she's holding; then she brings her downstage hand to her head, where THE COUNT pretends to adjust her wreath; she passes the note to him. THE COUNT slips it into his vest; the song comes to an end; the bride stands and curtsies deeply. FIGARO comes to receive her from the hands of THE COUNT, and withdraws to the other side of the room, next to MARCELINE. Meanwhile, the guests dance another reprise of the fandango. THE COUNT, anxious to read the note, moves downstage and takes it out; but in doing so, he stabs his finger with the pin that seals it; he shakes it, presses it, sucks it and, looking at the paper with its pin, he says, as the orchestra plays quietly underneath:

THE COUNT: Devil take these women, who stick pins everywhere! *(He throws the pin to the ground, reads the note and kisses it.)* 5

FIGARO: *(who has seen all this, says to his mother and to Suzanne)* I bet it's a love note that one of the girls slipped into his hand in passing. It was sealed 10 with a pin and gave him a nasty prick.

The dance begins again. THE COUNT, who has read the note, turns it over and he sees the invitation to return the seal in response. He searches for it on the ground and, finally finding it, pins it to his sleeve.

---

33 "Folies d'Espagne"] title of a dance tune, in three-quarter time, accompanied by castanets.

FIGARO: *(to Suzanne and Marceline)* From a loved one, everything is precious. Look, he's picked up the pin. Oh what a peculiar man!

Meanwhile, SUZANNE and THE COUNTESS are exchanging signals. The dance ends; the duet begins again. FIGARO leads MARCELINE to THE COUNT, the same way Suzanne had been led to him; just as THE COUNT takes up the wreath, during the opening bars of the duet, the action is interrupted by the following cries:

BAILIFF: *(shouting out the door)* Halt, messieurs! You can't all come in.... Guards! Guards! *(The guards run to the door.)*   15

THE COUNT: *(rising)* What is it?

BAILIFF: Monseigneur, it's Monsieur Bazile, surrounded by an entire village, because he's walking along....*singing.*   20

THE COUNT: Let him come in, alone.

THE COUNTESS: Allow me to withdraw.

THE COUNT: I won't forget your kindness.[34]

THE COUNTESS: Suzanne? She'll be right back.   25
    (Aside, to Suzanne.) Let's go and switch clothes. *(She goes out with Suzanne.)*

MARCELINE: He only comes here to spoil things.

FIGARO: Ah, I think you'll be surprised this time.

SCENE 10

Bazile, with his guitar, Grippe-Soleil, and all the previous characters, except The Countess and Suzanne

BAZILE: *(enters singing)*
    Sensitive and faithful hearts,
    Who blame capricious Love,
    Cease complaining of his darts—
    Is it a crime to change our mind?
    If Cupid comes equipped with wings,   5
    Are they not meant for flying blind?
    Are they not meant for flying blind?
    Are they not meant for flying blind?

FIGARO: *(approaching him)* Yes, that's exactly why he has wings on his back. My friend, what do you mean by this music?   10

---

34 kindness] for remaining for the ceremony against her will.

BAZILE: *(indicating Grippe-Soleil)* Having shown my respect for Monsiegneur by amusing this gentleman, who is part of his retinue, I may now in turn demand his justice.   15

GRIPPE-SOLEIL: Bah, sir, he ain't amused me at all with those lousy tunes!

THE COUNT: What do you want, then, Bazile?

BAZILE: That which belongs to me, Monseigneur, the hand of Marceline; and I've come to oppose—   20

FIGARO: *(approaching him)* Has it been long since Monsieur saw the face of a fool?

BAZILE: Monsieur, I'm looking at one now.

FIGARO: Since my eyes are serving you so well as a mirror, study there the effect of the following promise: if you so much as go near this woman—   25

BARTHOLO: *(laughing)* But why? Let him speak.

BRID'OISON: *(stepping between them)* N-n-ow, now, must two friends—

FIGARO: Us, friends!   30

BAZILE: That's a good one!

FIGARO: *(quickly)* Because he writes boring church music?

BAZILE: *(quickly)* And he writes poetry like a reporter?   35

FIGARO: *(quickly)* A saloon musician!

BAZILE: *(quickly)* A broadsheet spy!

FIGARO: *(quickly)* Opera grub!

BAZILE: *(quickly)* Diplomatic stableboy!

THE COUNT: *(sitting)* You're both insolent.   40

BAZILE: He insults me on every occasion.

FIGARO: I wish that was actually possible.

BAZILE: Telling everyone that I'm nothing but a fool.

FIGARO: You want me to be your echo?   45

BAZILE: Whereas I've never had a single student whose talent I didn't make *gleam.*

FIGARO: You mean scream.

BAZILE: There he goes again!

FIGARO: And why not, if it's true? Are you some Prince, on whom we must fawn? Accept the truth, scoundrel; you haven't the money to buy yourself a liar. Or, if you fear it from us, why have you come to ruin the wedding?   50

BAZILE: *(to Marceline)* Did you promise me, yes or no, that if, in four years, you weren't provided for, you'd consider me?   55

MARCELINE: On what condition did I promise that?

BAZILE: That if you recovered a certain lost son, I'd kindly agree to adopt him. 60

EVERYONE: He's found.

BAZILE: The offer holds.

EVERYONE: (indicating Figaro) And there he is!

BAZILE: (recoiling in horror) I've seen the devil! 65

BRID'OISON: (to Bazile) And y-y-you'll relinquish his dear mother?

BAZILE: What could be more horrifying than being taken for that loser's father?

FIGARO: —being taken for his son! No contest. 70

BAZILE: (indicating Figaro) Since Monsieur here is now a factor, I hereby declare that I no longer am! (He goes out.)

SCENE 11

All the previous characters, except Bazile

BARTHOLO: (laughing) Ha! Ha! Ha!

FIGARO: (jumping for joy) So in the end I *will* get my wife!

THE COUNT: (aside) And me, my mistress. (He stands.) 5

BRID'OISON: (to Marceline) And e-e-everybody's happy.

THE COUNT: Let both contracts be drawn up; I'll sign them.

EVERYONE: *Vivat!* (The ensemble goes out) 10

THE COUNT: I need an hour's rest. (He goes to leave along with the others.)

SCENE 12

Grippe-Soleil, Figaro, Marceline, The Count

GRIPPE-SOLEIL: (to Figaro) And I'm going to go help set up the fireworks under the big chestnut-trees, as I was told.

THE COUNT: (running back in) What fool told you to do that? 5

FIGARO: How's that wrong?

THE COUNT: (hotly) And the Countess, who's not feeling well, how's she supposed to see the fireworks? They should be on the terrace, facing her rooms. 10

FIGARO: Hear that, Grippe-Soleil? The terrace.

THE COUNT: Under the big chestnut-trees— ridiculous idea! (As he leaves, aside.) They nearly set fire to my rendezvous.

SCENE 13

Figaro, Marceline

FIGARO: How incredibly considerate of him. (He starts to leave.)

MARCELINE: (stopping him) A word or two, my son. I want to come clean with you. Led by a misguided suspicion, I've been unjust toward your 5 charming wife: I imagined her to be in league with the Count, even though Bazile told me that she always discouraged him.

FIGARO: You don't know much about your son if you think I'm rattled by these feminine impulses. 10 I defy the most cunning among you to deceive me.

MARCELINE: That's a wonderful attitude, my son, because jealousy—

FIGARO: —is but the foolish child of pride. That, 15 or the disease of a madman. Oh, on that point, Mother, I have a philosophy that's...imperturbable; and if Suzanne does deceive me one day, I forgive her in advance; she'll have been working on it for a long time...(He turns and sees Fanchette, who's 20 checking out both sides of the room.)

SCENE 14

Fanchette, Figaro, Marceline

FIGARO: Oh, ho!... My little cousin's eavesdropping on us.

FANCHETTE: Oh, not that, no; they say it's unethical.

FIGARO: That's true; but since it's also useful, we 5 often ignore the one for the sake of the other.

FANCHETTE: I was looking for someone.

FIGARO: Counterfeiting already, you little scamp! You know perfectly well he can't be here.

FANCHETTE: Who? 10

FIGARO: Chérubin.

FANCHETTE: I'm not looking for *him*; I know exactly where he is. It's my cousin Suzanne.

FIGARO: And what does my little cousin want with her? 15

FANCHETTE: I guess I can tell you, little cousin. It's...just a pin I want to give back to her.

FIGARO: (*agitated*) A pin? A pin?...And where'd you get it, you rascal? At your age, you're already employed as—(*He calms himself and speaks* 20 *gently.*)—you already do such a good job in everything you take on, Fanchette; and my pretty little cousin is so obliging—

FANCHETTE: What are you so angry about? I'm going. 25

FIGARO: (*stopping her*) No, no, I'm just kidding. Look, your little pin is the one that Monseigneur told you to give back to Suzanne, the one she used to seal a little note to him—you see, I'm perfectly well informed. 30

FANCHETTE: Then why did you ask, if you know all about it?

FIGARO: (*stalling*) Because it's just so much fun to learn how Monseigneur came to give you the job.

FANCHETTE: (*naively*) Exactly as you said: "Here, 35 little Fanchette, take this pin to your pretty cousin, and just say it's the seal for the big chestnut-trees."

FIGARO: The big?...

FANCHETTE: Chestnut-trees. It's true that he also added, "Make sure no one sees you." 40

FIGARO: You must obey, little cousin: fortunately, no one has seen you. Carry out your orders nicely, and don't say any more to Suzanne than Monseigneur told you to.

FANCHETTE: And why would I do that? Cousin, 45 you must think I'm a child! (*She goes out, hopping and skipping.*)

SCENE 15

Figaro, Marceline

FIGARO: Well, mother?

MARCELINE: Well, my son?

FIGARO: (*as if suffocating*) As for this....! There are in fact some things....

MARCELINE: "There are some things"? Well? Such 5 as...?

FIGARO: (*hands on his chest*) Mother, I just heard something—it's weighing on me, here, like lead.

MARCELINE: (*laughing*) So that heart that was so full of assurance was just an inflated balloon? A 10 single pin has burst it!

FIGARO: (*enraged*) But this pin, Mother, is the one he picked up!

MARCELINE: (*recalling what he'd said*) "Jealousy! Oh! on that point, Mother, I have a philosophy 15 that's imperturbable; and if one day Suzanne does deceive me, I forgive her—"

FIGARO: Oh, Mother, we speak from our feelings: when forced to speak in his own defence, even the iciest judge will misinterpret the law. Now I under- 20 stand why he threw such a fit over those fireworks! As for that cutie with her precious little pins, things are not going to turn out as planned, Mother, with her chestnut-trees. I may be married enough to have a right to be angry, but I'm still single enough to 25 abandon her yet and marry somebody else—

MARCELINE: Brilliant! Ruin everything for a suspicion. Tell me: what makes you so sure that she's tricking you and not the Count? Shouldn't you discuss the matter again with her, before you 30 condemn her out of hand? Do you really know that she's actually going to be there under the trees? Or what her intentions are, if she does go? What she'll say to him? What she'll do? I thought you had better judgement than that! 35

FIGARO: (*kissing her hands reverently*) She's right, my mother, she's right—right, right, always right. But, mom, you've got to make *some* allowance for human nature: in the end you're always glad you did. But we will investigate before we accuse or do 40 anything. I know where this rendezvous is. Mother—goodbye. (*He leaves*)

SCENE 16

Marceline, alone

MARCELINE: Good-bye. And I know where it is too. Now that I've stopped him, I'd better watch out for Suzanne—or rather, warn her. She's such a lovely creature. Ah! When vested interest doesn't turn us against each other, we're always so busy 5 supporting the other members of our poor oppressed sex against this fierce, this terrible— (*laughing*)—and ultimately a bit silly, race of men!

ACT V

*A chestnut grove, in a park; two pavilions, gazebos, or
summer houses, are to the right and left; upstage is an
ornamented clearing, with a lawn chair downstage.
The stage is dark.*

SCENE 1

FANCHETTE: *(alone, holding in one hand two
biscuits and an orange, in the other a lit paper
lantern)* The pavilion on the left, he said. That's
this one. If he doesn't come soon, my supporting
part—Those mean people in the kitchen—they   5
wouldn't give me anything but an orange and two
biscuits! "Who's this for, Mademoiselle?—Well,
Monsieur, it's for someone—Oh, sure, we know."
And what if it was? Just because Monseigneur
wishes not to see him, that doesn't mean he has   10
to starve to death! But even so it still cost me a
big fat kiss on the cheek! But who knows, maybe
he'll pay me back for it. *(She sees Figaro who has
just spotted her; she cries out.)* Ah!... *(She runs off,
into the pavilion on the left.)*   15

SCENE 2

*Figaro, with a big cape over his shoulders and a large
hat hiding his face. Bazile, Antonio, Bartholo,
Brid'oison, Grippe-Soleil; an ensemble of valets and
workmen.*

FIGARO: *(alone at first)* It's Fanchette! *(He inspects
the others as they arrive, and says, in a fierce, stand-
offish tone)* Good day, gentlemen; good evening.
Are you all here?

BAZILE: Everyone that you asked to come.   5

FIGARO: Roughly what time is it?

ANTONIO: *(looking up)* The moon should be up.

BARTHOLO: Hey, what shady plots are hatching?
He looks like a conspirator!

FIGARO: *(agitated)* Am I right that you've all come   10
to the chateau for the wedding?

BRID'OISON: We c-c-certainly did.

ANTONIO: We're going down there, in the park,
to wait for the festivities to start.

FIGARO: You need go no further, Messieurs; it's   15
right here under these chestnut-trees that we'll be

celebrating the honest woman I'm about to marry
and the chivalrous lord who's earmarked her for
himself.

BAZILE: *(thinking back on the day)* Ah! I know   20
exactly what this is. Believe me, we shouldn't be
here; it's about a rendezvous. Come, I'll explain it
to you over here.

BRID'OISON: *(to Figaro)* W-w-we'll be back.

FIGARO: When you hear me call, run back quickly,   25
all of you; and if I don't show you something
sensational, you can call me a liar.

BARTHOLO: Just remember, a wise man doesn't
meddle in the affairs of the great.

FIGARO: I'll remember.   30

BARTHOLO: Their position alone stacks the deck
against us, every time.

FIGARO: Oh no, you're forgetting their shrewdness.
But remember too, that the man who is known to be
timorous is at the mercy of every last scoundrel.   35

BARTHOLO: Very good!

FIGARO: And that, through the honoured blood-
line of my mother, I bear the name of Verte-Allure.

BARTHOLO: He's in the grip of the devil.

BRID'OISON: H-h-he sure is.   40

BAZILE: *(aside)* The Count and his Suzanne have
arranged things without me? Fine, this offensive
doesn't bother me one bit.

FIGARO: *(to the valets)* And as for you, you miscre-
ants, remember my orders: I want everything   45
around me lit up—and I swear that if I catch one
of you slacking... *(He grabs Grippe-Soleil's arm,
threateningly.)*

GRIPPE-SOLEIL: *(runs away crying and wailing)*
A—a—o—oh! Damned brute!   50

BAZILE: *(leaving)* May Heaven give you joy,
Monsieur bridegroom! *(They all leave.)*

SCENE 3

*Figaro, alone, walks about in the dark, speaking in the
most sombre tone.*

FIGARO: Oh, woman! woman! woman! what a
feeble and deceitful creature!...There isn't an animal
in all creation that acts contrary to its instinct—is
yours to cheat? After obstinately *refusing* when I
begged her in front of Madame; and then, at the   5

very moment when she said "I do," right in the middle of the ceremony...! He laughed when he read her note, the cad! And so did I, like an imbecile. No, Monsieur the Count, you will not have her...you will not have her. Just because you're a great Seigneur, you think you're a great genius. Nobility, fortune, rank and title—they make you so proud. But what have you done to deserve these goodies? You went to the trouble of being born, that's all; otherwise, you're a completely ordinary man. Whereas I—goddammit!—lost in the faceless crowd, I've had to employ more science and mathematics, merely to survive, than have been used to govern all of Spain for the last hundred years! And you think you can joust with me! Someone's coming—it's her—no, it's no one. The night is black as the devil, and here I am, already plying the ridiculous trade of a husband, even though I'm only half-married! *(He sits on a bench.)* Has there ever been anything more bizarre than my destiny? Born as the son of I-don't-know-who, stolen by bandits and raised in their ways, I grow disgusted and want to follow an honest profession—but in every direction, my way is blocked! I learn chemistry, pharmacology, and surgery—all of which, even with the help of a powerful patron, was barely enough to get me a veterinarian's licence![35] Tired of tormenting sick animals, and wanting to do quite the reverse, I throw myself, body and soul, into the theatre. I might as well have tied a stone around my neck! I slap together a comedy about life in a harem; as a Spanish writer, I figure I can lampoon Mahomet with impunity:[36] straightaway there's an envoy, from who-knows-where, complaining that my verses have offended the Ottoman Empire, Persia, a good part of India, all of Egypt, plus the kingdoms of Barca, Tripoli, Tunis, Algeria and Morocco: and there goes my play, up in smoke, just to please the Muslim princes, not one of whom, as far as I can tell, can even read, and all of whom slap us black-and-blue on the backs while calling us "dogs of Christians!" To make myself feel better, but mostly to make some money, I try my hand at composing a play about the destruction of the pagan cults of the Bards and Druids. I assure myself that no envoy is going to show up from these nations, which no longer exist, and that this time my play will get past the diplomats, the actors will act it, and I'll get paid a ninth of the receipts.[37] But I failed to see the venom lurking in this play, too: the analogies that could be drawn between the errors of a "false cult" and the revealed truths of a genuine religion. A Church official in a white linen collar understood it all much better than I did; I'm denounced for impiety and my play is banned at its third performance by the local Bishop.[38] If you can't humble human wit, you can always get your revenge by abusing it. My cheeks grew gaunt, my rent came due: from afar I saw the dreaded bailiff approaching, his pen sticking out of his wig like a pin in a pincushion. Trembling, I applied myself. A controversy arose over the nature of wealth; and, as it's not necessary to possess a thing in order to discuss it, I, without a penny to my name, write a book about the value and net result of money. At once, carriage-doors fly open to receive me, and I'm taken straight to prison,[39] at the gates of which I'm forced to abandon all my liberty and hope. I was, however, very well taken care of there: I got room and board for six months without ever receiving a bill, a great boon to me at the time. Looking on the bright side, I'd have to say that this economical rest-cure was the single greatest profit that literature ever brought me. *(He*

---

35 veterinarian's licence] lit., veterinarian's lancet.
36 lampoon ... with impunity] The Muslim Moors ruled Spain until the Renaissance, and many Moorish influences remained.
37 ninth of the receipts] Unlike the London theatres at this time, which paid authors mainly through benefit nights, the Comédie-Française of Paris divided profits from all performances among company members.
38 A short but complex passage follows here, having to do with the financial outcome of the withdrawn play: Figaro ends up owing the theatre money!
39 prison] In an earlier (uncensored) version, Beaumarchais actually named the Bastille, which is the prison evoked here; he himself spent some months in the For-l'Évêque prison in 1783, the year before the play's premiere.

stands up.) Oh, these power-brokers, so casual about the suffering they inflict, how I'd love to get my hands on one of them after a good disgrace has brought him down a notch! I'd point out...that annoying books only become a problem when you try to stop their circulation; that without the freedom to criticize, there's no real flattery in praise; and that it's only little men who fear a little writing. *(He sits back down.)* And then one day, tired of feeding an unknown hanger-on, they toss me into the street; and since one must eat, even out of prison, I sharpen my pen once more, and ask about the latest news. I'm told that, during my money-saving retreat, a free-market system had been established in Madrid for all consumer products, including those of the press; and that as long as I didn't write about the authorities, religion, politics, morals, people in high places, powerful corporations, the Opera, any other form of entertainment, or anyone affiliated with anything, I could freely publish whatever I wanted—subject to the approval of two or three censors. To take advantage of this sweet liberty, I announce a new magazine; and to ensure that none of the others feel their toes have been stepped on, I call it *The Useless Journal.* Phee-ew! A thousand wretched scribbling devils rise up against me; I'm shut down and out of work again. Despair was taking hold— when suddenly I was recommended for a position! Unfortunately, I was perfect for it: they needed someone to work out complex figures, so they hired a dancer. Stealing was all that was left; so I served as a banker for gamblers;[40] well, my friends, I dine out on the town, am graciously invited into the houses of all the most fashionable people, who of course keep three quarters of the profits for themselves. I might have risen quite high; I even began to understand that to get ahead, it's not *what* you know but *who* you know that counts. But since I was surrounded by crooked thieves who insisted that I remain honest, I was destined to sink once again. This time, I said goodbye to the world for good; and twenty fathoms of water would have separated me from it forever, had not a beneficent god pulled me back to my original calling. So I dust off my barber's kit and take up my English strop once again. Leaving the smoke to the fools who've a taste for it, and abandoning, as too heavy for a pedestrian, the shame of the mainstream, I go shaving from town to town, finally living carefree. A great lord stops by Seville; he recognizes me, I get him married; and to reward me for helping him to win his wife, he now tries to intercept mine! A subject for a storm and stress play.[41] And just as I'm ready to plunge into the abyss by marrying my mother, my parents materialize, one after the other. *(He gets up, hot and bothered.)* Everyone disagrees—it's you, it's him, it's me, no—not us; well, who is it then? *(He falls back into the seat.)* Oh, what a bizarre chain of events! Why has this happened to me? Why these things and not others? Who saddled me with all this? Forced to travel a road on which I set out unknowingly, just as I will depart it reluctantly, I've strewn it with as many flowers as my cheerfulness would permit. Mind you, I say "my cheerfulness" without knowing whether it's any more mine than the rest of it, nor even what this "me" is that I'm talking about: a random assortment of un-discovered talents? Or a stunted, idiotic fool? A frisky little animal? A young man eager for enjoyment and hungry for pleasure, a jack-of-all trades, just to survive—a master here, a valet there, according to the will of fate. Ambitious from vanity, industrious by necessity, but lazy—with relish! Orator when I have to, poet for recreation, musician on occasion, lover in demented out-bursts, I've seen it all, done it all, spent it all. And now, the fantasy is destroyed—to be so badly disillusioned.....Disillusioned! Suzanne, Suzanne, Suzanne! Oh how you torment me! ... I hear footsteps—someone's coming. Now comes the climax. *(He withdraws to the first set of wings, downstage right.)*

40 gamblers] lit., Faro, a card-game of pure chance played for money.

41 storm and stress play] lit., "intrigue, orage à ce sujet," but seemingly a reference to the hot new genre of *Sturm und Drang* (storm and stress) then sweeping Europe. See Schiller's *The Robbers* in this volume.

SCENE 4

*Figaro; The Countess dressed in Suzanne's clothes;
Suzanne wearing those of The Countess; Marceline*

SUZANNE: *(softly, to the Countess)* Yes, Marceline
  told me that Figaro would be here.
MARCELINE: And there he is; lower your voice.
SUZANNE: So, one of them is eavesdropping, the
  other's coming to find me. Here we go....   5
MARCELINE: I don't want to miss a word; I'll hide
  in the pavilion. *(She goes into the pavilion where
  Fanchette is hiding.)*

SCENE 5

Figaro, The Countess, Suzanne

SUZANNE: *(out loud)* Madame is shivering. Are you
  cold?
THE COUNTESS: *(out loud)* The night air is damp;
  I'm going to retire.
SUZANNE: *(out loud)* If Madame doesn't need me,   5
  I think I'll take the air for a while under these trees.
THE COUNTESS: *(out loud)* You'll catch cold out
  here.
SUZANNE: *(out loud)* I'm used to it.
FIGARO: *(aside)* Oh, you'll catch it all right!   10
  *(Suzanne withdraws to the wings stage left, opposite
  Figaro.)*

SCENE 6

*Chérubin, The Count, Figaro [hiding], The Countess,
Suzanne [hiding]*

CHÉRUBIN: *(wearing an officer's uniform, arrives
  singing gaily the refrain of his romance)* La, la, la, etc.
      Oh, my godmother
      Whom I've always adored.
THE COUNTESS: *(aside)* The little page!   5
CHÉRUBIN: *(stopping)* Someone's walking around
  here; I'd better get to my hideout quickly, where
  little Fanchette is... It's a woman!
THE COUNTESS: *(aside)* Oh my god!
CHÉRUBIN: *(crouching down, trying to see from afar)*   10
  Am I mistaken? All I can see in this darkness is
  the hair, with feathers in it, but I think it's
  Suzanne.

THE COUNTESS: *(aside)* What if the Count came
  now....!   15

(The Count arrives upstage.)

CHÉRUBIN: *(approaching and taking the hand of the
  Countess, who recoils)* Yes, it's that charming girl we
  call Suzanne. Ah! Could I ever mistake the softness
  of this hand, that little shiver that comes over it,
  or the beating of my heart? *(He tries to press the*   20
  back of the Countess's hand; she pulls away.)
THE COUNTESS: *(under her breath)* Go away!
CHÉRUBIN: Has pity brought you directly to the
  very part of the garden where I've been hiding for
  so long?   25
THE COUNTESS: Figaro's on his way.
THE COUNT: *(advancing, aside)* Isn't that Suzanne?
CHÉRUBIN: *(to The Countess)* I'm not afraid of
  Figaro at all, because that's not who you're waiting
  for.   30
THE COUNTESS: Oh really? Then who?
THE COUNT: *(aside)* She's with someone.
CHÉRUBIN: It's Monseigneur, you devil, who asked
  you for a rendezvous when I was behind the
  armchair this morning.   35
THE COUNT: *(aside, furiously)* It's that infernal
  page again!
FIGARO: *(aside)* And they say it's wrong to
  eavesdrop!
SUZANNE: *(aside)* The little tattletale.   40
THE COUNTESS: *(to the page)* Please; do me a
  favour and leave.
CHÉRUBIN: Not without receiving my reward for
  such obedience.
THE COUNTESS: *(terrified)* You want—?   45
CHÉRUBIN: *(passionately)* First, twenty kisses on
  your behalf, and then a hundred for your beautiful
  mistress.
THE COUNTESS: You dare?!
CHÉRUBIN: Oh yes, of course I dare. You're taking   50
  her place in the rendezvous with Monseigneur, just
  as I'm taking the Count's place here with you; and
  Figaro's the biggest sucker of all!
FIGARO: *(aside)* The brute!
SUZANNE: *(aside)* Cocky as a pageboy.   55

*(Chérubin tries to kiss The Countess; The Count steps
between them and receives the kiss.)*

THE COUNTESS: *(moving away)* Oh, heaven!

FIGARO: *(aside, having heard the kiss)* Nice girl I'm marrying! *(He listens.)*

CHÉRUBIN: *(feeling The Count's coat, aside)* It's Monseigneur! *(He flees into the pavilion where Fanchette and Marceline are hiding.)* 60

SCENE 7

Figaro, The Count, The Countess, Suzanne

FIGARO: *(approaching)*: I'm going to—

THE COUNT: *(thinking he's talking to the page)* Since you won't give me another kiss— *(He gives him a slap on the face.)*

FIGARO *(who is close enough, receives it)*: Ah! 5

THE COUNT: —that'll pay you for the first one.

FIGARO: *(aside, moving away and rubbing his cheek)* So eavesdropping isn't always that rewarding....

SUZANNE: *(laughs out loud, from the other side of the stage)* Ha! Ha! Ha! Ha! 10

THE COUNT: *(to The Countess, who he takes for Suzanne)* Who can understand that page? He gets the severest blow to the face, and he bursts out laughing.

FIGARO: *(aside)* If only he were feeling this one!... 15

THE COUNT: Strange! I can't seem to take a single step without....*(To The Countess.)* But let's forget that silliness; it'll only spoil my pleasure in finding you here in this grove.

THE COUNTESS: *(imitating Suzanne's voice)* 20 Weren't you expecting to?

THE COUNT: Thanks to your ingenious note! *(He takes her hand.)* You're trembling?

THE COUNTESS: I was frightened.

THE COUNT: Here: so that you're not deprived of 25 the kiss I intercepted..... *(He kisses her on the forehead.)*

THE COUNTESS: What liberties!

FIGARO: *(aside)* Hussy!

SUZANNE: *(aside)* Charming! 30

THE COUNT: *(taking his wife's hand)* What lovely soft skin; if only the Countess had such beautiful hands!

THE COUNTESS *(aside)*: Amazing what prejudice can accomplish! 35

THE COUNT: Does she have such firm and shapely arms? Such pretty fingers, so full of grace and mischief?

THE COUNTESS: *(in Suzanne's voice)* What about love....? 40

THE COUNT: Love...is only a romantic novel; the true story.....is pleasure. It's what brings me to your knees.

THE COUNTESS: You don't love her anymore?

THE COUNT: I love her very much; but three years 45 of marriage makes lovemaking so respectable!

THE COUNTESS: What *would* you desire from her?

THE COUNT: *(caressing her)* Just what I find in you, beautiful... 50

THE COUNTESS: But say what it is.

THE COUNT: I don't know—less predictability maybe, more spice in her behaviour, a certain something that breeds charm; an occasional refusal—who knows? Our wives believe they've 55 done all that's required when they love us—which is to say: once they love us (if they love us!), they just love us, period; and they become so kind, so consistently obliging, all the time and without exception, that one fine day, to our surprise, we 60 find only satiety where we'd looked again for happiness.

THE COUNTESS *(aside)*: Ah! How instructive!

THE COUNT: Truth is, Suzanne, I've often thought that if we do look elsewhere for the pleasure that 65 eludes us with them, it's because they don't apply themselves to the art of preserving our appetite, of renewing their lovemaking, of rekindling, so to speak, the pleasure of possessing them by adding variety. 70

THE COUNTESS: *(piqued)* So it's all their responsibility?...

THE COUNT: *(laughing)* And not the man's? You think you can change the course of nature? Our job is to win them, theirs.... 75

THE COUNTESS: Yes, theirs...?

THE COUNT: Is to keep us—all too easy to forget.

THE COUNTESS: Not by me it won't.

THE COUNT: Nor me.

FIGARO: *(aside)* Nor me. 80

SUZANNE: *(aside)* Nor me.

THE COUNT: *(taking his wife's hand)* There seems

to be an echo around here; let's speak lower. You don't have to worry about that—you, whom love has made so alive, so pretty! One drop of caprice and you could be the most bedevilling mistress! *(He kisses her on the brow.)* My Suzanne, as a Castilian I gave you my word. Here's all the gold I promised, with which I hereby buy back my renounced right to the delicious moment you're granting me. But since the favour you're bestowing on me is priceless, I add this diamond; I hope you'll wear it for love of me.

THE COUNTESS: *(curtseying)* Suzanne accepts it all.

FIGARO: *(aside)* It doesn't get any sluttier than that.

SUZANNE: *(aside)* More goodies for us.

THE COUNT: *(aside)* She's compromised now; all the better.

THE COUNTESS: *(looking upstage)* I see torches.

THE COUNT: The preparations for your wedding. Shall we go into one of these pavilions for a minute, and let them pass?

THE COUNTESS: Without a light?

THE COUNT: *(leading her gently)* What for? We're not going to be reading.

FIGARO: *(aside)* My God, she's going in! Just as I thought! *(He comes forward.)*

THE COUNT: *(raising his voice and turning around)* Who goes there?

FIGARO: *(angrily)* Going? I'm coming straight for you!

THE COUNT: *(under his breath, to the Countess)* It's Figaro!... *(He runs off.)*

THE COUNTESS: I'll follow you. *(She goes into the pavilion on the right, while the Count disappears into the woods upstage.)*

SCENE 8

Figaro, Suzanne, in the dark

FIGARO: *(trying to see where the Count and Countess went, taking the latter for Suzanne)* Now I don't hear anything; they've gone in, and here am I. *(With an altered tone.)* All you inept husbands, who hire expensive spies and spend whole months brooding over a suspicion without certain proof, you should follow my example. From day one I follow my wife

and listen carefully; before you know it, you're absolutely sure. It's wonderful—no more doubts; you know where you stand. *(Pacing vigorously.)* Luckily, I'm not too upset by it; no, her treachery means nothing to me. And at last, I've got them!

SUZANNE: *(who has come quietly out of the dark; aside)* You're going to pay for those beautiful suspicions. *(Taking on the voice of the Countess.)* Who goes there?

FIGARO: *(extravagantly)* "Who goes there?" Oh, only someone who wishes he'd been stifled at birth by the plague!

SUZANNE: *(in the Countess's voice)* Why, but it's Figaro!

FIGARO: Madame Countess!

SUZANNE: Not so loud.

FIGARO: *(fast)* Ah! Madame, heaven brought you with perfect timing. Where do you think Monseigneur is?

SUZANNE: Not that I care about the ingrate. Tell me—

FIGARO: *(faster)* And Suzanne, my bride—where do you think she is?

SUZANNE: Keep your voice down!

FIGARO: *(faster still)* This Suzanne, who's supposed to be so virtuous, who acted so demurely—they're together in there. I'm going to call them—

SUZANNE: *(puts her hand over his mouth, but forgets to disguise her voice)* No, don't call them!

FIGARO: *(aside)* It's Suzanne! God-*damn*!

SUZANNE: *(in the Countess's voice)* You seem nervous.

FIGARO: *(aside)* The traitor! Out to get me!

SUZANNE: We must avenge ourselves, Figaro.

FIGARO: Is this something you feel a keen desire to do?

SUZANNE: I'd hardly be a woman if I didn't! But men have hundreds more methods available to them.

FIGARO: *(confidingly)* Madame, there's no one else around. The women's method...beats all others.

SUZANNE: *(aside)* Oh, I'm going to smack him!

FIGARO: *(aside)* Wouldn't it be fun, before the wedding, if—?

SUZANNE: But that kind of vengeance is useless if it's not seasoned with a little love.

FIGARO: If you fail to detect it in anything, you must believe that my regard for you is merely concealed. 55

SUZANNE: *(piqued)* I don't know if you really mean that, but you don't say it with a very good grace.

FIGARO: *(with comic zeal, on his knees)* Oh, Madame, I adore you. Consider the hour, the 60 place, the circumstances, and let your spite supply me with those favours that eluded my prayers.

SUZANNE: *(aside)* My hand is itching.

FIGARO: *(aside)* My heart is racing.

SUZANNE: But Monsieur, have you imagined—? 65

FIGARO: Yes, Madame, yes; I have imagined.

SUZANNE: —that in anger and in love—

FIGARO: —deferral is death. Your hand, Madame?

SUZANNE: *(in her own voice, smacking his face)* There! 70

FIGARO: Ow! *Demonio!* What a smack!

SUZANNE: *(hitting him again)* What a smack? And this?

FIGARO: Ow! What the devil is this—some slapping festival? 75

SUZANNE: *(hitting him with every phase)* Ow? What is this? Suzanne? Here's for your suspicions; here's for your revenge and your treason; for your methods, your insults and your schemes! You call that love? Oh, tell it to me like you did this 80 morning!

FIGARO: *(laughing and getting up)* Santa Barbara! Yes, that's love for you. Oh, happiness! Oh, bliss! Oh, a hundred times happy Figaro! Beat me, my best-beloved, and never stop. But after you've 85 covered my entire body in bruises, look kindly, Suzanne, on the luckiest man to have ever been beaten by a woman.

SUZANNE: "The luckiest!" You total brat, your luck didn't prevent you from pouring forth such a 90 stream of lying babble to seduce the Countess that, truly forgetting myself, I gave in on her behalf.

FIGARO: Could I possibly mistake the sound of your lovely voice?

SUZANNE: *(laughing)* You recognized me? Oh! 95 You'll pay for that!

FIGARO: Isn't that just so female—to give a good thrashing and *still* hold a grudge. But tell me, by what good fortune do I find you here, when I thought you were with him; and how this outfit, 100 which really fooled me and which proves that you were innocent—

SUZANNE: Ha! It's you who's innocent, to come and walk right into a trap set for somebody else! Is it our fault that we set out to muzzle one fox 105 and ended up trapping two?

FIGARO: Then who got the other?

SUZANNE: His wife.

FIGARO: His wife?

SUZANNE: His wife. 110

FIGARO: *(wildly)* Oh, Figaro, you die! You never guessed that one! His wife? Oh these witty, these hundred, thousand times witty females! So, the kisses under the trees?

SUZANNE: Went to Madame. 115

FIGARO: And the page's?

SUZANNE: *(laughing)* To Monsieur.

FIGARO: And earlier, behind the armchair?

SUZANNE: To nobody.

FIGARO: Are you sure? 120

SUZANNE: *(laughing)* Watch it Figaro—it's raining blows.

FIGARO: *(kissing her hand)* And they're delivered by jewels. But the one from the Count—that was no joke. 125

SUZANNE: Come on, you narcissist, humble yourself.

FIGARO: *(doing each thing he says)* Fair is fair; on my knees, head bent, prostrate, navel to the ground.

SUZANNE: *(laughing)* Ah, the poor Count! What 130 trouble he's gone to—

FIGARO: *(getting back onto his knees)* —to seduce his own wife!

SCENE 9

The Count, enters from upstage and heads straight for the pavilion on the right; Figaro, Suzanne

THE COUNT: *(to himself)* I've looked for her everywhere in the woods; maybe she went in here.

SUZANNE: *(whispering to Figaro)* It's him.

THE COUNT: *(opening the door)* Suzanne, are you in there? 5

FIGARO: *(whispering)* He's looking for her, and I believe—

SUZANNE: That he didn't recognize her.

FIGARO: Let's finish him off; you want to? *(He kisses her hand.)*   10

THE COUNT: *(turning around)* A man at the Countess's feet!...Ah! I'm unarmed. *(He comes forward.)*

FIGARO: *(standing up quickly and disguising his voice)* Forgive me, Madame; I didn't realize that our   15
regular meeting-place was to be used for a wedding party tonight.

THE COUNT: *(aside)* It's the man from her closet this morning! *(He slaps his forehead.)*

FIGARO: *(continuing)* But it shall not be said that   20
we allowed such a trivial obstacle to hinder our pleasures.

THE COUNT: *(aside)* Slaughter, death, hell!

FIGARO: *(leading her toward the pavilion; whispering)* He's swearing. *(Out loud.)* Shall we then   25
hasten, Madame, and correct the injury done to us earlier, when I jumped from your window?

THE COUNT: *(aside)* Ah, ha! Discovered at last.

SUZANNE: *(near the pavilion on the left)* Before you come, make sure nobody's followed us. *(He kisses   30
her brow.)*

THE COUNT: *(crying out)* Vengeance! *(Suzanne flies into the pavilion, where Fanchette, Marceline and Chérubin are hiding.)*

SCENE 10

The Count, Figaro, the Count grabbing Figaro by the arm.

FIGARO: *(pretending to be terrified)* It's my master.

THE COUNT: *(recognizing him)* Ah! It's you, you degenerate! Ho there! Somebody! Anybody!

SCENE 11

Pédrille, The Count, Figaro

PÉDRILLE: *(in his riding boots)* Oh, Monseigneur, there you are—finally!

THE COUNT: Good, Pédrille. Are you alone?

PÉDRILLE: Rode my horse into the ground all the way from Seville.   5

THE COUNT: Get over here and holler as loud as you can.

PÉDRILLE: *(hollering at the top of his lungs)* No more sign of the page there than in my hand; here's his commission.   10

THE COUNT: *(pushing him away)* You stupid idiot!

PÉDRILLE: Monseigneur told me to holler.

THE COUNT: For help. Ho there, somebody! Whoever can hear me, come running!

PÉDRILLE: Figaro and me, we're both here; what   15
could happen to you?

SCENE 12

The previous characters, Brid'oison, Bartholo, Bazile, Antonio, Grippe-Soleil, all the wedding guests run on with torches.

BARTHOLO: *(to Figaro)* See? At your very first signal—

THE COUNT: *(pointing to the pavilion on the left)* Pédrille, grab that door. *(Pédrille does so.)*

BAZILE: *(whispering, to Figaro)* Did you catch him   5
with Suzanne?

THE COUNT: *(pointing to Figaro)* And now, vassals, I want you to surround this man for me, and answer for him with your lives.

BAZILE: Ha! Ha!   10

THE COUNT: *(furious)* Keep quiet! *(To Figaro in a frosty tone.)* Now, my cavalier, will you answer my questions?

FIGARO: *(icily)* Hm! How could I refuse, Monseigneur? You command everyone here—except   15
yourself.

THE COUNT: *(containing himself)* Except myself!

ANTONIO: What a way to talk.

THE COUNT: *(venting his anger again)* Oh, if anything could make me more enraged, it's that   20
phoney air of calm he adopts!

FIGARO: Are we soldiers, who kill and get killed for reasons we don't understand? Me, I like to know what's going on before I get angry.

THE COUNT: *(beside himself)* Oh, fury! *(Containing himself.)* A righteous man, feigning innocence!   25
Will you at least do us the favour of telling us who it was you just led into that pavilion?

FIGARO: *(indicating the other one, maliciously)* Which, this one?   30

THE COUNT: *(fast)* No, this one!

FIGARO: *(cooly)* Ah, that's different...a certain young lady who honours me with certain favours.

BAZILE: *(surprised)* Ah, ha!

THE COUNT: You hear that, gentlemen? 35

BARTHOLO: *(surprised)* We hear it!

THE COUNT: *(to Figaro)* And this young lady: does she have any other involvements that you might know of?

FIGARO: *(coldly)* I know that a great seigneur was 40 interested in her once; but either because he neglected her or because I please her better than the more desirable one, she did me the honour, today, of giving me preference.

THE COUNT: *(hotly)* Prefere—! *(He controls* 45 *himself.)* At least he's too simple to lie. Because I swear to you gentlemen that what he just confessed to, I heard from the mouth of his accomplice herself!

BRID'OISON: *(stupefied)* H-h-his accomplice! 50

THE COUNT: *(in a fury)* When a dishonour is public, so too must be the revenge. *(He goes into the pavilion.)*

SCENE 13

The previous characters, except The Count

ANTONIO: It's only fair.

BRID'OISON: *(to Figaro)* W-w-who did he say got the wife of "the other one"?

FIGARO: *(laughing)* Neither one had the pleasure.

SCENE 14

The previous characters, The Count, Chérubin

THE COUNT: *(inside the pavilion, dragging someone out whom we don't yet see)* All your efforts are wasted; you are lost, Madame, and your hour has finally come! *(He comes out, without looking behind him.)* Thank god that at least this loathsome 5 marriage hasn't yet produced any—

FIGARO: *(crying out)* Chérubin!

THE COUNT: My page?

BAZILE: Ha! Ha!

THE COUNT: *(beside himself, aside)* Always—this 10 diabolical page! *(To Chérubin.)* What were you doing in there?

CHÉRUBIN: *(cringing)* I was hiding, as you instructed me to.

PÉDRILLE: Great! And I almost knackered my horse 15 for him!

THE COUNT: Go in there, Antonio; and bring before her judge this vile traitor by whom I'm dishonoured

BRID'OISON: Are you referring to Madame? 20

ANTONIO: By jiminy, there's a god in heaven after all! You've done so much of that around here yourself—

THE COUNT: *(furious)* Get in there! *(Antonio goes in.)* 25

SCENE 15

The previous actors, except Antonio

THE COUNT: You will see, Messieurs, that the page was not alone in there.

CHÉRUBIN: *(bashfully)* My fate would have been too cruel, had some kind soul not been there to soothe the pain. 5

SCENE 16

The previous actors, Antonio, Fanchette

ANTONIO: *(dragging someone by the arm whom we don't yet see)* Come along, Madame; we all know you're in here so you don't have to make us beg.

FIGARO: *(crying out)* The little cousin!

BAZILE: Ha! Ha! 5

THE COUNT: Fanchette!

ANTONIO: *(turning around, cries out)* Ah! Jesus-blood, Monseigneur, that was nice of you—choosing me to make public that it's my daughter who's to blame for this pile-up! 10

THE COUNT: *(outraged)* How did I know she was in there? *(He starts to go in.)*

BARTHOLO: *(steps in front of him)* Allow me, Monsieur Count; things aren't getting any clearer. But I, for one, am cool and collected...*(He goes in.)* 15

BRID'OISON: Again, I'm c-c-completely confused...

SCENE 17

The previous actors, Marceline

BARTHOLO: *(speaking from inside, as he comes out)* Have no fear, Madame, we will do you no harm, or I will answer for it personally. *(He turns around and cries out.)* Marceline!

BAZILE: Ha! Ha! 5

FIGARO: *(laughing)* Hee hee, what lunacy! My mother's in on it?

ANTONIO: It's like a "Who's Worse" competition!

THE COUNT: *(outraged)* What does that matter to me? The Countess— 10

SCENE 18

The previous actors, Suzanne, her face covered with her fan

THE COUNT: —Ah, and here she comes. *(He violently takes her by the arm.)* What, Messieurs, do you think such odiousness deserves? *(Suzanne throws herself on her knees, lowering her head.)* No, no! *(Figaro throws himself on his knees on the other side. Louder:)* No, no! *(Marceline throws herself on her knees in front of him. Louder still:)* No, no! *(All the others fall to their knees, except Brid'oison. Beside himself:)* There could be a hundred of you! No! 5

SCENE 19 (FINAL)

All the previous actors; The Countess, emerging from the other pavilion.

THE COUNTESS: *(falling to her knees)* Here's one more, at least.

THE COUNT: *(looking at the Countess and Suzanne)* Ah! What am I seeing?

BRID'OISON: *(laughing)* Hee hee—it's Madame, by golly! 5

THE COUNT: *(trying to get the Countess to stand)* What—it was you, Countess? *(With a suppliant's tone.)* Nothing but the most generous pardon—

THE COUNTESS: *(laughing)* In my place, you'd say "No, no!"; but I—for the third time today!—I grant it to you unconditionally. *(She rises.)* 10

SUZANNE: *(rising)* So do I.

MARCELINE: *(rising)* So do I.

FIGARO: *(rising)* So do I—I think there's an echo in here. *(The others all rise.)* 15

THE COUNT: An echo! I was trying to hoodwink them; and they've manipulated me like a child!

THE COUNTESS: *(laughing)* Be glad we did, Monsieur. 20

FIGARO: *(brushing off his knees with his hat)* All in a day's work for an ambassador-in-training!

THE COUNT: *(to Suzanne)* But that note, sealed with the pin?...

SUZANNE: Madame dictated it. 25

THE COUNT: Then the response is surely due to her. *(He kisses the Countess's hand.)*

THE COUNTESS: To everyone, what belongs to them. *(She gives the purse to Figaro and the diamond to Suzanne.)* 30

SUZANNE: *(to Figaro)* Another dowry.

FIGARO: *(smacking the purse with his hand)* Number three—and a tough one to pull off, too.

SUZANNE: Just like our marriage.

GRIPPE-SOLEIL: And the bride's wedding-garter— can I have it? 35

THE COUNTESS: *(pulling out the ribbon she's been hiding in her bodice and preparing to throw it)* The garter? It's here in her dress; there! *(The boys all try to catch it.)* 40

CHÉRUBIN: *(most alert, succeeds)* Anyone who wants this will have to fight me for it!

THE COUNT: *(laughing, to the page)* I'm surprised that such an over-sensitive gentleman as yourself found it so funny to be given a certain slap in the face. 45

CHÉRUBIN: *(flinching and half-drawing his sword)* In my face, you say?

FIGARO: *(with comic mock anger)* But it was on my cheek that he got slapped; isn't that just the way the mighty dispense their justice! 50

THE COUNT: *(laughing)* On your cheek! Ha ha ha—what do you say to that, my beloved Countess?

THE COUNTESS: *(absorbed elsewhere, she returns to herself and says, sensitively)* Ah! Yes, my beloved Count, and for life, without let or hindrance, I swear. 55

THE COUNT: *(slapping the judge on the shoulder)* And you, Don Brid'oison—your opinion now? 60

BRID'OISON: Ab-b-bout everything, Monsieur?...
On my life, as for me, I would have to......agree.
That's my thinking.

ALL THE OTHERS: Well judged!

FIGARO: When I was poor, they ignored me; when 65
I showed some spirit, their hate followed quickly
behind. Now, with a lovely wife and some
money—

BARTHOLO: *(laughing)* Whole mobs of people will
clutch you to their hearts. 70

FIGARO: You think so?

BARTHOLO: Oh, I know them.

FIGARO: *(saluting the audience)* Well, my wife and
my fortune aside, I'll be delighted and honoured
to make them my guests. *(The introduction to the* 75
vaudeville starts to play.[42]*)*

---

42 The play is followed by a musical number, called a vaudeville, sung in rhymed verse by the central characters, and
then danced by the whole company. Vaudevilles, usually
sung to well-known tunes, were associated with the
popular fairground theatres of Paris.

FRIEDRICH SCHILLER

The Robbers

The Robbers is the teenage outburst of an inexperienced 19-year-old medical student, and it shows. The characters are at times laughably implausible, or worse: the sole female in the play convinces us only that Friedrich Schiller (1759–1805), having spent his entire life to that point in a military academy, hadn't yet met any actual women; the "vermin" Spiegelberg, the back-stabbing Judas among Moor's disciples, is a crude cliché from the most hackneyed tradition of German anti-Semitism. The Biblical references are heavy-handed, the Shakespearean borrowings obvious, the plotting clumsy. But Schiller's visceral loathing for the brutality, waste, greed and hypocrisy of his times gives this play a rare and irresistible urgency. Written in 1778, the same year as *The Marriage of Figaro*, *The Robbers* managed to beat Beaumarchais's play to the stage by two years, premiering in Mannheim on January 13, 1782. Like Beaumarchais after *Figaro*'s premiere, Schiller was rewarded for his success with prompt arrest and imprisonment. But unlike Beaumarchais, for whom a play about the French nobility could be conceived as a comedy, Schiller saw the German dukedoms of his day as catastrophically diseased.

This play was one of the most influential works of the *Sturm und Drang* ("storm and stress"), the literary movement that launched Romanticism. Taking its name from F. M. von Klinger's play *Confusion; or, Storm and Stress* (1776), *Sturm und Drang* swept across Europe and into America like rock-and-roll after centuries of classical music, bristling with ferocious energy and radical ideas. Its works drew hysterical sobbing fits from wildly emotional audiences, who made idols out of Schiller and fellow playwright Goethe (1749–1832). Rejecting the rationality and restraint of neoclassical art, *Sturm und Drang* celebrated intense subjectivity, extreme contrasts, untamed nature, and feeling above thought, exulting in visions of rebellion, violence, and suicide. The ruined castle, the hooting owls, the dark dungeon, the haunted forests of Bohemia, the good-and-evil brothers, the last-minute liberation—all the hallmarks of nineteenth-century Romantic and Gothic melodrama are already here in Schiller's first play.

Schiller's band of robbers also epitomizes the outlaw brotherhood that would later flourish in American pop-culture depictions of frontier cowboys and urban gangsters. Whether on the lam from corrupt law-makers, in voluntary exile from a dehumanizing society, or just determined to go out in a blaze of glory, such brooding rebels seek solace in the camaraderie of loyal brothers-in-arms and in the validating love of a charismatic leader. Viewers tend to admire these youthful forest- or canyon-dwelling gunslingers for their idealism, bravery, and defiance of pernicious social conventions—even though, by rejecting the law, these terrorists inevitably become the tyrants they despise. Schiller and Goethe intended their Storm and Stress works as cautionary tales, as warnings against the futility of such naive self-indulgence, but their rebel-heroes earned them fanatical cult followings regardless—as well as moralizing criticism for allegedly inspiring fans to commit copycat crimes and imitative suicides.

A poet, playwright, philosopher, and theatrical theorist, Schiller was also a professor of history at the University of Jena and co-artistic director, with Goethe, of the Weimar Court Theatre during its golden age. Author of a series of outstanding historical plays before his death at 46 of tuberculosis, Schiller is considered, like Shakespeare, his country's national dramatist. He continued to explore the relationship between personal and political freedom throughout his life. And in theoretical works such as *On the Aesthetic Education of Mankind* and "The Stage Considered as a Moral Institution," he argues that the theatre does not just give us a fleeting vision of freedom, as other arts might; rather, because of its unique combination of material and spiritual elements, it can actually make us free.

[J.W.]

FRIEDRICH SCHILLER
The Robbers

Translated by F.J. Lamport[1]

What drugs cure not, iron will cure;
what iron cures not, fire will cure.

HIPPOCRATES

CHARACTERS
COUNT MAXIMILIAN VON MOOR
KARL } his sons
FRANZ }
AMALIA VON EDELREICH, his niece
SPIEGELBERG }
SCHWEITZER }
GRIMM }
RATZMANN } libertines and bandits
SCHUFTERLE }
ROLLER }
SCHWARZ }
KOSINSKY }
HERRMANN, bastard son of a nobleman
DANIEL, Count Moor's servant
PASTOR MOSER
A PRIEST
ROBBERS, and others

*The scene of the action is Germany;
the duration about two years.*

ACT ONE SCENE 1
A room in OLD MOOR'S castle in Franconia.

FRANZ VON MOOR, OLD MOOR.

FRANZ: But are you sure you are well, father? You look so pale.

OLD MOOR: Quite well, my boy; what did you have to tell me?

FRANZ: The post's arrived; a letter from our informant in Leipzig. 5

OLD MOOR: *(eagerly)* News of my son Karl?

FRANZ: H'm, h'm!—Yes, indeed. But I'm afraid— I don't know—whether I should—your health— Father, are you really quite well? 10

OLD MOOR: As fit as a fiddle! Is it about my son, his letter?—why are you so anxious? That's twice you've asked me.

FRANZ: If you're not well—if you've the slightest suspicion that you're not well, then let me—I'll tell 15 you at some more appropriate moment. *(Half aside)* This is no news for a delicate constitution.

---

1 I have modernized the translation slightly, contracting many of Lamport's formal verb constructions and updating the punctuation. [J.W.]

OLD MOOR: God in Heaven, what can it be?

FRANZ: Let me first turn aside and shed a tear of pity for my lost brother—I should hold my peace forever, for he's your son; I should conceal his disgrace forever, for he's my brother. But to obey you is my first, sad duty; and so forgive me. [20]

OLD MOOR: Oh, Karl, Karl! If only you knew how your wild ways torture your old father's heart; if only you knew how a single piece of good news of you would add ten years to my life—would make me young again; while now—ah, every word brings me a step nearer the grave. [25]

FRANZ: If that's so, old man, then goodbye—this very day we'll all be tearing our hair over your coffin. [30]

OLD MOOR: Wait! It's only one single short step more—let him have his will. *(Sitting down)* The sins of the fathers are visited upon the third and the fourth generations—let it be accomplished. [35]

FRANZ: *(taking the letter from his pocket)* You know our informant. Look! I'd give the finger of my right hand to be able to say he was a liar, a black and venomous liar—Be prepared! Forgive me if I don't give you the letter to read for yourself—you shouldn't hear everything at once. [40]

OLD MOOR: Everything, everything—my son, you'll save me the need for crutches.

FRANZ: *(reading)* "Leipzig, May 1st—If it were not that the most solemn promise binds me not to conceal the slightest piece of information I can come by regarding the fate of your brother, then, my dear friend, never should my innocent pen have exercised such tyranny over you. From a hundred of your letters I can tell how news of this kind must pierce a brother's heart like a dagger; it's as if I could see the worthless wretch—" [45] [50]

(OLD MOOR covers his face.)

Father, look! it's only the mildest parts I'm reading—"see the wretch already costing you a thousand bitter tears"—ah, they flowed, they poured streaming down my cheeks in pity—"it's as if I could see your good old father, deathly pale already"—Dear God! and so you are, already, before you've heard anything at all? [55] [60]

OLD MOOR: Go on. Go on.

FRANZ: —"deathly pale already, reeling in his chair, and cursing the day those childish lips first framed the name 'father.' I couldn't find out everything, and of the little that I know it's only a little that I tell. Your brother, it seems, has run the whole gamut of infamy; I at any rate know nothing worse than the things he's done, though his imagination may well surpass the bounds of mine. Last night at midnight he made a grand resolution—since he'd run up debts of forty thousand ducats"—a pretty sum, father—"and as he'd robbed a rich banker's daughter here in town of her honour, and fatally wounded her fiancé, a fine young fellow of good birth, in a duel—to flee with seven others whom he'd depraved like himself, and escape the arm of the law"—father! In heaven's name, father! What's the matter? [65] [70] [75]

OLD MOOR: It's enough. Stop, my son.

FRANZ: I'll spare you—"he's been declared a wanted man, his victims are crying out for satisfaction, a price has been put on his head—the name of Moor"—no! my miserable lips shall never be my father's murderers! *(Tearing up the letter)* Don't believe it, father! Don't believe one syllable he writes! [80] [85]

OLD MOOR: *(weeping bitterly)* My name! my honourable name!

FRANZ: *(throwing his arms round his neck)* Shameful, thrice shameful Karl! Didn't I suspect it, when he was still a boy, and was always following after girls, chasing up hill and down dale with street-urchins and ruffians, shunning the sight of the church as a miscreant shuns the jail, and tossing the pennies he had wheedled from you to the first beggar he met, while we sat at home improving our minds with prayer and with reading pious sermons? Didn't I suspect it, when he would rather read the adventures of Julius Caesar and Alexander the Great and other such benighted heathens than the story of the penitent Tobias?[2] A hundred times I prophesied to you—for my love for him always [90] [95] [100]

---

2 The Book of Tobias: exemplarily righteous, god-fearing Jew who, although poor, gave alms generously and endangered himself by burying the dead against the decrees of the ruling Assyrian King. He was rewarded for his piety with great joy in later life.

kept the limits set by a son's duty to his father—that the boy would one day bring shame and misery on us all! Oh, if only he didn't bear the name of Moor! if only my heart didn't beat so warmly for him! The sinful love for him, that I cannot suppress, will one day bear witness against me before the judgement seat of God.

OLD MOOR: Ah—my hopes, my golden dreams!

FRANZ: I know; that's what I was saying. The fiery spirit that burns in the boy, so you always said, that makes him yearn so keenly for every kind of beauty and grandeur; the frankness that mirrors his soul in his eyes, the tender feeling that melts him to tears of sympathy at any sight of suffering, the manly courage that sends him climbing hundred-year-old oak trees and leaping ditches and fences and foaming rivers; the youthful ambition, the implacable constancy; all these shining virtues that took root in his father's favourite son, one day will make him a friend's true friend, a model citizen, a hero, a great, great man—and now, father, look! the fiery spirit has grown, has burgeoned, has brought forth glorious fruit. See how this frankness has so neatly turned to insolence, see how this tenderness coos for any coquette, so readily yields to the seduction of a Phryne![3] See how this fiery genius has burnt up the oil of its life in six short years, to the last drop, so that to his very face people can say "Voila, c'est l'amour qui a fait ça!"[4] No, just look at this bold imagination, just look at the plans it makes and carries out, so that the heroic deeds of a Cartouche or a Howard[5] pale into insignificance beside them! And only let these magnificent beginnings grow to full maturity—for after all, who can expect perfection at such a tender age? Perhaps, father, you will live to see the glorious day when he's the commander of an army,

---

[3] famous Greek courtesan (fourth century B.C.E.).

[4] "See—it's love that's done that."

[5] Louis-Dominique Cartouche, a feared robber and murderer, came to be admired as a romantic figure. Famous for his "wit and merriment" and the veritable army of followers he inspired, he was finally betrayed, captured, and executed in Paris on November 27, 1721—but not before he informed on all his accomplices.

ensconced in the stillness of the forests, ready to ease the weary wanderer's journey by taking half his burden from him—perhaps before you're laid to rest you'll be able to visit his monument, that he will have erected for him between heaven and earth—perhaps, oh father, father, father—find yourself another name, or shopkeepers and street-urchins will point their fingers at you, for they'll have seen your fine son's portrait at Leipzig fair![6]

OLD MOOR: And you too, my Franz, you too? Oh, my children. How they pierce my heart.

FRANZ: You see, I have my wits about me too; but my wit is the bite of scorpions.—And then that everyday dullard, that cold, wooden Franz, and all the other names that the contrast between the two of us so often prompted, when he sat on your lap or pinched your cheek—one day he'll die within the walls of his own estate, and rot and be forgotten, while the fame of this virtuoso flies from pole to pole—ah! gracious Heaven, see him join his hands in gratitude to you, that dry, cold, wooden Franz—that he's so unlike him!

OLD MOOR: Forgive me, my son; don't be angry with a father whose expectations have been dashed. The God who sends me tears through Karl will wipe them away, my Franz, by your hand.

FRANZ: Yes, father, my hand will wipe them away. Your Franz will make it his life's work to lengthen your days. Your life will be the oracle that I'll consult above all else in all my doings; the glass in which I'll see all things; no duty will be too sacred for me to break it in the service of your precious life. Will you believe me?

OLD MOOR: You bear a heavy burden of duty, my son—God bless you for what you have been and for what you will be to me!

FRANZ: But tell me, now—If you didn't have to call this son your own, would you be a happy man?

OLD MOOR: Oh, still!—when the midwife brought him to me, I lifted him up to Heaven and cried: am I not a happy man?

FRANZ: So you said. And now, do you find it so? You envy the wretchedest of your peasants, that he's not the father of this son—Sorrow will be

---

[6] i.e., on a poster for "Wanted" criminals.

yours as long as you have this son. That grief will grow with Karl. That sorrow will undermine your days. 185

OLD MOOR: Oh! it's made me like a man of fourscore years.

FRANZ: Why, then—if you were to disown this son of yours?

OLD MOOR: *(starting up)* Franz! Franz! What are you saying? 190

FRANZ: Isn't your love for him what brings you all this grief? Without that love, he no longer exists for you. Without this criminal love, this sinful love, he's dead for you—he was never born to you. Not flesh and blood, but the heart makes father and son. Love him no more, and this degenerate is no longer your son, even if he were cut from the flesh of your own body. He was the apple of your eye, but it is written, if thine eye offend thee, pluck it out; it's better for thee to enter into the kingdom of God with one eye, than having two eyes to be cast into hell fire. Better to enter childless into the kingdom of God, than that father and son should both be cast into hell fire. It's the word of God! 195 200 205

OLD MOOR: You want me to curse my son?

FRANZ: Not so, not so! It's not your son that I'd have you curse. What is he that you call your son? he whom you gave his life, while he spares no effort to shorten yours? 210

OLD MOOR: Oh, it's true, it's all too true! it's a judgement on me! The Lord wills it so!

FRANZ: See how the child of your bosom treats its father. Through your father's sympathy he strangles you, murders you through your love, has importuned your father's heart itself to strike the final blow. Once you're no more, he's master of your estates and king of his passions. The dam is broken, and the torrent of his desires can rage freely on. Imagine yourself in his place! How often he must wish them under the earth, his father, his brother, who stand pitiless in the way of his excesses? But is that love for love? Is that filial gratitude for a father's tenderness? When he sacrifices ten years of your life to a moment's lust? when he gambles the good name of his fathers, unspotted for seven centuries, on the pleasure of a fleeting minute? Is that he whom you call your son? Answer! Do you call that a son? 215 220 225

OLD MOOR: An unloving child! oh! but still my child! still my child! 230

FRANZ: A precious, darling child, whose sole pursuit it is, not to know it has a father. Oh, if only you would learn to see it as it is! if only the scales would fall from your eyes! But your indulgence can only confirm him in his depravity, your support give it legitimacy. Yes, indeed, you'll turn aside the curse from his head; on you, father, on you the curse of damnation will fall. 235

OLD MOOR: It's just! it's only just! Mine, mine is all the fault! 240

FRANZ: How many thousands who have drained the cup of pleasure to the dregs have been brought by suffering to see the error of their ways! And doesn't the bodily pain which accompanies every excess bear the fingerprint of the divine will? Should man by cruel mercifulness turn it aside? Should a father let go to eternal damnation what's entrusted to him?—Think, father, if you deliver him up to his misery for a little while, will he not have to mend his ways and learn to be a better man? or will he remain a scoundrel, even in that great school of misery, and then—woe to the father who flouted the decrees of a higher wisdom by his tenderness!—What then, father? 245 250

OLD MOOR: I'll write and say that my hand is turned from him— 255

FRANZ: What you do is just and wise.

OLD MOOR: —that he shall not show his face before me.

FRANZ: It will work to his salvation. 260

OLD MOOR: *(tenderly)* Until he mend his ways!

FRANZ: Very well, very well! But if then he should come with the mask of the hypocrite, should gain your pity by his tears and your forgiveness by his flattery, and the next day should mock your weakness in the arms of his whores? No, father! He'll come of his own accord, when his conscience tells him he's free. 265

OLD MOOR: Then I'll write this moment and tell him so. 270

FRANZ: Stop—just one more word, father. Your indignation, I fear, might dictate too harsh words for your pen, words that would rend his heart— and then—don't you think he might even take it

as a token of forgiveness that you deign to write 275
to him with your own hand? It'll be better to let
me write for you.

OLD MOOR: Do so, my son.—Ah! it would have
broken my heart! Tell him—

FRANZ: *(quickly)* Shall I, then? 280

OLD MOOR: Tell him that a thousand tears of
blood—tell him that a thousand sleepless nights—
But do not drive my son to despair.

FRANZ: Shouldn't you go to bed, father? This was
hard for you to bear. 285

OLD MOOR: Tell him that his father's bosom—I
tell you, do not drive my son to despair. *(Exit,
sadly.)*

FRANZ: *(watching him go, and laughing)* Console
yourself, old man, you'll never clasp him to that 290
bosom; the way to it is firmly barricaded to him,
as heaven is to hell.—He was torn from your arms
before you knew that you could will it so—I
should be a poor hand at it, if I couldn't manage
to prise a son from his father's heart, even if he 295
were bound to it with fetters of brass—I've drawn
a magic circle of curses around you, that he won't
be able to cross—Good luck, Franz! The favourite
is gone; things are looking brighter. I must pick
up all these pieces of paper, someone might easily 300
recognize my hand—*(collecting the torn pieces of
the letter)*. And the old man's grief will soon put
an end to him; and *she*—I must drive her precious
Karl from her thoughts too, even if he is half her
life to her. I have every right to be resentful of 305
nature; and by my honour, I will make my rights
known! Why was I not the first to creep out of
our mother's womb? Why not the only one? Why
did nature burden me with this ugliness? why me?
Just as if she had been bankrupt when I was born. 310
Why should I have this Laplander's nose? Why
should I have these blackamoor's lips, these
Hottentot's eyes? I truly think she made a heap of
the most hideous parts of every human kind as
the ingredients for me. Death and damnation! 315
Who gave her the power to make him like that,
and to keep it from me? Could anyone pay court
to her before she made him? Or offend her, before
he existed? Why was she so partial about her own
creation? No, no! I do her an injustice. After all, 320

she gave us the gift of ingenuity too when she set
us naked and miserable upon the shores of this
great ocean of the world: swim who can, and let
sink who is too clumsy! She gave me nothing;
what I can make of myself is my affair. Each man 325
has the same right to the greatest and the least;
claim destroys claim, impulse destroys impulse,
force destroys force. Might is right, and the limits
of our strength our only law. It's true; there are
certain conventions men have made, to rule the 330
pulses that turn the world. Honourable
reputation! A valuable coin indeed, one to drive
a fine bargain with for the man who knows how
to use it. Conscience—yes, indeed! an excellent
scarecrow, to keep the sparrows from the cherry- 335
trees! and a well-written cheque to help the
bankrupt too at the last moment. Yes indeed,
most admirable devices to keep fools respectful
and to hold down the mob, so that clever people
can live in better comfort. It must be admitted, 340
most ingenious devices! They remind me of the
hedges my peasants plant so cunningly around
their fields, so that the rabbits cannot jump
over—no, not on your life, not one single
rabbit!—But their lord and master sets spur to his 345
horse, and gallops away where the crops were
standing. Poor little rabbit! It's a sad part to play,
to be a rabbit in this world! But your lord and
master needs his rabbits! So, away we go! Fear
nothing, and you're as powerful as if all fear you. 350
It's the fashion nowadays to lace one's breeches so
that one can wear them tight or loose as one
pleases. We'll have ourselves a conscience made in
the latest style, so that we can let it out nicely as
we grow. How can we help it? Go to the tailor! 355
I've heard a great deal of idle talk about something
called love of one's kin, enough to turn a sound
man's head.—He's your brother! which, being
interpreted, is: he was baked in the same oven that
you were; so let him be sacred to you!—Just 360
consider this extraordinary conclusion, this
ridiculous argument from the proximity of bodies
to the harmony of minds; from the identity of
domicile to the identity of feeling; from the
uniformity of diet to the uniformity of 365
inclination. But there's more to it—he's your

father! He gave you life, you're his flesh and blood; so let him be sacred to you! Another cunning conclusion! I should like to know *why* he made me? Not out of love for me, surely, since there was no *me* to love? Did he know me before he made me? Or did he think of me while he was making me? Or did he wish for me as he was making me? Did he know what I should be like? I hope not, or I should want to punish him for making me regardless! Can I feel any gratitude to him for my being a man? No more than I could grudge it him if he'd made me a woman. Can I acknowledge any love that does not rest on respect for my person? Could respect for my person exist, when my person could only come into being through that for which it must be the condition? And what is so sacred about it all? The act itself through which I was created? As if that were anything but the animal gratification of animal desires? Or the result of that act, when that is nothing but brute necessity, that one would gladly be rid of if one could, if it were not at the cost of flesh and blood. Am I to speak well of him for loving me? That is vanity, the professional sin of all artists, who fancy their own work, however ugly it may be.—There it is then, the witchcraft that they veil in clouds of holy incense to abuse our fearful natures. Am I too to let myself be led along by it, like a little boy? Very well, then! courage, and to work! I will crush everything that stands in the way of my becoming master. And master I must be, to force my way to goals that I shall never gain through kindness. *(Exit.)*

SCENE 2
A tavern on the borders of Saxony.

(KARL VON MOOR deep in a book, SPIEGELBERG drinking at the table.)

MOOR: *(laying the book aside)* I hate this age of scribblers, when I can pick up my Plutarch[7] and read of great men.

SPIEGELBERG: *(puts a glass before him. Drinking)* Josephus[8] is the man you should read.

MOOR: The bright spark of Promethean fire is burnt out. All we have now is a flash of witch-meal—stage lightning, not flame enough to light a pipe of tobacco. Here we scratch about like rats at Hercules' club, and addle our miserable brains with speculation over what he had between his legs. A French cleric proclaims that Alexander was a coward; a consumptive professor with a bottle of smelling-salts under his nose gives lectures on energy. Fellows who faint when they've had a girl write commentaries on the tactics of Hannibal—boys still wet behind the ears crib their proses from Livy[9] on the battle of Cannae,[10] and snivel over Scipio's victories because they have to construe them.

SPIEGELBERG: You go on in the grand style.

MOOR: A fine reward for your valour on the battlefield, to live on in the grammar-school, and be dragged around, immortal, in a schoolboy's satchel. A worthy repayment for the blood you shed, to be wrapped round buns by a Nuremberg confectioner, or if you're lucky, to be hoisted on stilts by a French tragedian, and pulled about like puppets on a string! Haha!

SPIEGELBERG: *(drinking)* I tell you, you should read Josephus.

MOOR: Pah! An age of eunuchs, fit for nothing but chewing over the deeds of bygone days, mutilating the heroes of old with their learned interpretations and mocking them with their tragedies. The strength of their loins is dried up, and the dregs of a beer-barrel must help to propagate mankind.

---

7 Greek historian and philosopher (c. 46–c. 120 C.E.) who wrote a famous series of biographies comparing the most eminent Greek and Roman statesman and soldiers.

8 historian of the Jewish revolt against the Roman domination of Jerusalem (c. 66 C.E.). Josephus fought against the Romans as a commander, and was captured and spared; among the most famous passages in his *History of the Jewish War* are those that describe the suicides of the cornered rebels on Masada.

9 Roman historian (59 B.C.E.—17 C.E.) who wrote about Hannibal's military exploits; Book 35 of his writings contains a conversation between Hannibal and Scipio about great military leaders.

10 Italian village where the Romans sustained a major defeat at Hannibal's hands in 216 B.C.E., reportedly suffering 50,000 fatalities.

SPIEGELBERG: Tea, brother, tea!

MOOR: There they go, smothering healthy nature with their ridiculous conventions. Haven't the courage to drain a glass, because they'd have to wish 'Good health!' Fawn on the man who polishes His Highness's boots, and make life a misery for the wretch they have no need to fear. Praise each other to the skies for the sake of a dinner, and gladly poison each other when they lose a bedstead at an auction. Damn the Sadducee[11] who doesn't show himself enough in church, and reckon up their filthy lucre at the altar; fall on their knees so that they can show off their coat-tails the better; don't take their eye off the preacher, so as not to miss the cut of his wig.—Fall in a faint if they see a goose bleeding, and clap their hands when their rival goes bankrupt—No, however much I pleaded—"Just one more day!"—no! to jail with him, the dog!—Pleas! Oaths! Tears! *(Stamping his foot)* Hell and damnation!

SPIEGELBERG: And all for a few thousand miserable ducats—

MOOR: No, I'll not think of it. I'm supposed to lace my body in a corset, and strait-jacket my will with laws. The law has cramped the flight of eagles to a snail's pace. The law never yet made a great man, but freedom will breed a giant, a colossus. They ensconce themselves in a tyrant's belly, humour every whim of his digestion, and draw in their breath when his guts rumble.—Oh, if only Arminius's[12] spirit still glowed in the ashes!—Give me an army of fellows like me to command, and I'll turn Germany into a republic that will make Rome and Sparta look like nunneries. *(Tosses his sword onto the table and stands up.)*

---

11 empiricist Jewish sect, around the time of Christ, that did not believe in the resurrection of dead bodies or in the existence of angels and devils.

12 national hero of Germany who led a revolt against the Romans and defeated Varus's army in 9 C.E. In Schiller's time, and under the name Hermann der Cherusker, he began to be celebrated in German art, serving as the subject of works by J. E. Schlegel, Klopstock, and Kleist among other authors of the Romantic era.

SPIEGELBERG: *(jumping up)* Bravo! bravissimo! just what I wanted to talk to you about! Look, Moor, I'll tell you something I've been thinking about for a long time, you're just the man for it—drink up, have another—suppose we all turned Jews, and started talking about the Kingdom again?

MOOR: *(laughing out loud)* Ha! I see, I see! You want to put foreskins out of fashion, because the barber has had yours already?

SPIEGELBERG: You clown! It's true, I do happen, strangely enough, to be circumcised in advance. But look, isn't it a brave and cunning plan? We'll send out a manifesto to all the corners of the world and summon everyone who won't eat pork to Palestine. I shall have authentic documents to prove that Herod the Tetrarch was my great-great-grandfather, and so on. Man, what a jubilation, when they find their feet again, and can build Jerusalem anew. Then clear the Turks out of Asia while the iron is still hot, cut down the cedars of Lebanon, build ships, and flog ribbons and old tat to all the nations. And then—

MOOR: *(smiling, and taking him by the hand)* Now, friend! No more pranks of that kind.

SPIEGELBERG: *(taken aback)* Bah, you're not going to play the prodigal son now, are you? A fellow like you, who has written enough on faces with his sword to fill three attorneys' books in a leap year? Do you want me to tell the tale of the dog's funeral? What? I shall have to remind you of your own doings; that'll put a spark into you again, if nothing else can stir you up. Do you remember? Those fellows on the Council had had your mastiff's leg shot off, and to pay them back, you proclaimed a fast in the whole town. People grumbled about it. But you lost no time, bought up all the meat in Leipzig, so that in eight hours there wasn't a bone left to gnaw in the whole place, and the price of fish began to rise. The town council and the worthies were plotting revenge. Seventeen hundred of us lads out on the streets, and you leading us, and butchers and tailors and grocers following, and publicans and barbers and all the tradesmen, and swore they would wreck the town if anyone touched a hair of our heads. So they drew a blank, and went off with their tails between their legs. You sent for a whole panel of doctors, and offered three ducats to the one who would write a prescription for the dog. We thought the gentlemen would think it beneath their dignity and say no, and had already agreed we were going to force them to do it. But that wasn't necessary; they fought for the three ducats, even when it was knocked down to threepence, and they wrote a dozen prescriptions in the hour that soon finished the brute off.

MOOR: Miserable creatures!

SPIEGELBERG: The funeral was arranged with all pomp and ceremony, there were odes in honour of the departed dog, and we went out at night, nearly a thousand of us, a lantern in one hand and sword in the other, and so on through the town with bells and music till we had buried the dog. Then we stuffed ourselves with food till it was broad daylight, and you thanked the gentlemen for their heartfelt sympathy, and sold all the meat at half price. *Mort de ma vie!*[13] They respected us then, like a garrison in a conquered fortress—

MOOR: And you're not ashamed to boast of such a thing? Haven't even shame enough to be ashamed of playing such tricks?

SPIEGELBERG: Go along with you! I don't recognize Moor any longer. Don't you remember how you've railed a thousand times against the old skinflint, and said: let him pinch and scrape, so that you could swill to your heart's content! Don't you remember? eh? don't you remember? Oh, you Godforsaken coxcomb, that was spoken like a man, like a man of breeding, but now—

MOOR: Curse you for reminding me of it! Curse myself for saying it! But it was only in the heat of the wine, and my heart knew not the vain things my tongue spoke.

SPIEGELBERG: (*shaking his head*) No, no, no! it cannot be! No, brother, you can never be in earnest. My dear fellow, is it hardship that makes you so downcast? Come, let me tell you one of my exploits when I was a boy. There beside my house was a

ditch, eight feet wide at least, and we used to have contests, trying to jump across it. But it was no good. Flop! there you lay, and they hissed you and laughed at you, and threw snowballs at you, one after the other. Next door to our house a ranger kept his dog on a chain, a bad-tempered brute that used to bite; it would catch the girls by the skirt in no time if they didn't look out and went a shade too close. It was the best thing I knew to tease that dog whenever I could, and I would laugh till I was half dead to see the creature glowering so and longing to take a jump at me, if it could only get free. What happened? Another time I was giving it my usual treatment, and threw a stone and hit it so hard in the ribs, that it broke the chain, it was so furious, and was at me, and I was off and away like greased lightning. But hell's bells! there was the damned ditch in my way. What then? The dog at my heels, mad with rage, so never say die, a quick run up and—over I go. That jump saved my skin; the brute would have torn me to pieces.

MOOR: But why are you telling me this?

SPIEGELBERG: Why, to make you see—that necessity brings out the best in us! That's why I won't be afraid if it comes to the worst. Danger fortifies our courage; our strength grows in adversity. Fate must intend to make a great man of me, since it crosses me so often.

MOOR: (*irritated*) What should we need courage for, that we have not dared already?

SPIEGELBERG: What? So you'll let your talents moulder? Hide your light under a bushel? Do you really think your tomfooleries in Leipzig exhaust the range of human wit? Just wait till we've seen the wide world! Paris and London!—where you earn a box on the ears for calling anyone an honest man. It's a sight for sore eyes, to see business done on the grand scale!—I'll make you stare! I'll make your eyes pop! How to forge a signature—how to load dice—how to pick a lock—how to see the insides of a safe—just wait, and Spiegelberg will show you! The first gallows we come to, for the milksop who'd rather go hungry than get his fingers dirty.

MOOR: (*absently*) What? You've done all that, and more, I suppose?

---

13 "Death of my life," as in "on my life" or "it was almost the death of me."

SPIEGELBERG: I do believe you don't trust me. Just wait, let me really get warmed up; you'll have the surprise of your life, your brain will turn somersaults in your head, when my wits are delivered of their progeny. *(Standing up, heatedly)* Why, I see it all now! Great thoughts are taking shape in my soul! Mighty plans are fermenting in my ingenious mind! Curse me for sleeping! *(striking his forehead)* for letting my energies lie fettered, my prospects barred and thwarted; I am awake, I feel what I am—what I must and shall be! 215

MOOR: You're a fool. The wine's gone to your head.

SPIEGELBERG: *(in greater excitement)* Spiegelberg, they'll say, are you a magician, Spiegelberg? What a pity you didn't become a general, Spiegelberg, the King will say, you would have beaten the Austrians into a cocked hat. Yes, I can hear the doctors complaining, it's wicked that he didn't take up medicine, he would have discovered a cure for the clap.14 Ah! and that he didn't study economics, the Sullys15 will sigh in their treasuries, he would have conjured *louis d'or*16 from stones. And Spiegelberg will be the name, in east and west, and into the mud with you, cowards and toads, as Spiegelberg spreads his wings and flies high into the temple of fame. 220 225 230

MOOR: Good fortune to you! Climb up on pillars of shame to the summits of glory. In the shady groves of my father's home, in my Amalia's arms a nobler pleasure waits for me. Over a week ago I wrote to my father begging his forgiveness. I didn't conceal the slightest detail from him, and where there's honesty, there's also compassion and a helping hand. Let's say good-bye, Moritz. We'll see no more of each other after today. The post has arrived. My father's forgiveness is already within the walls of this town. 235 240

Enter SCHWEITZER, GRIMM, ROLLER, SCHUFTERLE, RATZMANN.

---

14 Schiller changed this line to "a new powder for goitre" in the published version.
15 Maximilien de Béthune, Duc de Sully (1599–1641), who revolutionized the economy of France with his financial policies and reforms.
16 French gold coins.

ROLLER: Do you know they're looking for us already? 245

GRIMM: That we're not safe from arrest at any minute?

MOOR: I'm not surprised. Let it be as it will. Didn't you see Schwarz? Didn't he say anything about a letter he had for me? 250

ROLLER: He's been looking for you for a long time—I think it's something of the kind.

MOOR: Where is he, where, where? *(Making as if to hurry away.)*

ROLLER: Don't go! We told him to come here. You're shaking? 255

MOOR: I'm not shaking. Why should I be shaking? Comrades! that letter—rejoice with me! I'm the happiest man on earth; why should I tremble?

Enter SCHWARZ.

MOOR: *(rushing to meet him)* Brother! brother—the letter, the letter! 260

SCHWARZ: *(giving him the letter, which he hurriedly opens)* What is it? You're as white as a sheet!

MOOR: My brother's hand!

SCHWARZ: What's the matter with Spiegelberg? 265

GRIMM: The fellow's crazy. He looks as though he's caught St. Vitus's dance.

SCHUFTERLE: He must be out of his mind. I think he's composing verses.

RATZMANN: Spiegelberg! Hey Spiegelberg!—The brute won't listen. 270

GRIMM: *(shaking him)* Man, are you dreaming, or—?

SPIEGELBERG: *(who has all the while been miming a mountebank's act in the corner of the room, jumping up wildly)* La bourse ou la vie!17 275

(He seizes SCHWEITZER by the throat; SCHWEITZER calmly pushes him back against the wall. MOOR drops the letter on the ground and runs out. All start back.)

ROLLER: *(after him)* Moor! Where are you going, Moor? What are you doing?

GRIMM: What's the matter, what's the matter? He's as pale as a corpse! 280

---

17 "Your money or your life." (Fr.)

SCHWEITZER: Fine news that must be! Let's see!

ROLLER: *(picks up the letter, and reads)* "Unfortunate brother!" That's a jolly way to begin. "I'm obliged to tell you in brief that your hopes are in vain; Father asks me to tell you that you are to go wherever your disgraceful deeds may take you. He also says that you are to entertain no hope of ever weeping your way to forgiveness at his feet, unless you are prepared to live on bread and water in the deepest of his dungeons, till your hairs are grown like eagles' feathers, and your nails like birds' claws. These are his very words. He commands me to write no more. Farewell for ever! I pity you—Franz von Moor." 285 290

SCHWEITZER: A sweet, charming brother! Indeed, Franz is the creature's name? 295

SPIEGELBERG: *(creeping up quietly)* Bread and water, do I hear? That's a fine life! But I have made other plans for you! Didn't I say I'd have to think for you all one day? 300

SCHWEITZER: What does he say, the donkey? He think for us all, the sheep's-head?

SPIEGELBERG: Cowards, cripples, lame dogs is what you are, all of you, if you haven't the courage for a great venture! 305

ROLLER: Well, that's true, so we would be; but is it going to get us out of this damned fix, your great venture? Is it?

SPIEGELBERG : *(laughing contemptuously)* You poor fool! Get you out of this fix? Ha, ha! out of this fix? Is that all your thimbleful of brain can think of? Is that enough to see your horses home? Don't call me Spiegelberg, if that was all I had in mind. Heroes, I tell you, lords, princes, gods it will make of you! 310 315

RATZMANN: That's enough to be getting on with, to be sure! But it'll be a breakneck job; it'll cost us our heads at least.

SPIEGELBERG: It'll cost nothing but courage, for I'll supply what wits are needed. Courage, I say, Schweitzer! Courage, Roller, Grimm, Ratzmann, Schufterle! Courage! 320

SCHWEITZER: Courage? Is that all? I've enough courage to go barefoot through hell.

SCHUFTERLE: Courage enough to scrap with the devil at the gallows' foot for a poor sinner's soul. 325

SPIEGELBERG: That's what I like to hear! If you have courage, let one among you say he still has anything to lose, and not everything to gain!

SCHWARTZ: Indeed, there would be plenty to lose, if I were to lose what I still have to gain! 330

RATZMANN: Yes, in hell's name! and plenty to gain, if I were to gain what I can't lose!

SCHUFTERLE: If I were to lose everything I have on me that's borrowed, then by tomorrow I'd have nothing left to lose. 335

SPIEGELBERG: Very well, then! *(He takes his place in the midst of them, and adopts an imperious tone.)* If there's still one drop of heroic German blood running in your veins—then come! We'll hide in the forests of Bohemia, raise a robber band, and—why are you staring at me? Has your little bit of courage melted away already? 340

ROLLER: I don't suppose you're the first rogue to overlook the gallows—and yet—what else is there we can do? 345

SPIEGELBERG: What else? Nothing else! There's no choice in the matter! Do you want to sit starving in the debtors' prison till the last trump blows? Do you want to scratch with spade and hoe for a scrap of stale bread? Do you want to beg for alms, singing ballads at people's windows? Do you want to take the King's shilling—if they would trust the looks of you, that's the first question—and do your stint in Purgatory while you're still on earth, at the mercy of some splenetic tyrant of a corporal? Or be drummed out to run the gauntlet, or tramp the galleys and drag the whole arsenal of Vulcan's smithy behind you? That's what else there is; that's all the choice you have! 350 355 360

ROLLER: It's not such a bad idea of Spiegelberg's. I've been making plans too, but it's the same kind of thing. How would it be, I thought, if you all sat down and cooked up an anthology or an almanac or something like that, or wrote reviews for a shilling or two? It's all the rage nowadays. 365

SCHUFTERLE: I'll be hanged if your plans aren't very much like mine. I was thinking to myself, what if you were to turn evangelical, and hold weekly classes in spiritual improvement? 370

GRIMM: That's it! and if that was no good, turn atheist, blaspheme against the four gospels, have our book burnt by the hangman, and we should do a roaring trade.

RATZMANN: Or we could set up to cure the pox— I know a doctor who built himself a house on a foundation of mercury, so the motto over the door says. 375

SCHWEITZER: *(stands up and gives SPIEGEL-BERG his hand)* Moritz, you're a great man—or a blind pig has found an acorn. 380

SCHWARZ: Excellent plans! most reputable professions! How great minds think alike! All that's left now is to turn into women and become bawds, or even sell our own virginity on the streets. 385

SPIEGELBERG: Nonsense, nonsense! And what's to stop you being most of these things in one person? My plan will still do the best for you, and make you famous and immortal too! Look, you poor things! As far ahead as that you must think! Think of the fame that'll live after you, the sweet feeling that you'll never be forgotten— 390

ROLLER: And at the top of the list of honest people! You're a master orator, Spiegelberg, when it comes to turning an honest man into a villain.—But doesn't anyone know where Moor is? 395

SPIEGELBERG: Honest, you say? What, do you think it will make you any less of an honest man than you are today? What do you call being honest? Relieving rich skinflints of the third of their worries that only disturbs their golden slumbers; bringing idle money into circulation, restoring the fair distribution of wealth, in a word bringing back the golden age; taking away some of the good Lord's burdens, so that he can be rid of them without war, pestilence, famine and doctors—that's what I call being an honest man, that's what I call being a worthy instrument in the hand of Providence; and with every joint you roast to be able to flatter yourself with the thought that it's your own cunning, your own lion's courage, your own long vigils that have earned it; to be respected by great and small— 400 405 410

ROLLER: And in the end to be hoisted up to heaven in the flesh, and come wind come weather, in spite of old father time and his greedy appetite, to swing there with sun and moon and all the stars in the firmament, while the birds sing a heavenly concert 415

at the feast and the long-tailed angels sit in sacred council? What? And while monarchs and potentates make a feast for moths and worms, to have the honour of being visited by Jove's royal bird?[18] Moritz, Moritz, Moritz! Beware, beware the three-legged beast! 420

SPIEGELBERG: And that frightens you, coward? Why, there's many a virtuoso rotting on the gibbet who might have reformed the world, and won't such a one be spoken of for hundreds and thousands of years, while many a king and many an elector might be left out of history altogether, if it weren't that the historians were afraid to leave a gap in the line of succession, and if it weren't that it made their books a few pages thicker and brought in more cash from the publisher. And if the passer-by does see you floating back and forth in the wind, why, he'll think to himself, that must have been no ordinary fellow, and he'll sigh that the world has gone to the dogs. 425 430 435

SCHWEITZER: *(slapping him on the back)* Superb, Spiegelberg! Superb! Why the devil do you stand there hesitating? 440

SCHWARZ: And even if it meant degradation— What more can there be? One can always have a pinch of powder with one, to speed one across the Acheron[19] if it should come to that, so that one will never hear the cock crow again. No, friend Moritz! it's a good proposal. That's my catechism too. 445

SCHUFTERLE: Hell! And mine as well. Spiegelberg, I'm your man!

RATZMANN: Like another Orpheus,[20] you have sung my howling brute of a conscience to sleep. Take me as I am! 450

GRIMM: *Si omnes consentiunt ego non dissentio.*[21]

---

18 i.e., to be pecked by an eagle while hanging on the scaffold rather than gobbled by lesser animals in the grave.

19 river or sometimes lake that dead souls in Greek mythology crossed on their way to Hades.

20 legendary Greek musician (supposedly pre-Homeric) who could calm wild beasts, protect against dangers, and even cheat death with his singing.

21 *Trans. note:* "If all give their assent, I do not withhold mine." A comma after *non* gives the sense "I do not, I withhold mine."

With no comma, mind. They're holding an auction in my head: evangelist, quack-doctor, reviewer and rogue. I'm to be had for the best offer. Here, Moritz, my hand!

ROLLER: And you too, Schweitzer? *(Offering SPIEGELBERG his right hand)* Then the devil can take my soul.

SPIEGELBERG: But your name will be written in the stars! What does it matter where your soul goes? When troops of couriers gallop ahead to announce our descent, so that the devils put on their Sunday best, rub the soot of millennia out of their eyes, and homed heads in their thousands poke from the smoky chimneys of their sulphur-ovens to see our arrival? Comrades! *(jumping up)* Away! Comrades! Is there anything in the world so glorious, so thrilling? Come, comrades, and away!

ROLLER: Gently now, gently! where are you going? the beast must have its head, children!

SPIEGELBERG: *(venomously)* What words of hesitation are these? Wasn't the head there before a single limb stirred? follow me, comrades!

ROLLER: Easy, I say. Even liberty must have its master. Without a head, Rome and Sparta were destroyed.

SPIEGELBERG: *(ingratiatingly)* Yes—wait, Roller is right. And the head must be a brilliant one. Do you understand? A shrewd political head it must be. Yes, if I think of what you were an hour ago, and what you are now—are by virtue of a single lucky idea—Yes, of course, of course you must have a chief—and the man who thought up that idea, tell me, mustn't he have a brilliant, political head?

ROLLER: If we could only hope—if we could only dream—but I'm afraid he won't do it.

SPIEGELBERG: Why not? Speak your mind, friend! Heavy though the task may be of steering the struggling ship against the gale, heavy though the weight of a crown may weigh—speak without fear, Roller! Perhaps he will do it after all.

ROLLER: And the whole thing falls to pieces if he won't. Without Moor we're a body without a soul.

SPIEGELBERG: *(turning away from him in disgust)* Idiot.

(Enter MOOR in wild agitation. He paces violently up and down the room, talking to himself.)

MOOR: Men, men! False breed of hypocrites and crocodiles! Their eyes water, but their hearts are iron! Kisses on their lips, but swords in their bosom! Lions and leopards feed their young, ravens take their chicks to feast on corpses, and *he, he*—Wickedness I have learnt to endure. I can smile while my arch-enemy is drinking my heart's blood; but when blood kinship turns traitor, when a father's love becomes a raging fury; oh, then catch fire, manly resignation, be as a ravening tiger, gentle lamb, and let every fibre stiffen to hatred and destruction!

ROLLER: Listen, Moor! What do you think? A robber's life is better than bread and water in the deepest dungeon after all, isn't it?

MOOR: Why was this spirit not formed into a tiger, that fastens its savage jaws in human flesh? Is this a father's devotion? Is this love for love? Would that I were a bear, and could raise the bears of the north against this race of murderers—repentance, and no forgiveness! Oh, that I might poison the ocean, that they might drink death from every spring! Trust, submission that none could turn away, and no pity!

ROLLER: Moor, listen to what I'm saying!

MOOR: It's unbelievable, it's a dream, a delusion—such moving pleas, such keen representation of my misery and my melting repentance—a brute beast would have wept in compassion! Stones would have shed tears, and yet—it would be thought a wicked slur on all mankind, if I were to say so—and yet, and yet—oh, if I could blow the trumpet of rebellion throughout the realm of nature, and stir up earth, sky and sea to battle against this brood of hyenas!

GRIMM: Listen, will you! You're so mad you don't hear.

MOOR: Get away from me! Are you not a man? Are you not born of woman? Out of my sight, you creature with man's face!—I loved him so unspeakably! no son loved so, my life I would a thousand times—*(foaming, stamping on the ground)* ha! he who should put a sword into my hand, to deal a deadly blow to this generation of vipers! he who should say to me: if I can pierce the heart of its life, crush it, strangle it—that man shall be my friend, my angel, my god—I will worship him! 545

ROLLER: We want to be those friends of yours, let us tell you!

SCHWARZ: Come with us into the forests of Bohemia! We're going to raise a band of robbers, and you— 550

(MOOR stares at him.)

SCHWEITZER: You are to be our captain! you must be our captain!

SPIEGELBERG: *(hurling himself into a chair in fury)* Slaves and cowards! 555

MOOR: Who gave you that idea? Listen, fellow! *(Seizing SCHWARZ fiercely)* It did not come from your man's soul! Who prompted you? Yes, by the thousand arms of death! we shall, we must! a thought fit for gods! Robbers and murderers! As 560 sure as my soul breathes, I am your captain!

ALL: *(shouting aloud)* Long live our captain!

SPIEGELBERG: *(jumping up, aside)* Until I see him off!

MOOR: See, the scales have fallen from my eyes! 565 What a fool I was, to seek to return to the cage! My spirit thirsts for deeds, my lungs for freedom— murderers, robbers! at that word I trampled the law beneath my feet—men showed me no humanity, when to humanity I appealed; so let me forget 570 sympathy and human feeling! I have no father now, I have no love now, and blood and death shall teach me to forget that I ever held anything dear! Oh, my amusement shall be the terror of the earth—it's agreed, I'll be your captain, and good 575 fortune to the champion among you who lights the fiercest fires, who does the foulest murders, for I say to you, he shall have a kingly reward! Gather round me every one, and swear loyalty and obedience till death! Swear by this right hand of 580 mine!

ALL: *(reaching him their hands)* We swear loyalty and obedience to you till death!

MOOR: Now, and by this right hand of mine! I swear to you to remain your captain in loyalty and 585 constancy till death! If any show cowardice or

hesitation or retreat, this arm shall strike him down on the spot; the same fate meet me from any and every one of you, if I offend against my oath! Are you agreed? 590

(SPIEGELBERG paces furiously up and down.)

ALL: *(throwing their hats in the air)* We're agreed!

MOOR: Very well then, let's go! Fear not death or danger, for an inflexible fate rules over us all. We must endure our going hence, be it on soft pillows of down, be it in the hurly-burly of battle, or be 595 it on the gallows and the wheel! One or the other must be our lot! *(Exeunt.)*

SPIEGELBERG: *(watching them go, after a pause)* There's one missing in your list: you forgot poison. *(Exit.)* 600

SCENE 3
OLD MOOR'S castle. AMALIA'S rooms.

FRANZ, AMALIA.

FRANZ: You look away, Amalia? Am I less worthy than he whom my father has cursed?

AMALIA: Away!—oh, merciful, loving father, who will cast his son to the wolves and the wild beasts! while he at home is refreshed with sweet, precious 5 wine, and cossets his feeble limbs in pillows of eiderdown, while his great and glorious son may perish! Shame on you, inhuman creatures! shame on you, you monsters, you abomination of mankind! His only son! 10

FRANZ: I thought he had two.

AMALIA: Yes, it's sons like you that he deserves. On his deathbed he'll stretch out his withered hands in vain to seek his Karl, and start back in horror when he catches the icy hand of his Franz—oh, it 15 is sweet, it is a sweet and noble thing, to earn your father's curse! Speak, Franz, good soul, good brother, what must one do if one would earn his curse?

FRANZ: My poor love, your fantasy is leading you 20 astray.

AMALIA: Oh, I beg you—do you pity your brother? No, inhuman creature, you hate him! and you hate me too?

FRANZ: I love you as I love myself, Amalia. 25

AMALIA: If you love me, can you refuse me one request?

FRANZ: Not one, not one—if it's not more than my life.

AMALIA: Oh, if that's true! One request, that you'll 30 fulfil so easily, so gladly—(Proudly) Hate me! I cannot but blush crimson with shame, if I think of Karl and realize that you do not hate me. You promise me? Now go, and leave me—let me be alone! 35

FRANZ: My sweet dreamer! how I adore your gentle loving heart. (Touching her breast) Here, here Karl reigned like a god in his temple, Karl stood before you while you were awake, Karl ruled your dreams, all creation seemed to you to be dissolved in him, 40 to reflect him, to echo him and him alone.

AMALIA: (moved) Yes, it's true, I admit it. In spite of you, barbarians, I confess it to all the world—I love him!

FRANZ: Inhuman, cruel! To reward such love like 45 this! To forget the one—

AMALIA: (starting up) What, to forget me?

FRANZ: Did you not put a ring on his finger? a diamond ring, as a pledge of your constancy? But after all, how can a young man withstand a 50 courtesan's charms? Who can blame him when he had nothing left to give away? And did she not pay him with interest for it, with her embraces, with her caresses?

AMALIA: (indignantly) A courtesan, my ring? 55

FRANZ: Pah! it's shameful. But if that was all! A ring, however precious, any Jew can replace, if it comes to that—perhaps he didn't like the setting, perhaps he changed it for a better one.

AMALIA: (angrily) But my ring, my ring, I say? 60

FRANZ: The very same, Amalia—ah, such a jewel, on my finger—and from Amalia!—death itself couldn't have torn it from me—is it not so, Amalia? it isn't the size of the diamond, it isn't the skill of the cutting—it's love that makes it pre- 65 cious—dearest child, you're weeping? Cursed be he who makes these heavenly eyes shed their precious drops—oh, and if only you knew everything, if only you could see him, as he is now!—

AMALIA: Monster! What do you mean, as he is 70 now?

FRANZ: Be still, sweet creature, don't ask me! (As if to himself, but aloud) If only there were some veil that could hide it, that filthy vice, so that it could creep out of sight of the world! But no! it shows 75 in all its vileness, in the yellow leaden ring round the eye; the deathly pallor of the sunken cheeks betrays it, and the hideous protruding bones—the stifled, strangled voice mutters of it—the tottering, decrepit frame proclaims it aloud in all its horror— 80 it gnaws the very marrow of the bones, and saps the bold youth's strength—there, there! the suppurating juices start forth from forehead and cheeks and lips and cover the whole body with their loathsome sores, and fester in the dark 85 hollows of bestial disgrace—pah! it revolts me. Nose, ears, eyes shudder at it—you saw him, Amalia, that wretch who coughed out his soul in our infirmary, the modest eye of shame seemed to turn aside from the sight of him—alas for him, you 90 cried! Think of it, summon up that vision once more before your mind's eye, and it is Karl that you see!—His kisses are a pestilence, his lips would poison yours!

AMALIA: (striking him) Shameless slanderer! 95

FRANZ: Does it fill you with horror, the thought of such a Karl? Does even my pale sketch disgust you? Go, gape at him himself, your handsome, angelic, divine Karl! Go, breathe in the perfume of his breath, let the sweet vapours that his throat 100 streams forth envelop you; one breath from his lips, and you would feel the same black swoon of death upon you as if you smelt a rotting corpse, or saw the carrion of a battlefield.

(AMALIA turns her face away.)

FRANZ: What surging tide of love! What bliss in his 105 embrace!—But is it not unjust to damn a man for the sickness of his body? Even the most miserable cripple of an Aesop may hide a great and noble soul, as the mud hides the ruby. (Smiling maliciously) Even scabbed lips may breathe of 110 love—But yet, if vice has sapped the strength of his character as well, if virtue has fled with chastity, as the perfume fades from the withered rose—if with the body the spirit too is crippled—

AMALIA: (starting up, joyfully) Ah, Karl! Now I see 115

you truly again! you are still your own true self! It was all a lie! Do you not know, wicked creature, that these things can never touch my Karl?

(FRANZ stands for a while deep in thought, then turns suddenly as if to go.)

Where are you hurrying to; would you fly from your own shame? 120

FRANZ: (hiding his face) Let me go, let me go! let my tears flow—tyrant of a father! to cast the best of your sons into such misery—to expose him to shame on every side—let me go, Amalia! I will fall on my knees at his feet, I will implore him to let 125 me, me bear the curse that he spoke—to disinherit me—me—to—my life, my blood—everything—

AMALIA: (throwing her arms round his neck) Oh, my Karl's brother, dearest, most precious Franz!

FRANZ: Oh, Amalia! how I love you for your 130 unshakeable constancy to my brother—forgive me, for presuming to put your love to so harsh a test! How perfectly you vindicate my hopes! With these your tears, these your sighs, this your heavenly displeasure—for me, me too—our souls were 135 always as one.

AMALIA: No, they were never that!

FRANZ: Oh, they were as one, in such sweet harmony, I always thought that we should have been twins! and if it were not for the unhappy 140 difference in outward looks between us, which I admit is not to his advantage, then ten times the one might have been taken for the other. Yes, you are, I said to myself so often, you are Karl himself, his echo, his living image! 145

AMALIA: (shaking her head) No, no! by the chaste light of Heaven! not one drop of his blood, not one spark of his spirit!

FRANZ: So alike in all our tastes: the rose was his favourite flower—what flower did I ever rate above 150 the rose? He loved music more than words can tell, and I! you stars are my witnesses, how often you have heard me at the keyboard in the silence of the night, when all around me lay buried in shadows and sleep—how can you doubt it still, 155 Amalia, when our love coincided in the same point of perfection, and if love is one, how can its children deny their ancestry?

(AMALIA stares at him in amazement.)

FRANZ: It was a clear, still evening, the last night before he set off for Leipzig, when he took me with 160 him to the arbour where you so often sat together, dreaming of love—we sat there long in silence—at last he took my hand and spoke softly and with tears in his eyes: I'm leaving Amalia, I don't know—I feel that it may be for ever—don't leave 165 her, brother! be her friend—her Karl—if Karl should—not—return—! (He falls on his knees before her and kisses her hand passionately.) No, he will not return, never, never, and I have promised him with a sacred oath! 170

AMALIA: (drawing back sharply) Traitor, I've found you out! In this same arbour he made me swear, never to love another—if he should not—see, how blasphemously, how vilely you—out of my sight!

FRANZ: You mistake me, Amalia, you're quite 175 mistaken in me!

AMALIA: Oh, I'm not mistaken in you; I know you from this moment—and you would be his equal? And you say it was to you he wept for my sake? To you? He would sooner have written my name 180 upon the pillory! Go, this instant!

FRANZ: You do me an injustice!

AMALIA: Go, I say! You've robbed me of a precious hour; let your life be so much the shorter.

FRANZ: You hate me. 185

AMALIA: I despise you, go!

FRANZ: (stamping his foot) Wait! I will make you tremble before me! To sacrifice me to a beggar? (Exit, angrily.)

AMALIA: Go, base creature!—now I'm with Karl 190 again—a beggar, did he say? Why then, the world is turned upside-down, beggars are kings and kings are beggars! I wouldn't change the rags he wears for the purple of the anointed—the look with which he begs for alms must be a noble and a 195 kingly look—a look to wither the pomp and splendour, the triumphs of the great and rich! Into the dust with you, idle jewels! (Tearing the pearls from her throat.) Be condemned, you great and rich, to wear your gold and silver and your precious 200 stones, to glut yourselves at feasts and banquets, to stretch your limbs on the soft couch of ease! Karl! Karl! You see that I am worthy of you. (Exit.)

ACT TWO SCENE I

(FRANZ VON MOOR, brooding in his room.)

FRANZ: It's taking too long for my liking—the doctor says he's on the mend—an old man's life is an eternity! And now my path would be clear and smooth before me, but for this miserable lump of tough flesh that bars the way to my treasures like the magic subterranean dog in the fairytale. But must my plans submit to the iron yoke of mechanical laws? Is my high-flying spirit to be bound to the snail's pace of material necessity?—Blow out a light that in any case is only stretching the last drop of oil—that's all there is to it; and yet I'd rather not have done it myself, on account of what people will say. I would not have him killed, but put down. I'd like to do it like a skilled doctor—only the other way around: not to put a spoke in Nature's wheel, but to help her in her own designs. And if we can prolong the conditions of life as we can, why should we not be able to abbreviate them? Doctors and philosophers have taught me how finely the motions of the mind are attuned to those of the machine that houses it. Convulsive attacks are accompanied by dissonant vibrations in the machine; passions disturb the vital force; the overburdened spirit weighs down its vehicle. What then? If one could discover how to smooth death this untrodden path into the citadel of life? to destroy the body through the soul?—ha! a masterpiece! The man who could do that—? A work of genius! Think, Moor! An art that deserved you for its discoverer! After all, poisoning has now been raised almost to the rank of a full-blown science, and experiments have forced nature to make known her limitations, so that the beats of the heart can now be reckoned out years in advance and one can say to the pulse: thus far, and no farther![22] Is not this a field where one might try one's wings? And how must I set about it, now, to disturb the sweet peace and harmony of body and soul? What species of sensation shall I have to choose? Which will be the deadliest enemies of the flower of life? Anger?—a ravening wolf that devours its prey too quickly. Nagging care?—a worm that gnaws too slowly. Sorrow?—a snake that creeps too sluggishly. Fear?—when hope will always check its growth? What? Has man no other executioners? Is the arsenal of death so soon exhausted? *(Brooding)* What? Well? No!—Ah! *(Starting up)* Terror! What can terror not accomplish? What can reason or religion do to stay the monster's icy embrace?—And yet?—if he could withstand that assault? If he could?—Oh, then come to my aid, grief, and you, repentance, Fury of hell, burrowing serpent that chew again what you have already devoured, and feed again on your own filth; eternal destroyers and eternal breeders of your poison; and you, howling self-reproach, who make desolate your own house, and wound your own mother's heart—And come you too to my aid, you beneficent Graces yourselves, soft smiling Past, and Future with your cornucopia overflowing with blossoms, show him in your glass the joys of heaven, and then let your fleeting foot escape his greedy arm—Blow upon blow, storm upon storm I will bring down on this fragile life, till at last there comes, to crown the troop of furies—despair! Triumph! triumph! The plan is made—Tight and cunning as can be—safe—foolproof; for *(mockingly)* there will be no trace of a wound nor corrosive poison for the anatomist's knife to reveal. *(Resolutely)* Very well, then! *(Enter HERRMANN.)* —Ha! *Deus ex machina.*[23] Herrmann!

HERRMANN: At your service, young master!

FRANZ: *(giving him his hand)* I'm not ungrateful for it.

HERRMANN: I have proofs of that.

FRANZ: You shall have more very soon—very soon, Herrmann!—I have something to tell you, Herrmann.

HERRMANN: I'm all ears.

---

22 *Schiller's note:* A woman in Paris is said to have achieved such success in systematic experiments with doses of poison that she could give the date of death in advance with some measure of reliability. Shame on our doctors, that this woman excels them in prognosis!

23 lit., "the god from the machine," or the unmotivated and sudden appearance of a theatrically contrived aid to the plot.

FRANZ: I know you, you're a resolute fellow—a soldier's heart—a man of courage.—My father did you a great injustice, Herrmann! 80

HERRMANN: The devil take me if I ever forget it!

FRANZ: Spoken like a man! Revenge is sweet, and a man deserves it. I like you, Herrmann. Take this purse, Herrmann. It would be heavier, if only I were lord here. 85

HERRMANN: That's my only wish, young master. I thank you.

FRANZ: Truly, Herrmann? do you truly wish that I was lord?—But my father's as strong as a lion, and I'm the younger son. 90

HERRMANN: I wish you were the elder son, and I wish your father were as strong as a consumptive girl.

FRANZ: Oh, how the elder son would reward you then! how he would raise you from this ignoble dust, 95 that suits so ill your spirit and nobility, raise you up into the light!—Then you should be covered with gold, just as you are, and rattle through the streets with four horses, indeed you should!—but I'm forgetting what I wanted to say to you. Have you 100 forgotten the Lady Amalia, Herrmann?

HERRMANN: Damnation! why do you remind me of that?

FRANZ: My brother whisked her away from you

HERRMANN: He'll pay for it! 105

FRANZ: She turned you down. I believe he even threw you down the stairs.

HERRMANN: I'll hurl him into hell for it.

FRANZ: He said people were whispering that you were got between the roast beef and the horse- 110 radish,[24] and your father could never look at you without beating his breast and sighing: God have mercy on me, miserable sinner!

HERRMANN: (furiously) By the burning fiery furnace! be silent! 115

FRANZ: He told you to auction your patent of nobility, and have your breeches patched with it.

HERRMANN: By all the devils! I'll tear out his eyes with my nails!

---

24 got between … the horseradish] that is, conceived be-tween courses at dinner, by the lord of the house, upon a servant.

FRANZ: What? you are angry? what can make you 120 angry with him? What can you do to him? How can a rat hurt a lion? Your anger will only make his triumph sweeter. You can do nothing but grit your teeth, and vent your rage on a piece of stale bread.

HERRMANN: (stamping on the floor) I'll grind him 125 to dust.

FRANZ: (clapping him on the shoulder) Pah, Herrmann! You're a gentleman. You mustn't be content to bear these insults. You must not let the lady go, no, you must not do that for all the world, 130 Herrmann! Hell and damnation! I'd stop at nothing if I were in your shoes.

HERRMANN: I won't rest till I have him, and have him under the ground.

FRANZ: Not so wild, Herrmann! Come closer—you 135 shall have Amalia!

HERRMANN: I must, come Satan himself! I must!

FRANZ: You will have her, I tell you, and I'll help you to her. Come closer, I say!—perhaps you didn't know that Karl's as good as disinherited? 140

HERRMANN (coming closer) Incredible! It's the first I've heard of it.

FRANZ: Keep calm, and listen. I'll tell you more about it another time—yes, I say, as good as banished, eleven months ago. But the old man is 145 already regretting his hasty step—and after all (laughing), I believe it wasn't his own doing. And my Lady Amalia besieges him every day with her reproaches and her lamentations. Sooner or later he'll send to the four corners of the earth to look 150 for him and then good night, Herrmann! if he finds him. You can swallow your pride and hold the carriage door for him, when he drives to church with her for their wedding.

HERRMANN: I'll throttle him before the altar! 155

FRANZ: Father will soon hand affairs over to him, and retire to live in peace on his estates. Then the proud hothead will have the reins in his hands, then he'll laugh at those who hated him and envied him—and I, Herrmann, I who would have made 160 you a great man, a man to be looked up to, will be bowing my knee at his door—

HERRMANN: (heatedly) No! as true as my name is Herrmann, you will not! not if a spark of wit still glimmers in my brain! you will not! 165

FRANZ: Will you be able to stop it? you too, my dear Herrmann, will be feeling his whip; he'll spit in your face if you meet him in the street, and woe betide you then if you shrug your shoulder or curl your lip—there, that's what will come of your suit to the lady, of your prospects, of your designs.   170

HERRMANN: Tell me, what should I do?

FRANZ: Listen, then, Herrmann! so that you may see what a good friend I am to you, how nearly your fate touches my heart—go, put on different clothes, disguise yourself so that no one will know you, and have yourself announced to the old man—say that you've come straight from Bohemia, that you were with my brother at the battle of Prague, that you saw him breathe his last on the battlefield—   175   180

HERRMANN: Will they believe me?

FRANZ: Aha, let me take care of that! Take this packet. Here you'll find everything set out for you to do. And documents that would convince doubt itself—look to it now, be on your way, and don't be seen! through the back door into the courtyard, jump over the garden wall—leave the climax of this tragicomedy to me!   185

HERRMANN: And that will be: long live our new lord and master, Franciscus von Moor!   190

FRANZ: (stroking his cheek) Clever, are you not?—for do you see, in this way we'll achieve all our goals at once, and quickly. Amalia will give up all hope of him. The old man will blame himself for his son's death, and—he's sickly—a rickety building doesn't need an earthquake to bring it crashing down—he won't survive the news. Then I'll be his only son—Amalia will have lost all support, and will be the plaything of my will, you can imagine—in short, everything will be as we would have it—but you mustn't take back your word!   195   200

HERRMANN: What are you saying? (Jubilant) Sooner may the bullet turn in its flight and tear the marksman's own bowels—count on me! Leave everything to me—Adieu!   205

FRANZ: (calling after him) The harvest is yours, my dear Herrmann!—When the ox has carted the corn to the barn, he has to make do with hay. A stable-maid for you, and no Amalia! (Exit.)   210

SCENE 2
OLD MOOR'S *bedroom*

OLD MOOR, asleep in an armchair; AMALIA

AMALIA: (creeping softly in) Softly, softly, he's asleep! (Standing before him as he sleeps) How handsome, how venerable!—venerable like the portrait of a saint—no, I cannot be angry with you! Dear white head, with you I cannot be angry! Rest asleep, wake joyfully—I alone will go my way in suffering.   5

OLD MOOR: (dreaming) My son! my son! my son!

AMALIA: (taking his hand) Listen! listen! his son is in his dreams.   10

OLD MOOR: Is it you? is it really you? ah, how wretchedly you look! Don't turn that sorrowful gaze on me! I'm wretched enough!

AMALIA: (waking him quickly) Look about you, sweet old man! You only dreamt. Have courage!   15

OLD MOOR: (half awake) He wasn't here? Did I not hold his hands in mine? Cruel Franz! will you tear him even from my dreams?

AMALIA: Do you hear, Amalia?

OLD MOOR: (more cheerfully) Where is he? where? Where am I? You here, Amalia?   20

AMALIA: How are you? You were asleep; your rest has refreshed you.

OLD MOOR: I was dreaming of my son. Why couldn't I dream on? I might have heard his lips speak forgiveness.   25

AMALIA: Angels bear no grudge—he has forgiven you, (taking his hands sorrowfully) Father of my Karl! I forgive you.

OLD MOOR: No, my daughter! His father stands condemned by the deathly pallor of your face. Unhappy girl! I robbed you of the joys of your youth—oh, do not curse me!   30

AMALIA: (kissing his hand tenderly) You?

OLD MOOR: Do you know this portrait, my daughter?   35

AMALIA: Karl's!

OLD MOOR: So he looked, when he was sixteen. Now he's different—Oh, my breast is aflame—this gentleness is wrath, this smile despair—Is it not so, Amalia? It was his birthday when you painted   40

him, in the jasmine arbour?—Oh, my daughter!
Your love brought me such joy.

AMALIA : *(not taking her eyes off the portrait)* No,
no! It isn't him. In Heaven's name, that isn't Karl.
Here, here—*(pointing to her heart and her forehead)*
The whole, so different. These dull colours cannot
reflect the divine spirit that shone in his fiery eyes.
Away with it! this is a mere man. I was just a
bungler.

OLD MOOR: This warm look of devotion—if he'd
stood before my bed, in the midst of death I would
have lived! Never, never should I have died!

AMALIA: Never, never should you have died? A leap
it would have been, as one springs from one
thought to another and a finer—this look would
have lighted your path beyond the grave. This look
would have borne you on beyond the stars!

OLD MOOR: It's sad, hard to endure! I'm dying,
and my son Karl isn't here—I'll be carried to my
grave, and he won't be at my grave to weep—how
sweet it is to be lulled into the sleep of death by a
son's prayer—it's like a lullaby.

AMALIA: *(rapturously)* Yes, sweet, sweet as heaven,
to be lulled into the sleep of death by a lover's
song—perhaps we may dream on still in the
grave—one long eternal never-ending dream of
Karl until the bell tolls for the day of resurrection
(leaping to her feet in ecstasy) and from that moment
on, in his arms for ever. *(Pause. She goes to the
keyboard, and plays.)*
Hector, will you bid farewell forever,
Now Achilles, with his murd'rous quiver,
Fearful vengeance for Patroclus swears?
Who will teach your tender son to fight,
To cast his spear, and fear the Gods of right,
When your corpse grim Xanthus downward bears?

OLD MOOR: A beautiful song, my daughter. You
must play it for me before I die.

AMALIA: It's the farewell of Andromache and
Hector[25]—Karl and I have often sung it to the lute
together. *(Continuing)*

Dearest wife, go, fetch the fateful lance,
Let me go to tread war's horrid dance,
On my back the weight of Ilium[26]
The Gods shield Astyanax[27] with their hand!
Hector falls, to save his fatherland,
We shall greet each other in Elysium.[28]

(Enter DANIEL)

DANIEL: There's a man waiting for you outside. He
asks to be allowed to see you, says he has an
important piece of news for you.

OLD MOOR: Only one thing in the world is
important to me, you know what that is, Amalia—
is it a man fallen on ill-luck, who has need of help
from me? He will not go sighing on his way.

AMALIA: If it's a beggar, make haste and send him
up.

(Exit DANIEL.)

OLD MOOR: Amalia, Amalia! have pity on me—

AMALIA: *(continuing to play)*
Never shall I hear your weapons sing,
In your hall your arms lie mouldering;
Priam's[29] race of heroes is passed by!
You are gone where daylight never gleams,
Where Cocytus[30] through the desert streams,
In dread Lethe's[31] flood your love will die.
All my thoughts, ambition's crown
Shall dread Lethe's flood in blackness drown,
But never yet my love!
Listen, now! at the walls, the wild one raving—
Gird my sword about me, cease your grieving!
Lethe shall not drown thy Hector's love!

(Enter FRANZ, HERRMANN in disguise, DANIEL.)

FRANZ: Here's the man. Terrible news, he says,
awaits you. Can you bear to hear it?

---

25 from the famous leave-taking scene between Hector, the
greatest fighter on the Trojan side, and his wife, before
he goes off to battle and to his death, from Homer's epic
the *Iliad*.

26 Troy.

27 their son, who in fact was not spared, according to the
myth, but rather killed by the conquering Greeks when
they took Troy.

28 i.e., in death.

29 king of Troy.

30 river in the underworld in Greek mythology.

31 lit., "forgetfulness"; an underworld river of forgetting.

OLD MOOR: It can be only one thing. Come here, friend, and do not spare me! Give him a cup of wine. 115

HERRMANN: *(disguising his voice)* My lord! do not punish a poor man, if against his own will he should pierce your heart. I'm a stranger in this land, but I know you well; you're Karl von Moor's father. 120

OLD MOOR: How do you know?

HERRMANN: I knew your son.

AMALIA: *(starting up)* He's alive? alive? You know him? where is he, where, where?

OLD MOOR: Can you tell me what's happened to my son? 125

HERRMANN: He was a student in Leipzig. From there he went on his wanderings, I don't know how far. He wandered all over Germany, bareheaded, as he told me, and without shoes, and begged his bread at men's doors. Five months later, the hateful war broke out between Prussia and Austria, and as he had nothing left to hope for in this world, King Frederick's victorious drum summoned him to Bohemia. Let me die, he said, to the great Schwerin, let me die the death of a hero, as I have no father any more! 130 135

OLD MOOR: *(burying his face in the pillows)* Oh, peace, oh peace!

HERRMANN: A week later came the great fight at Prague—I can tell you, your son stood his ground like a true warrior. He did miracles before the army's eyes. Five times they had to relieve the regiment beside him; he stood firm. Grenades fell to left and to right of him; your son stood firm. A bullet shattered his right hand; your son took the standard in his left, and stood firm— 140 145

AMALIA: *(ecstatically)* Hector, Hector! Stood firm, you hear it, stood firm—

HERRMANN: I found him on the evening of the battle, lying there with the bullets whistling around, with his left hand trying to stem the flow of blood, his right he had buried in the ground. Brother! he cried out when he saw me, there was a rumour in the ranks that the general was killed an hour ago—killed! I cried; and you?—Why then, he cried, and took his left hand away, let every true soldier follow his general with me! Soon 150 155

after he breathed out his mighty soul, to follow where the hero led. 160

FRANZ: *(attacking HERRMANN savagely)* May death seal your accursed lips! Have you come here to deal our father his death-blow?—Father! Amalia! Father!

HERRMANN: It was my dying comrade's last wish. Take my sword, he groaned, take it, give it to my old father, it's stained with his son's blood, he is revenged, let him rejoice. Tell him it was his curse that drove me to battle, war and death, tell him I am fallen in despair! His last gasp was—Amalia! 165 170

AMALIA: *(as if roused from a sleep of death)* His last gasp, Amalia!

OLD MOOR: *(crying out horribly, tearing his hair)* My curse that drove him to death! fallen in despair!

FRANZ: *(pacing about the room)* Oh, father, what have you done? My Karl, my brother! 175

HERRMANN: Here's the sword, and here too is a portrait that he took from his bosom! It is this lady, to the life! Give this to my brother Franz, he said— I don't know what he meant by it. 180

FRANZ: *(as if amazed)* To me? Amalia's portrait? To me, Karl, Amalia? Me?

AMALIA: *(attacking HERRMANN furiously)* Vile deceiver, who's paid you, who's bribed you? *(Seizing him.)* 185

HERRMANN: No one, my lady. See for yourself if it's not your portrait—you must have given it to him yourself

FRANZ: Dear God, Amalia, it is yours! It is truly yours! 190

AMALIA: *(returning the portrait)* Mine, mine! Oh, heaven and earth!

OLD MOOR: *(crying out, clawing at his face)* Woe, woe! my curse that drove him to death! fallen in despair! 195

FRANZ: And he could think of me in the last terrible hour of his departing, of me! Soul of an angel—as death's black banner already swept over him—of me!

OLD MOOR: *(babbling)* My curse that drove him, to death, fallen, my son, in despair! 200

HERRMANN: This grief is more than I can bear. Farewell, old lord! *(Softly to FRANZ)* Why did you have to go so far, young master? *(Exit, quickly.)*

AMALIA: *(jumping up, running after him)* Stay, stay! 205
What were his last words?
HERRMANN: *(calling over his shoulder)* His last
gasp was Amalia. *(Exit.)*
AMALIA: His last gasp was Amalia!—No, you're not
deceiving us! So it's true—true—he's dead—dead! 210
*(Swaying to and fro, and finally falling to the
ground.)* Dead—Karl is dead—
FRANZ: What do I see? What's this on the sword?
words written in the blood—Amalia!
AMALIA: His words? 215
FRANZ: Do I see aright, or am I dreaming? Look
there, letters of blood: Franz, do not desert my
Amalia! Look, look! and on the other side: Amalia,
all-powerful death releases you from your oath—
Do you see, do you see? He wrote it as his fingers 220
stiffened, wrote it in his heart's warm blood, wrote
it upon the solemn brink of eternity! his fleeting
spirit stayed a moment, that Franz and Amalia
might be joined.
AMALIA: God in Heaven! it is his hand.—He never 225
loved me! *(Hurrying off.)*
FRANZ: *(stamping on the floor)* Desperation! all my
art is foiled by such obstinacy!
OLD MOOR: Woe, woe! Do not leave me, my
daughter!—Franz, Franz! give me back my son! 230
FRANZ: Who was it that cursed him? Who was it
that drove his son to battle and death and
despair?—Oh! he was an angel! a jewel in heaven's
crown! Curses upon them that slew him! Curses,
curses upon you yourself!— 235
OLD MOOR: *(striking breast and forehead with his
clenched fist)* He was an angel, a jewel in heaven's
crown! Curses, curses, destruction and curses upon
myself! I am the father that slew his mighty son!
Me, me he loved unto death! To avenge me he 240
hurled himself into battle and death! Monster,
monster! *(Venting his rage upon himself)*
FRANZ: He's gone; it's too late for remorse!
(Laughing scornfully) It's easier to murder than to
bring to life. You'll never raise him from his grave 245
again.
OLD MOOR: Never, never, never raise him from
his grave again! Gone, gone, lost forever!—And it
was you who talked me into cursing him, you—
you—Give me back my son! 250

FRANZ: Don't tempt my wrath! I'll leave you to die!
OLD MOOR: Vampire! vampire! give me my son
again!

*(Springing up from his chair and attempting to seize
FRANZ by the throat; FRANZ hurls him back.)*

FRANZ: Feeble old bag of bones! You dare—die!
despair! 255
OLD MOOR: A thousand curses ring about your
ears! You stole my son from my very arms.
(Twisting and turning in his chair in despair) Woe,
woe! To despair, but not to die! They flee, they
leave me to die—my good angels flee from me, all 260
that is holy flees the cold grey murderer—Woe!
woe! is there no one to hold my head, is there no
one to free my struggling soul from its prison? No
sons! no daughters! no friends!—only men—is
there none, alone—abandoned—woe! woe!—To 265
despair, but not to die!

(Enter AMALIA, her eyes red with weeping.)

OLD MOOR: Amalia! Messenger of heaven! Have
you come to free my soul?
AMALIA: *(in a gentler tone)* You've lost a glorious
son. 270
OLD MOOR: Murdered him, you mean. Laden
with this accusation shall I step before God's
judgement-seat!
AMALIA: Not so, old man who grieves so greatly!
Our heavenly Father summoned him. We should 275
have been too happy in this world.—There, there
beyond the stars—we'll see him again.
OLD MOOR: See him again, see him again! Oh,
it will be like a sword to smite my soul—if I
find him, a saint among the ranks of the saints— 280
in the midst of heaven I shall be encompassed
with the terrors of hell! In the sight of the
Eternal, bowed down as I recall: it was I that slew
my son!
AMALIA: Oh, he'll smile the recollection and the 285
pain from your soul; be of good cheer, dear father,
as I am! Has he not already sung the name Amalia
to the angel's harp, for the heavenly hosts to hear,
and the hosts of heaven whispered it after him? His
last gasp was—Amalia; will he not cry out in his 290
jubilation: Amalia! before all?

OLD MOOR: Heavenly comfort drops from your lips! He will smile, you say? forgive me? You must stay at my side, my Karl's true love, when I'm dying. 295

AMALIA: To die is to fly to his arms! Oh, happy— I envy you. Why aren't my bones as brittle? Why aren't the hairs of my head as grey? Alas, for the strength of youth! Welcome, feeble old age! to bring me nearer to heaven and my Karl. 300

(Enter FRANZ.)

OLD MOOR: Come to me! my son! Forgive me if I was too harsh with you before! I forgive you everything. I would so gladly breathe my last in peace.

FRANZ: Have you done with weeping for your son?—as far as I can see, you have only one. 305

OLD MOOR: Jacob's sons were twelve, but for one he wept tears of blood.

FRANZ: Humph!

OLD MOOR: Go and fetch the Bible, my daughter, and read me the story of Jacob and Joseph! It moved me always to hear it—and I wasn't even a Jacob yet. 310

AMALIA: What part shall I read you? *(She takes the Bible and turns the pages.)* 315

OLD MOOR: Read me the grief of him in his bereavement, when he could not find him among his children—and waited in vain for him, in the circle of the eleven—and his lamentation, as he heard his Joseph was taken from him forever— 320

AMALIA: *(reads)* "And they took Joseph's coat, and killed a kid of the goats, and dipped the coat in the blood; and they rent the coat of many colours, and they brought it to their father; and said, This have we found: know now whether it be thy son's 325 coat or no?" *(FRANZ hurries suddenly away.)* "And he knew it, and said, It is my son's coat; an evil beast hath devoured him: Joseph is without doubt rent in pieces."

OLD MOOR: *(falls back upon the pillow)* Rent in 330 pieces! An evil beast hath devoured him!

AMALIA: *(reading on)* "And Jacob rent his clothes, and put sackcloth upon his loins, and mourned for his son many days. And all his sons and all his daughters rose up to comfort him; but he refused 335

to be comforted; and he said, For I will go down into the grave unto my son mourning.—"

OLD MOOR: Stop, stop! I'm not well!

AMALIA: *(rushing to his side, dropping the book)* Heaven protect us! What's this? 340

OLD MOOR: It's death! Black—swimming— before—my eyes—I beg you—call the pastor— that I may—take the sacrament—Where's—my son Franz?

AMALIA: He's fled! God have mercy on us! 345

OLD MOOR: Fled—fled from the bedside of the dying?—And this all—all—two sons, full of hope—the Lord gave—the Lord hath—taken away—blessed be the name of—

AMALIA: *(crying out suddenly)* Dead! All dead! *(Exit,* 350 *in despair; Enter FRANZ, skipping for joy.)*

FRANZ: Dead! they cry, dead! Now I'm your lord and master. A hue and cry in all the castle: dead!— But what, perhaps he's only asleep? to be sure! a sleep that will never hear a good-morning again— 355 sleep and death are but twins. Let's just confuse the names! Welcome, brave sleep! We'll call you death. *(Closing his father's eyes.)* Who will come now, and dare to summon me before the courts? Or say to my face: you're a villain? Away then with 360 this burdensome mask of gentleness and virtue! Now you'll see Franz naked, as he is, and cringe in terror! My father sugared his commands, made his territories one happy family, sat smiling at the gate, and called everyone brother and sister.—My 365 brows will beetle over you like storm-clouds, my imperious name hover like a threatening comet over these mountain-tops, my forehead will be your barometer! He stroked and fondled the necks that would not bow, but rose in spite against him. 370 I'm not one for stroking and fondling. I'll set my pointed spurs into your flesh, and see what a keen whip will do.—In my lands the day will come when potatoes and small beer make a holiday feast, and woe betide any I meet with full and rosy 375 cheeks! The ashen-white of poverty and slavish fear is my favourite colour: that's the livery I'll have you wear! *(Exit.)*

SCENE 3
The forest of Bohemia.

SPIEGELBERG, RATZMANN, ROBBERS

RATZMANN: Are you there? Is it really you? Ah, Moritz, Moritz, brother of my heart, I could hug you to pulp! Welcome to the forest of Bohemia! Why, you've grown big and strong. Hell's bells, buckets of blood! New men, too, a whole gang you've brought! That's what I call recruiting! 5

SPIEGELBERG: Isn't it, brother, isn't it? And fine fellows too!—Don't you think the hand of God is upon me, poor hungry wretch that I was, with my staff I passed over this Jordan, and now there are 10 seventy-eight of us; mostly bankrupt shopkeepers, bachelors who've failed their disputations, clerks from the Swabian[32] provinces, what a body of men! charming fellows, who'd steal each other's fly-buttons, and won't sleep beside each other without 15 their guns loaded—who keep their pistols primed, and have a reputation for a hundred miles around, you'd never believe it. You won't find a newspaper without a little item about Spiegelberg the master-mind—it's the only reason I read them— 20 descriptions of me from head to toe, you'd think you could see me with your own eyes—they haven't left out the buttons on my jacket. But we've been leading them a terrible dance. One day I went to a printer's, told him I'd seen the notorious 25 Spiegelberg, and dictated to a scribbler that was sitting there the spitting likeness of some miserable quack doctor in the town; the thing gets around, the fellow is arrested, shown the instruments, and the fool's so frightened that damn me if he doesn't 30 confess that he is your notorious Spiegelberg! Hell's teeth! I almost went to complain to the magistrates about the scurvy creature abusing my name—anyhow, three months later, there he swings. I had to take a strong pinch of snuff, I can tell you, when 35 I strolled by the gibbet and saw pseudo-Spiegelberg up there in all his glory—and while Spiegelberg dangles, Spiegelberg slips quietly out of the noose,

and cocks a snook at wise-owl Justice behind her back—it's enough to make you weep! 40

RATZMANN: *(laughing)* You're still the same as ever.

SPIEGELBERG: I am indeed, as you see, body and soul. Fool!—I must tell you the trick I played at St. Cecilia's convent. I reached the convent on my wanderings one evening as it was getting dark, and 45 as I hadn't fired a single shot that day—you know I hate the thought of *diem perdidi*[33] like poison, so it was high time to brighten up the night with some escapade, even if it meant singeing the devil's ears! We wait quietly until late at night. 50 Everything's as quiet as a mouse. The lights go out. We reckon the nuns will be between the sheets. Now I take my comrade Grimm with me, tell the others to wait outside the gate until they hear my whistle—take care of the convent porter, get his 55 keys off him, creep in where the girls are sleeping, whisk their clothes away, and pile them all up outside the gate. On we go, one cell after the other, take all the sisters' clothes in turn, last of all the abbess's—then I whistle, and my fellows outside 60 kick up a commotion as if it was the Day of Judgement, and into the sisters' cells, roaring like wild beasts!—ha, ha, ha! you should have seen the sport we had, the poor creatures fumbling around in the dark for their petticoats, and weeping and 65 wailing, when they found the devil had taken them! and us upon them like a whirlwind, and them rolling themselves up in their blankets, so surprised and scared they were, or creeping under the stove like cats, and some of them wetting 70 themselves with fright, poor things, you could have learnt to swim in there, and the hue and cry and lamentation, and last of all the old hag of an abbess, dressed like Eve before the Fall—brother, you know there's no creature in all this world I hate 75 more than a spider and an old woman, and just imagine now that wizened, hairy old dragon dancing about in front of me, conjuring me by her maiden's honour—the devil! I was already putting my fists up to knock her last few teeth all the way 80 through her guts—make up your mind! either out with the silver, the treasure-chest and all those dear

---

32 Swabian provinces] the part of Germany where Schiller was born.

---

33 a wasted or lost day.

little shiny sovereigns, or—my fellows knew what I meant—I tell you, I cleaned out that convent of more than a thousand's-worth, and had the fun too, and my fellows left them a memento to carry around for the next nine months. 85

RATZMANN: Damnation, why wasn't I there?

SPIEGELBERG: You see? Go on, tell me, isn't that a life of luxury? and it keeps you fit and strong, and the corpus is all in one piece, and growing every hour like a bishop's belly—I don't know, there must be something magnetic about me, that attracts all the rogues and vagabonds on God's earth like iron and steel. 90 95

RATZMANN: A fine magnet you are! But hang me, I'd like to know what witchcraft you use!

SPIEGELBERG: Witchcraft? No need of witch-craft—you must just have your wits about you! A certain practical expertise, that doesn't grow on trees, I admit—what I always say is, you see: you can make an honest man out of any old stick, but for a villain, you need grey matter—and you want a certain national talent too, a kind of, so to speak, villain's climate—and I'll tell you what, go to Swit-zerland: the Grisons, that's the Mecca of rogues today. 100 105

RATZMANN: Ah, brother! Italy, they tell me, is a good place altogether.

SPIEGELBERG: Oh yes, yes! everyone must have his due; Italy has had its share of good men, and if Germany goes on as it's going today, and they abol-ish the Bible completely, as there is every appearance, then Germany may produce some-thing worthwhile too, in time—but overall, let me tell you, climate makes very little difference; gen-ius will thrive in any soil, and the rest, brother—well, you know, a crab won't turn into a pineapple even in the Garden of Eden—but, as I was explaining to you—where was I? 110 115 120

RATZMANN: You were coming to the tricks of the trade.

SPIEGELBERG: Yes, the tricks of the trade! Well then, the first thing you must do, when you come to any town, is to find out from the police, the jailor and the poor-house keeper who it is they see most of, who comes to present his compliments most often, and these are the customers you must 125

look for—then, you establish yourself in the coffeehouses, the brothels, and the inns, keep your eyes open, sound people out, see who complains the loudest about their miserable five per cent these days, or about the pestilential increase in law and order, who curses the government most, or holds forth about the fashion for physiognomy and that kind of thing! Then you know where you are, brother! Honesty wobbles like a hollow tooth; just get out your pincers—Or, better and quicker: you go and drop a purse full of money in the street where everyone can see it, hide yourself somewhere by, and see who picks it up; then after a bit you come chasing after, looking around, and crying out, and ask him, just as it might be in passing, did the gentleman not find a purse of money? If he says yes, well, then the devil was watching; but if he denies it? "You'll excuse me, Sir—I really can't remember—I'm sorry." *(jumping up)* Victory, brother, victory! Put out your light, cunning Diogenes![34]—you've found the man you wanted. 130 135 140 145 150

RATZMANN: You are an expert practitioner.

SPIEGELBERG: My God! as if I'd ever doubted it.—Now you've got your man on the hook, you must be careful how you go about landing him. Look, my lad, this is how I've always done it. As soon as I was on the trail, I stuck to my candidate like a burr, drank and swore friendship with him, and *nota bene!*[35] you must pay for every round! It'll cost you a tidy penny, but you mustn't care—on you go, introduce him to gaming and doubtful company, get him involved in a fight, and mischief of one kind and another, till he's bankrupt of strength and resistance and money and conscience and good name; and by the way, I must tell you, you'll get nowhere unless you destroy both body and soul—believe me, brother! I must have drawn the conclusion fifty times in my extensive operations, that once the honest man is driven from his nest, the devil is master—it's as easy a 155 160 165

---

34 Cynic philosopher (c. 400–325 B.C.E.) who supposedly carried a lantern as he walked through Athens during the day, looking in vain for an honest man.

35 *nota bene*] "note well." (Ital.)

step—oh, as easy a step as from a whore to a pious 170
old maid.—But listen! was that a shot?

RATZMANN: It was the thunder; go on!

SPIEGELBERG: A still quicker, better way is this: you
rob your man of house and home, till he hasn't a
shirt left to his back, then he'll come to you of his 175
own accord—don't ask *me* the tricks, brother, just
ask that red-faced fellow over there—the pox! I got
him tangled up a treat—I showed him forty ducats,
said they were his if he'd take a pressing of his master's keys in wax for me—imagine! the stupid brute 180
does it, devil take me if he doesn't bring me the keys
and ask for his money—My good fellow, says I, let
me tell you that I'll take these keys straight to the
superintendent of police and book you a place on
the gibbet!—Strike me dead! you should have seen 185
the fellow: his eyes popped and he shivered like a wet
poodle—"In heaven's name! will the gentleman not
be reasonable? I'll—I'll—" "What, man? Will you
tuck up your pigtail and go to the devil with me?"—
"Oh yes, with pleasure, anything you say"—ha, ha, 190
ha! poor simpleton, mice like cheese, don't they?—
Have a good laugh at him, Ratzmann! ha, ha!

RATZMANN: Yes, yes, I must admit. I'll inscribe
your lesson in golden characters on the tablets of
my memory. Satan must know his man, choosing 195
you for his scout.

SPIEGELBERG: Don't you think so, brother? And
I reckon if I catch ten more for him he'll let me
go free—a publisher gives his agent one free copy
in ten, why should the devil be such a Jew?— 200
Ratzmann! I smell powder.

RATZMANN: Confound it! I've smelt it for a long
time. Mark my words, something will be up not
far from here!—Yes, yes, I tell you, Moritz—the
Captain will be glad to see you and your recruits— 205
he's enlisted some fine fellows, too.

SPIEGELBERG: But mine! mine! Pah—

RATZMANN: Yes, they look light-fingered
enough—but I tell you, our Captain's reputation
has led honest men into temptation too. 210

SPIEGELBERG: I hope not!

RATZMANN: *Sans* jest![36] and they're not ashamed
to serve under him. He doesn't murder for plunder

as we do—he doesn't seem to care about the
money, as long as he can keep his pistols primed, 215
and even his third of the booty, that's his by right,
he gives away to orphans, or to promising kids
from poor homes so that they can study. But if
there's a squire to be fleeced, one that drives his
peasants like cattle, or if we get hold of some gold- 220
braided scoundrel who twists the laws to his own
advantage, and makes justice wink with silver, or
any fine fellow of that kind—man! then he's in his
element, and the devil's in him, as if every nerve
of his body was a fury. 225

SPIEGELBERG: Hm, hm.

RATZMANN: Not long ago, we were at an inn, and
got wind that a rich count was on his way from
Regensburg, who'd just won a case worth a million,
thanks to a crafty lawyer—he was sitting at the table 230
playing backgammon—How many of us are there?
he asked me, and jumped to his feet; I saw him
biting his lip, as he only does when he's in a real
rage—five at the most, I said—It's enough! he said,
threw the money for the landlady on the table, left 235
the wine that he had ordered untouched—we set off
on our way. The whole time he didn't speak a word,
went aside by himself, only asked us from time to
time whether we could hear anything yet, and told
us to put our ears to the ground. At last, there comes 240
the count, riding along, his carriage weighed down
with baggage, the lawyer sitting inside with him,
one man riding ahead, two servants alongside—
then you should have seen the man, bounding up to
the carriage ahead of us, with two pistols in his 245
hand! and his voice, as he shouted Stop! The
coachman didn't want to stop, but he had to take a
dive from the box; the count shot out of the carriage
door, but it was useless, the riders fled—your
money, scum! he cried, in a voice like thunder—he 250
lay like a bullock under the axe—Are you the villain
who makes a whore of justice? The lawyer shook so
you could hear his teeth chattering—then there was
a dagger in his belly, sticking up like a stake in a
vineyard—I've done my part! he cried, and turned 255
away from us in his proud fashion—Plundering is
your business. And with that he disappeared into the
woods—

SPIEGELBERG: Hm, hm—brother, what I told you

---

[36] no joke.

just now was between ourselves, he needn't know 260
about it. Do you understand?

RATZMANN: Right, right, I understand!

SPIEGELBERG: You know what he's like. He has
his whims. You understand me,

RATZMANN: Very well, I understand. *(Enter* 265
SCHWARZ, at full speed.)

SCHWARZ: Quick, quick! where're the others? By
all the sacraments! you standing there, and talking?
Don't you know—don't you know, then?—and
Roller— 270

RATZMANN: What then, what?

SCHWARZ: Roller's been hanged, and four others
too.

RATZMANN: Roller? The plague! but when—how
do you know? 275

SCHWARZ: Three weeks and more he was inside,
and we heard nothing; three times they had him
up, and we heard nothing, they tortured him to
find out where the captain was—he gave nothing
away, stout lad; yesterday they tried him and this 280
morning he was sent express to the devil.

RATZMANN: Damnation! Does the captain know?

SCHWARZ: He heard about it yesterday. He was
foaming like a wild boar. You know Roller was
always his favourite, and now, torture—he had 285
ropes and ladders brought to the prison, but it was
no use—he dressed up as a friar himself and got
in there, and wanted to take Roller's place, but
Roller turned it down flat; now he's sworn an oath
that made our blood freeze, that he'll light him a 290
funeral pyre such as no king ever had, one that will
burn them black and blue. I wouldn't like to be
in that town. He's had it in for them for a long
time, because they're such miserable bigots, and
you know, when he says, I'll do it, it's as much as 295
if you or I had already done it.

RATZMANN: That's true. I know the captain. If
he'd given the devil his word that he'd go to hell,
he'd never say a prayer, even though he could save
himself with half an Our Father! But oh! poor 300
Roller! poor Roller!

SPIEGELBERG: *Memento mori!* But it makes no
difference to me. *(Singing.)*

As I go past the gallows tree,
I turn my head and blink my eye, 305

And think, as you swing there so free,
Who's the fool now, you or I?

RATZMANN: *(jumping up)* Listen! a shot. *(Shooting
and noises off.)*

SPIEGELBERG: Another! 310

RATZMANN: And another! the captain!

VOICES: *(singing offstage)*

In Nuremberg you'll never hang,
Unless they catch you first. *(Da capo[37])*

SCHWEITZER, ROLLER: *(offstage)* Hey, hallo! 315
halloo, ho!

RATZMANN: Roller, Roller! Ten devils take me!

SCHWEITZER, ROLLER: *(offstage)* Ratzmann!
Schwarz! Spiegelberg! Ratzmann!

RATZMANN: Roller! Schweitzer! Death, devils, hell 320
and damnation! *(Running to meet them.)*

*(Enter ROBBER MOOR on horseback;
SCHWEITZER, ROLLER, GRIMM,
SCHUFTERLE, and a troop of ROBBERS, covered
with dust and dirt.)*

MOOR: *(jumping down from his horse)* Freedom,
freedom!—you're home and dry, Roller!
Schweitzer, take my horse and wash him down
with wine. *(Throwing himself on the ground)* That 325
was warm work!

RATZMANN: *(to ROLLER)* By Pluto's fiery furnace!
are you resurrected from the wheel?

SCHWARZ: Are you his ghost? or am I a fool? or is
it really you? 330

ROLLER: *(recovering his breath)* It is. Flesh and
blood, entire. Where do you think I've come from?

SCHWARZ: Ask the Sibyl![38] the judge had put on
his black cap for you.

ROLLER: That he had, and that's not all. I've come 335
express from the gallows. Just let me get my breath
back. Schweitzer here will tell you. Get me a glass
of brandy!—you here again too, Moritz? I thought
I should be seeing you in another place—get me
a glass of brandy, will you? my bones are falling 340
apart—oh, captain! where's the captain?

SCHWARZ: Straight away, straight away!—but tell
us, say! how did you get away? how have we got

---

37 back to the top; repeat.
38 generic name for a female prophet or fortune-teller.

you again? My head is spinning. From the gallows, you say?

ROLLER: *(drinking a bottle of brandy)* Ah, that's good, that warms your heart! Straight from the gallows, I tell you! There you stand gasping, and can't imagine it—I was only three steps from the blessed ladder that was going to take me up to Abraham's bosom—so near, so near! sold to the dissecting-theatre already, head to foot, inside and out! you could've had my life for a pinch of snuff, but I owe the captain breath, life and liberty. 350

SCHWEITZER: It's a tale worth telling. The day before, we'd heard from our spies that Roller was in a pretty pickle, and if the skies didn't fall in time, then the next morning, at break of day—that would be today—he would have to go the way of all flesh.—Up! says the captain, what won't we do for a friend. We'll save him, or if we can't save him, then at least we'll light him a funeral pyre such as no king ever had, one that'll burn them black and blue. The whole band turned out. We sent a messenger express to him, with a note of what we were going to do, to drop in his soup. 355

ROLLER: I never believed they'd succeed.

SCHWEITZER: We bided our time till all the alleyways were empty. All the town had gone out to see the show, on horseback and on foot and in carriages all jostling together, you could hear the din and the penitential psalm a long way off. Now, says the captain, set alight, set alight! Our fellows flew like arrows, set fire to the town in thirty-three places at once, threw down burning firebrands near the powder-magazine, in the churches and the barns—by God, before a quarter of an hour was up, the north-east wind came and served us a treat—he must have had his grudge against the town too!—and helped the fire on its way to the topmost gables. And us meanwhile up and down the streets like furies—fire, fire! all through the town—shrieks and howls and rampage—the fire-bells start to ring, then up goes the arsenal in the air, as if the earth was split in two, and heaven burst, and hell sunk ten thousand fathoms deeper. 370 375 380 385

ROLLER: And now my escorts looked over their shoulders—there lay the town like Sodom and Gomorrha,[39] the whole horizon was fire and smoke and brimstone, forty hills echoing the hellish blast all around, everyone falls to the ground in panic—I seize the opportunity, and whish! like the wind—they'd untied me, we were as close to it as that—with my company staring back petrified like Lot's wife,[40] away! through the crowds, and off! Sixty yards further and I throw off my clothes, jump into the river, swim under the water till I thought I was out of their sight. The captain ready and waiting with clothes and horses—and so I escaped. Moor, Moor! I only hope you land in such a stew, so I can repay you in the same coin! 390 395 400

RATZMANN: A brute of a wish, that you deserve to be hanged for—but what a trick to pull off! 405

ROLLER: It was rescue in my darkest hour, you'll never know what it was like. You should have been there, with the rope around your neck, marching wide awake to the grave like me, and all their accursed rituals and hangman's ceremonies, and every tottering, frightened step nearer and nearer to the loathsome contrivance where I was going to be installed, rising in the hideous glow of the morning sun, and the hangman's assistants lurking, and the horrible music—I can still hear it ringing in my ears—and the hungry ravens croaking, thirty of them perched there on my half-rotten predecessor, and all that, all that—and the foretaste of the eternal bliss that was waiting for me too! Brother, brother! and all of a sudden, the password to freedom—a bang as if heaven had burst its hoops—listen, you vermin! I tell you, if you were to jump from the glowing furnace into icy water, you wouldn't feel such a difference as I did when I reached the opposite bank. 410 415 420 425

SPIEGELBERG: *(laughing)* Poor bastard! Now it's out of your system. *(Drinks to him)* Here's to your happy resurrection!

---

39 iniquitous biblical cities destroyed by divine fire (Genesis 18, 19).

40 The one family spared the above conflagration was Lot's, but his wife looked back at the blaze, contrary to God's commandment, and turned into a pillar of salt (Genesis 19:26).

ROLLER: *(throwing his glass away)* No, by all the treasures of Mammon![41] I shouldn't care to live through that again. Dying is more than a harlequinade,[42] and the fear of death is worse than dying itself. 430

SPIEGELBERG: And the arsenal blown up—you see now, Ratzmann? That's why the air smelt of sulphur for miles around, as if Moloch's[43] privy had been tipped out beneath the firmament—it was a master-stroke, captain! I envy you for it. 435

SCHWEITZER: If the town makes a holiday out of seeing my comrade done away with like a baited pig, why the devil should we have any qualms at setting off the town for the sake of our comrade? And on top of that, our fellows had the chance of plundering scot free. Tell us, what did you get? 440

ONE OF THE BAND: I crept into St. Stephen's in the confusion and cut the gold trimmings off the altar-cloth—the good Lord is a rich man, I said, and can spin gold out of old rope. 445

SCHWEITZER: Well done!—What's the use of that stuff in a church? They dedicate it to the Creator, who laughs at their trumpery—and his creatures go hungry—And you, Spangeler—where did you cast your nets? 450

ANOTHER: Bügel and I raided a chandler's, and have brought enough gear for fifty of us. 455

A THIRD: Two golden fob-watches I've spirited away, and a dozen silver spoons too.

SCHWEITZER: Good, good! And we've given them enough to keep them busy for a fortnight. If they want to put the fire out, they'll have to ruin the town with water.—Schufterle, didn't you hear how many dead there were? 460

SCHUFTERLE: Eighty-three, they say. The magazine alone blew sixty to smithereens.

MOOR: *(very gravely)* Roller, your life is dearly bought. 465

SCHUFTERLE: Pah! what do you mean? Now if it had been men; but it was only babes in arms still dirtying their linen, wrinkled grandmothers chasing the flies from them, shrivelled old stay-at-homes who couldn't find their way to the door—hypochondriacs whining for the doctor, while he'd gone out to follow the mob at his own solemn pace—Everyone with a sound pair of legs had run to see the spectacle, and only the dregs of the town was left behind to mind the houses. 470 475

MOOR: Oh, the poor, miserable creatures! Children, you say, the old and the sick?—

SCHUFTERLE: Yes, the devil take them! and women in childbed, and pregnant ones afraid of aborting under the gallows, and young wives who thought the hangman's tricks might give them a shock, and brand the child in their womb with a gallows-mark—poor poets who had no shoes to put on because their only pair was at the mender's, and riff-raff of that kind, not worth the trouble of talking about. I happened to be going past a row of cottages there, and heard a howling and peeped in, and when I took a good look, what was it? A baby, lying there as right as rain under the table, and the table just about to catch fire—Poor little brute! I said, you're freezing! and threw it into the flames— 480 485 490

MOOR: Did you, Schufterle? And may those flames burn in your breast till the day eternity grows grey!—Away, monster! Never let me see you in my band again! What, are you murmuring? Are you hesitating? Who can hesitate when I command? Away with him, I say—there are others among you who are ripe for my wrath. I know you, Spiegelberg. But I shall come amongst you, and terrible will be my judgement on you. 495 500

(Exeunt ROBBERS, trembling, leaving MOOR alone, pacing violently up and down.)

MOOR: Hear them not, avenger in Heaven! How can I prevent it? How can you prevent it, when your pestilence, your famine, your floods devour the just man with the wicked? Who can command the flame, and bid it spare the hallowed crops when it destroys the hornet's nest? Oh shame upon the murder of children! of women! of the sick! How this deed bows my head! It's poisoned my finest works—see the boy standing there, flushed 505 510

---

41 personified symbol of evil materialism.
42 theatrical genre combining spectacular magic effects and *commedia dell'arte* characters.
43 Canaanite idol for whom humans were burnt as sacrificial offerings (Leviticus 18:21).

with disgrace and mocked before the eyes of Heaven, he who ventured to play with Jove's thunderbolt, and hurled down pygmies when his task was to shatter titans—go, go! you're not the man to wield the highest tribunal's avenging sword; the first stroke was too much for your strength—here I renounce the impertinent plan, go to hide myself in some crevice of the earth, where the daylight shrinks before my shame. *(As if to flee. Enter ROBBERS, in haste.)*

A ROBBER: Look out, captain! The forest is alive! Whole troops of Bohemian cavalry are on the rampage—Hell's constable must have put them up to it.

MORE ROBBERS: Captain, captain! They've trailed us here—thousands of them are cordoning off the woods around us!

MORE ROBBERS: Help, help! They've caught us; we'll be hanged and quartered! Thousands and thousands of hussars and dragoons and scouts are riding up the hillside, and have cut off our bolt-holes.

(Exit MOOR. Enter SCHWEITZER, GRIMM, ROLLER, SCHWARZ, SCHUFTERLE, SPIEGEL-BERG, RATZMANN, and the ROBBER BAND.)

SCHWEITZER: Have we shaken them out of their beds? Cheer up, Roller! That's what I've been waiting for for a long time, a set-to with some of these cookhouse champions—where's the captain? Is the whole band together? We have powder enough, haven't we?

RATZMANN: Powder and plenty to spare. But there are no more than eighty of us—we're scarcely one to twenty.

SCHWEITZER: All the better! and if it was fifty of them to my finger-nail! Didn't they sit tight till we'd set fire to the straw under their arses? Brothers! brothers! there's nothing to worry about! They gamble their lives for ten kreutzers; aren't we fighting for our necks and our freedom? We'll be on them like the Flood and rain down on their heads like thunder-bolts—Where in the Devil's name is the captain?

SPIEGELBERG: He's left us in our hour of need. Can't we get away?

SCHWEITZER: Get away?

SPIEGELBERG: Oh, why didn't I stay in Jerusalem!

SCHWEITZER: Why, then I hope you drown in a sewer, you miserable rat! When it's naked nuns you've enough to say for yourself, but when you see a pair of fists—Coward, let's see now what you're made of, or we'll sew you into a sow's skin and set the dogs on you!

RATZMANN: The captain, the captain!

(Enter MOOR)

MOOR: *(slowly, aside)* I've let them encircle us completely; now these fellows will have to fight in desperation. *(Aloud)* Now, children! Now's the time! We're lost, or we must fight like wild boars at bay.

SCHWEITZER: Ha! I'll rip their bellies with my tusks till their tripes come bursting out by the yard! Lead on, captain! We'll follow you into the jaws of death!

MOOR: Load all weapons. There's no shortage of powder?

SCHWEITZER: *(bounding up)* No, powder enough to blow the earth sky-high!

RATZMANN: Every man has five pairs of pistols loaded, every man three rifles as well.

MOOR: Good, good! And now some of you must climb the trees, or hide among the thickets, and fire at them from the rear—

SCHWEITZER: That's your place, Spiegelberg!

MOOR: The rest of us, like furies, will fall upon their flank.

SCHWEITZER: That's the place for me!

MOOR: At the same time everyone must let them hear him whistle, and move around in the woods, so that our numbers will seem more formidable; and we must let all the dogs loose, and set them amongst their ranks, to separate and spread them out and drive them into your fire. We three, Roller, Schweitzer and I, will fight in the thick of it.

SCHWEITZER: Masterly, superb! We'll beat them so they won't know where the blows are coming from. I can shoot a cherry out of a man's mouth—just let them come!

(SCHUFTERLE tugs at SCHWEITZER'S sleeve; SCHWEITZER goes to one side with the captain and speaks quietly with him.)

MOOR: Silence! 595

SCHWEITZER: I beg you—

MOOR: Away! Let him thank his disgrace; it's saved his life. He will not die when I and my Schweitzer die, and my Roller. Take his clothes from him; I'll say he was a passer-by and I robbed him—Calm yourself, Schweitzer! I swear he'll yet be hanged one day. 600

(Enter a PRIEST)

PRIEST: *(aside, taken aback)* Is this the dragon's lair?—By your leave, gentlemen! I'm a servant of the Church, and out there are seventeen hundred men, set to guard every hair of my head. 605

SCHWEITZER: Bravo, bravo! a fine speech to keep one's belly warm.

MOOR: Silence, comrade!—Speak, father, and be brief! What business have you with us?

PRIEST: I'm sent by the authorities, whose word is life and death—you thieves—you murderous incendiaries—you scoundrels—poisonous brood of vipers, that creep in darkness, and sting where no man sees—plague upon the face of mankind—generation of hell—feast for ravens and vermin—colony for the gallows and the wheel— 610 615

SCHWEITZER: Dog! enough of your abuse, or—
(thrusting a rifle-butt into his face)

MOOR: Shame on you, Schweitzer! You've spoilt his peroration—he's learnt his sermon so perfectly by heart—go on, Sir!—"for the gallows and the wheel..."? 620

PRIEST: And you, glorious captain! Duke of cutpurses! King of villains! Great Mogul of all the scoundrels under the sun! Image of that first loathsome rabble-rouser, who stirred up a thousand legions of innocent angels to fiery rebellion, and dragged them down with him to the pit of damnation—the accusing cries of abandoned mothers howl at your heels, blood is the water you drink, men weigh on your murderous dagger no more than a bubble of air— 625 630

MOOR: Very true, very true! Go on!

PRIEST: What? Very true, very true? That's your answer? 635

MOOR: What, sir? That wasn't quite what you expected? Go on, go on! What more did you have to say?

PRIEST: *(heatedly)* Terrible man! get thee behind me! Does not the murdered Count's blood stick to your accursed fingers? Have you not with thieving hands violated the Lord's sanctuary, and villainously seized the consecrated vessels of the sacrament? What? Did not you hurl brands of fire into our God-fearing city, and blow up its magazine over the heads of pious Christians? *(Clasping his hands together)* Hideous, hideous sins, that stink to high heaven, and call the Last Judgement to arms, that it may break upon you! Ripe for retribution, ready for the last trumpet! 640 645 650

MOOR: Masterly, so far! but to the matter—what would the right worshipful gentlemen have you tell me?

PRIEST: That which you are not worthy to hear!—Look about you, incendiary and murderer! As far as your eye can see, you're pinned in by our cavalry—there's no room for you to escape now—as sure as cherries will grow upon these oaks, and these pine-trees bear peaches, so surely will you turn your back upon these oaks and pines unharmed. 655 660

MOOR: Do you hear, Schweitzer?—But go on!

PRIEST: Hear then, how graciously, how patiently justice has borne with your iniquities. If you will crawl upon your knees to the cross, and beg for grace and mercy, then see, severity itself will yield to pity, justice will be as a loving mother—she'll turn a blind eye to half of your crimes, and—consider!—you'll only be broken on the wheel. 665

SCHWEITZER: Do you hear, captain! Shall I squeeze this worn-out sheepdog by the throat till he sweats blood from every pore?— 670

ROLLER: Captain! Death, devils and hell! Captain!—see how he chews his lip between his teeth! shall I turn the fellow upside-down beneath the firmament like a ninepin? 675

SCHWEITZER: Me, me! Let me kneel, let me beg at your feet! Let me have the pleasure of grinding him to powder! *(PRIEST cries out.)*

MOOR: Leave him alone! Let no one dare to touch him! *(to the PRIEST, drawing his sword)* Look, father! here stand seventy-nine men, whose captain I am, and none of them will fly at a command, or dance to the music of your cannons; and out there stand 680 seventeen hundred who have grown grey beneath their muskets—but hear me! thus says Moor, captain of murderers and incendiaries. It's true; I killed the Count, I plundered the Dominican church and set it alight, I cast firebrands into your city of bigots, I blew up the arsenal over the heads of pious Christians—but that's not all. *(Stretching out his right hand)* Look at these four precious rings that I wear, one on each finger—go and tell the worshipful gentlemen with their powers of life and death, tell them point by point, what you are about to see and hear.—This ruby I took from the finger of a minister whom I laid low at his prince's feet when he was hunting. He was a man of the common people, who'd made his way by flattery to his master's highest favour—his neighbour's fall was the footstool of his exaltation—orphan's tears bore him aloft. This diamond I took from a minister of finance, who sold offices and honours to the highest bidder, and turned the sorrowing patriot away from his door. This agate I wear in honour of one of your cloth, whom I strangled with my own hands after he'd lamented, at the pulpit, before his congregation, that the Inquisition had so declined.—I could tell you many more stories of my rings, if it were not that I already regret the few words I've wasted on you—

PRIEST: O Pharaoh, Pharaoh!

MOOR: Do you hear? Did you mark him groan? Does he not stand there as if he'd call down fire from Heaven upon the Korahites[44] with prayer? judging with a shrug of his shoulders, damning with a Christian sigh! Can a man be so blind? He who has Argus's[45] hundred eyes to spy out his brother's spots, can he be so blind to his own?— Gentleness and tolerance they thunder from their clouds, and offer the God of love human sacrifices like a fiery-armed Moloch—they preach the love of their neighbour, and they curse the blind octogenarian at their door—they fulminate against covetousness, and they've slaughtered Peru for the sake of golden brooches, and harnessed the pagans like beasts of burden to drag their wagons—they rack their brains in wonder that nature could have brought forth a Judas Iscariot, and he's not the meanest of them who would betray God's Holy Trinity for ten pieces of silver! Oh, you Pharisees,[46] you forgers of the truth, you apes and mockers of God! You're not ashamed to kneel before cross and altar, to flay your backs with scourges and to mortify your flesh with fasting, and you think these miserable mountebank's tricks will deceive Him whom you fools yet call all-knowing—just as one mocks the great most bitterly by flattering them that they hate flatterers; you boast of your honesty and upright life, and the God who looks into your hearts would be seized with rage against the creator, if it were not He himself who created the monster of the Nile. Take him out of my sight.

PRIEST: That the wicked can be so proud!

MOOR: Not enough!—now I will speak with pride. Go and tell the right worshipful gentlemen that dice for life and death—I'm no thief that conspires with midnight and with sleep, and plays the great man when he mounts the ladder—what I've done, doubtless I'll read one day in the ledgers of Heaven, but with their miserable hirelings I'll waste my words no more. Tell them my trade is retribution—vengeance is my calling. *(Turning his back on him.)*

PRIEST: So you don't seek grace and mercy? Very well, I've nothing more to say to you. *(Turning to the band)* You then, listen to what I have to tell you in the name of justice!—If you'll now lay hands on this condemned criminal, bind him and deliver him up, then see! you'll be spared punishment for the horrors you've committed— the memory of them will be wiped out—Holy Mother Church will receive you once again into her loving bosom like sheep that have strayed, and to each one of you the way to rank and honour shall be open. *(Smiling triumphantly)* What then! What do you say to that, your Majesty?—Hurry then! Bind him, and you are free!

---

44 Biblical: the sons of Korah, singers and porters in the Temple (see Chronicles).

45 Greek mythological herdsman whose body was covered with eyes; at his death, Argus's eyes were given to the peacock's tail.

46 ancient biblical sect hated for its traditionalism, formalism, and self-righteousness.

MOOR: Do you hear? Do you hear him? Why do you hesitate? Don't you know what to do? Justice offers you freedom, and you are in truth her prisoners.—She grants you your lives, and those are no empty words, for you are in truth condemned men.—She promises you rank and honour, and what can your lot be, even if you were to be victorious, other than shame and curses and persecution?—She speaks to you with Heaven's voice of reconciliation, and you are, in truth, damned. There's not a hair on your heads, not on one of you, that's not destined for hell. Will you still consider? Are you still in doubt? Is it so hard to choose between heaven and hell? Will you not help them, father! 770 775 780

PRIEST: *(aside)* Is the fellow mad?—What, do you think perhaps it's a trap to catch you all alive? Read for yourselves, here's the general pardon, signed and sealed. *(Handing SCHWEITZER a paper)* Can you still be in doubt? 785

MOOR: Look, look! What more can you ask? Signed with his own hand—mercy beyond bounds—or are you afraid they'll break their word, have you heard that no faith is kept with traitors?—Oh, have no fear! Politics could make them keep their word, even if they'd given it to Satan himself. Who would ever believe them again? Would they ever be able to play the trick again?—I'd swear that they mean it! They know it's I who stirred you up and embittered you; they think you're innocent. Your crimes they interpret as the errors of hasty youth. It's I alone whom they seek, I alone who must pay the penalty. Is it not so, father? 790 795 800

PRIEST: What's the devil called that speaks out of him?—Yes, yes, it is so—the fellow has me spinning.

MOOR: What, still no reply? Surely you don't think you can break out by force of arms? Look around you, look around you! surely you can't think that! such confidence would be mere childish folly.— Or do you flatter yourselves, thinking to die the death of heroes, because you saw how I rejoiced at the thought of battle?—Oh, don't believe it! You're not Moor.—You're nothing but a gang of thieves! Miserable instruments of my greater designs, like the contemptible rope in the 805 810

hangman's hand! Thieves can't die the death of heroes. Life is the thief's profit; after it come terrors.—Thieves have the right to be afraid of death.—Hear how their trumpets sound! See how their threatening sabres flash! What? Still undecided? are you mad? are you out of your minds?—It's unforgivable! I will not owe my life to you, I despise your sacrifice! 815 820

PRIEST: *(in astonishment)* He'll drive me mad; I must fly from this place! Whoever heard such things as this?

MOOR: Or are you afraid that I'll kill myself, and by my suicide invalidate the treaty that counted only while I was alive? No, children! that's an idle fear. Here I throw away my dagger; here my pistols and the vial of poison that I had in readiness— I'm so wretched, I've lost even the power of my own life.—What, still undecided? Or do you think I'll resist, if you attempt to bind me? Look! see me lash my right hand to this oak-tree's branch, I'm defenceless, a child can conquer me—Who'll be the first to abandon his captain in his hour of need? 825 830 835

ROLLER: *(in furious excitement)* Even if nine circles of hell surrounded us! *(Brandishing his sword)* Every man who's not a dog, save your captain!

SCHWEITZER: *(tearing up the pardon, and throwing the pieces in the PRIEST's face)* Pardon, in our bullets! Away, vermin! tell the magistrates who sent you that in Moor's band you couldn't find a single traitor.—Save, save the captain! 840

ALL: *(shouting)* Save, save, save the captain! 845

MOOR: *(tearing himself free, joyfully)* Now we're free—Comrades! I feel an army in my fist—death or liberty!—at least they'll take none of us alive!

(The trumpets sound the attack. Noise and tumult. Exeunt, with drawn swords.)

ACT THREE SCENE 1

AMALIA in her garden, playing upon the lute.

AMALIA: Fair as angels, full of heaven's delight,
Fairer far than other youths was he,
His gaze as Maytime sunbeams tender-bright,
Mirrored in the heavenly azure sea.

His embrace—oh, raging ecstasies!
Fiery hearts around each other furled,
Our lips and ears entranced—before our eyes
The night—and our two spirits heavenward
   whirled.
And his kiss—oh, taste of paradise!
As two burning flames will grasp and cling,
As two harps will join their melodies
And their heavenly harmonies will sing,
Plunging, racing, soaring, spirits bound,
Lip and cheek a-tremble and ablaze,
Soul joined with soul and heaven and earth
   around
The lovers lost and melted in the haze.
He is gone! alas, it is in vain
The timid sigh recalls him to our grasp!
He is gone—and life is now but pain,
All joy expiring in a dying gasp.

(Enter FRANZ.)

FRANZ: Here again, wilful dreamer? You crept away from our merry feast, and spoilt our guests' pleasure.

AMALIA: I'm sorry for these innocent delights—when the dirge that sang your father to his grave must still be ringing in your ears—

FRANZ: Will you mourn forever? Let the dead sleep, and make the living happy! I've come—

AMALIA: And when will you be gone again?

FRANZ: Oh, Amalia! Let me not see these black, proud looks! You grieve me. I've come to tell you—

AMALIA: I suppose I must hear that Franz von Moor has succeeded to the title.

FRANZ: Yes, I came to hear what you'd say—Maximilian has been laid to rest with his forefathers. I'm your lord and master. But Amalia, I would be so in every respect.—You remember what you've been to our family; Moor treated you as his daughter, his love for you lives on even after his death—can you ever forget that?

AMALIA: Never, never. Who could be so thoughtless as to drown those memories in feasting!

FRANZ: My father's love for you must be repaid to his sons, and Karl's dead—you wonder? you're giddy? Yes, truly, the thought of it is so grand, so flattering, that it must numb even a woman's pride.

Franz tramples upon the hopes of the noblest young ladies in the land, Franz comes and offers his heart and his hand to a poor orphan who would be helpless without him, and with it all his gold and all his castles and forests. Franz, whom men envy and fear, comes of his own free will to declare himself Amalia's slave—

AMALIA: Why doesn't the lightning split the blaspheming tongue that speaks such shameful words? You, you murdered my love, and Amalia should call you husband? you—

FRANZ: Not so hasty, your most gracious highness!—It's true, Franz can't mop and mow like a cooing Celadon[47] before you—true, he hasn't learnt to moan his lover's complaint to the echo of the rocks and caves like a languishing Arcadian swain—Franz speaks, and if he hears no answer, he will—command.

AMALIA: Command? You, reptile, command? command me?—and if I throw your command back in your face with scorn?

FRANZ: You won't do that. I know a way that will nicely tame your blind obstinate pride—a convent cell!

AMALIA: Bravo! excellent! in a convent cell, spared your basilisk's look forever, and with time enough to think of Karl, to cling to his memory. Welcome with your convent! Let your cell enfold me!

FRANZ: Ha! is it so!—beware! Now you've taught me the art of tormenting you—the sight of me will scourge this everlasting fancy of Karl from your head like a fury with locks of fire; the bogey-man Franz will lurk behind your lover's image like the dog in the fairy-tale, that lay on the underground treasure—by your hair I'll drag you into the chapel with my sword in my hand, force the oath of matrimony out of your soul, take your virgin bed by storm, and conquer your proud innocence with my greater pride.

AMALIA: *(striking him across the face)* Take this for your dowry!

---

47 chivalrous shepherd-hero of a long sentimental romance by Honoré d'Urfé (1607–27), *L'Astrée,* full of precious talk and poetry about virtuous love, fidelity and constancy.

THE ROBBERS 803

FRANZ: (provoked) Ha! ten times and ten times
more you'll be paid back for that! Not my wife—
you won't have the honour—no, I'll have you for
my mistress, and honest peasant women will point
their fingers at you if you dare to cross the street.
Yes, gnash your teeth—spit fire and venom from
your eyes—I like a woman to be angry, it makes
you more beautiful, more desirable. Come—your
struggling will be sauce to my triumph and spice
to my pleasure when I force my embraces on
you—Come with me to my room—I'm burning
with desire—now, this minute you will go with
me! (Attempting to drag her off)

AMALIA: (falling on him) Forgive me, Franz! (As he is
about to embrace her, she snatches his sword from his
side and steps quickly back.) Look, villain, what I can
do to you now! I'm a woman, but a woman in desperation—dare to lay your lustful hands on my
body—this steel will pierce your loathsome breast,
and my uncle's spirit will guide my hand! Away, this
minute! (Drives him away) Ah! how good, how
good—now I can breathe—I felt I was strong as a
fiery steed, fierce as the tigress pursuing the triumphant robber of her cubs—A convent, he said!
Thanks for that happy discovery! Now love betrayed
has found its resting-place—a convent—the Redeemer's cross is the resting-place for love betrayed.
(About to go; enter HERRMANN, timidly.)

HERRMANN: Lady Amalia! Lady Amalia!

AMALIA: Wretch, why do you disturb me?

HERRMANN: I must shed this weight from my
soul before it drags me down to hell—(Falling at
her feet) Forgive me! forgive me! I've wronged you
grievously, Lady Amalia!

AMALIA: Stand up! Leave me! I don't want to hear!

HERRMANN: (detaining her) No! Stay! In God's
name! In God's eternal name, you will hear it all!

AMALIA: Not another sound—I forgive you—go
home in peace! (Hurrying away.)

HERRMANN: Then hear me this one word—it will
give you peace again!

AMALIA: (comes back and looks at him in amazement) What, friend!—who, what on earth or in
heaven can give me peace again?

HERRMANN: One single word from my lips—
listen to me!

AMALIA: (seizing his hand with pity) Good fellow—
can a word from your lips draw back the bolts of
eternity?

HERRMANN: (standing up) Karl is alive!

AMALIA: (crying out) Miserable wretch!

HERRMANN: It's so—And one word more—Your
uncle—

AMALIA: (rushing at him) You're lying—

HERRMANN: Your uncle—

AMALIA: Karl is alive!

HERRMANN: And your uncle—

AMALIA: Karl is alive?

HERRMANN: Your uncle too—Do not betray me.
(Rushes off.)

AMALIA: (standing as if petrified, then starting up
wildly and rushing after him) Karl is alive!

SCENE 2
A country scene, near the Danube.

The ROBBERS, camped on rising ground beneath
trees. The horses are grazing downhill.

MOOR: Here I must lie and rest (throwing himself on
the ground). My limbs are shattered and my tongue
is dried up like a potsherd. (SCHWEITZER creeps off
unnoticed.) I would bid you fetch me a handful of
water from the river, but you're all weary unto death.

SCHWARZ: And the wine in our wineskins is no
more.

MOOR: See how fair the corn stands! The trees
almost breaking beneath their fruits. The vine full
of promise.

GRIMM: It'll be a fine harvest.

MOOR: You think so? Then one man is repaid for
the sweat of his brow. One!—And yet the night
may bring hail, and all be beaten to the ground.

SCHWARZ: It may well be. All can be beaten to the
ground, a few hours before the reapers come.

MOOR: It's as I say. All will be beaten to nothingness.
Why should man succeed when he imitates the ant,
when he's thwarted when he's like the gods? Or is
this the limit destined for his endeavour?

SCHWARZ: I don't know.

MOOR: Well said, and it were better still that you
should never seek to know!—Brother—I've seen
men, their insect worries and their giant designs;

their godlike schemes and their mouse's scurryings, their wondrous chasing after happiness; this one trusting the leap of his horse—another, his donkey's nose—another, his own legs; this many-coloured lottery of life, where so many stake their innocence, their hopes of heaven, to draw the winning number, and—blanks, blanks every one—there was no lucky number there. Brothers, a spectacle to draw tears from your eyes, just as it stirs your stomach to laughter!

SCHWARZ: How gloriously the sun goes down!

MOOR: *(lost in the sight)* Like a hero's death!— Worthy of worship!

GRIMM: Are you so moved?

MOOR: When I was a boy, my dearest wish was— to live like that, to die like that—*(Biting back his anguish)* A foolish boy's wish!

GRIMM: I should think so!

MOOR: *(pulling his hat down over his eyes)* There was a time—Leave me alone, comrades!

SCHWARZ: Moor, Moor! What, in the devil's name—? See how pale he's turned!

GRIMM: Why, confound it! what's the matter? is he sick?

MOOR: There was a time when I couldn't sleep at night if I hadn't said my prayers—

GRIMM: Have you lost your wits? Would you take lessons from when you were a boy?

MOOR: *(laying his head on GRIMM's breast)* Brother! brother!

GRIMM: What? look—are you a child?

MOOR: Oh, if I were—if only I were again.

GRIMM: Fie, shame.

SCHWARZ: Take courage. Look at the beauty of the landscape, see how fine the evening is.

MOOR: Yes, friends, this world is so fair.

SCHWARZ: Why, well spoken.

MOOR: This earth is so glorious.

GRIMM: Yes, yes—that's what I like to hear.

MOOR: *(sinking back)* And I so hideous in this fair world—and I, a monster on this glorious earth.

GRIMM: Oh, in God's name.

MOOR: My innocence, my innocence—See! all went out to sun themselves in the peaceful beams of spring—Why I, I alone to drain hell from the joys of heaven? All so happy, all kin through the

spirit of peace! the whole world one family, a father there above—a father, but not mine—I alone cast out, I alone set apart from the ranks of the blessed—not for me the sweet name of child—not for me the lover's melting glance—never, never more the bosom friend's embrace. *(Starting back wildly)* Surrounded by murderers, in the midst of hissing vipers—fettered to vice with bands of iron—rocked giddily over the abyss of destruction on the frail reed of vice—I, I alone cast out, a howling Abaddon[48] amidst the fair world's happy blossoms!

SCHWARZ: *(to the others)* Incredible! I've never seen him like this.

MOOR: *(sorrowfully)* Oh, that I might return to my mother's womb—oh, that I might be born a beggar. No! I'd ask for no more, oh you heavens— than that I might be one of these who earn their daily bread! Oh, I'd labour till the blood sprang from my brow—to buy the sweet joy of a single afternoon's rest—the bliss of a single tear.

GRIMM: *(to the others)* Patience! the fit will soon have left him.

MOOR: There was a time when they'd flow so freely—oh, you days when I was at peace! You, my father's castle—you green dreaming valleys! Oh, Elysium of my childhood!—Will you never return? never cool my burning breast with your sweet murmurings? Mourn with me, Nature—Never, never will they return, never cool my burning breast with their sweet murmurings—Gone! gone! gone beyond recall!— *(Enter SCHWEITZER, with water in his hat.)*

SCHWEITZER: Drink your belly full, captain— here's water in plenty, and cold as ice.

SCHWARZ: You're bleeding—what have you been doing?

SCHWEITZER: Fool, it might have cost me two broken legs—and a broken neck. There I was going along one of those sandbanks by the river, whoosh! the stuff slips away from under my feet and down I go, a good ten-foot drop—and when I'd picked myself up and got my wits back, there was the clearest water you could ask for, running

---

48 destructive angel of hell.

between the stones. Enough of a caper for now, I 115
thought; this is what the captain wants.

MOOR: *(giving him back his hat, and wiping his face for him)* Let me—we don't often see the scars the cavalrymen left on your forehead, back there in Bohemia—your water was good, Schweitzer— 120
these scars suit you well.

SCHWEITZER: Pah! there's room for thirty more!

MOOR: Yes, children—it was a warm afternoon's work—and only one man lost—my Roller died a fine death. There'd be a monument on his grave, if he 125
hadn't died for my sake. This will have to serve *(wiping his eyes)*. How many of our enemies did we kill?

SCHWEITZER: A hundred and sixty hussars—ninety-three dragoons, forty or so riflemen—three hundred in all. 130

MOOR: Three hundred against one!—Each one of you has claim on this head. *(Baring his head)* Here I raise my dagger—as truly as my soul draws breath I swear—swear I will never forsake you.

SCHWEITZER: Don't swear! One day, you don't 135
know! your good luck may return, and you'll regret it.

MOOR: By my Roller's bones, I swear I'll never forsake you. *(Enter KOSINSKY)*

KOSINSKY: *(aside)* They told me I'd find him 140
around here—hallo! what faces are these? Is it—might they—they are, they are! I'll speak to them.

SCHWARZ: Look out! Who goes there?

KOSINSKY: Gentlemen, forgive me. I don't know, is this the right way? 145

MOOR: And who might we be, if it is?

KOSINSKY: Men!

SCHWEITZER: Haven't we proved it, captain?

KOSINSKY: The men I'm seeking are ones who can look death in the face and let danger play around 150
them like a charmed snake, who value freedom more than life and honour, whose very name, sweet sound to the poor and the oppressed, strikes terror in the valiant and turns the tyrant pale.

SCHWEITZER: *(to the captain)* I like this guy. 155
Listen, friend. We're the ones you're looking for.

KOSINSKY: I think you are, and I hope we'll soon be brothers.—Then you can show me the way to the man I want, your captain I mean, the great Count Moor. 160

SCHWEITZER: *(giving him his hand, warmly)* You're a man after my own heart!

MOOR: *(Coming closer)* And do you know their captain?

KOSINSKY: You are he—these features—who could 165
look at them, and seek another? *(Gazing at him for a long time)* I've always wished that I could see the man with destruction in his eye, there as he sat upon the ruins of Carthage[49]—now I need wish it no longer. 170

SCHWEITZER: This is a fine fellow!

MOOR: And what brings you to me?

KOSINSKY: Oh, captain! my more than cruel destiny—I've been shipwrecked in the rough seas of this world, have seen my life's hopes sink 175
beneath the ocean, and nothing left to me but the memory of what I'd lost, a torment that would drive me insane if I'd not sought to stifle it in distractions.

MOOR: Another with a grievance against God!— 180
Go on.

KOSINSKY: I joined the army. Still my ill-luck pursued me—I went on a journey to the East Indies, my ship ran aground on the rocks—nothing but frustrated plans! At last, I heard tell 185
everywhere of your deeds—of your murder and arson, as they called them—and I've travelled thirty leagues firmly resolved to serve with you, if you'll accept my services—I beg you, noble captain, do not turn me away! 190

SCHWEITZER: *(with a bound)* Hurrah, hurrah! Roller again, a thousand times over! A real assassin for our band!

MOOR: What's your name—?

KOSINSKY: Kosinsky. 195

MOOR: What, Kosinsky? And do you realize that you're a rash and foolish boy, taking the great step of your life as thoughtlessly as a careless girl—This is no skittle-alley, as you may think.

KOSINSKY: I know what you mean—I'm twenty- 200
four years old, but I've seen swords flash, and bullets whistle by me.

---

49 i.e., Moor is being likened to a Roman conqueror; in 146 B.C.E., Rome destroyed Carthage utterly—a city that had been one of the greatest in the ancient world.

MOOR: Indeed, young Sir?—and have you only learnt to fence so that you can strike down poor travellers for a few shillings, or run women through from behind? Go, go! you've run away from your governess because she threatened to whip you.

SCHWEITZER: What the devil, captain! what are you thinking of? you're not going to send this Hercules away? Doesn't he look like the man to chase the Marshal of Saxony over the Ganges with a kitchen ladle?

MOOR: Because your rags and tatters of schemes have come to nothing, you come here to be a villain, a cut-throat? Murder, boy; do you know what the word means? You could chop off poppy-heads and go to sleep with a clear conscience, but to bear murder on your soul—

KOSINSKY: I'll answer for every murder you bid me commit.

MOOR: What? are you so clever? Do you think you can catch a man with your flatteries? How do you know that I never have bad dreams, or that I won't turn pale on my deathbed? What have you done, to make you think of answering for it?

KOSINSKY: Little indeed—but I've come to you, Count Moor!

MOOR: Has your tutor been telling you tales of Robin Hood?—They should clap such careless creatures in irons, and send them to the galleys—exciting your childish imagination, and infecting you with delusions of greatness? Do you itch for fame and honour? would you buy immortality with murder and arson? Be warned, ambitious youth! Murderers earn no laurels! Bandits win no triumphs with their victories—only curses, danger, death and shame—do you not see the gibbet on the hill-top there?

SPIEGELBERG: *(pacing up and down in irritation)* Senseless! hideously, unforgivably stupid! that's not the way! that's not how I used to do it!

KOSINSKY: What should I fear, if I don't fear death?

MOOR: Splendid! incomparable! You learnt your lessons like a good boy; I see you know your Seneca[50] by heart.—But my friend, fine phrases

like that will not talk away the sufferings of your flesh, will never blunt the darts of your pain. Consider well, my son! *(Taking him by the hand)* Let me advise you as a father—see how deep the abyss is, before you jump into it! If there's still one single joy known to you in this world—there could be moments, when you—wake up—and then—find it's too late. Here you step beyond the bounds of humanity—you must either be more than a man, or you're a devil—Once more, my son! if one single spark of hope gleams anywhere within your life, then leave this terrible alliance which only despair can make—unless a higher wisdom founded it—we can easily be mistaken—Believe me, a man can think it's strength of mind, and yet, in the end, it's despair—Believe me, me! and go back, as quickly as you can.

KOSINSKY: No, there's no turning back for me. If my pleas cannot move you, then hear the story of my misfortune. After that you'll thrust the dagger into my hand yourself; you will—sit around me here on the ground, and listen carefully!

MOOR: I'll listen.

KOSINSKY: Let me tell you, then, that I come from a noble family in Bohemia, and through my father's early death inherited a sizeable estate. My lands were like a paradise—for they contained an angel—a girl with all the charms that the bloom of youth can endow, and chaste as the light of heaven.—But why do I tell you this? it can only fall on deaf ears—you've never loved, never been loved—

SCHWEITZER: Be still! our captain is as red as fire.

MOOR: Stop! I'll hear it another time—tomorrow, soon, or—when I have seen blood.

KOSINSKY: Blood, blood—let me go on! My tale will fill your soul with blood. She was from Germany, a commoner's daughter—but the sight of her would melt any nobleman's prejudice. As shy and modest as could be, she accepted the ring from my hand, and within a few days I was to lead my Amalia to the altar. *(MOOR leaps to his feet.)* Amidst the dizziness of the joys that awaited me, in the middle of my wedding preparations, I was summoned to court by an express messenger. I presented myself. I was shown letters that I was supposed to have written,

---

50 Seneca (c.4 B.C.E.–65 C.E.) was a Roman philosopher, orator, senator and poet, the author of nine tragedies; he was forced to commit suicide, and died bravely.

full of treasonable utterances. I was inflamed at this wickedness—my sword was taken from me; I was thrown senseless into prison—

SCHWEITZER: And meanwhile—go on! I think I can tell what was brewing. 295

KOSINSKY: I lay there for a month, not knowing what was happening to me. I was afraid for my Amalia, who would be suffering the pains of death every minute on my account. At last the chief minister of the court appeared, congratulated me 300
with honeyed words on the establishment of my innocence, read me the proclamation of my release, gave me back my sword. Now in triumph to my castle, to fly to my Amalia's arms—she was gone. At midnight they said she'd been taken away, no 305
one knew where, and had not been seen since. It flashed across my mind like lightning—away! to the city, I sound them out at court—all eyes were on me, no one would tell me anything—at last I catch sight of her through a secret grating in the 310
palace—she threw me a note.

SCHWEITZER: Didn't I say so?

KOSINSKY: Death, hell and devils! there it was! they'd offered her the choice of seeing me die or of becoming the Prince's mistress. Forced to decide 315
between her honour and her love—she chose the second, and *(laughing)* I was saved!

SCHWEITZER: What did you do?

KOSINSKY: I stood there, thunderstruck. Blood! was my first thought, blood! my last. I run home, 320
foaming with rage, pick myself a three-edged sword, and off like a fury to the minister's house, for he, he alone was the infernal pander. I must have been seen in the street, for when I got there all the rooms were locked. I hunted, I asked for 325
him: he was with the prince, I was told. I hurry there straight away; they denied that they had seen anything of him. I go back, break down the doors, find him, was on the point—but then five or six of his men sprang out of hiding and robbed me 330
of my sword.

SCHWEITZER: *(stamping on the ground)* And he got off scot free, and all your efforts were in vain?

KOSINSKY: I was arrested, charged, tried for my life, banished—do you hear?—as a mark of special 335
consideration, banished from the country with

ignominy, my estates confiscated and given to the minister, my Amalia is still in the tiger's clutches, sighing and mourning her life away, while my vengeance must go hungry, and bow beneath the 340
yoke of despotism.

SCHWEITZER: *(standing up, whetting his sword)* Here's grist for our mill, captain! Here's a fire to be lit!

MOOR: *(who has been pacing up and down in violent* 345
agitation, starting suddenly, to the ROBBERS) I must see her!—away! strike camp!—you'll stay with us, Kosinsky—pack up quickly!

THE ROBBERS: Where? What?

MOOR: Where? who can ask, where? *(Violently, to* 350
SCHWEITZER) Traitor, would you hold me back? But by every hope of heaven!—

SCHWEITZER: I, a traitor?—lead us to hell and I'll follow you!

MOOR: *(embracing him)* Brother of my heart! you 355
will follow me—she weeps, she mourns her life away. Up! away! all! to Franconia! Within the week we must be there! *(Exeunt.)*

ACT FOUR SCENE I
A country scene, by OLD MOOR'S castle.

ROBBER MOOR, KOSINSKY in the distance

MOOR: Go ahead and announce me. You remember everything you have to say?

KOSINSKY: You're Count Brand, from Mecklen-burg, and I'm your groom—have no fear, I'll play my part well enough; good-bye! *(Exit)* 5

MOOR: Soil of my fatherland, I salute you! *(He kisses the ground)* Sky of my fatherland! Sun of my fatherland! meadows and hills and rivers and forests! I salute you, from my heart I salute you all!—how sweet the breezes blow from the 10
mountains of my home! with what joyous balm you greet the poor outcast! Elysium! a world of poetry! Stop, Moor! your feet tread the floor of a holy temple. *(coming closer)* See there, the swallows' nests in the castle courtyard—the little gate that 15
leads to the garden!—and the corner by the palisade, where so often you'd lie listening and mock your pursuer—and there below, the valley

with its meadows, where as Alexander the hero you led your Macedonians into the battle of Arbela, and the hill close by, where you repulsed the Persian satraps—and your victorious banner fluttered on high! *(Smiling)* Those golden years of boyhood's May come to life again in an outcast's soul—Oh, you were so happy, so full of pure unclouded joy—and now—there lie the ruins of your schemes! Here you were one day supposed to wander, a great man, dignified and renowned—here to live your boyhood once more in Amalia's blossoming children—here! here, the idol of your people—but the Enemy scowled at your plans! *(Starting up)* Why did I come here? To hear, like a prisoner, the clanking chain wake me with a start from dreams of freedom—no, let me return to my exile and misery!—the prisoner had forgotten the light, but the dream of freedom flashed past him like the lightning in the night that it leaves darker behind—Farewell, you valleys of my fatherland! once you saw Karl the boy, and Karl the boy was a happy and fortunate boy—now you've seen the man, and he's in despair. *(He turns and goes quickly to the furthest part of the scene, where he suddenly stops, stands still and gazes across at the castle with an expression of grief.)* Not to see her, not one glance?—And just a single wall between myself and Amalia—No! I must see her—and him—and let me be annihilated! *(Turning around)* Father! father! your son is coming—away, black, reeking blood! away, fearful, hollow, convulsive stare of death! This single hour I beg of you—Amalia! father! your Karl is coming! *(He goes quickly towards the castle.)*—Torment me when the daybreak comes; don't leave me when the night has fallen—torment me with dreams of horror! but do not poison my one last joy! *(At the gate)* What feelings are these? what is it, Moor? Be a man!—Pangs of death— Horror and foreboding—*(He goes in.)*

SCENE 2
A gallery in the Castle

Enter ROBBER MOOR and AMALIA

AMALIA: And do you believe that you can recognize his likeness amongst these pictures?

MOOR: Oh yes, definitely. His image was always fresh in my memory. *(Going around, looking at the pictures.)* This isn't him.

AMALIA: Rightly guessed! This is the first Count, the founder of the line, who was ennobled by Barbarossa[51] when he served under him against the corsairs.

MOOR: *(in front of the pictures)* Nor is *this* he, nor *this*—nor *that* one there—he's not among them.

AMALIA: Why, look more closely!—I thought you said you knew him—

MOOR: I shouldn't know my own father better! He lacks that cast of gentleness around the lips, which would distinguish him among thousands—it's not him.

AMALIA: You amaze me. What? Not seen him for eighteen years, and yet—

MOOR: *(quickly, his face suddenly flushed) This* is him! *(He stands as if thunderstruck.)*

AMALIA: A fine figure of a man!

MOOR: *(gazing, wrapt, at the portrait)* Father, father, forgive me!—Yes, a fine figure of a man!—*(Wiping his eyes)* A godlike figure of a man!

AMALIA: It seems you're deeply moved to think of him.

MOOR: Oh, a fine figure of a man! and he's gone?

AMALIA: Gone! as all our purest joys must go— *(gently taking his hand)* Dear Count, there's no happiness on this earth.

MOOR: True, very true—and can it be that you've already found out this sad truth? You can't be twenty-three years old.

AMALIA: And I have found it out. Everything that lives lives only to die a sorrowful death; nothing we care for, nothing we make our own, but one day we must grieve at its loss.

MOOR: And what can you have lost already?

AMALIA: Nothing. Everything. Nothing.—Shall we go further, my lord?

MOOR: In such haste?—Whose portrait is that on the right? I seem to read bad luck in his features.

AMALIA: The portrait on the left is the Count's son, the present holder of the title—will you not come?

MOOR: But the portrait on the right?

---

51 Italian name for Kaiser Friedrich I (1120–90).

AMALIA: Will you not see the garden?

MOOR: But the portrait on the right?—you're weeping, my Amalia? *(Exit AMALIA in haste.)*

MOOR: She loves me, she loves me!—her whole being began to stir, the telltale drops flowed down her cheeks. She loves me!—Wretch, was this what you deserved? Am I not standing here like a condemned man before the fatal block? Is that the couch where at her bosom I dissolved in rapture? Are these my father's halls? *(Catching the eye of his father's portrait, as if transfixed)* You, you—Flames of fire from your eye—Curses, curses and rejection!—Where am I? Night before my eyes—the terrors of God—I, I have killed him. *(He rushes off.)* 60

(Enter FRANZ VON MOOR, deep in thought.)

FRANZ: Away with this vision! away, miserable coward! why are you afraid, and of whom? does it not seem, these few hours that the Count has trodden these floors, as if a spy of hell were creeping at my back—I ought to know him! There's something grand, something familiar in his wild sunburnt face, something that makes me tremble—and Amalia is not indifferent to him! Does she not linger upon the fellow with greedy, pining glances, of a kind of which she is otherwise so niggardly?— Did I not see her let fall a few furtive tears into his wine, that he gulped down behind my back as hastily as if he would've swallowed the glass as well? Yes, I saw it, saw it in the mirror with my own two eyes. Ho there, Franz! beware! there lurks some monster pregnant with ruin! *(He stands studying KARL'S portrait.)* His long goose-neck—his black, fiery-flashing eyes—h'm, h'm!—his dark overhanging bushy eyebrows! *(With a sudden convulsion)* Cunning, malicious hell! is it you who prompt me with this suspicion? It's *Karl!* Yes! all his features spring to life once more—It's him! despite his disguise—it's him! Death and damnation! *(Pacing violently up and down.)* Was it for this that I sacrificed my nights—levelled rocks and filled in yawning chasms—rebelled against every instinct of humanity, all for this giddy vagrant to come blundering through my cunningest coils—Gently, gently! All that remains is child's play—Haven't I already waded up to my ears in mortal sin?—it'd 90

be folly to swim back when the shore lies so far behind me—There can be no thought of turning back—heavenly grace itself would be reduced to beggary, and God's infinite mercy bankrupted, if all that I've incurred should be paid—Forward then, like a man! *(He rings the bell.)* Let him be coupled with his father's ghost and come; I care nothing for the dead.—Daniel! hey, Daniel!— What do you say; have they already stirred him up against me too? He looks like a man with a secret. *(Enter DANIEL.)*

DANIEL: You wish, my lord?

FRANZ: Nothing. Go, fill this cup with wine, but hurry! *(Exit DANIEL.)* Just wait, old man! I'll catch you out, I'll look you in the eye, I'll fix you so that your startled conscience will pale beneath your mask!—He shall die!—A poor workman he, who leaves a job half-finished, and stands back idly watching for what will happen next. *(Enter DANIEL with wine.)* 110

FRANZ: Put it down here! Look me straight in the eye! How your knees are shaking! How you tremble! Confess, old man! What have you done?

DANIEL: Nothing, your lordship, as true as God's alive, and my poor soul! 115

FRANZ: Drink this wine! drain it!—What? You hesitate?—Out with it, quickly! What did you put in this wine?

DANIEL: So help me God!—What? I—in the wine?

FRANZ: Poison you put in the wine! Are you not as white as a sheet? Confess, confess! Who gave it to you? The Count, wasn't it, the Count gave it to you? 120

DANIEL: The Count? Mary and Jesus! the Count didn't give me anything. 125

FRANZ: *(seizing him violently)* I'll throttle you till you're blue in the face, you grizzled old liar! Nothing! And what were you doing with your heads together like that? You and him and Amalia? And what have you been whispering together? Out with it all! What were the secrets, what were the secrets he confided to you? 130

DANIEL: That God knows who knows everything. He didn't confide any secrets to me.

FRANZ: Will you deny it? What plots have you been hatching to get *me* out of the way? It's true, isn't 135 it? You're going to strangle me in my sleep? Cut my throat when you're shaving me? Put poison in my wine or my chocolate? Out with it, out with it!—Send me to eternal rest with my soup? Out with it, I say! I know everything! 140

DANIEL: Then may God help me in my hour of need, but it's nothing but the truth I'm telling you!

FRANZ: This time I'll forgive you. But isn't it true he put money in your purse? He shook your hand more firmly than is customary? Firmly, as if he were greeting an old friend? 145

DANIEL: Never, my lord.

FRANZ: He said to you, for example, that he thought he knew you of old?—that you ought almost to recognize him? That the time would come when the scales would fall from your eyes—that—what? Are you telling me he never said such things? 150

DANIEL: Not a word of them. 155

FRANZ: That circumstances prevented him—that one often had to wear a mask, to get within range of one's enemy—that he would take revenge, take the most terrible revenge?

DANIEL: Not a breath of any such thing. 160

FRANZ: What? Nothing at all? Think carefully—that he knew your former master well—knew him exceptionally well—that he loved him—loved him uncommonly—loved him like a son—

DANIEL: Something of the kind I do remember I heard him say. 165

FRANZ: (turning pale) He did, he did indeed? What, let me hear! He said he was my brother?

DANIEL: (taken aback) What, your lordship? No, he didn't say that. But when the young lady took him through the gallery—I was just dusting the frames of the pictures—suddenly he stood still before the late master's portrait, as if he was thunderstruck. Her ladyship pointed to it, and said: a fine figure of a man! Yes, a fine figure of a man! he answered her, and wiped his eye as he did so. 170 175

FRANZ: Listen, Daniel! You know I've always been a good master to you; I've fed you and clothed you, I've spared you tasks that were too hard for you in your old age— 180

DANIEL: And may God reward you for it!—and I've always served you well.

FRANZ: That was what I was going to say. You've never refused me anything all the days of your life, for you know too well that you owe me obedience in all that I command. 185

DANIEL: In everything and with all my heart, as long as it's not against God and my conscience.

FRANZ: Nonsense, nonsense! Are you not ashamed? An old man, still believing in Christmas fairy-tales! Away with you, Daniel! that was a foolish thought. I'm your master. God and conscience may punish me, if there are such things as God and conscience. 190

DANIEL: (clasping his hands together) Merciful heavens! 195

FRANZ: By the obedience you owe me! Do you understand? By the obedience you owe me, I tell you, by tomorrow the Count must no longer be in the land of the living.

DANIEL: Help, holy God! Why not? 200

FRANZ: By the blind obedience you owe me!—and I tell you, I'm depending on you.

DANIEL: On me! Help me, holy Mother of God! On me? What wrong has an old man like me done? 205

FRANZ: There's no time to think about it; your fate is in my hand. Would you sigh out the rest of your days in my deepest dungeon, where hunger will drive you to gnaw the flesh from your own bones, and burning thirst to drink your own water? Or would you rather eat your bread in peace, and live a quiet old age? 210

DANIEL: What, master? Peace, and a quiet old age—and a murderer?

FRANZ: Answer my question! 215

DANIEL: My grey hairs, my grey hairs!

FRANZ: Yes or no!

DANIEL: No!—God grant me mercy!

FRANZ: (about to go) Good; you'll need it.

(DANIEL holds him back and falls on his knees before him.)

DANIEL: Mercy, my lord, have mercy! 220

FRANZ: Yes or no!

DANIEL: Your lordship, I'm seventy-one years old today, and honoured my father and mother, and never knowingly cheated anyone of a penny all the days of my life, and have stood by my faith like a 225 true and honest man, and have served in your house for four and forty years, and look to die in peace and with a clear conscience, oh my lord, my lord! *(Embracing his knees violently.)* And you'd rob me of my last comfort at my end, and have the sting of conscience stifle my last prayer, and have me pass over as an abomination in the sight of God and men—No, no, my dear good dear gracious lord and master, you wouldn't do that, you couldn't want to do that to an old man of seventy-one. 230 235

FRANZ: Yes or no! What's this babbling?

DANIEL: I'll be an even better servant from this day on, I'll work my poor old fingers to the bone in your service like a common labourer, I'll get up earlier, I'll go to bed later—Oh, and I'll say a prayer for you too in the morning and in the evening, and God won't refuse to hear an old man's prayer. 240

FRANZ: To obey is better than sacrifice. Did you ever hear of the hangman putting on airs when he had a sentence to carry out? 245

DANIEL: Oh, no, no, I know! but to slaughter innocence—to—

FRANZ: Am I accountable to you? Does the axe ask the executioner, why strike here and not there?—but see how patient I am—I'll reward you for the loyalty you've sworn to me. 250

DANIEL: But I hoped to stay a Christian man when I swore loyalty to you.

FRANZ: No contradictions! look, I'll give you one more whole day to consider! Think on it again. Happiness and misery—do you hear, do you understand? The greatest happiness—and the depths of misery! I shall do miracles of torture. 255

DANIEL: *(after a little reflection)* I'll do it; tomorrow I'll do it. *(Exit.)* 260

FRANZ: Temptation is strong, and *he* wasn't born to be a martyr for his faith.—Your health then, Sir count! It looks very much as though tomorrow morning you'll be eating your hangman's breakfast!—Everything depends on how one looks at these things; and the man who does not look according to his own advantage is a fool. The father perhaps has drunk another bottle of wine, and—feels the itch; and the result is—one man more, and the man was surely the last thing to be thought of in the 265 270

whole Herculean labour. Now it so happens that I feel the itch; and the result is—one man less, and surely there is more intelligence and intention in the loss than there ever was in the increase—Is not the existence of the most of mankind largely the result of a hot July afternoon, or the tempting sight of bed-linen, of the horizontal position of some sleeping kitchen nymph, or the putting out of a light? And if a man's birth is the work of an animal desire, of a mere chance, who's to say that the negation of his birth is any very important matter? A curse on the folly of our nursemaids and governesses, who corrupt our fantasy with horrific fairy-tales, and impress our soft brains with hideous images of judgements and punishments, so that involuntary shudders will seize a grown man's limbs with the chill of dread—bar the way to our boldest resolutions, bind our awakening reason in fetters of superstitious darkness—Murder! a whole Hell full of furies swoops about the very word—Nature forgot to make another man—they didn't tie the umbilical cord—the father's guts were running on his wedding night—and the whole shadow-play is gone. There was *something* and there is *nothing*—isn't that just the same as: there was nothing and there is nothing and about nothing there is nothing to be said?—man is born of filth, and wades a little while in filth, and makes filth, and rots down again in filth, till at the last he's no more than the muck that sticks to the soles of his great-grandson's shoes. That's the end of the song—the filthy circle of human destiny, and so it goes—a pleasant journey, brother dear! Our gouty, splenetic moralist of a conscience may chase wrinkled hags out of brothels, and torture old usurers on their death-beds—it'll never get a hearing with me. *(Exit.)* 275 280 285 290 295 300 305

SCENE 3
Another room in the castle.

Enter ROBBER MOOR from one side, DANIEL from the other.

MOOR: *(hurriedly)* Where's the lady?

DANIEL: Your lordship! Will you permit an old man to make one request of you?

MOOR: It's granted. What do you want?

DANIEL: Nothing, and everything; only a little, and yet so much—let me kiss your hand! 5

MOOR: That you shall not, good old man! *(Embracing him)* Would that I might call you father!

DANIEL: Your hand, your hand! I beg you. 10

MOOR: You shall not.

DANIEL: I must! *(He seizes KARL's hand, looks at it quickly, and falls on his knees before him.)* My beloved, my precious Karl!

MOOR: *(startled, but coldly and with self-control)* 15 What are you saying, my good man? I don't understand you.

DANIEL: Yes, deny it, disguise yourself! Very well, very well! You're still my own dear good young master—Merciful God! I an old man, and live to 20 see—fool that I was, straight away I should have—oh, father in heaven! So you've come back, and the old master is under the ground, and there you are again—what a donkey I was, blind I must have been *(beating his forehead)* not to know you the 25 very—well, well, well! Who would have dreamt it—all that I prayed for—Christ Jesus! here he is, as large as life, in these old rooms again!

MOOR: What is this talk? Have you got some raging fever, or is it a part in some comedy you're 30 rehearsing?

DANIEL: Oh for shame, for shame! It's not right to play such tricks on your old servant—This scar! Look, you remember!—Great God, how you frightened me! I was always so fond of you, and 35 the pain you could have caused me—you were sitting on my lap—you remember? There in the round room—what, my chick? you've forgotten that, haven't you—and the cuckoo-clock that you liked to hear so much—think of it! the cuckoo- 40 clock's gone, smashed to smithereens—old Susie knocked it flying, when she was cleaning the room—Yes, that's right, there you were sitting on my lap, and called out horsey! and I ran off to fetch your horsey for you—oh sweet Jesus! why did I 45 have to run off so, old donkey that I am—and how it ran hot and cold down my back—hear the crying and shouting out there in the passage-way, come running in, and there's the blood all bright, and you on the floor, with—holy mother of God! 50

I felt as if a bucket of icy water was poured over me—but that's what happens with children, if you don't watch them all the time. Great God, if it had gone in your eye—And it was your right hand, too. As long as I live, I said, never again will I let a child 55 get hold of a knife or a pair of scissors or anything sharp like that, I said—thanks be, my lord and lady away—yes indeed, I'll let that be a warning to me, all the days of my life, I said—My godfathers! I could have lost my position, I could, 60 may the Lord forgive you, you godless child! but praise be! it all healed up well, but for that wicked scar.

MOOR: I don't understand a word of what you're saying. 65

DANIEL: Oh yes, those were the days, weren't they? Many's the cake and biscuit and sweetmeat I've tucked into your hand, you were always my favourite, and do you remember what you said, down there in the stable, when I put you on the 70 old master's sorrel horse, and let you gallop all around the great meadow? Daniel, you said, just wait till I'm a great man, Daniel, and you shall be my bailiff, and ride with me in my coach—Yes, I said and laughed, if the good Lord give life and 75 health, and if you're not ashamed of an old man, I said, then I'll ask you to let me have the cottage there in the village that's been standing empty for so long, and lay in a cask of wine, and play host in my old age. Yes, go on, laugh! Forgotten all 80 about it, hadn't you, young master—don't want to know an old man, behave like a stranger, so grand—and still you're my precious young gentleman—a bit of a wild one you were, to be sure—don't take it amiss! Young blood will have 85 its day—and it can all turn out well in the end.

MOOR: *(throwing his arms around his neck)* Yes, Daniel! I won't conceal it any longer! I am your Karl, your long-lost Karl! And what about my Amalia? 90

DANIEL: *(beginning to weep)* Oh, that I should live to see this happy day, old sinner that I am!—and the master—God rest his soul!—wept for nothing! Down, down, old white head and weary old bones, go to your grave rejoicing! My lord and master is 95 alive, I've seen him with my own eyes!

MOOR: And he will keep the promises he made—take this, you honest greybeard, for the sorrel horse in the stable. *(Thrusts a heavy purse of money into his hand.)* No, I hadn't forgotten you, old man. 100

DANIEL: Stop, what are you doing? Too much! You didn't mean it!

MOOR: Yes, I meant it, Daniel! *(DANIEL is about to fall on his knees.)* Stand up; tell me, what about my Amalia? 105

DANIEL: God reward you! God reward you! Oh, good Lord!—Your Amalia, oh, it'll be the end of her; she'll die of joy!

MOOR: *(eagerly)* She hasn't forgotten me?

DANIEL: Forgotten? What talk is that? Forgotten you?—you should have been there, you should have seen her when she heard the news that you were dead, the news his lordship gave out— 110

MOOR: What did you say? my brother—

DANIEL: Yes, your brother, his lordship, your brother—I'll tell you about it another day, when there's time—and the ticking-off she gave him, every time he came, day after day, paying her his compliments and wanting to make her his lady. Oh, I must go, I must go, I must tell her, bring her the news. *(Going)* 115

120

MOOR: Stop, stop! she mustn't know, no one must know, nor my brother either—

DANIEL: Your brother? No, not he, heaven forbid that he should know, he of all people!—If he doesn't already know more than he ought to—Oh, let me tell you, there are wicked people, wicked brothers, wicked masters—but for all my master's gold I wouldn't be a wicked servant—his lordship thought you were dead. 125

130

MOOR: H'm! What are you muttering?

DANIEL: *(more softly)* And to be sure, with you coming alive again so uninvited—Your brother was the late master's only heir—

MOOR: Old man! What are you mumbling between your teeth, as if some monstrous secret was on the tip of your tongue, not wanting to come out—and yet it should come out! Speak more clearly! 135

DANIEL: But I will rather gnaw the flesh from my old bones for hunger, and drink my own water for thirst, than earn a life of plenty by doing murder. *(He hurries off.)* 140

MOOR: *(starting up, after a pause of horror)* Betrayed, betrayed! it flashes upon my soul like lightning!—*A villain's trickery!* Heaven and hell! not you, my father! *A villain's trickery!* A robber, a murderer, through a villain's trickery! Slandered by him! my letters forged, intercepted—full of love his heart—oh, monstrous fool that I've been—full of love his father's heart—oh, knavery, knavery! It would have cost me a single step, it would have cost me a single tear—oh, fool, fool, fool, blind fool that I've been! *(Running against the wall)* I could have been happy—oh villainy, villainy! my life's happiness vilely, vilely betrayed. *(Raging up and down)* A murderer, a robber through a villain's trickery!—He wasn't even angry. Not the thought of a curse in his heart—oh, fiend! unbelievable, creeping, loathsome fiend! *(Enter KOSINSKY.)* 145

150

155

KOSINSKY: Captain, where are you? What is it? You want to stay here longer, I see? 160

MOOR: Up! Saddle the horses! Before sunset we must be over the borders.

KOSINSKY: You're joking.

MOOR: *(imperiously)* Hurry, hurry! Don't hesitate; leave everything here! and let no man catch sight of you. *(Exit KOSINSKY.)* I must flee from within these walls. The slightest delay could drive me to frenzy, and he's my father's son—oh my brother, my brother! You've made me the most miserable outcast on earth; I've done nothing to offend you; it was not a brotherly deed—Reap the fruits of your wickedness in peace; my presence will no longer sour your enjoyment—but truly, it was not a brotherly deed. Let it be veiled forever in darkness, let death not disturb it! 165

170

175

(Enter KOSINSKY.)

KOSINSKY: The horses are saddled; you may mount as soon as you will.

MOOR: Such haste, such haste! Why do you harry me so? Am I not to see her again? 180

KOSINSKY: I'll unharness again right away if you bid me; you made me run, head over heels.

MOOR: Once more! one more farewell! I must drain this poisoned bliss to the last drop, and then—stop, Kosinsky! Ten minutes more—behind, by the courtyard gate—and we'll gallop away! 185

SCENE 4
The garden.

AMALIA

AMALIA: *You are weeping, my Amalia?*—and his voice as he said it! his voice! I felt as if nature were reborn—all the happy spring-times of love awakened again in his voice! The nightingale sang as it did then—the blossoms breathed perfume as they did then—and I lay in ecstasy upon his breast—Ah, false, faithless heart! how you seek to flatter your treachery! No, no, away, flee from my soul, deceitful image!—my own, my only one, I haven't broken my oath! Flee from my soul, treacherous, godless desires! in the heart where Karl reigns there is no place for mortal man—But why, my soul, why do you seek this stranger against my will? Why does he stand so close beside the image of my own, my only one? why is he his constant companion? You are weeping, *my* Amalia? Ah, I will flee him, flee him! Never shall my eye behold this stranger more!

(MOOR opens the garden gate.)

AMALIA: *(with a shudder)* Listen! Listen! did I not hear the gate? *(She sees MOOR, and springs to her feet.)* Him?—where?—what?—here I stand rooted and cannot flee—don't forsake me, God in Heaven!—No, you will not rob me of my Karl! My soul hasn't room for two divinities, and I'm a mortal woman! *(Taking out KARL's portrait)* O my Karl, be my angel to guard me against this stranger, this intruder on my love! You, you, let me gaze at you unceasing—no more these blasphemous glances at the other—*(She sits in silence, her gaze fixed on the portrait.)*

MOOR: You here, my lady?—and in sorrow?—and a tear upon this picture?—*(AMALIA doesn't answer.)* And who's the fortunate man for whose sake an angel's eye will glisten? may I see the idol of your—*(Trying to see the portrait.)*

AMALIA: No, yes, no!

MOOR: *(starting back)* Ah!—and does he deserve such adoration?—does he deserve it?

AMALIA: If you'd known him!

MOOR: I'd have envied him.

AMALIA: Worshipped him, you mean!

MOOR: Ah!

AMALIA: Oh, you would have loved him so—there was so much, in his face—in his eyes—in the tone of his voice—so much like you—so much that I love—*(MOOR stands with downcast eyes.)* Here, where you're standing, he stood a thousand times—and beside him she who at his side forgot all heaven and earth—here his eyes feasted on the glorious scene about him—Nature seemed to feel his generous, approving gaze, and to grow even more beautiful in the approbation of her master-piece—here he'd make heavenly music, and hold an airy audience captive—here from this bush he'd pluck roses, would pluck roses for me—here he lay upon my bosom, here his burning lips touched mine, and the flowers were glad to be crushed beneath the feet of lovers—

MOOR: He is no more?

AMALIA: He sails on stormy seas—Amalia's love sails with him—he treads the pathless sandy desert—Amalia's love makes the burning sand grow green beneath him, and the thorny bushes blossom—the noonday sun scorches his bare head, the arctic snows blister his feet, hailstorms beat about his brow, and Amalia's love soothes him in the tempest—oceans and mountains and horizons between the lovers, but their souls escape the dusty prison, and are united in the paradise of love—You seem sorrowful, count?

MOOR: These words of love stir my love, too, to life.

AMALIA: *(turning pale)* What do I hear? You love another?—Alas for me, what have I said?

MOOR: She believed me dead, and was true to him she thought dead—she learnt that I was alive, and would sacrifice for me the diadem of a saint. She knows that I roam an outcast, a wanderer in the desert, and her love flies through exile and desert to be with me. And her name is Amalia like yours, my lady.

AMALIA: How I envy your Amalia!

MOOR: Oh, she is an unhappy lady; she gives her love to one who's lost, and never in all eternity will she be rewarded.

AMALIA: No, no, she will be rewarded in heaven. Aren't we told that there's a better world, where the sorrowful will rejoice, and lovers recognize each other again?

MOOR: Yes, a world where all veils are rent, and love sees itself again, in terror—Eternity is its name— my Amalia is an unhappy lady. 90

AMALIA: Unhappy, and she loves you?

MOOR: Unhappy because she loves me! Why, what if I were a murderer? What, my lady? What if your lover could count a man killed for each one of your kisses? Alas for my Amalia! she's an unhappy lady. 95

AMALIA: (joyfully, springing to her feet) Ah! and I, I am happy! My one and only is like the light of heaven itself, and heaven is grace and mercy! He couldn't bear to hurt the merest insect—his soul is as far from thoughts of blood as the pole of day from midnight. 100

(MOOR turns quickly away between the bushes, gazing fixedly into the distance.)

AMALIA: (takes her lute, plays and sings)
Hector, will you bid farewell forever, 105
Now Achilles, with his murd'rous quiver
Fearful vengeance for Patroclus swears?
Who will teach your tender son to fight,
To cast his spear, and fear the Gods of right,
When your corpse grim Xanthus downward bears? 110

MOOR: (takes the lute silently from her, and plays)
Dearest wife, go, fetch the fateful lance,
Let me go—to tread—war's horrid dance—

(He throws down the lute, and rushes off.)

SCENE 5

A nearby forest: night.
In the centre, an old ruined castle.

The ROBBERS encamped on the ground, singing

CHORUS: Thieving, whoring, killing, fighting,
So we live from day to day,
For every one the hangman's waiting,
Let's be merry while we may.
We lead a life of liberty, 5
A life of merry joys,
Our lodging is the forest free,
In gale and tempest us you'll see,
The moon's our sun, my boys!
To Mercury we say our prayer, 10
The god of thieves, and light as air.
Today we'll be the farmer's guest,
Tomorrow the priest's so fat,
And for the next, we think it best
To let the Lord take care of that! 15
And every time the tale is told
Of drinking and of toasting,
We're fellows stout enough and bold
To join the enemy of old,
Who sits in hell a-roasting! 20
The stricken father's cries and groans,
The anguished mother's fearful moans,
The lonely bride's despairing tears,
Are joy and music to our ears!
Ha! see them twitch when their heads we lop, 25
Like oxen they bellow, like flies they drop,
That's a pleasure to our sight,
That's what gives our ears delight!
And when at last the tide has turned,
Then let the hangman take us; 30
It is but our reward we've earned,
We'll be gone before they make us.
A drop of Bacchus's juice to speed us as we go,
And up, my boys, away! and swifter than you know!

SCHWEITZER: It'll soon be night, and the captain's not back yet! 35

RATZMANN: And promised he'd be here with us again on the stroke of eight.

SCHWEITZER: If anything has happened to him— comrades! we'll burn the place down and kill every man, woman and child. 40

SPIEGELBERG: (taking RATZMANN on one side) A word in your ear, Ratzmann.

SCHWARZ: (to GRIMM) Shouldn't we be sending out scouts? 45

GRIMM: Let him be! He'll come back with a prize to shame us all.

SCHWEITZER: No, I swear by hell you're wrong there! He didn't look like a man planning a trick of that kind when he left us. Have you forgotten 50 what he told us as he led us over the heath? "Let one of you steal as much as a turnip from the field, if I find out then his head will fall on the spot—

as sure as my name is Moor."—He's forbidden us to rob! 55

RATZMANN: *(Softly, to SPIEGELBERG)* What are you driving at? Speak plainer.

SPIEGELBERG: Hush!—I don't know what sort of a price you or I put on our freedom, straining away like oxen at a wagon, and holding forth all the time 60 about our independence—I don't like it.

SCHWEITZER: *(to GRIMM)* What's that windbag brewing now?

RATZMANN: *(Softly, to SPIEGELBERG)* Do you mean the captain? 65

SPIEGELBERG: Hush, I say! He has his informers among us all the time—Captain, did you say? Who made him our captain? Didn't he usurp a title that by rights belongs to me?—What? is that why we gamble our lives—is that why we let fortune 70 vent her spleen on us, to count ourselves lucky at the last to be the bondsmen of a slave? Bondsmen, when we might be princes? By God, Ratzmann— I never liked it.

SCHWEITZER: *(to the others)* Yes, you're a hero— 75 good for squashing frogs with a stone.—Why, the sound of him blowing his nose would knock you flying—

SPIEGELBERG: *(to RATZMANN)* Yes—and for years now I've been thinking: things will have to 80 change. Ratzmann—if you're the man I've always taken you for—Ratzmann—he's disappeared—half given up for lost—Ratzmann—I do believe his hour of doom has struck—what? Not a flush, not a flicker when you hear the bells of freedom ring? 85 Have you not the spirit to take the hint?

RATZMANN: Ah, Satan! what snares are you laying for my soul?

SPIEGELBERG: Have I caught you?—Good! then follow me! I kept note of which way he crept— 90 come! Two pistols rarely miss, and then—we'll have struck the first blow! *(He is about to drag RATZMANN away with him.)*

SCHWEITZER: *(drawing his knife in fury)* Ha! Vermin! Just in time you remind me of the forests 95 of Bohemia! Were not you the coward whose teeth began to chatter when they cried "The enemy is here!" That day on my soul I swore—away with you, assassin. *(Stabs SPIEGELBERG to death.)*

ROBBERS: *(in agitation)* Murder! murder! 100 Schweitzer! Spiegelberg! Separate them!

SCHWEITZER: *(throwing his knife down on the body)* There! and that's the end of you! Calm now, comrades—take no notice of him—the vermin, he was always jealous of the captain, and he hadn't a scar on 105 his body—never mind, lads!—ah, the scoundrel! would he stab a man in the back? he, a man, in the back? Is that why we've felt the sweat glowing on our cheeks, to slink out of the world like rats? Vermin! Is that why we made our beds amidst fire and smoke, 110 to be put down like curs at the last?

GRIMM: But the devil—comrade—what was it between you? The captain will be furious.

SCHWEITZER: Let me take care of that. And you, you scoundrel *(to RATZMANN)*—you were his 115 right-hand man! Out of my sight with you— Schufterle tried that trick too, but now he's hanging there in Switzerland, as the captain prophesied he would.

(A shot is heard.)

SCHWARZ: *(jumping up)* Listen! a pistol-shot! 120 *(Another shot is heard.)* Another! Hurrah! The captain!

GRIMM: Patience! He must fire a third shot. *(Another shot is heard.)*

SCHWARZ: It is, it is! Look out for yourself, 125 Schweitzer—let us answer him! *(They fire.)*

(Enter MOOR and KOSINSKY.)

SCHWEITZER: *(going to meet them)* Welcome, captain!—I've been a little hasty while you were away. *(Leading him to the body)* You'll judge between the two of us—he wanted to stab you in 130 the back.

ROBBERS: *(in amazement)* What? The captain?

MOOR: *(gazing for a while at the body, then bursting out furiously)* O inscrutable hand of avenging Nemesis!—wasn't it him who sang me the siren 135 song?—Let this knife be consecrated to that dark spirit of retribution!—it wasn't you who did this, Schweitzer.

SCHWEITZER: By God! it was I who did it, and by the devil I swear it's not the worst thing I have 140 done in my life. *(Exit, with an ill grace.)*

MOOR: *(reflectively)* I understand—guiding hand of Heaven—I understand—the leaves are falling from the trees—and for me too it's autumn.—Take this from my sight. *(SPIEGELBERG's body is removed.)* 145

GRIMM: Give us the word, captain—what are we to do now?

MOOR: Soon—soon all shall be accomplished.— Give me my lute.—I've lost myself since I went in there—My lute, I say—I must nurse myself 150 back to strength—Leave me.

ROBBERS: It's midnight, captain.

MOOR: But those were only tears at a play—I must hear the Roman's song, to wake my sleeping spirit once more—My lute—Midnight, you said? 155

SCHWARZ: If not past already. Sleep weighs on us like lead. Three days since we closed an eye.

MOOR: What, does the balm of sleep fall even on the eyes of knaves? Why then should I not feel it? I've never been a coward or a base fellow—Lie 160 down and sleep—Tomorrow at daybreak we go on.

ROBBERS: Good night, captain! *(They lie down on the ground and go to sleep.) (Profound silence.)*

MOOR: *(takes up the lute and plays)*

> BRUTUS[52]
> Be ye welcome, fields of peace and calm,
> Where the last of Romans seeks his rest. 165
> From Philippi[53] with its wild alarm
> I come, with shame and anguish in my breast.
> Cassius, where art thou? Rome is gone,
> My band of brothers lying in their gore,
> To death's dark gate my steps are hurried on, 170
> The world no place for Brutus more.

CAESAR
> Who is that with steps so fierce and bold
> Comes to meet me from the rocks ahead?
> Can it be the truth my eyes have told?
> That must be a Roman's tread. 175
> Son of Tiber[54]—whence has come thy way?
> Stands the city on her seven hills?
> Often I have mourned the grievous day
> That she lacks a Caesar for her ills.

BRUTUS
> Ah, thou with wounds from three-and-twenty 180
> hands?
> Who summoned thee from death to light?
> Reel in horror, back where Hell-gate stands!
> Triumph not, proud mourner, in thy spite!
> Upon Philippi's brazen altar smokes
> The final sacrifice of freedom's blood; 185
> While Rome upon the bier of Brutus chokes.
> Brutus to Minos goes—Sink in thy flood!

CAESAR
> O fatal blow that Brutus's sword should deal!
> Thou also, Brutus, thou?
> My son—thy father—son, didst thou not feel, 190
> The earth entire to thee should homage vow?
> Go—thou as the noblest Roman art renowned,
> Since in thy father's breast thou plunged thy
> sword.
> Go—howl it till the gate of Hell resound.
> Brutus the noblest Roman is renowned 195
> Since in his father's breast he plunged his
> sword!
> Go—for now thou knowest by what hand
> I was kept on Lethe's strand;
> Come, dark ferryman, leave this land!

BRUTUS
> Father, stay!—Upon the earth so wide 200
> I have never known but one
> Fit to stand at mighty Caesar's side:
> It was he whom you called son.
> Only Caesar could have sought Rome's doom,
> Only Brutus Caesar would not fight. 205
> Where Brutus lives, for Caesar is no room,
> Go leftward, let me pass upon the right.

---

52 The following song takes the form of a dialogue in the underworld between Julius Caesar (100–44 B.C.E.), Roman military leader and dictator, and Brutus, leader of the successful Republican plot to assassinate him. It was said that when Caesar spied Brutus among his murderers, he lost his will to resist, saying, in Greek, "Even you, my child?" The parallel with Spiegelberg's attempted conspiracy is obvious.

53 Macedonian city and site of the famous defeat (42 B.C.E.) of Brutus and Cassius's Republican forces by Mark Antony and Octavian. Both defeated commanders committed suicide at this battle.

54 the main river of central Italy, which flowed beside Rome. A son of Tiber is therefore a Roman.

(He lays down the lute and paces up and down, deep in thought.)

Who'd be my protection?—Everything's so dark—labyrinths of confusion—no way out—no star to guide—if it were *over* with this last drawn breath—over like a shallow puppet-play—But why this burning hunger for happiness? Why this ideal of unattained perfection? This looking to another world for what we've failed to achieve in this—when one miserable touch of this miserable object *(holding his pistol to his forehead)* will make a wise man no better than a fool—a brave man no better than a coward—a noble man no better than a rogue? There's such divine harmony in the world of inanimate nature, why such discord in the world of reason?—No! no! there is something more, for I have not yet known happiness. Do you think that I'll tremble? Spirits of my slaughtered victims! I will not tremble. *(Trembling violently)* The terror of your dying moans—the blackness of your strangled faces—the hideous gaping of your wounds are but links in an unending chain of fate, and depend at the last on my idle moments, on the whims of my tutors and nursemaids, on my father's temperament and my mother's blood—*(Shuddering)* Why did my Perillus[55] make a brazen bull of me, to roast mankind in my glowing belly? *(He aims the pistol.)* Time and eternity—linked together by a single moment!—thou fearful key that will lock the prison of life behind me, and unbar before me the dwelling of eternal night—tell me—tell me—where, oh where wilt thou lead me?—Strange, undiscovered country! See, mankind grows weak before such visions, the tensile force of finitude is relaxed, and fancy, wilful ape of our senses, spins strange shadows to deceive our credulous mind—No, no! A man must not stumble—Be what you will, nameless *Beyond*—if but my own self to me is true—Be what you will, let me only take myself with me—Externals are

210

215

220

225

230

235

240

245

---

55 Perillus seems to have both devised and himself suffered a method of murder practised by Phalaris, a Sicilian tyrant (sixth century B.C.E.), who was known for roasting his enemies alive inside a bull's stomach.

only the varnish on a man—I'm my heaven and my hell. If you were to leave me nothing but some smoking desert, banished from your sight, where lonely night and everlasting desolation are all I must behold?—Then I'd people the silent emptiness with my imagination, and have all eternity to pick apart the tangled threads of universal misery.—Or will you lead me, born and reborn again, through ever-changing scenes of misery, step by step—to utter destruction? Can't I snap the threads of life that are woven for me there beyond, as easily as this present one?—You can make of me—nothing; of this freedom you cannot rob me. *(He loads the pistol. Suddenly he pauses.)* Am I going to die out of fear of a life of suffering? Am I going to grant misery this victory over me?—No! I will endure it! *(Throwing the pistol away)* Let suffering yield before my pride! It shall be accomplished! *(The darkness deepens. Enter HERRMANN through the forest.)*

250

255

260

265

HERRMANN: Listen, listen! fearful the owl's cry—twelve has struck in the village beyond—all is well, all is well—villainy sleeps—no spies listening in this wilderness. *(He comes to the ruined castle and knocks.)* Come out, man of sorrows, dungeon-dweller! Your meal is ready.

270

MOOR: *(drawing back quietly)* What can this mean?

A VOICE: *(from the tower)* Who knocks? Ho, Herrmann, my raven, is it you?

HERRMANN: I, Herrmann, your raven. Climb up to the grating and eat. *(Owls hoot.)* A dreary song they sing, the companions of your sleep—Is it good, old man?

275

THE VOICE: I was much hungered.—Thanks be to thee, sender of ravens, for this bread in the wilderness!—And what news of my dear child, Herrmann?

280

HERRMANN: Silence—listen—a sound like snoring! can't you hear it?

VOICE: What? can you hear something?

285

HERRMANN: The wind sighing in the crannies of your prison—a lullaby to make your teeth chatter and your nails turn blue—But listen, again—I keep thinking I hear men snoring—You have company, old man!—Oh, oh!

290

VOICE: Can you see anything?

HERRMANN: Fare you well—fare you well—a fearful place is this—Down into your hole—above, on high your help and your avenger—accursed son! *(Fleeing)* 295

MOOR: *(emerging, with horror)* Stand!

HERRMANN: *(cries out)* Ah!

MOOR: Stand, I say!

HERRMANN: Mercy! mercy! mercy! now all is betrayed! 300

MOOR: Stand! Speak! Who are you? What business have you here? Speak!

HERRMANN: Have pity, have pity on me, gracious master—hear one word before you kill me.

MOOR: *(drawing his sword)* What am I to hear? 305

HERRMANN: I know you forbade me on pain of death—I couldn't help—I couldn't do anything else—a God in Heaven—your own father there—I took pity—Strike me down!

MOOR: Here's some mystery—out with it! Speak! 310 I will hear everything.

THE VOICE: *(from the ruin)* Alas, alas! Is that you, Herrmann, speaking there? Who is it you're speaking to?

MOOR: Someone down there too—what's happen- 315 ing here? *(Running up to the castle.)* Is it some captive, cast aside?—I'll release his chains.—Voice! again! Where's the door?

HERRMANN: O have mercy, my lord—do not press further, my lord—for pity's sake, go by on 320 the other side! *(Blocking his way.)*

MOOR: A fourfold lock! Away!—It must out—Now for the first time, tricks of the thief's trade, come to my assistance. *(He takes housebreaking instru- ments and forces the lock of the grating. From below* 325 *an OLD MAN emerges, emaciated like a skeleton.)*

OLD MAN: Have pity on a miserable wretch! Have pity!

MOOR: *(starting back in terror)* That's my father's voice! 330

OLD MOOR: Thanks be to you, O God! The hour of my deliverance has come.

MOOR: Spirit of Count Moor! What has disturbed you in your grave? Did you take a sin with you into the other world, that has barred you entry to 335 the gates of Paradise? I'll have masses read that will speed the wandering spirit to its home. Did you

take the gold of widows and orphans and bury it in the earth, to drive you howling from your resting place at this midnight hour—then I'll tear 340 the buried treasure from the enchanted dragon's claws, and if he should vomit a thousand crimson flames upon me, and bare his pointed teeth against my sword—or have you come at my request, to answer the riddles of eternity? Speak, speak! I'm 345 no man to pale with fear.

OLD MOOR: I'm not a spirit—Touch me; I live, oh, a life of misery and wretchedness!

MOOR: What? Were you not buried?

OLD MOOR: I was buried—that's to say, a dead 350 dog is lying in the vault of my fathers; and I—for three months and more I have lain languishing in this dark underground chamber, with not a glimmer of light, with not a breath of warm air, with not a friend to visit me, with the croak of wild 355 ravens about me, and the hoot of owls at midnight.

MOOR. Heaven and earth! Who could do such a thing?

OLD MOOR: Don't curse him!—It was my son Franz who did it. 360

MOOR: Franz? Franz?—oh, everlasting chaos!

OLD MOOR: If you're a man, and have the heart of a man, oh my unknown deliverer, then hear, hear a father's sorrow, the sorrow his sons have brought upon him—for three months I've cried it 365 to these unhearing rocky walls, but there was only a hollow echo to mock my lamentations. And so, if you're a man, and have the heart of a man—

MOOR: A challenge to bring the wild beasts from their lairs! 370

OLD MOOR: There I lay upon my sickbed, and had scarcely begun to recover my strength after my grave illness, when they brought a man to me who told me my firstborn was dead on the field of battle, and brought with him a sword stained with his blood, 375 and his last farewell, and that it was my curse that had driven him to battle and death and despair.

MOOR: *(turning away with a violent movement)* It's revealed!

OLD MOOR: Hear me further! I fell into a swoon 380 at the message. They must have thought I was dead, for when I came to my senses again, I was lying in my coffin, and wrapped in my shroud like a dead man. I scratched at the lid of the coffin, and it opened. It was the dead of night, my son Franz stood before me.—What? he cried, in a terrible voice, will you live forever?—and straightway the lid was slammed shut again. The thunder of those words had robbed me of my senses; when I awoke once more I felt the coffin being lifted up and taken in a carriage, half an hour's journey. At last it was opened—I found myself at the entrance to this dungeon, my son before me, and the man who'd brought me Karl's bloodied sword—ten times I clasped his knees, and pleaded and implored him—his father's pleadings did not touch his heart—"down with him, the bag of bones!" his lips thundered, "he's lived for long enough"; and down I was thrust without pity, and my son Franz locked the door behind me. 385 390 395 400

MOOR: It's not possible, not possible! You must have been mistaken.

OLD MOOR: I may have been mistaken. Hear me further, but do not be angry! So I lay for a day and a night, and no man thought of me in my need. Nor did any man set foot in this wilderness, for the story goes that in these ruins the ghosts of my forefathers drag their rattling chains, and make deathly moan at midnight. At last I heard the door open again, this man brought me bread and water, and told me that I had been condemned to die of hunger, and that his life would be in danger if it were known that he was feeding me. And so I've clung feebly to life these many days, but the unrelenting cold—the foul air of my own filth—the boundless grief—my strength ebbed from me, my body withered, a thousand times with tears in my eyes I pleaded with God for death, but the measure of my punishment cannot yet be accomplished—or some joy must yet await me, that I've been so miraculously preserved. But my sufferings are earned—my Karl, my Karl!—and there was not a grey hair upon his head. 405 410 415 420

MOOR: That's enough. Up, you blocks, you lumps of ice! you dull unfeeling sleepers! Up! will none of you awake? *(He fires a pistol-shot over the sleeping robbers' heads.)* 425

THE ROBBERS: *(aroused)* Ho! hallo! hallo! What is it?

MOOR: Didn't this tale stir you in your slumbers? sleep everlasting would have been roused to wakefulness! Look, look! the laws of creation are made a game of dice, the bonds of nature are rent asunder, the ancient strife is let loose, the son has struck his father dead. 430 435

THE ROBBERS: What's the Captain saying?

MOOR: No, not struck him dead! the words are too kind! A thousand times the son has racked his father, flayed him, spitted him, broken him upon the wheel! no, these are words of men—has done what makes sin blush, what makes the cannibal shudder, what no devil in aeons could conceive.—His own son, his father—oh see, see, he's fallen in a swoon—his son, his own father, here in this dungeon he—cold—nakedness—hunger—thirst—oh look, oh see—he's my own father, it's the truth. 440 445

THE ROBBERS: *(running and gathering round the old man)* Your father? your father?

SCHWEITZER: *(approaches reverently and falls down before him)* Father of my captain! I kiss your feet! my dagger is yours to command. 450

MOOR: Vengeance, vengeance, vengeance shall be yours! venerable old man, so offended, so profaned! Thus from this moment I rend forever the band of brotherhood. *(Rending his garment from top to bottom)* Thus I curse every drop of brother's blood before the face of heaven! Hear me, moon and stars! Hear me, midnight heavens! who look down on this deed of shame! Hear me, thrice-terrible God, You who reign above the moon, and sit in judgement and retribution above the stars, and flame with fire above the night! Here I kneel—here I stretch forth my three fingers in the horror of the night—here I swear, and may nature spew me forth from her creation like a venomous beast if I break this oath, swear never to greet the light of day again, until the blood of my father's murderer, spilt before these stones, shall smoke beneath the sun. *(Standing up)* 455 460 465 470

THE ROBBERS: The very devil! Call us villains? No, in Belial's[56] name! we never did the like of this!

---

[56] personified spirit of wickedness, evil incarnate.

MOOR: Yes! and by the fearful groans of all who ever died beneath your daggers, of those my flames consumed and those my falling tower crushed— no thought of murder or of robbery shall find its place within your breasts, till all your garments are stained scarlet with the reprobate's blood—did you ever dream that you were the arm of a greater majesty? the tangled knot of our destinies is unravelled! Today, today an invisible power has conferred nobility upon our handiwork! Bow down in adoration before him who decreed you this sublime fate, who led you to this place, who deemed you worthy to be the terrible angels of his dark judgement! Uncover your heads! Kneel in the dust, that you may stand up sanctified! *(They kneel.)*

SCHWEITZER: Your command, captain! what are we to do?

MOOR: Stand up, Schweitzer! and touch these hallowed locks! *(He leads him to his father, and makes him hold a lock of his hair.)* Do you remember how you split the skull of that Bohemian cavalryman, just as he was raising his sabre over my head, and I had sunk to my knees, breathless and exhausted from my work? I promised you then that you should have a kingly reward, but till this moment I could not pay my debt.—

SCHWEITZER: You swore it, it's true, but let me not claim that debt from you in all eternity!

MOOR: No, I will pay it now. Schweitzer, no mortal man till this day was so honoured—Be my father's avenger!

SCHWEITZER: *(standing up)* My great captain! Today you make me proud for the first time! Your command! where, when, how shall he be struck down?

MOOR: Minutes are precious; you must hurry now—choose the worthiest men of our band, and lead them straight to the count's castle! Snatch him from his bed if he's asleep or lying in the arms of pleasure, drag him from table if he's gorged, tear him from the crucifix if you find him on his knees in prayer! But I tell you, and make no mistake of this! I do not want him dead! scratch his skin, or harm one hair of his head, and I will tear your flesh in pieces, and cast it to the hungry vultures for food! Alive and whole I must have him, and if you bring him to me alive and whole, you shall have a million for your reward; I'll steal it from a king at the risk of my own life, and you'll go as free as the air—if you understand me, hurry!

SCHWEITZER: Enough, captain—Here's my hand on it: either you'll see the two of us return, or neither. Schweitzer's angel of death is approaching! *(Exit, with a troop of robbers.)*

MOOR: You others, disperse in the woods—I'll remain.

ACT FIVE SCENE 1
A long vista of rooms—a dark night.

Enter DANIEL with a lantern and a bundle.

DANIEL: Good-bye, dear old home—so much joy and happiness I've seen here, when the good old master was still alive—tears on your mouldering bones! to ask such a thing of an old and faithful servant—it was a refuge for every orphan, and a haven for all with no one to care for them, and this son has made it a den of murderers—Good-bye, old floor! how many times Daniel has swept you—good-bye, old stove; it's hard for Daniel to take his leave after all these years—everything so familiar—it'll be painful, faithful old Eliezer[57]— But may God in his mercy protect me from the snares and wiles of the Evil One—Empty-handed I came—empty-handed I go—but my soul is saved.

(As he is about to go, FRANZ rushes in, in his dressing-gown.)

DANIEL: God be with me! The master! *(Blowing out his lantern.)*

---

57 Biblical: Eleazar, son of Aaron, was a priest responsible for the care of the sanctuary. (See Numbers, 4:15, 16, 17: "Eleazar … is to have charge of the oil for the light, the fragrant incense, the regular grain offering and the anointing oil. He is to be in charge of the entire tabernacle and everything in it, including its holy furnishings and articles.")

FRANZ: Betrayed! betrayed! Spirits spewed from their graves—roused from eternal sleep the kingdom of death cries to my face *Murderer! murderer!*—Who's there? 20

DANIEL: *(nervously)* Holy Mother of God! is it you, my lord, screaming through the passages so horribly that everyone starts from their sleep?

FRANZ: Sleep? who bade you sleep? Off with you, 25 and bring a light! *(Exit DANIEL. Enter another SERVANT.)* No one is to sleep tonight. Do you hear? Everyone must be up, and armed—all weapons loaded—Did you see them, there, along the gallery? 30

SERVANT: Who, your lordship?

FRANZ: Who, you fool, who? So coldly, so emptily you ask who? Why, it took hold of me like a fit! Who, you mule, who? Spirits and devils! How far on is the night? 35

SERVANT: The watchman just called two o'clock.

FRANZ: What? will this night last till the day of judgement? Didn't you hear a tumult close at hand? No shouts of triumph? No galloping horses' hooves? Where is Ka—I mean the Count? 40

SERVANT: I don't know, master!

FRANZ: You don't know? You're one of them as well? I will kick your heart out from between your ribs! you with your accursed *I don't know!* Be off, and fetch the pastor! 45

SERVANT: My lord!

FRANZ: Do you grumble? do you hesitate? *(Exit SERVANT, hurriedly.)* What? rogues and beggars conspired against me too? Heaven, hell, all conspired against me? 50

DANIEL: *(coming with a light)* Master—

FRANZ: No! I will not tremble! It was nothing but a dream. The dead are not yet risen—who says that I'm pale and trembling? I feel quite well, quite calm. 55

DANIEL: You're as pale as death, and your voice is quaking with fear.

FRANZ: I have a fever. Tell the pastor when he comes that I have a fever. I'll have myself bled tomorrow; tell the pastor. 60

DANIEL: Shall I bring you some drops of balsam and sugar?

FRANZ: Some drops of balsam and sugar! the pastor won't be here for a little while. My voice is weak and quaking, yes, balsam and sugar! 65

DANIEL: Give me the keys, so I can go and open the cupboard—

FRANZ: No, no, no! Stay! or I shall go with you. You see, I can't bear to be alone! how easily I might—you see—faint, if I'm alone. No, let me 70 be, let me be! It'll pass; you must stay.

DANIEL: Oh, you are sick, in earnest.

FRANZ: Yes, of course, of course! that's all.—And sickness turns the brain, and hatches strange fantastic dreams—but dreams mean nothing, 75 Daniel, do they? Dreams come from the belly, and dreams mean nothing—why, just now I had a merry dream—*(He collapses in a faint.)*

DANIEL: In the name of Jesus, what is this? George! Conrad! Sebastian! Martin! don't just lie there! 80 *(Shaking him)* Oh, Joseph and Mary Magdalen! can't you be sensible? They'll say I murdered him, God have pity on me!

FRANZ: *(in confusion)* Away—away! Why do you shake me like that, you hideous death's-head?—the 85 dead are not yet risen—

DANIEL: Oh, everlasting mercy! He's out of his mind.

FRANZ: *(raising himself, feebly)* Where am I?—you, Daniel? What have I been saying? Take no notice! I was lying, whatever it was—come, help me up!— 90 it was nothing but a fit of giddiness—because—I didn't sleep properly.

DANIEL: If only Johann was here! I'll call for help; I'll send for a doctor.

FRANZ: Stay! sit here beside me on this sofa— 95 there—you're a sensible man, a good man. Let me tell you about it!

DANIEL: Not now, another time! I'll put you to bed; rest will be better for you.

FRANZ: No, I beg you, let me tell you about it, and 100 laugh me to scorn!—See, I dreamt I had feasted like a king, and my heart was merry within me, and I lay drunken amidst the lawns of the castle gardens, and suddenly—it was the middle of the day—suddenly—but I tell you, laugh me to scorn! 105

DANIEL: Suddenly?

FRANZ: Suddenly a fearful thunderclap struck my slumbering ear; shuddering, I leapt up, and behold, I thought I saw the whole horizon stand ablaze

with fiery flames, and mountains and cities and 110
forests melted like wax in a furnace, and a howling
whirlwind swept away the sea and the earth and
the sky—and a voice rang out like a brazen
trumpet: Earth, give up thy dead, give up thy dead,
O sea! and the bare ground was in labour, and 115
began to cast up skulls and ribs and jaws and all
manner of bones that joined together and made
bodies of men, and they gathered in a great stream,
more than the eye could see, a living torrent! Then
I looked up, and behold, I stood at the foot of 120
Sinai, the mountain of thunder, and a throng
above me and below, and on the summit of the
mountain on three smoking thrones three men
before whose glance all creatures fled—

DANIEL: That's the very image of the Day of 125
Judgement.

FRANZ: Yes! the fantasies of a madman! Then there
came forth one who was like the starry night, and
he had in his hand a signet of iron, and he held it
between the place of sunrise and of sunset and 130
spoke: Everlasting, holy, just and incorruptible!
There is but one truth and there is but one virtue!
Woe, woe, woe to the creature that still dwells in
doubt!—Then there came forth another, who had
in his hand a looking-glass, and he held it between 135
the place of sunrise and of sunset and spoke: This
glass is truth; masks and hypocrisy shall be no
more—then I was afraid, as were all the people,
for we saw the faces of serpents and tigers and
leopards in the terrible glass reflected—Then there 140
came forth a third, who had in his hand a balance
of brass, and he held it between the place of sunrise
and sunset and spoke: come forth, you generation
of Adam—for I shall weigh your thoughts in the
balance of my wrath! and your works with the 145
weight of my anger!

DANIEL: God have mercy on me!

FRANZ: All stood as white as death, and each breast
beat with fearful expectation. Then it was as if I
heard my name named first in the thunder of the 150
mountain, and the marrow of my bones froze, and
my teeth chattered aloud. Right then the balance
began to ring, and the rocks to thunder, and the
hours went by, one by one, by the scale that hung on
the left, and one after another cast in a deadly sin— 155

DANIEL: Oh, may God forgive you!

FRANZ: But He didn't!—and the scale was piled
high like a mountain, but the other, filled with the
blood of atonement, kept it up in the air—at last
there came an old man, bent double with grief, his 160
own arm gnawed in his hunger; all eyes were cast
down in awe before him; I knew that man; he cut
a lock from the silvery hairs of his head, and cast
it upon the scale of sins, and lo! it sank, sank
suddenly into the pit, and the scale of atonement 165
flew up aloft!—Then I heard a voice that spoke
from the fiery rocks: forgiveness, forgiveness for
every sinner upon earth and in the pit! You only
are cast out! *(Pause; profound silence.)* Well, why
don't you laugh? 170

DANIEL: How can I laugh, when you make my skin
crawl? Dreams come from God.

FRANZ: Pah, nonsense! don't say that! Tell me that
I'm a fool, a crazy senseless fool! Say so, good
Daniel, I beg you; make mock of me! 175

DANIEL: Dreams come from God. I'll pray for you.

FRANZ: It's a lie, I say—go this instant, hurry, run,
see where the pastor is, tell him to make haste,
haste, but I tell you, it's a lie.

DANIEL: God be merciful to you! *(Exit.)* 180

FRANZ: Peasant's wisdom, peasant's fears!—No one
has yet discovered whether the past is not past, or
whether there is an eye watching beyond the
stars—h'm! Who prompted me to such thoughts?
Is there an Avenger there beyond the stars?—No, 185
no! Yes, yes! I hear a fearful hissing around me:
there is a judge beyond the stars! To go this very
night to face the Avenger beyond the stars! No, I
say!—a miserable corner where your cowardice
seeks to hide—empty, desolate it is beyond the 190
stars, and none to hear you—but if there should
be something more? No, no, there isn't! I command there not to be!—but if there is? Woe to you
if all has been accounted! if it should be counted
up before you this very night!—why do my bones 195
shiver?—To die!—why does the word catch my
throat so? To answer for myself to the Avenger beyond the stars—and if He's just, the widows and
the orphans, the tortured and the oppressed cry
out to Him, and if He's just?—Why did they suf- 200
fer? for what did you triumph over them?

(Enter PASTOR MOSER.)

MOSER: You sent for me, my lord. I'm astonished. The first time in my life! Do you have it in mind to make mock of religion, or are you beginning to tremble at its message? 205

FRANZ: To mock or to tremble, according to how you answer me.—Listen, Moser, I'll show you that you're a fool, or that you're making a fool of the whole world, and you'll answer me. Do you hear? By your life you will answer me. 210

MOSER: It's to One greater than me that you issue your summons; one day He'll surely give you your answer.

FRANZ: Now I will have it, now! this instant, so that I don't commit a shameful folly and call on the peasants' idol in my desperation, so often I've shouted and laughed to you as the wine flowed: There is no God!—Now I'm talking to you in earnest, I tell you, there is none! and you'll muster all the arguments you have at your command, but I'll blow them away with the breath of my lips. 215 220

MOSER: But if you could so easily blow away the thunder that will fall on your proud soul with a weight like ten thousand tons! that all-seeing God whom you, fool and villain, would banish from the midst of His creation, has no need of justification from the lips of common dust. For His greatness is as surely seen in your tyrannies, as in any smile of triumphant virtue. 225

FRANZ: Very good, priest! I like you like this. 230

MOSER: I stand here in the name of a greater master, and speak with another mere worm like myself, and have no business being liked. Indeed I'd have to be able to work miracles to wring confession from your obstinate wickedness—but if your convictions are so firm, why did you send for me? Tell me this—why did you send for me, at this hour of midnight? 235

FRANZ: Because I'm bored, and can find no pleasure at the chessboard. I want to amuse myself with a little priest-baiting. You will not unman my courage with your empty terrors. I know very well that those who have come off badly in this life put their trust in eternity; but they'll find themselves horribly cheated. I've always read that our being 240 245

is just a motion of the blood, and when the last drop of blood has ebbed, with it go mind and spirit too. They suffer all the infirmities of our body—won't they also cease when it's destroyed? go up in vapour as it rots? Let a drop of water find its way into your brain, and your life makes a sudden pause, and that pause is like the end of being, and its continuation is death. Our sensibility is the vibration of certain chords—and a broken instrument will sound no more. If I have my seven palaces demolished, if I smash this Venus[58] to pieces, then symmetry and beauty have ceased to exist. Look! there's your immortal soul for you! 250 255

MOSER: That's your philosophy of despair. But your own heart, that beats with anxious dread against your ribs even as you utter your proofs, gives the lie to them. These spiders' webs of systems can be torn to pieces with the single word: you must die!—I challenge you; that'll be the proof: if you still stand firm in death, if your principles do not desert you even then, then the victory is yours; but if in the hour of death you feel but the slightest qualm, then woe unto you! you've been deceived. 260 265

FRANZ: *(in confusion)* If in the hour of death I feel a qualm—? 270

MOSER: Oh, I've seen many such wretches, who until that moment had defied the truth like giants, but in death their delusions fluttered away. I'll stand by your bedside when you're dying—I'd really like to see a tyrant die—I'll stand there, and look you straight in the eye when the doctor takes your cold, damp hand, and can scarcely feel the limping, dwindling pulse, and with that fearful shrug of his shoulders looks up and says: mortal assistance is in vain! Then beware, oh then beware, that you don't look like a Nero or a Richard Crookback![59] 275 280

FRANZ: No, no!

MOSER: Even this No will then be turned into a howl of Yes—a tribunal within, that your sceptical 285

---

58 presumably a marble statue of Venus in the hall.

59 Although the circumstances of their death were dissimilar—Nero killed himself and Richard III died in battle—both historical figures were easily judged by posterity as murderous tyrants, and this seems to be Schiller's point.

speculations will not be able to silence, will then awake, and sit in judgement on you. But it will be an awakening as of one buried alive in the bowels of the churchyard, it will be a reluctant stirring—like that of the suicide who repents after the fatal stroke; it will be a flash of lightning that illuminates the midnight of your life; it will be a revelation, and if you still stand firm, then you will have won! 290

FRANZ: *(pacing up and down in agitation)* Priest's gossip, priest's gossip! 295

MOSER: Now for the first time the sword of eternity will cut through your soul, and now for the first time it will be too late.—The thought of God will arouse a fearful neighbour, called the judge. Moor, the lives of thousands hang upon your finger-tips, and of each of those thousands, nine hundred and ninety-nine you've made a misery. You would have been a Nero in the days of ancient Rome, in Peru a Pizarro. And now do you suppose that God will allow one man to dwell in His creation like a raging demon, and turn His works to nothing? Do you suppose that those nine hundred and ninety-nine were only there to be destroyed, puppets only for your devilish play? Oh, don't believe it! Every minute of theirs that you've murdered, every joy that you've poisoned, every perfection that you've kept from them, shall be demanded of you then, and if you can answer, Moor, then you will have won. 300 305 310

FRANZ: No more! not a word more! am I to be at the mercy of your liverish fancies? 315

MOSER: See, the destinies of men are held in a balance, fearful but beautiful to behold. Where the scale of this life falls, the scale of that will rise; where this rises, that will sink to the ground. But what, here, was only temporal affliction will there be made eternal triumph; what here was mortal triumph will there be made everlasting despair. 320

FRANZ: *(rushing at him furiously)* May the thunder strike you dumb, lying spirit! I'll tear out your accursed tongue by the roots! 325

MOSER: Do you feel the weight of truth so soon? But I've said nothing of proof as yet. Let me come to the proofs—

FRANZ: Be silent—go to Hell with your proofs! the soul is annihilated, I tell you; I'll hear no more of it! 330

MOSER: So the spirits of the pit do whimper, but God in Heaven shakes His head. Do you think you can escape the arm of His retribution in the empty realm of nothingness? ascend up into heaven, and He is there! make your bed in hell, and He is there! say to the night: hide me! and to the darkness: cover me! but the darkness shall be made bright around you, and the midnight shall be day around the damned—but your immortal spirit will refuse to hear the word, and shall be victorious over the blind thought. 335 340

FRANZ: But I don't want to be immortal—let those who do, live forever, I won't seek to hinder that! But I will compel him to annihilate me; I'll provoke him to rage, that in his rage he'll annihilate me. Tell me, what's the greatest sin, the sin that stirs him to the greatest wrath? 345

MOSER: I know but two. But they are not such as men commit, nor even dream of. 350

FRANZ: These two!—

MOSER: *(with a weight of meaning)* Parricide the one is called, fratricide the other—But why do you suddenly turn so pale?

FRANZ: What did you say, old man? Are you in league with Heaven or with Hell? Who told you that? 355

MOSER: Woe unto him who has both upon his conscience! Better it were for him that he had never been born! But be at ease; you have neither father nor brother more! 360

FRANZ: Aha!—what, you know of none greater? Think again—death, heaven, eternity, damnation hang on your lips—none greater than these?

MOSER: None greater than these. 365

FRANZ: *(collapsing into a chair)* Annihilation! annihilation!

MOSER: Rejoice, rejoice and be glad!—for all your abominations, you're still a saint compared with the parricide. The curse that will light upon you, compared with that awaiting him, is a song of love—the retribution— 370

FRANZ: *(leaping up)* Away! may a thousand catacombs swallow you up, screech-owl! who sent for you? go, I say, or I'll run you through and through! 375

MOSER: Can priest's gossip put a philosopher in

such a rage? Blow it away with the breath of your lips! *(Exit)*

(FRANZ writhes on his chair in fearful convulsions. Profound silence. Enter a SERVANT, in haste.)

SERVANT: Amalia has flown, the Count has suddenly disappeared.   380

(Enter DANIEL, terrified)

DANIEL: Your lordship, a troop of fiery horsemen galloping down the hill, crying murder, murder—the whole village is aroused.

FRANZ: Go and have all the bells rung at once, get   385
everyone to church—on their knees, everyone—They must pray for me—all the prisoners shall be freed—at liberty—the poor shall have their goods restored, everything twice, thrice over, I will—I will—go, go, call the confessor to bless my sins   390
away, are you not gone yet?

(The tumult becomes more audible.)

DANIEL: God have mercy on me, sinner that I am! How am I to make sense of this? You've always refused to hear a word of the comfort of prayer, thrown Bible and prayerbook at my head so often   395
when you caught me praying—

FRANZ: No more of that—To die! You see? Die? It'll be too late. *(SCHWEITZER is heard making a furious noise.)* Pray, I tell you, pray!

DANIEL: I always told you—you can be so scornful   400
of the comfort of prayer—but look out, look out! when your hour of need has come, when the waters rise about your soul, you'll give all the treasures of this world for a whisper of Christian prayer—Do you see? You cursed at me, but now do you see?   405

FRANZ: *(embracing him wildly)* Forgive me! Daniel, dear, good, precious, golden Daniel, forgive me! I'll clothe you from head to foot—will you pray?—I'll make you a bridegroom—I will—will you pray?—I beseech you—in the devil's name! will   410
you pray!

(Tumult in the street outside; cries, knocking.)

SCHWEITZER: *(in the street)* Take them by storm! Kill them! Break the doors down! I can see a light! he must be there.

FRANZ: *(on his knees)* Hear me pray, oh God in   415
Heaven!—It's the first time—and will never happen again—Hear me, God in Heaven!

DANIEL: Mercy, what are you saying? That's a godless prayer!

PEOPLE: *(rushing in)* Robbers! murderers! who's   420
making such a din at midnight?

SCHWEITZER: *(still outside)* Push them aside, comrade—it's the devil come to fetch your master—where's Schwarz and his band?—Surround the castle, Grimm—Storm the walls!   425

GRIMM: Brands and torches here—it's us up, or him down—I'll set his rooms on fire.

FRANZ: *(praying)* Lord God, I've been no common murderer—Lord God, I've never stooped to trifles—   430

DANIEL: God have mercy on us; his prayer itself's a sin.

(Stones and flaming brands fly through the air. The windows are broken. The castle is set on fire.)

FRANZ: I cannot pray—here, here! *(Beating his breast and forehead)* All dry, all withered. *(Standing up)* No, nor will I pray—Heaven will not have this   435
victory, hell will not make this mock of me—

DANIEL: Mary and Jesus! help—save us—the whole castle's in flames!

FRANZ: Here, take this sword. Quickly. Thrust it into my ribs from behind, so that these villains   440
cannot come and abuse me. *(The fire gains ground.)*

DANIEL: God forbid, God forbid! I don't want to send anyone to Heaven before his time, still less to—*(He runs away.)*

FRANZ: *(staring wide-eyed after him. After a pause)*   445
To Hell, were you going to say? In truth, I can smell something like—*(In a frenzy.)* Are those its twitterings? do I hear you hissing serpents of the pit?—They're forcing their way up—attacking the doors—why am I so afraid of this sharp steel?—   450
the doors give way—crash down—no way out—Ha! you then, take pity on me! *(He tears the golden cord from his hat and strangles himself. Enter SCHWEITZER with his men.)*

SCHWEITZER: Murdering scum, where are you?—   455
Did you see how they ran?—has he so few friends? Where has he crept to, the vermin?

GRIMM: *(coming upon the body)* Stop! what's this? Bring a light here—

SCHWARZ: He's stolen a march on us. Put up your swords, here he is, laid out like a dead cat. 460

SCHWEITZER: Dead? What? dead? Without me, dead? It's a lie, I tell you—see how quickly he'll jump up!—*(Shaking him.)* Hey, you there! There's a father to be murdered. 465

GRIMM: Spare yourself the trouble. He's as dead as a rat.

SCHWEITZER: *(leaving the body)* Yes! That's the end of him—He's as dead as a rat.—Go back and tell the Captain: He's as dead as a rat—he won't 470 see me again. *(Shoots himself)*

SCENE 2

The setting as in the last scene of the preceding Act.

OLD MOOR seated upon a stone; ROBBER MOOR opposite him; ROBBERS scattered in the woods.

ROBBER MOOR: He's not yet back? *(He strikes a stone with his dagger, making sparks.)*

OLD MOOR: Forgiveness be his punishment—my vengeance, redoubled love.

ROBBER MOOR: No, by the anger of my soul. It 5 shall not be. I won't have it. Such a deed of shame he'll drag behind him into eternity!—Why else should I have killed him?

OLD MOOR: *(bursting into tears)* Oh my child!

ROBBER MOOR: What?—you weep for him? here 10 by this dungeon?

OLD MOOR: Mercy! Oh have mercy! *(Wringing his hands violently.)* At this moment—at this moment my child is judged!

ROBBER MOOR: *(in fright)* Which one? 15

OLD MOOR: Ah! what do you mean by that?

ROBBER MOOR: Nothing. Nothing.

OLD MOOR: Have you come to laugh in mockery at my grief?

ROBBER MOOR: Oh, my treacherous con- 20 science!—Take no notice of what I say!

OLD MOOR: Yes, I had a son whom I tormented, and so a son must torment me in turn, it's the finger of God—oh my Karl! my Karl! if you hover about me in the raiment of peace, forgive me! Oh 25 forgive me!

ROBBER MOOR: *(quickly)* He forgives you. *(Checking himself)* If he's worthy to be called your son—he must forgive you.

OLD MOOR: Ah, he was too glorious for me—But 30 I'll go to meet him with my tears, with my sleepless nights and my torturing dreams, I'll embrace his knees and cry—will cry aloud: I've sinned in the sight of Heaven and before you. I'm not worthy to be called your father. 35

ROBBER MOOR: *(deeply moved)* He was dear to you, your other son?

OLD MOOR: Heaven's my witness! Why did I let myself be deceived by the wiles of a wicked son? Praised as a father I went among the fathers of 40 men. Fair about me blossomed my children, full of promise. But—Oh, unhappy the hour!—the evil spirit entered into the heart of my youngest, I believed the serpent—lost my children, both of them. *(Covering his face.)* 45

ROBBER MOOR: *(going away some distance from him)* Lost forever.

OLD MOOR: Oh, I feel it so deeply, what Amalia said; the spirit of vengeance spoke through her lips. In vain your dying hands you'll stretch out to 50 touch your son, in vain you'll think you grasp the warm hand of your Karl, who'll never come to stand at your bedside— *(ROBBER MOOR holds out his hand to him, with averted gaze.)*

OLD MOOR: Would that this were my Karl's hand! 55 But he lies far away in his narrow dwelling, is already sleeping his iron sleep, cannot hear the voice of my grief—woe to me! To die in the arms of a stranger—no son more—no son more to close my eyes— 60

ROBBER MOOR: *(in the most violent agitation)* Now it must be—now—leave me *(to the ROB-BERS)*. And yet—Can I give him back his son again?—I can no longer give him back his son— No! I won't do it. 65

OLD MOOR: What, my friend? What were you saying to yourself?

ROBBER MOOR: Your son—Yes, old man— *(stammering)* Your son—is—lost forever.

OLD MOOR: Forever? 70

ROBBER MOOR: *(looking up to heaven in anguish)* Oh but this once—let my soul not be weakened— sustain me just this once!

OLD MOOR: For ever, you say?

ROBBER MOOR: Ask no more. Forever, I said. 75

OLD MOOR: Stranger! Stranger! Why did you drag me out of my dungeon?

ROBBER MOOR: And what then?—What if I were to snatch his blessing—snatch it like a thief, and creep away with that godlike prize—a father's 80 blessing, they say, can never be lost.

OLD MOOR: And my Franz lost too?

ROBBER MOOR: (prostrating himself) It was I who broke the locks of your dungeon—Give me your blessing. 85

OLD MOOR: (with grief) That you had to destroy the son, to save the father!—See, the Divinity is unwearying in its mercy, and we poor worms let the sun go down on our wrath. (Laying his hand on the ROBBER's head.) Be happy, according as you 90 are merciful.

ROBBER MOOR: (standing up, tenderly) Oh— where's my manhood? My sinews grow slack, the dagger slips from my hand.

OLD MOOR: How good and how pleasant for 95 brethren to dwell together in unity, as the dew of Hermon, and as the dew that descended on the mountains of Zion—Learn to deserve such bliss, young man, and the angels of heaven will bask in the glory that shines about you. Let your wisdom 100 be the wisdom of grey hairs, but your heart—let your heart be the heart of an innocent child.

ROBBER MOOR: Oh, a foretaste of such bliss. Kiss me, godlike old man!

OLD MOOR: (kissing him) Imagine that it's a 105 father's kiss, and I'll imagine I'm kissing my son— can you also weep?

ROBBER MOOR: I thought it was a father's kiss— Alas for me if they should bring him now!

(Enter SCHWEITZER'S companions in silent mourning procession, with lowered heads and faces covered.)

ROBBER MOOR: Heavens! (Drawing back anx- 110 iously, and trying to hide. The procession passes him. He looks away from them. Profound silence. They stop.)

GRIMM: (in a subdued voice) Captain! (ROBBER MOOR does not answer, and draws further back.) 115

SCHWARZ: Beloved Captain!

(ROBBER MOOR draws still further back.)

GRIMM: We're innocent, captain.

ROBBER MOOR: (without looking at them) Who are you?

GRIMM: You won't look at us. We're your true and 120 faithful band.

ROBBER MOOR: Woe to you if you've been true to me!

GRIMM: The last farewell of your trusty servant Schweitzer—he'll come no more, your trusty 125 servant Schweitzer.

ROBBER MOOR: (springing to his feet) Then you didn't find him?

SCHWARZ: Found him dead.

ROBBER MOOR: (leaping up with joy) Thanks be to 130 Thee, guider of all things—Embrace me, my children—Mercy is the password from now on— So, even that might be overcome—all, all overcome!

(Enter more ROBBERS, and AMALIA.)

ROBBERS: Hurrah, hurrah! A catch, a magnificent catch! 135

AMALIA: (with hair flowing free) The dead, they cry, are resurrected at the sound of his voice—my uncle alive—in these woods—where is he? Karl! Uncle! Ah! (Rushing over to the old man.)

OLD MOOR: Amalia! My daughter! Amalia! 140 (Holding her tightly in his arms.)

ROBBER MOOR: (starting back) Who conjures up this vision before my eyes?

AMALIA: (tears herself away from the old man, runs to KARL and embraces him with rapture) He's mine, 145 oh you stars! he's mine!

ROBBER MOOR: (tearing himself loose, to the ROBBERS) Strike camp, all of you! The fiend has betrayed me!

AMALIA: Oh, my bridegroom, you're raving! Ah, for 150 rapture! Why am I so unfeeling, in this whirl of joy so cold?

OLD MOOR: (drawing himself upright) Bridegroom? Daughter! daughter! A bridegroom?

AMALIA: His forever! Mine for ever and forever and 155 forever!—oh, you heavenly powers, take from me this joy unto death, or I'll faint beneath its burden!

ROBBER MOOR: Tear her from my neck! Kill her! Kill him! me, yourselves! Everything! The whole world falls in ruins! *(Trying to escape.)* 160

AMALIA: Where are you going? what is it? Love, eternity! Rapture unending, and you would flee?

ROBBER MOOR: Away, away! Unhappiest of brides! See for yourself, ask for yourself and hear! Unhappiest of fathers! Let me flee this place forever! 165

AMALIA: Take me, in God's name, take me in your arms! It is as night before my eyes—He's running away!

ROBBER MOOR: Too late! In vain! Your curse, father—ask me no more! I am, I have—your curse—your curse, as I thought!—Who lured me to this place? *(Drawing his sword and rushing at the ROBBERS)* Which of you lured me to this place, you creatures of the pit? Swoon then, Amalia!—Die, father! Die through me a third time!—These your rescuers are robbers and murderers! Your Karl is their captain! 170

175

(OLD MOOR expires. AMALIA is silent, and stands like a statue. The whole band pauses in silent horror.)

ROBBER MOOR: *(running against an oak-tree)* The souls of those I strangled in the ecstasy of love—those I shattered in their blessed sleep—those—ha! Do you hear the arsenal exploding over the beds of those women in labour? Do you see the flames licking at the cradles of their nurselings?—our nuptial torch, our wedding music—oh, he doesn't forget, he knows how to join the links—so, not for me the joy of love! for me, love's a torment! it's retribution! 180

185

AMALIA: It's true! Great Lord in Heaven, it's true! What have I done, innocent lamb that I was! I loved him! 190

MOOR: This is more than a man can bear. I've heard death whistling towards me from more than a thousand musket-barrels, and without yielding a foot; and am I now to learn to quake like a woman? to quake before a woman?—No, no woman shall shake my manhood—Blood! blood! It's only something caught from a woman—give me blood to swill, and it'll pass. *(Trying to escape)* 195

AMALIA: *(falling into his arms)* Murderer! Devil! Angel—I can't leave you. 200

MOOR: *(hurling her away from him)* Away, you serpent, you'd mock a madman with your scorn, but I defy the tyrant, destiny—what, you are weeping? Oh you wicked, wanton stars! She's pretending to weep, pretending there's a soul that weeps for me. *(AMALIA throws her arms around his neck.)* Ah, what's this? She doesn't spit at me, she doesn't thrust me away—Amalia! Have you forgotten? do you know who it is you're embracing, Amalia? 205

210

AMALIA: My only one, I'll never leave you!

MOOR: *(in ecstatic joy)* She forgives me, she loves me! I'm pure as the heavenly ether—she loves me! Tears of gratitude to you, merciful God in Heaven! *(He falls on his knees, convulsed with weeping.)* Peace has returned to my soul, the raging torment is past, Hell is no more—See, oh see, the children of light weep upon the neck of the weeping devil—*(standing up, to the ROBBERS)* Why don't you weep too? weep, weep, for you are so blessed. Oh, Amalia! Amalia! Amalia! *(He hangs upon her lips; they remain silently embraced.)* 215

220

A ROBBER: *(approaching angrily)* Stop, traitor!—Let go of this arm immediately, or I'll tell you a word that'll make your ears ring and your teeth chatter with horror! *(He parts them with his sword.)* 225

AN OLD ROBBER: Remember the forests of Bohemia! Do you hear, do you hesitate—then remember the forests of Bohemia! Faithless man, where are your oaths? Do you forget wounds so quickly? When we set fortune, honour and life itself at a venture for you? When we stood around you like ramparts, bore like shields the blows that were aimed at your life—didn't you then raise your hand and swear an iron oath never to forsake us, as we had never forsaken you?—Have you no honour? have you no faith? Will you abandon us for a whining whore? 230

235

A THIRD ROBBER: Shame on your perjury! the spirit of Roller that died for you, Roller whom you summoned from the dead to be your witness, will blush for your cowardice, and rise armoured from his grave to punish you. 240

THE ROBBERS: *(all together, tearing open their clothes)* Look, look here! Do you recognize these scars? you belong to us! We bought you for our 245 bondsman with our heart's blood, you belong to us, and if the archangel Michael should fight with Moloch for you!—march with us, one sacrifice for another! Amalia for the band!

MOOR: *(letting go of her hand)* It's finished!—I sought to mend my ways and turn again to my father, but Heaven spoke, and said it should not be. *(Coldly)* Fool, and why did I seek it? Can so great a sinner still mend his ways? So great a sinner cannot mend his ways, that I should have known long ago.—Be calm, I beg you, be calm! it's as it should be—when he sought me, I would not, now when I seek him he will not—what could be more just than that?—Don't roll your eyes like that—he's no need of me. He's got creatures in abundance, he can so easily let one go, and that one am I. Come, comrades!

AMALIA: *(dragging him back)* Stop, stop! One stroke, one fatal stroke! Forsaken anew! Draw your sword, and have pity on me!

MOOR: Pity's flown to the wild beasts—I will not kill you!

AMALIA: *(clasping his knees)* Oh, in the name of God, in the name of all mercies! I ask no more for love, I know that our stars above flee one another in enmity—death is my only wish.—Forsaken, forsaken! Think of it in all its horror, forsaken! I cannot bear it. You can see, a woman cannot bear it. Death is my only wish! See, my hand is trembling! I haven't the heart to strike. I'm afraid of the flashing steel—for you it's so easy, you're a master in the art of slaughter, draw your sword, and I'll be happy!

MOOR: You want to be happy? Away with you, I kill no woman.

AMALIA: Ah, assassin! you can only kill those who are happy, those who are tired of life you pass by. *(Crawling to the ROBBERS.)* Then you must take pity on me, you hangman's apprentices!—There's such bloodthirsty pity in your looks, that's comfort for the wretched—your master's a vain, faint-hearted braggart.

MOOR: Woman, what are you saying?

(The ROBBERS turn away from her.)

AMALIA: No friend? not a friend among these

either? *(Standing up)* Then let Dido[60] teach me to die! *(She goes; one of the ROBBERS takes aim.)*

MOOR: Stop! Would you dare—Moor's love will die by Moor's hand alone! *(He kills her.)*

ROBBERS: Captain, captain! What have you done? are you mad?

MOOR: *(with gaze fixed on the body)* She's hit! This last convulsion, and it's over—Now, see! what more can you demand? You sacrificed to me a life that you could no longer call your own, a life of horror and disgrace—I've slaughtered an angel for you. Look, look, I say! Are you satisfied now?

GRIMM: You've paid your debts with interest. You've done more than any man would do for his honour. And now, come with us!

MOOR: You say that? The life of a saint for the lives of rogues—it's an unequal bargain, isn't it?—Oh, I tell you, if every one of you were to walk the scaffold, and have your flesh torn from your bones, piece by piece with red-hot pincers, if your torments were to last eleven summer days long, it would not make good these tears. *(With bitter laughter)* The scars, the forests of Bohemia! Yes, yes! of course, that had to be repaid.

SCHWARZ: Be calm, captain! Come with us; this is no sight for you. Lead us on!

MOOR: Stop—one word before we go on—Listen, you all-too-zealous executioners of my barbaric command—From this moment I cease to be your captain—With shame and loathing I lay down this bloodstained baton under whose sway you thought yourselves entitled to sin, and to affront the light of heaven with works of darkness—Draw aside to left and right—We shall never make common cause in all eternity.

ROBBERS: Ha! have you lost your courage? Where are your high-flying plans? Were they only soap-bubbles, that burst at a woman's breath?

MOOR: Oh, what a fool I was to suppose that I could make the world a fairer place through terror, and uphold the cause of justice through lawlessness. I called it revenge and right—I took

---

60 famous lover and Queen of Carthage who immolated herself on a pyre when her lover Aeneas abandoned her to pursue his imperial ambitions in Rome.

it upon myself, oh Providence, to smooth the jagged edges of your sword and make good your partiality—but—oh, childish vanity—here I stand at the limit of a life of horror, and see now, with weeping and gnashing of teeth, that *two men such as I would destroy the whole moral order of creation.* Mercy—mercy for the youth who sought to anticipate Your judgement—vengeance is yours alone. You have no need of man's hand. And now, truly, it's no longer in my power to make up for the past—what's ruined is ruined—what I've overthrown will never rise again. But still something remains that can reconcile me to the laws which I've offended, and restore the order which I've violated. They[61] must have a sacrifice—a sacrifice that will make manifest their invulnerable majesty to all mankind—and I myself will be the victim. For them I must surely die.

ROBBERS: Take his sword from him—He's going to kill himself.

MOOR: You fools! Damned to eternal blindness! Do you suppose a mortal sin can cancel out mortal sins, do you suppose the harmony of creation will be restored by such blasphemous discord? *(Throwing his weapons contemptuously at their feet.)* He shall have me alive. I'll go and give myself up, into the hands of the law.

ROBBERS: Tie him up, chain him! He's raving mad.

ROBBER MOOR: Not that they wouldn't find me soon enough, if the powers above so will it. But they might surprise me in my sleep, or catch me as I fled, or surround me by force and with swords, and then I'd have lost my one remaining merit, of dying for justice of my own free will. Why should I still seek like a common thief to keep hidden a life that in the eyes of Heaven has long been forfeit?

ROBBERS: Let him go! These are fantasies of greatness. He'll stake his life on empty admiration.

MOOR: I might be admired for it. *(After some reflection)* I remember speaking to a poor wretch as I came here—a day labourer, with eleven children—They're offering a thousand louis-d'ors' reward for handing over the great robber alive—I can help that man. *(Exit.)*

---

61 i.e., the laws.

Glossary of Dramatic Terms

absurdism, VOL. II: 8, 145, 277, 440. Associated with the minimalist style and bleak worldview of twentieth-century plays of the post-World-War-Two period (especially those of Ionesco, Pinter, and, problematically, Beckett). Such works seem set in a world stripped of faith in god or a rational cosmos, in which idealism has been lost, and human action and communication are futile. Absurdist characters are often portrayed as trapped in a pointless round of trivial, self-defeating acts of comical repetitiveness. For this reason, absurdism can verge on **farce** or **black comedy**. Connected with the shock and disillusionment that followed World War Two, absurdism was anticipated in parts of Büchner's *Woyzeck* (see Volume II). See also **existentialism**.

act [of a play], VOL. I: 438, VOL. II: 390. The sections into which a play or other theatrical work have been divided, either by the playwright or a later editor. Dividing plays into five acts became popular during the Renaissance in imitation of Roman tragedy; modern works are sometimes divided into three.

aestheticism, VOL. II: 108. Or "art for art's sake." A reaction to the **realism** and socially reforming agendas of late-nineteenth-century art. Associated in the theatre chiefly with Oscar Wilde, aestheticism asserted art's freedom to be separate and different from ordinary life and practical uses.

agōn, VOL. I: 3. Greek for contest or competition, from which we get prot*agon*ist, the first or main actor/character, as well as related words like agony, antagonize, etc. Plays were originally performed in competition, for prizes.

alexandrine couplets, VOL. I: 469. A rhymed verse form based on six-beat measures in which every second line rhymes with the one before. Alexandrines were used in French tragedy and comedy throughout the seventeenth and into the eighteenth century. They require highly skilled actors for their proper delivery.

"alienation effect," VOL. II: 170. Also known by the German term *verfremdungseffekt*, it is a Russian concept popularized by Bertolt Brecht to refer to any technique used in the theatre to distance spectators from the performance to the point where they can view it critically and ask questions about it. To alienate a phenomenon is to "make it strange," to make it seem odd or surprising. Actors do this when they keep their character at a distance rather than merging with it, or deliver their lines as if in quotation marks; directors use the "A-effect" when they interrupt the action or call attention to its artificiality with music, slides, or lighting. The opposite of "to alienate" is "to naturalize." See also **epic drama**.

allegory, VOL. I: xiii, 202, 240, VOL. II: xiii, 450. From the Greek for "speaking otherwise," allegories are generally **didactic** stories that consist of an accessible literal narrative that is meant to be taken symbolically as well. They often represent large-scale religious or political struggles in disguise. Allegorical characters frequently personify abstract values (Love, Charity, Greed, Big Business). Anima, the central figure in *The Play of the Virtues*, represents the human soul in general; see also *Everyman* (both in this volume).

allusion, VOL. I: 208, 469. A more or less veiled reference, within one work of art, to the ideas, words, images or even simply to the existence of another work of art or its creator.

anachronism, VOL. I: 208. Accidentally or intentionally attributing people, things, ideas and events to historical periods in which they do not and could not possibly belong.

antiquarianism, VOL. II: 4. The desire, particularly in nineteenth-century theatre, to avoid the above (**anachronism**) by meticulously researching the clothing, décor, music and architecture of various historical periods. Its goal is to ensure that the sets and costumes for a given play are accurate for the time and place in which the story is set.

apron, VOL. I: 500. The part of a stage that extends into the auditorium or audience beyond the **pro-scenium** arch; sometimes called a **forestage** or a thrust stage.

artistic director, VOL. I: 502, 771, VOL. II: 66, 167, 547, 588. The creative and administrative head of a theatre company, responsible for selecting plays and determining the style and mandate of the troupe. Before the twentieth century, this role was sometimes taken by the playwright, as in Molière's case, or by the leading actor, as in dozens of "actor-managers" of the English theatre.

asides, VOL. I: 147. Words delivered by actors to the audience, or by characters to themselves, which by **convention** are treated as if they were inaudible to the other characters on stage.

aulos, VOL. I: 5. The double-reeded pipe used on the ancient Greek stage as musical accompaniment for tragedy and comedy.

autos sacramentales, VOL. I: 258. Spanish religious plays. See also **Bible-cycle plays**, *carros*, and **mystery play**.

Bible-cycle plays, VOL. I: 186, 189. Medieval religious plays, usually performed outdoors, often on wheeled carts, dramatizing stories from the Bible. See also **mystery play** and **pageant-wagons**.

black comedy, VOL. II: 8. Humour based on death, horror, or any incongruously macabre subject matter.

"book," VOL. II: 169. The non-musical, verbal component of a musical (see **musical theatre**); in opera and **operetta**, the non-musical text is called the "libretto."

Boulevard, VOL. I: 498, VOL. II: 2. After the French Revolution, the largest theatre district in Paris, and for years the home of its **illegitimate theatre**. Sometimes called the "Boulevard of Crime" for its sensational true-crime stories and **melodrama**.

box-set, VOL. II: 4. A stage set consisting of three contiguous walls and a ceiling, realistic floor coverings, light fixtures, and practical windows and doors through which actors make their entrances and exits as if into a real room or building (see **realism**). Developed in the nineteenth century, it is still used occasionally by **scenographer**s today.

breeches roles, VOL. I: 552. Roles written or adapted for female actors in which they portray men or dress in male attire; especially popular during the English Restoration and throughout the eighteenth century, when men's trousers, or breeches, were form-fitting and reached only to the knee.

burlesque, VOL. II: 169. A comical imitation of an existing work which affectionately ridicules its sillier qualities, usually through exaggeration, substitution, and incongruity. The term is also used, in an unrelated sense, for a twentieth-century genre of American variety entertainment featuring music, pairs of comedians, and a succession of female striptease acts.

caricature, VOL. II: 277. An exaggerated and simplified depiction of character; the reduction of a personality to one or two telling traits at the expense of all other nuances and contradictions.

carros, VOL. I: 258. The wheeled parade floats on which religious plays were performed in Spain; similar mobile stages were called **pageant-wagons** in England.

catharsis, VOL. I: 92, VOL. II: 390. The infamously obscure medical term used by Aristotle in his *Poetics* to describe the purpose of **tragedy**: to stimulate pity and fear in the audience, and then bring about the purgation or purification (*catharsis*) of these and similar emotions. Since Aristotle, the term has been widely adopted to refer to the healthy and pleasurable effects of releasing strong emotions, not only by watching a play, but in life generally.

choral lyric, VOL. I: 1. A poem performed by a singing, dancing chorus; one of the early genres of Greek poetry out of which drama developed. See also **dithyramb**.

choral speech, VOL. II: 451. Text in a drama that is spoken simultaneously by a group of characters in a manner comparable to that of the ancient Greek **chorus**.

chorus, VOL. I: 1, 92. Originally, the choir of singing, dancing, masked young men who performed in ancient Greek tragedy and comedy. Treated in tragedy as a "character" within the story, the chorus often represents aggrieved groups (old men, foreign slaves, victims of the plague). The chorus berates, implores, advises, harasses, pursues, and sometimes even helps and commiserates with the main characters, but mostly bears witness to their doings and sayings. In **Old Comedy**, the chorus serves at times as the mouthpiece for the poet. It gradually disappeared from tragedy and comedy, but many attempts have been made to revive some version of it, notably during the Italian and English Renaissance, under **Weimar Classicism**, and by such twentieth-century playwrights as Jean Anouilh, T.S. Eliot, and Michel Tremblay. The singing and dancing chorus appears today most commonly in **musical theatre**, opera, and **operetta**.

collective creation, VOL. II: 172, 547. A theatrical work not written in isolation by a single author but jointly created through the rehearsal process by a group of performers, with or without the help of a writer to record and synthesize their ideas.

comedia capa y espada, VOL. I: 258. Spanish "cape and sword" plays, popular during the seventeenth century. Often featuring macho heroes who must sacrifice their love to preserve their honour, such works combined comedy, violence and adventure in a mix not unlike that of contemporary action films.

Comédie Française, VOL. I: 498, 501. The oldest state-funded theatre company still in existence. Formed in 1680, at the command of King Louis XIV, through the amalgamation of the two remaining French-language troupes in Paris, one of which was Molière's. Called the *Comédie Française* to distinguish it from the Italian company then resident in the capital (see *commedia dell'arte*), it was granted a monopoly on the performance of French drama. A symbol today of national conservatism.

comédies rosses, VOL. II: 4. Plays most closely associated with André Antoine's *Théâtre Libre* in late-nineteenth-century Paris. *Comédies rosses* featured sordid revelations of the depravity and bestiality of outwardly respectable but hypocritical upper- or middle-class characters.

comedy, VOL. I: xii, 2, 118–19, 190, 296, 366, 437–38, 468, 501, 504, 552, 605, VOL. II: xii, 66, 109, 168, 174, 440, 548. A play written to induce joy or laughter in the audience. Unlike **tragedy**, which generally takes characters from a condition of prosperity to a state of destruction or loss, comedy usually begins with a problem, and ends with its happy resolution. Comedy ranges from laughing genres like **satire** and **comedy of manners**, **parody**, **farce** and **burlesque**, to such weepy genres as sentimental and romantic comedy (see also **situation comedy**).

comedy of manners, VOL. I: xiii, 501, VOL. II: xiii. A type of comic play that flourished in the late seventeenth century in London, and elsewhere since, which bases its humour on the sexual and marital intrigues of "high society." It is sometimes contrasted with "comedy of character" as its **satire** is directed at the social habits and conventional hypocrisy of the whole leisured class. Also called **Restoration comedy**; exemplified by the plays of Behn, Wycherley and Congreve.

commedia dell'arte, VOL. I: 146, 257, 259, 502, 684, VOL. II: 7. A species of partly masked, highly physical, and almost completely improvised comic performance that emerged in Renaissance Italy and remained popular all across Europe for the next three hundred years. Its name, which essentially means "professional acting," distinguishes it from the scholarly amateur theatre that emerged at the same time (*commedia erudita*). Its characters were few in number and always more or less the same (see **stock characters**), but some remain in use today: Harlequin, Pierrot, Pulchinella, and others. See also *lazzi*.

commedia erudita, VOL. I: 257–58. The theatre of the scholarly academies that flourished in Renaissance Italy. Its practitioners, who were "erudite" or well-read, wrote plays in imitation of Greek and Roman **tragedies**, **satyr plays**, and **comedies**, staged them in new experimental indoor theatres, and in the process invented many aspects of post-classical theatre: the **proscenium** arch, illusionistic, changeable scenery, theatrical lighting, **pastoral drama**, and opera.

company, VOL. I: 295, 437, 468, VOL. II: 549, 588. Used to refer both to the members of a theatre-producing organization (including all creative and technical personnel), either travelling or resident in its own theatre building, and to the cast of an individual play.

convention, VOL. II: 206, 342. A device, technique, habit or practice that, through long usage, has come to be accepted as normal and expected regardless of how illogical or inappropriate it might otherwise seem. See, for example, **asides**.

corrales, VOL. I: 258. Name for the outdoor courtyard theatres of Spain during the Renaissance and beyond; similar in many ways to the public theatres of Elizabethan England.

cross-dressing, VOL. I: 184. The wearing of the clothing of the opposite sex, either on stage or in life, is typical of many single-gender theatrical traditions, such as those of ancient Greece and Shakespearean England, in which only men performed. See also **breeches roles**.

Dada, VOL. II: 169. A modernist "anti-art" art movement initially associated with Tristan Tzara, Zurich, and the first World War, but taken up by others elsewhere as well. Informed by a disgusted rejection of the civilization that produced that war, Dadaist artworks and cabaret-style performances attacked all the traditional values of European art by aggressively championing nonsense, randomness, vulgarity and anarchy. Along with the Italian Futurists, Dada expanded the language of modern theatre with its use of noise, chaos, spontaneity, and simultaneous, multi-media "happenings" in unconventional venues. See **modernism**.

determinism, VOL. II: 171. The idea that behaviour is shaped in advance, especially by the laws of heredity (genetics and the family) and environment (social and political factors). In contrast to a belief in **personal agency**, determinism implies that humans are not completely responsible for their actions.

Determinism in drama is associated particularly with nineteenth-century writers like Emile Zola, who argued, against the moralism of **melodrama**, for an objectively scientific study of humanity. See also **Naturalism**.

dialect, VOL. II: 450. A local variation of a given spoken language, such as Cockney English or Cajun French.

dialectic argument, VOL. II: 206. A mode of thought, associated with Socrates and with the nineteenth-century philosophers Hegel and Marx, in which terms are understood to contain their opposites, so that each one, being partial and only half the truth, should be annulled into a higher synthesis. The opposite of binary thinking (right or wrong, on or off), a dialectical argument has three terms (thesis, antithesis, synthesis), and says "yes, but also..., and therefore..." Brecht's "**alienation effect**" was based on and intended to induce dialectic thinking.

dialogue, VOL. II: 2, 67, 109, 170, 205–06, 277. Words spoken by actors, usually implying the exchange of language between two or more speakers.

didactic theatre, VOL. I: 189. Dramatic performances intended to teach a particular moral, political or religious lesson to the audience.

director, VOL. II: 170, 173, 390, 547. The individual or team responsible for interpreting, casting, and rehearsing a play, and making creative decisions regarding its staging. Before the twentieth century, these functions were performed not by a person who specialized in direction but by the leading actor in a troupe or by the playwright. See also *mise en scène*.

dithyramb, VOL. I: 1. A type of poem sung and danced in ancient Greece to celebrate the wine-god, Dionysus, and from which tragedy seems in some sense to have emerged. Dithyrambs performed by 50-member men's and boys' choirs competed for prizes during the Athenian theatre festivals (see also **choral lyric**).

double-casting, VOL. II: 548. Giving an actor two (or more) parts to play within a given production.

double entendre, VOL. I: 498. An utterance meant to be heard in two ways, one innocently literal and the other obscene or sexually suggestive. It is an important technique in comedy, especially **comedy of manners**.

downstage-centre, VOL. II: 167. A position on stage near the audience and halfway between each side wing. In order to aid the perspective illusion of painted scenery, theatre stages used to be raked upwards, with the horizon-line higher at the back of the stage than at the front. To move "downstage" is therefore to come closer to the audience.

dramaturgy, VOL. II: 341. The art or principles of playwriting.

dumb-show, VOL. I: 186. The silent representation of an action through physical mimicry and gestures only.

epic drama, VOL. II: 8. A term popularized by Bertolt Brecht (though invented by Erwin Piscator) to describe a style of theatrical storytelling that, for political reasons, pits itself against the conventional rules of **dramaturgy** as outlined by Aristotle, who distinguished "epic" from "dramatic" writing. Whereas traditional drama is supposed to make audiences empathize with the struggle of a single, psychologically self-contained protagonist, epic drama places characters against the backdrop of the largest possible historical and political context in order that their actions do not seem inevitable, or determined by private "human nature," but are revealed as part of a public, man-made, and therefore alterable set of historical facts. To prevent spectators from lapsing into an unthinking emotional stupor, epic theatre uses short, **episodic**, self-contained scenes, multi-media projections, written text, and music to interrupt and "alienate" the action rather than to emphasize its emotions. See "**alienation effect**," **epic poetry**, and **dialectic argument**.

epic poetry, VOL. I: 1. A form of oral verse, originally sung from memory to musical accompaniment by specialist bards, containing a vast panorama of human life in war and peace. The epics of ancient Greece, each tens of thousands of lines long, are known to us mainly through the works of Homer, the *Iliad* and the *Odyssey*. The stories of humans and gods contained in such poems provided most of the narrative material of Athenian **tragedy** and the **satyr play**.

epilogue, VOL. I: 365. A short, topical, often comic poem appended the end of a play and delivered directly to the audience by a popular actor.

episodic plot, VOL. II: 3. A play or literary work composed of a series of separate and to some degree interchangeable incidents (rather than of a single, unified, and continuously unfolding narrative) is said to have an episodic **plot**.

existentialism, VOL. II: 8. A kind of philosophy in which the meaning of human life is derived from the actual experience of the living individual. First detectable in the anti-systematic thinking of Kierkegaard in the nineteenth century, existentialism came to be associated with the playwrights, novelists and philosophers of post-World-War-Two France (especially Jean-Paul Sartre and Albert Camus). The existential worldview, in which life is assumed to have no essential or pre-existing meanings other than those we personally choose to endow it with, can produce an absurdist sensibility (see **absurdism**).

Expressionism, VOL. II: 8, 168, 170, 277. An influential art movement of the early twentieth century, c. 1907–1920s (see **modernism**). Associated with Germany, it was strongly visual in orientation; indeed, some of its pioneers in drama were visual artists (Kandinsky, Kokoschka). It aimed to give external expression to internal psychological states, usually of an extreme, nightmarish, or otherwise violent kind. Expressionist characters are often tormented by a hostile, overly mechanized, dehumanizing urban environment. Their paranoid or fearsome inner visions are represented visually on stage through distorted perspectives and uncanny colours, menacing lighting, unrealistic and exaggerated costumes, and confusing discontinuities of time and space. Expressionist plays can have a tendency to **allegory**.

fairytale, VOL. I: xiii, 684, VOL. II: xiii. An old and traditionally oral story, often assumed to be suitable only for children, in which the ordinary laws of nature are superseded by fantasy and the fulfillment of wishes. Fairytales are often surprisingly violent and typically composed of **convention**al elements such as handsome princes and sleeping beauties, enchanted forests, talking animals, wicked mothers and witches, and trials or enchanted objects that come in threes. Fairytale characters often use magic or guile to defeat rivals, marry a rich monarch, and live happily ever after.

farce, VOL. I: xiii, 186–87, 209, 222, 649, VOL. II: xiii, 174. Sometimes classed as the "lowest" form of **comedy**. Its humour depends not on verbal wit, but on physicality and sight gags: pratfalls, beatings, peltings with pies, malfunctioning equipment, unpleasant surprises, and sudden necessities to hide in boxes and closets. However, most comedy contains *some* elements of farce, which requires highly skilled actors for its effects. Also called "slapstick" in honour of the double-shafted baton carried by Arlecchino in *commedia dell'arte*, which when struck against another actor in a simulated beating made a loud slap.

folio edition, VOL. I: 365. A large-format printed version of a manuscript, often used in connection with Shakespeare's plays. After Shakespeare's death, two of his former partners in the King's Company, John Heminges and Henry Condell, collected thirty-six of his plays (excluding *Pericles* and *Two Noble Kinsmen*) and in 1623 published the collection in a volume that has since been called the First Folio. "Folio" refers to the size obtained when a sheet of paper of standard size is folded once, making two leaves or four pages, which can then be sewn together along the fold to make a book. When the sheet is folded twice—creating four leaves or eight pages—it is called a "**quarto**."

forestage, VOL. I: 500. See **apron**, above.

fringe theatre, VOL. II: 548. The production of plays and performance pieces outside or "on the margins" of mainstream theatre institutions.

Furies, VOL. I: 9. In the *Oresteia* trilogy, the spirits of vengeance. They were conceived in Greek mythology as underworld goddesses who punish murderers or incite the victim's surviving relatives to do so. Euphemistically called the Eumenides, "the kindly ones," out of fear of offending them as their cruelty was notorious, these frightful goddesses comprise the chorus of the final **tragedy** in Aeschylus's trilogy.

gallery, VOL. I: 501. Used in several senses to refer to an upper balcony in a theatre. In the Elizabethan public theatre, musicians sat in a "musicians' gallery" above the stage; indoor London theatre auditoriums of the next few centuries were divided in pit, boxes, and gallery, the last being the uppermost and least expensive seats. To "play to the gallery" is to pitch the level of one's performance to (what was assumed to be) the least discerning members of the audience, originally servants of those sitting below.

harlequinades, VOL. I: 501, 649. A form of theatrical entertainment popular in England in the eighteenth century, consisting of English versions of the **stock characters** of Italian *commedia dell'arte*. See also **pantomime**.

history play, VOL. I: 295, 366. A dramatic re-imagining of real people and events drawn from the annals of the past. Shakespeare and Schiller are considered among the greatest writers of history plays; Büchner and Strindberg are also noted for them. From time to time, such works have played important roles in the establishment of a nation's self-image and founding myths. Some degree of **anachronism** tends to be considered acceptable in historical dramas.

humorous comedy, VOL. I: 649. A play emphasizing laughter, and used in the context of eighteenth-century theatre in contrast with sentimental **comedy**. (Sentimental comedy was meant to induce "a joy too exquisite for laughter." Advanced by writers such as Richard Steele in the early eighteenth century, it was a wholesome, anti-aristocratic, middle-class alternative to the sex-and-adultery comedy of the Restoration.)

iambic dialogue, VOL. I: 2. Speech in a poetic drama that, with its unstressed/stressed rhythm (or short/long accent), most closely approximates the rhythm of everyday speech. Iambics were first used in Greek poetry in abusive poems that attacked particular individuals.

illegitimate theatre, VOL. II: 2. A historical term, now often used in quotation marks, to describe the many types of musical, variety, spectacular, and non-literary entertainment that exist alongside, or are seen as imperiling the survival of, more elevated and challenging forms. It derives from the monopolistic laws that regulated English and French theatre until the mid-nineteenth century, and which gave "licenses" to one or two companies only, along with protection from competition from other upstart enterprises. Known for their literary drama, serious opera and ballet, such theatres were called the legitimate houses; all others, technically illegal and therefore "illegitimate," avoided prosecution by steering clear of regular or classical plays, sometimes inventing new genres in the process (see, for example, **melodrama**).

improvisation, VOL. II: 548. The seemingly spontaneous invention of dramatic dialogue and/or a dramatic plot by actors without the assistance of a written text. All performers must generally be able do this in short bursts—to cover a mistake on stage, or to plumb the depths of a character during rehearsals. But improvisation is also a highly specialized art-form with its own rules and **conventions**. The actors of the *commedia dell'arte* tradition, who could extemporize on stage for hours on the basis of only a bare-bones scenario posted backstage, were said to be expert in it.

interlude, VOL. I: 186, 202. A short and often comical play or other entertainment performed between the **acts** of a longer or more serious work, particularly during the later Middle Ages and early Renaissance.

irony, VOL. I: 69, 93, VOL. II: 174. A contrast between what is said and what is known. Some speakers use it intentionally, as when Socrates feigned ignorance of things he knew quite well, to draw out other "philosophers." By contrast, dramatic irony occurs when characters utter statements whose full meaning is not understood by them (although it is clear to those who hear it, such as the audience or the other characters on stage). Many of Oedipus's remarks, which are true in ways he does not yet grasp, exemplify dramatic irony. Tragic irony, on the other hand, is said to occur when events turn out in an opposite way to what was expected and desired, yet so strangely fittingly that, in retrospect, it seems as if this outcome should have been predicted or known all along (see **tragedy**, with its "reversal and recognition"). Some forms of **satire** may also rely on irony.

jeu, VOL. I: 187. French for "play," as in a game; used in the titles of some French dramas (although not in the sense of "a theatrical play" in general, which is *une pièce*).

lazzi, VOL. I: 684. Italian for "turn" or "trick." Used of the comical gags, jokes, acrobatics, and **stock** gestures for which the servant characters of the *commedia dell'arte* were famous. Whenever the actors ran dry in their **improvisation**, Arlecchino or one of the other *zanni* (comic servants) would jump-start the action, drawing on a pre-perfected repertoire of tumbles, flips, beatings or other (usually physical) stage business.

legitimate theatre, VOL. II: 2. Historically, a state-licensed and legally protected monopoly theatre; metaphorically, by extension, the "high art" theatre world. See **illegitimate theatre**.

liturgical drama, VOL. I: 185–86. A play or playlet based on the text of the Catholic religious service that is performed as part of the service itself, originally staged in Latin by clerics, and eventually in various vernaculars. They were first documented in the tenth century, when Benedictine monks used gestures to act out the lines of the Easter Mass known as the "Quem Quaeritis" trope—a section of sung text depicting an exchange between an angel and the Marys who are looking for Jesus' body at the sepulchre. Over the next three centuries, such illustrations of key moments of the church service blossomed into semi-autonomous plays.

Liturgical drama declined after the Reformation, but can still be found today in some places, especially in Spain and South America.

make-up, VOL. I: 184. Any substance, usually in liquid, cream or powder form, that is used to disguise, transform, age, or decorate an actor's face. It includes the white lead reportedly used by Thespis in the sixth century B.C.E., as well as the "pancake," "powder," and "grease-paint" of later periods. In theatre traditions that do not use **masks**, and where distances or artificial lighting can impair visibility, make-up is sometimes used for the practical purpose of helping the audience to see the actors' features.

mansion, VOL. I: 188. Used in the Medieval period to describe the various locations represented, as part of the outdoor set, in some types of religious plays (see **passion play** and **miracle play**). For a piece about the Passion of Christ, for example, structures would be built to depict such locales as Heaven, Bethlehem, Jerusalem, Limbo, and Hell. Often elaborately decorated and equipped with sophisticated special-effects machines, such mansions were simultaneously visible throughout the play; the action advanced not through set changes but through the movement of actors from one mansion to the next.

mask, VOL. I: 2. Any removable and reusable material used to disguise, transform, obscure or decorate all or part of an actor's face. Many Western theatre traditions use masks as a **convention**. Greek and Roman actors always wore full masks with large, gaping mouth-holes (except in mimes); Italian actors of the *commedia dell'arte* wore coloured leather half-masks that covered their eyes, nose and upper cheeks. With the return of non-realistic performance styles in the twentieth century, the use of masks has become widespread again.

masques, VOL. I: 259. Spectacular entertainments performed at royal courts as part of special celebrations such as weddings and feast-days, chiefly during the Renaissance. Consisting of music, dance, technical wizardry, and extravagantly opulent costumes, masques celebrated the virtues of the reigning monarch in terms, images and alle-

gories drawn from Classical mythology. Members of the royal family and their entourage took part by joining in the dancing or allowing themselves to be carried aloft on "clouds" animated by hidden machines. In England, Ben Jonson provided the poetry for famous masques created in collaboration with architect and **scenographer** Inigo Jones.

melodrama, VOL. I: xii, xiii, 499, 770, VOL. II: xii, xiii, 1–3, 26, 66, 168, 206, 440. A type of storytelling that emerged in France and Germany in the wake of the French Revolution, and that is marked by many features of that event: a clear division of characters into the poor, weak, and good hero on one hand, often a child, woman, mute or slave; and a rich, powerful, and evil villain on the other, who schemes to exploit or harm the victim but who is triumphantly overthrown at the last possible minute, usually in a sensational fire, fight, avalanche, or other violent cataclysm. Literally "music-drama," melodrama originally used background music throughout the action, much like film soundtracks do, to emphasize the characters' emotions, warn of approaching danger, and shape the spectator's emotional response (especially at the ends of acts and scenes, when actors assumed particularly pathetic or frightening postures and held them, frozen, in **tableaux**). Melodrama was the most popular narrative genre in Europe and North America in the nineteenth century. It still retains its popularity today, but it has long since left the theatre, taking up residence in the Hollywood film.

minstrel show, VOL. II: 26. A type of musical variety entertainment consisting of racist **burlesque**s of African-American performance styles. Hugely popular in the United States from the mid-nineteenth to the early-twentieth century, minstrel shows were generally performed by white singers in "blackface" (black **make-up** with highlights applied to emphasize the lips and eyes), and were based on grotesquely exaggerated stereotypes. Minstrelsy developed elaborate **convention**s and achieved such wide mainstream acceptance that it attracted contributions from respectable composers such as Stephen Foster. There were even some instances in which African-American performers themselves adopted blackface and **caricature**-based mannerisms in order to appeal to popular taste. Long after minstrelsy's racist foundations were themselves recognized and denounced, variations on the minstrel show continued to appear, for example on British television (the BBC's "Black and White Minstrel Show" ran from 1958 to 1978).

miracle play, VOL. I: 185, 190. A type of medieval religious drama based on material drawn from stories and legends about the lives, works, suffering and martyrdom of Christian saints. Also called a **saint's play**.

mise en scène, VOL. II: 4, 168. French expression, literally meaning "the putting on stage," which has been adopted in other languages to describe the sum total of creative choices made in the staging of a play. Because these are nowadays usually made by a **director**, *mise en scène* can be used interchangeably with "direction," but the French term conveys a greater sense of the artistry involved, particularly with respect to the visual, stylistic, and conceptual aspects of a production that are not explicitly covered by the English term.

modernism, VOL. I: 241, VOL. II: 167ff, 439. A widespread movement in Western culture, datable perhaps to the Paris Exposition of 1889, which sought to sever all ties with the past and invent new modes of art, thought, and life that were consistent with (what was believed to be) an unprecedented new age of machines, speed, new possibility and change. Like the unadorned steel of the Eiffel Tower, like the architectural adage that "form follows function," like Futurist symphonies written for typewriter and vacuum cleaner, modernism rejected all ornamental beauty, challenged all recognizable artistic **conventions**, and tried to reinvent painting, music, theatre, architecture and other arts from scratch. Modernist sub-movements, such as **Symbolism**, Futurism, Constructivism, **Expressionism**, **Dada**, and **Surrealism**, advanced their own styles; but they all shared a desire to use artistic materials—light, colour, sound, space, time, bodies—in boldly new ways. From the early 1970s, the austerity and radicalism of modernism was rejected by many artists in favour of **postmodernism**.

monologue, VOL. II: 449–50. Used to refer to text that is spoken by an actor on stage alone, or to the audience, but not to another character. Can also be used in the sense of "a long uninterrupted speech."

morality play, VOL. I: xii, xiii, 185–89, 202, VOL. II: xii, xiii. A type of religious drama that flourished in the Middle Ages, usually cast in the form of an **allegory**, and intended to teach a clear moral lesson to the audience. *Everyman* (in this volume) is one of the most famous of all morality plays.

mumming, VOL. I: 187. The practice of disguising oneself in costume and, with other mummers, going door to door to entertain one's neighbours, usually in connection with an ancient seasonal festival or holiday. Modern-day Halloween approximates the practices of the earliest known mummers, who seem to have been common in England in the Middle Ages.

musical theatre, VOL. II: 169. Virtually all theatre, in all periods and places, features music. But the term "musical theatre" refers to a specific, often American genre of entertainment that dominated the commercial theatre districts of New York, London, and other cities through the twentieth century. Divided into songs, dances, and unsung spoken sections, and frequently featuring large dancing choruses, musicals can be hard to distinguish from some kinds of opera and **operetta**; but whereas the vocal parts of opera can usually be handled only by professional musicians, musical theatre **scores** are generally intended for actors (who happen to be able to sing). Very great musicals will tend to "cross over" and be taken into the **repertoires** of serious opera companies eventually.

mystery play, VOL. I: 185, 187–88, 208–09. A type of religious drama popular in the Middle Ages, based on narrative material taken from the Old and New Testaments. In England, mystery plays, also called **Bible-cycle plays**, were performed by the members of trade and craft guilds in the streets of market towns, often on Corpus Christi day. See **pageant-wagons**, *carros*, and *autos sacramentales*.

Naturalism, VOL. I: xiii, 685, VOL. II: xiii, 1, 4, 5, 8, 277. The term used by Emile Zola in the late nineteenth century to describe a new, scientific method of novel-writing and playwriting. Influenced by medical science—and a few naturalist playwrights were actually doctors—Naturalism aimed to diagnose human crimes and evils as dispassionately as a doctor would a disease. Like specimens in an experiment, Naturalist characters are placed within specific biological, political, and social conditions, conditions that are often referred to collectively as "heredity" and "environment." The goal is to observe, as objectively and unmoralistically as possible, what kind of behaviour results (see **determinism**). Naturalist works can be grim in tone and detailed in their **realism**, often focusing on the ugly or "pathological" side of life (suicide, infanticide, poverty, venereal disease, prostitution).

neoclassical dramaturgy, VOL. I: 259. The principles, rules and **conventions** of writing plays according to the precepts and ideals of **neoclassicism**. Often based on the so-called **unities** of time, place, and action.

neoclassicism, VOL. I: 469, 498–99, 501–02. Literally the "new classicism," the aesthetic style in drama and other art-forms that dominated high culture in Europe through the seventeenth and eighteenth centuries, and in some places into the nineteenth century, or until it was swept away by **Romanticism**. Its subject matter was often taken from Greek and Roman myth and history; but more important than its subject matter was its *style*, which was based on a selective and often downright false image of the ancient world. It valued order, reason, clarity and moderation; it rejected strong contrasts in tone as well as, usually, the supernatural and anything that cannot be rationally motivated within the plot of a play (such as the appearance of gods, witches, or a dancing chorus). Racine's *Phèdre* (in this volume) is considered one of the most perfectly realized neoclassical dramas. See also **unities**.

New Comedy, VOL. I: 5, 92, 146, 257, 438. A type of comic play that flourished in ancient Greece from the fourth century B.C.E., particularly under such playwrights as Menander. It was later imported into Rome, where its plots and characters were reworked in Latin. Replacing **Old Comedy** after Athens' defeat in the Peloponnesian War, it focused on private, everyday domestic situations involving parent-child disharmony, money, neighbours, and parental obstacles to love and marriage. Its young lovers, bad-tempered parents, scheming slaves and golden-hearted prostitutes quickly achieved the status of **stock characters**. Also known as **situation comedy**.

Old Comedy, VOL. I: 5, 92, 119, 147. The type of dramatic **satire** practiced in fifth-century Athens and equated today with the works of Aristophanes (see *Frogs* in this volume). The genre is known for its fantastical and unrealistic **episodic** plots, its frequent use of animal choruses (frogs, birds, wasps, horse-mounted knights), and particularly for its brilliant verbal wit, free obscenity, and fearless attacks on living Athenian politicians and other public figures (e.g., Euripides and Socrates). See also **chorus**.

operetta, VOL. II: 169. Also known as "light opera." A theatrical work that is mostly sung and intended to be performed by professional singers. Associated with the works of Franz Lehar and Johann Strauss II, operetta differs from opera in three ways: it features longer unsung spoken scenes, tends to treat lighter, frothier subjects, and uses less challenging and more popular musical idioms. See also **musical theatre**.

orchestra, VOL. I: 3. Lit., "the dancing place." In the ancient world it was the lower, flat, circular surface-area of the outdoor theatre where the **chorus** danced and sang. It was also used by fifty-member choirs in the performance of **dithyrambs**, which were danced in a circular formation. As the dancing chorus disappeared from drama, the orchestra shrank to a semi-circle below a raised stage; over the centuries, it was eventually given over to musicians. The term is mainly used in the theatre today to refer to this orchestra-pit, or to the ground-floor seats of the auditorium, also called the *parterre* or stalls.

pageant-wagons, VOL. I: 188. Wheeled and elaborately decorated parade floats used as mobile stages in England for the performance of **Bible-cycle plays**, or **mystery plays**. They were sometimes built on two levels, with trap doors and mechanical devices for raising angels or thrones up to heaven. Actors drew them through the streets of market towns along a prearranged route, either by hand or horse, stopping intermittently at fixed performance locations to enact their portion of the Biblical narrative. Many wagons were stored through the year in covered sheds and brought out on Corpus Christi day.

Panathenaia, VOL. I: 3. Lit., "all-Athenian," a large ancient Greek summer festival featuring contests, prizes, and religious rituals, specializing in the competitive recitation of **epic poetry**.

pantomime, VOL. I: 501, 649, VOL. II: 169. Originally a genre of virtuoso solo performance invented by the ancient Romans. It is usually used today to refer to a type of spectacular entertainment that emerged in London at the beginning of the eighteenth century, featuring *commedia dell'arte* characters, magical special-effects wizardry, music, dance, and fantastical **episodic** plots. It remained very popular into the nineteenth century, when it picked up certain features of **melodrama** and developed into the form it usually takes today, the "Christmas Panto," which involves some audience participation, often of children. Also used in the sense of "to enact silently," or mime (see **dumb-show**).

parable, VOL. I: 684, VOL. II: 482. A short story told to illustrate a moral principle. It differs from **allegory** in being shorter and simpler: parables do not generally function on two levels simultaneously.

parody, VOL. I: 208. A comic play or other work in which an institution, phenomenon, person, or artistic genre is ridiculed, usually through exaggeration, debasement, substitution, and incongruity. Unlike **burlesque**, which tends to target a specific work and imitate its tone, style, or oddities perfectly and even affectionately, parody is loose, general, and critical.

passion play, VOL. I: 188. A type of late medieval religious drama based on episodes from the life of Christ as related in the New Testament, similar to the **saint's play** or **miracle play** insofar as it dramatizes the persecution, suffering, and death of a martyr revered by Christians. Sometimes staged over many days, usually on an outdoor **mansion** set featuring Heaven on the left and a prominent and spectacularly equipped Hell Mouth on the right.

pastoral drama, VOL. I: 258. A type of play invented during the Renaissance by members of Italian scholarly academies in an attempt to revive the **satyr play** of ancient Greece (see *commedia erudita*). Filtering the lusty, drunken goat-men, ecstatic maenads, and rustic settings of the satyr play though their Christian worldview, such writers created a new theatrical genre in which innocent shepherds, nymphs, and shepherdesses gambol in an idealized natural landscape free from the pressures of city life and the corruptions of civilization.

personal agency, VOL. II: 171, 590. The power, as exercised by an individual, to originate and carry out his or her desires from sources within the self, free from or against the **determinism** of external forces.

playwright-in-residence, VOL. II: 549, 622. A writer or creator of plays who is engaged by a theatre company to work within their midst for a period of time, either for the purpose of nurturing a young talent, or gaining prestige from association with an established writer, and usually in the hope that he or she will produce new work for the company to perform.

plot, VOL. II: 205, 277. Not to be confused with the "story," the plot of a play or other literary work is the precise arrangement of incidents used to tell the story. The same story can give rise to countless plots, depending on the point at which the writer chooses to begin (at Oedipus's birth? or on the last day of his reign?), what he or she chooses to dramatize (the wedding night of Oedipus and Jocasta? the murder of Hamlet's father?), and how he chooses to bring the events about (a messenger? a lost letter? an epiphany? a gun-battle?).

poetic prose dramas, VOL. II: 67. Plays that employ symbolism, metaphor and heightened language to a degree normally associated with poetry, but that are written in prose rather than verse.

postmodernism, VOL. I: 241, 685. A movement in art and culture during the last quarter of the twentieth century named for its rejection of **modernism**. Characterized by its re-embrace of tradition, postmodern art incorporates styles and conventions from previous historical periods, usually in eclectic combinations that reveal new aspects of each one. Noted for its playfulness and ironic detachment (see **irony**), postmodernism has been accused of lacking political seriousness; but its tendency to bring different media, periods, and cultural values into contact with one another (Western and Eastern theatre traditions, puppets and live actors, classical sculptures and computers, etc.) suggests that it is committed to seeing the world "globally" and resisting the domination of imagery and ideas by any one group or ideology.

proagon, VOL. I: 93. Greek for "pre-contest." It refers to the point in the Athenian theatre festivals at which playwrights appeared before the public with their actors to advertise their upcoming play, functioning like the "trailer" of contemporary movies in generating audience interest. At first performed outdoors, such events came to be held in the Odeon, or music-hall. See *agōn*.

proscenium, VOL. I: 258, 259, 500, 501, VOL. II: 298. A Latin architectural term derived from the Greek *proskenion*, the front-most section of the theatre building (*skēnē*) as it developed in the post-Classical, Hellenistic period. During the Renaissance, when theatres were built indoors, artificial lighting, perspective painting, and changeable scenery were adopted in **scenography**. To hide the scene-shifting equipment and lighting instruments from view of the spectators, a single archway was constructed at the front of the acting area. (The first proscenium of this type was built for the Teatro Farnese in 1618.) Stages on which a pictorial illusion is created with the help of a three- or four-sided border or frame are called "proscenium arch," or "picture-frame"

theatres, and they reached their heyday during the nineteenth century, the age of **realism**.

protagonist, VOL. II: 1, 2, 170, 296, 298, 389. The central character in a drama or other literary work; see *agōn*.

quarto, VOL. I: 316, 318, 503, 552, 605. Refers to the size of a published book created from sheets of paper that have been folded twice. When sewn together along the second fold and ripped along the first, eight pages are produced. In the case of Shakespeare, the word is used of certain printed copies of his plays that appeared during his lifetime, usually in "bootleg" versions (see by contrast the **folio** edition). Before the advent of copyright laws, publication of plays during the author's life was strongly resisted, as this would have made the works available to rival companies. When such plays did appear, usually against the wishes of the playwright, they often did so in badly corrupted versions. For example, the first edition of *Hamlet* (1603) is believed to be a reconstruction of the play from memory by the actor who played Marcellus. Much of the text seems merely paraphrased, but the **stage directions** are probably authentic. The second edition of *Hamlet* (1604) is more reliable. These two editions of the play are known as the First and Second Quarto (or Q1 and Q2).

realism, VOL. I: 685, 713, VOL. II: 1, 4, 5, 8, 144, 167. The attempt to so faithfully duplicate the appearance of the real world in art that viewers might conceivably be fooled into accepting the imitation for the thing itself. In the theatre, realism usually refers to a style of production perfected in the nineteenth century, when vast expense and labour were devoted to achieving the kinds of all-consuming illusions that today are more commonly associated with movies. Because the theatre's technical equipment, and the audience, must be hidden from view to achieve such illusions, theatrical realism is often associated with darkened auditoriums and picture-frame or **proscenium**-arch stages.

repertoire, VOL. I: 437, 468, 503, VOL. II: 1, 66, 169, 205. Used to refer either, in general, to the sum total of plays that are considered stage-worthy at a given time, or to the particular list of plays that can be readied for performance by an individual theatre company (or performer).

repertory, VOL. II: 205. A system of scheduling plays non-consecutively by alternating them with other plays from a company's current **repertoire.** The repertory or "rep" system is very rare in North American commercial theatre.

Restoration comedy, VOL. I: 501, 605–06. A genre of witty and sexually uninhibited drama associated with the London theatres in the decades after 1660, when King Charles II was "restored" to the English throne. It was known for its pungent **satire,** obsession with the habits of the upper classes, and cynical depiction of human customs, particularly the institution of marriage. Also see **comedy of manners.**

role-playing, VOL. I: xiii, 146, 184, 190, VOL. II: xiii, 548. The pretended adoption of the identity or function of another person. All acting, of course, is a type of role-playing. The impersonation of others is a common theme in drama and appears within the plots of countless plays.

romance, VOL. I: xiii, 296, 366, VOL. II: xiii, 168. A dreamlike genre of fiction or storytelling in which the ordinary laws of nature are suspended, in which statues come to life, shipwrecked men emerge from the sea unharmed, and troubled or broken worlds are magically healed at the end, often by daughters, and often in **pastoral** settings.

Romanticism, VOL. I: 770, VOL. II: 1, 5. A widespread movement in art and culture, beginning in the later eighteenth century, that aimed to throw off the shackles of **neoclassicism.** Rejecting all rules and rational principles, Romantic art emphasized feeling, stark contrasts, extreme or abnormal psychological states, as well as the inner world of dreams, fantasies, and the supernatural. Natural and untutored "genius" was prized over technical mastery, untamed and "sublime" nature over civilization. Some Romantic poets did produce works for the stage, such as Goethe and Schiller, and Byron and Shelley, but Romanticism in the theatre

more often took the form of violently emotional acting, particularly the kind made famous by Edmund Kean. Romanticism also manifested itself throughout nineteenth-century theatre in **melodrama** and Gothic plays, with their intense villains, brooding heroes, spooky vampires, and dark medieval castles.

saint's play, VOL. I: xii, 185, 189, 190–91, VOL. II: xii. See **miracle play.**

satire, VOL. I: xiii, 119, VOL. II: xiii, 8, 341, 588. A humorous play or other work in which people, attitudes, or types of behaviour are ridiculed for the purpose of correcting their blameworthy qualities. Satirists differ from other types of comic writers in that they are often morally outraged by the follies and vices they depict. Of all types of **comedy,** satire is the most critical. It can also, paradoxically, be the most subtle, for satirists may mask their fury with humour so effectively that they can seem to be condoning the faults they abhor. Satire often makes use of **irony** and frequently targets politicians and other public figures. For this reason, satire tends to flourish in liberal societies where free speech is prized. See also **Old Comedy** and **comedy of manners.**

satyr play, VOL. I: 2, 258. Ancient Athenian genre of comical drama, usually a mythological **burlesque,** which was performed by a singing and dancing chorus dressed in satyr costume (a furry loincloth to which a goat's tail and artificial penis were attached, plus a mask depicting an ugly snubbed nose, high forehead, and goat's ears). In Greek myth, satyrs were the drunken, randy, rabble-rousing attendants of Dionysus, in whose honour all theatre was performed in ancient Greece. Satyr plays were staged as part of the Greek **tragic tetralogy,** either as the first or the last play of the four. See also **pastoral drama.**

scenography, VOL. I: 3. Also called "set design" or "stage design," scenography is often preferred today as a term to describe the visual and spatial aspects of a theatrical production. This is because many artists working in the theatre do not design only the sets, but also the costumes and sometimes even the lighting, too, for a unified effect. Scenography also implies that the creation of a beautiful and functional environment on stage is a specialized art-form, not merely a variant of other types of design.

score, VOL. II: 169. The musical text of an opera, **operetta** or **musical**, as written by a composer, containing parts for singers and musicians.

screenplay, VOL. II: 341, 390, 482, 622. The written text used in the making of a movie. It describes the sequence of shots and camera angles that will be used in the telling of the story, as well as what the characters do and say. Screenplays are often based on pre-existing stage-plays and novels.

set design, VOL. II: 3. See **scenography**.

situation comedy, VOL. I: xiii, 5, 146, 190, 500, 713. VOL. II: xiii. Humorous play or other performed story concerning everyday domestic trials and tribulations within families and/or between friends and neighbours. Love, marriage, wealth, and family or neighbourhood harmony are usually the focus of sitcoms. The jokes are generated by awkward or complex situations involving false assumptions, mistaken identities, and attempts to trick others out of money, prestige, or lovers. Sitcoms often feature **stock characters** such as the braggart, the parasite, the clever servant, the stupid servant, the violent cook, and so on. See also **New Comedy** and **convention**.

skēnē, VOL. I: 3. Greek for "scene house." Used of the covered, indoor portion of the Theatre of Dionysus in ancient Athens that was used by the actors for entrances, exits, and changes of costumes and **mask**s. The *skēnē* also housed the theatre's special-effects machinery. In fifth-century tragedy, the scene house generally represented a palace or temple with its large central doors. In later centuries, scene buildings were constructed with new architectural features such as multiple openings and rows of pillars for receiving painted scenery; in such Hellenistic theatres, the *skēnē* was expanded and divided into an upper and a lower stage (or *proskenion*; see **proscenium**).

"social problem" plays, VOL. II: 66–67. Dramas, usually from the late nineteenth and early twentieth centuries, that focused on specific topical and controversial issues such as prostitution, slum landlordism, venereal disease, and other malaises of modern society. Associated with Shaw and Ibsen in particular, and often closely related to the plays of **Naturalism**.

sound-scape, VOL. II: 170. Named by analogy with "landscape," a sound-scape is the totality of sound-effects, ambient noises and music used by a sound-designer or **director** as the aural background for a production.

stage design, VOL. II: 3. See **scenography**.

stage directions, VOL. I: 189, VOL. II: 390, 440. The written but unspoken parts of a play text, sometimes provided by the playwright and sometimes by later editors, that describe gestures, stage action or technical effects (set changes, music cues, etc.). It was very rare until the nineteenth century, when detailed staging instructions became routine. With the rise of the **director** in the twentieth century, the freedom of theatre artists to determine the stage action for themselves has been energetically asserted, and for this reason stage directions are considered nonessential parts of the play by many theatre practitioners today.

stichomythia, VOL. I: 2. One of the meters of Greek dramatic poetry, used for the rapid exchange of short lines of **dialogue** between two speakers, approximating the effect of a witness under cross-examination. Of all Greek verse forms, it is the most definitive of drama and most strongly contrasted with its long **monologue** passages, which remain closer to earlier forms of **epic poetry** and **choral lyric**. See also **iambic dialogue**.

stock characters, VOL. I: 684. Personality types in dramatic literature that recur so often that their particular collection of character traits, their professions, and sometimes even their names and costumes have become fixed. Some genres of theatre consist almost entirely of stock characters, such as the *commedia dell'arte*. Since this **convention** is much more typical of **comedy** than **tragedy**, great comic actors will often devote their entire careers to perfecting, developing, and even radically re-interpreting one of these stock characters, which are sometimes called "masks" in honour of the masked improvisers of the Italian comedy tradition. See also **caricature, New Comedy,** and **situation comedy.**

Sturm und Drang, VOL. I: 502, 770. German for "Storm and Stress." A literary movement that took its name from the title of an F.M. von Klinger play of 1776, and which was one of the earliest manifestations of **Romanticism,** it is associated particularly with the work of Goethe and Schiller (see *The Robbers* in this volume).

subplot, VOL. I: 7, 405, 469, 552. A secondary narrative embedded within the main one that usually comments on, contrasts with, or in some other way illuminates the primary line of action in a play or other literary work. Subplots usually mirror the events related in the main **plot,** except transposed to a different and often lower social plane or tone.

Surrealism, VOL. II: 169, 277. One of the many influential schools within **modernism.** Like **realism,** to which it obviously refers, surrealism incorporates elements of the true appearance of life and nature; but unlike realism, it combines these elements according to a logic more typical of dreams than waking life. Isolated aspects of surrealist art may create powerful illusions of reality, but the effect of the whole is to disturb or question our sense of reality rather than to confirm it.

symbolism, VOL. II: 5, 67, 168, 277. The use of signs, visible images or other sensuous effects to represent invisible or intangible ideas.

Symbolist theatre, VOL. II: 5, 144. A movement based in late-nineteenth-century Paris in which playwrights, following the lead of Symbolist poets and painters, tried to convey invisible emotional or spiritual truths through a careful orchestration of atmosphere and **symbolism.** Most of the works of the Symbolist theatre were presented at either Paul Fort's *Théâtre d'Art* or Aurélien Lugné-Poë's *Théâtre de l'Oeuvre.*

tableaux, VOL. I: 713. Plural of *tableau,* French for painting or picture. It is used in drama to refer to a visually pleasing and emotionally compelling arrangement of actors' bodies on stage. First recommended for wide use by theorist and playwright Denis Diderot in the eighteenth century, such consciously contrived stage pictures did gain prominence in the centuries that followed, particularly in **melodrama,** which often called for them in the **stage directions.**

theatron, VOL. I: 3. Greek word for theatre, literally "the viewing place."

tragedy, VOL. I: xiii, 2, 92, 118–19, 187, 296, 366, 468, 501, VOL. II: xiii, 1, 174. A Greek word believed to mean "song of the goat-singers" (see **satyr play** and **dithyramb**). Originating in the sixth century B.C.E., tragedy is the oldest dramatic genre and remains for many the "highest" form of poetry. Our knowledge of it derives mainly from the plays of Aeschylus, Sophocles, and Euripides, as well as from the little we know about the manner of its performance (see *agōn,* **chorus, mask, orchestra,** *skēnē,* and **tragic tetralogy**). Our understanding of it has also been shaped by Aristotle, whose description of Athenian tragedy in his *Poetics* remains a touchstone for tragic theory and practice to this day. According to Aristotle, tragedy is the imitation of an organically unified, serious action in which the **plot,** or arrangement of incidents, elicits the audience's pity and fear and then effects a **catharsis,** or purgation, of these and similar emotions. Tragic plots generally take the **protagonist** from a condition of good fortune to bad, often to his or her destruction, involve mental and/or physical suffering, and ideally take place within families, usually of a socially elevated or prominent type (royal families, for example). In Aristotle's view the most effective tragic plots also involve a simultaneous "reversal and recognition," a moment when the character's fortune turns for the worse and he or she is suddenly able to grasp a truth that was unavailable before. Tragedy has been reconceived by every subsequent age that has practiced it, beginning in the Renaissance. In the seventeenth century it was reinvented according to the principles of **neoclassicism**; in the eighteenth according to those of the Enlightenment ("middle-class" or "bourgeois tragedy"). **Romanticism** in turn created its own tragic forms, often inspired by Shakespeare. Notable re-thinkings of tragedy in the modern age include Arthur Miller's essay "Tragedy and the Common Man." See also **working-class tragedy**.

tragic tetralogy, VOL. I: 2, 8. A four-part **tragedy**. Mostly associated with the (non-comic) plays of Athens in the fifth-century B.C.E., it consisted of one **satyr play** and three tragedies written on related themes. Another famous tragic tetralogy, *The Ring of the Nibelung,* was written in the nineteenth century by composer Richard Wagner. This four-part "music drama," created in imitation of Greek tragedy, is based on the heroes and gods of Germanic myth.

tragi-comedy, VOL. I: xiii, VOL. II: xiii. A genre of drama in which many elements of **tragedy** are present, but which generally has a happy end. Corneille's *The Cid* is an excellent example of this genre, which was sometimes preferred to straight tragedy under **neoclassicism**. See in this volume *Fuenteovejuna*.

unities [of action, time and place], VOL. I: 257. A doctrine invented by the theorists of **neoclassicism**, who considered "the three unities" an essential rule of proper **tragedy**. It stipulates that the plot, the span of time it represents, and the amount of physical terrain it covers must together approximate the true unity of real space/time conditions (i.e., the single location and continuous two-hour time-period that prevails on stage during performance, during which one can realistically represent only so much action and no more). The concept was based on a misreading of Aristotle, and was soon ridiculed almost out of existence by writers such as G.E. Lessing and Samuel Johnson. But it did succeed in determining the form taken by tragedy during the seventeenth and eighteenth centuries. It also ensured that the *un*-unified plays of Shakespeare would remain beneath the contempt of many for over a hundred years. Despite their poor grounding in ancient theatre practice and the rigidity with which their (mostly French) advocates enforced them, the unities remain a useful concept in drama. Works of theatrical **realism** and **Naturalism**, for example, tend to observe them instinctively.

vomitorium, VOL. I: 7. In theatrical contexts, used to describe a ramp or raked hallway under the seats of the auditorium that allows spectators to ascend to their seats, or actors to the playing area, from below. The ancient Romans, who built their poured-concrete theatres on flat ground rather than nestled into naturally occurring hillsides, were the first to use "voms."

Weimar Classicism, VOL. I: 502. The style of playwriting, acting, and **scenography** associated with the Weimar Court Theatre during the late eighteenth century, when Schiller and Goethe were **playwright**s-in-residence and **artistic director**s there. Following their *Sturm und Drang* periods, both adopted an approach to writing and staging plays that was noted for its greater fidelity to Classical Greek culture than was common in **neoclassicism**. See also **antiquarianism**.

word-scenery, VOL. I: 498. The use of language alone, when spoken by actors on stage, to convey the locations depicted in a play without the help of sets, lighting, or other theatrical effects. It is typical of bare-stage traditions like those of Shakespeare. Superb examples of the effectiveness of word-scenery can be found in Shakespeare's Prologues to *Henry V*.

working-class tragedy, VOL. II: 8. A **tragedy** whose **protagonist** is drawn from the "proletarian" or working class. The genre does not appear until the nineteenth century (see Büchner's *Woyzeck* in Volume II), and is based on an implicit rejection of the traditional, Aristotelian assumption that only the "best" of a society's citizens were suitable for serious dramatic treatment.

workshop, VOL. II: 515, 588. The process of developing and improving a play through a collaboration between a playwright and a group of theatre artists with the goal of producing a script deemed ready for performance.

Sources

Anonymous. *The Farce of Master Pierre Pathelin*, translated by Alan E. Knight, from *The Semiotics of Deceit* by Donald Maddox. Lewisburg, PA: Bucknell University Press, 1984. Translation copyright © 1984 by Alan E. Knight. Reprinted by permission of the publisher.

Aeschylus. *Agamemnon*, from *The Complete Greek Tragedies*, edited by David Grene and Richmond Lattimore. Copyright © 1992 by The University of Chicago Press. Reprinted by permission of the publisher.

Aeschylus. *The Libation Bearers* and *Eumenides*, translated by Geoff W. Bakewell. Translation copyright © 2003 by Geoff W. Bakewell. Used with permission.

Aristophanes. *Frogs*, translated by Jennifer Wise. Translation copyright © 2003 by Jennifer Wise. Used with permission.

[Pierre-Augustin Caron de] Beaumarchais. *The Marriage of Figaro*, translated by John Van Burek and Jennifer Wise. Copyright © 2003 by John Van Burek and Jennifer Wise. Used with permission.

Aphra Behn. *The Rover*, edited by Anne Russell. Peterborough, Canada: Broadview Press, 1999. Copyright © 1999 by Anne Elizabeth Russell. Reprinted with permission.

Susanna Centlivre. *A Bold Stroke for a Wife*, edited by Nancy Copeland. Peterborough, Canada: Broadview Press, 1995. Copyright © 1995 by Nancy Copeland. Reprinted with permission.

William Congreve. *The Way of the World*, edited by Richard Kroll, from *The Broadview Anthology of Restoration and Early Eighteenth-Century Drama*, edited by J. Douglas Canfield. Peterborough, Canada: Broadview Press, 2001. Copyright © 2001 by Richard Kroll. Reprinted with permission.

Carlo Gozzi. *Turandot*, from *Five Tales for the Theatre*, edited and translated by Albert Bermel and Ted Emery. Chicago: University of Chicago Press, 1989. Copyright © 1989. Reprinted by permission of the publisher.

Euripides. *Hippolytus*, translated by Gilbert and Sarah Lawall, published by Bristol Classical Press. Copyright © 1986 by Gilbert and Sarah Lawall. Reprinted by permission of the translators.

Hildegard of Bingen. *The Play of the Virtues (Ordo Virtutum)*, translated by Peter Dronke. Copyright © 1981 by Peter Dronke. Reprinted with permission.

Hroswitha of Gandersheim. *The Conversion of Thais the Whore*, translated by Katharina M. Wilson as *The Conversion of the Harlot Thais*, from *The Plays of Hrotsvit of Gandersheim* (Garland Library of Medieval Literature, Volume 62, Series B). New York: Garland Publishing, 1989. Translation copyright © 1989 by Katharina M. Wilson. Reprinted by permission of the translator.

Christopher Marlowe. *Doctor Faustus*, edited by Michael Keefer. Peterborough, Canada: Broadview Press, 1991. Copyright © 1991 by Michael Keefer. Reprinted with permission.

Molière. *Tartuffe*, translated by Richard Wilbur. Copyright © 1963, 1962, 1961, and renewed 1991, 1990, 1989 by Richard Wilbur. Reprinted by permission of Harcourt Brace & Company. CAUTION: Professional and amateurs are hereby warned that this translation, being fully protected under the copyright laws of the United States of America, the British Empire, including the Dominion of Canada, and all other countries which are signatories to the Universal Copyright Convention and the International Copyright Union, is subject to royalty. All rights, including professional, amateur, motion picture, recitation, lecturing, public reading, radio broadcasting, and television, are strictly reserved. Particular emphasis is laid on the question of readings, permission for which must be secured from the author's agent in writing. Inquiries on professional rights (except for amateur rights) should be addressed to Mr. Gilbert Parker, Curtis Brown, Ltd., Ten Astor Place, New York, NY 10003; inquiries on translation rights should be addressed to Harcourt Brace & Company, Permissions Department, Orlando, FL 32887. The amateur acting rights of Tartuffe are controlled exclusively by the Dramatists Play Service, Inc., 440 Park Avenue South, New York, NY. No amateur performance of the play may be given without obtaining in advance the written permission of the Dramatists Play Service, Inc., and paying the requisite fee.

Plautus. *Miles Gloriosus*, from *Plautus: Three Comedies (Miles Gloriosus, Pseudolus, Rudens)*, translated by Peter L. Smith. Ithaca: Cornell University Press, 1991. Copyright © 1991 Cornell University. Used by permission of the publisher, Cornell University Press.

Racine. *Phèdre*, translated by William Packard. Copyright © 1966, and renewed 1994 by William Packard. Reprinted by permission of Samuel French, Inc. CAUTION: Professionals and amateurs are hereby warned that "Phèdre," being fully protected under the copyright laws of the United States of America, the British Commonwealth countries, including Canada, and the other countries of the Copyright Union, is subject to a royalty. All rights, including professional, amateur, motion picture, recitation, public reading, radio, television and cable broadcasting, and the rights of translation into foreign languages, are strictly reserved. Any inquiry regarding the availability of performance rights, or the purchase of individual copies of the authorized acting edition, must be directed to Samuel French, Inc., 45 West 25 Street, NY, NY 10010 with other locations in Hollywood and Toronto, Canada.

Friedrich Schiller. *The Robbers*, from *The Robbers and Wallenstein*, translated by F.J. Lamport. Middlesex, England: Penguin Books, 1979. Copyright © 1979 by F.J. Lamport.

William Shakespeare. *Hamlet*, edited by Craig S. Walker. Footnotes to *Hamlet* copyright © 2003 by Craig S. Walker. Used by permission.

William Shakespeare. *The Tempest*, edited by Craig S. Walker. Footnotes to *The Tempest* copyright © 2003 by Craig S. Walker. Used by permission.

Sophocles. *Oedipus Tyrannos*. Translated by Thomas F. Gould. Translation copyright © 1970 by Thomas F. Gould. Reprinted by permission of the Estate of Thomas F. Gould.

Lope de Vega. *Fuenteovejuna*, translated by Richard Sanger. Copyright © 2003 by Richard Sanger. Used with permission.

William Wycherley. *The Country Wife*, edited by Peggy Thompson, from *The Broadview Anthology of Restoration and Early Eighteenth-Century Drama*, edited by J. Douglas Canfield. Peterborough, Canada: Broadview Press, 2001. Copyright © 2001 by Peggy Thompson.